Italian Song Texts from the 17th through the 20th Centuries, Vol. I:

Italian Song Texts from the 17th Century

with

International Phonetic Alphabet Transliteration
Word-for-word Literal Translation, and
Idiomatic Translation

by

Martha Gerhart

LEYERLE
PUBLICATIONS

ITALIAN SONG TEXTS FROM THE
17th THROUGH THE 20th CENTURIES

Volume I
ITALIAN SONG TEXTS FROM THE 17th CENTURY
By
Martha Gerhart

This book may be ordered directly from

**LEYERLE
PUBLICATIONS**

**Box 384
Geneseo, New York 14454**

Dedicated to

my dear departed Lady,
who was my
unconditionally loving companion
during the first two years of work
on this book

Martha Gerhart

enjoyed a prestigious career as a vocal coach/pianist based in New York City until re-locating to Dallas, Texas in the fall of 1997. She teaches at Southern Methodist University, where her duties have included Italian and German Diction classes for singers, Techniques of Vocal Accompanying classes for pianists, Opera Theatre coaching, and individual curricular Vocal Coaching. In Dallas she continues her private coaching and her association with The Dallas Opera.

Ms. Gerhart was on the music staffs of the New York City Opera (spanning the Directorships of Julius Rudel and Beverly Sills), Chicago Lyric Opera, and The San Francisco Opera, and she was eight times a master coach with the San Francisco Opera's Merola Opera Training Program. Among other performing companies with which she has been associated are the Spoleto Festival, New York City's Mostly Mozart Festival, Glimmerglass Opera, and Chautauqua Opera. She has presented numerous master classes as guest at singers' training programs and at colleges and schools of music.

She is the translator of line-by-line translations in many of the Hal Leonard Publishing Corporation's Vocal Library Series, including their *Opera Anthologies*.

A graduate of Middlebury College (B.A. cum laude) and the University of Colorado (M.Mus.), Ms. Gerhart began her professional training in opera as a student of Boris Goldovsky at his Oglebay Opera Workshops, studied opera with Luigi Ricci in Rome, and piano with Seymour Bernstein in New York City.

Elena Servi

has been Italian language and diction coach at the San Francisco Opera since 1976.

Ms. Servi came to the United States from her native city of Milano, Italy. She has taught at the University of California (Berkeley), San Francisco State University, and Holy Names College (Oakland, California).

Ms. Servi was engaged on several occasions as Italian coach at the Paris Opera's Centre de formation lyrique. She has also served as Italian diction coach at the Salzburg Easter Festival and at the Shanghai Conservatory in China.

In addition to her work with the San Francisco Opera's artists, Ms. Servi is known for her work with the young singers of the San Francisco Opera Center: the Merola Program singers and the Adler Fellows.

Gastone Rossato

is a native of Padova, Italy, where he received degrees in science and the humanities. At the Università di Padova he received a doctorate in mechanical engineering, and he was further schooled in England at Cambridge University.

Mr. Rossato has translated numerous technical manuals for companies such as Beechcraft Raytheon, Piper, and Aero Commander, as well as books on oral pathology, pediatric orthodontics and articles on other subjects related to engineering, electronics, and physics. He is also translator of Kipling's *Gunga Din* (Milano, 1963) and T. S. Eliot, *Poems* (Milano, 1964), both in collaboration with D. Selvatico Estense.

Acknowledgements

First and foremost, thanks to my dear friend and esteemed colleague Elena Servi for her unfailingly expert help with problem-solving about the many puzzles concerning antiquated forms of the Italian language and context, and about their best possible modern translations. Though Elena modestly declined to be co-author of this book project at its inception, her willingness to be my "expert advisor" was a stipulation of my agreeing to undertake the project, as well as my inspiration for going on with it even when it became clear that Elena, given her otherwise busy professional schedule, could not possibly be my sole advisor. I cannot thank Elena enough for her help on a portion, at least a third, of the texts.

Second, thanks to Gastone Rossato for sharing the task of expert advisor. In our Sunday morning work sessions (after which he usually took to the skies for pleasure, also being a pilot and trainer of pilots), his enjoyment of the old Italian texts, and in solving the problems inherent in their translations, given his encyclopedic knowledge, was infectious.

Third, thanks to Elvia Puccinelli, for her last-minute translation help "in a pinch," and for her generosity and enthusiasm when making suggestions after proofreading a good part of my draft.

Fourth, but by no means last, thanks to Martin Friedman for his expert advice, in proofreading, about all things having to do with English language usage, as well as for his suggestions and the knowledge he shared regarding the *Glossary*.

Deep appreciation to William Leyerle for inviting me to prepare this huge project for inclusion in his series of volumes of vocal texts' translations. His commitment, trust, support and patience have been close to angelic.

Thanks also to:

Southern Methodist University, for a President's Partners Grant to purchase a laptop computer to use for work on the project when travelling.

Dr. David Mancini, Chair of the Department of Theory and Composition at Southern Methodist University. Author and scholar in his field, David also has a passion for the Italian language (both antiquated and modern), which I discovered was much more than the "hobby" he claimed.

Clayton Crenshaw, Head of Circulation Services at SMU's Hamon Arts Library, for his always gracious help with locating and lending resources.

Billie Stovall, Library Specialist for Interlibrary Loans at SMU's Fondren Library, who kindly and conscientiously filled every request for music books through the Interlibrary Loan service, without which the collection of texts for this project would have been impossible.

The SMU students who helped greatly with tasks such as xeroxing, filing, and proofreading, especially Laura Ayres, Erick Andrew Reich, and Margarita Roco.

Donata Schiannini, lexicographer supreme, of Milano, Italy.

Contents

Introduction and Explanations.. i.- iii.

About the use of the IPA, with
   Key to the IPA Symbols.. iv.- vi.

THE SONG TEXTS.. 1- 502

Glossary.. 503-511

Index... 512-517

Bibliography, with Numbering Key............................... 518-523

Introduction and Explanations

The purpose of this series of books is several-fold. First, to provide singers, teachers, stage directors, and other interested readers with reliable translations and guidelines for pronunciation of Italian songs. Second, to assist those who know modern Italian but who may be stumped by words of antiquated or poetic usage. And last but not least: to whet the appetites of singers, teachers, and students to further explore this repertoire.

My intention was to include songs the user is likely to come across in published music – that is, in performing editions; it was not my purpose to address manuscripts or unedited collections, however fascinating the study of them is. As new editions of vocal music are continually being published (and as the number of already published songs is enormous), some song texts will obviously be missing from this collection. Meanwhile, the large number of published songs for which the texts were, up to now, not translated into English – or, in some cases, published with erroneous translations – easily justifies the production of these volumes and William Leyerle's dedication to publishing them. Furthermore, to date, only a few publications have included IPA (International Phonetic Alphabet) transliterations.

Songs, here, are understood to be compositions for a solo voice with keyboard accompaniment or in reduction for voice and keyboard. Included are also the texts of songs originally found in collections for voice with guitar transcription, as the earliest seventeenth century songs were accompanied by instruments in the lute family. Occasionally, I have included texts of songs published in full orchestral score, when cleanly printed and easily adaptable in reduction to performance by one keyboard player. And, I have included songs which were composed for voice and keyboard along with obbligato instruments, as the addition of obbligato instruments was an important part of the development of the solo song during the seventeenth century.

In subsequent volumes "standard" opera arias for which translations and IPA transliterations are otherwise available will not be included. However, many of the Italian song texts in this volume are, in fact, of "arias" – i.e., solo pieces excerpted from operas composed during the birth and development of opera in the seventeenth century.

For the fascinating history of the beginnings and the development of solo song, I recommend the various excellent forewords in modern scholarly editions. Among the fine books in print on the subject, I recommend in particular Con che soavità: Studies in Italian Opera, Song, and Dance, 1580-1740, edited by Iain Fenlon and Tim Carter and published by Clarendon Press in 1995, and Monteverdi and his Contemporaries, edited by Tim Carter and published by Ashgate Publishing Company in 2000.

To assemble the list of composers for this volume I had to decide what to do about the composers whose lifetimes spanned the end of the the seventeenth century and the beginning of the eighteenth century. I decided, rather arbitrarily, on a birth date of 1675 as the cutoff for Volume I, making a composer's years of flourishing the priority of choice. Hence J.S. Bach (b.1685) and Antonio Vivaldi (b.1678) will be included in Volume II: Italian Song Texts from the 18th century; Alessandro Scarlatti (b.1660) is included in this volume, but his son Domenico (b.1685) will appear in Volume II.

Translating old Italian texts poses many problems. Words required for correct grammatical context are often missing, for poetic reasons or because of a need by the composer to adapt the text to the musical phrase, or perhaps simply by carelessness. Words of antiquated usage sometimes remain a mystery, even after old dictionaries and encyclopedias have been consulted, and some words used today had a different meaning in the seventeenth century. Old Italian script was easily misread (and often is, even now, by modern editors), the manuscripts having been at the mercy not only of copyists but also of foreign (especially German) publishers who functioned early on as editors as well as publishers. My goal was to translate the Italian accurately while also making the translation "make sense" in English – a sometimes nearly impossible task. My translations offer solutions which may not be the only possible ones.

While I have sought and received help from expert colleagues, I am solely responsible for the choices made, and for any errors.

એ

Notes about editing

While making every effort to retain the old Italian as printed, in order to preserve its flavor, I have

- Changed or corrected words which were clearly misprints.
- Modernized spelling by removing the "h" from words like "hor" (= or), and by changing "et" (from the Latin), when found, to the modern "e" or "ed."
- Occasionally modernized the spelling of common word forms such as "siccome" (instead of "sì come") and "eppure" (instead of "e pure"), although the latter were used in old Italian, and usually retained "da le," "de gli," etc., common in old Italian, sometimes with a note about their modern equivalents.
- Added (or changed) punctuation only when necessary to make sense of the context; many texts were printed on the music pages with very little punctuation – in some cases even with none at all. My purpose was not to be a text editor in the in the scholarly sense of what that would have entailed.
- Modernized (added or removed) capitalization; for example, the custom at the time was to capitalize each first line, however short, of the original poem.
- Added diacritical markings (accents) where missing: for example, on the word "sì" (when its meaning is, correctly, not the same as the word "si" without an accent), and on the word "ché" when its meaning is "perché."
- Replaced the grave accent (`) with the acute accent (´) on words such as "perché," in accordance with current modern editing practice.
- Replaced, occasionally, a completely unfamiliar word with its modern equivalent: for example, changing "russullo," which appeared in Albinonini's "Son qual Tantalo novello" with "ruscello" (= stream).
- Changed a word which does not make sense in context; in such cases I've included a note about it.
- Not added a "d," when missing, as would be proper in modern Italian for euphony in combinations of vowels such as in the words "e io," which become "ed io" if "edited."

Notes about formatting

The four-line format is similar to that used in other Leyerle texts volumes.

The numbers in brackets at the beginning of each song are the numbers I assigned to the publication(s) *(see Bibliography)* in which the song is printed. Without exception, I have copied the texts from published music rather than from any secondary source.

Listings of proper names in the *Glossary*, when there are such, are indicated by *GL* at the end of each text.

Abbreviations I've used within the translations are
alt., or var. = alternate or variant in different prints
(fig.) = figurative meaning
(lit.) = literary meaning
(poet.) = poetic meaning
(mod.) = modern equivalent.

In the literal translations I have occasionally used brackets to enclose pleonastic words, i.e., words in Italian which are not translatable as such in the idiomatic translation.

For *da capo* ("A-B-A") arias, I have not repeated the text of the "A" sections.

Though in the seventeenth century it was not a usual practice of the composers to identify their poets, when a poet or librettist is known, the name appears in italics at the top right of the translation. If an aria is known to be from a particular opera, that information appears in italics at the top left of the translation, as does the name of the character singing, when known. However, I am not listing the titles of the collections or manuscripts in which individual songs were originally found; that information may be found on the title pages of the songs, in editors' notes, or from the composers' biographical information in reliable sources.

I have made it no priority to preserve rhyme schemes when formatting the copied texts; this decision was made not only in the interest of saving space, but also because it would have involved a kind of research (doubtless a fascinating one) not germane to the purpose of this book.

The notes provided on the translation pages in "boxes" are intended to help the user identify words or word forms which he or she may not be able to find in a medium-sized good Italian dictionary.

Vocal compositions in the seventeenth century were often titled or subtitled "aria," "arietta," "canzonetta," "recitativo," "madrigal," "sonetto," etc. Because cross-referencing all such titles and subtitles in the Index would have been exhaustive, the reader is directed to search the *Index* not by the "generic" title, but rather by either the composer or the first line of the text.

When writing the biographical sketches of the composers, I found that available sources of information often differed in details. With a few exceptions, I have taken my facts from *Grove* (which sometimes even differs in details from its own printed version to its current on-line version) as the most reliable source. Biographical information about these composers is gathered from baptismal records, death certificates, letters of their contemporaries, preserved records regarding performances, preserved accounts of critiques of performances, and dedications on title pages of published music; musicologists are continuing to sort out this information and publish the results of their research in modern editions.

About understanding the translations

How many of us have read an English translation of an "old Italian song" and have been left without a clear understanding of what it was all about? No wonder, considering the dubiousness of accuracy in some of the original texts' transcriptions and the difficulty of deciphering them. It will help the reader to know that:

- Many of these Italian texts are "poor," most likely taken from "formulas" of the day. On the other hand, many are poetically elegant and inspired, and many are rich in symbolism and plays on words.
- Many of the texts are based on historical events or mythological events and characters; the reader will do well to be inspired to research those references.
- The texts reflect the beliefs of the period regarding astronomy and the structure of the world. Remember Dante, whose Paradise was made up of ten Circles or Heavens, and Ptomely's theories about the fixed stars. (There is a fine drawing of "A perfect description of the Celestial Orbs" appended to Leonard Digges' *A Prognostication Everlasting* [London, 1576, published in The Book of the Cosmos, edited by Dennis Richard Danielson, Cambridge, Mass.: Perseus Publishing, 2000] of the concentric circles of the planet, with the sun in the center.)
  Understanding such things, the user will understand what a poet is talking about when he writes about moving (or not) to another sphere, or another heaven.
- The stars (also referred to as comets) were thought to have the powers of destiny; "stelle" (stars) and "luci," or "lumi," (lights) usually refer, poetically, to "eyes."
- The image of the sun ("il sole," the center of the universe) is often used as referring to a person, meaning "the most dearly beloved one," rather than to the sun literally, and it is sometimes used poetically in both senses simultaneously.
- "Sospirare," which means "to sigh," has the connotation of "to feel love," "to yearn for love," or "to express or breathe love."
- The word "deh" as an invocative is common in Italian but not satisfactorily translatable into English. As it has the connotation of an expressive plea, I've translated it as "ah," or sometimes as "pray" or "please."
- "War" and "wounding" usually refer to the trials of love, and Love personified or the "archer god (Cupid)" is the culprit. Death, in these contexts, refers to the consummation of love, both painful and full of pleasure.

Almost a century after the International Phonetic Association met to codify the sounds of language into universal symbols (creating an International Phonetic Alphabet), Evelina Colorni's classic *Singers' Italian* was published, in 1970, using IPA as a tool for teaching lyric diction to non-Italian-speaking students who had previously learned by imitating Italian singers or native Italian teachers, coaches, or speakers. At least a half dozen other "diction for singers" books have been published since then, Italian diction is taught or coached at the major opera companies and at universities and schools of music, vocal music is being published with IPA symbols accompanying the texts, and volumes (including this one) of vocal music texts with IPA symbols are being published. Many linguistics sites, as well as IPA fonts, are accessible on the internet.

One result of this wealth of information is that there are some different opinions about some details of Italian pronunciation for singers. Though one can never be faulted for following pronunciation as indicated by phonetics in the finest dictionaries, assumed to reflect the highest form of the language, there are differences in phonetic spelling even among good dictionaries. Unlike the government of Germany, Italy is not currently concerned with establishing "correct" rules of pronunciation or the "correct" way of transcribing the language into phonetics; in fact, the latest edition (the eleventh) of the excellent Italian dictionary by Zingarelli (see *Bibliography*) does not include phonetic spellings.

The non-native singer of Italian must learn to be comfortable with discrepancies found in dictionaries, diction manuals, and published IPA transliterations. And therefore, the user of this book is due an explanation of the decisions I made when transliterating the Italian texts:

1. All unstressed *e's* and *o's* are "closed."
- This choice is based on the dictionary rules for the *spoken* language, with Zingarelli as my authority. Yet I remind the singer that IPA symbols are exactly that – symbols, not scientifically determinable quantities, which when turned into sound, may (and will) change from "closed" to "open," in the case of the *e's* and *o's* (in both stressed and unstressed syllables) in the interest of vocal needs or the best vocalism, or to avoid a "dreaded diphthong." There are also many Italian words (such as "sento," "cielo," "contento") for which, in practice, both "closed" and "open" vowel pronunciations in the stressed syllable are perfectly acceptable.
- As the repertoire in this volume will be sung by different voice types in different keys, the tessitura, hence the degree of adjusting "open" and "closed" vowel sounds, will vary with the individual singer.

2. I am not using the *nasal m* symbol [ɱ], whereby the letter *n* assimilates before the labiodentals *v* or *f* ("inferno" becomes im ˈfɛr no) or before *b*, *p*, or *m* ("un bel dì" becomes um bɛl di). This choice was a practical decision to avoid confusion on the part of the student who might wonder why "un" is transcribed as "um" unlike in any dictionary. However, the non-Italian student is encouraged to use the [ɱ] upon the advice of experts.

3. I am not transcribing as double consonants those which result from *phrasal doubling (raddoppiamento sintattico)* by which, for example, "a morte" becomes am ˈmɔrte, and "a dio" becomes ad ˈdio. The conscientious student should utilize this important aspect of Italian diction according to the rules about it and/or with the guidance of an expert, making phrasal doublings as expressively (or dramatically) called for.

4. I *am* using the symbol [ŋ], an important sound in Italian. The singer who prefers to use the frontal "n" in its place, however, will not be incorrect (as long as no "shadow vowel" is produced by doing so).

5. Regarding syllabication, I am making spaces between each syllable in the hope that seeing each syllable by itself will encourage the singer to lengthen the vowel before a single consonant rather than making an incorrect double consonant, and that when there are two consonants, the first of which is *l*, *m*, *n*, or *r*, the syllabic division will encourage the singer to give more strength to the first of those two consonants.

A special note about the intervocalic "s": The diction "rule" is that a single "s" between two vowels is voiced. But in purest Italian, the single "s" is pronounced unvoiced in many words: così, casa, gelosia, riposa, scherzosa, etc. Since preferred practice among singers is to voice the "s" in such words in the interest of legato, I am transliterating them as having the voiced "s" [z] sound.

• However, words which are combinations of a prefix and a stem beginning with an unvoiced "s" (risolvi, risanare, etc.) retain the unvoiced "s" in singing.

And a word about *ligatures* (the combining of two or more vowel sounds on one musical pitch): Modern editors, especially in America, often add slur marks under these combinations; since this book is of texts only, I have transliterated each word as though it stands alone. When transferring the IPA to the music pages, enlightened choices about which of the "multiple" sounds to stress and which to glide (or even omit) must be made by the singer in each case depending on the musical setting. Again, for the non-native Italian singer decisions about this may best be made by consulting an expert.

There are other many other details regarding the vocalization of Italian texts which simply can not be shown in IPA. For instance, how much should a "rolled r" be rolled? An "r" next to a consonant is never rolled as much as a true double "rr." "Barbaro fato!" would call for a stronger rolled first "r," for dramatic expression, than that in the name "Barbarina," though both "r's" are followed by consonants. Such decisions will provide many challenges, and pleasures, for the singer.

In sum, the IPA is a marvelous tool, but it is only that: a guide toward singing with beautiful Italian lyric diction. Buon viaggio!

Key to the IPA symbols

IPA symbol	approximate sound in American English	as in the Italian word
	Vowels	
[i]	f<u>ee</u>t	mio ['mi o]
[e]	pot<u>a</u>to	vedo ['ve do]
[ɛ]	b<u>e</u>d	bella ['bɛl: la]
[a]	f<u>a</u>ther	amo ['a mo]
[ɔ]	t<u>au</u>t	sposa ['spɔ za]
[o]	t<u>o</u>te	amore [a 'mo ɾe]
[u]	t<u>u</u>be	uno ['u no]
	Semi-vowels (also called Glides)	
[j]	<u>Y</u>ale	pieno ['pjɛ no]
[w]	<u>w</u>atch	quando ['kwan do]
	Plosive consonants (unaspirated)	
[b]	<u>b</u>eg	bene ['bɛ ne]
[p]	<u>p</u>et	petto ['pɛt: to]
[d]	<u>d</u>eep	dire ['di ɾe]

[t]	<u>t</u>op	tono [ˈtɔ no]
[g]	<u>G</u>ordon	gola [ˈgo la]
[k]	<u>k</u>it	caro [ˈka ɾo]

Fricative consonants

[v]	<u>v</u>et	vita [ˈvi ta]
[f]	<u>f</u>it	fare [ˈfa ɾe]
[ʃ]	<u>sh</u>e	scena [ˈʃɛ na]
[s]	<u>s</u>et	sole [ˈso le]
[z]	<u>z</u>ip	rosa [ˈrɔ za]

Lateral consonants

| [l] | <u>l</u>ip | libro [ˈli bro] |
| [ʎ] | mil<u>lio</u>n | figlio [ˈfiʎ: ʎo] |

Vibrant Consonants

| [ɾ] | *British* pronunciation of "ve<u>r</u>y" a flipped "r" | core [ˈkɔ ɾe] |
| [r] | no equivalent in English – a trilled or rolled "r" | crudo [ˈkru do] |

Nasal consonants

[n]	<u>n</u>ame	nome [ˈno me]
[m]	<u>m</u>op	mano [ˈma no]
[ŋ]	a<u>n</u>chor	anche [ˈaŋ ke]
[ɲ]	on<u>io</u>n	sogno [ˈsoɲ: ɲo]

Affricate consonants
(plosive consonants followed by a fricative consonant)

[tʃ]	<u>ch</u>eese	cielo [ˈtʃɛ lo]
[dʒ]	<u>G</u>eorge	gioco [ˈdʒɔ ko]
[dz]	fee<u>ds</u>	zelo [ˈdzɛ lo]
[ts]	fi<u>ts</u>	zio [ˈtsi o]

Other Symbols

[ː] the "lengthening" symbol, indicating a long vowel or consonant – in this book, used [only] to indicate double sounding consonants

[ˈ] primary stress indication: the syllable following the mark is stressed

Abbatini, Antonio Maria (1595-1679)

Teacher and theorist, Abbatini was *maestro di cappella* at Santa Maria Maggiore in Rome, where he trained boy sopranos, from 1640 intermittently until 1677. He published various books of sacred music – masses, psalms, and motets – and a dramatic cantata *Il pianto di Rodomonte*.

Of his three operas composed between 1650 and 1668, *Dal male il bene* is noteable for having two of the earliest examples of the ensemble finale. *La comica del cielo*, about a penitent Spanish actress, has as librettist Giulio Rospigliosi, pope Clement IX, in whose service Abbatini became employed in 1667.

[1, 2, 46]
from: *La comica del cielo (1668)*
character: *Baltasara*

Giulio Rospigliosi

'kwan to ɛ 'bɛl: lo il 'mio di 'lɛt: to
Quanto è bello il mio diletto
How handsome is my loved one

'kwan to	ɛ	'bɛl: lo	il	'mi o	di 'lɛt: to	'kwan to	ɛ	'dol tʃe	a	ki	la 'do ɾa
Quanto	**è**	**bello**	**il**	**mio**	**diletto,**	**quanto**	**è**	**dolce**	**a**	**chi**	**l'adora!**
how much	is	handsome	the	my	loved one	how much	is	sweet	to	the one who	him adores

How handsome my loved one is, how sweet he is to the one who adores him!

un	'su o	'lam po	i	'tʃe li	in 'dɔ ɾa	un	'su o	'rad: dʒo	'ar de	'oɲ: ɲi	'pɛt: to
Un	**suo**	**lampo**	**i**	**cieli**	**indora,**	**un**	**suo**	**raggio**	**arde**	**ogni**	**petto.**
a	his	light	the	heavens	gilds	a	his	ray	enflames	every	breast

His light gilds the heavens, his ray enflames every breast.

'sot: to	'du e	lu 'tʃen ti	'dʒi ɾi	'rɔ ze	e	'dʒiʎ: ʎi	in	'lu i	sod: 'dʒor na no
Sotto	**due**	**lucenti**	**giri**	**rose**	**e**	**gigli**	**in**	**lui**	**soggiornano,**
beneath	two	shining	eyes	roses	and	lilies	in	him	reside

Beneath his shining eyes roses and lilies dwell;

i	dʒa 'tʃin ti	e di	dzaf: 'fi ɾi	le	'su e	'ma ni	e	il	'se no	a 'dor na no
i	**giacinti**	**ed i**	**zaffiri**	**le**	**sue**	**mani**	**e**	**il**	**seno**	**adornano.**
the	hyacinths	and the	sapphires	the	his	hands	and	his	breast	adorn

hyacinths and sapphires adorn his hands and his breast.

tra	i	'fiʎ: ʎi	da 'da mo	si	'bɛl: lo	non	ɛ
Tra	**i**	**figli**	**d'Adamo**	**sì**	**bello**	**non**	**è;**
among	the	sons	of Adam	such a	fine one	not	is

Among the sons of Adam there is not a finer one;

'lu i	'tʃer ko	'lu i	'kja mo	ke	'rɛg: ga	il	'mi o	pjɛ
lui	**cerco,**	**lui**	**chiamo,**	**che**	**regga**	**il**	**mio**	**piè.**
him	I seek	to him	I call	that	he may guide	the	my	foot

I search for him [and] I call to him, that he may guide my way.

'eʎ: ʎi	ɛ	sol	del	'mi o	kɔr	'lu ni ko	od: 'dʒɛt: to
Egli	**è**	**sol**	**del**	**mio**	**cor**	**l'unico**	**oggetto!**
he	is	sole	of the	my	heart	the unique	object

He is the single, only object of my heart!

GL: **Adamo**

Agostini [Augustini], Pietro Simone (c.1635-1680)

Agostini led a notorious personal life. He studied music in Ferrara with Mazzaferrata and then joined the military, serving in Crete in the war against the Turks, for which he was made a Knight of the Golden Spur.

By 1664 he was in Genoa, where he was commissioned to write works for the Teatro del Falcone and also invited to compose for the Teatro Ducale in Milan. He was banned from Genoa for his involvement with a nun.

In the early 1670's he went to Rome, winning the prestigious post of music director at Sant'Agnese in the Piazza Navona. In 1679, the year before his death, he was invited to Parma to be *maestro di cappella* to Ranuccio II, the Duke of Parma.

Agostini was highly regarded as a composer, particularly for his cantatas, of which he wrote about thirty.

[57]

non sɔ 'ko me 'lal ma 'mi a
Non so come l'alma mia
I know not how my soul

non	sɔ	'ko me	'lal ma	'mi a	pju	re 'spi ɾi	in	'kwes to	'se no
Non	**so**	**come**	**l'alma**	**mia**	**più**	**respiri**	**in**	**questo**	**seno**
not	I know	how	the soul	mine	more	may breathe	in	this	breast

I know not how my soul still breathes within this breast

sa li 'men to	ʎi	ɛ	il	ve 'le no	du ne 'tɛr na	dʒe lo 'zi a
s'alimento	**gli**	**è**	**il**	**veleno**	**d'un'eterna**	**gelosia.**
if nourishment	to it	is	the	poison	of an eternal	jealousy

when its nourishment is the poison of an eternal jealousy.

per 'ke	a 'mor	se	fe 'ri	il	'kɔ ɾe	non	ben 'dɔ	kwe 'stɔk: ki	'mjɛ i
Perché	**Amor,**	**se**	**ferì**	**il**	**core,**	**non**	**bendò**	**quest'occhi**	**miei?**
why	Love	if	it wounded	the	heart	not	blindfolded	these eyes	mine

Why did Love, when it wounded my heart, not blindfold these eyes of mine?

ko 'zi	'skɔr dʒer	non	po 'trɛ i	i	'mjɛ i	'tɔr ti	e	il	'mi o	do 'lo ɾe
Così	**scorger**	**non**	**potrei**	**i**	**miei**	**torti**	**e**	**il**	**mio**	**dolore.**
thus	to perceive	not	I would be able	the	my	wrongs	and	the	my	sorrow

Then I would not be aware of my wrongs and my sorrow.

GL: **Amor**

Albinoni, Tomaso Giovanni (1671-1751)

Violinist and teacher, Albinoni spent most of his life in Venice, where he was born and where he died. Outside of Venice he visited Florence, where he was concertmaster for the premiere of his opera *Griselda*, and Munich, where he oversaw successful productions of *I veri amici* and *Il trionfo d'amore* during festivities surrounding the marriage of the electoral prince Karl Albrecht to the younger daughter of the late Emperor Joseph I.

As the eldest son of a prosperous stationer and manufacturer of playing cards, Tomaso would have been expected to inherit the responsibilities of the family business; fortunately for posterity, father Antonio's will, at his death in 1709, left the business management principally to two younger sons, reflecting Tomaso's total commitment to music by that time.

Albinoni had many patrons, and his output was huge: nine collections of instrumental works (sonatas, sinfonias, concertos), more than fifty operas, and at least forty-five solo cantatas.

[65]

a ˈmor ˈsɔr te de ˈsti no
Amor, Sorte, Destino!
Love, Fate, Destiny!

a ˈmor   ˈsɔr te   de ˈsti no   ˈtrɔp po   ˈfjɛ ri   ne ˈmi tʃi   ˈo ɾa   vi   ˈskɔ pro
Amor,   Sorte,   Destino!   Troppo   fieri   nemici,   ora   vi   scopro!
love   fate   destiny   too   cruel   enemies   now   you   I discover
Love, Fate, Destiny – now I discover you, enemies too cruel!

miŋ ko ɾadː ˈdʒia ste   un ˈtɛm po   a da ˈmar   ˈklɔ ɾi   or   ˈklɔ ɾi   a   me   toʎː ˈʎe te
M'incoraggiaste   un tempo   ad amar   Clori;   or   Clori   a   me   togliete,
me you encouraged   once   to to love   Clori   now   Clori   from   me   you take away
You once encouraged me to love Clori; now you take Clori away from me –

ˈan tsi   me   di   me   ˈstesː so   ˈo ɾa   pri ˈva te
anzi   me   di   me   stesso   ora   private.
in fact   me   of   me   myself   now   you deprive
in fact, you deprive me now of my very self.

pur   a ˈve te   il   tri ˈon fo   di   ve ˈder   su   kwe ˈstɔkː ki   il   ˈpjan to   a ˈfju mi
Pur   avete   il   trionfo   di   veder   su   quest'occhi   il   pianto   a fiumi;
indeed   you have   the   triumph   of   to see   upon   these eyes   the   weeping   like rivers
Indeed, you have the triumph of seeing rivers of tears from these eyes,

e   aŋ ˈkor   non   vi pla ˈka te
e   ancor   non   vi placate?
and   still   not   you are placated
and still you are not satisfied?

a ˈmor   de ˈsti no   ˈsɔr te   ren ˈde te mi   il   ˈmi o   bɛn   o   pur   la   ˈmɔr te
Amor,   Destino,   Sorte!   Rendetemi   il   mio   ben   o   pur   la   morte!
Love   Destiny   Fate   give back to me   the   my   dear one   or   else   the   death
Love, Destiny, Fate – give me back my dear one, or [give me] death!

o pur = (mod.) oppure

mɛ   pju   ˈka ɾo   o   ˈdi o   bam ˈbi no   ˈdelː la   ˈvi ta
M'è   più   caro,   o   dio   bambino,   della   vita
to me is   more   dear   o   god   child   than the   life
It is dearer to me, o child-god *[Cupid]*, than life

star   vi ˈtʃi no   al   ˈmi o   ˈdol tʃe   a ˈma to   bɛn
star   vicino   al   mio   dolce   amato   ben.
to be   near   to the   my   sweet   beloved   dear one
to be near my sweet beloved dear one.

se   da   ˈlu i   lon ˈtan   sen ˈmɔ ɾe   il   ˈmi o   afː ˈflitː to   a ˈman te   ˈkɔ ɾe
Se   da   lui   lontan   sen more,   il   mio   afflitto   amante   core
if   from   her   far   itself dies   the   my   afflicted   loving   heart
If, far from her, my afflicted, loving heart dies,

Though "lui" properly translates as "him," in this context Clori is a female and "lui" refers to the (masculine) "dolce amato ben" – hence masculine in the grammar but feminine in the translation.

ne   go ˈder   pwɔ   un   di   se ˈɾen
né   goder   può   un   dì   seren.
not   to enjoy   it can   one   day   serene
it cannot enjoy a single peaceful day.

ma   o i 'mɛ   kin 'van   so 'spi ɾo   'i o   'pjaŋ go   in 'va no
Ma   ohimè   ch'invan   sospiro;   io   piango   invano,
but   alas   [that] in vain   I sigh   I   I weep   in vain
But alas, I sigh in vain, I weep in vain;

e   a 'mor   're zo   i nu 'ma no   'gɔ de   del   'mi o   mar 'tir   del   'mi o   kor 'dɔʎ: ʎo
e   Amor   reso   inumano   gode   del   mio   martir,   del   mio   cordoglio,
and   Love   rendered   inhuman   enjoys   of the   my   suffering   of the   my   grief
and Love, rendered inhuman, enjoys my suffering [and] my grief

've de   ke   kon   lin 'tʃɛn so   din fo 'ka ti   so 'spi ɾi
vede   che   con   l'incenso   d'infocati   sospiri
sees   that   with   the incense   of fiery   sighs
[and] sees that with the incense of burning sighs

'ɔf: fro   a   un   'nu me   kɛ   'lun dʒi   la   'vit: ti ma   fe 'del   del   'dʒen jo   'mi o
offro   a   un   nume   ch'è   lungi   la   vittima   fedel   del   genio   mio.
I offer   to   a   deity   that is   far away   the   victim   faithful   of the   spirit   my
I am offering to a god that is far away the faithful victim – my spirit.

lo   've de   e   'lu i   sen 'ri de   e   pren 'dɛn do   il   'mi o   dwɔl   a   'sker no
Lo   vede   e   lui   sen ride.   E   prendendo   il   mio   duol   a   scherno
it   he sees   and   he   laughs about it   and   taking   the   my   sorrow   in   mockery
He [Love] sees it and laughs about it. And, taking my sorrow in mockery

e   'dʒɔ ko   'sɛm pre   pju   da   tor 'men to   al   'mi o   gran   'fɔ ko
e   gioco   sempre   più   dà   tormento   al   mio   gran   foco.
and   game   always   more   gives   torment   to the   my   great   ardor
and jest, he gives ever more torment to my great ardor.

sil   'mi o   pe 'nar   se il   so spi 'rar   ben 'da to   a 'mor   tɛ   'gra to
S'il   mio   penar,   se il   sospirar,   bendato   Amor,   t'è   grato,
if the   my   suffering   if the   sighing   blindfolded   Love   to you is   welcome
If my suffering and sighing is welcome to you, blindfolded Love,

kon 'tʃɛ di   al 'men   ke   del   'mi o   bɛn   non   'prɔ vi   il   kɔr   iŋ 'gra to
concedi   almen   che   del   mio   ben   non   provi   il   cor   ingrato.
grant   at least   that   of the   my   dear one   not   I may feel   the   heart   ungrateful
grant at least that I may not feel the ungrateful heart of my beloved.

GL: **Amor, Clori**

☙

[65]

ki   non   sa   'kwan to   i nu 'ma no
Chi   non   sa   quanto   inumano
Whoever does not know how inhuman

ki   non   sa   'kwan to   i nu 'ma no   'si a   in   un   'pɛt: to   il   'di o   da 'mor
Chi   non   sa   quanto   inumano   sia   in   un   petto   il   Dio   d'Amor,
Whoever   not   knows   how much   inhuman   may be   in   a   breast   the   God   of Love
Whoever does not know how inhuman the God of Love may be in a breast,

'kwan to 'kru do il 'fɔ ko in 'sa no lo di 'man di a 'kwes to kɔr
quanto **crudo** **il** **foco** **insano,** **lo** **dimandi** **a** **questo** **cor.**
how cruel the fire insane it let ask to this heart
how cruel his insane fire [is], should ask this heart.

dimandi = domandi

ʎi di 'ra ve ɾi 'tjɛ ro ke non si 'tɔ sto dun di 'vin sem 'bjan te ri 'ma ze pri dʒo 'njɛ ɾo
Gli **dirà** **veritiero** **che non sì tosto** **d'un** **divin** **sembiante** **rimase** **prigioniero,**
to him it will tell truthfully that not as soon as of a divine countenance it was prisoner
It will tell him truthfully that as soon as it [this heart] became prisoner of a divine countenance

ke 'ma i 'lar va di 'bɛ ne ma ske 'rɔ le 'su e 'pe ne
che **mai** **larva** **di** **bene** **mascherò** **le** **sue** **pene,**
that never semblance of well-being it masked the its sufferings
nevermore did a semblance of happiness mask its sufferings...

'koɲ ɲi a u 'rɔ ɾa no 'vɛl: la fu pre 'kor sa da 'swɔ i 'kal di so 'spi ɾi
ch'ogni **aurora** **novella** **fu** **precorsa** **da** **suoi** **caldi** **sospiri,**
that every dawn new was preceded by its hot sighs
that every new dawn was preceded by its burning sighs

e 'doɲ: ɲa u 'ra ta 'stel: la dal 'su o pe 'rɛn: ne 'pjan to
ed ogn'aurata **stella** **dal** **suo** **perenne** **pianto,**
and every gilded star by the its incessant tears
and every golden star by its incessant weeping...

ke 'lal ma kin se 'kju ze non fu 'ma i 'su a
che **l'alma** **ch'in** **se** **chiuse** **non** **fu** **mai** **sua,**
that the soul which in itself closed not was ever its
that the soul which it enclosed never belonged to it,

ma sol del 'suo do 'lo ɾe epː 'pur le 'lɔ di 'tɛsː so
ma **sol** **del** **suo** **dolore.** **Eppur** **le** **lodi** **tesso**
but only of the its sorrow And yet the praises I sing
but [rather] only [belonged to] its sorrow. And yet I sing praises

al 'mi o ne 'mi ko a 'mo ɾe 'mi ze ro 'laŋ gwo e da do 'ɾar non 'tʃesː so
al **mio** **nemico** **Amore,** **misero** **languo,** **e** **d'adorar** **non** **cesso?**
to the my enemy Love wretched I languish and of to adore not I cease
to my enemy Love; wretched, I languish, and I do not stop adoring?

'tan to 'dol tʃe ɛ 'kwelː la 'pja ga 'ka pre al kɔr pu 'pilː la 'va ga
Tanto **dolce** **è** **quella** **piaga,** **ch'apre** **al** **cor** **pupilla** **vaga,**
so sweet is that wound which opens to the heart eye pretty
So sweet is that wound which a pretty eye opens in the heart

kɛ di 'lɛtː to 'aŋ ko il pe 'nar
ch'è **diletto** **anco** **il** **penar.**
that is pleasure even the suffering
that even suffering is pleasure.

anco = (mod.) anche

'i o lo sɔ ke sebː 'bɛn 'ar do di 'ku pi do il 'fjɛ ro 'dar do
Io **lo** **so,** **che** **sebben** **ardo,** **di** **Cupido** **il** **fiero** **dardo,**
I it know that even though I burn of Cupid the cruel arrow
I know that, even though I burn from Cupid's cruel arrow,

pur	mɛ	ˈfɔr tsa		la do ˈrar
pur	**m'è forza**			**l'adorar.**
yet	to me it is necessary			him to adore

still I must adore him *[Cupid]*.

ko ˈzi	si	ˈkan dʒa	ˈa i	ˈra i	dun	ˈva go	ˈvi zo	lin ˈfɛr no	ˈdel: le	ˈpe ne
Così	**si**	**cangia**	**ai**	**rai**	**d'un**	**vago**	**viso**	**l'inferno**	**delle**	**pene**
thus	itself	changes	at the	eyes	of a	beautiful	face	the hell	of the	sufferings

in	pa ɾa ˈdi zo
in	**Paradiso.**
into	paradise

Thus is the hell of suffering changed into paradise by the eyes of a beautiful face.

𝒢ℒ: **Amor[e], Cupido**

&

[65]

dal: ˈlar ko dun bɛl ˈtʃiʎ: ʎo
Dall'arco d'un bel ciglio
From the bow of a beautiful eyebrow

dal: ˈlar ko	dun	bɛl	ˈtʃiʎ: ʎo	sa dʒit: ˈta ɾjo	da ˈmo ɾe	sem pli ˈtʃet: to	gar ˈdzon
Dall'arco	**d'un**	**bel**	**ciglio,**	**sagittario**	**d'amore,**	**semplicetto**	**garzon**
from the bow	of a	beautiful	eyebrow	archer	of love	simple	boy

From the bow of a beautiful eyebrow, archer of love *[Cupid]*, a simple boy

laŋ ˈgwi a	tra ˈfit: to	ne	tro ˈvan do	pje ˈta de	nel: la do ˈra ta	i ˈrɛ ne
languia	**trafitto,**	**né**	**trovando**	**pietade**	**nell'adorata**	**Irene**
was languishing	wounded	not	finding	compassion	in the adored	Irene

> *languia = languiva*
> *pietade = (mod.) pietà*

was wounded and languishing, not finding compassion from his adored Irene

ˈdel: le	ˈsu e	a ˈtʃer be	ˈpe ne	e	del	ˈsu o	im: ˈmɛn so	ar ˈdo ɾe
delle	**sue**	**acerbe**	**pene**	**e**	**del**	**suo**	**immenso**	**ardore;**
of the	his	bitter	pains	and	of the	his	immense	ardor

for his bitter pains and his immense ardor;

so spi ˈro zo	e	do ˈlɛn te	un	ˈdʒor no	in	ˈta li	ˈnɔ te	si laɲ: ˈɲɔ	kon
sospiroso	**e**	**dolente,**	**un**	**giorno**	**in**	**tali**	**note**	**si lagnò**	**con**
sighing	and	sorrowful	one	day	in	such	notes	himself complained	to

lar ˈtʃer	ˈnu me	iŋ kle ˈmɛn te
l'arcier	**nume**	**inclemente:**
the archer	deity	harsh

sighing and sorrowful, one day he complained to the harsh archer god in such a manner:

ke	tu	ˈmab: bja	iŋ ka te ˈna to	son	kon ˈtɛn to	o	ˈdi o	da ˈmor
Che	**tu**	**m'abbia**	**incatenato,**	**son**	**contento,**	**o**	**Dio**	**d'Amor.**
that	you	me have	put in chains	I am	content	o	God	of Love

"I am content that you have fettered me, o God of Love.

ma kil kɔr 'vɔʎ: ʎi zbra 'nar mi e le 'pja ge rinː no 'var mi
Ma ch'il cor vogli sbranarmi e le piaghe rinnovarmi,
but that the heart you wish to tear to pieces me and the wounds to renew me

But that you wish to tear my heart to pieces and renew my wounds

ɛ le 'strɛ mo del ri 'gor
è l'estremo del rigor.
is the extreme of the severity

is the height of severity.

si 'mi a 'bɛlː la ti 'ran: na kwa 'lor 'sɛn tsa pje 'ta mi 'vi bri il 'gwar do
Sì, mia bella tiranna, qual'or senza pietà mi vibri il guardo,
yes my beautiful tyrant whenever without pity to me you cast the glance

Yes, my beautiful tyrant, whenever you cast a pitiless glance at me,

a kwe 'sta ni ma e 'zaŋ gwe mi ze 'ra bil tro 'fɛ o di 'tu a fje 'retː tsa
a quest'anima esangue, miserabil trofeo di tua fierezza,
at this soul lifeless miserable trophy of your cruelty

at this lifeless soul, miserable trophy of your cruelty,

'vi bri 'u na 'nwɔ va 'pja ga 'on de a 'spɛr sa di 'saŋ gwe
vibri una nuova piaga, onde aspersa di sangue
you hurl a new wound from which splattered with blood

you hurl a new wound from which, splattered with blood,

'su i kon 'fin 'delː la 'vi ta da 'mjɛ i 'palː li di 'lu mi sta per fudː 'dʒir
sui confin della vita da miei pallidi lumi stà per fuggir
its limit of the life from my pallid eyes is about to to flee

it [my soul], on the edge of life, is about to flee from my pallid eyes

in 'ma ske ɾa di 'pjan to 'kwan do men 'fjɛ ɾa o 'bɛlː la
in maschera di pianto, quando men fiera, o bella,
in mask of tears unless less cruel o beautiful one

in a mask of tears unless, less cruel, o beautiful one,

la 'dɔʎː ʎa ke makː 'kɔ ɾa non radː dol 'tʃisː si e din mer 'tʃe
la doglia che m'accora non raddolcissi, ed in mercé
the pain that me grieves not you may sweeten and in mercy

you sweeten the pain that grieves me and, in mercy,

non 'do ni un 'tu o 'lam po a mo 'ro zo a ki ta 'do ɾa
non doni un tuo lampo amoroso a chi t'adora.
not you may give a your flash loving to the one who you adores

grant a loving glance to the one who adores you.

'va go a 'ma bi le 'mi o 'vi zo
Vago amabile mio viso,
pretty pleasing my face

My pretty, pleasing face,

'laʃː ʃa al 'men ke per te 'sɛn ta il pja 'tʃer del 'mi o pe 'nar
lascia almen che per te senta il piacer del mio penar.
let at least that for you I may feel the pleasure of the my suffering

at least allow me to feel the pleasure of suffering for you.

'laʃ: ʃa	o	'ka ɾa	e	ti ram: 'men ta	ke	non	pwɔ	nel	pa ɾa 'di zo
Lascia,	**o**	**cara,**	**e**	**ti rammenta**	**che**	**non**	**può**	**nel**	**Paradiso**
let	o	dear	and	yourself remember	that	not	is able	in the	Paradise

la	fje 'ret: tsa	'ma i	reɲ: 'ɲar
la	**fierezza**	**mai**	**regnar.**
the	cruelty	ever	to reign

Allow that, o dear one, and remember that cruelty can never reign in Paradise."

GL: **Amor**

ॐ

[65]

del 'kja ɾo 'ri o
Del chiaro rio
Of the clear brook

del	'kja ɾo	'ri o	il	mor mo 'ri o
Del	**chiaro**	**rio**	**il**	**mormorio**
of the	clear	brook	the	murmur

| rio (lit.) = rivo, ruscello |

The murmuring of the clear brook

tra	le	di 'lɛt: te	'su e	'fre sker 'bet: te	'ri zo	ɛ	da 'mor
tra	**le**	**dilette**	**sue**	**fresch'erbette**	**riso**	**è**	**d'amor.**
among	the	delightful	its	fresh grasses	laughter	is	of love

among its delightful fresh grasses is the laughter of love.

e	pur	'kwe i	'ri vi	di	'se no	'pri vi	son	'sɛn tsa	kɔr
E	**pur**	**quei**	**rivi**	**di**	**seno**	**privi**	**son**	**senza**	**cor.**
and	yet	those	streams	of	cove	lacking	are	without	heart

And yet those streams, lacking a cove, have no heart.

| *The poet puns with the word "seno"(= cove, or inlet, in the above context and breast, or bosom, in the next line).* |

e	tu	kru 'dɛl	'mi a	'fil: li	'ka i	'se no	e	kɔr	non	'sɛn ti
E	**tu,**	**crudel**	**mia**	**Filli,**	**ch'hai**	**seno**	**e**	**cor,**	**non**	**senti**
and	you	cruel	my	Filli	who you have	breast	and	heart	not	you feel

And you, my cruel Filli, who have [both] breast and heart, feel not

'fjam: ma	da 'mor	ne	'ku ɾi	'del: la	'fjam: ma	'ki o	'sɔf: fro	il	'fje ɾo	ar 'do ɾe
fiamma	**d'amor,**	**né**	**curi**	**della**	**fiamma**	**ch'io**	**soffro**	**il**	**fiero**	**ardore.**
flame	of love	nor	you care	of the	flame	that I	I suffer	the	fierce	ardor

the flame of love nor care that I suffer the fierce ardor of the flame.

kal 'men	dʒak: 'ke	ri 'sɔl vi	di	non	pje 'gar ti	iŋ 'gra ta
Ch'almen	**giacché**	**risolvi**	**di**	**non**	**piegarti,**	**ingrata,**
[that] at least	since	you resolve	of	not	to yield yourself	ungrateful

At least, since you resolve not to submit, ungrateful one,

ta 'lor	mi	kon tʃe 'des: si	di	po 'ter mi	fis: 'sar	ne	'two i	'bɛ i	'lu mi
talor	**mi**	**concedessi**	**di**	**potermi**	**fissar**	**ne'**	**tuoi**	**bei**	**lumi,**
sometimes	to me	you would grant	of	to be able me	to fix	on	your	beautiful	eyes

allow me at times to fix my gaze upon your beautiful eyes

kin   ri mi 'rar   'kwel: le   lu 'tʃɛn ti   'stel: le
ch'in   rimirar   quelle   lucenti   stelle
that in   contemplating   those   shining   stars
so that, in contemplating those shining stars *[eyes]*,

a 'vri a   'tre gwa   kwel dwɔl ke   mi   tor 'men ta
avria   tregua   quel duol che   mi   tormenta,
should have   respite   that grief which me   torments
the grief which torments me should have relief,

> *avria = (mod.)*
> *avrebbe*

e   'lal ma   nel   pe 'nar   sa 'ri a   kon 'tɛn ta
e   l'alma   nel   penar   saria   contenta.
and   the soul   in the suffering should be content
and my soul should be content in suffering.

> *saria = (mod.)*
> *sarebbe*

'sɛn tsa   of: 'fe za   del   'tu o   'bɛl: lo   'laʃ: ʃa   'dir ti   al 'men   'se i   'mi a
Senza   offesa   del   tuo   bello   lascia   dirti   almen   sei   mia.
without   offence   of the your   beauty   let   to tell you at least you are mine
Without offending your beauty, at least let me tell you [that] you are mine.

'dim: mi   'po i   ke   mi   'vwɔi   'spɛn to   ka   mo 'ri re   'i o   ɔon   kon 'tɛn to
Dimmi   poi   che   mi   vuoi   spento   ch'a   morire   io   son   contento
tell me   then   that me   you wish dead   because to to die   I   am   content
Tell me then that you wish me dead, for I am content to die

sol   di   'dɔʎ: ʎa   a 'tʃɛr ba   e   'ri a
sol   di   doglia   acerba   e   ria.
only of   grief   bitter   and cruel
of bitter and cruel grief alone.

ri 'spon di   o   'mi a   ti 'ran: na   'njɛ gi   di   kom pja 'tʃer mi   af: 'fe   'ka i 'tɔr to
Rispondi,   o   mia   tiranna.   Nieghi   di   compiacermi;   affé   ch'hai torto,
respond   o   my   tyrant   you refuse of   to satisfy me   in faith [that] you are wrong
Reply, o my tyrant. You refuse to satisfy me; in faith, you are wrong,

e 'dɛ   tri 'on fo   vil   vo 'ler mi   'mɔr to
ed è   trionfo   vil   volermi   morto.
and it is triumph   vile to wish me   dead
and it is a wicked triumph to wish me dead.

GL: **Filli**

[12, 53] In [53] is the Aria **In amar bellezza altera**, but not its preceding Recitative.

'fat: to   ber 'saʎ: ʎo   e 'tɛr no   in a 'mar   bel: 'let: tsa   al 'tɛ ra
Fatto bersaglio eterno...In amar bellezza altera
Eternal target...In loving proud beauty

'fat: to   ber 'saʎ: ʎo   e 'tɛr no   'del: li   'stra li   da 'mo re   ke   'fa i
Fatto   bersaglio   eterno   delli   strali   d'Amore,   che   fai?
made   target   eternal   of the   arrows   of Love   what you do
Eternal target of Love's *[Cupid's]* arrows, what are you doing,

> *delli = (mod.) degli*

ke   'pɛn si   e   ke   ri 'sɔl vi   o   'kɔ ɾe
che   pensi?   e   che   risolvi   o   core?
what   you think   and   what   you resolve   o   heart
what are you thinking, and what do you resolve, o heart?

kon   so 'a vi   lu 'ziŋ ge   a 'mi ka   'spɛ ne   pro 'met: te   'al: la   'tu a   'fe de
Con   soavi   lusinghe   amica   spene   promette   alla   tua   fede
with   sweet   enticements   friendly   hope   promises   to the   your   faithfullness

spene (poet.) =
speme (lit.) =
speranza

a mo 'ro za   mer 'tʃe de
amorosa   mercede,
loving   reward
With sweet enticements friendly hope promises loving reward for your faithfullness;

ma   tra   kon 'ti nu e   'pe ne   in 'tan to   oɲ: 'ɲor   tad: 'dʒi ɾi
ma   tra   continue   pene   intanto   ognor   t'aggiri,
but   among   continuous   sufferings   meanwhile   always   you wander
but meanwhile you ever wander among continuous sufferings,

e   i   pro 'mes: si   kon 'tɛn ti   aŋ 'kor   non   'mi ɾi
e   i   promessi   contenti   ancor   non   miri.
and   the   promised   happinesses   still   not   you see
and you do not yet see the promised happiness.

dɛ   'vo i   per   'luŋ ge   'prɔ ve   a 'man ti   e 'spɛr ti
Deh   voi   per   lunghe   prove   amanti   esperti,
ah   you   through   long   tests   lovers   expert
Ah, you, through long trials expert lovers,

I changed the printed "noi" to "voi," as
it makes more sense in context; "noi"
could easily have been a copying error.

per   sen 'tjɛ ɾi   si   in 'tʃɛr ti   kon 'fu zo   ri mi 'ran do   il   'pas: so   'mi o
per   sentieri   sì   incerti   confuso   rimirando   il   passo   mio;
through   paths   so   uncertain   confused   looking again   the   step   my
through paths so uncertain confusedly looking back upon my steps –

'di te mi   per pje 'ta   ke   far   dɛd: 'dʒi o
ditemi   per pietà   che   far   deggio?
tell me   for pity's sake   what   to do   I ought?
tell me, for pity's sake, what should I do?

in   a 'mar   bel: 'let: tsa   al 'tɛ ɾa   'te me   e   'spɛ ɾa   'kwe sto   'kɔ ɾe
In   amar   bellezza   altera,   teme   e   spera   questo   core.
in   loving   beauty   proud   fears   and   hopes   this   heart
In loving proud beauty, this heart fears and hopes.

mi   lu 'ziŋ ga   e   mi   spa 'vɛn ta   mi   kon 'so la   e   mi   tor 'men ta
Mi   lusinga   e   mi   spaventa,   mi   consola   e   mi   tormenta
me   entices   and   me   frightens   me   consoles   and   me   torments

in un 'tɛm po   il   'su o   splen 'do ɾe
in un tempo   il   suo   splendore.
at one time   the   its   splendor
Its splendor entices me and frightens me, consoles and torments me all at once.

GL: **Amore**

৯

[65]

'fil: li 'kjɛ di al 'mi o 'kɔ ɾe
Filli, chiedi al mio core
Filli, you ask my heart

'fil: li	'kjɛ di	al	'mi o	'kɔ ɾe	ke	'ta mi		e	ti do 'la tri
Filli,	**chiedi**	**al**	**mio**	**core**	**che**	**t'ami**		**e**	**t'idolatri,**
Filli	you ask	to the	my	heart	that	you I should love		and	you I should idolize

Filli, you ask my heart to love you and worship you,

ma	tʃɔ	ke	pju	sap: 'pret: tsa	in	a 'mor	non	os: 'sɛr vi
ma	**ciò**	**che**	**più**	**s'apprezza**	**in**	**amor**	**non**	**osservi:**
but	that	which	most	one esteems	in	love	not	you observe

but you do not observe that which is most valued in love:

la	'fe de	la	ko 'stan tsa	ke	di	ma 'tʃiɲ ɲo	aŋ 'kor	i	'kɔ ɾi	'spet: tsa
la	**fede,**	**la**	**costanza,**	**che**	**di**	**macigno**	**ancor**	**i**	**cori**	**spezza,**
the	faith	the	constancy	which	of	rock	even	the	hearts	breaks

fidelity [and] constancy, which break even hearts of stone,

'so no	a	te	'no mi	iɲ: 'ɲɔ ti
sono	**a**	**te**	**nomi**	**ignoti.**
are	to	you	names	unknown

are unknown to you.

e	pur	'fe de	e	ko 'stan tsa	kwan din 'sjɛ me	non	'reɲ: ɲa no	in	u 'nal ma
E	**pur**	**fede**	**e**	**costanza,**	**quand'insieme**	**non**	**regnano**	**in**	**un'alma,**
and	yet	faith	and	constancy	when together	not	they reign	in	a soul

And yet when fidelity and constancy do not reign together in a soul,

'per de	a 'mor	la	'su a	'fɔr tsa	ne	'ma i	da 'mor	pwɔ	ri por 'tar	la	'pal ma
perde	**amor**	**la**	**sua**	**forza,**	**né**	**mai**	**d'amor**	**può**	**riportar**	**la**	**palma.**
loses	love	the	its	power	nor	ever	of love	can	to win	the	palm

love loses its power, and [one] can never have love's victory.

'sɛn tsa	il	'van to	di	'kan di da	'fe de	'kjɛ di	in 'va no	al	'tu o	'bɛ ne	ke	'ta mi
Senza	**il**	**vanto**	**di**	**candida**	**fede,**	**chiedi**	**invano**	**al**	**tuo**	**bene**	**che**	**t'ami.**
without	the	merit	of	pure	faith	you ask	in vain	to	your	dear one	that	you he love

Without the merit of true fidelity, you ask in vain for your dear one to love you.

ma	se	'ʎɔf: fre	·	il	'tu o	'kɔ ɾe	la	'fe de
Ma	**se**	**gl'offre**		**il**	**tuo**	**core**	**la**	**fede,**
but	if	to him offers		the	your	heart	the	faith

But if your heart offers him fidelity,

pwɔ	spe 'rar	dot: te 'ner	tʃɔ	ke	'bra mi
può	**sperar**	**d'ottener**	**ciò**	**che**	**brami.**
it can	to hope	of to obtain	that	which	you desire

it can hope to obtain what you desire.

la	'fe de	ɛ	un	'tʃɛr to	iŋ 'kan to	ke	nel: la 'ma to	'se no
La	**fede**	**è**	**un**	**certo**	**incanto,**	**che**	**nell'amato**	**seno**
the	faith	is	a	certain	charm	which	in the beloved	breast

Fidelity is a certain charm which, in the beloved's breast,

afː faʃː 'ʃi na la 'men te e anː 'nɔ da il 'kɔ ɾe
affascina la mente e annoda il core,
enchants the mind and ties together the heart
enchants the mind and binds the heart,

e dɛ il 'latː te pri 'mjɛr ke 'sudː dʒe a 'mo ɾe
ed è il latte primier che sugge amore.
and it is the milk first which sucks love
and it is the first milk which love suckles.

'a ma pur 'kwan to 'sa i 'strudː dʒi ti 'kwan to 'vwɔ i
Ama pur quanto sai, struggiti quanto vuoi:
love then how much you know how pine away how much you wish
Love as much as you know how, pine away as much as you wish;

se la ka 'te na 'tu a 'fe de non 'van ta
se la catena tua fede non vanta,
if the chain your faith not boasts
if your obligation does not boast of fidelity,

il 'tu o a 'mor non a 'latː tʃo e non iŋ 'kan ta
il tuo amor non ha laccio e non incanta.
the your love not has knot and not charms
your love has no bond and will not charm.

im 'pa ɾa a ser 'bar 'fe de se 'va i tʃer 'kan do fe
Impara a serbar fede se vai cercando fé.
learn to to keep faith if you go searching for fidelity
Learn to keep faith if you seek fidelity,

fé = (poetic) fede	

ke 'mɛr ta ben ri 'stɔ ɾo ki al 'ka ɾo 'su o te 'zɔ ɾo
Ché merta ben ristoro chi al caro suo tesoro
because merits well compensation he who to the dear his treasure

'fi do in a 'mor si 'djɛ
fido in amor si diè.
devoted in love oneself gave
for he who has given himself devotedly in love to his dear treasure well deserves compensation.

GL: **Filli**

&

[65]

lon ta 'nan tsa kru 'dɛl
Lontananza crudel
Cruel separation

lon ta 'nan tsa kru 'dɛl mi 'skwar tʃi il 'kɔ ɾe
Lontananza crudel, mi squarci il core.
separation cruel me you tear apart the heart.
Cruel separation, you tear my heart apart.

alː 'la u ɾa ke re 'spi ɾo alː 'lon da ke ri 'mi ɾo 'di ko
All'aura che respiro, all'onda che rimiro, dico:
to the air that I breathe to the wave that I gaze at I say
To the air I breathe, to the waves at which I gaze, I say,

dal	'mi o	do 'lor	'prɛn di	un	so 'spi ɾo	'prɛn di	ke	di	'mi e	'pe ne
dal	**mio**	**dolor**	**prendi**	**un**	**sospiro,**	**prendi**	**che**	**di**	**mie**	**pene**
from the	my	sorrow	take	a	sigh	take	something	of	my	pains

te sti 'mɔn jo	fe 'del	el	'pɔr ta	a	i 'ɾɛ ne
testimonio	**fedel,**	**e'l**	**porta**	**a**	**Irene.**
testimony	faithful	and it	carry	to	Irene

"Take a sigh from my sorrow; take some faithful testament of my suffering and carry it to Irene."

ma	'vo la	o	'di o	kru 'dɛ le	iŋ 'gra ta	'la u ɾa
Ma	**vola,**	**o**	**Dio**	**crudele,**	**ingrata**	**l'aura,**
but	flies away	o	God	cruel	ungrateful	the breeze

But, o cruel God, the breeze flies away ungratefully,

e	'del: le	'mi e	kwe 'ɾɛ le	'sor da	'lon da	non	'ɔ de
e	**delle**	**mie**	**querele**	**sorda**	**l'onda**	**non**	**ode**
and	of the	my	complaints	deaf	the wave	not	hears

and the waves, deaf to my complaints, do not hear

'kwel: la	'vo tʃe	ke	'kju za	'nel: le	'viʃ: ʃe ɾe	a 'man ti	il	kɔr	mi 'ro de
quella	**voce**	**che**	**chiusa**	**nelle**	**viscere**	**amanti**	**il**	**cor**	**mi rode.**
that	voice	which	closed	in the	viscera	loving	the	heart	me eats into

that voice which, within my loving depths, consumes my heart.

'tʃɛ li	'stel: le	de 'sti no	i 'ɾɛ ne	a 'mo ɾe
Cieli!	**Stelle!**	**Destino!**	**Irene!**	**Amore!**
heavens	stars	fate	Irene	Love

Heavens! Stars! Fate! Irene! Love!

lon ta 'nan tsa	kru 'dɛl	mi	'skwar tʃi	il	'kɔ ɾe
Lontananza	**crudel,**	**mi**	**squarci**	**il**	**core.**
separation	cruel	me	you tear apart	the	heart.

Cruel separation, you tear my heart apart.

'kɔ ɾe	a 'ma bi le	del	'ka ɾo	'bɛ ne	ti sov: 'vɛŋ ga	ke	'sɛ i	'mi o
Core	**amabile**	**del**	**caro**	**bene,**	**ti sovvenga**	**che**	**sei**	**mio**
heart	lovable	of the	dear	dear one	yourself remember	that	you are	mine

Lovable heart of my beloved one, remember that you are mine

e	kɛ	'mi o	il	'tu o	do 'lor
e	**ch'è**	**mio**	**il**	**tuo**	**dolor.**
and	that is	mine	the	your	sorrow

and that your sorrow is mine.

se	lon 'ta no	a	'tan te	'pe ne	non	in 'tɛn di	dwɔl	si	'ri o
Se	**lontano**	**a**	**tante**	**pene**	**non**	**intendi**	**duol**	**sì**	**rio,**
if	far	from	so many	pains	not	you understand	grief	so	cruel

rio (lit.)
= reo

If, far from so many pains, you do not understand such cruel grief,

'sɛn ti	al 'me no	il	'tu o	do 'lor
senti	**almeno**	**il**	**tuo**	**dolor.**
feel	at least	the	your	sorrow

at least feel your [own] sorrow.

i 'rɛ ne a 'ma ta i 'rɛ ne 'te ko 'par la il 'mi o a 'mo re non per pje 'ta del 'fa to
Irene, **amata** **Irene:** **teco** **parla** **il** **mio** **amore** **non** **per** **pietà** **del** **fato,**
Irene beloved Irene you with speaks the my love not for pity of the fate
Irene, beloved Irene, my love speaks to you, [but] not to obtain pity for my fate,

    ke 'vi bra al: 'lal ma 'mi a il 'su o ri 'go re
    che **vibra** **all'alma** **mia** **il** **suo** **rigore.**
    which hurls at the soul mine the its severity
    which hurls its severity at my soul.

lon ta 'nan tsa kru 'dɛl mi 'skwar tʃi il 'kɔ re
Lontananza **crudel,** **mi** **squarci** **il** **core.**
separation cruel me you tear apart the heart.
Cruel separation, you tear my heart apart.

'pjan dʒer 'lun dʒi dal 'nu me ke 'sa ma ɛ un sat: 'tsja re di 'pjan to la 're na
Pianger **lungi** **dal** **nume** **che** **s'ama** **è** **un** **saziare** **di** **pianto** **l'arena,**
to weep far from the deity that one loves is a satiating of tears the sand
To weep, far from the deity one loves, is to quench the dry ground with tears,

    ɛ un dar 'le na a li 'stes: sa em pje 'ta
    è **un** **dar** **lena** **a** **l'istessa** **empietà.**
    is a giving strength to the itself impiety
    is to give strength to impiety itself.

'so lo 'pa ga pe 'nan do la 'bra ma 'kwan do in 'fat: tʃa al 'su o 'bɛ ne
Solo **paga** **penando** **la** **brama,** **quando** **in** **faccia** **al** **suo** **bene**
only paid for suffering the longing when in face of the his beloved
One's desire is only satisfied by suffering, when in front of his beloved

    si 'zve na e laŋ 'gwɛn do ri 'trɔ va pje 'ta
    si svena **e** **languendo** **ritrova** **pietà.**
    himself severs the veins and languishing finds pity
    he severs his veins and, languishing, finds pity.

GL: **Amore**

⇛

[65]

        mi da 'pe na 'kwan do 'spi ra
        Mi da pena quando spira
        It pains me when [the gentle breeze] breathes

mi da 'pe na 'kwan do 'spi ra dzef: fi 'ret: to a 'klɔ ri in 'se no
Mi **da** **pena** **quando** **spira** **Zeffiretto** **a** **Clori** **in** **seno,**
to me gives pain when blows little Zephyr to Clori on breast
It pains me when the gentle breeze breathes on Clori's breast,

    se ba 'tʃan do i 'bjaŋ ki a 'vo ri fa si 'tɛ pi di ʎar 'do ri
    se **baciando** **i** **bianchi** **avori** **fa** **sì** **tepidi** **gl'ardori**
    if kissing the white ivory skins makes so tepid the ardors
    when kissing that ivory-white makes my ardor so lukewarm

tepidi = tiepidi

ke	per	ˈdʒɛ lo	ˈi o	ˈvɛŋ go ˈme no
che	**per**	**gelo**	**io**	**vengo meno.**
that	through	chill	I	I faint

that I faint from the chill.

ˈfor se	te ˈmer	non	ˈdɛd: dʒo	ke	ra ˈpi ta	non	ˈsi a	ˈsi no	dal: ˈla u ɾe
Forse	**temer**	**non**	**deggio**	**che**	**rapita**	**non**	**sia**	**sino**	**dall'aure**
perhaps	to fear	not	I ought	that	ravished	not	be	even	by the breezes

la	ˈka ɾa	ˈa ni ma	ˈmi a	il	ˈmi o	te ˈzɔ ɾo	se	ˈvol to	ko ˈzi	ˈva go
la	**cara**	**anima**	**mia,**	**il**	**mio**	**tesoro,**	**se**	**volto**	**così**	**vago,**
the	dear	soul	mine	the	my	treasure	if	face	so	lovely

se	ko ˈzi	ˈbɛl: la	i ˈma go	ˈma i	non	for ˈmɔ	ˈku pi do
se	**così**	**bella**	**imago,**	**mai**	**non**	**formò**	**Cupido.**
if	so	beautiful	image	ever	not	formed	Cupid

> imago =
> (mod.)
> immagine

Perhaps I ought not fear that my dear soul, my treasure, will be ravished even by the breezes,
as Cupid never formed such a lovely face, such a beautiful image.

non	ˈsi a	ˈduŋ kwe	stu ˈpor	sa ˈmor	dʒe ˈlo zo	di	ˈdzɛf: fi ɾo	led ˈdʒɛr	mi	ˈfan: no
Non	**sia**	**dunque**	**stupor**	**s'Amor**	**geloso**	**di**	**Zeffiro**	**legger**	**mi**	**fanno**
not	it be	then	wonder	if Love	jealous	of	Zephyr	gentle	me	make

i	ˈba tʃi
i	**baci,**
the	kisses

> If the original were "d'Amor," rather than
> "s'Amor," the Italian would make more sense:
> ...the kisses of gentle Zephyr make me jealous of Love,...

No wonder, then, if the kisses of gentle Zephyr make my love a jealous love,

ˈmen tre	ki	ˈar de	a	un	tal	ˈvol to	pa ˈvɛn ta
mentre	**chi**	**arde**	**a**	**un**	**tal**	**volto**	**paventa**
while	he who	burns	to	a	such	face	fears

as he who burns with passion at [seeing] such a face fears

ke	ˈaŋ ke	kwel	ʎi	ˈvɛŋ ga	ˈtɔl to
che	**anche**	**quel**	**gli**	**venga**	**tolto.**
that	also	that	from him	may become	taken away

that even that may be taken away from him.

del	ˈmi o	kɔr	sa ˈɾɛ i	dʒe ˈlo zo	sil	ˈmi o	kɔr	non	ˈfos: se	ˈmi o
Del	**mio**	**cor**	**sarei**	**geloso**	**s'il**	**mio**	**cor**	**non**	**fosse**	**mio,**
of the	my	heart	I would be	jealous	if the	my	heart	not	were	mine

I would be jealous of my own heart, were it not mine,

ke	fud: ˈdʒen do	dal	ˈmi o	ˈpɛt: to	ˈvo la	in	sen	del	ˈva go	od: ˈdʒɛt: to
ché	**fuggendo**	**dal**	**mio**	**petto**	**vola**	**in**	**sen**	**del**	**vago**	**oggetto**
because	fleeing	from the	my	breast	it flies	to	breast	of the	lovely	object

ˈso vra	ˈla li	del	de ˈzi o
sovra	**l'ali**	**del**	**desio.**
upon	the wings	of the	desire

for, fleeing from my breast, it flies on the wings of desire to the breast of the lovely one.

ma	ke	por ˈtɛn to	ɛ	ˈkwe sto
Ma	**che**	**portento**	**è**	**questo**
but	what	marvel	is	this

But what a marvel this is,

ke	a ˈdon ta	del	ˈmi o	dʒɛl	ke	non	ɛ	ˈpɔ ko
che	**ad onta**	**del**	**mio**	**gel,**	**che**	**non**	**è**	**poco**
that	in spite	of the	my	cold	which	not	is	little

that in spite of my coldness, which is considerable,

ˈprɛn de	ˈsɛm pre	pju	ˈfɔr tsa	il	ˈmi o	gran	ˈfɔ ko
prende	**sempre**	**più**	**forza**	**il**	**mio**	**gran**	**foco.**
takes	always	more	strength	the	my	great	fire

my great ardor becomes ever greater.

> *foco = (mod.) fuoco*

GL: **Amor, Clori, Cupido, Zeffiretto, Zeffiro**

⮞

[65]

ˈo ve ri ˈvɔl go il ˈpjɛ de
Ove rivolgo il piede
Wherever I turn my step

ˈo ve	ri ˈvɔl go	il	ˈpjɛ de	o	ne	ˈpja ni	o	ne	ˈmon ti
Ove	**rivolgo**	**il**	**piede,**	**o**	**ne'**	**piani**	**o**	**ne'**	**monti,**
wherever	I turn	the	foot,	either	in the	plains	or	in the	mountains

Wherever I turn my step – either on the plains or in the mountains,

o	ne	ˈli di	o	ne	ˈfon ti	ˈsɛm pre	kwe ˈstal ma	ˈmi a	ˈpjan dʒe	e	so ˈspi ra
o	**ne'**	**lidi**	**o**	**ne'**	**fonti,**	**sempre**	**quest'alma**	**mia**	**piange**	**e**	**sospira.**
either	in the	shores	or	at the	springs	always	this soul	mine	weeps	and	sighs.

on the shores or at the springs – this soul of mine always weeps and sighs.

ˈpɔr ta	nel	kɔr	im ˈprɛsː sa	lim ˈmaˑ dʒi ne	kru ˈdɛl	ke	ˈfudː dʒe	e	a ˈdo ɾa
Porta	**nel**	**cor**	**impressa**	**l'immagine**	**crudel**	**che**	**fugge**	**e**	**adora,**
it carries	in the	heart	imprinted	the image	cruel	which	it flees	and	adores

It bears, stamped upon its heart, the cruel image, which it flees and adores,

per	ˈku i	laŋ ˈgwiʃː ʃe	oɲː ˈɲor	tra	le	ka ˈte ne
per	**cui**	**languisce**	**ognor**	**tra**	**le**	**catene,**
for	whom	languishes	always	among	the	chains

[of the one] for whom it always languishes in chains;

sofː ˈfri	gran	ˈtɛm po	il	ˈbar ba ɾo	ri ˈgo ɾe	ˈkwelː la	ke	a	ˈtutː te	ˈlo ɾe
soffrì	**gran**	**tempo**	**il**	**barbaro**	**rigore,**	**quella**	**che**	**a**	**tutte**	**l'ore,**
suffered	great	time	the	barbaric	severity	that one	which	at	all	the hours

it *[my soul]* suffered for a long time the barbaric severity of having her at all times,

o	ˈsi a	ˈnɔtː te	o	ˈsi a	ˈdʒor no
o	**sia**	**notte**	**o**	**sia**	**giorno,**
whether	it be	night	or	it be	day

whether night or day,

kol	ˈmi o	pen ˈsjɛr	a	me	sadː ˈdʒi ɾa	in ˈtor no
col	**mio**	**pensier**	**a**	**me**	**s'aggira**	**intorno.**
with the	my	thought	to	me	roams	around

haunt my thoughts.

'io   non   do 'vrε i   sen 'tir   pju   'pe na   'kwan do   lon 'ta no   son
Io   **non**   **dovrei**   **sentir**   **più**   **pena**   **quando**   **lontano**   **son**
I   not   ought   to feel   more   pain   when   far   I am
I ought not to feel pain anymore when I am far

da   ko 'lε i   ke   a 'do ɾa   il   kɔr
da   **colei**   **che**   **adora**   **il**   **cor.**
from   her   whom   adores   the   heart
from her whom my heart adores.

epː 'pur   pju   'fiɛ ɾo   kwe 'stal ma   'mi a   e   vi e 'pju   in 'sa no
Eppur   **più**   **fiero**   **quest'alma**   **mia,**   **e**   **vie più**   **insano**
and yet   more   harsh   this soul   mine   and   more and more   insane

del   'nu me   ar 'tʃɛro   'prɔ va   il   ri 'gor
del   **nume**   **arciero**   **prova**   **il**   **rigor.**
of the   god   archer   experiences   the   punishment
And yet this soul of mine experiences a harsher and ever more insane punishment from the archer god [Cupid].

'kja mo   lo   'zdeɲː ɲo   e   'li ɾa   in   a 'ju to   del   'kɔ ɾe
Chiamo   **lo**   **sdegno**   **e**   **l'ira**   **in**   **aiuto**   **del**   **core;**
I call to   the   scorn   and   the anger   in   help   of the   heart
I summon scorn and anger to help my heart;

printed:
agiuto =
(mod.) aiuto

'kja mo   'lɔ djo   el   fu 'ro ɾe   la   'rotː ta   'fe de   e   i   si mu 'la ti   afː 'fɛtː ti
chiamo   **l'odio**   **e'l**   **furore,**   **la**   **rotta**   **fede**   **e**   **i**   **simulati**   **affetti.**
I call to   the hate   and the   fury   the   broken   faith   and   the   feigned   affections
I summon hate and fury, broken faith and feigned affections.

ma   o i 'mε   ke   son   ko 'stretː to   dal   'su o   'dol tʃe   sem 'bjan te   e
Ma   **ohimè,**   **che**   **son**   **costretti**   **dal**   **suo**   **dolce**   **sembiante**   **e**
but   alas   [that]   they are   forced   by the   her   sweet   appearance   and
But, alas: they are compelled by her sweet countenance and

kwel   bel   'fɔ ko   a   laʃː 'ʃar   del   kɔr   'mi o   la   'sɛ de   e   il   'lɔ ko
quel   **bel**   **foco**   **a**   **lasciar**   **del**   **cor**   **mio**   **la**   **sede**   **e**   **il**   **loco;**
that   beautiful   fire   to   to leave   of the   heart   mine   the   seat   and   the   place
that beautiful ardor to leave the seat and place in my heart;

e   'i vi   'a i 'lasː so   kon   ti 'ranː no   im 'pɛ ɾo
e   **ivi,**   **ahi lasso,**   **con**   **tiranno**   **impero**
and   therein   woe is me   with   tyrannical   rule
and therein – woe is me – with tyrannical rule

si fa   'sɛm pre   pju   'kru do   e   pju   se 'vɛ ɾo
si fa   **sempre**   **più**   **crudo**   **e**   **più**   **severo.**
itself makes   always   more   cruel   and   more   severe
it [the punishment of the the archer god] always becomes more cruel and more harsh.

ko 'zi   laŋ 'gwir   mi   fa   'kwelː la   kru 'dɛl   bel 'ta   ke   minː na 'mo ɾa
Così   **languir**   **mi**   **fa**   **quella**   **crudel**   **beltà**   **che**   **m'innamora.**
thus   to languish   me   makes   that   cruel   beauty   who   me makes fall in love
Thus does that cruel beauty with whom I am in love make me languish.

pju   ke   la   'fudː dʒe   il   'kɔ ɾe   sin 'fjamː ma   pju   da 'mo ɾe   e   pju   la 'do ɾa
Più   **che**   **la**   **fugge**   **il**   **core,**   **s'infiamma**   **più**   **d'amore,**   **e**   **più**   **l'adora.**
more   that   her   flees   the   heart   catches fire   more   of love   and   more   her adores
The more my heart flees her, the more it becomes inflamed with love and the more it adores her.

☙

[65]

'par ti mi 'laʃ: ʃi
Parti, mi lasci
You are departing, you are leaving me

'par ti	mi	'laʃ: ʃi	a	'kwa le	mi	'laʃ: ʃi	'al: le	'mi e	'pe ne
Parti,	**mi**	**lasci,**	**ah'**	**quale**	**mi**	**lasci**	**alle**	**mie**	**pene,**
you depart	me	you leave	alas	such a	me	you leave	to the	my	pains

You are departing, you are leaving me; alas, you are leaving me in such a [state] to my pains

e	in 'prɛ da al	'mi o	do 'lor	'fjɛ ɾo	e	mor 'ta le
e	**in preda al**	**mio**	**dolor**	**fiero**	**e**	**mortale.**
and	prey to	my	sorrow	cruel	and	deadly

and prey to my cruel and deadly sorrow.

dɛ	bel: 'li do lo	'mi o	per 'ke	'lul ti mo	ad: 'di o	non	ɛ	per	me	fa 'ta le
Deh	**bell'idolo**	**mio,**	**perché**	**l'ultimo**	**addio**	**non**	**è**	**per**	**me**	**fatale,**
o	beautiful idol	mine	why	the last	farewell	not	is	for	me	fatal

O my beautiful idol, why is the last farewell not fatal to me

e	per	'mi a	'sɔr te	non	ɛ	'lul ti mo	ad: 'di o	so 'spir	di	'mɔr te
e	**per**	**mia**	**sorte,**	**non**	**è**	**l'ultimo**	**addio**	**sospir**	**di**	**morte?**
and	for	my	fate	not	is	the last	farewell	sigh	of	death

and to my fate; why is the last farewell not the sigh of death?

'van: ne	'ki o	're sto	a	'pjan dʒe ɾe	're sto	a	laŋ 'gwir	per	te
Vanne	**ch'io**	**resto**	**a**	**piangere,**	**resto**	**a**	**languir**	**per**	**te,**
go away	[that] I	I remain	to	to weep	I remain	to	to languish	for	you

Go; I will remain to weep and to languish for you –

vanne: antiquated form of "vattene," from "andarsene"

a	'pjan dʒe ɾe	per	te	'dol tʃe	bɛn	'mi o
a	**piangere**	**per**	**te,**	**dolce**	**ben**	**mio.**
to	to weep	for	you	sweet	dear one	mine

to weep for you, my sweet dear one.

a	per 'ki o	're sti	e 'za ni me	sol	re ste 'ra	kon	me	dwɔl	ko 'zi	'ri o
Ah',	**perch'io**	**resti**	**esanime,**	**sol**	**resterà**	**con**	**me**	**duol**	**così**	**rio.**
alas	even if	I may become	lifeless	only	will stay	with	me	sorrow	so	cruel

Alas, even if I die, such cruel sorrow will only stay with me.

diʃ: 'ʃɔl ta	in	a ma 'ris: si mi	so 'spi ɾi	'lal ma	'te ko	ne 'vjɛ ne
Disciolta	**in**	**amarissimi**	**sospiri,**	**l'alma**	**teco**	**ne viene;**
dissolved	in	most bitter	sighs	the soul	you with	away goes

Dissolved in bitterest sighs, my soul leaves with you;

kon	me	're stan	le	'pe ne	e	li	'mjɛ i	'kru di	e	'bar ba ɾi	mar 'ti ɾi
con	**me**	**restan**	**le**	**pene**	**e**	**li**	**miei**	**crudi**	**e**	**barbari**	**martiri.**
with	me	remain	the	pains	and	the	my	cruel	and	barbarous	torments

the pains and my cruel and barbarous torments remain with me.

e li miei = (mod.) ed i miei

a	se	mi	'laʃ: ʃi	al 'me no	ti ɾi 'kɔr da di	me	kɔr	del	'mi o	'kɔ ɾe
Ah',	**se**	**mi**	**lasci,**	**almeno**	**ti ricorda di**	**me,**	**cor**	**del**	**mio**	**core;**
alas	if	me	you leave	at least	you remember [of]	me	heart	of the	my	heart

Alas, if you leave me, at least remember me, heart of my heart;

in	ko 'zi	fjɛr	tor 'men to	sol	ti	ri 'kje de	il	'tɛ ne ɾo	a 'mor	'mi o
in	**così**	**fier**	**tormento**	**sol**	**ti**	**richiede**	**il**	**tenero**	**amor**	**mio;**
in	such	cruel	torment	only	you	asks	the	tender	love	mine

amidst such cruel torment my tender love only asks [that] of you;

se	'tut: ta	'pe ne	e	'tut: ta	dwɔl	son	'i o	e	se	per	te
se	**tutta**	**pene**	**e**	**tutta**	**duol**	**son**	**io,**	**e**	**se**	**per**	**te**
if	all	pains	and	all	sorrow	am	I	and	if	for	you

if [it is my fate to be] all suffering and sorrow, and if for you

mi	'strug: go	in	'me sto	'pjan to	dɛ	non	nje 'gar mi	il	'van to
mi	**struggo**	**in**	**mesto**	**pianto,**	**deh**	**non**	**niegarmi**	**il**	**vanto**
I am consumed		in	sad	weeping	ah	not	to deny me	the	reward

niegarmi = (mod.) negarmi

I am consumed by sad tears, ah, do not deny me the reward

e	si	'lje ve	ri 'stɔ ɾo	ke	'kwal ke	'vɔl ta	al 'me no
e	**sì**	**lieve**	**ristoro,**	**che**	**qualche**	**volta**	**almeno**
and	such	slight	comfort	that	sometimes		at least

and so slight a comfort: that at least sometimes

ti sov: 'vɛŋ ga	di	me	ke	sol	ta 'do ɾo
ti sovvenga	**di**	**me,**	**che**	**sol**	**t'adoro.**
you may remember	[of]	me	that	only	you I adore

you may remember me, who alone adores you.

dɛ	'ka ɾo	bɛn	'mi a	'vi ta	non ti skor 'dar	di	me	ke	per	te	'mɔ ɾo
Deh	**caro**	**ben**	**mia**	**vita,**	**non ti scordar**	**di**	**me,**	**che**	**per**	**te**	**moro.**
please	dear	dear one	my	life	do not forget	[of]	me	that	for	you	I die

Please, dearly beloved, my life, forget me not, as I am dying for you.

si	'lje ve	e	'dol tʃe	a 'i ta	sol	'kje de	la	'mi a	fe	per	'mi o	ri 'stɔ ɾo
Sì	**lieve**	**e**	**dolce**	**aita,**	**sol**	**chiede**	**la**	**mia**	**fé**	**per**	**mio**	**ristoro.**
such	slight	and	sweet	help	only	asks	the	my	faith	for	my	consolation

My faithfullness requires only such slight and sweet help for my consolation.

aita (poet.) = (mod.) aiuto

&

[65]

po i 'ke al 'va go se 'ren
Poiché al vago seren
Since from the charming serenity

po i 'ke	al	'va go	se 'ren	di	'du e	pu 'pil: le	'mil: le	fe 'ri te	e	'mil: le
Poiché	**al**	**vago**	**seren**	**di**	**due**	**pupille**	**mille**	**ferite**	**e**	**mille**
since	at the	charming	serenity	of	two	eyes	thousand	wounds	and	thousand

da mo 'ro ze	sa 'et: te	al	sen	ri 'pɔr to	a	so ste 'ne ɾe	oɲ: 'ɲora	il	do 'lor
d'amorose	**saette**	**al**	**sen**	**riporto,**	**a**	**sostenere**	**ognora**	**il**	**dolor**
of amorous	darts	to the	breast	I receive	to	to sustain	always	the	sorrow

Since from the charming serenity of two eyes I receive thousands of wounds and thousands of amorous darts in my breast, in order to perpetually sustain the sorrow

ke	mak: 'ko ɾa	la	'fe de	im 'peɲ: ɲo	e	la	ko 'stan tsa	e 'zɔr to
che	**m'accora,**	**la**	**fede**	**impegno**	**e**	**la**	**costanza**	**esorto.**
which	me breaks the heart	the	faith	I pledge	and	the	constancy	I exhort

which breaks my heart I pledge fidelity and I exhort constancy.

ko 'zi   dal: 'la spre   'pe ne ke   nel: 'la ni ma 'mi a no 'dri sko 'tan to
Così   **dall'aspre**   **pene,** **che**   **nell'anima** **mia** **nodrisco** **tanto,**
thus   from the bitter   pains which   in the soul   mine   I nourish   so much

> *nodrisco:*
> *from "nodrire" =*
> *(mod.) "nutrire"*

Thus, from the bitter pains I nourish so much in my soul

'veŋ go   a   mo 'strar kwal 'si a   'lal mo   a li 'men to del   'fɔ ko 'mi o
vengo   **a**   **mostrar** **qual** **sia**   **l'almo**   **alimento**   **del**   **foco** **mio,**
I come   to   to show what be   the life-giving   food   of the   fire   mine

will I show the fertile food of my passion

kol   bɛl   li 'kwor del   'pjan to
col   **bel**   **liquor** **del**   **pianto.**
with the   beautiful   liquor of the   weeping

with the beautiful liquor of my tears.

'fil: le   'ka ɾa il   'mi o tor 'men to fa   ko 'stan tsa 'al: la 'mi a fe
Fille   **cara,** **il**   **mio** **tormento** **fa**   **costanza** **alla** **mia** **fé.**
Fille   dear   the   my   torment makes   constancy at the my faithfulness

Fille dear, my torment makes my fidelity steadfast.

'nel: le   'pja ge ɔ   il   'mi o kon 'tɛn to e   go 'den do 'ar do per te
Nelle   **piaghe** **ho**   **il**   **mio** **contento,** **e**   **godendo** **ardo** **per** **te.**
in the   wounds I have   the   my comfort and   enjoying I burn for you

I take comfort from my wounds and, enjoying, I burn for you.

'mi ze ɾo   bɛn   'ved: dʒo al   ri 'gor de   'twɔ i 'lu mi
Misero,   **ben**   **veggio** **al**   **rigor** **de'**   **tuoi** **lumi,**
miserable   well   I see at the   severity of the   your eyes

Miserable, I well see from the severity of your eyes,

al: lo 'nor   di   'mi e 'pe ne   vi 'tʃi na la   'mi a 'mɔr te
all'onor   **di**   **mie** **pene,**   **vicina** **la**   **mia** **morte.**
to the honor   of   my pains   near the   my death

as reward for my pains, [that] my death draws near.

ma   il   mo 'rir ɛ   di   'glɔ ɾja a   ki   'a ma 'bɛ ne
Ma   **il**   **morir** **è**   **di**   **gloria** **a**   **chi**   **ama** **bene:**
but   the   dying is   of   glory to   who   loves well

But dying is glorious for one who loves well;

sol   per   'pɔ ko ri 'stɔ ɾo   del   'mi o 'kru do mo 'rir vor: 'rɛ i   mo 'ɾɛn do
sol   **per**   **poco** **ristoro**   **del**   **mio** **crudo** **morir** **vorrei**   **morendo**
only   for   little compensation   of the   my cruel dying I should like   dying

dying, I should only wish, as small compensation for my cruel death,

mi 'ɾar   il   'tu o bɛl   'tʃiʎ: ʎo e   'da ɾe al: 'li dol 'mi o
mirar   **il**   **tuo** **bel**   **ciglio,** **e**   **dare** **all'idol** **mio**
to gaze at   the   your beautiful   brow and   to give to the idol mine

to gaze upon your beautiful eyes and to give my idol,

in   'seɲ: ɲo di   'mi a fe   'lul ti mo ad: 'di o
in   **segno** **di**   **mia** **fé**   **l'ultimo** **addio.**
in   sign of   my faithfulness   the last farewell

as a sign of my fidelity, the last farewell.

'al ma   di   'kwe sto   'kɔ ɾe ti   'vɔʎː ʎo 'sɛm pre a 'mar
Alma   di   questo   core, ti   voglio sempre amar.
soul   of   this   heart you I want forever to love
Soul of this heart, I want to love you forever.

'si a   'fjɛ ɾa la 'mi a 'sɔr te 'si a 'tʃɛr ta la 'mi a 'mɔr te
Sia fiera la mia sorte, sia certa la mia morte,
be cruel the my fate be certain the my death
However cruel my fate, however certain my death,

ti   'vɔʎː ʎo i do la 'trar
ti   voglio idolatrar.
you I want to idolize
I want to worship you.

GL: **Fille**

∾

[65]

'rjɛ di a me
Riedi a me
Return to me

'rjɛ di a me 'lu tʃe gra 'di ta 'dol tʃe 'pe na del kɔr 'mi o
Riedi a me, luce gradita, dolce pena del cor mio.
return to me light welcome sweet sorrow of the heart mine
Return to me, welcomed light, sweet sorrow of my heart.

> *riedi: from "riedere"*
> *(lit.) = "redire"(poet.)*
> *= "ritornare"*

'sɛn tsa te ke 'sɛ i 'mi a 'vi ta 'ko me 'ma i 'vi ver pɔsː 'si o
Senza te, che sei mia vita, come mai viver poss'io?
without you who you are my life how ever to live can I
Without you, who are my life, how ever can I live?

'lun dʒi da kwe beʎː 'ʎɔkː ki in 'tor no al di 'ku i 'lu me
Lungi da que' begl'occhi, intorno al di cui lume
far from those beautiful eyes around [to] the of whose light
Far from those beautiful eyes, around whose illumination

in vi 'zi bil far 'falː la 'vo la e ri 'vo la oɲː 'ɲor kwe 'stal ma a 'man te
invisibil farfalla vola e rivola ogn'or quest'alma amante,
invisible butterfly flies and flies back always this soul loving
this loving soul, [like an] invisible butterfly, flutters to and fro,

un 'sɛ ko lo 'oɲː ɲi i 'stan te mi 'sem bra a 'ma to 'nu me
un secolo ogni istante mi sembra, amato nume.
a century every moment to me seems beloved deity
every moment seems a century to me, beloved deity.

e se la ri mem 'bran tsa di ri ve 'der ti in 'brɛ ve non tem 'prasː se
E se la rimembranza di rivederti in breve non temprasse
and if the remembrance of seeing you quickly not tempered
And if the memory of seeing you does not quickly mitigate

il ri 'gor de 'mjɛ i mar 'ti ɾi
il rigor de' miei martiri,
the severity of my torments
the severity of my torments,

nel	mar	del	'pjan to	'mi o	mor: 'rɛ i	'na u fra go		as: 'sɔr to
nel	**mar**	**del**	**pianto**	**mio,**	**morrei**	**naufrago**		**assorto.**
in the	sea	of the	weeping	mine	I should die	shipwrecked person		swallowed up

I should die, shipwrecked [and] swallowed up in the sea of my tears.

> *Printed is "absorto": a "b," rather than an "s," must have been transcribed in error. "assorto" is the (poet.) past participle of "assorbire."*

'vjɛ ni	'duŋ kwe	o	'mi o	'so le	in	'grɛm bo	'al: le	tem 'pɛ ste	a	'dar mi	il	'pɔr to
Vieni	**dunque,**	**o**	**mio**	**sole,**	**in**	**grembo**	**alle**	**tempeste**	**a**	**darmi**	**il**	**porto.**
come	then	o	my	sun	in	bosom	at the	tempests	to	to give me	the	harbor

Come then, o my sun, to grant me haven in the bosom of the tempests.

'so lo	'vo i	'lu tʃi	'mi e	'bɛl: le	mi	po 'te te	il	kɔr	be 'ar
Solo	**voi,**	**luci**	**mie**	**belle,**	**mi**	**potete**	**il**	**cor**	**bear.**
only	you	eyes	mine	beautiful	to me	you can	the	heart	to make happy

Only you, beautiful eyes of mine, can make my heart happy.

dɛ	tor 'na te	le	pro 'tʃɛl: le	del	'mi o	'dwɔ lo	a	traŋ kwil: 'lar
Deh	**tornate,**	**le**	**procelle**	**del**	**mio**	**duolo**	**a**	**tranquillar.**
please	return	the	storms	of the	my	grief	to	to quiet

Please return to quiet the storms of my grief.

&

[40]

ruʃ: ʃel: 'let: to	lim pi 'det: to
Ruscelletto	**limpidetto**
Limpid	little brook

ruʃ: ʃel: 'let: to	lim pi 'det: to	'kwan do	i 'rɛ ne	a	te	sen	'vjɛ ne
Ruscelletto	**limpidetto,**	**quando**	**Irene**	**a**	**te**	**sen'**	**viene,**
little brook	limpid	when	Irene	to	you	herself there	comes

Limpid little brook, when Irene comes there to [look into] you,

non	la	far	ko 'zi	vet: 'tso za	nɔ	non	la	far	ko 'zi	vet: 'tso za
non	**la**	**far**	**così**	**vezzosa.**	**No,**	**non**	**la**	**far**	**così**	**vezzosa.**
not	her	make	so	charming	no	not	her	make	so	charming

do not make her so charming. No, do not make her so charming.

se	ko 'noʃ: ʃe	i	'prɛ dʒi	'swɔ i
Se	**conosce**	**i**	**pregi**	**suoi**
if	she knows	the	attractions	her

If she knows her attractions

kon	ʎa 'man ti	'el: la	'fi a	'pɔ i	pju	kru 'dɛ le	e	pju	ri 'tro za
con	**gl'amanti**	**ella**	**fia**	**poi**	**più**	**crudele**	**e**	**più**	**ritrosa.**
with	the lovers	she	will be	then	more	cruel	and	more	coy

> *fia = (mod.) sarà*

she will then be more cruel with her lovers, and more coy.

&

[65]

son qwal ˈtan ta lo no ˈvɛlː lo
Son qual Tantalo novello
I am like a new Tantalus

son	kwal	ˈtan ta lo	no ˈvɛlː lo	ke	dun	ˈva go	e	bɛl	ruʃː ˈʃɛlː lo	ˈsulː la	ˈspon da
Son	**qual**	**Tantalo**	**novello**	**che**	**d'un**	**vago**	**e**	**bel**	**ruscello**	**sulla**	**sponda**
I am	like	Tantalus	new	who	of a	charming	and	beautiful	stream	on the	bank

I am like a new Tantalus who, from the edge of a charming and beautiful stream,

ˈse gwe	ˈlon da	ke	dal	ˈlabː bro	oɲː ˈɲor	sen ˈfudː dʒe
segue	**l'onda,**	**che**	**dal**	**labbro**	**ognor**	**sen fugge.**
follows	the wave	which	from the	lip	always	from it flees

pursues the water which always escapes from his lips.

ˈio	laŋ ˈgwi sko	in	ˈoɲː ni	i ˈstan te	beŋ ˈke	ˈprɛsː so	al	bɛl	sem ˈbjan te
Io	**languisco**	**in**	**ogni**	**istante,**	**benché**	**presso**	**al**	**bel**	**sembiante**
I	I languish	in	every	instant	even though	near	to the	beautiful	countenance

I languish at every moment, even though [I am] near the beautiful countenance

e	a	kwel	sen	ke	mi	di ˈstrudː dʒe
e	**a**	**quel**	**sen**	**che**	**mi**	**distrugge.**
and	to	that	breast	which	me	destroys

and that bosom which destroys me.

di	stra va ˈgan te	afː ˈfanː no	ˈsɔfː fro	ˈla spro	te ˈno ɾe
Di	**stravagante**	**affanno**	**soffro**	**l'aspro**	**tenore,**
of	extravagant	anguish	I suffer	the harsh	manner

I suffer the harshness of extraordinary anguish,

e	di	ˈstra no	do ˈlo ɾe	ˈsɛn te	kwe ˈstal ma	ˈmi a	ri ˈgor	ti ˈɾanː no
e	**di**	**strano**	**dolore**	**sente**	**quest'alma**	**mia**	**rigor**	**tiranno.**
and	of	strange	sorrow	feels	this soul	mine	severity	tyrannical

and my soul feels the tyrannical severity of a strange sorrow.

ˈal tri	ˈpe na	e	si ˈstrudː dʒe	per	belː ˈletː tsa	iŋ ko ˈstan te
Altri	**pena**	**e**	**si strugge**	**per**	**bellezza**	**incostante;**
another	suffers	and	himself pines	for	beauty	inconstant

Another suffers and pines for inconstant beauty;

> *altri: a singular pronoun = another, somebody else*

ˈal tri	si ˈve de	zven tu ˈra to	a ˈman te	dun	ˈi do lo	kru ˈdɛl	ke	ˈlo dja	e	ˈfudː dʒe
altri	**si vede**	**sventurato**	**amante**	**d'un**	**idolo**	**crudel**	**che**	**l'odia**	**e**	**fugge;**
another	himself sees	unlucky	lover	of an	idol	cruel	who	him hates	and	flees

another sees himself as the unlucky lover of a cruel idol who hates him and flees from him;

e	ˈprɔ va	ˈal tri	kwal	ˈsi a	il	ˈdʒɛ lo	e dil	ve ˈlen	di	dʒe lo ˈzi a
e	**prova**	**altri**	**qual**	**sia**	**il**	**gelo**	**ed il**	**velen**	**di**	**gelosia.**
and	experiences	another	what	is	the	ice	and the	poison	of	jealousy

and another feels what the ice and poison of jealousy is.

la	ˈpe na	del	ˈmi o	kɔr	a ˈvan tsa	ˈoɲː ɲi	do ˈlor	ke	fa	laŋ ˈgwi ɾe
La	**pena**	**del**	**mio**	**cor**	**avanza**	**ogni**	**dolor**	**che**	**fa**	**languire.**
the	pain	of the	my	heart	surpasses	every	sorrow	which	makes	languishing

The pain in my heart surpasses every sorrow which causes languishing.

'i o   'striŋ go   nel   'mi o   sen   il   so spi 'ra to   bɛn
Io   stringo   nel   mio   sen   il   sospirato   ben,
I   I press   to the   my   breast   the   longed-for   dear one

I press my longed-for dear one to my bosom,

e   il   'lab: bro   lu ziŋ 'gjɛr   ɛ   ver   'ki o   'ba tʃo
e   il   labbro   lusinghier   è   ver   ch'io   bacio;
and   the   lip   enticing   it is   true   that I   I kiss

and it is true that I kiss her enticing lips;

ma   'pɔ i   nɔ   non   'dʒun dʒe   'ma i   kwel   bɛl   dʒo 'ir
ma   poi   no,   non   giunge   mai   quel   bel   gioir.
but   then   no   not   arrives   never   that   beautiful   rapture

but then, no, that beautiful rapture is never reached.

GL: **Tantalo**

&

[50]

'vol to   'ka ɾo   del   'mi o   bɛl   'so le
Volto caro del mio bel sole
Dear face of my beautiful sun

'vol to   'ka ɾo   del   'mi o   bɛl   'so le   non fud: 'dʒir   da   ki   'ta ma   e   de 'zi a
Volto   caro   del   mio   bel   sole,   non fuggir   da   chi   t'ama   e   desia.
face   dear   of the   my   beautiful   sun   do not flee   from   one who   you loves   and   desires

Dear face of my beautiful sun, do not flee from the one who loves and desires you.

va ged: 'dʒan do   'kwe i   'va gi   splen 'do ɾi   del   'kri ne   fra   'fjo ɾi
Vagheggiando   quei   vaghi   splendori   del   crine   fra   fiori
gazing at   those   lovely   splendors   of the   hair   among   flowers

By making me gaze at the lovely splendor of your hair among the flowers,

'va i   le 'gan do   kwe 'stal ma   'mi a
vai   legando   quest'anima   mia.
you go   binding   this soul   mine

you are enslaving this soul of mine.

> *"noi," printed, may likely have been, rather,*
> *"vai," which makes sense gramatically*
> *in the context (as "noi" does not).*

'li djo   'ka ɾo   e   a do 'ra to   'gran de   iŋ 'kan to   da 'mo ɾe   e   di   bel: 'let: tsa
Lidio   caro   e   adorato,   grande   incanto   d'Amore   e   di   Bellezza,
Lidio   dear   and   adored   great   pleasure   of Love   and   of   Beauty

Dear and adored Lidio, great delight of Love and Beauty,

'vwɔ i   ke   per   te   mo 'ren do   'vwɔ i   ke   per   te   vi 'vɛn do   'sɔf: fra   'pe ne
vuoi   che   per   te   morendo,   vuoi   che   per   te   vivendo,   soffra   pene
you wish   that   for   you   dying   you wish   that   for   you   living   that I suffer   pains

you want me, dying and living for you, to suffer pains

e   tor 'men ti   e   'ma i   non   'gɔ da   un   mo 'men to   di   'pa tʃe   al: 'lal ma   a 'man te
e   tormenti,   e   mai   non   goda   un   momento   di   pace   all'alma   amante.
and   torments   and   ever   not   that I enjoy   one   moment   of   peace   to the soul   enamored

and torments, and never to enjoy one moment of peace to my enamored soul.

se   tu   'sɛ i   pur   ko 'stan te   di   ve 'der mi   mo 'rir   fra   'tan te   'pe ne
Se   tu   sei   pur   costante   di   vedermi   morir   fra   tante   pene,
if   you   are   indeed   steadfast   of   to see me   to die   among   so many   sufferings

If you are indeed steadfast about seeing me die among so many sufferings,

'laʃː ʃa	ka	te	'mi a	'vi ta	'pɔsː sa	dir	so spi 'ran do	adː 'di o	'mi o	'bɛ ne
lascia	**ch'a**	**te**	**mia**	**vita**	**possa**	**dir**	**sospirando**	**addio**	**mio**	**bene.**
allow	that to	you	my	life	I be able	to say	sighing	farewell	my	dear one

let me say to you, my life, with my last breath: "Farewell, my dear one."

si	kru 'dɛl	ke	'sɛ i	'mi o	'bɛ ne	ke	'sɛ i	'lal ma	di	kwe 'stal ma
Sì	**crudel**	**che**	**sei**	**mio**	**bene,**	**che**	**sei**	**l'alma**	**di**	**quest'alma,**
so	cruel	[that]	you are	my	dear one	who	you are	the soul	of	this soul

So cruel you are, my dear one, you who are the soul of my soul

ke	'sɛ i	'kɔ ɾe	del	'mi o	kɔr
che	**sei**	**core**	**del**	**mio**	**cor,**
who	you are	heart	of the	my	heart

[and] the heart of my heart.

'vwɔ i	ke	'pe ni	pe ne 'rɔ	'vwɔ i	ke	'gɔ da	go de 'rɔ
Vuoi	**che**	**peni**	**penerò,**	**vuoi**	**che**	**goda**	**goderò,**
you want	that	I may suffer	I shall suffer	you want	that	I may enjoy	I shall enjoy

If you want me to suffer, I shall suffer; if you want me to enjoy, I shall enjoy;

e	in	un	'pun to	pro ve 'rɔ	tʃɔ	ke	'si a	'dʒɔ ja	e	do 'lor
e	**in**	**un**	**punto**	**proverò**	**ciò**	**che**	**sia**	**gioia**	**e**	**dolor.**
and	in	one	moment	I shall experience	that	which	may be	joy	and	pain

and in a single moment I shall experience what is joy and [what is] pain.

GL: **Amore**

Aldrovandini, Giuseppe Antonio Vincenzo (1671-1707)

Of the late 17th century Bolognese school of composers and with an individual originality, Aldrovandini wrote some half dozen serious operas, several oratorios, and numerous cantatas and motets, as well as instrumental sonatas and concerti. He studied composition with Perti in Bologna, became *principe* of the Accademia Filarmonica in 1702, and in the same year was named honorary *maestro di cappella* to the Duke of Mantua.

Aldrovandini's comic operas in Bolognese dialect (*Gl'inganni amorosi scoperti in villa*, *Amor torna in s'al so'*, and *Dafni*) were popular at the time and widely performed. They are historically important in the regional development of opera buffa as a genre outside of the Neapolitan school. The music has been lost, but the style is suggested by episodes in the surviving *Cesare in Alessandria* (1699).

Aldrovandini had intemperate habits. He lived in poverty and died by drowning when he fell into the Canale Navile after a night of drinking at a waterfront tavern.

---

[47]

di 'stelː la in 'fɛ sta
Di stella infesta
Of a hostile star

di	'stelː la	in 'fɛ sta	'la spra	iŋ kle 'mɛn tsa	'tutː to	min 'vo la
Di	**stella**	**infesta**	**l'aspra**	**inclemenza**	**tutto**	**m'invola;**
of	star	hostile	the harsh	inclemency	everything	from me steals

The harsh mercilessness of a hostile star steals everything from me;

'mi o	kɔr	pat: 'tsjɛn tsa
mio	**cor,**	**pazienza!**
my	heart	patience

my heart, have patience!

il	pju	mi	'rɛ sta	ke	se bɛn	'so la	ɛ	lin: no	'tʃɛn tsa
Il	**più**	**mi**	**resta,**	**che,**	**se ben**	**sola,**	**è**	**l'innocenza.**	
the	most	to me	remains	which	even though	(the) only (thing)	it is	the innocence	

The best remains for me, though it is the only thing: innocence.

❧

[53]

vor: 'rɛi po 'ter mo 'ri re

Vorrei poter morire

I should like to be able to die

vor: 'rɛi	po 'ter	mo 'ri re	non	dʒa	per	non	pe 'na re
Vorrei	**poter**	**morire**	**non**	**già**	**per**	**non**	**penare,**
I should wish	to be able	to die	not	indeed	in order to	not	to suffer

I should like to be able to die – not, indeed, to cease suffering,

ma	per	ve 'der	kon 'tɛn to	'li do lo	del	'mi o	kɔr
ma	**per**	**veder**	**contento**	**l'idolo**	**del**	**mio**	**cor.**
but	in order to	to see	content	the idol	of the	my	heart

but in order to see the idol of my heart content.

ko 'zi	ve 'dri a	dʒo 'i re	'kwel: le	pu 'pil: le	'ka re
Così	**vedria**	**gioire**	**quelle**	**pupille**	**care**
thus	I would see	to rejoice	those	eyes	dear

Thus I would see rejoice those dear eyes

> *vedria (from "vedere")*
> *= (mod.) vedrei*

per	'ku i	mo 'rir	mi	'sɛn to	kon	'bar ba ro	do 'lor
per	**cui**	**morir**	**mi**	**sento**	**con**	**barbaro**	**dolor.**
through	which	to die	myself	I feel	with	cruel	sorrow

for which I feel myself dying with cruel sorrow.

 # *Anonimo [Anonymous – composers unknown]*

---

[40]

a 'mar il 'ka ro 'bɛ ne

Amar il caro bene

To love one's dearly beloved

a 'mar	il	'ka ro	'bɛ ne	aŋ 'kor	in	lon ta 'nan tsa
Amar	**il**	**caro**	**bene**	**ancor**	**in**	**lontananza**
to love	the	dear	dear one	even	in	distance

To love one's dearly beloved even when from afar

ɛ	gran	'fe de	dun	kɔr	e	gran	ko 'stan tsa
è	**gran**	**fede**	**d'un**	**cor**	**e**	**gran**	**costanza.**
is	great	faith	of a	heart	and	great	constancy

is a heart's great faith and constancy.

se	in	mar	di	fjɛr	tor 'men to	som: 'mɛr so	'oɲ: ɲi	kon 'tɛn to
Se	**in**	**mar**	**di**	**fier**	**tormento**	**sommerso**	**ogni**	**contento,**
if	in	sea	of	fierce	torment	submerged	every	happiness

If, in the sea of fierce torment, every happiness is submerged,

ε 'pɔr to del mar 'tir sol la spe 'ran tsa
è porto del martir sol la speranza.
is haven from the agony only the hope
hope alone is a haven from the agony.

ma 'dim: mi o 'tʃɛ ko 'di o per 'ke kol 'tu o fi 'len ko 'zi spje 'ta to
Ma dimmi, o cieco dio, perché, col tuo Filén così spietato,
but tell me o blind god why with the your Fileno so unmerciful
But tell me, o blind god *[Cupid]*, why, so unmercifully to your Fileno,

per 'ke da 'kwe sto 'pɛt: to mal: lon ta 'na sti 'lal ma
perché da questo petto m'allontanasti l'alma?
why from this breast me you distanced the soul
why did you take my soul away from my breast?

a ke fra 'mil: le 'pe ne mi 'sɛn to or 'mai laŋ 'gwi ɾe se tu
Ah, che fra mille pene mi sento ormai languire, se tu,
ah [that] among thousand pains me I feel now to languish if you
Ah, amidst a thousand pains I now feel I shall languish if you,

'ka ɾo il 'mi o 'bɛ ne non 'tor ni a da ni 'mar 'kwe sto 'tu o 'se no
caro il mio bene, non torni ad animar questo tuo seno;
dear the my dear one not you return to animate this your breast
my dearly beloved, do not return to revive this breast which belongs to you;

sa 'ra 'fɔr tsa il pe 'ri ɾe ke non pwɔ
sarà forza il perire, ché non può,
will be necessity the perishing because not can

printed is " puol,"an antiquated form of "potere" = (mod.) può

beŋ 'ke 'fɔr te ɾe 'star di 'vi zo un kɔr 'sɛn tsa la 'mɔr te
benché forte, restar diviso un cor senza la morte.
although strong to stay divided a heart without the death
I will necessarily perish, for a heart, however strong, can not stay divided without dying.

'duŋ kwe o 'bɛl: la ke 'sɛ i la 'mi a 'vi ta
Dunque, o bella, che sei la mia vita,
therefore o beautiful one who you are the my life
Therefore, o beautiful one, you who are my life,

non laʃ: 'ʃar mi kwe 'stal ma mo 'rir se kwel 'zgwar do
non lasciarmi quest'alma morir! se quel sguardo
not to let to me this soul to die if that glance
do not let my soul die, as that glance

kon 'ku i ma fe 'ri ta ε ba 'stan te per 'far mi dʒo 'ir
con cui m'ha ferita è bastante per farmi gioir.
with which me has wounded is enough for to make me to rejoice
which wounded me suffices to give me joy.

ma ke fa 'vɛl: lo o 'tʃe li aŋ 'kor dal: 'li dol 'mi o 'spe ɾo pje 'ta ri 'stɔ ɾo
Ma che favello, o cieli, ancor dall'idol mio spero pietà, ristoro?
but what I speak o heavens still from the idol mine I hope pity reward
But what am I saying, o heavens! Am I still hoping for pity, reward from my idol?

a   ke   non   pwɔ   kon so 'lar mi   il   'mi o   bɛn
Ah,   che   non   può   consolarmi   il   mio   ben,
ah   [that]   not   is able to console me   the   my   dear one
Ah, my dear one can not console me

se   non   ma 'skol ta
se   non   m'ascolta.
if   not   me she listens to
if she does not listen to me.

dɛ   'vo i   'a u ɾe pje 'to ze ku 'di te i   'pjan ti 'mjɛ i le   'mi e   kwe 'ɾɛ le
Deh,   voi   aure   pietose,   ch'udite   i   pianti   miei,   le   mie   querele,
pray   you   breezes merciful   who hear   the   tears   mine   the   my   laments
Please, you merciful breezes who hear my weeping and my laments,

'vo i   'di te   al   'mi o   'bɛ ne   ke   'lun dʒi dal   'su o   bɛl
voi,   dite   al   mio   bene,   che   lungi   dal   suo   bel
you   say   to the   my   dear one that   far   from the her   beauty
tell my dear one that, far from her beauty,

'i o   'vi vo   in   'pe ne
io   vivo   in   pene!
I   I live   in   sufferings
I live in suffering!

non   a   dʒa   tor 'men to   un   'kɔ ɾe   pju   ped: 'dʒo ɾe   kwan 'tɛ   a 'mar
Non   ha   già   tormento   un   core   più   peggiore   quant'è   amar
not   has   [indeed] torment   a   heart   more   worse   so much as it is   loving
A heart has no torment worse than loving

in   lon ta 'nan tsa   se   pe 'nan do   in   'du ɾe   'tem pre   'vi ve   'sɛm pre
in   lontananza,   se   penando   in   dure   tempre   vive   sempre
in   distance   if   suffering   in   harsh   conditions lives   always
from afar; suffering in harsh conditions, it lives always

fra   il   ti 'mor   e   la   spe 'ran tsa
fra   il   timor   e   la   speranza.
between the   fear   and   the   hope
between fear and hope.

ಜ

[47]

a 'mor a 'mor 'fam: mi go 'der
Amor, Amor, fammi goder
Love, Love, make me enjoy

a 'mor   a 'mor   'fam: mi go 'der
Amor,   Amor,   fammi   goder!
love   love   make me to enjoy
Love, Love, make me enjoy!

'fam: mi   ba 'tʃar   kwel   'lab: bro   a 'spɛr so   di   tʃi 'na bro
Fammi   baciar   quel   labbro,   asperso   di   cinabro,
make me   to kiss   that   lip   sprinkled   with   cinnabar
Make me kiss those lips, sprinkled with cinnabar,

ke   'sɛr ve   'dar ko   a   te   ben 'da to   ar 'tʃɛr
che   serve   d'arco   a   te,   bendato   arcier!
which   serves   as arch   to   you   blindfolded   archer
which serve as an arch to you, blindfolded archer!

GL: **Amor**

Care mie selve
See *Rontani*

[51]   *Annibale Pocaterra [?]*

'do ve   'do ve   'kor: ri   'mi o   'kɔ ɾe
Dove, dove corri, mio core?
Where, where are you running, my heart?

'do ve   'do ve   'kor: ri   'mi o   'kɔ ɾe   di 'vɔl dʒi   di 'vɔl dʒi   i   'pas: si
Dove,   dove   corri,   mio   core?   Divolgi,   divolgi   i   passi!
where   where   you run   my   heart   turn away   turn away   the   steps
Where, where are you running, my heart? Divert, divert your steps,

ke   per   'kwe sto   sen 'tje ɾo   a   'mɔr te   'va si
ché   per   questo   sentiero   a   morte   va si!
because   through   this   path   to   death   one goes
for this path leads to death!

> *va si = si va; however, the*
> *original may have been "va, si!"*
> *(= leads to death – yes!)*

'sɛ i   di 'spo sto   a da 'ma ɾe
Sei   disposto   ad amare?
you are   prepared   to love
Are you prepared to love?

'ɛk: ko ti   il   've ɾo   a 'mo ɾe   il   've ɾo   a 'man te   ke   tʃɔ   'si a   il   've ɾo
Eccoti   il   vero   amore,   il   vero   amante,   che   ciò   sia   il   vero:
here is to you   the   true   love   the   true   lover   because   this   be   the   truth
Behold your true love, your true lover, for this is the truth:

kwel   'pal: li do   sem 'bjan te   e   'kwel: le   'pja ge   dol tʃe 'men te   a 'ma ɾe   'spi ɾa no
quel   pallido   sembiante   e   quelle   piaghe   dolcemente   amare   spirano
that   pale   face   and   those   wounds   sweetly   bitter   breathe
that pale face and those sweetly bitter wounds express

a 'du na   'vo tʃe
ad una   voce:
at one   voice
in a single voice:

so 'vɛr kjo   a 'mor   mi   fa   mo 'rir   in   'kro tʃe
"Soverchio   amor   mi   fa   morir   in   croce."
excessive   love   me   makes   to die   on   cross
"Excessive love makes me die in *[sweet]* agony."

[51]   *Cataneo[?]*

'fud: dʒi 'fud: dʒi 'fud: dʒi di 'lɛt: ta a 'man te

Fuggi, fuggi, fuggi, diletta amante

Flee, flee, flee, beloved lover

'fud: dʒi   'fud: dʒi   'fud: dʒi   di 'lɛt: ta   a 'man te   'em pja   'dɔn: na   ka 'dʒon   di   'pjan te

Fuggi,   fuggi,   fuggi,   diletta   amante   empia   donna,   cagion   di   piante,

flee   flee   flee   beloved   lover   pitiless   woman   cause   of   tears

Flee, flee, flee, beloved lover, pitiless woman, cause of tears,

ke   non   dʒa   per   'ɛs: ser   kru 'dɛ le   ma   per   'ɛs: ser   iŋ 'gra ta   e   in fi 'dɛ le

ché,   non   già   per   esser   crudele,   ma   per   esser   ingrata   e   infidele,

because   not   already   for   to be   cruel   but   for   to be   ungrateful   and   unfaithful

because not only for being cruel, but for being ungrateful and unfaithful,

'oɲ: ɲi   'kɔ ɾe   ta   in   or: 'ro ɾe

ogni   core   t'ha   in   orrore.

every   heart   you has   in   horror

every heart loathes you.

'fud: dʒi   'fud: dʒi   'fud: dʒi   ke   ki   ti   'mi ɾa   per 'ke   'vi vi   'pjan dʒe   e   so 'spi ɾa

Fuggi,   fuggi,   fuggi,   che   chi   ti   mira   perché   vivi   piange   e   sospira.

flee   flee   flee   because   he who   you   sees   because   you live   weeps   and   sighs

Flee, flee, flee, as whoever sees you weeps and sighs because you live.

> *A second verse is printed as text only:*

'fud: dʒi   'fud: dʒi   'fud: dʒi   fal: 'la tʃe   'fɛ ɾa   'frɔ de   in fer 'nal

Fuggi,   fuggi,   fuggi,   fallace   fera,   frode   infernal,

flee   flee   flee   deceptive   beast   fraud   infernal

Flee, flee, flee, deceptive beast, hellish fraud,

> *fera =*
> *(mod.)*
> *fiera*

em 'pi ɾa   me 'dʒɛ ɾa   ke   seb: 'bɛ ne   'a i   di   'dɔn: na   la 'spɛt: to

empira   megera,   che   sebbene   hai   di   donna   l'aspetto

sublime   shrew   who   although   you have   of   woman   the aspect

sublime shrew who, although you have the appearance of a woman,

> *empira =*
> *(mod.) empirea*

di   'fu ɾja   un   'kɔ ɾe   na 'skon di   nel   'pɛt: to   'tut: ta   'dɔn: na   'tut: to   iŋ 'gan: no

di   furia   un   core   nascondi   nel   petto: tutta   donna,   tutto   inganno.

of   fury   a   heart   you hide   in the   breast   all   woman   all   deception

hides in your breast the heart of a fury: all woman, all deceit.

'fud: dʒi   'fud: dʒi   'fud: dʒi   koɲ: 'ɲun   ke   'ta ma

Fuggi,   fuggi,   fuggi,   ch'ognun   che   t'ama

flee   flee   flee   because each one   who   you loves

Flee, flee, flee, because everyone who loves you

il   'tu o   bɛn   'pjan dʒe   il   'tu o   mal   'bra ma

il   tuo   ben   piange,   il   tuo   mal   brama.

the   your   happiness   weeps   the   your   woe   longs for

bewails your happiness and desires your woe.

☙

This song is attributed in five of the publications to Pergolesi, and in two of them to Ciampi. John Glenn Paton, in [60], gives the background of the song and establishes the composer as anonymous.

[12, 20, 25, 29, 36, 54, 59, 60, 64]   Alternately titled **Tre Giorni**.

'ni na
Nina
Nina

tre	'dʒor ni	son	ke	'ni na	in	'lɛt: to	se ne 'sta
Tre	**giorni**	**son**	**che**	**Nina**	**in**	**letto**	**se ne sta.**
three	days	are	that	Nina	in	bed	herself stays

For three days Nina has been in bed.

in [25] and [36]:
a letto = in letto

> *In [60] and [36] the verse continues as follows:*

il	'son: no	las: sas: 'si na	zveʎ: 'ʎa te la	per	pje 'ta
Il	**sonno**	**l'assassina,**	**svegliatela**	**per**	**pietà!**
the	sleep	her murders	awaken her	for	pity's sake

Sleep is killing her; awaken her, for pity's sake!

> *and then [60] continues as follows:*

e	'tʃim ba li	e	'tim pa ni	e	'pif: fe ri	zveʎ: 'ʎa te mi	ni 'net: ta
E	**cimbali**	**e**	**timpani**	**e**	**pifferi,**	**svegliatemi**	**Ninetta,**
and	cymbals	and	drums	and	fifes	awaken to me	dear Nina

Cymbals and drums and fifes, awaken dear Nina for me.

per 'ke	non	'dɔr ma	pju
perché	**non**	**dorma**	**più.**
so that	not	she may sleep	more

so she will sleep no longer.

> *but [36] continues as follows:*

'tʃɛm ba li	'pif: fe ri	'tim pa ni	zveʎ: 'ʎa te	'mi a	ni 'net: ta
Cembali,	**pifferi,**	**timpani!**	**Svegliate**	**mia**	**Ninetta,**
cymbals	fifes	drums	awaken	my	dear Nina

Cymbals, fifes, drums! Awaken my dear Nina,

at: 'tʃɔ	non	'dɔr ma	pju
acciò	**non**	**dorma**	**più.**
so that	not	she may sleep	more

so she will sleep no longer.

'pif: fe ri	'tim pa ni	'tʃem ba li	zveʎ: 'ʎa te	'mi a	ni 'net: ta
Pifferi,	**timpani,**	**cembali,**	**svegliate**	**mia**	**Ninetta,**
fifes	drums	cymbals	awaken	my	dear Nina

Fifes, drums, cymbals, awaken my dear Nina,

> *alt. in [25]:*

'pif: fe ri	'tʃem ba li	'tim pa ni	zveʎ: 'ʎa te mi	ni 'net: ta
Pifferi,	**cembali,**	**timpani,**	**svegliatemi**	**Ninetta,**
fifes	cymbals	drums	awaken to me	dear Nina

Fifes, cymbals, drums, awaken dear Nina for me,

at: 'tʃɔ   non   'dɔr ma   pju
acciò   non   dorma   più.
so that   not   she may sleep   more
so she will sleep no longer.

In [60] is a second verse:

e   'men tre   il   sjor   dot: 'to ɾe   a   vi zi 'tar la   va
E   mentre   il   sior   dottore   a   visitarla   va,
and   while   the   sir   doctor   to   to visit her   goes
And while the doctor is going to visit her,

sior =
sor =
signore

ni 'net: ta   per   a 'mo ɾe   in   lɛt: to   se ne 'sta
Ninetta   per   amore,   in   letto   se ne sta.
dear Nina   for   love   in   bed   herself stays
dear Nina, for love, is staying in bed.

e   'tim pa ni   e   'pif: fe ɾi   e   'tʃim ba li   zveʎ: 'ʎa te mi   ni 'net: ta
E   timpani   e   pifferi   e   cimbali,   svegliatemi   Ninetta,
and   drums   and   fifes   and   cymbals   awaken to me   dear Nina
Drums and fifes and cymbals, awaken dear Nina for me,

at: 'tʃɔ   non   'dɔr ma   pju
acciò   non   dorma   più.
so that   not   she may sleep   more
so she will sleep no longer.

[51]

non te 'mer 'fil: li 'mi a
Non temer, Filli mia
Fear not, my Filli

non   te 'mer   'fil: li   'mi a   ke   il   'mi o   'kɔ ɾe   'si a   dal 'tru i
Non   temer,   Filli   mia,   che   il   mio   core   sia   d'altrui,
not   to fear   Filli   mine   that   the   my   heart   may be   of another
Fear not, my Filli, that my heart may belong to another,

ke   'ɛs: ser   'vɔʎ: ʎo   per   te   kwal   'sɛm pre   'fu i
ché   esser   voglio   per   te,   qual   sempre   fui.
because   to be   I want   for   you   like   always   I was
for I want to be for you as I always was.

ne   'fi a   ke   'vɔl ta   'nwɔ va   a da 'mar   la   'mi a   'mwɔ va
Né   fia   che   volta   nuova   ad amar   la   mia   muova
nor   will be   that   turn   new   to love   the   mine   may move
Nor will it be that a new circumstance may move [my heart] to love,

fia = (mod.) sarà

"volta nuova," above, is problematic: the intention is more likely "Nor will a new face stir mine to love," which would correctly require "volto nuovo" ['vol to 'nwɔ vo]. Perhaps the feminine endings on "volta" and "nuova" are poetic license to rhyme with "muova."

ke   non   pwɔ   kɔr   dʒen 'til   ne   've ɾo   a 'man te
ché   non   può   cor   gentil   né   vero   amante
because   not   is able   heart   kind   nor   true   lover
for neither a kind heart nor a true lover can

'rom per	'su a	'fe de	per	no 'vɛl	sem 'bjan te
romper	**sua**	**fede**	**per**	**novel**	**sembiante.**
to break	its	faith	for	new	countenance

break its faith for a new countenance.

> "sua" refers both to the heart and the true lover
> lover; but in English one can not say "neither...
> nor... can break _their_ faith"– Hence, "its"...

GL: **Filli**

❧

[36]

'ɔk: ki 'bɛl: li
Occhi belli
Beautiful eyes

'ɔk: ki	'bɛl: li	'ɔk: ki	a do 'ra ti	non	mi	'fa te	pju	laŋ 'gwir
Occhi	**belli,**	**occhi**	**adorati,**	**non**	**mi**	**fate**	**più**	**languir.**
eyes	beautiful	eyes	adored	not	me	make	more	to languish

Beautiful eyes, adored eyes, do not make me languish more.

'va gi	'lu mi	i do la 'tra ti	se re 'na te vi	al	'mi o	dʒo 'ir
Vaghi	**lumi**	**idolatrati**	**serenatevi**	**al**	**mio**	**gioir.**
charming	eyes	idolized	become serene	at the	my	joy

Charming, idolized eyes, become serene at my joy.

> *serenare (lit.)* =
> *rasserenare*

❧

[55]

'ɔk: ki del: 'lal ma 'mi a
Occhi dell'alma mia
Eyes of my soul

'ɔk: ki	del: 'lal ma	'mi a	vi 'va tʃi	e	'so li
Occhi	**dell'alma**	**mia,**	**vivaci**	**e**	**soli,**
eyes	of the soul	mine	bright	and	unique

Eyes of my soul, bright and unique,

dɛ	'si o	'ar do	per	'vo i	'den tro	e	di 'fwɔ ra
deh,	**s'io**	**ardo**	**per**	**voi**	**dentro**	**e**	**di fuora,**
ah	as I	I burn	for	you	within	and	without

ah, as I burn for you inside and out,

> *fuora (poet.)* = *fuori*

laʃ: 'ʃa te	'ki o	vi	'ba tʃi	'aŋ ke	'ki o	'mɔ ra
lasciate	**ch'io**	**vi**	**baci,**	**anche**	**ch'io**	**mora.**
let	that I	you	may kiss	even	that I	may die

let me kiss you, even if I die.

'ɔk: ki	'vi vi	da 'mor	fjam: 'mɛl: li	ar 'dɛn ti
Occhi	**vivi,**	**d'amor**	**fiammelli**	**ardenti,**
eyes	bright	of love	flames	ardent

Bright eyes, ardent flames of love,

dɛ	se	un	'luŋ go	ser 'vir	'mɛr ta	mer 'tʃe de
deh,	**se**	**un**	**lungo**	**servir**	**merta**	**mercede,**
ah	if	a	long	servitude	merits	reward

ah, if a long servitude merits reward,

mi 'ra te   se   nɛ   'deɲ: ɲa   la   'mi a   'fe de
mirate   se   n'è   degna   la   mia   fede.
see   if   of it is   worthy   the   my   faith
see if my fidelity is worthy of it.

'ɔk: ki   si   'dol tʃɛ   il   bɛn   ke   si de 'zi a
Occhi,   sì   dolc'è   il   ben   che   si desia
eyes   so   sweet is   the   well-being   that   is desired
Eyes, so sweet is the happiness desired

desia: from "desiare" (lit.) = " desiderare"

del   a 'ma to   te 'zɔr   'kwan do   si 'mɔ ɾe
del   amato   tesor'   quando   si more.
of the   beloved   treasure   when   one dies
from the beloved treasure when one is dying;

dɛ   spar 'dʒe te ne   un   'pɔ ko   'en tro   al   'mi o   'kɔ ɾe
Deh!   spargetene   un   poco   entro   al   mio   core.
ah   sprinkle of it   a   little   inside   to the   my   heart
ah, shed a little of it upon my heart.

'ɔk: ki   se   per   pje 'ta   non 'ke   per   'mi o   'mɛr to
Occhi,   se   per   pietà   non ché   per   mio   merto,
eyes   if   through   pity   as well as   for   my   merit
Eyes, if through pity as well as for my merit

merto = (mod.) merito

non   im 'pɛ tro   da   'vo i   'kwal ke   kon 'fɔr to
non   impetro   da   voi   qualche   conforto,
not   I obtain   from   you   some   comfort
I do not obtain some comfort from you,

'vo i   'dol tʃi   'ɔk: ki   'vo i   mi   a 've te   'mɔr to
voi,   dolci   occhi,   voi   mi   avete   morto.
you   sweet   eyes   you   me   have   dead
you, sweet eyes, will have me dead.

❧

[40] In [40]: "by Monteverdi?"

'ɔk: ki   'fon ti   del   'kɔ ɾe
Occhi, fonti del core
Eyes, wellsprings of the heart

'ɔk: ki   'fon ti   del   'kɔ ɾe   'ɔk: ki   pjan 'dʒe te
Occhi,   fonti   del   core,   occhi   piangete;
eyes,   fountains   of the   heart   eyes   weep
Eyes, wellsprings of the heart – eyes, weep;

'vɔl dʒe   'mi o   'so le   in   'al tra   'par tel   'pjɛ de
volge   mio   sole   in   altra   parte'l   piede.
turns   my   sun   to   other   place the   foot
my sun turns her step elsewhere.

'al tro   da   'vo i   ke   'pjan to   il   kɔr   non   'kjɛ de
Altro   da   voi   che   pianto   il   cor   non   chiede;
other   from   you   than   weeping   the   heart   not   asks
My heart asks from you nothing other than weeping;

*printed is "Altra";
grammatically correct
is "Altro"*

'la kri ma 'mil: le a 'mil: le   'ɔk: ki   spar 'dʒe te
lacrim' a mill' a mille,   **occhi,**   **spargete!**
tears at thousands and thousands   eyes   shed
eyes, shed tears by the thousands!

pje 'ta	kol	'vo stro	'pjan to	al 'tru i	mo 've te	'del: la	'kan di da	'mi a	sin 'tʃɛ ɾa	'fe de
Pietà	**col**	**vostro**	**pianto**	**altrui**	**movete**	**della**	**candida**	**mia**	**sincera**	**fede;**
pity	with the	your	weeping	others	move	of the	pure	my	sincere	faith

With your weeping, move others to pity for my pure, sincere faith;

'di te	kwal	in dʒu 'stis: si ma	mer 'tʃe de	del	ti 'ɾan: no	del	kor	mi 'ze ɾja	a 've te
dite	**qual**	**ingiustissima**	**mercede**	**del**	**tiranno**	**del**	**cor**	**miseria**	**avete.**
say	what	most unjust	reward	of the	tyrant	of the	heart	misery	you have

tell what misery you have, a most unjust reward from the tyrant of the heart *[Cupid]*.

'ɔk: ki	da	'no i	si 'par te	il	'nɔ stro	'so le	ne	vwɔl	'mi ze ɾo	me
Occhi,	**da**	**noi**	**si parte**	**il**	**nostro**	**sole,**	**né**	**vuol,**	**misero**	**me,**
eyes	from	us	departs	the	our	sun	nor	wishes	miserable	mc

Eyes, our sun leaves us; miserable me: nor does she wish –

laf: 'fan: no	'ri o	kal	e 'stɾe mo	par 'tir	'far mi	pa 'rɔ le
l'affanno	**rio**	**ch'al**	**estremo**	**partir**	**farmi**	**parole.**
the anguish	cruel	that at the	final	parting	to make me	words

cruel anguish – to speak to me at the final parting.

> rio
> *(lit.)* =
> reo

'vo i	do 'lɛn ti	'ɔk: ki	'mjɛ i	se	non	pos: 'si o	'men tre	'la ni ma	'mi a	par 'tir
Voi,	**dolenti**	**occhi**	**miei,**	**se**	**non**	**poss'io,**	**mentre**	**l'anima**	**mia**	**partir**
you	sorrowful	eyes	mine	if	not	am able I	when	the soul	mine	to depart

si 'vwɔ le	'ɔk: ki	'liŋ gwe	del	kor	'di te	ad: 'di o
si vuole,	**occhi,**	**lingue**	**del**	**cor,**	**dite**	**addio!**
itself wishes	eyes	tongues	of the	heart	say	farewell

O sorrowful eyes of mine, if I am not able to do so, when my soul wishes to depart – eyes, tongues for my heart, say farewell for me!

ʃ

[10, 19]

o led: 'dʒa dri 'ɔk: ki 'bɛl: li
O leggiadri occhi belli
O beautiful lovely eyes

o	led: 'dʒa dri	'ɔk: ki	'bɛl: li	'ɔk: ki	'mjɛ i	'ka ɾi
O	**leggiadri**	**occhi**	**belli,**	**occhi**	**miei**	**cari,**
o	lovely	eyes	beautiful	eyes	mine	dear

O beautiful lovely eyes, my dear eyes,

'vi vi	'rad: dʒi	del	'tʃɛl	se 're ni	e	'kja ɾi
vivi	**raggi**	**del**	**ciel**	**sereni**	**e**	**chiari,**
bright	rays	of the	sky	serene	and	clear

bright rays serene and clear as the sky,

po i 'ke	'tan to	bra 'ma te	di	ve 'der mi	laŋ 'gwi ɾe	di	ve 'der mi	mo 'ri ɾe
poiché	**tanto**	**bramate**	**di**	**vedermi**	**languire,**	**di**	**vedermi**	**morire,**
since	so much	you desire	of	to see me	to languish	of	to see me	to die

since you desire so much to see me languish, to see me die,

'ɔk: ki   'bɛl: li   ke   a 'do ɾo   mi 'ra te   'ki o   'mɔ ɾo
occhi   belli   che   adoro,   mirate   ch'io   moro.
eyes   beautiful which I adore   look at   that I   I die
beautiful eyes I adore, look: I am dying.

o   se 'ɾe ne   'mi e   'lu tʃi   o   'lu tʃi   a 'ma te
O   serene   mie   luci,   o   luci   amate,
o   serene   my   eyes   o   eyes   loved
O my serene eyes, o beloved eyes,

'tan to   'kru de   al   'mi o   a 'mor   'kwan to   spje 'ta te
tanto   crude   al   mio   amor   quanto   spietate,
so much   cruel   to the my   love   as much   pitiless
as cruel to my love as pitiless,

po i 'ke   'tan to   go 'de te   'del: la   'fjam: ma   'ki o   'sɛn to   del   'mi o   'gra ve   tor 'men to
poiché   tanto   godete   della   fiamma   ch'io   sento   del   mio   grave   tormento,
since   so much   you enjoy   of the   flame   that I   I feel   of the my   grave   torment
since you enjoy so much the flame I feel in my deep torment,

dɛ   mi 'ra te mi   un   'pɔ ko   e   dʒo 'i te   al   'mi o   'fɔ ko
deh   miratemi   un   poco   e   gioite   al   mio   foco.
ah   look at me   a   little   and have pleasure at the my   fire
ah, look at me a little and take pleasure from my fire.

> In [19] are two more verses, printed as text only:

o   tʃe 'lɛ sti   fa 'tʃɛl: le   ar 'dor   de   'kɔ ɾi   'vi vi   al 'bɛr gi   da 'mor
O   celesti   facelle   ardor   de'   cori   vivi   alberghi   d'amor,
o   heavenly   little torches ardor   of the hearts   living   refuges   of love
O heavenly little lights, ardor of hearts, living refuges of love,

da 'mor   te 'zo ɾi   se   vi   'pja tʃe   mi 'ra ɾe   u na 'man te   fe 'ri to
d'amor   tesori   se   vi   piace   mirare   un amante   ferito,
of love   treasures   if   you it pleases to see   a lover   wounded
treasures of love, if it pleases you to see a lover wounded,

u na 'man te   tra 'di to   'lu tʃi   'kru de   e   spje 'ta te   me   'stes: so   mi 'ra te
un amante   tradito,   luci   crude   e   spietate   me   stesso   mirate.
a lover   betrayed   eyes   cruel   and pitiless   me   myself   look at
a lover betrayed, cruel and pitiless eyes, look at me.

---

lu ziŋ 'gjɛ ɾe   pu 'pil: le   'ɔk: ki   fa 'ta li   de   'mjɛ i   'pjan ti   mi 'ni stre
Lusinghiere   pupille,   occhi   fatali   de'   miei   pianti   ministre
flattering   eyes   eyes   fateful   of the my   tears   ministers
Flattering eyes, fateful eyes, ministers of my tears

e   de   'mjɛ i   'ma li   dɛ   mi 'ra te mi   al 'me no
e   de'   miei   mali,   deh   miratemi   almeno
and of the my   woes   ah   look at me   at least
and of my woes, ah, at least look at me,

al   'mi o   'luŋ go   pe 'na ɾe   al   'mi o   gran   la gri 'ma ɾe
al   mio   lungo   penare   al   mio   gran   lagrimare,
at the my   long   suffering   at the my   great   weeping
at my long suffering [and] my great weeping;

> *lagrimare =
> (mod.) lacrimare*

ke	son	'fju mi	kor: 'rɛn ti	kwe 'stɔk: ki	do 'lɛn ti
che	**son**	**fiumi**	**correnti**	**quest'occhi**	**dolenti.**
because	are	rivers	flowing	these eyes	sorrowful

for my sorrowful eyes are flowing rivers [of tears].

❧

[51]

o 'mi a 'fil: li gra 'di ta
O mia Filli gradita
O my pleasing Filli

o	'mi a	'fil: li	gra 'di ta	'ɛk: ko	ke	pur	ri 'tor no	a	'prɛn der	'led: dʒe
O	**mia**	**Filli**	**gradita,**	**ecco**	**che**	**pur**	**ritorno**	**a**	**prender**	**legge**
o	my	Filli	pleasing	here is	that	[indeed]	I return	to	to take	command

O my pleasing Filli, I return here to take commands

e	'vi ta	da	'bɛ i	'vo stri	'ɔk: ki	e	far	kon	'vo i	sod: 'dʒor no
e	**vita**	**da'**	**bei**	**vostri**	**occhi,**	**e**	**far**	**con**	**voi**	**soggiorno.**
and	life	from	beautiful	your	eyes	and	to make	with	you	sojourn

and life from your beautiful eyes, and to spend time with you.

dɛ	pje 'ta de	vat: 'tʃen da	var: 'rɛn da	vet: 'tso za	pje 'to za	di	me
Deh,	**pietade**	**v'accenda,**	**v'arrenda**	**vezzosa**	**pietosa**	**di**	**me,**
ah	pity	you may arouse	you may yield	graceful	compassionate	of	me

> *pietade =*
> *(mod.) pietà*

Ah, may pity stir in you; may you yield, graceful [and] compassionate to me,

ka 'man te	pen 'ti to	dʒa	'gri da	mer 'tʃe
ch'amante	**pentito**	**già**	**grida**	**mercé.**
because lover	repentant	now	cries	mercy

for a repentant lover now cries for mercy.

o	'mi o	'dol tʃe	kon 'fɔr to	'ɛk: ko	ke	pur	mi 'trɔ vo	'ko me
O	**mio**	**dolce**	**conforto,**	**ecco**	**che**	**pur**	**mi trovo**	**come**
o	my	sweet	comfort	here is	that	[indeed]	me I find	like

O my sweet comfort, I find myself here as

in	si 'ku ɾo	'pɔr to	'a i	'vo stri	'pjɛ di	el	'mi o	ser 'vir	rin: 'no vo
in	**sicuro**	**porto**	**ai**	**vostri**	**piedi;**	**e'l**	**mio**	**servir**	**rinnovo.**
in	safe	haven	at the	your	feet	and the	my	serving	I renew

in a safe haven at your feet; and I renew my servitude.

> *Also in* [51] *is a variant version, which includes the following different or additional text:*

dɛ	pje 'ta de	lat: 'tʃɛt: ti	pro 'met: ti	vo 'ler si	do 'ler si	di	me
Deh	**pietade**	**l'accetti**	**prometti**	**volersi**	**dolersi**	**di**	**me,**
ah	pity	it accept	promises	wishes	sorrows	from	me

Please, for pity's sake, accept my promises, my good will, [and] my sorrows,

ka 'man te	pen 'ti to	dʒa	'gri da	mer 'tʃe
ch'amante	**pentito**	**già**	**grida**	**mercè.**
because lover	repentant	now	cries	mercy

for a repentant lover now cries for mercy.

o	'bɛl: la	'al ma	dʒen 'til	'ɛk: ko	'ki o	pur	ne	'vɛɲ: ɲo
O	**bella**	**alma**	**gentil**	**ecco**	**ch'io**	**pur**	**ne**	**vegno**
o	beautiful	soul	kind	here is	that I	[indeed]	from there	I come

*vegno =
(mod.)
vengo*

O beautiful kind soul, hence I come,

ri ve 'rɛn te	e	u 'mi le	per	la	'mi a	'fe de	a	'dar vi	il	kɔr	in	'peɲ: ɲo
riverente	**e**	**umile**	**per**	**la**	**mia**	**fede**	**a**	**darvi**	**il**	**cor**	**in**	**pegno.**
reverent	and	humble	for	the	my	faith	to	to give you	the	heart	in	pledge

reverent and humble, to pledge my heart to you in faith.

dɛ	pje 'ta de	vi 'spi ra	non	'i ra	ven 'det: ta	val: 'let: ta	di	me
Deh	**pietade**	**v'ispira**	**(non**	**ira,**	**vendetta)**	**v'alletta**	**di**	**me,**
ah	pity	you inspires	not	anger	revenge	you attracts	of	me

Ah, pity (not anger [or] revenge) inspires you [and] attracts you to me,

ka 'man te	pen 'ti to	dʒa	'gri da	mer 'tʃe
ch'amante	**pentito**	**già**	**grida**	**mercé.**
because lover	repentant	now	cries	mercy

for a repentant lover now cries for mercy.

GL: **Filli**

&

[36]

'par te il 'pjɛ
Parte il piè
I depart

'par te	il	pjɛ	ma	're sta	il	'kɔ re	pri dʒo 'njer	del	'tu o	bɛl	krin
Parte	**il**	**piè,**	**ma**	**resta**	**il**	**core,**	**prigionier**	**del**	**tuo**	**bel**	**crin.**
departs	the	foot	but	stays	the	heart	prisoner	of the	your	beautiful	head of hair

I depart, but my heart remains, a prisoner of your beautiful tresses.

da	kwel	'lab: bri	laʃ: ʃi 'vet: ti	da	kweʎ: 'ʎɔk: ki	a mo ro 'zet: ti
Da	**quel**	**labbri**	**lascivetti,**	**da**	**quegl'occhi**	**amorosetti,**
on	those	lips	dear lustful	on	those eyes	dear amorous

'pɛn de	o	'bɛl: la	il	'mi o	de 'stin
pende	**o**	**bella,**	**il**	**mio**	**destin.**
hangs	o	beautiful one	the	my	destiny

My destiny, o beautiful one, depends upon those dear lustful lips, those dear loving eyes.

&

[51]   *Lodovico Torti [?]*

pen 'sjɛ ri kwje 'ta te
Pensieri quietate
Thoughts, be still

pen 'sjɛ ri	kwje 'ta te	non	pju	in	'va no	pen 'sa te	a	kwel	ke	dʒa	fu
Pensieri	**quietate,**	**non**	**più**	**in**	**vano**	**pensate**	**a**	**quel**	**che**	**già**	**fu.**
thoughts	be quiet	not	more	in	vain	think	of	that	which	before	was

Thoughts, be still; think no more, in vain, of what was before.

son	'fɔl: li	spe 'ran tse	'mu ta	ɛ	lu 'zan tsa	e	'kor: re	'lɔd: dʒi	di
Son	**folli**	**speranze;**	**muta**	**è**	**l'usanza**	**e**	**corre**	**l'oggi**	**dì,**
they are	foolish	hopes	changed	is	the habit	and	runs	the present	day

il	no 'vɛl: lo	a 'man te	e	'ʎe ne	'do na	il	si
il	**novello**	**amante**	**e**	**gliene**	**dona**	**il**	**"sì."**
the	new	lover	and	to him of it	gives	the	yes

They are foolish hopes; the routine has changed, and today the new lover is current, and she gives him her "yes."

[51]   *Diacinta Fedele [?]*

'si o mor: 'rɔ ke di 'ra
S'io morrò, che dirà
If I die, what will she say

'si o	mor: 'rɔ	ke	di 'ra	la	kru 'dɛl	ne 'mi ka	'mi a
S'io	**morrò,**	**che**	**dirà,**	**la**	**crudel**	**nemica**	**mia,**
if I	I will die	what	will say	the	cruel	enemy	mine

kɛ	il	'mi o	mal	'tan tɔ	de 'zi a
che	**il**	**mio**	**mal**	**tanto**	**desia?**
who	the	my	harm	so much	desires

If I die, what will my cruel enemy, who desires my misfortune so much, say?

pjan dʒe 'ra	'si o	mor: 'rɔ	si	e	me	lo	'spɛ ro	kol	'tɛm po
Piangerà	**s'io**	**morrò,**	**sì,**	**e**	**me**	**lo**	**spero**	**col**	**tempo**
will weep	if I	I will die	yes	and	me	it	I hope	with the	time

ke	sa	se	mo 'ves: se	'u na	'vɔl ta	pje 'ta
che	**sa,**	**se**	**movesse**	**una**	**volta**	**pietà.**
that	knows	if	may have moved	one	time	pity

She will weep if I die, yes; and I hope that she knows it, in time, if pity will have moved her for once.

> *If "che sa," printed, was originally "chi sa," it would make more sense:*
> ...and I hope that with time – who knows – pity may have moved her for once.

> "Star vicino" had been attributed to Salvator Rosa until John Glenn Paton
> explained, in [60], that it is correctly by an anonymous composer. See *Rosa*.

[21, 24, 29, 30, 52, 60]

star vi 'tʃi no
Star vicino
To be near

star	vi 'tʃi no	al	bel: 'li dol	ke	'sa ma
Star	**vicino**	**al**	**bell'idol,**	**che**	**s'ama,**
to be	near	to the	beautiful idol	whom	one loves

To be near the beautiful idol one loves

ɛ	il	pju	'va go	di 'lɛt: to	da 'mor
è	**il**	**più**	**vago**	**diletto**	**d'amor!**
is	the	most	charming	delight	of love

is the most charming delight of love!

> *in* [30]: *dolce* ['dol tʃe]
> (= sweet) *instead of "vago":*
> ...is the sweetest delight...

From here on, as the prints which continue with additional texts differ as to the number of verses and the order of the lines, the reader is asked, when searching for a translation, to use from the following whichever are found on the music pages he or she is using.

ɛ	un	iŋ ˈkan to	u neb ˈbret: tsa	ˈu na	ˈbra ma	ke	ˈdu e	ˈkɔ ɾi	kon ˈdʒun dʒe	in un	kɔr
È	**un**	**incanto,**	**un'ebbrezza,**	**una**	**brama,**	**che**	**due**	**cori**	**congiunge**	**in un**	**cor.**
it is	an	enchantment	an intoxication	a	yearning	what	two	hearts	joins	in one	heart

It is an enchantment, an intoxication, [and] a yearning, that which unites two hearts as one.

for tu ˈna to	ki	in ˈtɛn de	ʎi	at: ˈtʃɛn ti	di	u naf: ˈfet: to	sin ˈtʃe ɾo	e	fe ˈdel
Fortunato	**chi**	**intende**	**gli**	**accenti**	**di**	**un affetto**	**sincero**	**e**	**fedel!**
fortunate	he who	hears	the	words	of	an affection	sincere	and	faithful

Fortunate is he who hears the expression of a sincere and faithful affection!

ˈeʎ: ʎi	ˈprɔ va	vi ˈvɛn do	i kon ˈtɛn ti	sol	kon ˈtʃes: si	ˈa i	be ˈa ti	nel	tʃɛl
Egli	**prova**	**vivendo**	**i contenti**	**sol**	**concessi**	**ai**	**beati**	**nel**	**ciel!**
he	experiences	living	the contentments	only	granted	to the	blessed souls	in the	heaven

He experiences, living, the contentments granted only to the blessed souls in heaven!

"ai beato" is in some prints; grammatically correct would be either "al beato" or "ai beati," and I've chosen the latter as best in the context.

a	ke	ˈdʒo va	le ˈta te	fjo ˈɾi ta	ˈoɲ: ɲi	ˈbe ne	ke	il	ˈtʃe lo	ne	dje
A	**che**	**giova**	**l'etate**	**fiorita?**	**Ogni**	**bene**	**che**	**il**	**cielo**	**ne**	**diè.**
to	what	is useful	the age	flowered	every	good	that	the	heaven	to it	gave

Of what good is the bloom of youth? Every good that heaven gave to it.

etate = (mod.) età

diè (lit.) = diede (from "dare")

non	si ˈkon ti	fra	i	ˈdʒor ni	di	ˈvi ta	kwel	ke	ˈskor so	in	a ˈman do	non	ɛ
Non	**si conti**	**fra**	**i**	**giorni**	**di**	**vita**	**quel**	**che**	**scorso**	**in**	**amando**	**non**	**è.**
not	one may count	among	the	days	of	life	that	which	past by	in	loving	not	is

Let one not count among his days of living one day which has not been spent in loving.

In [21] is a note that the following verse – the 2nd verse in this print – was "added at a later date by Count Pepoli of Bologna."

star	lon ˈta no	dal	bɛn	ke	si ˈbra ma
Star	**lontano**	**dal**	**ben**	**che**	**si brama,**
to be	far	from the	dear one	whom	one desires

To be far from the desired dear one

	star	lon ˈtan	da	ko ˈlɛ i	ke	si ˈbra ma
var.:	**Star**	**lontan**	**da**	**colei**	**che**	**si brama,**
	to be	far	from	her whom	that	one desires

To be far from her whom one desires

ɛ	da ˈmo ɾe	il	pju	ˈvi vo	do ˈlor
è	**d'amore**	**il**	**più**	**vivo**	**dolor!**
is	of love	the	most	acute	sorrow

is the deepest sorrow of love!

	ɛ	da ˈmo ɾe	il	pju	ˈme sto	do ˈlor
var.:	**è**	**d'amore**	**il**	**più**	**mesto**	**dolor!**
	is	of love	the	most	sad	sorrow

is the saddest sorrow of love!

Ariosti, Attilio (1666-1729)

Singer, organist, harpsichordist, and violist, Ariosti joined the monastic Order of Servites in 1688 (as Frate Ottavio) and was organist at their basilica, Santa Maria dei Servi, in his native Bologna.

By 1696 he was in the service of the Duke of Mantua, who sent him in 1697 to serve as *maître de musique* at the Berlin court of Sophie Charlotte, Electress of Brandenburg. Despite political pressure to return to his Catholic order he remained, being a skillful courtier and diplomat as well as musician, under royal patronage for six years in Berlin and then for seven and a half in Vienna, where in 1707 Joseph I pronounced him imperial minister and agent for all the princes and states of Italy.

Records attest that as of 1716 Ariosti was in London, where he spent most of the rest of his life. He was one of a "renowned triumverate" [Burney, quoted in *Grove*] of composers employed by the Royal Academy, Handel and Giovanni Bononcini being the other two. Though he was not as prolific (or successful) as the other two, in London he published a collection of six cantatas and six lessons for the viola d'amore printed in a unique scordatura system allowing their performance with violin fingerings on the viola d'amore. His total output included some twenty operas, many cantatas, several oratorios, and instrumental divertimenti for violin and violoncello, as well as the libretto for Bononcini's opera *Polifemo*.

[90]

for tu 'na te pas: 'sa tc
Fortunate passate
Happily go by

for tu 'na te	pas: 'sa te	'mi e	'pe ne	se	un	bɛl	'lat: tʃo
Fortunate	**passate**	**mie**	**pene**	**se**	**un**	**bel**	**laccio**
fortunate	pass by	my	sufferings	if	a	beautiful	bond

O my sufferings, go by happily, as a beautiful bond

or	in	'brat: tʃo	al	'mi o	'be ne	pju	ko 'stan te	pju	a 'man te	mi	fa
or	**in**	**braccio**	**al**	**mio**	**bene**	**più**	**costante**	**più**	**amante**	**mi**	**fa.**
now	in	arm	at the	my	dear one	more	constant	more	loving	me	makes

now makes me more faithful [and] more loving in the arms of my beloved.

'si a	pur	da 'mo ɾe	'fjɛ ɾa	la 'spret: tsa	'brɛ ve	dol 'tʃet: tsa	la	pla ke 'ra
Sia	**pur**	**d'amore**	**fiera**	**l'asprezza**	**breve**	**dolcezza**	**la**	**placherà.**
may be	yet	of love	cruel	the bitterness	brief	sweetness	it	will placate

However cruel the bitterness of love may be, a brief sweetness will placate it.

> *I changed the printed "lo" to "la," to refer to "dolcezza"; however, "lo" could have referred back to "mio bene," above.*

son	gra te	al	'kɔ ɾe	'la spre	vi 'tʃɛn de	'kwan do	sar: 'rɛn de	kru 'dɛl	bel 'ta
Son	**grate**	**al**	**core**	**l'aspre**	**vicende**	**quando**	**s'arrende**	**crudel**	**beltà.**
are	pleasing	to the	heart	the harsh	events	when	itself surrenders	cruel	beauty

Harsh times are pleasing to the heart when cruel beauty surrenders.

[91]   *Paolo Rolli [?]*

la 'rɔ za
La rosa
The rose

da	pro 'tʃɛl: la	tem pe 'sto za	'tok: ka	un	di	la	'bɛl: la	'rɔ za
Da	**procella**	**tempestosa**	**tocca**	**un**	**dì**	**la**	**bella**	**rosa,**
by	storm	tempestuous	touched	one	day	the	beautiful	rose

Touched by a tempestuous storm one day, the beautiful rose

tocca (lit.) =
toccata

'tut: ta   'mɛ sta   se ne 'sta va   sko lo 'ri ta   e   'sɛn tsa   o 'dor
tutta   **mesta**   **se ne stava,**   **scolorita**   **e**   **senza**   **odor.**
all   sad   she was   discolored   and   without   fragrance
was altogether sad, discolored and without fragrance.

la   spret: 'tsa van   'ni tʃe   e   'klɔ ri   lab: bo 'ri an   'la u ɾe   i   pa 'sto ɾi
La   **sprezzavan**   **Nice**   **e**   **Clori,**   **l'abborìan**   **l'aure,**   **i**   **pastori,**
her   scorned   Nice   and   Clori   her loathed   the breezes   the   shepherds
Nice and Clori, the breezes and the shepherds, loathed her;

> *abborìan: from (mod.) aborrire, = (mod.) abborivano*

ne   pju   'la pe   a   kɔr   nan 'da va   il   'su o   'gra to   e   'dol tʃe   u 'mor
né   **più**   **l'ape**   **a**   **cor**   **n'andava**   **il**   **suo**   **grato**   **e**   **dolce**   **umor.**
nor   more   the bee   to   heart   there went   the   her   pleasing   and   sweet   nectar
and the bees no longer visited her [for] her pleasing and sweet nectar.

'kwan do   un   'rad: dʒo   di   sol   sul   bɛl   mat: 'ti no
Quando   **un**   **raggio**   **di**   **sol**   **sul**   **bel**   **mattino,**
when   a   ray   of   sun   on the   beautiful   morning
When a ray of sun, upon the beautiful morn,

'dal: le   laŋ 'gwɛn ti   'fɔʎ: ʎe   suk: 'kjan do   il   'gra ve   u 'mor
dalle   **languenti**   **foglie**   **succhiando**   **il**   **grave**   **umor**
from the   languishing   foliage   sucking up   the   heavy   liquid
drawing from the drooping foliage the heavy liquid

ke   la   ren 'de a   ki 'na ta   al   swɔl   'kwal ke   vi 'gor   le   'pɔr se
che   **la**   **rendea**   **chinata**   **al**   **suol,**   **qualche**   **vigor**   **le**   **porse:**
which   her   made   bent down   to the   ground   some   vitality   to her   gave
which was bending her down to the ground gave her some strength,

> *rendea = rendeva*

ri sto 'ra ta   'el: la   al: 'lo ɾa   a 'pɔ ko a 'pɔ ko   iŋ ko min 'tʃan do   ar 'di ta   a   ri al 'tsar   la   'fron te
ristorata   **ella**   **allora**   **a poco a poco**   **incominciando**   **ardita**   **a**   **rialzar**   **la**   **fronte,**
refreshed   she   then   little by little   beginning   bold   to   to raise   the   forehead
then, refreshed little by little, boldly beginning to raise her brow,

'tɔ sto   si 'vi de   in 'tor no   di 'nwɔ vo   a   va ged: 'dʒa ɾe   il   'su o   ko 'lo ɾe
tosto   **si vide**   **intorno**   **di nuovo**   **a**   **vagheggiare**   **il**   **suo**   **colore**
soon   one saw   around   again   to   to admire   the   her   color

'la pe   la u 'rɔ ɾa   la   'nin fa   e   il   bɛl   pa 'sto ɾe
l'ape,   **l'aurora,**   **la**   **ninfa**   **e**   **il**   **bel**   **pastore.**
the bee   the dawn   the   nymph   and   the   handsome   shepherd
soon she saw around her the bees, the dawn, the nymphs and the handsome shepherd again admiring her color.

dʒa   di 'nwɔ vo   fa 'sto za   kam 'ped: dʒa   e   di 'spred: dʒa   de   'fjo ri   la   'skjɛ ɾa
Già   **di nuovo**   **fastosa**   **campeggia,**   **e**   **dispregia**   **de'**   **fiori**   **la**   **schiera,**
now   again   with pomp   takes the field   and   scorns   of the   flowers   the   rank
Now, once again, she stands high and scorns the multitude of [the other] flowers;

ko 'zi   al 'tɛ ɾa   lor   'dɔn: na   si fa
così   **altera**   **lor**   **donna**   **si fa.**
thus   proud   their   lady   herself makes
thus she proudly makes herself their queen.

e	se	'klɔ ri	sa: 'pres: sa	o	fi 'le no	per	tok: 'kar lel	ver 'miʎː ʎo	'su o	'se no
E	se	Clori	s'appressa	o	Fileno	per	toccarle'l	vermiglio	suo	seno,
and	if	Clori	approaches	or	Fileno	for	to touch her the	vermilion	her	breast

And if Clori or Fileno approach to touch her vermilion breast,

'fjɛ ɾe	'pun te	di	'spi ne	ʎi	da
fiere	punte	di	spine	gli	da.
harsh	pricks	of	thorns	to him	gives

she gives them harsh pricks with her thorns.

GL: **Clori**

&

[1, 3, 46]
from: *Lucio Vero (1727)*   *Nicola Francesco Haym, after Apostolo Zeno*

'vwɔ i ke 'par ta
Vuoi che parta!
You want me to leave!

'vwɔ i	ke	'par ta	'i o	par ti ɾo	ma	sov: 'vɛŋ ga ti	kru 'dɛl
Vuoi	che	parta!	Io	partirò;	ma	sovvengati,	crudel,
you want	that	I leave	I	I will leave	but	remember	cruel one

You want me to leave! I will leave; but remember, cruel one,

ke	vjɛn	'me ko	il	'mi o	ros: 'sor
che	vien	meco	il	mio	rossor!
that	comes	me with	the	my	shame

that my shame comes with me.

'smɔr tsi	in 'tan to	'kwe sto	'pjan to	kwel	af: 'fɛt: to	ke	nel	'pɛt: to
Smorzi	intanto	questo	pianto,	quel	affetto,	che	nel	petto,
may lessen	meanwhile	this	weeping	that	affection	which	in the	breast

May my weeping, meanwhile, diminish that feeling in my breast

ke	vi	'po ze	un	'tʃɛ ko	a 'mor
che	vi	pose	un	cieco	amor.
which	there	put	a	blind	love

which a blind love put there.

Badalla, Rosa Giacinta *(c.1660-c.1710)*

A Benedictine nun at the musical convent of Santa Radegonda in Milan, Badalla took her vows around 1678. Little else is known about her, which is unfortunate since "Badalla's 1684 book of solo motets is perhaps the most interesting – and certainly one of the most virtuostic – of the late seventeenth-century Lombard repertory" *[from notes by Robert L. Kendrick, in [63], pg.264].*
Apart from Badalla's *Motetti a voce sola*, on Latin texts, two secular cantatas survive: "Vuò cercando" (below) and "O fronde care."

[63]   *Rosa Giacinta Badalla [?]*

vwɔ tʃer 'kan do
Vuò cercando
I wish, searching

vwɔ	tʃer ˈkan do	ˈkwel: la	ˈspɛ me	ke	ver ˈded: dʒa	per	o ˈnor
Vuò	**cercando**	**quella**	**speme**	**che**	**verdeggia**	**per**	**onor.**
I wish	seeking	that	hope	which	becomes verdant	through	honor

I wish, searching, for that hope which will blossom through honor.

> speme (lit.) = speranza
>
> vuò = (mod.) voglio

ˈkwe sta	ˈso la	mi	da	ˈpa tʃe
Questa	**sola**	**mi**	**da**	**pace;**
this	alone	to me	gives	peace

This alone will give me peace;

sol	di	ˈkwe sta	si kom ˈpja tʃe	kwa ˈlor	ˈlaŋ gwe	laf: ˈflit: to	ˈmi o	kɔr
sol	**di**	**questa**	**si compiace**	**qual'or**	**langue**	**l'afflitto**	**mio**	**cor.**
only	of	this	takes delight	which now	languishes	the afflicted	my	heart

only from this will my afflicted heart, which now languishes, have delight.

ˈɛk: ko	ˈki o	dʒa	la	ˈve do	spun ˈtar	dal	ˈtu o	gran	ˈmɛr to
Ecco,	**ch'io**	**già**	**la**	**vedo,**	**spuntar**	**dal**	**tuo**	**gran**	**merto,**
behold	[that] I	already	it	I see	to rise	from the	your	great	merit

Behold, I already see it [that hope] emerging from your great merit,

> merto= (mod.) merito

ke	fa	del	ˈmi o	ser ˈvir	ˈam bi to	in ˈtʃer to
che	**fa**	**del**	**mio**	**servir**	**ambito**	**incerto.**
which	makes	of the	my	serving	striving	uncertain

which makes of my searching an uncertain striving.

> printed is "inserto," which makes no sense; I've changed it, guessing a miscopying, to "incerto"

dʒar di ˈnjɛ ɾa	for tu ˈna ta	al ˈfin	ri ˈtrɔ vo	in	ˈgrɛm bo	ˈa i	ˈfjo ɾi
Giardiniera	**fortunata,**	**alfin**	**ritrovo**	**in**	**grembo**	**ai**	**fiori,**
gardener	fortunate	at last	I find	in	bosom	at the	flowers

A fortunate gardener, at last I find in the lap of the flowers

kwel	bɛl	fjor	ˈdel: la	spe ˈɾan tsa
quel	**bel**	**fior**	**della**	**speranza,**
that	beautiful	flower	of the	hope

that beautiful flower of hope

ke	si ˈnu tre	e	pju	sa ˈvan tsa	ˈkol: le	ˈpjɔd: dʒa	ˈde i	fa ˈvo ɾi
che	**si nutre**	**e**	**più**	**s'avanza**	**colle**	**pioggia**	**dei**	**favori.**
which	feeds	and	more	grows	with the	rain	of the	favors

which is nourished and grows from the watering of your favors.

siɲ: ˈɲor	se	dun	tal	ˈfjo ɾe	ne	ˈfa i	ˈprɔ di go	ˈdo no	al	ˈmi o	de ˈzi o
Signor,	**se**	**d'un**	**tal**	**fiore,**	**ne**	**fai**	**pròdigo**	**dono**	**al**	**mio**	**desio**
lord	if	of a	such	flower	of it	you make	lavish	gift	to the	my	desire

Lord, if with such a flower you make a lavish gift to my desire,

vɔ	pre zen ˈtar ti	aŋ ˈki o	beŋ ˈke	vil	kon trak: ˈkam bjo	a	ˈtan to ˈno ɾe
vo	**presentarti**	**anch'io**	**benché**	**vil**	**contraccambio**	**a**	**tant'onore,**
I go	to present to you	also I	although	humble	in exchange	to	so much honor

I will present to you – though humble in recompense for so much honor –

un	mat: ˈtset: to	di	ˈrɔ ze	e	di	dʒa ˈtʃin ti	ˈkɔl ti	ˈne i	ˈmjɛ i	re ˈtʃin ti
un	**mazzetto**	**di**	**rose**	**e**	**di**	**giacinti,**	**colti**	**nei**	**miei**	**recinti.**
a	bouquet	of	roses	and	of	hyacinths	gathered	in the	my	enclosed walls

a bouquet of roses and hyacinths picked from within my cloistered walls.

> Mr. Kendrick, in [63], points out that the "mazzetto di rose e di giacinti" illude to Badalla's own name Rosa Giacinta.

tu	ke	'sɛ i	la	pju	bel: la u 'ɔ ɾa	ke	ri 'splɛn da	nel	'tʃe lo	da 'mor
Tu	**che**	**sei**	**la**	**più**	**bell'aurora,**	**che**	**risplenda**	**nel**	**cielo**	**d'amor,**
you	who	are	the	most	beautiful dawn	which	may shine	in the	heaven	of love

You who are the most beautiful dawn which shines in the heaven of love,

saŋ 'kor	'lal ba	di	'rɔ ze	sin 'fjo ɾa	non	zdɛɲ: 'ɲar	'pik: kol	'do no	di	fjor
s'ancor	**l'alba**	**di**	**rose**	**s'infiora,**	**non**	**sdegnar**	**piccol**	**dono**	**di**	**fior.**
if even	the dawn	of	roses	itself adorns	not	to disdain	small	gift	of	flowers

even though the dawn adorns itself with roses, do not disdain my small gift of flowers.

✻ *Bassani, Giovanni Battista (c.1650-1716)*

Composer, organist, and celebrated violinist, Bassani is believed to have studied in Venice with Castrovillari and in Ferrara with Legrenzi.

By 1667 he was associated with the Accademia della Morte, Ferrara, where he was organist; in 1677 he became a member of the Accademia Filarmonica in Bologna; in 1680 he was *maestro di cappella* at the court of Duke Alessandro II della Mirandola; in 1682 he was elected *principe* of the Accademia Filarmonica, Bologna and in 1683 elected *maestro di cappella* of the Accademia della Morte; in 1712 he was called to teach at the music school of the Congregazione di Carità and direct the music at Santa Maria Maggiore in Bergamo, where he is buried.

Bassani composed a great number of masses, motets, and solo cantatas in the predominant concertato style of the middle baroque Bolognese school. Of at least fifteen oratorios, three have survived.   Of some dozen operas only some arias from *Gli amori alla moda* are extant.

Though prolific in sacred and secular vocal music, Bassani has been best known for his trio sonatas for strings.

---

[11]
from: *Mosè risorto dall'acque (1694)* (an Oratorio)
character: *Faraone* (the Pharaoh)

ke 'nar: ri 'i te o 'fu ɾje
Che narri?...Ite, o furie
What are you saying?...Go, o furies

ke	'nar: ri	e 'di o	ke	'sɛn to	in	'plɛ be	ko 'zi	'vi le
Che	**narri?**	**Ed io**	**che**	**sento**	**in**	**plebe**	**così**	**vile**
what	you say	[and] I	[that]	I hear	in	proletariat	so	vile

What are you saying?   I am hearing among such miserable common people

si	te me 'ra ɾjo	ar 'di ɾe	di spret: 'tsar	le	'mi e	'led: dʒi
sì	**temerario**	**ardire**	**disprezzar**	**le**	**mie**	**leggi?**
such	rash	boldness	to scorn	the	my	laws

a boldness so rash, scorning my laws?

a	se	pur	'spɛn to	non	ɛ	il	po 'ter	del	'mi o	te 'mu to	'ʃet: tro
Ah!	**se**	**pur**	**spento**	**non**	**è**	**il**	**poter**	**del**	**mio**	**temuto**	**scettro,**
ah	if	indeed	spent	not	is	the	power	of the	my	feared	sceptre

Ah, if indeed the power of my feared sceptre is not extinguished,

kon	me mo 'ran di	e 'zɛm pi	'si an	pu 'ni ti	'kwe sti	'em pi
con	**memorandi**	**esempi**	**sian**	**puniti**	**questi**	**empi!**
by	remembered	examples	may be	punished	these	impious ones

by memorable examples may these impious ones be punished!

'mɔ ɾa	'tut: to	i zra 'ɛ le	'vit: ti ma	'del: lo	'zdɛɲ: ɲo	e	'mi o	tro 'fɛ o	'mɔ ɾa	le 'brɛ o
Mora	**tutto**	**Israele**	**vittima**	**dello**	**sdegno**	**e**	**mio**	**trofeo;**	**mora**	**l'Ebreo.**
may die	all	Israel	victim	of the	scorn	and	my	trophy	let die	the Jew

May all Israel die, victim of my scorn and my trophy; let the Jew die.

'i te	o	'fu ɾje	ke	ma dʒi 'ta te	del: lo 'lim po	'aʎ: ʎi	'al ti	'kul mi ni
Ite,	**o**	**furie**	**che**	**m'agitate**	**dell'Olimpo**	**agli**	**alti**	**culmini.**
go	o	furies	who	me you shake	from Olympus	to the	high	summits

Go, o furies, you who shake me to the high summits of Olympus.

<table>
<tr><td>ite: imperative
of "ire" =
(mod.) "andare"</td></tr>
</table>

'i te	'ra pi de	e din vo 'la te	al	to 'nan te	i	'pro pri	'ful mi ni
Ite	**rapide**	**ed involate,**	**al**	**tonante**	**i**	**propri**	**fulmini.**
go	swiftly	and fly	to the	thundering [of Zeus]*	the	own	thunderbolts

Go swiftly, and fly at Zeus' thunderbolts.

*see **Giove**, in the *Glossary.*

GL: **Olimpo**

❧

[53]

'dim: mi	'ka ɾa
Dimmi cara	

Tell me, dear

'dim: mi	'ka ɾa	'ko me	'ma i	si pwɔ	a 'mar	la	kru del 'ta
Dimmi	**cara,**	**come**	**mai**	**si può**	**amar**	**la**	**crudeltà.**
tell me	dear	how	ever	it is possible	to love	the	cruelty

Tell me, dear, how it is ever possible to love cruelty.

ɛ	un	far	'tɔr to	al	'di o	'ku pi do	ɛ	un	mo 'stra ɾe	a 'mor	in 'fi do
È	**un**	**far**	**torto**	**al**	**dio**	**Cupido;**	**è**	**un**	**mostrare**	**amor**	**infido;**
it is	a	doing	wrong	to the	god	Cupid	it is	a	showing	love	treacherous

It is wronging the god Cupid; it shows treacherous love;

ɛ	un	vo 'le ɾe	un em pje 'ta
è	**un**	**volere**	**un'empietà.**
it is	a	wishing	an impiety

it is to wish a sacrilege.

GL: **Cupido**

❧

[5, 9, 42]

'dɔr mi	'bɛl: la
Dormi, bella	

Are you asleep, beautiful one

'dɔr mi	'bɛl: la	'dɔr mi	tu	se	'dɔr mi	'soɲ: ɲa ti	'dɛs: ser	men	'kru da
Dormi,	**bella,**	**dormi**	**tu?**	**Se**	**dormi,**	**sognati**	**d'esser**	**men**	**cruda;**
you sleep	beautiful one	you sleep	you	if	you sleep	dream	of to be	less	cruel

Are you asleep, beautiful one? If you are asleep, dream of being less cruel;

se	'veʎ: ʎi	'pɔr dʒi mi	'kwal ke	pje 'ta
se	**vegli,**	**porgimi**	**qualche**	**pietà.**
if	you are awake	offer me	some	pity

if you are awake, offer me some pity.

so 'spi ɾi	pro 'fon di	tra 'man do	dal	kɔr	e	tu	non	ri 'spon di
Sospiri	**profondi**	**tramando**	**dal**	**cor**	**e**	**tu**	**non**	**rispondi,**
sighs	deep	I transport	from the	heart	and	you	not	you respond

I send deep sighs from my heart, and you do not respond,

'a i   'bar ba ɾo   a 'mor
ahi,   barbaro   amor.
alas   barbarous   love
alas, barbarous love.

'bɛ i   'lu mi   ru 'bɛl: li   ki   'ma i   ki   va 'pri va
Bei   lumi   rubelli   chi   mai,   chi   v'apriva?
beautiful   eyes   rebellious   who   ever   who   you opened
Beautiful, rebellious eyes, who has ever opened you?

> rubelli = (mod.) ribelle

e   tu   non   fa 'vɛl: li   'a i   'bar ba ɾo   a 'mor
E   tu   non   favelli,   ahi,   barbaro   amor.
[and]   you   not   you speak   alas   barbarous   love
You do not speak, alas, barbarous love.

❧

[5, 9, 12, 42]

po 'za te dor 'mi te
Posate, dormite
Rest, sleep

a   se   tu   'dɔr mi   aŋ 'ko ɾa   e   se   dor 'mɛn do   'tan te   'pe ne
Ah   se   tu   dormi   ancora,   e   se   dormendo   tante   pene
ah   if   you   you sleep   still   and   if   sleeping   so many   pains

> *alt. in* [12]:
>
> ma   se   tu   'dɔr mi   aŋ 'ko ɾa
> **Ma   se   tu   dormi   ancora,**
> but   if   you   you sleep   still
> But if you are still sleeping,

mi   'da i   non   de 'star ti   dʒam: 'ma i   ke
mi   dai,   non   destarti   giammai,   ché
to me   you give   not   wake up you   never   because
Ah, if you are still sleeping, and asleep you give me such pain, never wake up, because

non   sa 'ɾi a   ba 'stan te   a   sof: 'frir ti   zveʎ: 'ʎa ta   un   'kɔ ɾe   a 'man te
non   saria   bastante   a   soffrirti   svegliata   un   core   amante.
not   would be   enough   to   to suffer you   awake   a   heart   loving
a loving heart could not endure you awake.

> saria = (mod.) sarebbe

> *in* [12]: **"soffrirsi"** *must be a printing or copying error.*

po 'za te   dor 'mi te   pu 'pil: le   gra 'di te
Posate,   dormite,   pupille   gradite;
rest   sleep   eyes   lovely
Rest, sleep, lovely eyes,

e   il   'vɔ stro   ri 'go ɾe   'laʃ: ʃi   aŋ 'ko ɾa   po 'za ɾe   un   'staŋ ko   'ko ɾe
e   il   vostro   rigore   lasci   ancora   posare   un   stanco   core.
and   the   your   severity   may let   [even]   to rest   a   tired   heart
and may your severity allow a tired heart to rest.

dor 'mi te   po 'za te   pu 'pil: le   a do 'ɾa te
Dormite,   posate,   pupille   adorate;
sleep   rest   eyes   adored
Sleep, rest, adored eyes;

e	il	'vɔ stro	ri 'go re	'laʃ: ʃi	aŋ 'ko ɾa	po 'za ɾe	un	'staŋ ko	'ko ɾe
e	**il**	**vostro**	**rigore**	**lasci**	**ancora**	**posare**	**un**	**stanco**	**core.**
and	the	your	severity	may let	[even]	to rest	a	tired	heart

and may your severity allow a tired heart to rest.

dor 'mi te	po 'za te	pu 'pil: le	a do 'ra te
Dormite,	**posate,**	**pupille**	**adorate;**
sleep	rest	eyes	adored

Sleep, rest, adored eyes;

e	in	'pla tʃi do	o 'bli o	'dɔr ma	il	'vɔ stro	fu 'ror	'ki o	'par to
e	**in**	**placido**	**oblio**	**dorma**	**il**	**vostro**	**furor,**	**ch'io**	**parto.**
and	in	peaceful	oblivion	may sleep	the	your	fury	because I	I depart

and may your fury sleep in peaceful oblivion, for I am departing.

ad: 'di o
Addio.
farewell

Farewell.

&

[5, 9, 42]

'se gwi ta a 'pjan dʒe ɾe
Seguita a piangere
Keep on weeping

nɔ	non	te 'me te	o	'pjan ti	a	non	ve 'de te
No,	**non**	**temete,**	**o**	**pianti;**	**ah**	**non**	**vedete**
no	not	fear you	o	tears	ah	not	see you

No, do not fear, o tears; ah, do you not see

ke	'ri de	la	pje 'ta	'so pral	'su o	'vi zo
che	**ride**	**la**	**pietà**	**sopra'l**	**suo**	**viso?**
that	smiles	the	pity	upon the	her	face

that pity smiles upon her face?

stan	a 'fɔr tsa	in	bɛl: 'lɔk: ki	or 'goʎ: ʎo	e 'di ɾa
Stan	**a forza**	**in**	**bell'occhi**	**orgoglio**	**ed ira,**
are	necessarily	in	beautiful eyes	pride	and anger

[Though] pride and anger are, necessarily, in her beautiful eyes,

> bell'occhi =
> (mod.) begl'occhi

'sɛm pre	'dal: la	pje 'ta	kle 'mɛn tsa	'spi ɾa
sempre	**dalla**	**pietà**	**clemenza**	**spira.**
always	from the	pity	mercy	breathes

mercy always emanates from [her] pity.

'se gwi ta	a	'pjan dʒe ɾe	'pɔ ve ɾo	kɔr	e	'spe ɾa	'fran dʒe ɾe	il	'tu o	ri 'gor
Seguita	**a**	**piangere,**	**povero**	**cor,**	**e**	**spera**	**frangere**	**il**	**tuo**	**rigor.**
continue	to	to weep	poor	heart	and	hope	to break	the	your	severity

Keep on weeping, poor heart, and hope to break your severity.

> "suo rigor" (= her severity) *would make more sense*
> *than "tuo rigor" in the context; perhaps a miscopying?*

un	've ro	dwɔl	lin te ne 'riʃː ʃe		e	'mol tʃe
Un	**vero**	**duol**	**l'intenerisce**		**e**	**molce:**
a	real	sorrow	her, or it (the heart) softens		and	placates

in one source "intenerita" is printed here, rather than "intenerisce" – a printing or copying error...

A real sorrow softens and placates:

'i o	sɔ	di	'filː li	il	kɔr	'qwan to	'si a	'dol tʃe
io	**so**	**di**	**Filli**	**il**	**cor**	**quanto**	**sia**	**dolce.**
I	I know	of	Filli	the	heart	how much	it be	sweet

I know how sweet Filli's heart is.

se	in fe 'de le	mi	a	sofː 'fɛr to	si pla ke 'ra
Se	**infedele**	**mi**	**ha**	**sofferto,**	**si placherà:**
if	unfaithful	me	has	suffered	will be appeased

If she has suffered my infidelity, she will be appeased:

'i o	sɔ	bɛn	ke	non	lo	'mɛr to	ma	lo	fa 'ra
io	**so**	**ben**	**che**	**non**	**lo**	**merto,**	**ma**	**lo**	**farà.**
I	I know	well	that	not	it	I merit	but	[it]	she will do

I well know that I do not merit it, but she will.

vo 'le a	'tir si	pju	'di re	ma	'filː li	in te ne 'ri ta	a	si	'dol tʃe	par 'lar
Volea	**Tirsi**	**più**	**dire,**	**ma**	**Filli**	**intenerita**	**a**	**sì**	**dolce**	**parlar:**
wanted	Tirsi	more	to say	but	Filli	made tender	at	such	sweet	speaking

volea = voleva

Tirsi wanted to say more; but Filli, moved by such sweet words,

dɛ	'disː se	'ta tʃi	e	i	so 'spi ɾi	arː re 'stɔ	kol	swɔn	de	'ba tʃi
deh,	**disse,**	**taci!**	**e**	**i**	**sospiri**	**arrestò**	**col**	**suon**	**de'**	**baci.**
please	she said	be silent	and	the	sighs	arrested	with the	sound	of	kisses

said: "please, be silent!" And she stopped his sighs with the sound of kisses.

GL: **Filli, Tirsi**

☙

[49]

ti	'laʃː ʃo	e u 'rilː la
Ti	**lascio**	**Eurilla**

I am leaving you, Eurilla

ti	'laʃː ʃo	e u 'ril: la	or	ke	di 'ver so	il	'fa to	vwɔl	ke	'dal tra	dʒe 'lo zo
Ti	**lascio**	**Eurilla,**	**or**	**che**	**diverso**	**il**	**fato**	**vuol**	**che**	**d'altra**	**geloso**
you	I leave	Eurilla	now	that	cruel	the	fate	wishes	that	of another	jealous

I am leaving you, Eurilla, now that cruel fate wishes that, jealous of another,

'i o	tabː ban 'do ni
io	**t'abbandoni.**
I	you I abandon

I abandon you.

ma	'sapː pi	al	'fi ne	o	'kru da	ke	a	'tu a	ka 'dʒo ne
Ma	**sappi**	**al**	**fine**	**o**	**cruda**	**che**	**a**	**tua**	**cagione**
but	know	in the	end	o	cruel one	that	by	your	cause

un   a ma 'tor   per 'de sti   per 'ke   a 'ma ɾe   ta 'tʃer   tu   non   sa 'pe sti
un   amator   perdesti   perché   amare   tacer   tu   non   sapesti.
a   lover   you lost   because   loving   silence   you   not   you knew how

But know in the end, o cruel one, that you lost a lover because of yourself, because you knew not how to keep silent about loving.

bi 'zoɲː ɲa   'fin dʒe ɾe   ki   vwɔl   go 'der   non   'ba sta   'fin dʒe ɾe
Bisogna   fingere   chi   vuol   goder.   Non   basta   fingere.
it is necessary   to pretend   he who   wants   to have satisfaction   not   is enough   to pretend

The one who wants to be satisfied must pretend. Pretending is not enough.

un   sen   a 'man te   kon 'vjɛn   ko 'stan te   kon   'fin to   afː 'fɛtː to
Un   sen   amante   convien   costante   con   finto   affetto
a   breast   loving   is better   constant   with   feigned   affection

A loving breast had better be constant with feigned affection,

sa 'per   diʃː 'ʃer ne ɾe   lal 'tru i   vo 'ler
saper   discernere   l'altrui   voler.
to know how   to discern   the other's   wish

to know how to discern the other's wish.

'duŋ kwe   im 'pa ɾa   da 'ma ɾe   e   se   'pɔr ti   nel   sen   'lu ni ko   odː 'dʒɛtː to
Dunque   impara   d'amare   e   se   porti   nel   sen   l'unico   oggetto
then   learn   of to love   and   if   you bear   in the   breast   the sole   object

Then learn to love; and if you bear in your breast the one object [of love],

non   far   'kal tro   ri 'va le   'a vi do   del   'tu o   'bɛlː lo
non   far   ch'altro   rivale   avido   del   tuo   bello
not   to make   that other   rival   eager   of the   your   beauty

do not allow that another rival, eager for your beauty,

ti 'skɔ pra   'trɔpː po   'fi da   a   kwel   ke   a 'do ɾi
ti scopra   troppo   fida   a   quel   che   adori
you may discover   too   loyal   to   the one   who   you adore

may discover you [to be] too loyal to the one you adore;

ma   kon   'sadː dʒo   o pe 'rar   di   'dʒe njo   'skal tro
ma   con   saggio   operar   di   genio   scaltro.
but   with   wise   to act   with   talent   clever

rather, act with wisdom, with clever talent.

se   so 'spi ɾi   per   un   'fin dʒi   kon   'lal tro
Se   sospiri   per   un   fingi   con   l'altro.
if   you sigh   for   one   pretend   with   the other

If you sigh for one, pretend with the other.

se   per   te   dʒa   'visː si   a 'man te   or   pju   'va go   un   krin   manː 'nɔ da
Se   per   te   già   vissi   amante   or   più   vago   un   crin   m'annoda.
if   for   you   already   I lived   lover   now   more   lovely   a   head of hair   me entangles

Though I have already lived for you as [your] lover, now more lovely tresses entangle me.

son   ka 'pa tʃe   'dal tro   afː 'fɛtː to   'tʃer ki   oɲː 'ɲu no   'al tro   di 'lɛtː to
Son   capace   d'altro   affetto.   Cerchi   ogn'uno   altro   diletto
I am   capable   of other   affection   may search for   each one   other   delight

| ogn'uno = |
| (mod.) ognuno |

I am capable of other affection. May each one search for another delight,

e	a	'su a	'vɔʎ: ʎa	in	sen	lo	'gɔ da
e	**a**	**sua**	**voglia**	**in**	**sen**	**lo**	**goda.**
and	at	his	desire	in	breast	it	may enjoy

and, at his desire, enjoy it in his breast.

tu	're sta	o	'bɛl: la	'i o	in 'tan to	'spɛ ɾo	mi 'ɾar	le	'dʒɔ je	'mi e	ri 'sor te
Tu	**resta**	**o**	**bella,**	**io**	**intanto**	**spero**	**mirar**	**le**	**gioie**	**mie**	**risorte.**
you	stay behind	o	beauty	I	in the meantime	I hope	to see	the	joys	mine	revived

Stay there, o beautiful one; I, meanwhile, hope to see my joys flourish again.

ki	si 'mu ta	in	a 'mor	'kan dʒa	la	'sɔr te
Chi	**si muta**	**in**	**amor**	**cangia**	**la**	**sorte.**
he who	is transformed	in	love	changes	the	destiny

He who is transformed in love changes destiny.

✵ *Belli, Domenico (c.1590-1627)*

LIttle Is known about the life of Belli, one of the earliest composers in the new monodic style. From 1610 to 1613 he was music tutor to the clerics of San Lorenzo in Florence, succeeding Marco da Gagliano. In 1619 both he and his wife Angelica, a singer, were enrolled as musicians in the service of the Medici court; Angelica continued in court service after her husband's death in 1627.

All of Belli's surviving music was published in 1616. The five scenes of his *Orfeo dolente* were performed that year as "intermedi" between the acts of Tasso's *Aminta*, produced by the Rinaldi family at their Palazzo della Gherardesca in Florence. The music of another theatre work, *Andromeda (1618)*, has been lost, but it was highly praised by Caccini in a letter to the secretary of the Grand Duke of Tuscany the day after its performance.

Belli's primo libro of thirty-five *Arie per suonarsi con il chitarrone*, dedicated to the Duke of Mantua, attests to his harmonic and formal adventurousness.

[44]

di 'vɔ stri 'ɔk: ki
Di vostri occhi
From your eyes

di	'vɔ stri	'ɔk: ki	le	fa 'tʃɛl: le	ke	dan	'fjam: me	'a i	kɔr	di	'dʒɛ lo
Di	**vostri**	**occhi**	**le**	**facelle,**	**che**	**dan**	**fiamme**	**ai**	**cor**	**di**	**gelo,**
of	your	eyes	the	sparks	which	give	flames	to the	heart	of	ice

The sparks from your eyes, which ignite icy hearts,

van	pod: 'dʒan do	'si no	al	'tʃɛ lo	e	la	'dʒun te	'so no	'stel: le
van	**poggiando**	**sino**	**al**	**cielo**	**e**	**là**	**giunte**	**sono**	**stelle.**
go	rising	up to	to the	heaven	and	there	reached	are	stars

rise up to heaven and, having arrived there, are stars.

se	splen 'de te	e	ʃin til: 'la te	rav: vi 'va te	'lal me	e	i	'kɔ ɾi
Se	**splendete**	**e**	**scintillate,**	**ravvivate**	**l'alme**	**e**	**i**	**cori,**
if	you shine	and	you sparkle	you revive	the souls	and	the	hearts

When you shine and sparkle, you revive souls and hearts,

e	ne	'vɔ stri	'pu ɾi	ar 'do ɾi	'lal me	'nɔ stre	im pri dʒɔ 'na te
e	**ne'**	**vostri**	**puri**	**ardori**	**l'alme**	**nostre**	**imprigionate.**
and	in the	your	pure	ardors	the souls	our	you imprison

and within your pure ardor you confine our souls.

'ar don	ʎi	pju	ar 'dɛn ti	'kɔ ɾi	o	bɛʎ: 'ʎɔk: ki	'a i	'vɔ stri	'zgwar di
Ardon	**gli**	**più**	**ardenti**	**cori,**	**o**	**begl'occhi,**	**ai**	**vostri**	**sguardi.**
they burn	the	most	ardent	hearts	o	beautiful eyes	at the	your	glances

The most ardent hearts burn, o beautiful eyes, at your glances.

'vi bra	a 'mor	fa 'ta li	'dar di	'tut: ti	'fjam: me	'tut: ti	ar 'do ɾi
Vibra	**amor**	**fatali**	**dardi,**	**tutti**	**fiamme,**	**tutti**	**ardori.**
hurls	love	fatal	darts	all	flames	all	ardors

Love hurls fatal arrows, all of flames, all of passion.

Bembo, Antonia (c.1640-c.1720)

Composer (a student of Francesco Cavalli) and singer, Bembo was born in Venice. Around 1676 she left her husband and three children and moved to Paris, where her reputation as a musician, and her singing, so impressed King Louis XIV that he gave her a pension allowing her to stay in France in the service of his court.

Her first collection of vocal music, *Produzioni armoniche*, consists of forty-one arias and cantatas on Italian, French, and Latin texts. Besides other collections of both sacred and secular music, she also wrote an opera, *Ercole amante*, to the same libretto her teacher Cavalli had set years before for the marriage of Louis XIV.

---

[34]   *Aurelia Fedeli*

in a 'mor tʃi vwɔl ar 'dir
In amor ci vuol ardir
Loving takes courage

in	a 'mor	tʃi vwɔl	ar 'dir	'trɔp: po	'ti mi do	'mi o	kɔr
In	**amor**	**ci vuol**	**ardir,**	**troppo**	**timido**	**mio**	**cor!**
in	love	it takes	courage	too	timid	my	heart

Loving takes courage, o my too timid heart!

'skat: tʃa	o 'ma i	'skat: tʃa	il	ti 'mor	se	tu	'bra mi	di	dʒo 'ir	*omai*
Scaccia	**omai,**	**scaccia**	**il**	**timor**	**se**	**tu**	**brami**	**di**	**gioir!**	*(poet.)*
drive out	now	drive out	the	fear	if	you	you long for	of	to be delighted	*= ormai*

Now dispel, dispel the fear if you long to have delight!

Berti, Giovanni Pietro (?-1638)

Singer, organist and composer, Berti sang as a tenor in the choir of San Marco in Venice. In 1624 he became second organist there, and held that position until his death.

Two collections of twenty-six *Cantade et arie* (1624, 1627) show a wide stylistic range and depth which mark Berti as one of the most important composers of secular song of the time; his synthesis of aria, arioso and recitative was, in effect, the beginnings of the chamber cantata. His varied use of metrical, harmonic, and melodic changes and affective devices resulted from his interest in setting sophisticated poetic texts.

Many of Berti's strophic arias were published before 1618 as texts with Spanish guitar tablature, and are thus some of the earliest extant Venetian examples of monody.

Grove identifies "Dove sei gita" (1634) as being perhaps the earliest example of a da capo aria.

---

[40]

'do ve 'sɛ i 'dʒi ta
Dove sei gita
Where have you gone

'do ve	'sɛ i	'dʒi ta	o	li ber 'ta	gra 'di ta
Dove	**sei**	**gita,**	**oh,**	**libertà**	**gradita?**
where	you are	gone	o	freedom	enjoyed

Where have you gone, o enjoyed freedom?

> *gita: past participle of "gire" = (mod.) "andare"*

dal	di	ke	'sɛpː pa 'mo ɾe	fu 'gar ti	dal	'mi o	'kɔ ɾe
Dal	**dì,**	**che**	**sepp' Amore**	**fugarti**	**dal**	**mio**	**core,**
from the	day	that	knew how Love	to drive away you	from the	my	heart

Since the day that Love drove you from my heart,

'on de	fudː 'dʒɛn do	a	'vo lo	tu	mi	laʃː 'ʃa sti	'so lo
onde	**fuggendo**	**a**	**volo**	**tu**	**mi**	**lasciasti**	**solo,**
whence	fleeing	at	flight	you	me	you left	alone

whence, by taking flight, you left me alone,

un	'ta tʃi to	ve 'ne no	ke	mɛ 'kor so	nel	'se no
un	**tacito**	**veneno,**	**che**	**m'è corso**	**nel**	**seno,**
a	hidden	poison	which	me has run	in the	breast

a hidden poison which flowed through my breast

> *tacito = (lit.) nascosto*
> *veneno = (mod.) veleno*

di	fu 'nɛ ste	a ma 'retː tse	kɔn tri 'stɔ	'mi e	dol 'tʃetː tse
di	**funeste**	**amarezze**	**contristò**	**mie**	**dolcezze.**
of	funereal	bitternesses	afflicted	my	sweet tastes

saddened my sweet pleasures with mournful bitterness.

adː 'di o	per	'sɛm pre	adː 'di o	li ber 'ta	dal	kɔr	'mi o
Addio	**per**	**sempre**	**addio,**	**libertà,**	**dal**	**cor**	**mio.**
farewell	for	always	farewell	freedom	from the	heart	mine

Take leave forever, freedom, from my heart.

GL: **Amore**

✳ *Biancosi, Gerardo (c.1600-?)*

The only information found about Biancosi is in Jeppesen's "Notes on the composers," in *La Flora, Vol.2.* Jeppesen wrote that Gerardo Biancosi is an "unknown composer by whom the Venetian editor Alessandro Vincenti published an aria with guitar tablature in 1634."

---

[40]

ben 'kin	me	'dʒi ɾi
Bench'in	**me**	**giri**

Though you turn to me

ben 'kin	me	'dʒi ɾi	i	laʃː ʃi 'vet ti	'zgwar di	'dɛʎː ʎa
Bench'in	**me**	**giri**	**i**	**lascivetti**	**sguardi,**	**Delia,**
even though to	me	you turn	the	flirtatious	glances	Delia

Though you turn your flirtatious glances to me, Delia,

sɔ	ke	non	'ar di
so	**che**	**non**	**ardi.**
I know	that	not	you burn

I know you are not burning [with passion].

ko 'no sko	i	'fin ti	'vet: tsi	kon	'kwa li	mak: ka 'ret: tsi
Conosco	**i**	**finti**	**vezzi,**	**con**	**quali**	**m'accarezzi.**
I recognize	the	feigned	charms	with	which	me you caress

I recognize the feigned charms with which you caress me.

sɔ	ke	ti 'ri di	e	sɔ	'kal tri	tu	'bra mi
So	**che**	**ti ridi**	**e**	**so**	**ch'altri**	**tu**	**brami.**
I know	that	you laugh	and	I know	that another	you	you desire

I know that you are laughing and that you desire someone else.

> *altri: a singular
> pronoun = another,
> somebody else*

fa	pur	'kwan to	tu	'sa i	sɔ	ke	non	'ma mi
Fa	**pur**	**quanto**	**tu**	**sai,**	**so**	**che**	**non**	**m'ami.**
do	then	as much as	you	you know how	I know	that	not	me you love

Go ahead as much as you know how; I know you do not love me.

'kwel: la	'tu a	'bel: la	'bok: ka	ɛ	men ti 'tri tʃe	oɲ: 'ɲor	'kes: ser	'mi a	'di tʃe
Quella	**tua**	**bella**	**bocca**	**è**	**mentitrice,**	**ognor**	**ch'esser**	**mia**	**dice.**
that	your	beautiful	mouth	is	liar	always	that to be	mine	it says

That beautiful mouth of yours is a liar, always saying that you are mine.

se	ta 'lor	tu	mi	'ba tʃi	son	'frɔ di	i	'twɔ i	'ba tʃi
Se	**talor**	**tu**	**mi**	**baci**	**son**	**frodi**	**i**	**tuoi**	**baci,**
if	at times	you	me	you kiss	are	frauds	the	your	kisses

When at times you kiss me, your kisses are deceits,

e	ben 'ke	'vi ta	e 'da ni ma	mi	'kja mi
e	**benché**	**vita**	**ed anima**	**mi**	**chiami.**
and	even though	life	and soul	me	you call

even though you call me your life and soul.

fa	pur	'kwan to	tu	'sa i	sɔ	ke	non	'ma mi
Fa	**pur**	**quanto**	**tu**	**sai,**	**so**	**che**	**non**	**m'ami.**
do	then	as much as	you	you know how	I know	that	not	me you love

Go ahead as much as you know how; I know you do not love me.

Bononcini [Buononcini], Giovanni (1670-1747)

Some confusion exists as to which Bononcini composed which songs, as some publications simply print the name "Bononcini." Only one of the texts in this volume is that of a song clearly identified as being by Giovanni Maria, the father.

Giovanni Bononcini, son of Giovanni Maria Bononcini, and sometimes incorrectly referred to as Giovanni Battista Bononcini, was a cellist, engaged in 1732 as cellist at the court of Louis XV in Paris, and an extremely famous, successful composer in his time.

Born in Modena, he moved to Bologna at the age of eight, after his father's death; he began to publish his compositions by the age of fifteen. In 1691 he entered the service of Filippo Colonna in Rome; in 1697 he entered the service of Leopold I in Vienna. By 1719 he was in Rome again; and in 1720 he was invited to join the Royal Academy of Music in London, of which Handel was the director. Handel and Bononcini became rivals; accounts of their rivalry, also concerning the famous singers of the day for which both composers wrote music, have been preserved.

Bononcini's fortunes changed for the worse upon the death of his major supporter in London and due to other adversities. In 1732 he went to Paris, then to Lisbon, then to Vienna; reduced to poverty, he died in Vienna.

His output was huge: a total of dramatic works, cantatas, and sacred works numbering in the hundreds, as well as instrumental works.

[26]

ben 'ke spe 'ran tsa
Benché speranza
Although hope

ben 'ke	spe 'ran tsa	'si a	men tsoɲ: 'ɲe ɾa	iŋ gan: na 'tri tʃe	non	mi	sa 'ra	nɔ	nɔ
Benché	**speranza**	**sia**	**menzognera**	**ingannatrice**	**non**	**mi**	**sarà,**	**no,**	**no.**
although	hope	may be	liar	deceiver	not	to me	it will be	no	no

Although hope may be a liar, it will not deceive me, no, no.

in	me	sa 'van tsa	e	'pɔ i	mi	'di tʃe	si	'spɛ ɾa	ka 'vra i	pje 'ta
In	**me**	**s'avanza**	**e**	**poi**	**mi**	**dice**	**sì,**	**spera,**	**ch'avrai**	**pietà.**
in	me	it increases	and	then	to me	says	yes	hope	because you will have	mercy

It increases in me and then says to me: "Yes, do hope, as you will have mercy."

seb: 'bɛn	fal: 'la tʃe	si 'mo stri	oɲ: 'ɲo ɾa	'del: le	'su e	'frɔ di	non	'te me	il kɔr	nɔ	nɔ
Sebben	**fallace**	**si mostri**	**ognora**	**delle**	**sue**	**frodi**	**non**	**teme**	**il cor,**	**no,**	**no.**
although	fallacious	itself may show	always	of the	its	frauds	not	fears	the heart	no	no

Although it may always be deceptive, my heart does not fear its frauds, no, no.

mal: 'let: ta	e	'pja tʃe	mi	'di tʃe	aŋ 'ko ɾa	si	'gɔ di	al	'di o	da 'mor
M'alletta	**e**	**piace,**	**mi**	**dice**	**ancora**	**sì,**	**godi**	**al**	**dio**	**d'amor.**
me it entices	and	pleases	to me	says	even	yes	take pleasure	at the	god	of love

It entices and pleases me; it even says to me: "Yes, take pleasure in the god of love."

[35, 64]

da te se ti 'pja tʃe
Da te...Se ti piace
From you...If you would like

da	te	ke	'paʃ: ʃi	oɲ: 'ɲo ɾa	di	'zdeɲ: ɲo	'lal ma
Da	**te,**	**che**	**pasci**	**ognora**	**di**	**sdegno**	**l'alma**
from	you	who	you feed	always	with	scorn	the soul

From you who always feed your soul with scorn

e	di	fje 'ret: tsa	il	'gwar do	'kon tro	me	ke	ta 'ma i	'sɛm pre	ko 'stan te
e	**di**	**fierezza**	**il**	**guardo**	**contro**	**me,**	**che**	**t'amai**	**sempre**	**costante,**
and	with	haughtiness	the	glance	toward	me	who	you I loved	always	constant

and your glance with haughtiness toward me who always loved you faithfully,

'ʃɔl to	da 'mo ɾe	e	'fe de	'mwɔ vo	al 'pa ɾi del	kɔr	'li be ɾo	il	'pjɛ de
sciolto	**d'amore**	**e**	**fede,**	**muovo**	**al pari del**	**cor**	**libero**	**il**	**piede!**
released	from love	and	fidelity	I move	at the equal of the	heart	free	the	foot

I go, released from love and fidelity, my foot free as my heart!

se	ti	'pja tʃe	di	'far mi	mo 'ri ɾe
Se	**ti**	**piace**	**di**	**farmi**	**morire**
if	you	it pleases	of	to make me	to die

If you would like me to die

vɔ   mo ˈrir   ma   lon ˈta no   da   te
vo'   **morir,**   **ma**   **lontano**   **da**   **te,**
I am going   to die   but   far   from   you
I will die, but far away from you,

ke   di   ˈmɔr te   ɛ   pju   ˈkru do   il   mar ˈti ɾe
ché   **di**   **morte**   **è**   **più**   **crudo**   **il**   **martìre**
because   than   death   is   more   harsh   the   torment
for torment is harsher than death

> *martire =*
> *(mod.)*
> *martirio*

ˈkwan do   ˈpɛn so   ke   ˈmaŋ ki   di   fe
quando   **penso**   **che**   **manchi**   **di**   **fe'.**
when   I think   that   you are lacking   of   fidelity
when I think that you lack fidelity.

[45]
from: *Astianatte (1727)*
character: *Andromaca*

                               Nicola Francesco Haym

de ˈlaʃ: ʃa o ˈkɔ ɾe di re spi ˈɾar
Deh lascia o core di respirar
Ah, stop breathing, o heart

dɛ   ˈlaʃ: ʃa   o   ˈkɔ ɾe   di   re spi ˈɾar   per   un   mo ˈmen to
Deh   **lascia**   **o**   **core**   **di**   **respirar**   **per**   **un**   **momento.**
ah   leave off   o   heart   of   to breathe   for   a   moment
Ah, stop breathing for a moment, o heart.

dɛ   ˈlaʃ: ʃa   o   ˈkɔ ɾe   di   so spi ˈɾar   per   un   mo ˈmen to
Deh   **lascia**   **o**   **core**   **di**   **sospirar**   **per**   **un**   **momento.**
ah   leave off   o   heart   of   to sigh   for   a   moment
Ah, stop sighing for a moment, o heart.

o   ˈtor na   e   ˈtor na   ˈpɔ i   kon   pju   do ˈlor   a   la kri ˈmar   ˈki o   mi kon ˈtɛn to
O   **torna,**   **e**   **torna**   **poi**   **con**   **più**   **dolor**   **a**   **lacrimar**   **ch'io**   **mi contento.**
oh   come back   and   come back   then   with   more   sorrow   to   weeping   that I   I am content
Oh come back; and come back then with more sorrow, as I am content in weeping.

[4, 6, 8, 19, 22, 24, 34]
from: *Eraclea (1692)* (a pasticcio by Antonio Draghi to which arias by Bononcini were added)
character: *Mirena*
                              Silvio Stampiglia, after Nicolò Minato

dɛ pju a me non va skon ˈde te
Deh, più a me non v'ascondete
Ah, do not hide from me any longer

dɛ   pju   a   me   non   va skon ˈde te   ˈlu tʃi   ˈva ge   del   ˈmi o   sol
Deh   **più**   **a**   **me**   **non**   **v'ascondete,**   **luci**   **vaghe**   **del**   **mio**   **sol.**
ah   more   to   me   not   yourself you hide   eyes   lovely   of the   my   sun
Ah, do not hide from me any longer, lovely eyes of my sun.

kon   zve ˈlar vi   se ˈvo i   ˈsjɛ te   ˈvo i   po ˈte te   trar   kwe ˈstal ma
Con   **svelarvi,**   **se voi**   **siete,**   **voi**   **potete**   **trar**   **quest'alma**
with   revealing yourselves   if you   are   you   are able   to draw   this soul
By revealing yourselves, you can take this soul

> *in some prints:*
> *"suelarvi": the "u"*
> *= (mod.) "v"*

fwɔr	di	dwɔl
fuor	**di**	**duol.**
away	from	sorrow

away from sorrow.

> *var in* [19]: **Con svelarmi se voi siete,** [kon zve 'lar mi se 'vo i 'sjɛ te] =
> By revealing [yourselves] to me,...
>
> *in* [8] *and* [24]: **voi potete far quest'alma fuor...** *the "f" in "far" was surely a miscopying of "tr," as "far fuori" (= to murder) makes no sense in the context.*

❧

[35]

la spe 'ran tsa i 'kɔ ɾi af: 'fi da
La speranza i cori affida
Hope sustains hearts

la	spe 'ran tsa	i	'kɔ ɾi	af: 'fi da	tra	le	'pe ne	e	tra	i	do 'lor
La	**speranza**	**i**	**cori**	**affida**	**tra**	**le**	**pene**	**e**	**tra**	**i**	**dolor;**
the	hope	the	hearts	makes firm	among	the	pains	and	among	the	sorrows

Hope sustains hearts among pains and sorrows;

ma	se	'man ka	'do ve	an: 'ni da	la	ko 'stan tsa	'tʃɛ de	a 'mor
ma	**se**	**manca**	**dove**	**annida,**	**la**	**costanza,**	**cede**	**amor.**
but	if	lacks	where	it nests	the	constancy	cedes	love

but if it lacks constancy where it nests, love gives up.

❧

[21, 25]
from: *Astarto (1715)*
character: *Nino*

Paolo Antonio Rolli

le 'spɛr to nok: 'kjɛ ɾo
L'esperto nocchiero
The expert helmsman

le 'spɛr to	nok: 'kjɛ ɾo	per 'ke	'tor na	al	'li do	ap: 'pe na	par 'ti
L'esperto	**nocchiero**	**perché**	**torna**	**al**	**lido,**	**appena**	**partì?**
the expert	helmsman	why	he returns	to the	shore	scarcely	he departed

Why does the expert helmsman return to the shore from which he has just departed?

del	'vɛn to	kan 'dʒa to	del	'flut: to	tur 'ba to	sak: 'kor se	e	fud: 'dʒi
Del	**vento**	**cangiato,**	**del**	**flutto**	**turbato**	**s'accorse**	**e**	**fuggì!**
of the	wind	changed	of the	wave	turbulent	he noticed	and	fled

He noticed the changing wind [and] the turbulent wave, and fled!

se	il	mar	lu ziŋ 'gje ɾo	sa 'pe a	'kɛ ɾa	in 'fi do	per 'ke	'ma i	sal 'pɔ
Se	**il**	**mar**	**lusinghiero**	**sapea**	**ch'era**	**infido,**	**perché**	**mai**	**salpò?**
if	the	sea	enticing	he knew	that it was	unfaithful	why	ever	he set sail

> *alt.:*
> *S'il =*
> *Se il*
>
> *sapea = sapeva*

If he knew that the enticing sea was unfaithful, why ever did he set sail?

sal 'pɔ	ma	iŋ gan: 'na to	al	'li do	laʃ: 'ʃa to	in 'brɛ ve	tor 'nɔ
Salpò,	**ma**	**ingannato,**	**al**	**lido**	**lasciato**	**in breve**	**tornò.**
he set sail	but	deceived	to the	shore	left	shortly	he returned

He set sail but, deceived, he soon returned to the shore he had left.

❧

[35, 64]

'lun dʒi da te
Lungi da te
Far from you

'lun dʒi da te ben   'mi o   'mɔr to   al   pja 'tʃer   son   'i o
Lungi   da   te   ben   mio,   morto   al   piacer   son   io,
far   from you dear one mine dead   to the pleasure I am   I

Far from you, my dear one, I am dead to pleasure

son   'vi vo   al   'mi o   do 'lor
son   vivo   al   mio   dolor.
I am   alive   to the   my   sorrow

[but] alive to my sorrow.

ep: 'pur   la   'spɛ me   'i o   'sɛn to   'dir mi
Eppur   la   speme   io   sento   dirmi:
yet   the   hope   I   I hear   to say to me

Yet I hear hope saying to me:

speme (lit.)	E pur =
= speranza	(mod.) Eppure

sa 'ra i   kon 'tɛn to   se   'tor ni   a   ri ve 'der   sul: 'la li   del   pen 'sjɛr
Sarai   contento   se   torni   a   riveder   sull'ali   del   pensier
you will be happy   if   you return to   to see   on the wings of the thought

lod: 'dʒet: to   del   'tu o   a 'mor
l'oggetto   del   tuo   amor.
the object   of the your   love

"You will be happy if you return, on the wings of thought, to see the object of your love."

[5, 9, 19, 43, 54, 59, 60, 64] This song is incorrectly attributed in some prints to S. DeLuca.
from: *Eraclea (1692)* (a pasticcio by Antonio Draghi to which arias by Bononcini were added)
character: *King Romulus of Rome*   *Silvio Stampiglia, after Nicolò Minato*

non   'pɔs: so   di spe 'rar
Non posso disperar
I cannot despair

non   'pɔs: so   di spe 'rar   'sɛ i   'trɔp: po   'ka ɾa   al   kɔr
Non   posso   disperar,   sei   troppo   cara   al   cor.
not   I am able   to despair   you are too   dear   to the heart

I cannot despair; you are too dear to my heart.

il   'so lo   spe 'ra ɾe   da 'ver   a   dʒo 'i ɾe
Il   solo   sperare   d'aver   a   gioire
the   only   hoping   of to have to   to enjoy

Just the hope of having joy

mɛ   un   'dol tʃe   laŋ 'gwi ɾe   mɛ   un   'ka ɾo   do 'lor
m'è   un   dolce   languire,   m'è   un   caro   dolor.
to me is a   sweet   languishing to me is a   dear   sadness

is for me a sweet languishing, is for me a dear sadness.

in some	do 'lor	a	si
prints:	**dolor,**	**ah,**	**sì!**
	sadness	ah	yes

...sadness – ah, yes!

[49]

o fron 'do zo ar boʃ: 'ʃɛl: lo

O frondoso arboscello

O leafy sapling

o	fron 'do zo	ar boʃ: 'ʃɛl: lo	ke	in	'ri va	del	ruʃ: 'ʃɛl: lo
O	**frondoso**	**arboscello**	**che**	**in**	**riva**	**del**	**ruscello**
o	leafy	sapling	which	on	bank	of the	brook

	le	'ver di	'fron de	va ged: 'dʒan do	'sta i	'dim: mi	sas: 'si ze	'ma i
	le	**verdi**	**fronde**	**vagheggiando**	**stai**	**dimmi,**	**s'assise**	**mai**
	the	green	leaves	dominating	you are	tell me	sat herself	ever

	'al: la	'dol tʃe	'om bra	'tu a	'li do lo	'mi o
	alla	**dolce**	**ombra**	**tua**	**l'idolo**	**mio.**
	in the	sweet	shade	yours	the idol	mine

O leafy sapling, you whose green leaves overlook the bank of the brook, tell me if my idol ever sat in your sweet shade.

e	tu	'lim pi do	'ri o	'ka i		di	'vɛr di	zme 'ral di	'am be	le	'spon de
E	**tu**	**limpido**	**rio**	**ch'hai**		**di**	**verdi**	**smeraldi**	**ambe**	**le**	**sponde**
and	you	limpid	brook	which you have		of	green	emeralds	both	the	shores

And you, limpid brook, who have shores of green emerald

	e	dɔr	la 're ne	e	di	kri 'stal: lo	'a i	'lon de	'dim: mi
	e	**d'or**	**l'arene**	**e**	**di**	**cristallo**	**ai**	**l'onde**	**dimmi,**
	and	of gold	the sands	and	of	crystal	in the	the waves	tell me

and sands of gold, and ripples of crystal, tell me,

	'spɛk: kja si		'ma i	la	'va ga	'fil: le	nel: 'lon de	'tu e	traŋ 'kwil: le
	specchiasi		**mai**	**la**	**vaga**	**Fille**	**nell'onde**	**tue**	**tranquille?**
	looks at her reflection		ever	the	lovely	Fille	in the waters	your	tranquil

does the lovely Fille ever look at her reflection in your tranquil waters?

ma	'vo i	non	ri spon 'de te	e	a 'va ɾi	in 'tan to	vi	pren 'de te
Ma	**voi,**	**non**	**rispondete**	**e**	**avari**	**intanto**	**vi**	**prendete**
but	you	not	you respond	and	avaricious	meanwhile	you	take

But you do not respond and, avaricious, you meanwhile take

	da	me	so 'spi ɾi	e	'pjan to
	da	**me**	**sospiri**	**e**	**pianto.**
	from	me	sighs	and	weeping

from me sighs and tears.

ver: 'ra	un	di	ke	la	'mi a	'bɛl: la	fud: dʒi 'ti va	pa sto 'rɛl: la
Verrà	**un**	**dì**	**che**	**la**	**mia**	**bella**	**fuggitiva**	**pastorella**
will come	a	day	that	the	my	beautiful	fugitive	shepherdess

A day will come when my beautiful fugitive shepherdess

	al	'mi o	'gred: dʒe	tor ne 'ɾa
	al	**mio**	**gregge**	**tornerà.**
	to the	my	flock	will return

will return to my flock.

'vɔʎ: ʎo	al: 'lo ɾa	o	'pjan ta	o	'ri o	'far le	'nɔ to	il	do 'lor	'mi o
Voglio	**allora**	**o**	**pianta**	**o**	**rio**	**farle**	**noto**	**il**	**dolor**	**mio**
I want	at that time	o	tree	o	brook	to make to her	known	the	pain	mine

I want, then, o tree, o brook, to make known to her my pain

e	la	'vɔ stra	kru del 'ta
e	**la**	**vostra**	**crudeltà.**
and	the	your	cruelty

and your cruelty.

al: 'lor ke	'tor na	a 'pri le	di	'nwɔ ve	'foʎ: ʎe	a	ri ve 'stir	le	'pjan te
Allorché	**torna**	**aprile**	**di**	**nuove**	**foglie**	**a**	**rivestir**	**le**	**piante**
When	returns	april	with	new	foliage	to	to clothe	the	trees

When April returns to clothe the trees with new foliage

te	sol	'nu do	di	'fjor	ne 'glɛt: to	e	'vi le
te	**sol**	**nudo**	**di**	**fior**	**negletto**	**e**	**vile**
you	only	naked	of	flower	neglected	and	shoddy

e	'zvɛl to	'po i	da	'tur bi ne	se 've ɾo	o	ar boʃ: 'ʃɛl: lo	kru 'dɛl	ve 'der	'i o 'spe ɾo
e	**svelto**	**poi**	**da**	**turbine**	**severo**	**o**	**arboscello**	**crudel**	**veder**	**io spero.**
and	uprooted	then	by	whirlwinds	severe	o	sapling	cruel	to see	I I hope

I hope to see only you bare of flowers, uncared for and shoddy, and then uprooted by severe winds,
o cruel sapling.

e	tu	'bar ba ɾo	'ri o	ke	si	su 'per bo	al	'ma ɾe	'pɔr ti	'lon de
E	**tu**	**barbaro**	**rio**	**che**	**sì**	**superbo**	**al**	**mare**	**porti**	**l'onde**
and	you	barbarous	brook	who	so	proud	to the	sea	you carry	the waters

'tu e	'kja ɾe	'nel: la	sta 'dʒo ne	e 'sti va	'ko i	'fre ski	u 'mor	non	baɲ: ɲe 'ra i
tue	**chiare**	**nella**	**stagione**	**estiva,**	**coi**	**freschi**	**umor**	**non**	**bagnerai**
yours	clear	in the	season	summer	with the	fresh	humors	not	you will bathe

la	'ri va	ke	'dʒu sti	e	non	kru 'dɛ li	'lak: kwe	ti	nje ge 'ran: no
la	**riva**	**ché**	**giusti**	**e**	**non**	**crudeli**	**l'acque**	**ti**	**niegheranno**
the	shore	because	just	and	not	cruel	the waters	you	will refuse

i	'ma ɾi	e	i	'tʃɛ li
i	**mari**	**e**	**i**	**cieli.**
the	seas	and	the	skies

And you, barbarous brook who so proudly carry your clear waters to the sea in the
summertime, you will not bathe your shore with fresh humors because, justly and not
cruelly, the seas and skies will deny you water.

> umor[i] = as in
> English: i.e.,
> vital liquids

e	in	'fi ne	'a ri do	in	'tut: to	ti	pas: se 'ra	il	pa 'stor	kon	'pjɛ de	aʃ: 'ʃut: to
E	**in**	**fine**	**arido**	**in**	**tutto**	**ti**	**passerà**	**il**	**pastor**	**con**	**piede**	**asciutto.**
and	at	end	arid	in	all	you	will pass	the	shepherd	with	foot	dry

And finally, [when you are] completely arid, the shepherd will pass by you with dry feet.

'kwan do	sa 'ra i	sɛn 'tson de	o	'bar ba ɾo	ruʃ: 'ʃɛl: lo	la	'nin fa	e
Quando	**sarai**	**senz'onde**	**o**	**barbaro**	**ruscello**	**la**	**ninfa**	**e**
when	you will be	without waters	o	barbarous	brook	the	nymph	and

When you are without water, o barbarous brook, the nymph and

il	pa sto 'rel: lo	a	te	pju	non	ver: 'ra
il	**pastorello**	**a**	**te**	**più**	**non**	**verrà.**
the	shepherd	to	you	more	not	will come

the shepherd will no longer come to you.

e	'kwan do	'sɛn tsa	'fron de	sa 'ra i	'kru do	ar boʃ: ʃɛl: lo	la	'nin fa
E	**quando**	**senza**	**fronde**	**sarai,**	**crudo**	**arboscello,**	**la**	**ninfa**
and	when	without	leaves	you will be	cruel	sapling	the	nymph

And when you are without leaves, cruel sapling, the nymph

e	il	pa sto 'rɛl: lo	kol	pjɛ	ti	pre me 'ra
e	**il**	**pastorello**	**col**	**piè**	**ti**	**premerà.**
and	the	shepherd	with the	foot	you	will press upon

and the shepherd will stomp on you.

GL: **Fille**

☙

[5, 9, 25, 26, 31, 54, 59, 60, 64]   Alternately titled **Per la gloria**.
from: *Griselda (1722)*
character: *Ernesto*

Paolo Antonio Rolli

per la 'glɔ rja da do 'rar vi
Per la gloria d'adorarvi
For the glory of adoring you

per	la	'glɔ rja	da do 'rar vi	'vɔʎ: ʎo	a 'mar vi	o	'lu tʃi	'ka rɛ
Per	**la**	**gloria**	**d'adorarvi**	**voglio**	**amarvi,**	**o**	**luci**	**care.**
for	the	glory	of to adore you	I want	to love you	o	eyes	dear

For the glory of adoring you I want to love you, o dear eyes.

a 'man do	pe ne 'rɔ	ma	'sɛm pre	va me 'rɔ	si	nel	'mi o	pe 'na re
Amando	**penerò,**	**ma**	**sempre**	**v'amerò,**	**sì,**	**nel**	**mio**	**penare.**
loving	I will suffer	but	always	you I will love	yes	in the	my	suffering

In loving I will suffer; but always I will love you, yes, in my suffering.

pe ne 'rɔ	va me 'rɔ	'lu tʃi	'ka rɛ
Penerò,	**v'amerò,**	**luci**	**care.**
I will suffer	you I will love	eyes	dear

I will suffer, I will love you, dear eyes.

> *var.:* ...v'amerò, care care.
> = ...I will love you, dear, dear ones.

'sɛn tsa	'spe me	di	di 'lɛt: to	'va no	af: 'fɛt: to	ɛ	so spi 'ra re
Senza	**speme**	**di**	**diletto**	**vano**	**affetto**	**è**	**sospirare,**
without	hope	of	pleasure	futile	affection	is	yearnng

Without the hope of pleasure, yearning is a futile affection;

> *speme (lit.) = speranza*

ma	i	'vɔ stri	'dol tʃi	'ra i	ki	va ɡed: 'dʒar	pwɔ	'ma i	e	non	va 'ma re
ma	**i**	**vostri**	**dolci**	**rai**	**chi**	**vagheggiar**	**può**	**mai**	**e**	**non**	**v'amare?**
but	the	your	sweet	eyes	who	to gaze at	is able	ever	and	not	you to love

but who can ever contemplate your sweet glances and not love you?

pe ne 'rɔ	va me 'rɔ	'lu tʃi	'ka rɛ
Penerò,	**v'amerò,**	**luci**	**care!**
I will suffer	you I will love	eyes	dear

I will suffer, I will love you, dear eyes!

> *var.: as above*

☙

[50]

'pjaŋ go in 'van dal: 'li dol
Piango invan dal[l']idol
I weep in vain [because of the separation] from my idol

'pjaŋ go	in 'van	dal: 'li dol	'mi o	la	pe 'no za	lon ta 'nan tsa
Piango	**invan**	**dal[l']idol**	**mio**	**la**	**penosa**	**lontananza,**
I weep	in vain	from the idol	mine	the	painful	separation

I weep in vain [because of the] painful separation from my idol;

e   lu 'ziŋ go   il   'mi o   de 'zi o   kon   la   'ka ɾa   ri mem 'bran tsa
e   **lusingo** **il** **mio** **desio**   **con** **la** **cara** **rimembranza.**
and   I satisfy   the   my   longing   with   the   dear   rimembrance
and I satisfy my longing with the dear memory of her.

> *The translation could also be "of him," as there is nothing in the Italian to identify the speaker specifically as a man or a woman.*

la   bel: 'lis: si ma   sem 'bjan tsa   'kɔ   skol 'pi ta   in   'mɛd: dzo   al   'kɔ ɾe
La **bellissima**   **sembianza**   **ch'ho** **scolpita** **in** **mezzo**   **al** **core**
the   most beautiful   features   which I have engraved in   middle   at the heart
The most beautiful face, engraved in the depths of my heart,

'pɔ ko   'tɛm pra   il   'mi o   do 'lo ɾe   ke   mad: 'dʒo ɾe   in   me   san: 'nan tsa
poco **tempra** **il** **mio** **dolore**   **che** **maggiore**   **in** **me** **s'annanza.**
little   tempers   the   my   sorrow   that   greater   in   me   itself announces
little assuages my sorrow, which increases in me.

> *"s'annanza" is a puzzle I could not solve with research; the verb "annanzare" may likely be an antiquated variant of "annunziare" = to announce, foretell.*

'lun dʒi   'dal: la   'su a   'sfe ɾa   'sa dʒi ta   il   'fɔ ko   e   'stri da   e   par   ke
Lungi   **dalla** **sua** **sfera** **s'agita**   **il** **foco** **e**   **strida** **e** **par** **che**
far   from the   its   sphere   agitates   the   fire   and   crackles   and   it seems that
Far from its sphere the fire stirs and crackles, and it seems that

'dʒɛ ma   'lon da   pas: sad 'dʒɛ ɾa   per 'ke   a 'fɔr tsa dal   'fon te   si di 'vi de
gema   **l'onda** **passaggiera**   **perché** **a forza dal**   **fonte** **si divide.**
groans   the wave   passing over   because   necessarily from the source   it parts
the passing wave groans because it must separate from its source.

> *passaggiera = (mod.) passeggiera*

ko 'zi   'prɔ vo   aŋ 'kor 'i o   'dɔʎ: ʎa   o mi 'tʃi da   'sɛn tsa   di   te   'mi o   'bɛ ne
Così   **provo**   **ancor** **io** **doglia** **omicida,**   **senza**   **di** **te** **mio** **bene,**
thus   I experience still   I   suffering murderous   without   of   you   my   dear one
Thus do I still experience deadly suffering without you, my dear one;

kon   du 'ris: si me   'pe ne   tor 'men ta   'lal ma   'mi a   lon ta 'nan tsa   kru 'dɛ le   e   dʒe lo 'zi a
con   **durissime**   **pene** **tormenta**   **l'alma** **mia** **lontananza**   **crudele**   **e** **gelosia.**
with   harshest   pains   torments   the soul mine   separation   cruel   and   jealousy
cruel separation and jealousy torment my soul with the harshest of pains.

lon 'tan   dal   'vol to   ke   min: na 'mo ɾa   maf: 'flid: dʒe   oɲ: 'ɲo ɾa   'fred: do   ti 'mor
Lontan **dal** **volto** **che** **m'innamora**   **m'affligge**   **ognora**   **freddo**   **timor.**
far away   from the face   that   me enamors   me afflicts   always   cold   fear
Far away from the face that enamors me, cold fear constantly afflicts me.

'te mo   ka 'man te   'dal tro   sem 'bjan te   la   'su a   mer 'tʃe de   'rub: bil   'mi o   kɔr
Temo   **ch'amante**   **d'altro** **sembiante**   **la** **sua** **mercede**   **rubbi'l**   **mio** **cor.**
I fear   that lover   of other   countenance   the   its   prize   may rob the   my   heart
I fear that a lover of different countenance may rob my heart of its prize.

☙

[1, 2]
from: *Mario Fuggitivo (1710)*
character: *Dalinda*

Silvio Stampiglia

pju   non   ti   'vɔʎ: ʎo   'kre de ɾe
Più **non** **ti** **voglio**   **credere**
I no longer wish to believe you

pju	non	ti	'vɔʎː ʎo	'kre de ɾe	pe 'no za	dʒe lo 'zi a
Più	**non**	**ti**	**voglio**	**credere,**	**penosa**	**gelosia!**
more	not	you	I wish	to believe	painful	jealousy

I no longer wish to believe you, painful jealousy!

tu	'vwɔ i	kon	'fredː do	'dʒe lo	e 'stiŋ gwe ɾe	il	'mi o	'fɔ ko
Tu	**vuoi**	**con**	**freddo**	**gelo**	**estinguere**	**il**	**mio**	**foco,**
you	want	with	icy	cold	to extinguish	the	my	fire

You want to extinguish my fire with icy cold;

ma	per	lar 'dor	'ki o	'tʃe lo	'kwe sto	'tu o	'dʒe lo	ɛ	'pɔ ko
ma	**per**	**l'ardor,**	**ch'io**	**celo,**	**questo**	**tuo**	**gelo**	**è**	**poco.**
but	for	the ardor	which I	I conceal	this	your	cold	is	little

but, for the ardor which I conceal, this cold of yours is slight.

ne	'ma i	ʎi	sa 'pra	'tʃe de ɾe	la	'bɛlː la	'fjamː ma	'mi a
Né	**mai**	**gli**	**saprà**	**cedere**	**la**	**bella**	**fiamma**	**mia.**
not	ever	to it	it will know how	to yield	the	beautiful	flame	mine

My beautiful flame will never yield to it.

&

[35]

pju 'va ga e vetː tso 'zetː ta
Più vaga e vezzosetta
More pretty and charming

pju	'va ga	e	vetː tso 'zetː ta	sa 'ra i	se	nel	'tu o	'kɔ ɾe
Più	**vaga**	**e**	**vezzosetta**	**sarai**	**se**	**nel**	**tuo**	**core**
more	pretty	and	charming	you will be	if	in the	your	heart

'da i	'lwɔ go	'alː la	pje 'ta
dai	**luogo**	**alla**	**pietà!**
you give	place	to the	pity

You will be more pretty and charming if you make room in your heart for pity!

non	've di	o	sem pli 'tʃetː ta	ke	'ʃe ma	il	'tu o	ri 'go ɾe
Non	**vedi,**	**o**	**semplicetta,**	**che**	**scema**	**il**	**tuo**	**rigore**
not	you see	o	silly girl	that	lessens	the	your	severity

Do you not see, o silly girl, that your severity lessens

i	'pre dʒi	'alː la	bel 'ta
i	**pregi**	**alla**	**beltà.**
the	merits	to the	beauty

the merits of your beauty?

&

[25]
from: *Calfurnia (1724)*   *Nicola Haym*

se 'ma i vjɛn 'tokː ka
Se mai vien tocca
Whenever [a wound] touches

se	'ma i	vjɛn	'tokː ka	'pja ga	mor 'ta le	'a spro	'fi a	il	'ma le
Se	**mai**	**vien**	**tocca**	**piaga**	**mortale,**	**aspro**	**fia**	**il**	**male**
if	ever	comes	touches	wound	mortal	sharp	will be	the	hurt

Whenever a mortal wound touches, the hurt will be sharp

> fia =
> (mod.)
> sarà

e   vi e 'pju   'kreʃ: ʃe   'fjɛ ɾo   il   do 'lor
e   viepiù   cresce   fiero   il   dolor!
and   all the more   grows   fierce   the   pain
and the pain will grow even more fierce!

e   vi e 'pju   'kreʃ: ʃe   pju   'kreʃ: ʃe   'fjɛ ɾo   il   do 'lor
E   viepiù   cresce,   più   cresce   fiero   il   dolor!
and   all the more   grows   more   grows   fierce   the   pain
And the more the pain increases, the more cruel it becomes!

'ta le   aŋ 'ki o   'so no   ke   se   ram: 'men to   il   'mi o   tor 'men to
Tale   anch'io   sono   che   se   rammento   il   mio   tormento
such   also I   I am   [that]   if   I remember   the   my   torment
And so it is with me: if I remember my torment,

'tan to   sak: 'kreʃ: ʃe   kop: 'pri me   il   kɔr
tanto   s'accresce,   ch'opprime   il   cor.
so much   it increases   that it crushes   the   heart
it increases so much that it crushes my heart.

❧

[26]

si   ke   fe 'de le
Sì, che fedele
Yes, faithful [eyes]

si   ke   fe 'de le   pu 'pil: le   a 'ma te   ben 'ke   spje 'ta te   va do ɾe 'ɾo
Sì,   che   fedele   pupille   amate   benché   spietate   v'adorerò.
yes   [that]   faithful   eyes   beloved   although   pitiless   you I will adore
Yes, faithful beloved eyes, even though [you are] pitiless, I will adore you.

e   se   kru 'dɛ le   ɛ   il   'nu me   in 'fan te   'dɛs: ser   ko 'stan te   non   laʃ: ʃe 'ɾo
E   se   crudele   è   il   nume   infante   d'esser   costante   non   lascierò.
and   if   cruel   is   the   deity   infant   of to be   constant   not   I shall leave off
And if the infant deity *[Cupid]* is cruel, I will not stop being faithful.

❧

[34]
from: *Calfurnia (1724)*
character: *Giulia*

Nicola Haym

u 'nom bra   di 'pa tʃe
Un'ombra di pace
A hint of peace

u 'nom bra   di   'pa tʃe   si   'mo stra   al   'mi o   kɔr
Un'ombra   di   pace   si   mostra   al   mio   cor.
a hint   of   peace   itself   shows   to the   my   heart
A hint of peace appears in my heart.

af: 'fan: no   ke   'pja tʃe   mi   'vjɛ ne   a   be 'ar   a
Affanno   che   piace   mi   viene   a   bear.   [Ah!]
anxiety   which   is pleasing   to me   comes   to   to make happy   ah
A pleasing anxiety comes to make me happy. [Ah!]

mi	par	ke	si ˈkan dʒi	in	ˈdʒɔ ja	il	do ˈlor
Mi	**par**	**che**	**si cangi**	**in**	**gioia**	**il**	**dolor,**
to me	it seems	that	may change	into	joy	the	sorrow

It seems to me that my sorrow is changing into joy

e	ˈdi ka	tu	ˈpjan dʒi	ma	ˈdɛ vi	spe ˈrar
e	**dica:**	**tu**	**piangi,**	**ma**	**devi**	**sperar.**
and	it says	you	you weep	but	you ought	to hope

and is saying: you weep, but you should hope.

[10, 25, 38, 60] This song was formerly attributed to Salvator Rosa.

ˈva do bɛn ˈspes: so kan ˈdʒan do ˈlɔ ko
Vado ben spesso cangiando loco
I go very often from place to place

ˈva do	bɛn	ˈspes: so	kan ˈdʒan do	ˈlɔ ko	ma	non	sɔ	ˈma i	kan ˈdʒar	de ˈzi o
Vado	**bɛn**	**spesso**	**cangiando**	**loco,**	**ma**	**non**	**so**	**mai**	**cangiar**	**desio.**
I go	very	often	changing	place	but	not	I know how	ever	to change	desire

I go very often from place to place, but I can never change my desire.

ˈsɛm pre	li ˈstes: so	sa ˈra	il	ˈmi o	ˈfɔ ko	e	sa ˈrɔ	ˈsɛm pre	li ˈstes: so	aŋ ˈki o
Sempre	**l'istesso**	**sarà**	**il**	**mio**	**foco,**	**e**	**sarò**	**sempre**	**l'istesso**	**anch'io.**
always	the same	will be	the	my	fire	and	I will be	always	the same	also I

My passion will always be the same, and I too will always be the same.

✦ *Bononcini, Giovanni Maria (1642-1678)*

Violinist, composer, and theorist, he was born in Montecorone, near Modena, and went to Modena as a young boy to study. He became violinist at the Cathedral of Modena and chamber musician to the Dowager Duchess Laura d'Este. He and his wife Anna Maria Prezii had eight children, of whom only two survived: Giovanni (see *Bononcini, G.*) and Antonio Maria (b.1677).

Grove mentions a sketch drawn in a copy of Bononcini's *Varii Fiori* showing that he also played the *violoncello da spalla*, a large instrument held over the shoulder and sometimes strapped to the chest.

His theoretical treastise *Musico prattico*, first printed in 1673, was widely distributed at the time and influential in the decades after his death.

Up until the last years of his life he composed only instrumental music; his sonatas "represent the highest achievement of the late 17th century Modenese instrumental school *[Grove]*." Beginning in 1675 he composed arias and solo cantatas, madrigals, and a chamber opera.

[24, 44]

pje ˈta ˈmi o ˈka ɾo ˈbɛ ne
Pietà, mio caro bene
Have pity, my dearly beloved

pje ˈta	ˈmi o	ˈka ɾo	ˈbɛ ne	o	ˈi dol	ˈmi o	pje ˈta
Pietà,	**mio**	**caro**	**bene!**	**O**	**idol**	**mio,**	**pietà!**
have pity	my	dear	dear one	o	idol	mine	have pity

Have pity, my dearly beloved! O my idol, have pity!

	pje 'ta	'mi o	'ka ɾo	'bɛ ne	'i dol	'mi o	pje 'ta	
in [44]:	**Pietà**	**mio**	**caro**	**bene,**	**idolo**	**mio,**	**pietà!**	
	have pity	my	dear	dear one	idol	mine	have pity	

Have pity, my dearly beloved; my idol, have pity!

iŋ 'kon tro	un	kɔr	ke	'laŋ gwe	dʒa	'vin to	'kwa zi	e 'zan gwe
Incontro	**un**	**cor**	**che**	**langue,**	**già**	**vinto,**	**quasi**	**esangue,**
toward	a	heart	which	languishes	already	defeated	nearly	dead

Toward a heart which languishes, already defeated, nearly dead,

	'kon tro	dun	kɔr	ke	'laŋ gwe
in [44]:	**Contro**	**d'un**	**cor**	**che**	**langue, ...**
	toward	[of] a	heart	which	languishes

Toward a heart which languishes, ...

u 'zar	pju	non	kon 'vjɛ ne	fje 'ret: tsa	e	kru del 'ta
usar	**più**	**non**	**conviene**	**fierezza**	**e**	**crudeltà.**
to use	more	not	is necessary	pride	and	cruelty

it is no longer necessary to act with pride and cruelty.

> [24] *ends with* ..**e crudeltà, ah!**
> (...and cruelty – ah!)

✿ *Bottegari, Cosimo* (1554-1620)

Composer, singer, and lutenist, he was born in Florence. By 1573 he was in Munich, appointed a gentleman of the chamber (*gentiluomo della camera*, or *Kammerherr*), at the court of Duke Albrecht V of Bavaria, who ennobled him and bestowed many favors upon him.

Bottegari edited an anthology of music by composers in the service of the Duke, to which he himself contributed two madrigals. His *Arie e canzoni in musica* (known as *The Bottegari Lutebook*) is a collection of some one hundred and twenty-seven works for voice and lute by various composers; it includes some of the earliest known monodies, of which about forty are his own.

Following the death of Duke Albrecht in 1579, Bottegari returned to Florence and joined the Medici court as a performer. He was not salaried, other than with horse, stabling, food and the services of a groom; apparently he was independently wealthy as a result of various commercial enterprises.

[7, 36]

mi 'par to
Mi parto
I am leaving

mi	'par to	'a i	'sɔr te	'ri a
Mi	**parto,**	**ahi!**	**sorte**	**ria,**
me	I depart	alas	fate	cruel

I am leaving – alas, cruel fate,

e	il	kɔr	vi	'laʃ: ʃo	e	laf: 'flit: ta	'al ma	'mi a
e	**il**	**cor**	**vi**	**lascio**	**e**	**l'afflitta**	**alma**	**mia.**
and	the	heart	to you	I leave	and	the afflicted	soul	my

and I am leaving you my heart and my grieving soul.

ne	mor: 'rɔ	nɔ	ke	a 'mor	non	'vwɔ le	ad: 'di o	dol 'tʃis: si mo	bɛn	'mi o
Né	**morrò,**	**no,**	**ché**	**amor**	**non**	**vuole;**	**addio,**	**dolcissimo**	**ben**	**mio.**
not	I will die	no	because	love	not	wishes	farewell	sweetest	dear	my

I shall not die, for love does not wish it; farewell, my sweetest dear one.

> *The following two lines are not in* [36].

mi	'par to	e	vɔ	lon 'ta no	'sɛm pre	kja 'man do	il	'vɔ stro	'no me	in 'va no
Mi	**parto**	**e**	**vo**	**lontano**	**sempre**	**chiamando**	**il**	**vostro**	**nome**	**invano.**
me	I depart	and	I go	far away	always	calling	the	your	name	in vain

I am leaving, and I am going far away always calling your name in vain.

ne	mor: 'rɔ	nɔ	ke	il	dwɔl	ma 'i ta	ad: 'di o	dol 'tʃis: si ma	'mi a	'vi ta
Né	**morrò,**	**no,**	**che**	**il**	**duol**	**m'aita;**	**addio,**	**dolcissima**	**mia**	**vita.**
not	I will die	no	because	the	grief	me helps	farewell	sweetest	my	life

I shall not die, for grief sustains me; farewell, my sweetest life.

mi	'par to	o	'mi a	siɲ: 'ɲo ɾa	ke	dja	del	'mi o	par 'tir	ɛ	'dʒun ta	'lo ɾa
Mi	**parto,**	**o**	**mia**	**signora,**	**ché**	**già**	**del**	**mio**	**partir**	**è**	**giunta**	**l'ora.**
me	I depart	o	my	lady	because	already	of the	my	departing	is	reached	the hour

I am leaving, o my lady, for the hour for my departure has arrived.

ne	mor: 'rɔ	nɔ	ke	a 'mor	non	'vwɔ le	ad: 'di o	dol 'tʃis: si mo	bɛn	'mi o
Né	**morrò,**	**no,**	**ché**	**amor**	**non**	**vuole;**	**addio,**	**dolcissimo**	**ben**	**mio.**
not	I will die	no	because	love	not	wishes	farewell	sweetest	dear	my

I shall not die, for love does not wish it; farewell, my sweetest dear one.

> *var. in* [36]*:* ...**ch'il** (= **che il**) **duol m'aita.** *See line 2, above, for translation.*

[55] Titled **Morte da me**.   *Baldassarre Castiglione*

'mɔr te da me 'tan ta spet: 'ta ta
Morte, da me tant'aspettata
Death, so long awaited

'mɔr te	da	me	'tan ta spet: 'ta ta	'vjɛ ni
Morte,	**da**	**me**	**tant'aspettata,**	**vieni:**
death	by	me	so much awaited	come

Death, so long awaited, come:

e	fa	ke	'vɛŋ ga	si	se 'kre ta	e	'lɛn ta
e	**fa**	**che**	**venga**	**sì**	**secreta**	**e**	**lenta,**
and	make	that	you come	so	secretly	and	slowly

and come so stealthily and slowly

kel	'tu o	ve 'nir	il	'mi o	mo 'rir	non	'sɛn ta
che'l	**tuo**	**venir**	**il**	**mio**	**morir**	**non**	**senta.**
that the	your	coming	the	my	dying	not	I may feel

that I may not feel the moment of my dying.

o	vjɛn	kon	'kwel: la	'fret: ta	'ko me	da	'tʃɛl	sa 'et: ta
O	**vien!**	**con**	**quella**	**fretta**	**come**	**da**	**ciel**	**saetta,**
o	come	with	that	haste	like	from	heaven	thunderbolt

O come, as swiftly as a thunderbolt from heaven

ke	'twɔ na	e	'lam pa	e	'ful mi na	in un 'pun to
che	**tuona**	**e**	**lampa**	**e**	**fulmina**	**in un punto;**
which	roars	and	flashes	and	strikes	at the same time

that roars and flashes and strikes all at once;

ko 'zil   'mi o   'kɔ ɾe   'si a   da   te   diz 'dʒun to
così'l   mio   core   sia   da   te   disgiunto.
thus the   my   heart   may be   by   you   *(lett.)* torn away
thus may my heart be taken away by you.

&

[55]

non ε 'pe na mad 'dʒor
Non è pena maggior
There is no greater suffering

non   ε   'pe na   mad: 'dʒor   kor 'te zi   a 'man ti
Non   è   pena   maggior,   cortesi   amanti,
not   is   suffering   greater   courtly   lovers
There is no greater suffering, courtly lovers,

'vo i   ke   do 'na ste   a   'du o   beʎ: 'ʎɔk: kil   'kɔ ɾe
voi   che   donaste   a   duo   begl'occh'il   core,
you   who   gave   to   two   beautiful eyes the   heart
you who have given your hearts to two beautiful eyes,

> *duo =*
> *(mod.)*
> *due*

ke   'kwan do   'lwɔ mo   'al: la   'su a   'dɔn: na   in: 'nan ti
che   quando   l'uomo   alla   sua   Donna   innanti
than   when   the man   of the   his   Lady   in front
than when a man, in the presence of his Lady,

far   pa 'le ze   non   'pɔs: sil   'su o   do 'lo ɾe
far   palese   non   poss'il   suo   dolore,
to make   manifest   not   he may the   his   grief
can not make his grief known

e   kwan tuŋ 'kwel: la   il   kɔr   'ved: dʒa i   sem 'bjan ti
e   quantunqu'ella   il   cor   vegg'ai   sembianti
and   although she   the   heart   may look at the   expressions
and [when], though she may see the face of his heart,

> *vegg' [vegga]*
> *(poet.) = veda*

non   si 'mwɔ va   pje 'ta   di   ki   si 'mɔ ɾe
non   si muov'a   pietà   di   chi   si more:
not   herself is moved to   pity   for   he who   himself is dying
she is not moved to pity for the one who is dying.

gran   mi 'zε ɾjal   'su o   a 'mor   'te ner   tʃe 'la to
Gran   miseria'l   suo   amor   tener   celato
great   misery the   his   love   to keep   hidden
Great misery it is to keep one's love hidden

e   a 'man dal 'tru i   non   'εs: ser   'pun to   a 'ma to
e,   amand'altrui,   non   esser   punto   amato.
and   loving another   not   to be   at all   loved
and, loving someone, not to be loved at all.

Busatti, Cherubino (?-c.1644)

All that is known about Busatti's life is that he was a priest who in 1638 was organist at the Church of San Sebastiano in Venice.

Though most of his secular songs are lost, Busatti is credited with the collections *Arie a voce sola commode da cantarsi nel clavicembalo* (1638), *Arie* (books two through six, not dated), and *Settimo libro d'ariette a voce sola* (1644).

[39]

'di te 'ki o 'kan ti
Dite ch'io canti
Tell me to sing

'di te	'ki o	'kan ti	'i o	kan te 'rɔ	'kan to	sɛn 'tsar te	e	sɛn tsiŋ 'gan: no
Dite	**ch'io**	**canti,**	**io**	**canterò.**	**Canto**	**senz'arte**	**e**	**senz'inganno.**
say	that I	I should sing	I	I will sing	I sing	without art	and	without deceit

Tell me to sing, and I will sing. I will sing without artfulness or deceit.

ki	'dis: se	'dɔn: na	'vol se	dir	'dan: no
Chi	**disse:**	**donna**	**volse**	**dir:**	**danno.**
who	said	woman	meant	to say	ruin

Whoever said "woman" intended to say "ruin."

de	la	kan 'tso ne	'kwe stɛ	'u na	'par te	ma	'i o	pe 'rɔ	non	sɔ
De	**la**	**canzone**	**quest'è**	**una**	**parte,**	**ma**	**io**	**però**	**non**	**so**
of	the	song	this is	a	part	but	I	nevertheless	not	I know

de la = (mod.) della

This is part of the song; but I still do not know

sil	'tɔ no	vi	'pjat: tʃa	o	si	o	nɔ
s'il	**tono**	**vi**	**piaccia,**	**o**	**sì,**	**o**	**no?**
if the	tone	to you	is pleasing	either	yes	or	no

tuono = (mod.) tono

if the tone pleases you – yes or no?

'di te	'ki o	'kan ti	'i o	kan te 'rɔ	'kwan do	ke	'mo stra	'dɔn: na	da 'mar ci
Dite	**ch'io**	**canti,**	**io**	**canterò.**	**Quando**	**che**	**mostra**	**donna**	**d'amarci,**
say	that I	I should sing	I	I will sing	when	[that]	shows	woman	of to love us

Tell me to sing, and I will sing. When a woman shows us love,

al: 'lo ra	'pen sa	pju	diŋ gan: 'nar tʃi	lef: 'fet: to	'kja ro	tʃe	lo	di 'mo stra
allora	**pensa**	**più**	**d'ingannarci;**	**l'effetto**	**chiaro**	**ce**	**lo**	**dimostra.**
[in that case]	she thinks	more	of to deceive us	the effect	clear	to us	it	she demonstrates

she is thinking more about deceiving us; she clearly demonstrates the effect on us.

ma	o i 'mɛ	non	sɔ	se	pju	bra 'ma te	'ki o	'kan ti	o	nɔ
Ma	**ohimè,**	**non**	**so**	**se**	**più**	**bramate**	**ch'io**	**canti,**	**o**	**no?**
But	alas	not	I know	if	more	you desire	that I	I sing	or	no

But alas, I don't know if you want me to sing more, or not.

'di te	'ki o	'kan ti	'i o	kan te 'rɔ	le	'dɔn: ne	'kru de	kol	lu ziŋ 'ga re
Dite	**ch'io**	**canti,**	**io**	**canterò.**	**Le**	**donne**	**crude**	**col**	**lusingare**
say	that I	I should sing	I	I will sing	the	women	cruel	with the	flattering

Tell me to sing, and I will sing. Cruel women, with their flattering,

an   un   fin   'em pjo   lon 'tan   da 'ma ɾe
han   un   fin   empio   lontan   d'amare,
have   a   purpose   wicked   far   from loving
have a wicked purpose far from loving,

e   un   'pɛt: to   'in fi do   ke   'tɔs ko   'kju de
e   un   petto   infido,   che   tosco   chiude.
and   a   breast; *(fig.)* heart   unfaithful   which   poison   contains
and an unfaithful heart which contains poison.

or 'su   non   sɔ   se   pju   di 'ɾe te   'ki o   'kan ti   o   nɔ
Orsù,   non   so   se   più   direte   ch'io   canti,   o   no?
come now   not   I know   if   more   you will say   that I   I sing   or   no
Come now, I don't know if you will tell me to sing more, or not!

'di te   'ki o   'tat: tʃa   'i o   ta tʃe 'rɔ   per 'ke   non 'pɔs: so   kan 'tan do   il   've ɾo
Dite   ch'io   taccia,   io   tacerò;   perché   non posso   cantando   il   vero
say   that I   I be quiet   I   I will be quiet   because   not I am able   singing   the   truth
Tell me to be quiet, and I will be quiet; because in singing the truth I can not

far   ap: pa 'ri ɾe   'bjaŋ ko   per   'ne ɾo   e dil   'mi o   'kan to   da   'vo i   ɛ   'mɔs: so
far   apparire   bianco   per   nero,   ed il   mio   canto   da   voi   è   mosso.
to make   to appear   white   for   black   and the   my   song   by   you   is   aroused
make black appear white, and my song is inspired by you.

ma   'tʃɛr to   sɔ   ke   la   kan 'tso ne   non   vi   gu 'stɔ
Ma   certo   so   che   la   canzone   non   vi   gustò!
But   certainly   I know   that   the   song   not   to you   was pleasing
But I know for sure that you did not like the song!

ès

[40]

ɛ   tor 'na to   il   'mi o   bɛn
È tornato il mio ben
My dear one has returned

ɛ   tor 'na to   il   'mi o   bɛn
È   tornato   il   mio   ben,
has   returned   the   my   dear one
My dear one has returned,

si ɛ 'fat: to   il   tʃɛl   se 'ren   'a i   'mjɛ i   tor 'men ti
si è fatto   il   ciel   seren   ai   miei   tormenti;
itself has made   the   sky   serene   to the   my   torments
[and] the sky has become serene to my torments;

pju   non   'te mo   do 'lor   or   ke   mi   'pɔr dʒe   a 'mor   'dʒɔ je   e   kon 'tɛn ti
più   non   temo   dolor,   or   che   mi   porge   Amor   gioie   e   contenti.
more   not   I fear   suffering   now   that   to me   offers   Love   joys   and   contentments
no longer do I fear suffering, now that Love offers me joy and contentment.

'ɛk: ko   ke   pur   lab: 'bratʃ tʃo   e   per   so 'ver kja   'dʒɔ ja   'i o   mi di 'sfat: tʃo
Ecco,   che   pur   l'abbraccio   e   per   soverchia   gioia   io   mi disfaccio.
here   [that]   now   her I embrace   and   through   excessive   joy   I   myself consume
Here, now, I embrace her and am consumed with excessive joy.

'veŋ ga   pur   kwel   ke   vwɔl
Venga   pur   quel   che   vuol,
may come   [yet]   that   which   it wishes
Come what may,

kɔ   vi 'tʃi no   il   'mi o   sol   'ko i   'swo i   'bɛ i   'ra i
ch'ho   vicino   il   mio   sol   coi   suoi   bei   rai.
[that] I have   near   the   my   sun   with the   its   beautiful   rays
I have near me my sun with her beautiful rays.

> "il mio sole," grammatically masculine, =
> my beloved one, hence "her[beautiful rays]"

non   ɔ   pju   ke   laŋ 'gwir   non   ɔ   pju   ke   sof: 'frir
Non   ho   più   che   languir,   non   ho   più   che   soffrir
not   I have   more   [that]   languishing   not   I have   more   [that]   suffering
I have no more languishing, no more suffering

e   'pe ne   e   'gwa i   ke   la   'su a   'vi sta   a 'ma ta
e   pene   e   guai,   ché   la   sua   vista   amata
both   pains   and   woes   because   the   her   sight   beloved
from pains and woes, because her beloved countenance

a   dʒa   'la ni ma   'mi a   rak: kon so 'la ta
ha   già   l'anima   mia   racconsolata.
has   already   the soul   my   comforted
has already comforted my soul.

o   bɛn 'spar si   so 'spir   o   so 'a vi   mar 'tir   o   'dol tʃi   'pe ne
O   ben sparsi   sospir,   o   soavi   martir,   o   dolci   pene,
o   spread about sparingly   sighs   o   gentle   torments   o   sweet   pains
O rare sighs, o gentle torments, o sweet pains

kɔ   sof: 'fer te   lon 'tan   'las: so   ma   non   in   van   dal   'mi o   kar   'bɛ ne
ch'ho   sofferte   lontan,   lasso,   ma   non   in   van   dal   mio   car   bene,
that I have   suffered   far   miserable   but   not   in   vain   from the   my   dear   dear one
which I, miserable, have suffered far from my dear one, but not in vain,

> car = caro

lor   mi   'me na   il   do 'lo ɾe   mar 'ti ɾe   in: na mo 'ra to   al   tʃɛl   da 'mo ɾe
l'or   mi   mena   il   dolore,   martire   innamorato,   al   ciel   d'Amore.
the hour   me   leads   the   sorrow   martyr   enamored   to the   heaven   of Love
sorrow now guides this loving martyr to the heaven of Love.

𝒢𝓛: **Amor[e]**

❧

[40]

'mɔr to   son   'io
Morto son io
I am dead

'mɔr to   son   'i o   'ka ɾo   'dol tʃe   ben   'mi o   or 'su   'pren di mi   al 'me no
Morto   son   io,   caro   dolce   ben   mio.   Orsù   prendimi   almeno,
dead   am   I   dear   sweet   dear one   my   come now   take me   at least
I am dead, my sweet dear one.
Now at least take me,

> Printed is "prendem," not a possible verb form in context;
> I've changed it to "prendimi," guessing a copying error.

se   'vi vo   non   mi   'vwɔ i   'mɔr to   nel   'se no
se   vivo   non   mi   vuoi,   morto   nel   seno.
if   alive   not   me   you wish   dead   to the   breast
dead, to your breast, if you do not wish me alive.

e	ˈkwin tʃi	per	ˈmi a	ˈsɔr te	a ˈvrɔ	la	ˈtom ba	in	ˈmɔr te
E	**quinci**	**per**	**mia**	**sorte,**	**avrò**	**la**	**tomba**	**in**	**morte.**
and	here	for	my	fate	I will have	the	grave	in	death

And hence will be, as my fate, the grave.

tul	ˈnjɛ ɡi	o	ˈkru da	o	in dʒu ˈrjo zi	ˈtɔr ti
Tu'l	**nieghi**	**o**	**cruda;**	**o**	**ingiuriosi**	**torti,**
you it	you refuse	o	cruel one	oh	injurious	wrongs

You refuse, o cruel one? Oh, what an injurious wrong,

> *nieghi = (mod.)*
> *negi, from "niegare" =*
> *(mod.) "negare"*

ne ˈɡar	in ˈfin	la	se pol ˈtu ɾa	ˈa i	ˈmɔr ti
negar	**in fin**	**la**	**sepoltura**	**ai**	**morti!**
to deny	in the end	the	burial place	to the	dead

to deny, in the end, a burial place to the dead!

&

[40]

pu pil: ˈlet: te
Pupillette
Little eyes

pu pil: ˈlet: te	non	man tʃi ˈde te	nɔ
Pupillette,	**non**	**m'ancidete,**	**no,**
little eyes	not	me you kill	no

Little eyes, you do not kill me, no,

> *ancidete =*
> *(mod.) uccidete*

ke	non	pwɔ	mo ˈrir	kwel	kɔr	ke	ˈprɔ va	i	ˈvɔ stri	ˈdar di
ché	**non**	**può**	**morir**	**quel**	**cor,**	**che**	**prova**	**i**	**vostri**	**dardi.**
because	not	is able	to die	that	heart	which	feels	the	your	arrows

because that heart which feels your arrows cannot die.

beŋ ˈke	ar ˈtʃe ri	ˈvo i	ˈsja te	non	sa ˈpe te	fe ˈrir	ke	non	sa ˈnja te
Benché	**arcieri**	**voi**	**siate,**	**non**	**sapete**	**ferir**	**che**	**non**	**saniate.**
although	archers	you	you are	not	you know how	to wound	that	not	you heal

Although you are archers, you do not know how to wound without healing.

zdeɲ: ɲo ˈzet: te	im pa ˈɾa te	a	fe ˈrir
Sdegnosette,	**imparate**	**a**	**ferir,**
haughty little ones	learn	to	to wound

Haughty little ones, learn to wound,

ke	mo ˈrir	ve ˈdre te	a	ˈvo i	ri ˈvɔl to	ˈoɲ: ɲi	mor ˈta le
che	**morir**	**vedrete**	**a**	**voi**	**rivolto**	**ogni**	**mortale.**
that	to die	you will see	to	you	turned	every	mortal

so that you will see every mortal turned toward you dying.

e	se	pja ˈɡar	vo ˈle te	ar ˈma te vi	di	ˈstra li	non	ar ˈde te
E	**se**	**piagar**	**volete,**	**armatevi**	**di**	**strali,**	**non**	**ardete!**
and	if	to injure	you want	arm yourselves	with	arrows	not	you burn

And if you want to injure, arm yourselves with arrows [but] do not burn!

fu ɾjo ˈzet: te	mi nat: ˈtʃa te mi	pur
Furiosette,	**minacciatemi**	**pur;**
little angry ones	threaten me	then

Angry little ones, go ahead and threaten me;

son	si ˈkur	ne	le	ˈgwɛrː re	da ˈmor	da	ˈvɔ stri	ˈzdeɲː ɲi
son	**sicur**	**ne**	**le**	**guerre**	**d'Amor**	**da**	**vostri**	**sdegni,**
I am	safe	of	the	wars	of Love	from	your	scorns

I am safe from your scorn in the wars of Love

> ne le = (mod.) nelle

kɔ	per	ri ˈpa ɾi	e	ˈsku di
ch'ho	**per**	**ripari**	**e**	**scudi**
because I have	for	shelters	and	shields

because I have, as refuge and shield

ˈkon tro	i	ˈvɔ stri	ˈɔkː ki	ar ˈtʃɛr	du ˈɔ i	ˈlabː bri	iɲː ˈɲu di
contro	**i**	**vostri**	**occhi**	**arcier**	**duoi**	**labbri**	**ignudi.**
against	the	your	eyes	archer	two	lips	naked

against your archer eyes, two naked lips.

> duoi = (mod.) due

GL: Amor

 # Buzzoleni, Giovanni (fl.1682-1722)

Neither birth nor death dates are given in *Grove* for Buzzoleni. It is known that he was a tenor and was in the service of Ferdinando Carlo Gonzaga, Duke of Mantua, in 1682, when he sang four roles in Legrenzi's *Ottaviano Cesare Augusto*. As a singer he is named in the libretti of three theatre works in Naples and, as "a musician of the emperor," in one libretto in Parma.

Buzzoleni appears as composer of a solo cantata, *Clorinda idolo mio*, in a collection of Duke Francesco II d'Este. Jeppesen, in [40], identifies the songs translated below as being from manuscripts in the Royal Library in Copenhagen, and writes that Buzzoleni is an "unknown composer, probably of the Modenese school, who lived in the second half of the seventeenth century."

---

[40]

non fudː dʒi ˈra i
Non fuggirai
You will not flee

non	fudː dʒi ˈra i	nɔ	ˈsoɲː ɲo	o	va ˈnedː dʒo	si	ke	fudː ˈdʒi	la	ˈkru da
Non	**fuggirai,**	**no,**	**sogno**	**o**	**vaneggio,**	**sì**	**che**	**fuggì**	**la**	**cruda,**
not	you will flee	no	dream	or	fantasy	as	that	fled	the	cruel one

You will not flee, no, you dream or fantasy, like the cruel one fled

e	di	spe ˈran tsa	ˈnu da	laʃː ˈʃɔ	ˈla ni ma	ˈmi a
e	**di**	**speranza**	**nuda**	**lasciò**	**l'anima**	**mia,**
and	of	hope	bare	left	the soul	mine

and left my soul devoid of hope;

e	makː ˈkɔr go	ˈo ɾa	sol	ke	ˈde sto	e	al	ˈlu me
e	**m'accorgo**	**ora**	**sol**	**che**	**desto**	**e**	**al**	**lume**
and	I realize	now	only	that	I awake	and	in the	light

I realize now only that I awaken and, in the light,

in ˈve tʃe	del	ˈmi o	bɛn	ˈstriŋ go	le	ˈpju me
invece	**del**	**mio**	**ben**	**stringo**	**le**	**piume.**
instead	of the	my	beloved	I clasp	the	feathers

I am embracing the pillow instead of my beloved.

ˈkan dʒi	a ˈman te	pen ˈsjɛr	le	ki ˈmɛ ɾe	del	kɔr	ˈzvɛlː li	e di ˈzgom bra
Cangi,	**amante,**	**pensier,**	**le**	**chimere**	**del**	**cor**	**svelli**	**ed isgombra,**
change	lover	thought	the	fancies	of the	heart	pull out	and clear out

Change your thinking, lover; pull away and free yourself from the fancies of the heart,

> ed isgombra = (mod.) e sgombra

ke	'spes: so	kwel	pja 'tʃer	ke	ti	pro 'po ne	a 'mor
ché	**spesso**	**quel**	**piacer,**	**che**	**ti**	**propone**	**amor,**
because	often	that	pleasure	which	to you	suggests	love

because often the pleasure which love suggests to you

ε	un	'soɲː ɲo	e	u 'nom bra
è	**un**	**sogno**	**e**	**un'ombra.**
is	a	dream	and	a shadow

is [but] a dream and an illusion.

❧

[39]

si ke 'mɔr te
Sì che morte
As death

si	ke	'mɔr te	ε	lon ta 'nan tsa	'prɔ vi	in	kɔr	'pe na	in fi 'ni ta
Sì	**che**	**morte**	**è**	**lontananza,**	**provi**	**in**	**cor**	**pena**	**infinita,**
as	that	death	is	distance	let experience	in	heart	pain	infinite

> *sì che (lit.)* = *sicché*

As death is distance, let the heart feel infinite pain;

ke	sol	'pɛr de	al: 'lor	la	'vi ta	'kwan do	'lal ma	al 'tro ve	a	'stan tsa
ché	**sol**	**perde**	**allor**	**la**	**vita,**	**quando**	**l'alma**	**altrove**	**ha**	**stanza.**
because	only	loses	then	the	life	when	the soul	elsewhere	has	residence

for one only loses life when one's soul resides elsewhere.

❧

[39]

'vɔl dʒi mi o 'ka ɾa 'fil: li
Volgimi, o cara Filli
Turn to me, o dear Filli

'vɔl dʒi mi	o	'ka ɾa	'fil: li	pje 'to za	un	'gwar do	al 'me no	se	non	'vwɔ i
Volgimi,	**o**	**cara**	**Filli,**	**pietosa**	**un**	**guardo**	**almeno,**	**se**	**non**	**vuoi**
turn to me	o	dear	Filli	compassionate	a	glance	at least	if	not	you want

At least turn a compassionate glance to me, o dear Filli, if you do not want

ke	kwe 'stal ma	'sɛm pre	in	kon 'ti nu o	'pjan to	si 'strug: ga	e	'mɔ ɾa
che	**quest'alma**	**sempre**	**in**	**continuo**	**pianto**	**si strugga**	**e**	**mora;**
that	this soul	always	in	continuous	weeping	may waste away	and	may die

this soul to waste away and die in ceaseless weeping.

le	'mi e	'pe ne	ri 'stɔ ɾa	il	'mi o	'dwɔ lo	kon 'so la
le	**mie**	**pene**	**ristora,**	**il**	**mio**	**duolo**	**consola,**
the	my	pains	comfort	the	my	sorrow	console

Comfort my pain, console my sorrow;

e	kon	'dol tʃe	pje 'ta de	'pla ka	del	'tu o	ri 'gor	le	'du ɾe	'tɛm pre
e	**con**	**dolce**	**pietade**	**placa**	**del**	**tuo**	**rigor**	**le**	**dure**	**tempre,**
and	with	sweet	pity	alleviate	of the	your	severity	the	stern	hardnesses

and with sweet pity lessen the stern harshness of your severity

> *pietade = (mod.) pietà*

se	non	'vwɔ i	kil	'mi o	kɔr	'pjaŋ ga	per	'sɛm pre
se	**non**	**vuoi**	**ch'il**	**mio**	**cor**	**pianga**	**per**	**sempre.**
if	not	you want	that the	my	heart	may weep	for	ever

if you do not want my heart to weep forever.

dɛ	'pla ka	lo	'zdeɲ ɲo	vet: 'tso za	ti 'ran: na	se	'vwɔ i
Deh,	**placa**	**lo**	**sdegno,**	**vezzosa**	**tiranna,**	**se**	**vuoi**
please	alleviate	the	anger	charming	tyrannical one	if	you want

Please calm your anger, charming tyrant, if you want

del	'mi o	'kɔ ɾe	tem 'pra ɾe	lar 'do ɾe	kin	'se no	mi	sta
del	**mio**	**core**	**temprare**	**l'ardore**	**ch'in**	**seno**	**mi**	**sta.**
of the	my	heart	to temper	the ardor	which in	breast	of me	is

to temper in my breast the ardor of my heart.

o	al 'me no	pje 'to za	su 'pɛr ba	or goʎ: 'ʎo za
O	**almeno**	**pietosa,**	**superba,**	**orgogliosa,**
or	at least	pitious	haughty one	proud one

Or at least, being pitious, proud and haughty one,

ri 'tor na	a	'kwe sta	'al ma	la	'su a	li ber 'ta
ritorna	**a**	**questa**	**alma**	**la**	**sua**	**libertà.**
return	to	this	soul	the	its	freedom

give this soul back its freedom.

𝒢ℒ: **Filli**

🞵 *Caccini, Francesca* (1587-c.1641[?])

Elder daughter of Giulio Caccini, nicknamed "la cecchina" ("the little magpie"), was born in Florence and enjoyed the benefits of training with her father and growing up at the Medici court when the "new style" (monody) was being developed. She became a most gifted singer – while still in her teens, she sang in Peri's and Giulio Caccini's settings of *Euridice* – and poet, as well as a gifted player on the lute, guitar, harp, and harpsichord.

As musician and composer, she was one of the highest paid members of the Medici court. She was the first woman to compose an opera (*La liberazione di Ruggiero dall'isola d'Alcina*, 1625). Of the five operas and many sacred and secular songs she composed, only the opera mentioned above and her *Primo Libro (1618)*, which includes nineteen sacred solos, thirteen secular solo songs, and four duets for soprano and bass, have survived. She also taught, in various convents as well as at court, and she and her daughter Margherita often performed together.

---

[34]　　　　　　　　　　　　　　　　　　　　　　　　　　*Francesca Caccini [?]*

ke tɔ fat: 'ti o
Che t'ho fatt'io
What have I done to you

ke	tɔ	fat: 'ti o	ke	'tan to	'bra mi	la	'mɔr te	'mi a
Che	**t'ho**	**fatt'io,**	**che**	**tanto**	**brami**	**la**	**morte**	**mia**
what	to you I have	done I	that	so much	you desire	the	death	mine

What have I done to you, that you so greatly desire my death

per 'ke   'i o   non   'ta mi
perché   **io**   **non**   **t'ami?**
so that   I   not   you I may love
in order to keep me from loving you?

non   'sa i   'ki o   'vi vo   sol   del   'tu o   splen 'do ɾe   'a i   'du ɾo   'kɔ ɾe
Non   **sai**   **ch'io**   **vivo**   **sol**   **del**   **tuo**   **splendore?**   **Ahi,**   **duro**   **core!**
not   you know   that I   I live   only   for the   your   splendor   alas   hard   heart
Do you not know that I live only for your splendor? Alas, callous heart!

o i 'mɛ   'pjɛ ga   il   de 'zi o   ke   tɔ   fat: 'ti o
Ohimè,   **piega**   **il**   **desio!**   **Che**   **t'ho**   **fatt'io?**
alas   subdue   the   desire   what   to you I have   done I
Alas, subdue your desire! What have I done to you?

se   'sprɛt: tsi   a 'mo ɾe   iŋ 'gra to   'se no   dʒa   non   vo 'ler   'ki o   'vɛŋ go 'me no
Se   **sprezzi**   **amore,**   **ingrato**   **seno,**   **già**   **non**   **voler**   **ch'io**   **vengo meno.**
if   you scorn   love   ungrateful   breast   now   not   to wish   that I   I expire
If you scorn love, ungrateful breast, do not wish for my demise.

gra 'diʃ: ʃi   al 'men   'ki o   'ta mi   e   kwel   tor 'men to   a
Gradisci   **almen**   **ch'io**   **t'ami,**   **e**   **quel**   **tormento,**   **ah,**
accept   at least   that I   you I may love   and   that   torment   [ah]
At least accept that I love you, and the torment

'ki o   per   te   'sɛn to   'a i   di spje 'ta to   'kɔ ɾe   se   'sprɛt: tsi   a 'mo ɾe
ch'io   **per**   **te**   **sento,**   **ahi,**   **dispietato**   **core,**   **se**   **sprezzi**   **amore!**
that I   for   you   I feel   ah   pitiless   heart   if   you scorn   love
that I feel for you, ah, pitiless heart, [even] if you scorn love!

Two more verses, the 2nd and 3rd stanzas of the poem (see notes in [34]), are printed as text only:

---

ke   'van to   a 'vra i   'ki o   mi kon 'su mi   al   'kja ɾo   sol
Che   **vanto**   **avrai**   **ch'io**   **mi consumi**   **al**   **chiaro**   **sol**
what   advantage   you will have   that I   I may be consumed   at the   bright   sun
What will you have to gain if I waste away in the bright sun

de   'twɔ i   'bɛ i   'lu mi
de'   **tuoi**   **bei**   **lumi?**
of   your   beautiful   eyes
of your beautiful eyes?

dɛ   'vɔl dʒi   al   'mi o   do 'lor   pje 'to zo   il   'gwar do   'ki o   'mɔ ɾo   e 'dar do
Deh,   **volgi**   **al**   **mio**   **dolor**   **pietoso**   **il**   **guardo,**   **ch'io**   **moro**   **ed ardo.**
pray   turn   to the   my   sorrow   mercifully   the   glance   that I   I die   and I burn
Please, turn your glance mercifully to my sorrow, as I am dying and burning.

'a i   se   mo 'rir   mi   'fa i   ke   'van to   a 'vra i
Ahi,   **se**   **morir**   **mi**   **fai,**   **che**   **vanto**   **avrai?**
alas   if   to die   me   you make   what   advantage   you will have
Alas, if you make me die, what will you have to gain?

dun   'al ma   al 'tɛ ɾa   'ri a   kru del 'ta te   'prɛ dʒo   non 'si a   'dal ta   bel 'ta te
D'un   **alma**   **altera,**   **ria**   **crudeltate,**   **pregio**   **non sia**   **d'alta**   **beltate,**
of a   soul   proud   harsh   cruelty   prize   not may be   of great   beauty
Let the harsh cruelty of a proud soul be not the prize of great beauty,

ria (lit.) = rea
crudeltate = (mod.) crudeltà
pregio = (mod.) premio, prezzo
beltate = (mod.) beltà

ma   di   fe ˈde le   a ˈmor   di   ˈpu ɾa   ˈfe de   ˈem pja   mer ˈtʃe de

ma   di   fedele   amor,   di   pura   fede   empia   mercede,

but   of   faithful   love   of   pure   fidelity   cruel   reward

but the cruel reward of faithful love and pure fidelity –

ˈa i   kɔr   di   ˈkru do   ˈse no   dun   ˈal ma   al ˈtɛ ɾa

ahi   cor   di   crudo   seno,   d'un   alma   altera.

alas   heart   of   cruel   breast   of a   soul   proud

alas, heart of a cruel breast, of a proud soul.

‽

[62, 66]   *Francesca Caccini [?]*

ki de ˈzi a di sa ˈper

Chi desia di saper

Whoever wants to know

ki   de ˈzi a   di   sa ˈpɛr   ke   ˈkɔ za   ɛ   a ˈmo ɾe   ˈi o   di ˈɾɔ

Chi   desia   di   saper   che   cosa   è   amore,   io   dirò,

whoever   desires   of   to know   what   thing   is   love   I   I will say

To whomever wants to know what love is, I will say

ke   non   ˈsi a   se   non   ar ˈdo ɾe   ke   non   ˈsi a   se   non   do ˈlo ɾe

che   non   sia   se   non   ardore,   che   non   sia   se   non   dolore,

that   not   it be   if   not   passion   that   not   it be   if   not   sorrow

that it is [nothing] if not passion, sorrow,

ke   non   ˈsi a   se   non   ti ˈmo ɾe   ke   non   ˈsi a   se   non   fu ˈɾo ɾe

che   non   sia   se   non   timore,   che   non   sia   se   non   furore.

that   not   it be   if   not   fear   that   not   it be   if   not   fury.

fear, and fury.

ki   mi   do man de ˈɾa   sa ˈmor   ˈi o   ˈsɛn to   ˈi o   di ˈɾɔ

Chi   mi   domanderà   s'amor   io   sento,   io   dirò

whoever   to me   will ask   if love   I   I feel   I   I will say

To whomever will ask me if I feel love, I will say

kel   ˈmi o   ˈfɔ ko   ɛ   ˈtut: to   ˈspɛn to

che'l   mio   foco   è   tutto   spento,

that the   my   fire   is   all   burned out

that my passion is all spent,

ˈki o   non   ˈprɔ vo   pju   tor ˈmen to   ˈki o   non   ˈtre mo   ne   pa ˈvɛn to

ch'io   non   provo   più   tormento,   ch'io   non   tremo,   né   pavento,

that I   not   I experience   more   torment   that I   not   I tremble   nor   I fear

that I feel no more torment, that I neither tremble nor fear,

ˈki o   ne   ˈvi vo   oɲ: ˈɲor   kon ˈtɛn to

ch'io   ne   vivo   ogn'or   contento.

that I   of it   I live   every hour   content

[and] that I live every hour content with that.

ki   mi   kon siʎ: ʎe ˈra   ˈki o   ˈdɛb: ba ˈma ɾe   ˈi o   di ˈɾɔ

Chi   mi   consiglierà   ch'io   debb'amare,   io   dirò

whoever   me   will advise   that I   ought to love   I   I will say

To whomever will advise me that I should love, I will say

ke	pju	'dol tʃe	ɛ	a 'mor	fud: 'dʒi ɾe	ne		te 'me ɾe	ne	spe 'ɾa ɾe
che	**più**	**dolce**	**è**	**amor**	**fuggire**	**né**		**temere,**	**né**	**sperare,**
that	more	sweet	it is	love	to flee	neither		to fear	nor	to hope

that it is sweeter to flee from love than to fear, to hope,

ne	av: vam 'pa ɾe	ne	dʒe 'la ɾe	ne	laŋ 'gwi ɾe	ne	pe 'na ɾe
né	**avvampare,**	**né**	**gelare,**	**né**	**languire,**	**né**	**penare;**
nor	to burn	nor	to freeze	nor	to languish	nor	to suffer

to burn, to freeze, to langush or to suffer;

'i o	di 'ɾɔ	ke	non	vɔ	pju	so spi ɾa ɾe
io	**dirò**	**che**	**non**	**vo'**	**più**	**sospirare.**
I	I will say	that	not	I wish	more	to sigh

I will say that I do not wish to sigh anymore.

ki	da 'mor	kre de 'ra	'dol tʃe	il	dʒo 'i ɾe	'i o	di 'ɾɔ
Chi	**d'amor**	**crederà**	**dolce**	**il**	**gioire,**	**io**	**dirò**
whoever	of love	will believe	sweet	the	enjoying	I	I will say

To whomever will believe the enjoyment of love to be sweet, I will say

ke	pju	'dol tʃe	ɛ	a 'mor	fud: 'dʒi ɾe	ne	pje 'gar si	al	'su o	de 'zi ɾe
che	**più**	**dolce**	**è**	**amor**	**fuggire,**	**né**	**piegarsi**	**al**	**suo**	**desire,**
that	more	sweet	it is	love	to flee	neither	to submit oneself	to the	its	desire

that it is sweeter to flee from love than to yield to its desire,

ne	ten 'tar	'swo i	'zdeɲ: ɲi	e 'di ɾe	ne	pro 'va ɾe	il	'su o	mar 'ti ɾe	*martire =*
né	**tentar**	**suoi**	**sdegni**	**ed ire,**	**né**	**provare**	**il**	**suo**	**martire.**	*(mod.)*
nor	to tempt	its	scorns	and wraths	nor	to experience	the	its	agony	*martirio*

tempt its wrath and scorn, or experience its agony.

❧

[62, 66]   *Francesca Caccini [?]*

ki	ɛ	ko 'stɛ i
Chi	**è**	**costei**
Who		is she

ki	ɛ	ko 'stɛ i	ke	kwal	sor 'dʒen te	a u 'ɾɔ ɾa	i	'pas: si	'mwɔ ve
Chi	**è**	**costei**	**che**	**qual**	**sorgente**	**aurora**	**i**	**passi**	**muove**
who	is	she	who	like	rising	dawn	the	steps	moves

Who is she who, like the rising dawn, moves her steps

a 'par del		'so le	e 'lɛt: ta	'bɛl: la	'ko me	la	'lu na
a par del		**sole**	**eletta,**	**bella**	**come**	**la**	**luna,**
on an equal with the		sun	proud	beautiful	like	the	moon

proud as the sun, beautiful as the moon,

e	kwal	sa 'spɛt: ta	'skjɛ ɾa	dar 'ma ti	e 'ɾɔ i	'trom ba	so 'nɔ ɾa
e	**qual**	**s'aspetta**	**schiera**	**d'armati**	**eroi**	**tromba**	**sonora.**
and	like	one awaits	host	of armed	heroes	trumpet	resounding

like one who expects the resounding trumpet of a host of armed heroes?

'kwe sta	ɛ	ko 'lɛ i	kel	'tʃɛ lo	'ar de	e	in: na 'mo ɾa
Questa	**è**	**colei**	**che'l**	**cielo**	**arde**	**e**	**innamora**
this one	is	she	who the	heaven	burns	and	enchants

It is she who inflames and enchants heaven,

e	kon	un	de	'beʎ: ʎi	'ɔk: ki	il	kɔr	sa 'et: ta
e	**con**	**un**	**de'**	**begli**	**occhi**	**il**	**cor**	**saetta**
and	with	one	of the	beautiful	eyes	the	heart	wounds with an arrow

and with a single beautiful eye pierces the heart,

did 'di o	ma 'dʒon	'so pra	kwel	'mon ti	e 'rɛt: ta	'san ti
d'Iddio	**magion**	**sopra**	**quel**	**monti**	**eretta**	**santi**
of God	dwelling	above	those	mountains	elevated	holy

Iddio =
(mod.) Dio

I've changed the printed "menti" to "monti" (guessing a miscopying or misprint) to help make sense of this in context...

kaŋ 'kor	le ter ni 'ta de	o 'no ɾa
ch'ancor	**l'eternitade**	**onora.**
as even	the eternity	honors

eternitade = (mod.) eternità

as even eternity honors the house of God elevated above those holy mountains.

pre 'dʒa to	'dɛ va	av: ven tu 'ro zo	'skɔr no	del: 'lan dʒel	non	se	kon
Pregiato	**d'Eva**	**avventuroso**	**scorno**	**dell'Angel**	**non**	**se**	**con**
esteemed	of Eve	fateful	scorn	of the Angel	not	if	by

"storno," rather than
"scorno," is printed
on the music page

di 'vɛr sa	'sɔr te	'e i	fe	men	'bɛl: lil	'tʃe lo	'el: la	la	a 'dor no
diversa	**sorte**	**ei**	**fé**	**men**	**bell'il**	**cielo,**	**ella**	**l'ha**	**adorno.**
different	fate	he	made	lo00	beautiful the	heaven	she	it has	adorned

Though by the fateful scorn of the Angel esteemed by Eve, rather than by a different fate, he made heaven less beautiful, she *[Mary]* has adorned it.

Instead of "fé," on the music page is printed "te" in one place and
"se" in another; "fé" seems to be the correct alternative in the context.

ko 'zi	di 'tʃe a	la	for tu 'na ta	'kɔr te	di	pa ɾa 'di zo	in	kwel	fe 'li tʃe	'dʒor no
Così	**dicea**	**la**	**fortunata**	**corte**	**di**	**paradiso**	**in**	**quel**	**felice**	**giorno**
thus	said	the	blessed	court	of	paradise	on	that	happy	day

Thus spoke the blessed court of paradise on that happy day

dicea = diceva

kel: la 'pɛr se	a	ma 'ri a	let: 'tʃɛl se	'pɔr te
ch'ell'aperse	**a**	**Maria**	**l'eccelse**	**porte.**
that it opened	to	Mary	the lofty	gates

when it opened its lofty gates to Mary.

G𝓛: **Eva, Maria**

❧

[48]

Francesca Caccini [?]

di spje 'ga te 'gwan tʃe a 'ma te
Dispiegate, guancie amate
Show, beloved cheeks

dis pje 'ga te	'gwan tʃe	a 'ma te	'kwel: la	'pɔr po ɾa	a 'tʃer 'bet: ta
Dispiegate,	**guancie**	**amate,**	**quella**	**porpora**	**acerbetta**
show	cheeks	loved	that	purple	youthful

ke	per 'dɛn ti	ke	do 'lɛn ti	'si an	le	'rɔ ze	in su	ler 'bet: ta
che	**perdenti,**	**che**	**dolenti,**	**sian**	**le**	**rose**	**in su**	**l'erbetta.**
that	fading	that	sorrowful	may be	the	roses	above	the grass

Show, beloved cheeks, that youthful purple which may put the fading and sorrowful roses in the grass to shame.

'a pra	il	'lab: bro	di	tʃi 'na bro	un	sor: 'ri zo	aŋ 'kor tra	il	've lo
Apra	**il**	**labbro**	**di**	**cinabro**	**un**	**sorriso**	**ancor tra**	**il**	**velo**
may open	the	lip	of	cinnabar	a	smile	[even] between	the	veil

May your cinnabar lips open in a smile beneath your veil,

ke	a da 'prir lo	ke	a	sko 'prir lo
ché	**ad aprirlo,**	**ché**	**a**	**scoprirlo,**
because	at the opening it	because	at	the uncovering it

for when they are opened and uncovered,

ri de 'ran	la	'tɛr: ra	e	il	'tʃɛ lo
rideran	**la**	**terra**	**e**	**il**	**cielo.**
will smile	the	earth	and	the	heaven

earth and heaven will smile.

[62, 66] Titled "Aria romanesca." "Romanesca" was a compositional formula popular in the late sixteenth and early seventeenth centuries having a standard chordal progression whose bass moved by fourths.

'ɛk: ko 'ki o 'vɛr so il 'saŋ gwe
Ecco ch'io verso il sangue
Here I spill my blood

'ɛk: ko	'ki o	'vɛr so	il	'saŋ gwe	'ɛk: ko	ka	'mɔr ti o	'vɛɲ: ɲo
Ecco	**ch'io**	**verso**	**il**	**sangue,**	**ecco**	**ch'a**	**mort'io**	**vegno.**
here	[that] I	I spill	the	blood	here	[that] to	death I	I come

vegno =
(mod.)
vengo

Here I spill my blood; here I meet my death.

'pla ka	'i zra el	lo	'zdɛɲ: ɲo	dʒa	've din	'kro tʃe	il	'tu o	siɲ: 'ɲo ɾe	e 'zaŋ gwe
Placa	**Israel**	**lo**	**sdegno;**	**già**	**ved'in**	**croce**	**il**	**tuo**	**Signore**	**esangue,**
placate	Israel	the	anger	already	you see on	cross	the	your	Lord	pale

Calm your anger, Israel; already you see your Lord pale on the cross,

"io," printed, must be a misprint for "lo"

'pɔ pol	ko 'tan to	a 'ma to
popol	**cotanto**	**amato.**
people	so much	loved

o greatly beloved people.

'pɔ pol	ko 'tan to	iŋ 'gra to	ri 'spon di	ri 'spon di	o	'pɔ pol	'mi o
Popol	**cotanto**	**ingrato,**	**rispondi;**	**rispondi**	**o**	**popol**	**mio:**
people	so much	ungrateful	answer	answer	o	people	mine

People so thankless, answer; answer, o my people.

in	ke	tof: 'fe zi	'ma i	ke	tɔ	fat: 'ti o
In	**che**	**t'offesi**	**mai,**	**che**	**t'ho**	**fatt'io?**
in	what	you I offended	ever	what	to you I have	done I

However have I offended you? What have I done to you?

"mei," printed, must be a misprint for "mai"

o i 'mɛ	ke	per	'tu o	'bɛ ne	ar 'man do	il	'brat: tʃo	in 'vit: to
Ohimè,	**che**	**per**	**tuo**	**bene**	**armando**	**il**	**braccio**	**invitto**
alas	[that]	for	your	good	arming	the	arm	invincible

Alas, for your sake, armed invincibly,

'lem pje	tʃit: 'ta	de 'dʒit: to	kon	'pja ge	fla dʒel: 'la i	dor: 'ri bil	'pe ne
l'empie	**città**	**d'Egitto**	**con**	**piaghe**	**flagellai**	**d'orribil**	**pene;**
the evil	city	of Egypt	with	wounds	I lashed	of horrible	pains

I lashed the evil city of Egypt with wounds of horrible pain;

tu   mim 'pja gi   le   'mɛm bra   ne   di   tʃɔ   ti ri 'mɛm bra
tu   m'impiaghi   le   membra   né   di   ciò   ti rimembra.
you   me cover with wounds   the   limbs   nor   of   that   to you it remembers
you cover my limbs with wounds [and] do not remember [that I did] that.

te   da   ser 'vad: dʒo   a 'tʃɛr bo   'tras: si   fwɔr   di   pe 'riʎ: ʎo
Te   da   servaggio   acerbo   trassi   fuor   di   periglio,
you   from   servitude   bitter   I drew   out   of   danger
I drew you away from the danger of bitter servitude,

e   'den tro   al   mar   ver 'miʎ: ʎo   per   te   som: 'mɛr si   fa ɾa 'on   su 'per bo
e   dentro   al   mar   vermiglio   per   te   sommersi   faraon   superbo;
and   into   to the   sea   vermilion   for   you   I submerged   pharaoh   proud
and I submerged the proud pharaoh into the Red Sea for you;

tu   mi   'da i   per   mer 'tʃe de   in   'prɛ da   a   ki   mi   'kjɛ de
tu   mi   dai   per   mercede   in   preda   a   chi   mi   chiede.
you   me   you give   for   reward   in   prey   to   he who   me   asks for
in reward, you give me as prey for the asking.

'sa i   pur   ke   per   'tu o   'skam po   del   'ma ɾe   a 'per si   'lon de
Sai   pur   che   per   tuo   scampo   del   mare   apersi   l'onde,
you know   indeed   that   for   your   escape   of the   sea   I opened   the waves
You know, indeed, that I opened the waves of the sea for your escape

e   si 'ku ɾo   'al: le   'spon de   ti   'tras: si   fwɔr   del   tem pe 'sto zo   'kam po
e   sicuro   alle   sponde   ti   trassi   fuor   del   tempestoso   campo;
and   safe   at the   shores   you   I drew   out   of the   tempestuous   plain
and, safely on shore, I led you out of the tempestuous plain;

tu   per 'ki o   'vɛn ga 'me no   'ma pri   kol   'fɛr: ro   il   'se no
tu   perch'io   venga meno   m'apri   col   ferro   il   seno.
you   though I   I may swoon   me you open   with the   sword   the   breast
even though I faint, you open my breast with the sword.

> antiquated (lit.)
> meaning for
> "perché" = sebbene

in   ko 'lon: na   di   'fɔ ko   per   la   de 'zɛr ta   'vi a   in: 'nan tsi   a   te
In   colonna   di   foco   per   la   deserta   via   innanzi   a   te
in   pillar   of   fire   through   the   deserted   way   in front   of   you
At the forefront through the desert, in a pillar of fire

men   dʒa   del   bɛl   'kar: ro   im: mor 'tal   seɲ: 'ɲan do   il   'lɔ ko
men   già   del   bel   carro   immortal   segnando   il   loco;
I led   once   of the   beautiful   chariot   immortal   marking   the   place
I once led the beautiful, immortal chariot to mark the spot;

> men = menò
> (from "menare")

tu   'den tro   i 'ni kwe   'pɔr te   'ma i   kwi   'da to   'al: la   'mɔr te
tu   dentro   inique   porte   m'hai   qui   dato   alla   morte.
you   into   iniquitous   doors   me you have   here   given   to the   death
through iniquitous portals you have now given me to death.

> "alle," printed,
> must be a
> misprint of "alla"

[62, 66]

la pa sto ˈrɛl: la ˈmi a

La pastorella mia

My little shepherdess

la	pa sto ˈrɛl: la	ˈmi a	tra	i	ˈfjo ɾi	ɛl	ˈdʒiʎ: ʎo
La	**pastorella**	**mia**	**tra**	**i**	**fiori**	**è'l**	**giglio,**
the	little shepherdess	mine	among	the	flowers	is the	lily

Among the flowers my little shepherdess is the lily,

ˈan tsi	la	ˈrɔ za	di	pju	gra to ˈdo ɾe
anzi	**la**	**rosa**	**di**	**più**	**grat'odore.**
or rather	the	rose	of	more	agreeable fragrance

or rather the rose, with its even more pleasing fragrance.

tra	le	ˈdʒɛm: me	il	ru ˈbin	ˈva go	e	ver ˈmiʎ: ʎo
Tra	**le**	**gemme**	**il**	**rubin**	**vago**	**e**	**vermiglio,**
among	the	gems	the	ruby	lovely	and	vermilion

Among the gems [she is] the lovely, vermilion ruby,

ˈsi o	ˈmi ɾo	ˈdel: le	ˈlab: bra	il	bɛl	ko ˈlo ɾe
s'io	**miro**	**delle**	**labbra**	**il**	**bel**	**colore.**
if I	I look at	of the	lips	the	beautiful	color

when I consider the beautiful color of her lips.

e	tra	i	ˈpo mi	al	gra ˈna to	las: si ˈmiʎ: ʎo
E	**tra**	**i**	**pomi**	**al**	**granato**	**l'assimiglio,**
and	among	the	fruits	to the	pomegranate	her I compare

And among the fruits, I compare her to the pomegranate,

> assimiglio: form of
> the verb
> " assimigliare" =
> (mod.) assomigliare

ki	a	la	ko ˈro na	a	deʎ: ˈʎal tri	ɛ	siɲ: ˈɲo ɾe
chi	**ha**	**la**	**corona,**	**a**	**degl'altri**	**è**	**signore.**
who	has	the	crown	to	of the others	is	sovereign

which has a crown [and] is king of the others.

re ˈdʒi naŋ ˈkel: la	par	tra	le	don ˈdzɛl: le
Regin' anch'ella	**par**	**tra**	**le**	**donzelle,**
queen also she	she seems	among	the	damsels

She also seems like a queen among the damsels,

ˈan tsi	la	ˈdɛ a	da ˈmor	tra	ˈlal tre	ˈstel: le
anzi	**la**	**Dea**	**d'Amor**	**tra**	**l'altre**	**stelle.**
or rather	the	Goddess	of Love	among	the other	stars

or rather the Goddess of Love among the other stars.

GL: **Amor**

❧

Francesca Caccini

[33]

ma ˈri a ˈdol tʃe ma ˈri a

Maria, dolce Maria

Mary, sweet Mary

ma 'ɾi a	'dol tʃe	ma 'ɾi a	'no me	so 'a ve	'tan to ke	a	pro nun 'tʃar
Maria,	**dolce**	**Maria,**	**nome**	**soave**	**tanto che**	**a**	**pronunciar**
Mary	sweet	Mary	name	sweet	so much that	to	to pronounce

*pronunciar[e]
= (mod.)
pronunziar[e]*

ti	im 'pa ɾa	'dis: se	il	'kɔ ɾe
ti	**impara**	**disse**	**il**	**core.**
you	learn	said	the	heart

*Printed is "di sil," for which
most likely correct is "disse il."*

Mary, sweet Mary, name so sweet that my heart told me to learn to pronounce it –

'no me	sa 'kra to	e	'san to	kel	kɔr	min 'fjam: mi	di	tʃe 'lɛ ste	a 'mo ɾe
Nome	**sacrato,**	**e**	**santo**	**che'l**	**cor**	**m'infiammi**	**di**	**celeste**	**amore,**
name	sacred	and	holy	which the	heart	me you inflame	with	celestial	love

Sacred and holy name which inflames my heart with celestial love –

ma 'ɾi a	'ma i	se 'pri o	'kan to	ne	pwɔ	la	'liŋ gwa	'mi a	pju	fe 'li tʃe	pa 'rɔ la
Maria,	**mai**	**sepr'io**	**canto**	**né**	**può**	**la**	**lingua**	**mia**	**più**	**felice**	**parola.**
Mary	never	separate I	song	nor	is able	the	tongue	mine	more	happy	word

Mary, never will I separate my song [from your name], nor can my tongue [utter] a happier word.

'trar mi	dal	sen	dʒa 'ma i	ke	dir	ma 'ɾi a	'no me	'koɲ: ɲi	do 'lor
Trarmi	**dal**	**sen**	**già mai**	**che**	**dir**	**Maria**	**nome**	**ch'ogni**	**dolor**
to take away me	from the	breast	never	that	to say	Mary	name	that every	sorrow

Printed in error are "trormi," rather than "trarmi," and "gio" rather than "già."

'tem pra	e	kon 'so la	'rɔ ko	traŋ 'kwil: la	'koɲ: ɲi	af: 'fan: no	ak: 'kwɛ ta
tempra	**e**	**consola,**	**roco**	**tranquilla**	**ch'ogni**	**affanno**	**acqueta**
lessens	and	consoles	faint	quiets	that every	trouble	assuages

Never will I remove from my breast the quiet whisper of "Mary," name that lessens and consoles every sorrow, that assuages every trouble,

'koɲ: ɲi	kɔr	fa	se 'rε no	'koɲ: ɲi	kɔr	fa	se ɾe 'noɲ: 'ɲal ma	'lje ta
ch'ogni	**cor**	**fa**	**sereno,**	**ch'ogni**	**cor**	**fa**	**seren'ogn'alma**	**lieta.**
that every	heart	makes	serene	that every	heart	makes	serene every soul	happy

[and] that makes every heart serene – that makes every heart serene and every soul happy.

GL: **Maria**

&

[62, 66] Titled with the spelling **Nel camino.**

nel kam: 'mi no
Nel cammino
Along the journey

printed "camino" = (mod.) cammino

nel	kam: 'mi no	'a spro	e	'er to	di	'kwe sta	'val: le	'del: la	mor 'tal	'vi ta
Nel	**cammino**	**aspro**	**e**	**erto**	**di**	**questa**	**valle**	**della**	**mortal**	**vita,**
on the	journey	harsh	and	arduous	of	this	vale	of the	mortal	life

Along the harsh and arduous journey in this vale of mortal life,

sok: 'kor: ri	al	'pɔ pol	'tu o	'pɔr dʒi li	a 'i ta
soccorri	**al**	**popol**	**tuo,**	**porgili**	**aita.**
give aid	to the	people	yours	offer them	help

aid your people; offer them help.

tu	'du tʃe	tu	pa 'sto ɾe	u 'mil	gwal 'bɛr to
Tu	**duce,**	**tu**	**pastore**	**umil**	**Gualberto,**
you	leader	you	shepherd	humble	Gualberto

*printed (in error)
is "pastora"*

You, leader – you, humble shepherd Gualberto –

tu	tʃi	ˈa i	del	pa ɾa ˈdi zo	il	ˈkal: le	a ˈpɛr to
tu	**ci**	**hai**	**del**	**paradiso**	**il**	**calle**	**aperto;**
you	to us	have	of the	paradise	the	path	opened

you have opened for us the path to paradise;

ma	se	ˈtu a	ˈsan ta	man	non	tʃi	so ˈstjɛ ne	ka ˈdrem	ˈmi ze ɾi	ˈno i
ma	**se**	**tua**	**santa**	**man**	**non**	**ci**	**sostiene,**	**cadrem**	**miseri**	**noi.**
but	if	your	holy	hand	not	us	sustains	we will fall	wretched	us

but if your holy hand does not sustain us, we will fall – woe to us.

e	se	kon	i	ˈprɛ gi	ˈtwɔ i	non	tʃim ˈpɛ tri	pje ˈta	del	ˈsom: mo	ˈbɛ ne
E	**se**	**con**	**i**	**preghi**	**tuoi**	**non**	**c'impetri**	**pietà**	**del**	**sommo**	**bene,**
and	if	with	the	prayers	yours	not	for us you obtain	mercy	from the	greatest	good

And if, with your prayers, you do not obtain God's mercy upon us,

> preghi (lit.) = preghieri

> impetri: from "impetrare" = (mod.) impietrare

> il sommo bene = il Dio = God

il	ˈtu o	dʒu ˈdit: tsjo	e ˈtɛr no	a	se	mi	ˈkja mi
il	**tuo**	**giudizio**	**eterno**	**a**	**sé**	**mi**	**chiami**
the	your	judgement	eternal	to	itself	me	may call

may your eternal judgement summon me

e	ˈtɔl ga il	ˈkru do	in ˈfɛr no
e	**tolga'il**	**crudo**	**inferno.**
and	may take away the	merciless	hell

and deliver me from merciless hell.

> In both prints [62, 66] *the text on the music page ends with* "sommo bene." *The rest of the text, as above, is included on the text and translation page printed in* [62].
> *An alternative translation, should the song end with* "sommo bene," *could be:* ...but if your holy hand does not sustain us and if, with your prayers, you do not obtain God's mercy upon us, we will fall – woe to us.

[1, 2, 17, 47, 33]
from: *La liberazione di Ruggiero dall'isola d'Alcina (1625)*
character: *the Shepherd*

Ferdinando Saracinelli

per la pju ˈva ga e ˈbɛl: la
Per la più vaga e bella
For the most desirable and beautiful

per	la	pju	ˈva ga	e	ˈbɛl: la	ter: ˈre na	ˈstel: la	ke	ˈɔd: dʒi	o ˈsku ɾi
Per	**la**	**più**	**vaga**	**e**	**bella**	**terrena**	**stella,**	**che**	**oggi**	**oscuri**
for	the	most	desirable	and	beautiful	terrestrial	star	which	today	may obscure

di	ˈfɛ bo	i	ˈrad: dʒi	ˈdɔ ro	ˈmi o	ˈkɔ re	ar ˈde va
di	**Febo**	**i**	**raggi**	**d'oro,**	**mio**	**core**	**ardeva;**
of	Phoebus	the	rays	of gold	my	heart	was burning

For the most desirable and beautiful star on earth, who today obscures Phoebus' golden rays, my heart was burning.

a ˈmor	ri ˈde va	ˈva go	di	ri mi ˈra re	il	ˈmi o	mar ˈtɔ ɾo
Amor	**rideva,**	**vago**	**di**	**rimirare**	**il**	**mio**	**martoro.**
Love	was laughing	eager	of	to see	the	my	torment

> martoro = (mod.) martorio

Love was laughing, eager to see my torment.

ma	da 'ver mi	sker 'ni to	'tɔ sto	pen 'ti to	kon	la	pje 'ta	di	'lɛ i
Ma	**d'avermi**	**schernito,**	**tosto**	**pentito,**	**con**	**la**	**pietà**	**di**	**lei**
but	of having me	mocked	soon	repented	with	the	mercy	of	her

mi	'sa na	il	'pɛt: to
mi	**sana**	**il**	**petto.**
me	heals	the	breast

But, soon repented for having mocked me, he *[Love]* heals my breast with her *[the most beautiful star's]* mercy.

on 'di o	fɔ	'fe de	a	ki	nol	'kre de
Ond'io	**fo**	**fede,**	**a**	**chi**	**nol**	**crede,**
Whence I	I make	proof	to	whoever	not it	believes

Thus do I bear witness for whomever does not believe it,

ke	a 'mo ɾe	ɛ	'so lo	il	'di o	'doɲ: ɲi	di 'lɛt: to
che	**Amore**	**è**	**solo**	**il**	**dio**	**d'ogni**	**diletto.**
that	Love	is	alone	the	god	of all	delight

that Love alone is the god of all delight.

> *alt. in* [33]: *ch'Amore*
> [ka 'mo ɾe] = *che Amore*

GL: Amor[e], Febo

Caccini, Giulio (c.1545-1618)

Singer, composer, teacher, and instrumentalist (on harp, harpsichord, theorbo, and chitarrone), he was born in Tivoli or Rome. By 1565 he was in the service of the Medici court in Florence, where he was based until his death. In Florence he studied singing and playing with the famed virtuoso Scipione delle Palle, and he became very famous as a singer. Later, among the artists and literati of the Florentine "Camerata," under the patronage of Giovanni de' Bardi, Count of Vernio, he was inspired to compose the solo vocal music in recitative style ("musica in stile rappresentativo") for which he is known as the "father of monody."

The first of his two collections of arias and madrigals, *Le nuove musiche (1602)*, was the first such collection of solo vocal music. Caccini also wrote dramatic scenes and operas; both his and Peri's settings of *Euridice* have laid claim to being the first opera to have appeared in print.

With his wife Lucia di Filippo Gagnolanti, a singer, he had two daughters, Francesca and Settimia, both of whom became singer-composers.

---

[11] Titled "Aria di romanesca." See the *note* on page 80.

'a i di spje 'ta to a 'mor
Ahi! dispietato Amor
Alas, pitiless Love

'a i	di spje 'ta to	a 'mor	'ko me	kon 'sɛn ti
Ahi!	**dispietato**	**Amor**	**come**	**consenti**
alas	pitiless	Love	how	you allow

Alas, pitiless Love, how can you allow

'ki o	'me ni	'vi ta	si	pe 'no ze	'ri a
ch'io	**meni**	**vita**	**sì**	**penos'e**	**ria.**
that I	may lead	life	so	painful and	cruel

me to lead a life so painful and cruel?

GL: Amor

[41]

al 'fon te al 'pra to
Al fonte, al prato
To the spring, to the meadow

al	'fon te	al	'pra to	al	'bɔ sko	al: 'lom bra	al	'fre sko	'fja to
Al	**fonte,**	**al**	**prato,**	**al**	**bosco,**	**all'ombra,**	**al**	**fresco**	**fiato,**
to the	spring	to the	meadow	to the	woods	to the shade	to the	cool	breath of wind

To the spring, to the meadow, to the woods, to the shade, to the cool breath of wind

printed is "al'ombra"; gramatically correct is "all'ombra"

kil	'kal do	'zgom bra	pa 'stor	kor: 're te
ch'il	**caldo**	**sgombra,**	**pastor**	**correte;**
which the	heat	clears away	shepherd	hurry

which dispels the heat, shepherd, hasten;

tʃa 'skun	ka	'se te	tʃa 'skun	kɛ	'staŋ ko	ri 'pɔ zil	'fjaŋ ko
ciascun	**ch'ha**	**sete,**	**ciascun**	**ch'è**	**stanco**	**ripos'il**	**fianco!**
each	who has	thirst	each	who is	tired	let rest the	flank (side, hip)

let everyone who is thirsty, everyone who is weary, rest!

'fug: ga	la	'nɔ ja	'fug: ga	il	do 'lo ɾe	sol	'ri zo	e	'dʒɔ ja
Fugga	**la**	**noia,**	**fugga**	**il**	**dolore,**	**sol**	**riso**	**e**	**gioia,**
let flee	the	tedium	let flee	the	sorrow	only	laughter	and	joy

Let tedium [and] sorrow flee; may only laughter and joy,

sol	'ka ɾo	a 'mo ɾe	'nɔ sko	sod: 'dʒor ni	ne	'ljɛ ti	'dʒor ni
sol	**caro**	**Amore,**	**nosco**	**soggiorni,**	**ne'**	**lieti**	**giorni,**
only	dear	Love	with us	may sojourn	in the	happy	days

only dear Love stay with us; in the happy days

nosco (poet.) = con noi

non	'sɔ da	'ma i	kwe 'ɾɛ le	o	'la i
non	**s'oda**	**mai**	**querele**	**o**	**lai!**
not	one may hear	ever	quarrels	or	lamentations

may quarrels or laments never be heard!

ma	'dol tʃe	'kan to	di	'va gi	ut: 'tʃɛl: li	pel	'ver de	'man to	'deʎ: ʎi	ar buʃ: 'ʃɛl: li
Ma	**dolce**	**canto**	**di**	**vaghi**	**uccelli**	**pe'l**	**verde**	**manto**	**degli**	**arbuscelli**
but	sweet	song	of	pretty	birds	through the	green	mantle	of the	young trees

ri 'swo ni	'sɛm pre	kon	'nwɔ ve	'tɛm pre	'men tre	kal: 'lon de	'ɛk: ko	ri 'spon de
risuoni	**sempre**	**con**	**nuove**	**tempre,**	**mentre**	**ch'all'onde**	**Ecco**	**risponde.**
let resound	always	with	new	timbres	while	[that] to the waves	Echo	answers

But let the sweet song of pretty birds ever resound in the green mantle
of the young trees with new tones, while Echo answers the waves.

arbuscelli = (mod.) arboscelli
Ecco = (mod.) Eco

printed is "ch'al'onde"; gramatically correct is "ch'all'onde"

e	'men tre	al: 'let: ta	'kwan to pju 'pwɔ te	la	tʃi ca 'let: ta	kon	'rɔ ke	'nɔ te
E	**mentre**	**alletta**	**quanto più puote**	**la**	**cicaletta**	**con**	**roche**	**note**
and	while	entices	as much as it can	the	little cicada	with	hoarse	notes

puote = (mod.) può

il	'son: no	'dol tʃe	kel	'kal do	'mol tʃe
il	**sonno**	**dolce**	**ch'el**	**caldo**	**molce**
the	slumber	sweet	which the	heat	alleviates

el = (mod.) il

And while the little cicada, with throaty notes, entices as much as it can the sweet slumber
which relieves the heat,

e	'no i	pjan 'pja no	kon	'lɛ i	kan 'tja mo
e	noi	pian piano	con	lei	cantiamo.
[and]	we	very softly	with	her	we sing

we sing very softly with her.

GL: **Amore, Ecco**

&

Alternately titled **Amarilli mia bella**.
[5, 9, 11, 19, 20, 24, 31, 32, 36, 38, 39, 45, 54, 59, 60, 64]   *Giovanni Battista Guarini*

a ma 'ril: li
Amarilli
Amarilli

a ma 'ril: li	'mi a	'bɛl: la	non	'kre di	o	del	'mi o	kɔr	'dol tʃe	de 'zi o
Amarilli,	**mia**	**bella,**	**non**	**credi,**	**o**	**del**	**mio**	**cor**	**dolce**	**desio,**
Amarilli	my	beautiful one	not	you believe	o	of the	my	heart	sweet	desire

Amarilli, my beautiful one, do you not believe, o sweet desire of my heart,

'dɛs: ser	tu	la 'mor	'mi o
d'esser	**tu**	**l'amor**	**mio?**
of to be	you	the love	mine

that you are my love?

'kre di lo	pur	e	se	ti 'mor	tas: 'sa le
Credilo	**pur:**	**e**	**se**	**timor**	**t'assale,**
believe it	certainly	and	if	fear	you-assails

Do believe it; and if fear assails you

du bi 'tar	non	ti	'va le
dubitar	**non**	**ti**	**vale.**
to doubt	not	to you	is worth

doubting will not avail you.

> The following alternate phrase is in a few prints. According to Paton (see [60]), Parisotti, in his 1885 *Arie Antiche* edition, changed the original phrase, below, to "dubitar non ti vale," above; other editions followed suit, to avoid the sexual connotation.

'pren di	'kwe sto	'mi o	'stra le
prendi	**questo**	**mio**	**strale.**
take	this	my	arrow

take my arrow.

'a pri mi	il	'pɛt: to	e	ve 'dra i	'skrit: to	iŋ	'kɔ ɾe
Aprimi	**il**	**petto**	**e**	**vedrai**	**scritto**	**in**	**core:**
open me	the	breast	and	you will see	written	in	heart

Open my breast and you will see written on my heart:

a ma 'ril: li	ɛ	il	'mi o	a 'mo ɾe
Amarilli	**è**	**il**	**mio**	**amore.**
Amarilli	is	the	my	love

"Amarilli is my love."

GL: **Amarilli**

&

[10, 19, 41, 42]

a 'mor kat: 'tɛn di
Amor, ch'attendi?
Love, what are you waiting for?

a 'mor	kat: 'tɛn di	a 'mor	ke	'fa i
Amor,	**ch'attendi,**	**Amor,**	**che**	**fai?**
Love	what you wait for	Love	what	you do

Love, what are you waiting for? Love, what are you doing?

su	ke	non	'prɛn di	ʎi	'stra li	o 'ma i
Su,	**ché**	**non**	**prendi**	**gli**	**strali**	**omai?**
come on	why	not	you take	the	arrows	now

Come on, why do you not take up your arrows now?

omai (poet.)
= ormai

a 'mor	ven 'det: ta	a 'mor	sa 'et: ta		kwel	kɔr
Amor	**vendetta,**	**Amor**	**saetta**		**quel**	**cor,**
Love	vengeance	Love	shoot with arrows		that	heart

Love, take revenge! Love, with your arrows pierce that heart

kal 'tɛ ɾo	'zdeɲ: ɲal	'tu o	im 'pɛ ɾo
ch'altero	**sdegna'l**	**tuo**	**impero!**
which haughty	scorns	your	empire

which haughtily scorns your empire!

alt.: sdegna il = sdegna'l
(sdegn'al: a misprint)

> *The following verse is not in* [10] *or* [42]*; in those prints the*
> *next (and last) verse is "Dall'alto cielo...ogni altro avanza."*

a 'mor	pos: 'sɛn te	a 'mor	kor 'te ze	di 'ra	la	'dʒen te	pur	'ar se	e	'pre ze
Amor	**possente,**	**Amor**	**cortese,**	**dirà**	**la**	**gente**	**pur**	**arse**	**e**	**prese,**
Love	mighty	Love	kind	will say	the	people	indeed	burned	and	conquered

Mighty Love, kind Love, people will say [that] she indeed burned and conquered,

'kwel: la	kru 'dɛ le	ke	di	kwe 'rɛ le	'va ga	e	di	'pjan ti
quella	**crudele,**	**che**	**di**	**querele**	**vaga,**	**e**	**di**	**pianti,**
that	cruel one	who	of	complaints	desirous	and	of	tears

that cruel one who, desirous of complaints and tears,

sker 'ni a	ʎi	a 'man ti
schernìa	**gli**	**amanti.**
sneered at	the	lovers.

sneered at her lovers.

schernìa =
scherniva

dal: 'lal to	'tʃɛ lo	'ful mi na	'dʒɔ ve	lar 'tʃɛr	di	'dɛ lo	sa 'et: te	'pjɔ ve
Dall'alto	**cielo**	**fulmina**	**Giove,**	**l'arcier**	**di**	**Delo**	**saette**	**piove,**
from the high	heaven	sends lightning	Jove	the archer	of	Delos	arrows	rains

From the high heavens Jove sends lightning bolts, the archer of Delos rains arrows;

ma	lo	stral	'dɔ ro	'sor ni	dal: 'lo ro
ma	**lo**	**stral**	**d'oro**	**s'orni**	**d'alloro:**
but	the	arrow	of gold	may be adorned	with laurel

but may the arrow of gold be adorned with laurel,

ke	di	pos: 'san tsa	'oɲ: ɲi	'al tro	a 'van tsa
ché	**di**	**possanza**	**ogni**	**altro**	**avanza.**
because	of	power	each	other	it exceeds

for it surpasses all others in power.

The following verses are printed as additional texts in [19]:

o	'pom pa	o	'glɔ rja	o	'spɔʎː ʎe	al 'tɛ ɾe	'nɔ bil	vitː 'tɔ rja	sa 'mor	la	'fɛ ɾe
O	**pompa,**	o	**gloria,**	o	**spoglie**	**altere,**	**nobil**	**vittoria**	**s'Amor**	**la**	**fere;**
o	pomp	o	glory	o	spoils	proud	noble	victory	if Love	her	wounds

O pomp, o glory, o proud spoils, noble victory if Love wounds her –

fere (lit.) = ferisce

a 'mor	ar 'diʃ ʃi	a 'mor	fe 'riʃ ʃi	a 'mor	e 'dɔ di	kwal	a 'vra	i	'lɔ di
amor	**ardisci,**	**amor**	**ferisci,**	**amor**	**ed odi**	**qual**	**avrà**	**i**	**lodi?**
love	dare	love	wound	love	and hate	which	will have	the	lauds

odi = odio

dare, love; wound, love; [between] love and hate, which will win the prize?

kwel	kɔr	su 'pɛr bo	'laŋ gwe	e	so 'spi ɾa
Quel	**cor**	**superbo**	**langue**	**e**	**sospira,**
that	heart	proud	languishes	and	sighs

That proud heart languishes and sighs;

kwel	'vi zo	a 'tʃɛr bo	pje 'ta te	'spi ɾa
quel	**viso**	**acerbo**	**pietate**	**spira.**
that	face	unripe	pity	inspires

pietate = (mod.) pietà

that young face inspires pity.

'fatː ti	du 'ɔ i	'fju mi	'kwe i	'kru di	'lu mi	pur	'ver san	'fɔ ɾe	'pjan to	da 'mo ɾe
Fatti	**duoi**	**fiumi**	**quei**	**crudi**	**lumi,**	**pur**	**versan**	**fore**	**pianto**	**d'amore.**
made	two	rivers	those	cruel	eyes	indeed	pour	out	weeping	of love

duoi = (mod.) due

fore = (mod.) fuori

Having become two rivers, those cruel eyes indeed shed tears of love.

se	'kru da	e	'ri a	ne 'gɔ	mer 'tʃe de	'u mi le	e	'pi a	'mer tʃe de	or	'kjɛ de
Se	**cruda**	**e**	**ria**	**negò**	**mercede,**	**umile**	**e**	**pia**	**mercede**	**or**	**chiede.**
if	harsh	and	cruel	she denied	reward	humble	and	pious	pity	now	she asks

If harshly and cruelly she denied reward, humbly and piously now she asks for pity.

GL: **Amor, Delo, Giove**

❧

[41]

'a u ɾa mo 'ro za
Aur'amorosa
Amorous breeze

'a u ɾa mo 'ro za	ke	dol tʃe 'men te	'spi ɾi	al	bɛl	matː 'tin
Aur'amorosa,	**che**	**dolcemente**	**spiri**	**al**	**bel**	**mattin**
breeze amorous	who	sweetly	you blow	at the	beautiful	morning

Amorous breeze, you who blow sweetly in the beautiful morning

'men tre	'sor dʒe	la u 'ro ɾa	dɛ	spi 'roɲː ɲi	'o ɾa
mentre	**sorge**	**l'aurora,**	**deh,**	**spir' ogni**	**ora!**
while	rises	the dawn	ah	blow every	hour

as the dawn rises, ah, blow forever!

'zgom bra ne	o 'ma i	lar 'dor	kin tʃe ne 'riʃː ʃe	il	'mon te	el	'pja no
Sgombrane	**omai**	**l'ardor**	**ch'incenerisce**	**il**	**monte**	**e'l**	**piano**
clear away from it	now	the burning heat	which reduces to ashes	the	mountain	and the	plain

Dispel the burning heat which reduces the mountain and the plain to ashes,

omai (poet.) = ormai

e	fa	kal	'tu o	va 'lo ɾe	re 'spi ɾi		il	'kɔ ɾe
e	**fa**	**ch'al**	**tuo**	**valore**	**respiri**		**il**	**core!**
and	make	that at	your	prowess	may breathe again		the	heart

so that, due to your prowess, the heart may breathe again!

'a pri ne		un	'dʒor no	vi e 'pju		ke	'ma i	traŋ 'kwil: lo
Aprine		**un**	**giorno,**	**vie più**		**che**	**mai**	**tranquillo,**
open up for us		a	day	more and more		than	ever	tranquil

Open up for us a day more tranquil than ever,

si 'ke	'oɲː ɲi	'spir to	'tu a	mer 'tʃe	rav: 'vi ve	in	'kwe ste	'ri ve
sì che	**ogni**	**spirto**	**tua**	**mercé**	**ravvive**	**in**	**queste**	**rive!**
so that	every	spirit	your	grace	may revive	on	these	shores

so that your grace may revive every spirit on these shores!

> the "e" ending of
> "ravvive" (from
> "ravvivare") is an
> archaic variant

[37]

'bɛl: le 'rɔ ze pur pu 'ri ne
Belle rose purpurine
Beautiful crimson roses

'bɛl: le	'rɔ ze	pur pu 'ri ne	ke	fra	'spi ne	su	la u 'rɔ ra	non	a 'pri te
Belle	**rose**	**purpurine,**	**che**	**fra**	**spine**	**su**	**l'aurora**	**non**	**aprite,**
beautiful	roses	crimson	[that]	among	thorns	upon	the dawn	not	you open

Beautiful crimson roses *[lips]*, among thorns you do not open at the dawn

ma	mi 'ni stre	'deʎː ʎi	a 'mo ɾi	'bɛi	te 'zɔ ɾi	di	'bɛi	'dɛn ti	ku sto 'di te
ma,	**ministre**	**degli**	**amori,**	**bei**	**tesori,**	**di**	**bei**	**denti**	**custodite.**
but	ministers	of the	loves	beautiful	treasures	of	beautiful	teeth	you guard

but rather, as ministers of love, you guard beautiful treasures of beautiful teeth.

'di te	'rɔ ze	pret: 'tsjo ze	a mo 'ro ze	'di te	on 'dɛ	ke	'si o	maf: 'fis: so
Dite,	**rose**	**preziose,**	**amorose,**	**dite,**	**ond'è**	**che**	**s'io**	**m'affisso**
say	roses	precious	amorous	say	whence it is	that	if I	fix my eyes

Tell me, precious, amorous roses: tell me how it is that, when I fix my eyes

nel	bɛl	'gwar do	at: 'tʃe zo	ar 'dɛn te
nel	**bel**	**guardo**	**acceso**	**ardente,**
in the	beautiful	look	on fire	ardent

'vo i	re 'pɛn te	diʃː ʃoʎː 'ʎe te	un	bɛl	sor: 'ri zo
voi	**repente**	**disciogliete**	**un**	**bel**	**sorriso.**
you	suddenly	you melt	a	beautiful	smile

in a beautiful, burning, ardent glance, you suddenly melt into a beautiful smile.

ε	tʃɔ	'for se	per	a 'i ta	di	'mi a	'vi ta	ke	non	'rɛd: dʒe	'al: le	'vɔ stre	'i ɾe
È	**ciò**	**forse**	**per**	**aita**	**di**	**mia**	**vita**	**che**	**non**	**regge**	**alle**	**vostre**	**ire,**
is	that	perhaps	for	help	of	my	life	that	not	bears	to the	your	angers

Is it perhaps to help my life, which cannot bear your wrath,

o	pur	ε	per 'ke	'vo i	'se te	'tut: te	'lje te	me	mi 'ran do	in	sul	mo 'ri re
o	**pur**	**è**	**perché**	**voi**	**sete**	**tutte**	**liete**	**me**	**mirando**	**in**	**su'l**	**morire?**
or	perhaps	it is	because	you	are	all	happy	me	seeing	in	upon the	dying

or perhaps it is because you are utterly happy seeing me on the verge of death?

> sete = (mod.) siete

'bɛl: le	'rɔ ze	o	fe ɾi 'ta te	o	pje 'ta te	del	si	far	la	ka 'dʒon	'si a
Belle	**rose,**	**o**	**feritate,**	**o**	**pietate,**	**del**	**sì**	**far**	**la**	**cagion**	**sia,**
beautiful	roses	either	you wound	or	you have pity	of the	so	making	the	reason	be

Beautiful roses, whether you wound or have pity, that is why you do so;

'i o	vɔ	dir	in	'nɔ vi	'mɔ di	'vɔ stre	'lɔ di	ma	ri 'de te	tut: ta 'vi a
Io	**vo'**	**dir**	**in**	**novi**	**modi**	**vostre**	**lodi,**	**ma**	**ridete**	**tuttavia.**
I	want	to say	in	new	ways	your	praises	but	you laugh	however

I want to speak your praises in new ways; but you, however, keep on laughing.

se	bɛl	'ri o	se	bel: la u 'ret: ta	tra	ler 'bet: ta
Se	**bel**	**rio,**	**se**	**bell'auretta,**	**tra**	**l'erbetta**
if	beautiful	brook	if	beautiful breeze	among	the young grass

sul	mat: 'tin	mor mo 'ran 'dɛr: ra
su'l	**mattin**	**mormorand'erra,**
upon the	morn	murmuring wanders

If a beautiful brook, if a beautiful breeze, wanders murmuring among the young grass at morn,

se	di	'fjo ɾi	un	pra ti 'tʃɛl: lo	si	fa	'bɛl: lo
se	**di**	**fiori**	**un**	**praticello**	**si**	**fa**	**bello,**
if	of	flowers	a	meadow	itself	makes	beautiful

'no i	di 'tʃam	'ri de	la	'ter: ra
noi	**diciam,**	**ride**	**la**	**terra.**
we	say	smiles	the	earth

if a meadow adorns itself with flowers, we say that the earth is smiling.

'kwan do	av: 'vjɛn	ke	un	dzef: fi 'ret: to	per	di 'let: to
Quando	**avvien**	**che**	**un**	**zeffiretto**	**per**	**diletto,**
when	happens	that	a	zephyr	for	pleasure

'mɔ va	il	pjɛ	su	'lon de	'kja ɾe
mova	**il**	**piè**	**su**	**l'onde**	**chiare**
moves	the	foot	over	the waves	bright

When a zephyr happens to move, for pleasure, over the sparkling wave

si	ke	'la kwa	in	su	la 'ɾe na	'sker tsi	ap: 'pe na
sì	**che**	**l'acqua**	**in**	**su**	**l'arena**	**scherzi**	**appena,**
so	that	the water	on	upon	the sand	may play	scarcely

so that the water plays gently on the sand,

'no i	di 'tʃam	ke	'ri de	il	'ma ɾe
noi	**diciam**	**che**	**ride**	**il**	**mare.**
we	say	that	smiles	the	sea

we say that the sea is smiling.

se	dʒa 'ma i	fra	i	fjor	ver 'miʎ: ʎi
Se	**già mai**	**fra**	**i**	**fior**	**vermigli,**
if	(lit.) at times	among	the	flowers	vermilion

se	tra	'dʒiʎ: ʎi	've ste	'lal ba	un	'a u ɾe o	've lo
se	**tra**	**gigli**	**veste**	**l'alba**	**un**	**aureo**	**velo,**
if	among	lilies	dresses	the dawn	a	gold	veil

If at times, among the vermilion flowers and the lilies, the dawn dresses in a golden veil,

e	su	'rɔ te	di	'dzɛf: fi ɾo	'mɔ ve	in 'dʒi ɾo
e	su	rote	di	Zeffiro	move	in giro,
and	upon	wheels	of	Zeffiro	moves	around

rote =	move =
(mod.) ruote	(mod.) muove

'no i	di 'tʃam	ke	'ri de	il	'tʃe lo
noi	diciam	che	ride	il	cielo.
we	say	that	smiles	the	heaven

and moves upon the wheels of Zeffiro, we say that the heaven is smiling.

bɛn	ɛ	ver	'kwan dɛ	dʒo 'kon do	'ri de	il	'mon do
Ben	è	ver,	quand'è	giocondo	ride	il	mondo,
well	it is	true	when it is	joyful	smiles	the	world

It is very true [that] the world smiles when it is joyful,

'ri de	il	tʃɛl	'kwan dɛ	dʒo 'ko zo
ride	il	ciel	quand'è	giocoso,
smiles	the	heaven	when it is	jovial

[and] the heaven smiles when it is jovial;

bɛn	ɛ	ver	ma	non	san	'pɔ i	'ko me	'vo i
ben	è	ver,	ma	non	san	poi	come	voi,
well	it is	true	but	not	they know how	then	like	you

'fa ɾe	un	'ri zo	grat: 'tso zo
fare	un	riso	grazioso.
to make	a	smile	charming

it is very true, but then they do not know how to make a charming smile like you do.

GL: **Zeffiro**

❧

[11]

ki mi kon 'fɔr ta i 'mɛ
Chi mi confort'ahimè!
Who will comfort me, alas!

ki	mi	kon 'fɔr ta i 'mɛ	ki	pju	kon 'so la mi
Chi	mi	confort'ahimè!,	chi	più	consolami,
who	me	comforts alas	who	more	consoles

Who will comfort me? Alas, who will still console me

or	kel	'mi o	sol	ke	si	'bɛ i	'rad: dʒi	a 'dor na no
or	che'l	mio	sol	che	sì	bei	raggi	adornano,
now	that the	my	sun	who	so	beautiful	rays	they adorn

now that my sun, who is adorned by such beautiful rays,

il	de zi 'a to	'lu me	'a i 'las: so	in 'vo la mi
il	desiato	lume,	ahi lasso,	involami.
the	desired	light	miserable me	steals from me

steals from me – ah, woe – my desired light?

la	'bel: lis: si ma	a u 'rɔ ɾa	'on de	sad: 'dʒor na no	'mi e	'nɔt: ti
La	bellissima	Aurora,	onde	s'aggiornano	mie	notti,
the	most beautiful	dawn	whence	turn to day	my	nights

The most beautiful Dawn, through which my nights become days,

in: 'nan tsi 'tɛm po   'ɛk: ko   ab: ban 'do na mi
innanzi tempo   ecco   abbandonami,
before time   here   abandons me
abandons me here before [it is] time,

ne 'pɛn sa ke 'kwe ste 'o ɾe 'unkwa non 'tor na no
né pensa, che queste ore unqua non tornano.
nor thinks that these hours ever not they return
nor does she think these hours will ever return.

*unqua (poet.)
= mai*

'kwin tʃi si 'tri sta in kɔr 'vo tʃe ri 'swɔ na mi
Quinci sì trista in cor, voce risuonami,
hence so sad in heart voice resounds to me
Hence a voice resounds so sadly in my heart

ke 'tut: ti i 'mjɛ i pen 'sjɛr dol 'tʃet: tsa o 'bli a no
che tutti i miei pensier dolcezza obliano.
that all the my thoughts sweetness they forget
that all my thoughts forget sweetness.

e 'ri o so 'spɛt: to a 'ri e kwe 'ɾɛ le 'spro na mi
E rio sospetto a rie querele spronami.
and cruel suspicion to cruel complaints urges me on
And cruel suspicion urges me on to cruel complaints.

*rio, rie (lit.) =
reo, rei*

'di va ke ʎi 'ɔk: ki 'mjɛ i 'tan to de 'zi a no
Diva, che gli occhi miei tanto desiano,
goddess whom the eyes mine so much they desire
Goddess, whom my eyes desire so much,

*diva (lit.)
= dea*

e ke 'nwɔ ve va 'get: tse 'ɔd: dʒi in te 'sor go no
e che nuove vaghezze oggi in te sorgono,
[and] what new charms today in you rise
what new charms are born in you today,

ke dal 'mɛ sto ti 'ton si ti de 'zi a no
che dal mesto Titon sì ti desiano?
that from the sad Titon thus you they desire
that [my eyes] desire you as though from the sad Titon?

*desiano: from "desiare"
(lit.) = "desiderare"*

GL: **Aurora, Titon**

&

[39]

dɛ 'do ve son fud: 'dʒi ti
Deh, dove son fuggiti
Ah, where have they fled

dɛ 'do ve son fud: 'dʒi ti dɛ 'do ve son spa 'ri ti 'ʎɔk: ki
Deh, dove son fuggiti, deh, dove son spariti gl'occhi
ah where are fled ah where are vanished the eyes

de 'kwa li er: 'ra i 'i o son 'tʃe ner o 'ma i
de' quali errai? Io son cener omai.
of which I strayed I I am ash now
Ah, where have the eyes from which I strayed gone? I am now [reduced to] ashes.

*omai (poet.)
= ormai*

'a u ɾe   di 'vi ne   ker: 'ra te   pe ɾe 'gri ne   in   'kwe sta   'par te   in   'kwel: la
Aure   divine,   ch'errate   peregrine   in   questa   part'e   in   quella,
breezes   divine   who rove   wandering   in   this   place and   in   that one

Divine breezes, you who rove wandering here and there,

 peregrine =
(mod.) pellegrine

de   re 'ka te   no 'vel: la   del: 'lal ma   'lu tʃe   'lo ro
deh,   recate   novella   dell'alma   luce   loro,
pray   bring   news   of the glorious   light   their

please bring [me] news of their glorious light,

'a u ɾe   'ki o   me ne 'mɔ ɾo
aure   ch'io   me ne moro!
breezes   because I   I from it die

o breezes, for [otherwise] I will die.

❧

[11]

dɛ se 'tu e 'bɛl: le 'tʃiʎ: ʎa
Deh! Se tue belle ciglia
Ah, if your beautiful eyes

de   se   'tu e   'bɛl: le   'tʃiʎ: ʎa   'o ɾa   mi   'skɔr go no
Deh!   Se   tue   belle   ciglia   ora   mi   scorgono
ah   if   your   beautiful   eyelashes   now   me   perceive

Ah, if your beautiful eyes now perceive me,

'mi ɾa   ke   'ʎɔk: ki   'mjɛ i   'la kri me   'pjɔ vo no
mira   che   gl'occhi   miei   lacrime   piovono,
see   that   the eyes   mine   tears   rain

see that my eyes are raining tears

e   ke   'men tre   dal   kor   'prɛ gi   ti   'pɔr go no
e   che   mentre   dal   cor   preghi   ti   porgono
and   that   while   from the   heart   prayers   to you   offer

 preghi (lit.)
= preghiere

'mi e   'vo tʃi   'ko i   so 'spir   'la ɾja   kom: 'mɔ vo no
mie   voci   coi   sospir   l'aria   commovono.
my   words   with the   sighs   the air   they stir

and that, while my words offer you prayers from the heart, they stir the air with sighs.

❧

[24, 39, 44]   *Francesco Cini*

'fɛ ɾe sel 'vad: dʒe
Fere selvaggie
Savage wild beasts

'fɛ ɾe   sel 'vad: dʒe   ke   per   'mon ti   er: 'ra te
Fere   selvaggie,   che   per   monti   errate,
wild beasts   savage   who   through   mountains   rove

Savage wild beasts who rove through the mountains,

 in [44]: selvagge
= selvaggie   fere =
(mod.) fiere

il   pjɛ   fer 'ma te   in   'kwe ste   'ver di   'pjad: dʒe
il   piè   fermate   in   queste   verdi   piaggie.
the   foot   halt   on   these   green   slopes

halt on these green slopes.

u 'di til	'mi o	la 'men to	ka	ta 'lor	per	pje 'ta	fer 'ma to	il	'vɛn to
Udit'il	**mio**	**lamento,**	**ch'ha**	**talor**	**per**	**pietà**	**fermato**	**il**	**vento.**
hear the	my	lament	which has	sometimes	for	pity	stopped	the	wind

alt.:
Udite il =
Udit'il

Hear my lament, which has sometimes stopped the wind out of pity.

'fil: li de	'mi a	'mi a	'fil: li de	'bɛl: la	mɛ	si	ru 'bɛl: la	si	spje 'ta te	'ri a
Fillide	**mia,**	**mia**	**Fillide**	**bella,**	**m'è**	**sì**	**rubella,**	**sì**	**spietat'e**	**ria,**
Fillide	mine	my	Fillide	beautiful	to me is	so	ricalcitrant	so	pitiless and	cruel

My Fillide, my beautiful Fillide, is so ricalcitrant, so pitiless and cruel to me,

rubella = ribella | *ria (poet.) = rea*

ke	mi	've de	mo 'ri re	ne	vwɔl	mo 'rɛn dil	'mi o	kor 'dɔʎ: ʎo	u 'di re
che	**mi**	**vede**	**morire,**	**né**	**vuol**	**morend'il**	**mio**	**cordoglio**	**udire.**
that	me	sees	to die	nor	wishes	dying the	my	grief	to hear

alt.:
morendo il
= morend'il

that she sees me dying but does not wish to hear my grief in the dying.

[24] ends with this (alternate) text:

si	spje 'ta ta	e	'ri a	'di te le	ke	ri 'mi ri
sì	**spietata**	**e**	**ria!**	**Ditele**	**che**	**rimiri,**
so	pitiless	and	cruel	tell her	that	may she look at

'men tre	'ki o	'mɔ ro	al 'men	i	'mjɛ i	mar 'ti ri
mentre	**ch'io**	**moro**	**almen**	**i**	**miei**	**martiri!**
while	that I	I die	at least	the	my	sufferings

...[is] so pitiless and cruel! Tell her to see at least, as I die, my suffering!

[39] continues as follows; in [44] the next text (after "...cordoglio udire," above) is "Diteli voi,..." continuing to the end.

per	'lɛ i	mi 'strug: go	'ko me	'tʃe ral	'fɔ ko	ne	'trɔ vo	'lo ko	'si o	mas: 'si do
Per	**lei**	**mi struggo**	**come**	**cer'al**	**foco,**	**né**	**trovo**	**loco**	**s'io**	**m'assid'o**
for	her	myself I consume	like	wax at the	fire	nor	I find	repose	if I	I take my seat or

'fug: go	tal	ko 'ma i	'vin te	'stan ko	'sen to	lo	'spir to
fuggo,	**tal**	**ch'omai**	**vint'e**	**stanco**	**sento**	**lo**	**spirto**
I flee	such	that now	vanquished and	weary	I feel	the	spirit

el	kɔr	ve 'nir mi 'maŋ ko
e'l	**cor**	**venir mi manco.**
and the	heart	failing me

For her I waste away like wax exposed to a fire; I find no repose whether I stay or flee;
so vanquished and weary am I that I feel my spirit and my heart failing.

'di te le	'vo i	se	di	me	vi	'ka le
Ditele	**voi,**	**se**	**di**	**me**	**vi**	**cale,**
tell her	you	if	of	me	to you	it matters

Tell her, if I matter to you,

kel	'mi o	gran	'ma le	vjen	da	'ʎɔk: ki	'swɔ i
che'l	**mio**	**gran**	**male**	**vien**	**da**	**gl'occhi**	**suoi.**
that the	my	great	woe	comes	from	the eyes	hers

alts.: ch'il = che'l;
dagli occhi = da gl'occhi

that my great woe comes from her eyes.

'di te le	ke	ri 'mi ri	'men tre	'ki o	'mɔ ro	al 'me no	i	'mjɛ i	mar 'ti ri
Ditele	**che**	**rimiri,**	**mentre**	**ch'io**	**moro,**	**almeno**	**i**	**miei**	**martiri.**
tell her	that	may she look at	while	that I	I die	at least	the	my	sufferings

Tell her to see at least, as I die, my suffering.

GL: **Fillide**

&

[61]
from: *Euridice (1602)*
character: *Orfeo*

Ottavio Rinuccini

non 'pjaŋ go e non so 'spi ɾo
Non piango e non sospiro
I am not weeping and I am not sighing

non	'pjaŋ go	e	non	so 'spi ɾo	o	'mi a	'ka ɾa	e u ɾi 'di tʃe
Non	**piango**	**e**	**non**	**sospiro,**	**o**	**mia**	**cara**	**Euridice,**
not	I weep	and	not	I sigh	o	my	dear	Euridice

I am not weeping and I am not sighing, o my dear Euridice,

ke	so spi 'rar	ke	la gri 'mar	non	'pɔs: so
ché	**sospirar,**	**ché**	**lagrimar**	**non**	**posso.**
because	to sigh	because	to weep	not	I am able

for I cannot sigh, I cannot weep.

ka 'da ve ɾe	in fe 'li tʃe	o	'mi o	'kɔ ɾe	o	'mi a	'spɛ me	o	'pa tʃe	o	'vi ta
Cadavere	**infelice,**	**o**	**mio**	**core,**	**o**	**mia**	**speme,**	**o**	**pace,**	**o**	**vita!**
corpse	unlucky	o	my	heart	o	my	hope	o	peace	o	life

speme (lit.) = speranza

Unlucky corpse: o my heart, o my hope, o peace, o life!

o i 'mɛ	ki	mi	ta	'tɔl to	o i 'mɛ	'do ve	sɛ	'dʒi ta
Ohimè!	**chi**	**mi**	**t'ha**	**tolto,**	**ohimè!**	**dove**	**se'**	**gita?**
alas	who	from me	you has	taken away	alas	where	are you	gone

gita: from "gire" (lit.) = "andare"

Alas, who has taken you from me? Alas, where have you gone?

'tɔ sto	ve 'dra i	kin 'va no	non	kja 'ma sti	mo 'rɛn do	il	'tu o	kon 'sɔr te
Tosto	**vedrai**	**ch'invano**	**non**	**chiamasti**	**morendo**	**il**	**tuo**	**consorte.**
soon	you will see	that in vain	not	you called	dying	the	your	spouse

Soon you will see that you, dying, did not call to your spouse in vain.

non	son	lon 'ta no	'i o	'vɛŋ go	o	'ka ɾa	'vi ta	o	'ka ɾa	'mɔr te
Non	**son**	**lontano:**	**Io**	**vengo,**	**o**	**cara**	**vita,**	**o**	**cara**	**morte!**
not	I am	far away	I	I come	o	dear	life	o	dear	death

I am not far away; I am coming, o dear life, o dear death!

GL: **Euridice**

☙

[41]

o ke fe 'li tʃe 'dʒor no
O, che felice giorno
Oh, what a happy day

o	ke	fe 'li tʃe	'dʒor no
O,	**che**	**felice**	**giorno!**
oh	what	happy	day

Oh, what a happy day!

o	ke	'lje to	ri 'tor no	rav: 'vi va	il	kɔr	dʒa	'spɛn to
O,	**che**	**lieto**	**ritorno**	**ravviva**	**il**	**cor**	**già**	**spento!**
oh	what	joyous	return	enlivens	the	heart	formerly	lifeless

Oh, what a joyous return enlivens my formerly lifeless heart!

'kwan ta   dol 'tʃet: tsa   'sɛn to   o   'mi a   'vi ta   o   'mi a   'dʒɔ ja   in fi 'ni ta
Quanta   **dolcezza**   **sento,**   **o,**   **mia**   **vita,**   **o,**   **mia**   **gioia**   **infinita!**
how much   sweetness   I feel   o   my   life   o   my   joy   infinite
How much sweetness I feel, o my life, o my infinite joy!

'ɛk: kol   'mi o   bɛn   ri 'tor na   e   'kwe ste   'ri ve   a 'dor na
Ecco'l   **mio**   **ben**   **ritorna**   **e**   **queste**   **rive**   **adorna.**
here is the   my   dear one   returns   and   these   shores   adorns
Here my dear one returns and adorns these shores.

'ɛk: ko ne   'lje to   il   'dʒi ɾo   del   bɛl   'gwar do   'ki o   'mi ɾo
Eccone   **lieto**   **il**   **giro**   **del**   **bel**   **guardo**   **ch'io**   **miro,**
here is of it   happy   the   turn   of the   beautiful   glance   that I   I look at
Here is, happily, the beautiful glance at which I gaze –

'ɔk: ki   'bɛl: li   'ɔk: ki   'ka ɾi   'ɔk: ki   del   sol   pju   'kja ɾi
occhi   **belli,**   **occhi**   **cari,**   **occhi**   **del**   **sol**   **più**   **chiari.**
eyes   beautiful   eyes   dear   eyes   than the   sun   more   shining
beautiful eyes, dear eyes, eyes more luminous than the sun.

or   bɛn   prɔ 'vi o   nel   'pɛt: to   non   do 'lor   ma   di 'lɛt: to
Or   **ben**   **prov'io**   **nel**   **petto**   **non**   **dolor,**   **ma**   **diletto.**
now   well   feel I   in the   breast   not   sorrow   but   delight
Now I truly feel in my breast not sorrow, but delight.

'tor na   la   'kja ɾa   e   'bɛl: la   'mi a   ri lu 'tʃɛn te   'stel: la
Torna   **la**   **chiara**   **e**   **bella,**   **mia**   **rilucente**   **stella.**
returns   the   shining   and   beautiful   my   resplendant   star
My shining and beautiful resplendant star returns.

'tor na   il   sol   'tor na   'la u ɾa   'tor na   ki   mi   re 'sta u ɾa
Torna   **il**   **sol,**   **torna**   **l'aura,**   **torna**   **chi**   **mi**   **restaura.**
returns   the   sun   returns   the air   returns   the one who   me   restores
The sun returns, the air returns, the one who restores me returns.

'dol tʃe   or   'mi a   'vi ta   'rɛn de   kwel   'di o   ki   'kɔ ɾi   at: 'tʃɛn de
Dolce   **or'**   **mia**   **vita**   **rende**   **quel**   **dio**   **ch'i**   **cori**   **accende.**
sweet   now   my   life   makes   that   god   who the   hearts   inflames
That god who inflames hearts makes my life sweet now.

a 'mor   ke   la 've a   'tɔl to   or   mi   'rɛn de   il   bɛl   'vol to
Amor,   **che**   **l'avea**   **tolto,**   **or**   **mi**   **rende**   **il**   **bel**   **volto,**   *avea =*
Love   who   it had   taken away   now   to me   gives back   the   beautiful   face   *aveva*
Love, who had taken it away, now gives me back the beautiful face,

il   'mi o   kɔr   il   'mi o   'bɛ ne   il   'mi o   kon 'for to   e   'spe ne   *spene (poet.)*
il   **mio**   **cor,**   **il**   **mio**   **bene,**   **il**   **mio**   **conforto**   **e**   **spene.**   *= speme (lit.)*
the   my   heart   the   my   dear one   the   my   comfort   and   hope   *= speranza*
my heart, my dear one, my comfort and hope.

GL: **Amor**

[13]

'ɔ di e u 'tɛr pe il 'dol tʃe 'kan to

Odi, Euterpe, il dolce canto

Hear, Euterpe, the sweet song

'ɔ di	e u 'tɛr pe	il	'dol tʃe	'kan to	ka	lo	stil	a 'mor	mim 'pɛ tra
Odi,	**Euterpe,**	**il**	**dolce**	**canto**	**ch'a**	**lo**	**stil**	**Amor**	**m'impetra,**
hear	Euterpe	the	sweet	song	which at	the	style	Love	me entreats

odi: from "odire" = (mod.) "udire"

Hear, Euterpe, the sweet song which Love inspires me to compose

e dak: 'kɔr da	al	'dol tʃe	'kan to	'la u re o	swɔn	'del: la	'mi a	'tʃe tra
ed accorda	**al**	**dolce**	**canto**	**l'aureo**	**suon**	**della**	**mia**	**cetra,**
and tune	at the	sweet	song	the golden	sound	of the	my	cithara

and tune, to the sweet song, the golden sound of my cithara,

ke	a	dir	kwel	'ke i	mi	ra 'dʒo na	'trɔp: po	'dol tʃe	a 'mor	mi	'spro na
ché	**a**	**dir**	**quel**	**ch'ei**	**mi**	**ragiona**	**troppo**	**dolce**	**amor**	**mi**	**sprona.**
because	to	to say	that	which it	to me	reasons	too	sweet	love	me	urges

for exceedingly sweet love urges me to say what goes through my mind.

di	not: 'tur no	e	'ka sto	've lo	la	'mi a	'li dja	il	sen	ko 'pri a
Di	**notturno**	**e**	**casto**	**velo**	**la**	**mia**	**Lidia**	**il**	**sen**	**copria;**
with	nocturnal	and	chaste	veil	the	my	Lidia	the	breast	was covering

copria = copriva

My Lidia's breast was covered with a nocturnal and chaste veil;

ma	la	'lu na	in	'mɛd: dzo	il	'tʃe lo	dol tʃe 'men te	il	sen	ma 'pri a
ma	**la**	**luna**	**in**	**mezzo**	**il**	**cielo**	**dolcemente**	**il**	**sen**	**m'apria,**
but	the	moon	in	middle	the	sky	sweetly		the	breast	to me opened

apria = apriva

ka	mi 'rar	si	bɛl	te 'zɔ ro	lam ped: 'dʒɔ	di	'fjam: me	'dɔ ro
ch'a	**mirar**	**sì**	**bel**	**tesoro**	**lampeggiò**	**di**	**fiamme**	**d'oro.**
in order to	to see	so	beautiful	treasure	flashed	with	flames	of gold

but in the middle of the sky the moon, as it flashed with flames of gold to illuminate such a beautiful treasure, was sweetly opening her breast to me.

e	ve 'de a	so 'a ve	e	'pu ra	la	'su a	'ne ve	il	'pɛt: to	a 'pri re
E	**vedea**	**soave**	**e**	**pura**	**la**	**sua**	**neve**	**il**	**petto**	**aprire;**
and	I saw	delicate	and	pure	la	her	snow	the	breast	to open

the "a" ending of "vedea" (= "vedeva") is an antiquated alternate for the "o" ending ("vedevo")

And I saw the delicate and pure snow of her breast uncover;

e	sen 'ti a	di	'dol tʃe	'ku ra	nel	'mi o	'pɛt: to	il	kɔr	laŋ 'gwi re
e	**sentia**	**di**	**dolce**	**cura**	**nel**	**mio**	**petto**	**il**	**cor**	**languire,**
and	I felt	of	sweet	care	in the	my	breast	the	heart	to languish

sentia: same note as above, about "vedea"

and I felt the heart in my breast languish with sweet caring

e	sa 'lir	ve 'lo tʃe	e	'lɛ ve	il	'mi o	kɔr	tra	'ne ve	e	'ne ve
e	**salir**	**veloce**	**e**	**leve**	**il**	**mio**	**cor**	**tra**	**neve**	**e**	**neve.**
and	to rise	quick	and	gently	the	my	heart	among	snow	and	snow

leve = (mod.) lieve

and my heart rise quickly and gently between snow and snow.

e	da	'kwe i	so 'a vi	al 'bo ri	sfa vil: 'la va	un	'dol tʃe	'fɔ ko
E	**da**	**quei**	**soavi**	**albori**	**sfavillava**	**un**	**dolce**	**foco;**
and	from	those	gentle	dawns	sparkled	a	sweet	fire

And from those gentle dawnings sparkled a sweet fire;

e	le	'grat: tsje	kon	ʎi	a 'mo ɾi	a 've an	'kwi vi	un	'dol tʃe	'lɔ ko
e	le	grazie	con	gli	amori	avean	quivi	un	dolce	loco,
and	the	graces	with	the	loves	had	therein	a	sweet	place

avean = avevan[o]

and therein the graces and loves had a sweet home,

e	se	'kwi vi	il	kɔr	dʒun 'dʒe a	su	la	'ne ve	il	kɔr	mar 'de a
e	se	quivi	il	cor	giungea,	su	la	neve	il	cor	m'ardea.
and	if	therein	the	heart	reached	on	the	snow	the	heart	me burned

giungea = giungeva

ardea = ardeva

and when my heart reached it, my heart burned upon the snow.

GL: **Amor, Euterpe**

&

[55]

o i 'mɛ se 'tan ta 'ma te
Ohimè, se tant'amate
Alas, if you love so much

o i 'mɛ	se	'tan ta 'ma te	di	sen 'tir	dir	o i 'mɛ
Ohimè,	**se**	**tant'amate**	**di**	**sentir**	**dir**	**"ohimè,"**
alas	if	so much you love	of	to hear	to say	"alas"

Alas, if you love so much hearing "alas" spoken,

dɛ	per 'ke	'fa te	ki	'di tʃe	o i 'mɛ	mo 'ɾi ɾe
deh,	**perché**	**fate**	**chi**	**dice**	**"ohimè"**	**morire?**
ah	why	you make	who	says	"alas"	to die

ah, why do you make the one who says "alas" die?

'si o	'mɔ ɾo	un	sol	po 'tre te	'laŋ gwi do	e	do lo 'ro zo i 'mɛ	sen 'ti ɾe
S'io	**moro,**	**un**	**sol**	**potrete**	**languido**	**e**	**doloros' "ohimè"**	**sentire;**
if I	I die	one	only	you will be able	faint	and	sorrowful "alas"	to hear

If I die, you will be able to hear only one faint and sorrowful "alas";

ma	se	kɔr	'mi o	vor: 're te	ke	'vi tabː 'bi o	da	'vo i
ma	**se,**	**cor**	**mio,**	**vorrete**	**che**	**vit'abb'io**	**da**	**voi,**
but	if	heart	mine	you will want	that	life may have I	from	you

but, my beloved, if you wish me to have life from you,

e	'vo i	da	me	a 'vre te	'milː le	'dol tʃe	o i 'mɛ
e	**voi**	**da**	**me,**	**avrete**	**mille**	**dolce**	**"ohimè."**
and	you	from	me	you will have	thousand	sweet	"alas"

and you from me, you will have a thousandfold sweet "alas."

&

[53]

per fi 'disː si mo 'vol to
Perfidissimo volto
Most treacherous face

per fi 'disː si mo	'vol to	bɛn	lu 'za ta	bel: 'letː tsa	in	te	si 've de
Perfidissimo	**volto,**	**ben**	**l'usata**	**bellezza**	**in**	**te**	**si vede,**
most treacherous	face	well	the customary	beauty	in	you	one sees

Most treacherous face, in you is easily seen the customary beauty,

ma   non   lu 'za ta   'fe de
ma   non   l'usata   fede.
but   not   the customary   faith
but not the customary faithfulness.

dʒa   mi   pa 're vi   dir   kwe sta mo 'ro ze   'lu tʃi   ke   dol tʃe 'men te
Già   mi   parevi   dir: Quest'amorose   luci   che   dolcemente
formerly   to me   you seemed   to say   these amorous   eyes   which   sweetly

ri 'vɔl go   a   te   si   'bɛl: le   e   si   pje 'to ze
rivolgo   a   te   sì   belle   e   sì   pietose,
I turn   to   you   so   beautiful   and   so   compassionate
You once seemed to say to me: These so beautiful and so compassionate eyes which I sweetly turn to you –

'pri ma   ve 'dra i   tu   'spɛn te   ke   'si a   'spɛn to   il   de 'zi o
prima   vedrai   tu   spente   che   sia   spento   il   desio
before   you will see   you   spent   than   may be   spent   the   desire

ka   te   le   'dʒi ɾa
ch'a   te   le   gira.
which to   you   them   turns
you will sooner see them lifeless than will the desire which turns them to you be extinguished.

'a i   ke   'spɛn to   'ɛl   de 'zi o   ma   non   ɛ   'spɛn to   kwel
Ahi!   che   spento   è'l   desio,   ma   non   è   spento   quel,
alas   [that]   spent   is the   desire   but   not   is   spent   that one

per   'ku i   'i o   'spi ɾo   ab: ban do 'na to   'kɔ ɾe
per   cui   io   spiro,   abbandonato   core.
for   which   I   I breathe   abandoned   heart
Alas, dead is your desire; but my abandoned heart, which keeps me alive, is not dead.

o   'vol to   'trɔp: po   'va go   e   'trɔp: po   'ri o   per 'ke   se   'pɛr di   a 'mo ɾe
Oh!   volto   troppo   vago   e   troppo   rio,   perchè   se   perdi   amore
oh   face   too   charming   and   too   cruel   why   if   you lose   love

> *rio (lit.)*
> *= reo*

non   'pɛr di   aŋ 'kor   va 'get: tsa
non   perdi   ancor   vaghezza?
not   you lose   also   charm
Oh, face too charming and too cruel, why, if you lose [your] love [for me], do you not also lose your charm?

o   non   'a i   'pa ɾi   a   la   bel 'ta   fer 'met: tsa
Oh!   non   hai   pari   a   la   beltà   fermezza.
oh   not   you have   equal   to   the   beauty   steadiness
Oh, you have not faithfulness equal to your beauty!

❧

[55, 37]   *Ottavio Rinuccini*

sfo 'ga va kon le 'stel: le
Sfogava con le stelle
[A lovesick man] found relief among the stars

sfo 'ga va   kon   le   'stel: le   u nin 'fer mo   da 'mo ɾe   'sot: to   not: 'tur no   'tʃe lo
Sfogava   con   le   stelle   un infermo   d'amore   sotto   notturno   cielo
found relief   with   the   stars   an infirm one   of love   beneath   nocturnal   sky
A lovesick man found relief among the stars beneath the night sky

il	'su o	do 'lo ɾe	e	di 'tʃe a	'fis: so	in	'lo ɾo
il	**suo**	**dolore;**	**e**	**dicea,**	**fisso**	**in**	**loro:**
the	his	sorrow	and	he said	fixed	on	them

for his sorrow; and, with his gaze fixed on them, he said:

*dicea =
diceva*

o	im: 'ma dʒi ni	'bɛl: le	del	'i dol	'mi o	ka 'do ɾo	si 'ko me	a	me	mo 'stra te
O,	**immagini**	**belle**	**del**	**idol**	**mio**	**ch'adoro,**	**sì come**	**a**	**me**	**mostrate,**
o	images	beautiful	of the	idol	mine	whom I adore	*(lit.)* as	to	me	you show

O beautiful images of my idol whom I adore, as you show me,

'men tre	ko 'zi	splen 'de te	la	'su a	'ra ɾa	bel 'ta te
mentre	**così**	**splendete**	**la**	**sua**	**rara**	**beltate,**
while	thus	you shine	the	her	rare	beauty

while you shine thus, her rare beauty,

*beltate =
beltade =
(mod.) beltà*

ko 'zi	mo 'stra te	a	'le i	'men tre	ko 'tan to	ar 'de te	i	'vi vi	ar 'do ɾi	'mjɛ i
così	**mostrate**	**a**	**lei,**	**mentre**	**cotanto**	**ardete**	**i**	**vivi**	**ardori**	**miei.**
thus	show	to	her	while	so much	you burn	the	burning	ardors	mine

also show her, while you burn so much, my blazing ardors.

la	fa 'ɾe ste	kol	'vɔ stro	'a u ɾe o	sem 'bjan te
La	**fareste**	**col**	**vostro**	**aureo**	**sembiante**
her	you would make	with the	your	golden	countenance

With your golden countenance you would make her

*in [37]: vostr'aureo
= vostro aureo*

pje 'to za	si 'ko me	me	'fa te	a 'man te
pietosa	**sì come**	**me**	**fate**	**amante.**
compassionate	*(lit.)* as	me	you make	lover

compassionate, as you make me a lover.

&

[10, 14, 19, 24]

tu	'ka i	le	'pen: ne	a 'mo ɾe
Tu ch'hai le penne, Amore
You who have wings, Love

tu	'ka i	le	'pen: ne	a 'mo ɾe	e	'sa i	spje 'gar le	a	'vo lo
Tu	**ch'hai**	**le**	**penne,**	**Amore,**	**e**	**sai**	**spiegarle**	**a**	**volo,**
you	who have	the	feathers	Love	and	you know how	to spread them	in	flight

You who have wings, Love, and know how to spread them in flight,

dɛ	'mwɔ vi	'rat: to	un	'vo lo	fin	la	do 'vɛl	'mi o	'kɔ ɾe
deh	**muovi**	**ratto**	**un**	**volo**	**fin**	**là**	**dov'è'l**	**mio**	**core,**
pray	move	swiftly	a	flight	up to	there	where is the	my	heart

please, fly swiftly to where my heart is;

e	se	non	'sa i	la	'vi a	'ko i	'mjɛ i	so 'spir	tin 'vi a
e	**se**	**non**	**sai**	**la**	**via**	**coi**	**miei**	**sospir**	**t'invia.**
and	if	not	you know	the	way	with the	my	sighs	you sends

and if you do not know the way, my sighs will show you.

*in [19]: co' miei
= coi miei*

va	pur	kel	tro ve 'ra i	tral	've lo	el	'bjaŋ ko	'se no
Va	**pur:**	**che'l**	**troverai**	**tra'l**	**velo**	**e'l**	**bianco**	**seno,**
go	then	[that] it	you will find	between the	veil	and the	white	breast

Then go: you will find it between the veil and the white breast,

*in [24]: fra = tra;
e il = e'l;
che il = che'l*

in [19]: ch'il = che'l

o   tral   'dol tʃe   se 're no   de   lu mi 'no zi   'ra i
o   tra'l   dolce   sereno   de'   luminosi   rai,
or   among the   sweet   serenity   of the luminous   eyes
or in the sweet serenity of the luminous eyes,

> in [24]: *fra = tra;*
> *dei = de'*

o   tra   'bɛi   'nɔ di   'dɔ ɾo   del   'mi o   'dol tʃe   te 'zɔ ɾo
o   tra   bei   nodi   d'oro   del   mio   dolce   tesoro.
or   among   beautiful knots   of gold of the   my   sweet   treasure
or among the beautiful golden tresses of my sweet treasure.

> in [24]: **del dolce mio tesoro (same translation)**

> *The following additional verses are printed as text only in [19]:*

'van: ne   lu 'ziŋ ga   e   'prɛ ga   per 'ke   dal   bɛl   sod: 'dʒor no
Vanne,   lusinga,   e   prega   perché   dal   bel   soggiorno
go   charm   and   beg   so that from the beautiful sojourn
Go, charm, and beg, so that from its lovely sojourn

'fat: tʃa   il   'mi o   kɔr   ri 'tor no   e   sel   ve 'nir   pur   'njɛ ga
faccia   il   mio   cor   ritorno,   e   se'l venir   pur   niega,
may make   the   my   heart return   and   if it coming   still refuses
my heart may return; and if it still refuses,

ri 'vɔl to   al   'nɔ stro   'so le   'diʎ: ʎi   ko 'tal   pa 'ɾɔ le
rivolto   al   nostro   sole,   digli   cotal   parole:
turned   to the our   sun   tell it   such   words
turned to our sun, say these words to it:

kwel   'tu o   fe 'de le   a 'man te   tra   'ljɛ ta   a 'mi ka   'dʒɛn te
Quel   tuo   fedele   amante,   tra   lieta   amica   gente,
that   your   faithful   lover   among   happy   friendly   people

'vi ve   'mɛ sto   e   do 'lɛn te   e   kol   'tri sto   sem 'bjan te
vive   mesto   e   dolente,   e   col   tristo   sembiante
lives   sad   and   sorrowful   and   with the wretched   countenance
That faithful lover of yours lives sad and sorrowful among happy, friendly people; and with downcast
countenance,

'doɲ: ɲi   al: le 'gret: tsa   'spɛn to   'tur ba   lal 'tru i   kon 'tɛn to
d'ogni   allegrezza   spento   turba   l'altrui   contento.
of every   joy   spent   clouds   the others' happiness
drained of every joy, clouds others' happiness.

di   ke   fral   'kan to   el   'ri zo   'spar go   so 'spir   di   'fɔ ko
Di' che fra'l canto   e'l   riso   spargo   sospir   di   foco,
say that among the song   and the laughter I pour out sighs   of   fire
Say that among the songs and laughter I pour out sighs of passion,

ke   fral   di 'lɛt: to   el   'dʒɔ ko   non   'ma i   se 're no   il   'vi zo
che fra'l diletto   e'l   gioco   non   mai   sereno   il   viso,
that among the pleasure   and the play   not   ever   serene   the face
that my face is never serene among pleasure and play,

ke   'dal ma   e   di   kɔr   'pri vo   'stɔm: mi   fra   'mɔr to   e   'vi vo
che d'alma   e   di   cor   privo   stommi   fra   morto   e   vivo.
that of soul   and   of   heart deprived I am   between dead   and   alive
[and] that I am, deprived of soul and heart, between death and life.

'sen tro	'al: le	'tɛ pi de	'on de	'dar no	fra	'la u ri	e	'fad: dʒi
S'entro	alle	tepide	onde	d'Arno,	fra	lauri	e	faggi
if within	at the	tepid	wave	of Arno	among	laurels	and	beeches

tepido =
(mod.)
tiepido

'fug: gon	ʎi	e 'sti vi	'rad: dʒi
fuggon	gli	estivi	raggi,
flee	the	summer	rays

When the summer rays on the tepid waves of the Arno, among laurels and beeches, flee,

'i o	su	lom 'bro ze	'spon de	o [i]n su	lar 'dɛn te	a 're na	're sto	'kar ko	di	'pe na
io,	su	l'ombrose	sponde	o'n su	l'ardente	arena,	resto	carco	di	pena.
I	on	the shady	banks	or up on	the burning	sand	I remain	weighed down	with	pain

I, whether on the shady banks or the burning sand, remain burdened with pain.

> The following lines, through "accresco," defy a clear translation; they remain questionable.

se	dal	sas: 'so zo	'fon do	il	krin	stil: 'lan te	e	'mɔl: le
Se	dal	sassoso	fondo	il	crin	stillante	e	molle
if	from the	stony	bottom	the	hair	dripping	and	wet

If, from the rocky depths, with hair dripping and soggy,

'or ke no	il	'ka po	'e i	'stɔl: le	di	'prɛ da	il	sen	fe 'kon do
Orcheno,	il	capo	ei	stolle	di	preda	il	sen	fecondo
of Orco	the	head	he	raises	of	prey	the	breast	replete

stolle: from
(antiquated)
"stollere"

Orco, his belly full of prey, raises his head

'o ve	oɲ: 'ɲun	un	'kor: rer	'mi ro	a 'pe na	un	'gwar do	'i o	'dʒi ro
ove	ognun	un	correr	miro	a pena	un	guardo	io	giro.
where	everyone	a	running	I see	scarcely	a	look	I	I turn

and I see everyone run [from him], I scarcely glance at him.

'men tre	per	'pjad: dʒe	e	'kɔl: li	'se gwon	fu 'ga tʃi	'fje re
Mentre	per	piagge	e	colli	seguon	fugaci	fiere
while	through	slopes	and	hills	pursue	fleeting	wild animals

le	kat: tʃa 'tri tʃi	'fje re	las: 'si o	kon	ʎi	'ɔk: ki	'mɔl: li
le	cacciatrici fiere	lass'io	con	gli	occhi	molli
the	beasts of prey	become weary I	with	the	eyes	wet

While over the slopes and hills the beasts of prey pursue fleeting wild animals, I, weary, with moist eyes,

or	del	'tʃe sto	or	del	're sko	'lon da	pjan 'gɛn do	ak: 'kre sko
or	del	cesto,	or	del	resco	l'onda	piangendo	accresco.
now	from the	basket	now	from	rush	the wave	weeping	I increase

now from my basket and now from the rushes, raise the water level with my weeping.

> *Problems: "cesto" and "resco." "Cesto" could be "cesta" (a light river craft); "resco," if "resca," would be either a thread or a marsh river plant. Perhaps "or del cesto, or del resco" is an (antiquated) idiom?*

non	'deʎ: ʎi	a u 'dʒe i	vo 'lan ti	'mi ro	le	'prɛ de	e	i	'vo li
Non	degli	augei	volanti	miro	le	prede	e	i	voli
not	of the	birds	flying	I gaze at	the	preys	and	the	flights

augei =
augelli (poet.)
= uccelli

sol	per 'ke	mi	kon 'so li	ver 'sar	so 'spi ri	e	'pjan ti
sol	perché	mi	consoli	versar	sospiri	e	pianti
only	because	me	it may console	to shed	sighs	and	tears

I gaze at the prey and the flight of the flying birds only because it may console me to shed sighs and tears;

ma	di	'ki o	non	vor: 'rɛ i	far	'nɔ ti	i	do 'lor	'mjɛ i
ma	di'	ch'io	non	vorrei	far	noti	i	dolor	miei.
but	say	that I	not	I should like	to make	known	the	sorrows	mine

but tell [my heart] that I do not wish to make my sorrows known.

a 'mor	kor 'te ze	im 'pɛ tra	ka	me	'tor ni	il	kɔr	'mi o
Amor	**cortese**	**impetra**	**ch'a**	**me**	**torni**	**il**	**cor**	**mio**
love	kind	implores	that to	me	may return	the	heart	mine

Kind Love, convince my heart to return to me,

o	'kel: la	il	'man di	on 'di o	pju	non	'sem bri	'wɔm	di	'pjɛ tra
o	**ch'ella**	**il**	**mandi,**	**ond'io**	**più**	**non**	**sembri**	**uom**	**di**	**pietra**
or	that she	it	may send	whence I	more	not	may seem	man	of	stone

or else may she send it back, so that I may no longer seem to be a man of stone,

ne	pju	kon	'tri sto	a 'spɛt: to	'tur bi	lal 'tru i	di 'lɛt: to
né	**più**	**con**	**tristo**	**aspetto**	**turbi**	**l'altrui**	**diletto.**
nor	more	with	wretched	appearance	may cloud	the others'	pleasure

nor any longer cloud others' pleasure with my wretched appearance.

ma	se	per	'mi a	ven 'tu ra	del	'su o	tor 'nar	dub: 'bjo za
Ma	**se**	**per**	**mia**	**ventura**	**del**	**suo**	**tornar**	**dubbiosa**
but	if	through	my	luck	of the	its	return	doubtful

man 'dar lo	a	me	non	'ɔ za	a 'mor	pro 'met: ti	e	'dʒu ra
mandarlo	**a**	**me**	**non**	**osa,**	**Amor**	**prometti**	**e**	**giura,**
to send it	to	me	not	dares	Love	promise	and	swear

But if perchance its return is doubtful, or she dares not send it back, Love, promise her

ke	'su o	fu	'sɛm pre	e	'si a	il	'kɔ re	e	'lal ma	'mi a
che	**suo**	**fu**	**sempre,**	**e**	**sia**	**il**	**core**	**e**	**l'alma**	**mia.**
that	hers	was	always	and	may be	the	heart	and	the soul	mine

that my heart and soul were always, and always will be, hers.

GL: **Amor[e], Arno, Orcheno**

&

[37, 39]   *Ottavio Rinuccini*

u 'di te a 'man ti
Udite, amanti
Hear, lovers

u 'di te	a 'man ti	u 'di te	o	'fɛ re	er: 'ran ti	o	'tʃɛ lo	o	'stel: le
Udite,	**amanti,**	**udite,**	**o**	**fere**	**erranti,**	**o**	**cielo,**	**o**	**stelle,**
Hear	lovers	hear	o	wild beasts	roving	o	heaven	o	stars

fere =
(mod.)
fiere

Hear, lovers – hear, o roving wild beasts, o heaven, o stars,

o	'lu na	o	'so le	'dɔn: ne	don 'dzɛl: le	le	'mi e	pa 'rɔ le
o	**luna,**	**o**	**sole,**	**donn'e**	**donzelle,**	**le**	**mie**	**parole!**
o	moon	o	sun	women and	girls	the	my	words

in [37]: donne e
= donn'e

o moon, o sun, women and girls, my words!

e	sa ra 'dʒon	mi	'dɔʎ: ʎo	pjan 'dʒe te	al	'mi o	kor 'dɔʎ: ʎo
E,	**s'a ragion**	**mi**	**doglio,**	**piangete**	**al**	**mio**	**cordoglio!**
and	if rightly	me	I lament	weep	at the	my	grief

in [37]: se a = s'a;
il mio cordoglio
(same translation)

And if I lament justifiably, weep at my grief!

la 'bɛl: la 'dɔn: na 'mi a dʒa si kor 'te ze e 'pi a
La bella donna mia, già sì cortese e pia,
the beautiful lady mine formerly so kind and devout
My beautiful lady, formerly so kind and devout,

non sɔ per 'ke sɔ bɛn ke 'ma i non 'vɔl dʒe a me
non so perché, so ben che mai non volge a me
not I know why I know well that ever not she turns to me

'kwe i 'dol tʃi 'ra i e 'di o pur 'vi vo e 'spi ɾo sen 'ti te ke mar 'ti ɾo
quei dolci rai, ed io pur vivo e spiro, sentite che martiro!
those sweet eyes and I yet I live and I breathe hear what agony
never turns those sweet eyes to me – well I know, though I know not why – and yet
I live and breathe; hear: what agony!

> *martiro =*
> *(mod.) martirio*

'ka ɾe a mo 'ro ze 'stel: le 'vo i pur kor 'te zi e 'bɛl: le kon 'dol tʃi 'zgwar di
Care amorose stelle, voi pur cortesi e belle con dolci sguardi
dear amorous stars you indeed kind and beautiful with sweet glances
Dear amorous stars, kind and beautiful indeed, with sweet glances

te 'ne stin 'vi ta da 'mil: le 'dar di 'lal ma fe 'ri ta
tenest'in vita da mille dardi l'alma ferita,
kept in life from thousand darts the soul wounded
you kept my soul, wounded from a thousand darts, alive,

> *in [37]: teneste in*
> *= tenest' in*

e 'dor pju non vi 'mi ɾo sen 'ti te ke mar 'ti ɾo
ed or più non vi miro, sentite che martiro!
and now more not you I see hear what agony
and now I see you no more; hear: what agony!

o i 'mɛ ke 'tri sto e 'so lo so 'li o 'sɛn tol 'mi o 'dwɔ lo
Ohimè, che tristo e solo, sol'io sento'l mio duolo,
alas [that] unhappy and alone only I I feel the my sorrow
Alas, unhappy and alone, I feel only my sorrow;

> *in [37]: triste (= tristo);*
> *sol io sento il mio =*
> *sol' io sento'l mio*

'lal ma lo 'sen te 'sen te lol 'kɔ ɾe e lo kon 'sɛn te in 'dʒu sto a 'mo ɾe
l'alma lo sente, sentelo'l core, e lo consente ingiusto amore,
the soul it feels feels it the heart and it consents unjust love
my soul feels it, my heart feels it, and unjust love allows it;

> *in [37]: sentelo il = sentelo'l*

a 'mor sel 've de e 'ta tʃe e da pur 'ar ko e 'fa tʃe
Amor sé'l vede e tace ed ha pur arco e face.
Love himself it sees and is quiet and has yet bow and torch
Love *[Cupid]* himself sees it and is silent, and yet he has his bow and torch.

GL: **Amor**

❧

[11]

vo ka 'lid: dzo
Vocalizzo
Vocalise

a i 'mɛ 'ki o 'mɔ ɾo 'par to
Ahimè ch'io moro. Parto.
alas [that] I I die I depart
Alas, I am dying. I am departing.

Caccini, Settimia (1591-c.1660?)

Born in Florence, younger daughter of Giulio, sister of Francesca, Settimia sang at an early age with her family at the Medici court in Florence and accompanied them in 1604 to Paris, where she performed for king Henry IV. After returning to Florence, in 1609 she married the musician Alessandro Ghivizzani and went with him in 1612 to the Gonzaga court at Mantua. In 1622 Ghivizzani was named *maestro di cappella* in Parma; Settimia appeared in many performances in Parma and in Lucca.

Following the death of her husband (c.1634), Settimia returned to Florence and to the service of the Medici court. Apparently an outstanding singer, she sang the role of Venus in the first performance of Monteverdi's *Arianna* (1608, in Mantua), and she was admired for her performance in the same composer's *Mercurio e Marte*, produced in 1628 for the inauguration of the Teatro Farnese in Parma.

Her few surviving compositions are strophic arias with anonymous texts.

[62]

'kan tan ʎa u 'dʒɛl: li
Cantan gl'augelli
The birds are singing

'kan tan	ʎa u 'dʒɛl: li	in: na mo 'ra ti	e	'so no	i	'pra ti	fjo 'ri ti	e	'bɛl: li
Cantan	**gl'augelli**	**innamorati**	**e**	**sono**	**i**	**prati**	**fioriti**	**e**	**belli.**
they sing	the birds	enamoured	and	are	the	meadows	flowered	and	beautiful

The enamoured birds are singing, and the meadows are in flower and beautiful. | augelli (poet.) = uccelli |

'so vra	'rɔ ze	e	vi 'ɔ le	'spar dʒe	'swɔ i	'rad: dʒi	'dɔr	lu 'tʃɛn te	il	'so le
Sovra	**rose**	**e**	**viole**	**sparge**	**suoi**	**raggi**	**d'or**	**lucente**	**il**	**sole,**
upon	roses	and	violets	spreads	its	rays	of gold	shining	the	sun

The shining sun sheds its golden rays upon roses and violets,

e	'strut: te	al 'fi ne	'pɔr ton	tri 'bu to	al	'fin	le	'ne vi	al 'pi ne
e	**strutte**	**al fine**	**porton**	**tributo**	**al**	**fin**	**le**	**nevi**	**alpine.**
and	melted	at last	they bring	tribute	at the	end	the	snows	Alpine

and the Alpine snows, melted at last, bring their final tribute.

nel	'tu o	bɛl	'se no	o	'bɛl: la	'klɔ ɾi	'ʎa spri	ri 'go ɾi	non	'veŋ gon 'me no
Nel	**tuo**	**bel**	**seno,**	**o**	**bella**	**Clori,**	**gl'aspri**	**rigori**	**non**	**vengon meno.**
in the	your	beautiful	breast	o	beautiful	Clori	the harsh	rigors	not	are lacking

In your beautiful breast, o beautiful Clori, harsh rigors are not lacking.

'mi ɾo	nel	'tu o	bɛl	'vol to	di	pri ma 've ɾa	'oɲ: ɲi	te 'zɔr	rak: 'kol to
Miro	**nel**	**tuo**	**bel**	**volto**	**di**	**primavera**	**ogni**	**tesor**	**raccolto,**
I see	in the	your	beautiful	face	of	spring	every	treasure	gathered

I see every treasure of spring gathered in your beautiful countenance,

ma	'pɔ i	diʃ: 'ʃɛr no	nel	'tu o	dʒe 'la to	sen	ri 'gor	di	'vɛr no
ma	**poi**	**discerno**	**nel**	**tuo**	**gelato**	**sen**	**rigor**	**di**	**verno.**
but	then	I discern	in the	your	icy	breast	harshness	of	winter

but then I discern the harshness of winter in your icy breast.

'skor: ro no	'lo ɾe	ma	'tu a	bɛl: 'let: tsa	ma	'tu a	fje 'ret: tsa	si fa	mad: 'dʒo re
Scorrono	**l'ore**	**ma**	**tua**	**bellezza,**	**ma**	**tua**	**fierezza**	**si fa**	**maggiore.**
they run	the hours	but	your	beauty	but	your	cruelty	becomes	greater

The hours run by, but your beauty and your cruelty become greater.

'skor: ron	ve 'lo tʃe	'ʎan: ni	ma	son	e 'tɛr ni	i	'mjɛ i	doʎ: 'ʎo zi	af: 'fan: ni
Scorron	**veloci**	**gl'anni**	**ma**	**son**	**eterni**	**i**	**miei**	**dogliosi**	**affanni**
they run	fast	the years	but	are	eternal	the	my	mournful	woes

The years rush by, but eternal are my mournful woes

e	la	'mi a	'fe de	'nel: la	sta 'dʒon	da 'mor	'sɛn tsa	mer 'tʃe de
e	**la**	**mia**	**fede**	**nella**	**stagion**	**d'amor**	**senza**	**mercede.**
and	the	my	faith	in the	season	of love	without	reward

and my faith, without reward, in the season of love.

GL: **Clori**

&

[62]

'kɔ ɾe di 'kwe sto 'kɔ ɾe
Core di questo core
Heart of this heart

'kɔ ɾe	di	'kwe sto	'kɔ ɾe	af: 'fe	mor: 'rɔ	ne 'ga ɾe	a	me	pje 'ta	ɛ	'trɔp: pa	kru del 'ta
Core	**di**	**questo**	**core,**	**affé**	**morrò;**	**negare**	**a**	**me**	**pietà**	**è**	**troppa**	**crudeltà.**
heart	of	this	heart	in faith	I shall die	to deny	to	me	pity	is	too much	cruelty

Heart of this heart, in faith I shall die; to deny me pity is too much cruelty.

soɲ: 'ɲor	mi	'vwɔ i	af: 'flid: dʒe ɾe	'tan to	mi	'pwɔ i	tra 'fid: dʒe ɾe
S'ogn'or	**mi**	**vuoi**	**affliggere**	**tanto**	**mi**	**puoi**	**trafiggere**
if every hour	me	you want	to afflict	so much	me	you can	to stab

If you always want to afflict me so much, you can stab me;

ke	vo len 'tjɛr	per	te	'lal ma	kju 'drɔ
che	**volentier**	**per**	**te**	**l'alma**	**chiudrò.**
that	willingly	for	you	the soul	I will close

for I will gladly, for you, close off my soul.

'vi ta	'del: la	'mi a	'vi ta	o i 'me	pje 'ta	a	'tan ta	ser vi 'tu	'a spe	non	'ɛs: ser	pju
Vita	**della**	**mia**	**vita,**	**ohimè**	**pietà;**	**a**	**tanta**	**servitù**	**aspe**	**non**	**esser**	**più.**
life	of the	my	life,	alas	pity	to	such	servitude	viper	not	to be	more

Life of my life, alas, have pity; to such servitude be no longer a viper.

> *aspe = (mod.) aspide*

soɲ: 'ɲor	mi	'vwɔ i	far	'pjan dʒe ɾe	kru 'dɛ le	il	kɔr	'pwɔ i	'fran dʒe ɾe
S'ogn'or	**mi**	**vuoi**	**far**	**piangere,**	**crudele,**	**il**	**cor**	**puoi**	**frangere**
if every hour	me	you want	to make	to weep	cruel one	the	heart	you can	to break

If you always want to make me weep, cruel one, you can break my heart;

ke	vo len 'tjɛr	per	te	'lal ma	si 'mwɔr
che	**volentier**	**per**	**te**	**l'alma**	**si muor.**
that	willingly	for	you	the soul	itself dies

for gladly, for you, my soul will die.

'al ma	del: 'lal ma	'mi a	pje 'ta de	al	kɔr
Alma	**dell'alma**	**mia,**	**pietade**	**al**	**cor.**
soul	of the soul	my	pity	to the	heart.

Soul of my soul, have pity on my heart.

&

[62]

'du e 'lu tʃi ri 'dɛn ti
Due luci ridenti
Two smiling eyes

'du e	'lu tʃi	ri 'dɛn ti	kon	'gwar do	se 're no	di	'dol tʃi	tor 'men ti	miŋ 'gom bra no	il	'se no
Due	**luci**	**ridenti**	**con**	**guardo**	**sereno**	**di**	**dolci**	**tormenti**	**m'ingombrano**	**il**	**seno.**
two	eyes	smiling	with	glance	serene	of	sweet	torments	me take over	the	breast

Two smiling eyes fill my breast with their serene glance, with sweet torments.

ma	'lam pi	da 'mo re	ra 'pi sko no	il	'kɔ re	kon	'fur to	dʒen 'ti le	la	li ber 'ta
Ma	**lampi**	**d'amore**	**rapiscono**	**il**	**core**	**con**	**furto**	**gentile**	**la**	**libertà.**
but	flashes	of love	rob		the	heart	with	theft	gentle	the	liberty

But beams of love, with gentle theft, rob my heart of liberty.

pur	'lje to	vi 'vra	kwe 'stal ma	kan 'tan do	sa 'do ra	pe 'nan do	tʃe 'lɛs te	bel 'ta
Pur	**lieto**	**vivrà**	**quest'alma**	**cantando**	**s'adora**	**penando**	**celeste**	**beltà.**
yet	happy	will live	this soul	singing	if it adores	suffering	celestial	beauty

Yet will this singing soul live happily if it adores, while suffering, heavenly beauty.

'du e	'lab: bra	di	'rɔ ze	kon	'dol tʃi	ros: 'so ri	le	'pa tʃi	a mo 'ro ze
Due	**labbra**	**di**	**rose**	**con**	**dolci**	**rossori**	**le**	**paci**	**amorose**
two	lips	of	roses	with	sweet	blushes	the	peaces	amorous

pro 'met: to no	'a i	'kɔ ri
promettono	**ai**	**cori.**
promise	to the	hearts

Two lips of roses promise, with sweet blushing, loving peace to hearts.

ma	in	kwel	bɛl	'se re no	san: 'ni da	il	ve 'le no	ke	ut: 'tʃi de	del: 'lal me	la	li ber 'ta
Ma	**in**	**quel**	**bel**	**sereno**	**s'annida**	**il**	**veleno**	**che**	**uccide**	**dell'alme**	**la**	**libertà.**
but	in	that	beautiful	serenity	nests	the	poison	which	kills	of the souls	the	liberty

But in that beautiful serenity nests the poison which kills the freedom of souls.

'du e	'brat: tʃa	so 'a vi	'mi e	'dol tʃi	ka 'te ne	far	'pɔs: son	men	'gra vi
Due	**braccia**	**soavi,**	**mie**	**dolci**	**catene**	**far**	**posson**	**men**	**gravi**
two	arms	gentle	my	sweet	chains	to make	can	less	severe

a 'tʃɛr be	'mi e	'pe ne
l'acerbe	**mie**	**pene.**
the bitter	my	pains

Two gentle arms, my sweet chains, can make my bitter pains less severe.

da	'kwe 'sti o	de 'zi o	'si a	'sɛr vo	il	kɔr	'mi o	si 'pɛr da	la	li ber 'ta
Da	**quest'io**	**desio**	**sia**	**servo**	**il**	**cor**	**mio,**	**si perda**	**la**	**libertà.**
from	this I	I desire	may be	servant	the	heart	my	may itself lose	the	liberty

From this I wish that my heart be a servant, though it lose its freedom.

'du e	'ri zi	'du e	'zgwar di	'du e	'ka re	pa 'rɔ le	'si an	'fjam: me	'si an	'dar di
Due	**risi,**	**due**	**sguardi,**	**due**	**care**	**parole**	**sian**	**fiamme,**	**sian**	**dardi;**
two	laughs	two	glances	two	dear	words	may be	flames	may be	arrows

May two laughs, two glances, two dear words be flames [and] darts;

mo 'rir	non	mi 'dwɔ le
morir	**non**	**mi duole.**
dying	not	me make sorrowful

dying does not grieve me.

morː ˈrɔmː mi	be ˈa to	morː ˈrɔ	for tu ˈna to	e		per de ˈrɔ	ˈljɛ to	la	li ber ˈta	
Morrommi	**beato,**	**morrò**	**fortunato**	**e**		**perderò**	**lieto**	**la**	**libertà.**	
I shall die	blessed	I shall die	fortunate	and		I shall lose	happy	the	liberty	

I shall die blessed, I shall die fortunate, and I shall happily lose my freedom.

❧

[62]

d͡ʒa spe ˈra i
Già sperai
Once I hoped

d͡ʒa	spe ˈra i	non	ˈspe ɾo	or	pju
Già	**sperai,**	**non**	**spero**	**or'**	**più;**
once	I hoped	not	I hope	now	more

Once I hoped, now I hope no more;

ˈri zo	e	ˈdjɔ ko	ˈdol t͡ʃe	ˈfɔ ko	a ˈmor	d͡ʒa	fu
riso	**e**	**gioco,**	**dolce**	**foco,**	**amor**	**già**	**fu.**
laughter	and	play	sweet	fire	love	once	was

love was once laughter, play, and sweet ardor.

or	ka	ˈmɔr te	ˈe i	ti	sa ˈetː ta	kɔr	tra ˈdi to	ˈvanː ne	ar ˈdi to	ˈalː la	ven ˈdetː ta
Or	**ch'a**	**morte**	**ei**	**ti**	**saetta,**	**cor**	**tradito,**	**vanne**	**ardito**	**alla**	**vendetta.**
now	that to	death	he	you	wounds	heart	betrayed	go	bold	to the	revenge

Now that he wounds you to death, betrayed heart, go boldly to take revenge.

ei = egli

d͡ʒa	ˈfu i	ˈljɛ to	or	ˈgri do	o i ˈmɛ
Già	**fui**	**lieto,**	**or**	**grido**	**oimè;**
once	I was	happy	now	I cry	alas

Once I was happy, now I cry "alas";

ˈpe ne	e	ˈgwa i	ˈdɔʎː ʎe	o ˈma i	ˈlun d͡ʒi	da	me
pene	**e**	**guai,**	**doglie**	**omai**	**lungi**	**da**	**me.**
pains	and	troubles	sorrows	now	far	from	me

pains, troubles, and sorrows, now [go] away!

omai (poet.)
= ormai

per	sotː ˈtrar mi	al	ˈd͡ʒo go	in ˈdeɲː ɲo	su	kɔr	ˈmi o
Per	**sottrarmi**	**al**	**giogo**	**indegno**	**su,**	**cor**	**mio;**
in order to	to remove from me	to the	yoke	undeserving	come on	heart	my

So as to remove my undeserved yoke, come on, my heart:

ˈtu o	de ˈzi o	ˈvɔl d͡ʒi	ˈalː lo	ˈzdeɲː ɲo
tuo	**desio**	**volgi**	**allo**	**sdegno.**
your	desire	turn	to the	indignation

turn your desire into indignation.

ˈzdeɲː ɲo	a ˈma to	oɲː ˈɲun	di ˈra	son	ˈtu e	ˈpal me	tor ˈnar	ˈlal me	in	li ber ˈta
Sdegno	**amato,**	**ogn'un**	**dirà,**	**son**	**tue**	**palme,**	**tornar**	**l'alme**	**in**	**libertà.**
indignation	beloved	each one	will say	are	your	palms	returning	the souls	to	liberty

Beloved indignation, everyone will say that returning souls to freedom is your victory.

gran	posː ˈsan tsa	in	te	si ˈserː ra	per ˈke	ˈsfi di
Gran	**possanza**	**in**	**te**	**si serra**	**perché**	**sfidi**
great	power	in	you	is united	because	you defy

Great power is within you because you defy,

'pɔ i kut: 'tʃi di   a 'mo re   in   'gwɛr: ra
poich'uccidi   **Amore**   **in**   **guerra.**
then [that] you kill   love   in   war.
[and] then kill, Love in war.

GL: **Amore**

Caldara, Antonio (c.1670-1736)

Born in Venice (no record of his date of birth has been found), composer, keyboard player, violinist, and cellist, he probably studied with Legrenzi, who was *maestro di cappella* at St.Mark's in Venice from 1681 to 1690, and perhaps also with the cello virtuoso Domenico Gabrielli.

In 1699 Caldara was made *maestro di cappella da chiesa e dal teatro* to Ferdinando Carlo, the last Gonzaga Duke of Mantua; financial and political difficulties besieged the Mantuan court until 1708, when Carlo died mysteriously. By 1709 Caldara was in Rome as *maestro di capella* to Prince Ruspoli, a lavish Roman patron of the arts for whom (in company with Alessandro Scarlatti, Pasquini, Corelli, and other eminent composers in Rome) he worked until 1716, when he received the appointment of *vice-kapellmeister* for Charles VI in Vienna, where he remained for the rest of his life. In Vienna he was paid handsomely; yet his widow was destitute a few weeks after his death, inviting speculation about his personal spending habits.

Caldara was extremely prolific. Of his more than three thousand estimated compositions, the majority are vocal works: operas, oratorios, cantatas, masses, motets, arias, madrigals, and canons.

[1, 3, 4, 12, 5, 25, 46, 54, 59, 60, 64]
from: *La costanza in amor vince l'inganno (1710)*
character: *Clizia*

'al ma del 'kɔ ɾe
Alma del core
Soul of my heart

'al ma   del   'kɔ ɾe   'spir to   del: 'lal ma   'sɛm pre   ko 'stan te   ta do ɾe 'rɔ
Alma   **del**   **core,**   **spirto**   **dell'alma,**   **sempre**   **costante**   **t'adorerò.**
soul   of the   heart   spirit   of the soul   always   constant   you I will adore
Soul of my heart, spirit of my soul, I will always faithfully adore you.

sa 'rɔ   kon 'tɛn to   nel   'mi o   tor 'men to   se   kwel   bɛl   'lab: bro   ba 'tʃar   po 'trɔ
Sarò   **contento**   **nel**   **mio**   **tormento,**   **se**   **quel**   **bel**   **labbro**   **baciar**   **potrò.**
I will be   content   in the   my   torment   if   that   beautiful   lip   to kiss   I shall be able
I will be content, in my torment, if I will be able to kiss those beautiful lips.

[4, 6, 8, 21, 25, 29, 30, 32, 54, 59, 60, 64]

'ko me 'rad: dʒo di sol
Come raggio di sol
As a ray of sunlight

'ko me   'rad: dʒo   di   sol   'mi te   e   se 'ɾe no   'so vra   'pla tʃi di   'flut: ti   si ri 'pɔ za
Come   **raggio**   **di**   **sol**   **mite**   **e**   **sereno**   **sovra**   **placidi**   **flutti**   **si riposa,**
like   ray   of   sun   mild   and   serene   over   placid   waves   itself reposes
As a ray of sunlight, mild and serene, reposes upon placid waves

'men tre   del   'ma ɾe   nel   pro 'fon do   'se no   sta   la   tem 'pe sta   a 'sko za
mentre   **del**   **mare**   **nel**   **profondo**   **seno**   **sta**   **la**   **tempesta**   **ascosa:**
while   of the   sea   in the   profound   breast   is   the   tempest   hidden
while within the deep bosom of the sea lies the hidden tempest,

ko 'zi	'ri zo	ta 'lor	'ga jo	e	pa 'ka to	di	kon 'tɛn to
così	**riso**	**talor**	**gaio**	**e**	**pacato**	**di**	**contento,**
thus	laughter	at times	cheerful	and	calm	with	contentment

so does laughter, sometimes cheerful and calm with contentment,

di	'dʒo ja	un	'lab: bro	in 'fjo ɾa	'men tre	nel	'su o	se 'gre to
di	**gioia**	**un**	**labbro**	**infiora,**	**mentre**	**nel**	**suo**	**segreto**
with	joy	a	lip	adorns	while	in the	its	secret

adorn lips with joy while, in its depths,

il	kɔr	pja 'ga to	saŋ 'gɔʃ: ʃa	e	si mar 'to ɾa
il	**cor**	**piagato**	**s'angoscia**	**e**	**si martora.**
the	heart	wounded	itself grieves	and	itself tortures

the wounded heart grieves and tortures itself.

[50]

e 'kwan do 'ma i kɔr 'mi o go 'dra i

E quando mai cor mio godrai

And whenever, my heart, will you enjoy

For whatever reasons, this text is especially poorly edited; lines 4-8 have "problems" about which I've made "educated guesses."

e	'kwan do	'ma i	kɔr	'mi o	go 'dra i	la	li ber 'ta
E	**quando**	**mai**	**cor**	**mio**	**godrai**	**la**	**libertà.**
and	when	ever	heart	mine	you will enjoy	the	liberty

And whenever, my heart, will you enjoy liberty?

tav: vin se	il	'tʃɛ ko	'di o	kon	si	'kru da	ka 'te na
T'avvinse	**il**	**cieco**	**dio**	**con**	**sì**	**cruda**	**catena**
you surrounded	the	blind	god	with	so	harsh	chain

The blind god *[Cupid]* surrounded you with such a harsh chain

printed (in error) instead of "cieco" is "cisco"

'keʎ: ʎi	ɛ	u ne 'tɛr na	'pe na	ser 'vir	'al: la	bel 'ta
ch'egli	**è**	**un'eterna**	**pena**	**servir**	**alla**	**beltà.**
that it	it is	an eternal	punishment	to serve	to the	beauty

that it is an eternal punishment to serve beauty

'toʎ: ʎe ɾe	il	'son: no	al	'tʃiʎ: ʎo	il	'tʃi bo	al	'lab: bro
Togliere	**il**	**sonno**	**al**	**ciglio,**	**il**	**cibo**	**al**	**labbro**
to take away	the	sleep	from the	brow	the	food	from the	lip

e	'al: le	'pjan te	il	'mo to	im pri dʒo 'nar	la	'vo tʃe	e
e	**alle**	**piante**	**il**	**moto,**	**imprigionar**	**la**	**voce**	**e**
and	from the	feet	the	motion	to imprison	the	voice	and

'nel: la	'men te	le 'gar	'si no	il	pen 'sjɛ ɾo	e	'po ko	af: 'fɛt: to	e	'po ko
nella	**mente**	**legar**	**sino**	**il**	**pensiero,**	**è**	**poco**	**affetto**	**e**	**poco**
in the	mind	to bind	even	the	thought	is	little	affected	and	little

I changed the printed "e," after "pensiero," to "è" in order to help make sense in the context.

se	'mil: le	'vɔl te	il	'kɔ ɾe	fra	'spa zmi	de li 'ran ti	o	'di o	non	'mɔ ɾe
se	**mille**	**volte**	**il**	**core**	**fra**	**spasmi**	**deliranti**	**o**	**Dio**	**non**	**more.**
if	thousand	times	the	heart	among	spasms	frenzied	oh	God	not	dies

when a thousand times the heart, in frenzied spasms, oh God, is little affected if it does not die even after sleep has been taken from the brow, food from the lips, movement from the feet, sound from the voice, and freedom from the thoughts.

si	si	ke	no	laʃ:	'ʃar vi	'ka ɾa	pu 'pil: la
Sì	sì	che	no'	lasciarvi,		cara	pupilla.
yes	yes	[that]	not wants	to leave here		dear	eye

Yes, yes, [your] dear eyes do not want to go away.

> "no'" comes from "nolle": = (lit.) non volere
> printed is "caro pupilla," which must be
> either "cara pupilla" or "care pupille"

ko 'zi	'fjɛ ɾo	ɛ	il	'vɔ stro	'zgwar do	ke	da 'mor	la 'ku to	'dar do
Così	fiero	è	il	vostro	sguardo	che	d'Amor	l'acuto	dardo
thus	cruel	is	the	your	glance	that	of Love	the sharp	dart

So cruel is your glance that the sharp dart of Love

> printed is "nostro,"
> which I've changed to
> the more likely "vostro"

'tan to	un	'mi ze ɾo	kɔr	'ma i	non	fe 'ri
tanto	un	misero	cor	mai	non	ferì.
so much	a	miserable	heart	ever	not	wounded

never wounded a miserable heart so much.

GL: Amor

&

[67]

il dʒel zo 'mi no
Il gelsomino
The jasmin

al: lap: pa 'ɾir	di	ri splen 'dɛn te	a u 'ɾɔ ɾa	'spun ta	dal	'ver de	'stɛ lo	il	dʒel zo 'mi no
All'apparir	**di**	**risplendente**	**aurora**	**spunta**	**dal**	**verde**	**stelo**	**il**	**gelsomino,**
at the appearance	of	resplendent	dawn	sprouts	from the	green	stalk	the	jasmin

At the appearance of resplendent dawn the jasmin sprouts from its green stalk

e	ap: 'pe na	'pom pa	fa	di	'su e	bel: 'let: tse	ke	'fil: li de	sa 'dor na
e	**appena**	**pompa**	**fa**	**di**	**sue**	**bellezze**	**che**	**Fillide**	**s'adorna**
and	barely	display	makes	of	its	beauties	that	Fillide	herself adorns

and, as soon as it displays its beauty, Fillide adorns [with it]

il	'bjan ko	'pet: to	'o ve	'nu tre	'oɲ: ɲi	'grat: tsja	'oɲ: ɲi	di 'let: to
il	**bianco**	**petto,**	**ove**	**nutre**	**ogni**	**grazia,**	**ogni**	**diletto.**
the	white	breast	where	nourishes	every	grace	every	delight

her white breast, where she nurtures every grace and delight.

> printed is
> gratia =
> (mod.) grazia

ma	iŋ 'ka u to	'kwan to	'sɛ i	'kan di do	'fjo ɾe	se	'kre di	di	tro 'var
Ma	**incauto**	**quanto**	**sei,**	**candido**	**fiore,**	**se**	**credi**	**di**	**trovar**
but	imprudent	how much	you are	innocent	flower	if	you believe	of	to find

But how imprudent you are, innocent flower, if you believe you will find

fra	'kwel: le	'ne vi	ri 'stɔ ɾo	'al: le	'tu e	'fjam: me	bɛn 'prɛ sto	pro ve 'ɾa i
fra	**quelle**	**nevi**	**ristoro**	**alle**	**tue**	**fiamme;**	**ben presto**	**proverai**
among	those	snows	relief	to the	your	flames	very soon	you will experience

relief, amid those snows, from your passions; very soon you will feel

lar 'dor	vo 'ɾa tʃe	dun	'fɔ ko	'koɲ: ɲi	kɔr	di 'vo ɾa	e	'sfa tʃe
l'ardor	**vorace**	**d'un**	**foco**	**ch'ogni**	**cor**	**divora**	**e**	**sface.**
the ardor	voracious	of a	fire	that every	heart	devours	and	destroys

the voracious ardor of a fire that devours and destroys every heart.

dʒel zo 'mi no	kan di 'det: to	non	tal: 'let: ti		sem pli 'tʃet: to
Gelsomino	**candidetto,**	**non**	**t'alletti**		**semplicetto,**
jasmin	little innocent	not	yourself may let be tempted		little simpleton

Simple, little, innocent jasmin, may you not be tempted

di	kwel	'se no	il	bɛl	kan 'dor
di	**quel**	**seno**	**il**	**bel**	**candor.**
of	that	breast	the	beautiful	whiteness

by the beautiful whiteness of that breast.

fra	le	'ne vi	di	kwel	'pɛt: to
Fra	**le**	**nevi**	**di**	**quel**	**petto**
among	the	snows	of	that	breast

Among the snows of that breast

vɛ	na 'sko sto	or goʎ: ʎo 'zet: to	di	'ku pi do	il	'fjɛ ɾo	ar 'dor
v'è	**nascosto**	**orgogliosetto**	**di**	**Cupido**	**il**	**fiero**	**ardor.**
there is	hidden	proudly	of	Cupid	the	fierce	ardor

is proudly hidden the fierce ardor of Cupid.

ma	'kwan to	pju	fe 'li tʃe	a 'ma to	'fjo ɾe	tu	'sɛ i	di	'kwe sto	'kɔ ɾe
Ma	**quanto**	**più**	**felice,**	**amato**	**fiore,**	**tu**	**sei**	**di**	**questo**	**core**
but	how much	more	happy	beloved	flower	you	you are	than	this	heart

But how much happier you are, beloved flower, than this heart,

se	in	'tan ti	'two i	tor 'mɛn ti	'prɔ vi	la	in	kwe	splen 'do ɾi
se	**in**	**tanti**	**tuoi**	**tormenti**	**provi**	**là**	**in**	**que'**	**splendori**
if	in	so many	your	torments	you experience	there	in	those	splendors

if in your many torments you feel there, in those splendors,

il	pja 'tʃer	di	'tu a	'spɛ me	'a spri	mar 'tɔ ɾi
il	**piacer**	**di**	**tua**	**speme,**	**aspri**	**martori.**
the	pleasure	of	your	hope	bitter	agonies

the pleasure of your hope and bitter agonies.

> speme (lit.) = speranza
> martori = (mod.) martiri

sol	'i o	so 'spi ɾo	e	'pe no	e	al	lam ped: 'dʒar	di	kwel	e 'bur ne o	'se no
Sol	**io**	**sospiro**	**e**	**peno,**	**e**	**al**	**lampeggiar**	**di**	**quel**	**eburneo**	**seno**
only	I	I sigh	and	I suffer	and	at the	gleaming	of	that	ivory	breast

Only I sigh and suffer; and at the glow of that ivory breast

'sɛn to	ke	'lal ma	'mi a	saf: 'fan: na	dal	do 'lo ɾe
sento	**che**	**l'alma**	**mia,**	**s'affanna**	**dal**	**dolore**
I feel	that	the soul	mine	is anguished	from the	pain

I feel that my soul is anguished by pain

e	at: 'tʃe za	da	lar 'do ɾe	di	'tan to	a 'ma ɾo	'fɔ ko
e	**accesa**	**da**	**l'ardore**	**di**	**tanto**	**amaro**	**foco,**
and	set on fire	by	the ardor	of	so much	bitter	fire

and, on fire from the ardor of so much bitter passion,

si va	'mɛ sta	strud: 'dʒen do	a 'pɔ ko a 'pɔ ko
si va	**mesta**	**struggendo**	**a poco a poco.**
itself goes	sad	consuming	little by little

is sadly, gradually, being destroyed.

son	'ko me	far fal: 'let: ta	in 'tor no al	'va go	'lu me	ke	'dʒi ɾa	sem pli 'tʃet: ta
Son	**come**	**farfalletta**	**intorno al**	**vago**	**lume**	**che**	**gira**	**semplicetta,**
I am	like	little butterfly	around the	charming	light	which	circles	simple little one

I am like an innocent little butterfly which circles around the luring light

e	in 'fi ne	a	'mɔr te	va
e	**infine**	**a**	**morte**	**va.**
and	in the end	to	death	goes

and finally goes to its death.

kwal	'fi da	na vi 'tʃɛl: la	fra	'lɔr: ri da	pro 'tʃɛl: la
Qual	**fida**	**navicella**	**fra**	**l'orrida**	**procella,**
like a	faithful	little boat	among	the fearsome	tempest

Like a faithful little boat in a fearsome tempest

on 'ded: dʒa	iŋ 'ka u to	il	'kɔ ɾe	'sɛn tsa	spe 'rar	pje 'ta
ondeggia	**incauto**	**il**	**core**	**senza**	**sperar**	**pietà.**
sways	incautious	the	heart	without	hoping	pity

my heart wavers incautiously, without hoping for pity.

𝒢ℒ: **Cupido, Fillide**

ॐ

[67]

'lun dʒi dal: 'li dol 'mi o
Lungi dall'idol mio
Far from my idol

'lun dʒi	dal: 'li dol	'mi o	fra	'mil: le e 'mil: le	'pe ne	'vi ve ɾe	o i 'mɛ	dɛd: 'dʒi o
Lungi	**dall'idol**	**mio**	**fra**	**mille e mille**	**pene**	**vivere,**	**ohimè,**	**degg'io?**
far	from the idol	mine	among	thousand and thousand	sufferings	to live	alas	must I

Far from my idol must I live, alas, amidst thousands and thousands of sufferings?

ε	'trɔp: po	gran	mar 'ti ɾe	il	'pɛr de ɾe	il	'su o	'bɛ ne
È	**troppo**	**gran**	**martire**	**il**	**perdere**	**il**	**suo**	**bene,**
it is	too much	great	agony	the	losing	the	one's	dear one

Losing one's beloved is too great an agony;

ma	il	'pɛr der lo	per	'sɛm pre	eʎ: 'ʎɛ	un	mo 'ri ɾe
ma	**il**	**perderlo**	**per**	**sempre**	**egl'è**	**un**	**morire.**
but	the	losing it	for	ever	it is	a	dying

but losing her [or "him"] forever is death.

> The "lo" in "perderlo" is gramatically masculine because it refers to "il bene," but there is nothing in the text to identify the beloved one as specifically a "him" or a "her."

'pjan dʒi	'mi ze ɾo	kɔr	il	so spi 'ra to	a 'mor	pju	non	ve 'dra i
Piangi	**misero**	**cor;**	**il**	**sospirato**	**amor**	**più**	**non**	**vedrai.**
weep	miserable	heart	the	longed-for	love	more	not	you will see

Weep, miserable heart; you will see your longed-for love no more.

per	e ter 'nar	ʎaf: 'fan: ni	son	pur	'fje ɾi	e	ti 'ran: ni	un	'sɛm pre	un	'ma i
Per	**eternar**	**gl'affanni**	**son**	**pur**	**fieri**	**e**	**tiranni**	**un**	**sempre**	**un**	**mai.**
for	to perpetuate	the woes	are	yet	cruel	and	tyrannical	an	always	a	never

Still, the cruel and tyrannical "always" and "never" are [the words] which perpetuate pain.

a	bɛn	pre 'vi de	il	kɔr	ka	'dar mi	'pe ne	'sta bi li	il	'fa to
Ah'	**ben**	**previde**	**il**	**cor,**	**ch'a**	**darmi**	**pene**	**stabili**	**il**	**fato**
alas	well	foresaw	the	heart	that to	to give me	sufferings	permanent	the	fate

a 'ver	do 've a	le	'tɛm pre	e	al: 'lor ke	'dis: se	il	'lab: bro
aver	**dovea**	**le**	**tempre;**	**e**	**allor ché**	**disse**	**il**	**labbro,**
to have	had	the	hardenings	and	when	said	the	lip

dovea =
doveva

Alas, well did my heart foresee that fate must have had its mind set on giving me perpetual suffering; and when your lips said

ad: 'di o	'mi o	'bɛ ne	'mɛ sta	sod: 'dʒun se	'lal ma	ad: 'di o	per	'sɛm pre
addio	**mio**	**bene,**	**mesta**	**soggiunse**	**l'alma,**	**addio**	**per**	**sempre.**
farewell	my	dear one	sad	added	the soul	farewell	for	ever

"farewell, my dear one," my soul sadly added, "farewell forever."

'ɛk: ko	'dol tʃe	kor	'mi o	'lun dʒi	da	te nan 'da i		'lun dʒi	da	te	son	'i o
Ecco,	**dolce**	**cor**	**mio:**	**lungi**	**da**	**te n'andai,**		**lungi**	**da**	**te**	**son**	**io.**
see	sweet	heart	mine	far	from	from you I went away		far	from	you	am	I

See, my sweet beloved: I have gone far away from you; I am far from you.

nɔ	nɔ	'lun dʒi	da	te	non	sa 'rɔ	'ma i
No,	**no,**	**lungi**	**da**	**te**	**non**	**sarò**	**mai!**
no	no	far	from	you	not	I will be	ever

No, no, I will never be far from you!

'dar vi	un	'gwar do	'so lo	'so lo	'si o	po 'tes: si	o	'va gi	'ra i
Darvi	**un**	**guardo**	**solo,**	**solo**	**s'io**	**potessi,**	**o**	**vaghi**	**rai,**
to give you	a	glance	only	only	if I	I were able	o	lovely	eyes

Were I only able to give you a single glance, o lovely eyes,

kwal	kon 'for to	a 'vrɛb: be	il	kor
qual	**conforto**	**avrebbe**	**il**	**cor!**
what	comfort	would have	the	heart

what comfort my heart would have!

ma	il	de 'sti no	'a ma	il	'su o	'dwɔ lo	e	non	vwɔl
Ma	**il**	**destino**	**ama**	**il**	**suo**	**duolo**	**e**	**non**	**vuol**
but	the	destiny	loves	the	its	sorrow	and	not	wishes

But destiny loves the sorrow it has caused, and does not wish

'ki o	'spɛ ri	'ma i	'tan ta	'pa tʃe	al	'mi o	do 'lor
ch'io	**speri**	**mai**	**tanta**	**pace**	**al**	**mio**	**dolor.**
that I	I may hope	ever	so much	peace	in the	my	pain

that I may ever hope for so much peace in my pain.

[1, 3, 47]

'mir ti 'fad: dʒi
Mirti, faggi
Myrtles, beeches

'mir ti	'fad: dʒi	'troŋ ki	e	'fron de	'mon ti	'kɔl: li	'fju mi	e	'spon de
Mirti,	**faggi,**	**tronchi**	**e**	**fronde,**	**monti,**	**colli,**	**fiumi**	**e**	**sponde**
myrtles	beeches	tree trunks	and	branches	mountains	hills	rivers	and	shores

Myrtles, beeches, trees and branches, mountains, hills, rivers and shores,

ki	di	'vo i	'fil: li	mad: 'di ta	la	'mi a	'vi ta	per pje 'ta
chi	**di**	**voi**	**Filli**	**m'addita,**	**la**	**mia**	**vita**	**per pietà!**
who	of	you	Filli	me points out	the	my	life	for pity

which of you, out of pity for my life, will show me where Filli is?

'an tri   'bɔ ski   'ru pi   e   'sel ve   'or si   'ti gri   'fjɛ ɾe   e   'bel ve
Antri,   boschi,   rupi   e   selve,   orsi,   tigri,   fiere   e   belve,
caves   woods   cliffs   and   forests   bears   tigers   wild beasts   and   savage beasts
Caves, woods, cliffs and forests, bears, tigers, wild and savage beasts,

ven ti 'tʃɛl: li   'a u ɾe   gra 'di te   'vo i   mel   'di te   iŋ   ka ɾi 'ta
venticelli,   aure   gradite,   voi   mel   dite   in   carità!
little winds   breezes   pleasing   you   to me it   say   in   kindness
gentle winds, pleasant breezes: kindly tell me!

GL: **Filli**

☙

[67]

par 'tɛn tsa
Partenza
Departure

'dʒun to   ɛ   il   'dʒor no   fa 'tal   do 'ril ne   a 'ma ta   in   'ku i   ti 'ɾan: no   il   'fa to
Giunto   è   il   giorno   fatal,   Dorilne   amata,   in   cui   tiranno   il   fato
arrived   is   the   day   fatal   Dorilne   beloved   in   which   tyrannical   the   fate
The fatal day has arrived, beloved Dorilne, on which tyrannical fate

fra   'tan te   a 'ma ɾe   'pe ne   mi   ko 'strin dʒe   a   par 'tir   da   te   'mi o   'bɛ ne
fra   tante   amare   pene   mi   costringe   a   partir   da   te,   mio   bene.
among   so many   bitter   pains   me   forces   to   to depart   from   you   my   dear one
forces me, among so many bitter pains, to leave you, my dear one.

pju   non   ti   ri ve 'drɔ   mi   'di tʃe   il   'kɔ ɾe
Più   non   ti   rivedrò,   mi   dice   il   core,
more   not   you   I will see   to me   says   the   heart
I will see you no more, my heart tells me,

se   'mi ze ɾo   e   do 'len te   pas: se 'ɾɔ   i   'dʒor ni   'mjɛ i   'sot: to   'al tro   'tʃe lo
se   misero   e   dolente   passerò   i   giorni   miei   sotto   altro   cielo.
if   miserable   and   sorrowful   I shall pass   the   days   mine   beneath   other   heaven
if, miserable and sorrowful, I shall pass my days beneath another heaven.

spet: 'ta ko lo   fu 'nɛ sto   'de vo   'dar ti   per 'fin   'lul ti mo   ad: 'di o
Spettacolo   funesto   devo   darti   per fin   l'ultimo   addio.
spectacle   funereal   I must   to give you   finally   the last   farewell
A mournful sight, I must finally give you the last farewell.

in dʒu 'stis: si mi   'nu mi   ad: 'di o   do 'ril ne   ti   'laʃ: ʃo
Ingiustissimi   numi!   Addio   Dorilne;   ti   lascio,
most unjust   gods   farewell   Dorilne   you   I leave
Most unjust gods! Farewell, Dorilne; I leave you

e   nel   par 'ti ɾe   'sɛm pre   a 'man te   fe 'del   'va do   a   mo 'ri ɾe
e   nel   partire   sempre   amante   fedel   vado   a   morire.
and   in the   departing   always   lover   faithful   I go   to   to die
and, in departing, I go to death an ever faithful lover.

'dɛ vo   laʃ: 'ʃar ti   al 'fin   'dol tʃe   'mi a   'vi ta   pju   non   vi   ri ve 'drɔ
Devo   lasciarti   alfin,   dolce   mia   vita;   più   non   vi   rivedrò,
I must   to leave you   at last   sweet   my   life   more   not   you   I will see
I must leave you at last, my sweet life; I will see you no more,

pu 'pil: le   a 'ma te   se   'fi da   'lal ma   'mi a   'kor: re   a   mo 'ri ɾe
pupille   **amate,**   **se**   **fida**   **l'alma**   **mia**   **corre**   **a**   **morire.**
eyes   beloved   if   faithful   the soul   mine   runs   to   to die
beloved eyes, if my faithful soul rushes to death.

'sen tsa   di   te   dol 'tʃis: si mo   kɔr   'mi o   fra   'tan ti   af: 'fan: ni
Senza   **di**   **te,**   **dolcissimo**   **cor**   **mio,**   **fra**   **tanti**   **affanni**
without   of   you   sweetest   heart   mine   among   so many   woes

'vi ver   non   pɔs: 'si o   se   mi   'sfɔr tsa   il   de 'stin   doɲ: 'nor   laŋ 'gwi ɾe
viver   **non**   **poss'io**   **se**   **mi**   **sforza**   **il**   **destin**   **d'ognor**   **languire.**
to live   not   can I   if   me   compels   the   destiny   of always   to languish
Without you, my sweetest heart, I cannot live among so many woes, if destiny compels me to languish forever.

non   'pjan dʒe ɾe   'mi o   'kɔ ɾe   da   'tre gwa   a   'twɔ i   so 'spi ɾi
Non   **piangere,**   **mio**   **core;**   **da'**   **tregua**   **a**   **tuoi**   **sospiri**
not   to weep   my   heart   give   respite   to   your   sighs
Do not weep, my heart. Give pause to your sighs;

ne   mak: 'kreʃ: ʃer   kol   'tu o   mad: 'dʒor   do 'lo ɾe
né   **m'accrescer**   **col**   **tuo**   **maggior**   **dolore.**
nor   me to increase   with the   your   greater   grief
do not increase [my own grief] with your greater grief.

ma   'pri a ke   'lal ma   a 'man te   'par ta   da   te   'mi a   'ka ɾa   a 'skol ta   al 'me no
Ma   **pria che**   **l'alma**   **amante**   **parta**   **da**   **te,**   **mia**   **cara,**   **ascolta**   **almeno**
but   before   the soul   loving   may depart   from   you   my   dear   listen to   at least
But before my loving soul parts from you, my dear one, at least listen to

> pria (poet.) = prima

le   sin 'tʃe ɾe   pro 'tɛ ste   del   'tu o   fe 'del   del   'tu o   'ka ɾo   fal 'tʃe ste
le   **sincere**   **proteste**   **del**   **tuo**   **fedel,**   **del**   **tuo**   **caro**   **Falceste.**
the   sincere   protests   of the   your   faithful one   of the   your   dear   Falceste
the sincere protestations of your faithful one, of your dear Falceste.

mar de 'ɾa   'sɛm pre   in   'pɛt: to   lar 'dor   ke   mi   tor 'men ta
M'arderà   **sempre**   **in**   **petto**   **l'ardor**   **che**   **mi**   **tormenta,**
in me will burn   always   in   breast   the ardor   that   me   torments
The ardor that torments me will always burn in my breast,

e   fra   lom 'bro ze   'sel ve   de ste 'ɾɔ   aŋ 'kor   pje 'ta   'si no   'al: le   'bel ve
e   **fra**   **l'ombrose**   **selve**   **desterò**   **ancor**   **pietà**   **sino**   **alle**   **belve.**
and   among   the shady   forests   I shall awaken   even   pity   even   to the   wild beasts
and I shall awaken pity even from the wild beasts in the shadowy forests.

'lul ti mo   ad: 'di o   ti   'do na   il   kɔr   'mi o
L'ultimo   **addio**   **ti**   **dona**   **il**   **cor**   **mio.**
the last   farewell   to you   gives   the   heart   mine
My heart gives you its last farewell.

non   'pjan dʒer   'mi a   'vi ta   da   'pa tʃe   al   do 'lor
Non   **pianger**   **mia**   **vita;**   **da'**   **pace**   **al**   **dolor.**
not   to weep   my   life   give   peace   to the   grief
Do not weep, my life; give peace to your grief.

ti   'laʃ: ʃo   e   non   'mɔ ɾo   'i o   'par to   e   aŋ 'kor   'vi vo
Ti   **lascio**   **e**   **non**   **moro;**   **io**   **parto**   **e**   **ancor**   **vivo.**
you   I leave   and   not   I die   I   I depart   and   yet   I live
I leave you and do not die; I depart and yet I live.

'a i   'strat: tsjo   i na u 'di to   'a i   'fje ɾo   mar 'tɔr
Ahi   strazio   inaudito!   Ahi   fiero   martor!
alas   torture   unheard-of   alas   cruel   agony
Alas, unheard-of torture! Alas, cruel agony!

❧

[4, 6, 8, 16, 52, 54, 59, 60, 64]
from: *La costanza in amor vince l'inganno (1710)*
character: *Aminta*

seb: 'bɛn kru 'dɛ le
Sebben, crudele
Although, cruel one

seb: 'bɛn   kru 'dɛ le   mi   'fa i   laŋ 'gwir   'sɛm pre   fe 'de le   ti   'vɔʎ: ʎo   a 'mar
Sebben,   crudele,   mi   fai   languir,   sempre   fedele   ti   voglio   amar.
although   cruel one   me   you make   to languish always   faithful   you   I want   to love
Although, cruel one, you make me languish, I will always love you faithfully.

kon   la   luŋ 'get: tsa   del   'mi o   ser 'vir
Con   la   lunghezza   del   mio   servir
with   the   length   of the my   serving
With the length of my servitude

la   tua   fje 'ret: tsa   sa 'prɔ   staŋ 'kar
la   tua   fierezza   saprò   stancar.
the   your   pride   I will know how   to wear down
I shall wear down your pride.

❧

[4, 6, 8, 22, 25, 34, 37]
from: *La costanza in amor vince l'inganno (1710)*
character: *Silvia*

'sel ve a 'mi ke
Selve amiche
Friendly woods

'sel ve   a 'mi ke   om 'bro ze   'pjan te   'fi do   al 'bɛr go   del   'mi o   'kɔ ɾe
Selve   amiche,   ombrose   piante,   fido   albergo   del   mio   core,
woods   friendly   shady   plants   faithful   refuge   of the my   heart
Friendly woods, shady trees, trusted refuge for my heart,

'kjɛ de   a   'vo i   kwe 'stal ma   a 'man te   'kwal ke   'pa tʃe   al   'su o   do 'lo ɾe
chiede   a   voi   quest'alma   amante   qualche   pace   al   suo   dolore.
asks for   to   you   this soul   loving   some   peace   to the its   sorrow
this loving soul begs you for some peace in its sorrow.

❧

[35, 64]

si tin 'tɛn do
Sì t'intendo
Yes, I hear you

si   tin 'tɛn do   'ɛk: ko   tin 'tɛn do   il   'mi o   dwɔl   non   sker 'nir   pju
Sì   t'intendo,   ecco   t'intendo,   il   mio   duol   non   schernir   più;
yes   you I hear   here   you I hear   the   my   grief   not   mock   more
Yes, I hear you; I do hear you. Do not mock my grief anymore.

la   'tu a   'sɔr te   'i o   bɛn   kom 'prɛn do   ke   'al: la   'mi a   'si mil   dʒa   fu
la   tua   sorte   io   ben   comprendo,   che   alla   mia   simil   già   fu.
the   your   fate   I   well   I understand   because   to the   my   similar   before   was
I well understand your fate, because mine was similar.

di   nar 'tʃis: so   il   kɔr   spret: 'tsan te   so   ke   in   'ru pe   ti   kan 'dʒɔ
Di   Narcisso   il   cor   sprezzante   so   che   in   rupe   ti   cangiò.
of   Narcisso   the   heart   scornful   I know   that   into   rock   you   changed
I know that the scornful heart of Narcisso transformed you into a rock.

aŋ 'kor   'i o   tra 'di ta   a 'man te   'nwɔ vo   'sas: so   'ɛs: ser   do 'vrɔ
Ancor   io   tradita   amante   nuovo   sasso   esser   dovrò.
also   I   betrayed   lover   new   stone   to be   I shall have to
Also I, a betrayed lover, shall have to become a new stone.

GL: **Narcisso**

❧

[1, 3, 47, 57]

'va ge   'lu tʃi
Vaghe luci
Lovely eyes

'va ge   'lu tʃi   ɛ   'trɔp: po   'kru do   il   de 'sti no   del   'mi o   'kɔ ɾe
Vaghe   luci,   è   troppo   crudo   il   destino   del   mio   core,
lovely   eyes   is   too   harsh   the   destiny   of the   my   heart
Lovely eyes, too harsh is the destiny of my heart

ke   laŋ 'gwɛn do   al   'vo stro   ar 'do ɾe   'dɛ e   la   'fjam: ma   in   sen   tʃe 'lar
che   languendo   al   vostro   ardore   dee   la   fiamma   in   sen   celar.
which   languishing   at the   your   ardor   must   the   flame   in   breast   to hide
which, languishing from your ardor, must conceal the flame in my breast.   dee = deve

si   ti 'ran: na   ɛ   la   'mi a   'sɔr te   ke   sof: 'frir   do 'vrɔ   la   'mɔr te
Sì   tiranna   è   la   mia   sorte,   che   soffrir   dovrò   la   morte,
so   tyrannical   is   the   my   fate   that   to suffer   I shall have   the   death
So tyrannical is my fate that I shall have to suffer death

'pri a ke   al   'mi o   fa 'ta le   a 'mo ɾe   'prɛm jo   un   di   'pɔs: sa   spe 'rar
pria che   al   mio   fatale   amore   premio   un   dì   possa   sperar.
before   to the   my   fatal   love   reward   one   day   I may be able   to hope
before I may hope for reward, one day, for my fatal love.   *pria = (poet.) prima*

in [57]: pria ch'al = pria che al

Calestani, Vincenzo (1589-in or after 1617)

Calestani dedicated his only known volume of songs, *Madrigali et arie…parto primo*, to Isabella Mastiani, a member of a leading family in Pisa whom he accompanied and to whom he taught music.
Grove calls Calestani's volume, containing twenty-five solos and three duets of his own composition, "one of the most attractive and varied Italian songbooks of the early seventeenth century."
In a few of his most interesting songs Calestani exhibited his contribution to the development of the short strophic song into the more sophisticated aria of the later seventeenth century cantata.

[14, 39]

ak: ˈkɔr ta lu ziŋ ˈgjɛ ɾa
Accorta lusinghiera
Cunning flatterer

ak: ˈkɔr ta	lu ziŋ ˈgjɛ ɾa	dʒa	man: no ˈda sti	il	kɔr
Accorta	**lusinghiera,**	**già**	**m'annodasti**	**il**	**cor,**
cunning	flattering one	already	me you entangled	the	heart

Cunning flatterer, you have already entangled my heart,

e ˈdor	at: ˈtʃɔ	ˈki o	ˈpɛ ɾa	in	me	non	ˈkre di	a ˈmor
ed or'	**acciò**	**ch'io**	**pera**	**in**	**me**	**non**	**credi**	**amor.**
and now	so that	that I	may perish	in	me	not	you believe	love

and now, so I may perish, you do not believe my love.

> *The following verse is not in [14]; in [39] it is the 2nd verse:*

ne ˈgar	non	ˈpwɔ i	ˈa i	ˈkru da	ˈa i	di zle ˈal
Negar	**non**	**puoi,**	**ahi,**	**cruda,**	**ahi,**	**disleal,**
to deny	not	you are able	alas	cruel woman	alas	unfaithful one

You cannot – alas, cruel, unfaithful woman – deny

ˈkol pa	de	ˈʎɔk: ki	ˈtwɔ i	la	ˈmi a	ˈpja ga	mor ˈtal
colpa	**de**	**gl'occhi**	**tuoi:**	**la**	**mia**	**piaga**	**mortal.**
fault	of	the eyes	yours	the	my	wound	mortal

your eyes' fault for my mortal wound.

> *The following verse is the 2nd verse in [14] , the 3rd in [39]:*

in	ˈpjan to	mi	di ˈstil: lo	diʃ: ˈʃol to	ˈa i	ˈlu mi	il	fren
In	**pianto**	**mi**	**distillo,**	**disciolto**	**ai**	**lumi**	**il**	**fren;**
in	weeping	myself	I exude	dissolved	at the	eyes	the	restraint

My tears overflow, restraint gone from my eyes;

di ˈfwɔ ɾi	ˈar do	e	sfa ˈvil: lo	kol ˈmɔ	di	ˈfjam: me	il	sen
di fuori	**ardo**	**e**	**sfavillo,**	**colm'ò**	**di**	**fiamme**	**il**	**sen.**
outside	I burn	and	I spark	filled I have	with	flames	the	breast

I burn and blaze; my breast is filled with flames.

ò =
(mod.) ho

> *The following verse is not in [14]; in [39] it is the 4th verse:*

e	se	la	ˈtu a	bel: ˈlet: tsa	mi	tjɛn	las: so	pri ˈdʒon
E	**se**	**la**	**tua**	**bellezza**	**mi**	**tien,**	**lasso,**	**prigion,**
and	if	the	your	beauty	me	keeps	miserable	prisoner

And if your beauty keeps me, miserable, a prisoner,

ko 'zi	la	'tu a	fje 'ret: tsa	ɛ	del	'mi o	mal	ka 'dʒon
così	**la**	**tua**	**fierezza**	**è**	**del**	**mio**	**mal**	**cagion.**
thus	the	your	pride	is	of the	my	pain	reason

then your pride is the reason for my pain.

> *The following verse is the 3rd and last verse in [14], the 5th verse in [39]:*

---

ko 'zi	'pjan se	un	pa 'sto ɾe	kon	'mil: le	e	'mil: le	o i 'mɛ
Così	**pianse**	**un**	**pastore**	**con**	**mille**	**e**	**mille**	**ohimè,**
thus	wept	a	shepherd	with	thousand	and	thousand	alas

Thus did a shepherd lament, with thousands and thousands of sighs,

del	'su o	non	fi 'ni to	a 'mo ɾe	la	non	kre 'du ta	fe
del	**suo**	**non**	**finito**	**amore**	**la**	**non**	**creduta**	**fé.**
for the	his	not	finished	love	the	not	believed in	faithfulness

his unrequited love and untrusted faithfulness.

[14, 41]

'fer ma do 'ɾin da 'mi a
Ferma, Dorinda mia
Stop, my Dorinda

'fer ma	do 'ɾin da	'mi a	dɛ	'fer ma	il	'pje de	'kan dʒa	pen 'sjer	ri 'vol dʒi	'pas: si
Ferma,	**Dorinda**	**mia,**	**deh,**	**ferma**	**il**	**piede,**	**cangia**	**pensier,**	**rivolg'i**	**passi!**
stop	Dorinda	my	pray	stop	the	foot	change	thought	turn back the	steps

Stop, my Dorinda, please stop; change your thinking, turn back your steps!

ɛ	'tor na in 'dje tro	'mi a	do 'ɾin da	'tor na	ɛ	'nin fa	'bɛl: le	'mi o	bɛl	sol
Eh!	**Torna in dietro,**	**mia**	**Dorinda,**	**torna,**	**eh,**	**ninfa**	**bell'e**	**mio**	**bel**	**sol.**
ah	come back	my	Dorinda	return	ah	nymph	beautiful and	my	beautiful	sun

Ah, come back, my Dorinda; return, beautiful nymph and my beautiful sun.

ɛ	'fer ma	il	pjɛ	ve 'lo tʃe	ɛ	'fer ma	ɛ	'po za	ɛ	'vol dʒi	'ʎɔk: ki	kru 'dɛl
Eh	**ferma**	**il**	**piè**	**veloce,**	**eh**	**ferma,**	**eh**	**posa;**	**eh**	**volgi**	**gl'occhi,**	**crudel,**
ah	stop	the	foot	fleeting	ah	stop	ah	alight	ah	turn	the eyes	cruel one

Ah, stop fleeing; ah, stop; ah, alight; ah, turn your eyes, cruel one,

'vol dʒi	le	'pjan te	al	'tu o	fe 'del	'kwan to	doʎ: 'ʎo zo	a 'man te
volgi	**le**	**piante**	**al**	**tuo**	**fedel**	**quanto**	**doglioso**	**amante!**
turn	the	(soles of) feet	to the	your	faithful	as much as	sorrowful	lover

turn your steps toward your lover, who is as faithful as he is sorrowful!

Campana, Francesca (c.between 1605 and 1610-1665)

Campana's reputation during her lifetime rests on a letter addressed to Francesco I of Modena from the poet Fulvio Testi in 1633 praising her as a composer, keyboard player, and singer. Her collection of twelve vocal pieces in a variety of styles, *Arie a una, due, e tre voci*, was published in 1629; but, apart from a solo aria and a two-part madrigal also published in 1629, no other of her works were published.

She was probably born in Rome. She married Giovan Carlo Rossi, at least seven years her junior, who was an organist and the youngest brother of the composer Luigi Rossi. She died in Rome while her husband was, from 1661 to 1666, in Paris.

She was influenced stylistically by the monodies of Monteverdi and Giulio Caccini, whose *Nuove Musiche* seems to have been a model for her own published collection.

[63]   sem pli ˈtʃet: to a u dʒel: ˈlin
                              Semplicetto augellin
                               Simple little bird

sem pli ˈtʃet: to	a u dzel: ˈlin	ke	ˈmen tre	ˈkan ti	ˈkja mi	lar ˈtʃer
Semplicetto	**augellin,**	**che**	**mentre**	**canti**	**chiami**	**l'arcier**
simple	little bird	that	while	you sing	you call	the archer

augellin[o] = (mod.) uccellin[o]

Simple little bird, you who in your singing summon the archer

ke	ti per ˈkwɔ ta	il	ˈpet: to	ˈtor na	dɛ	ˈtor na	a	tʃe le ˈbrar	ˈtwɔ i	ˈvan ti
che	**ti percuota**	**il**	**petto,**	**torna,**	**deh**	**torna**	**a**	**celebrar**	**tuoi**	**vanti**
who	you may wound	the	breast	go back	please	go back	to	to celebrate	your	virtues

who may wound you in the breast, please go back and extol your virtues

ˈden tro ˈal: le	ˈfron di	del	na ˈti o	bo ˈsket: to
dentro alle	**frondi**	**del**	**natio**	**boschetto.**
inside of the	foliage	of the	native	little woods

natio (poet.) = nativo

within the foliage of your native woodlands.

ke	ˈo ve	il	ˈmon do	su ˈpɛr bo	a	ʎa bi ˈtan ti	ˈpje ni	diŋ ˈgan: no	e
Ché	**ove**	**il**	**mondo**	**superbo**	**ha**	**gl'habitanti**	**pieni**	**d'inganno**	**e**
because	where	the	world	proud	has	the inhabitants	full	of deceit	and

For wherever the proud world's inhabitants are full of deceit and

di	mal ˈva dʒo	af: ˈfɛt: to	ˈkwan to	spje ge ˈɾa i	tu	pju	ˈdol tʃi	ˈkan ti
di	**malvagio**	**affetto,**	**quanto**	**spiegherai**	**tu**	**più**	**dolci**	**canti**
of	evil	feeling	as much	you will put forth	you	most	sweet	songs

evil feelings, the more you expound your most sweet songs,

ˈtan to	men	tro ve ˈɾa i	ˈfi do	ri ˈtʃet: to
tanto	**men**	**troverai**	**fido**	**ricetto.**
so much	less	you will find	trusted	refuge

the less you will find a safe shelter.

ˈmi ze ɾo	tu	non	ˈsa i	ˈkwan ti	lat: ˈtʃɔ li	por ˈtan do	in ˈvi dja
Misero	**tu**	**non**	**sai**	**quanti**	**lacciuoli**	**portando**	**invidia**
poor	you	not	you know	how many	little snares	bearing	envy

Poor you – you know not how many little snares, envious

ˈal: la	ˈtu a	ˈlje ta	ˈsɔr te	si na ˈskon dan	fra	i	ˈra mi	ˈo ve	tu	ˈvo li
alla	**tua**	**lieta**	**sorte,**	**si nascondan**	**fra**	**i**	**rami**	**ove**	**tu**	**voli.**
at the	your	happy	fate	themselves hide	among	the	branches	wherein	you	you fly

of your happy lot, are hidden among the branches wherein you fly.

ˈvat: te ne ˈvi a	ˈdal: le	men ˈti te	ˈskɔr te	ke	non	ˈpwɔ i	ˈmi zer	se	non
Vattene via	**dalle**	**mentite**	**scorte**	**ché**	**non**	**puoi**	**miser**	**se**	**non**
go you away	from the	lying	escorts	because	not	you can	poor one	if	not

ti ˈmwɔ vi	o	sal ˈvar	li ber ˈta de	o	fud: ˈdʒir	ˈmɔr te
ti muovi	**o**	**salvar**	**libertade**	**o**	**fuggir**	**morte.**
you move	either	to preserve	liberty	or	to escape	death

libertade = (mod.) libertà

Get away from false companions, for if you do not fly away, poor one, you can neither keep your freedom nor escape death.

[63]

'si o ti 'gwar do
S'io ti guardo
If I look at you

'si o	ti	'gwar do	ti 'zdeɲː ɲi	'si o	ti	'par lo	tu	'fudː dʒi
S'io	**ti**	**guardo**	**ti sdegni,**	**s'io**	**ti**	**parlo**	**tu**	**fuggi;**
If I	you	I look at	you are disdainful	if I	to you	I speak	you	flee

If I look at you, you are disdainful; if I speak to you, you flee;

e	zdeɲː 'ɲo za	e	fu 'ga tʃe	oɲː ɲor	mi	'strudː dʒi
e	**sdegnosa**	**e**	**fugace**	**ogn'or**	**mi**	**struggi.**
and	disdainful	and	fugitive	always	me	you consume

and disdainful and fugitive, you always make me suffer.

se	'mɔ di	per 'ke	've di	'palː li do	il	'vol to	e	dʒa
Se	**m'odi**	**perché**	**vedi**	**pallido**	**il**	**volto**	**e**	**già**
If	me you hate	because	you see	pale	the	face	and	already

If you hate me because you see that my face is pale and already

> printed *"odii"*
> = *(mod.) odi*

ka 'nu to	il	'kri ne	non	di spred: 'dʒar	'mi o	ben	le	pelː le 'gri ne	belː 'letː tse
canuto	**il**	**crine,**	**non**	**dispregiar**	**mio**	**ben**	**le**	**pellegrine**	**bellezze**
white	the	hair	not	to undervalue	my	dear one	the	uncommon	beauties

my hair is white *[with age]*, do not underestimate, my dear, the uncommon beauties

ke	posː 'sje di	ke	se	tʃa 'sku na	ɛ	nel	'mi o	'kɔ ɾe	im 'prɛsː sa
che	**possiedi**	**ché**	**se**	**ciascuna**	**è**	**nel**	**mio**	**core**	**impressa,**
which	you possess	because	if	each	is	in the	my	heart	engraved

which you possess, because as each of them is engraved in my heart,

di spretː 'tsan do	il	'mi o	'kɔ ɾe	'sprɛtː tsi	te	'stesː sa
disprezzando	**il**	**mio**	**core**	**sprezzi**	**te**	**stessa.**
spurning	the	my	heart	you spurn	you	yourself

in spurning my heart you spurn yourself.

Caproli [del Violino], Carlo (before 1620-after 1675)

Born in Rome, he was a composer, organist, and violinist. A student of Luigi Rossi, in 1653 he went to Paris, where his opera *Le nozze di Peleo e di Theti* was well received in 1654; the young Louis XIV himself participated in the ballets between the scenes of the opera.

In 1655 Caproli returned to Rome to direct musical activities on special occasions; he was appointed *guardiano* of the instrumentalists of the Congregazione dei Musici di Roma (later the Accademia di S. Cecelia).

Regarded as one of the best violinists in Rome, he was also recognized by his contemporaries as one of the best cantata composers.

"Tu mancavi a tormentarmi" is attributed in some sources to Cesti (see *Cesti*).

[19, 34]

tu maŋ 'ka vi a tor men 'tar mi
Tu mancavi a tormentarmi
All I needed was for you to torture me

tu	maŋ 'ka vi	a	tor men 'tar mi	kru de 'lisː si ma	spe 'ɾan tsa
Tu	**mancavi**	**a**	**tormentarmi,**	**crudelissima**	**speranza,**
you	failed	to	to torture me	most cruel	hope

All I needed was for you to torture me, cruelest hope,

e	kon	'dol tʃe	ri mem 'bran tsa	'pɔ i	di 'nwɔ vo	avː ve le 'nar mi
e	**con**	**dolce**	**rimembranza**	**poi**	**di nuovo**	**avvelenarmi.**
and	with	sweet	remembrance	then	again	to poison me

and then, with sweet memories, to poison me again!

aŋ 'kor	'du ra	la	sven 'tu ra	'du na	'fjamː ma	in tʃe ne 'ri ta
Ancor	**dura**	**la**	**sventura**	**d'una**	**fiamma**	**incenerita:**
still	lasts	the	misfortune	of a	flame	burned out

The misfortune from a burned out passion still endures:

la	fe 'ri ta	aŋ 'kor	a 'pɛr ta	pur	mavː 'vɛr ta	'nwɔ ve	'pe ne
la	**ferita**	**ancor**	**aperta**	**pur**	**m'avverta**	**nuove**	**pene;**
the	wound	still	open	yet	me may warn	new	sufferings

the wound, still open, may yet warn me of new sufferings;

dal	ru 'mor	'delː le	ka 'te ne	'ma i	non	've do	alː lon ta 'nar mi
dal	**rumor**	**delle**	**catene**	**mai**	**non**	**vedo**	**allontanarmi.**
from the	noise	of the	chains	ever	not	I see	to draw away

I will never see myself drawing away from the noise of the chains.

> *Printed in [19] are two additional verses:*

'sɛm pre	in 'tor no a	ki	mutː 'tʃi de	va	dʒi 'ran do	il	'mi o	pen 'sjɛ ro
Sempre	**intorno a**	**chi**	**m'uccide**	**va**	**girando**	**il**	**mio**	**pensiero,**
always	around	the one who	me kills	goes	turning	the	my	thought

My thoughts are always turning around the one who is killing me,

el	ri 'gor	dun	'vol to	'fjɛ ro	mi	ri 'kja ma	'alː le	di 'sfi de
e'l	**rigor**	**d'un**	**volto**	**fiero**	**mi**	**richiama**	**alle**	**disfide.**
and the	severity	of a	face	proud	me	again calls	to the	challenges

and the severity of a proud face recalls me to its challenges.

sɛ	de 'sti no	dun	me 'ski no	'lɛsː ser	'pre zo	in	man	de	'mɔ ri	tra di 'to ri
S'è	**destino**	**d'un**	**meschino**	**l'esser**	**preso**	**in**	**man**	**de'**	**Mori**	**traditori,**
if it is	destiny	of a	wretched one	the being	taken	into	hand	of the	Moors	traitorous

If it is the destiny of a wretched one to be taken into the hands of the traitorous Moors,

'zgwar di	'fjɛ ri	vo len 'tje ri	miŋ ka 'te no	'ka i	tor 'men ti	del	'mi o	'se no
sguardi	**fieri**	**volentieri**	**m'incateno**	**ch'ai**	**tormenti**	**del**	**mio**	**seno**
glances	proud	gladly	me I fetter	because at the	torments	of the	my	breast

di bwɔn 'gu sto	il	'fa to	arː 'ri de
di buon gusto	**il**	**fato**	**arride.**
with good taste	the	fate	smiles on

I will gladly chain myself to the proud glances, as fate smiles happily upon the torments of my breast.

aŋ 'kor	'fu ma	il	'fɔ ko	e 'stin to	fra	le	'tʃe ne ri	del	'pɛtː to
Ancor	**fuma**	**il**	**foco**	**estinto,**	**fra**	**le**	**ceneri**	**del**	**petto,**
still	smokes	the	fire	extinguished	among	the	ashes	of the	breast

The extinguished passion still smokes among the ashes of my breast;

e	te 'na tʃe	a 'mi o di 'spɛt: to	un	bɛl	krin	mi	'tje ne	avː 'vin to
e	**tenace**	**a mio dispetto**	**un**	**bel**	**crin**	**mi**	**tiene**	**avvinto.**
and	tenacious	despite myself	a	beautiful	head of hair	me	holds	bound

and firmly, despite myself, beautiful tresses keep me bound.

vɔ	fin	'dʒen do	vɔ	fud:	'dʒen do	ma	sal:	'la mo	ɛ	'pre zo	il	'peʃ: ʃe
Vo	**fingendo,**		**vo**	**fuggendo,**		**ma**	**s'all'amo**		**è**	**preso**	**il**	**pesce**
I go	pretending		I go	fleeing		but	if at the hook		is	taken	the	fish

I keep pretending, I keep fleeing; but if the fish is hooked,

non	ri	'ɛʃ: ʃe	la	di	'fe za	ma	lim	'pre za	ɛ	av: ven tu	'rar mi
non	**riesce**		**la**	**difesa,**		**ma**	**l'impresa**		**è**	**avventurarmi;**	
not	succeeds		the	defense		but	the undertaking		is	to venture	

he has no defense – rather, the adventure is in the braving of it;

e	pur	'sker tso	kon	kwel:	'lar mi	de	beʎ:	'ʎɔk: ki	ke	man	'vin to
e	**pur**	**scherzo**	**con**	**quell'armi**		**de'**	**begl'occhi**		**che**	**m'han**	**vinto.**
and	yet	I play	with	those weapons		of	beautiful eyes		which	me have	vanquished

and yet I am playing with those weapons, the beautiful eyes, which have vanquished me.

✿ *Carissimi, Giacomo* (1605-1674)

Born in Marino, near Rome, he was one of the most important and influential seventeeth century composers, highly esteemed by his contemporaries.

From 1625 to 1627 he was organist at the Cathedral of Tivoli; in 1628 he was *maestro di cappella* at the Cathedral of S. Rufino in Assisi. From 1629 until his death he was *maestro di cappella* back in Rome, at the Collegio Germanico, a Jesuit seminary; services were held, and music performed, in the adjoining church of S. Apollinare.

He declined offers, during his career, to leave Rome for prestigious posts in Venice and Brussels.

Though not a great deal is known about Carissimi's life, he was apparently "very frugal in his domestic circumstances, very noble in his manners towards his friends and others... *[Grove]*."

His composition centered on masses, motets, oratorios, and cantatas. Unfortunately, most of his manuscripts at the Collegio Germanico were destroyed or lost; among extant works are many solo cantatas, but the total quantity of his output is uncertain.

---

[24]

a mo 'ri ɾe
A morire!
To death!

a	mo 'ri ɾe	per	ser 'bar	dʒu 'stit: tsja	e	'fe de	pju	non	'val gon
A	**morire!**	**Per**	**serbar**	**giustizia**	**e**	**fede,**	**più**	**non**	**valgon**
to	dying	in order	to preserve	justice	and	faith	more	not	have power

le	ko 'ro ne	ke	seb: 'bɛ ne	'i o	'rɛ sto	e 'zaŋ gwe
le	**corone**	**ché**	**sebbene**	**io**	**resto**	**esangue**
the	crowns	because	even though	I	I remain	drained of blood

To death! The crowns no longer have the power to preserve justice and faith because, though I am drained of blood,

la	ko 'stan tsa	al	'mi o	kɔr	'meʃ: ʃi	e li 'zi ɾe
la	**costanza**	**al**	**mio**	**cor**	**mesce**	**elisire!**
the	constancy	to the	my	heart	pours out	elixir

constancy pours elixir into my heart!

a	mo 'ri ɾe
A	**morire!**
to	dying

To death!

☙

[68]   *Domenico Benigni*

a ˈmor ˈmi o ke ˈkɔ za ɛ ˈkwe sta
Amor mio, che cosa è questa?
My love, what is this?

a ˈmor	ˈmi o	ke	ˈkɔ zɛ	ˈkwe sta	ˈtutː to	il	di	ˈsja mo	da ˈka po
Amor	**mio,**	**che**	**cos'è**	**questa?**	**Tutto**	**il**	**dì**	**siamo**	**da capo.**
love	mine	what	thing is	this	all	the	day	we are	from the beginning

My love, what is this? All day long we start all over again.

tu	ti la ˈmen ti	e	a	me	mi ˈdwɔ le	il	ˈka po
Tu	**ti lamenti,**	**e**	**a**	**me**	**mi duole**	**il**	**capo.**
you	you complain	and	to	me	me hurts	the	head

You complain, and my head aches.

ˈsa i	ke	ko ˈzɛ	per	for ˈnir	ˈkwe sta	ˈfɛ sta	oɲː ˈɲun	ˈfatː tʃa	da se
Sai	**che**	**cos'è**	**per**	**fornir**	**questa**	**festa?**	**Ognun'**	**faccia**	**da sé.**
you know	what	thing it is	for	to provide	this	festivity	each one	let do	by himself

Do you know what it's like to provide this entertainment? Let each of us be on our own.

ˈsɛ i	ˈbɛlː le	ˈbwɔ no	ma	non	ˈfa i	per	me
Sei	**bell'e**	**buono,**	**ma**	**non**	**fai**	**per**	**me.**
you are	handsome and	good	but	not	you do	for	me

You are handsome and good, but you do not do for me.

le ˈvjam	ˈpu ɾe	alː le gra ˈmen te	il	komː ˈmɛr tʃo	tra	di	ˈno i
Leviam	**pure**	**allegramente**	**il**	**commercio**	**tra**	**di**	**noi.**
let us remove	[yet]	cheerfully	the	business	between	of	us

Let's cheerfully get rid of the business between us.

ˈvɛr bi	ˈgrat tsja	oɲː ˈɲun	ˈfat tʃa	i	ˈfatː ti	ˈswɔ i
Verbi	**grazia,**	**ognun'**	**faccia**	**i**	**fatti**	**suoi.**
by the grace of the words		each one	let do	the	matters	his

Please, let's both mind our own business.

ˈsi a	pur	ko ˈzi	e	ˈkwelː lo	ke	si ˈpɛn te
Sia	**pur**	**così,**	**e**	**quello**	**che**	**si pente,**
may it be	yet	thus	and	that one	who	repents

ˈstrilː li	e	ˈpjaŋ ga	ˈoɲː ɲi	di	ˈi o	non	mi mo ve ˈrɛ i	da	kwi	a	li
strilli	**e**	**pianga**	**ogni**	**dì.**	**Io**	**non**	**mi moverei**	**da**	**qui**	**a**	**lì.**
may scream	and	may weep	every	day	I	not	I would not move	from	here	to	there

So may it be, and may the one who has second thoughts scream and weep every day. I would not budge.

ki	si ˈpo ne	a	dʒo ˈkar	ˈte ko	kon	pen ˈsjer	di	ˈfar la	ˈpatː ta
Chi	**si pone**	**a**	**giocar**	**teco,**	**con**	**pensier**	**di**	**farla**	**patta,**
who	sets about	to	to play	you with	with	thought	of	to make it	even

Whoever sets out to play with you, with the thought of getting even,

pwɔ	riŋ grat ˈtsjar	idː ˈdi o	se	ʎi	vjen	ˈfatː ta
può	**ringraziar**	**Iddio**	**se**	**gli**	**vien**	**fatta.**
is able	to thank	God	if	to him	comes	done

can thank God if it comes out that way.

Iddio = (mod.) Dio

'i o	bɛn	lo	sɔ	ke	'fin dʒi	'dɛs: ser	'tʃɛ ko
Io	**ben**	**lo**	**so**	**che**	**fingi**	**d'esser**	**cieco,**
I	well	it	I know	that	you pretend	of to be	blind

I know well that you are pretending to be blind,

ma	non	mi	'bur li	nɔ
ma	**non**	**mi**	**burli,**	**no.**
but	not	me	you fool	no

but you aren't fooling me, no.

'fat: tʃa	'pas: so	ki	vwɔl	'ki o	me ne 'stɔ
Faccia	**passo**	**chi**	**vuol',**	**ch'io**	**me ne sto.**
let make	step	who	wishes	[that] I	I stay

Let whoever wishes take a step; I will stay put.

&

[68]

Domenico Benigni

a 'pri te vi in 'fɛr ni
Apritevi, inferni
Open up, infernos

a 'pri te vi	in 'fɛr ni	se	al	re	'del: le	'stel: le	kon	'vɔʎ: ʎe	ru 'bɛl: le
Apritevi,	**inferni,**	**se**	**al**	**re**	**delle**	**stelle,**	**con**	**voglie**	**rubelle,**
open up	infernos	if	to the	king	of the	stars	with	wishes	rebellious

'i o	non	kon 'sa kro	i	'mjɛi	pen 'sjɛ ri	in 'tɛr ni
io	**non**	**consacro**	**i**	**miei**	**pensieri**	**interni.**
I	not	I consecrate	the	my	thoughts	internal

Open up, infernos, if I, with rebellious wishes, do not consecrate my innermost thoughts to the king of the stars.

u 'di te mi	o	'tʃe li	nel: la spre	sa 'et: te	skok: 'ka te	ven 'det: te
Uditemi	**o**	**cieli.**	**Nell'aspre**	**saette**	**scoccate**	**vendette,**
hear me	o	heavens	in the sharp	arrows	shoot	revenges

Hear me, o heavens. Hurl revenge with sharp arrows,

se	'fi a	ke	del	'mi o	kɔr	'di o	si kwe 'rɛ li
se	**fia**	**che**	**del**	**mio**	**cor**	**Dio**	**si quereli.**
if	will be	that	of the	my	heart	God	complains

if God complains about my heart.

> *fia =*
> *(mod.) sarà*

si	do 'le va si	un	're o	ke	al 'fin	ri 'mɔr so	'dal: le	'kol pe	kom: 'mes: se
Sì	**dolevasi**	**un**	**reo,**	**che**	**al fin**	**rimorso**	**dalle**	**colpe**	**commesse,**
thus	bewailed	a	guilty one	who	finally	remorseful	by the	sins	committed

Thus bewailed a guilty one who, finally remorseful about the sins he committed,

su	le	pu 'pil: le	i 'stes: se	man 'da va	il	'dwo lo	a	men di 'kar	sok: 'kor so
su	**le**	**pupille**	**istesse**	**mandava**	**il**	**duolo**	**a**	**mendicar**	**soccorso;**
over	the	eyes	themselves	sent	the	pain	to	to beg for	help

let pain emit from his eyes, to beg for help;

> *istesse = (mod.) stesse*

e	kon	i 'ra to	'kan to	ʃoʎ: 'ʎe a	le	'vo tʃi	e	lo	se 'gwi va	il	'pjan to
e	**con**	**irato**	**canto,**	**sciogliea**	**le**	**voci,**	**e**	**lo**	**seguiva**	**il**	**pianto.**
and	with	angry	song	loosed	the	voices	and	it	followed	the	weeping

and he loosed his voice in angry song, and he followed it with weeping.

> *sciogliea = scioglieva*

ma   tra   kon 'fu zi od: 'dʒɛt: ti   e   di   'zdeɲ: ɲo   e   da 'mo ɾe
Ma   tra   confusi   oggetti,   e   di   sdegno,   e   d'amore,
but   among   confused   objects   and   of   anger   and   of love
But, with confused purposes of anger and love,

'kon tro   se   'vɛr so   un   'di o   'kol mo   daf: 'fɛt: ti
contro   sé,   verso   un   Dio,   colmo   d'affetti,
against   himself   toward   a   God   filled   with affections
against himself, toward a God, filled with feelings,

il   'sad: dʒo   pek: ka 'to ɾe   per   dar   al   'su o   do 'lor   'for tse   e lo 'kwɛn ti
il   saggio   peccatore,   per   dar   al   suo   dolor   forze   eloquenti,
the   wise   sinner   for   to give   to the   his   sorrow   powers   eloquent
the wise sinner, in order to give eloquent powers to his sorrow,

sol   di   'la gri me   ar 'mɔ   'kwe sti   la 'men ti
sol   di   lagrime   armò   questi   lamenti.
only   with   tears   he armed   these   laments
armed these laments only with tears.

> lagrime =
> (mod.)
> lacrime

a   ki   'di o   non   'se gwe   in   'tɛr: ra   'ar mi   il   tʃɛl   'u na   kon 'dʒu ɾa
A   chi   Dio   non   segue   in   terra,   armi   il   ciel   una   congiura;
to   he who   God   not   follows   on   earth   let arm   the   heaven   a   conspiracy
Let heaven provide arms for a conspiracy against whomever does not follow God on earth;

e   zdeɲ: 'ɲa ta   la   na 'tu ɾa   non   ʎin 'ti mi   'al tro   ke   'gwɛr: ra
e   sdegnata   la   natura   non   gl'intimi   altro   che   guerra.
and   indignant   the   nature   not   to him let summon   other   than   war
and let indignant nature not summon for him anything other than war.

'i o   ke   'sɛm pre   tra   pja 'tʃe ɾi   'dem pjo   'mon do   il   pje   ri 'vɔl si
Io,   che   sempre   tra   piaceri   d'empio   mondo   il   piè   rivolsi,
I   who   always   among   pleasures   of wicked   world   the   foot   turned
I, who always turned to the pleasures of a wicked world,

e   non   'vɔl si   'por: re   il   'fre no   a   'mjɛ i   pen 'sje ɾi
e   non   volsi   porre   il   freno   a   miei   pensieri,
and   not   turned   to put   the   restraint   to   my   thoughts
and did not restrain my thoughts –

or   de   'sɛn si   al: 'lwɔ mo   ti 'ɾan: ni   bɛn   rav: 'vi zo   le   ka 'te ne
or   de'   sensi   all'uomo   tiranni,   ben   ravviso   le   catene;
now   of the   senses   to the man   tyrannical   well   I recognize   the   chains
now I well recognize the chains of the senses tyrannical to men,

ne   kon 'vje ne   a do 'rar   'nu mi   daf: 'fan: ni
né   conviene   adorar   numi   d'affanni.
nor   it is fitting   to adore   deities   of woes
[and know that] it is not fitting to worship gods of woe.

em pje 'ta   ke   di   ko 'tʃi to   su   la 'ɾe ne   mi   tra 'e sti
Empietà,   che   di   Cocito   su   l'arene   mi   traesti,
impiety   which   of   Cocito   on   the sands   me   you drew
Impiety, you who led me to the banks of Cocito,

non	son	'kwe sti	i	de 'zir	dun	kɔr	pen 'ti to
non	**son'**	**questi**	**i**	**desir**	**d'un**	**cor**	**pentito.**
not	are	these	the	desires	of a	heart	repentant

these are not the desires of a repentant heart.

'kon tro	il	'su o	re den 'tor	'lal ma	non	'ɛr: ra
Contro	**il**	**suo**	**Redentor**	**l'alma**	**non**	**erra.**
against	the	its	Redeemer	the soul	not	makes a mistake

The soul will not err against its Redeemer.

GL: **Cocito**

&

[68]

bɛl	'tɛm po	per	me	se nan 'dɔ
Bel tempo per me se n'andò				

Good times have left me

bɛl	'tɛm po	per	me	se nan 'dɔ	dak: 'ke	la	bel 'ta	mo 'stran do	pje 'ta
Del	**tempo**	**per**	**me**	**se n'andò,**	**dacché**	**la**	**beltà,**	**mostrando**	**pietà,**
good	time	for	me	went away	since	the	beauty	showing	pity

Good times have left me since the beautiful one, showing pity,

il	'kɔ re	ad	a 'ma re	al: let: 'tɔ
il	**core**	**ad**	**amare**	**allettò.**
the	heart	to	to love	lured

lured my heart to loving.

'i o	vi 've a	ko 'zi	kon 'tɛn to	'ʃɔl to	il	sen	'li be ɾo	il	pjɛ
Io	**vivea**	**così**	**contento,**	**sciolto**	**il**	**sen,**	**libero**	**il**	**piè,**
I	I used to live	so	content	unbound	the	breast	free	the	foot

I used to live so contentedly, breast unbound and footloose,

> *the "a" ending of "vivea" is an antiquated variant; = (mod.) "vivevo"*

ke	le	'nɔ je	e dil	tor 'men to	per	ti 'mor	fud: 'dʒi an	da	me
che	**le**	**noie**	**ed il**	**tormento**	**per**	**timor**	**fuggian**	**da**	**me.**
that	the	pains	and the	torment	for	fear	fled	from	me

that pain and torment fled from me out of fear.

> *fuggian[o] = (mod.) fuggivan[o]*

se 're ni	i	'dʒor ni	le	'nɔt: ti	traŋ 'kwil: le	'ɛ ɾa no	a	'mi e	pu 'pil: le
Sereni	**i**	**giorni,**	**le**	**notti**	**tranquille,**	**erano**	**a**	**mie**	**pupille.**
serene	the	days	the	nights	tranquil	were	to	my	eyes

The days were serene, the nights tranquil, to my eyes.

e	fra	dʒo 'ko zi	'kan ti	ri 'de va	'i o	sol	'kwan do	pjan 'dʒe an	ʎa 'man ti
E	**fra**	**giocosi**	**canti,**	**rideva**	**io**	**sol,**	**quando**	**piangean**	**gl'amanti.**
and	among	playful	songs	I laughed	I	only	when	wept	the lovers

And among playful songs I alone laughed when lovers wept.

> *piangean[o] = piangevan[o]*

ma	ke	prɔ	'las: so	ke	prɔ
Ma	**che**	**pro?**	**Lasso,**	**che**	**pro?**
but	what	use	miserable	what	use

But what for? Miserable me, what for?

di	se 'gwir	bel: 'let: tse	'va ne	al: lat: 'tʃa to	in	ser vi 'tu
Di	**seguir**	**bellezze**	**vane,**	**allacciato**	**in**	**servitù,**
of	pursuing	beauties	vain	tied	in	servitude

'i o   fud: 'dʒi a   ka   'men ti   'sa ne   li ber 'ta   'va le un pe 'ru
io   fuggia   ch'a   menti   sane,   libertà   vale un Perù.
I   I fled   because to   minds   sane   freedom   is worth a fortune

I fled from pursuing vain beauties, being bound in servitude, because to sound minds freedom is worth a fortune.

fuggia =
fuggiva

ko 'zi   le   'dʒo je   de   'lal ma   e   del   'ko ɾe   non   tur 'ba va   al 'kun   ti 'mo ɾe
Così   le   gioie   de   l'alma   e   del   core   non   turbava   alcun   timore.
thus   the joys   of   the soul and of the heart   not   disturbed   any   fear

Thus, no fear disturbed the joys of my heart and soul.

e   fra   dʒo 'ko zi   'kan ti   ri 'de va   'i o   sol   'kwan do   pjan 'dʒe an   ʎa 'man ti
E   fra   giocosi   canti,   rideva   io   sol, quando   piangean   gl'amanti.
and among playful   songs   I laughed   I   only when   wept   the lovers

And among playful songs I alone laughed when lovers wept.

ma   ke   pro   'las: so   ke   pro
Ma   che   pro?   Lasso,   che   pro?
but what use   miserable what use

But what for? Miserable me, what for?

☙

[15, 39]   *Domenico Benigni*

'ko me   'se te   im por 'tu ni
Come sete importuni
How importunate you are

'ko me   'se te   im por 'tu ni   a mo 'ɾo zi   pen 'sjɛ ɾi
Come   sete   importuni,   amorosi   pensieri!
how   you are importunate   amorous   thoughts

How importunate you are, amorous thoughts!

sete =
(mod.)
siete

'pri vo   'doɲ: ɲi   pje 'ta de   ke   vo 'le te   'ki o   'spe ɾi
Privo   d'ogni   pietade,   che   volete   ch'io   speri?
deprived of every   pity   what   you want   that I   I may hope

What do you want me, deprived of all pity, to hope?

pietade =
(mod.) pietà

laʃ: 'ʃa te   o i 'mɛ   'ki o   nel   'mi o   'pɛt: to   a 'du ni
Lasciate,   ohimè,   ch'io   nel   mio   petto   aduni
let   alas   that I   in the my   breast   I may gather

Let me, alas, gather in my breast

'kwan ta   il   'reɲ: ɲo   da 'mor   'pe ne   e   tor 'men ti
quant'ha   il   regno   d'Amor   pene   e   tormenti!
how much has the kingdom   of Love   sufferings and torments

as many sufferings and torments as has the kingdom of Love!

ki   de 'zi a   di   mo 'rir   non   si la 'men ti
Chi desia   di   morir   non   si lamenti.
who desires   of   to die   not   may complain

May he who wants to die not complain.

non   vɛ   pju   'spe me   al 'ku na   ke   lu 'ziŋ gi   il   'mi o   'ko ɾe
Non   v'è   più   speme   alcuna   che   lusinghi   il   mio   core,
not   there is more hope   any   which may lure   the my   heart

There is no longer any hope which may lure my heart;

speme (lit.)
= speranza

'tut: te per me spa 'ri te son le 'dʒɔ je da 'mo ɾe
tutte **per** **me** **sparite** **son** **le** **gioie** **d'amore.**
completely for me vanished are the joys of love
the joys of love have completely vanished for me.

non 'di te o i 'mɛ ke si 'kan dʒi for 'tu na
Non **dite,** **ohimè,** **che** **si cangi** **Fortuna,**
not say alas that may change fortune
Do not say, alas, that Fortune may change;

'tan to spe 'ra ɾe al 'mi o de 'zir non 'li tʃe
tanto **sperare** **al** **mio** **desir** **non** **lice.**
so much hoping to the my desire not is allowed
my desire is not allowed such hope.

non si 'vɔl dʒe la 'sɔr te a un in fe 'li tʃe
Non **si volge** **la** **sorte** **a** **un** **infelice.**
not turns the destiny to an unfortunate
The destiny of an unfortunate one does not change.

e ke 'for se pen 'san do al swɔn 'da spre kwe 'ɾɛ le
E **che** **forse** **pensando** **al** **suon** **d'aspre** **querele,**
and [that] perhaps thinking at the sound of bitter laments
And, perhaps thinking of the sound of bitter laments,

in te ne 'rir kre 'de te 'du ɾo 'sas: so kru 'dɛ le
intenerir **credete** **duro** **sasso** **crudele?**
to soften you believe hard stone cruel
you believe [that one can] soften a cruel, hard stone?

ta 'tʃe te o 'ma i 'do ve sin 'te zi e 'kwan do
Tacete **omai,** **dove** **s'intese** **e** **quando,**
be silent now where was understood and when
Be silent now; where and when has it been understood

ke sen 'tis: se pje 'ta de 'al ma din 'fɛr no
che **sentisse** **pietade** **alma** **d'inferno?**
that may have felt pity soul of hell
that a hellish soul may have felt pity?

ki 'su e 'pe ne a do 'rɔ 'pe ni in e 'tɛr no
Chi **sue** **pene** **adorò** **peni** **in** **eterno.**
he who his sufferings adored let suffer in eternity
Let he who has loved his sufferings suffer in eternity.

GL: **Amor, Fortuna**

> omai (poet.)
> = ormai

❧

[1, 2]

ko 'zi vo 'le te ko 'zi sa 'ra
Così volete, così sarà!
If you want it like this, like this it will be!

ko 'zi vo 'le te ko 'zi sa 'ra 'bɛl: la ti 'ran: na ke 'tʃin ta 'sje te di kru del 'ta
Così **volete,** **così** **sarà,** **bella** **tiranna,** **che** **cinta** **siete** **di** **crudeltà!**
like this you want like this will be beautiful tyrant that girded you are with cruelty
If you want it like this, like this it will be, beautiful tyrant, for you are girded with cruelty!

se   dal   'fon te   del   'tu o   'kɔ ɾe   ne   di 'stil: la no   i   mar 'ti ɾi
Se   dal   fonte   del   tuo   core   ne   distillano   i   martiri,
if   from the   fountain   of the   your   heart   of it   distill   the   sufferings
If suffering drips from the fountainhead of your heart,

'tu o   ri 'go ɾe   nel   do 'lo ɾe   'fat: tʃa   'pa go   i   'mjɛ i   so 'spi ɾi
tuo   rigore   nel   dolore   faccia   pago   i   miei   sospiri!
your   rigidity   in the   sorrow   may do   content with   the   my   sighs
your cruelty's thirst for sorrow may be satisfied by my sighs!

se   go 'de te   a   'mjɛ i   tor 'men ti   il   pe 'nar   mi   sa 'ɾa   'dʒɔ ko
Se   godete   a   miei   tormenti,   il   penar   mi   sarà   gioco;
if   you delight   at   my   torments   the   suffering   to me   will be   game
If you delight in my torments, suffering will be a game for me;

il   'mi o   'let: to   'si a   ri 'tʃet: to   dun   in 'fer mo   e   sa 'ɾa   'pɔ ko
il   mio   letto   sia   ricetto   d'un   infermo,   e   sarà   poco!
the   my   bed   let be   refuge   of an   infirm one   and   will be   little
may my bed be the refuge of a sick man, and that will be little [to ask]!

se   vɛr   me   'sɛm pre   se 've ɾa   'dɛs: ser   'kru da   al 'fin   ti 'van ti
Se   ver   me   sempre   severa   d'esser   cruda   alfin   ti vanti,
if   toward   me   always   severe   of to be   cruel   in the end   you may boast
If, always severe towards me, in the end you boast about being cruel,

ver (poet.)
= verso

tra   ka 'te ne   'di an   le   'pe ne   sol   ri 'mɛ djo   'a i   'tri sti   'pjan ti
tra   catene   dian   le   pene   sol   rimedio   ai   tristi   pianti!
among   chains   let give   the   sufferings   only   remedy   to the   sad   tears
let my suffering in chains be the only cure for my sad tears!

[21, 24]

dɛ kon ten 'ta te vi
Deh, contentatevi
Ah, be satisfied

dɛ   kon ten 'ta te vi   'ki o   mi la 'men ti
Deh,   contentatevi,   ch'io   mi lamenti!
ah   be content   that I   myself lament
Ah, be satisfied that I am lamenting!

'kɛs: ser   'ta tʃi to   pju   non   si 'pwɔ   nɔ
Ch'esser   tacito   più   non   si può,   no!
[that] to be   silent   more   not   is possible   no
It is no longer possible for me to be silent, no!

'a tro   'nem bo   al 'lor ke   'twɔ na   par   ke   in 'seɲ: ɲi   a   'kjɛ der   a 'i ta
Atro   nembo   allor che   tuona,   par   che   insegni   a   chieder   aita!
dark   cloud   when   thunders   seems   that   teaches   to   to ask for   help
When a dark cloud thunders, it seems to make one call for help!

allor che =
(mod.) allorché

e   la   'bok: ka   'del: la   fe 'ɾi ta   ben 'ke   'mu ta
E   la   bocca   della   ferita,   benché   muta,
and   the   mouth   of the   wound   although   mute
And the open wound, although mute,

pje 'ta	ri 'swɔ na	pje 'ta	pje 'ta	ri 'swɔ na
pietà	**risuona!**	**Pietà!**	**Pièta**	**risuona!**
pity	echos	pity	pity	echos

echos "have pity"! It echos "have pity, pity"!

risuona: from "risuonare"
= (mod.) "risonare"

☙

[68]

dɛ me 'mɔ rja
Deh, memoria
Ah, memory

dɛ	me 'mɔ rja	e	ke	pju	'kjɛ di	'ki o	ram: 'men ti	il	'pri mo	af: 'fɛt: to
Deh,	**memoria,**	**e**	**che**	**più**	**chiedi?**	**Ch'io**	**rammenti**	**il**	**primo**	**affetto?**
ah	memory	[and]	what	more	you ask	that I	I may remember	the	first	affection

Ah, memory, what more do you ask? That I should remember my first affection?

se	man: 'ni di	e 'tɛr na	in	'pɛt: to	bɛn	il	'sa i	'men tre	lo	've di
Se	**m'annidi**	**eterna**	**in**	**petto,**	**ben'**	**il**	**sai**	**mentre**	**lo**	**vedi.**
if	me you hide	eternal	in	breast	well	it	you know	while	it	you see

If you lurk eternally in my breast you will know it well, for you will see it.

'a i	par 'tir	non	pwɔ	dal: 'lal ma	kwel: li 'ma dʒi ne	gra 'di ta
Ahi,	**partir**	**non**	**può**	**dall'alma**	**quell'imagine**	**gradita.**
alas	to depart	not	is able	from the soul	that image	pleasing

Alas, that pleasing image cannot leave my soul.

e	so 'spe za	kon	'lɛ i	la	'vi ta	'rɛ sta	'dʒe li da	la	'sal ma
E	**sospesa**	**con**	**lei**	**la**	**vita,**	**resta**	**gelida**	**la**	**salma.**
and	sospended	with	it	the	life	remains	ice cold	the	corpse

And, life being suspended with it [my soul], my body is ice cold.

tu	da	me	ke	'vwɔ i	pen 'sjɛ ɾo	'ki o	so 'spi ɾi	il	'mi o	te 'zɔ ɾo
Tu	**da**	**me,**	**che**	**vuoi,**	**pensiero?**	**Ch'io**	**sospiri**	**il**	**mio**	**tesoro?**
you	from	me	what	you want	thought	that I	I may sigh	the	my	treasure

What do you want from me, thoughts? That I should yearn for my treasure?

'eʎ: ʎi	ɛ	'spɛn to	'i o	'sɛm pre	'mɔ ɾo	ke	ve 'der	pju	non	lo	'spe ɾo
Egli	**è**	**spento.**	**Io**	**sempre**	**moro,**	**che**	**veder**	**più**	**non**	**lo**	**spero.**
He	is	dead	I	always	I die	that	to see	more	not	him	I hope

He is dead. I am forever dying because I do not hope to see him again.

o	sa 'pes: si	'kwan te	'vɔl te	'kja mo	'lom bra	del	'mi o	'bɛ ne
O	**sapessi**	**quante**	**volte**	**chiamo**	**l'ombra**	**del**	**mio**	**bene.**
oh	if you knew	how many	times	I call to	the spectre	of the	my	dear one

Oh, if you knew how often I call to the spectre of my dear one.

e	ʎi	'mo stro	le	ka 'te ne	ke	kon 'sɛr vo	al	'kɔ ɾe	av: 'vɔl te
E	**gli**	**mostro**	**le**	**catene**	**che**	**conservo**	**al**	**core**	**avvolte.**
and	to him	I show	the	chains	which	I keep	at the	heart	wrapped

And I show him the chains which I keep wrapped around my heart.

'vjɛ ni	'di ko	e	'tram: mi	'te ko	'nel: la	'tom ba	in	'ku i	di 'mɔ ɾi
Vieni,	**dico,**	**e**	**trammi**	**teco**	**nella**	**tomba**	**in**	**cui**	**dimori.**
come	I say	and	draw me	you with	into the	tomb	in	which	you dwell

Come, I say, and draw me with you into the tomb where you dwell.

ka	ve ˈder ti	in	ˈkweʎː ʎorː ˈro ɾi	ˈaŋ ko	a ˈmor	vwɔl	ve ˈnir	ˈme ko
Ch'a	**vederti**	**in**	**quegl'orrori,**	**anco**	**Amor**	**vuol'**	**venir**	**meco.**
[that] to	to see you	in	those horrors	also	Love	wants	to come	me with

anco =
(mod.)
anche

To see you in those horrors, Love also wants to come with me.

ma	sil	tʃɛl	a	ri tar ˈda ta	la	for ˈtu na	del	mo ˈri ɾe
Ma	**s'il**	**Ciel'**	**ha**	**ritardata**	**la**	**fortuna**	**del**	**morire,**
but	if the	heaven	has	delayed	the	fortune	of the	dying

But if heaven has delayed the fate of dying,

stɔ	se ˈpol ta	kol	de ˈzi ɾe	in	kwe ˈlur na	so spi ˈɾa ta
sto	**sepolta**	**col**	**desire**	**in**	**quel'urna**	**sospirata.**
I stay	buried	with the	desire	in	that urn	longed-for

I will stay buried with desire in that longed-for urn.

GL: **Amor**

☙

[49]

ɛ ˈbɛlː lo lar ˈdi ɾe
È bello l'ardire
The courage is laudable

ɛ	ˈbɛlː lo	lar ˈdi ɾe	dun	ˈa ni ma	ˈfɔr te	kiŋ ˈkon tra	la	ˈmɔr te
È	**bello**	**l'ardire**	**d'un**	**anima**	**forte**	**ch'incontra**	**la**	**morte**
it is	fine	the courage	of a	soul	strong	which meets	the	death

per	ˈnɔ bil	de ˈzi ɾe
per	**nobil**	**desire.**
through	noble	desire

The courage of a strong soul which meets death through a noble aspiration is laudable.

a	ki	non	ˈfu ɾa	i	ˈgwar di	ˈi ka ɾo	a u ˈda tʃe	ˈkwan do	spje ˈgar	pre ˈzu me
A	**chi**	**non**	**fura**	**i**	**guardi**	**Icaro**	**audace**	**quando**	**spiegar**	**presume**
to	he who	not	steals	the	glances	Icarus	bold	when	to spread	presumes

To the one who does not look at Icarus, when he presumes to spread

del	dʒe ni ˈtor	se ˈgwa tʃe	per	in ˈsɔ li te	ˈvi e	non	ˈsu e	le	ˈpju me
del	**genitor**	**seguace**	**per**	**insolite**	**vie**	**non**	**sue**	**le**	**piume**
of the	father	follower	through	strange	paths	not	his	the	feathers

the wings that were not his, as follower of his father's untrodden paths –

se	ˈpɔ i	pre tʃi pi ˈtan do	va	del	mar	tra	vo ˈra dʒi ni	pro ˈfun de
se	**poi**	**precipitando**	**va**	**del**	**mar**	**tra**	**voragini**	**profunde,**
if	then	plunging	goes	of the	sea	among	vortexes	deep

when then, plunging into the deep vortexes of the sea,

ˈlaʃː ʃa	ˈno me	a	kwelː ˈlon de	ˈkodː dʒi aŋ ˈkor	mor mo ˈran do
lascia	**nome**	**a**	**quell'onde**	**ch'oggi ancor**	**mormorando**
leaves	name	to	those waves	that today still	murmuring

he gives his name to those waves *[the Icarian Sea]* which murmur to this day –

par	ki	ˈvan ti	di	ˈlu i	ˈvɔʎː ʎon	ri ˈdi ɾe
par	**ch'i**	**vanti**	**di**	**lui**	**voglion**	**ridire:**
it seems	that the	merits	of	him	want	repeating

it seems that his merits bear repeating:

ɛ	'bɛl: lo	lar 'di ɾe	dun	'a ni ma	'fɔr te	kiŋ 'kon tra	la	'mɔr te
È	**bello**	**l'ardire**	**d'un**	**anima**	**forte**	**ch'incontra**	**la**	**morte**
it is	fine	the courage	of a	soul	strong	which meets	the	death

per	'nɔ bil	de 'zi ɾe
per	**nobil**	**desire.**
through	noble	desire

The courage of a strong soul which meets death through a noble aspiration is laudable.

se	un	en 'tʃɛ la do	ru 'bɛl: le	'so vra	'ku mu lo	de	'mon ti	de	ti 'ta ni
Se	**un**	**Encelado**	**rubelle**	**sovra**	**cumulo**	**de'**	**monti**	**de'**	**Titani**
if	an	Enceladus	rebellious	over	mass	of the	mountains	of the	Titans

If a rebellious Enceladus, standing over the Titans' mountain mass,

'ar ma	le	'fron ti	'kon tro	i	'dɛ i	'kon tro	le	'stel: le
arma	**le**	**fronti**	**contro**	**i**	**dei,**	**contro**	**le**	**stelle**
arms	the	heads	against	the	gods	against	the	stars

shows his hostile face against the gods, against the stars –

ki	per	la	me ɾa 'viʎ: ʎa	non	i 'nar ka	le	'tʃiʎ: ʎa
chi	**per**	**la**	**meraviglia**	**non**	**inarca**	**le**	**ciglia**
who	through	the	marvel	not	arches	the	brows

who would not arch his brow in amazement

se	'pɔ i	di 'ste zo	a	'tɛr: ra	da	'brat: tʃo	'oɲ: ɲi	po 'ten te
se	**poi**	**disteso**	**a**	**terra**	**da**	**braccio**	**ogni**	**potente,**
if	then	laid out	on	earth	from	arm	all	powerful

if, though felled to earth from the almighty arm [of Zeus] –

se 'pol to	'aŋ ko	fa	'gwɛr: ra	e	vo mi 'tan do	oɲ: 'ɲor	'sol fo	ko 'tʃɛn te
sepolto	**anco**	**fa**	**guerra**	**e**	**vomitando**	**ogn'or**	**solfo**	**cocente**
buried	even	makes	war	and	spewing	always	sulphur	scalding

even buried, he still makes war and, continuously spewing scalding fire

anco = (mod.) anche
solfo = (mod.) zolfo

'kon tro	il	ne 'mi ko	tʃɛl	'sfo ga	pur	'li ɾe
contro	**il**	**nemico**	**ciel**	**sfoga**	**pur**	**l'ire:**
against	the	enemy	heaven	vents	yet	the wraths

vents his wrath against the hostile heaven:

ɛ	'bɛl: lo	lar 'di ɾe	dun	'a ni ma	'fɔr te	kiŋ 'kon tra	la	'mɔr te
È	**bello**	**l'ardire**	**d'un**	**anima**	**forte**	**ch'incontra**	**la**	**morte**
it is	fine	the courage	of a	soul	strong	which meets	the	death

per	'nɔ bil	de 'zi ɾe
per	**nobil**	**desire.**
through	noble	desire

The courage of a strong soul which meets death through a noble aspiration is laudable.

'kwan to	ko 'lu i	siŋ 'gan: na	ke	kwe 'sta ni ma	a 'man te	per	'nɔ bi le	sem 'bjan te
Quanto	**colui**	**s'inganna**	**che**	**quest'anima**	**amante**	**per**	**nobile**	**sembiante**
how much	he who	is mistaken	that	this soul	loving	through	noble	appearance

per	'trɔp: po	te me 'ra ɾja	'ɔd: dʒi	kon 'dan: na
per	**troppo**	**temeraria**	**oggi**	**condanna.**
through	too	reckless	today	condemns

How much mistaken is he who today condemns as too reckless this [my] loving soul,
in love with a noble appearance.

ɛ	u 'na kwi la	il	'mi o	'kɔ ɾe	ke	'lɔk: kjo	del	pen 'sjɛr	'fis: sa	nel	'so le
È	**un'aquila**	**il**	**mio**	**core**	**che**	**l'occhio**	**del**	**pensier**	**fissa**	**nel**	**sole**
is	an eagle	the	my	heart	which	the eye	of the	mind	fixes	on the	sun

My heart is an eagle which fixes the eye of its mind on the sun   *(Eagles could stare at the sun without becoming blind.)*

ne	di	sof: 'frir	ʎi	'dwɔ le	'oɲ: ɲi	'strat: tsjo	da 'mo ɾe
né	**di**	**soffrir**	**gli**	**duole**	**ogni**	**strazio**	**d'amore.**
not	of	to suffer	to it	suffers	every	torture	of love

[and] does not regret to suffer every torture of love.

se	kon 'dʒu ɾi	'kon tro	me	la	for 'tu na	'kwan to	sa	'lar mi	a 'dan: ni
Se	**congiuri**	**contro**	**me**	**la**	**fortuna**	**quanto**	**sa**	**l'armi**	**a danni**
if	may conspire	against	me	the	fortune	how much	knows	the arms	to damages

di	'mi a	fe	in dʒeɲ: 'ɲo za	kru del 'ta	per	si	'deɲ: ɲa	ka 'dʒon	'glɔ ɾja	ɛ	mo 'ɾi ɾe
di	**mia**	**fé**	**ingegnosa**	**crudeltà**	**per**	**sì**	**degna**	**cagion**	**gloria**	**è**	**morire.**
of	my	faith	ingenious	cruelty	through	so	worthy	cause	glory	it is	to die

If fortune, with its knowledge of warfare, conspires a crafty cruelty against my faith *[love]*, it will be glorious to die for such a worthy cause.

ɛ	'bɛl: lo	lar 'di ɾe	dun	'a ni ma	'for te	kiŋ 'kon tra	la	'mɔr te
È	**bello**	**l'ardire**	**d'un**	**anima**	**forte**	**ch'incontra**	**la**	**morte**
it is	fine	the courage	of a	soul	strong	which meets	the	death

per	'nɔ bil	de 'zi ɾe
per	**nobil**	**desire.**
through	noble	desire

The courage of a strong soul which meets death through a noble aspiration is laudable.

GL: **Encelado, Icaro, Titani**

☙

[22, 24]

'fil: li	non	'ta mo	pju
Filli, non t'amo più			

Filli, I do not love you anymore

'fil: li	non	'ta mo	pju	e	se	nol	'kre di	a	me
Filli,	**non**	**t'amo**	**più,**	**e**	**se**	**nol**	**credi**	**a**	**me,**
Filli	not	you I love	anymore	and	if	not it	you believe	to	me

Filli, I do not love you anymore; and if you do not believe it,

've di	ke	ɔ	'ʃɔl to	il	pjɛ	'dal: la	'tu a	ser vi 'tu
vedi,	**che**	**ho**	**sciolto**	**il**	**piè,**	**dalla**	**tua**	**servitù.**
see	that	I have	freed	the	foot	from the	your	servitude

see that I have freed my step from your servitude.

'fil: li	non	'ta mo	pju
Filli,	**non**	**t'amo**	**più!**
Filli	not	you I love	anymore

Filli, I do not love you anymore!

ne 'ga to	'oɲ: ɲi	ri 'stɔ ɾo	del	'mi o	fe 'del	ser 'vi ɾe
Negato	**ogni**	**ristoro**	**del**	**mio**	**fedel**	**servire,**
denied	any	compensation	of the	my	faithful	serving

Denied any recompense for my faithful serving,

il	'tu o	'vol to	kru 'dɛl	pju	non	a 'do ɾo
il	**tuo**	**volto**	**crudel**	**più**	**non**	**adoro.**
the	your	face	cruel	more	not	I worship

I do not worship your cruel face anymore.

'fil: li	non	'ta mo	pju	nɔ	nɔ	non	'ta mo	pju
Filli,	**non**	**t'amo**	**più,**	**no,**	**no,**	**non**	**t'amo**	**più.**
Filli	not	you I love	anymore	no	no	not	you I love	anymore

Filli, I do not love you anymore – no, no, I do not love you anymore.

GL: **Filli**

☙

[39]   *Count Teodoli*

fud: 'dʒi te fud: 'dʒi te
Fuggite, fuggite
Flee, flee

fud: 'dʒi te	fud: 'dʒi te	pen 'sje ɾi	gwer: 'rje ɾi	kin	'va no	as: sa 'li te	kon	'ar mi
Fuggite,	**fuggite,**	**pensieri**	**guerrieri,**	**ch'in**	**vano**	**assalite**	**con**	**armi**
flee	flee	thoughts	warring	who in	vain	you assail	with	weapons

Flee, flee, warring thoughts, you who in vain assail with weapons

di	'pa tʃe	kwel	kwɔr	ke	si 'sfa tʃe	tra	'pe ne	in fi 'ni te
di	**pace**	**quel**	**cuor**	**che**	**si sface**	**tra**	**pene**	**infinite.**
of	peace	that	heart	which	comes undone	among	pains	infinite

of peace that heart which is being demolished among infinite pains.

tʃes: 'sa te	tʃes: 'sa te	ru 'bɛl: le	'mi e	'stel: le	dal 'tsar vi	spje 'ta te	a	'spɛ me	gra 'di ta
Cessate,	**cessate,**	**rubelle**	**mie**	**stelle,**	**d'alzarvi**	**spietate**	**a**	**speme**	**gradita,**
cease	cease	rebellious	my	stars	of to rise	merciless	at	hope	welcomed

Cease, cease, my rebellious stars, to rise merciless at welcomed hope,

speme (lit.) = speranza

ke	'mɔr te	ɛ	la	'vi ta	del: 'lal me	spret: 'tsa te
ché	**morte**	**è**	**la**	**vita**	**dell'alme**	**sprezzate.**
because	death	is	the	life	of the souls	scorned

for the life of scorned souls is like death.

kor: 're te	kor: 're te	po 'tɛn ti	tor: 'rɛn ti	fe 'ri te	ut: tʃi 'de te	la	'spɛ me
Correte,	**correte,**	**potenti**	**torrenti,**	**ferite**	**uccidete**	**la**	**speme**
run	run	mighty	torrents	wound	kill	the	hope

Rush, rush, mighty torrents; wound [and] kill the hope

e	la	'bra ma	dun	kwɔr	ke	trɔp: 'pa ma	'du e	'stel: le	ko 'me te
e	**la**	**brama**	**d'un**	**cuor**	**che**	**tropp'ama**	**due**	**stelle**	**comete.**
and	the	yearning	of a	heart	which	too much loves	two	stars comets	(= comets)

and the yearning of a heart which immoderately loves two comets *[eyes]*.

☙

[68]

in un mar di pen 'sje ɾi
In un mar di pensieri
In a sea of thoughts

in   un   mar   di   pen 'sjɛ ɾi   'lal ma   'so la   sad: 'dʒi ɾa
In   un   mar   di   pensieri,   l'alma   sola   s'aggira,
in   a   sea   of   thoughts   the soul   alone   wanders
In a sea of thoughts my soul wanders alone

e   kon   do 'lor   si   'fjɛ ɾi   nel   'su o   mar 'tir   so 'spi ɾa
e   con   dolor   sì   fieri,   nel   suo   martir   sospira.
and   with   sorrows   so   terrible   in the   its   agony   sighs
and, with such terrible sorrow, sighs in its agony.

per 'ke   il   'fa to   dun   zven tu 'ɾa to   nɔ   non   si 'pwɔ   'fran dʒe ɾe
Perché   il   fato   d'un   sventurato,   no,   non   si può   frangere,
because   the   fate   of an   unfortunate   no   not   is possible   to break
Because the fate of an unfortunate one – no – cannot be broken,

'tok: ka a me   'sɛm pre   di   'pjan dʒe ɾe
tocca a me   sempre   di   piangere.
it befalls me   always   of   to weep
I must weep forever.

non   a   'ma i   'tre gwa   o   'pa tʃe   di   'ku ɾe   il   'mi o   kɔr   'pjɛ no
Non   ha   mai   tregua   o   pace,   di   cure   il   mio   cor   pieno.
not   has   ever   respite   or   peace   of   concerns   the   my   heart   full
My heart, full of concerns, never has respite or peace.

ko 'zi   da u 'dʒel   ra 'pa tʃe   'e ska   ɛ   'sɛm pre   il   'mi o   'se no
Così   d'augel'   rapace,   esca   è   sempre   il   mio   seno.
thus   of bird   predatory   bait   is   always   the   my   breast
Thus, my breast is always bait for a predatory bird.

> *augel[lo] =*
> *(mod.) uccel[lo]*

per 'ke   le   'stel: le   'em pje   e   ru 'bɛl: le   nɔ   non   si 'pwɔ   'fran dʒe ɾe
Perché   le   stelle   empie   e   rubelle,   no,   non   si può   frangere,
because   the   stars   wicked   and   rebellious   no   not   is possible   to break
Because the wicked and rebellious stars – no – cannot be quelled,

'tok: ka a me   'sɛm pre   di   'pjan dʒe ɾe
tocca a me   sempre   di   piangere.
it befalls me   always   of   to weep
I must weep forever.

kwal   di   'si zi fo   il   'sas: so   il   'mi o   de 'zir   si 'tro va   or   'al to   in   'tʃi ma
Qual   di   Sisifo   il   sasso,   il   mio   desir   si trova   or   alto   in   cima,
like   of   Sisyphus   the   stone   the   my   desire   is found   now   high   at   summit
Like Sisyphus' stone, my desire is now at the top of the summit,

or   'bas: so   ma   'nul: la   al 'fin   ʎi   'dʒo va
or   basso,   ma   nulla   al fin   gli   giova.
now   low   but   nothing   in the end   to it   is of help
now at the bottom; but, in the end, nothing helps it.

ke   'ri a   zven 'tu ɾa   'sɛm pre   pju   'du ɾa   nɔ   non   si 'pwɔ   'fran dʒe ɾe
Ché   ria   sventura,   sempre   più   dura,   no,   non   si può   frangere,
because   cruel   misfortune   always   more   harsh   no   not   is possible   to break
Because cruel misfortune, ever more harsh – no – cannot be defied,

'tok: ka a me   'sɛm pre   di   'pjan dʒe ɾe
tocca a me   sempre   di   piangere.
it befalls me   always   of   to weep
I must weep forever.

𝒢ℒ: **Sisifo**

ॐ

[1, 2, 46]

la 'mi a 'fe de
La mia fede
My fidelity

la   'mi a   'fe de   al 'tru i   dʒu 'ra ta   'al: la   'fu ga   oɲ: 'ɲor   maf: 'fret: ta
La   mia   fede   altrui   giurata   alla   fuga   ognor   m'affretta;
the   my   fidelity   other person   sworn   to the   flight   always   hastens
The fidelity I have sworn to another always hastens my flight;

ma   la   'di va   ke   mal: 'lɛt: ta   'tjɛ ne   'lal ma   iŋ ka te 'na ta
ma   la   diva,   cho   m'alletta,   tiene   l'alma   incatenata.
but   the   goddess   who   me lures   keeps   the soul   chained
but the goddess who lures me keeps my soul enchained.

> diva (lit.)
> = dea

in   un   'dub: bjo   si   mo 'lɛ sto   in fe 'li tʃe   ke   fa 'ɾɔ
In   un   dubbio   sì   molesto,   infelice,   che   farò!
in   a   doubt   so   troublesome   unhappy   what   I will do
In such a troublesome uncertainty, unhappy me, what shall I do?

'so no   in 'fi do   se   kwi   'ɾɛ sto   son   kru 'dɛl   se   me ne 'vɔ
Sono   infido,   se   qui   resto,   son   crudel,   se   me ne vo.
I am   unfaithful   if   here   I remain   I am   cruel   if   I go away
I am unfaithful if I remain here; I am cruel if I go away.

se   da   te   'bɛl: la   min 'vo lo   dun   'te ze o   son   pju   ti 'ran: no
Se   da   te,   bella,   m'involo,   d'un   Teseo   son   più   tiranno;
if   from   you   beautiful one   I take flight   than a   Theseus   I am   more   tyrannical
If I take flight from you, beautiful one, I am more tyrannical than a Theseus;

se   mi 'fer mo   in   'kwe sto   'swɔ lo   'trɔp: po   o i 'mɛ   flo 'ɾin da   iŋ 'gan: no
se   mi fermo   in   questo   suolo,   troppo   ohimè   Florinda   inganno.
if   me I come to a stop   on   this   soil   too much   alas   Florinda   I deceive
if I stay on this soil, alas, I deceive Florinda too much.

'fat: tʃa   'i o   'pu ɾe   o   kwel   o   'kwe sto   'sɛm pre   'ɾɛ o   mi kja me 'ɾɔ
Faccia   io   pure   o   quel   o   questo,   sempre   reo   mi chiamerò:
I may do   I   [yet]   either   that   or   this   always   guilty   I will consider myself
Whether I do this or that, I will always consider myself guilty:

'so no   in 'fi do   se   kwi   'ɾɛ sto   son   kru 'dɛl   se   me ne 'vɔ
Sono   infido,   se   qui   resto,   son   crudel,   se   me ne vo.
I am   unfaithful   if   here   I remain   I am   cruel   if   I go away
I am unfaithful if I remain here; I am cruel if I go away.

𝒢ℒ: **Teseo**

ॐ

[39]

ma nɔ non fud: ˈdʒir
Ma no, non fuggir
No, do not flee

ma	nɔ	non	fud: ˈdʒir	nɔ	nɔ
Ma	**no!**	**Non**	**fuggir,**	**no,**	**no!**
[but]	no	not	to flee	no	no

No, do not flee, no, no!

ˈpja ga	ke	ˈpja tʃe	fud: ˈdʒir	non	si ˈpwɔ	nɔ	non	si ˈpwɔ
Piaga	**che**	**piace**	**fuggir**	**non**	**si può,**	**no,**	**non**	**si può!**
wound	which	pleases	to flee	not	is possible	no	not	is possible

It is not possible to escape a wound which gives pleasure – no, it is not possible!

❧

[27]

ˈmɛ sto in sen
Mesto in sen
Sad in the bosom

ˈmɛ sto	in	sen	dun	ˈan tro	om ˈbro zo	ˈda to	in	ˈprɛ da	a	ˈpe na	ˈrɛ a
Mesto	**in**	**sen**	**d'un**	**antro**	**ombroso**	**dato**	**in**	**preda**	**a**	**pena**	**rea**
sad	in	bosom	of a	cavern	gloomy	given	in	prey	to	pain	cruel

Sad, in the bosom of a gloomy cavern, prey to cruel pain,

la	ˈsu a	ˈbɛl: la	ga la ˈtɛ a	so spi ˈro zo	la gri ˈmo zo	ˈtir si	un	di	ko ˈzi	pjan ˈge a
la	**sua**	**bella**	**Galatea**	**sospiroso**	**lagrimoso**	**Tirsi**	**un**	**dì**	**così**	**piangea.**
the	his	beautiful	Galatea	melancholy	tear-filled	Tirsi	one	day	thus	was weeping

Tirsi, melancholy and full of tears, was weeping one day for his beautiful Galatea [*piangea = piangeva*]
as follows *[with the following thoughts]*:

del	sol	ˈlu tʃi do	e	so ˈvran o	i	lu ˈtʃen ti	ˈa u ɾe i	splen ˈdo ɾi
Del	**sol**	**lucido**	**e**	**sovrano**	**i**	**lucenti**	**aurei**	**splendori**
of the	sun	shining	and	sovereign	the	bright	golden	splendors

The bright golden splendors of the shining and sovereign sun

son	per	me	mor ˈta li	or: ˈro ɾi	or	ke	a	te	ˈvi vo	lon ˈta no
son	**per**	**me**	**mortali**	**orrori**	**or**	**che**	**a**	**te**	**vivo**	**lontano.**
are	for	me	deadly	horrors	now	that	from	you	I live	distant

are deadly horrors for me now that I live far from you.

ˈdol tʃe	ˈpjan dʒe	in	sul: lal ˈbo ɾe	lu ziɲ: ˈɲol	ˈsu a	ˈpe na	ˈri a
Dolce	**piange**	**in**	**sull'albore**	**l'usignol**	**sua**	**pena**	**ria,**
sweetly	weeps	at	upon the dawn	the nightingale	his	suffering	sad

The nightingale, upon the dawn, weeps sweetly in his sad suffering; [*ria (lit.)* = *rea*]

> *The nightingale often appears in literary texts as the sad herald of the dawn which parts illicit lovers, or as the evoker of painful memories of past or lost love. According to one legend, the nightingale leans its breast upon a thorn when it sings.*

ma	si	ˈdol tʃe	me lo ˈdi a	non	lu ˈziŋ ga	il	ˈmi o	do ˈlo ɾe
ma	**sì**	**dolce**	**melodia**	**non**	**lusinga**	**il**	**mio**	**dolore.**
but	so	sweet	melody	not	is gratified	the	my	sorrow

but my sorrow is not gratified by such sweet melody.

GL: **Galatea, Tirsi**

❧

[24, 55]

nɔ nɔ ˈmi o ˈkɔ ɾe
No, no, mio core
No, no, my heart

nɔ	nɔ	ˈmi o	ˈkɔ ɾe	nɔ	nɔ	nɔ	non	iŋ gol ˈfar ti
No,	**no,**	**mio**	**core,**	**no!**	**No,**	**no!**	**Non**	**ingolfarti!**
no	no	my	heart	no	no	no	not	entrap yourself

No, no, my heart – no! No, no, do not become trapped!

In [24] *the next text is "Non lasciarti..."*

se	da ˈmor	tɛ	ˈnɔ to	il	ˈma ɾe	non	fi ˈdar ti	a	ˈkwe sta	ˈkal ma
Se	**d'amor**	**t'è**	**noto**	**il**	**mare,**	**non**	**fidarti**	**a**	**questa**	**calma**
if	of love	to you is	known	the	sea	not	to trust yourself	to	this	calm

If the sea of love is known to you, do not entrust yourself to this calm

ka	ri ˈdot: ta	pju	dun	ˈal ma	di spe ˈra ta	a	na u fra ˈga ɾe
ch'ha	**ridotta**	**più**	**d'un**	**alma**	**disperata**	**a**	**naufragare.**
which has	driven	more	than one	soul	desperate	to	to be shipwrecked

which has brought more than one desperate soul to shipwreck.

non	laʃ: ˈʃar ti	lu ziŋ ˈga ɾe	da	si	ˈdol tʃe	pro spet: ˈti va
Non	**lasciarti**	**lusingare,**	**da**	**sì**	**dolce**	**prospettiva,**
not	to let yourself	to be deceived	by	such	sweet	prospect

Do not let yourself be deceived by such a sweet prospect,

ke	lon ˈta no	ˈdal: la	ˈri va	ˈkor: ri	il	ˈri skjo	dan: ne ˈgar ti
ché	**lontano**	**dalla**	**riva**	**corri**	**il**	**rischio**	**d'annegarti!**
because	far	from the	coast	you run	the	risk	of to drown yourself

because, far from the coast, you run the risk of drowning!

in [55]: **porti rischio** [ˈpɔr ti ˈris kjo] = you take the risk...

In [55] *are the following additional texts:*

non	ti ˈfi ḍi	a	ˈstel: le	a	ˈlu na	il	nok: ˈkjer	del	ˈtu o	pen ˈsjɛ ɾo
Non	**ti fidi**	**a**	**stelle,**	**a**	**luna**	**il**	**nocchier**	**del**	**tuo**	**pensiero,**
not	you may entrust	to	stars	to	moon	the	helmsman	of the	your	thought

May the helmsman of your thoughts not trust the stars and the moon,

ke	in	kwel	ˈpɛ la go	si	ˈfjɛ ɾo	ˈsɛm pre	ˈkor: re si	for ˈtu na
ché	**in**	**quel**	**pelago**	**sì**	**fiero**	**sempre**	**corresi**	**fortuna.**
because	in	that	open sea	so	fierce	always	navigates itself in a storm	fortune

for in that most fierce open sea a storm is always brewing.

par ti ˈra i	kon	ˈvo lo	ar ˈdi to	del	de ˈzi o	su	la	ˈtu a	ˈna ve
Partirai	**con**	**volo**	**ardito**	**del**	**desio**	**su**	**la**	**tua**	**nave,**
you will depart	with	flight	bold	of the	desire	on	the	your	ship

You will depart in bold flight on the ship of your desire,

e	kon	ˈvɛn to	il	pju	so ˈa ve	laʃ: ʃe ˈra i	la ˈmi ko	ˈli do
e	**con**	**vento**	**il**	**più**	**soave**	**lascerai**	**l'amico**	**lido.**
and	with	wind	the	most	gentle	you will leave	the friendly	shore

and with the most gentle wind you will leave the friendly shore.

☙

[1, 2, 17, 20, 24, 47]

nɔ nɔ non si ˈspɛ ɾi

No, no, non si speri

No, no, do not be hopeful

nɔ	nɔ	non	si	ˈspɛ ɾi	ɛ	ˈmɔr ta	la	ˈspɛ me	pjan ˈdʒe te	pen ˈsjɛ ɾi
No,	**no,**	**non**	**si**	**speri!**	**È**	**morta**	**la**	**speme!**	**Piangete,**	**pensieri!**
no	no,	not	one may hope		is	dead	the	hope	weep	thoughts

No, no, do not be hopeful! Hope is dead! Weep, thoughts!

speme (lit.) = speranza

a	ˈbru no	ve ˈsti ti	nel	ˈvɔ stro	do ˈlo ɾe	de ˈzi ɾi	tra ˈdi ti	laʃː ˈʃa te	il	ˈmi o	ˈkɔ ɾe
A	**bruno**	**vestiti,**	**nel**	**vostro**	**dolore,**	**desiri**	**traditi,**	**lasciate**	**il**	**mio**	**core!**
in	black	dressed	in the	your	sorrow	desires	betrayed	leave	the	mio	heart

Betrayed desires, clothed in mourning because of your sorrow, leave my heart!

le	ˈdʒɔ je	da ˈmo ɾe	son	ˈlam pi	fu ˈga tʃi	men ˈda tʃi	ledː ˈdʒe ɾi
Le	**gioie**	**d'amore**	**son**	**lampi**	**fugaci,**	**mendaci,**	**leggieri!**
the	joys	of love	are	flashes	fleeting	lying	fickle

The joys of love are fleeting, lying, fickle flashes!

leggieri = (mod.) leggeri

In several of the prints are additional verses:

kon	ˈdɛ stra	pje ˈto za	so ˈa ve	kor ˈte ze	pje ˈta te	a mo ˈro za	nel	ˈpɛtː to	latː ˈtʃe ze
Con	**destra**	**pietosa**	**soave,**	**cortese**	**pietate**	**amorosa**	**nel**	**petto**	**l'accese.**
with	right hand	compassionate	gentle	kind	pity	amorous	in the	breast	it inflamed

With compassionate and gentle hand, kind and loving pity inflamed my breast.

pietate = (mod.) pietà

ma	ˈzdeɲː ɲo	lofː ˈfe ze	kon	ˈri dʒi di	ˈstra li	mor ˈta li	se ˈve ɾi
Ma	**sdegno**	**l'offese**	**con**	**rigidi**	**strali,**	**mortali,**	**severi.**
but	scorn	it hurt	with	rigid	arrows	deadly	harsh

But scorn hurt it with rigid, deadly, harsh arrows.

a	ˈmɔr te	fe ˈri ta	kon	ˈar mi	di	ˈpa tʃe
A	**morte**	**ferita**	**con**	**armi**	**di**	**pace,**
to	death	wounded	with	weapons	of	peace

Mortally wounded by weapons of peace,

do ˈvɛbː be	la	ˈvi ta	se ˈpol ta	sen	ˈdʒa tʃe
dov'ebbe	**la**	**vita,**	**sepolta**	**sen**	**giace**
where had	the	life	buried	breast	lies

my buried breast lies where it had its life:

nel	kɔr	ke	si ˈsfa tʃe	per	ˈfjamː me	e	so ˈspi ɾi	mar ˈti ɾi	pju	ˈfjɛ ɾi
nel	**cor,**	**che**	**si sface,**	**per**	**fiamme**	**e**	**sospiri,**	**martiri**	**più**	**fieri.**
in the	heart	which	comes undone	through	flames	and	sighs	tortures	more	cruel

in the heart which is being destroyed by flames and sighs, [which are] crueler tortures.

I changed the printed "a sospiri" to "e sospiri," which makes more sense, guessing the "a" to be a copying error.

nɔ	nɔ	non	si	ˈspɛ ɾi	ɛ	ˈmɔr ta	la	ˈspɛ me	pjan ˈdʒe te	pen ˈsjɛ ɾi
No,	**no,**	**non**	**si**	**speri!**	**È**	**morta**	**la**	**speme!**	**Piangete,**	**pensieri!**
no	no,	not	one may hope		is	dead	the	hope	weep	thoughts

No, no, do not be hopeful! Hope is dead! Weep, thoughts!

⌘

[12, 23, 39]

non 'pɔs: so 'vi ve ɾe
Non posso vivere
I cannot live

non	'pɔs: so	'vi ve ɾe	'sɛn tsa	il	'mi o	bɛn	nɔ	nɔ
Non	**posso**	**vivere**	**senza**	**il**	**mio**	**ben,**	**no,**	**no!**
not	I am able	to live	without	the	my	dear one	no	no

I cannot live without my dear one, no, no!

a 'mor	pje 'to zo	'dam: mi	le	'pju me
Amor	**pietoso,**	**dammi**	**le**	**piume;**
Love	merciful	give to me	the	feathers

Merciful Love, give me wings;

del	'mi o	bɛl	'nu me	'gwi da mi	in	sen
del	**mio**	**bel**	**nume**	**guidami**	**in**	**sen.**
of the	my	beautiful	deity	guide me	to	breast

guide me to the breast of my beautiful deity.

GL: **Amor**

[26]

pjan 'dʒe te
Piangete
Weep

pjan 'dʒe te	'a u ɾe	pjan 'dʒe te	ɔ	per 'du to	il	'mi o	'bɛ ne
Piangete	**aure,**	**piangete,**	**ho**	**perduto**	**il**	**mio**	**bene**
weep	breezes	weep	I have	lost	the	my	dear one

'tʃin to	del	'su o	splen 'do ɾe	'del: la	'su a	'lu tʃe	a 'dor no
cinto	**del**	**suo**	**splendore**	**della**	**sua**	**luce**	**adorno;**
encircled	of the	her	splendor	of the	her	light	adorned

Weep, breezes, weep. I, [who was] encircled by her splendor and adorned by her light, have lost my dear one;

da	'kwe ste	'pjad: dʒe	a 'mɛ ne	ɛ	spa 'ri to	kwel	'so le
da	**queste**	**piaggie**	**amene**	**è**	**sparito**	**quel**	**sole**
from	these	shores	pleasant	has	disappeared	that	sun

ke	'al: le	'tɛ ne bre	'mi e	por 'ta va	il	'dʒor no
che	**alle**	**tenebre**	**mie**	**portava**	**il**	**giorno.**
which	to the	darknesses	mine	brought	the	day

from these pleasant shores that sun who used to bring daylight to my darkness has vanished.

o	'du ɾa	'sɔr te	o	'di o	ɛ	par 'ti to	il	kɔr	'mi o
O	**dura**	**sorte**	**o**	**Dio**	**è**	**partito**	**il**	**cor**	**mio;**
o	harsh	fate	o	God	is	departed	the	heart	mine

O harsh fate, o God, my heart [beloved one] has departed;

ɛ	par 'ti ta	ko 'lɛ i	'kɛ ɾa	sol	del	'mi o	bɛn	'dol tʃe	'kwjɛ te
è	**partita**	**colei**	**ch'era**	**sol**	**del**	**mio**	**ben**	**dolce**	**quiete.**
is	departed	she	who was	only	of the	my	well-being	sweet	peacefulness

she who was the only sweet peace of my happiness has departed.

pjan 'dʒe te	'a u ɾe	pjan 'dʒe te	la kri 'mo ze	din 'tor no	ʃoʎ: 'ʎe te	il	'vɔ stro	'vo lo
Piangete	**aure,**	**piangete.**	**Lacrimose**	**d'intorno**	**sciogliete**	**il**	**vostro**	**volo**
weep	breezes	weep	tearful	around	unloose	the	your	flight

e	pje 'to zo	sul	'la le	ke	'mjɛ i	'kal di	so 'spi ɾi	'vo i	por 'ta te
e	**pietoso**	**sul**	**l'ale**	**ché**	**miei**	**caldi**	**sospiri**	**voi**	**portate**
and	merciful	upon	the wing	because	my	hot	sighs	you	carry

Weep, breezes, weep. Tearful, take flight mercifully, as you bear my feverish sighs,

il	'mi o	'dwɔ lo	il	'mi o	af: 'fan: no	i	mar 'ti ɾi
il	**mio**	**duolo**	**il**	**mio**	**affanno**	**i**	**martiri**
the	my	grief	the	my	woe	the	agonies

my grief, my woe, and my agonies;

e	'do ve	'dɔr me	a 'mo ɾe	'de sti	al 'me no	pje 'ta de	il	'mi o	do 'lo ɾe
e	**dove**	**dorme**	**amore**	**desti**	**almeno**	**pietade**	**il**	**mio**	**dolore.**
and	where	sleeps	love	let awaken	at least	pity	the	my	pain

and wherever love is sleeping, let my pain at least awaken pity.

pietade = (mod.) pietà

'mi ze ɾo	ma	ke	'kjɛg: go	'a i	ke	'trɔp: po	va 'ned: dʒo
Misero	**ma**	**che**	**chieggo**	**ahi**	**che**	**troppo**	**vaneggio;**
miserable	[but]	what	I ask	alas	that	too much	I rave

Miserable me, what am I asking for? Alas, I am raving too much.

chieggo = (mod.) chiedo

'lun dʒi	'del: la	'mi a	'vi ta	'a u ɾa	'dol tʃe	di	'spɛ me	non	mi	lu 'ziŋ gi	pju
lungi	**della**	**mia**	**vita**	**aura**	**dolce**	**di**	**speme**	**non**	**mi**	**lusinghi**	**più,**
far away	from the	my	life	breeze	sweet	of	hope	not	me	may entice	more

Far from my life *[my beloved]*, may the sweet breeze of hope no longer entice me;

speme (lit.) = speranza

ne	le	mi 'zɛ ɾje	e 'stre me	pju	non	'spɛ ɾo	al	'mi o	'ma le
ne	**le**	**miserie**	**estreme**	**più**	**non**	**spero**	**al**	**mio**	**male**
in	the	miseries	extreme	more	not	I hope	to the	my	hurt

ne le = (mod.) nelle

'o ɾe	traŋ 'kwil: le	e	'ljɛ te
ore	**tranquille**	**e**	**liete.**
hours	tranquil	and	happy

in my extreme misery I no longer hope for tranquil and happy hours to [relieve] my pain.

pjan 'dʒe te	'a u ɾe	pjan 'dʒe te
Piangete	**aure,**	**piangete.**
weep	breezes	weep

Weep, breezes, weep.

&

[10, 19, 34]   In [34] titled **Piangete**.

pjan 'dʒe te	o i 'mɛ	pjan 'dʒe te
Piangete, ohimè, piangete		

Weep, alas, weep

pjan 'dʒe te	o i 'mɛ	pjan 'dʒe te	'a ni me	in: na mo 'ra te
Piangete,	**ohimè**	**piangete,**	**anime**	**innamorate,**
weep	alas	weep	souls	enamored

Weep – alas, weep, enamored souls,

e	sok: 'kor so	e	pje 'ta te	so spi 'ran do	pjan 'dʒɛn do	al 'tru i	kje 'de te
e	**soccorso**	**e**	**pietate,**	**sospirando,**	**piangendo,**	**altrui**	**chiedete.**
and	help	and	pity	sighing	weeping	of others	ask for

pietate = (mod.) pietà

and, sighing and weeping, ask others for help and pity.

'kwan do	sa 'di ra	bel 'ta	se 're na	ki	non	so 'spi ra	in 'dar no	'spɛ ra
Quando	**s'adira**	**beltà**	**serena**	**chi**	**non**	**sospira**	**indarno**	**spera;**
when	gets angry	beauty	serene	he who	not	sighs	in vain	hopes

indarno = (mod.) invano

When a serene beauty gets angry, he who does not sigh hopes in vain;

ki	non	'pjan dʒe	da 'mar	non	si 'di a	'van to
chi	**non**	**piange**	**d'amar**	**non**	**si dia**	**vanto:**
he who	not	weeps	of loving	not	himself may give	boast

he who does not weep cannot boast of loving:

ɛ	'fɔ ko	a 'mor	e	lo	so 'stje ne	il	'pjan to
è	**foco**	**amor**	**e**	**lo**	**sostiene**	**il**	**pianto.**
is	fire	love	and	it	sustains	the	weeping

Love is fire, and weeping fuels it.

The following additional texts appear, variously, in [19] *and/or* [34]:

laŋ 'gwi te	o i 'mɛ	laŋ 'gwi te	o	se 'gwa tʃi	da 'mo re
Languite,	**ohimè**	**languite,**	**o**	**seguaci**	**d'Amore!**
languish	alas	languish	o	disciples	of Love

Languish – alas, languish, o disciples of Love!

il	tor 'men to	il	do 'lo re	ne	so 'spi ri	ne	'pjan ti	al 'tru i	ri 'de te
Il	**tormento,**	**il**	**dolore**	**né**	**sospiri,**	**né**	**pianti**	**altrui**	**ridete.**
the	torment	the	pain	nor	sighs	nor	tears	of others	laugh

Do not laugh at the torment, pain, sighs, or tears of others.

laŋ 'gwi te	o i 'mɛ	laŋ 'gwi te	se	'di ra	ɛ	'pje no	un	bɛl	sem 'bjan te
Languite,	**ohimè**	**languite.**	**Se**	**d'ira**	**è**	**pieno,**	**un**	**bel**	**sembiante,**
languish	alas	languish	if	of anger	is	full	a	beautiful	countenance

Languish – alas, languish. If a beautiful face is full of anger,

ki	non	vjɛn 'me no	ɛ	'fal so	a 'man te
chi	**non**	**vien meno**	**è**	**falso**	**amante.**
he who	not	swoons	is	false	lover

he who does not swoon is a false lover.

ki	non	'pjan dʒe	da 'mar	non	si 'di a	'van to
Chi	**non**	**piange**	**d'amar**	**non**	**si dia**	**vanto:**
he who	not	weeps	of loving	not	himself let give	boast

He who does not weep should not boast of loving:

ko 'noʃ: ʃe	a 'mor	i	'swɔ i	se 'gwa tʃi	al	'pjan to
conosce	**Amor**	**i**	**suoi**	**seguaci**	**al**	**pianto.**
knows	Love	the	his	followers	by the	weeping

Love knows his disciples by their weeping.

𝒢ℒ: **Amor[e]**

&

[1, 2, 16, 46]   sok: ko 're te mi 'ki o 'mɔ ɾo
                                   Soccorretemi, ch'io moro
                                   Help me, as I am dying

sok: ko 're te mi   sok: ko 're te mi   'ki o   'mɔ ɾo
Soccorretemi,   **soccorretemi,**   **ch'io**   **moro!**
help me   help me   [that] I   I die
Help me, help me – I am dying!

'ɔk: ki   'bɛl: li   o   'di o   pje 'ta
Occhi   **belli,** **oh** **Dio,** **pietà!**
eyes   beautiful   oh   God   pity
Beautiful eyes, – oh God, – have pity!

ne ge 're te   'vo i   ri 'stɔ ɾo   a   ki   per   'vo i   pjan 'dʒɛn do   a   mo 'rir   va
Negherete **voi** **ristoro** **a** **chi** **per** **voi** **piangendo** **a** **morir** **va?**
you will deny you   relief   to   one who for   you   weeping   to   dying   goes
Will you deny relief to one who, weeping for you, is going to die?

| **[16]** *ends here; the other prints continue:* |

il   ti 'mor   la   dʒe lo 'zi a   mi   kon 'du ko no   'al: la   'mɔr te
Il **timor,** **la** **gelosia**   **mi** **conducono**   **alla**   **morte;**
the   fear   the   jealousy   me   lead   to the   death
Fear and jealousy lead me to death;

dʒa   del   'se no   'a pron   le   'pɔr te   per   ke   'fug: ga   'lal ma   'mi a | *per che =* |
già **del** **seno** **apron** **le** **porte,** **per** **che** **fugga** **l'alma**   **mia.** | *(mod.) perché* |
already of the   breast   open   the   doors   for   that   may flee   the soul   mine
they are already opening the doors of my breast, so that my soul may flee.

'ɔk: ki   'bɛl: li   e   ke   sa 'ri a   se   in   'tan to   'dwɔ lo   un   'gwar do   'so lo | *saria =* |
Occhi **belli,** **e** **che** **saria,** **se** **in** **tanto** **duolo** **un** **guardo** **solo** | *sarebbe* |
eyes   beautiful   [and] what   it would be if   in   so much   grief   one   glance   only
mi   vol 'dʒe ste   per   mer 'tʃe
mi **volgeste**   **per** **mercé!**
to me   you would turn for   mercy
Beautiful eyes, what would happen if, in my great sorrow, you would turn just one merciful glance to me?

a   non   tar 'da te   o i 'mɛ   ke   mut: 'tʃi de   il   gran   mar 'tɔ ɾo
Ah, **non** **tardate,** **ohimè,** **ché** **m'uccide**   **il** **gran** **martoro!**
ah   not   delay   alas   because me kills   the   great   agony
Ah, do not delay, alas, as the great agony is killing me!

la   spe 'ran tsa   zbi got: 'ti ta   per   fud: 'dʒir   a   'pron te   'la le
La **speranza**   **sbigottita**   **per** **fuggir**   **ha** **pronte** **l'ale,**
the   hope   dismayed   for   to fly   has   ready   the wing
My dismayed hope has its wings poised for flight,

per 'ke   've de   ke   mor 'ta le   ɛ   del   'fjan ko   la   fe 'ɾi ta
perché **vede,**   **che** **mortale**   **è** **del** **fianco** **la** **ferita.**
because   it sees   that   mortal   is   of the   hip   the   wound
for it sees that my wound is mortal.

'ɔk: ki 'bɛl: li e ki ma 'i ta
Occhi belli, e chi m'aita?
eyes beautiful [and] who me helps
Beautiful eyes, who will help me?

'kru di sa 're te se ne ge 're te un sol 'gwar do per mer 'tʃe
Crudi sarete, se negherete un sol guardo per mercé!
cruel you will be if you will deny one only glance for mercy
You will be cruel if you deny just one merciful glance!

❧

[68]   *Domenico Benigni*

swo ne 'ra 'lul ti ma 'trom ba
Suonerà l'ultima tromba
The last trumpet will sound

swo ne 'ra 'lul ti ma 'trom ba ne vi 'pen sa no i mor 'ta li
Suonerà l'ultima tromba; né vi pensano i mortali.
will sound the last trumpet not of it think the mortals
The last trumpet will sound, and mortal beings are not thinking about it.

a la 'mɔr te al 'tɛr go 'la li e dap: per 'tut: to il 'no me 'su o rim 'bom ba
Ha la morte al tergo l'ali, e dappertutto il nome suo rimbomba.
has the death at the back the wings and on all sides the name her resounds
Death has wings on her back, and her name resounds on all sides.

o da kwal 'tʃe ka 'nu be 'ɛ gri vi 'vɛn ti sof: 'fu ska il 'vɔ stro 'kɔ ɾe
Oh da qual cieca nube, egri viventi, s'offusca il vostro core?
oh from what blind cloud weak living ones clouds over the your heart
Oh, by what blind cloud are your hearts darkened, you weak living beings?

sa tʃa 'skun ke si 'mɔ ɾe ne si 'trɔ va fra 'no i ki ne pa 'vɛn ti
Sa ciascun che si more; né si trova fra noi chi ne paventi.
knows each one that one dies not is found among us one who of it may be afraid
Each of us knows that he must die; there is not one among us who is afraid of it.

son do 'mɛ sti tʃi spa 'vɛn ti i ter: 'ro ɾi 'del: la 'mɔr te kre 'doɲ: 'ɲwɔm da 've ɾe in 'sɔr te
Son' domestici spaventi i terrori della morte; cred' ogn'uom d'avere in sorte
are common frights the terrors of the death believes each man of to have in destiny

'vi ver pju deʎ: ʎe le 'men ti pur non 'pas: sa no mo 'men ti ki se 'pol kri a 'pɛr ti 'so no
viver più degl'elementi; pur non passano momenti ch'i sepolchri aperti sono;
to live more than the elements yet not pass moments that the sepulchres opened are
The terrors of death are everyday fears; each man believes it is his destiny to live longer than the elements,
yet no moments pass in which sepulchres are opened;

> *The four elements (earth, air, fire, and water) were commonly represented by the various deities who had domain over them.*

e men 'tri o ko 'zi ra 'dʒo no 'kwan ti an 'dran 'mɔr ti 'al: la 'tom ba
e mentr'io così ragiono, quanti andran' morti alla tomba?
and while I thus I reason how many will be going dead ones to the tomb
and while I am thinking this way, how many will die and go to the tomb?

ke 'no i sjam 'tʃe ne ɾe e 'pol ve ke 'bre ve ɛ 'kwe sta 'vi ta
Che noi siam' cenere e polve, che breve è questa vita,
that we are ashes and dust that brief is this life
That we are ashes and dust, that this life is brief,

> *polve =*
> *(mod.)*
> *polvere*

kal	dʒi 'rar	di	po 'ko re	il	tʃɛl	dis: 'sɔl ve	la	va ni 'ta
ch'al	**girar**	**di**	**poch'ore,**	**il**	**ciel**	**dissolve**	**la**	**vanità,**
that at the	turning	of	few hours	the	heaven	dissolves	the	vanity

that at the turning of a few hours heaven dispels the vanity

si	fol: le 'men te	'am bi ta	si sa	kɛ	ve ri 'ta	'ʃe za	da	'tʃe li
sì	**follemente**	**ambita;**	**si sa**	**ch'è**	**verità,**	**scesa**	**da**	**cieli.**
so	foolishly	coveted	one knows	that it is	truth	descended	from	heavens

so foolishly coveted... – it is known that these are truths sent down from the heavens.

e	pur	'soɲ: ɲi	par: 'ra	'ki o	vi	ri 've li
E	**pur**	**sogni**	**parrà**	**ch'io**	**vi**	**riveli:**
and	yet	dreams	it will seem	which I	to you	may reveal

And yet it will seem that what I reveal to you are dreams:

ke	'kwan to	ɛ	di	'va go	a	'kre du la	'dʒen te
Che	**quanto**	**è**	**di**	**vago**	**a**	**credula**	**gente**
that	what	is	of	desirous	to	credulous	people

That what is pleasing to credulous people

ɛ	'sem pli tʃe	im: 'ma go	dun	'bɛ ne	ap: pa 'rɛn te
è	**semplice**	**immago**	**d'un**	**bene**	**apparente.**
is	simply	image	of a	good	apparent

is merely the image of a seeming good...

ke	'kwan to	ri 'splɛn de	neʎ: 'ʎɔ stri	dun	'vol to	da	'brɛ vi	vi 'tʃɛn de
Che	**quanto**	**risplende**	**negl'ostri**	**d'un**	**volto**	**da**	**brevi**	**vicende**
that	what	shines	in the purples	of a	face	by	brief	alterations

That what glows in rosy cheeks *[made-up with purple tints, from oysters]* is, in a brief time,

neʎ: 'ʎom bre	ɛ	se 'pol te
negl'ombre	**è**	**sepolte.**
in the shadows	is	buried

buried in the shadows...

ke a	'rɛd: dʒa	for 'tu na	din 'vit: to	mo 'nar ka	kru 'dɛl	im por 'tu na	non	'tʃe de	la	'par ka
Che a	**reggia**	**fortuna**	**d'invitto**	**monarca**	**crudel',**	**importuna**	**non**	**cede**	**la**	**Parca.**
that to	royal	fortune	of invincible	monarch	cruel	troublesome	not	yields	the	Fate

That cruel, troublesome Fate does not yield to the royal fortunes of an invincible monarch.

par 'la te	'vo i	par 'la te	ka 'da ve ri	se 'pol ti	e	'kon tro	'no i	ri 'vɔl ti
Parlate	**voi,**	**parlate**	**cadaveri**	**sepolti,**	**e**	**contro**	**noi**	**rivolti,**
speak	you	speak	corpses	buried	and	toward	us	turned

spet: 'ta ko li	dor: 'ror	'lɔs: sa	mo 'stra te
spettacoli	**d'orror',**	**l'ossa**	**mostrate.**
spectacles	of horror	the bones	show

Speak – speak, you buried corpses; and, turned toward us, spectacles of horror, show your bones.

par 'la te	'vo i	par 'la te	e	'di te	fra	pja 'tʃe ri	'kwan ti	'dʒat: tʃo no	kwi	tras: 'sar
Parlate	**voi,**	**parlate,**	**e**	**dite,**	**fra**	**piaceri**	**quanti**	**giacciono**	**qui**	**trassar**
speak	you	speak	and	say	among	pleasures	how many	are lying	here	passed

la	'vi ta	di	dʒo ven 'tu	fjo 'ri ta	spe 'ran do	al	'vol to	lor	'se ko li	in 'te ri
la	**vita**	**di**	**gioventù**	**fiorita,**	**sperando**	**al**	**volto**	**lor**	**secoli**	**interi.**
the	life	of	youth	flowered	hoping	at the	turn	their	centuries	entire

Speak, you – speak, and tell how many who are lying here passed their lives, blossomed with youth, among pleasures, hoping in their turn to live for whole centuries.

trassar = trassarono ("trassare" = "transitare")

'mɔr te	al	fin	tra	kwe 'stom bre	'ɛk: ko	ʎin 'vɔl ve
Morte	**al**	**fin**	**tra**	**quest'ombre**	**ecco**	**gl'involve,**
death	at the	end	among	these shadows	here	them envelops

In the end, death envelops them here among these shadows,

e	non	're sta	di	'lo ɾo	'al tro	ke	'pol ve
e	**non**	**resta**	**di**	**loro**	**altro**	**che**	**polve.**
and	not	remains	of	them	other	than	dust

and there remains of them nothing but dust.

in	fre ske 'ta	'kwe i	ke	si 'fi da no	mal	si kon 'fi da no
In	**fresch'età**	**quei**	**che**	**si fidano**	**mal**	**si confidano;**
in	young age	those	who	trust	badly	open their hearts

In youth those who trust open up their hearts unwisely;

dʒo 'ir	si 'kre da no	ma	'pɔ i	sav: 've da no	ke	va ni 'ta
gioir	**si credano**	**ma**	**poi**	**s'avvedano**	**ch'è**	**vanità.**
to enjoy	themselves believe	but	then	they realize	that it is	vanity

they think they're enjoying themselves, but then they realize that it is vanity.

dun	'so lo	di	'kwe i	ke	si 'pɛn ta no	non	si di 'spɛn sa no
D'un	**solo**	**dì**	**quei**	**che**	**si pentano**	**non**	**si dispensano.**
of one	single	day	those	who	may repent	not	are absolved

Those who may repent are not absolved of a single day [of Purgatory].

'lo ɾe	ke	'sɔ na no	'sɛm pre	vin 'tɔ na no	'vi ver	ko 'zi
L'ore	**che**	**sonano**	**sempre**	**v'intonano**	**viver**	**così.**
the hours	which	sound	always	you attune	to live	thus

The hours which ring out always attune you so to live.

'jɛ ɾi	dʒa	fu	'ko me	vi	'las: sa no	'ʎan: ni	ke	'pas: sa no
Ieri	**già**	**fu;**	**come**	**vi**	**lassano**	**gl'anni**	**che**	**passano.**
yesterday	already	was	how	you	leave	the years	which	pass

Yesterday is gone; how the passing years leave you!

> *lassano: from the verb "lassare," = "lasciare"*

le	'tom be	in 'seɲ: ɲa no	ke	mal	sim 'peɲ: ɲa no	'lal me	kwa	dʒu
Le	**tombe**	**insegnano**	**che**	**mal**	**s'impegnano**	**l'alme**	**qua**	**giù.**
the	tombs	teach	that	badly	are engaged	the souls	here	below

The tombs teach that the souls down here are badly utilized.

'i o	dal: 'lɔs: sa	se 'pol te	e	in tʃe ne 'ri te	'tʃer ko	ri 'trar	kon 'siʎ: ʎo
Io,	**dall'ossa**	**sepolte**	**e**	**incenerite,**	**cerco**	**ritrar'**	**consiglio**
I	from the bones	buried	and	reduced to ashes	I seek	to obtain	advice

I, from the bones buried and reduced to ashes, seek to find advice

per	'lal me	non	pen 'ti te
per	**l'alme**	**non**	**pentite.**
for	the souls	not	repentant

for unrepentant souls.

e	'pu ɾe	in	'va no	'kjɛ do	a 'ju to	lon 'ta no
E	**pure**	**in**	**vano**	**chiedo**	**aiuto**	**lontano,**
and	yet	in	vain	I call for	help	distant

And yet I call in vain to afar for help,

se fre 'kwɛn ti kwa dʒu 'so no i pe 'riʎ: ʎi
se frequenti qua giù sono i perigli.
if frequent here below are the perils
as the perils down here are many.

a 'mi ko a 'ku i pɔ 'kan tsi su le 'gwan tʃe fjo 'ri van li 'gu stri e 'rɔ ze
Amico, a cui poc'anzi su le guancie fiorivan ligustri e rose,
friend at whom a short while ago upon the cheeks blossomed privets and roses
Friend, upon whose cheeks just a short while ago bloomed privet and roses [i.e., the white of privet
flowers and the pink of roses],

tra ʎin fe 'li tʃi a 'van tsi 'du na 'mɔr te kru 'dɛl le 'mɛm bra a 'sko zi
tra gl'infelici avanzi, d'una morte crudel le membra ascosi.
among the unfortunate remains of a death cruel the limbs I concealed
I hid your limbs among the unfortunate remains of a cruel death.

'a i ke ve 'du to e 'zɛm pjo non 'va le a 'mɔ ver 'lem pjo
Ahi, che veduto esempio non vale a mover' l'empio,
alas [that] seen example not has influence to to move the impious one
Alas, the shown example does not move the impious one,

ke ne 'fal: li se 'pol to in 'va ɾje 'for me
che ne' falli sepolto in varie forme.
who in the sins buried in various forms
who [is] buried in sins of various kinds.

ben 'ke il 'tʃɛ lo lo 'de sti kon av: 'vi zi fu 'nɛ sti
Benché il cielo lo desti con avvisi funesti,
although the heaven him may arouse with warnings deadly
Though heaven may arouse him with dire warnings,

dal le 'tar go 'de i 'vit: tsi op: 'prɛs: so 'dɔr me
dal letargo dei vizi oppresso, dorme.
from the lethargy of the vices oppressed sleeps
he sleeps, oppressed in the lethargy of his vices.

GL: **Parca**

&

[39] *Domenico Benigni*

zven 'tu ɾa kwɔr 'mi o
Sventura, cuor mio
Alas, my heart

zven 'tu ɾa kwɔr 'mi o non vɛ pju kon 'fɔr to
Sventura, cuor mio; non v'è più conforto.
misfortune heart mine non there is more comfort
Alas, my heart: there is no more comfort.

ne 'vi vo ne 'mɔr to mi 'laʃ: ʃa il de 'zi o
Né vivo, né morto mi lascia il desio,
neither alive nor dead me leaves the desire
Desire leaves me neither alive nor dead;

la 'spɛ me si o 'bli o al: 'la spra 'mi a 'doʎ: ʎa ak: 'kreʃ: ʃe il mar 'tɔ ɾo
la speme, si oblio all'aspra mia doglia accresce il martoro.
the hope if I forget to the bitter my grief increases the agony

speme (lit.) = *speranza*	

hope, if I forget, increases the agony of my cruel pain.

non   sɔ   ke   mi   'vɔʎ: ʎa
Non   so,   che   mi   voglia.
not   I know what   to me is wanting
I know not what I want.

    non   sɔ   ke   mi   'vɔʎ: ʎa   sɔ   bɛn   ke   mi 'mɔ ɾo
Chorus: **Non   so   che   mi   voglia,   so   ben   che   mi moro.**
    not   I know what   to me is wanting I know well that I am dying
  I know not what I want, [but] I know well that I am dying.

      | *var. at the end:* **ch'io mi moro** ['ki o mi 'mɔ ɾo] (same translation) |

ma   'sɛm pre   mofː 'fɛn de   un   'nɔ bil   pen 'sjɛ ɾo   e   'si o   mi di 'spɛ ɾo
Ma   sempre   m'offende   un   nobil   pensiero,   e   s'io   mi dispero
but   always   me strikes   a   noble   thought   and   if I   I despair
Yet a noble thought always strikes me; and if I despair

  a 'mor   non   min 'tɛn de
  Amor   non   m'intende.
  Love   not   me hears
  Love does not hear me.

'ma i   mi   difː 'fɛn de   da   stral   ke   si 'ʃɔʎ: ʎa
Mai   mi   diffende   da   stral,   che   si scioglia,
never   me   defends   from   arrow   which   may come loose
He never defends me from the arrow which is loosed

  'dalː li   'ɔkː ki   ka 'do ɾo
  dalli   occhi   ch'adoro.
  by the   eyes   which I adore
  from the eyes I adore.

              | *dalli (poet.) = dagli* |

non   sɔ   ke   mi   'vɔʎ: ʎa
Non   so,   che   mi   voglia.
not   I know what   to me is wanting
I know not what I want.

fra   'du ɾe   ka 'te ne   il   'pjan to   mɛ   'dʒɔ ko
Fra   dure   catene   il   pianto   m'è   gioco,
among   harsh   chains   the   weeping   to me is play
Among harsh chains weeping is play for me;

  dʒo 'i sko   nel   'fwɔ ko   ser 'vɛn do   il   'mi o   'bɛ ne
  gioisco   nel   fuoco   servendo   il   mio   bene.
  I delight   in the fire   serving   the   my   dear one
  I delight in the fire, serving my dear one.

ma   'pɔ i   fra   le   'pe ne   il   'pɛtː to   sin 'vɔʎ: ʎa
Ma   poi   fra   le   pene   il   petto   s'invoglia,
but   then   among the   pains   the   breast   becomes desirous
But then, among the pains, my breast becomes desirous,

  e 'di o   pju   makː 'kɔ ɾo
  ed io   più   m'accoro.
  and I   more   am heartbroken
  and I am more heartbroken.

non   sɔ   ke   mi   'voʎ: ʎa
Non   so,   che   mi   voglia.
not   I know   what   to me   is wanting
I know not what I want.

GL: **Amor**

&

Alternately titled **Vittoria, Vittoria!** or **Vittoria, Vittoria mio core!**
[4, 6, 8, 11, 19, 20, 24, 26, 30, 37, 39, 44, 54, 59, 60, 64]   *Domenico Benigni*

vit: 'tɔ ɾja   'mi o   'kɔ ɾe
Vittoria, mio core!
Victory, my heart!

vit: 'tɔ ɾja   vit: 'tɔ ɾja   'mi o   'kɔ ɾe   non   la gri 'mar   pju
Vittoria!   Vittoria,   mio   core!   Non   lagrimar   più;
victory   victory   my   heart   not   to weep   more
Victory! Victory, my heart! Weep no more;

ɛ   'ʃɔl ta   da 'mo ɾe   la   vil   ser vi 'tu   ɛ   'ʃɔl ta   da 'mo ɾe   la   ser vi 'tu
è   sciolta   d'Amore   la   vil   servitù,   è   sciolta   d'Amore   la   servitù.
is   released   of Love   the   vile   servitude   is   released   of Love   the   servitude
the miserable bondage of love is liberated – liberated is the bondage of love.

> *Many prints repeat* **"la vil servitù"** *(rather than* **"la servitù"**) *at the end of this phrase.*

dʒa   'lem pja   a   'twɔ i   'dan: ni   fra   'stwɔ lo   di   'zgwar di
Già   l'empia   a'   tuoi   danni,   fra   stuolo   di   sguardi,
before   the evil woman   to   your   harms   among   multitude   of   glances
Formerly the evil woman, to your detriment, among a multitude of glances,

kon   'vet: tsi   bu 'dʒar di   di 'spɔ ze   ʎiŋ 'gan: ni
con   vezzi   bugiardi   dispose   gl'inganni.
with   charms   lying   arranged   the deceptions
with false charms, planned the deceptions.

le   'frɔ de   ʎi af: 'fan: ni   non   'an: no   pju   'lɔ ko
Le   frode,   gli affanni   non   hanno   più   loco;
the   frauds   the anxieties   not   they have   more   place
The frauds and anxieties exist no more;

del   'kru do   'su o   'fɔ ko   ɛ   'spɛn to   lar 'do ɾe
del   crudo   suo   foco   è   spento   l'ardore!
of the   cruel   her   fire   is   extinguished   the intense heat
the flame of her cruel fire is extinguished!

> *Almost all prints continue with a 2nd verse:*

da   'lu tʃi   ri 'dɛn ti   non   'ɛʃ: ʃe   pju   'stra le
Da   luci   ridenti   non   esce   più   strale,
from   eyes   smiling   not   comes out   more   dart
From smiling eyes come no more darts

ke   'pja ga   mor 'ta le   nel   'pɛt: to   mav: 'vɛn ti
che   piaga   mortale   nel   petto   m'avventi:
which   wound   mortal   in the   breast   to me you hurl
with which you hurl a deadly wound to my breast:

nel	dwɔl	ne	tor 'men ti	'i o	pju	non	mi	'sfat: tʃo
nel	**duol,**	**ne'**	**tormenti**	**io**	**più**	**non**	**mi**	**sfaccio;**
in the	grief	in	torments	I	more	not	myself	tear apart

in grief and torment I no longer tear myself apart;

> *In some prints, "io" incorrectly appears as "Io." "Jo," which also appears occasionally, = (mod.) Io*
> *in [19]: ne = (correct) ne'*

ε	'rot: to	'oɲ: ɲi	'lat: tʃo	spa 'ri to	il	ti 'mo ɾe
è	**rotto**	**ogni**	**laccio,**	**sparito**	**il**	**timore!**
is	broken	every	noose	vanished	the	fear

broken is every tie, vanished is fear!

> *In [26] is a 3rd verse; in [19] it is printed at the bottom of the page as the 2nd verse:*

kon	'fin to	se 'ɾe no	spe 'ɾan tsa	o mi 'tʃi da	a	'mɔr te	non	'sfi da
Con	**finto**	**sereno**	**speranza**	**omicida**	**a**	**morte**	**non**	**sfida.**
with	feinged	calm	hope	murderous	to	death	not	defies

With false calm, murderous hope does not defy death.

> *sereno = (mod.) serenità*
> *printed in [26] is "Amor te" = (correct) "a morte"*

> *var. in [19]:*

kon	'spir to	se 'ɾe no	spe 'ɾan tsa	o mi 'tʃi da	a	'mɔr te	mi	'sfi da
Con	**spirto**	**sereno**	**speranza**	**omicida**	**a**	**morte**	**mi**	**sfida.**
with	spirit	calm	hope	murderous	to	death	me	challenges

With calm spirit murderous hope challenges me to death.

pju	'la ni ma	in	'se no	dʒa	'fud: dʒe	vjen 'me no
Più	**l'anima**	**in**	**seno**	**già**	**fugge**	**vien meno**
[more]	the soul	in	breast	already	flees	fails

The soul in my breast is fleeing, is failing;

e	'zdeɲ: ɲo	e	ra 'dʒo ne	fra	'lar mi	in	ten 'tso ne	tri 'on fa	la 'mo ɾe
e	**sdegno,**	**e**	**ragione**	**fra**	**l'armi**	**in**	**tenzone**	**trionfa**	**l'Amore.**
and	anger	and	reason	among	the weapons	in	conflict	triumphs	the Love

and among the battling weapons – anger and reason – Love triumphs.

> *In order to make sense of this, I've changed the printed "è" to "e" and the printed "d"("d'Amore") to "l" ("l'Amore").*

> *var. in [19]:*

e	zdeɲ: 'ɲa ta	ka 'dʒo ne	fra	'lar mi	in	ten 'tso ne	tri 'on fa	la 'mo ɾe
e	**sdegnata**	**cagione**	**fra**	**l'armi**	**in**	**tenzone**	**trionfa**	**l'Amore.**
and	angry	cause	among	the weapons	in	conflict	triumphs	the Love

and [in its] angry cause among the battling weapons, Love triumphs.

> *As above, I've changed the printed "d'Amore" to "l'Amore."*

GL: **Amore**

Cavalli, Francesco [Caletti-Bruni] (1602-1676)

Born in Crema, his father Giovanni Battista Caletti (known also as Bruni) provided his early musical instruction. Impressed by Francesco's singing and musical accomplishments, Federico Cavalli, governor of Crema from 1614 to 1616, took him to Venice and the choir of S. Marco there; as was a custom, the Cavalli (sponsor's) surname was adopted.

During Cavalli's early years at S. Marco the music was directed by Monteverdi, with whom he most likely studied; his association with S. Marco continued for the rest of his life. In 1665 he was finally granted the post of first organist there, and in 1668 he became *maestro di cappella*.

Cavalli's opera *Le nozze di Teti e di Peleo (1639)* was the first of more than forty operas for which he was acclaimed and upon which his reputation as a historically significant Italian opera composer is based. His opera *Giasone (1648)* became, according to *Grove*, the most frequently performed opera of the seventeenth century.

Cavalli's extant sacred works are probably only a small portion of those he composed during his career.

[10, 19, 43, 45]
from: *Serse [Xerse] (1654)*
character: *Clito*

Nicolò Minato

af: 'fe mi 'fa te 'ri de ɾe
Affé, mi fate ridere
Really, you make me laugh

	af: 'fe	mi	'fa te	'ri de ɾe	a	a
Refrain:	**Affé,**	**mi**	**fate**	**ridere**	**ah....**	**ah!**
	in faith	me	you make	to laugh	ah	ah!

Really, you make me laugh – ha ha!

alt.: A fè = Affé

a mo 'ro zi	laʃ: ʃi 'vet: ti	'doɲ: ɲi	'da ma	ke	mi 'ra te	vin fjam: 'ma te
Amorosi	**lascivetti**	**d'ogni**	**dama**	**che**	**mirate**	**v'infiammate.**
amorous	little lustful ones	of every	lady	whom	you see	you burst into flames

Amorous little lustful ones, you are inflamed by every lady you see.

'ko me	in	'tʃen to	af: 'fɛt: ti	un	sol	kɔr	si	pwɔ	di 'vi de ɾe
Come	**in**	**cento**	**affetti**	**un**	**sol**	**cor**	**si**	**può**	**dividere?**
how	in	hundred	affections	one	only	heart	itself	is able	to divide

How can a single heart be divided among a hundred affections?

Here, in [19], is included a line – an "aside" – sung by the character Amastre:

e	skal 'tri to	ko 'stu i	'tʃer to	ɛ	di	'kor te
E	**scaltrito**	**costui**	**certo**	**è**	**di**	**corte.**
[and]	clever	he	certainly	is	of	court

He is certainly shrewd about the ways of the court.

vim pri 'dʒo na	viɲ ka 'te na	'oɲ: ɲi	krin	kun	'pɔ ko	a 'dor no	'va da	in 'tor no
V'imprigiona,	**v'incatena**	**ogni**	**crin**	**ch'un**	**poco**	**adorno**	**vada**	**intorno.**
you imprisons	you enchains	every	head of hair	that a	little	adorned	goes	around

Every head of hair *[every woman's tresses]* going around, however little made up *[decorated with ornaments]*, imprisons you and enchains you.

da	bel 'ta	ve 'du ta	ap: 'pe na	vi laʃ: 'ʃa te	il	kɔr	di 'vi de ɾe
Da	**beltà**	**veduta**	**appena**	**vi lasciate**	**il**	**cor**	**dividere.**
by	beauty	seen	scarcely	yourself you let	the	heart	to divide

By just a glimpse of beauty you allow your heart to be split.

alt. in [19, 43]:
... **il cor uccidere** [ut: 'tʃi de ɾe]
= ...your heart to be killed.

❧

[45]
from: *Serse [Xerse] (1654)*
character: *Periarco*

Nicolò Minato

be 'a to ki pwɔ
Beato chi può
Fortunate is the one who is able

be 'a to	ki	pwɔ	lon 'tan	'del: le	'kor ti	go 'der	'kwel: le	'sɔr ti
Beato	**chi**	**può**	**lontan**	**delle**	**corti**	**goder**	**quelle**	**sorti**
fortunate	who	is able	far away	from the	courts	to enjoy	those	destinies

Fortunate is the one who is able, far away from the palaces, to enjoy the destiny

kil	tʃɛl	li	do 'nɔ
ch'il	**ciel**	**li**	**donò.**
which the	heaven	to him	gave

heaven has bestowed on him.

li = (mod.) gli

tʃer 'kan do   si va   i   fjor   tra   le   'spi ne
Cercando   si va   i   fior   tra   le   spine,
Searching for   he goes   the   flowers   among   the   thorns
He searches for flowers among the thorns,

e   in 'tan to   di   'bri ne   tʃi   'spar dʒe   le 'ta
e   intanto   di   brine   ci   sparge   l'età.
and   meanwhile   of   frosts   there   it sheds   the age
and meanwhile age scatters frost *[the white hair of old age]* upon him.

&

[26]
from: *Eritrea (1652)*   *Giovanni Faustini*

ki   si   'paʃ: ʃe
Chi si pasce
He who is nourished

ki   si 'paʃ: ʃe   di   spe 'ran tsa   'sɛm pre   in   'kor te   sten te 'ra
Chi   si pasce   di   speranza   sempre   in   corte   stenterà.
the one who   feeds   on   hope   always   in   courtship   will have difficulty
He who is nourished by hope will always have difficulty in courtship.

se   si 'man dʒa   il   'frut: to   in 'ɛr ba
Se   si mangia   il   frutto   in erba
if   one eats   the   fruit   green
If one eats unripe fruit,

la   for 'tu na   'sɛm pre   a 'tʃer ba   la   'su a   'mɛs: se   ven de 'ra
la   fortuna   sempre   acerba   la   sua   messe   venderà.
the   fortune   always   unripe   the   its   harvest   will sell
fortune will always sell its harvest while still green.

&

[5, 9, 19]
from: *Giasone (1648)*   *Giacinto Andrea Cicognini*

de 'lit: tsje   kon 'tɛn te
Delizie contente
Pleasing delights

de 'lit: tsje   kon 'tɛn te   ke   'lal ma   be 'a te   fer 'ma te
Delizie   contente   che   l'alma   beate   fermate.
delights   pleasing   that   the soul   you make happy   stop
Pleasing delights, you who make the soul happy, stop.

su   'kwe sto   'mi o   'kɔ re   dɛ   pju   non   stil: 'la te   le   'dʒɔ je   da 'mo re
Su   questo   mio   core   deh   più   non   stillate   le   gioie   d'amore.
on   this   my   heart   ah   more   not   drip   the   joys   of love
Ah, upon this heart of mine no longer trickle the joys of love.

de 'lit: tsje   'mi e   'ka re   fer 'ma te vi   kwi   non   sɔ   pju   bra 'ma re
Delizie   mie   care,   fermatevi   qui;   non   so   più   bramare,
delights   mine   dear   stop you   here   not   I know how   more   to desire
My dear delights, stop here. I know not how to desire anymore;

mi   'ba sta   ko 'zi
mi   basta   così.
to me   is enough   like this
this is enough for me.

in   'grɛm bo   'aʎ: ʎi   a 'mo ɾi   fra   'dol tʃi   ka 'te ne   mo 'rir   mi   kon 'vjɛ ne
In   grembo   agli   amori   fra   dolci   catene,   morir   mi   conviene.
in   lap   of the   loves   among   sweet   chains   to die   to me is better
In the lap of love, among sweet chains, it is better for me to die.

> *in* [19]: *agl'amori*
> [aʎ: ʎa 'mo ɾi]
> = *agli amori*

dol 'tʃet: tsa   o mi 'tʃi da   a   'mɔr te   mi   'gwi da   in   'brat: tʃo   al   'mi o   'bɛ ne
Dolcezza   omicida,   a   morte   mi   guida   in   braccio   al   mio   bene.
sweetness   murderous   to   death   me   guide   into arms   to the my   dear one
Murderous sweetness, lead me to death in the arms of my dear one.

> *in* [19]: *dolcezz'omicida*
> [dol 'tʃet: tso mi 'tʃi da]
> = *dolcezza omicida*

☙

[30, 32, 44]
from: *Giasone (1648)*
character: *Medea*

Giacinto Andrea Cicognini

del: 'lan tro   'ma dʒi ko
Dell'antro magico
Of the magical cave

del: 'lan tro   'ma dʒi ko   stri 'dɛn ti   'kar di ni   il   'var ko   a 'pri te mi
Dell'antro   magico   stridenti   cardini   il   varco   apritemi
of the cave   magical   shrieking   hinges   the opening   open to me
Open to me, shrieking hinges, the passage to the magical cave

e   fra   le   'tɛ ne bre   del   'ne gro   os 'pit: tsjo   laʃ: 'ʃa te mi
e   fra   le   tenebre   del   negro   ospizio   lasciatemi.
and   among the   darknesses   of the black   abode   leave me
and leave me in the darkness of the black abode.

> *"le tenebri"* is printed;
> correct is *"le tenebre"*

sul: 'lar ka   or: 'ri bi le   del   'la go   'sti dʒo   i   'fwɔ ki   'splɛn di no
Sull'arca   orribile   del   lago   Stigio   i   fuochi   splendino
on the coffer   horrible   of the lake   Stygian   the fires   let sparkle
On the horrible coffer of the Stygian lake let the fires sparkle

e   su   ne   'man di no   'fu mi   ke   'tur bi no   la   'lu tʃe   al   di
e   su   ne   mandino   fumi   che   turbino   la   luce   al   dì.
and   above of it let send   fumes   which let cloud   the   light   to the day
and send up fumes which will cloud the light of day.

GL: **Stigio**

☙

[57]

dis: ser: 'ra te vi a me
Disserratevi a me
Open yourselves to me

dis: ser: 'ra te vi   a   me   pro 'fon di   a 'bis: si   ke   la   'vɔ stra   fe ɾi 'ta
Disserratevi   **a**   **me,**   **profondi**   **abissi,**   **ché**   **la**   **vostra**   **ferità**
open yourselves   to   me   deep   abysses   because   the   your   *(lit.)* cruelty
Open yourselves to me, deep abysses, for your cruelty,

al par di   tal   ri 'gor   sa 'ra   'dol tʃe   pje 'ta
al par di   **tal**   **rigor**   **sarà**   **dolce**   **pietà.**
as equal to   such   severity   it will be   sweet   mercy
compared to such severity, will be sweet mercy.

del   sol   i   'rad: dʒi   dɔr   'njɛ gi   'al: le   'lu tʃi   'mi e   per 'pɛ tu a   e 'klis: si
Del   **sol**   **i**   **raggi**   **d'or**   **nieghi**   **alle**   **luci**   **mie**   **perpetua**   **eclissi.**
of the   sun   the   rays   of gold   let deny   to the   eyes   mine   perpetual   eclipse
Let an everlasting eclipse deny my eyes the golden rays of the sun.

> *nieghi: from "niegare" = (mod.) negare*

se   le   'stel: le   al   'mi o   dwɔl   'pa jon   di   'sas: so   e   non   vɛ   pje 'ta
Se   **le**   **stelle**   **al**   **mio**   **duol**   **paion**   **di**   **sasso**   **e**   **non**   **v'è**   **pietà**
if   the   stars   to the   my   sorrow   seem   of   stone   and   not   there is   pity
If the stars seem hard as stone to my sorrow and there is no pity

per   me   nem: 'men   de   'mjɛ i   mar 'tir   'pɔs: so   spe 'rar   mer 'tʃe
per   **me,**   **nemmen**   **de'**   **miei**   **martir**   **posso**   **sperar**   **mercé,**
for   me   neither   from the   my   agony   I am able   to hope for   mercy
for me, neither can I hope for mercy in my agony;

se   per   'far mi   laŋ 'gwir   'so no   e 'tɛr ni   ri 'go ɾi   in   tʃɛl   pre 'fis: si
se   **per**   **farmi**   **languir**   **sono**   **eterni**   **rigori**   **in**   **ciel**   **prefissi,**
if   in order to   to make me   to languish   are   eternal   rigors   in   heaven   predestined
if eternal rigors are predestined in heaven to make me languish,

dis: ser: 'ra te vi   a   me   pro 'fon di   a 'bis: si
disserratevi   **a**   **me,**   **profondi**   **abissi!**
open yourselves   to   me   deep   abysses
open yourselves to me, deep abysses!

↊

[24, 48]

'dol tʃe a 'mor ben 'da to 'di o
Dolce Amor, bendato dio
Sweet Love, blindfolded god

'dol tʃe   a 'mor   ben 'da to   'di o   non   mi   far   pju   so spi 'ɾar   a
Dolce   **Amor,**   **bendato**   **dio,**   **non**   **mi**   **far**   **più**   **sospirar,**   **ah!**
sweet   Love   blindfolded   god   not   me   to make   more   to sigh   ah
Sweet Love, blindfolded god *[Cupid]*, do not make me sigh anymore – ah!

il   'tu o   'dar do   'si a   'la sta   da 'kil: le
Il   **tuo**   **dardo**   **sia**   **l'asta**   **d'Achille,**
il   your   arrow   may be   the javelin   of Achilles
May your arrow be [as infallible as] Achilles' javelin,

ke   mi   'sa ni   la   'pja ga   del   kɔr
che   **mi**   **sani**   **la**   **piaga**   **del**   **cor!**
which   me   may heal   the   wound   of the   heart
which will heal my heart's wound!

o	kol	'lu tʃi do	ri 'gor	'tʃɛ ko	ar 'tʃer	di	'du e	pu 'pil: le
O	**col**	**lucido**	**rigor**	**cieco**	**arcier**	**di**	**due**	**pupille,**
or	with the	shining	harshness	blind	archer	of	two	eyes

'kwe sto	sen	non	sa et: 'tar		a	'kwe sto	kɔr	non	sa et: 'tar
questo	**sen**	**non**	**saettar,**		**ah,**	**questo**	**cor**	**non**	**saettar!**
this	breast	not	to shoot with an arrow		ah	this	heart	not	to shoot with an arrow

Or [else], o blind archer, do not pierce this breast; ah, do not pierce this heart with the shining hardness of two eyes!

	non	sa et: 'tar		a	'kwe sto	sen	non	sa et: 'tar	nɔ
var.	**non**	**saettar,**		**ah,**	**questo**	**sen**	**non**	**saettar,**	**no.**
in [48]:	not	to shoot with an arrow		ah	this	breast	not	to shoot with an arrow	no

...[do] not pierce this breast; ah, do not pierce this breast – no.

𝒢ℒ: **Achille, Amor**

❧

[20, 24, 27]

don 'dzɛl: le fud: 'dʒi te
Donzelle, fuggite
Damsels, flee

don 'dzɛl: le	fud: 'dʒi te	pro 'ka tʃe	bel 'ta	fud: 'dʒi te	fud: 'dʒi te	fud: 'dʒi te
Donzelle,	**fuggite**	**procace**	**beltà!**	**Fuggite,**	**fuggite,**	**fuggite!**
damsels	flee	provocative	beauty	flee	flee	flee

> *var. in [27]:*
> ... **lasciva beltà.**
> [laʃ: 'ʃi va bel 'ta]
> = ... lustful beauty.

Damsels, flee from provocative beauty! Flee, flee, flee!

se	'lu tʃi do	'zgwar do	vi	'pɛ ne tra	il	'kɔ ɾe
Se	**lucido**	**sguardo**	**vi**	**penetra**	**il**	**core,**
if	bright	glance	you	penetrates	the	heart,

> *in [27]:*
> cor = core

If a bright glance penetrates your heart,

laʃ: 'ʃa te	kwel	'dar do	del	'pɛr fi do	a 'mo ɾe
lasciate	**quel**	**dardo**	**del**	**perfido**	**amore,**
leave	that	arrow	of the	perfidious	love

> *in [27]:*
> amor = amore

let go of that arrow of perfidious love

ke	in 'si dje	skal 'tri te	tra 'man do	vi 'sta
che	**insidie**	**scaltrite**	**tramando**	**vi sta!**
which	snares	cunning	scheming	there lies

> *var. in [27]:*
> ... **vi va.** [vi 'va]
> = there goes
> (same translation)

which is scheming cunning deceptions!

❧

[26]
from: *Eritrea (1652)*

Giovanni Faustini

gran pat: 'tsi a
Gran pazzia
Great folly

gran	pat: 'tsi a	lin: na mo 'ɾar si	'sɛn to	i	'sad: dʒi	a	dir	ko 'zi
Gran	**pazzia**	**l'innamorarsi**	**sento**	**i**	**saggi**	**a**	**dir**	**così.**
great	folly	the falling in love	I hear	the	sages	to	to say	thus

Falling in love is great folly, I hear the sages say.

si so 'spi ɾa   'nɔt: te   e   di   ma   kon 'vjɛn   'pɔ i   di spe 'ɾar si
Si sospira   notte   e   dì   ma   convien   poi   disperarsi?
one sighs   night   and   day   but   it is reasonable   then   to despair
People sigh night and day; but is it reasonable, then, to despair?

❧

[26]
from: *Eritrea (1652)*   *Giovanni Faustini*

in a 'mor
In amor
In love

in   a 'mor   tʃi 'vwɔl   spe 'ran tsa   'al ma   'mi a   'kre di lo   a   me
In   amor   ci vuol   speranza   alma   mia   credilo   a   me.
in   love   it takes   hope   soul   mine   believe it   to   me
In love it takes hope, my soul – believe me.

a   ti 'mo ɾe   ki   a 'do ɾa   'di a 'ban do   ke   ser 'vɛn do   ta 'tʃen do   spe 'ran do
A   timore   chi   adora   dia bando   che   servendo   tacendo   sperando
to   fear   he who   adores   let give exile to   because   serving   being silent   hoping
He who adores should banish fear, because by serving, being silent, hoping,

a do 'ran do   si 'trɔ va   mer 'tʃe
adorando   si trova   mercé.
adoring   one finds   reward
[and] adoring one finds reward.

❧

[26]
from: *Eritrea (1652)*   *Giovanni Faustini*

ma le 'det: to
Maledetto
Cursed

ma le 'det: to   il   ser 'vir   e   ki   li   'pja tʃe
Maledetto   il   servir   e   chi   li   piace.
cursed   the   serving   and   one who   to him   it pleases | *li = (mod.) gli* |
Cursed be serving and whomever it pleases.

u 'no ɾa   di   'bɛ ne   'ma i   'gɔ de   ki   'sɛr ve
Un'ora   di   bene   mai   gode   chi   serve.
an hour   of   happiness   never   enjoys   he who   serves
He who serves never enjoys an hour of happiness.

daf: 'fan: ni   ka 'tɛr ve   sof: 'frir   ʎi   kon 'vjɛ ne   ne   'trɔ va   'ma i   'pa tʃe
D'affanni   caterve   soffrir   gli   conviene   né   trova   mai   pace.
of woes   masses   to suffer   for him   it is necessary   nor   he finds   ever   peace
For him it is necessary to suffer a multitude of woes and never find peace.

❧

[14, 38, 39]

son aŋ 'kor par go 'let: ta
Son ancor pargoletta
I am still a little girl

son	aŋ 'kor	par go 'let: ta	e	a 'mor	non	'prɔ vo	ma	kwal	'tɛ ne ɾa	'pjan ta
Son	**ancor**	**pargoletta**	**e**	**amor**	**non**	**provo,**	**ma**	**qual**	**tenera**	**pianta**
I am	still	little girl	and	love	not	I experience	but	what	young	plant

I am still a little girl and know not love; but what young plant

fe	la	'fɔʎ: ʎa	per 'tut: to	'sɛn tsa	fjor	'sɛn tsa	'frut: to
fe'	**la**	**foglia**	**per tutto**	**senza**	**fior,**	**senza**	**frutto.**
made	the	leaf	completely	without	flower	without	fruit

fe' =
(mod.)
feci

ever made foliage completely without flower, without fruit?

	ko 'zi	'lil: la	da 'mor	si 'ri de	e	'kan ta
Refrain:	**Così**	**Lilla**	**d'amor**	**si ride**	**e**	**canta,**
	thus	Lilla	of love	herself laughs	and	sings

Thus Lilla laughs and sings to herself about love.

The following 2nd verse is not in [14]:

'o ve	'dʒi ɾo	le	'lu tʃi	a 'man ti	'i o	'trɔ vo	ma	ko 'lu i ke
Ove	**giro**	**le**	**luci**	**amanti**	**io**	**trovo,**	**ma**	**colui che**
whereto	I turn	the	eyes	lovers	I	I find	but	the man who

Wherever I turn my eyes I find lovers; but the man who

si 'van ta	da 'ver mi	va ged: 'dʒa ta	non	ma	si 'nor	pro 'va ta
si vanta	**d'avermi**	**vagheggiata**	**non**	**m'ha**	**sinor**	**provata.**
brags about	of having me	courted	not	me has	up to now	experienced

brags about having courted me has not known me so far.

'o ve	un	'tʃen: no	mi	'kja ma	il	'vo lo	'i o	'mɔ vo
Ove	**un**	**cenno**	**mi**	**chiama**	**il**	**volo**	**io**	**movo,**
whereto	a	sign	me	calls	the	flight	I	I move

Wherever a nod beckons me, thereto I fly;

ma	kon	bal 'det: tsa	'tan ta	'ma no	aŋ 'kor	non	mi	'strin se
ma	**con**	**baldezza**	**tanta**	**mano**	**ancor**	**non**	**mi**	**strinse,**
but	with	boldness	so much	hand	yet	not	me	clasped

but with such boldness no hand has yet clasped me,

'brat: tʃo	aŋ 'kor	non	mi	'tʃin se
braccio	**ancor**	**non**	**mi**	**cinse.**
arm	yet	not	me	encircled

no arm yet embraced me.

❧

[37, 41]

Nicolò Minato

so 'spi 'ri di 'fɔ ko
Sospiri di foco
Fiery sighs

so 'spi ɾi di 'fɔ ko ke   'la u ɾe   in fjam: 'ma te   led: 'dʒɛ ɾi   vo 'la te   in 'tor no al   'mi o 'bɛ ne

Sospiri di foco, che l'aure infiammate, leggieri volate intorno al mio bene

sighs of fire who the breezes you inflame light fly around my dear one

Fiery sighs, you who inflame the breezes, fly lightly around my dear one

e   'la spre 'mi e 'pe ne nar: 'ra te ʎi un 'pɔ ko so 'spi ɾi di 'fɔ ko

e l'aspre mie pene narrategli un poco, sospiri di foco!

and the bitter my pains tell him a little sighs of fire

and tell him a little of my bitter pains, fiery sighs!

a u 'ret: te led: 'dʒɛ ɾe ku 'di te il 'mi o 'dwɔ lo por 'ta te vi a 'vo lo

Aurette leggiere, ch'udite il mio duolo, portatevi a volo

little breezes light who hear the my grief take yourselves at flight

Little light breezes, you who hear my grief, fly

> *in* [37]:
> *che udite*
> [ke u 'di te]
> = *ch'udite*

> *leggiere = (mod.) leggere*

al sen di ka 'do ɾo e 'di te 'ki o 'mo ɾo in 'dɔʎ: ʎe se 've ɾe

al sen di ch'adoro, e dite ch'io moro in doglie severe,

to the breast of who I adore and say that I I die in sufferings severe

to the breast of the one I adore and say that I am dying in deep suffering,

> *in* [37]:
> *di chi adoro*
> [di ki a 'do ɾo]
> = *di ch'adoro*

a u 'ret: te led: 'dʒɛ ɾe

aurette leggiere!

little breezes light

little light breezes!

☙

[41]   *Aurelio Aureli*

spe 'ran tse

Speranze

Hopes

spe 'ran tse 'vo i ke 'sjɛ te av: 'vet: tse a lu ziŋ 'gar

Speranze, voi, che siete avvezze a lusingar,

hopes you who you are accustomed to to to flatter

Hopes, you who are used to flattering,

dal 'se no 'mi o par 'ti te vi non mi 'sta te a iŋ gan: 'nar

dal seno mio partitevi, non mi state a ingannar!

from the breast mine leave you not to me stay to to deceive

leave my breast; do not remain to deceive me!

a nɔ fer 'ma te il 'vo lo 'vɔʎ: ʎo 'vi ver spe 'ran do e mi kon 'so lo

Ah, no, fermate il volo, voglio viver sperando e mi consolo!

ah no stop the flight I want to live hoping and myself I console

Ah, no: stop your flight! I want to live in hope, and I console myself!

'sɛn to il kɔr ke mi 'di tʃe 'sof: fri in a 'mor

Sento il cor, che mi dice: soffri in amor!

I hear the heart which to me says suffer in love

I hear my heart, which says to me: "Suffer in love!

la 'sɔr te un di mu 'ta bi le ti sa ne 'ra il do 'lor

La sorte un dì, mutabile, ti sanerà il dolor!

the fate one day changeable you will heal the pain

One day fickle fate will heal your pain!"

a   si   ˈsta te mi   in ˈse no vi tratː ˈteŋ go spe ˈran tse e   viŋ ka ˈte no
Ah, sì, statemi   in seno, vi trattengo, speranze, e v'incateno!
ah   yes remain with me in breast you I keep   hopes   and you I enchain
Ah, yes, stay in my breast; I will keep you, hopes, and I will enchain you!

❧

[55]
from: *Didone (1641)*
character: *Hecuba*

Giovanni Francesco Busenello

ˈtrɛ mu lo ˈspi ɾi to
Tremulo spirito
Trembling spirit

ˈtrɛ mu lo ˈspi ɾi to ˈflɛ bi le e   ˈlaŋ gwi do ˈɛʃː ʃi vi ˈsu bi to
Tremulo   spirito,   flebile e   languido,   escivi subito.
trembling   spirit   mournful and languid   leave you at once
Trembling spirit, mournful and languid, leave at once.

escivi: old form of "uscire"

ˈvo la ti ˈla ni ma ˈkɛ ɾe bo   ˈtor bi do ˈku pi do a ˈspɛtː ta la
Volati,   l'anima   ch'Erebo   torbido, cupido, aspetta là.
fly you   the soul   because Erebus dark   greedy   waits   there
Fly, soul, for dark and greedy Erebus awaits.

ˈpɔ ve ɾo ˈpri a mo ˈskɔr da ti ˈdɛ ku ba ˈve do va ˈmi ze ɾa
Povero   Priamo, scordati   d'Ecuba, vedova misera.
poor   Priam   forget   [of] Hecuba widow   miserable
Poor Priam, forget Hecuba, your miserable widow.

"Ecuba" is printed with the classical Greek spelling beginning with "H."

ˈka u za no ˈlul ti mo ˈɔrː ri do e ˈzil jo ˈpa ɾi de e ˈdɛ le na
Causano   l'ultimo orrido   esilio   Paride ed Elena.
they cause the final horrid   exile   Paris   and Helen
Paris and Helen cause the final terrible exile.

𝒢ℒ: Ecuba, Elena, Erebo, Paride, Priamo

❧

[24]
from: *Giasone (1648)*
character: *Delfa*

Giacinto Andrea Cicognini

ˈtrɔpː po so ˈa vi i ˈgu sti
Troppo soavi i gusti
Too sweet are the pleasures

ˈtrɔpː po so ˈa vi i   ˈgu sti a ˈmor pro ˈmetː te e   da
Troppo   soavi   i   gusti Amor   promette, e   da!
too   sweet   the tastes Love   promises   and gives
Too sweet are the pleasures Love promises and gives!

in ˈter min ˈtrɔpː po aŋ ˈgu sti di don ˈdzɛlː la lo ˈnor rakː ˈkju zo sta
In termin   troppo   angusti di donzella l'onor   racchiuso sta.
in boundaries too   narrow   of damsel   the honor contained stays
The honor of a damsel is enclosed within boundaries too narrow.

ˈspe ɾi del   mar spu ˈman te rakː ˈkɔʎː ʎer ˈlon da in sen
Speri   del   mar spumante   raccoglier l'onda in sen
may hope of the sea   foaming   to gather   the wave to breast

ki	vwɔl	'te ne ɾe a 'fren	'fe mi na	a 'man te
chi	**vuol**	**tenere a fren**	**femina**	**amante!**
who	wishes	to keep in check	female	lover

femina (poet.)
= femmina

Whoever wants to keep a woman in love harnessed may as well hope to gather the frothy wave of the sea to his breast!

se	la	'fɛb: bre	da 'mo ɾe	a	me	nel	'kɔ ɾe	si 'djɛ de
Se	**la**	**febbre**	**d'amore,**	**a**	**me**	**nel**	**core**	**si diede,**
if	the	fever	of love	to	me	to the heart	gave itself

"deto," not "diede," is printed; as "deto" was not found either in modern Italian or old Italian, I'm suggesting that the intention was "diede," from "dare."

If the fever of love entered my heart,

un	led: 'dʒa dro	a ma 'to ɾe	mi	'strin si	al	'se no	e 'doɲ: ɲi	mal	sa 'nɔ
un	**leggiadro**	**amatore**	**mi**	**strinsi**	**al**	**seno,**	**ed ogni**	**mal**	**sanò!**
a	fair	lover	me	I clasped	to the	breast	and every	ill	it healed

I clasped a fair lover to my breast, and every ill was healed!

GL: **Amor**

ও

[41]   *Aurelio Aureli*

'va ge 'stel: le
Vaghe stelle
Charming stars

'va ge	'stel: le	'lu tʃi	'bɛl: le	non	dor 'mi te
Vaghe	**stelle,**	**luci**	**belle,**	**non**	**dormite!**
charming	stars	lights	beautiful	not	you sleep

Charming stars, beautiful lights, do not sleep!

a 'pri te	il	se 're no	de	'vo stri	beʎ: 'ʎɔk: ki
Aprite	**il**	**sereno**	**de**	**vostri**	**begl'occhi,**
open	the	clear light	of	your	beautiful eyes

Open up the sunshine of your beautiful eyes;

laʃ: 'ʃa te	'ke	'skɔk: ki	in	'kwe sto	'mi o	'se no	a 'mo ɾe	i	'swɔ i	'dar di
lasciate	**che**	**scocchi**	**in**	**questo**	**mio**	**seno,**	**Amore**	**i**	**suoi**	**dardi.**
let	that	may shoot	into	this	my	breast	Love	the	his	arrows

let Love [Cupid] shoot his arrows into my breast.

I changed the printed "ch'io" to "che," to make sense of the grammar in the context.

'bɛ i	'lu tʃi di	'zgwar di	i	'lu mi	dɛ	a 'pri te
Bei	**lucidi**	**sguardi,**	**i**	**lumi,**	**deh,**	**aprite!**
beautiful	shining	glances	the	lights	ah	open

Beautiful shining glances, ah, open your light [eyes]!

GL: **Amore**

Cesarini, Carlo Francesco (1666-after 1741)

Composer and violinist, also called "Carlo del Violino," he was born near Urbino and apparently spent all of his life in or around Rome in the service of Cardinal Benedetto Pamphili, except for the years 1690-93 when he was in Bologna with Pamphili, who was the papal legate.

Cesarini was probably also *maestro di cappella* at the church of Il Gesù from 1704 to 1741.

His gifts as a composer were best known from his cantatas, of which at least fifty-five are extant; most of the texts are by Pamphili. He also wrote operas and oratorios, as well as other sacred music. He was a wealthy man, as attested by a record of large gifts given to his daughters in 1735.

[1, 3, 46]
from: *La gelosia* (A solo cantata)

'fil: li   'fil: li   nol   'njɛ go   kom pa 'ti te mi

Filli, Filli, nol niego...Compatitemi

Filli, Filli, I do not deny it...Have pity on me

'fil: li	'fil: li	nol	'njɛ go	'i o	'dis: si	ke	'ne i	pro 'fon di	a 'bis: si
Filli,	**Filli,**	**nol**	**niego,**	**io**	**dissi,**	**che**	**nei**	**profondi**	**abissi**
Filli	Filli	not it	I deny	I	I said	that	into the	deep	abysses

> *nol = non + il*
> *niego = (mod.) nego*
> *(form of "negare")*

Filli, Filli, I do not deny it: I said that into the deep absysses

'ka da	ki	per	te	'sɛr ba	ar 'do ɾe	in	'pɛt: to
cada	**chi**	**per**	**te**	**serba**	**ardore**	**in**	**petto,**
may fall	he who	for	you	keeps	ardor	in	breast

may fall the one who has ardor for you in his breast,

ke	kon	'tor bi di	e 'klis: si	ri 'mi ɾa	il	sol	ki	te	ri 'mi ɾa
che	**con**	**torbidi**	**eclissi**	**rimira**	**il**	**sol,**	**chi**	**te**	**rimira.**
that	with	dark	eclipses	looks at	the	sun	he who	to you	looks

that whoever looks at you looks [as if looking] at the sun in dark eclipse.

'i o	'dis: si	ke	non	'trɔ vi	ri 'pɔ zo	ki	lo	'spe ɾa	da	te
Io	**dissi,**	**che**	**non**	**trovi**	**riposo,**	**chi**	**lo**	**spera**	**da**	**te;**
I	I said	that	not	may find	repose	he who	it	hopes	from	you

I said that he who hopes for repose will not find it from you;

lo	'dis: si	ɛ	've ɾo
lo	**dissi,**	**è**	**vero!**
it	I said	it is	true

I said it – it is true!

ma	ke	'di ɾe	non	'ɔ za	kon 'fu za	nel	'su o	dwɔl	'liŋ gwa	dʒe 'lo za
Ma	**che**	**dire**	**non**	**osa,**	**confusa**	**nel**	**suo**	**duol,**	**lingua**	**gelosa!**
but	what	to say	not	it dares	confused	in the	its	grief	tongue	jealous

But my jealous tongue dares not speak, confused in its grief!

kom pa 'ti te mi	'so no	in 'fer mo	tol: le 'ɾa te mi	il	'mi o	'ma le	ɛ	mal	da 'mor
Compatitemi,	**sono**	**infermo;**	**tolleratemi,**	**il**	**mio**	**male**	**è**	**mal**	**d'amor!**
have pity on me	I am	infirm	tolerate me	the	my	illness	is	sickness	of love

Have pity on me; I am ill. Put up with me; my illness is lovesickness!

un	in 'fer mo	ke	sa 'di ɾa	fa	pje 'ta	non	'mwɔ ve	a 'di ɾa
Un	**infermo,**	**che**	**s'adira,**	**fa**	**pietà,**	**non**	**muove**	**ad ira.**
an	infirm one	who	gets angry	makes	pity	not	moves	to anger

An angry, sick man elicits pity, not anger.

'nel: la	'kol pa	a	la	di 'skol pa	per	et: 'tʃɛs: so	di	fu 'ror
Nella	**colpa**	**ha**	**la**	**discolpa**	**per**	**eccesso**	**di**	**furor.**
in the	fault	has	the	excuse	through	excess	of	frenzy

His excuse for his sin is an excess of enthusiasm.

GL: **Filli**

❧

[58]

un di la ˈbɛlː la ˈklɔ ɾi
Un dì la bella Clori
One day the beautiful Clori

un	di	la	ˈbɛlː la	ˈklɔ ɾi	sker ˈtsan do	kon	a ˈmor	ˈlar ko	ʎi	ˈpre ze
Un	**dì**	**la**	**bella**	**Clori**	**scherzando**	**con**	**Amor**	**l'arco**	**gli**	**prese.**
one	day	the	beautiful	Clori	playing	with	Love	the bow	from him	took

One day the beautiful Clori, playing with Love *[Cupid]*, took his bow from him.

sa ˈetː ta		or	ˈtutː ti	i	ˈkɔ ɾi	fe ˈriʃː ʃe
Saetta		**or**	**tutti**	**i**	**cori,**	**ferisce,**
she pierces with arrows		now	all	the	hearts	wounds

Now she shoots arrows and wounds all hearts;

ma	il	ˈsu o	kɔr	ˈsal vo	lo	ˈre ze
ma	**il**	**suo**	**cor**	**salvo**	**lo**	**rese.**
but	the	her	heart	safe	it	she rendered

but she has kept her own heart safe.

GL: **Clori, Amor**

 Cesti, Antonio (1623-1669)

Sometimes incorrectly referred to as Marc' Antonio Cesti, his baptismal name was Pietro. He was a choirboy in Arezzo and then, upon joining the Franciscan order shortly before his sixteenth birthday, he adopted the name (Brother) Antonio.

He is reported to have studied with Abbatini and with Carissimi in Rome. The painter and writer Salvator Rosa, one of a Florentine literary circle, provided texts for some of Cesti's cantatas; from 1649 onwards, Rosa's letters are a major source of information about Cesti. As Brother Antonio, Cesti apparently led a life that was anything but religious in its details.

He held a regular position at the court of Archduke Ferdinand Karl in Innsbruck from 1652 to 1657. Then he was back in Rome as a tenor in the papal choir, having secured a release from his monastic vows. By 1666 he was at the Habsburg court in Vienna; in 1668 he planned to return to Italy; he died in Florence.

Cesti was one of the most important vocal composers of his time. He composed over sixty secular cantatas as well as some sacred music. His operas, numbering about fifteen, were competition for those of Cavalli.

[1, 2, 46]
from: *Orontea (1656)*
character: *Silandra*

Giacinto Andrea Cicognini

adː ˈdi o ko ˈrin do ˈvje ni a li ˈdɔ ro
Addio Corindo...Vieni, Alidoro
Farewell, Corindo...Come, Alidoro

adː ˈdi o	ko ˈrin do	adː ˈdi o	ri ˈvɔl to	a ˈdal tra	ˈsfɛ ɾa
Addio	**Corindo,**	**addio!**	**Rivolto**	**ad altra**	**sfera,**
Farewell	Corindo	farewell	turned	to other	sphere

ˈdel la	ˈfjamː ma	pri ˈmje ɾa	non	si ramː ˈmen ta	pju	ˈle gro	kɔr	ˈmi o
della	**fiamma**	**primiera,**	**non**	**si rammenta**	**più**	**l'egro**	**cor**	**mio.**
of the	flame	first	not	itself remembers	more	the weak	heart	mine

Farewell, Corindo, farewell! Turned to another passion, my weak heart no longer remembers its first love.

primiera (poet.) = prima

'vjɛ ni a li 'dɔ ɾo 'vjɛ ni   kon 'so la ki   si 'mwɔ ɾe
Vieni, Alidoro,   vieni! Consola chi   si more!
come   Alidoro   come   console   one who is dying
Come, Alidoro, come! Console one who is dying!

e   tem 'pran do il 'mi o ar 'do ɾe   'gɔ di in 'grɛm bo a si 'lan dra i di   se 're ni
E   temprando   il   mio   ardore   godi   in grembo   a Silandra   i dì   sereni!
and   strengthening the my   ardor   enjoy in bosom   of Silandra the days   serene
And, strengthening my ardor, enjoy serene days at the bosom of Silandra!

'vjɛ ni   'mi a   'vi ta   'vjɛ ni
Vieni,   mia   vita,   vieni!
come   my   life   come
Come, my life, come!

[17, 21, 24]
from: *Il pomo d'oro (1668)*
character: *Venus*

Francesco Sbarra

a 'kwan to ɛ 've ɾo
Ah! quanto è vero
Ah, how true it is

a   'kwan to   ɛ   've ɾo   ke   il   'nu do   ar 'tʃɛ ɾo   'fɔr tsa   non a
Ah!   quanto   è   vero,   che   il   nudo   arciero   forza   non ha!
ah   how much it is true   that the naked   archer   power   not has
Ah, how true it is that the naked archer *[Cupid]* does not have power!

il   'nɔ stro   'kɔ ɾe   'oɲː ɲi vi 'go ɾe   'so lo   ʎi   da
Il   nostro   core   ogni   vigore   solo   gli   da!
the   our   heart   every   strength only to him gives
Only our hearts give him whatever strength he has!

lat: 'tʃe za   'fa tʃe   per   'ku i   si 'sfa tʃe   'mi ze ɾo   sen
L'accesa   face   per   cui   si sface   misero   sen,
the ignited torch   through which is undone miserable breast
The burning torch by which the miserable breast is undone

ɛ   sol   del   'sɛn so   lar 'do ɾe   in 'ten so   ke   non a   fren
è   sol   del   senso   l'ardore   intenso,   che   non ha   fren!
is only of the senses   the ardor intense   which not has retraint
is only the intense ardor of the senses, which has no restraint!

[49]

a 'man ti 'i o vi di 'sfi do
Amanti, io vi disfido
Lovers, I defy you

a 'man ti   'i o vi   di 'sfi do   a   ki   pju   'sɛr ve   e 'da ma
Amanti,   io   vi   disfido,   a   chi   più   serve   ed ama,
lovers   I   you I defy   as   one who most serves   and loves
Lovers, I defy you, as one who serves and loves the most,

> *disfido:* from
> *"disfidare"* =
> (mod.) *"diffidare"*

a   ki   ɛ   pju   'fi do
a   chi   è   più   fido.
as   one who   is   most   faithful
as one who is most faithful.

in   'kam po   a 'pɛr to   a 'spɛt: to   'oɲ: ɲi   fe 'ri to   'pɛt: to   oɲ: 'ɲal ma   at: 'tʃe za
In   campo   aperto   aspetto   ogni   ferito   petto,   ogn'alma   accesa
on   field   open   I await   every   wounded   breast   every soul   on fire
On the open field *[of the tournament]* I await every wounded breast, every inflamed soul;

e   'si a   'dʒu di tʃe   a 'mor   di   tal   kon 'te za
e   sia   giudice   Amor   di   tal   contesa.
and   may be   judge   Love   of   such   contest
and may Love be the judge of such a contest.

al: 'lar mi   'al: la   ten 'tso ne   'vɛŋ gan   ʎa 'man ti   'fi di   al   pa ɾa 'go ne
All'armi,   alla   tenzone,   vengan'   gl'amanti   fidi   al   paragone.
to arms   to the   duel   let come   the lovers   faithful   to the   comparison
To arms, to battle *[duel of honor]*; let the faithful lovers come to the competition.

il   'mon do   il   'kam po   'si a   'sku do   la   'fe de   'mi a   'trom ba   la   'fa ma
Il   mondo   il   campo   sia,   scudo   la   fede   mia,   tromba   la   fama,
the   world   the   field   may be   shield   the   fidelity   mine   trumpet   the   fame
May the world be my battlefield, my fidelity the shield, my renown the trumpet,

e   gwer: 'rjɛ ɾo   gwer: 'rjɛ ril   'mi o   kɔr   'ka ma   e   ri 'a ma
e   guerriero,   guerrier' il   mio   cor   ch'ama   e   riama.
and   warrior   warrior the   my   heart   which loves   and   rearms
and my heart, which loves time and again, the warrior.

si   'glɔ rja   il   'fi do   'kwɔ ɾe   kin 'seɲ: ɲa   il   bɛn   a 'mar   'aŋ ka da 'mo ɾe
Si'   gloria   il   fido   cuore   ch'insegna   il   ben   amar   anch'ad Amore
may be   glory   the   faithful   heart   which teaches   the   well   loving   even to Love
May glory be the faithful heart that teaches the art of loving to Love himself;

e   sal 'kun   non   mel   'kre de   'prɔ vi   'del: la   'mi a   'fe dɛ
e   s'alcun   non   me'l   crede   provi   della   mia   fede
and   if anyone   not   me it   believes   may he experience   of the   my   fidelity

i   'prɛ dʒi   e   i   'van ti
i   pregi   e   i   vanti.
the   merits   and the   virtues
and if anyone does not believe me, let him experience the merits and the virtues of my fidelity.

a   bat: 'taʎ: ʎa   mor 'tal   vi   'sfi do   a 'man ti
A   battaglia   mortal   vi   sfido,   amanti.
to   battle   mortal   you   I challenge   lovers
I challenge you, lovers, to battle to the death.

GL: **Amor[e]**

❧

[55]

'bɛl: la   'klɔ ɾi
Bella Clori
Beautiful Clori

'bɛl: la   'klɔ ɾi   aŋ 'kor   non   'kre di   tʃɔ   ke   've di
Bella   Clori,   ancor   non   credi   ciò   che   vedi.
beautiful   Clori   still   not   you believe   that   which   you see
Beautiful Clori, you still do not believe what you see.

se   non   'ku ɾi   il   par 'lar   'mi o   've di   il   'pra to   e   'sɛn ti   il   'ri o
Se   non   curi   il   parlar   mio,   vedi   il   prato   e   senti   il   rio,
if   not   you pay attention to   the   speaking   mine   see   the   meadow   and   hear   the   brook
If you do not heed what I say, see the meadow and hear the brook,

e da 'skol ta   le   pa 'ɾɔ le   ke   ti   'di tʃe   il   'ma ɾe   el   'so le
ed ascolta   le   parole   che   ti   dice   il   mare   e'l   sole.
and listen to   the   words   which   to you   says   the   sea   and the   sun
and listen to the words the sea and the sun say to you.

da ma 'ɾan to   'rik: ko   'man to   se   miŋ 'gan: na   a 'pril   ri 'dɛn te
D'amaranto   ricco   manto   se   m'inganna   april'   ridente,
of red   rich   mantle   if   me deceives   april   smiling
If smiling april deceives me with its rich rosy mantle,

'pɔ ko   'du ɾa   'mi a   ven 'tu ɾa   al   sof: 'fjar   di   'bok: ka   al 'dʒen te
poco   dura   mia   ventura   al   soffiar   di   bocca   algente.
little   lasts   my   good fortune   at the   blowing   of   mouth   icy
at the breath of an icy mouth my good fortune does not last.

e   tu   'klɔ ɾi   nol   kom 'prɛn di   tʃɔ   kin 'tɛn di
E   tu   Clori   nol   comprendi   ciò   ch'intendi.
and   you   Clori   not it   you understand   that   which you hear
And you, Clori, do not understand what you hear.

nol = non + il

ma   sel   'pra to   sel   'ri o   sel   'ma ɾe   el   'so le   non   a   'vo tʃe   ba 'stan te
Ma   se'l   prato,   se'l   rio,   se'l   mare   e'l   sole   non   ha   voce   bastante
but   if the   meadow   if the   brook   if the   sea   and the   sun   not   have   voice   enough
But if the voices of the meadow, the brook, the sea and the sun are not sufficient

a   'dir ti   il   've ɾo   at: 'tɛn di   il   'mi o   pen 'sjɛ ɾo
a   dirti   il   vero,   attendi   il   mio   pensiero.
to   to tell you   the   truth   consider   the   my   thought
to tell you the truth, consider my thoughts:

antiquated translaton of the verb "attendere" = to consider, be attentive

si ri 'skja ɾa   il   'ri o   tur 'ba to   e   pju   'va go   il   sol   ri 'sor dʒe
Si rischiara   il   rio   turbato   e   più   vago   il   sol   risorge;
clears up   the   brook   turbid   and   more   lovely   the   sun   rises again
The turbid brook will clear up, the sun will rise again more lovely;

vjɛn   traŋ 'kwil: lo   il   'ma ɾe   i 'ɾa to   e dil   'pra to   'nu do   un   'tɛm po
vien   tranquillo   il   mare   irato,   ed il   prato,   nudo   un   tempo,
comes   tranquil   the   sea   angry   and the   meadow   bare   one   time
the angry sea will become tranquil and the meadow, once bare,

di   'fjor   sa 'dor na   ma   la   bel: 'let: tsa   'tu a   'par te   non   'tor na
di   fior   s'adorna;   ma   la   bellezza   tua   parte,   non   torna.
with   flowers   itself adorns   but   the   beauty   yours   departs   not   returns
will adorn itself with flowers; but your beauty will go away and not return.

GL: **Clori**

[24]
from: *Il pomo d'oro (1668)*
character: *Eufrosina*

Francesco Sbarra

ke aŋ 'gɔʃ: ʃa ke af: 'fan: no
Che angoscia, che affanno!
What anguish, what anxiety!

ke aŋ 'gɔʃ: ʃa ke af: 'fan: no
Che   angoscia,   che   affanno!
what   anguish   what   anxiety
What anguish, what anxiety!

nel   'kɔ ɾe   pja 'ga to   a 'mo ɾe   ti 'ran: no   a   'skrit: to   il   'mi o   'fa to
Nel   core   piagato   Amore   tiranno   ha   scritto   il   mio   fato!
in the   heart   wounded   Love   tyrannical   has   written   the   my   fate
In my wounded heart tyrannical Love has written my fate!

o   'kru do   tor 'men to   ke   'pe na   'ki o   'sɛn to
O   crudo   tormento,   che   pena   ch'io   sento!
oh   cruel   torment   what   pain   [that] I   I feel
Oh, cruel torment – what pain I feel!

dal: 'lal ma   ke   'dʒɛ me   la   'pa tʃe   ɛ   fud: 'dʒi ta
Dall'alma   che   geme   la   pace   è   fuggita!
from the soul   which   laments   the   peace   is   flown
Peace has flown from my lamenting soul!

ɛ   'mɔr ta   la   'spɛ me   mɛ   'gra ve   la   'vi ta
È   morta   la   speme,   m'è   grave   la   vita!
is   dead   the   hope   to me is   harsh   the   life
Hope is dead; my life is harsh!

speme (lit.) = speranza	

o   'kru do   tor 'men to   ke   'pe na   'ki o   'sɛn to
O   crudo   tormento!   Che   pena   ch'io   sento!
oh   cruel   torment   What   pain   [that] I   I feel
Oh, cruel torment – what pain I feel!

𝒢ℒ: **Amore**

❧

[21, 24]
from: *Il pomo d'oro (1668)*
character: *Proserpina*

Francesco Sbarra

e 'do ve tad: 'dʒi ɾi
E dove t'aggiri
And why are you wandering

e   'do ve   tad: dʒi ɾi   tra   'lal me   do 'lɛn ti
E   dove   t'aggiri   tra   l'alme   dolenti,
and   why   you wander   among   the souls   sorrowful
And why are you wandering among the sorrowful souls

dove (antiquated meaning) = perché	

se   'pjan ti   e   so 'spi ɾi   non   'al tro   kwi   'sɛn ti
se   pianti   e   sospiri,   non   altro   qui   senti?
if   tears   and   sighs   not   other   here   you hear
when you hear nothing but weeping and sighing here –

se   'pe ne   e   tor 'men ti   iŋ 'gom bra no   il   'tut: to
Se   pene   e   tormenti   ingombrano   il   tutto
if   sufferings   and   torments   clutter   the   all
when suffering and torments encumber everything

dor: 'ror   di   'stri da   di   kwe 'rɛ le   e   'lut: to   di 'lut: to
d'orror,   di   strida,   di   querele,   e   lutto!   **di lutto!**
of horror   of   shrieks   of   laments   and   mourning   *added in the last repeat:*   with mourning!
with horror, shrieking, lamenting, and mourning!

[27]

in seɲ: 'ɲa te mi a mo 'ri ɾe
Insegnatemi a morire
Teach me to die

in seɲ: 'ɲa te mi   a   mo 'ri ɾe   kru de 'lis: si me   'stel: le
Insegnatemi   a   morire,   crudelissime   stelle.
teach me   to   to die   most cruel   stars
Teach me to die, cruelest stars.

'vo i   per   mad: 'dʒor   mar 'ti ɾe   mi   ri ser 'ba te   in   'vi ta
Voi   per   maggior   martire   mi   riserbate   in   vita,
you   for   greater   agony   me   you keep   in   life
You, in order to make me suffer more, preserve my life;

e 'di o   ke   'dʒo ko   son   di   'kru da   'sɔr te   'ɛ zu le   mi ri 'trɔ vo
ed io   che   gioco   son   di   cruda   sorte   esule   mi ritrovo
and I   who   joke   I am   of   cruel   fate   exile   myself I find
and I, who am a joke of cruel fate, find myself an exile

dal   'reɲ: ɲo   'del: la   'vi ta   e   'del: la   'mɔr te
dal   regno   della   vita   e   della   morte.
from the   realm   of the   life   and   of the   death
from the realms of life and death.

o   'sfɛ ɾe   se 'vɛ ɾe   al 'men   per   non   ve 'der mi   si   ko 'stan te   sof: 'fri ɾe
O   sfere   severe,   almen   per   non   vedermi   sì   costante   soffrire,
o   spheres   severe   at least   for   not   to see me   so   constantly   to suffer
O austere stars, at least in order not to see me suffer so constantly,

in seɲ: 'ɲa te mi   a   mo 'ri ɾe
insegnatemi   a   morire.
teach me   to   to die
teach me to die.

[4, 6, 8, 19, 24, 34, 36, 42, 45, 54]
from: *Orontea (1656)*
character: *Orontea*

Giacinto Andrea Cicognini

in 'tor no al: 'li dol 'mi o
Intorno all'idol mio
Around my idol

in 'tor no al: 'li dol	'mi o	spi 'ra te	pur	spi 'ra te	'a u ɾe	so 'a vi	e	'gra te
Intorno all'idol	**mio**	**spirate**	**pur,**	**spirate,**	**aure**	**soavi**	**e**	**grate;**
around the idol	mine	blow	[then]	blow	breezes	gentle	and	pleasant

Blow, gentle and pleasant breezes, around my idol;

e	'nel: le	'gwan tʃe	e 'lɛt: te	ba 'tʃa te lo	per	me	kor 'te zi	a u 'ɾet: te
e	**nelle**	**guancie**	**elette**	**baciatelo**	**per**	**me,**	**cortesi**	**aurette!**
and	on the	cheeks	chosen	kiss him	for	me	kind	little breezes

and kiss his precious cheeks for me, kind little breezes!

al	'mi o	bɛn	ke	ri 'po za	sul: 'la li	'del: la	'kwjɛ te
Al	**mio**	**ben,**	**che**	**riposa**	**sull'ali**	**della**	**quiete,**
to the	my	dear one	who	sleeps	on the wings	of the	repose

> *in some prints:*
> *su l'ali =*
> *sull'ali*

'gra ti	'soɲ: ɲi	as: si 'ste te
grati	**sogni**	**assistete,**
pleasant	dreams	aid

Aid my dear one, who sleeps on the wings of repose, with pleasant dreams

e	il	'mi o	rak: 'kju zo	ar 'do ɾe	zve 'la te ʎi	per	me	o	'lar ve	da 'mo ɾe
e	**il**	**mio**	**racchiuso**	**ardore**	**svelategli**	**per**	**me,**	**o**	**larve**	**d'amore!**
and	the	my	enclosed	ardor	reveal to him	for	me	o	shadows	of love

and reveal to him for me my inner ardor, o spirits of love!

> *in some prints: e 'l [el] = e il*
> *in some prints: ... per me, larve d'amore!*

[45] *prints a continuation of this aria, including recitatives:*

o i 'mɛ	non	son	pju	'mi a
Oimè,	**non**	**son**	**più**	**mia;**
alas	not	I am	more	mine

Alas, I am no longer my own;

se	mi 'sprɛt: tsa	a li 'do ɾo	sa 'ɾa	la	'vi ta	'mi a	'pɾe da	di	'mɔr te
se	**mi sprezza**	**Alidoro**	**sarà**	**la**	**vita**	**mia**	**preda**	**di**	**morte.**
if	me scorns	Alidoro	will be	the	life	mine	prey	of	death

if Alidoro scorns me, my life will be prey to death.

'kwe sto	di a 'dɛ ma	'dɔ ɾo	'ki o	ti	'pɔ zo	sul	'kri ne
Questo	**diadema**	**d'oro**	**ch'io**	**ti**	**poso**	**sul**	**crine,**
this	diadem	of gold	which I	on you	place	on the	hair

This gold diadem which I place on your head,

'kwe sto	'ʃɛt: tro	re 'al	'na kwe	per	te
questo	**scettro**	**real**	**nacque**	**per**	**te.**
this	scepter	royal	was born	for	you

[and] this royal scepter, were destined for you.

tu	'sɛ i	'la ni ma	'mi a	tu	'sɛ i	la	'vi ta	'mi a
Tu	**sei**	**l'anima**	**mia,**	**tu**	**sei**	**la**	**vita**	**mia,**
you	are	the soul	mine	you	are	the	life	mine

You are my soul, you are my life,

tu	'sɛ i	'mi o	re	o	'di o	ki	'vi de	'ma i
tu	**sei**	**mio**	**re;**	**oh**	**Dio,**	**chi**	**vide**	**mai**
you	are	my	king	oh	God	who	saw	ever

you are my king; oh God, who has ever seen

pju	'bɛl: la	ma e 'sta	pju	bɛl	reɲː 'ɲan te
più	**bella**	**maestà,**	**più**	**bel**	**regnante?**
more	beautiful	majesty	more	handsome	sovereign

a more beautiful majesty, a more handsome sovereign?

di 'vi no	ɛ	kwel	sem 'bjan te	inː na 'mo ra no	il	tʃɛl	'kwe i	'kju zi	'ra i
Divino	**è**	**quel**	**sembiante;**	**innamorano**	**il**	**ciel**	**quei**	**chiusi**	**rai.**
divine	is	that	countenance	they charm	the	heaven	those	closed	eyes

That countenance is divine; those closed eyes charm heaven.

pju	'bɛl: la	ma e 'sta	ki	'vi de	'ma i
Più	**bella**	**maestà**	**chi**	**vide**	**mai?**
more	beautiful	majesty	who	saw	ever

Who has ever seen a more beautiful majesty?

ma	nel	'mi o	kɔr	se 'pol to	non	vɔ	te 'ner	lo	stral
Ma	**nel**	**mio**	**cor**	**sepolto**	**non**	**vò**	**tener**	**lo**	**stral**
but	in the	my	heart	buried	not	I want	to keep	the	arrow

But I do not want to keep buried in my heart the arrow

ke	mi	fe 'ri
che	**mi**	**ferì.**
that	me	wounded

that wounded me.

'u na	re 'dʒi na	a 'man te	non	vwɔl	pe 'nar	non	vwɔl	mo rir	ko 'zi
Una	**regina**	**amante**	**non**	**vuol**	**penar,**	**non**	**vuol**	**morir**	**così.**
a	queen	loving	not	wants	to suffer	not	wants	to die	thus

A loving queen does not want to suffer and die like this.

'lɛdː dʒi	o	'mi o	'ka ro	in	'ne gre	'nɔ te	i	'mjɛ i	sin 'tʃe ri	a 'mo ri
Leggi,	**o**	**mio**	**caro**	**in**	**negre**	**note**	**i**	**miei**	**sinceri**	**amori,**
read	o	my	dear	in	black	notes	the	my	sincere	affections

Read, o my dear, in my writing *[my note]*, of my sincere affections –

in	'bre vi	atː 'tʃɛn ti	imː men si 'ta	dar 'do ri
in	**brevi**	**accenti**	**immensità**	**d'ardori.**
in	brief	words	immensity	of ardors.

[read,] in brief words, of the immensity of my ardors.

'dɔr mi	bɛn	'mi o	per	te	've ʎː ʎa	o ron 'tɛ a	'mi a	'vi ta	adː 'dio
Dormi,	**ben**	**mio.**	**Per**	**te**	**veglia**	**Orontea.**	**Mia**	**vita,**	**addio.**
sleep	dear one	mine	for	you	keeps watch	Orontea	my	life	farewell

Sleep, my dear one. Orontea keeps watch over you. My life, farewell.

જી

[24, 43]
from: *Il Pomo d'oro (1668)*
character: *Paride*

. Francesco Sbarra

o	del	bɛn	ke	akː kwi ste 'rɔ
	O	**del**	**ben**	**che acquisterò**

Oh, what good I will gain

o	del	bɛn	ke	akː kwi ste 'rɔ	'ka ɾa	e	'bɛlː la	a 'ma ta	idː 'dɛa
O	**del**	**ben**	**che**	**acquisterò,**	**cara**	**e**	**bella**	**amata**	**iddea,**
oh	of the	good	that	I will gain	dear	and	beautiful	beloved	goddess

Oh, what good I will gain, dear and beautiful beloved goddess,

iddea = (mod.) dea

se	'tua	'vi sta	'ɔdː dʒi	mi 'bɛ a	e	ke	'fi a	'kwan do	ta 'vrɔ
se	**tua**	**vista**	**oggi**	**mi bea,**	**e**	**che**	**fia**	**quando**	**t'avrò!**
if	your	glance	today	me makes happy	and	that	will be	when	you I shall have

if today your glance makes me happy; and how [good] it will be when I have you!

fia = (mod.) sarà

par 'tjam	pur	pasː 'sja mo	il	mar	non	si 'te man	'flutː ti	o	'vɛn ti
Partiam	**pur,**	**passiamo**	**il**	**mar!**	**Non**	**si teman**	**flutti**	**o**	**venti,**
let us depart	then	let us cross	the	sea	not	one fears	waves	or	winds

Let us depart, then; let us cross the sea! We will not fear waves or winds,

ke	nel	'pɔr to	'de i	kon 'tɛn ti	ɔ	bɛn	'pre sto	da	arː ri 'var
ché	**nel**	**porto**	**dei**	**contenti**	**ho**	**ben**	**presto**	**da**	**arrivar!**
because	in the	port	of the	happinesses	I have	well	soon	at	to arrive

for I will soon arrive in the harbor of happiness!

in [43]: d'arrivar = da arrivar

❧

[34]
from: *Alessandro, vincitor di se stesso (1651)*
character: *Efestione*

Francesco Sbarra

si man 'tjɛ ne il 'mi o a 'mor
Si mantiene il mio amor
My love sustains itself

si man 'tjɛ ne	il	'mi o	a 'mor	di	do 'lor	dafː 'fanː ni	e	'pe ne
Si mantiene	**il**	**mio**	**amor**	**di**	**dolor,**	**d'affanni**	**e**	**pene,**
itself maintains	the	my	love	with	sorrow	with woes	and	pains

My love sustains itself with sorrow, woes, and pain,

ke	dʒo 'i re	del	'mi o	'bɛ ne	nemː 'men	'pɔsː so	kol	pen 'sjɛ ɾo
ché	**gioire**	**del**	**mio**	**bene**	**nemmen**	**posso**	**col**	**pensiero.**
because	to delight	of the	my	dear one	not even	I am able	with the	thought

for I am unable to delight in my dear one even in my thoughts.

'a ɾo	pur	sebː 'bɛn	non	'spɛ ɾo
Amo	**pur,**	**sebben**	**non**	**spero.**
I love	yet	even though	not	I hope

Yet I love, even though I do not hope.

❧

[27]

si 'vɔʎː ʎo mo 'rir
Sì, voglio morir
Yes, I want to die

si	'vɔʎː ʎo	mo 'rir	'na kwe	'li be ɾo	il	'mi o	kɔr	ma	sodː 'dʒa tʃe
Sì,	**voglio**	**morir;**	**nacque**	**libero**	**il**	**mio**	**cor**	**ma**	**soggiace**
yes	I want	to die	was born	free	the	my	heart	but	is subjected

Yes, I want to die; my heart was born free but is subjected

per   a 'mor   a   ti 'ranː ni ko   mar 'tir
per   amor   a   tirannico   martir.
by   love   to   tyrannical   agony
by love to tyrannical agony.

o   'ka ɾa   li ber 'ta   ke   'vi vo   'pɛr si   e   'dalː la   'mɔr te   'spɛ ɾo
O   cara   libertà   che   vivo   persi   e   dalla   morte   spero,
o   dear   freedom   which   alive   I lost   and   from the   death   I hope
O dear freedom, which I lost when alive and hope for from death,

dɛ   madː 'di ta   il   sen 'tjɛ ɾo   'on da   mo 'rir   si 'va
deh   m'addita   il   sentiero   ond'a   morir   si va.
ah   to me show   the   path   whence to   to die   one goes
ah, show me the path to where one dies.

ɛ   la   'vi a   da ke 'ron te   a   'tutː ti   a 'pɛr ta
È   la   via   d'Acheronte   a   tutti   aperta,
is   the   course   of Acheron   to   everyone   open
Acheron's course is open to everyone,

e   ki   mo 'rir   non   sa   'vi ta   non   'mɛr ta
e   chi   morir   non   sa   vita   non   merta
and   he who   to die   not   knows how   life   not   merits
and whoever does not know how to die does not merit life.

GL: **Acheronte**

[5, 9, 19, 34, 42, 44, 54; in [19] and [34] attributed to *Caproli*]

tu maŋ 'ka vi a tor men 'tar mi
Tu mancavi a tormentarmi
All I needed was for you to torture me

tu maŋ 'ka vi a tor men 'tar mi kru de 'lisː si ma spe 'ɾan tsa
Tu mancavi a tormentarmi, crudelissima speranza,
you failed to to torment me most cruel hope
All I needed was for you to torture me, cruelest hope,

e   kon   'dol tʃe   ri mem 'bran tsa   'vwɔ i   di 'nwɔ vo   avː ve le 'nar mi
e   con   dolce   rimembranza   vuoi   di nuovo   avvelenarmi.
and   with   sweet   remembrance   you wish   anew   to poison me
and then, with sweet memories, to poison me again!

> *var. in* [44], *instead of "vuoi":* **puoi** ['pwɔ i] = you are able (to poison me....)

aŋ 'kor   'du ɾa   la   zven 'tu ɾa   du na   'fjamː ma   in tʃe ne 'ri ta
Ancor   dura   la   sventura   d'una   fiamma   incenerita;
still   lasts   the   misfortune   of a   flame   reduced to ashes
The misfortune of a burned out passion still endures;

> *alt.:* **d'una fiamma intenerita** [in te ne 'ri ta] = of a passion made tender

la   fe 'ri ta   aŋ 'ko ɾa   a 'pɛr ta   par   mavː 'vɛr ta   'nwɔ ve   'pe ne
la   ferita   ancora   aperta   par   m'avverta   nuove   pene.
the   wound   still   open   seems   me it warns   new   pains
the wound, still open, seems to warn me of new suffering.

dal	ru ˈmor	ˈdel: le	ka ˈte ne	ˈma i	non	ˈve do	al: lon ta ˈnar mi
Dal	**rumor**	**delle**	**catene**	**mai**	**non**	**vedo**	**allontanarmi.**
from the	noise	of the	chains	ever	not	I see	to distance myself

I do not see myself ever drawing away from the noise of the chains.

[58]

ˈvjɛ ni o ˈma i dɛ ˈvjɛ ni o ˈmɔr te
Vieni omai, deh, vieni, o morte
Come now, ah come, o death

ˈvjɛ ni	o ˈma i	dɛ	ˈvjɛ ni	o	ˈmɔr te	ˈkwe sto	ˈkɔ ɾe	a	kon so ˈlar
Vieni	**omai,**	**deh,**	**vieni,**	**o**	**morte,**	**questo**	**core**	**a**	**consolar.**
come	now	ah	come	o	death	this	heart	to	to console

Come now; ah come, o death, to console this heart.

la	ˈmi a	ˈvi ta	la	ˈmi a	ˈsɔr te	tu	sa ˈɾa i
La	**mia**	**vita,**	**la**	**mia**	**sorte**	**tu**	**sarai,**
the	my	life	the	my	fate	you	you will be

You will be my life and my destiny

se	fa ˈɾa i	ˈkab: bja	ˈfi ne	ˈu na	ˈvɔl ta	il	ˈmi o	pe ˈnar
se	**farai**	**ch'abbia**	**fine**	**una**	**volta**	**il**	**mio**	**penar.**
if	you will make	that I may have	end	one	time	the	my	suffering

if you will once allow my suffering to end.

 Cifra, Antonio (1584-1629)

Born near Terracina, he was a choirboy at S. Luigi dei Francesi in Rome, and for about a year was *maestro di cappella* at the Collegio Germanico, from which post he was dismissed for his "evil habits with women" and his neglect of his duties with the choirboys *[Grove]*. In 1609 he became *maestro di cappella* at Santa Casa di Loreto, which position he occupied for most of the rest of his life.

Stylistically, Cifra was essentially a member of the Roman school of church composers in the early seventeenth century; as such he was the most prolific. His output includes five books of motets, three books of psalms, five of masses, sacred as well as secular "scherzi" *(Li diversi scherzi)*, and madrigals.

[12, 41]   *Gabriello Chiabrera*

la vi o ˈlet: ta
La violetta
The little violet

> Although "little violet" is the common translation of "violetta," this text refers to the flower's red and white colors, which are not characteristic of violets; a rare literary translation for "viola" ("violet") is "garofano," which means "carnation," so this text may in fact be referring to "the little carnation."

la	vi o ˈlet: ta	ken ˈsu	ler ˈbet: ta	ˈa pre	al	mat: ˈtin	no ˈvɛl: la	
La	**violetta**	**ch'en su**	**l'erbetta**	**apre**	**al**	**mattin**	**novella,**	*en su =*
the	little violet	which upwards	the little grass	opens	at the	morning	new	*(mod.)*
								in su

The little violet, which opens up from the young grass at the new morning –

di	non	ɛ	ˈkɔ za	ˈtut: ta	o do ˈro za	ˈtut: ta	led: ˈdʒa dra	e	ˈbɛl: la
di',	**non**	**è**	**cosa**	**tutta**	**odorosa,**	**tutta**	**leggiadra**	**e**	**bella?**
say	not	it is	thing	all	fragrant	all	elegant	and	beautiful

say, is it not an absolutely fragrant, absolutely elegant and beautiful thing?

The following is in [12]:

'a i	ken	'brɛ ve	'o ɾa	'ko me	la u 'rɔ ɾa	'lun dʒe	da	'no i	sen 'vo la
Ahi,	che'n	breve	ora,	come	l'aurora	lunge	da	noi	sen vola,
alas	[that] in	brief	hour	like	the dawn	far	from	us	flies away

Alas, in a brief hour, as the dawn vanishes far from us,

'ɛk: ko	laŋ 'gwi ɾe	'ɛk: ko	pe 'ri ɾe	la	'mi ze ɾa	vi 'ɔ la
ecco	languire,	ecco	perire,	la	misera	viola.
here is	to languish	here is	to perish	the	poor	violet

here languishes, here perishes the poor violet.

The following is in both prints:

si	tʃer ta 'men te	ke	dol tʃe 'men te	'el: la	ne 'spi ɾa	o 'do ɾi
Sì,	certamente,	che	dolcemente	ella	ne spira	odori
yes	certainly	[that]	sweetly	it	from it emanates	fragrances

Yes, certainly, it sweetly emanates fragrances

e	'nem pje	il	'pɛt: to	di	bɛl	di 'lɛt: to	'ko i	'bɛ i	de	'swɔ i	ko 'lo ɾi
e	n'empie	il	petto	di	bel	diletto	coi	bei	de'	suoi	colori.
and	of it fills	the	breast	with	pleasant	delight	with the	beauties	of	its	colors

and fills one's breast with pleasant delight, with the beauty of its colors.

The following is in [12]:

tu	'ku i	bel: 'let: tsa	e	dʒo vi 'net: tsa	'ɔd: dʒi	'fan	si	su 'pɛr ba
Tu,	cui	bellezza	e	giovinezza	oggi	fan	sì	superba,
you	whose	beauty	and	youth	today	make	so	proud

You, whose beauty and youth make so proud now,

so 'a ve	'pe na	'dol tʃe	ka 'te na	di	'mi a	pri 'dʒo ne	a 'tʃer ba
soave	pena	dolce	catena	di	mia	prigione	acerba.
sweet	suffering	gentle	chain	of	my	prison	bitter

[are] the sweet suffering, the gentle chain, in my bitter imprisonment.

The following is in both prints:

'va ga	ros: 'sed: dʒa	'va ga	bjan 'ked: dʒa	tra	'la u ɾe	mat: tu 'ti ne
Vaga	rosseggia,	vaga	biancheggia	tra	l'aure	mattutine,
graceful	it reddens	graceful	it turns white	among	the breezes	morning

It reddens gracefully, it whitens gracefully, among the morning breezes,

'prɛ dʒo	da 'pri le	'vi e pju	dʒen 'ti le
pregio	d'Aprile	vie più	gentile,
prize	of April	more and more	gentle

the gentlest prize of April;

| *pregio =* | *in [12]: via più =* |
| *(mod.) premio* | *(mod.) vie più* |

ma	ke	di 'vɛ ne	al	'fi ne
ma	che	divene	al	fine?
but	what	it becomes	at the	end

but what becomes of it in the end?

| *divene =* |
| *(mod.)* |
| *diviene* |

The following is in [12]:

dɛ	kon	kwel	'fjo ɾe	kon 'siʎ: ʎa	il	'kɔ ɾe	tu	la	'su a	'fre ska	e 'ta de
Deh	**con**	**quel**	**fiore**	**consiglia**	**il**	**core**	**tu**	**la**	**sua**	**fresca**	**etade;**
ah	with	that	flower	advise	the	heart	you	the	its	fresh	age

etade =
(mod.)
età

Ah you, with that flower counsel your heart about its young age,

> *Perhaps "tu" is a misprint for "su" (= on, regarding) in which case the translation*
> *would easily be:* Ah, with that flower counsel your heart about its young age,

ke	'tan to	'du ɾa	'lal ta	ven 'tu ɾa	di	'kwe sta	'tu a	bel 'ta de
che	**tanto**	**dura**	**l'alta**	**ventura**	**di**	**questa**	**tua**	**beltade.**
that	so much	endures	the high	good fortune	of	this	your	beauty

beltade =
(mod.)
beltà

so that the great good fortune of this beauty of yours will last.

 ## *da Gagliano, Marco* (1582-1643)

Born in Florence to Zanobi and Camilla da Gagliano, he may never have seen the village of Gagliano from which the family had taken its name. He was active from early youth in musical performances. In 1608 he succeeded his former teacher Luca Bati as *maestro di cappella* of the cathedral S. Maria del Fiore in Florence; in 1609 he was given that title at the Medici court as well. Taking holy orders, in 1610 he joined the canons of S. Lorenzo, and in 1615 was elevated to protonotary apostolic.

In 1607 Gagliano founded the Accademia degli Elevati, whose members included the city's finest composers, performers, and literati; among them were Peri, Caccini, Giovanni de' Bardi, and Ottavio Rinuccini; Cardinal Ferdinando Gonzaga was the academy's patron.

Gagliano prepared, directed, composed, and performed (as singer, and on the theorbo and keyboard instruments) a great variety of music for the Medici court: operas, ballets, oratorios, masses, motets, and madrigals. He was among the first to compose in the new style, the "stile rappresentativo," and his opera *Dafne (1608)* is a milestone in the early history of opera.

[61]
from: *Dafne (1608)*

ki da 'lat: tʃi da 'mor
Chi da' lacci d'Amor
He who from the bonds of Love

ki	da	'lat: tʃi	da 'mor	'vi ve	diʃ: 'ʃol to	'del: la	'su a	li ber 'ta	'gɔ da	pur	'lje to
Chi	**da'**	**lacci**	**d'Amor**	**vive**	**disciolto,**	**della**	**sua**	**libertà**	**goda**	**pur**	**lieto,**
who	from	bonds	of Love	lives	untied	of the	his	freedom	may enjoy	indeed	happy

May he who lives free from the bonds of Love indeed enjoy his freedom happily,

su 'pɛr bo	nɔ	do 'sku ɾa	'nu be	in 'vɔl to	'stas: si	per	'no i	del	tʃɛl	'lal to	de 'kre to
superbo	**no:**	**d'oscura**	**nube**	**involto,**	**stassi**	**per**	**noi**	**del**	**ciel**	**l'alto**	**decreto:**
proud	no	with dark	cloud	wrapped	is	for	us	of the	heaven	the high	decree

but not proudly; wrapped in a dark cloud for us is the high decree from heaven:

sor	non	'sɛn ti	da 'mor	'pɔ ko	ne	'mol to	a 'vra i	di 'ma ni	il	kɔr
S'or	**non**	**senti**	**d'amor**	**poco,**	**né**	**molto,**	**avrai**	**dimani**	**il**	**cor**
If now	not	you feel	of love	little	nor	much	you will have	tomorrow	the	heart

If now you feel neither little nor much of love, tomorrow your heart will be

tur 'ba to	e	iŋ 'kwɛ to	e	siɲ: 'ɲor	pro ve 'ra i	'kru do	e	se 've ɾo
turbato	**e**	**inqueto,**	**e**	**Signor**	**proverai**	**crudo**	**e**	**severo,**
troubled	and	restless	and	Lord	you will experience	cruel	and	harsh

troubled and restless, and you will experience a cruel and harsh master:

a ˈmor   ke   ˈdjan tsi   di sprɛtː ˈtsa sti   al ˈtɛ ɾo
Amor,   che   dianzi   disprezzasti   altero.
Love,   whom   a short time ago   you spurned   haughty
Love, whom you haughtily spurned a short time ago.

GL: **Amor**

☙

[24]
from: *La Flora (1628)*   *Andrea Salvadori*

ˈdɔr mi a ˈmo ɾe
Dormi, Amore
Sleep, Love

ˈdɔr mi   a ˈmor   ke   pa ˈzi te a   kon   le   ˈgratː tsje   ˈsu e   so ˈrɛlː le
Dormi,   Amor,   ché   Pasitea   con   le   Grazie,   sue   sorelle,
sleep   Love   because   Pasitea   with   the   Graces   her   sisters
Sleep, Love *[Cupid]*, because Pasitea, with the Graces, her sisters,

vwɔl   ba ˈtʃar   ˈtu e   ˈlu tʃi   ˈbɛlː le   ˈo ve   ˈlje ta   ˈelː la   si ˈbe a
vuol   baciar   tue   luci   belle,   ove   lieta   ella   si bea!
wants   to kiss   your   eyes   beautiful   where   happy   she   rejoices
wants to kiss your beautiful eyes, where she happily rejoices!

tu   non   ˈdɔr mi   e ˈdi o   il   vorː ˈrɛ i
Tu   non   dormi,   ed io   il   vorrei,
you   not   you sleep   and I   it   should like
You are not sleeping, and I would like you to [do so];

ˈdɔr mi   o   ˈdʒɔ ja   ˈdeʎː ʎi   ˈdɛ i   ˈdɔr mi   a ˈmor   e   il   ˈdwɔ lo   iŋ ˈganː na
dormi,   o   gioia   degli   Dei,   dormi,   Amor,   e   il   duolo   inganna!
sleep   o   joy   of the   Gods   sleep   Love   and   the   sorrow   elude
sleep, o joy of the Gods – sleep, Love, and elude sorrow!

fa la ˈninː na   fa la ˈnanː na
Fa la ninna,   fa la nanna!
go to sleep   go to sleep
Go to sleep, go to sleep!

ninnananna = lullaby

ˈdɔr mi   a ˈmor   ke   in ˈtan to   a ˈgla ja   ke   ˈtu a   ˈkjɔ ma   akː ˈkɔʎː ʎe   in   ˈnɔ di
Dormi,   Amor,   che   intanto   Aglaia,   che   tua   chioma   accoglie   in   nodi,
sleep   Love   that   meanwhile   Aglaia   who   your   hair   gathers   in   knots
Sleep, Love, so that Aglaia, who will gather your hair into plaitlets,

accogliere (lit.) = raccogliere

lo de ˈratː ti   in   ˈmilː le   ˈmɔ di   kol   dʒen ˈtil   ˈfiʎː ʎo   di   ˈma ja
loderatti   in   mille   modi,   col   gentil   figlio   di   Maia.
will praise you   in   thousand   ways   with the   gentle   son   of   Maia
will praise you in a thousand ways, along with the gentle son of Maia.

ˈvegː go   ˈkju zi   i   ˈdu e   ˈbɛ i   ˈdʒi ɾi   ˈɔ do   i   ˈdol tʃi   ˈtwɔ i   re ˈspi ɾi
Veggo   chiusi   i   due   bei   giri,   odo   i   dolci   tuoi   respiri!
I see   closed   the   two   beautiful   orbits   I hear   the   sweet   your   breaths
I see your two beautiful eyes closed; I hear your sweet breathing!

'dɔr mi   a 'mor   e   il   'dwɔ lo   iŋ 'gan: na
Dormi,   Amor,   e   il   duolo   inganna!
sleep   Love   and   the   sorrow   elude
Sleep, Love, and elude sorrow!

fa la 'nin: na   fa la 'nan: na
Fa la ninna,   fa la nanna!
go to sleep   go to sleep
Go to sleep, go to sleep!

GL: **Aglaia, Amor[e], Grazie, Maia, Pasitea**

&

[27]
from: *La Flora (1628)*
character: *Corilla*

Andrea Salvadori

'i o   'ɛ ɾa   par go 'let: ta
Io era pargoletta
I was a little girl

'i o   'ɛ ɾa   par go 'let: ta   kwan 'dal tri   mi   nar: 'rɔ
Io   era   pargoletta   quand'altri   mi   narrò
I   was   baby girl   when another   me   told
I was a little girl when someone told me

era =	altri: a singular pronoun
(mod.) ero	= another, somebody else

ke   a 'mor   ɛ   vi pe 'ret: ta   ke   'mɔr de   'kwan to   pwɔ
che   amor   è   viperetta   che   morde   quanto   può.
that   love   is   little viper   that   bites   as much as   it can
that love is a little viper that bites as much as it can.

kwel   dir   si   miŋ gan: 'nɔ   ke   a 'mor   gran   'tɛm po
Quel   dir   sì   m'ingannò   che   amor   gran   tempo
that   talk   so   me deceived   that   love   great   time

o 'dja i   te 'mɛn do   af: 'fan: ni   e   'gwa i
odiai   temendo   affanni   e   guai.
I hated   fearing   woes   and   troubles
Those words deceived me so much that I hated love for a long time, fearing woes and troubles.

ma   'pɔ i   kun   'dʒor no   'vi di   li 'rin do   e 'deʎ ʎi   me
Ma   poi   ch'un   giorno   vidi   Lirindo   ed egli   me
but   then   when one   day   I saw   Lirindo   and he   me
But then one day, when I saw Lirindo and he [saw] me,

bɛn   'kja ɾo   al: 'lor   mav: 'vi di   ke   'sɛr pe   a 'mor   non   ɛ
ben   chiaro   allor   m'avvidi   che   serpe   amor   non   è
well   clear   at that moment   I realized   that   snake   love   not   is
I realized very clearly, at that moment, that love is not a snake

serpe (lit.) =
serpente

ma   'bɛ ne   ɛ   per   'mi a   fe   un   'ka ɾo   un   'dol tʃe   af: 'fɛt: to
ma   bene   è   per   mia   fé   un   caro,   un   dolce   affetto,
but   well   is   for   my   faith   a   dear   a   sweet   affection
but is very much, upon my word, a dear and sweet affection,

un   bɛl   de ˈzi o   del   ˈpɛt: to
un **bel**   **desio**   **del** **petto.**
a   beautiful   desire   of the breast; *(fig.)* heart
a beautiful desire of the heart.

al: ˈlo ɾa   il   ˈmi o   te ˈzɔ ɾo   sti ˈma i   la   ˈsu a   bel ˈta
Allora   **il** **mio** **tesoro**   **stimai**   **la** **sua** **beltà,**
then   the   my   treasure   I considered the   his   beauty
Then I considered the beauty of my treasure;

or   ˈar do   e   non   mi ˈmɔ ɾo   ke   ˈmɔr te   a ˈmor   non   da
or **ardo** **e** **non** **mi moro** **ché**   **morte**   **amor** **non** **da.**
now   I burn   and   not   I die   because   death   love   not   gives
now I burn and do not die, for love does not cause death.

ˈdi ka   ˈal tri   ˈkwan to   sa   da ˈmor   ˈmil: le   tor ˈmen ti
Dica   **altri**   **quanto** **sa**   **d'amor** **mille**   **tormenti,**
may say   another   how much   knows   of love   thousand   torments

ˈi o   ˈprɔ vo   oɲː ˈɲor   kon ˈtɛn ti
io **provo** **ognor**   **contenti.**
I   I experience always   contentments
Someone else may say how much he knows about love's thousands of torments, [but] I always feel contentment.

lo ˈdar   vɔ   ˈsɛm pre   il   ˈgwar do   ke   ˈlal ma   min va ˈgi
Lodar   **vo'** **sempre**   **il** **guardo** **che**   **l'alma** **m'invaghì,**
to praise   I want always   the   glance   which   the soul   me enamored
I always want to praise the glance which enamored my soul –

> guardo *(poet.)*
> = *sguardo*

lo ˈdar   la   ˈfjam: ma   e   il   ˈdar do   ke   ˈmar se   e   mi fe ˈɾi
lodar   **la** **fiamma**   **e** **il** **dardo** **che**   **m'arse**   **e** **mi ferì.**
to praise   the   flame   and   the   arrow   which   me burned   and   me wounded
to praise the flame and the arrow which burned me and wounded me.

o   ˈka ɾo   o   ˈdol tʃe   di   ˈki o   ˈvi di   il   bɛl   sem ˈbjan te
Oh **caro,** **oh** **dolce** **dì** **ch'io**   **vidi** **il** **bel**   **sembiante,**
oh   dear   oh   sweet   day   that I   I saw   the   beautiful   countenance
Oh, dear and sweet day when I saw the beautiful face

ˈki o   ne   di ˈven: ni   a ˈman te
ch'io **ne** **divenni**   **amante.**
that I   of it I became   lover
of the one of whom I became the lover.

non   ɛ   pju   ˈmi o   il   kɔr   ke   ˈmi o   dʒa   fu
Non **è** **più** **mio** **il** **cor**   **che**   **mio** **già**   **fu,**
not   is   more   mine   the   heart   that   mine   formerly   was
The heart which used to be mine is mine no more;

lɔ   ˈda to   al   ˈmi o   de ˈzi o   e   kɔr   ˈi o   non   ɔ   pju
l'ho **dato** **al** **mio** **desio**   **e** **cor**   **io**   **non** **ho** **più.**
it I have given   to the my   desire   and   heart   I   not   I have more
I have given it to my desired one, and I have a heart no more.

a 'mor	or	'narː ra	tu	'narː ra	il	'mi o	dʒo 'i ɾe
Amor	**or**	**narra**	**tu,**	**narra**	**il**	**mio**	**gioire;**
love	now	tell	you	tell	the	my	enjoying

Love, do tell now – tell about my joy;

lo	'prɔ vo	e	nol	sɔ	'di ɾe
lo	**provo**	**e**	**nol**	**so**	**dire.**
it	I experience	and	not it	I know how	to say

I feel it and do not know how to describe it.

GL: **Amor**

[7, 40] In [7] titled **Mie speranze lusinghiere**.

'mi e spe 'ran tse
Mie speranze
My hopes

'mi e	spe 'ran tse	lu ziŋ 'gje ɾe	de zi 'a te	in	van	pja 'tʃe ɾe
Mie	**speranze**	**lusinghiere,**	**desiate**	**in**	**van**	**piacere;**
my	hopes	deceptive	you desire	in	vain	pleasure

My deceptive hopes, you wish in vain for pleasure;

desiate: from "desiare"
(lit.) = "desiderare"

'fal si	'zgwar di	beŋ 'ke	'tar di	da	'vo i	'ʃɔl to	pur	mi 'vɔl to	al	sen 'tjɛr
falsi	**sguardi,**	**benché**	**tardi,**	**da**	**voi**	**sciolto**	**pur**	**mi volto**	**al**	**sentier**
false	glances	although	late	from	you	released	[yet]	I turn	to the	path

false glances, although late in coming, released from you I turn to the path

di	li ber 'ta de	e	da 'mo ɾe	'zgom brol	'kɔ ɾe	ke	laŋ 'gwi	'sen tsa	pje 'ta de
di	**libertade,**	**e**	**d'Amore**	**sgombro'l**	**core,**	**che**	**languì**	**senza**	**pietade.**
of	freedom	and	from Love	I clear out the	heart	which	languished	without	pity

of freedom, and I empty my heart, which languished without pity, of Love.

libertade = (mod.) libertà;
pietade = (mod.) pietà

In [40] are the following 2nd and 3rd verses:

'bakː ko	a 'mi ko	a	de 'zir	'mje i	fu ga 'tor	de	pen 'sjɛr	're i	sol	marː 'ri da
Bacco,	**amico**	**a**	**desir**	**miei,**	**fugator**	**de'**	**pensier**	**rei,**	**sol**	**m'arrida,**
Bacchus	friend	to	desires	mine	purger	of	thoughts	evil	only	me may smile upon

May Bacchus, friend to my desires, purger of evil thoughts, but smile upon me –

'me ko	arː 'ri da	fe sted: 'dʒan te	fjamː medː 'dʒan te	tra	le	'tatː tse	ru bi 'no ze
meco	**arrida**	**festeggiante,**	**fiammeggiante**	**tra**	**le**	**tazze**	**rubinose,**
me with	may smile	joyfully	glowingly	among	the	cups	of ruby

smile with me joyfully, glowingly, among ruby goblets,

e	min 'vi ti	co	'swɔ in 'vi ti	'tʃin to	in	krin	'de de ɾa	e	'rɔ ze
e	**m'inviti**	**co'**	**suo' inviti,**	**cinto**	**in**	**crin**	**d'edera**	**e**	**rose.**
and	me may entice	with	his exhortations	crowned	on	hair	with ivy	and	roses

suo'
=
suoi

and entice me with his exhortations, his head crowned with ivy and roses.

ki	da 'mor	mal	for tu 'na to	'pɔr tal	'kɔ ɾe	'ar so	e	pja 'ga to	i	'swɔ i	'dwɔ li
Chi	**d'Amor**	**mal**	**fortunato**	**porta 'l**	**core**	**arso**	**e**	**piagato,**	**i**	**suoi**	**duoli**
he who	of Love	not	fortunate	bears the	heart	burned	and	wounded	the	his	sorrows

ɾi kon ˈso li   ˈko i   pos: ˈsɛn ti   le ni ˈmen ti   di   ke   ˈbak: ko   ˈsa na   ˈlal me
riconsoli   co'i   possenti   lenimenti,   di   che   Bacco   sana   l'alme,
may console   with the   potent   reliefs   of   which   Bacchus   heals   the souls

May the one who, unlucky, has a heart burned and wounded by Love console his sorrows with the potent remedies by which Bacchus heals souls –

ˈbak: ko   ˈpi o   ˈbak: ko   ˈdi o   do na ˈtor   di   ˈla u ɾi   e   ˈpal me
Bacco   pio,   Bacco   dio,   donator   di   lauri   e   palme.
Bacchus   devout   Bacchus   god   giver   of   laurels   and   palms

devout Bacchus, god Bacchus, giver of laurels and palms.

In [7] are the following 2nd and 3rd verses, printed as text only:

ˈfug: go   a ˈmo ɾe   ˈem pjo   ti ˈɾan: no   ˈki o   ser ˈvi i   sol   per   ˈmi o   ˈdan: no
Fuggo   Amore,   empio   tiranno,   ch'io   servìi   sol   per   mio   danno;
I flee   love   cruel   tyrant   whom I   served   only   for   my   harm

I flee from Love, cruel tyrant, whom I have served only to my detriment;

i   mar ˈti ɾi   i   so ˈspi ɾi   le   kwe ˈɾɛ le   del   kru ˈdɛ le   non   ˈfi a   pju | *fia =*
i   martiri,   i   sospiri,   le   querele   del   crudele   non   fia   più | *(mod.)*
the   agonies   the   sighs   the   complaints   of the   cruel one   not   will be   more | *sarà*

ˈki o   ˈprɔ vi   ˈma i   si   di ˈvɛr si   ˈi o   sof: ˈfɛr si   dʒa   per   ˈlu i
ch'io   provi   mai,   sì   diversi   io   soffersi   già   per   lui
that I   may experience   never   so   different   I   I suffered   already   through   him

tor ˈmen ti   e   ˈgwa i
tormenti   e   guai.
torments   and   woes

no more will I experience the agonies, the sighs, the complaints of the cruel one, as I have already suffered so many different torments and woes because of him *[Love]*.

ˈmi o   di ˈlɛt: to   e   ˈmi o   kon ˈtɛn to   ˈprɛs: so   un   ˈri o   di   ˈpu ɾo   ar ˈdʒɛn to
Mio   diletto   e   mio   contento,   presso   un   rio   di   puro   argento,
my   pleasure   and   my   contentment   beside   a   brook   of   pure   silver

My pleasure and my contentment, beside a brook of pure silver,

ˈfi a   sul: ˈlɛr be   ˈver di   a ˈtʃer be   di   ri ˈpɔ zo   o bli ˈo zo   kon for ˈtar   laf: ˈflit: ta   ˈmen te
fia   sull'erbe   verdi acerbe,   di riposo   oblioso   confortar   l'afflitta   mente,
shall be   upon the grasses   green young   of repose   oblivious   to comfort   the afflicted   mind

upon the new green grass, shall be, in the repose of oblivion, comfort for my afflicted mind,

ˈo ve   ˈla u ɾa   ne   re ˈsta u ɾa   ke   tra   i   fjor   spi ˈɾar   si ˈsɛn te
ove   l'aura   ne   restaura,   che   tra   i   fior   spirar   si sente.
where   the breeze   of it   restores   that   among   the   flowers   to blow   is felt

where the breeze that I feel wafting among the flowers will restore me.

GL: **Amor[e], Bacco**

☙

[40]

pu ˈpil: le   ar ˈtʃɛ ɾe
Pupille arciere
Archer eyes

pu ˈpil: le   ar ˈtʃɛ ɾe   pu ˈpil: le   ˈne ɾe   ˈrɛ dʒo   al ˈbɛr go   da ˈmo ɾe
Pupille   arciere,   pupille   nere,   regio   albergo   d'Amore,
eyes   archer   eyes   dark   royal   residence   of Love

Archer eyes, dark eyes, royal abode of Love,

'vo i   'kwel: le   'se te   ke   tra fid: 'dʒe te   ke   sa et: 'ta te   il   'kɔ ɾe
voi   **quelle**   **sete,**   **che**   **trafiggete,**   **che**   **saettate**   **il**   **core.**
you   those   are   that   pierce   that   wound with an arrow   the   heart

| | sete = |
| | (mod.) siete |

you are they who pierce and wound my heart.

o   'lu tʃi   a 'ma te   'lu tʃi   be 'a te   'kjɛd: dʒo   mer 'tʃe de   aŋ 'ki o
O   **luci**   **amate,**   **luci**   **beate,**   **chieggio**   **mercede**   **anch'io,**
o   eyes   loved   eyes   blessed   I ask for   mercy   also I

| | chieggio = |
| | (mod.) chiedo |

O beloved eyes, blessed eyes, I too ask for mercy;

'da te mi   a 'i ta   'da te mi   'vi ta   non   pju   tor 'men ti   o   'di o
datemi   **aita,**   **datemi**   **vita,**   **non**   **più**   **tormenti,**   **o**   **Dio!**
give me   help   give me   life   not   more   torments   o   God

give me help – give me life, not more torments, o God!

'i o   per   'vo i   'sɛn to   'gra ve   tor 'men to   kru del: 'lis: si mi   'lu mi
Io   **per**   **voi**   **sento**   **grave**   **tormento,**   **crudellissimi**   **lumi.**
I   through   you   I feel   grave   torment   most cruel   eyes

I feel grave torment from you, cruelest eyes.

pur   'va mo   e   in 'tan to   da 'ma ɾo   'pjan to   'ver so   fon 'ta ne   e   'fju mi
Pur   **v'amo**   **e**   **intanto**   **d'amaro**   **pianto**   **verso**   **fontane**   **e**   **fiumi!**
yet   you I love   and   meanwhile   of bitter   weeping   I shed   fountains   and   rivers

Yet I love you and, meanwhile, I am shedding fountains and rivers of bitter tears!

GL: **Amore**

&

[39, 45]   In [45] titled **Il dannato.**

'val: li   pro 'fon de
Valli profonde
Deep valleys

'val: li   pro 'fon de   al   sol   ne 'mi ke   'ru pi   kel   tʃɛl   su 'pɛr be   mi nat: 'tʃa te
Valli   **profonde,**   **al**   **sol**   **nemiche,**   **rupi,**   **ch'el**   **ciel**   **superbe**   **minacciate,**
valleys   deep   to the   sun   hostile   cliffs   which the   sky   proud   you threaten

Deep valleys, hostile to the sun, cliffs which proudly threaten the sky,

| el (poet.) = il | in [45]: che'l = ch'el |

'grɔt: te   'on de   non   'par te   'ma i   si 'len tsjo   e   'nɔt: te
grotte,   **onde**   **non**   **parte**   **mai**   **silenzio**   **e**   **notte,**
grottos   whence   not   departs   ever   silence   and   night

grottos from which silence and night never depart,

'a er   ke   'da tra   'nu be   il   tʃɛl   'ɔk: ku pi   pre tʃi pi 'tan ti   'sas: si
aer   **che**   **d'atra**   **nube**   **il**   **ciel**   **occupi,**   **precipitanti**   **sassi,**
air   that   of dark   cloud   the   sky   you fill up   precipitating   rocks

| aer = aere |
| (poet.) = |
| aria, atmosfera |

air that fills the sky with a dark cloud, falling rocks,

'al te   di 'ɾu pi   'ɔs: sa   in se 'pol te   er 'bo ze   'mu ɾa   e   'rot: te
alte   **dirupi,**   **ossa**   **insepolte,**   **erbose**   **mura**   **e**   **rotte,**
tall   crags   bones   unburied   grass-covered   walls   and   broken

tall crags, unburied bones, broken walls overgrown with grass –

'dwɔ mi ni al 'bɛr go dʒa
d'uomini **albergo** **già,**
of men abode formerly
former abode of men

or	pur	kon 'dot: te	ke	'te mon	dʒir	tra	'vo i	ser 'pɛn ti	e	'lu pi
or	**pur**	**condotte**	**che**	**temon**	**gir**	**tra**	**voi**	**serpenti**	**e**	**lupi,**
now	yet	reduced	that	they fear	to go	among	you	serpents	and	wolves

> *gir = gire = (mod.) andare*

but now reduced [to a condition] where [even] serpents and wolves fear to go among you,

'er me	kam 'paɲ: ɲe	i na bi 'ta ti	'li di	'o ve	'vo tʃe	dwɔm	'ma i	'la er	non	'fjɛ de
erme	**campagne,**	**inabitati**	**lidi,**	**ove**	**voce**	**d'uom**	**mai**	**l'aer**	**non**	**fiede,**
remote	countrysides	uninhabited	shores	where	voice	of man	ever	the air	not	strikes

remote countrysides, uninhabited shores where the voice of man never cuts the air,

> *fiede: from "fiedere" = (mod.) "ferire"*

'om bre	son	'i o	dan: 'na ta	al	'pjan to	e 'tɛr no	ke	tra	'vo i	'vɛŋ go
ombre,	**son**	**io**	**dannata**	**al**	**pianto**	**eterno,**	**che**	**tra**	**voi**	**vengo**
shadows	am	I	damned	to the	weeping	eternal	that	among	you	I come

a	de plo 'rar	'mi a	'fe de	e	'spɛ ɾo	al	swɔn	de	la kri 'mo zi	'stri di
a	**deplorar**	**mia**	**fede**	**e**	**spero**	**al**	**suon**	**de'**	**lacrimosi**	**stridi,**
to	deplore	my	faith	and	I hope	at the	sound	of	tearful	cries

se	non	si 'pjɛ ga	il	tʃɛl	'mɔ ver	lin 'fɛr no
se	**non**	**si piega**	**il**	**ciel,**	**mover**	**l'inferno.**
if	not	submits	the	heaven	to move to pity	the hell

> *in [45]: muover[e] (= mover[e])*

shadows, I, who come among you to deplore my faith, am damned to eternal weeping; and I hope, if heaven does not yield to the sound of tearful cries, to move hell to pity.

✤ de' Cavalieri, Emilio (c.1550-1602)

Also known as del Cavaliere, he was born into a noble Roman family. In addition to being a composer, organist, and singer, he was a diplomat involved in secret missions for votes leading to the election of popes Innocent IX (in 1591) and Clement VIII (in 1592).

In 1587, when Cardinal Ferdinando de' Medici became Grand Duke of Tuscany, Cavalieri was made "overseer of artists and craftsmen and of vocal and instrumental musicians" at the Florence court. For the wedding of Ferdinando to Christine of Lorraine in 1589, he oversaw the production of the most lavish series of *intermedi* conceived to date, involving poets, composers, set designers, and costume designers including Caccini, Peri, Rinuccini, G. B. Strozzi, and Bardi.

He was an important contributor to pre-operatic genres, and he was composer of the first surviving play set entirely to music, *La Rappresentazione di Anima, et di Corpo,* which was produced in Rome in February 1600 and published later that year; the score is the earliest one printed with a figured bass.

Whether or not Cavalieri can be credited as "inventor" of the new style of monody (*stile rappresentativo*) was debated at the time. Caccini boasted in 1600 that he had been composing in this style for fifteen years; but Peri, in 1601, wrote in the preface to his score for *Euridice* that it was Cavalieri who "before any other so far as I know, enabled us with marvelous invention to hear our kind of music upon the stage *[Grove]*."

[13, 37]
from: *La Rappresentazione di Anima, e di Corpo (1600)*

mo 'nɔ lo go del 'tɛm po
Monologo del "Tempo"
Monologue of "Time"

il	'tɛm po	'fud: dʒe	la	'vi ta	si di 'strud: dʒe	e	dʒa	mi par	sen 'ti ɾe
Il	**tempo**	**fugge,**	**la**	**vita**	**si distrugge,**	**e**	**già**	**mi par**	**sentire**
the	time	flies	the	life	is being consumed	and	already	to me it seems	to hear

'lul ti ma   'trom ba   e   'di ɾe
l'ultima   tromba   e   dire:
the last   trumpet   and   to say

Time flies by, life is wasting away; and I already seem to hear the last trumpet saying:

uʃ: 'ʃi te   'dal: la   'fɔs: sa   'tʃe ne ɾi   'spar se   e 'dɔs: sa
"Uscite   dalla   fossa,   ceneri   sparse,   ed ossa;
come out   from the   grave   ashes   dispersed   and bones

"Come out of your graves, scattered ashes and bones;

sor 'dʒe te   'a ni me   aŋ 'ko ɾa   pren 'de te   i   'kɔr pi   o 'ro ɾa
sorgete,   anime   ancora,   prendete   i   corpi   or ora;
rise   souls   again   take   the   bodies   now

rise up again, souls, re-enter your bodies now;

> *in* [37]: *var. of "or ora":*
> *ognora* [oɲ: 'ɲo ɾa] = always

ve 'ni te   a   dir   il   've ro   se   fu   miʎ: 'ʎor   pen 'sjɛ ro
Venite   a   dir'   il   vero,   se   fu   miglior   pensiero
come   to   to say   the   truth   if   was   better   thought

Come, tell the truth: was it a better idea

ser 'vi ɾe   al   'mon do   'va no   o   al   re   del   tʃɛl   so 'pra no
servire   al   mondo   vano,   o   al   Re   del   Ciel   soprano?
to serve   to the   world   vain   or   to the   King   of the   Heaven   sovereign

to serve the vain world or the sovereign King of Heaven?

si   ke   tʃa 'skun   in 'tɛn da   'a pra   ʎi   'ɔk: ki   e   kom 'prɛn da
Sì,   che   ciascun   intenda,   apra   gli   occhi   e   comprenda
yes   [that]   everyone   let heed   let open   the   eyes   and   let understand

Yes, let everyone take heed, open their eyes and understand

ke   'kwe sta   'vi ta   ɛ   'vɛn to   ke   'vo la   in   un   mo 'men to
che   questa   vita   è   vento   che   vola   in   un   momento.
that   this   life   is   wind   which   blows away   in   a   moment

that this life is a wind which blows away in an instant.

'ɔd: dʒi   vjɛn 'fɔ ɾe   do 'man   si 'mɔ ɾe   'ɔd: dʒi   nap: 'pa ɾe   do 'man   di 'spa ɾe
Oggi   vien fore,   doman   si more;   oggi   n'appare,   doman   dispare.
today   comes forth   tomorrow   dies   today   to us appears   tomorrow   disappears

Today it emerges, tomorrow it dies; today it appears, tomorrow it disappears.

> *in* [37]: *fuore* ['fwɔ ɾe] = *fore* = (mod.) *fuori; ne appare* [ne ap: 'pa ɾe] = *n'appare*

'fat: tʃa   'duŋ kwe   oɲ: 'ɲun   'prɔ va   'men tril   'tɛm po   ʎi   'dʒo va
Faccia   dunque   ognun   prova,   mentr'il   tempo   gli   giova,
let make   then   each one   trial   while the   time   to him   avails

Let each one then try, while time is still on his side,

> *in* [37]: *mentre il*
> ['men tre il]
>   = *mentr'il*

laʃ: 'ʃar   kwan 'tɛ   nel   'mon do   kwan 'tuŋ kwin   se   dʒo 'kon do
lasciar   quant'è   nel   mondo,   quantunqu'in   sé   giocondo,
to leave   so much is   in the   world   even if in   himself   merry

to leave whatever is in this world, however merry in itself,

> *in* [37]:
> *quantunque in*
> [kwan 'tun kwe in]
> = *quantunqu'in*

e 'dɔ pri   kon   la   man   'ɔ pri   kol   'kɔ ɾe
ed opri   con   la   man,   opri   col   core,
and may work   with   the   hand   may work   with the   heart

and work with his hands, work with his heart,

> *opri: from*
> *"oprare"* =
> (mod.) *"operare"*

per	'ke	del	bɛn	o 'prar	'frut: to	ɛ	lo 'no ɾe
perché	**del**	**ben**	**oprar**	**frutto**	**è**	**l'onore."**	
because	of the	good	to perform	fruit	is	the honor	

because honor is the fruit of doing good deeds."

var. in [37]:
bene = ben

 ## della **Ciaia**, *Azzolino Bernardino* (1671-1755)

Organist, composer, and organ builder, he was born in Siena into a wealthy family and became at a very young age a page of the Gran Maestro of the Pisan Cavalieri di S. Stefano, the Grand Duke of Tuscany. In 1678 he joined that order of knights. During a tour of sea duty with them his ship often stopped in Marseilles, where he heard and examined organs by Flemish builders.

After being called back to Pisa to be part of the governing council, he was sent to Rome in 1713 as secretary to the Colonna-Barbaglia family; in 1730 he returned permanently to Pisa.

In 1733 he began the design and execution, soliciting the help of many of the principal Italian organ makers of the time, of a magnificent organ for S. Stefano – "the best organ in Tuscany and one of the most beautiful in Italy" *[Grove]* – with four manuals and more than sixty stops. It was first played on November 28, 1737, at the funeral of Giovangastone de' Medici.

Though della Ciaia is known today mostly for his instrumental music (sonatas, toccatas, and ricercares), he also wrote sacred vocal music (psalms, masses, and an oratorio) and solo cantatas.

---

[57]

se mi di 'tʃes: si o 'va ga
Se mi dicessi, o vaga
If you said to me, o pretty one

se	mi	di 'tʃes: si		o 'va ga		nɔ	non	map: 'pa ga	'lɔk: kjo
Se	**mi**	**dicessi,**		**o**	**vaga:**	**No,**	**non**	**m'appaga**	**l'occhio,**
if	to me	you said		o	pretty one	no	not	me gratifies	the eye

il	'lab: bro	il	'ri zo	il	pjɛ	non	pjan dʒe 'rɛ i
il	**labbro,**	**il**	**riso,**	**il**	**pie',**	**non**	**piangerei.**
the	lip	the	laughter	the	foot	not	I would weep

If you said to me, o pretty one, "No, your eyes, your lips, your laughter, your feet do not gratify me,"
I would not weep.

ma	il	dir	kɛ	tra di 'to ɾe	'kwe sto	'mi o	'kɔ ɾe
Ma	**il**	**dir**	**ch'è**	**traditore**	**questo**	**mio**	**core**
but	the	saying	that is	traitor	this	my	heart

ti par		'prɛ mjo	'al: la	'mi a	fe	kru 'dɛl	ke	'sɛ i
ti par		**premio**	**alla**	**mia**	**fe',**	**crudel**	**che**	**sei?**
to you seems		prize	to the	my	fidelity	cruel one	that	you are

But to say that my heart is untrue – do you think this is reward for my faithfulness, o cruel one?

 ## de **Rochechouart**, *Gabriel* (? - ?)

The Rochechouart family had several branches, the most famous of which is that of Mortemart. The only information found about this composer is printed in notes in [51]: "The Marquis of Mortemart, mentioned in 'The Burwell Lute Tutor' as composer of the concordance to the song 'Se voi, luci amate,' was Gabriel de Rouchechouart, Marquis de Mortemart, 'premier gentilhomme de la Chambre du Roi,' made duke and peer in 1650. He was the father of Madame de Montespan, mistress of Louis XIV."

[51]

se 'vo i 'lu tʃi a 'ma te
Se voi, luci amate
If you, beloved eyes

se	'vo i	'lu tʃi	a 'ma te	mi	'so lo	mi 'ra te	fe 'li tʃe	vi 'vrɔ
Se	**voi,**	**luci**	**amate,**	**mi**	**solo**	**mirate**	**felice**	**vivrò!**
if	you	eyes	beloved	to me	only	you look	happy	I will live

If you, beloved eyes, will only look at me, I will live happily!

ma	se	in	'al tra	'par te	lo	'zgwar do	dʒi 'ra te	sɛn 'tsal tro	mor: 'rɔ
Ma	**se**	**in**	**altra**	**parte**	**lo**	**sguardo**	**girate**	**senz'altro**	**morrò.**
but	if	to	other	side	the	glance	you turn	certainly	I will die

But if you turn your glance elsewhere, I will certainly die.

e	se	non	lo	kre 'de te	pro 'var lo	po 'te te	kol	'vɔl dʒer ve lo
E	**se**	**non**	**lo**	**credete**	**provarlo**	**potete**	**col**	**volgervelo.**
and	if	not	it	you believe	to test it	you can	with the	turning away you it

And if you do not believe it, you can try it by turning away.

ma	'so lo	pen 'sar lo	o i 'mɛ	non	ve 'de te	non	ve 'de te	ke	'mɔ ɾo	di 'dʒa
Ma	**solo**	**pensarlo –**	**Ohimè!**	**Non**	**vedete?**	**Non**	**vedete**	**che**	**moro**	**di già?**
but	only	think of it	alas	not	you see	not	you see	that	I die	already

But just think of it – alas, don't you see? Do you not see that I am already dying?

> moro = muoio

> In [51] *are two versions of this song; the "variant" version does not include the following 3rd verse:*

a	'fɔl: le	va 'ned: dʒo	non	've do	ke	'kjɛ do	kwel	ke	non	si 'pwɔ
Ah!	**Folle**	**vaneggio!**	**Non**	**vedo**	**che**	**chiedo**	**quel**	**che**	**non**	**si può?**
ah	foolish	I rave	not	I see	that	I ask	that	which	not	is possible

Ah, I am raving foolishly! Do I not see that I am asking the impossible?

ke	'sɔʎ: ʎon	le	'dɔn: ne	far	'sɛm pre	al: la 'pɛd: dʒo	'i o	'duŋ kwe	'mɔ ɾo
Ché	**soglion**	**le**	**donne**	**far**	**sempre**	**alla peggio,**	**io**	**dunque**	**moro.**
because	are accustomed	the	women	to do	always	at the worst	I	therefore	I die

As women are used to always acting carelessly, I am therefore dying.

✦ d'*India, Sigismondo* (c.1580-1629)

Of noble Sicilian birth, by 1600 he was in Florence, where famous singers such as Giulio Caccini and Vittoria Archilei performed his songs. From 1611 to 1623 he was *maestro della musica di camera* at the court of Carlo Emanuele I, Duke of Savoy, in Turin. After a short time at the Este court in Modena he moved on to Rome, where he was under the patronage of Cardinal Maurizio of Savoy. In 1626 he took a permanent position at the Este court; he spent his last years either in Rome or in Modena.

The originality of d'India's monodies attest to his thorough schooling in the techniques and expressive devices of the late Renaissance polyphonic madrigal. His eighty-four chamber monodies are in genres of the time: strophic arias, variations, madrigals, and laments. His strophic arias (either dance-songs or canzonettas) are set to light verses by poets such as Chiabrera; his solo madrigals are typically settings of serious, sophisticated poetry by poets such as Rinuccini and Guarini.

---

[14]

'ka ɾa 'mi a 'tʃe tran 'dja mo
Cara mia cetr' andiamo
Let's go, my dear cither

'ka ɾa　'mi a　'tʃe tran 'dja mo　a　ri tro 'var　ko 'lɛ i　kɛ　'mi o　'so lo　de 'zi o
Cara   mia   cetr' andiamo   a   ritrovar   colei   ch'è   mio   solo   desio,
dear   my   cither let us go   to   to find   her   who is   my   sole   desire

Let's go, my dear cither, to find her who is my sole desire,

'tu o   sol   od: 'dʒɛt: to
tuo   sol   oggetto.
your   sole   object

your sole object *[of your intentions]*.

'kwi vi   a   te   da   le   'kɔr de   a   me
Quivi   a   te   da'   le   corde   a   me,
therein   at   you   give   the   strings   to   me

Therein lend your strings to me;

dal   'pɛt: to   'ɛ skan   ʎat: 'tʃen ti   'twɔ i   ʎaf: 'fan: ni   'mjɛ i
dal   petto   escan   gl'accenti   tuoi   gl'affanni   miei,
from the   breast; *(fig.)* heart   may come out   the inflections   your   the afflictions   mine

may your inflections and my afflictions come from the heart,

ke   pje 'to zar mo 'ni a   pwɔ   'for sim pe 'trar   'pa tʃe   a   'lal ma   'mi a
ché   pietos' armonia   può   fors' impetrar   pace   a   l'alma   mia.
because   merciful harmony   is able   perhaps to implore   peace   to   the soul   mine

for a merciful harmony may perhaps beg peace for my soul.

ॐ

[55]   *Francesco Petrarca*

'men tre kel kɔr
Mentre che'l cor
While my heart

'men tre kel   kɔr   'daʎ: ʎi a mo 'ro zi   'vɛr mi   fu   kon su 'ma to   en   'fjam: ma mo 'ro 'zar se
Mentre che'l   cor   dagli amorosi   vermi   fu   consumato   e'n   fiamm' amoros' arse,
while   [that] the   heart   by the   amorous   worms   was   consumed   and in   flames amorous burned

While my heart was being consumed by amorous worms and burned in amorous flames

di   'va ga   'fɛ ɾa   le   ve 'sti dʒa   'spar se   tʃer 'ka i
di   vaga   fera   le   vestigia   sparse   cercai
of   lovely   cruel woman   the   traces   scattered   I searched for

| *fera =* |
| *(mod.)* |
| *fiera* |

I searched for the scattered traces of the lovely, cruel woman

per   'pɔd: dʒi   so li 'ta ɾi   e 'der mi   e 'dɛb: bi   ar 'dir   kan 'tan do   di   do 'ler mi   da 'mor
per   poggi   solitari   ed ermi;   ed ebbi   ardir,   cantando,   di   dolermi   d'amor,
through   hills   solitary   and remote   and I had   courage   singing   of   to complain   of Love

throughout solitary and remote hills; and I had the courage, singing, to complain about love,

printed "solitarii" = (mod.) "solitari"

di   'lɛ i   ke   si   'du ɾa   map: 'par se   ma   lin 'dʒeɲ: ɲo   e   le   'ri 'mɛ ɾa no
di   lei,   che   sì   dura   m'apparse;   ma   l'ingegno   e   le   rim' erano
of   her   who   so   harsh   to me showed   but   the mind   and   the   rhymes were

about her who was so harsh to me; but my mind and poetry were

apparse = (mod.) apparì

'skar se   in   kwel: le 'ta de   'a i   pen 'sjer   'nwɔ vi   e   in 'fer mi
scarse   in   quell'etade   ai   pensier   nuovi   e   infermi.
scanty   in   that age   at the   thoughts   new   and   infirm

slight at that age, as my thoughts were young and weak.

etade =
(mod.) età

kwel	'fɔ ko	ɛ	'mɔr tel 'kɔ prun		'pit: tʃol	'mar mo
Quel	**foco**	**è**	**mort' e'l copr' un**		**picciol**	**marmo:**
that	fire	is	dead and it covers a		small	marble

That passion is dead, and a small marble *[gravestone]* covers it.

ke	se	kol	'tɛm po	'fos: se	'i to	a van 'tsan do	'ko me	dʒa	in	'al tri
che	**se**	**col**	**tempo**	**fosse**	**ito**	**avanzando**	**come**	**già**	**in**	**altri,**
[that]	if	with the	time	were	gone	advancing	like	now	in	others

If, with time, it *[the passion]* had grown, as it has in others,

> *ito: from "ire" (lit.) = "andare"*

in 'fi no	'al: la	vek: 'kjet: tsa	di	'ri me	ar 'ma to	on 'ɔd: dʒi	mi di 'zar mo
in fino	**alla**	**vecchiezza,**	**di**	**rime**	**armato**	**ond'oggi**	**mi disarmo,**
until	to the	old age	with	rhymes	armed	which today	I surrender

to old age, I, armed with rhymes which today I discard,

kon	stil	ka 'nu to	a 'vrɛ i	'fat: to	par 'lan do	'rom per	le	'pjɛ tre
con	**stil**	**canuto**	**avrei**	**fatto,**	**parlando,**	**romper**	**le**	**pietre,**
with	style	of old age	I would have	made	speaking	to break	the	stones

e	'pjan dʒer	di	dol 'tʃet: tsa
e	**planger**	**di**	**dolcezza.**
and	to weep	with	sweetness

would have made the rocks split and weep with sweetness at my words in mature style.

[55]

o del 'tʃɛ lo da 'mor
O del Cielo d'Amor
O, of the Heaven of Love

o	del	'tʃɛ lo	da 'mor	'u ni ko	'so le	'spɛk: kjo	de	se mi 'dɛ i	'al	'tu o	'rad: dʒo
O	**del**	**Cielo**	**d'Amor**	**unico**	**sole,**	**specchio**	**de'**	**semidei,**	**al**	**tuo**	**raggio**
o	of the	Heaven	of Love	unique	sun	mirror	of	demigods	at	your	ray

al	'tu o	'lu me	al	'tu o	'dar do	a	'ki o	'ar do
al	**tuo**	**lume**	**al**	**tuo**	**dardo,**	**ah**	**ch'io**	**ardo!**
at the	your	light	at the	your	arrow	ah	that I	I burn

O unique sun of the Heaven of Love, mirror of the demigods, ah, how I burn in your rays, in your light, at your arrow *[piercing beam]*!

dɛ	'mi ra min	'vi zo	'mi a	'dʒɔ ja	'mi a	'vi ta	'mi o	'ka ro	te 'zɔ ro
Deh,	**mirami'n**	**viso,**	**mia**	**gioia,**	**mia**	**vita,**	**mio**	**caro**	**tesoro,**
pray	look at me in	face	my	joy	my	life	my	dear	treasure

Pray look into my face, my joy, my life, my dear treasure.

sat: 'tʃe zo	son	'i o	'a i	ke	mi 'strug: go	mi 'sfat: tʃo	mi 'mo ro	kɔr	'mi o
s'acceso	**son**	**io,**	**ahi,**	**che**	**mi struggo,**	**mi sfaccio,**	**mi moro**	**cor**	**mio!**
set on fire	am	I	alas	[that]	I waste away	I come undone	I die	heart	mine

I am on fire; alas, I am wasting away, I am fading, I am dying, my beloved!

GL: **Amor**

Falconieri, Andrea (1585 or 1586-1656)

Brought up in Parma by the Duke in the house of Farnese, by 1610 Falconieri had succeeded his teacher Santino Garsi as official court lutenist in Parma. From 1614 through 1639, when he was appointed lutenist for the royal chapel at Naples, he was in Florence, Modena, Spain, France, and Genoa in the various capacities of chitarrone player, court musician, or music teacher. In 1647 he was appointed *maestro di cappella* at the court of the King of Naples, his birthplace, and he held this post until his death from the plague.

Though it is known from historical writings that Falconieri was a prolific songwriter, his surviving songs – among the first to distinguish stylistically in the same song between recitative or arioso and aria – are few. They include songs published in Rome in 1616 in the collection *Libro primo di villanelle*, and in *Il quinto libro delle musiche* (in three volumes) published in Florence in 1619.

[11]

ar ˈmil: la iŋ ˈgra ta
Armilla ingrata
Ungrateful Armilla

ar ˈmil: la	iŋ ˈgra ta	ki	ˈmjɛ i	so ˈspi ɾi	pju	non	ˈmi ɾi
Armilla	**ingrata,**	**ch'i**	**miei**	**sospiri**	**più**	**non**	**miri.**
Armilla	ungrateful	[that] the	my	sighs	more	not	you see

Ungrateful Armilla, you will no longer see my sighs.

non	ti stu ˈpi ɾe	ˈki o	non	vɔ	pju	laŋ ˈgwi ɾe
Non	**ti stupire,**	**ch'io**	**non**	**vò**	**più**	**languire.**
not	yourself be surprised	that I	not	want	more	to languish

Do not be surprised that I wish to languish no more.

ˈal tra	ˈfjam: ma	ˈar de	il	kɔr	ˈmi o	non	tel	dis: ˈsi o
Altra	**fiamma**	**arde**	**il**	**cor**	**mio;**	**non**	**te'l**	**diss'io.**
other	flame	burns	the	heart	my	not	you it	told I

Another passion ignites my heart; didn't I tell you [this would happen]?

ta ˈmɔ	il	kɔr	ˈmi o	tra	ˈmil: le	ˈgwa i	e	tul	ˈsa i
T'amò	**il**	**cor**	**mio**	**tra**	**mille**	**guai,**	**e**	**tu'l**	**sai.**
you I loved	the	heart	my	among	thousand	complaints	and	you it	know

My heart loved you despite a thousand complaints, and you know that.

ma	al ˈfin	sag: ˈgi ɾa	ko ˈlɛ i	ke	trɔp: po	a ˈspi ɾa
Ma	**alfin'**	**s'aggira**	**colei**	**che**	**troppo**	**aspira.**
but	finally	herself deceives	she	who	too much	aspires to

But in the end she who aspires to too much deceives herself.

[11, 48]

beʎ: ˈʎɔk: ki lu ˈtʃɛn ti
Begl'occhi lucenti
Beautiful bright eyes

bɛʎ: 'ʎɔk: ki	lu 'tʃɛn ti	ka 'fɔr tsa di	'fɔ ko	in	'ri zo	e	in	'dʒɔ ko
Begl'occhi	**lucenti,**	**ch'a forza di**	**foco,**	**in**	**riso,**	**e**	**in**	**gioco,**
beautiful eyes	bright	which by dint of	fire	in	laughter	and	in	fun

Beautiful bright eyes which, because of your fire, in laughter and in play,

in [48]: che a = ch'a

tor 'na te	i	tor 'men ti	bɛʎ: 'ʎɔk: ki	lu 'tʃɛn ti	se	'tan to	vo 'no ɾo
tornate	**i**	**tormenti,**	**begl'occhi**	**lucenti,**	**se**	**tanto**	**v'onoro,**
return	the	torments	beautiful eyes	bright	as	so much	you I honor

bring back [to me] your torments, beautiful bright eyes, as I honor you so much,

vol 'dʒe te	pje 'to zi	'kwɛ i	'rad: dʒi	a mo 'ɾo zi	ve 'de te	'ki o	'mɔ ɾo
volgete	**pietosi**	**quei**	**raggi**	**amorosi.**	**Vedete**	**ch'io**	**moro.**
turn	compassionate	those	rays	amorous	see	that I	I die

turn those loving rays [toward me] compassionately. See that I am dying.

in [48]: che moro = ch'io moro

a 'pe na	re 'spi ɾo	nel	'gra ve	'mi o	'dwɔ lo	e	'lal ma	sul	'vo lo
A pena	**respiro,**	**nel**	**grave**	**mio**	**duolo,**	**e**	**l'alma**	**sul**	**volo,**
with difficulty	I breathe	in the	deep	my	grief	and	the soul	on the	flight

I hardly breathe in my deep grief, and my soul in its flight

in [48]: Appena = (lit.) a pena

si 'sta	dun	so 'spi ɾo
si sta	**d'un**	**sospiro;**
stays	of a	sigh

is suspended on a sigh;

	nel	'gra ve	'mi o	'fɔ ko	e	'lal ma	sul	'vo lo
var. in [48]:	**nel**	**grave**	**mio**	**foco**	**e**	**l'alma**	**sul**	**volo**
	in the	deep	my	fire	and	the soul	on the	flight

...in my deep passion, and my soul in its flight

sen 'sta	dun	so 'spi ɾo
sen sta	**d'un**	**sospiro;**
stays	of a	sigh

is suspended on a sigh;

ap: 'pe na	re 'spi ɾo	e	pur	'i o	non	'mi ɾo	se non	fe ɾi 'ta te
appena	**respiro**	**e**	**pur'**	**io**	**non**	**miro,**	**se non**	**feritate.**
scarcely	I breathe	and	yet	I	[not]	I see	[if not] only	cruelty

I scarcely breathe, and yet I only see cruelty.

in [48]: feritade; feritate, feritade = (mod.) ferità (lit.) = crudeltà

kan 'dʒa te	ko 'stu mi	o	'ful dʒi di	'lu mi	por 'ta te	pje 'ta te
Cangiate	**costumi,**	**o**	**fulgidi**	**lumi.**	**Portate**	**pietate.**
change	customs	o	shining	eyes	bring	pity

Change your ways, o shining eyes. Have pity.

pietate, pietade = (mod) pietà

in [48]: ... e pur io non miro se non feritade. O fulgidi lumi pietade.
= ... and yet I only see cruelty. O shining eyes, [have] pity.

❧

[41, 48]

'bɛl: la fan 'tʃul: la
Bella fanciulla
Beautiful maiden

'bɛl: la fan 'tʃul: la dal 'vi zo ro 'za to ke 'ma i pri 'va to di 'mi a li ber 'ta de
Bella fanciulla dal viso rosato, che m'hai privato di mia libertade,
beautiful young girl with the face rosy who me you have deprived of my liberty
Beautiful maiden with rosy face, you who have deprived me of my freedom,

in [48]: libertatede = libertade = (mod.) libertà

'ab: bi pje 'ta de al 'mi o 'gra ve mar 'ti ɾe 'bɛl: la fan 'tʃul: la non mi far mo 'ri ɾe
abbi pietade al mio grave martire; bella fanciulla, non mi far morire!
have pity to the my grave suffering beautiful young girl not me to make to die
have pity on my deep suffering; beautiful maiden, do not make me die!

in [48]: pietate = pietade = (mod.) pietà

o fan tʃul: 'let: ta da 'ʎɔk: ki ri 'dɛn ti ke si lu 'tʃen ti 'mos tri i 'two i 'bɛ i 'ra i
O fanciulletta da gl'occhi ridenti, che sì lucenti mostri, i tuoi bei rai,
o dear young girl of the eyes laughing which so bright you show the your beautiful eyes
O dear maiden with laughing eyes which you show off so brightly, your beautiful eyes

dagli, in [48] = da gl'

pon 'fi ne o 'ma i al 'mi o 'gra ve mar 'ti ɾe o fan tʃul: 'let: ta non mi far mo 'ri ɾe
pon' fine omai al mio grave martire; o fanciulletta, non mi far morire!
put end now to the my grave suffering o dear young girl not me to make to die
must now put an end to my grave suffering; o dear maiden, do not make me die!

omai (poet.) = ormai

[48] ends here; in [41] are two more verses:

o par go 'let: ta 'dal: la 'bɛl: la 'bok: ka 'on de tra 'bok: ka di dol 'tʃet: tsa un 'ma ɾe
O pargoletta dalla bella bocca, onde trabocca di dolcezza un' mare,
o child with the beautiful mouth where overflows of sweetness a sea
O child with the beautiful mouth from which overflows a sea of sweetness,

dɛh non ne 'ga ɾe a 'i ta al 'mi o mar 'ti ɾe o par go 'let: ta non mi far mo 'ri ɾe
deh non negare aita al mio martire; o pargoletta, non mi far morire!
please not to deny help to the my suffering o child not me to make to die
please do not refuse help for my suffering; o child, do not make me die!

o don dzel: 'let: ta 'del: le 'tʃiʎ: ʎa 'bɛl: le 'do ve 'du e 'stel: le an 'tʃi da no il 'mi o 'kɔ ɾe
O donzelletta delle ciglia belle, dove due stelle ancidano il mio core,
o dear damsel of the brows beautiful where two stars kill the my heart
O dear damsel with the beautiful brows beneath which two eyes are killing my heart,

ancidano: from "ancidere" (lit.) = "uccidere"

'ab: bi do 'lo ɾe al 'mi o 'gra ve mar 'ti ɾe o don dzel: 'let: ta non mi far mo 'ri ɾe
abbi dolore al mio grave martire; o donzelletta, non mi far morire!
have sorrow to the my grave suffering o dear damsel not me to make to die
be sorry for my deep suffering; o dear damsel, do not make me die!

℅

[10, 19, 22, 24, 37, 41]

'bɛl: la 'pɔr ta di ru 'bi ni
Bella porta di rubini
Beautiful ruby portal

'bɛl: la 'pɔr ta di ru 'bi ni 'ka pri il 'var ko 'a i 'dol tʃi at: 'tʃen ti
Bella porta di rubini, ch'apri il varco ai dolci accenti,
beautiful portal of rubies that opens the way to the sweet words
Beautiful ruby portal, which opens to sweet words

ke	'ne i	'ri zi	pe ɾe 'gri ni	'skɔ pri	'pɛr le	ri lu 'tʃɛn ti
che	**nei**	**risi**	**peregrini**	**scopri**	**perle**	**rilucenti,**
that	in the	smiles	rare	uncovers	pearls	shining

and reveals, in rare smiles, shining pearls,

tu	da 'mor	'dol tʃe	'a u ra	'spi ri	re fri 'dʒɛ ɾjo	'a i	'mjɛ i	mar 'ti ɾi
tu	**d'amor**	**dolce**	**aura**	**spiri,**	**refrigerio**	**ai**	**miei**	**martiri.**
you	of love	sweet	air	breathe	relief	to the	my	torments

you breathe the sweet air of love, comfort to my sufferings.

> *vars.:*
> *dolc'aura =*
> *dolce aura;*
> *a' miei = ai miei*

> *The following 2ⁿᵈ verse does not appear in [10], [22], or [24]:*

in	te	'kju ze	a 'mor	sa 'ga tʃe	i	dol 'tʃis: si mi	di 'lɛt: ti
In	**te**	**chiuse**	**Amor**	**sagace**	**i**	**dolcissimi**	**diletti,**
in	you	enclosed	Love	sagacious	the	sweetest	delights

Shrewd Love enclosed in you the sweetest delights,

'po ze	il	'sɛɲ: ɲo	in	te	di	'pa tʃe	'ri zi	'ba tʃi	e	'ka ɾi	'det: ti
pose	**il**	**segno**	**in**	**te**	**di**	**pace,**	**risi,**	**baci**	**e**	**cari**	**detti.**
put	the	sign	in	you	of	peace	smiles	kisses	and	dear	words

placed in you the signals for peace: smiles, kisses, and endearing words.

'e i	per	te	tri 'on fa	e	'reɲ: ɲa	vin tʃi 'tri tʃe	ar 'dɛn te	in 'seɲ: ɲa
Ei	**per**	**te**	**trionfa**	**e**	**regna,**	**vincitrice**	**ardente**	**insegna.**
He	through	you	triumphs	and	reigns	conquering	ardent	emblem

He triumphs and reigns through you, [his] ardent, victorious emblem.

> *In [19] the following verse is printed as text for a 4ᵗʰ verse:*

vet: tso 'zet: ta	e	'fre ska	'rɔ za	u mi 'det: to	e	'dol tʃe	'lab: bro
Vezzosetta	**e**	**fresca**	**rosa,**	**umidetto**	**e**	**dolce**	**labbro,**
charming	and	fresh	rose	moist	and	sweet	lip

Charming fresh rose, moist sweet lips

'ka i	la	'man: na	ru dʒa 'do za	sul	bel: 'lis: si mo	tʃi 'na bro
ch'hal	**la**	**manna**	**rugiadosa**	**sul**	**bellissimo**	**cinabro,**
which has	the	manna	dewy	on the	most beautiful	crimson

> *alt: "su'l" = "sul"*

with dewy manna upon your most beautiful crimson,

> *alt:* **manna spiritosa** [spi ɾi 'to za] *(antiquated spelling: spirituosa) =* ...with sparkling manna...

non	par 'lar	ma	'ri di	e	'ta tʃi	'si an	ʎi	at: 'tʃɛn ti	i	'nɔ stri	'ba tʃi
non	**parlar,**	**ma**	**ridi**	**e**	**taci,**	**sian**	**gli**	**accenti**	**i**	**nostri**	**baci.**
not	to speak	but	smile	and	be silent	may be	the	words	the	our	kisses

do not speak, but [rather] smile and be silent; may our kisses be our words.

> *alt: sien = (mod.) sian*

> *In [19] the following verse is printed as text for a 3ʳᵈ verse:*

tu	'sɛ	'lan tro	on 'dɛʃ: ʃe 'fwɔ ɾi	un	bɛl	'dzɛf: fi ro	o do 'ra to	e	in	te
Tu	**se'**	**l'antro**	**ond'esce fuori**	**un**	**bel**	**zeffiro**	**odorato;**	**e**	**in**	**te**
you	are	the cavern	where comes out	a	beautiful	zephyr	fragrant	and	in	you

You are the chamber from which emanates a beautiful fragrant breath; in you

'naʃ: ʃe	e	in	te	si 'mwɔ re	kwel	so 'spir	ke	mɛ	si	'gra to
nasce,	**e**	**in**	**te**	**si muore**	**quel**	**sospir**	**che**	**m'è**	**sì**	**grato;**
is born	and	in	you	dies	that	sigh	which	to me is	so	welcome

is born and dies that sigh which is so welcome to me;

di   te   'stes: sa   'sɛ i   la   'trom ba   e   de   'ba tʃi   a 'ma ta   'tom ba
di   te   stessa   sei   la   tromba,   e   de'   baci   amata   tomba.
of   you   yourself   you are   the   trumpet   and   of   kisses   beloved   tomb

you are the passage to your very self, and the receptacle of beloved kisses.

GL: **Amor**

ॐ

[43]

'ka ɾa ɛ la 'rɔ za e 'va ga
Cara è la rosa, e vaga
Dear and lovely is the rose

'ka ɾa   ɛ   la   'rɔ za   e   'va ga   pur   se   in   dʒar 'din   do 'vel: la   ɛ   'pɔ sta
Cara   è   la   rosa,   e   vaga,   pur   se   in   giardin   dov'ella   è   posta,
dear   is   the   rose   and   lovely   even   if   in   garden   where it   is   placed

Dear and lovely is the rose even if, in the garden where it is situated

ɛ   'so la   kon   la   bel: 'let: tsa   'su a   'lɔk: kjo   men   'pa ga
è   sola.   Con   la   bellezza   sua   l'occhio   m'en   paga,
it is   alone   with   the   beauty   its   the eye   me of it   satisfies

it is alone. With its beauty my eyes are content;

ma   se   'mi sto   ɛ   kon   'kwel: la   il   kan di 'det: to   'dʒiʎ: ʎo
ma   se   misto   è   con   quella   il   candidetto   giglio,
but   if   mixed   it is   with   that one   the   pure white   lily

but if it is combined with [the beauty of] the pure white lily,

o   'ko me   'bɛl: la   o   'ko me   ɛ   'bɛl: la
o   come   bella,   o   come   è   bella!
oh   how   beautiful   oh   how   it is   beautiful

oh, how beautiful – oh, how beautiful it is!

o   'ko me   il   de 'zir   'vo la   'den tro   a   kwel   'mi sto
O   come   il   desir   vola   dentro   à   quel   misto,
oh   how   the   desire   flies   within   to   that   mixture

Oh, how my desire flies to that combination

e   'gɔ de   'a u ɾe   a mo 'ro ze   re 'stan do   'pa go   in   mi 'ɾar   'dʒiʎ: ʎi   e   'rɔ ze
e   gode   aure   amorose,   restando   pago   in   mirar   gigli   e   rose.
and   enjoys   breaths   loving   being   satisfied   in   looking at   lilies   and   roses

and enjoys loving breaths, satisfied by looking at the lilies and roses.

ko 'zi   la   'vi va   'rɔ za   ke   nel   kan 'dor   di   'bɛl: la   'gwan tʃa   'splɛn de
Così   la   viva   rosa   che   nel   candor   di   bella   guancia   splende
thus   the   alive   rose   which   in the   whiteness   of   beautiful   cheek   is radiant

Thus does the living rose, which glows in the whiteness of beautiful cheeks,

kon   la   va 'get: tsa   'su a   'la ni ma   at: 'tʃɛn de
con   la   vaghezza   sua   l'anima   accende;
with   the   beauty   its   the soul   ignites

ignite the soul with its beauty;

ma   se   'maŋ ka   il   bɛl   'saŋ gwe   del   por po 'ra to   'fjo ɾe   o   'ko me   'laŋ gwe
ma   se   manca   il   bel   sangue   del   porporato   fiore,   o   come   langue.
but   if   is lacking   the   beautiful   blood   of the   crimson   flower   oh   how   languishes

but if the beautiful life-blood of the crimson flower is lacking, oh how [the soul] languishes.

dɛ	'sɛm pre	il	kan 'dor	'va go	di 'skɔ pra	a 'mor	nel	'tu o	dʒen 'til	ver 'miʎ: ʎo
Deh	**sempre**	**il**	**candor**	**vago**	**discopra**	**Amor**	**nel**	**tuo**	**gentil**	**vermiglio,**
ah	always	the	whiteness	lovely	may reveal	Love	in the	your	gentle	vermilion

Ah, may Love always reveal the lovely whiteness in your gentle vermilion,

re stan 'di o	'pa go	in	mi 'rar	'rɔ za	e	'dʒiʎ: ʎo
restand'io	**pago**	**in**	**mirar**	**rosa,**	**e**	**giglio.**
remaining I	satisfied	in	looking at	rose	and	lily

while I remain content looking at the rose and lily.

GL: **Amor**

&

[14, 40]

'dɔn: niŋ 'gra ta
Donn'ingrata
Ungrateful woman

'dɔn: niŋ 'gra ta	'sɛn tsa	a 'mo ɾe	dʒa	per	te	'lal ma	si 'mo ɾe
Donn'ingrata,	**senza**	**amore,**	**già**	**per**	**te**	**l'alma**	**si more,**
woman ungrateful	without	love	[already]	for	you	the soul	itself dies

Ungrateful unloving woman, my soul is dying for you;

e	tu	oɲ: 'ɲor	kon 'stan te	e	'fɔr te	'pɔ ko	'ku ɾi	la	'su a	'mɔr te
e	**tu**	**ognor**	**constante**	**e**	**forte**	**poco**	**curi**	**la**	**sua**	**morte.**
and	you	always	constant	and	strong	little	heed	the	its	death

> *constante*
> *= (mod.)*
> *costante*

and you, always firm and strong, care little about its death.

ko 'zi	va	ki	a	'ma la	'sɔr te
Così	**va**	**chi**	**ha**	**mala**	**sorte!**
thus	goes	he who	has	bad	luck

So it goes for him who has bad luck!

se	ti	'sɛr vo	e	son	fi 'dɛ lɛ	tu	mi	'fudː dʒi	e	'sɛ ı	kru 'dɛ le
Se	**ti**	**servo**	**e**	**son**	**fidele,**	**tu**	**mi**	**fuggi**	**e**	**sei**	**crudele.**
if	you	I serve	and	I am	faithful	you	me	flee	and	you are	cruel

When I serve you and am faithful, you flee from me and are cruel.

> *fidele = (mod.) fedele*

'kwe sta	'duŋ kwe	ɛ	la	mer 'tʃe de	del	'mi o	a 'mor	'delː la	'mi a	'fe de
Questa	**dunque**	**è**	**la**	**mercede**	**del**	**mio**	**amor,**	**della**	**mia**	**fede.**
this	then	is	the	reward	of the	my	love	of the	my	faithfulness

This, then, is the reward for my love, my faithfulness.

ko 'zi	va	ki	a	'dɔn: na	'kre de
Così	**va**	**chi**	**a**	**donna**	**crede!**
thus	goes	he who	in	woman	believes

So it goes for him who believes in a woman!

> *In* [40] *is a 3rd verse:*

da	te	iŋ 'gra ta	non	voʎː 'ʎi o	'al tro i 'mɛ	kun	'zgwar do	'pi o
Da	**te,**	**ingrata,**	**non**	**vogl'io**	**altr', ohimè,**	**ch'un**	**sguardo**	**pio.**
from	you	ungrateful one	not	want I	other alas	than a	glance	compassionate

From you, ungrateful one, I wish for nothing other, alas, than a compassionate glance.

e	pur	'sɛm pre	mal	mi 'ra to	mal	gra 'di to	e	mal	trat: 'ta to
E	**pur**	**sempre**	**mal**	**mirato,**	**mal**	**gradito**	**e**	**mal**	**trattato.**
and	yet	always	badly	looked at	badly	appreciated	and	badly	treated

And yet I am always poorly seen, unappreciated, and badly treated.

ko 'zi	va	ki	ɛ	zven tu 'ra to
Così	**va**	**chi**	**è**	**sventurato!**
thus	goes	he who	is	unlucky

So it goes for him who is unlucky!

&

[11]

'fil: li vet: 'tso za 'fil: li a mo 'ro za
Filli vezzosa, Filli amorosa
Charming Filli, amorous Filli

'fil: li	vet: 'tso za	'fil: li	a mo 'ro za	del	'va go	a 'pri le	vi	ɛ	pju	dʒen 'ti le
Filli	**vezzosa,**	**Filli**	**amorosa,**	**del**	**vago**	**aprile**	**vi**	**è**	**più**	**gentile**
Filli	charming	Filli	amorous	of the	lovely	april	[here]	is	more	gracious

Charming Filli, amorous Filli, you are more gracious than lovely April,

ma	pju	spje 'ta ta	ke	'fjɛ ɾa	i 'ra ta
ma	**più**	**spietata,**	**che**	**fiera**	**irata.**
but	more	merciless	than	wild beast	angry

but more merciless than an angry wild beast.

se	nel	'tu o	'vi zo	ri 'mi ɾo	'fi zo	un	'tʃɛl	se 're no	di	'stel: le	'pjɛ no
Se	**nel**	**tuo**	**viso**	**rimiro**	**fiso,**	**un**	**ciel'**	**sereno**	**di**	**stelle**	**pieno**
if	in the	your	face	I look at	fixed	a	heaven	serene	of	stars	full

'splɛn dan	pju	as: 'sa i	i	'twɔ i	'bɛ i	'ra i
splendan'	**più**	**assai**	**i**	**tuoi**	**bei**	**rai.**
shine	more	much	the	your	beautiful	eyes

When I gaze in your face, much more than a serene heaven full of stars shines in your beautiful eyes.

GL: **Filli**

&

[24, 27]

non pju da 'mo ɾe
Non più d'amore
No more suffering of love

non	pju	da 'mo ɾe	non	pju	dar 'do ɾe	'pe ne	e	tor 'men ti	doʎ: 'ʎo zi	at: 'tʃen ti
Non	**più**	**d'amore,**	**non**	**più**	**d'ardore,**	**pene**	**e**	**tormenti,**	**dogliosi**	**accenti;**
not	more	of love	not	more	of passion	sufferings	and	torments	sorrowful	words

No more suffering, torment, and sorrowful words of love and passion;

'al: la	'mi a	'dʒɔ ja	'fug: ga	'oɲ: ɲi	'no ja
alla	**mia**	**gioia**	**fugga**	**ogni**	**noia!**
at the	my	joy	may flee	every	trouble

may all troubles flee at my joy!

di	'kwe i	'bɛ i	'ra i	non	'si an	pju	'ma i	ʎi	'zgwar di	a 'ma ti
Di	**quei**	**bei**	**rai**	**non**	**sian**	**più**	**mai**	**gli**	**sguardi**	**amati**
of	those	beautiful	eyes	not	may be	more	ever	the	glances	beloved

May the beloved glances from those beautiful eyes nevermore be

'fjɛ ɾi	o	spje 'ta ti	ma	da 'mor	'pjɛ ni	'splen dan	se 're ni
fieri	**o**	**spietati,**	**ma**	**d'amor**	**pieni**	**splendan**	**sereni.**
proud	or	pitiless	but	of love	full	may shine	serenely

proud or pitiless; rather may they shine serenely, full of love.

in [27]: splendin[o]
= (mod.) splendan[o]

The following is the 4ᵗʰ verse in [27]:

i	so spi 'ra ti	'dʒor ni	be 'a ti	men vɔ	pas: 'san do	'dol tʃe	kan 'tan do
I	**sospirati**	**giorni**	**beati**	**men vo**	**passando**	**dolce**	**cantando.**
the	longed-or	days	blessed	I go	passing	sweet	singing

I spend the longed-for blessed days in sweet song –

o	'dol tʃe	'vi ta	a	me	gra 'di ta
O	**dolce**	**vita**	**a**	**me**	**gradita.**
o	sweet	life	to	me	pleasing

o sweet life, pleasing to me.

The following is the 3ʳᵈ verse in [27]:

al	'mi o	dʒo 'i ɾe	'fug: ga	il	laŋ 'gwi ɾe	e	nel	'mi o	'pet: to	'vi va	il	di 'let: to
Al	**mio**	**gioire**	**fugga**	**il**	**languire.**	**E**	**nel**	**mio**	**petto**	**viva**	**il**	**diletto;**
at	my	rejoicing	may flee	the	languishing	and	in the	my	breast	may live	the	delight

May languishing flee at my rejoicing, and may delight live in my breast;

e 'tɛr na	'si a	la	'dʒɔ ja	'mi a
eterna	**sia**	**la**	**gioia**	**mia!**
eternal	may be	the	joy	my

may my joy be eternal!

❧

[24, 27]

'nu do ar 'tʃɛ ɾo

Nudo arciero

Naked archer

'nu do	ar 'tʃɛ ɾo	ke	si	al 'tje ɾo	'va i	dʒo 'kan do	'va i	sker 'tsan do
Nudo	**arciero,**	**che**	**sì**	**altiero,**	**vai**	**giocando,**	**vai**	**scherzando.**
naked	archer	who	so	proud	you go	playing	you go	joking

Naked archer *[Cupid]*, you who go around playing [and] joking so proudly –

in [27]: ...vai giocando e scherzando. = you go around playing and joking.

tu	ke	i	'kɔ ɾi	ut: 'tʃi di	e	'strud: dʒi	'vi a	lon 'ta no	o 'ma i	ten 'fud: dʒi
Tu,	**che**	**i**	**cori**	**uccidi**	**e**	**struggi,**	**via**	**lontano**	**omai**	**ten fuggi!**
you	who	the	hearts	kill	and	consume	away	far	now	yourself flee

you who destroy and consume hearts, now flee far away!

The following is the 2ⁿᵈ verse in [27]:

non	tar 'da ɾe	di	spje 'ga ɾe	vɛr	le	'stel: le	'la li	'bɛl: le
Non	**tardare**	**di**	**spiegare**	**ver**	**le**	**stelle**	**l'ali**	**belle;**
not	to delay	of	to spread	toward	the	stars	the wings	beautiful

Do not delay spreading your beautiful wings toward the stars;

ver (poet.) = verso

e	tra	i	'dɛ i	'vi vi	im: mor 'ta li	'ɔ pra	'lar ko	'ɔ pra	ʎi	'stra li
e	**tra**	**i**	**dei**	**vivi**	**immortali**	**opra**	**l'arco,**	**opra**	**gli**	**strali.**
and	among	the	gods	living	immortal	may open	the bow	may open	the	arrows

and among the living, immortal gods may you unloose your bow and arrows.   *opra: from "oprire" = (mod.) "aprire"*

The following is the 3rd verse in [27], the 2nd in [24]:

'nɔ va	ar 'tʃɛ ɾa	'ɔd: dʒi	im 'pɛ ɾa	ke	il	'tu o	'fɔ ko	'prɛn de	in	'dʒɔ ko
Nova	**arciera**	**oggi**	**impera,**	**che**	**il**	**tuo**	**foco**	**prende**	**in**	**gioco,**
new	archeress	today	rules	who	the	your	fire	takes	in	play

A new archeress rules today who makes a mockery of your fire

e	'de i	'two i	son	pju	pos: 'sɛn ti	i	'swo i	'stra li	'a spri	e	puŋ 'dʒɛn ti
e	**dei**	**tuoi**	**son**	**più**	**possenti,**	**i**	**suoi**	**strali**	**aspri**	**e**	**pungenti.**
and	than the	yours	are	more	powerful	the	her	arrows	sharp	and	stinging

and whose sharp and stinging arrows are more powerful than yours.   *in [27]: de' = dei*

The following is the 3rd (and last) verse in [24]:

non	tar 'da ɾe	di	spje 'ga ɾe	vɛr	le	'stel: le	'la li	'bɛl: le
Non	**tardare**	**di**	**spiegare**	**ver**	**le**	**stelle**	**l'ali**	**belle.**
not	to delay	of	to spread	toward	the	stars	the wings	beautiful

Do not delay spreading your beautiful wings toward the stars;

tu	ke	i	'kɔ ɾi	ut: 'tʃi di	e	'strud: dʒi	'vi a	lon 'ta no	o 'ma i	ten 'fud: dʒi
Tu,	**che**	**i**	**cori**	**uccidi**	**e**	**struggi,**	**via**	**lontano**	**omai**	**ten fuggi!**
you	who	the	hearts	kill	and	consume	away	far	now	yourself flee

you who destroy and consume hearts, now flee far away!

The following is the 4th verse in [27]:

'su o	va 'lo ɾe	ɛ	mad: 'dʒo ɾe	ne	per	'pro va	si ri 'trɔ va	ki
Suo	**valore**	**è**	**maggiore;**	**né**	**per**	**prova**	**si ritrova**	**chi**
her	strength	is	greater	nor	through	test	is found	one who

il	'su o	'fɔ ko	'ɔd: dʒi	non	'sɛn ta	on 'doɲ: 'ɲal ma	'ar de	e	spa 'vɛn ta
il	**suo**	**foco**	**oggi**	**non**	**senta**	**ond' ogn'alma**	**arde**	**e**	**spaventa.**
the	her	fire	today	not	feels	wherefrom every soul	burns	and	frightens

Her strength is greater; and it is proven that no one can be found today who does not feel her fire, which burns and frightens every soul. *("Her" refers to the "Nova arciera," above.)*

The following is the 5th (and last) verse in [27]:

tra	le	'rɔ ze	'tjɛ ne	a 'sko ze	'spi ne	a 'ma ɾe	ke	pe 'na ɾe	'fan: no
Tra	**le**	**rose**	**tiene**	**ascose**	**spine**	**amare**	**che**	**penare**	**fanno**
among	the	roses	holds	hidden	thorns	bitter	which	to suffer	make

oɲ: 'ɲor	'la ni me	e	i	'kɔ ɾi	tra	le	aŋ 'gɔʃ: ʃe	e	tra	i	do 'lo ɾi
ognor	**l'anime**	**e**	**i**	**cori**	**tra**	**le**	**angosce**	**e**	**tra**	**i**	**dolori.**
always	the souls	and	the	hearts	among	the	anguishes	and	among	the	sorrows

Hidden among the roses are sharp thorns which always make souls and hearts suffer in anguish and sorrow.

[10, 19, 21, 24, 42]

o	bel: 'lis: si mi	ka 'pel: li
	O bellissimi capelli	
	O most beautiful tresses	

o	bel: 'lis: si mi	ka 'pel: li	'mjɛ i	dol 'tʃis: si mi	di 'lɛt: ti	a mo 'ro zi	ser pen 'tɛl: li
O	**bellissimi**	**capelli,**	**miei**	**dolcissimi**	**diletti,**	**amorosi**	**serpentelli,**
o	most beautiful	tresses	my	sweetest	delights	amorous	little snakes

O most beautiful tresses – my sweetest delights, amorous little snakes

ke	ri 'tɔr ti	in	a nel: 'let: ti	diʃː ʃen 'de te	in fra	le	'rɔ ze	'del: le	'gwan tʃe	ru dʒa 'do ze
che	**ritorti**	**in**	**anelletti,**	**discendete**	**in fra**	**le**	**rose**	**delle**	**guancie**	**rugiadose.**
[that]	twisted	in	ringlets	you descend	among	the	roses	of the	cheeks	dewy

twisted into ringlets – you fall down amidst the roses of her dewy cheeks.

> de le = (mod.) delle

The following 2nd verse is the 3rd verse in [19]:

'tret: tʃe	om 'bro ze	ove	sa 'skon de	per	fe 'rir	la 'la to	ar 'tʃe ro
Treccie	**ombrose,**	**ove**	**s'asconde,**	**per**	**ferir,**	**l'alato**	**arciero,**
locks	shady	where	himself hides	for	to strike	the winged	archer

Shady locks where the winged archer *[Cupid]* hides, waiting to strike,

'tʃe dan	pju	le	'kjo me	'bjon de	'bɛl: le	'tret: tʃe	al	'vɔ stro	'ne ro
cedan	**più**	**le**	**chiome**	**bionde,**	**belle**	**treccie,**	**al**	**vostro**	**nero,**
let yield	more	the	hair	blond	beautiful	locks	to the	your	dark

may locks of blond hair yield more to your beautiful dark ones

> *in [19]: cedin[o] (poet.) = cedan[o]*

> *in [19]:* **pur** [pur], *rather than* **più,** *is printed.* = may locks of blond hair indeed yield to your beautiful dark ones...

ke	sker 'tsan do	al	'vi zo	in 'tor no	'nɔt: te	'sje te	e	ʎi	'ɔk: ki	'dʒor no
che	**scherzando**	**al**	**viso**	**intorno,**	**notte**	**siete**	**e**	**gli**	**occhi**	**giorno.**
which	playing	at the	face	around	night	are	and	the	eyes	day

which, playing around your face, are like the night, and your eyes like the day.

> *in [19]: gl'occhi = gli occhi*

In [19] the following is the 2nd verse:

'vi ve	'fjam: me	'on dil	kɔr	'ar se	'bɛl: le	'kjo me	pel: le 'gri ne
Vive	**fiamme**	**ond'il**	**cor**	**arse,**	**belle**	**chiome**	**pellegrine**
bright	flames	where the	heart	burned	beautiful	hair	wandering

Bright flames with which my heart burned, beautiful wandering tresses

kon ded: 'dʒa te	al: 'la u ɾa	'spar se	su	le	'gwan tʃe	por po 'ri ne
ch'ondeggiate	**all'aura**	**sparse**	**su**	**le**	**guance**	**porporine,**
which waved	at the air	spilled	on	the	cheeks	purple

which, wavy in the breeze, spilled upon your rosy cheeks,

al: lat: 'tʃa te	il	'pɛt: to	'mi o	li ber 'ta de	ad: 'di o
allacciate	**il**	**petto**	**mio:**	**libertade**	**addio.**
(lit.) you seduce	the	breast	mine	liberty	farewell

you seduce my breast: liberty, farewell!

> libertade = (mod.) libertà

> printed "a Dio" =
> (mod.) "addio"

In [19] the following is a 4th verse:

'dol tʃi	'nɔ di	del	'mi o	'kɔ ɾe	'ca ɾi	'lat: tʃi	del	'mi o	'pɛt: to
Dolci	**nodi**	**del**	**mio**	**core,**	**cari**	**lacci**	**del**	**mio**	**petto,**
sweet	bonds	of the	my	heart	dear	snares	of the	my	breast

Sweet bonds of my heart, dear snares of my breast,

'sɛn tsa	'vo i	non	ɔ	va 'lo ɾe	fwɔr	di	'vo i	non	ɛ	di 'lɛt: to
senza	**voi**	**non**	**ho**	**valore,**	**fuor**	**di**	**voi**	**non**	**è**	**diletto,**
without	you	not	I have	worth	away	from	you	not	is	delight

without you I have no worth; away from you there is no delight.

'sɛr vo	son	'ɛk: ko vi	il	'brat: tʃo	'si a	ka 'te na	un	'vɔ stro	'lat: tʃo
servo	**son**	**eccovi**	**il**	**braccio**	**sia**	**catena**	**un**	**vostro**	**laccio.**
servant	I am	here is to you	the	arm	be it	chain	a	your	snare

I am your servant; here is my arm – may your snare be a chain.

&

[10, 19, 24, 27, 38, 41]

ok: 'kjet: ti a 'ma ti
Occhietti amati
Beloved eyes

ok: 'kjet: ti	a 'ma ti	ke	min tʃen 'de te	per 'ke	spje 'ta ti	or 'ma i	pju	'sje te
Occhietti	**amati**	**che**	**m'incendete,**	**perché**	**spietati**	**ormai**	**più**	**siete?**
eyes	beloved	which	me ignite	why	pitiless	now	more	you are

alt.: omai (poet.) = ormai

Beloved eyes, which set me on fire, why are you more pitiless now?

'splen dan	se 'ɾe ni	di	'dʒɔ ja	'pjɛ ni	'vɔ stri	splen 'do ɾi	'fjam: me	'de i	'kɔ ɾi
Splendan	**sereni,**	**di**	**gioia**	**pieni,**	**vostri**	**splendori,**	**fiamme**	**dei**	**cori.**
let shine	serene	of	joy	full	your	splendors	flames	of the	hearts

in [27]:
Splendin[o]
(poet.)
= Splendan[o]
alt.: de' = dei

Let your splendors, which inflame hearts, shine serenely and full of joy.

'bok: ka	ver 'miʎ: ʎa	'ka i	per	kon 'fi ni	o	me ɾa 'viʎ: ʎa	'pɛr le	e	ru 'bi ni
Bocca	**vermiglia**	**ch'hai**	**per**	**confini,**	**o**	**meraviglia,**	**perle**	**e**	**rubini,**
mouth	vermilion	that has	for	boundaries	oh	wonder	pearls	and	rubies

Red mouth bordered – oh wonder – with pearls and rubies,

in [27]: che hai = ch'hai

'kwan do	ri 'dɛn te	'kwan do	kle 'mɛn te	di 'ɾa i	ben	'mi o	'i o	'ar do	aɲ 'ki o
quando	**ridente,**	**quando**	**clemente,**	**dirai:**	**ben**	**mio,**	**io**	**ardo**	**anch'io?**
when	smiling	when	merciful	you will say	dear one	my	I	burn	also I

when, smiling and merciful, will you say, "My dear one, I too am burning with love"?

[10] *and* [24] *end here; following is the 3rd (and last) verse in* [38] *and* [41], *the 4th (and last) verse in* [27] *and* [19]:

'si o	non	laŋ 'gwi sko	per	te	'mi a	'dʒɔ ja	'si o	non	pa 'ti sko	'i o	'tɔ sto	'mwɔ ja
S'io	**non**	**languisco**	**per**	**te,**	**mia**	**gioia,**	**s'io**	**non**	**patisco,**	**io**	**tosto**	**muoia;**
if I	not	I languish	for	you	my	joy	if I	not	I suffer	I	soon	I may die

If I do not languish for you and suffer, my joy, I may soon die;

ma	'si o	to 'no ɾo	o	'mi o	te 'zɔ ɾo	'kan dʒa	in	pje 'ta te	'tu a	fe ɾi 'ta te
ma	**s'io**	**t'onoro,**	**o**	**mio**	**tesoro,**	**cangia**	**in**	**pietate**	**tua**	**feritate.**
but	if I	you honor	o	my	treasure	change	into	pity	your	cruelty

but if I honor you *[your wishes]*, o my treasure, [then] change your cruelty to pity.

alt.: pietade = pietate = (mod.) pietà   *alt.: feritade = feritate = (mod.) ferità = crudeltà*

The following is the 3rd verse in [27] *and* [19]:

'kre di	'mi o	'kɔ ɾe	ke	oɲ: 'ɲor	pju	'fɔr te	'fi a	in	me
Credi,	**mio**	**core,**	**che**	**ognor**	**più**	**forte**	**fia**	**in**	**me**
believe	my	heart	that	always	more	strong	will be	in	me

in [19]: ch'ogn'or
= che ognor
fia = (mod.) sarà

lar 'do ɾe	'si no 'al: la	'mor te
l'ardore	**sino alla**	**morte.**
the passion	up until to the	death

Believe, my darling, that my passion will be ever stronger until death.

ne	'si a	ki	'tɛn ti	far	'me no	ar 'dɛn ti	i	'mjɛ i	so 'spi ɾi	i	'mjɛ i	mar 'ti ɾi
Né	**sia**	**chi**	**tenti**	**far**	**meno**	**ardenti**	**i**	**miei**	**sospiri,**	**i**	**miei**	**martiri.**
not	may be	who	may try	to make	less	ardent	the	my	sighs	the	my	tortures

May no one attempt to make my sighs and torments less ardent.

☙

[10, 19, 43]

'se gwi 'se gwi do 'lɛn te 'kɔ ɾe
Segui, segui, dolente core
Follow, follow, aching heart

'se gwi	'se gwi	do 'lɛn te	'kɔ ɾe	ʎi	'ɔk: ki	'fon ti	del	'vi vo	ar 'do ɾe
Segui,	**segui,**	**dolente**	**core,**	**gli**	**occhi**	**fonti**	**del**	**vivo**	**ardore,**
follow	follow	aching	heart	the	eyes	sources	of the	living	passion

Follow, follow, aching heart, the eyes which are the source of my living passion –

'stel: le	'kja ɾe	'stel: le	lu 'tʃɛn ti	a mi 'ɾar si	'ful mi ni	ar 'dɛn ti
stelle	**chiare,**	**stelle**	**lucenti,**	**a mirarsi,**	**fulmini**	**ardenti.**
stars	bright	stars	shining	to look at	lightnings	burning

bright stars, shining stars, [which are] like looking at lightning flashes.

e	se	a	'ra i	'tan to	se 're ni	'for tsa	ɛ	pur	'ki o	'pjaŋ ga	e	'pe ni
E	**se**	**a**	**rai**	**tanto**	**sereni**	**forza**	**è**	**pur**	**ch'io**	**pianga**	**e**	**peni**
and	if	at	eyes	so	serene	necessary	it is	yet	that I	weep	and	suffer

And if I must yet weep and suffer from eyes so serene

vɔ	pe 'na ɾe	kɔr	'mi o	per	bɛn	a 'ma ɾe
vo'	**penare,**	**cor**	**mio,**	**per**	**ben**	**amare.**
I want	to suffer	heart	my	in order to	well	to love

I want to suffer, my heart, so as to love well.

'fug: ga	'fug: ga	sik: 'ko me	il	'vɛn to	'kwe sta	'va ga	del	'mi o	tor 'men to
Fugga,	**fugga**	**siccome**	**il**	**vento**	**questa**	**vaga**	**del**	**mio**	**tormento;**
may flee	may flee	as	the	wind	this	charming one	of the	my	torment

May this charming one flee like the wind from my torment;

'ko me	'tʃɛ ka	non	'ma i	ri 'mi ɾi	'lal to	'pe zo	de	'mjɛ i	mar 'ti ɾi
come	**cieca**	**non**	**mai**	**rimiri**	**l'alto**	**peso**	**de'**	**miei**	**martiri:**
like	blind	not	ever	may she see	the high	weight	of	my	agonies

may she, as though blind, never know the profundity of my sufferings;

'ki o	per	me	non	'ma i	pen 'ti to	del	do 'lor	'kwa zi	in fi 'ni to
ch'io	**per**	**me,**	**non**	**mai**	**pentito**	**del**	**dolor**	**quasi**	**infinito,**
because I	for	myself	not	ever	repentant	of the	sorrow	almost	infinite

for I, never regretful of my nearly infinite sorrow,

vɔ	pe 'na ɾe	kɔr	'mi o	per	bɛn	a 'ma ɾe
vo'	**penare,**	**cor**	**mio,**	**per**	**ben**	**amare.**
I want	to suffer	heart	my	in order to	well	love

want to suffer, my heart, so as to love well.

☙

[9, 19, 34, 54]

vet: tso 'zet: te e 'ka ɾe pu pil: 'let: te
Vezzosette e care pupillette
Pretty and dear little eyes

vet: tso	'zet: te	e	'ka ɾe	pu pil: 'let: te	ar 'dɛn ti
Vezzosette		**e**	**care**	**pupillette**	**ardenti,**
pretty		and	dear	little eyes	ardent

Pretty and dear little ardent eyes,

ki	va	'fat: to	a 'va ɾe	'de i	'bɛ i	'ra i	lu 'tʃen ti
chi	**v'ha**	**fatto**	**avare**	**dei**	**bei**	**rai**	**lucenti?**
who	you has	made	miserly	of the	beautiful	rays	shining

who has made you miserly with your beautiful shining rays?

> var.:
> de' = dei

'si o	ri 'mi ɾo	i	'vos tri	'zgwar di	'skɔr go	sol	'ful mi ni	e	'dar di
S'io	**rimiro**	**i**	**vostri**	**sguardi**	**scorgo**	**sol**	**fulmini**	**e**	**dardi;**
If I	I gaze at	the	your	glances	I perceive	only	lightning bolts	and	arrows

If I gaze at your glances I see only flashes and darts;

ne	ve 'der	sɔ	pju	kwel	'ri zo	ke	ren 'de a	si	'va go	il	'vi zo	a
né	**veder**	**so**	**più**	**quel**	**riso**	**che**	**rendea**	**sì**	**vago**	**il**	**viso.**	**Ah!**
nor	to see	I know how	more	that	smile	which	made	so	charming	the	face.	Ah!

I can no longer see that smile which used to make your face so charming. Ah!

> [19] and [34] omit the "Ah!"
> rendea = rendeva

> [9] and [54] end here; [19] prints the following verses as text only:

ki	va	'fat: to	o 'sku ɾe	pu pil: 'let: te
Chi	**v'ha**	**fatto**	**oscure,**	**pupillette**
who	you has	made	dark	little eyes

'bɛl: le	ke	se 'ɾe ne	e	'pu ɾe	ras: sem bra 'va te	'stel: le
belle	**che**	**serene,**	**e**	**pure**	**rassembravate**	**stelle?**
beautiful	as	serene	and	indeed	you resembled	stars

Who darkened you, little eyes as beautiful as serene,
which indeed shone [before] like stars?

> I changed the printed "rassembravi" to "rassembravate," because "pupillette" needs a plural verb.
> Paton, in [34], prints "rassembrami" which, if the correct original, is not a plural verb form either...

ki	ma	'tɔl to	i	'dol tʃi	'ra i
Chi	**m'ha**	**tolto**	**i**	**dolci**	**rai?**
who	me has	taken away	the	sweet	rays

Who has taken your sweet glances away from me?

'dil: lo	a 'mor	se	tu	lo	'sa i	'dil: lo
Dillo,	**amor,**	**se**	**tu**	**lo**	**sai,**	**dillo,**
say it	love	if	you	it	you know	say it

Say it, love, if you know; say it,

e	'si a	kwel	ke	si	'si a	o	di 'sprɛt: tso	o	dʒe lo 'zi a
e	**sia**	**quel**	**che**	**si**	**sia**	**o**	**disprezzo,**	**o**	**gelosia.**
and	be it	that	which	itself	be	either	contempt	or	jealousy

and be it what it is, whether contempt or jealousy.

> In [34]: quel che si fia ['fi a] = (and be it) what will be; fia = (mod.) sarà

> The following is printed in [34] as the 2nd verse, which is the 3rd verse of the original poem:

non	pju	zdeɲ: ɲo 'zet: te	ri mi 'rar	vi	'vɔʎ: ʎo
Non	**più**	**sdegnosette**	**rimirar**	**vi**	**voglio,**
not	more	scornful little ones	to gaze at	you	I wish

I do not wish, scornful little ones, to gaze at you anymore

ne	pju	su per 'bet: te	sof: 'frir	'tanto	or 'goʎ: ʎo
né	**più**	**superbette**	**soffrir**	**tanto**	**orgoglio,**
nor	more	proud little ones	to suffer	so much	arrogance

nor anymore, proud little ones, to suffer so much arrogance;

ke	ve 'der	'si o	non	vof: 'fe zi	'vɔ stri	'ra i	di	'zdeɲ: ɲo	at: 'tʃe zi
ché	**veder**	**s'io**	**non**	**v'offesi**	**vostri**	**rai**	**di**	**sdegno**	**accesi,**
because	to see	if I	not	you I offended	your	eyes	of	scorn	ignited

pu pil: 'let: te	ɛ	in 'dʒu sto	'dwɔ lo	o	ri 'de te	o	'i o	'prɛn do	il	'vo lo
pupillette,	**è**	**ingiusto**	**duolo**	**o**	**ridete,**	**o**	**io**	**prendo**	**il**	**volo.**
little eyes	is	unjust	pain	either	smile	or	I	I take	the	flight

for to see, when I did not offend you, your eyes lit up with scorn, little eyes, is unjust pain.
Either smile, or I will flee.

[34] *omits the "io" of "io prendo"*

❋ *Fasolo, Giovanni Battista* (c.1598-c.1664)

Composer, organist, organ teacher, and a Franciscan friar, Fasolo spent much of his time in Sicily, where by 1645 he enjoyed the patronage of the Prince of Paterno. From 1659 to 1664 he was *maestro di cappella* to the Archbishop of Monreale, near Palermo.

Among his sacred music output, his important *Annuale (1645)* contains music to provide a parish organist with enough pieces (hymns, masses, ricercares, canzonas, fugues) for services of an entire ecclesiastical year.

Fasolo's earliest printed collections are of secular arias for voice and guitar: *La barchetta passaggiera*, renamed *Misticanza di vigna alla bergamasca* after the title of its first aria, and *Il carro di Madama Lucia*, which begins with a lament of Lucia in the *commedia dell'arte* tradition.

[5, 9]

'kan dʒa 'kan dʒa 'tu e 'vɔʎ: ʎe
Cangia, cangia tue voglie
Change, change your wishes

'kan dʒa	'kan dʒa	'tu e	'vɔʎ: ʎe	o	'mi o	kɔr	ke	fe 'de le	'fo sti
Cangia,	**cangia**	**tue**	**voglie,**	**o**	**mio**	**cor,**	**che**	**fedele**	**fosti**
change	change	your	wishes	o	my	heart	because	faithful	you were

a	'dɔn: na	kru 'dɛ le
a	**donna**	**crudele.**
to	woman	cruel

Change, change your wishes, o my heart, for you were faithful to a cruel woman.

	non	tak: 'kɔr dʒi	me 'skin	ke	'sɛ i	fe 'ri to
Refrain:	**Non**	**t'accorgi,**	**meschin,**	**che**	**sei**	**ferito?**
	not	you realize	wretch	that	you are	wounded

Do you not realize, o wretched one, that you are wounded?

'laʃ: ʃa	'laʃ: ʃa	da 'mar	ki	ta	tra 'di to
Lascia,	**lascia**	**d'amar**	**chi**	**t'ha**	**tradito.**
leave	leave	of to love	the one who	you has	betrayed

Cease, cease loving the one who has betrayed you.

'laʃ: ʃa	'laʃ: ʃa	da 'ma ɾe	ki	ti	'fin dʒe	kol	'ri zo
Lascia,	**lascia**	**d'amare**	**chi**	**ti**	**finge**	**col**	**riso,**
leave	leave	of to love	the one who	to you	pretends	with the	smile

Cease, cease loving the one who deceives you with her smile,

kol   mo 'strar ti   il   bɛl   'vi zo
col   mostrarti   il   bel   viso.
with the   showing you   the   beautiful face
showing you her beautiful face.

In [9] a 3rd verse is printed as text only:

've di   pur   'ko me   il   'kan to   ɛ   ka 'dʒon   di   'tu e   'dɔʎː ʎe
Vedi   pur   come   il   canto   è   cagion   di   tue   doglie!
see   indeed how   the   song   is   cause   of   your   sufferings
See, indeed, how the song is the cause of your sufferings!

'kan dʒa   'kan dʒa   'tu e   'vɔʎː ʎe
Cangia,   cangia   tue   voglie.
change   change   your   wishes
Change, change your wishes.

&

[10]

'lun dʒi 'lun dʒi ɛ a 'mor da me
Lungi, lungi è amor da me
Love is far, far away from me

'lun dʒi   'lun dʒi   ɛ   a 'mor   da   me   da 'ke   'fu i   tra 'di to
Lungi,   lungi   è   amor   da   me   da che   fui   tradito...
far   far   is   love   from me   since   I was   betrayed | *da che = (mod.) dacché* |
Love is far, far away from me since I was betrayed...

dʒa   da   te   'dɔnː na   'sɛn tsa   fe
già   da   te   donna   senza   fé.
now   from   you   woman   without   faith
now [I am far] from you, faithless woman.

'vanː ne   pur   su 'pɛr ba   va   do 'vɛ   a 'mor   kon   'lar ko   al 'tɛ ro
Vanne   pur,   superba,   va   dov'è   Amor   con   l'arco   altero,
go away   then   haughty one go   where is love   with   the bow   proud
Go away then, haughty one – go where Love is, with his proud bow

'koɲː ɲi   kɔr   fa   pri dʒo 'nje ro
ch'ogni   cor   fa   prigioniero.
which every heart makes   prisoner
which makes every heart a prisoner.

pju   non   'a mo   non   'bra mo   a i 'mɛ
Refrain: **Più   non   amo,   non   bramo   ahimè**
more   not   I love   not   I desire   alas
I love no more; I do not desire, alas,

da 'mar   'dɔnː na   kɛ   'sɛn tsa   fe
d'amar   donna   ch'è   senza   fé.
of to love woman   who is   without   faith
to love a faithless woman.

la	ka 'dʒon	tu	'sa i		per 'ke	da	te	'lun dʒi	il	pje	ri 'vɔl si
La	**cagion**	**tu**	**sai**		**perché**	**da**	**te**	**lungi**	**il**	**piè**	**rivolsi,**
the	reason	you	you know		why	from	you	far	the	foot	I turned

You know the reason why I turned my steps far away from you,

'dɔn: na	're a	'sen tsa	mer 'tʃe	e	'da i	'lat: tʃi	il	kɔr	diʃ: 'ʃɔl si
donna	**rea,**	**senza**	**mercé,**	**e**	**dai**	**lacci**	**il**	**cor**	**disciolsi**
woman	cruel	without	pity	and	from the	ties	the	heart	I untied

cruel, pitiless woman, and [why] I undid my heart's ties

e	spret: 'tsa i	da 'mor	il	'reɲ: ɲo	per	se 'gwir	'li ɾa	e	lo	'zdeɲ: ɲo
e	**sprezzai**	**d'amor**	**il**	**regno**	**per**	**seguir**	**l'ira**	**e**	**lo**	**sdegno.**
and	I scorned	of love	the	realm	for	to follow	the anger	and	the	contempt

and scorned the realm of love to follow anger and contempt.

GL: **Amor**

🏵 *Fedeli, Ruggiero* (c.1655-1722)

Composer, singer, and violist, he played in Venetian theatre orchestras and at S. Marco in Venice. In 1674 he joined the choir at S. Marco, but he was dismissed in 1677 because of repeated absences.
He went to Germany, where he sang in operas at Bayreuth and Dresden and held various court and theatre positions: at the Berlin court chapel, in Kassel, Brunswick, and Wolfenbüttel. In 1709 he returned to Kassel, where he had been *Kapellmeister* from 1700 to 1702, for the rest of his life.
In addition to sacred music, Fedeli wrote arias, an opera (*Almira*), and eight Italian cantatas.

[25, 35]   In [35] titled **Il mio core**, by "Riggiero Fedelli."

il	'mi o	'kɔ ɾe	non	ɛ	kon	me
Il mio core non è con me						
My heart is not with me						

il	'mi o	'kɔ ɾe	non	ɛ	kon	me	nɔ
Il	**mio**	**core**	**non**	**è**	**con**	**me,**	**no,**
the	my	heart	not	is	with	me	no

My heart is not with me, no –

ne	sa 'prɛ i	ki	mel	ra 'pi
né	**saprei**	**chi**	**mel**	**rapì!**
nor	I would know	who	from me it	stole

nor would I know who stole it from me!

se	la 'mo ɾe	op: 'pur	la	fe	non	sɔ	dir	ki	'tan to	ar 'di
Se	**l'amore**	**oppur**	**la**	**fé,**	**non**	**so**	**dir**	**chi**	**tanto**	**ardì.**
if	the love	or else	the	fidelity	not	I know how	to say	who	so much	dared

Whether [it was] love or fidelity, I cannot say which dared so much.

🏵 *Freschi, Domenico* (c.1634-1710)

Composer, singer, and priest at the Cathedral of Vicenza, he became *maestro di cappella* there in 1656 and remained in that post for the rest of his life.
In addition to composing sacred music (psalms, masses, and at least three oratorios) and dramatic cantatas, he was active as an opera composer in Venice and for a private theatre near Padua; of his fifteen operas much of the music has been lost.

---

[57]
from: *Olimpia vendicata (1681)*   *Aurelio Aureli*

a ˈmo ɾe ti ˈsɛn to kal ˈvar ko ˈmat: ten di
Amore, ti sento ch'al varco m'attendi
Love, I feel that you are waiting in ambush for me

a ˈmo ɾe   ti   ˈsɛn to   kal   ˈvar ko   mat: ˈten di
Amore, **ti** **sento** **ch'al** **varco**   **m'attendi,**
Love   you   I feel   that at the opening   me you await
Love, I feel that you are waiting in ambush for me;

    ma   in ˈva no   pre ˈtɛn di   fe ˈɾir   ˈkwe sto   ˈkɔ ɾe
    ma   **invano**   **pretendi**   **ferir**   **questo**   **core.**
    but   in vain   you expect   to wound   this   heart
    but in vain do you expect to wound this heart.

a   le   sa ˈet: te   ˈtu e   sa ˈɾɔ   di   ˈskɔʎ: ʎo
A   **le**   **saette**   **tue**   **sarò**   **di**   **scoglio,**
to   the   arrows   your   I will be   of   stone
I will be like stone to your arrows,

    ne   min: na mo ɾe ˈɾɔ   kwan ˈdi o   non   ˈvɔʎ: ʎo
    né   **m'innamorerò**   **quand'io**   **non**   **voglio.**
    nor   I will fall in love   when I   not   I want
    and I will not fall in love when I do not want to.

ˈku pi do   tin ˈtɛn do   ke   ˈvwɔ i   tor men ˈtar mi   ma   ˈva ne   son   ˈlar mi
Cupido,   **t'intendo**   **che**   **vuoi**   **tormentarmi,**   **ma**   **vane**   **son**   **l'armi**
Cupid   you I understand   that   you want   to torment me   but   futile   are   the weapons
Cupid, I understand that you want to torment me; but futile are the weapons

    ke   ˈva i   di spo ˈnɛn do
    che   **vai**   **disponendo.**
    which   you go   preparing
    you are preparing.

GL: **Amore, Cupido**

Frescobaldi, Girolamo (1583-1643)

"Prince of Italian organists," he was a famous keyboard composer who, in his innovative variation techniques and daring harmonic progressions, had a significant influence on early Baroque style. His output of keyboard works was huge.

Apparently a child prodigy both as singer and instrumentalist, he was organist at the Accademia della Morte in his native Ferrara at the age of fourteen. In 1608 he became organist of the Cappella Giulia, the resident musical establishment at S. Pietro in Rome; he retained that post until his death except for the years 1628 to 1634, when he was organist to the young Ferdinando II, Grand Duke of Tuscany, in Florence.

In addition to instrumental works and sacred vocal works, Frescobaldi composed a considerable amount of solo vocal music which he titled in a variety rich even for the early seventeenth century: song, sonnet, aria, canzona, romanesca, recitativo, etc. Two collections of solo vocal music (*Primo libro d'arie*, *Secondo libro d'arie*) were published simultaneously in 1630; other songs date from 1621.

Frescobaldi was criticized by some for being "uncultured"; the theorist Giovanni Battista Doni wrote, in 1640, that Frescobaldi "failed to set the text properly and did not even know the meaning of words that are somewhat uncommon *[Grove]*."

[69]

'al: la 'glɔ ɾja
Alla gloria
To glory

'al: la	'glɔ ɾja	'al: li	o 'no ɾi	kor: 're te	pa sto 'ɾel: le	'ɛk: ko	'lɛr 'bɛk: ko
Alla	**gloria,**	**alli**	**onori**	**correte**	**pastorelle,**	**ecco**	**l'erb' ecco**
to the	glory	to the	honors	run	shepherdesses	here is	the grass here is

alli =
(mod.) agli

Hasten, shepherdesses, to glory and honors; behold the grass and

li	'fjo ɾi	di 'nɔ ve	e 'tɛr ne	e	'bɛl: le	ke	ne	ri 'pɔr ta
li	**fiori**	**di nove,**	**eterne,**	**e**	**belle**	**che**	**ne**	**riporta**
the	flowers	again	eternal	and	beautiful	that	to us	brings back

nove	*li =*
(poet.) =	*(mod.)*
nuove	*i*

il	'rad: dʒo	dun	pju	se 're no	'mad: dʒo
il	**raggio**	**d'un**	**più**	**sereno**	**maggio.**
the	ray	of a	more	serene	May

the flowers which the sun of a more serene May brings back to us again, eternal and beautiful.

'ɛk: ko	la	pri ma 've ɾa	'ɛk: ko	'lom bre	ʎa u 'dʒɛl: li
Ecco	**la**	**primavera,**	**ecco**	**l'ombr'c**	**gl'augelli,**
here is	the	spring	here is	the shade and	the birds

augelli (poet.) = uccelli

Behold the springtime, behold the shade [of leafy trees] and the birds;

'ɛk: ko	la 'ma ta	'skje ɾa	di	'fon ti	e	di	ruʃ: 'ʃɛl: li
ecco	**l'amata**	**schiera**	**di**	**fonti,**	**e**	**di**	**ruscelli,**
here is	the beloved	array	of	fountains	and	of	streams

behold the lovable array of fountains and streams

ke	kon	lor	'rad: dʒi	a 'ma ti	fan	dʒo 'ir	'kɔl: li	e	'pra ti
che	**con**	**lor**	**raggi**	**amati**	**fan**	**gioir**	**colli,**	**e**	**prati.**
which	with	their	rays	beloved	make	to rejoice	hills	and	meadows

which, with their lovely reflections, make hills and meadows rejoice.

'ɛk: ko	'flɔ ɾa	vet: 'tso za	'kar ka	'dɛr be	e	vi 'ɔ le	'ɛk: ko	il	'dʒiʎ: ʎo
Ecco	**Flora**	**vezzosa,**	**carca**	**d'erbe,**	**e**	**viole,**	**ecco**	**il**	**giglio,**
here is	Flora	charming	loaded	with grasses	and	violets	here is	the	lily

Behold Flora, her arms full of grasses and violets; behold the lily

carca = (mod.) carica (from "caricare")

e	la	'rɔ za	kon	la	fjo 'ri ta	'prɔ le
e	**la**	**rosa,**	**con**	**la**	**fiorita**	**prole,**
and	the	rose	with	the	flowering	offspring

and the rose, with their flowering broods

ke	kon	se 're ni	'lam pi	fan	dʒo 'ir	'sel ve	e	'kam pi
che	**con**	**sereni**	**lampi**	**fan**	**gioir**	**selve,**	**e**	**campi.**
which	with	clear	flashes	make	to rejoice	woods	and	fields

which, with clear, bright colors make woods and fields rejoice.

per	'lu i	fjo 'riʃ: ʃe	il	'pra to	per	'lɛ i	ver 'ded: dʒa	il	'kɔl: le
Per	**lui**	**fiorisce**	**il**	**prato,**	**per**	**lei**	**verdeggia**	**il**	**colle,**
for	him	flowers	the	meadow	for	her	becomes green	the	hill

For him [the lily] the meadow flowers, for her [the rose] the hill becomes verdant;

per 'lu i   di 'vjɛn   be 'a to   il   dʒar 'din   'gra te   'mɔlː le
per lui   divien   beato   il   giardin   grat'e   molle,
for   him   becomes   blissful   the   garden   pleasant and   moist
for him the pleasant and dewy garden becomes blissful;

per 'am bi   'san to   'dzɛ lo   dʒo 'iʃː ʃil   'mon del   'tʃɛ lo
per ambi   santo   zelo   gioisc' il   mond' e'l   cielo.
for   both   pious   zeal   rejoices the   world and the   heaven
for both their pious zeal, earth and heaven rejoice.

la 'vedː dʒo   il   'pra to   a 'dor no   di   'stelː le   il   tʃɛl   di   'fjo ɾi
Là   veggio   il   prato   adorno   di   stelle,   il   ciel   di   fiori,
there   I see   the   meadow   adorned   with   stars   the   sky   with   flowers

> veggio =
> *vedo*

There I see the meadow adorned with stars, the sky with flowers;

kwi 'tutː to   in 'tor no   ri 'mi ɾo   'al mi   splen 'do ɾi
qui   tutto   intorno   rimiro   almi   splendori,
here   all   all around   I see   great   splendors
here, all around, I see the great splendors,

ma non sɔ   'do ve   'si a   ko 'ɾilː la   'a ni ma   'mi a
ma non so   dove   sia   Corilla   anima   mia.
but   not   I know   where   may be   Corilla   soul   my
but I know not where Corilla, my soul, is.

a i 'mɛ   ki   mi   ta 'skon de   ko 'ɾilː la   'a i   'fjɛ ɾa   'sɔr te
Ahimè, chi   mi   t'asconde,   Corilla,   ahi   fiera   sorte,
alas   who   from me   you hides   Corilla   ah   cruel   fate

> asconde:
> *from "ascondere"*
> *= "nascondere"*

Alas, who is hiding you from me, Corilla? Ah, cruel fate;

ti 'tʃɛ li   tra   le   'fron de   'for se   per 'ke   la   'mɔr te
ti celi   tra   le   fronde   forse   perché   la   morte,
yourself you conceal   among   the   foliage   perhaps   so that   the   death

> celi: from
> *"celare" (lit.)*
> *= "nascondere"*

perhaps you are concealing yourself among the foliage so that death

kon pju   'gra vi   mar 'ti ɾi   mi 'fatː tʃa   o 'ror   mo 'ri ɾe
con più   gravi   martiri,   mi faccia   or or   morire.
with   most   grave   agonies   me may make   just now   to die
may now make me die with deepest agony.

GL: **Flora**

&

[69]

a 'mjɛ i 'pjan ti
A' miei pianti
By my tears

a 'mjɛ i   'pjan ti   al 'fi ne   un   di   kwel   kɔr   'a spro
A' miei   pianti   alfine   un   dì   quel   cor   aspro,
at   my   tears   at last   one   day   that   heart   relentless

kwel di 'a spro   samː molː 'li   sin te ne 'ri   'i ol   pre 'ga i   la kri 'ma i
quel diaspro   s'ammollì,   s'intenerì: io 'l   pregai,   lacrimai,
that   hardness   softened   was moved   I it   I begged   I shed tears
Finally, one day, the relentless hardness of that heart softened, was moved by my tears;
I begged it, I shed tears,

so spi 'ra i	el	'mi o	sol	non	mi	spa 'ri
sospirai,	**e'l**	**mio**	**sol**	**non**	**mi**	**sparì.**
I lamented	and it	my	sun	not	from me	vanished

I lamented, and my sun did not vanish from me.

> *"sol[e]" (= sun) in contexts such as this, has the figurative (poet.) meaning of "most dearly beloved one."*

Two more verses are printed as text only:

la	'su a	'lu tʃe	in	me	spje 'gɔ	'mjɛ i	la 'men ti	'mjɛ i	tor 'men ti	kon so 'lɔ
La	**sua**	**luce**	**in**	**me**	**spiegò,**	**miei**	**lamenti,**	**miei**	**tormenti**	**consolò,**
the	her	light	to	me	opened out	my	laments	my	torments	consoled

She spread her light to me; she consoled my laments [and] my torments;

pju	kon for 'tɔ	dzo i 'ra i	ri de 'ra i	kan te 'ra i
più	**confortò:**	**- Gioirai,**	**riderai,**	**canterai -**
more	comforted	you will rejoice	you will laugh	you will sing

furthermore, she comforted: "You will rejoice, you will laugh, you will sing,"

'pɔ i	mi	'dis: se	e	so spi 'rɔ
poi	**mi**	**disse,**	**e**	**sospirò.**
then	to me	said	and	she sighed

she said to me then, and she sighed.

kon	kwe 'sta u ɾa	di	pje 'ta	la	'mi a	'vi ta	dʒa	zmar: 'ri ta	tor ne 'ra
Con	**quest'aura**	**di**	**pietà,**	**la**	**mia**	**vita**	**già**	**smarrita**	**tornerà,**
with	this breath	of	pity	the	my	life	formerly	lost	will return

With this breath of pity my formerly lost life will return,

re spi ɾe 'ra	la kri 'man do	so spi 'ran do	sup: pli 'kan do	'doɲ: ɲi	kɔr	vit: to ɾja	sa
respirerà:	**lacrimando,**	**sospirando,**	**supplicando,**	**d'ogni**	**cor**	**vittoria**	**s'ha.**
will breathe again	weeping	sighing	supplicating	of every	heart	victory	one has

will breathe again: [through] weeping, sighing, [and] supplicating, every heart is won over.

[38, 69, 70] Also titled **Maddalena alla Croce.**

a pjɛ 'del: la gran 'kro tʃe
A' piè della gran croce
At the foot of the great cross

a	pjɛ	'del: la	gran	'kro tʃe	in	'ku i	laŋ 'gwi va	vi 'tʃi no	a	'mɔr te
A'	**piè**	**della**	**gran**	**croce**	**in**	**cui**	**languiva**	**vicino**	**a**	**morte**
at	foot	of the	great	cross	on	which	languished	near	to	death

il	bwɔn	dʒe 'zu	spi 'ran te	ska piʎ: 'ʎa ta	ko 'zi	'pjan dʒer	su 'di va
il	**buon**	**Gesù**	**spirante,**	**scapigliata**	**così**	**pianger**	**s'udiva**
the	good	Jesus	expiring	with hair disheveled	thus	to weep	one heard

At the foot of the great cross on which the good Jesus languished near death was heard weeping thus, she with disheveled hair,

> *Mary Magdalen is associated with both tears and [copious] hair based on the Bible story in which she anoints Jesus' feet after washing them with her tears and drying them with her hair.*

la	'su a	fe 'de le	ad: do lo 'ra ta	a 'man te
la	**sua**	**fedele**	**addolorata**	**amante,**
the	his	faithful	anguishing	lover

his faithful, anguished lover [Mary Magdalen];

e	del: lu 'mor	ke	da	'beʎ: ʎi	'ɔk: ki	uʃ: 'ʃi va	e
e	**dell'umor,**	**che**	**da'**	**begli**	**occhi**	**usciva,**	**e**
and	of the liquid (humor)	which	from the	beautiful	eyes	flowed out	and

> *humor: one of the vital vital liquids in the constitution of the body*

del: 'lɔr	'del: la	'kjɔ ma	on 'do za	er: 'ran te	non	man 'dɔ	'ma i	da ke	la	'vi ta
dell'or	della	chioma	ondosa,	errante	non	mandò	mai,	da che	la	vita
of the gold	of the	hair	undulating	rambling	not	sent	ever	ever since	the	life

ε	'vi va	'per le	e 'dɔ ro	pju	bɛl	lin 'di a	o	la 'tlan te
è	viva	perle	ed oro	più	bel	l'India	o	l'Atlante:
is	alive	pearls	and gold	more	beautiful	the India	or	the Africa

and neither India nor Africa ever sent to us, from the beginning of life, pearls and gold more beautiful than those of her tears and her wavy, flowing hair.

> *in* [69]:
> **perle, od oro** = pearls or gold

> *in* [29]: **la vita è vita** (the life is life) = *same translation*
>
> *da che* = (mod.) *dacché*

'ko me	far	di 'tʃe a	'las: sa	o	siɲ 'ɲor	'mi o
Come	far,	(dicea)	lassa,	o	Signor	mio,
how	to make	she said	weary	o	Lord	mine

> *dicea* = *diceva*

'pwɔ i	'sɛn tsa	me	kwe 'stul ti ma	par 'ti ta
puoi	senza	me	quest'ultima	partita?
you are able	without	me	this last	departure

How can you make, o my Lord – she said wearily – this last departure without me?

> *partita (lit.)* = *partenza*

'ko me	mo 'rɛn do	tu	'vin tʃer	pos: 'si o	ke	se	mo 'rir	pur	'vwɔ i
Come,	morendo	tu,	vincer	poss'io?	Che	se	morir	pur	vuoi,
how	dying	you	to win	can I	for	if	to die	still	you wish

How can I survive, with you dying? For, if you still wish to die,

> *in* [69]:
> **viver poss'io** = [how] can I live...

'la ni ma	u 'ni ta	ɔ	'te ko	il	'sa i	'mi o	re den 'tor	'mi o	'di o
l'anima	unita	ho	teco,	(il	sai,	mio	Redentor,	mio	Dio),
the soul	united	I have	you with	it	you know	my	Redeemer	my	God

I have united my soul with you (you know it, my Redeemer, my God);

pe 'rɔ	'te ko	a 'ver	'dɛd: dʒo	e	'mɔr te	e	'vi ta
però	teco	aver	deggio	e	morte,	e	vita.
therefore	you with	to have	I must	and	death	and	life

therefore, I must share both death and life with you.

GL: **Atlante**

❧

[69]

'ar do e 'tat: 'tʃo il 'mi o mal
Ardo, e taccio il mio mal
I am burning, and I am silent about my hurt

'ar do	e	'tat: tʃo	il	'mi o	mal	per 'ki o	pa 'vɛn to	ke	'si o	'skɔ pro	lar 'dor
Ardo,	e	taccio	il	mio	mal,	perch'io	pavento	che	s'io	scopro	l'ardor,
I burn	and	I am silent	the	my	hurt	because I	I am afraid	that	if I	I reveal	the burning he

I am burning, and I am silent about my hurt because I am afraid that if I reveal the fire

'ken tro	mi	'sfat: tʃe	'fɔ ko	di	'zdeɲ: ɲo	e	non	da 'mo ɾe	at: 'tʃɛn da
ch'entro	mi	sface,	foco	di	sdegno,	e	non	d'Amore	accenda.
which within	me	destroys	fire	of	scorn	and	not	of Love	I may ignite

which is destroying me within, I might ignite fire of scorn rather than of Love.

'i o	'te mo	a 'mor	ke	non	of: 'fɛn da	pju	ko 'lɛ i	ke	me	'stes: so
Io	temo,	Amor,	che	non	offenda	più	colei,	che	me	stesso,
I	I fear	Love	that	not	may offend	more	her	than	me	self

il	'mi o	tor 'men to	ke	di	pja 'tʃer	a	me	'for se	le	'spja tʃe
il	**mio**	**tormento,**	**ché**	**di**	**piacer**	**a**	**me**	**forse**	**le**	**spiace,**
the	my	torment	because	of	to be pleasing	to	me	perhaps	to her	is displeasing

I fear, Love, that my torment may offend her more than myself, because perhaps she does not like being pleasing to me,

on 'di o	so 'stɛɲː ɲo	in	'pa tʃe	la	'gwerː ra	ke	mi 'fanː no
ond'io	**sostegno**	**in**	**pace**	**la**	**guerra,**	**che**	**mi fanno**
whence I	I bear	in	peace	the	war	which	to me make

> *sostegno =*
> *(mod.) sostengo*

i	'mjɛ i	pen 'sjɛ ɾi	e	'si o	'tɛn to	for 'mar	'prjɛ gi	o	pa 'rɔ le
i	**miei**	**pensieri,**	**e**	**s'io**	**tento**	**formar**	**prieghi,**	**o**	**parole,**
the	my	thoughts	and	if I	I try	to form	prayers	or	words

> *prieghi =*
> *(mod.) preghi*

whence I bear peacefully the war that my thoughts wage against me;
and if I try to form prayers or words,

'fe de	e	ti 'mor	non	'vwɔ le	'ki o	pro 'ku ɾi	sa 'lu te	o	'ki o	la	'spe ɾi
fede,	**e**	**timor**	**non**	**vuole**	**ch'io**	**procuri**	**salute,**	**o**	**ch'io**	**la**	**speri:**
faith	and	fear	not	wishes	that I	I may obtain	well-being	or	that I	it	I may hope

faith and fear do not allow me to obtain, nor hope for, well-being.

'mɔ ɾo	'sɛn tsa	sko 'prir	kwal	son	kwal	'fu i	e	non	'fugː go	il	mo 'rir
moro	**senza**	**scoprir**	**qual**	**son,**	**qual**	**fui,**	**e**	**non**	**fuggo**	**il**	**morir,**
I die	without	to reveal	what	I am	what	I was	and	not	I flee	the	dying

I am dying without revealing who I am, who I was; and I flee not death

ma	'li ɾa	al 'tru i
ma	**l'ira**	**altrui.**
but	the anger	another's

but another's anger.

pur	nel	si 'lɛn tsjo	i	'mjɛ i	pen 'sjɛ ɾi	a 'skon do	'vi vo	pe 'nan do
Pur	**nel**	**silenzio**	**i**	**miei**	**pensieri**	**ascondo:**	**vivo**	**penando,**
still	in the	silence	the	my	thoughts	I conceal	I live	suffering

> *ascondo: from*
> *"ascondere" (lit.)*
> *= "nascondere"*

Still I conceal my thoughts in silence: I live in suffering,

en	la gri 'mar	mi 'sfat: tʃo	e	'mɔ ɾo	'alː le	spe 'ran tse	al	dwɔl	ri 'na sko
e'n	**lagrimar**	**mi sfaccio**	**e**	**moro**	**alle**	**speranze,**	**al**	**duol**	**rinasco,**
and in	weeping	I dissolve	and	I die	at the	hopes	at the	grief	I am reborn

and dissolve in weeping; and I am dead to hope, born again to grief.

sol	di	pen 'sjɛ ɾi	e	di	so 'spir	mi 'pa sko
sol	**di**	**pensieri,**	**e**	**di**	**sospir**	**mi pasco.**
only	with	thoughts	and	with	sighs	myself I nourish

I feed only on thoughts and sighs.

e	ser 'ban do	il	'mi o	dwɔl	'kju zo	e	pro 'fon do	'den tro	son	'tutː to	'fɔ ko
E	**serbando**	**il**	**mio**	**duol**	**chiuso,**	**e**	**profondo**	**dentro**	**son**	**tutto**	**foco,**
and	keeping	the	my	grief	closed up	and	deep	within	I am	all	fire

And, keeping my grief deeply enclosed, I am all afire within

e	'fwɔ ɾi	un	'gjat: tʃo	vorː 'rɛ i	par 'lar	ma	'tatː tʃo
e	**fuori**	**un**	**ghiaccio:**	**vorrei**	**parlar,**	**ma**	**taccio,**
and	outside	an	ice	I would like	to speak	but	I am silent

and ice-cold without; I would like to speak, but I am silent

per 'ki o   non sɔ   bɛn dir kwel 'ki o   vorː're i
perch'io non so   ben dir quel ch'io vorrei,
because I not I know how well to say that which I I would like
because I do not know well how to say what I would like:

kwan 'di o son   'lun dʒi ar 'di sko apː 'prɛsː so i 'trɛ mo
quand'io son lungi ardisco, appresso i' tremo.
when I I am far away I dare nearby I I tremble
when I am distant I am daring; nearby I tremble.

or 'fugː go or 'tor no or 'te mo e son 'mɔr to in me 'stesː so
Or fuggo, or torno, or temo, e son morto in me stesso,
now I flee now I return now I fear and I am dead in me self
Now I flee, now I return; now I fear, and am dead within myself

e 'vi vo in 'lɛ i e di 'vi za da me
e vivo in lei, e divisa da me
and alive in her and divided from me

'la ni ma 'mi a per se gwi 'tar al 'tru i se 'stesː sa o 'bli a
l'anima mia per seguitar altrui se stessa oblia.
the soul mine for to pursue another it itself forgets
and alive in her; and my soul, separated from me, forgets itself in order to pursue someone else.

GL: **Amor[e]**

❧

[69]   *Giacomo Marmitta*

bɛn 'vedː dʒo
Ben veggio
Well I see

bɛn 'vedː dʒo 'donː na o 'ma i ke pju non 'so no 'zdeɲː ɲi a mo 'ro zi
Ben veggio, donna omai, che più non sono sdegni amorosi
well I see woman now that more not are indignations amorous

> *veggio = (mod.) vedo; omai = (mod.) ormai*

'kwe i kal   'mi o de 'zi ɾe ol 'tradː dʒo 'fanː no ma son 'zdeɲː ɲi e 'di ɾe
quei ch'al mio desire oltraggio fanno; ma son sdegni, ed ire
those which to the my desire insult make but are indignations and angers
Now I well see, woman, that amorous indignations are no longer those which insult my desire; but they are indignations and angers

di 'ki o 'trɛ mo kwa 'lor pju ne ra 'dʒo no
di ch'io tremo qual'or più ne ragiono.
of which I I shudder when more of it I think
from which I shudder the more I think about them.

> *qual'or [qualora] (lit.) = allorché*

'ɛkː ko il 'lam po apː pa 'rir dʒa 'sɔ de il 'twɔ no el 'fol go ɾe diʃː 'ʃen de
Ecco il lampo apparir, già s'ode il tuono, e'l folgore discende,
here is the lightning flash to appear now is heard the thunder and the thunderbolt descends

ke 'la tra 'nu be 'fen de ne di 'fe za per me 'trɔ vo o per 'do no
che l'atra nube fende, né difesa per me trovo, o perdono;
which the dark cloud rends not defense for me I find or forgiveness
Here appears a flash of lightning, now the thunder is heard, and the thunderbolt which cuts into the dark cloud comes down. I find no defense or forgiveness;

'an tsi	dal 'tsar	la	'vi sta	pju	non	ar 'di sko	in	'kwel: lal 'tɛ ro	'tʃiʎ: ʎo
anzi	**d'alzar**	**la**	**vista**	**più**	**non**	**ardisco**	**in**	**quell'altero**	**ciglio,**
in fact	of to raise	the	sight	more	not	I dare	to	that proud	brow

in fact, I dare no more to raise my eyes to that proud brow

ke	'fred: da	dʒe lo 'zi a	'tur ba	e	kon 'tri sta	ma	sol	kje 'dɛn do	vo	'pa tʃe
che	**fredda**	**gelosia**	**turba,**	**e**	**contrista,**	**ma**	**sol**	**chiedendo**	**vo'**	**pace,**
which	cold	jealousy	troubles	and	afflicts	but	only	seeking	I wish	peace

which cold jealousy troubles and afflicts. But seeking only peace

e	kon 'siʎ: ʎo	e	la gri 'man do	il	'dʒor no	la	'nɔt: te
e	**consiglio,**	**e**	**lagrimando**	**il**	**giorno,**	**la**	**notte**
and	advice	and	weeping	the	day	the	night

and advice, and weeping all day, at night

a	'mjɛ i	pen 'sjɛr	'tri sti	ri 'tor no
a'	**miei**	**pensier**	**tristi**	**ritorno.**
to	my	thoughts	sad	I return

I return to my sad thoughts.

'ko me	'pɔs: so	o	me	'mi ze ro	e	in fe 'li tʃe	'du o	di 'ver si	va 'po ri
Come	**posso,**	**o**	**me**	**misero,**	**e**	**infelice?**	**Duo**	**diversi**	**vapori**
how	I can	o	me	miserable	and	unfortunate	two	different	flames

duo = (mod.) due

How is it possible, o miserable and unfortunate me? Two different flames

al	'tʃe lo	aʃ: 'ʃe zi	del	'vɔ stro	ar 'dɛn te	'kɔ re	e	'kwi vi	at: 'tʃe zi
al	**cielo**	**ascesi**	**del**	**vostro**	**ardente**	**core,**	**e**	**quivi**	**accesi**
to the	heaven	ascended	of the	your	ardent	heart	and	therein	ignited

ascended to the heaven of your ardent heart and, ignited there,

han	'mi a	spe 'ran tsa	'zvɛl ta	da	ra 'di tʃe	per 'ku i	la	'do ve
han	**mia**	**speranza**	**svelta**	**da**	**radice;**	**per cui**	**là**	**dove**
have	my	hope	pulled up	from	root	whereby	there	where

han = hanno

they have uprooted my hope; whereby there where

'i o	mi	vi 've a	fe 'li tʃe	or	son	kon 'dot: to	a	'ta le	ke	'mɔr te
io	**mi**	**vivea**	**felice**	**or**	**son**	**condotto**	**a**	**tale**	**che**	**morte**
I	me	I lived	happy	now	I am	reduced	to	such	that	death

vivea = viveva; the "eva" ending is an antiquated variant of "evo"

I was living a happy life, now I am reduced to such [a state] that death

ɛ	mi 'nor	'ma le	sel	've ro	dir	di	'mi a	zven 'tu ra	'li tʃe
è	**minor**	**male,**	**se'l**	**vero**	**dir**	**di**	**mia**	**sventura**	**lice.**
is	less	evil	if the	truth	to say	of	my	misfortune	is permitted

lice: from "licere" (poet.) = essere permesso

is the lesser evil, if the truth be permitted to be said about my misfortune.

ke	tro 'van do mi	'pri vo	del: la 'mor	'vɔ stro	vi a 'pju	'prɔ vo	'pe ne
Ché,	**trovandomi**	**privo**	**dell'amor**	**vostro,**	**via più**	**provo**	**pene**
because	finding myself	deprived	of the love	your	all the more	I experience	pains

via più = (mod.) viepiù

Because, finding myself deprived of your love, I feel more pain

ke	kwal	si 'vɔʎ: ʎa	'al ma	pro 'dot: ta	in	'vi vo
che	**qual**	**si voglia**	**alma**	**prodotta**	**in**	**vivo;**
than	what	wishes	soul	born	in	living flesh

than a soul born in living flesh may wish for;

ke	'i o	son	'vi vo	al	de 'zi o	'mɔr to	'al: la	'spe ne
ché	io	son	vivo	al	desio,	morto	alla	spene,
because	I	I am	alive	to the	desire	dead	to the	hope

spene (poet.) = speme (lit.) = speranza

because I am alive to desire [but] dead to hope,

ne	'kol pa	mi	kon 'dan: na	ma	'kwel: ler: 'ror	kel	ve 'der	'vɔ stro	ap: 'pan: na
né	colpa	mi	condanna,	ma	quell'error,	che'l	veder	vostro	appanna.
not	guilt	me	condemns	but	that error	which it	seeing	your	obscures

it is not guilt that condemns me but that error *[of hope]* which is obscured by the sight of you.

'ki o	non	'vɔl si	dʒam: 'ma i	pur	un	sol	'zgwar do	in	'par te	'o ve	non	'fu ste
Ch'io	non	volsi	giammai	pur	un	sol	sguardo	in	parte	ove	non	fuste,
Because I	not	turned	ever	yet	a	single	glance	to	place	where	not	you were

Because I have never yet turned a single glance to a place were you were not [there],   *fuste = (mod.) foste*

o	've ɾa	o	'fin ta	dal	pen 'sjɛr	'mi o	da	'ku i	'sja te	di 'pin ta
o	vera,	o	finta	dal	pensier	mio,	da	cui	siate	dipinta,
either	real	or	feigned	from the	thought	mine	from	which	you are	depicted

whether real or imagined in my thoughts in which you are depicted,

'an tsi	'vi va	for 'ma ta	o 'vuŋ kwe	'i o	'zgwar do	e	seb: 'bɛ ne	a	se 'gwir vi
anzi	viva	formata	ovunque	io	sguardo:	e	sebbene	a	seguirvi
or rather	alive	formed	wherever	I	I look	and	even though	to	to follow you

or rather formed as alive wherever I look: and even though in pursuing you

'ɛb: bi	il	pjɛ	'tar do	'kwe sti	'rat: to	vi	'dʒun se	ne	da	'vo i
ebbi	il	piè	tardo	questi	ratto	vi	giunse,	né	da	voi
I had	the	foot	slow	this one	swiftly	you	reached	not	from	you

questi: usage as a singular pronoun

si diz 'dʒun se	ke	pju	ve 'lo tʃe	as: 'sa i	ke	'dam: ma	o	'par do
si disgiunse	ch'è	più	veloce	assai,	che	damma,	o	pardo.
itself severed	because it is	more	swift	much	than	fawn	or	leopard

damma = daino
pardo = leopardo

my foot was slow, nevertheless it reached you swiftly; it did not sever itself from you,
because it is much more swift than a fawn or a leopard.

ko 'zi	vi	'fus: se	'da to	po 'ter lo	u 'di ɾe	e	ra dʒo 'nar	kon	'lu i
Così	vi	fusse	dato	poterlo	udire,	e	ragionar	con	lui,
thus	to you	was	given	to be able it	to hear	and	to reason	with	him

fusse = fosse

Thus were you able to hear that and to reason with him

kor	vi	di 'rɛb: be	il	'mi o	doʎ: 'ʎo zo	'sta to
ch'or	vi	direbbe	il	mio	doglioso	stato:
who now	to you	should speak	the	my	sorrowful	state

who would now tell you of my sorrowful state:

'kwan to	kan 'dʒa to	son	da	kwel	'ki o	'fu i
quanto	cangiato	son	da	quel	ch'io	fui,
how much	changed	I am	from	that	which I	I was

how much I have changed from what I was,

po i 'ke a 'tɔr to	mi	'ved: dʒo	skat: 'tʃa to	del	'mi o	an 'ti ko	a 'ma to	'sɛd: dʒo
poich'a torto	mi	veggio	scacciato	del	mio	antico	amato	seggio.
since unjustly	myself	I see	banished	of the	my	old	beloved	seat

since I see myself unjustly banished from my old, beloved seat *[place in your heart]*.

☙

[69]
ko 'zi mi di spret: 'tsa te
Così mi disprezzate?
You scorn me like this?

ko 'zi	mi	di spret: 'tsa te	ko' zi	'vo i	mi	bur 'la te
Così	**mi**	**disprezzate?**	**Così**	**voi**	**mi**	**burlate?**
thus	me	you scorn	thus	you	me	you make fun of

You scorn me like this? You make fun of me like this?

'tɛm po	ver: 'ra	ka 'mo re	fa 'ra	di	'vɔ stro	'kɔ re	kwel	ke	'fa te	del	'mi o
Tempo	**verrà,**	**ch'Amore**	**farà**	**di**	**vostro**	**core**	**quel**	**che**	**fate**	**del**	**mio;**
time	will come	that Love	will make	of	your	heart	that	which	you make	of the	mine

The time will come when Love will do with your heart what you are doing to mine;

non	pju	pa 'rɔ le	ad: 'di o	ad: 'di o	ad: 'di o
non	**più**	**parole,**	**addio,**	**addio,**	*addio.*
not	more	words	farewell	farewell	farewell

no more words: farewell, farewell, *farewell.*

'da te mi	pur	mar 'ti ri	bur 'la te	i	'mje i	so 'spi ri	ne 'ga te mi	mer 'tʃe de
Datemi	**pur**	**martiri,**	**burlate**	**i**	**miei**	**sospiri,**	**negatemi**	**mercede,**
give me	then	agonies	laugh at	the	my	sighs	deny me	reward

Go ahead and give me agony, laugh at my sighs, deny me reward,

ol trad: 'dʒa te	'mi a	'fe de	kin	'vo i	ve 'dre te	'po i	kwel	ke	mi	'fa te	'vo i
oltraggiate	**mia**	**fede,**	**ch'in**	**voi**	**vedrete**	**poi**	**quel**	**che**	**mi**	**fate**	**voi.**
profane	my	faith	that in	you	you will see	then	that	which	to me	do	you

profane my faith, as you will then see in yourself what you do to me.

bel 'ta	'sɛm pre	non	'reɲ: ɲa	e	'sel: la	pur	vin 'seɲ: ɲa	a	di spre 'dʒar
Beltà	**sempre**	**non**	**regna,**	**e**	**s'ella**	**pur**	**v'insegna**	**a**	**dispregiar**
beauty	always	not	reigns	and	if it	still	you it teaches	to	to scorn

Beauty does not reign forever; and if it still makes you scorn

> *dispregiar[e] = disprezzar[e]*

'mi a	fe	kre 'de te	pur	a	me	ke	'sɔd: dʒi	man tʃi 'de te	do 'man	vi pen ti 're te
mia	**fé**	**credete**	**pur**	**a**	**me,**	**ché**	**s'oggi**	**m'ancidete,**	**doman**	**vi pentirete.**
my	fidelity	believe	then	to	me	because	if today	me you kill	tomorrow	it you will repent

my fidelity, then believe me: because if you kill me today,
you will repent it tomorrow.

> *ancidete: from "ancidere"*
> *(lit.) = "uccidere"*

non	'ne go	dʒa	kin	'vo i	a 'mor	a	i	'prɛ dʒi	'swɔ i
Non	**nego**	**già,**	**ch'in**	**voi**	**Amor**	**ha**	**i**	**pregi**	**suoi,**
not	I deny	now	that in	you	Love	has	the	merits	its

I do not deny now that Love has its merits in you;

ma	sɔ	kil	'tɛm po	'kas: sa	bel 'ta	ke	'fud: dʒe	e	'pas: sa
ma	**so**	**ch'il**	**tempo**	**cassa**	**beltà,**	**che**	**fugge,**	**e**	**passa.**
but	I know	that the	time	erases	beauty	which	flees	and	passes

but I know that time erases beauty, which is fleeting and passes away.

se	non	vo 'le te	a 'ma re	'i o	non	'voʎ: ʎo	pe 'na re
Se	**non**	**volete**	**amare,**	**io**	**non**	**voglio**	**penare.**
If	not	you want	to love	I	not	I want	to suffer

If you do not want to love, I do not want to suffer.

il	'vɔ stro	'bjon do	'kri ne	le	'gwan tʃe	pur pu 'ri ne	ve 'lo tʃi	pju	ke	'mad: dʒo
Il	vostro	biondo	crine,	le	guance	purpurine	veloci	più	che	maggio
the	your	blond	head of hair	the	cheeks	rosy	fast	more	than	May

'tɔ sto	fa 'ran	pas: 'sad: dʒo	pret: 'tsa teʎ: ʎi	pur	'vo i
tosto	faran	passaggio:	prezzategli	pur	voi,
quickly	will make	passage	value it	then	you

'ki o	ri de 'ro	bɛn	'pɔ i
ch'io	riderò	ben	poi.
because I	I will laugh	well	then

Your blond tresses and rosy cheeks will quickly fade away faster than May: value them, as I will then laugh well.

GL: **Amor[e]**

&

[69]

'deɲ: ɲa ti o gran fer 'nan do
Degnati, o gran Fernando
Deign, o great Fernando

> The Fernando addressed in this song is Ferdinand II, Grand Duke of Tuscany; the song is contained in Frescobaldi's *Primo libro delle Canzoni (1628)*, with a dedication "to his most Serene Highness / Ferdinand II / Grand Duke of Tuscany." For more information, see the excellent notes in [69].

'deɲ: ɲa ti	o	gran	fer 'nan do	tu	ke	'sɛm pre	a bor: 'ri sti
Degnati,	**o**	**gran**	**Fernando,**	**tu,**	**che**	**sempre**	**aborristi,**
deign	o	great	Fernando	you	who	always	you loathed

e	'mar sja	e	'mi da	pje 'gar	lo 'rek: kje	e	ri kja 'mar	dal	'ban do
e	**Marsia,**	**e**	**Mida,**	**piegar**	**l'orecchie,**	**e**	**richiamar**	**dal**	**bando**
both	Marsyas	and	Midas	to bend	the ears	and	to call back	from the	exile

O great Fernando, you who always loathed Marsyas and Midas, deign to lend your ear and call back from exile

'bɛl: la	vir 'tu	ke	in	'kwe ste	'kar te	an: 'ni da
bella	**Virtù,**	**che**	**in**	**queste**	**carte**	**annida.**
beautiful	Virtue	who	in	these	papers	is nested

beautiful Virtue, nested in these papers.

a 'skol ta	il	swɔn	gra 'di to	la	'fe de	in	'kwe sto	aɲ 'kor	vjen	dal: lu 'di to
Ascolta	**il**	**suon**	**gradito:**	**la**	**fede**	**in**	**questo**	**ancor**	**vien**	**dall'udito.**
listen to	the	sound	pleasant	the	faith	in	this	still	comes	from the heard

Listen to the pleasant sound; believing in this still comes from the hearing.

ma	se	'lɔk: kjo	vi	'kjɛ de	aɲ 'ke i	'kwal ke	kon 'tɛn to	o	'kwal ke	'par te
Ma	**se**	**l'occhio**	**vi**	**chiede**	**anch'ei**	**qualche**	**contento,**	**o**	**qualche**	**parte,**
but	if	the eye	you	asks for	also it	some	content	or	some	part

But if the eye also asks you for some contentment, or some portion,

'bɛ ne	ɛ	'tʃɛ ko	kwel: 'lwɔm	'kɔd: dʒi	non	've de	e 'sprɛs: so	il	'tu o	va 'lor
bene	**è**	**cieco**	**quell'uom**	**ch'oggi**	**non**	**vede**	**espresso**	**il**	**tuo**	**valor**
well	is	blind	that man	who today	not	sees	expressed	the	your	prowess

very blind is that man who today does not see your prowess expressed

'den tro a	kwe 'star te	'men tre	ak: 'kɔr di	in	te	'stes: so	si	bɛn	ʎi	af: 'fɛt: ti
dentro a	**quest'arte,**	**mentre**	**accordi**	**in**	**te**	**stesso**	**sì**	**ben**	**gli**	**affetti**
within	this art	while	you tune	in	you	yourself	so	well	the	affections

in this art, as you attune in yourself the affections

'al: la	ra 'dʒo ne	ap: 'prɛs: so	o	be 'a ta	ar mo 'ni a	dun	kwɔr	so 'a ve
alla	**ragione**	**appresso:**	**o**	**beata**	**armonia**	**d'un**	**cuor**	**soave,**
to the	reason	in the presence	o	blessed	harmony	of a	heart	gentle

according to reason: o blessed harmony of a gentle heart,

ke	'tɛm pra	in	'kwe sta	'vi ta	kol	'dol tʃe	del: le 'ta	del	'sen: no	il	'gra ve
che	**tempra**	**in**	**questa**	**vita**	**col**	**dolce**	**dell'età**	**del**	**senno**	**il**	**grave.**
which	tempers	in	this	life	with the	sweetness	of the age	of the	mind	the	serious

which in this life tempers the seriousness of mind with the sweetness of age.

ma	'for se	or	la	'mi a	'liŋ gwa	ɛ	'trɔp: po	ar 'di ta
Ma	**forse**	**or**	**la**	**mia**	**lingua**	**è**	**troppo**	**ardita:**
but	perhaps	now	the	my	tongue	is	too	bold

But perhaps my tongue is now too bold;

'tat: tʃo	e da	dir	sol	'prɛn do	kwel	ke	da	'sad: dʒo	in 'ten do
taccio,	**ed a**	**dir**	**sol**	**prendo**	**quel**	**che**	**da**	**saggio**	**intendo,**
I am silent	and to	to say	only	I treat	that	which	from	example	I understand

I will be silent, and I will only say what I know from experience:

ke	ki	kwad: 'dʒu	de'	'kan ti	il	'swɔ no	ap: 'prɛt: tsa
che	**chi**	**quaggiù**	**de'**	**canti**	**il**	**suono**	**apprezza**
that	who	here below	of the	songs	the	sound	appreciates

that he who appreciates the sound of songs in this world

al: lar mo 'ni a	del	tʃɛl	'la ni ma	av: 'vet: tsa
all'armonia	**del**	**ciel**	**l'anima**	**avvezza.**
to the harmony	of the	heaven	the soul	trains

prepares his soul for the harmony of heaven.

GL: **Marsia, Mida, Virtù**

&

[69]

di	'li kɔ ɾi	un	'gwar do	al 'tɛ ɾo
di 'li kɔ ɾi un 'gwar do al 'tɛ ɾo

Di Licori un guardo altero

A haughty glance from Licori

di	li 'kɔ ɾi	un	'gwar do	al 'tɛ ɾo	do va 'mor	'swɔ i	'stra li	in 'do ɾa
Di	**Licori**	**un**	**guardo**	**altero,**	**dov'Amor**	**suoi**	**strali**	**indora,**
from	Licori	a	glance	haughty	where Love	his	arrows	gilds

min: na 'mo ɾa	ben 'ke	'si a	tur 'ba to	e	'fɛ ɾo
m'innamora,	**benché**	**sia**	**turbato,**	**e**	**fero;**
me enamors	even though	it be	angry	and	cruel

fero = (mod.) fiero

A haughty glance from Licori, wherein Love gilds his arrows, enamors me even though angry and cruel;

ke	fa 'ɾi a	'kwan do	pje 'to zo	pro met: 'tes: se	al	kɔr	ri 'pɔ zo
che	**faria**	**quando**	**pietoso**	**promettesse**	**al**	**cor**	**riposo?**
what	I would do	when	merciful	it may promise	to the	heart	peace

faria = (mod.) farei

what would I do if, merciful, it promised peace to my heart?

> *Three more verses are printed as text only:*

ma	pju	'sor da	e	pju	kru 'dɛ le	ke	fred: 'da spe
Ma	**più**	**sorda,**	**e**	**più**	**crudele**	**che**	**fredd'aspe,**
but	more	deaf	and	more	cruel	than	cold snake

aspe = (mod.) aspide

But more deaf and more cruel than a cold snake,

e	'ti gre	ir 'ka na	i nu 'ma na	'zdeɲː ɲa	u 'dir	le	'mi e	kwe 'rɛ le
e	tigre	Ircana,	inumana,	sdegna	udir	le	mie	querele,
and	tiger	from Ircania	inhuman	disdains	to hear	the	my	complaints

stony-hearted and inhuman, she disdains to hear my complaints,

ne	ri 'vɔl dʒe	a	'tan to	'dwɔ lo	de	'beʎː ʎi	'ɔkː ki	un	'dʒi ro	'so lo
né	rivolge	a	tanto	duolo	de'	begli	occhi	un	giro	solo.
nor	turns	to	so much	grief	of the	beautiful	eyes	one	turn	only

nor does she turn a single glance of her beautiful eyes toward so much grief.

'a i	ke	'par lo	'a i	ke	va 'ned ʒo	'ko me	pwɔ	li 'kɔ ri	'mi a
Ahi,	che	parlo,	ahi,	che	vaneggio,	come	può	Licori	mia
ah	what	I speak	ah	what	I rave	how	is able	Licori	mine

Ah, what am I saying; ah, how I am raving. How can my Licori

'ɛsː ser	'pi a	'si o	nulː 'lo zo	e	'nulː la	'kjɛdː dʒo
esser	pia,	s'io	null'oso,	e	nulla	chieggio?
to be	compassionate	if I	nothing I dare	and	nothing	I ask for

be compassionate if I dare nothing and ask for nothing?

> chieggio =
> (mod.)
> chiedo

non	sa	'for se	il	'gra ve	ar 'do re	ke	min 'fjamː ma	e	'strudː dʒe	il	'kɔ re
Non	sa	forse	il	grave	ardore,	che	m'infiamma,	e	strugge	il	core.
not	knows	perhaps	the	deep	ardor	which	me inflames	and	consumes	the	heart

Perhaps she does not know the deep ardor which inflames me and consumes my heart.

ma	kwe 'stɔkː ki	'kwa zi	'spen ti	'pɔnː no	'dir ʎi	i	'mje i	mar 'ti ri
Ma	quest'occhi	quasi	spenti	ponno	dirgli	i	miei	martiri,
but	these eyes	almost	lifeless	are able	to say to her	the	my	agonies

> ponno =
> (mod.) possono
>
> "gli," here (dialect) = a lei

But these nearly lifeless eyes can tell her my agony;

da	i	so 'spi ri	pwɔ	sa 'per	'mi e	'fjamː me	ar 'den ti
da	i	sospiri	può	saper	mie	fiamme	ardenti,
from	the	sighs	is able	to know	my	flames	ardent

from my sighs she can know my ardent fervor;

e	dal	'palː li do	sem 'bjan te	pwɔ	ve 'der	'ki o	'so no	a 'man te
e	dal	pallido	sembiante	può	veder	ch'io	sono	amante.
and	from the	pale	countenance	is able	to see	that I	I am	lover

and from my pale face she can see that I am a lover.

GL: **Amor, Ircana, Licori**

 ❧

[69]

'dɔnː na sjam 'rɛi di 'mɔr te
Donna, siam rei di morte
Woman, we are guilty of death

'dɔnː na	sjam	'rɛ i	di	'mɔr te	erː 'ra sti	erː 'ra i
Donna,	siam	rei	di	morte,	errasti,	errai,
woman	we are	guilty	of	death	you erred	I erred

Woman, we are guilty of death. You erred, I erred;

di	per 'dɔn	non	son	'deɲː ɲi	i	'nɔ stri	erː 'ro ri
di	perdon	non	son	degni	i	nostri	errori:
of	pardon	not	are	worthy	the	our	errors

our mistakes are not worthy of forgiveness:

tu   kav: ven 'ta sti   in   me   si   'fjɛ ɾi   ar 'do ɾi   'i o   ka   si   'ka ɾo   sol
tu,   ch'avventasti   in   me   sì   fieri   ardori,   io,   ch'a   sì   caro   sol
you   who flung   to   me   so   raging   passions   I   whom to   so   dear   sun
you who hurled such raging passions upon me, I to such a dear sun

ʎi   'ɔk: ki   le 'va i   'i o   ke   'u na   'fɛ ɾa   'ri dʒi da   a do 'ra i   tu   ke
gli   occhi   levai;   io,   che   una   fera   rigida   adorai,   tu,   che
the   eyes   I raised   I   who   a   beast   cruel   I adored   you   who
turned my eyes; I who adored a cruel beast, you who

> fera =
> (mod.)
> fiera

'fu sti   sor 'da spe   a   'mjɛi   do 'lo ɾi   tu   nel: 'li ɾe   o sti 'na ta   'i o   'neʎ: ʎi   a 'mo ɾi
fusti   sord'aspe   a'   miei   dolori;   tu   nell'ire   ostinata,   io   negli   amori;
were   deaf snake   to the   my   pains   you   in the anger   stubborn   I   in the   affections
were a snake deaf to my pains; you stubborn in anger, I in affections;

> fusti = (mod.) fosti

tu   pur 'trɔp: po   zdeɲ: 'ɲa sti   'i o   'trɔp: po   a 'ma i
tu   pur troppo   sdegnasti,   io   troppo   amai.
you   [yet] too much   you scorned   I   too much   I loved
you scorned me too much, [and] I loved [you] too much.

or   la   'pe na   lad: 'dʒu   nel   'fjɛ ɾo   a 'vɛr no   'pa ɾi   al   'fal: lo   na 'spɛt: ta
Or   la   pena   laggiù   nel   fiero   Averno   pari   al   fallo   n'aspetta,
now   the   suffering   down there   in the   cruel   Avernus   equal   to the   offence   us awaits
Now, suffering equal to the offence awaits us down there in the cruel Avernus;

ar de 'ra   'po i   ki   'vis: se   in   'fɔ ko   in   'vi vo   'fɔ ko   e 'tɛr no
arderà   poi   chi   visse   in   foco,   in   vivo   foco   eterno;
will burn   then   he who   lived   in   passion   in   blazing   fire   eternal
he who lived in passion will, then, burn in the blazing eternal fire;

'kwi vi   sa 'mor   'fi a   'dʒu sto   am be 'du e   'no i   tra   le   'fjam: me
quivi,   s'Amor   fia   giusto,   ambedue   noi   tra   le   fiamme
there   if Love   will be   just   both   us   among   the   flames

> fia =
> (mod.)
> sarà

dan: 'na ti   a 'vrem   lin 'fɛr no
dannati   avrem   l'inferno:
damned   will have   the inferno
there, if Love is just, damned among the flames, we will both have hell:

tu   nel   'mi o   kɔr   e 'di o   'neʎ: ʎi   'ɔk: ki   'two i
tu   nel   mio   cor,   ed io   negli   occhi   tuoi.
you   in the   my   heart   and I   in the   eyes   your
you in my heart, and I in your eyes.

GL: **Amor, Averno**

☙

[69]   *Giovanni Della Casa*

'do po   si   'luŋ go   er: 'ror
Dopo sì lungo error
After such longtime sinning

'do po   si   'luŋ go   er: 'ror   'do po   le   'tan te   si   'gra vi   of: 'fe ze
Dopo   sì   lungo   error,   dopo   le   tante   sì   gravi   offese,
after   such   long   error   after   the   so many   such   grave   offences
After such longtime sinning, after so many such grave offences

on 'da i   oɲ: 'ɲor   sof: 'fɛr to   lan 'ti ko   'fal: lo   e   'lem pjo   'mi o   de 'mɛr to
ond'hai   ogn'or   sofferto   l'antico   fallo,   e   l'empio   mio   demerto,
whence you have   always   borne   the old   mistake   and   the impious   my   unworthiness
whence you have always borne the original sin and my impious unworthiness,

> demerto = (mod.) demerito

kon   la   pje 'ta   'del: le   'tu e   'lu tʃi   'san te   'mi ɾa   'pa dre   tʃe 'lɛ ste
con   la   pietà   delle   tue   luci   sante,   mira,   Padre   celeste,
with   the   mercy   of the   your   eyes   holy   look   Father   heavenly
see, heavenly Father, with the mercy of your holy eyes,

o 'ma i   kon   'kwan te   'la gri me   a   te   de 'vo to   i   mi kon 'vɛr to
omai   con   quante   lagrime   a   te   devoto   i'   mi converto,
now   with   how many   tears   to   you   devoted   I   I am converted
with how many tears now, devoted to you, I am converted,

> omai (poet.) = ormai

e   'spi ɾa   al   'vi ver   'mi o   'brɛ ve   e din 'tʃɛr to   'grat: tsja   kal   bwɔn   ka 'min
e   spira   al   viver   mio   breve,   ed incerto,   grazia,   ch'al   buon   camin
and   breathe   to the   life   mine   brief   and uncertain   grace   that to the   good   path
and shed grace upon my brief and uncertain life, that to the righteous path

> camin[o] = (mod.) cammin[o]

'vol ga   le   'pjan te   'mo stra   ʎi af: 'fan: ni   il   'saŋ gwe   e   i   su 'dor   'spar si
volga   le   piante: mostra   gli affanni   il   sangue,   e   i   sudor   sparsi
I may turn   the   feet   shows   the woes   the   spirit   and   the   sweats   shed
I may turn my steps: your spirit demonstrates its sufferings and the toils expended

or   'vol gon   ʎi   'an: ni   e   'la spro   'tu o   do 'lo ɾe   'a i   'mjɛ i   pen 'sjɛ ri
(or   volgon   gli   anni),   e   l'aspro   tuo   dolore   ai   miei   pensieri,
now   turn   the   years   and   the harsh   your   grief   at   my   thoughts
(now [that] the years turn), and your deep grief at my thoughts,

a 'dal tro   od: 'dʒɛt: to   av: 'vet: tsi   raf: 'fred: da   siɲ: 'ɲor   'mi o   kwel   'fɔ ko
ad altro   oggetto   avvezzi;   raffredda,   Signor   mio,   quel   foco,
to other   object   accustomed   cool off   Lord   mine   that   fire
which were used to [being directed at] another object. Cool, my Lord, that fire

on 'dar si   kol   'mon do   e   kon su 'ma i   la   'vi ta   e   'lo ɾe
ond' arsi   col   mondo,   e   consumai   la   vita,   e   l'ore,
in which I burned   with the   world   and   I wasted   the   life   and   the hours
in which I burned with the world and wasted my life and my time,

tu   ke   kon 'tri to   kɔr   dʒam: 'ma i   non   'sprɛt: tsi
tu,   che   contrito   cor   giammai   non   sprezzi.
you   who   contrite   heart   never   not   you spurn
o you who never spurns a contrite heart.

☙

[38, 69, 70]

Francesco Della Valle

'do ve 'do ve siɲ: 'ɲor
Dove, dove, Signor
Where, where, Lord

'do ve   'do ve   siɲ: 'ɲor   'kwje to   ri 'tʃet: to   'fi a   'ma i   ke   'tro vi
Dove,   dove,   Signor,   quieto   ricetto   fia   mai   che   trovi,
where   where   Lord   peaceful   refuge   will be   ever   that   I may find
Where, where, Lord, may I ever find peaceful refuge –

> fia = (mod.) sarà

'a i	'koɲː ɲi	'vi a	mɛ	'kju za	per	fud: 'dʒir	'li ɾa	'tu a
ahi,	**ch'ogni**	**via**	**m'è**	**chiusa.**	**Per**	**fuggir**	**l'ira**	**tua,**
ah	[that] every	path	to me is	closed	in order	to flee	the wrath	your

ah, every way is closed to me. To flee your wrath

ne	'dʒo va	i 'sku za	'koɲː ɲi	'kɔ za	ɛ	pa 'le ze	al	'tu o	ko 'spɛt: to
né	**giova**	**iscusa,**	**ch'ogni**	**cosa**	**è**	**palese**	**al**	**tuo**	**cospetto.**
not	avails	excuse	because every	thing	is	manifest	to the	your	sight

excuses do not avail, because all things are manifest in your eyes.

> *iscusa = (mod.) scusa*

tʃɔ	ke	a 'mi ko	mi	dje	'va no	di 'let: to
Ciò	**che**	**amico**	**mi**	**diè**	**vano**	**diletto,**
that	which	friend	to me	gave	vain	pleasure

What as a friend gave me vain pleasure,

> *var.: ch'amico*
> *= che amico*

'fat: to	or	ne 'mi ko	i	'mjɛ i	de 'lit: ti	ak: 'ku za
fatto	**or**	**nemico**	**i**	**miei**	**delitti**	**accusa.**
made	now	enemy	the	my	offences	accuses

having now become an enemy, denounces my crimes,

> *var.:* **accusai** (= I accused) : *makes much less sense... perhaps a dialect variant of "accusa," or a misprint.*

'on de	'da i	'swɔ i	pja 'tʃer	'lal ma	de 'lu za
Onde	**dai**	**suoi**	**piacer**	**l'alma**	**delusa**
whence	by the	its	pleasures	the soul	deluded

Wherefore, deluded by its pleasures, my soul

'rom per	de 'zi a	'la tra	pri 'dʒon	del	'pɛt: to
romper	**desia**	**l'atra**	**prigion**	**del**	**petto.**
to break through	desires	the dark	prison	of the	breast

desires to break out of the dark prison of my breast.

fan	ʎi	e le 'men ti	'o ve	di 'let: to	'pre zi	te sti 'mɔn jo	'apː po	te
Fan	**gli**	**elementi**	**ove**	**diletto**	**presi**	**testimonio**	**appo**	**te**
make	the	elements	where	pleasure	I took	testimony	*(lit.)* by	you

> *var.:* **gli clementi** : *surely a mis-copying....*

del	fal: 'lir	'mi o	e	'kon tri	mi 'vedː dʒo	i	di	mal	'spe zi
del	**fallir**	**mio,**	**e**	**contr'i'**	**mi veggio**	**i**	**dì**	**mal**	**spesi.**
of the	failing	mine	and	against them	I see myself	the	days	badly	spent

> *veggio = (mod.) vedo*

The elements from which I took pleasure make testimony to you of my failing; and, faced with them, I see my days ill-spent.

sol	tu	'sɛ i	'pɔr to	di	sa 'lu te
Sol	**tu**	**sei**	**porto**	**di**	**salute,**
only	you	you are	haven	of	*(lit.)* salvation

You alone are the haven of salvation,

on 'di o	'tan to	ti	pre ge 'rɔ	'kwan to	tof: 'fe zi
ond'io	**tanto**	**ti**	**pregherò,**	**quanto**	**t'offesi,**
whence I	so much	to you	I will pray	as much	you I offended

whence I shall pray to you as much as I have offended you;

e	'do ve	an 'drɔ	se	non	a	te	'mi o	'di o
e	**dove**	**andrò,**	**se**	**non**	**a**	**Te,**	**mio**	**Dio?**
and	where	I will go	if	not	to	You	my	God

and where will I go, my God, if not to You?

> *var.:*
> *dov'andrò =*
> *dove andrò*

☙

[69]

'do ve 'do ve spa 'rir si 'rat: to

Dove, dove sparir sì ratto

Where, where disappeared so quickly

'do ve	'do ve	spa 'rir	si	'rat: to	i	di	se 're ni	ke	'fol: le
Dove,	**dove**	**sparir**	**sì**	**ratto**	**i**	**dì**	**sereni,**	**che,**	**folle,**
where	where	disappeared	so	quickly	the	days	serene	which	foolish

sparir = sparirono

	in tor bi 'da i	kol	fal: 'lir	'mi o
	intorbidai	**col**	**fallir**	**mio?**
	I muddled	with the	failing	mine

Where, oh where, have the serene days, which I foolishly muddled with my failings, gone so quickly?

'a i	kel	'vi ver	del: 'lwɔm	'ra pi do	'ri o	ras: 'sem bra
Ahi,	**che'l**	**viver**	**dell'uom**	**rapido**	**rio**	**rassembra,**
ah	[that] the	living	of the man	rapid	brook	*(lit.)* is like

Ah, the life of man is like a rushing brook,

	e dal	fud: 'dʒir	ʎi	'an: ni	ba 'le ni
	ed al	**fuggir**	**gli**	**anni**	**baleni.**
	and at the	fleeing	the	years	lightning flashes

and in fleeting, the years [are like] lightning flashes.

dʒa	'vis: si	'tʃɛ ko	del	'mi o	'pjan to	'pjɛ ni	or	'a pro	i	'lu mi
Già	**vissi**	**cieco,**	**del**	**mio**	**pianto**	**pieni**	**or**	**apro**	**i**	**lumi**
formerly	I lived	blind	of the	my	weeping	full	now	I open	the	eyes

Before, I lived blindly; now I open my eyes, full of weeping,

a	te	'mi o	sol	'mi o	'di o	ke	mil: 'lu stra	un	'tu o	'rad: dʒo
a	**te,**	**mio**	**Sol,**	**mio**	**Dio,**	**ché**	**m'illustra**	**un**	**tuo**	**raggio,**
to	you	my	Sun	my	God	because	me illuminates	a	your	ray

to you, my Sun, my God, because a ray of yours illuminates me

'on de	ved: 'dʒi o	ke	lan 'ti ke	dol 'tʃet: tse	'ɛ ran	ve 'le ni
onde	**vegg'io**	**che**	**l'antiche**	**dolcezze**	**eran**	**veleni.**
whence	see I	that	the old	sweetnesses	were	poisons

whereby I see that the old sweetnesses were poison.

vegg'io = (mod.) vedo io

'vo la no	ʎi	'an: ni	e	de	'mjɛ i	'fal: li	il	'pɔn do	pju	'kreʃ: ʃe
Volano	**gli**	**anni,**	**e**	**de'**	**miei**	**falli**	**il**	**pondo**	**più**	**cresce,**
fly	the	years	and	of	my	failings	the	*(lit.)* weight	more	grows

The years fly by, and the weight of my failings becomes greater;

e	'kwa i	sa 'ran	'kol pe	se 'gre te	sɛ	nel	'tu o	'zgwar do
e	**quai**	**saran**	**colpe**	**segrete,**	**s'è**	**nel**	**tuo**	**sguardo**
and	what	will be	sins	secret	if is	in the	your	glance

	un	'pit: tʃol	'pun to	il	'mon do
	un	**picciol**	**punto**	**il**	**mondo?**
	a	little	point	the	world

and what will be of secret sins if, in your sight, the world is but a tiny point?

'del: la	mal	'ka u ta	e 'ta	'lɔ pre	in di 'skre te	'on de	tof: 'fe zi	o 'bli a
Della	**mal**	**cauta**	**età**	**l'opre**	**indiscrete**	**onde**	**t'offesi**	**oblia,**
of the	badly	prudent	age	the deeds	indiscreet	where	you I offended	forget

opre: plural of opra (poet.) = (mod.) opera

Forget the indiscreet deeds of my imprudent years, by which I offended you,

qwel	'tu o	pro 'fon do	o tʃe 'an	di	pje 'ta	'si a		per	me	'lɛ te
quel	**tuo**	**profondo**	**ocean**	**di**	**pietà,**	**sia**		**per**	**me**	**Lete.**
that	your	deep	ocean	of	pity	may be		for	me	Lethe

[and] let your deep ocean of pity be Lethe for me.

GL: **Lete**

❧

[69]

'duŋ kwe do 'vrɔ
Dunque dovrò
Then I shall have to

'duŋ kwe	do 'vrɔ	del	'pu ro	ser 'vir	'mi o	kru 'dɛl
Dunque	**dovrò**	**del**	**puro**	**servir**	**mio,**	**crudel,**
then	I shall have to	of the	pure	serving	mine	cruel one

or	ri por 'tar	tor 'men ti	e	'pe ne
or	**riportar**	**tormenti,**	**e**	**pene:**
now	to receive	torments	and	pains

Then I shall now have to receive torments and pains in exchange for my chaste servitude, o cruel one:

o	tra 'di te	spe 'ran tse	o	van	de 'zi o
O	**tradite**	**speranze,**	**o**	**van**	**desio,**
o	betrayed	hopes	o	vain	desire

O betrayed hopes, o vain desire,

ke	se 'pol ta	nel	dwɔl	'lal ma	mi	'tjɛ ne
che	**sepolta**	**nel**	**duol**	**l'alma**	**mi**	**tiene!**
which	buried	in the	grief	the soul	me	keeps

which keep my soul buried in grief!

te	a 'mor	te	'so lo	'o ra	iŋ kol 'par	dɛd: 'dʒi o	ke	min 'vo li
Te,	**Amor,**	**te**	**solo**	**ora**	**incolpar**	**degg'io,**	**che**	**m'involi,**
you	Love	you	only	now	to blame	ought I	who	from me you steal

You, Love – I must now blame only you, who rob me,

ti 'ran: no	'oɲ: ɲi	'mi o	'bɛ ne
tiranno,	**ogni**	**mio**	**bene;**
tyrant	every	my	good thing

o tyrant, of every happiness.

te	te	iŋ kol 'par	dɛd: 'dʒi o	ke	'prɛn di	a	'dʒɔ ko
Te,	**te**	**incolpar**	**degg'io,**	**che**	**prendi**	**a**	**gioco**
you	you	to blame	ought I	who	you take	as	game

You – I must blame you, who take it as a joke

ke	'mar da	il	kɔr	di	kru del 'ta de	il	'fɔ ko
che	**m'arda**	**il**	**cor**	**di**	**crudeltade**	**il**	**foco.**
that	me may burn	the	heart	with	cruelty	the	fire

> *foco* = (mod.) *fuoco*
> *crudeltade* = (mod.) *crudeltà*

that the fire of cruelty is burning my heart.

GL: **Amor**

❧

[69]

'en tro 'na ve do 'ra ta
Entro nave dorata
In a golden ship

'en tro 'na ve do 'ra ta sol 'kjam 'fil: li de il 'ma ɾe
Entro   nave   dorata   solchiam,   Fillide,   il   mare,
within   ship   golden   we plough   Fillide   the   sea
We cut through the waves, Fillide, in a golden ship;

've di un 'nem bo kap: 'pa ɾe 'mi ɾa 'la ɾja in fo 'ka ta
vedi   un   nembo   ch'appare,   mira   l'aria   infocata.
see   a   cloud   which appears   look at   the air   fiery
see a cloud appear; look at the fiery air.

i 'vɛn ti 'sof: fja no e 'lon de in: 'nal tsa no el dʒa 'pla tʃi do mar
I   venti   soffiano,   e   l'onde   innalzano,   e'l   già   placido   mar
the   winds   blow   and   the waves   rise up   and the   formerly   placid   sea
The winds blow and the waves rise, and the formerly calm sea

di 'vjɛn se 've ɾo 'tor na in 'dje tro nok: 'kje ɾo
divien   severo: torna   indietro,   nocchiero.
becomes   severe   turn   back   helmsman
becomes severe: turn back, helmsman.

> *Three more verses are printed as text only:*

'fil: li 'mi a tu pa 'vɛn ti lo 'tu o 'spir to vjɛn 'me no
Filli   mia,   tu   paventi,   lo   tuo   spirto   vien meno
Filli   mine   you   you fear   the   your   spirit   faints
My Filli, you are afraid; your spirit is failing

> *spirto =*
> *(mod.) spirito*

e strin 'dʒɛn do mi al 'se no 'for mi 'laŋ gwi di at: 'tʃɛn ti
e   stringendomi   al   seno   formi   languidi   accenti.
and   pressing me   to the   breast   you shape   languid   words
and, pressing me to your breast, you form languid words.

tem 'pɛ ste e 'tur bi ni 'tɛ ti kon 'fon do no e pre 'tʃi pi ta il tʃɛl
Tempeste,   e   turbini   Teti   confondono,   e   precipita   il   ciel
tempests   and   turmoils   Tethys   stir up   and   precipitates   the   sky

kon 'vɛr so in 'on de
converso   in   onde:
changed into   in   waves
Tempests and turmoils stir up the sea; and the sky falls in waves:

'tor na 'al: le 'spon de
torna   alle   sponde.
return   to the   shores
go back to shore.

'fil: li kɔr del 'mi o 'kɔ ɾe 'fil: li 'dol tʃe 'mi o 'bɛ ne
Filli,   cor   del   mio   core,   Filli   dolce   mio   bene,
Filli   heart   of the   my   heart   Filli   sweet   my   dear one
Filli, heart of my heart – Filli, my sweet beloved one,

'i o	nel	mar	di	'mi e	'pe ne	'prɔ vo		'dop: pjo	lor: 'ro ɾe
io	**nel**	**mar**	**di**	**mie**	**pene**	**provo**		**doppio**	**l'orrore.**
I	in the	sea	of	my	pains	I experience		twofold	the horror

in the sea of my pains I doubly feel the horror.

'tʃɛ lo	im pla 'ka bi le		'neb: bja	fol 'tis: si ma	'dal: la	'lu tʃe	del	di
Cielo	**implacabile,**		**nebbia**	**foltissima**	**dalla**	**luce**	**del**	**dì**
heaven	implacable		fog	most dense	from the	light	of the	day

'tut: ti	ne	'pri va
tutti	**ne**	**priva:**
everyone	of it	deprives

An implacable heaven [and] the densest of fogs deprive everyone of the light of day:

'tor na	'al: la	'ri va
torna	**alla**	**riva.**
return	to the	coast

go back to the coast.

ma	'tu e	'ra ɾe	bel: 'let: tse	'skɔr dʒe	il	'ma ɾe	a di 'ra to
Ma	**tue**	**rare**	**bellezze**	**scorge**	**il**	**mare**	**adirato,**
but	your	rare	beauties	perceives	the	sea	angry

But the angry sea perceives your rare beauties,

e	dʒa	'laʃ: ʃa	pla 'ka to	'su e	te 'mu te	fje 'ret: tse
e	**già**	**lascia**	**placato**	**sue**	**temute**	**fierezze.**
and	already	lets	calmed	its	feared	cruelties

and has already calmed its frightful cruelty.

'dzɛf: fi ɾi	'spi ɾa no	'lon de	sin 'kre spa no	e	la	'lu tʃe	del	sol
Zeffiri	**spirano,**	**l'onde**	**s'increspano,**	**e**	**la**	**luce**	**del**	**sol**
zephyrs	blow	the waves	ripple	and	the	light	of the	sun

Gentle breezes are blowing, the waves are rippling, and the light of the sun

pju	non	si 'tʃe la	'spje ga	la	've la
più	**non**	**si cela:**	**spiega**	**la**	**vela.**
more	not	is hidden	unfurl	the	sail

is hidden no longer: unfurl the sails.

> *cela: from*
> *"celare" (lit.) =*
> *"nascondere"*

𝒢𝓛: **Filli, Fillide, Teti**

❦

[69]   *Francesco Balducci*

la	'mi a	'pal: li da	'fat: tʃa
La mia pallida faccia
My pale face

la	'mi a	'pal: li da	'fat: tʃa	ɛ	'liŋ gwa	di	pje 'ta
La	**mia**	**pallida**	**faccia**	**è**	**lingua**	**di**	**pietà,**
the	my	pale	face	is	tongue	of	pity

My pale face is the voice of pity,

e	kwal	per	'vo i	mi 'sfat: tʃa		a	'vo i	nar: 'ran do	va
e	**qual**	**per**	**voi**	**mi sfacia**		**a**	**voi**	**narrando**	**va.**
and	how	for	you	may come undone		to	you	speaking	goes

and it is telling you how I may melt away for you.

ɛ   bɛn   'ki o   'tat: tʃa   del   'pɛt: to   'mi o   lin 'tʃɛn djo   'ri o
È   ben   ch'io   taccia   del   petto   mio   l'incendio   rio,
it is   well   that I   be silent   of the   breast   mine   the fire   cruel
It is well that I be silent about the cruel fire in my breast;

> reo (lit.)
> = rio

pur   oɲ: 'ɲu no   sel   've de   oɲ: 'ɲwɔ mo   il   sa
pur   ogn'uno   se'l   vede   ogn'uomo   il   sa;
yet   each one   if it   sees   each man   it   knows
yet anyone, if they see it, knows it:

sol   da   'vo i   non   si 'kre de   in fi 'ni ta   bel: 'let: tsa   e   'pɔ ka   'fe de
sol   da   voi   non   si crede,   infinita   bellezza,   e   poca   fede.
only   from   you   not   is believed   infinite   beauty   and   little   faith
you are the only one who does not believe [it], o woman of infinite beauty and little faith.

Two more verses are printed as text only:

i   'mjɛ i   so 'spi ri   ar 'dɛn ti   del   'kju zo   ar 'dor   fan   fe
I   miei   sospiri   ardenti   del   chiuso   ardor   fan   fé,
the   my   sighs   ardent   of the   enclosed   ardor   make   faith
My burning sighs are proof of the fire within me;

le   'la gri me   ko 'tʃɛn ti   son   pur   fa 'vil: le   o i 'mɛ
le   lagrime   cocenti   son   pur   faville,   ohimè.
the   tears   burning   are   yet   sparks   alas
alas, my burning tears are like sparks.

ɛ   bɛn   'ki o   'tɛn ti   in   'par te   o 'sku ra   tʃe 'lar   lar 'su ra
È   ben   ch'io   tenti   in   parte   oscura   celar   l'arsura,
it is   well   that I   I may try   in   part   dark   to hide   the scorching heat
It is well that I try to hide the scorching heat in a dark place;

pju   'kja ro   del   'mi o   'fɔ ko   il   sol   non   ɛ
più   chiaro   del   mio   foco   il   sol   non   è;
more   bright   of the   my   fire   the   sun   not   is
the sun is not brighter than my fire;

pur   da   'vo i   non   si 'kre de   in fi 'ni ta   bel: 'let: tsa   e   'pɔ ka   'fe de
pur   da   voi   non   si crede,   infinita   bellezza,   e   poca   fede.
yet   from   you   not   is believed   infinite   beauty   and   little   faith
yet you do not believe [it], o woman of infinite beauty and little faith.

'mo stra   la   'gwan tʃa   e 'zaŋ gwe   kwal   'pja ga   il   sen   ma 'pri
Mostra   la   guancia   esangue   qual   piaga   il   sen   m'aprì,
shows   the   cheek   bloodless   what   wound   the   breast   me opened
My bloodless cheeks show what wound split my breast,

per   'ku i   fud: 'dʒɛn do   il   'saŋ gwe   'tan to   si sko lo 'ri
per   cui,   fuggendo   il   sangue,   tanto   si scolorì.
through   which   fleeing   the   blood   so much   lost color
for which reason, the blood having escaped, they *[my cheeks]* lost so much color.

il   kɔr   ke   'laŋ gwe   'skɔ pre   il   do 'lo re   del   'mi o   pal: 'lo re
Il   cor,   che   langue,   scopre   il   dolore   del   mio   pallore,
the   heart   which   languishes   reveals   the   pain   of the   my   pallor
My languishing heart reveals the pain of my pallor,

per	'ke	'tʃɛ li		lo	stral	ke	lo	fe 'ri
perché	**celi**		**lo**	**stral,**	**che**	**lo**	**ferì;**
so that	it may conceal	the	arrow	which	it	wounded

so that it may conceal the arrow which wounded it:

pur	da	'vo i	non	si 'kre de	in fi 'ni ta	bel: 'let: tsa	e	'pɔ ka	'fe de
pur	**da**	**voi**	**non**	**si crede**	**infinita**	**bellezza,**	**e**	**poca**	**fede.**
yet	from	you	not	is believed	infinite	beauty	and	little	faith

yet you do not believe [it], o woman of infinite beauty and little faith.

ক

[69]

non mi ne 'ga te
Non mi negate
Do not refuse me

non	mi	ne 'ga te	o i 'mɛ	'lu mi	se 're ni	'ki o	vi	'mo stri	la	'mi a	fe
Non	**mi**	**negate,**	**ohimè,**	**lumi**	**sereni,**	**ch'io**	**vi**	**mostri**	**la**	**mia**	**fé,**
not	me	refuse	alas	eyes	serene	that I	to you	may show	the	my	faith

Do not refuse, alas, serene eyes, my showing you my faithfulness,

vi	'nar: ri	il	'mi o	de 'zi o	mi 'strug: go		ar 'den do	'vi vo	pjan 'dʒɛn do
vi	**narri**	**il**	**mio**	**desio;**	**mi struggo**		**ardendo,**	**vivo**	**piangendo,**
to you	I may tell	the	my	desire	I am being consumed	burning	I live	weeping

telling you my desire; I am being consumed in flames; I live in weeping,

e	'kjɛd: dʒo	al	'mi o	ser 'vir	'kwal ke	mer 'tʃe
e	**chieggio**	**al**	**mio**	**servir**	**qualche**	**mercé.**
and	I beg for	to	my	serving	some	mercy

and I beg for some mercy in my servitude.

chieggio =
(mod.) chiedo

Two other verses are printed as text only:

'pɛn so	koɲ: 'ɲor	sof: 'fri	'fɔ ko	im: mor 'tal	il	'se no
Penso,	**ch'ogn'or**	**soffrì**	**foco**	**immortal**	**il**	**seno,**
I think	that always	suffered	fire	immortal	the	breast

I think my breast has always suffered immortal passion;

'pɛn so	kin	'va no	un	di	bra 'ma i	'lje to	e	se 're no
penso,	**ch'in**	**vano**	**un**	**dì**	**bramai**	**lieto,**	**e**	**sereno;**
I think	that in	vain	one	day	I yearned	happy	and	serene

I think I yearned in vain, once happy and carefree;

ne	'vɔl: li	'ma i	'lu tʃi di	'ra i	sko 'vrir	la	'fjam: ma	kil	'mi o	kɔr	nu 'tri
né	**volli**	**mai,**	**lucidi**	**rai,**	**scovrir**	**la**	**fiamma,**	**ch'il**	**mio**	**cor**	**nutrì.**
not	I wished	ever	bright	eyes	to reveal	the	flame	which the	my	heart	fed

I never wished, bright eyes, to reveal the flame which my heart nurtured.   scovrir[e] = (mod.) scoprir[e]

ma	'po i 'ki o	'sɛn to	dʒa	ka	'mɔr te	il	dwɔl	min 'vi ta
Ma,	**poi ch'io**	**sento**	**già**	**ch'a**	**morte**	**il**	**duol**	**m'invita,**
but	since I	I feel	now	that to	death	the	grief	me invites

But, since I now feel that grief invites me to death,

'kjɛd: dʒo	pje 'ta	'kjɛd: dʒo	o	'beʎ: ʎi	'ɔk: ki	a 'i ta
chieggio	**pietà,**	**chieggio,**	**o**	**begli**	**occhi,**	**aita;**
I beg for	pity	I beg for	o	beautiful	eyes	help

I beg for pity; I beg, o beautiful eyes, for help.

un	'gwar do	'so lo	tem pre 'ra	il	'dwɔ lo	un	'gwar do	'so lo	in	'vi ta	mi	ter: 'ra
un	**guardo**	**solo**	**temprerà**	**il**	**duolo,**	**un**	**guardo**	**solo**	**in**	**vita**	**mi**	**terrà.**
one	glance	only	will temper	the	grief	one	glance	alone	in	life	me	will hold

A single glance will mitigate my grief; a single glance will keep me alive.

❧

[69]

o bɛl: 'lɔk: ki
O bell'occhi
O beautiful eyes

o	bɛl: 'lɔk: ki	ke	gwer: 'rjɛ ɾi	sa et: 'ta te	i	'kɔ ɾi	a 'man ti
O	**bell'occhi,**	**che**	**guerrieri**	**saettate**	**i**	**cori**	**amanti,**
o	beautiful eyes	which	warriors	you shoot darts to	the	hearts	loving

bell'occhi:
= (mod.)
begl'occhi

'dol tʃi	'lje ti	e	sfa vil: 'lan ti	'stra li	ar 'ma ti	ak: 'kɔr ti	ar 'tʃe ɾi
dolci,	**lieti,**	**e**	**sfavillanti**	**strali**	**armati,**	**accorti**	**arcieri,**
sweet	happy	and	sparkling	arrows	armed	cunning	archers

O beautiful eyes, which like warriors shoot darts into sweet, loving, and happy hearts and, armed with sparkling arrows as cunning archers,

'men tre	ar 'dɛn do	'o ɾa	dʒo 'i te	dɛ	mi 'ɾa te	e	non	fe 'ɾi te
mentre	**ardendo**	**ora**	**gioite**	**deh**	**mirate,**	**e**	**non**	**ferite.**
while	burning	now	you rejoice	ah	look	and	not	wound

while burning, now you rejoice – ah, look and do not wound.

'lu mi	'va gi	ka mo 'ro zi	'dol tʃe	'spɛ me	al 'tru i	por 'dʒe te
Lumi	**vaghi,**	**ch'amorosi**	**dolce**	**speme**	**altrui**	**porgete,**
eyes	lovely	which amorously	sweet	hope	others	you offer

speme (lit.)
= speranza

Lovely eyes, which amorously offer sweet hope to others,

or	ka 'man do	'vo i	ri 'de te	non	pju	'kru di	ma	pje 'to zi
or	**ch'amando**	**voi**	**ridete**	**non**	**più**	**crudi,**	**ma**	**pietosi,**
now	that loving	you	laugh	not	more	harsh	but	compassionate

now that in loving you laugh, no longer harsh, but compassionate,

'men tre	ar 'dɛn do	aŋ 'kor	dʒo 'i te	dɛ	mi 'ɾa te	e	non	fe 'ɾi te
mentre	**ardendo**	**ancor**	**gioite**	**deh**	**mirate,**	**e**	**non**	**ferite.**
while	burning	still	you rejoice	ah	look	and	not	wound

while burning, still you rejoice – ah, look and do not wound.

'stel: le	a 'ma te	'al me	pu 'pil: le	ke	pren 'de te	'al ta	va 'get: tsa
Stelle	**amate,**	**alme**	**pupille,**	**che**	**prendete**	**alta**	**vaghezza**
stars	beloved	glorious	eyes	who	you take	great	pleasure

Beloved stars, glorious eyes, you who derive great pleasure

nel	mi 'ɾar	'nɔ bil	bel: 'let: tsa	'kal: le	'fjam: ma	'mil: le a 'mil: le
nel	**mirar**	**nobil**	**bellezza,**	**ch'alle**	**fiamm' a**	**mille a mille**
in the	looking at	noble	beauty	which to the	flames in	thousand by thousand

'men tre	ar 'dɛn do	ne	dʒo 'i te	dɛ	mi 'ɾa te	non	fe 'ɾi te
mentre	**ardendo**	**ne**	**gioite**	**deh**	**mirat'e**	**non**	**ferite.**
while	burning	of it	you rejoice	ah	look and	not	wound

in looking at noble beauty [and] rejoice in the burning of thousands of flames – ah, look and do not wound.

❧

[69]   *Francesco Della Valle*

o i ˈmɛ ke fur
Ohimè, che fur
Alas, what were

o i ˈmɛ	ke	fur	ke	ˈso no	e	ke	sa ˈran: no	kwe ˈstem pje	ˈmɛm bra
Ohimè,	**che**	**fur,**	**che**	**sono,**	**e**	**che**	**saranno**	**quest'empie**	**membra?**
alas	what	were	what	are	and	what	will be	these ungodly	limbs

fur = furono

Alas, what were, what are, and what will be of these ungodly limbs?

ˈa i	ri mem ˈbran tsa	ˈdu ɾa	ˈʃe ze	ˈlal ma	dal	tʃɛl	ˈkan di da	e	ˈpu ɾa
Ahi	**rimembranza**	**dura!**	**Scese**	**l'alma**	**dal**	**ciel**	**candida,**	**e**	**pura,**
alas	remembrance	harsh	descended	the soul	from the	heaven	innocent	and	pure

Alas, cruel memory! My soul descended from heaven innocent and pure,

e	kon	le	ˈkol pe	lor	mak: ˈkja ta	ˈlan: no
e	**con**	**le**	**colpe**	**lor**	**macchiata**	**l'hanno.**
and	with	the	sins	their	blemished	it they have

and they have besmirched it with their sins.

ˈlas: so	in	ˈbrɛ ve	di	ˈmɔr te	e ˈspo ste	al	ˈdan: no	ˈpɔ ka	ˈpol ve ɾe	ˈfi en
Lasso!	**in**	**breve,**	**di**	**morte**	**esposte**	**al**	**danno,**	**poca**	**polvere**	**fien,**
woe	in	short	of	death	exposed	to the	damage	little	dust	they will be

Woe is me! Shortly, exposed to the damage of death, they will be but a little dust,   *fien[o] = (mod.) saranno*

ˈfred: da	e do ˈsku ɾa	e	le ˈtɛr no	pe ˈnar	ˈkwel: la	non	ˈku ɾa
fredda,	**ed oscura,**	**e**	**l'eterno**	**penar**	**quella**	**non**	**cura,**
cold	and dark	and	the eternal	suffering	that	not	cares about

cold and dark; and eternal suffering cares nothing about it [my dust],

ˈtan to	il	ˈsɛn so	ɛ	di	ˈlɛ i	ˈfat: to	ti ˈran: no
tanto	**il**	**senso**	**è**	**di**	**lei**	**fatto**	**tiranno.**
so much	the	lust	is	of	it	made	tyrant

so much has lust become its tyrant.

ˈpri a ke	ˈda tro po	ˈrɛ a	ˈprɛ da	ri ˈman ga	ˈspi ɾa	o	siɲ: ˈɲor
Pria che	**d'Atropo**	**rea**	**preda**	**rimanga,**	**spira,**	**o**	**Signor,**
before	of Atropo	cruel	prey	I may remain	breathe	o	Lord

pria (poet.) = prima

Before I remain the cruel prey of Atropo, o Lord, breathe

le	ˈfjam: me	ˈtu e	so ˈa vi	kil	ˈdʒe lo	del	ˈmi o	kwɔr
le	**fiamme**	**tue**	**soavi,**	**ch'il**	**gielo**	**del**	**mio**	**cuor**
the	flames	yours	gentle	that the	ice	of the	my	heart

gielo = (mod.) gelo

your gentle flames, so that the ice of my heart

si ˈskal di	e	ˈfran ga
si scaldi	**e**	**franga.**
itself may warm	and	may break

may thaw and break.

ˈved: dʒo	e dak: ˈku zo	o ˈma i	le	ˈkol pe	ˈgra vi	ˈon de	kon ˈvjɛn
Veggio,	**ed accuso**	**omai**	**le**	**colpe**	**gravi;**	**onde**	**convien**
I look at	and I accuse	now	the	sins	grave	wherefore	it is fitting

veggio = (mod.) vedo

omai (poet.) = ormai

Now I look at and charge my grave sins, wherefore it is fitting

ke ter na 'men te	'pjaŋ ga	per 'ke	le	'mak: kje	di	kwe 'stal ma	'i o	'la vi
ch'eternamente	pianga,	perché	le	macchie	di	quest'alma	io	lavi.
that eternally	I may weep	so that	the	stains	of	this soul	I	I may cleanse

that I should eternally weep in order to cleanse the stains of this soul.

GL: **Atropo**

☙

[69] In two parts ("Prima parte" and "Seconda parte"); each part is an Aria.

o 'mi o kɔr
O mio cor
O my heart

o	'mi o	kɔr	'dol tʃe	'mi a	'vi ta	po i 'ke	'las: so	il	'tu o	'pas: so
O	mio	cor,	dolce	mia	vita,	poiché,	lasso,	il	tuo	passo
o	my	heart	sweet	my	life	since	alas	the	your	step

'vɔl dʒe	al 'tro ve	'in vi da	'stel: la	al 'men	'sɛn ti	'pri a	ke	'par ti
volge	altrove	invida	stella,	almen	senti,	pria	che	parti,
turns	elsewhere	envious	star	al least	hear	before	that	you depart

O my heart, my sweet life, since, alas, an envious star turns your path elsewhere,
at least hear, before you depart,

i	'mjɛ i	la 'men ti
i	miei	lamenti.
the	my	laments

my laments.

> *invida (lit.) =*
> *= invidiosa*
>
> *pria (poet.) =*
> *prima*

Three other verses are printed as text only:

'trɔp: po	a i 'mɛ	'rat: to	ten 'fud: dʒi
Troppo,	ahimè,	ratto	ten fuggi.
too	alas	quickly	you flee

Too quickly, alas, you flee.

'fer ma	un	'pɔ ko	e	kwel	'fɔ ko	kon	ke	il	kɔr	mab: 'bru dʒi
Ferma	un	poco,	e	quel	foco	con	che	il	cor	m'abbrugi,
stop	a	little	and	that	fire	with	which	the	heart	me you burn

> *abbrugi: from*
> *"abbrugiare" =*
> *"abbruciare" = "bruciare"*

e	'strud: dʒi	'spen dʒi	'pri a	e	'pɔ i	'par ti	'a ni ma	'mi a
e	struggi,	spengi	pria,	e	poi	parti,	anima	mia.
and	you consume	extinguish	first	and	then	leave	soul	mine

> *spengi (lit.)*
> *= spegni*

Stop for a little while, and first extinguish that fire with which you burn and consume my heart;
and then leave, my soul.

'i o	per	te	sol	'vi vo	e	'spi ɾo	sol	ri 'vɔl to	nel	'tu o	'vol to
Io	per	te	sol	vivo,	e	spiro,	sol	rivolto	nel	tuo	volto
I	for	you	only	I live	and	I breathe	only	turned	in the	your	face

'oɲ: ɲi	bɛn	'gɔ do	e	ri 'mi ɾo	da	te	'lun dʒe	'dwɔ lo
ogni	ben	godo,	e	rimiro,	da	te	lunge	duolo,
every	good thing	I enjoy	and	I see	from	you	far away	sorrow

I live and breathe only for you; I enjoy and see every happiness only when turned toward your face;
and, far away from you, sorrow

e	'no ja	il	kɔr	mi	'pun dʒe
e	noia	il	cor	mi	punge.
and	affliction	the	heart	me	stings

and affliction sting my heart.

vor: 'ra i	'duŋ kwe	kol	par 'ti ɾe	a	ki	'ta ma	e	ti	'bra ma
Vorrai	**dunque**	**col**	**partire**	**a**	**chi**	**t'ama,**	**e**	**ti**	**brama**
you will want	then	with the	departing	from	one who	you loves	and	you	desires

dar	ka 'dʒo ne	al	'su o	mo 'ri ɾe
dar	**cagione**	**al**	**suo**	**morire?**
to give	reason	to the	his	dying

Will you then want, in departing, to give reason to one who loves and desires you, to die?

de	sok: 'kor so	se	non	'a i	kɔr	'da spe	o	'dor so
Deh,	**soccorso!**	**se**	**non**	**hai**	**cor**	**d'aspe,**	**o**	**d'orso.**
ah	help	if	not	you have	heart	of snake	or	of bear

Ah, offer assistance, if you have not the heart of a snake or a bear!

> *aspe =*
> *(mod.) aspide*

> The following Aria is the "Seconda Parte":

tu	'sa i	pur
Tu	**sai**	**pur**
You	know	indeed

tu	'sa i	pur	'dol tʃe	'mi o	'bɛ ne	kɔ	nel	'kɔ ɾe	tan tar 'do ɾe
Tu	**sai**	**pur,**	**dolce**	**mio**	**bene,**	**ch'ho**	**nel**	**core**	**tant'ardore**
you	you know	indeed	sweet	my	dear one	that I have	in the	heart	so much ardor

You know indeed, my sweet dear one, that I have in my heart as much ardor

'kwan ta	il	mar	'stɛ ɾi la 'ɾe ne	ke	il	'mi o	'pɛt: to
quant'ha	**il**	**mar**	**steril'arene,**	**ch'è**	**il**	**mio**	**petto**
as much as has	the	sea	barren sands	because is	the	my	breast

as the sea has barren sands, for my breast is

din fi 'ni to	a 'mor	ri 'tʃet: to
d'infinito	**amor**	**ricetto.**
of infinite	love	shelter

a refuge of infinite love.

> Three other verses are printed as text only:

ma	ke	'fat: tʃo	i	'pre gi	el	'pjan to	'spar go	in	'va no
Ma,	**che**	**faccio?**	**I**	**preghi,**	**e'l**	**pianto**	**spargo**	**in**	**vano,**
but	what	I do	the	entreaties	and the	weeping	I shed	in	vain

> *preghi: pl. of*
> *prego (lit.) =*
> *preghiera*

But what am I doing? I pour out entreaties and tears in vain,

ke	'e i	lon 'ta no	pju	non	'mɔ de	e	'fud: dʒe	in 'tan to
ché	**ei**	**lontano**	**più**	**non**	**m'ode,**	**e**	**fugge**	**intanto.**
because	he	far away	more	not	me hears	and	flees	meanwhile

because he, far away, no longer hears me, and all the while he is fleeing.

'a i	for 'tu na	del	'mi o	mal	'sɛm pre	di 'dʒu na
Ahi,	**fortuna!**	**del**	**mio**	**mal**	**sempre**	**digiuna.**
alas	fortune	of the	my	illness	always	abstains

Alas, o fortune, always ignorant of my hurt!

'a u ɾe	'vo i	pje 'to ze	al 'me no	kin ten 'de te	e	ve 'de te	il	do 'lor
Aure	**voi**	**pietose**	**almeno,**	**ch'intendete,**	**e**	**vedete**	**il**	**dolor,**
breezes	you	merciful	at least	that understand	and	see	the	pain

At least you, merciful breezes who understand and see the pain

kɔ	'den tro	al	'se no	ri fe 'ri te	al	kru 'dɛl	kwel	'ko ɾa	u 'di te
ch'ho	dentro	al	seno,	riferite	al	crudel	quel	ch'ora	udite.
that I have	within	at the	breast	relate	to the	cruel one	that	which now	you hear

that I have within my breast, tell the cruel one what you are now hearing.

ri fe 'ri te	ke	vi 'tʃi no	'al: le	'pɔr te	'del: la	'mɔr te	ma	kon 'dot: to
Riferite	che	vicino	alle	porte	della	morte	m'ha	condotto
relate	that	near	to the	gates	of the	death	me has	lead

il	'mi o	de 'sti no
il	mio	destino,
the	my	destiny

Tell him that my destiny has led me close to the gates of death,

dal: la 'i ta	di	'lu i	sol	'pɛn de	'mi a	'vi ta
dall'aita	di	lui	sol	pende	mia	vita.
from the help	of	him	alone	hangs on	my	life

[that] my life depends upon his help alone.

&

[69]   *Desiderio Cavalcabò*

o 'sku ɾe 'sel ve
Oscure selve
Somber forests

o 'sku ɾe	'sel ve	'o ve	dʒam: 'ma i	non	'lu tʃe	'rad: dʒo	di	'so le
Oscure	selve,	ove	giammai	non	luce	raggio	di	sole,
somber	forests	where	never	not	light	ray	of	sun

e	spa ven 'to zi	'bɔ ski	'lɔ ki	de 'zɛr ti	i na bi 'ta ti	e	'fo ski
e	spaventosi	boschi,	lochi	deserti,	inabitati,	e	foschi
and	frightening	woods	places	deserted	uninhabited	and	dark

vɔ	tʃer 'kan 'di o	per	ri tro 'var	la	'lu tʃe
vo	cercand'io,	per	ritrovar	la	luce.
I go	searching I	for	to find again	the	light

I am searching somber forests, where there is never a ray of sunlight, and frightening woods,
[and] deserted, dark and uninhabited places, in order to find the light again.

de 'zir	mi	'spro na	a 'mor	mi	ɛ	'gwi da	e	'du tʃe
Desir	mi	sprona,	Amor	mi	è	guida	e	duce:
desire	me	urges on	Love	to me	is	guide	and	leader

Desire urges me on; Love is my guide and leader:

lun	'tut: ti	i	'sɛn si	'mjɛ i	fa	in 'fer mi	e	'lo ski	'lal tro	mab: 'baʎ: ʎa
l'un	tutti	i	sensi	miei	fa	infermi,	e	loschi,	l'altro	m'abbaglia,
the one	all	the	senses	mine	makes	infirm	and	weak-sighted	the other	me blinds

the one makes all my senses infirm and weak-sighted, the other blinds me;

e	per 'ki o	non	ko 'noʃ: ʃi	'mi o	mal	so 'vɛn te	a	la gri 'mar	min 'du tʃe
e	perch'io	non	conosci	mio	mal,	sovente	a	lagrimar	m'induce.
and	although I	not	I know	my	illness	often	to	weeping	me leads

and although I do not know what my illness is, it often brings me to tears.

printed is "conosci" (mod. "conosci"): poetic license taken to rhyme with "loschi"? grammatically correct would be "conosco."

ko 'zi	pjan 'dʒɛn do	in	'kwe sta	'par te	en	'kwel: la	'fug: go	le	'dʒɛn ti
Così	piangendo,	in	questa	parte,	e'n	quella,	fuggo	le	genti,
thus	weeping	in	this	place	and in	that	I flee	the	people

Thus weeping, in this place and that, I flee from people

en	so li 'ta ɾjo	al 'bɛr go	'tʃer ko	in	'par te	af: fre 'nar	lin 'tɛr na	'dɔʎ: ʎa
e'n	**solitario**	**albergo**	**cerco**	**in**	**parte**	**affrenar**	**l'interna**	**doglia.**
and in	solitary	refuge	I search	in	part	*(lit.)* to restrain	the internal	suffering

and in solitary refuge I search in part to restrain my internal suffering.

'mil: le	'kar te	al	di	'skwar tʃo	e	'mil: le	a 'spɛr go	di	'la gri me	e	diŋ 'kjo stro
Mille	**carte**	**al**	**dì**	**squarcio,**	**e**	**mille**	**aspergo**	**di**	**lagrime,**	**e**	**d'inchiostro.**
thousand	papers	by	day	I tear up	and	thousand	I sprinkle	with	tears	and	with ink

I tear up a thousand pages a day, and sprinkle a thousand with tears and ink.

o	'fɛ ra	'stel: la	i	vo	'dje tro al	'mi o	mal	per	'prɔ prja	'vɔʎ: ʎa
O	**fera**	**stella!**	**I'**	**vo**	**dietro al**	**mio**	**mal**	**per**	**propria**	**voglia.**
o	cruel	star	I	I go	back to the	my	illness	through	own	desire

O cruel destiny! I return to my illness by my own volition.

> fera =
> *(mod.)*
> fiera

GL: **Amor**

[20, 24, 36, 39, 48, 57, 69]

se 'la u ra 'spi ra
Se l'aura spira
When the breeze blows

se	'la u ra	'spi ra	'tut: ta	vet: 'tso za	la	'fre ska	'rɔ za	ri 'dɛn te	sta
Se	**l'aura**	**spira**	**tutta**	**vezzosa,**	**la**	**fresca**	**rosa**	**ridente**	**sta;**
if	the breeze	blows	all	charming	the	fresh	rose	smiling	is

When the breeze blows so enchantingly, the fresh rose is smiling;

la	'sjɛ pe	om 'bro za	di	'bɛ i	zme 'ral di	de 'sti vi	'kal di	ti 'mor	non	a
la	**siepe**	**ombrosa**	**di**	**bei**	**smeraldi**	**d'estivi**	**caldi**	**timor**	**non**	**ha.**
the	hedge	shady	of	beautiful	emeralds	of summers	hot	fear	not	has

the shady hedge of beautiful emeralds does not fear hot summers.

a	'bal: li	'lje te	ve 'ni te	'nin fe	gra 'di te	fjor	di	bel 'ta
A'	**balli,**	**liete**	**venite,**	**ninfe**	**gradite,**	**fior**	**di**	**beltà.**
to	dances	happy	come	nymphs	gracious	flowers	of	beauty

Come happily to the dances, gracious nymphs, flowers of beauty.

> *var.:* ai balli = a' balli
>
> *in* [57]: A canti lieti venite
> [a 'kanti...] =
> Come happily to the singing,

or	ke	si	'kja ro	il	'va go	'fon te	dal: 'al to	'mon te	al	mar	sen 'va
Or	**che**	**sì**	**chiaro**	**il**	**vago**	**fonte**	**dall'alto**	**monte**	**al**	**mar**	**sen' va,**
now	that	so	clear	the	pretty	stream	from the high	mountain	to the	sea	leaves

Now that the pretty stream, so clear, flows from the high mountain [down] to the sea,

'swɔ i	'dol tʃi	'vɛr si	'spje ga	la u 'dʒel: lo	e	lar boʃ: 'ʃel: lo	fjo 'ri to	sta
suoi	**dolci**	**versi**	**spiega**	**l'augello,**	**e**	**l'arboscello**	**fiorito**	**sta.**
its	sweet	verses	tells	the bird	and	the sapling	flowered	is

the birds sing their sweet verses, and the saplings are in bloom.

> augello
> *(poet.)*
> = uccello

> *in* [48]: arbuscello = (mod.) arboscello

un	'vol to	'bɛl: lo	al: 'lom bra	ak: 'kan to	sol	si 'di a	'van to	da 'ver	pje 'ta
Un	**volto**	**bello**	**all'ombra**	**accanto**	**sol**	**si dia**	**vanto**	**d'aver**	**pietà.**
a	face	beautiful	in the shade	nearby	only	let give itself	boast	of to have	pity

May a beautiful face, in the nearby shade, boast only of having compassion.

al	'kan to	'nin fe	ri 'dɛn ti	skat: 'tʃa te	i	'vɛn ti	di	kru del 'ta
Al	**canto,**	**ninfe**	**ridenti,**	**scacciate**	**i**	**venti**	**di**	**crudeltà!**
to the	song	nymphs	merry	dispel	the	winds	of	cruelty

Strike up the song, merry nymphs; drive away the winds of cruelty!

[69]

se 'lon de o i 'mɛ
Se l'onde, ohimè
If the sea [of tears], alas

se	'lon de	o i 'mɛ	ke	da	kwe 'stɔk: ki	'pjɔ vo no	se	i	ko 'tʃɛn ti	so 'spir
Se	**l'onde,**	**ohimè,**	**che**	**da**	**quest'occhi**	**piovono,**	**se**	**i**	**cocenti**	**sospir,**
if	the waves	alas	which	from	these eyes	pour	if	the	burning	sighs

If the sea [of tears] which pours from these eyes, if the burning sighs

ke	dal	sen	'mɛ sko no	pje 'ta	non	pju	de	'mjɛ i	mar 'tir
che	**dal**	**sen**	**m'escono,**	**pietà**	**non**	**più**	**de'**	**miei**	**martir**
which	from the	breast	from me exit	pity	not	more	of the	my	agonies

non	'tro va no	ma	no 'vɛl: la	im pje 'ta de	in	'fil: li	ak: 'kre ska no
non	**trovano,**	**ma**	**novella**	**impietade**	**in**	**Filli**	**accrescano,**
not	find	but	new	cruelties	in	Filli	may increase

which leave my breast find no more pity for my agony, but [rather may] increase new cruelties in Filli,

tʃer ke 'rɔ	kol	mo 'rir	tor 'nar	pla 'ka bi le	'lem pja	'on de	'lal ma
cercherò	**col**	**morir**	**tornar**	**placabile**	**l'empia,**	**onde**	**l'alma,**
I will seek	with the	dying	to get back	placable	the pitiless one	wherefrom	the soul

I will seek, with my death, to placate the pitiless woman for whom my soul

el	kɔr	'sɛm pre	laŋ 'gwi ska no	'ɛk: ko	il	fin	pjɛn	daf: 'fan: ni
e'l	**cor**	**sempre**	**languiscano:**	**ecco**	**il**	**fin**	**pien**	**d'affanni,**
and the	heart	always	languish	here is	the	end	full	of woes

and heart always languish. This is the end, full of woes and

e	mi ze 'ra bi le	ka	se 'gwa tʃi	da 'mo re	i	'fa ti	or 'di ska no
e	**miserabile,**	**ch'a'**	**seguaci**	**d'Amore**	**i**	**Fati**	**ordiscano.**
and	miserable	which to the	followers	of Love	the	Fates	plan

miserable, which the Fates plan for the followers of Love.

se	per	a 'mar	ki	'tan to	'ɔ dja	il	'mi o	'vi ve re	mor 'tal	dʒɛl	'sɛn to
Se	**per**	**amar**	**chi**	**tanto**	**odia**	**il**	**mio**	**vivere**	**mortal**	**giel**	**sento,**
if	through	loving	the one who	so much	hates	the	my	living	mortal	ice	I feel

If, through loving the one who hates my being alive so much, I feel a deathly cold,

> giel = gielo = (mod.) gelo

el	'kɔ re	ar 'dɛn do	'sfa tʃe si	'a i
e'l	**core**	**ardendo**	**sfacesi,**	**ahi!**
and the	heart	burning	dissolves	alas

and my burning heart dissolves in flames, alas,

> sface [in "sfacesi"] = (mod.) sfa

bɛn	po 'tras: si	al	'mi o	se 'pol kro	'skri ve re
ben	**potrassi**	**al**	**mio**	**sepolcro**	**scrivere:**
well	one will be able	on the	my	sepulchre	to write

one may well inscribe on my tombstone:

'kwe sti	in	'pre mjo	da 'mor	sot: 'tɛr: ra	'dʒa tʃe si
questi	**in**	**premio**	**d'Amor**	**sotterra**	**giacesi.**
this man	in	prize	of Love	underground	lies himself

this man lies beneath the ground as Love's reward.

> questi = costui

GL: **Amor[e], Fati, Filli**

[69]

siɲː ˈɲor ˈko ɾa fra ʎi ˈɔ stri
Signor, c'ora fra gli ostri
Dear Sir, who now among the purples

siɲː ˈɲor	ˈko ɾa	fra	ʎi	ˈɔ stri	ˈo ɾa	fra	ˈlar mi	ˈmɔ vi
Signor,	**c'ora**	**fra**	**gli**	**ostri,**	**ora**	**fra**	**l'armi**	**movi**
sir	who now	among	the	purples	now	among	the weapons	you move

ˈga ɾa	per	te	fra	ˈpal: la	e	ˈmar te	e	ˈdʒun to	a
gara	**per**	**te**	**fra**	**Palla,**	**e**	**Marte,**	**e**	**giunto**	**a**
competition	through	you	between	Athena	and	Mars	and	arrived	at

Dear Sir, you who, among the purples *[togas]*, provoke contests now in the field of knowledge, now in warfare, and having reached

ˈkwan to	pwɔ	na ˈtu ɾa	e ˈdar te	ˈkon tro al	gran	ˈno me	ˈtu o	ˈmɔr te	di ˈzar mi
quanto	**può**	**natura,**	**ed arte**	**contro al**	**gran**	**nome**	**tuo**	**morte**	**disarmi.**
as much	can	nature	and art	against the	great	name	your	death	may yield

the limits of nature and art, even death is powerless against your great name.

se	ˈmɔ lː	et: ˈtʃɛl se	di	su ˈper bi	ˈmar mi	a	ˈkwe sta	ˈdɛ stɾa
Se	**moli**	**eccelse**	**di**	**superbi**	**marmi**	**a**	**questa**	**destra**
if	masses	lofty	of	proud	marbles	to	this	right hand

ˈu mil	non	ˈli tʃe	al ˈtsar te	ˈu mil	tri ˈbu to	di	de ˈvo te	ˈkar te
umil	**non**	**lice**	**alzarte,**	**umil**	**tributo**	**di**	**devote**	**carte**
humble	not	is permitted	raised	humble	tribute	of	devoted	pages

If this humble hand is not permitted to raise lofty masses of proud marble to you, a humble tribute of devoted pages

ti	ˈpɔr go	in	ˈvo to	e	ti	kon ˈsa kro	i	ˈkar mi
ti	**porgo**	**in**	**voto,**	**e**	**ti**	**consacro**	**i**	**carmi.**
to you	I offer	in	vow	and	to you	I consecrate	the	poems

I offer you as a vow, and to you I consecrate my poems.

nel	ˈpit: tʃol	ˈdo no	il	gran daf: ˈfɛt: to	ˈmi o	ri ˈmi ɾa	u ˈma no	e	le	pri ˈmit: tsje
Nel	**picciol**	**dono**	**il**	**grand'affetto**	**mio**	**rimira**	**umano,**	**e**	**le**	**primizie**
in the	small	gift	the	great affection	mine	see	human	and	the	first fruits

ak: ˈkɔʎ: ʎi	del	ˈpi gro	in ˈdʒeɲː ɲo	i mi ta ˈtor	di	ˈdi o
accogli	**del**	**pigro**	**ingegno**	**imitator**	**di**	**Dio.**
receive	of the	sluggish	mind	imitator	of	God

> an "imitator of God": i.e., as a creator, one who creates something out of nothing

In this small present see my great human affection, and receive the youthful fruits of a languorous creative mind.

ke	ˈtɛm po	ˈfi a	kal	ˈtra tʃe	ˈem pjo	ʎi	or ˈgoʎː ʎi	tu
Che	**tempo**	**fia,**	**ch'al**	**Trace**	**empio**	**gli**	**orgogli**	**tu**
that	time	will be	that at the	people of Thrace	impious	the	proud ones	you

> fia = (mod.) sarà

do me ˈra i	vit: to ˈrjo zo	e ˈdi o	spje ge ˈrɔ	le	ˈtu e	ˈglɔ ɾje	in	ˈmilː le	ˈfɔʎː ʎi
domerai	**vittorioso,**	**ed io**	**spiegherò**	**le**	**tue**	**glorie**	**in**	**mille**	**fogli.**
you will prevail	victorious	and I	I will spread	the	your	glories	on	thousand	pages

There will be a time when you will prevail over the arrogance of the impious Thracians, and I will expound your glories on a thousand pages.

𝒢ℒ: **Marte, Palla, Trace**

☙

[69]

son fe 'ri to
Son ferito
I am wounded

son   fe 'ri to   son   'mɔr to   e   di 'fe za   non   fɔ
Son   ferito,   son   morto,   e   difesa   non   fo,
I am   wounded   I am   dead   and   defense   not   I make
I am wounded, I am dead, and I have no defense,

> *fo =*
> *(mod.) faccio*

'ɔk: ki   'duŋ kwe   a   gran   'tɔr to   'nwɔ vo   dwɔl   so fri 'rɔ
occhi,   dunque   a   gran   torto   nuovo   duol   sofrirò;
eyes   therefore   at   great   wrong   new   sorrow   I will suffer
o eyes; therefore, I will unjustly suffer new sorrow.

dɛ   kweʎ: 'ʎar ki   al: len 'ta te   dɛ   non   pju   sa et: 'ta te   il   'mi o   kɔr
deh   quegl'archi   allentate,   deh   non   più   saettate   il   mio   cor,
pray   those bows   slacken   pray   not   more   shoot with arrows the   my   heart
Please slacken those bows; please do not any longer pierce my heart

ke   si   'ka ɾo   a   'vo i   dʒa   fu   non   mi   fe 'ri te   pju
che   sì   caro   a   voi   già   fu: non   mi   ferite   più.
which so   dear   to   you   formerly was   not   me   wound   more
which was once so dear to you: do not wound me anymore.

> *Two more verses are printed as text only:*

son   e 'zaŋ gwe   son   'spɛn to   'dal: la   'vɔ stra   im pje 'ta
Son   esangue,   son   spento   dalla   vostra   impietà,
I am   drained of blood I am spent   from the   your   impiety
I am drained of blood, I am spent from your lack of pity;

> *impietà =*
> *(mod.) empietà*

ne   pwɔ   'dar si   tor 'men to   a   ki   'vi ta   non   a
né   può   darsi   tormento   a   chi   vita   non   ha;
not   is able to give itself torment   to   he who life   not   has
torment can not be inflicted on one who is not alive.

'a i   kin   van   mof: fen 'de te   e   in   van   'lar mi   ten 'de te
ahi,   ch'in   van   m'offendete,   e   in   van   l'armi   tendete,
ah   [that] in vain   me you offend   and in   vain   the weapons you aim
Ah, in vain you offend me and in vain you aim your weapons;

'me ko   'lal ma   non   ɛ   'ko me   dʒa   fu   non   mi   fe 'ri te   pju
meco   l'alma   non   è,   come   già   fu: non   mi   ferite   più.
me with   the soul   not   is   how   formerly was   not   me   wound   more
my soul is not with me, as it once was: do not wound me anymore.

son   un   dʒɛl   'so no   u 'nom bra   dun   ke   'vi ve   di   fe
Son   un   giel,   sono   un'ombra   d'un,   che   vive   di   fé,
I am   an   ice   I am   a shadow   of one   who   lives   of   faith
I am ice; I am a shadow of one who lives by faith;

> *giel[o] =*
> *(mod.) gel[o]*

'mɔr te   'tut: to   ma 'dom bra   'nul: la   're sta   di   me
morte   tutto   m'adombra,   nulla   resta   di   me;
death   completely me veils   nothing   remains   of   me
death completely veils me; nothing remains of me.

or	ke	a 'ves: si mi		ut: 'tʃi zo	rad: dop: 'pja te		il	bɛl	'ri zo
or,	**che**	**avessimi**		**ucciso,**	**raddoppiate**		**il**	**bel**	**riso,**
now	that	you may have me		killed	double		the	beautiful	laughter

Now that you may have killed me, double the beautiful laughter

ke	'del: la	'dʒɔ ja	'mi a	'seɲ: ɲo	dʒa	fu	non	mi	fe 'ri te	pju
che	**della**	**gioia**	**mia**	**segno**	**già**	**fu:**	**non**	**mi**	**ferite**	**più.**
which	of the	joy	mine	mark	formerly	was	not	me	wound	more

which was once the mark of my joy: do not wound me anymore.

❧

[69]

Girolamo Preti

ti 'laʃ: ʃo 'a ni ma 'mi a

Ti lascio, anima mia

I am leaving you, my soul

ti	'laʃ: ʃo	'a ni ma	'mi a	'dʒun ta	ɛ	kwel: 'lo ɾa
Ti	**lascio,**	**anima**	**mia,**	**giunta**	**è**	**quell'ora,**
you	I leave	soul	mine	arrived	is	that hour

I am leaving you, my soul; that hour has come –

printed "quall'ora" must be, correctly, "quell'ora"

'lo ɾa	o i 'mɛ	ke	mi	'kja ma	'al: la	par 'ti ta
l'ora,	**ohimè,**	**che**	**mi**	**chiama**	**alla**	**partita.**
the hour	alas	that	me	calls	to the	departure

the hour, alas, which calls me to the departure.

partita (lit.) = partenza

'i o	'par to	o i 'mɛ	kon 'vjɛn	'ki o	'mɔ ɾa
Io	**parto,**	**ohimè,**	**convien**	**ch'io**	**mora,**
I	I depart	alas	it is necessary	that I	I may die

I am departing – alas, I must die,

per 'ke	kon 'vjɛn	par 'tir	da	te	'mi a	'vi ta
perché	**convien**	**partir**	**da**	**te,**	**mia**	**vita.**
because	it is necessary	to depart	from	you	my	life

for I must depart from you, my life.

a	pur 'trɔp: po	ɛl	do 'lor	'ken tro	mak: 'kɔ ɾa
Ah	**pur troppo**	**è'l**	**dolor**	**ch'entro**	**m'accora;**
ah	[yet] too much	is the	pain	which within	breaks my heart

Ah, excessive is the pain which breaks my heart;

non	mi	dar	kol	'tu o	dwɔl	'nɔ va	fe 'ri ta
non	**mi**	**dar**	**col**	**tuo**	**duol**	**nova**	**ferita.**
not	to me	to give	with the	your	sorrow	new	wound

do not give me, with your sorrow, a new wound.

nova = (mod.) nuova

dɛ	non	laŋ 'gwir	kɔr	'mi o	kal	'mi o	par 'ti ɾe
Deh	**non**	**languir,**	**cor**	**mio,**	**ch'al**	**mio**	**partire**
pray	not	to languish	heart	mine	because at	my	departing

mi	'dwɔ le	il	'tu o	do 'ler	pju	kel	mo 'ri ɾe
mi	**duole**	**il**	**tuo**	**doler**	**più**	**che'l**	**morire.**
to me	causes pain	the	your	pain	more	than the	dying

Please do not languish, my heart; because your pain at my parting causes me more pain than the dying.

❧

[69]

'trɔpː po 'sotː to 'du e 'stelː le

Troppo, sotto due stelle

Too much, beneath two stars

'trɔpː po	'sotː to	'du e	'stelː le	'al me	e	dol 'tʃisː si me	'sotː to	un	bɛl	krin
Troppo,	**sotto**	**due**	**stelle**	**alme,**	**e**	**dolcissime,**	**sotto**	**un**	**bel**	**crin,**
too much	beneath	two	stars	glorious	and	sweetest	beneath	a	beautiful	head of hair

Too much, beneath two glorious and sweetest stars, beneath beautiful tresses,

'sotː to	un	sem 'bjan te	'nɔ bi le	'vɔʎː ʎe	'tʃe lon si	o i 'mɛ	'kru de
sotto	**un**	**sembiante**	**nobile,**	**voglie**	**celonsi,**	**ohimè,**	**crude,**
beneath	a	countenance	noble	desires	conceal themselves	alas	cruel

e	a 'sprisː si me	e	'mɛn te	sol	'neʎː ʎi	al 'tru i	'danː ni	imː 'mɔ bi le
e	**asprissime,**	**e**	**mente**	**sol**	**negli**	**altrui**	**danni**	**immobile.**
and	most bitter	and	mind	only	of the	others'	damages	motionless

celonsi: the "on" (celono) ending is an antiquated variant ending for "an" (celano)

beneath a noble countenance, do cruel and bitterest desires conceal themselves, alas, and with unwavering mind only [desire] other peoples' ills.

tʃɔ	bɛn	prɔ 'vi o	kin	van	so 'spi ɾo	e	'dɔʎː ʎo mi
Ciò	**ben**	**prov'io,**	**ch'in**	**van**	**sospiro,**	**e**	**dogliomi,**
this	well	experience I	that in	vain	I sigh	and	I lament

This I feel very much: that in vain I sigh and lament,

a 'man te	'fatː to	di	bel 'ta	in di 'tʃi bi le	in	van	mafː 'fli go
amante	**fatto**	**di**	**beltà**	**indicibile,**	**in**	**van**	**m'affligo,**
lover	made	of	beauty	indescribable	in	vain	I grieve

having been made a lover of indescribable beauty; in vain I grieve;

in	van	di	'vi ta	'spɔʎː ʎo mi	ke	pju	li 'na spra
in	**van**	**di**	**vita**	**spogliomi,**	**ché**	**più**	**l'inaspra**
in	vain	of	life	I strip myself	because	more	it embitters

'oɲː ɲi	'mi o	'stratː tsjo	orː 'ri bi le
ogni	**mio**	**strazio**	**orribile.**
every	my	torture	horrible

in vain I strip myself of life, because every horrible torture of mine makes it [life] more bitter.

e 'di o	pju	'la mo	e	'men tre	ʎi	'ɔkː ki	'stilː la no
Ed io	**più**	**l'amo,**	**e**	**mentre**	**gli**	**occhi**	**stillano**
and I	more	her I love	and	while	the	eyes	exude

kol	'pjan to	'lal ma	e	'kwe ste	man	mutː 'tʃi do no	'fjamː me	pju	'vi ve
col	**pianto**	**l'alma,**	**e**	**queste**	**man**	**m'uccidono,**	**fiamme**	**più**	**vive**
with the	weeping	the soul	and	these	hands	me they kill	flames	more	alive

And I love her more; and while my eyes exude tears from my soul, and these hands kill me, flames more alive

in	me	'sɛm pre	sfa 'vilː la no	i	'mjɛ i	pen 'sjɛr	da	'le i	'ma i	si di 'vi do no
in	**me**	**sempre**	**sfavillano,**	**i**	**miei**	**pensier**	**da**	**lei**	**mai**	**si dividono.**
in	me	always	spark	the	my	thoughts	from	her	never	part

in me are continuously being stoked, [and] my thoughts never leave her.

☙

[69]

Girolamo Preti

'van: ne o 'kar ta a mo 'ro za
Vanne, o carta amorosa
Go, o love-note

'van: ne	o	'kar ta	a mo 'ro za	'van: ne	a	ko 'lɛ i	per	'ku i	ta 'tʃɛn do	'i o	'mɔ ɾo
Vanne,	**o**	**carta**	**amorosa,**	**vanne**	**a**	**colei,**	**per**	**cui**	**tacendo**	**io**	**moro:**
go	o	paper	amorous	go	to	she who	for	whom	being silent	I	I die

Go, o love-note – go to the one for whom, being silent, I am dying:

dɛ	'mi a	'ti mi da	'kar ta	ar 'diʃ: ʃi	e	'spe ɾa	e	'prjɛ ga	'kjɛ di a
deh	**mia**	**timida**	**carta,**	**ardisci,**	**e**	**spera,**	**e**	**priega,**	**chiedi a**
pray	my	timid	paper	be bold	and	hope	and	implore	ask to

> *priega*
> *(poet.)*
> *= prega*

please, my timid note, be bold, and hope and implore; ask from

ko 'lɛ i	di	'mi o	a 'mor	di	'mi a	'fe de	pje 'ta	ma	non	mer 'tʃe de
colei	**di**	**mio**	**amor**	**di**	**mia**	**fede**	**pietà,**	**ma**	**non**	**mercede.**
her	of	my	love	of	my	fidelity	pity	but	not	reward

her pity for my love and my fidelity, but not reward.

non	'kjɛd: dʒo	nɔ	non	'kjɛd: dʒo	ka	'mje i	so 'spir	so 'spi ɾi
Non	**chieggio**	**no,**	**non**	**chieggio**	**ch'a'**	**miei**	**sospir**	**sospiri,**
not	I ask	no	not	I ask	that to	my	sighs	she may sigh

> *chieggio =*
> *(mod.) chiedo*

I do not ask, no – I do not ask that she sigh to my sighs;

non	'kjɛd: dʒo	nɔ	non	'kjɛd: dʒo	kal	'mi o	laŋ 'gwir	laŋ 'gwi ska
non	**chieggio**	**no,**	**non**	**chieggio**	**ch'al**	**mio**	**languir**	**languisca:**
not	I ask	no	not	I ask	that at the	my	languishing	she may languish

I do not ask, no – I do not ask that she languish at my languishing:

ah	'kru do	ɛ	ben	kwel	'kɔ ɾe	'bɛ nɛ	in 'deɲ: ɲo	a ma 'to ɾe
ah	**crudo**	**è**	**ben**	**quel**	**core,**	**ben'è**	**indegno**	**amatore,**
ah	harsh	is	well	that	heart	well is	unworthy	lover

ah, harsh indeed is that heart, unworthy indeed is that lover

ki	di	ve 'der	de 'zi a	la 'ma ta	'dɔn: na	so spi 'rar	da 'mo ɾe
chi	**di**	**veder**	**desia**	**l'amata**	**donna**	**sospirar**	**d'amore.**
he who	of	to see	wishes	the loved	woman	to sigh	of love

who wishes to see his beloved woman sigh for love.

'lun dʒi	'lun dʒi	da	'lɛ i	'si en	le	'pe ne	a mo 'ro ze
Lungi,	**lungi**	**da**	**lei**	**sien**	**le**	**pene**	**amorose:**
far	far	from	her	let be	the	sufferings	amorous

Let my amorous sufferings be far, far away from her:

do 'lor	'pjan ti	so 'spir	'tut: ti	'si en	'mje i
dolor,	**pianti,**	**sospir,**	**tutti**	**sien**	**miei.**
pain	tears	sighs	all	let be	mine

pain, tears, sighs – let them all be mine.

'an tsi	o	'nwɔ vo	stu 'por	del: la 'mor	'mi o	'i o	non	'bra mo	'i o	non	'kjɛd: dʒo
Anzi	**(o**	**nuovo**	**stupor**	**dell'amor**	**mio)**	**io**	**non**	**bramo,**	**io**	**non**	**cheggio**
indeed	oh	new	marvel	of the love	mine	I	not	I desire	I	not	I ask

Indeed (oh, new marvel of my love), I do not desire, I do not ask,

ke   la 'mor   'mi o   ri 'a mi   ke   sa 'mo ɾe   a   do 'lor
che   l'amor   mio   riami: ché,   s'amore   ha   dolor,
that   the love mine   may love in return   because   if love   has pain
that my love should love me in return: because if love is painful,

non   vwɔ   ke   'ma mi
non   vuò   che   m'ami.
not   I want that me she may love
I do not want her to love me.

> *vuò =*
> *(mod.) voglio*

'i o   'bra mo   'i o   'kjɛd: dʒo   'so lo   kel   'mi o   a 'mor   non   i 'zdeɲː ɲi
Io   bramo,   io   cheggio   solo   che'l   mio   amor   non   isdegni,
I   I desire   I   I ask   only   that the   my   love   not   may disdain

> *the "i" before "sdegni"*
> *was added for euphony*

I desire, I ask only that my love not disdain [me];

e   'vɔʎː ʎa   per   mer 'tʃe   de   'mjɛ i   do 'lo ɾi   sol
e   voglia   per   mercé   de'   miei   dolori   sol
and   I may wish   for   reward   of   my   pains   only

> *mercé =*
> *mercede*

and I wish, in reward for my pains, only

'ki o   'la mi   e   la 'do ɾi
ch'io   l'ami,   e   l'adori.
that I   her may love   and   her may adore
to love her and adore her.

> There are two Aria settings of the following text printed. The first was originally published in the *Primo Libro d'arie musicali*, the second in the *Secondo libro d'arie musicali*. See the editor's notes in [69].

[69]

Francesco Balducci

'voi par 'ti te
Voi partite
You are departing

'vo i   par 'ti te   'mi o   'so le   e   'pɔr ta   il   'vɔ stro   'lu me   al 'tro ve   il   'dʒor no
Voi   partite,   mio   sole, e   porta   il   vostro   lume   altrove   il   giorno.
you   you depart   my   sun   and   takes   the   your   light   elsewhere   the   day
You are departing, my sun; and the day is taking your light elsewhere.

ki   sa 'ra   ke   kon 'so le   la   'mi a   'nɔt: te   do 'lɛn te
Chi   sarà,   che   console   la   mia   notte   dolente,
who   will be   that   may console   the   my   night   sorrowful
Who may console my sorrowful night,

> *console: the "e" (rather*
> *than "i") on this subjunctive*
> *verb form is an archaic*
> *variant verb form ending*

se   'vo i   non   'fa te   al   'nɔ stro   tʃɛl   ri 'tor no
se   voi   non   fate   al   nostro   ciel   ritorno?
if   you   not   you make   to the   our   heaven return
if you do not return to our heaven?

o   'mi e   spe 'ran tse   'spɛn te   'a i   'bɛl: le   'lu tʃi   'on de   ne 'dʒi vo   al 'tɛ ɾa
O   mie   speranze   spente: ahi   belle   luci,   onde   ne givo   altera,
o   my   hopes   wasted   alas   beautiful eyes   whence   I went   proud
O, my wasted hopes: alas, beautiful eyes to which I was proudly going

> *ne givo: from "gir[se]ne"*
> *= "andar[se]ne"*

'ko me	su	'lal ba	o i 'mɛ	'vi di	la	'se ɾa
come	**su**	**l'alba,**	**ohimè,**	**vidi**	**la**	**sera!**
as	upon	the dawn	alas	I saw	the	evening

when at dawn, alas, I saw the evening!

Two other verses are printed as text only. Following is the 2nd verse in the "Primo Libro":

'vo i	par 'ti te	'mi o	'be ne	e	'me ko	in	kom paɲ: 'ɲi a	're sta no	i	'ma li
Voi	**partite,**	**mio**	**bene,**	**e**	**meco**	**in**	**compagnia**	**restano**	**i**	**mali.**
you	you depart	my	dear one	and	me with	in	company	rest	the	hurts

You are departing, my dear one, and the hurts remain with me.

kon	'vo i	'par te	la	'spɛ ne	'del: la	spe 'ra ta	'dʒɔ ja
Con	**voi**	**parte**	**la**	**spene**	**della**	**sperata**	**gioia,**
with	you	leaves	the	hope	of the	hoped for	joy

With you leaves the hope of hoped-for joy,

spene (poet.) = speme
(lit.) = speranza

e	'lal ma	per	sɛ 'gwir vi	a 'pɛr to	a	'la li
e	**l'alma**	**per**	**seguirvi**	**aperto**	**ha**	**l'ali;**
and	the soul	for	to follow you	open	has	the wings

and my soul spreads its wings to follow you;

ɛ	'dʒun to	il	di	'ki o	'mɔ ja	'a i	'du ɾo	'ka zo
è	**giunto**	**il**	**dì**	**ch'io**	**moia:**	**ahi**	**duro**	**caso,**
is	arrived	the	day	that I	I may die	alas	harsh	fate

the day for me to die has come: alas, harsh fate,

'a i	'fɛ ɾa	di par 'ti ta	po i 'ke	kol	'vɔ stro	pje	'par te	la	'vi ta
ahi	**fera**	**dipartita,**	**poiché**	**col**	**vostro**	**piè**	**parte**	**la**	**vita.**
alas	cruel	departure	since	with the	your	foot	departs	the	life

fera =
(mod.) fiera

alas, cruel separation, as with your departure my life departs.

Following is the 2nd verse in the "Secondo Libro":

'vo i	par 'ti te	e	por 'ta te	kon	'vo i	la	'dʒɔ ja	lal: le 'gret: tsa	el
Voi	**partite,**	**e**	**portate**	**con**	**voi**	**la**	**gioia,**	**l'allegrezza,**	**e'l**
you	you depart	and	you take	with	you	the	joy	the gladness	and the

You are departing; and you are taking with you joy, gladness, and

'ri zo	'mi ze ɾo	e	kwi	laʃ: 'ʃa te	laf: 'fan: no	il	'dwɔ lo	il	'pjan to
riso,	**misero!**	**e**	**qui**	**lasciate**	**l'affanno,**	**il**	**duolo,**	**il**	**pianto**
laughter	miserable me	and	here	you leave	the woe	the	grief	the	weeping

laughter – miserable me! And here you are leaving woe, grief, and weeping;

e	si 'kan dʒa	in	in 'fɛr no	il	pa ɾa 'di zo
e	**si cangia**	**in**	**inferno**	**il**	**paradiso;**
and	itself changes	into	hell	the	paradise

and paradise changes into hell.

'a i	'ko me	ɛ	'bre ve	il	'kan to	deʎ: ʎin fe 'li tʃi	e	'zven tu 'ɾa ti	a 'man ti
ahi,	**come**	**è**	**breve**	**il**	**canto**	**degl'infelici,**	**e**	**sventurati**	**amanti,**
alas	how	is	brief	the	song	of the wretched ones	and	unfortunate	lovers

Alas, how brief is the song of wretched and unfortunate lovers;

'ko me	son	'luŋ gi	e	'sɛn tsa	'fi ne	i	'pjan ti
come	**son**	**lunghi,**	**e**	**senza**	**fine**	**i**	**pianti.**
how	are	long	and	without	end	the	tears

how long-lasting and endless are the tears.

> *The 3rd verse is the same in both versions:*

'vo i	par 'ti te	ma	're sta	'mi ze ɾa	in	me	di	'vo i	la	ri mem 'bran tsa
Voi	**partite,**	**ma**	**resta,**	**misera!**	**in**	**me**	**di**	**voi**	**la**	**rimembranza;**
you	you depart	but	remains	miserable	in	me	of	you	the	memory

You are departing, but the sad memory of you stays with me;

sol	'kwe sta	il	'vo lo	ar: 'rɛ sta	al: 'la ni ma	ke	'fud: dʒe
sol	**questa**	**il**	**volo**	**arresta**	**all'anima,**	**che**	**fugge,**
only	this	the	flight	arrests	to the soul	which	flees

only this stops the flight of my soul, which is fleeing,

e	'vi ve	a 'mor	se	'mɔr ta	ɛ	la	spe 'ran tsa
e	**vive**	**amor,**	**se**	**morta**	**è**	**la**	**speranza.**
and	lives	love	if	dead	is	the	hope

and love is alive even though hope is dead.

ma	'nwɔ vo	dwɔl	mi 'strud: dʒe	ke	'vo i	kan 'dʒan do	tʃɛl
Ma	**nuovo**	**duol**	**mi strugge**	**ché**	**voi**	**cangiando**	**ciel**
but	new	sorrow	me consumes	because	you	changing	heaven

But new sorrow consumes me; for in changing heavens

kan 'dʒa te	a 'mo ɾe	'lun dʒe	'daʎ: ʎi	'ɔk: ki	o i 'mɛ	'lun dʒe	dal	'kɔ ɾe
cangiate	**amore,**	**lunge**	**dagli**	**occhi,**	**ohimè,**	**lunge**	**dal**	**core.**
you change	love	far	from the	eyes	alas	far	from the	heart

you are changing love, far from my eyes – alas, far from my heart.

> *var.: da gl'occhi =*
> *(mod.) dagli occhi*

🏵 *Gabrielli, Domenico (1651-1690)*

Renowned cellist, he was nicknamed "Menghino dal violoncello," "Menghino" being a regional diminutive of the name Domenico; he was born, and he died, prematurely of an incurable illness, in Bologna. He studied composition with Legrenzi in Venice and cello with Petronio Franceschini, whom he succeeded in 1680 as cellist at S. Petronio, in Bologna. He travelled a great deal, often performing at the Este court in Modena. He became president of the Accademia Filarmonica in Bologna in 1683.

Gabrielli was not only a composer of some of the earliest music for cello, which he also employed as an obbligato instrument in various instrumental forms, but also a composer of vocal music: some twelve operas, which were premiered in Bologna, Modena, Turin, and Venice, four oratorios, solo cantatas, and over fifty other secular and sacred works.

---

[47]

from: *Clearco in Negroponte (1685)*   *Antonio Arcoleo*

bel: 'let: tsa ti 'ran: na
Bellezza tiranna
Tyrannical beauty

bel: 'let: tsa	ti 'ran: na	laŋ 'gwi sko	per	te
Bellezza	**tiranna,**	**languisco**	**per**	**te!**
beauty	tyrannical	I languish	for	you

Tyrannical beauty, I languish for you!

mi	'sprɛt: tsi	'i o ta 'do ɾo	mi	'fud: dʒi	e 'di o	'mwɔ ɾo	kru 'dɛ le	per 'ke
Mi	**sprezzi,**	**io t'adoro,**	**mi**	**fuggi,**	**ed io**	**muoro,**	**crudele,**	**perché?**
me	you scorn	I you I adore	me	you flee	and I	I die	cruel one	why

> *muoro =*
> *(mod.)*
> *muoio*

You scorn me; I adore you; you flee me, and I am dying, cruel one – why?

Gaffi, (Tommaso) Bernardo (1667-1744)

Roman composer, organist, and harpsichordist, he studied with Pasquini and held various positions as organist in Rome between 1688 and 1710 when, upon the death of Pasquini, he was appointed to succeed him as organist at S. Maria in Aracoeli.
Gaffi wrote at least seven oratorios in addition to some sacred pieces and various secular cantatas. His twelve chamber cantatas, Op.1, include several arias with obbligato instruments, unusual for the time; the obbligato parts were allowed to be played on the harpsichord.
Gaffi also wrote a short treatise, *Regole per sonare con la parte*, which is interesting for its unusually detailed classification of cadences according to the movement of the bass line.

[22, 24, 27]

ˈlu tʃi vetː ˈtso ze
Luci vezzose
Charming eyes

ˈlu tʃi	vetː ˈtso ze	ˈduŋ kwe	sa ˈɾe te	ˈsɛm pre	zdeɲː ˈɲo ze	ko ˈzi	vɛr	me
Luci	**vezzose,**	**dunque**	**sarete**	**sempre**	**sdegnose**	**così**	**ver**	**me?**
eyes	charming	then	you will be	always	scornful	thus	toward	me

Charming eyes, will you then always be scornful like this toward me?

ˈsɛm pre	spje ˈta te	mi	ne ge ˈɾe te	ˈkwal ke	mer ˈtʃe
Sempre	**spietate,**	**mi**	**negherete**	**qualche**	**mercé?**
always	pitiless	to me	you will deny	any	favor

Ever pitiless, you will deny me any favor?

ˈsɛm pre	spje ˈta te	ˈlu tʃi	a do ˈɾa te	mi	ne ge ˈɾe te	ˈkwal ke	mer ˈtʃe
Sempre	**spietate,**	**luci**	**adorate,**	**mi**	**negherete**	**qualche**	**mercé!**
always	pitiless	eyes	adored	to me	you will deny	any	favor

Ever pitiless, adored eyes, you will deny me any favor!

[52]

si ˈpwɔ ri mi ˈɾar
Si può rimirar
May I gaze upon

si ˈpwɔ	ri mi ˈɾar	ˈva gi	ˈɾa i	ke	mi	ˈdi te	si ˈpwɔ
Si può	**rimirar**	**vaghi**	**rai,**	**che**	**mi**	**dite,**	**si può?**
one can	to gaze at	lovely	eyes	what	to me	you say	one can

May I gaze upon lovely eyes? What do you say to me – may I?

ˈsi o	ˈkjɛ do	al	ˈmi o	bɛn	mi ˈsɛn to	nel	sen	ri ˈspon der	di	nɔ
S'io	**chiedo**	**al**	**mio**	**ben,**	**mi sento**	**nel**	**sen**	**risponder**	**di**	**no!**
if I	I ask	to the	my	dear one	I feel	in the	breast	to answer	of	no

If I ask my dear one, I feel in my breast the answer "no"!

si ˈpwɔ	va gedː ˈdʒar	ˈva go	ˈtʃiʎː ʎo	si ˈpwɔ	ke	mi	di	si ˈpwɔ
Si può	**vagheggiar**	**vago**	**ciglio,**	**si può,**	**che**	**mi**	**di',**	**si può?**
one can	to look at fondly	lovely	brow	one can	what	to me	you say	one can

May I look fondly at a lovely brow? What do you say to me – may I?

'si o   'kje do   a da 'mor   mi 'sɛn to   nel   kɔr   ri 'spon der   di   si
S'io   chiedo   ad Amor,   mi sento   nel   cor   risponder   di   sì.
if I   I ask   to Love   I feel   in the   heart   to answer   of   yes
If I ask Love, I feel in my heart the answer "yes".

GL: **Amor**

 Gasparini, Francesco (1668-1727)

Born near Lucca, he was active in 1682 as organist at Madonna dei Monti in Rome. In 1687 he was active at the Roman palace of Cardinal Benedetto Pamphili as a violinist and as a composer of arias and cantatas to texts by Pamphili. In 1701, having achieved some reputation, he was appointed to the important post of *maestro di coro* at the Ospedale della Pietà in Venice. In 1713 he re-settled in Rome; in 1725 he was named *maestro di cappella* at S. Giovanni in Laterano, but he did not take up the post because of poor health.

He was highly regarded as a teacher. Alessandro Scarlatti sent his son Domenico to Venice in 1705 to study with him; Benedetto Marcello was his most famous student.

Gasparini at his best was "a composer of the first rank *[Grove]*." He composed more than forty operas, at least ten masses, chamber duets, and solo cantatas.

His practical manual of figured bass accompaniment, *L'armonico pratico*, remains an important source of information about continuo realization at the time.

[10, 54]

a u dʒel: 'lin   'va go   e   ka 'nɔ ro
Augellin vago e canoro
Pretty little songbird

a u dʒel: 'lin	'va go	e	ka 'nɔ ro	tu	so 'spi ri	il	'kɔl: le
Augellin	**vago**	**e**	**canoro**	**tu**	**sospiri**	**il**	**colle,**
little bird	pretty	and	singing	you	you sigh for	the	hill

augellin: diminutive of augello (poet.) = uccello

Pretty little songbird, you yearn for the hills [and]

il	'pra to	e	pur	'sɛ i	tra	'lat: tʃi	'dɔ ro	dol tʃe 'men te	im pri dʒo 'na to
il	**prato**	**e**	**pur**	**sei**	**tra**	**lacci**	**d'oro**	**dolcemente**	**imprigionato.**
the	meadow	and	yet	you are	among	ties	of gold	sweetly	imprisoned

the meadow; and yet you are sweetly imprisoned in golden ties.

pur	'sɛn tsa	'ma i	po 'za ɾe	e	'la li	el	'pje de
Pur	**senza**	**mai**	**posare**	**e**	**l'ali**	**e'l**	**piede,**
[yet]	without	ever	to put down	[and]	the wings	and the	foot

Without ever alighting

'sɛm pre	in	per 'pɛ tu i	'dʒi ɾi	'va go	a u 'dʒel	ti rad: 'dʒi ɾi
sempre	**in**	**perpetui**	**giri**	**vago**	**augel**	**ti raggiri,**
always	in	perpetual	turns	pretty	bird	you circle

you continuously circle in perpetual turns, pretty bird;

e	i	'two i	kon 'tʃen ti	'sem bran	'nɔ te	di	'dʒɔ ja	e	son	la 'men ti
e	**i**	**tuoi**	**concenti**	**sembran**	**note**	**di**	**gioia**	**e**	**son**	**lamenti.**
and	the	your	harmonies	seem	notes	of	joy	and	are	laments

and your harmonies, [which] seem to be notes of joy, are laments.

'i o	tin 'tɛn do	ka 'nɔ ɾo	a u dʒel: 'let: to	tu	'va i	pjan 'dʒɛn do	la	'tu a	ser vi 'tu
Io	**t'intendo,**	**canoro**	**augelletto,**	**tu**	**vai**	**piangendo**	**la**	**tua**	**servitù:**
I	you I understand	singing	little bird	you	you go	weeping	the	your	servitude

I understand you, little song-bird: your are lamenting your servitude,

> *augelletto (poet.) = uccelletto*
> *(diminutive of "uccello")*

e	vor: 're sti	da 'mɛ no	bo 'sket: to	le	bɛl: 'lom bre	go 'de ɾe	aŋ 'kor	tu
e	**vorresti**	**d'ameno**	**boschetto**	**le**	**bell'ombre**	**godere**	**ancor**	**tu.**
and	you would like	of pleasant	grove	the	lovely shadows	to enjoy	even	you

and you too would like to enjoy the lovely shade of a pleasant grove.

&

[5, 9, 42]

'ka ɾo   'lat: tʃo   'dol tʃe   'nɔ do
Caro laccio, dolce nodo
Dear noose, dear knot

'ka ɾo	'lat: tʃo	'dol tʃe	'nɔ do	ke	le 'ga sti	il	'mi o	pen 'sjɛr
Caro	**laccio,**	**dolce**	**nodo,**	**che**	**legasti**	**il**	**mio**	**pensier,**
dear	noose	dear	knot	that	you bound	the	my	thought

Dear noose, dear knot, you that have bound my thoughts,

sɔ	'ki o	'pe no	e	pur	ne	'gɔ do	son	kon 'tɛn to	e	pri dʒo 'njɛr
so	**ch'io**	**peno**	**e**	**pur**	**ne**	**godo,**	**son**	**contento**	**e**	**prigionier.**
I know	that I	I suffer	and	yet	of it	I take pleasure	I am	content	and	prisoner

I know that I suffer, and yet I take pleasure in it; I am content, and a prisoner.

&

[53]

dɛ laʃ: 'ʃa te mi il ne 'mi ko
Deh, lasciatemi il nemico
Please leave me the enemy

dɛ	laʃ: 'ʃa te mi	il	ne 'mi ko	se	toʎ: 'ʎe ste	a	me	la 'man te
Deh,	**lasciatemi**	**il**	**nemico**	**se**	**toglieste**	**a**	**me**	**l'amante,**
pray	leave to me	the	enemy	if	you took away	from	me	the lover

Please leave me the enemy, since you took the lover away from me,

'stel: le	a 'mi ke	per	pje 'ta
stelle	**amiche,**	**per**	**pietà.**
stars	friendly	for	pity

friendly stars, for pity's sake.

e dal: 'lor	'kwe sto	ne 'mi ko	se	non	'pɔs: so	a 'ma ɾe	la 'man te
Ed allor	**questo**	**nemico,**	**se**	**non**	**posso**	**amare**	**l'amante,**
and then	this	enemy	if	not	I am able	to love	the lover

po 'trɔ	o 'djar	kon	li ber 'ta
potrò	**odiar**	**con**	**libertà.**
I will be able	to hate	with	freedom

And then, if I cannot love the lover, I will freely be able to hate this enemy.

&

[5, 9, 25] Alternately titled **Lasciar d'amarti per non penar**.

laʃː ˈʃar da ˈmar ti
Lasciar d'amarti
To stop loving you

laʃː ˈʃar   da ˈmar ti   per   non   pe ˈnar
Lasciar   d'amarti   per   non   penar,
to leave   of loving you   for   not   to suffer
To stop loving you in order not to suffer,

ˈka ɾo   ˈmi o   ˈbɛ ne   non   si ˈpwɔ   far   nɔ
caro   mio   bene,   non   si può   far,   no.
dear   my   dear one   not   one is able   to do   no
my dearly beloved one, is not possible – no.

a ˈfɔr tsa di   ˈpe ne   di   ˈstra li   e   ka ˈte ne
A forza di   pene,   di   strali   e   catene,
at the power of   pains   of   arrows   and   chains
Even at the mercy of pain, arrows, and chains,

non   ˈvɔʎ ʎo   laʃː ˈʃar ti   ti   ˈvɔʎ ʎo   a do ˈɾar   si   a si
non   voglio   lasciarti;   ti   voglio   adorar,   sì,   ah sì.
not   I want   to leave you   you   I want   to adore   yes   ah yes
I do not want to leave you; I want to adore you – yes, ah yes.

✿ *Ghivizzani, Alessandro* (c.1572-c.1634)

Born in Lucca, in 1609 he married Settimia Caccini, Giulio's younger daughter, and joined the musicians at the Florentine court.   Banished from Tuscany in 1611 (*Grove* does not say why), he returned to Lucca but left for the Mantuan court in 1613. In 1620 he was appointed *maestro di cappella* in Lucca; in 1622 he went to Parma (where Settimia sang) at the request of Cardinal Odoardo Farnese, in whose service he probably remained until his death. His surviving compositions are few. It is known, at least, that he wrote motets, secular songs, and arias.

[27]

ˈfilː li ˈmi a se vi pen ˈsa te
Filli mia, se vi pensate
My Filli, if you think

ˈfilː li ˈmi a   se   vi   pen ˈsa te   ˈki o   mi ˈmɔ ra   ˈki o   mi ˈstrugː ga   in   ˈvi vo   ar ˈdor
Filli   mia,   se   vi   pensate   ch'io   mi mora,   ch'io   mi strugga   in   vivo   ardor
Filli   mine   if   you   think   that I   I may die   that I   I may be consumed   in   burning   ardor
My Filli, if you think that I am dying, that I am being consumed in burning ardor,

viŋ ganː ˈna te   o   ˈmi a   siɲː ˈɲo ɾa   ke   per   ˈvo i   ˈpatː tso   ɛ   ki   mwɔr
v'ingannate   o   mia   signora,   ché   per   voi   pazzo   è   chi   muor.
you deceive yourself   o   my   lady   because   for   you   mad   is   he who   dies
you deceive yourself, o my lady; because mad is he who would die for you.

ˈvo i   pren ˈde te   oɲː ˈɲor   di ˈletː to   diŋ ganː ˈna ɾe   ki   da   ˈvo i   ˈspɛ ɾa   mer ˈtʃe
Voi   prendete   ognor   diletto   d'ingannare   chi   da   voi   spera   mercé;
you   take   always   pleasure   from to deceive   he who   from   you   hopes   pity
You always take pleasure in deceiving the one who hopes for pity from you;

son	ko 'stret: to	ab: ban do 'na ɾe	ki	non	'prɛt: tsa	a 'mor	ne	fe
son	**costretto**	**abbandonare**	**chi**	**non**	**prezza**	**amor**	**né**	**fé.**
I am	compelled	to abandon	one who	not	values	love	nor	fidelity

I must abandon one who values neither love nor fidelity.

> *prezza: from "prezzare" = "apprezzare"*

laŋ gwi 'ɾa	kwal	fjor	da 'pri le	per	'ku i	'sjɛ te	si	su 'pɛr ba	in	dʒo ven 'tu
Languirà	**qual**	**fior**	**d'aprile**	**per**	**cui**	**siete**	**sì**	**superba**	**in**	**gioventù;**
will languish	that	flower	of April	for	which	you are	so	proud	in	youth

That flower of April, of which you are so proud in your youth, will languish;

'tut: ta	u 'mi le	'dɔn: na	al: 'lor	mer 'tʃe	kje 'dre te
tutta	**umile**	**donna**	**allor**	**mercé**	**chiedrete**
all	humble	woman	then	pity	you will ask

> the pronunciation of "umile"
> is the poetic variant appropriate
> because of the musical stress

a	ki	'sɛr vo	un	di	vi	fu
a	**chi**	**servo**	**un**	**dì**	**vi**	**fu.**
to	he who	servant	one	day	to you	was

then, a completely humble woman, you will ask for pity from the one who was once a servant to you.

ri de 'rɔm: mi	al: 'lor	'deʎ: ʎi	'an: ni	ke	a 'vran	'tɔl to	'oɲ: ɲi	'prɛ dʒo	'al: la	bel 'ta
Riderommi	**allor**	**degli**	**anni**	**che**	**avran**	**tolto**	**ogni**	**pregio**	**alla**	**beltà;**
I will laugh at	then	of the	years	which	will have	taken away	every	value	to the	beauty

Then I will laugh about the years which will have taken away all value from your beauty;

'daʎ: ʎi	af: 'fan: ni	al 'fin	diʃ: 'ʃol to	di 'rɔ	'vek: kja	in	'pa tʃe	va
dagli	**affanni**	**alfin**	**disciolto**	**dirò**	**vecchia**	**in**	**pace**	**va.**
from the	woes	finally	released	I will say	old woman	in	peace	go

finally released from my woes, I will say "be gone *[go in peace],*" old woman.

GL: **Filli**

Kapsberger, Johann (c.1580-1651)

In Italy from his youth because his father, a noble military official with the Imperial House of Austria, settled in Venice, he was called "Giovanni Geronimo Tedesco della Teorba" because of his prowess on instruments of the lute family. He was also a virtuoso performer on the trumpet.

Soon after 1605 Kapsberger was in Rome, where he moved among the nobility and, in 1624, entered the service of Cardinal Francesco Barberini, working alongside Frescobaldi, Luigi Rossi, Domenico Mazzocchi, and the poets of the day.

He was a prolific and original composer, largely responsible for the the development of the theorbo as a solo instrument. His instrumental music includes virtuoso toccatas, variations, dances, and sinfonie. His vocal music includes motets, a mass, solo madrigals, arias, and seven books of villanellas.

---

[36]

'tʃin ta di 'rɔ ze
Cinta di rose
Encircled by roses

'tʃin ta	di	'rɔ ze	lo do 'ra ta	'flɔ ɾa	'lje ta	le	'pjad: dʒe	ko lo 'ri te	in 'fjo ɾa
Cinta	**di**	**rose**	**l'odorata**	**Flora**	**lieta**	**le**	**piagge**	**colorite**	**infiora.**
encircled	of	roses	the sweet-smelling	Flora	happy	the	slopes	colorful	adorns

Encircled by roses, sweet-smelling Flora happily adorns the colorful slopes.

e	'dʒiʎː ʎi	'de sta	su sur: 'ran do	'fwɔ ɾa	'la u ɾa	ka 'nɔ ɾa
E	**gigli**	**desta**	**susurrando**	**fuora**	**l'aura**	**canora.**
and	lilies	awakens	whispering	outside	the air	singing

*susurrando =
(mod.) sussurrando*
fuora (poet.) = fuori

And the song-filled air awakens the lilies with whispers.

Two more verses are printed as text only:

al	'nwɔ vo	'pɔr to	dol tʃe 'men te	in 'ten to	il	'ri vo	'gɔ de	nel	fu 'ga tʃe	ar 'dʒen to
Al	**nuovo**	**porto**	**dolcemente**	**intento**	**il**	**rivo**	**gode**	**nel**	**fugace**	**argento:**
to the	fresh	harbor	sweetly	attentive	the	brook	delights	in the	fleeting	silver

Purposely, sweetly flowing to its new harbor, the brook delights in its fleeting silver;

e	kon	ri 'skon tro	di	so 'nɔ ɾo	at: 'tʃen to	'mor mo ɾa	il	'ven to
E	**con**	**riscontro**	**di**	**sonoro**	**accento**	**mormora**	**il**	**vento.**
and	with	reply	of	resonant	word	murmurs	the	wind

and the wind murmurs reply in resonant words.

'tor nan	'a i	'kam pi	'lu tʃi di	ko 'lo ɾi	il	'pra to	'sor na	do do 'ɾa ti	'fjo ɾi
Tornan	**ai**	**campi**	**lucidi**	**colori,**	**il**	**prato**	**s'orna**	**d'odorati**	**fiori:**
return	to the	fields	bright	colors	the	meadow	is adorned	with fragrant	flowers

Bright colors return to the fields; the meadow is adorned with fragrant flowers;

e	il	'tʃɛ lo	'spi ɾa	di	no 'vɛlː lo 'no ɾi	'rikː ki	te 'zɔ ɾi
E	**il**	**cielo**	**spira**	**di**	**novell'onori**	**ricchi**	**tesori.**
and	the	heaven	exudes	of	new glories	rich	treasures

and heaven exudes new glories [and] rich treasures.

GL: **Flora**

☙

[36]

in te la 'vi ta
In te la vita
The life in you

in	te	la	'vi ta	'fra le	'spir to	ter: 're no	kwal	ve 'lo tʃe
In	**te**	**la**	**vita,**	**frale**	**spirto**	**terreno,**	**qual**	**veloce**
in	you	the	life	frail	spirit	earthly	like a	swift

ba 'le no	'fudː dʒe	'rat: ta	dal	'se no
baleno	**fugge**	**ratta**	**dal**	**seno.**
lightning flash	flees	rapidly	from the	breast

Frail, earthly spirit, the life in you is rapidly escaping from your breast like a swift flash of lightning.

il	'vol to	a 'dor no	di	'vi vi	ko 'lor	'pɛr din	un	'dʒor no
Il	**volto**	**adorno**	**di**	**vivi**	**color'**	**perd'in**	**un**	**giorno**
the	face	adorned	with	bright	colors	loses in	one	day

The face adorned with bright color loses in a day

il	su	bɛl	fjor	ne	fa	ri 'tor no
il	**su'**	**bel**	**fior,**	**né**	**fa**	**ritorno.**
the	its	beautiful	flower	nor	makes	return

its beautiful bloom, which does not come back.

'na to   a   mo 'rir   'mi ra   i   'twɔi   'dan: ni
Nato   a   morir,   mira   i   tuoi   danni,
born   to   to die   see   the   your   faults
[O mortal], born to die, look at your faults:

va   fu 'ga tʃe   la   bel 'ta   e   le 'ta   'fud: dʒe   'ljɛ ve   il   dʒo 'ir
va   fugace   la   beltà   e   l'età   fugge   lieve   il   gioir.
goes   fleeting   the   beauty   and   the old age   runs from   easily   the   enjoying
beauty is fleeting, and joy easily avoids old age.

're stan   sol   ʎaf: 'fan: ni
Restan'   sol   gl'affanni.
remain   only   the woes
Only woes remain.

kwel   ke   tu   'mi ri   bɛl   te 'a tro   din 'tor no
Quel   che   tu   miri,   bel   teatro   d'intorno,
that   which   you   you see   beautiful   scene   around
What you see – a beautiful scene all around,

'va go   'kam po   del   'dʒor no   sɔl   di   'pe na   ɛ   sod: 'dʒor no
vago   campo   del   giorno,   sol   di   pena   è   soggiorno.
lovely   field   of the   day   only   of   suffering   is   sojourn
a lovely place – is but a sojourn of suffering.

tʃɔ   'ki vi   'dʒi ra   si 've ste   di   fral
Ciò   ch'ivi   gira   si veste   di   fral,
that   which therein   goes around   dresses itself   of   *(poet.)* the human corporal body
What goes around therein is dressed in human form;

in   'kam po   'di ra   'vi ta   ɛ   mor 'tal   ke   'ljɛ ve   'spi ra.
in   campo   d'ira   vita   è   mortal   che   lieve   spira.
in   field   of sorrow   life   is   mortal   which   lightly   breaths
in a state of sorrow, life is a mortal being which is barely alive.

> *ira (antiquated meaning) = afflizione, dolore*

del   'fal so   bɛn   'fud: dʒi   ʎiŋ 'gan: ni   ke   da   'no i   kol   di
Del   falso   ben   fuggi   gl'inganni,   ché   da   noi   col   dì
of the   false   happiness   flee   the deceptions   because   from   us   with the   day

kol   sol   'par te   a   vol   'oɲ: ɲi   'nɔ stro   se 'ren
col   sol   parte   a   vol   ogni   nostro   seren'.
with the   sun   departs   in   flight   every   our   serenity
Flee from the deceptions of a false happiness, because our every serenity flies from us with the day and the sun.

're stan   sol   ʎaf: 'fan: ni
Restan'   sol   gl'affanni.
remain   only   the woes
Only woes remain.

[55]   *Giovanni Battista Guarini*

in ter: 'rot: te   spe 'ran tse
Interrotte speranze
Interrupted hopes

in ter: 'rot: te   spe 'ran tse   e   'fer ma   'fe de
Interrotte   speranze,   e   ferma   fede,
interrupted   hopes   and   firm   faith
Interrupted hopes and firm faith,

'fjam: me   e   'stra li   pos: 'sɛn ti   in   'de bil   'kɔ ɾe
fiamme   e   strali   possenti   in   debil   core,
flames   and   arrows   mighty   in   weak   heart
flames and mighty arrows in a weak heart,

> *debil[e]* =
> *(mod.) debol[e]*

nu 'drir   sol   di   so 'spir   un   fɛ ɾar 'do ɾe
nudrir   sol   di   sospir   un   fer' ardore,
to nourish   only   of   sighs   a   fierce passion
to nourish a fierce passion only with sighs,

> *fer[o]* =
> *(mod.) fier[o]*

e   tʃe 'lar   il   'tu o   mal   kwal   'al tri   il   've de
e   celar   il   tuo   mal   qual   altri   il   vede,
and   to hide   the   your   hurt   as   another   it   sees
and to hide the outer signs of your hurt...

> *altri (singular)*
> *= another, someone else*

se 'gwir   di   'va go   e   fud: dʒi 'ti vo   'pje de   'lor me   ri 'vɔl te
Seguir   di   vago   e   fuggitivo   piede   l'orme   rivolte
to follow   with   wandering   and   fleeting   foot   the footsteps   turned

a   vo lun 'ta ɾjo   er: 'ro ɾe
a   voluntario   errore;
at   voluntary   error
To follow, wandering and fleeting, footsteps voluntarily erring,

> *voluntario* =
> *(mod.) volontario*

'per der   del   'se me   'spar sel   'frut: to   el   'fjo ɾe
perder   del   seme   spars' e'l   frutto,   e'l   fiore,
to lose   of the   seed   sown and the   fruit   and the   flower
to lose the fruit and flower of the sown seed

e   la   spe 'ra ta   gran   laŋ 'gwir   mer 'tʃe de
e   la   sperata   gran   languir   mercede,
and   the   hoped   great   languishing   reward
and the hoped-for reward of great languishing...

far   'du no   'zgwar do   sol   'led: dʒe   'a i   pen 'sje ɾi
Far   d'uno   sguardo   sol   legge   ai   pensieri,
to make   of one   glance   only   law   to the   thoughts
To make a single glance rule your thoughts,

e   dun   'ka sto   vo 'ler   'fre no   al   de 'zi o
e   d'un   casto   voler   freno   al   desio,
and   with a   chaste   will   restraint   to the   desire
and to restrain your desire with a chaste will,

e   'spen der   la gri 'man do   i   'lu stri   in 'tje ɾi
e   spender   lagrimando   i   lustri   intieri,
and   to spend   weeping   the   lusters   entire
and to spend entire lusters *[periods of five years]* in weeping...

> *intieri (lit.)*
> *= interi*

'kwe sti   ka   'vo i   'kwa zi   gran   'faʃ: ʃi   in 'vi o   'dɔn: na   kru 'dɛl
Questi   ch'a   voi   quasi   gran   fasci   invio,   donna   crudel',
these   which to   you   as if   great   bundles   I send   woman   cruel
These [are] what I send you, cruel woman, like great bundles of kindling;

'da spri	tor 'men ti	e	'pe ne	sa 'ran	i	tro 'fɛ i	'vɔ stril	'rɔ go	'mi o
d'aspri	**tormenti,**	**e**	**pene**	**saran**	**i**	**trofei**	**vostr', il**	**rogo**	**mio.**
of bitter	torments	and	pains	will be	the	trophies	your the	funeral pyre	mine

they will be your trophies of bitter torments and pain, and my funeral pyre.

Keiser, Reinhard (1674-1739)

Keiser was schooled at the Thomasschule in Leipzig and then went to Brunswick, where the court opera was flourishing. He began writing operas, the total number of which probably exceeded a hundred in his lifetime, and around 1696 he moved to Hamburg to be director and chief composer of the Hamburg Opera. In 1704, when the theater was temporarily closed, he produced his *Almira* in Weissenfels; his partner passed its libretto on to the young Handel, who was in the opera orchestra, and the success of Handel's own setting of the libretto led to strained relations between the two composers.

As a musical dramatist Keiser gave each of his operas an individual style reflecting its dramatic character, and he experimented with varieties of instrumental scoring.

He was called "perhaps the most original musical genius that Germany has ever produced" at the time *[Grove]*, though his operas were rarely performed outside Hamburg and Brunswick. He retains his reputation for being the first great figure in German operatic history.

---

[55]
from: *L'inganno fedele (1714)*   *Johann Ulrich von König*

per kom pja 'tʃer ti o 'ka ɾa
Per compiacerti, o cara
To satisfy you, o dear one

per	kom pja 'tʃer ti	o	'ka ɾa	o	'ka ɾa	'tut: to	fa 'ra	il	'mi o	kɔr
Per	**compiacerti,**	**o**	**cara!**	**O**	**cara,**	**tutto**	**farà**	**il**	**mio**	**cor.**
for	to satisfy you	o	dear one	o	dear one	everything	will do	the	my	heart

To satisfy you, o dear one – o dear one, my heart will do everything!

gra 'di to	o	non	a 'ma to	sker 'ni to	ov: 'ver	spret: 'tsa to
Gradito,	**o**	**non**	**amato,**	**schernito,**	**ovver**	**sprezzato,**
welcomed	or	not	loved	mocked	or else	scorned

Whether welcomed or unloved, mocked or scorned,

a do ɾe 'rɔ	ko 'stan te	'tu o	a 'ma bi le	ri 'gor
adorerò	**costante**	**tuo**	**amabile**	**rigor.**
I will adore	constant	your	lovable	severity

I will faithfully adore your lovable severity.

Landi, Stefano (1587-1639)

Singer, composer, and teacher born in Rome, he entered the Collegio Germanico in Rome as a boy soprano in 1595; in 1602 he began studies at the Seminario Romano; by 1614 he was *maestro di cappella* at S. Maria della Consolazione, and by the end of 1624 was *maestro di cappella* at S. Maria ai Monti. In 1629 he joined the Sistine Chapel choir as a contralto.

During his career he was in the service of various benefactors: Marco Cornaro, Bishop of Padua, Prince Paolo Savelli, Duke of Albano, Cardinal Scipione Borghese, Cardinal Ludovico Ludovisi, and Urban VIII (Barberini).

Landi was the first to be buried in the common tomb for Sistine singers in the Chiesa Nuova, the church of the Oratorians in Rome.

He wrote at least two operas, *a cappella* masses, and seven books of solo arias.

[55]
                                    su 'pɛr bi 'kɔl: li
                                    Superbi colli
                                    Proud hills

su 'pɛr bi   'kɔl: li   e   'vo i   'sa kre   ru 'i ne
Superbi   colli,   e   voi,   sacre   ruine,
proud   hills   and   you   sacred   ruins
Proud hills and you, sacred ruins,

        kil   gran   'no me   di   'ro ma   aŋ 'kor   te 'ne te
        ch'il   gran   nome   di   Roma   ancor   tenete,
        which the great name   of   Rome   still   you keep
        which still bear the great name of Rome,

        'a i   ke   re 'li kwe   mi ze 'ran da 've te
        ahi,   che   reliquie   miserand' avete
        ah   what relics   miserable you have
        ah, what miserable relics you contain

        di   'tan te   'ɔ pe ɾe   et: 'tʃɛl se   e   pel: le 'gri ne
        di   tante   opere   eccelse   e   pellegrine.
        of   so many   works   glorious   and   transient
        of so many glorious and transient works.

ko 'lɔs: si   'ar ki   e   te 'a tri   'ɔ pre   di 'vi ne
Colossi,   archi   e   teatri,   opre   divine,
colossi   arches   and theaters   works   divine
Colossi *[gigantic statues]*, arches and theaters, divine works,

        tri on 'fal   'pom pe   glo ɾi 'o ze   e   'ljɛ te
        trionfal   pompe   gloriose   e   liete,
        triumphal   pomps   glorious   and   joyous
        glorious and joyous triumphal displays,

        in   'pɔ ka   'pol ve   o 'ma i   kon 'vɛr se   'se te
        in   poca   polve   omai   converse   sete,
        in   little   dust   now   turned   you are
        you are now become but dust

polve = (mod.) polvere
omai (poet.) = ormai
sete = (mod.) siete

        e   'fat: te   al   'mon do   vil   'fa vo la   al   'fi ne
        e   fatte   al   mondo   vil'   favola   al   fine.
        and made   to the world   vulgar fable   at the end
        and, in the end, rendered a fable to the vulgar world.

al fine (lit)
= alfine

Lanier, Nicholas (1588-1666)

Born (and died) in London, he was a composer, singer, lutenist, and performer on the viol. He was the first to hold the position, from at least 1626, of Master of the King's Music, to Charles I. In the mid-1620's the King sent him to Italy several times to purchase a large portion of the art collection of the Dukes of Mantua. Lanier himself was also a painter and a print maker, and a poet.

Little of his music survives, but he is known to have introduced the new style of Italian monody to England, and to have been an innovative composer of songs. He is claimed by some to have been the first composer of opera in England, based on descriptions of several of his court masques, especially those to texts of Ben Jonson.

[51]

Pietro Benedetti

a mo 'ro za par go 'let: ta
Amorosa pargoletta
Amorous little girl

a mo 'ro za	par go 'let: ta	zdeɲ: ɲo 'zet: ta	ke	da 'mor	'sprɛt: tsa	lim 'pɛ ro	tu	non	'sa i
Amorosa	**pargoletta,**	**sdegnosetta,**	**che**	**d'amor**	**sprezza**	**l'impero,**	**tu**	**non**	**sai**
amorous	little girl	contemptuous	who	of love	spurns	the command	you	not	you know

Amorous, contemptuous little girl, who spurns the command of love, you do not know

kon	kwal	ar 'do re	'oɲ: ɲi	'ko re	sa	fe 'rir	'kru da	se 've ro
con	**qual**	**ardore**	**ogni**	**core**	**sa**	**ferir,**	**cruda,**	**severo.**
with	what	fervor	every	heart	knows how	to wound	cruel one	considerable

with what great fervor every heart knows how to wound, cruel one.

ri tro 'zet: ta	tu	non	'kre di	e	pur
Ritrosetta,	**tu**	**non**	**credi**	**e**	**pur**
recalcitrant little one	you	not	you believe	and	yet

Recalcitrant little girl, you do not believe [me]; and yet,

've dil	'mi o	do 'lor	nel	'pɛt: to	a 'skol to
vedi'l	**mio**	**dolor**	**nel**	**petto,**	**ascolto.**
you see	my	pain	in the	breast	I listen to

you see, I listen to the pain in my breast.

sem pli 'tʃet: ta	tu	non	'sa i	'ko me	'fa i	sof: fe 'rir	dun	'va go	'vol to
Semplicetta,	**tu**	**non**	**sai**	**come**	**fai**	**sofferir**	**d'un**	**vago**	**volto.**
simple little one	you	not	you know	how	you make	to suffer	by a	pretty	face

Simple little one, you do not know how you cause suffering
because of a pretty face.

> *sofferir[e] = (mod.) soffrir[e]*

Legrenzi, Giovanni (1626-1690)

Born near Bergamo, son of a violinist and minor composer, his rise to fame, honor, and wealth was remarkable; as a young man his resources were so meagre that he required a title of patrimony, granted in 1649, in order to be ordained. He became one of the most important opera composers in Venice; his music represents the final stages of formation of the late baroque style.

After serving as organist at S. Maria Maggiore in Bergamo, he went to Ferrara and then, by 1670, settled in Venice, where he became *maestro di cappella* at S. Marco in 1681.

In addition to solo cantatas, he wrote eighteen operas, three in Ferrara and most of the others under the patronage of the Grimani family in Venice. His operas often incorporated a great deal of spectacle and special effects such as fires or storms, and they were well received.

Legrenzi was otherwise known as a composer of liturgical music and violin sonatas.

[4, 6, 8, 19, 21, 24, 26, 29, 30, 38, 45, 54, 59, 60, 64]

ke 'fjɛ ro ko 'stu me
Che fiero costume
What a cruel habit

ke	'fjɛ ro	ko 'stu me	da 'li dʒe ro	'nu me	ke	a 'for tsa di	'pe ne	si 'fat: tʃa	a do 'rar
Che	**fiero**	**costume**	**d'aligero**	**nume,**	**che**	**a forza di**	**pene**	**si faccia**	**adorar!**
what	cruel	habit	of winged	deity	that	through	sufferings	himself makes	to adore

What a cruel habit of the winged deity [Cupid], that through suffering he makes us adore him!

e   pur   nel: lar 'do ɾe   il   'di o   tra di 'to ɾe   un   'va go   sem 'bjan te   mi   fe   i do la 'trar
E **pur** **nell'ardore** **il** **dio** **traditore** **un** **vago** **sembiante** **mi** **fe'** **idolatrar.**
and   yet   in the passion   the   god   treacherous   a   lovely   countenance   me   made   to idolize
And yet, in passion, the treacherous god made me idolize a lovely face.

alt.: eppur = e pur

ke   'kru do   de 'sti no   ke   un   'tʃɛ ko   bam 'bi no
Che **crudo** **destino** **che** **un** **cieco** **bambino**
what   cruel   destiny   that   a   blind   child
What cruel destiny, that a blind child,

alt.: ch'un = che un

kon   'bok: ka   di   'lat: te   si 'fat: tʃa   sti 'mar
con **bocca** **di** **latte** **si faccia** **stimar!**
with   mouth   of   milk   himself makes   to esteem
barely weaned, makes himself esteemed!

ma   'kwe sto   ti 'ran: no   kon   'bar ba ɾo   iŋ 'gan: no   'bar ba ɾo af: 'fan: no
Ma **questo** **tiranno** **con** **barbaro** **inganno,**   **barbaro** **affanno**
but   this   tyrant   with   barbarous   deception   barbarous damage
But this tyrant, with barbarous deception,

var. in [59]:

en 'tran do   per   ʎi   'ɔk: ki   mi   fe   so spi 'ɾar
entrando **per** **gli** **occhi,** **mi** **fe'** **sospirar.**
entering   through   the   eyes   me   made   to sigh
entering through my eyes, made me sigh.

alt.: gl'occhi = gli occhi

[19] includes the following Recitative and Aria:

or   ke   'ʃol to   da 'mo ɾe   'spi ɾo   di   li ber 'ta   'la u ɾe   vi 'ta li
Or **che** **sciolto** **d'amore** **spiro** **di** **libertà** **l'aure** **vitali;**
now   that   set free   of love   I breathe   of   liberty   the airs   vital
Now freed from love, I breathe the life-giving air of liberty;

ko 'no sko   e   'veg: go   al 'fi ne   ke   fjo 'ri ta   bel 'ta   non a ke   'spi ne
conosco **e** **veggo** **alfine** **che** **fiorita** **beltà** **non ha che** **spine.**
I recognize   and   I see   at last   that   flowering   beauty   has only   thorns
I see at last that flowering beauty has only thorns.

'i o   vi   'laʃ: ʃo   'lu tʃi   'bɛl: le   pju   non   'ar do   al   'vo stro   ar 'dor
o **vi** **lascio,** **luci** **belle,** **più** **non** **ardo** **al** **vostro** **ardor;**
I   you   I leave   eyes   beautiful   more   not   I burn   at the   your   ardor
I am leaving you, beautiful eyes; no longer do I burn at your ardor.

vi van 'ta te   'dɛs: ser   'stel: le   e   men 'ti te   lo   splen 'dor
vi vantate **d'esser** **stelle** **e** **mentite** **lo** **splendor.**
you brag   of to be   stars   and   you lie   the   splendor
You boast of being stars, and you lie [with] your splendor.

a 'man ti   siŋ 'ke   po 'te te   non   ar 'de te
Amanti, **sin che** **potete** **non** **ardete.**
lovers   as long as   you are able   not   you burn
Lovers, as long as you can, do not burn [with ardor].

e   ki   non   sa   kef: 'fi me ɾa   del   'tɛm po   ɛ   la   bel 'ta
E **chi** **non** **sa** **ch'effimera** **del** **tempo** **è** **la** **beltà.**
and   who   not   knows   that ephemeral   of the   time   is   the   beauty
And who does not know that beauty is short-lived?

su	la	'se ɾa	'pjan dʒe	il	'fjo ɾe	beŋ	ke	'ri ze	sul	mat: 'tin
Su	**la**	**sera**	**piange**	**il**	**fiore**	**ben**	**che**	**rise**	**sul**	**mattin.**
upon	the	evening	weeps	the	flower	even	though	it smiled	upon the	morning

ben che = (mod.) benché

The flower weeps in the evening even though it smiled in the morning.

ko 'zi	fa	la 'man te	'kɔ ɾe	'kju de	in	'pjan to	il	'su o	de 'stin
Così	**fa**	**l'amante**	**core:**	**chiude**	**in**	**pianto**	**il**	**suo**	**destin.**
thus	does	the loving	heart	closes	in	weeping	the	its	destiny

Thus does the loving heart: its destiny ends in tears.

&

[44]

'far tʃi 'pat: tso
Farci pazzo
It makes us crazy

'far tʃi	'pat: tso	da	ka 'te na	a	non	far	kon 'tɛn to	il	'kɔ ɾe
Farci	**pazzo**	**da**	**catena**	**a**	**non**	**far**	**contento**	**il**	**core.**
to make us	crazy	from	chain	to	not	to make	content	the	heart

It makes us crazy *["fit to be tied"]* not to content our hearts.

il	ko 'ɾal	di	'bɛl: la	'bok: ka	mi	kon 'strin se	a	in: na mo 'ɾar mi
Il	**coral**	**di**	**bella**	**bocca**	**mi**	**constrinse**	**a**	**innamorarmi**
the	coral	of	beautiful	mouth	me	compelled	to	to fall in love

The coral of a beautiful mouth compelled me to fall in love,

'on de	vwɔ	per	ven di 'kar mi	ke	sul	'lab: bro	di	tʃi 'na bro
onde	**vuò**	**per**	**vendicarmi**	**che**	**sul**	**labbro**	**di**	**cinabro**
whence	wished	for	to take revenge on me	that	upon	lip	of	cinnabar

mi	di 'spɛn si	i	'stra li	a 'mo ɾe
mi	**dispensi**	**i**	**strali**	**Amore.**
to me	may dispense	the	arrows	Love

whereby Love wished to take revenge on me by bestowing his arrows upon lips of cinnabar.

'far tʃi	'pat: tso	da	ka 'te na	a	non	far	kon 'tɛn to	il	'kɔ ɾe
Farci	**pazzo**	**da**	**catena**	**a**	**non**	**far**	**contento**	**il**	**core.**
to make us	crazy	from	chain	to	not	to make	content	the	heart

It makes us crazy *["fit to be tied"]* not to content our hearts.

il	ko 'lor	di	'ne ve	in 'tat: ta	mi	de 'stɔ	le	'fjam: me	in	'pɛt: to
Il	**color**	**di**	**neve**	**intatta**	**mi**	**destò**	**le**	**fiamme**	**in**	**petto**
the	color	of	snow	virginal	me	aroused	the	flames	in	breast

The complexion of virginal snow aroused the flames in my breast,

'on de	vwɔ	per	'mi o	di 'lɛt: to	ke	'ku pi do	'di o	di	'kni do
onde	**vuò**	**per**	**mio**	**diletto**	**che**	**Cupido**	**Dio**	**di**	**Cnido**
whence	wished	for	my	pleasure	that	Cupid	God	of	Cnido

printed "Gnido" = Cnido

mi	di 'strug: ga	in	kwel: lar 'do ɾe
mi	**distrugga**	**in**	**quell'ardore.**
me	may destroy	in	that fire

whereby Cupid, God of Cnido, wished, for my pleasure, to destroy me in that fire.

'far tʃi	'pat: tso	da	ka 'te na	a	non	far	kon 'tɛn to	il	'kɔ ɾe
Farci	**pazzo**	**da**	**catena**	**a**	**non**	**far**	**contento**	**il**	**core.**
to make us	crazy	from	chain	to	not	to make	content	the	heart

It makes us crazy *["fit to be tied"]* not to content our hearts.

GL: **Amore, Cnido, Cupido**

❧

[27]

mi nu 'dri te di spe 'ran tsa
Mi nudrite di speranza
You feed me with hope

mi	nu 'dri te	di	spe 'ran tsa	'lu tʃi	'bɛl: le	'va ge	'stel: le
Mi	**nudrite**	**di**	**speranza,**	**luci**	**belle**	**vaghe**	**stelle.**
me	you feed	with	hope	eyes	beautiful	charming	stars

You feed me with hope, beautiful eyes, charming stars.

> *nudrite: from "nudrire" = (mod.) "nutrire"*

ma	da 'mor	ko 'me te	a u 'ra te	li be 'ra te	'kwe sto	kɔr
Ma	**d'amor**	**comete**	**aurate**	**liberate**	**questo**	**cor**
but	from love	comets	colored with gold	liberate	this	heart

But, gilded comets *[transient stars]*, free this heart from love;

non	'spɛ ɾa	pju	non	pju	non	'spɛ ɾa	pju
non	**spera**	**più,**	**non**	**più,**	**non**	**spera**	**più.**
not	hopes	more	not	more	not	hopes	more

it does not hope any longer – no more, it hopes no more.

❧

[57]

non tʃɛ ke 'di ɾe la 'vɔʎ: ʎo ko 'zi
Non c'è che dire, la voglio così
There is nothing to say – I want it that way

non	tʃɛ	ke	'di ɾe	nɔ	la	'vɔʎ: ʎo	ko 'zi
Non	**c'è**	**che**	**dire,**	**no,**	**la**	**voglio**	**così.**
not	there is	what	to say	no	it	I want	thus

There is nothing to say, no – I want it that way.

al: 'lɛt: to	kol	'gwar do	kol	'ri zo	lu 'ziŋ go	ma	'fiŋ go
Alletto	**col**	**guardo,**	**col**	**riso**	**lusingo,**	**ma**	**fingo**
I entice	with the	glance	with the	laughter	I flatter	but	I pretend

I entice with my glance, I flatter with my laughter; but I am pretending,

e	sol	tra	'pjan ti	'gɔ do	ʎi	a 'man ti	ve 'der	laŋ 'gwi ɾe
e	**sol**	**tra**	**pianti**	**godo**	**gli**	**amanti**	**veder**	**languire**
and	only	among	tears	I enjoy	the	lovers	to see	to languish

and only in tears do I enjoy seeing lovers languish

la	'nɔt: tel	di
la	**nott'e'l**	**dì.**
the	night and the	day

night and day.

se	'spɛ me	vi		'pɔr go	kon	'dʒen jo	ti 'ran: no	viŋ 'gan: no
Se	**speme**	**vi**		**porgo**	**con**	**genio**	**tiranno,**	**v'inganno;**
if	hope	to you		I offer	with	genius	tyrannical	you I deceive

If, with tyrannical genius, I offer you hope, I am deceiving you;

speme (lit.) = *speranza*

or	se	vi	'pja tʃe	'al: la	'mi a	'fa tʃe	in tʃe ne 'ri ɾe	ve 'ni te	si
or	**se**	**vi**	**piace**	**alla**	**mia**	**face**	**incenerire,**	**venite,**	**sì.**
now	if	you	it pleases	to the	my	torch	to reduce to ashes	come	yes

now if you would like to be reduced to ashes by my flame, do come, yes, do.

[1, 2, 46]

non mi dir di pa le 'zar
Non mi dir di palesar
Do not tell me to reveal

non	mi	dir	di	pa le 'zar	o	'mi o	kɔr	ad: do lo 'ra to
Non	**mi**	**dir**	**di**	**palesar,**	**o**	**mio**	**cor**	**addolorato,**
not	to me	to say	of	to reveal	o	my	heart	saddened

Do not tell me to reveal, o my grieving heart,

al	bel: 'li do lo	spje 'ta to	la	ka 'dʒon	del	'tu o	pe 'nar
al	**bell'idolo**	**spietato**	**la**	**cagion**	**del**	**tuo**	**penar!**
to the	beautiful idol	pitiless	the	reason	of the	your	suffering

to my beautiful, pitiless idol, the reason for your suffering!

non	ɛ	'deɲ: ɲo	di	sa 'lir	il	'tu o	'fɔ ko	a 'dal ta	'sfe ɾa
Non	**è**	**degno**	**di**	**salir**	**il**	**tuo**	**foco**	**ad alta**	**sfera.**
not	is	worthy	of	to rise	the	your	fire	to high	sphere

Your passion is not worthy of rising to a high sphere.

ɛ	fal: 'la tʃe	kon siʎ: 'ʎɛ ɾa	la	'spe me	a	ri sa 'nar	'em pjo	mar 'tir
È	**fallace**	**consigliera**	**la**	**speme**	**a**	**risanar**	**empio**	**martir.**
is	fallacious	advisor	the	hope	to	to heal	cruel	agony

Hope is a deceptive advisor in the healing of cruel agony.

speme (lit.) = *speranza*

'pe na	so 'spi ɾa	e	'ta tʃi	e	sol	ta 'van tsa
Pena,	**sospira**	**e**	**taci!**	**E**	**sol**	**t'avanza,**
suffer	sigh	and	be quiet	[and]	only	to you is left

Suffer, sigh, and stay quiet! It only remains for you

'vin tʃer	'la spro	do 'lor	kon	la	ko 'stan tsa
vincer	**l'aspro**	**dolor**	**con**	**la**	**costanza.**
to conquer	the bitter	pain	with	the	constancy

to conquer the bitter pain through constancy.

'sot: to	il	'man to	del	ta 'tʃer	del: lar 'dor	'kɔ pri	la	'fɔr tsa
Sotto	**il**	**manto**	**del**	**tacer**	**dell'ardor**	**copri**	**la**	**forza,**
beneath	the	mantle	of the	being silent	of the ardor	conceal	the	strength

Beneath the guise of silence, conceal the strength of your passion;

ke	se 'pol ta	pju	rin 'for tsa	'oɲ: ɲi	'fjam: ma	il	'su o	po 'ter
ché	**sepolta**	**più**	**rinforza**	**ogni**	**fiamma**	**il**	**suo**	**poter!**
because	buried	more	reinforces	each	flame	the	its	power

because, buried, each flame grows more in its power!

ke	se	'po i	taf: 'flid: dʒe	il	dwɔl	tu	kon	'pjɔd: dʒa	di	gran	'pjan to
Ché,	**se**	**poi**	**t'afflige**	**il**	**duol,**	**tu**	**con**	**pioggia**	**di**	**gran**	**pianto,**
because	if	then	you grieves	the	sorrow	you	with	rain	of	great	weeping

ke	'daʎ: ʎi	'ɔk: ki	'skor: ra	in 'tan to	'pɔr ta	'la ni ma	'tu a	stil: 'la ta	al	swɔl
che	**dagli**	**occhi**	**scorra**	**intanto,**	**porta**	**l'anima**	**tua**	**stillata**	**al**	**suol.**
which	from the	eyes	may flow	meanwhile	carries	the soul	your	distilled	to the	ground

Because then, if sorrow grieves you, you will take your distilled soul to the ground in a torrential rain of tears which, meanwhile, flow from my eyes.

'mu to	'pjan dʒer	ta 'lor	pje 'ta de	im 'pɛ tra
Muto	**pianger**	**talor**	**pietade**	**impetra;**
silent	weeping	sometimes	pity	obtains

Silent weeping sometimes obtains pity;

pietade =
(mod.) pietà

'rɛn de	'mɔl: le	la	'pjɔd: dʒa	'aŋ ko	la	'pjɛ tra
rende	**molle**	**la**	**pioggia**	**anco**	**la**	**pietra.**
makes	soft	the	rain	even	the	stone

rain will soften even stone.

anco =
(mod.) anche

 # Lonati, Carlo Ambrogio (c.1645-c.1710-15)

Born in Milan, composer, impresario, violinist, and singer, he is first mentioned in records as violinist of the royal chapel in Naples. By 1668 he was in Rome; he served the expatriate Queen Christina of Sweden as leader of her string orchestra, acquiring the nickname "Il gobbo della regina (the queen's hunchback)."
There is speculation about his friendship with Stradella, who joined him at the Teatro del Falcone in Genoa in 1677; Lonati was deported from Genoa in 1682 after the murder of Stradella, and was denied return. He apparently spent his late years in Milan.
Much of his music has been lost. He is known for his violin sonatas and trio sonatas, but he also contributed to opera, both as performer and composer. He performed as a singer primarily in comic roles, but as composer his operas belong to the more serious genre of *dramma per musica*. Cantatas and canzonettas (such as "Tu partisti") were also among his vocal contributions.

[1, 2, 15, 46]

tu par 'ti sti
Tu partisti
You have departed

tu	par 'ti sti	'i do lo	a 'ma to	me	laʃ: 'ʃa sti	fra	le	'pe ne
Tu	**partisti,**	**idolo**	**amato;**	**me**	**lasciasti**	**fra**	**le**	**pene!**
you	departed	idol	beloved	me	you left	among	the	sufferings

You have departed, beloved idol; you have left me among sufferings!

"me" instead of "mi":
an antiquated usage
(if not a misprint)

'du ri	'lat: tʃi	e	'ri e	ka 'te ne	'sɔf: fre	un	'pɛt: to	in: na mo 'ra to
Duri	**lacci**	**e**	**rie**	**catene**	**soffre**	**un**	**petto**	**innamorato.**
harsh	bonds	and	cruel	chains	suffers	a	breast	enamored

An enamored breast suffers harsh bonds and cruel chains.

rie: feminine
plural of "rio"
(lit.) = "reo"

Lori, Arcangelo (1615-1679)

A leading lutenist of the mid-17th century, he was called Arcangelo del leuto ("Archangel of the lute"); "Dimmi, Amor" has been attributed until recently to a composer named del Leuto.

Lori was also an organist, at S. Luigi dei Francesi, probably until 1633, and a voice teacher. Yet he was mostly involved as a performer on the lute, participating in many patronal festivals and church performances. As far as is known, he spent his whole career in Rome.

Few of his compositions are extant: a motet for soprano (with violin, lute and continuo), some arias, and some solo cantatas.

[5, 9, 19, 34, 44]

'dim: mi a 'mor
Dimmi, Amor
Tell me, Love

'dim: mi	a 'mor	'dim: mi	ke	fa	la	'mi a	'ka ɾa	li ber 'ta
Dimmi	**Amor,**	**dimmi**	**che**	**fa**	**la**	**mia**	**cara**	**libertà?**
tell me	Love	tell me	what	does	the	my	dear	freedom

> *"cara" is not in the text in* [44]

Tell me, Love – tell me, what is my dear freedom doing?

dak: 'ke	an 'dɔ	'ko me	'sa i	tu	a	le 'gar si	a dun	bel	'kri ne
Dacché	**andò,**	**come**	**sai**	**tu,**	**a**	**legarsi**	**ad un**	**bel**	**crine,**
ever since	it went	as	know	you	to	to tie itself	to a	beautiful	head of hair

> *in* [9] *and* [19]: *Da che = Dacché*

Ever since it went away, as you know, to bind itself to beautiful tresses,

'kwe sto	kɔr	pjɛn	di	ru 'i ne	non	la	'po i	ri 'vi sta	pju
questo	**cor,**	**pien**	**di**	**ruine**	**non**	**l'ha**	**poi**	**rivista**	**più!**
this	heart	full	of	ruins	not	it has	then	seen again	more

> *in* [34]: *non ha = not has*
> *ruine = rovine*

this heart, full of havoc, has never seen it again!

ʊn	pen 'sjɛr	il	kɔr	man 'dɔ	a	tro 'var la	in	'su e	ka 'te ne
Un	**pensier**	**il**	**cor**	**mandò**	**a**	**trovarla**	**in**	**sue**	**catene;**
a	thought	the	heart	sent	to	to find it	in	its	chains

My heart sent off a thought to find it, in its chains;

ma	per	'kreʃ ʃer	le	'mi e	'pe ne	il	pen 'sjɛr	'ma i	non	tor 'nɔ
ma	**per**	**crescer**	**le**	**mie**	**pene**	**il**	**pensier**	**mai**	**non**	**tornò!**
but	for	to increase	the	my	pains	the	thought	ever	not	returned

but, to add to my suffering, the thought has never returned!

The following text appears in [19] *as a 2ⁿᵈ verse printed as text only, and in* [34] *as a 3ʳᵈ verse below the music:*

kwel	pen 'sjɛr	ke	ti	par 'ti	re 'stɔ	'for se	pri dʒo 'njɛ ɾo
Quel	**pensier**	**che**	**ti**	**partì,**	**restò**	**forse**	**prigioniero,**
that	thought	which	to you	left	remained	perhaps	prisoner

> *alt. in* [34]: *...che si partì = ...which left,*

That thought which left [in search of] you perhaps remained a prisoner,

kin: na 'mo ɾa	'oɲ: ɲi	pen 'sjɛ ɾo	la	bel 'ta	ke	mi	fe 'ri
ch'innamora	**ogni**	**pensiero,**	**la**	**beltà**	**che**	**mi**	**ferì.**
because ensnares	every	thought	the	beauty	who	me	wounded

because the beauty who wounded me ensnares every thought.

'dim: mi   a 'mor   'dim: mi   ke   fa   la   'mi a   'ka ɾa   li ber 'ta
Dimmi,   Amor,   dimmi   che   fa   la   mia   cara   libertà?
tell me   Love   tell me   what   does   the   my   dear   freedom

Tell me, Love – tell me, what is my dear freedom doing?

| var. in [34]: ...che fa il pensier, la libertà? = ...what are my thoughts [and] my freedom doing? |

GL: **Amor**

 Lotti, Antonio (1666 or 1667-1740)

Born in Hanover, where his father was *Kapellmeister*, by 1683 Lotti was in Venice studying with Legrenzi; as a teacher himself, his pupils included Bassani, Gasparini, and Marcello. Singer and organist, he began as a choirboy at St. Mark's basilica in Venice in 1687; he became first organist there in 1704 and held that position until 1736, when he was named *primo maestro di cappella*.

A prolific composer of sacred music, madrigals, and motets, Lotti has been cited as bridging late baroque and early classical style. Unfortunately, much of his music has been lost.

He wrote many operas for the Venetian theatres and, between 1717 and 1719 on a leave of absence from St. Mark's, three operas for Dresden, all to public success.

---

[57]

'pjan dʒe   il   'fjo ɾe   e   'dʒɛ me   il   'pra to
Piange il fiore e geme il prato
The flower weeps and the meadow laments

'pjan dʒe   il   'fjo ɾe   e   'dʒɛ me   il   'pra to
Piange   il   fiore   e   geme   il   prato
weeps   the   flower   and   laments   the   meadow

The flower weeps and the meadow laments

al   ri 'gor   di   'bɔ re a   i 'ra to   ke   tra   'tʃep: pi   tan: no 'dɔ
al   rigor   di   Borea   irato   che   tra   ceppi   t'annodò.
at the   harshness   of   north wind   angry   which   among   fetters   you entangled

at the harshness of the angry North Wind which entangled you in fetters.

e   la u 'dʒɛl   ke   in 'tor no   'dʒi ɾa   kol   kan 'tar
E   l'augel   che   intorno   gira   col   cantar
and   the bird   which   around   turns   with the   singing

And the bird which flies around, singing,

| *augel[lo] (poet.)* = *uccel[lo]* |

par   ke   so 'spi ɾa   ke   il   kru 'dɛ le   ti   dʒe 'lɔ
par   che   sospira   ché   il   crudele   ti   gelò.
seems   that   it sighs   because   the   cruel one   you   froze

seems to sigh because the cruel one made you ice-cold.

GL: **Borea**

[4, 6, 8, 20, 25, 26, 29, 30, 31, 44, 54, 59, 60, 64]

pur di 'tʃe sti   o   'bok: ka   'bɛl: la
Pur dicesti, o bocca bella
Indeed you said, o beautiful mouth

pur	di	'tʃe sti	o	'bok: ka	'bɛl: la	kwel	so	'a ve	e	'ka ɾo	si
Pur	**dicesti,**		**o**	**bocca**	**bella,**	**quel**	**soave**		**e**	**caro**	**sì,**
indeed	you said		o	mouth	beautiful	that	sweet		and	dear	yes

Indeed you said, o beautiful mouth, that sweet and dear "yes"

ke	fa	'tut: to	il	'mi o	pja 'tʃer
che	**fa**	**tutto**	**il**	**mio**	**piacer.**
which	makes	all	the	my	pleasure

which causes all my pleasure.

per	o 'nor	di	'su a	fa 'tʃɛl: la	kon	un	'ba tʃo	a 'mor	ta 'pri
Per	**onor**	**di**	**sua**	**facella**	**con**	**un**	**bacio**	**Amor**	**t'aprì**
through	honor	of	his	little torch	with	a	kiss	Love	you opened

In honor of his flame, Love opened you with a kiss,

'dol tʃe	'fon te	del	go 'der	a	si	del	go 'der
dolce	**fonte**	**del**	**goder,**	**ah!**	**sì,**	**del**	**goder.**
sweet	fount	of the	taking pleasure	ah	yes	of the	taking pleasure

sweet fount of pleasure – ah, yes, of pleasure.

> *"ah!" is not included in all the prints.*

G𝓛: Amor

Mancini, Francesco (1672-1737)

Composer and organist, he was born and educated in Naples, studying with Francesco Provenzale and Gennaro Ursino, and he died in Naples. First organist at the royal chapel from 1704 to 1706, he became *vice-maestro* upon the arrival of Alessandro Scarlatti; in 1725, upon Scarlatti's death, he became its *maestro di cappella* for the rest of his life. He was also a teacher, and *maestro di cappella* from 1720 to 1735 at the Conservatorio di S. Maria di Loreto.

Mancini achieved a notable reputation as an opera composer, composing some twenty of them. Arias and intermezzos of his were added, as was the custom of the time, to others' operas, including ones by such famous composers as Bononcini and Handel.

[25, 35, 64]

dir 'ki o 'ta mi
Dir ch'io t'ami
To say that I love you

dir	'ki o	'ta mi		o	'ka ɾa	ɛ	'pɔ ko
Dir	**ch'io**	**t'ami,**		**o**	**cara,**	**è**	**poco**
to say	that I	you I may love		o	dear one	is	little

To say that I love you, o dear one, is little

se	in	te	'pɔ za	il	'mi o	pen 'sjɛr
se	**in**	**te**	**posa**	**il**	**mio**	**pensier.**
if	in	you	rests	the	my	thought

when my thoughts rest in you.

ma	se	'pɛn si	al	'mi o	bɛl	'fɔ ko
Ma	**se**	**pensi**	**al**	**mio**	**bel**	**foco,**
But	if	you think	of the	my	beautiful	fire

But if you think about my beautiful passion,

bɛn	sa 'pra i	ke	'so no	i	'ra i	del	'tu o	'tʃiʎ: ʎo	lu ziŋ 'gjer
ben	**saprai,**	**che**	**sono**	**i**	**rai**	**del**	**tuo**	**ciglio**	**lusinghier.**
well	you will know	that	are	the	rays	of the	your	eyebrow	charming

you will well know that [it is from] the rays of your charming eyes.

[37]

'men tre il kɔr si 'stil: la in 'pjan to
Mentre il cor si stilla in pianto
While my heart melts in tears

'men tre	il	kɔr	si 'stil: la	in	'pjan to
Mentre	**il**	**cor**	**si stilla**	**in**	**pianto**
while	the	heart	itself distills	in	weeping

While my heart melts in tears

'lal ma	'mi ze ɾa	in	so 'spi ɾi	la	diʃ: 'ʃɔʎ: ʎe	a 'mor	dal	sen
l'alma	**misera**	**in**	**sospiri**	**la**	**discioglie**	**amor**	**dal**	**sen.**
the soul	sad	in	sighs	[it]	releases	love	from the	breast

love detaches my sad soul from my breast in sighs.

di	ko 'stan tsa	al: 'lor	per	'van to	ko 'zi	'kju do	i	'mjɛ i	re 'spi ɾi
Di	**costanza**	**allor**	**per**	**vanto**	**così**	**chiudo**	**i**	**miei**	**respiri**
of	constancy	then	for	merit	thus	I close off	the	my	breaths

And thus, in the cause of faithfulness, I will stop breathing

se	per 'du to	ɔ	il	'ka ɾo	bɛn
se	**perduto**	**ho**	**il**	**caro**	**ben.**
if	lost	I have	the	dear	dear one

if I have lost my dearly beloved.

[40]

son pri dʒo 'njɛ ɾo
Son prigioniero
I am prisoner

son	pri dʒo 'njɛ ɾo	del	'nu me	ar 'tʃɛ ɾo	e	dʒa	per 'de i	la	li ber 'ta
Son	**prigioniero**	**del**	**nume**	**arciero,**	**e**	**già**	**perdei**	**la**	**libertà.**
I am	prisoner	of the	deity	archer	and	now	I lost	the	freedom

I am prisoner of the archer god *[Cupid]*, and have now lost my freedom.

ma	non	sɔ	'ko me	'del: le	'mi e	'pe ne
Ma	**non**	**so**	**come**	**delle**	**mie**	**pene**
but	not	I know	how	of the	my	sufferings

al	'ka ɾo	'bɛ ne	'kjɛ der	pje 'ta
al	**caro**	**bene**	**chieder**	**pietà.**
to the	dear	dear one	to ask for	pity

But I know not how to ask pity from my dearly beloved for my sufferings.

Manzi [Manzia, Mancia], Luigi (c.1665-after 1708)

Few details about his life and work are known. Probably born in Brescia, his first known dramatic composition, *Paride in Ida*, was composed for the electoral court in Hanover in 1687, and the last extant libretto which names him as composer is that of a performance of his opera *Partenope* in Brescia in 1710.

In 1698 he was composing operas in Naples; beginning in 1701 he was in Düsseldorf, where he was *consigliere della camera* to the Elector Palatine Johann Wilhelm. By 1708 he was back in Italy.

He wrote instrumental music as well as solo vocal pieces, for several of which he also wrote the texts, and at least nine operas.

[35]

ˈa i   ˈkɔ ɾe   o   kru ˈdɛ le
Hai core, o crudele
You have the heart, o cruel one

ʃoʎ: ˈʎe te mi   pje ˈto ze   ˈlal ma   di   ˈkwe sto   sen   ˈfja le   vi ˈta li
Scioglietemi   pietose   l'alma   di   questo   sen,   fiale   vitali
untie me   mercifully   the soul   from   this   breast   vials   vital
Free my soul mercifully from this breast, vials [of deadly liquids],

per ˈke   non   ˈrɛ sti   in   ˈvi ta   u na ˈman te   sker ˈni ta
perché   non   resti   in   vita   un'amante   schernita.
so that   not   may remain   in   life   a lover   scorned
so that a scorned lover may not remain alive.

ˈa i   ˈkɔ ɾe   o   kru ˈdɛ le   per   ˈfar mi   mo ˈrir
Hai   core,   o   crudele,   per   farmi   morir!
you have   heart   o   cruel one   for   to make me   to die
You have the heart, o cruel one, to make me die!

ˈa i   ˈlal mɑ   si   ˈfjɛ ɾa   e   ˈsɔfː frɨ   ke   ˈpe ɾa
Hai   l'alma   sì   fiera   e   soffri   che   pera,
you have   the soul   so   proud   and   you endure   that   may perish

un   sen   ke   pje ˈto zo   tin ˈvi ta   a   dʒo ˈir
un   sen   che   pietoso,   t'invita   a   gioir.
a   breast   which   compassionate   you invites   to   to delight
You have such a proud soul, and you can bear to let perish a breast which compassionately invites you to delight.

> pera = (mod.)
> *perisca*

&

[39]

son   ˈpɔ ve ɾa   don ˈdzɛlː la
Son povera donzella
I am a poor damsel

son   ˈpɔ ve ɾa   don ˈdzɛlː la   ˈal tro   non   hɔ   ke   il   ˈkɔ ɾe
Son   povera   donzella,   altro   non   ho   che   il   core,
I am   poor   damsel   other   not   I have   than   the   heart
I am a poor damsel; I have nothing other than my heart,

e   il   ˈkɔ ɾe   ti   ˈdo no
e   il   core   ti   dono.
and   the   heart   to you   I give
and my heart I give to you.

non   ˈmɛ ɾi to   il   ˈtu o   a ˈmo ɾe   ma   pur   se   ma me ˈɾa i
Non   merito   il   tuo   amore,   ma   pur   se   m'amerai,
not   I merit   the   your   love   but   yet   if   me you will love
I do not merit your love; but yet if you will love me,

alː ˈlor   ve ˈdra i   ˈkwan to   fe ˈde le   ˈi o   ˈso no
allor   vedrai,   quanto   fedele   io   sono.
then   you will see   how   faithful   I   I am
then you will see how faithful I am.

&

from: *Medea tradita* (a Cantata)

[39]

toʎː 'ʎe te mi pje 'to zi

Toglietemi, pietosi

Take away from me, merciful ones

toʎː 'ʎe te mi	pje 'to zi	'lal ma	da	'kwe sto	sen	'fja ti	vi 'ta li
Togletemi,	**pietosi,**	**l'alma**	**da**	**questo**	**sen,**	**fiati**	**vitali,**
take away from me	merciful ones	the soul	from	this	breast	breaths	vital

Take away from this breast, merciful ones, my soul and mortal breath,

per 'ke	non	'rɛ sti	in	'vi ta	u na 'man te	sker 'ni ta
perché	**non**	**resti**	**in**	**vita**	**un'amante**	**schernita.**
so that	not	may not remain	in	life	a lover	scorned

so that a scorned lover may not remain alive.

'tɛsː sa lo	'sɛn tsa	fe	dʒa 'zo ne	iŋ 'gra to	ko 'zi	'duŋ kwe	ri 'fju ti
Tessalo	**senza**	**fé,**	**Giasone**	**ingrato,**	**così**	**dunque**	**rifiuti**
Thessalian	without	faith	Jason	ungrateful	thus	then	you reject

Faithless Thessalian, ungrateful Jason, thus you reject

la	reɲː 'ɲan te	di	'kɔl ko	e	si	'tɔ sto	abː bandː 'do ni	un	'fi do	'pɛtː to
la	**Regnante**	**di**	**Colco,**	**e**	**sì**	**tosto**	**abbandoni**	**d'un**	**fido**	**petto**
the	Queen	of	Colchis	and	so	quickly	you abandon	of a	faithful	breast

i	de zi 'a ti	am 'plɛsː si	'a i	spe 'ran tse	da 'mor	'ko me	fudː 'dʒi te
i	**desiati**	**amplessi,**	**ahi,**	**speranze**	**d'amor,**	**come**	**fuggite!**
the	desired	embraces	alas	hopes	of love	how	you flee

the Queen of Colchis, and so quickly you abandon the desired embraces of a faithful breast?
Alas, hopes of love, how you flee!

'ka ɾe	'dʒɔ je	del	kɔr	'ko me	spa 'ri te
Care	**gioie**	**del**	**cor,**	**come**	**sparite!**
dear	joys	of the	heart	how	you vanish

Dear joys of the heart, how you vanish!

'a i	'kɔ ɾe	o	kru 'dɛ le	per	'far mi	mo 'ɾir
Hai	**core,**	**o**	**crudele,**	**per**	**farmi**	**morir?**
you have	heart	o	cruel one	for	to make me	to die

Have you the heart, o cruel one, to make me die?

'a i	'lal ma	si	'fjɛ ɾa	e	'sofː fri	ke	'pɛ ɾa
Hai	**l'alma**	**sì**	**fiera**	**e**	**soffri**	**che**	**pera**
you have	the soul	so	proud	and	you endure	that	may perish

> *pera (poet.)*
> = *perisca*

un	sen	ke	pje 'to zo	tin 'vi ta	a	dʒo 'ir
un	**sen**	**che**	**pietoso**	**t'invita**	**a**	**gioir?**
a	breast	which	compassionate	you invites	to	to delight

Have you such a proud soul, and can you bear to let perish a breast which compassionately invites you to delight?

𝒢ℒ: **Colco, Giasone, Tessalo**

[12, 39]

'vɔʎː ʎo 'far ti 'di ɾe il 've ro

Voglio farti dire il vero

I want to make you tell the truth

'vɔʎː ʎo	'far ti	'di ɾe	il	've ɾo	men tsoɲː	'ɲje ɾo	'korː ro	'vo lo	al	'nwɔ vo	a 'mor
Voglio	**farti**	**dire**	**il**	**vero,**	**menzogniero,**		**corro,**	**volo**	**al**	**nuovo**	**amor.**
I want	to make you	to tell	the	truth	liar		I run	I fly	to the	new	love

I want to make you tell the truth, liar; I am running, flying to my new love.

> *menzogniero = (mod.) menzognero*

son	dʒa	'pre za	'so no	atː 'tʃe za	da	kwel	krin	da	kwelː lar 'dor
Son	**già**	**presa,**	**sono**	**accesa**	**da**	**quel**	**crin**	**da**	**quell'ardor.**
I am	already	caught	I am	on fire	from	that	head of hair	from	that ardor

I am already caught; I am on fire from those locks, from that ardor.

❋ *Manzolo, Domenico (fl.1623-1639)*

He was in the service of the city of Bologna, and his name appears on a list of professional singers employed by the Anziani and Confaloniero families in Bologna in 1639.

As a composer Manzolo is known only by his book of *Canzonette*: forty-one songs, mostly secular, and mostly for solo voice and continuo, published in Venice in 1623.

---

[43]

se pje 'ta de in te non 'trɔ vi
Se pietade in te non trovi
If you do not find pity in yourself

se	pje 'ta de	in	te	non	'trɔ vi	'bɛlː la	e	'fje ɾa
Se	**pietade**	**in**	**te**	**non**	**trovi,**	**bella**	**e**	**fiera,**
if	pity	in	yourself	not	you find	beautiful one	and	proud

If you do not find pity in yourself, beautiful and proud one –

> *pietade = (mod.) pietà*

sal	'mi o	'pjan to	non	ti	'mwɔ vi	'kru de	al 'tɛ ɾa
s'al	**mio**	**pianto**	**non**	**ti**	**muovi,**	**crud'e**	**altera,**
if at the	my	weeping	not	you	are moved	harsh and	haughty

if, harsh and haughty, you are not moved by my tears,

ke	spe 'ɾar	pɔsː 'si o	dʒamː 'ma i	da	'two i	'ra i
che	**sperar**	**poss'io**	**giammai**	**da**	**tuoi**	**rai?**
what	to hope	am able I	ever	from	your	rays

what can I ever hope from your glances?

'sɛn tsa	'spɛ me	non	sanː 'ni da	'en tro	il	'kɔ ɾe
Senza	**speme**	**non**	**s'annida**	**entro**	**il**	**core,**
without	hope	not	itself nests	within	the	heart

> *speme (lit.) = speranza*

o	di 'vjɛn	'tɔ sto	o mi 'tʃi da	'em pjo	a 'mo ɾe
o	**divien**	**tosto**	**omicida,**	**empio**	**Amore;**
or	becomes	quickly	murderous	cruel	Love

Without hope, cruel Love will not nest in the heart or quickly become murderous;

'duŋ kwe	'prɛ mjo	a	me	si 'sɛr ba	'mɔr te	a 'tʃɛr ba
dunque	**premio**	**a**	**me**	**si serba**	**morte**	**acerba.**
therefore	reward	to	me	remains	death	bitter

therefore, bitter death remains my reward.

GL: **Amore**

Marini, Biagio (1594-1663)

Composer and violinist born into an established family in Brescia, he was a violinist under Monteverdi at S. Marco in Venice in 1615. By 1620 he was back in Brescia as music director of the Accademia degli Erranti; in 1621 he was a violinist at the Farnese court in Parma; between 1623 and 1649 he served the courts at Neuburg and Düsseldorf in Germany and travelled, probably as performer as well as composer. In 1649 he was *maestro di cappella* at S. Maria della Scala in Milan, and in 1652 he was music director of the Accademia della Morte in Ferrara.
Though Marini is best known for his instrumental music, in all the genres of the time, he also composed vocal music of great variety: arias, monodies, canzonettas, and secular concerted madrigals, as well as sacred music.

[27] "Allegrezza del nuovo maggio (Joy at the new May)."

or ke 'lal ba
Or che l'alba
Now that daybreak

or	ke	'lal ba	or	ke	la u 'rɔ ra	'man da 'fwɔr	del: lo 'rjɛn te
Or	**che**	**l'alba**	**or**	**che**	**l'aurora**	**manda fuor**	**dell'oriente**
now	that	the daybreak	now	that	the dawn	sends forth	from the east

Now that daybreak, now that dawn, sends forth from the east

il	bɛl	sol	ke	'tut: to	in 'dɔ ra	kol	'su o	'rad: dʒo	'al mo	e	lu 'tʃɛn te
il	**bel**	**sol**	**che**	**tutto**	**indora**	**col**	**suo**	**raggio**	**almo**	**e**	**lucente**
the	beautiful	sun	which	everything	gilds	with the	its	ray	glorious	and	shining

the beautiful sun, which gilds everything with its glorious and shining rays,

e	kwi	'do ve	tra spa 'rɛn te	ve 'djam	'par ma	far	pas: 'sad: dʒo
e	**qui**	**dove**	**trasparente**	**vediam**	**Parma**	**far**	**passaggio,**
and	here	where	clear	we see	Parma	to make	way

and here where we see Parma becoming clearly visible,

	su	su	kan 'tja mo	'mad: dʒo
Refrain:	**su**	**su**	**cantiamo**	**maggio.**
	come on	come on	let us sing	May

Come on, come on: let's celebrate May.

tra ste	'spon de	gir lan 'da te	di	pret: 'tsjo zi	e	'va ri	'fjo ri
Tra 'ste	**sponde**	**ghirlandate**	**di**	**preziosi**	**e**	**vari**	**fiori**
between these	banks	garlanded	with	precious	and	various	flowers

`'ste = queste`

Between these banks garlanded with precious flowers of various kinds

'kor: ron	'lon de	in: na mo 'ra te	al	'su o	'di o	di	'va gi	a 'mo ri
corron	**l'onde**	**innamorate**	**al**	**suo**	**dio**	**di**	**vaghi**	**amori;**
run	the waves	enamoured	to the	its	god	of	charming	loves

flows the sea, enamoured by its god of charming loves;

ke	fa 'ran: no	i	'nɔ stri	'kɔ ri	aŋ 'kɔr	'lak: kwe	an	da 'mor	'sad: dʒo
che	**faranno**	**i**	**nostri**	**cori**	**s'ancor**	**l'acque**	**han**	**d'amor**	**saggio,**
what	will do	the	our	hearts	if even	the waters	have	of love	sample

what will our hearts do if even the waters fall in love?

aŋ 'kɔr	'no i	in	'ri va	al: 'lon de	de sti	'kja ri	e	'pu ri	ar 'dʒɛn ti
Ancor	**noi**	**in**	**riva**	**all'onde**	**de 'sti**	**chiari**	**e**	**puri**	**argenti**
now	us	on	bank	at the waves	of these	clear	and	pure	silvers

`'sti = questi`

Now, on the bank of this river of clear and pure silver

a skol	'tjam	tra	'kwe ste	'fron de	'deʎ: ʎi	a u 'dʒɛl: li	'dol tʃi	at: 'tʃɛn ti
ascoltiam	**tra**	**queste**	**fronde**	**degli**	**augelli**	**dolci**	**accenti**
let us listen to	among	these	foliages	of the	birds	sweet	accents

augelli (poet.)
= uccelli

let's listen, among the foliage, to the sweet voices of the birds,

'o ve	il	'vɛr no	e	ʎi	'a spri	'vɛn ti	pju	non	'dan: no
ove	**il**	**verno**	**e**	**gli**	**aspri**	**venti**	**più**	**non**	**danno**
where	the	winter	and	the	bitter	winds	more	not	give

verno =
inverno

a	'no i	ol 'trad: dʒo
a	**noi**	**oltraggio.**
to	us	damage

where the winter and the bitter winds do not ravage anymore.

GL: **Parma**

&

[27] "Chiome inanellate della sua pargoletta (His little girl's ringlets)."

rit: tʃu 'tɛl: la par go 'let: ta
Ricciutella pargoletta
Curly-headed little girl

rit: tʃu 'tɛl: la	par go 'let: ta	pju	del	sol	lu 'tʃen te	e	'bɛl: la
Ricciutella	**pargoletta**	**più**	**del**	**sol**	**lucente**	**e**	**bella,**
curly-headed	little girl	more	than the	sun	shining	and	beautiful

Curly-headed little girl, brighter and more beautiful than the sun,

'va ga	si	ma	ri tro 'zet: ta	del	'mi o	kɔr	'vi va	fa 'tʃɛl: la
vaga	**sì**	**ma**	**ritrosetta**	**del**	**mio**	**cor**	**viva**	**facella,**
pretty	yes	but	bashful	of the	my	heart	vivid	torch

pretty, yes, but bashful – vivid torch of my heart,

'sem bri	'rɔ za	ver miʎ: 'ʎet: ta	nel	'tu o	'vi zo	'al ma	don 'dzɛl: la
sembri	**rosa**	**vermiglietta**	**nel**	**tuo**	**viso**	**alma**	**donzella**
you seem	rose	little vermilion	in the	your	face	glorious	damsel

your face is like a little vermilion rose, o glorious damsel,

ma	ti	'mo stri	zdeɲ: ɲo 'zet: ta	rit: tʃu 'tɛl: la	par go 'let: ta
ma	**ti**	**mostri**	**sdegnosetta**	**ricciutella**	**pargoletta.**
but	yourself	you show	disdainful	curly-headed	little girl

but you prove to be disdainful, curly-headed little girl.

rit: tʃu 'tɛl: la	par go 'let: ta	i	'twɔ i	krin	son	'fi li	'dɔ ɾo
Ricciutella	**pargoletta**	**i**	**tuoi**	**crin**	**son**	**fili**	**d'oro,**
curly-headed	little girl	the	your	head of hair[s]	are	threads	of gold

Curly-headed little girl, your locks are threads of gold;

la	'tu a	'bok: ka	ver miʎ: 'ʎet: ta	di	ko 'ɾal: li	ɛ	il	'mi o	te 'zɔ ɾo
la	**tua**	**bocca**	**vermiglietta**	**di**	**coralli**	**è**	**il**	**mio**	**tesoro.**
the	your	mouth	little vermilion	of	corals	is	the	my	treasure

your little vermilion mouth is my treasure trove of corals.

le	'tu e	'lu tʃi	son	sa 'et: te	al	'mi o	kɔr	on 'di o	ne	'mo ɾo
Le	**tue**	**luci**	**son**	**saette**	**al**	**mio**	**cor**	**ond'io**	**ne**	**moro,**
the	your	eyes	are	darts	to the	my	heart	whence I	of them	I die

Your eyes are darts [shot] to my heart, from which I am dying;

la	'tu a	'vi sta	oɲː 'ɲor	mal: 'lɛt: ta	rit: tʃu 'tɛl: la	par go 'let: ta
la	**tua**	**vista**	**ognor**	**m'alletta**	**ricciutella**	**pargoletta.**
the	your	sight	always	me attracts	curly-headed	little girl

the sight of you always attracts me, curly-headed little girl.

rit: tʃu 'tɛl: la	par go 'let: ta	ke	da 'mor	non	'sɛn ti	il	'fɔ ko
Ricciutella	**pargoletta**	**che**	**d'amor**	**non**	**senti**	**il**	**foco**
curly-headed	little girl	who	of love	not	you feel	the	fire

Curly-headed little girl, you who do not feel the fire of love,

ne 'ma i	'dʒun se	'su a	sa 'et: ta	al	'tu o	kɔr	kel	'prɛn di	a	'dʒɔ ko
né mai	**giunse**	**sua**	**saetta**	**al**	**tuo**	**cor**	**ché'l**	**prendi**	**a**	**gioco.**
never	reached	its	dart	at the	your	heart	because it	you take	as	joke

> *né mai =*
> *(mod.)*
> *non mai*

never has its dart reached your heart, because you mock it.

e	non	'te mi	'su a	ven 'det: ta	ne	'swɔ i	'stra i	ne	'ar ko	ne	'fɔ ko
E	**non**	**temi**	**sua**	**vendetta**	**né**	**suoi**	**strai**	**né**	**arco**	**né**	**foco**
and	not	you fear	its	revenge	nor	its	arrows	nor	bow	nor	fire

> *printed "strai"*
> *= strali*

And you are not afraid of its revenge, nor of its [Cupid's] arrows, bow, or fire;

ma	zdeɲ 'ɲo za	'fud: dʒi	in 'fret: ta	rit: tʃu 'tɛl: la	par go 'let: ta
ma	**sdegnosa**	**fuggi**	**in fretta**	**ricciutella**	**pargoletta.**
but	disdainful	you flee	in haste	curly-headed	little girl

but, disdainful, you flee in haste, curly-headed little girl.

rit: tʃu 'tɛl: la	par go 'let: ta	'fud: dʒi	pur	'kwan to	tu	'sa i
Ricciutella	**pargoletta**	**fuggi**	**pur**	**quanto**	**tu**	**sai**
curly-headed	little girl	you flee	then	as much as	you	you know

Curly-headed little girl, you flee; flee, then, as much as you know how,

ke	da 'mor	'la spra	sa 'et: ta	nel	'tu o	'pɛt: to	al 'fin	a 'vra i
ché	**d'amor**	**l'aspra**	**saetta**	**nel**	**tuo**	**petto**	**alfin**	**avrai.**
because	of love	the sharp	dart	in the	your	breast	finally	you will have

> *in the repeat:*
> *alfine [al 'fi ne]*
> *= alfin*

because, in the end, you will have the sharp dart of love in your breast.

e	sa 'ra	per	'mi a	ven 'det: ta	kel	'su o	'fɔ ko	pro ve 'ra i
E	**sarà**	**per**	**mia**	**vendetta**	**che'l**	**suo**	**foco**	**proverai**
and	will be	for	my	vengeance	that the	its	fire	you will experience

And my vengeance will be that you will feel its fire

ne	sa 'ra i	pju	ri tro 'zet: ta	rit: tʃu 'tɛl: la	par go 'let: ta
né	**sarai**	**più**	**ritrosetta**	**ricciutella**	**pargoletta.**
nor	you will be	more	bashful	curly-headed	little girl

and will no longer be bashful, curly-headed little girl.

❦

[27]

sem pli 'tʃet: te ver dʒi 'nɛl: le
Semplicette verginelle
Innocent little virgins

sem pli 'tʃet: te	ver dʒi 'nɛl: le	ke	dʒa 'ma i	'lar te	vi	djɛ
Semplicette	**verginelle**	**che**	**già mai**	**l'arte**	**vi**	**diè**
simple little	little virgins	who	ever	the art	to you	gave

Innocent little virgins, whoever gave you the skill

di   fe 'rir   'kwan to   pju   im 'bɛl: le   kɔr   ar 'ma to   u 'ni to   a   fe
di   ferir   quanto   più   imbelle   cor   armato   unito   a   fé,
of   to wound   how much   most   unwarlike   heart   armed   united   by   faith
to wound such an unwarlike, faithful heart

ke   da   'vo i   'lun dʒi   sen 'va   ne   de 'zi a   'vɔ stra   bel 'ta
che   da   voi   lungi   sen va   né   desia   vostra   beltà.
that   from   you   far   goes away   nor   desires   your   beauty
that goes far away from you and does not desire your beauty.

ki   dʒi 'rar   'kwe i   'lu tʃi 'dɔk: ki   e   a   'no i   'lal me   fe 'rir
Chi   girar   quei   lucid'occhi   e   a   noi   l'alme   ferir
who   to turn   those   shining eyes   and   to   us   the souls   to wound
Who [gave you the skill] to turn those shining eyes and wound our souls,

'po i   kja 'mar ne   in 'fi di   e   'ʃɔk: ki   e   ki   'lan gwe   aŋ 'kor   sker 'nir
poi   chiamarne   infidi   e   sciocchi,   e   chi   langue   ancor   schernir
then   to call us   unfaithful   and   foolish   and   who   languishes   even   to deride
[and] then to call us unfaithful and foolish, and even to deride the languishing,

ki   se 'gwir   ri 'tro zo   kɔr   e   fud: 'dʒir   ki   per   'vo i   mwɔr
chi   seguir   ritroso   cor   e   fuggir   chi   per   voi   muor.
who   to follow   recalcitrant   heart   and   to flee   he who   for   you   dies
to pursue a recalcitrant heart, and to flee from the one who is dying for you.

'for se   a 'mor   ko 'zi   vin 'seɲ: ɲa   dar   al 'tru i   'frɔ de   per   se
Forse   amor   così   v'insegna   dar   altrui   frode   per   sé
perhaps   love   thus   you teaches   to give   others'   frauds   for   itself
Perhaps love, for its own sake, teaches you others' deceptions,

e   per   'vi ta   'mɔr te   in 'deɲ: ɲa   a   ke   a 'mor   'ta le   non   ɛ
e   per   vita   morte   indegna   ah   che   amor   tale   non   è
and   for   life   death   undeserved   ah   [that]   love   such   not   is
and to give in exchange for life an undeserved death. Ah, love is not like that;

ma   'vo i   'sjɛ te   ke   'ar te   tal   in ven 'ta te   'doɲ: ɲi   mal
ma   voi   siete   che   arte   tal   inventate   d'ogni   mal.
but   you   are   that   art   such   you invent   of every   evil
but you are such that you invent the skill of every evil.

dɛ   kan 'dʒa te   sem pli 'tʃet: te   'kwe sto   'vɔ stro   in 'sa no   stil
Deh   cangiate   semplicette   questo   vostro   insano   stil.
pray   change   simple little ones   this   your   insane   style
Oh please change, innocent little ones, these insane ways of yours.

non   fud: 'dʒi te   ri tro 'zet: te   'al ma   ar 'dɛn te   a 'man te   u 'mil
Non   fuggite   ritrosette   alma   ardente   amante   umil,
not   flee   little ricalcitrant ones   soul   ardent   lover   humble
Do not, little recalcitrant ones, flee an ardent soul, a humble lover,

ke   dʒa   'vo i   kol   'vɔ stro   a 'mor   le   in vo 'la ste   'ʃɔl to   il   kɔr
ché   già   voi   col   vostro   amor   le   involaste   sciolto   il   cor.
because   already   you   with the   your   love   from them   you stole   freed   the   heart
because you have already, with your love, stolen from him *[the soul and lover]* his free heart.

Matteis, Nicola (?-c.1700)

Italian composer, violinist, guitarist, and teacher, he apparently settled in London around 1670. While his circumstances were poor in early years, he was noticed for his violin playing in London in 1674 and soon earned a reputation for virtuosity. He was also a master on the five-course guitar.

An important figure in the development of violin playing in England, he published four books of violin pieces: airs, preludes, fugues, allemandes, etc.

He also published a collection of songs, in two volumes, which included some airs for violin and bass; and he may have been the composer of a 1696 St. Cecelia Day Ode performed in London and Oxford, the music for which is now lost.

He authored *The False Consonances of Music*, an important treatise on thorough-bass realization for the guitar.

[1, 2, 16, 46]

'ka ɾo 'vol to pal: li 'det: to
Caro volto pallidetto
Dear little pale face

'ka 'ɾo	'vol to	pal: li 'det: to	'dol tʃe	'fjam: ma	del	'mi o	kɔr
Caro	**volto**	**pallidetto,**	**dolce**	**fiamma**	**del**	**mio**	**cor!**
dear	face	little pale	sweet	flame	of the	my	heart

Dear little pale face, sweet flame of my heart!

a	si	'tɛ ne ɾo	pal: 'lor	'tʃɛ da	pur	'tin ta	di	'skɔr no	'lal ba	al: 'lor
A	**sì**	**tenero**	**pallor**	**ceda**	**pur**	**tinta**	**di**	**scorno**	**l'alba**	**allor,**
to	such	delicate	pallor	may yield	indeed	tinged	with	humiliation	the dawn	then

To such delicate pallor may the dawn then indeed concede, tinged with humiliation –

ke	ne	'a pre	il	'dʒor no	ke	non	a	pju	bɛl	ko 'lor
che	**ne**	**apre**	**il**	**giorno,**	**che**	**non**	**ha**	**più**	**bel**	**color.**
which	to us	opens	the	day	which	not	has	more	beautiful	color

[the dawn] which opens up the day for us, [and] which has not a more beautiful color.

'va go	'vi zo	in	'ku i	per 'vet: tso	'laŋ gwe	a 'mor	ke	'mar de	il	sen
Vago	**viso,**	**in**	**cui**	**per vezzo**	**langue**	**amor,**	**che**	**m'arde**	**il**	**sen!**
lovely	face	in	which	by force of habit	languishes	love	that	me burns	the	breast

Lovely face, in which love habitually languishes [and] which inflames my breast,

a	si	'pla tʃi do	ba 'len	'mi ɾo	la	su	'lal ta	'mɔ le	o sku 'ɾar si	i	'ra i
A	**sì**	**placido**	**balen**	**miro**	**là**	**su**	**l'alta**	**mole**	**oscurarsi**	**i**	**rai**
at	such	peaceful	glow	I see	there	upon	the high	mass	to eclipse	the	rays

del	'so le	e	di	'tʃin tsja	il	bɛl	se 'ren
del	**sole**	**e**	**di**	**Cinzia**	**il**	**bel**	**seren.**
of the	sun	and	of	Cynthia	the	beautiful	serenity

> *the printed "Cintia"*
> *= (mod.) Cinzia*

I see in such a peaceful sunset the rays of the sun disappear behind the tall mountain and the beautiful light of the moon [Cynthia] appear.

GL: **Cinzia**

Mazzaferrata, Giovanni Battista (?-1691)

Composer, organist, and teacher, he was *maestro di cappella* of the Accademia della Morte in Ferrara by at least 1668. In the early 1680's it is probable that he moved to Tuscany, as an oratorio of his was performed in Siena in 1684. At some point he returned to Ferrara, where he died.

He wrote sonatas for two violins and continuo of interest, foreshadowing early classical style, and is otherwise known as a composer of both sacred and secular music. For solo voice his *Primo libro delle cantate da camera* (1673), which included "Presto io m'innamoro," was his major contribution.

[21, 24, 27]

'prɛ sto 'i o min: na 'mo ɾo
Presto io m'innamoro
I fall in love easily

'prɛ sto	'i o	min: na 'mo ɾo	ma	pju	'prɛ sto	il	kɔr	nɛ	ʃɔl to
Presto	**io**	**m'innamoro,**	**ma**	**più**	**presto**	**il**	**cor**	**n'è**	**sciolto!**
easily	I	I fall in love	but	more	easily	the	heart	of it is	freed

I fall in love easily; but more easily is my heart freed from it!

ri ve 'ri sko	'ɔd: dʒi	un	bɛl	'vol to	ma	di 'man	pju	non	la 'do ɾo
Riverisco	**oggi**	**un**	**bel**	**volto,**	**ma**	**diman**	**più**	**non**	**l'adoro!**
I revere	today	a	beautiful	face	but	tomorrow	more	not	it I adore

Today I revere a beautiful face, but tomorrow I no longer adore it!

> vars.: *bell volto,*
> *bello volto*
> = *bel volto*

ɛ	un	ef: 'fi me ɾo	e	ka 'dɛn te	kwel: la 'mor	ke	ma	pja 'ga to
È	**un**	**effimero**	**e**	**cadente**	**quell'amor**	**che**	**m'ha**	**piagato,**
is	an	ephemeral thing	and	ruined thing	that love	which	me has	wounded

That love which has wounded me is an ephemeral and ruinous thing;

'ɔd: dʒi	'so no	'ɛ gro	e	laŋ 'gwen te	ma	di 'man	son	ri sa 'na to
oggi	**sono**	**egro**	**e**	**languente,**	**ma**	**diman**	**son**	**risanato!**
today	I am	ill	and	languishing	but	tomorrow	I am	cured

today I am ill and languishing, but tomorrow I am cured!

Mazzocchi, Domenico (1592-1665)

Born in Civita Castellana, he was ordained a priest and, by 1619, was made a Doctor of Laws in Rome. In 1621 he entered the service of Cardinal Ippolito Aldobrandini, whose brother Giovanni Giorgio commissioned his only surviving opera, *La catena d'Adone*. After the death of the Cardinal, Mazzocchi remained in the service of the Cardinal's niece and heir, Olimpia Aldobrandini Borghese, receiving support from the powerful Borghese family. Pope Urban VIII (Maffeo Barberini) was a patron, as was the next pope, Innocent X (Giambattista Pamphili).

Besides the surviving opera, he wrote at least one other opera, madrigals for four to eight voices, seven Latin oratorios, motets, cantatas, dramatic dialogues, sonnets, and – his last collection of vocal music – *Musiche sacre, e morali (1640)*, from a modern edition of which almost all of the texts included here below are copied.

[71] "Nella Santissima Natività di N.S. (On the most holy birth of our Lord)."   *Claudio Achillini*

a tra ve 'stir si
A travestirsi
To invest himself

a	tra ve ˈstir si	di	pas: ˈsi bil	ˈve lo	e	a	pa ˈgar	ˈdel: le	ˈmi e	ˈkol pe	il	ˈfi o
A	**travestirsi**	**di**	**passibil**	**velo**	**e**	**a**	**pagar**	**delle**	**mie**	**colpe**	**il**	**fio,**
to	to invest himself	of	suffering	veil	and	to	to pay	of the	my	sins	the	penalty

To invest himself with a mortal veil [of suffering], and to pay the price for my sins,

ˈpas: sa	per ˈke	dal	ˈfaŋ go	ˈi o	ˈpas: si	in	ˈdi o
passa,	**perché**	**dal**	**fango**	**io**	**passi**	**in**	**Dio**
passes	so that	from the	mire	I	may pass	to	God

da	le	ˈstel: le	ˈal: la	ˈstal: la	il	re	del	ˈtʃɛ lo
da	**le**	**stelle**	**alla**	**stalla**	**il**	**Re**	**del**	**Cielo.**
from	the	stars	to the	stable	the	King	of the	Heaven

> da le =
> (mod.) dalle

the King of Heaven goes from the stars to the stable, so that I may pass from the mire to God.

ˈkwi vi	su	ˈfred: di	ˈstek: ki	ˈar de	di	ˈdzɛ lo	nel	pju	ˈfit: to	ri ˈgo ɾe
Quivi	**su**	**freddi**	**stecchi**	**arde**	**di**	**zelo**	**nel**	**più**	**fitto**	**rigore,**
therein	on	cold	twigs	burns	with	zeal	in the	most	fixed	severity

e	nel	pju	ˈri o	e	se non ˈkwan do	ˈe i	ˈsɛn te	un	ˈfja to	ˈpi o
e	**nel**	**più**	**rio,**	**e**	**se non quando**	**ei**	**sente**	**un**	**fiato**	**pio**
and	in the	most	cruel	and	unless	he	feels	a	breath	pious

> rio (lit.)
> = reo

There, upon cold twigs [straw], he burns with zeal in the most cruel, severe conditions; and unless he hears a pious breath,

> I've changed the printed "quanto" to
> "quando" in order to make more sense
> of the context, thus guessing a copying error.

fra	ʎin ˈtʃen di	da ˈmor	ˈtre ma	di	ˈdʒɛ lo
fra	**gl'incendi**	**d'amor**	**trema**	**di**	**gielo.**
among	the fires	of love	trembles	with	ice

> gielo =
> (mod.) gelo

he trembles with cold among the fires of [worldly] love.

u ˈdi te	o	ˈter: ra	o	tʃɛl	le	ˈmi e	pa ˈɾo le	per	fud: ˈdʒir	la	pju	ˈkru da
Udite	**o**	**terra,**	**o**	**ciel,**	**le**	**mie**	**parole.**	**Per**	**fuggir**	**la**	**più**	**cruda**
hear	o	earth	o	heaven	the	my	words	for	to flee	the	most	harsh

Hear, o earth, o heaven, my words. To escape the harshest

ˈi ɾa	del	ˈvɛr no	al	re spi ˈɾar	dun	ˈbu e	si ˈskal da	il	ˈso le
ira	**del**	**verno**	**al**	**respirar**	**d'un**	**bue**	**si scalda**	**il**	**Sole.**
wrath	of the	winter	at the	breathing	of an	ox	itself warms	the	Sun

wrath of winter, the Sun [Jesus] warms itself [himself] at the breathing of an ox.

ma	per ke	ˈvwɔ le	im po ve ˈɾir	lin ˈfɛr no	ˈpas: sa
Ma	**per che**	**vuole**	**impoverir**	**l'Inferno,**	**passa,**
but	because	wants	impoverish	the Hell	pass

> per che =
> (mod.) perché

But because he wants to impoverish Hell, he passes,

e	la	ˈli bra	ˈsu a	tok: ˈkar	non	ˈvwɔ le
e	**la**	**Libra**	**sua**	**toccar**	**non**	**vuole,**
and	the	Libra	her	to touch	not	wants

ˈdal: la	ˈver dʒi ne	al	ˈta u ɾo	il	ˈso le	e ˈter no
dalla	**Vergine**	**al**	**Tauro**	**il**	**Sole**	**eterno.**
from the	Virgo	to the	Taurus	the	Sun	eternal

> tauro =
> (mod.)
> toro

the eternal Sun, between Virgo and Taurus, but does not want to touch [without touching] Libra.

> To help understand this [difficult] text: Christmas (the birth of Jesus) comes between Virgo (the Virgin:
> late August) and Taurus (the Bull: late April); the sun enters Libra at the end of September.

GL: Libra, Tauro, Vergine

☙

[71] "Moralità presa dall'Aurora (The moral of Dawn)."   *Francesco Carducci*

kon gir 'lan da di 'rɔ ze
Con ghirlanda di rose
Garlanded with roses

kon	gir 'lan da	di	'rɔ ze	e 'da u re o	am: 'man to	da	la	'fɔʎ: ʎa	dʒem: 'ma ta
Con	**ghirlanda**	**di**	**rose,**	**ed aureo**	**ammanto**	**da**	**la**	**foglia**	**gemmata**
with	garland	of	roses	and golden	cloaked	by	the	foliage	bejeweled

'ɛʃ: ʃe	la u 'rɔ ra	ve	'ko me	il	'va go	tʃɛl	di	'ra i	sin 'dɔ ra
esce	**l'Aurora,**	**vè**	**come**	**il**	**vago**	**ciel**	**di**	**rai**	**s'indora,**
appears	the Dawn	look	how	the	lovely	sky	with	rays	itself gilds

> *vè: from "vedi"*
> *(= look!)*

Garlanded with roses, bejeweled by the foliage, and cloaked in gold, Dawn appears;
see how the lovely sky gilds itself with rays;

ve	'ko me	'lom bra	si di 'le gwa	in 'tan to
vè	**come**	**l'ombra**	**si dilegua**	**intanto.**
look	how	the dark	vanishes	meanwhile

see how the darkness, meanwhile, vanishes.

'pjan dʒe	la	'bɛl: la	ma	son	'pɛr le	il	'pjan to
Piange	**la**	**bella,**	**ma**	**son**	**perle**	**il**	**pianto,**
weeps	the	beautiful one	but	are	pearls	the	weeping

The beautiful one *[Dawn]* weeps, but her tears are pearls

'on de	il	'pra to	ne	'ri de	e	se nin 'fjo ra
onde	**il**	**prato**	**ne**	**ride,**	**e**	**se n'infiora.**
whence	the	meadow	of them	smiles	and	itself with them adorns

that make the meadow smile and with which it adorns itself.

per	le	kam 'paɲ: ɲe	in su per 'biʃ: ʃe	'flɔ ra
Per	**le**	**campagne**	**insuperbisce**	**Flora,**
through	the	countrysides	becomes superb	Flora

Throughout the countryside Flora grows in beauty,

ke	di	'dʒɛm: me	o do 'ro ze	a	'kar ko	il	'man to
che	**di**	**gemme**	**odorose**	**ha**	**carco**	**il**	**manto.**
who	with	jewels	fragrant	has	loaded	the	mantle

> *carco =*
> *(mod.) carico*

and her mantle is covered with fragrant buds.

ma	ke	'tɔ sto	'de i	fjor	'lɔ stro	naʃ: 'ʃen te	im pal: li 'diʃ: ʃe
Ma	**che?**	**tosto**	**dei**	**fior**	**l'ostro**	**nascente**	**impallidisce,**
But	what	before long	of the	flowers	the purple	dawning	pales

What now? Before long the dawning purple of the flowers pales;

a 'pe na	uʃ: 'ʃi	lal 'bo re	ke	se ne 'vo la	il	'dʒor no	al: lot: tʃi 'dɛn te
a pena	**uscì**	**l'albore,**	**che**	**se ne vola**	**il**	**giorno**	**all'occidente.**
scarcely	came out	the dawn	that	itself from it flies	the	day	to the west

scarcely has the dawn come when the day flies away into the west.

> *a pena (lit.) = appena*

ko 'zi	il	bɛn	di	kwa 'dʒu	'maŋ ka	kwal	'fjo re
Così	**il**	**ben**	**di**	**qua giù**	**manca**	**qual**	**fiore,**
thus	the	happiness	of	here below	fails	like a	flower

> *qua giù (lit.)*
> *= quaggiù*

Thus does the happiness of the world here below wilt like a flower;

'brɛ ve   'lu tʃe   e   la   'dʒɔ ja   e   di re 'pɛn te
breve   **luce**   **e**   **la**   **gioia,**   **e**   **di repente**
brief   light   and   the   joy   and   suddenly
joy is [like] a brief day, and suddenly

'pɔr ta   a dun   'ljɛ to   di   'nɔt: te   il   do 'lo ɾe
porta   **ad un**   **lieto**   **dì,**   **notte**   **il**   **dolore.**
brings   to a   happy   day   night   the   sorrow
night brings sorrow to a happy day.

GL: **Aurora, Flora**

❮

[71] "Contro la gelosia (Against jealousy)."   *Giovanni Della Casa*

'ku ɾa ke di ti 'mor
Cura, che di timor
Worry, who with fear

'ku ɾa ke di ti 'mor ti 'nu tri e 'kreʃ: ʃi e pju te 'mɛn do mad: 'dʒor
Cura, **che** **di** **timor** **ti** **nutri,** **e** **cresci** **e** **più** **temendo** **maggior**
worry who with fear yourself you feed and you grow and more fearing greater

'fɔr tsa ak: 'kwi sti e 'men tre kon la 'fjam: ma il 'dʒɛ lo 'meʃ: ʃi
forza **acquisti,** **e** **mentre** **con** **la** **fiamma** **il** **gelo** **mesci,**
power you gain and while with the flame the ice you mix
Worry, you who feed yourself with fear and grow in power with more fearing, mixing fire and ice,

'tut: to il 'reɲ: ɲo da 'mor 'tur bi e kon 'tri sti
tutto **il** **regno** **d'Amor** **turbi,** **e** **contristi.**
all the kingdom of Love you disturb and you sadden
you disturb and sadden the entire kingdom of Love.

po i 'ke in 'brɛ ve 'o ɾa 'en tro il 'mi o 'dol tʃe 'a i 'mi sti
Poiché **in** **breve** **ora** **entro** **il** **mio** **dolce** **hai** **misti**
since in short hour within the my sweet you have mixed
Since you have, within a short time, mingled with my sweet feelings

'tut: ti ʎi a 'ma ɾi 'twɔ i dal 'mi o kɔr 'ɛʃ: ʃi 'tor na a ko 'tʃi to
tutti **gli** **amari** **tuoi** **dal** **mio** **cor** **esci,** **torna** **a** **Cocito**
all the bitternesses your from the my heart leave return to Cocytus
all your bitternesses, leave my heart; return to Cocytus,

a i la gri 'mo zi e 'tri sti 'cam pi din 'fɛr no 'i vi a te 'stes: sa iŋ 'kreʃ: ʃi
a i **lagrimosi** **e** **tristi** **campi** **d'inferno,** **ivi** **a** **te** **stessa** **incresci.**
to the tearful and sad fields of hell there to you yourself be disagreeable
to the tearful and sad fields of hell; there, be disagreeable to yourself.

> *lagrimosi = (mod.) lacrimosi*

'i vi 'sɛn tsa ri 'pɔ zo i 'dʒor ni 'me na 'sɛn tsa 'son: no le 'nɔt: ti
Ivi **senza** **riposo** **i** **giorni** **mena** **senza** **sonno** **le** **notti,**
there without rest the days lead without sleep the nights
There, lead your days without repose, your nights without sleep;

'i vi ti 'dwɔ li non men di 'dub: bja ke di 'tʃɛr ta 'pe na
ivi **ti duoli** **non** **men** **di** **dubbia,** **che** **di** **certa** **pena.**
there suffer not less of doubt than of certain pain
there, suffer no less from doubt than from certain pain.

> *dubbia:*
> *from "dubbiare"=*
> *(mod.) "dubitare"*

'vat: te ne a ke pju 'fɛ ɾa ke non 'swɔ li
Vattene, **ah** **che** **più** **fera,** **che** **non** **suoli**
go away ah [that] more fierce than not you are used to
Go away! Ah, more fierce than usual,

> *fera =
> (mod.)
> fiera*

sel 'tu o ve 'nen mɛ 'kor so in 'oɲː ɲi 've na
se'l **tuo** **venen** **m'è** **corso** **in** **ogni** **vena,**
as the your poison to me has run in every vein
as your poison has run through my every vein,

> *venen[o] =
> (mod.)
> velen[o]*

kon 'nwɔ ve 'lar ve a me ri 'tor ni e 'vo li
con **nuove** **larve** **a** **me** **ritorni** **e** **voli?**
with new deceptive appearances to me you return and you fly
you fly and return to me with new phantoms?

GL: **Amor, Cocito**

❧

[71] "Ottave per la Natività di N.S. (Ottavas [stanzas with a specific rhyme pattern] for the birth of our Lord)."
Giulio Rospigliosi

'dʒun to 'alː la 'ku na
Giunto alla cuna
Arrived at the cradle

'dʒun to 'alː la 'ku na 'o ve al 'su o 'fiʎː ʎo 'vi vo 'ledː dʒi di 'mɔr te
Giunto **alla** **cuna,** **ove** **al** **suo** **figlio** **vivo** **leggi** **di** **morte**
arrived at the cradle where at the his son living laws of death

> *cuna (lit.)
> = culla*

il 'somː mo re pre 'skrisː se kon 'fu zo un pa sto 'relː lo
il **sommo** **Re** **prescrisse,** **confuso** **un** **pastorello,**
the supreme king prescribed confused a shepherd
A shepherd, confused, arrived at the cradle where the supreme King prescribed the laws of death to his living son

e 'kwa zi 'pri vo di mo vi 'men to a dʒe 'zu ʎi 'ɔkː ki afː 'fisː se
e **quasi** **privo** **di** **movimento,** **a** **Giesù** **gli** **occhi** **affisse.**
and almost without of movement to Jesus the eyes fixed
and, almost motionless, fixed his eyes upon Jesus.

> *Giesù =
> (mod.) Gesù*

e dafː 'fɛtː to zgor 'gan do un 'lar go 'ri vo in un de 'vɔ to o i 'mɛ
E **d'affetto** **sgorgando** **un** **largo** **rivo,** **in** **un** **devoto,** **ohimè,**
and of affection pouring out a large stream in a devout alas
And, pouring out a great and devout stream of affection, alas,

pro 'rupː pe e 'disː se o 'mi o 'dol tʃe siɲ 'ɲor pje 'to zo 'tan to
proruppe, **e** **disse,** **o** **mio** **dolce** **Signor** **pietoso** **tanto,**
burst out and said o my sweet Lord merciful so much
burst out and said: o my sweet and greatly merciful Lord,

ke per far 'ljɛ to il 'mon do or 'vɛr si il 'pjan to
che **per** **far** **lieto** **il** **mondo** **or** **versi** **il** **pianto,**
who for to make happy the world now you shed the tear
you who will now shed tears to make the world happy,

tu	ʎi	ˈstra li	pun ˈdʒɛn ti	e	le	vi ˈva tʃi	ˈfjam: me	dal	tʃɛl	ne	ˈpɔr ti
tu	**gli**	**strali**	**pungenti,**	**e**	**le**	**vivaci**	**fiamme**	**dal**	**ciel**	**ne**	**porti,**
you	the	arrows	sharp	and	the	vivid	flames	from the	heaven	to us	you bring

you bring the sharp arrows and the vivid flames to us from heaven,

e ˈtɛr no	a ˈmo ɾe	e	bɛn	sɛn ˈti o	kon	di zu ˈza te	ˈfa tʃi
eterno	**amore,**	**e**	**ben**	**sent'io**	**con**	**disusate**	**faci**
eternal	love	and	well	feel I	with	unused	torches

tra	kwe ˈstom bre	dʒe ˈla te	ˈar der mil	ˈkɔ ɾe
tra	**quest'ombre**	**gelate**	**arderm'il**	**core.**
among	these shadows	cold	to burn me the	heart

eternal love, and well do I feel my heart burning in these cold shadows with fire to which it is unaccustomed.

dɛ	ˈprɛn di	i	ˈmjɛ i	so ˈspi ɾi	e	ˈkwe sti	ˈba tʃi	ˈprɛn di
Deh	**prendi**	**i**	**miei**	**sospiri,**	**e**	**questi**	**baci**	**prendi,**
pray	take	the	my	sighs	and	these	kisses	take

Please take my sighs and these kisses,

ˈki o	ˈbaɲ: ɲo	di	pje ˈto ze	u ˈmo ɾe	e	ˈsi o	per	te
ch'io	**bagno**	**di**	**pietose**	**umore,**	**e**	**s'io**	**per**	**te**
that I	I bathe	with	compassionate	humor	and	if I	for	you

humor: one of the essential fluids in the constitution of the body

which I bathe with compassionate tears; and if for you

dʒa	mi di ˈstrug: go	al ˈme no	ˈrɛ sta	a ˈmor	ˈsan to	a da bi ˈtar mi	in	ˈse no
già	**mi distruggo**	**almeno**	**resta**	**amor**	**santo**	**ad abitarmi**	**in**	**seno.**
now	I dissolve	at least	remains	love	holy	[to] to live in me	in	breast

I now melt, at least holy love remains in my breast.

ˈrɛ sta	a ˈmor	ˈsan to	a	rav: vi ˈvar mi	e	ˈdʒi ra	ʎi	ˈɔk: ki	di	ˈtu a	kle ˈmɛn tsa
Resta	**amor**	**santo**	**a**	**ravvivarmi,**	**e**	**gira**	**gli**	**occhi**	**di**	**tua**	**clemenza**
remain	love	holy	to	to revive me	and	turn	the	eyes	of	your	clemency

Stay, holy love, and revive me, and turn the eyes of your clemency

ˈal: le	ˈmi e	ˈspɔʎ: ʎe	er: ˈra i	nol	ˈne go	er: ˈra i	ma	ˈtʃes: si	ˈli ɾa
alle	**mie**	**spoglie.**	**Errai,**	**no'l**	**nego,**	**errai,**	**ma**	**cessi**	**l'ira,**
to the	my	mortal remains	I erred	not it	I deny	I erred	but	may cease	the wrath

ˈken tro	a	tʃe ˈlɛ ste	kɔr	mal	si rak: ˈkɔʎ: ʎe	per ˈdo na	il	ˈmi o	fal: ˈlir
ch'entro	**a**	**celeste**	**cor**	**mal**	**si raccoglie.**	**Perdona**	**il**	**mio**	**fallir,**
that within	at	celestial	heart	wrongly	gathers	forgive	the	my	failing

to my mortal remains. I erred – I do not deny it – I erred; but let the wrath, which hardly can be contained in a celestial heart, cease. Forgive my failings;

ke	sol	re ˈspi ɾa	in	ˈkwe sta	ˈspɛ me	il	kɔr	fra	le	ˈmi e	ˈdɔʎ: ʎe
ché	**sol**	**respira**	**in**	**questa**	**speme**	**il**	**cor**	**fra**	**le**	**mie**	**doglie,**
because	only	breaths	in	this	hope	the	heart	among	the	my	sorrows

speme (lit.) = speranza

for my heart breaths only in this hope, among my sorrows,

fa	ˈki o	ˈmɔ ɾa	per	te	ne	ti	ˈsi a	ˈnɔ ja
fa	**ch'io**	**mora**	**per**	**te**	**né**	**ti**	**sia**	**noia,**
make	that I	I may die	for	you	nor	to you	it may be	annoyance

mora = muoia

let me die for you, and be it no trouble to you

ke	se	ˈlun dʒi	a	te	ˈvis: si	or	per	te	ˈmɔ ja
che	**se**	**lungi**	**a**	**te**	**vissi,**	**or**	**per**	**te**	**moia.**
that	if	far	from you	I lived	now	for	you	I may die	

moia = muoia

that, although I lived far from you, now I may die for you.

☙

[71] "Sonetto – Consideratione nella morte di Christo (Reflection on the death of Christ)."

Abbate Saracini

o ˈma i le ˈlu tʃi erː ˈran ti
Omai le luci erranti
Now the errant eyes

o ˈma i	le	ˈlu tʃi	erː ˈran ti	ˈa ni ma	ˈdʒi ɾa	al	ˈtu o	fatː ˈto ɾe
Omai	**le**	**luci**	**erranti**	**anima**	**gira**	**al**	**tuo**	**fattore,**
now	the	eyes	errant	soul	turn	to the	your	creator

omai (poet.) = ormai

Now, o my soul, turn your errant eyes to your creator,

e	ˈso vra	ˈkwe sto	ˈleɲː ɲo	de	lan ˈti ke	ru ˈi ne	ˈal to	ri ˈteɲː ɲo
e	**sovra**	**questo**	**legno**	**de**	**l'antiche**	**ruine**	**alto**	**ritegno**
and	above	this	wood	of	the old	failings	high	support

ruine = (mod.) rovine; sovra = (mod.) sopra

ne	le	ˈsu e	ˈpe ne	i	ˈfalː li	ˈtwo i	ri ˈmi ɾa
ne	**le**	**sue**	**pene**	**i**	**falli**	**tuoi**	**rimira.**
in	the	his	sufferings	the	mistakes	your	look at

and consider your [own] sins in light of His sufferings upon the cross, the high standard, for our past sins.

in	van	pur ˈtrɔpː po	il	ˈsa i	ˈsan dʒe	e	so ˈspi ɾa
In	**van,**	**pur troppo**	**il**	**sai,**	**s'ange**	**e**	**sospira**
in	vain	unfortunately	it	you know	suffers	and	sighs

s'ange: from angere (lit.) = affliggere

per	ka ˈdu ko	de ˈzi o	ka ˈdu ko	in ˈdʒeɲː ɲo	ˈduŋ kwe	a spi ˈɾan do	al	sem pi ˈtɛr no
per	**caduco**	**desio**	**caduco**	**ingegno,**	**dunque**	**aspirando**	**al**	**sempiterno**
for	perishable	desire	perishable	mind	therefore	aspiring	to the	(lit.) eternal

ˈreɲː ɲo	so ˈspi ɾa ·	al ˈmen	per	ˈdi o	ˈse i	per	te	ˈspi ɾa
regno	**sospira**	**almen**	**per**	**Dio,**	**s'ei**	**per**	**te**	**spira.**
kingdom	sigh	at least	for	God	if he	for	you	breaths his last

Alas, you know that a mortal mind suffers and sighs in vain with transitory desire; therefore, if you aspire to the eternal kingdom, at least suffer for God, for he dies for you.

ma	non	te ˈmer	ben ˈke	tre ˈman te	ˈfasː si	limː ˈmɔ bil	ˈtʃen tro
Ma	**non**	**temer,**	**ben che**	**tremante**	**fassi**	**l'immobil**	**centro**
but	not	to fear	even though	trembling	makes itself	the motionless	center

But fear not, even though the earth's motionless center starts to tremble

e	in	un	ˈfran dʒe	e	disː ˈsɛrː ra	le	ˈpje tre
e	**in**	**un**	**frange**	**e**	**disserra**	**le**	**pietre,**
and	in	one	breaks	and	throws open	the	rocks

and at once breaks and scatters the rocks,

e	i	ˈlu mi	a	il	tʃɛl	ˈtor bi di	e	ˈkasː si
e	**i**	**lumi**	**ha**	**il**	**ciel**	**torbidi,**	**e**	**cassi,**
and	the	lights	has	the	heaven	dark	and	switched off

and heaven has darkened and obscured its eyes –

ke	per	fer ˈmetː tsa	ˈtu a	ˈtre ma	la	ˈtɛrː ra
ché	**per**	**fermezza**	**tua**	**trema**	**la**	**terra,**
because	for	resoluteness	your	trembles	the	earth

for the earth trembles in order to make you resolute,

per 'ke	tu	'spe tri	il	kɔr	'fraŋ gon si	i	'sas: si
per che	**tu**	**spetri**	**il**	**cor,**	**frangonsi**	**i**	**sassi,**
in order that	you	you may free yourself	the	heart	they break	the	stones

per che =
(mod.) perché

the rocks shatter so that you may free your heart,

e	per	a 'prir ti	ʎi	'ɔk: ki	il	tʃel	ʎi	'ser: ra
e	**per**	**aprirti**	**gli**	**occhi**	**il**	**ciel**	**gli**	**serra.**
and	for	to open to you	the	eyes	the	heaven	them	closes

and heaven closes its [own] eyes in order to open yours.

ક્ર

[71]

Francesco Bracciolini

pat: tsa 'rɛl: lo a u dʒel: 'lin

Pazzarello augellin

Foolish little bird

pat: tsa 'rɛl: lo	a u dʒel: 'lin	ke	'men tre	'kan ti	'kja mi	lar 'tʃer
Pazzarello	**augellin,**	**che**	**mentre**	**canti,**	**chiami**	**l'Arcier**
foolish	little bird	who	while	you sing	you call	the archer

augellin[o] (poet.)
= uccellin[o]

ke	ti	per 'kwɔ ta	il	'pet: to	'tor na	de	'tor na	a	tʃe le 'brar	'two i	'van ti
che	**ti**	**percuota**	**il**	**petto,**	**torna,**	**deh**	**torna**	**a**	**celebrar**	**tuoi**	**vanti**
who	you	may strike	the	breast	return	pray	return	to	extol	your	virtues

Foolish little bird, who in your singing summon the Archer *[Cupid]*, who may strike your breast,
return – please, return – to extol your virtues

'den tro	le	'fron di	del	na 'ti o	bo 'sket: to
dentro	**le**	**frondi**	**del**	**natio**	**boschetto.**
within	the	foliage	of the	native	grove

natio = (mod.) nativo

in the foliage of your native grove.

'ko ve	il	'mon do	fal: 'la tʃe	a	ʎi	a bi 'tan ti	'pjɛ ni	diŋ 'gan: no
Ch'ove	**il**	**mondo**	**fallace**	**ha**	**gli**	**abitanti**	**pieni**	**d'inganno**
because where	the	world	fallacious	has	the	inhabitants	full	of deceit

Whereas the people in the fallacious vain world are full of deceit

e	di	mal 'va dʒo	af: 'fet: to	'qwan to	tu	spje ge 'ra i	pju	'dol tʃi	'kan ti
e	**di**	**malvagio**	**affetto**	**quanto**	**tu**	**spiegherai**	**più**	**dolci**	**canti,**
and	of	wicked	feeling	as much	you	you will expound	most	sweet	songs

and wicked feelings, the more you expound your most sweet songs,

'tan to	men	tro ve 'ra i	'fi do	ri 'tʃet: to
tanto	**men**	**troverai**	**fido**	**ricetto.**
so much	less	you will find	trusted	refuge

the less you will find a safe shelter.

'sem pli tʃe	tu	non	'sa i	'kwan ti	lat: 'tʃwɔ li	por 'tan do	in 'vi dja
Semplice,	**tu**	**non**	**sai**	**quanti**	**lacciuoli,**	**portando**	**invidia**
simple-hearted one	you	not	you know	how many	little snares	bearing	envy

Simple-hearted one, you do not know how many little snares, envious

'al: la	'tu a	'lje ta	'sɔr te	si na 'skon don	tra	'ra mi	'o ve	tu	'vo li
alla	**tua**	**lieta**	**sorte,**	**si nascondon**	**tra**	**rami,**	**ove**	**tu**	**voli.**
to the	your	happy	fate	are hiding	among	branches	wherein	you	you fly

of your happy lot, are hiding among the branches wherein you fly.

'kar tʃe ɾe sap: pa 'ɾek: kja aŋ 'gu sto e 'fɔr te e non 'pwɔ i mi ze 'rɛl
Carcere s'apparecchia angusto e forte, e non puoi miserel,
prison itself prepares narrow and strong and not you can poor little one

se non tin 'vo li kam 'par si 'ku ɾo o ser vi 'tu te o 'mɔr te
se non t'involi, campar sicuro, o servitute, o morte.
if not you take flight to live safe either servitude or death

> *servitute = (mod.) servitù*

A strong and narrow prison *[a cage]* is being prepared for you; and you, poor little one, cannot live safely if you don't fly away; [your choices are] either servitude or death.

❧

[71] "Sonetto contro Amore (Sonnet against Love)."   *Cardinale Ubaldini*

'pɛr fi do ke kja 'ma ɾe
Perfido, che chiamare
Wicked [you are], to call [yourself Love]

'pɛr fi do ke kja 'ma ɾe a 'mor ti 'fa i e 'spɛn di 'kon tro 'no i 'li ɾe
Perfido, che chiamare Amor ti fai e spendi contro noi l'ire,
wicked that to call Love yourself you make and you spend against us the angers
Wicked [you are], to call yourself Love; against us you employ anger

e le 'frɔ di sol del 'pjan dʒer ti 'paʃ: ʃi e sol ti 'gɔ di
e le frodi, sol del pianger ti pasci e sol ti godi
and the deceptions only of the weeping yourself you feed and only yourself you enjoy
and deceptions; you feed only on weeping, and you only enjoy

del laŋ 'gwir 'nɔ stro e non ti 'sat: tsi 'ma i
del languir nostro, e non ti sazi mai.
of the languishing our and not yourself you satisfy ever
our languishing; and you are never satisfied.

or di ' gjat: tʃo or di 'fɔ ko ar 'ma to 'va i or di kwa 'drɛl: la
Or di ghiaccio, or di foco armato vai, or di quadrella,
now of ice now of fire armed you go now with *(lit.)* arrows
Armed now with ice, now with fire, you go around – now with arrows,

or di ka 'te na e 'no di e 'pɔ i ke 'luŋ go 'strat: tsjo
or di catena e nodi, e poi che lungo strazio
now with chains and knots and then when long torment

> *printed "stratio" = (mod.) strazio*

in 'mil: le 'mo di fat: 'ta i dun 'al ma al 'fin 'mɔr te le 'da i
in mille modi fatt'hai d'un alma, alfin morte le dai.
in thousand ways made you have of a soul at last death to it you give
now with chains and knots; and then, when you have caused torment in a thousand ways, in the end you make a soul die.

o 'mo stro e 'pu ɾe o 'zɔ di 'mu za ar 'dʒi va kon 'tar 'fa ma bu 'dʒar da
O mostro, e pure osò di musa Argiva contar fama bugiarda,
o monster and yet dared of muse Greek to count fame false
O monster, though you dared gain ill-deserved fame from the Greek muse,

> *Argiva (old meaning) = Greca*

e din fe 'de le kin tʃɛl ti par to 'ri la 'tʃi prja 'di va
ed infedele ch'in ciel ti partorì la Cipria Diva;
[and] infidel who in heaven to you gave birth the of Cyprus Queen *[Venus]*
infidel heavenly son of Venus,

> *diva (lit.) = dea*

te	lin 'fɛr no	pro 'dus: se	e	te	kru 'dɛ le	nu 'trir	le 'rin: ni
te	**l'inferno**	**produsse,**	**e**	**te**	**crudele**	**nutrir**	**l'Erinni**
you	the hell	bred	and	you	cruel	nourished	the Erinyes

nutrir = nutrirono

hell bred you, and the Erinyes nourished you, cruel one,

in su	la	'sti dʒa	'ri va	e	fu	il	'tu o	'lat: te	sol	ve 'le no	e	'fjɛ le
in su	**la**	**Stigia**	**riva,**	**e**	**fu**	**il**	**tuo**	**latte**	**sol**	**veleno,**	**e**	**fiele.**
on	the	Stygian	shore	and	was	the	your	milk	only	poison	and	gall

on the Stygian shore; and your milk was only poison and gall.

GL: **Amor, Erinni, Stigia**

&

[1, 2]

pju non 'si a
Più non sia
May it not be

pju	non	'si a	ke	min: na 'mo ɾi	'va ga	'rɔ za	in	'nɔ bil	'vi zo
Più	**non**	**sia,**	**che**	**m'innamori**	**vaga**	**rosa**	**in**	**nobil**	**viso!**
more	not	it may be	that	I fall in love	pretty	rose	in	nobil	face

May it not be that I fall in love anymore with a pretty rose in a noble face!

'spes: so	'dʒa tʃe	'aŋ gwe	tra	'fjo ɾi	ke	'al tri	'poi
Spesso	**giace**	**angue**	**tra**	**fiori,**	**che**	**altri**	**poi**
often	lies	snake	among	flowers	that	someone	then

altri (singular)
= another, someone else
angue (lit.) = serpente

ne	're stan 'tʃi zo
ne	**rest'anciso.**
from it	may be killed

anciso (from "ancidere") (lit.) = ucciso (from "uccidere")

A snake often lies among the flowers, so that one may be killed by it.

'ɔ stro	e 'dɔr	di	'fre ska	e 'ta de	non	lu 'ziŋ gi	un kɔr	fe 'de le
Ostro	**ed or**	**di**	**fresca**	**etade**	**non**	**lusinghi**	**un cor**	**fedele!**
pink	and gold	of	fresh	age	not	may entice	a heart	faithful

ostro (lit.) = the rosy
color of a complexion
etade = (mod.) età

May the pink [cheeks] and gold [hair] of youth not entice a faithful heart!

'vɛ ste	pur	'spɔʎː ʎe	do 'ra te	per le 'pjad: dʒe	'aŋ gwe	kru 'dɛ le
Veste	**pur**	**spoglie**	**dorate**	**per le piagge**	**angue**	**crudele.**
dresses	indeed	cast-off skins	golden	on the slopes	snake	cruel

Indeed, a cruel snake in the fields is [deceptively] clothed in golden skin.

non	vi	'mɔ va	o	'ri zo	o	'kan to	di	bel: 'let: tsa	al: let 'ta 'tri tʃe
Non	**vi**	**mova**	**o**	**riso**	**o**	**canto**	**di**	**bellezza**	**allettatrice!**
not	you	may move	either	smile	or	song	of	beauty	alluring

"mi mova"
(...move me)
would make
more sense in the context; perhaps a
copying error at some point?

May neither a smile or a song from an alluring beauty move you!

pur	kan 'tan do	in 'vi ta	al	'pjan to	la	si 'rɛ na	iŋ gan: na 'tri tʃe
Pur	**cantando**	**invita**	**al**	**pianto**	**la**	**sirena**	**ingannatrice.**
indeed	singing	invites	to the	weeping	the	siren	deceptive

Indeed, the deceptive seductress invites tears when she sings.

&

[71] "Comparatione della nostra vita ad un horologio a polvere (Comparison of our life to an hourglass)."

Francesco Bonisegni

'kwe sti kal par del tʃɛl
Questi, ch'al par del ciel
These, [shiny] as the sky

'kwe sti	kal	par	del	tʃɛl	'glɔ bi	lu 'tʃɛn ti	'splɛn di di	si	ma	'fra li
Questi,	**ch'al**	**par**	**del**	**ciel**	**globi**	**lucenti,**	**splendidi**	**sì,**	**ma**	**frali,**
these	which at	equal	of the	sky	globes	shiny	splendid	so	but	frail

These globes, shiny as the sky, so splendid yet frail, which

il	'mon do	am: 'mi ra	'ɛb: be ro	di	vul 'ka no	e 'spo sti	al: 'li ra
il	**mondo**	**ammira,**	**ebbero**	**di**	**Vulcano**	**esposti**	**all'ira**
the	world	admires	had	of	Vulcan	exposed	to the anger

'kru do	na 'ta le	'en tro	le	'fjam: me	ar 'dɛn ti
crudo	**natale**	**entro**	**le**	**fiamme**	**ardenti.**
cruel	birth	within	the	flames	burning

the world admires, had a cruel birth within the burning flames exposed to Vulcan's wrath.

'kwel: la	ke	'kwa zi	in	'ri vo li	ka 'dɛn ti	'ra pi da	oɲ: 'ɲor	pre tʃi pi 'tar
Quella,	**che**	**quasi**	**in**	**rivoli**	**cadenti,**	**rapida**	**ogn'or**	**precipitar**
that	which	almost	in	streams	falling	rapid	always	to fling

si 'mi ra	a 're na	fu	'ko ve	pjul	mar	sa 'di ra
si mira,	**arena**	**fu,**	**ch'ove**	**più'l**	**mar**	**s'adira,**
one sees	sand	was	that where	most the	sea	flies into a rage

fu	lu 'di brjo	de	'lon de	e	'sker tso	'a i	'vɛn ti
fu	**ludibrio**	**de**	**l'onde,**	**e**	**scherzo**	**ai**	**venti.**
was	mockery	of	the waves	and	joke	at the	winds

That which is seen falling ever rapidly, as in little cascades, was sand exposed to the waves
where the sea is most furious, and mocked by the winds.

ko 'zi	da 'mor	e	di	for 'tu na	a 'va ra	tra	il	'fɔ ko	e	'lon de	si rad: 'dʒi ra
Così	**d'Amor,**	**e**	**di**	**fortuna**	**avara,**	**tra**	**il**	**foco,**	**e**	**l'onde**	**si raggira,**
thus	of Love	and	of	fortune	stingy	among	the	fire	and	the water[s]	wanders around

e	'vɔl ve	'kwe sta	'mi ze ra	'vi ta	al 'tru i	si	'ka ra
e	**volve**	**questa**	**misera**	**vita**	**altrui**	**sì**	**cara.**
and	turns	this	miserable	life	others'	so	dear

> volve: from "volvere"
> = (mod.) "volgere

Thus this miserable life, to others so dear, wanders around lacking love and [good] fortune,
between fire and water.

'brɛ ve	mo 'men to	'oɲ: ɲi	po 'ter	dis: 'sɔl ve	kwi	ti	'spɛk: kja
Breve	**momento**	**ogni**	**poter**	**dissolve;**	**qui**	**ti**	**specchia,**
brief	moment	every	power	dissolves	here	yourself	reflect

A brief moment dissipates every power; mirror yourself here,

o	mor 'ta le	e	'kwin di	im 'pa ra	ke	di	've tro	ɛ	la	'vi ta
o	**mortale,**	**e**	**quindi**	**impara,**	**che**	**di**	**vetro**	**è**	**la**	**vita,**
o	mortal	and	hence	learn	that	of	glass	is	the	life

o mortal, and hence learn that life is made of glass,

e   'lwɔ mo   ɛ   'pol ve
e   **l'uomo**   **è** **polve.**
and   the man   is   dust
and man is dust.

polve =
(mod.) polvere

GL: **Amor, Vulcano**

&

[71] "Traductione di 'Dulces exuviae' (Translation of 'Dulces exuviae') from [Virgil's] the *Aeneid*, 4."
character: *Dido*   *Cardinale Ubaldini*

'spoʎː ʎe ke 'fo sti un 'tɛm po
Spoglie, che fosti un tempo
Mortal remains, which were once

'spoʎː ʎe   ke   'fo sti un   'tɛm po   e   'dol tʃi   e   'ka ɾe
Spoglie,   **che**   **fosti** **un** **tempo,** **e**   **dolci,** **e**   **care**
mortal remains which   were   one   time   both   sweet   and   dear
Mortal remains, which were once both sweet and dear

'men tril   tʃɛl   lo   per 'mi ze   el   'vɔlː le   il   'fa to   pren 'de te   o 'ma i
mentr'il **ciel** **lo** **permise,** **e'l** **volle** **il** **fato** **prendete** **omai**
while the   heaven   it   permitted   and it wished   the   fate   take   now
as long as heaven permitted it and fate wished it, now take

kwe 'stal ma   e   del: la 'ma ɾe   'ku ɾe   ʃoʎː 'ʎe te   il   'pɛtː to   in: na mo 'ɾa to
quest'alma, **e**   **dell'amare**   **cure**   **sciogliete** **il** **petto** **innamorato.**
this soul   and   of the bitter   cares   free   the   breast   enamoured
this soul and free my enamoured breast of its painful cares.

omai =
(mod.)
ormai

'visː si   e   lo   'spat tsjo   kal   'mi o   'kor so   'da ɾe
Vissi, **e**   **lo** **spazio,**   **ch'al** **mio** **corso** **dare**
I lived   and   the   length of time that at the my   course   to give

printed "spatio"
= (mod.) spazio

'vɔlː le   for 'tu na   i 'ni kwa   ɔ   dʒa   var 'ka to   e   son   'tʃer ta   o ɾa 'ma i
volle **fortuna**   **iniqua,**   **ho**   **già** **varcato,** **e**   **son** **certa**   **ora mai**
wished   fortune   unjust   I have already exceeded   and   I am   certain   now
I lived, and have already exceeded the length of time which unjust fortune wished to give me;
and I am now certain

ke   'gran de   e   'kja ɾa   pas: se 'ɾa   'lom bra   'mi a   la   'ri pa   a 'va ɾa
che   **grande,** **e**   **chiara**   **passerà**   **l'ombra** **mia** **la** **ripa** **avara.**
that   great   and   bright   will pass   the shadow mine   the   shore   greedy
that, grand and bright, my spirit will pass the greedy shore [i.e., the shore of the Styx].

ripa =
(mod.) riva

fon 'da i   tʃitː 'ta   fa 'mo za   in   'stra no   'li do
Fondai   **città**   **famosa**   **in** **strano**   **lido,**
I founded   city   famous   in   foreign   (poet.) country
I founded a famous city in a foreign land;

'vi di   su 'pɛr be   le   no 'vɛlː le   'mu ɾa
vidi **superbe**   **le** **novelle**   **mura,**
I saw   magnificent the new   walls
I saw its magnificent new walls;

e	ven di 'ka i	'kon tro	il	fra 'tɛl: lo	in 'fi do	del	kon 'sɔr te	fe 'del
e	**vendicai**	**contro**	**il**	**fratello**	**infido**	**del**	**consorte**	**fedel**
and	I avenged	against	the	brother	unfaithful	of the	husband	faithful

la	'mɔr te	'du ra
la	**morte**	**dura.**
the	death	harsh

and I took revenge on my unfaithful brother for the harsh death of my faithful husband.

fe 'li tʃe	o i 'mɛ	'trɔp: po	fe 'li tʃe	'di do	se	non	a 'vɛs: si	'ma i
Felice,	**oimè,**	**troppo**	**felice**	**Dido,**	**se**	**non**	**avessi**	**mai**
happy	alas	too	happy	Dido	if	not	had I	never

Happy – alas, too happy Dido would have been – had I never,

per	'mi a	zven 'tu ra	nok: 'kjɛ ro	'a i	'li di	'mjɛ i	do 've u ro	il 'vɔl se
per	**mia**	**sventura**	**nocchiero**	**ai**	**lidi**	**miei,**	**dov'Euro**	**il volse,**
for	my	misfortune	helmsman	to the	shores	mine	where *(lit.)* sirocco	it turned

le 'ga to	il	'leɲ: ɲo	ke	da	'trɔ ja	'ʃɔl se
legato	**il**	**legno,**	**che**	**da**	**Troia**	**sciolse.**
bound	the	ship	which	from	Troy	cast off

to my misfortune, given harbor on my shores, to which sirocco turned its helmsman, to the ship cast off from Troy.

GL: **Dido, Euro, Troia**

Melani, Alessandro (1639-1703)

Born in Pistoia to Domenico, bell ringer of the Cathedral, and Camilla Melani, Alessandro was their seventh surviving son. The parents made the most of social and political opportunities for advancement; Atto and Francesco Maria, the second and third sons, were castrated and achieved fame as castrato singers. By the beginning of the eighteenth century the Melani family was registed among Tuscan nobility.

Alessandro was a choirboy at the Cathedral of Pistoia at age eleven. In 1667 he went with his brother Jacopo to Rome, attracted by its richness of musical life under Giulio Rospigliosl (who became Pope Clement IX in 1667), and was almost immediately elected *maestro di cappella* of S. Maria Maggiore there. In addition to the patronage of successive popes after Clement IX, Alessandro Melani had a great many secular patrons, including Prince Ferdinando de' Medici.

His career in Rome as a composer was mainly in opera. In addition to at least a dozen operas, he wrote oratorios, sacred music, arias, and at least thirty-one solo cantatas, the later ones foreshadowing those of Alessandro Scarlatti.

[12, 40]

vet: 'tso za a u 'rɔ ra
Vezzosa Aurora
Lovely dawn

vet: 'tso zo	a u 'rɔ ra	dɛ	'sor dʒi	si
Vezzosa	**Aurora,**	**deh,**	**sorgi,**	**sì,**
lovely	dawn	ah	rise	yes

Lovely dawn, ah, rise, yes,

e	il	'pra to	in 'dɔ ra	por 'tan do	il	di
e	**il**	**prato**	**indora**	**portando**	**il**	**dì.**
and	the	meadow	gild	bringing	the	day

and gild the meadow, heralding the day.

'al ba   dʒen 'ti le   afː 'fretː ta   il   pjɛ
Alba   **gentile,**   **affretta**   **il**   **piè,**
daybreak   gentle   hasten   the   foot
Gentle daybreak, hasten your step,

ke   il   'mon do   ɛ   'vi le   'sɛn tsa di   te
ché   **il**   **mondo**   **è**   **vile**   **senza di**   **te.**
because   the   world   is   miserable   without   you
as the world is miserable without you.

GL: **Aurora**

 # *Melani, Jacopo* (*1623-1676*)

First son of Domenico and Camilla Melani and brother of Alessandro, he was an organist and opera composer. *Maestro di cappella* at the Pistoia (city of his birth) Cathedral in 1657, he moved to Rome in 1667; around 1673 he returned to Pistoia as organist at the Cathedral, and he remained there until his death.
Jacopo Melani was the leading composer of the time of comic operas, of which only two of his survive. Most of his operas were mounted in Florence; the most important among them were *Il podestà di Colognole (1656)*, *Ercole in Tebe (1661)*, and *Il Girello*, which was performed at the Palazzo Colonna in Rome in 1668 and staged throughout Italy between 1669 and 1676 by a touring group of which Melani may have been a part.

[1, 2, 46]
from: *Il Girello (1668)*
character: *Doralba*

Filippo Acciaiuoli

iŋ ko 'stan te mu sta 'fa
Incostante Mustafa?
Is Mustafa inconstant?

iŋ ko 'stan te   mu sta 'fa
Incostante   **Mustafa?**
inconstant   Mustafa
Is Mustafa inconstant?

'bjon de   'kjɔ me   e   bɛl   sem 'bjan te   la   for 'tu na   e   il   tʃɛl   tʃi   da
Bionde   **chiome**   **e**   **bel**   **sembiante**   **la**   **fortuna**   **e**   **il**   **ciel**   **ci**   **da;**
blond   hair   and   beautiful   face   the   fortune   and   the   heaven   to us   gives
Fortune and heaven bestow blond hair and a beautiful face on us;

ma   de 'ledː dʒer si   un   a 'man te   'laʃː ʃa   al   kɔr   la   li ber 'ta
ma,   **d'eleggersi**   **un**   **amante,**   **lascia**   **al**   **cor**   **la**   **libertà.**
but   of to choose   a   lover   leave   to the   heart   the   liberty
but, in choosing a lover, let the heart have freedom.

'duŋ kwe   'sɔr te   ɛ   la   bel 'ta   ke   mu 'tar   'tɔ sto   si 'mi ɾa
Dunque   **sorte**   **è**   **la**   **beltà,**   **che**   **mutar**   **tosto**   **si mira,**
Well then   luck   is   the   beauty   which   to change   quickly   one sees
So beauty, which one sees changing quickly, is luck;

e   kwal   'rwɔ ta   aŋ 'kelː la   'dʒi ɾa   kon   il   'kor so   delː le 'ta
e   **qual**   **ruota**   **anch'ella**   **gira**   **con**   **il**   **corso**   **dell'età.**
and   like a   wheel   also it   turns   with   the   course   of the age
and, like a wheel, it also turns in the course of the years.

from: *Il Girello (1668)*   *Filippo Acciaiuoli*
character: *Doralba*

[1, 2, 46]

skon siʎ: ˈʎa ta do ˈral ba ˈo ve tad: ˈdʒi ri
Sconsigliata Doralba, ove t'aggiri?
Rash Doralba, where are you wandering?

skon siʎ:	ˈʎa ta	do ˈral ba	ˈo ve	tad: ˈdʒi ri	non	ˈve di
Sconsigliata		**Doralba,**	**ove**	**t'aggiri?**	**Non**	**vedi**
rash		Doralba	where	you wander	not	you see

Rash Doralba, where are you wandering? Do you not see

a	ˈtwɔ i	so ˈspi ri	ˈmu to	il	tʃɛl	ˈsor do	un	ˈskja vo	e	ˈtʃɛ ko	a ˈmo re
a	**tuoi**	**sospiri**	**muto**	**il**	**ciel,**	**sordo**	**un'**	**schiavo**	**e**	**cieco**	**Amore!?**
at	your	sighs	mute	the	heaven	deaf	an	enslaved	and	blind	love

the heaven silent, an enslaved and blind Love deaf to your sighs!?

del	ˈtu o	ser ˈvi le	ar ˈdo re	son	ki ˈmɛ re	ʎi	af: ˈfan: ni
Del	**tuo**	**servile**	**ardore**	**son**	**chimere**	**gli**	**affanni,**
of the	your	servile	passion	are	fantasies	the	anxieties

Your anxieties are fantasies of your servile passion;

son	a ˈbɔr ti	i	pen ˈsjɛ ri	son	ʎi	af: ˈfɛt: ti	bu ˈdʒi e	le	spe ˈran tse	de ˈli ri
son	**aborti**	**i**	**pensieri,**	**son**	**gli**	**affetti**	**bugie,**	**le**	**speranze**	**deliri.**
are	aborted	the	thoughts	are	the	affections	lies	the	hopes	ravings

your thoughts come to nothing, your affections are lies, and your hopes are ravings.

ma	se	del: ˈlal ma	ˈmi a	ˈu no	ˈskja vo	ɛ	la	ˈspɛ ne
Ma,	**se**	**dell'alma**	**mia**	**uno**	**schiavo**	**è**	**la**	**spene,**
but	if	of the soul	mine	a	slave	is	the	hope

But if hope is a slave of my soul,

> *spene (poet.) = speme (lit.) = speranza*

pa ven ˈtar	le	ka ˈte ne	o	ˈmi o	kɔr	ɛ	pat: ˈtsi a
paventar	**le**	**catene,**	**o**	**mio**	**cor,**	**è**	**pazzia!**
to fear	the	shackles	o	my	heart	is	folly

to fear the shackles, o my heart, is folly!

mu sta ˈfa	ˈdo ve	ˈse i	ˈdo ve	sod: ˈdʒor na	il	sol	ˈdeʎ: ʎi	ˈɔk: ki	ˈmje i
Mustafa,	**dove**	**sei?**	**dove**	**soggiorna**	**il**	**sol**	**degli**	**occhi**	**miei?**
Mustafa	where	you are	where	sojourns	the	sun	of the	eyes	mine

Mustafa, where are you? Where is the light of my eyes *[i.e., my beloved one]* sojourning?

ˈtor na	bɛn	ˈmi o	dɛ	ˈtor na	a	be ˈar	ˈkwe sto	ˈpɛt: to
Torna,	**ben**	**mio,**	**deh**	**torna**	**a**	**bear**	**questo**	**petto,**
come back	dear one	mine	ah	come back	to	to make happy	this	breast

Come back, my dear one; ah, come back to make this breast happy

ˈpri a	ke	di ˈven ti	od: ˈdʒɛt: to	ˈde i	mar ˈti ri	pju	ˈrɛ i
pria	**che**	**diventi**	**oggetto**	**dei**	**martiri**	**più**	**rei!**
before	that	I may become	object	of the	torments	more	cruel

before I become the object of more cruel torments!

> *pria (poet.) = prima*

GL: **Amore**

Milanuzzi, Carlo (?- c.1647)

Composer and organist born near Camerino, also known as a preacher and author of literary collections, he became an Augustinian monk; sometime before 1618 he was organist at the Augustinian church in Perugia; by 1622 he was in northern Italy as *maestro di cappella* at S. Eufemia in Verona. He held posts in Venice and Modena between 1623 and 1643; his last known appointment, in 1643, was again in Venice as organist and *maestro di cappella* at S. Mauro, Noventa di Piave.
Milanuzzi wrote numerous sacred vocal works in concertato style, and he contributed to the genre of the secular solo aria with at least nine books of “ariose vaghezze,” eight of which survive. “Gia morta è la fiamma” is from the sixth of those nine books.

[27]

dʒa ˈmɔr ta ɛ la ˈfjamː ma
Già morta è la fiamma
Now the flame is dead

dʒa	ˈmɔr ta	ɛ	la	ˈfjamː ma	dʒa	ˈspɛn to	ɛ	lar ˈdo ɾe
Già	**morta**	**è**	**la**	**fiamma,**	**già**	**spento**	**è**	**l’ardore.**
now	dead	is	the	flame	now	spent	is	the ardor

Now the flame is dead, now the ardor is spent.

non	ˈka de	pjul	ˈkɔ ɾe	ke	a ˈmor	non	lin ˈfjamː ma
Non	**cade**	**più’l**	**core**	**ché**	**amor**	**non**	**l’infiamma,**
not	falls	more the	heart	because	love	not	it enflames

My heart no longer fails, because love does not enflame it,

ke	a ˈmor	nel	ˈmi o	sen	pju	ˈfɔr tsa	non	a	ko ˈzi	va
ché	**amor**	**nel**	**mio**	**sen**	**più**	**forza**	**non**	**ha.**	**Così**	**va.**
because	love	in the	my	breast	more	power	not	has	thus	goes

because love no longer has power in my breast. And so it goes.

non	ˈsɛn to	pju	il	ˈfɔ ko	ke	son	ˈtutː to	ˈgjatː tʃo
Non	**sento**	**più**	**il**	**foco**	**ché**	**son**	**tutto**	**ghiaccio.**
not	I feel	more	the	fire	because	I am	all	ice

I no longer feel the fire, because I am all ice-cold.

per	ˈlɛ i	pju	magː ˈgjatː tʃo	per	ˈlɛ i	non	min ˈfɔ ko
Per	**lei**	**più**	**m’agghiaccio,**	**per**	**lei**	**non**	**m’infoco,**
for	her	more	I turn to ice	for	her	not	I become enflamed

For her I freeze more and more, for her I do not become enflamed,

ke	a ˈmor	nel	ˈmi o	sen	pju	ˈfɔr tsa	non	a	ko ˈzi	va
ché	**amor**	**nel**	**mio**	**sen**	**più**	**forza**	**non**	**ha.**	**Così**	**va.**
because	love	in the	my	breast	more	power	not	has	thus	goes

because love no longer has power in my breast. And so it goes.

tu	ˈvi vi	su ˈpɛr ba	tu	ˈgɔ di	zdeɲː ˈɲo za	ke	pju	non	sa ˈtʃɛr ba
Tu	**vivi**	**superba,**	**tu**	**godi**	**sdegnosa**	**che**	**più**	**non**	**s’acerba**
you	you live	proudly	you	you rejoice	haughtily	that	more	not	intensifies

ˈmi a	ˈpja ga	a mo ˈɾo za	ke	a ˈmor	nel	ˈmi o	sen
mia	**piaga**	**amorosa,**	**che**	**amor**	**nel**	**mio**	**sen**
my	wound	amorous	that	love	in the	my	breast

pju	'fɔr tsa	non	a	ko 'zi	va						
più	**forza**	**non**	**ha.**	**Così**	**va.**						
more	power	not	has	thus	goes						

You live proudly, you rejoice haughtily in the fact that my love-wound is no longer enflamed, that love no longer has power in my breast. And so it goes.

dʒo 'i sko	ri 'na sko	se	un	'tɛm po	'fu i	'pri vo	di	'vi ta
Gioisco,	**rinasco.**	**Se**	**un**	**tempo**	**fui**	**privo**	**di**	**vita**
I have joy	I am reborn	if	one	time	I was	deprived	of	life

I am joyful, I am reborn. If I was once deprived of life,

or	son	'vi vo	di	'dʒo ja	mi 'pa sko
or	**son**	**vivo,**	**di**	**gioia**	**mi pasco,**
now	I am	alive	with	joy	myself I nourish

now I am alive; I feed on joy,

ke	a 'mor	nel	'mi o	sen	pju	'fɔr tsa	non	a	ko 'zi	va
ché	**amor**	**nel**	**mio**	**sen**	**più**	**forza**	**non**	**ha.**	**Così**	**va.**
because	love	in the	my	breast	more	power	not	has	thus	goes

because love no longer has power in my breast. And so it goes.

Miniscalchi, Guglielmo (fl.1616-1630)

Born in Venice, he was an Augustinian monk at S. Stefano in Venice, and by 1622 he was *maestro di cappella* there.

Though Miniscalchi wrote liturgical music (psalms, motets, etc.), he was most popular for his secular solo songs, most of which are contained in three books of arias published in Venice between 1625 and 1630.

[57]

		so 'spi ɾo si		
		Sospiro, sì		
		I am sighing, yes		

so 'spi ɾo	si	ma	pur	ke	'dʒo va mi	il	so spi 'rar
Sospiro,	**sì,**	**ma**	**pur**	**che**	**giovami**	**il**	**sospirar**
I sigh	yes	but	[yet]	what	does good for me	the	sighing

I am sighing, yes; but what good does sighing do me

se	la	kru 'dɛl	ke	mi	fe 'ri	non	da	ri 'stɔ ɾo	al	'mi o	pe 'nar
se	**la**	**crudel**	**che**	**mi**	**ferì**	**non**	**da**	**ristoro**	**al**	**mio**	**penar?**
if	the	cruel one	who	me	wounded	not	gives	comfort	to the	my	suffering

if the cruel woman who wounded me does not comfort my suffering?

sofː 'frir	il	'ko ɾe	non	pwɔ	tal	ar 'do ɾe	e	pur	sa 'ɾɔ	co 'stan te
Soffrir	**il**	**core**	**non**	**può**	**tal**	**ardore**	**e**	**pur**	**sarò**	**costante.**
to suffer	the	heart	not	is able	such	ardor	and	yet	I will be	constant

My heart is not able to endure such ardor, and yet I will be constant.

nɔ	pju	nɔ	non	'vɔʎː ʎo	'ɛsː ser	a 'man te
No,	**più**	**no,**	**non**	**voglio**	**esser**	**amante.**
no	more	no	not	I want	to be	lover

No, no more do I want to be a lover.

laŋ ˈgwi sko	si	ma	pur	ke	ˈdʒo va mi	il	ˈmi o	laŋ ˈgwir
Languisco,	**sì,**	**ma**	**pur**	**che**	**giovami**	**il**	**mio**	**languir**
I languish	yes	but	[yet]	what	does good for me	the	my	languishing

I am languishing, yes; but what good does languishing do me

se	la	bel ˈta	ke	mi	ra ˈpi	non	ˈpor dʒe	ˈpa tʃe	a	ˈmjɛ i	mar ˈtir
se	**la**	**beltà**	**che**	**mi**	**rapì**	**non**	**porge**	**pace**	**a’**	**miei**	**martir?**
if	the	beauty	who	me	enraptured	not	offers	peace	to	my	torments

if the beautiful one who enraptured me does not offer peace to my torments?

sofː ˈfrir	il	ˈkɔ ɾe	non	pwɔ	tal	ar ˈdo ɾe	e	pur	sa ˈɾɔ	co ˈstan te
Soffrir	**il**	**core**	**non**	**può**	**tal**	**ardore**	**e**	**pur**	**sarò**	**costante.**
to suffer	the	heart	not	is able	such	ardor	and	yet	I will be	constant

My heart is not able to endure such ardor, and yet I will be constant.

nɔ	pju	nɔ	non	ˈvɔʎː ʎo	ˈɛsː ser	a ˈman te
No,	**più**	**no,**	**non**	**voglio**	**esser**	**amante.**
no	more	no	not	I want	to be	lover

No, no more do I want to be a lover.

ke	ˈpar lo	o i ˈmɛ	ˈa i	ke	va ˈnedː dʒo	nel	ˈmi o	do ˈlor
Che	**parlo,**	**ohimè?**	**Ahi,**	**che**	**vaneggio**	**nel**	**mio**	**dolor;**
what	I say	alas	ah	[that]	I rave	in the	my	pain

What am I saying, alas! Ah, I am delirious in my pain;

ˈvɔʎː ʎo	mo ˈɾir	ˈli dja	per	te	fe ˈɾiʃː ʃi	il	sen	fe ˈɾiʃː ʃi	il	kɔr
voglio	**morir,**	**Lidia,**	**per**	**te;**	**ferisci**	**il**	**sen,**	**ferisci**	**il**	**cor.**
I want	to die	Lydia	for	you	wound	the	breast	wound	the	heart

I want to die for you, Lydia. Wound my breast, wound my heart.

ˈi o	vɔ	sofː ˈfri ɾe	kon ˈtɛn to	mar ˈti ɾe	ˈi o	ˈvɔʎː ʎo	ˈɛsː ser	co ˈstan te
Io	**vo’**	**soffrire**	**contento**	**martire;**	**io**	**voglio**	**esser**	**costante**
I	I want	to suffer	contented	torment	I	I want	to be	constant

I want to endure torment, contented; I want to be constant

nel	ˈmi o	dwɔl	e	ˈsɛm pre	ˈɛsː ser	a ˈman te
nel	**mio**	**duol**	**e**	**sempre**	**esser**	**amante.**
in the	my	suffering	and	always	to be	lover

in my suffering, and to be a lover forever.

Monteverdi, Claudio (1567-1643)

Organist and player of viols and theorbo, and composer of tremendous importance, he was born in Cremona. Musically precocious, he published his first volume of compositions at the age of fifteen. In 1590 he was employed at the court of Vincenzo Gonzaga, Duke of Mantua, where he became *maestro di cappella* in 1601; in 1612, after the death of Vincenzo, he was dismissed (or resigned), and in 1613, upon the death of Giovanni Gabrieli, was appointed Gabrieli's successor as *maestro di cappella* at S. Marco in Venice. He remained in that prestigious post for the rest of his life, responsible for providing music for civic events and for patrons among the aristocracy as well as the sacred music for S. Marco. He had some thirty singers and twenty instrumentalists at his disposal; he was an innovator in the variety of his orchestrations and instrumental effects.

The list of his compositions fills more than three pages in *Grove*. Monteverdi's "favola in musica," *Orfeo*, first performed in 1607, is considered an example, if not the first, of the new genre to be called opera. From his *Arianna (1608)* only the famous "Lament" survives; its success contributed to the practice of other composers' regularly including laments in their operas.

In his early madrigals, Monteverdi employed musical devices to achieve heights of human emotions, characterization, and text painting which are a characteristic of his later solo dramatic works.

[12]
from: *L'Incoronazione di Poppea (1642)*
character: *Arnalta*   *Giovanni Francesco Busenello*

a ˈda dʒa ti   pop: ˈpɛ a   o bli ˈvjon   so ˈa ve
Adagiati, Poppea…Oblivion soave
Rest well, Poppea…Gentle oblivion

a ˈda dʒa ti	pop: ˈpɛ a	ak: ˈkwjɛ ta ti	ˈa ni ma	ˈmi a	sa ˈra i	bɛn	ku sto ˈdi ta
Adagiati,	**Poppea,**	**acquietati**	**anima**	**mia,**	**sarai**	**ben**	**custodita.**
rest comfortably	Poppea	be calm	soul	mine	you will be	well	guarded

Rest well, Poppea; be calm, my dear; you will be well protected.

o bli ˈvjon	so ˈa ve	i	ˈdol tʃi	sen ti ˈmen ti	in	te	ˈfiʎ: ʎa	ad: dor ˈmen ti
Oblivion	**soave,**	**i**	**dolci**	**sentimenti**	**in**	**te,**	**figlia,**	**addormenti.**
oblivion	gentle	the	sweet	feelings	in	you	daughter	may lull you

May gentle oblivion lull sweet thoughts in you, daughter.

po ˈza te vi	ˈɔk: ki	ˈla dri	a ˈpɛr ti	dɛ	ke	ˈfa te	se	ˈkju zi	aŋ ˈkor	ru ˈba te
Posatevi,	**occhi**	**ladri,**	**aperti,**	**deh,**	**che**	**fate,**	**se**	**chiusi**	**ancor**	**rubate.**
rest you	eyes	roguish	open	ah	that	you do	if	closed	even	you rob

Rest, thieving eyes; ah, what are you doing open, when you rob [hearts] even when closed?

pop: ˈpɛ a	ri ˈman ti	in	ˈpa tʃe	ˈlu tʃi	ˈka ɾe	e	gra ˈdi te	dor ˈmi te	o ˈma i	dor ˈmi te
Poppea,	**rimanti**	**in**	**pace;**	**luci**	**care**	**e**	**gradite,**	**dormite,**	**omai**	**dormite.**
Poppea	stay you	in	peace	eyes	dear	and	pleasing	sleep	now	sleep

Poppea, rest in peace; sleep now – sleep, dear and pleasing eyes.

> omai (poet.) = ormai

a ˈman ti	va ged: ˈdʒa te	il	mi ˈra ko lo	ˈnɔ vo	ɛ	lu mi ˈno zo	il	di
Amanti,	**vagheggiate**	**il**	**miracolo**	**novo,**	**è**	**luminoso**	**il**	**dì**
lovers	gaze admiringly at	the	miracle	new	is	luminous	the	day

Lovers, gaze admiringly at the new miracle; the day is luminous

si ˈko me	ˈswɔ le	e	pur	ve ˈde te	ad: dor men ˈta to	il	ˈso le
sì come	**suole,**	**e**	**pur**	**vedete**	**addormentato**	**il**	**sole.**
like	is usual	and	yet	you see	put to sleep	the	sun

as usual, and yet you see the sun sleeping [...you see the night bright as day].

&

[20, 24, 53, 74]
from: *Il Ballo [Il Balletto] delle Ingrate (1608)*
character: *Una delle ingrate* (One of the ungrateful women)   *Ottavio Rinuccini*

ˈa i   ˈtrɔp: po   ɛ   ˈdu ɾo
Ahi! troppo è duro
Alas, it is too harsh

ˈa i	ˈtrɔp: po	ɛ	ˈdu ɾo	kru ˈdɛl	sen ˈtɛn tsa	e	vi e ˈpju	ˈkru da	ˈpe na
Ahi!	**troppo**	**è**	**duro,**	**crudel**	**sentenza,**	**e**	**vie più**	**cruda**	**pena**
alas	too much	it is	harsh	cruel	sentence	and	all the more	severe	punishment

Alas, the cruel sentence is too harsh, and the punishment all the more severe,

tor ˈna ɾe	a	la gri ˈmar	nel: ˈlan tro	o ˈsku ɾo
tornare	**a**	**lagrimar**	**nell'antro**	**oscuro!**
to return	to	to weep	in the cave	gloomy

to return to weeping in the gloomy cave!

> var.: tornar =
> tornare

'a er   se 're no   e   'pu ɾo   ad: 'di o   per   'sɛm pre

Aer   sereno   e   puro,   addio   per   sempre!

air   serene   and   pure   farewell   for   always

Clear, pure air, farewell forever!

> *aer[e] (poet.) =*
> *aria, atmosfera*

ad: 'di o   per   'sɛm pre   ad: 'di o   o   'tʃɛ lo   o   'so le   ad: 'di o   'lu tʃi de   'stel: le

Addio,   per   sempre   addio,   o   cielo,   o   sole,   addio,   lucide   stelle!

farewell   for   always   farewell   o   heaven   o   sun   farewell   shining   stars

Farewell – farewell forever, o heaven, o sun; farewell, shining stars!

ap: pren 'de te   pje 'ta   'dɔn: ne   e   don 'dzɛl: le

Apprendete   pietà,   donne   e   donzelle!

learn   pity   ladies   and   maidens

Learn to show pity, ladies and maidens!

❧

[92]

'ar do e sko 'prir
Ardo e scoprir
I am burning and [I dare not] reveal

'ar do   e   sko 'prir   'a i 'las: so   non   ar 'di sko   kwel   ke   'pɔr to   in   sen

Ardo   e   scoprir,   ahi lasso!   Non   ardisco   quel   che   porto   in   sen:

I burn   and   to reveal   woe is me   not   I dare   that   which   I bear   in   breast

I am burning – woe is me! – and I dare not reveal what I bear in my breast:

riŋ 'kju zo   ar 'do ɾe

rinchiuso   ardore.

locked up   ardor

repressed passion.

e   'tan to   pju   do 'lɛn te   oɲ: 'ɲor   laŋ 'gwi sko   'kwan to   pju   sta   tʃe 'la to

E   tanto   più   dolente   ognor   languisco,   quanto   più   sta   celato,

and   so much   more   painful   always   I languish   how much   more   stays   hidden

il   'mi o   do 'lo ɾe

il   mio   dolore.

the   my   pain

And the more painfully I continue to languish, the more my pain stays hidden.

fra   me   ta 'lor   'mil: le   di 'zeɲ: ɲi   or 'di sko   'kol: la   'liŋ gwa   diʃ 'ʃɔr

Fra   me   talor   mille   disegni   ordisco   colla   lingua   discior,

in   me   sometimes   thousand   intentions   I plan   with the   tongue   to dissolve

Sometimes I have a thousand resolutions to dispel, by speaking,

> *discior[re] =*
> *(mod.)*
> *disciogliere*

'aŋ ke   il   ti 'mo ɾe   e dal: 'lor   'fat: to   ar 'di to   'i o   non   pa 'vɛn to   gri 'dar   sok: 'kor so

anche   il   timore;   ed allor,   fatto   ardito   io   non   pavento   gridar   soccorso

[even]   the   fear   and then   made   bold   I   not   I fear   to cry out   relief

my fear; and then, emboldened, I am not afraid to cry out for relief

a   mi tʃi 'djal   tor 'men to

a   micidial   tormento!

at   deadly   torment

from my deadly torment!

ma	sav: 'vjɛn	'ki o	map: 'prɛs: so	a	'lɛ i	da 'van ti	per	pro 'var
Ma,	**s'avvien**	**ch'io**	**m'appresso**	**a**	**lei**	**davanti**	**per**	**provar**
but	if it happens	that I	I draw near	to	her	in front of	for	to experience

But if I happen to come before her presence, to feel

al	'mi o	mal	'pa tʃe	e	di 'lɛt: to	di 'vɛŋ go	'tɔ sto	'pal: li do	in	sem 'bjan te
al	**mio**	**mal,**	**pace**	**e**	**diletto,**	**divengo**	**tosto**	**pallido**	**in**	**sembiante**
to the	my	pain	peace	and	pleasure	I become	at once	pale	in	face

peace and pleasure in my pain, suddenly my face pales

e	ki 'nar	ʎi	'ɔk: ki	a	'tɛr: ra	son	ko 'stret: to
e	**chinar**	**gli**	**occhi**	**a**	**terra**	**son**	**costretto.**
and	to bow	the	eyes	to	ground	I am	compelled

and I am compelled to lower my eyes.

dir	vor 're i	ma	non	'ɔ zo	'in di	tre 'man te	ko 'min tʃo	a	e	mi ri 'tɛŋ go
Dir	**vorrei!**	**ma**	**non**	**oso!**	**Indi,**	**tremante**	**[comincio]**	**ah**	**e**	**mi ritengo.**
to say	I would like	but	not	I dare	then	trembling	[I begin]	ah	and	I hold back

I would like to speak, but I don't dare! Then, trembling, [I begin; and] ah, [then] I restrain myself.

The (missing) word "comincio" was added by the editor of [92] *to complete the context gramatically.*

al 'fin	laf: 'fɛt: to	sa 'prir	'nun tsja	del	kor	la	'liŋ gwa	'vwɔ le
Alfin	**l'affetto**	**s'aprir**	**nunzia**	**del**	**cor**	**la**	**lingua**	**vuole!**
at last	the affection	to open up	messenger	of the	heart	the	tongue	wants

At last my tongue, spokesman of my heart, wants to express my affection;

si	'troŋ kan	'sul: le	'lab: bra	le	pa 'rɔ le
si	**troncan**	**sulle**	**labbra**	**le**	**parole!**
themselves	they cut short	on the	lips	the	words

[but] the words are broken off on my lips!

❧

[93]

'kjɔ ma 'dɔ ɾo
Chioma d'oro
Golden hair

'kjɔ ma	'dɔ ɾo	bɛl	te 'zɔ ɾo	tu	mi	'le gi	in	'mil: le	'no di
Chioma	**d'oro,**	**bel**	**tesoro,**	**tu**	**mi**	**leghi**	**in**	**mille**	**nodi,**
hair	of gold	beautiful	treasure	you	me	you tie	in	thousand	knots

Golden hair, beautiful treasure, you tie me in a thousand knots,

se	tan: 'nɔ di	se	ti 'szɔ di
se	**t'annodi,**	**se**	**ti snodi.**
if	you become knotted	if	you become unknotted

whether you are in plaits or whether you are loose.

kan di 'det: te	'pɛr le	e 'lɛt: te	se	le	'rɔ ze	ke	ko 'pri te	di sko 'pri te
Candidette	**perle**	**elette,**	**se**	**le**	**rose**	**che**	**coprite**	**discoprite,**
snow-white little	pearls	precious	if	the	roses	which	you cover	you uncover

Little precious snow-white pearls *[teeth]*, when you reveal the roses which you conceal,

mi	fe 'ɾi te
mi	**ferite.**
me	you wound

you wound me.

'vi ve   'stel: le   ke   si   'bɛl: le   e   si   'va ge   ri splen 'de te
Vive   stelle   che   sì   belle   e   sì   vaghe   risplendete,
lively   *(fig.)* eyes   which   so   beautiful   and   so   pretty   you sparkle
Bright eyes which sparkle so beautifully and prettily,

se   ri 'de te   man tʃi 'de te
se   ridete   m'ancidete.
if   you laugh   me you kill
when you laugh, you kill me.

> *ancidete: from "ancidere" = (mod.) "uccidere"*

pret: 'tsjo ze   a mo 'ro ze   ko ɾal: 'li ne   'lab: bra   a 'ma te   se   par 'la te   mi   be 'a te
Preziose,   amorose   coralline   labbra   amate,   se   parlate   mi   beate.
precious   loving   coral   lips   beloved   if   you speak   me   you make happy
Precious, loving, beloved coral lips, when you speak you make me happy.

o   bɛl   'nɔ do   per   'ku i   'gɔ do   o   so 'a ve   uʃ: 'ʃir   di   'vi ta
O   bel   nodo   per   cui   godo   o   soave   uscir   di   vita,
o   beautiful   knot   through   which   I take pleasure   o   sweet   leaving   of   life
O beautiful knot through which I take pleasure, o sweet death,

o   gra 'di ta   'mi a   fe 'ri ta
O!   Gradita   mia   ferita.
o   welcome   my   wound
oh, welcome [is] my wound!

&

[1, 2, 47]   *Giovanni Battista Guarini*

kon ke so a vi 'ta
Con che soavità
With what sweetness

kon   ke   so a vi 'ta   'lab: bra   o do 'ra te   e   vi   'ba tʃo   e   va 'skol to
Con   che   soavità,   labbra   odorate,   e   vi   bacio   e   v'ascolto;
with   what   sweetness   lips   scented   both   you   I kiss   and   you I listen to
With what sweetness, fragrant lips, do I both kiss you and listen to you;

ma   se   'gɔ do   un   pja 'tʃer   'lal tro   mɛ   'tɔl to
ma   se   godo   un   piacer,   l'altro   m'è   tolto,
but   if   I enjoy   one   pleasure   the other   from me is   taken away
but if I enjoy one pleasure, the other is taken away from me,

'ko me   i   'vɔ stri   di 'lɛt: ti   san 'tʃi do no   fra   lor
come   i   vostri   diletti   s'ancidono   fra   lor,
as   the   your   delights   themselves kill   among   them
as your delights kill each other

> *ancidono: from ancidere = (mod.) uccidere*

se   dol tʃe 'men te   'vi ve   per   am be 'du e   'la ni ma   'mi a
se   dolcemente   vive   per   ambedue   l'anima   mia.
if   agreeably   lives   for   both   the soul   mine
even though my soul lives agreeably for both.

ke   so 'a ve   ar mo 'ni a   fa 'ɾe ste   o   'ka ɾi   'ba tʃi
Che   soave   armonia   fareste,   o   cari   baci,
what   sweet   harmony   you would make   o   dear   kisses
What sweet harmony you would make, o dear kisses,

ke   so 'a ve   ar mo 'ni a   fa 're ste   o   'dol tʃi 'det: ti
che   soave   armonia   fareste,   o   dolci   detti,
what   sweet   harmony   you would make   o   gentle   words
what sweet harmony you would make, o gentle words,

se   'fo ste   u ni ta 'men te   dam be 'du e   le   dol 'tʃet: tse   'am bo   ka 'pa tʃi
se   foste   unitamente   d'ambedue   le   dolcezze   ambo   capaci,
if   you were   in unison   of both   the   sweetnesses   both   capable
if you were both capable of uniting your sweetnesses –

ba 'tʃan do   i   'det: ti   e   ra dʒo 'nan do   i   'ba tʃi
baciando   i   detti   e   ragionando   i   baci!
kissing   the   words   and   speaking   the   kisses
the words kissing and the kisses speaking!

&

[39]
from: *Orfeo (1607)* Alternately titled **L'Orfeo Prologo**.
character: *La Musica*   *Alessandro Striggio*

dal 'mi o   per 'mɛs: so   a 'ma to
Dal mio Permesso amato
From my beloved Permessos

dal   'mi o   per 'mɛs: so   a 'ma to   a   'vo i   ne 'veɲ: ɲo   'iŋ kli ti   e 'rɔ i
Dal   mio   Permesso   amato   a   voi   ne vegno   incliti   eroi,
from the   my   Permessos   beloved   to   you   from I come   illustrious   heroes
From my beloved Permessos I come to you, illustrious heroes,

> *vegno (poet.)*
> *= vengo*

'saŋ gwɛ   dʒɛn 'til   de   're dʒi   di   'ku i   'nar: ra   la   'fa ma   et: 'tʃɛl si   'prɛ dʒi
sangue   gentil   de'   regi,   di   cui   narra   la   Fama   eccelsi   pregi
blood   noble   of the   kings   of   whom   speaks   the   Fame   excellent   merits
you with the noble blood of kings, of whom Fame speaks your excellent merits

ne   'dʒun dʒe   al   ver   per 'kɛ   trɔp: 'pal to   il   'seɲ: ɲo
né   giunge   al   ver   perch'è   tropp'alto   il   segno.
nor   reaches   to the   truth   because is   too lofty   the   aim
though does not reach the truth, because too lofty is the aim.

'i o   la   'mu zi ka   son   'ka i   'dol tʃi   at: 'tʃɛn ti   sɔ   far   traŋ 'kwil: lo
Io   la   Musica   son,   ch'ai   dolci   accenti   so   far   tranquillo
I   the   Music   I am   who at the   sweet   accents   I know how   to make   tranquil
I am Music, who with my sweet accents knows how to calm

'oɲ: ɲi   tur 'ba to   'kɔ ɾe   e dor   di   'nɔ bil   'i ɾa   e dor   da 'mo ɾe   pɔs: sin fjam: 'mar
ogni   turbato   core   ed or   di   nobil   ira   ed or   d'amore   poss'infiammar
every   troubled   heart   and now   with   noble   fury   and now   with love   can inflame
every troubled heart and, now with noble fury and now with love, can inflame

le   pju   dʒe 'la te   'men ti
le   più   gelate   menti.
the   most   frozen   minds
the most ice-cold minds.

'i o   su   'tʃe te ɾa   dɔr   kan 'tan do   'sɔʎ: ʎo
Io   **su** **cetera**   **d'or** **cantando**   **soglio**
I   upon   cithara   of gold   singing   I am in the habit of

Singing upon a golden lyre, I am in the habit of

<table>
<tr><td>cetera =
(mod.) cetra</td></tr>
</table>

mor 'tal   o 'rek: kjo   lu ziŋ 'gar   ta 'lo ɾa   e   in   'kwe sta   'gwi za   lar mo 'ni a   so 'no ɾa
mortal **orecchio** **lusingar** **tal' ora** **e** **in** **questa** **guisa** **l'armonia** **sonora**
mortal   ear   to entice   at times   and   in   this   manner   the harmony   sonorous

de   la   'li ɾa   del   tʃel   pju   'lal me   in 'vɔʎ: ʎo
de **la** **lira** **del** **ciel** **più** **l'alme** **invoglio.**
of   the   lyre   of the   heaven   most   the souls   I inspire

enticing mortal ears at times; and in doing so I most inspire souls with the sonorous harmony of the
lyre of heaven.

'kwin tʃi   a   'dir vi   dor 'fɛ o   de 'zi o   mi   'spro na
Quinci   **a** **dirvi**   **d'Orfeo** **desio** **mi** **sprona,**
hence   to   to tell you of Orfeo   desire   me   urges

Hence, desire urges me to tell you about Orfeo –

dor 'fɛ o   ke   'tras: se   al   'su o   kan 'tar   le   'fɛ ɾe
d'Orfeo, **che** **trasse** **al** **suo** **cantar** **le** **fere**
of Orfeo   who   drew   at the   his   singing   the   wild beasts

about Orfeo, who drew the wild beasts [to him] with his singing

<table>
<tr><td>fere (plural of
fera) = (mod.) fiere</td></tr>
</table>

e   'sɛr vo   fe   lin 'fɛr no   a   'su e   pre 'gje ɾe
e **servo** **fè** **l'inferno** **a** **sue** **preghiere,**
and   servant   made   the hell   at   his   entreaties

and made hell his servant with his entreaties –

<table>
<tr><td>fè =
(mod.) fece</td></tr>
</table>

'glɔ rja   im: mor 'tal   di   'pin do   e   de li 'ko na
gloria **immortal** **di** **Pindo** **e** **d'Elicona.**
glory   immortal   of   Pindus   and   of Helicon

[Orfeo], the immortal glory of Pindus and of Helicon.

or   'men tre   i   'kan ti   al 'tɛr no   or   'lje ti   or   'mɛ sti
Or   **mentre** **i** **canti** **alterno,** **or** **lieti** **or** **mesti,**
now   while   the   songs   I alternate   now   happy   now   sad

Now while I vary my songs – now happy, now sad –

non   si 'mɔ va   a u dʒel: 'lin   fra   'kwe ste   'pjan te
non **si mova** **augellin**   **fra** **queste** **piante,**
not   may stir   little bird   among   these   bushes

may nary a little bird stir among these bushes,

<table>
<tr><td>augellin[o] (poet.)
= uccellin[o]
mova: from "movere"
= (mod.) "muovere"</td></tr>
</table>

ne   'sɔ da   in   'kwe ste   'ri ve   'on da   so 'nan te
né **s'oda** **in** **queste** **rive** **onda** **sonante**
nor   may be heard on   these   shores   wave   sounding

nor a wave be heard playing on these shores,

e 'doɲ: ɲi   a u 'ret: ta   in   'su o   ka 'min   sar: 'rɛ sti
ed ogni **auretta**   **in** **suo** **camin** **s'arresti.**
and every   little breeze   on   its   path   may come to a stop

and may every little breeze stop in its path.

<table>
<tr><td>camin[o] =
(mod.) cammino</td></tr>
</table>

GL: **Elicona, Fama, Musica, Orfeo, Permesso, Pindo**

[37]
from: *Il ritorno d'Ulisse in patria (1640)*
character: *Penelope*

Giacomo Badoaro

di 'mi ze ɾa re 'dʒi na
Di misera regina
Of the unhappy queen

di	'mi ze ɾa	re 'dʒi na	non	ter mi 'na ti	'ma i	do 'lɛn ti	afː 'fanː ni
Di	**misera**	**Regina**	**non**	**terminati**	**mai**	**dolenti**	**affanni!**
of	unhappy	queen	not	ended	ever	painful	woes

O never-ending painful woes of the unhappy queen!

la spetː 'ta to	non	'dʒun dʒe	e	pur	'fugː go no	ʎi	'anː ni
L'aspettato	**non**	**giunge**	**e**	**pur**	**fuggono**	**gli**	**anni.**
the awaited one	not	arrives	and	yet	flee	the	years

The awaited one does not come, and yet the years fly by.

la	'sɛ ɾje	del	pe 'nar	ɛ	'luŋ ga	'a i	'trɔpː po
La	**serie**	**del**	**penar**	**è**	**lunga,**	**ahi,**	**troppo:**
the	succession	of the	suffering	is	long	alas	too much

The measure of suffering is, alas, too great;

a	ki	'vi ve	in	aŋ 'gɔʃː ʃa	il	'tɛm po	ɛ	'tsɔpː po
a	**chi**	**vive**	**in**	**angoscia**	**il**	**tempo**	**è**	**zoppo.**
to	one who	lives	in	anguish	the	time	is	lame in legs or feet

for one who lives in anguish, time does not move on.

falː la 'tʃisː si ma	'spe me	spe 'ran tse	non	pju	'ver di	ma	ka 'nu te
Fallacissima	**speme,**	**speranze**	**non**	**più**	**verdi,**	**ma**	**canute,**
most fallacious	hopes	hopes	not	more	green	but	white (haired)

Falsest hopes, hope no longer youthful but aged,

speme (lit.)
= *speranze*

alː lin vekː 'kja to	'ma le	non	pro metː 'te te	pju	'pa tʃe	o	sa 'lu te
all'invecchiato	**male**	**non**	**promettete**	**più**	**pace**	**o**	**salute.**
to the grown-old	pain	not	you promise	more	peace	or	salvation

you promise no more peace or salvation to my pain grown old.

skor 'se ɾo	'kwatː tro	'lu stri	dal	me mo 'ra bil	'dʒor no	in	'ku i
Scorsero	**quattro**	**lustri**	**dal**	**memorabil**	**giorno**	**in**	**cui**
passed	four	lusters	from the	memorable	day	on	which

Twenty years have passed since the memorable day when,

scorsero =
scorserono

lusters: periods of five years

kon	'su e	ra 'pi ne	il	su 'pɛr bo	tro 'ja no	kja 'mɔ	'lal ta	'su a	'pa trja	'alː le	ru 'i ne
con	**sue**	**rapine**	**il**	**superbo**	**Trojano**	**chiamò**	**l'alta**	**sua**	**patria**	**alle**	**ruine.**
with	his	plunders	the	proud	Trojan	called	the noble	his	homeland	to the	ruins

with his plunder, the proud Trojan *[Paris]* brought ruin to his noble homeland.

a ra 'dʒon	'ar se	'trɔ ja	po i 'ke	la 'mo ɾe	im 'pu ɾo
A ragion	**arse**	**Troja,**	**poichè**	**l'amore**	**impuro,**
rightly	burned	Troy	since	the love	impure

Rightly did Troy burn, since impure love,

kɛ	de 'litː to	di	'fɔ ko	si 'pur ga	kon	le	'fjamː me
ch'è	**delitto**	**di**	**foco**	**si purga**	**con**	**le**	**fiamme.**
which is	crime	of	fire	one purges	with	the	flames

which is a crime of passion, is purged with flames.

ma	bɛn	ˈkon tro	ra ˈdʒo ne	per	lal ˈtru i	ˈfal: lo	kon dan: ˈna ta
Ma	**ben**	**contro**	**ragione**	**per**	**l'altrui**	**fallo**	**condannata,**
but	well	against	reason	for	the others'	error	condemned

But, condemned most unjustifiably for the errors of others,

in: no ˈtʃɛn te	del: lal ˈtru i	ˈkol pe	ˈi o	ˈso no	laf: ˈflit: ta	pe ni ˈtɛn te
innocente	**dell'altrui**	**colpe**	**io**	**sono**	**l'afflitta,**	**penitente.**
innocent	of the others'	guilts	I	I am	the afflicted one	penitent

innocent of others' guilt, I am the afflicted one, in penance.

u ˈlis: se	ak: ˈkɔr to	e	ˈsad: dʒo	tu	ke	pu ˈnir	ʎi	a ˈdul te ri	ti ˈvan ti
Ulisse	**accorto**	**e**	**saggio,**	**tu**	**che**	**punir**	**gli**	**adulteri**	**ti vanti,**
Ulysses	astute	and	wise	you	who	to punish	the	adulterers	you boast

Astute and wise Ulysses, you who boast of punishing the adulterers,

a ˈgut: tsi	ˈlar mi	e	ˈsuʃ: ʃi ti	le	ˈfjam: me	per	ven di ˈkar	ʎi	er: ˈro ri
aguzzi	**l'armi**	**e**	**susciti**	**le**	**fiamme**	**per**	**vendicar**	**gli**	**errori**
you sharpen	the weapons	and	you stir up	the	flames	for	to avenge	the	errors

you sharpen your weapons and you incite the flames to avenge the errors

ˈdu na	ˈprɔ fu ga	ˈgre ka	e	in ˈtan to	ˈlaʃ: ʃi	la	ˈtu a	ˈka sta	kon ˈsɔr te
d'una	**profuga**	**greca;**	**e**	**intanto**	**lasci**	**la**	**tua**	**casta**	**consorte**
of a	refugee	Greek	and	meanwhile	you leave	the	your	chaste	wife

of a fugitive Greek *[Helen]*; [and] meanwhile, you leave your chaste wife

fra	i	ne ˈmi tʃi	ri ˈva li	in	ˈdub: bjo	del: lo ˈnor	in ˈfor se	a	ˈmɔr te
fra	**i**	**nemici**	**rivali**	**in**	**dubbio**	**dell'onor,**	**in forse**	**a**	**morte!**
among	the	enemy	rivals	in	doubt	of the honor	in danger	to	death

among hostile enemies, in danger to her honor, to death!

ˈoɲ: ɲi	par ˈtɛn tsa	at: ˈtɛn de	de zi ˈa to	ri ˈtor no
Ogni	**partenza**	**attende**	**desiato**	**ritorno.**
Every	departure	expects	desired	return

Every departure supposes a longed-for return;

tu	sol	del	ˈtu o	tor ˈnar	per ˈde sti	il	ˈdʒor no
Tu	**sol**	**del**	**tuo**	**tornar**	**perdesti**	**il**	**giorno.**
you	only	of the	your	returning	you missed	the	day

you alone have missed the day of your return.

non	ɛ	ˈduŋ kwe	per	me	ˈva ɾja	la	ˈsɔr te
Non	**è**	**dunque**	**per**	**me**	**varia**	**la**	**sorte?**
not	is	then	for	me	changeable	the	fate

Is my fate unchangeable, then?

kan ˈdʒo	ˈfor se	for ˈtu na	la	vo ˈlu bi le	ˈrwɔ ta	in	ˈsta bil	ˈsɛd: dʒo
Cangiò	**forse**	**Fortuna**	**la**	**volubile**	**ruota**	**in**	**stabil**	**seggio?**
changed	perhaps	fortune	the	changeable	wheel	into	fixed	seat

Has Fortune perhaps changed her moving wheel into an immoveable seat?

e	la	ˈsu a	ˈpron ta	ˈve la	ke	ˈoɲ: ɲi	u ˈman	ˈka zo	ˈpɔr ta
E	**la**	**sua**	**pronta**	**vela,**	**che**	**ogni**	**uman**	**caso**	**porta**
and	the	her	ready	sail	which	every	human	event	brings

fra	liŋ ko ˈstan tsa	a	ˈvo lo
fra	**l'incostanza**	**a**	**volo,**
among	the variability	in	flight

And does her ready sail, which brings variability to every human event in flight,

sol	per	me	non	rak: 'kɔʎ: ʎe	un	'fja to	'so lo
sol	**per**	**me**	**non**	**raccoglie**	**un**	**fiato**	**solo?**
only	for	me	not	gathers	a	breath	single

not gather a single breath of air only for me?

'kan dʒan	per	'al tri	pur	a 'spɛt: to	il	'tʃɛ lo	le	'stel: le er: 'ran ti	e	'fis: se
Cangian	**per**	**altri**	**pur**	**aspetto**	**il**	**cielo,**	**le**	**stelle erranti**	**e**	**fisse.**
change	for	others	yet	aspect	the	heaven	the	stars moving	and	fixed

Yet the heaven, the moving stars and fixed planets [stars] change configuration for others.

'tor na	dɛ	'tor na	u 'lis: se	pe 'nɛ lo pe	ta 'spɛt: ta
Torna	**deh!**	**torna,**	**Ulisse!**	**Penelope**	**t'aspetta!**
return	pray	return	Ulysses	Penelope	you awaits

Return, please! Return, Ulysses! Penelope awaits you!

lin: no 'tʃɛn te	so 'spi ɾa	'pjan dʒe	lof: 'fe za
L'innocente	**sospira,**	**piange**	**l'offesa,**
the innocent one	sighs	weeps	the offended one

The innocent one is sighing; the offended one is weeping,

e	'kon tro	il	te 'na tʃe	of: fen 'sor	ne	pur	sa 'di ɾa
e	**contro**	**il**	**tenace**	**offensor**	**né**	**pur**	**s'adira.**
and	against	the	tenacious	offender	nor	yet	gets angry

and yet is not angry with the tenacious offender.

al: 'la ni ma	af: fan: 'na ta	'pɔr to	le	'su e	di 'skol pe	at: 'tʃɔ	non	're sti
All'anima	**affannata**	**porto**	**le**	**sue**	**discolpe,**	**acciò**	**non**	**resti**
at the soul	troubled	I bear	the	his	defences	so that	not	may remain

In my troubled soul I bear his defence, so that it may not

di	kru del 'ta	mak: 'kja to	ma	'fab: bro	'de i	'mjɛ i	'dan: ni	iŋ 'kol po	il	'fa to
di	**crudeltà**	**macchiato,**	**ma,**	**fabbro**	**dei**	**miei**	**danni,**	**incolpo**	**il**	**Fato.**
with	cruelty	stained	but	creator	of the	my	damages	I blame	the	Fate

be stained with cruelty; but I blame Fate as the cause of my deep grief.

ko 'zi	per	'tu a	di 'spɛn sa	kol	de 'sti no
Così	**per**	**tua**	**dispensa,**	**col**	**destino,**
thus	for	your	dispensation	with the	destiny

kol	'tʃe lo	fo 'men to	'gwɛr: ra	e	sta bi 'li sko	'ris: se
col	**cielo**	**fomento**	**guerra**	**e**	**stabilisco**	**risse.**
with the	heaven	I incite	war	and	I establish	disputes

Instead of laying blame on you, I war and dispute with destiny and heaven.

'tor na	dɛ	'tor na	u 'lis: se
Torna,	**deh!**	**torna,**	**Ulisse!**
return	pray	return	Ulysses

Return, please! Return, Ulysses!

'tor na	il	traŋ 'kwil: lo	al	'ma ɾe	'tor na	il	'dzɛf: fi ɾo	al	'pra to
Torna	**il**	**tranquillo**	**al**	**mare,**	**torna**	**il**	**zeffiro**	**al**	**prato,**
returns	the	calmness	to the	sea	returns	the	breeze	to the	meadow

Calm returns to the sea, the breeze returns to the meadow;

la u 'rɔ ɾa	'men tre	al	sol	fa	'dol tʃe	in 'vi to	a	un	ri 'tor no
l'aurora	**mentre**	**al**	**sol**	**fa**	**dolce**	**invito**	**a**	**un**	**ritorno**
the dawn	meanwhile	to the	sun	makes	sweet	invitation	to a		return

the dawn, meanwhile, sweetly invites the sun to a return

printed "è"
must be a
misprint for "a"

del   di   kɛ   'pri a   par 'ti to
del   dì   ch'è   pria   partito.
of the   day   that is   before   departed
of the day previously departed.

*pria =
(mod.) prima*

'tor nan   le   'bri ne   in   'tɛr: ra   'tor na no   al   'tʃɛn tro   i   'sas: si   e
Tornan   le   brine   in   terra,   tornano   al   centro   i   sassi   e,
return   the   frosts   on   earth   return   to the   center   the   rocks   and
Frosts return to earth, rocks return to the center *[the earth, the ground]*, and

kon   'lu bri tʃi   'pas: si   'tor na   al: lo 'tʃe a no   il   'ri vo
con   lubrici   passi,   torna   all'oceano   il   rivo.
with   slippery   steps   returns   to the ocean   the   stream
the stream returns, in smooth flow, to the ocean.

'lwɔ mo   kwad: 'dʒu   kɛ   'vi vo   'lun dʒe   'da i   'swɔ i   prin 'tʃi pi
L'uomo   quaggiù,   ch'è   vivo,   lunge   dai   suoi   principi
the man   here below   who is   alive   far   from the   his   beginnings
Man, alive in this world far from his origins,

*printed "principii"
= (mod.) principi*

'pɔr ta   u 'nal ma   tʃe 'lɛ ste   e   un   'kɔr po   'fra le
porta   un'alma   celeste   e   un   corpo   frale.
bears   a soul   heavenly   and   a   body   mortal
bears a heavenly soul and a mortal body.

'tɔ sto   'mɔ ɾe   il   mor 'ta le   e   'tor na   'lal ma   in   'tʃe lo
Tosto   more   il   mortale   e   torna   l'alma   in   cielo,
soon   dies   the   mortal   and   returns   the soul   to   heaven
The mortal soon dies, and the soul returns to heaven;

*more =
muore*

e   'tor na   il   'kɔr po   in   'pol ve   'do po   'brɛ ve   sod: 'dʒor no
e   torna   il   corpo   in   polve,   dopo   breve   soggiorno.
and   returns   the   body   to   dust   after   brief   sojourn
and the body returns to dust after a brief sojourn.

*polve =
(mod.) polvere*

tu   sol   del   'tu o   tor 'nar   per 'de sti   il   'dʒor no
Tu   sol   del   tuo   tornar   perdesti   il   giorno.
you   only   of the   your   returning   you missed   the   day
You alone have missed the day of your return.

'tor na   ke   'men tre   'pɔr ti   'em pje   di 'mɔ ɾe   al   'mi o   'fjɛ ɾo   do 'lo ɾe
Torna,   ché   mentre   porti   empie   dimore   al   mio   fiero   dolore,
return   because   while   you bring   cruel   abodes   to the   my   fierce   pain
Return, because while you bring cruel lodging to my fierce pain

"di more," rather than "dimore," may have been the original; but if so, that doesn't really help in translation...

'ved: dʒo   del   'mi o   mo 'rir   'lo ɾa   pre 'fis: se
veggio   del   mio   morir   l'ora   prefisse.
I see   of the   my   dying   the hour   pre-arranged
I foresee the pre-arranged hour of my death.

*veggio (poet.)
= vedo*

'tor na   dɛ   'tor na   u 'lis: se
Torna,   deh!   torna,   Ulisse!
return   pray   return   Ulysses
Return, please! Return, Ulysses!

GL: **Fortuna, Penelope, Troja, Ulisse**

੭

[75, 76]

'ɛk: ko di 'dol tʃi 'rad: dʒi
Ecco di dolci raggi
Behold, with sweet rays

'ɛk: ko	di	'dol tʃi	'rad: dʒi	il	sol	ar 'ma to	del	'vɛr no	sa et: 'tar
Ecco	**di**	**dolci**	**raggi**	**il**	**sol**	**armato**	**del**	**verno**	**saettar**
here is	of	sweet	rays	the	sun	armed	of the	winter	to throw arrows at

la	sta 'dʒon	'flɔ ɾi da
la	**stagion**	**florida;**
the	season	blooming

Behold the sun, armed with sweet rays, transforming the winter into the blooming season;

di	dol 'tʃis: si ma 'mor	i ne bri 'a to	'dɔr me	'ta tʃi to	'vɛn to	in	sen	di	'klɔ ɾi da
di	**dolcissim'amor**	**inebriato**	**dorme**	**tacito**	**vento**	**in**	**sen**	**di**	**Clorida,**
of	sweetest love	drunk	sleeps	silent	wind	in	breast	of	Clorida

drunk with sweetest love, the wind sleeps silently in the breast of Clorida,

ta 'lor	pe 'rɔ	laʃ: 'ʃi vo	e	o do 'ra to	on ded: 'dʒar	tre mo 'lar
talor	**però**	**lascivo**	**e**	**odorato,**	**ondeggiar,**	**tremolar**
sometimes	however	lascivious	and	scented	to sway	to quiver

fa	'lɛr ba	'flɔ ɾi da
fa	**l'erba**	**florida.**
it makes	the grass	flourishing

though at times, wanton and perfumed, it makes the flourishing grass waver and quiver.

'la ɾja	la	'tɛr: ra	il	tʃɛl	'spi ɾan	a 'mo ɾe	'ar da	'duŋ kwe	da 'mor
L'aria,	**la**	**terra,**	**il**	**ciel**	**spiran**	**amore,**	**arda**	**dunque**	**d'amor,**
the air	the	earth	the	sky	breathe	love	may burn	then	of love

'ar da	'oɲ: ɲi	'kɔ ɾe
arda	**ogni**	**core.**
may burn	every	heart

The air, the earth, [and] the sky breathe love; and so may every heart burn with love.

GL: **Clorida**

❧

[61]
from: *Orfeo (1607)*
character: *Orfeo*

Alessandro Striggio

'ɛk: ko pur ka 'vo i ri 'tor no
Ecco pur ch'a voi ritorno
I return here to you

'ɛk: ko	pur	ka	'vo i	ri 'tor no	'ka ɾe	'sel ve	e	'pjad: dʒe	a 'ma te
Ecco	**pur**	**ch'a**	**voi**	**ritorno,**	**care**	**selve**	**e**	**piaggie**	**amate,**
here	[indeed	that] to	you	I return	dear	woods	and	shores	beloved

I return here to you, dear woods and beloved shores,

da	kwel	sol	'fat: te	be 'a te	per	'ku i	sol	'mi e	'nɔt: tan	'dʒor no
da	**quel**	**sol**	**fatte**	**beate,**	**per**	**cui**	**sol**	**mie**	**nott'han**	**giorno.**
from	that	sun	made	blessed	through	which	only	my	nights have	day

blessed by that sun through which alone my nights are [turned into] days.

a play on words: sol[e] (sun = figuratively, beloved one), and sol[e] = only

❧

[73]

e dɛ pur ˈduŋ kwe ˈve ɾo
Ed è pur dunque vero
Then it is indeed true

e ˈdɛ	pur	ˈduŋ kwe	ˈve ɾo	di zu ma ˈna to	kɔr	ˈa ni ma	ˈkru da		
Ed è	**pur**	**dunque**	**vero,**	**disumanato**	**cor,**	**anima**	**cruda,**		
[and] it is	indeed	then	true	dehumanized	heart	soul	cruel		

Then it is indeed true, o heart rendered inhuman, cruel woman,

The title in [73] is **Et è pur vero.** *"Et" = (mod.) "E."*

ke	kan ˈdʒan do	pen ˈsjɛ ɾo	e	di	ˈfe de	e	da ˈmor	tu	ˈrɛ sti	iɲ: ˈɲu da
che	**cangiando**	**pensiero**	**e**	**di**	**fede**	**e**	**d'amor**	**tu**	**resti**	**ignuda?**
that	changing	thought	and	of	faith	and	of love	you	you remain	naked

that in changing your mind you are bereft of faith and love?

da ˈver	tra ˈdi to	me	ˈda ti	pur	ˈvan to	
D'aver	**tradito**	**me**	**dati**	**pur**	**vanto,**	
of to have	betrayed	to me	give yourself	yet	credit	

Yet, do boast of having betrayed me,

ke	la	ˈtʃe te ɾa	ˈmi a	ri ˈvɔl go	in	ˈpjan to	
ché	**la**	**cetera**	**mia**	**rivolgo**	**in**	**pianto.**	
because	the	cithara	mine	I turn	in	weeping	

for I have turned my cithara to weeping.

cetera = (mod.) cetra

ɛ	ˈkwe sto	il	gwi der ˈdo ne	de	la mo ˈɾo ze	ˈmi e	ˈtan te	fa ˈti ke	
È	**questo**	**il**	**guiderdone**	**de**	**l'amorose**	**mie**	**tante**	**fatiche?**	
is	this	the	reward	of	the amorous	my	so many	efforts	

Is this the reward for so many amorous efforts of mine?

ko ˈzi	mi	fa	ra ˈdʒo ne	il	ˈvɔ stro	ˈrɛ o	de ˈstin	ˈstel: le	ne ˈmi ke	
Così	**mi**	**fa**	**ragione,**	**il**	**vostro**	**reo**	**destin,**	**stelle**	**nemiche?**	
thus	to me	makes	reason	the	your	wicked	fate	stars	hostile	

To this does your wicked fate resign me, hostile stars?

ma	sel	ˈtu o	kɔr	ɛ	ˈdoɲ: ɲi	fe	ri ˈbɛl: le	
Ma	**se'l**	**tuo**	**cor**	**è**	**d'ogni**	**fe'**	**ribelle,**	
but	if the	your	heart	is	of every	faithfulness	rebel	

But if your heart rebels against all faithfulness,

ˈli dja	la	ˈkol pa	ɛ	ˈtu a	non	ˈdel: le	ˈstel: le	
Lidia,	**la**	**colpa**	**è**	**tua,**	**non**	**delle**	**stelle.**	
Lydia	the	fault	is	yours	not	of the	stars	

Lydia, the fault is yours, not the stars'.

be ve ˈɾɔ	sfor tu ˈna to	ʎas: sas: si ˈna ti	ˈmje i	ˈtor bi di	ˈpjan ti		
Beverò,	**sfortunato,**	**gl'assassinati**	**miei**	**torbidi**	**pianti,**		
I will swallow	unlucky	the tormented	my	troubled	tears		

I, unlucky one, will swallow my tormented, troubled tears

e	ˈsɛm pre	ad: do lo ˈra to	a	ˈtut: ti	ˈʎal tri	ab: ban do ˈna ti	a ˈman ti	
e	**sempre**	**addolorato**	**a**	**tutti**	**gl'altri**	**abbandonati**	**amanti,**	
and	always	saddened	to	all	the other	abandoned	lovers	

and, saddened forever, to all the other abandoned lovers

e skol pi 'rɔ sul 'mar mo 'al: la 'mi a 'fe de
e scolpirò sul marmo alla mia fede:
and I will sculpt upon the marble to the my faith
I will carve on the tombstone of my faith:

'ʃɔk: ko ɛ kwel kɔr kin 'bɛl: la 'dɔn: na 'kre de
Sciocco è quel cor ch'in bella donna crede.
foolish is that heart which in beautiful woman believes
"Foolish is the heart that believes in a beautiful woman."

'pɔ ve ɾo di kon 'fɔr to men 'di ko di spe 'ran tsa an 'drɔ ra 'min go
Povero di conforto, mendico di speranza, andrò ramingo;
lacking of comfort beggar of hope I shall go wandering
Lacking comfort, begging for hope, I shall wander;

e 'sɛn tsa 'sal ma o 'pɔr to fra tem 'pe ste vi 'vrɔ 'me sto e so 'lin go
e senza salma o porto, fra tempeste vivrò mesto e solingo.
and without armor or harbor among tempests I will live sad and lonely
and without armor or harbor, among tempests I will live sad and lonely.

ne a 'vrɔ la 'mɔr te di pre 'tʃi pi ti a 'ski vo
Né avrò la morte di precipiti a schivo
not I shall have the death of precipices reluctant to
I shall not die afraid of the depths,

per 'ke non pwɔ mo 'rir ki non ɛ 'vi vo
perché non può morir chi non è vivo.
because not is able to die he who not is alive
for he who is not alive cannot die.

il 'nu me ɾo de ʎi 'an: ni kal sol di 'tu e bel: 'let: tse
Il numero de gli anni ch'al sol di tue bellezze
the number of the years that at the sun of your beauties

de gli =
(mod.) degli

'i o 'fu i di 'ne ve
io fui di neve,
I I was of snow
The number of years I was snow beneath the sunshine of your beauties,

il 'kol mo deʎ: ʎaf: 'fan: ni ke non mi 'dje ɾo 'ma i ri 'pɔ zo 'brɛ ve
il colmo degl'affanni che non mi diero mai riposo breve:
the height of the woes which not to me gave ever repose brief
the enormity of the woes which never gave me repose, however brief –

diero =
diedero
(from the
verb "dare")

in seɲ: ɲe 'ran: no a mor mo 'rar i 'vɛn ti le 'tu e per 'fi dje
insegneranno a mormorar i venti le tue perfidie,
they will teach to to whisper the winds the your treacheries
they will teach the winds to whisper your treacheries,

o 'kru da e i 'mjɛ i tor 'men ti
o cruda, e i miei tormenti.
o cruel one and the my torments
o cruel one, and my torments.

'vi vi   kol   kɔr   di   'gjat: tʃo   e   liŋ kon 'stan tsa   'tu a   'la u ɾa   dif: 'fi di
Vivi   col   cor   di   ghiaccio,   e   l'inconstanza   tua   l'aura   diffidi;
live   with the   heart   of   ice   and   the inconstancy   your   the breeze   let distrust
Live with a heart of ice, and let the breeze distrust your inconstancy;

> *inconstanza = (mod.) incostanza*

'strin dʒi   il   'tu o   bɛn   in   'brat: tʃo
stringi   il   tuo   ben   in   braccio
clasp   the   your   dear one   in   arm
embrace your dear one

e   del   'mi o   mal   kon   'lu i   tri 'on fa   e   'ri di
e   del   mio   mal   con   lui   trionfa   e   ridi;
and   of the   my   hurt   with   him   exult   and   laugh
and exult and laugh with him about my hurt,

e   'am bi   in   u 'njon   'dol tʃe   gra 'di ta   fab: bri 'ka te   il   se 'pol kro   'al: la   'mi a   'vi ta
e   ambi   in   union   dolce   gradita   fabbricate   il   sepolcro   alla   mia   vita.
and   both   in   unity   sweet   pleasant   make   the   sepulchre   to the   my   life
and both [of you], in sweet and pleasant unity, build a sepulchre for my life.

a 'bis: si   u 'di te   di   'mi a   di spe ɾa 'tsjon   ʎi   'ul ti mi   at: 'tʃen ti
Abissi   udite,   di   mia   disperazion   gli   ultimi   accenti,
abysses   hear   of   my   despair   the   final   words
Hear, abysses, the final words of my despair,

da   'pɔ i   ke   son   for 'ni te   le   'mi e   'dʒɔ je   e   ʎa 'mor
da   poi   che   son   fornite   le   mie   gioie   e   gl'amor
from   since   are   finished   the   my   joys   and   the loves

> *poi che =*
> *(mod.) poiché*

e   i   'mjɛ i   kon 'tɛn ti
e   i   miei   contenti.
and   the   my   contentments
since my joys and loves and contentments are over.

'tan to   ɛl   'mi o   mal   ke   no mi 'nar   'i o   'vɔʎ: ʎo
Tanto   è'l   mio   mal   che   nominar   io   voglio
so much   is the   my   hurt   that   to name   I   I wish
So great is my hurt that I wish to name

'ɛ mu lo   del   in 'fɛr no   il   'mi o   kor 'dɔʎ: ʎo
emulo   del   inferno   il   mio   cordoglio.
emulator   of the   hell   the   my   grief
my grief emulator of hell.

☙

[72, 73, 75, 76]

'ɛ ɾi dʒa 'tut: ta 'mi a
Eri già tutta mia
You were once all mine

'ɛ ɾi   dʒa   'tut: ta   'mi a   'mi a   kwel: 'lal ma   e   kwel   'kɔ ɾe
Eri   già   tutta   mia,   mia   quell'alma   e   quel   core;
you were   once   all   mine   mine   that soul   and   that   heart
You were once all mine – mine, that soul and that heart;

ki	da	me	ti	de 'zvi a	'nɔ vo	'lat: tʃo	da 'mo ɾe
chi	**da**	**me**	**ti**	**desvia:**	**novo**	**laccio**	**d'amore?**
who	from	me	you	diverts	new	snare	of love

who turns you away from me? A new snare of love?

desviare = (mod.)
disviare = deviare

o	bel: 'let: tsa	o	va 'lo ɾe	o	mi 'ra bil	kon 'stan tsa	'do ve	'sɛ i	tu
O	**bellezza,**	**o**	**valore,**	**o**	**mirabil**	**constanza,**	**dove**	**sei**	**tu?**
o	beauty	o	virtue	o	wonderful	constancy	where	are	you

O beauty, o virtue, o wondrous constancy, where are you?

constanza = (mod.) costanza | *in [76]: ove = dove*

	'ɛ ɾi	dʒa	'tut: ta	'mi a	or	non	'sɛ i	pju	non	pju
Chorus:	**Eri**	**già**	**tutta**	**mia;**	**or**	**non**	**sei**	**più,**	**non**	**più.**
	you were	once	all	mine	now	not	you are	more	not	more

You were once all mine; now you are mine no longer.

a	ke	'mi a	non	'sɛ i	pju
Ah,	**che**	**mia**	**non**	**sei**	**più.**
ah	[that]	mine	not	you are	more

Ah, you are no longer mine.

sol	per	me	'ʎɔk: ki	'bɛl: li	ri vol 'dʒe vi	ri 'dɛn ti
Sol	**per**	**me**	**gl'occhi**	**belli**	**rivolgevi**	**ridenti,**
only	for	me	the eyes	beautiful	you turned	smiling

You used to turn your smiling eyes only to me;

var.: gli occhi = gl'occhi

per	me	'dɔ ɾo	i	ka 'pel: li	si spje 'ga van	'a i	'vɛn ti
per	**me**	**d'oro**	**i**	**capelli**	**si spiegavan**	**ai**	**venti.**
for	me	of gold	the	hair	themselves spread out	at the	winds

for me your golden hair spread open in the winds.

o	fu 'ga tʃi	kon 'tɛn ti	o	fer 'met: tsa	dun	'kɔ ɾe	'do ve	'sɛ i	tu
O	**fugaci**	**contenti,**	**o**	**fermezza**	**d'un**	**core,**	**dove**	**sei**	**tu?**
o	fleeting	contentments	o	steadfastness	of a	heart	where	are	you

O fleeting contentments, o heart's steadfastness, where are you?

il	dʒo 'ir	nel	'mi o	'vi zo	a	ke	pju	non	ri 'mi ɾi
Il	**gioir**	**nel**	**mio**	**viso,**	**ah**	**che**	**più**	**non**	**rimiri;**
the	rejoicing	in the	my	face	ah	[that]	more	not	you look at

Ah, no more do you see joy in my face;

il	'mi o	'kan to	il	'mi o	'ri zo	ɛ	kon 'vɛr so	in	mar 'ti ɾi
il	**mio**	**canto,**	**il**	**mio**	**riso**	**è**	**converso**	**in**	**martiri.**
the	my	song	the	my	laugh	is	changed	into	agonies

my song [and] my laughter have been changed to suffering.

o	di 'spɛr si	so 'spi ɾi	o	spa 'ri ta	pje 'ta te	'do ve	'sɛ i	tu
O	**dispersi**	**sospiri,**	**o**	**sparita**	**pietate,**	**dove**	**sei**	**tu?**
o	dissipated	sighs	o	vanished	devotion	where	are	you

O wasted sighs, o vanished devotion, where are you?

pietate = (mod.) pietà

&

[38]
from: *Il ritorno d'Ulisse in patria (1640)*
character: *Penelope*

Giacomo Badoaro

il: lu 'stra te vi o 'tʃɛ li
Illustratevi, o cieli
Shine, o heavens

il: lu 'stra te vi	o	'tʃɛ li	rin fjo 'ra te vi		o	'pra ti	'a u ɾe	dʒo 'i te
Illustratevi,	**o**	**cieli,**	**rinfioratevi,**		**o**	**prati!**	**Aure,**	**gioite!**
light up	o	heavens	cover yourselves again with flowers		o	meadows	breezes	rejoice

Shine, o heavens; bloom, o meadows! Breezes, rejoice!

ʎi	a u dʒel: 'let: ti	kan 'tan do	i	'ri vi	mor mo 'ran do	or	si ral: 'le gri no
Gli	**augelletti**	**cantando,**	**i**	**rivi**	**mormorando,**	**or**	**si rallegrino!**
the	little birds	singing	the	brooks	murmuring	now	let be happy

augelletti (poet.)
= uccelletti

Now let the little singing birds [and] the murmuring brooks be happy!

kwel: 'lɛr be	ver ded: 'dʒan ti	kwel: 'lon de	su sur: 'ran ti	or	si kon 'so li no
Quell'erbe	**verdeggianti,**	**quell'onde**	**sussurranti**	**or**	**si consolino,**
those grasses	verdant	those waters	purling	now	let be consoled

Now let those verdant grasses and those purling waters be consoled,

dʒa 'kɛ	'sor ta	fe 'li tʃe	dal	'tʃe ne ɾe	tro 'jan	la	'mi a	fe 'ni tʃe
già ch'è	**sorta**	**felice**	**dal**	**cenere**	**trojan**	**la**	**mia**	**fenice.**
since is	risen	happy	from the	ashes	Trojan	the	my	phoenix

as my phoenix has happily risen from the ashes of Troy.

GL: **Fenice**

❧

[10, 19]
from: *Orfeo (1607)*
character: *Messagiera*

Alessandro Striggio

in un fjo 'ri to 'pra to
In un fiorito prato
In a flowering meadow

in	un	fjo 'ri to	'pra to	kon	'lal tre	'su e	kom 'paɲ: ɲe
In	**un**	**fiorito**	**prato**	**con**	**l'altre**	**sue**	**compagne**
in	a	flowering	meadow	with	the other	her	companions

In a flowering meadow, along with her other companions,

'dzi va	koʎ: 'ʎen do	'fjo ɾi	per	'far ne	'u na	gir 'lan da	a	le	'su e	'kjɔ me
giva	**cogliendo**	**fiori**	**per**	**farne**	**una**	**ghirlanda**	**a**	**le**	**sue***	**chiome,**
went	gathering	flowers	for	to make of them	a	garland	to	the	her	head of hair

she was gathering flowers to make a garland for her hair,

giva: from "gire" (lit.) = "andare"

kwan 'daŋ gwe	in si 'djo zo	'kɛ ra	fra	'lɛr be	a 'sko zo
quand'angue	**insidioso,**	**ch'era**	**fra**	**l'erbe**	**ascoso,**
when snake	cunning	which was	among	the grasses	hidden

when a cunning snake [which had been] hidden in the grass

angue (lit.)
= serpente

le	'pun se	un	'pjɛ	kon	ve le 'no zo	'dɛn te
le	**punse**	**un**	**piè**	**con**	**velenoso**	**dente.**
her	stung	a	foot	with	poisonous	tooth

in [19]: pie' =
piè (= piede)

bit her foot with poisonous tang.

e ˈdɛk: ko   im: man ti ˈnɛn te   sko lo ˈrir si   il   bɛl   ˈvi zo   e   ne
Ed ecco   **immantinente**   **scolorirsi**   **il**   **bel**   **viso,**   **e**   **ne'**
and [here]   *(lit.)* at once   turned pale   the beautiful   face   and   in

> *in [19]: nei = ne'*
> *scolorir = scolorirono*

ˈswɔ i   ˈlu mi   spa ˈrir   kwe ˈlam pi   ˈon de   ˈel: la   al   sol   ˈfe a   ˈskɔr no
suoi   **lumi**   **sparir**   **que' lampi**   **onde**   **ella**   **al**   **sol**   **fea**   **scorno.**
her   eyes   disappeared   those flashes   by which   she   at the   sun   made   humiliation

And at once her beautiful face turned pale; and the
sparkle in her eyes, which humbled the sun, was gone.

> *in [19]: ond'ella = onde ella*   *fea = (mod.) faceva*
> *sparir = sparirono*

al: ˈlor   ˈno i   ˈtut: te   zbi got: ˈti te   e   ˈmɛ ste   le   ˈfum: mo   in ˈtor no   ri kja ˈmar   ten ˈtan do
Allor   **noi**   **tutte**   **sbigottite**   **e**   **meste**   **le**   **fummo**   **intorno**   **richiamar**   **tentando**
then   we   all   stunned   and   sad   her   were   around   to call back   trying

Then, utterly stunned and sad, we surrounded her, trying to revive

ʎi   ˈspir ti   in   ˈlɛ i   zmar: ˈri ti   kon   ˈlon da   ˈfre ska   e   co   pos: ˈsɛn ti   ˈkar mi
gli   **spirti**   **in**   **lei**   **smarriti**   **con**   **l'onda**   **fresca**   **e**   **co'**   **possenti**   **carmi.**
the   spirits   in   her   lost   with   the water   fresh   and   with   powerful   incantations

the spirit gone from her with fresh water and powerful incantations.

> *in [19]: con = co'; li [li] = gli*

ma   ˈnul: la   ˈval se   ˈa i ˈlas: sa   ˈkɛl: la   i   ˈlaŋ gwi di   ˈlu mi   al ˈkwan to   a ˈprɛn do
Ma   **nulla**   **valse,**   **ahi lassa,**   **ch'ella**   **i**   **languidi**   **lumi**   **alquanto**   **aprendo**
but   nothing   availed   alas woe to her   that she   the   listless   eyes   somewhat   opening

a   te   kja ˈman do   or ˈfɛ o   or ˈfɛ o   ˈdo po   un   ˈgra ve   so ˈspi ɾo
e   **te**   **chiamando**   **Orfeo,**   **Orfeo,**   **dopo**   **un**   **grave**   **sospiro**
and   to you   calling   Orpheus   Orpheus   after   a   deep   sigh

spi ˈɾɔ   fra   ˈkwe ste   ˈbrat: tʃa
spirò   **fra**   **queste**   **braccia**
she expired   among   these   arms

But nothing availed – alas, woe to her; and having somewhat opened her listless eyes, she expired
in these arms, after a deep sigh, calling you, Orpheus;

e ˈdi o   ri ˈma zi   ˈpjɛ na   il   kɔr   di   pje ˈta de   e   di   spa ˈvɛn to
ed io   **rimasi**   **piena**   **il**   **cor**   **di**   **pietade**   **e**   **di**   **spavento.**
and I   I remained   full   the   heart   of   pity   and   of   terror

> *pietade =*
> *(mod.) pietà*

and I was left with my heart full of pity and terror.

𝓖𝓛: **Orfeo**

---

*the following note is from <u>The Operas of Monteverdi</u> (London: John Calder Limited, 1992; published in
association with English National Opera with English singing version by Anne Ridler), p.42:
"The 1609 score has 'sue chiome,' but both 1607 librettos have 'tue chiome.' John Whenham writes: 'The difference is that
the librettos' version suggests that Eurydice lingers behind after thanksgiving at the temple in order to gather flowers to
garland Orpheus's hair ('tue chiome'); the score has her lingering to gather flowers for her own hair ('sue chiome').
The former seems dramatically more plausible, and I suspect that 'sue' in the score is an error.'"

[75, 76]

ˈi o kar ˈma to sin ˈor
Io ch'armato sin or
I, who armed up to now

'i o   kar 'ma to   sin 'or   dun   'du ɾo   'dʒɛ lo   'deʎː ʎi   as: 'sal ti   da 'mor
Io   ch'armato   sin or   d'un   duro   gelo   degli   assalti   d'amor
I   who armed   up until now   with a   harsh   cold   from the   assaults   of love

po 'te i   di 'fɛn der mi
potei   difendermi,
I was able   to defend myself

I who, armed with a harsh chill, was able to defend myself against love's assaults until now –

ne   lin fo 'ka to   'su o   pun 'dʒɛn te   'tɛ lo   'pwɔ te   'lal ma   pas: 'sar
né   l'infocato   suo   pungente   telo   puote   l'alma   passar
nor   the on fire   its   sharp   arrow   is able   the soul   to pass through

puote = può

ol   'pɛtː to   of: 'fɛn der mi
o'l   petto   offendermi?
or the   breast   to hurt me

can its *[love's]* sharp, fiery arrow not pierce my soul or hurt my breast?

or   ke   il   'tutː to   si 'kan dʒa   al   'nɔ vo   'tʃɛ lo
Or   che   il   tutto   si cangia   al   novo   cielo,
now   that   the   everything   changes   at the   new   sky

Now that everything changes with the new day,

a   'due   'beʎː ʎi   'ɔkː ki   aŋ 'kor   non   do 've a   ar: 'ren der mi
a   due   begli   occhi   ancor   non   dovea   arrendermi?
to   two   beautiful   eyes   even   not   I ought to have   to yield myself

should I not have surrendered to two beautiful eyes?

in [76]:
begl'occhi
= begli occhi
dovea = (mod.) dovevo

si   di 'zar ma   il   'sɔ li to   ri 'go ɾe
Sì,   disarma   il   solito   rigore,
yes   disarm   the   usual   severity

Yes, disarm my usual severity;

'ar da   'duŋ kwe   da 'mor   'ar da   il   'mi o   'kɔ ɾe
arda   dunque   d'amor,   arda   il   mio   core.
let burn   then   of love   let burn   the   my   heart

let my heart burn with love – let it burn.

☙

[74]

'i o   ke   nelː 'lɔtː tsjo   'na kwi   e   'dɔtː tsjo   'visː si
Io che nell'ozio naqui e d'ozio vissi
I, who was born in idleness and lived in idleness

'i o   ke   nelː 'lɔtː tsjo   'na kwi   e   'dɔtː tsjo   'visː si   ke   'va go   sol
Io   che   nell'ozio   naqui   e   d'ozio   vissi,   che   vago   sol
I   who   in the idleness   I was born   and   of idleness   I lived   who   desirous   only

printed "otio" =
(mod.) ozio

I, who was born in idleness and lived in idleness, and who, desiring only

di   ri po 'za ta   'kwjɛ te   tra pas: 'sa va   non   pur   'lo ɾe   notː 'tur ne
di   riposata   quiete   trapassava   non   pur   l'ore   notturne
of   rest   quiet   passed   not   only   the hours   nocturnal

peaceful rest, passed not only the hours of night

ma   i   'dʒor ni   in 'tjɛ ɾi   aŋ 'kor   tra   'mɔlː li   'pju me
ma   i   giorni   intieri   ancor   tra   molli   piume
but   the   days   entire   even   among   soft   feathers

but even entire days in [my feather] bed,

e	tra	gra 'tom bre	'doɲ: ɲi 'ku ɾa	'skar ko	il	'fre sko	mi go 'de a
e	tra	grat'ombre,	d'ogni cura	scarco	il	fresco	mi godea
and	among	pleasant shades	of every care	untroubled	the	cool	I enjoyed

scarco = (mod.) scarico

and in pleasant shade, free from every care, enjoyed the coolness

godea = godeva; the "a" ending, rather than "o" for the first person singular, is an antiquated variant.

du 'na u ɾa	'lje ve	kol	'rɔ ko	mor mo 'rar	dun	'pit tʃɔl	'ri vo
d'un'aura	lieve	col	roco	mormorar	d'un	picciol	rivo
of a breeze	gentle	with	faint	murmuring	of a	little	stream

of a gentle breeze, along with the faint murmur of a little stream

ke	'fe a	te 'nor	'deʎ: ʎi	a u dʒel 'let: ti	al	'kan to
che	fea	tenor	degli	augelletti	al	canto
which	made	tenor	of the	little birds	to the	singing

fea = faceva

augelletti (poet.) = uccelletti

which added the tenor *[voice part]* to the singing of the little birds –

'i o	'stes: so	po i 'ke	dʒe ne 'ro za	'ku ɾa	di	bel: 'lis: si mo	a 'mor
Io	stesso	poi che	generosa	cura	di	bellissimo	Amor
I	myself	after	generous	concern	of	most beautiful	Love

poi che = (mod.) poiché

I myself, after the generous concern of most beautiful Love

mi	'pun se	il	'kɔ ɾe	al: 'lor	kel	'gwar do	'vɔl si	al	di 'vin	'lu me
mi	punse	il	core,	allor	ch'el	guardo	volsi	al	divin	lume
to me	stung	the	heart	at the moment	that the	glance	I turned	to the	divine	light

stung my heart, at the moment when I turned my glance to the divine light

el = (mod.) il

ke	sfa vil: 'lar	vi 'di o	da	'kwe i	'bɛl: li	'ɔk: ki	el	'swɔ no	u 'di
che	sfavillar	vid'io	da	quei	belli	occhi	e'l	suono	udì
which	to sparkle	saw I	from	those	beautiful	eyes	and the	sound	I heard

which I saw sparkling from those beautiful eyes, and [when] I heard the sound

ke	da	ru 'bi ni	e	'per le	mi	'dʒun se	al	kɔr	dan 'dʒe li ka	fa 'vel: la
che	da	rubini	e	perle	mi	giunse	al	cor	d'angelica	favella,
which	from	rubies	and	pearls	me	reached	to the	heart	of angelic	speech

of angelic words which reached my heart from [a mouth of] rubies *[lips]* and pearls *[teeth]*,

spret: 'tsan do	ʎi	'a dʒi	di	traŋ 'kwil: la	'vi ta	non pur	'kjug: go
sprezzando	gli	agi	di	tranquilla	vita	non pur	chiuggo
scorning	the	comforts	of	tranquil	life	no longer	I shut

chiuggo: from "chiudere"

scorning the comforts of a tranquil life, I no longer close

al	gran	di	tra	il	'son: no	i	'lu mi
al	gran	dì	tra	il	sonno	i	lumi,
at the	broad	day	in	the	sleep	the	eyes

my eyes in slumber during broad daylight;

ma	bɛn	so 'vɛn te	aŋ 'kor	e	'stel: le	e	'se ɾa	kan 'dʒar	'vi dʒi le	a 'man te
ma	ben	sovente	ancor	e	stelle	e	sera	cangiar	vigile	amante
but	well	often	[also]	and	stars	and	evening	to change	watchful	lover

but often, a wakeful lover, I turn stars and night

in	'so le	in	'al ba
in	sole	in	alba.
into	sun	into	dawn

into sunlight and dawn.

'spes: so 'kar ko di 'fɛr: ro al: 'lom bra o 'sku ɾa men 'vɔ si 'kur
Spesso carco di ferro all'ombra oscura men vo sicur
often laden with sword to the shadows dark I go out confidently
Often, armed with sword, I go confidently into the dark shadows

'o ve il de 'zi o mi 'spin dʒe e 'tan te 'sɔf: fro 'oɲ: ɲi or
ove il desio mi spinge, e tante soffro ogni or
where the desire me urges and so many I endure every hour
where desire urges me; and all the time I endure so many

'du ɾe fa 'ti ke a mo 'ro zo gwer: 'rjɛr kas: 'sa i men 'grɛ ve mi 'zu ɾa
dure fatiche, amoroso guerrier, ch'assai men greve misura
difficult labors amorous warrior that much less heavy measure
difficult tasks, as warrior of love, as it is much easier

in un kol va lo 'ro zo i 'spa no ten 'tar puɲ: 'ɲan do lo sti 'na to 'bɛl ga
in un col valoroso Ispano tentar pugnando l'ostinato Belga
on a hillside brave Spaniard to test combatting the stubborn Belgian
for the brave Spaniard to war against the stubborn Belgian on a hillside,

o pur la 'do ve in: 'nun da i 'lar gi 'kam pi
o pur là dove innunda i larghi campi
or [rather] there where floods the broad fields

o pur = (mod.) oppure
innunda: from (mod.) "inondare"

'li stro re 'al 'tʃin to di 'fɛr: ro il 'bu sto
l'Istro Real, cinto di ferro il busto,
the Danube (River) surrounded with iron the doublet
or where the Danube floods the vast plains, breast enclosed in armor –

se 'gwir tra 'lar mi il 'kja ɾo e 'no bil 'saŋ gwe di kwel gran re
seguir tra l'armi il chiaro e nobil sangue di quel gran re
to follow among the weapons the clear and noble blood of that great king
to follow, in warfare, the clear and noble blood of that great king

kor su la 'sa kra 'tɛ sta 'pɔ za il splen 'dor del di a 'dɛ ma a u 'gu sto
ch'or su la sacra testa posa il splendor del diadema augusto,
who now upon the sacred head places the splendor of the diadem august
who now places upon his sacred head the splendor of the august diadem

di kwel gran re kal: le ko 'ro ne 'a i 'la u ɾi 'al: le 'spɔʎ: ʎi
di quel gran re ch'alle corone, ai lauri, alle spogli,
of that great king who to the crowns to the laurels to the spoils

e 'a i tri 'on fi il tʃɛl de 'sti na
e ai trionfi il ciel destina.
and to the triumphs the heaven destines
of that great king for whom heaven destines crown, laurel, spoils, and triumphs.

o 'sɛm pre glo 'rjo zo o 'sɛm pre in 'vit: to 'se gwi fe 'li tʃe e
O sempre glorioso, o sempre invitto, segui felice e
o ever glorious o ever invincible pursue happy and

for tu 'na to a 'pje no 'lal te vit: 'to ɾje e glo 'rjo ze im 'pre ze
fortunato a pieno l'alte vittorie e gloriose imprese,
fortunate fully the grand victories and glorious deeds
O forever glorious one, o forever invincible one, pursue, fully happy and fortunate, your great victories and glorious deeds,

ke	'for se	un	di	'kwe sta	'mi a	'rɔ ka	'tʃe tra
che	**forse**	**un**	**dì**	**questa**	**mia**	**roca**	**cetra**
that	perhaps	one	day	this	my	faint	cithera

so that perhaps one day this faintly-sounding cithera of mine

ri to ne 'ɾa	non	vil	'ne i	'two i	gran	'prɛ dʒi	al: 'lor	kal	swɔn
ritornerà	**non**	**vil**	**nei**	**tuoi**	**gran**	**pregi**	**allor**	**ch'al**	**suon**
will return	not	humble	in the	your	great	rewards	at the moment	that at the	sound

will return not inglorious into your great favor, when at the sound

de	'lar mi	kan te 'ɾɔ	le	'tu e	'pal me	e	i	'kja ɾi	al: 'lɔ ɾi
de	**l'armi**	**canterò**	**le**	**tue**	**palme**	**e**	**i**	**chiari**	**allori.**
of	the arms	I will sing	the	your	palms	and	the	bright	laurels

of battle I will sing of your victories and bright laurels.

'kwan do	lo 'stil	fu 'ɾor	de 'prɛs: so	e	'do mo	dal	'tu o	in 'vit: to	va 'lor
Quando	**l'ostil**	**furor**	**depresso**	**e**	**domo**	**dal**	**tuo**	**invitto**	**valor,**
when	the hostile	fury	subsided	and	suppressed	by the	your	invincible	valor

When the hostile fury [of the enemy will have been] curbed and vanquished
by your invincible valor,

> *domo (lit.) = domato*

dal	'tu o	gran	'sen: no	u 'dra	pjen	di	spa 'ven to	e	di	ter: 'ro ɾe
dal	**tuo**	**gran**	**senno**	**udrà**	**pien**	**di**	**spavento**	**e**	**di**	**terrore**
by the	your	great	mind	will hear	full	of	fright	and	of	terror

lo 'rjɛn te	so 'nar	'bɛl: 'li ke	'skwil: le
l'oriente	**sonar**	**belliche**	**squille,**
the East	to sound	warlike	blares (of trumpets)

[and] by your great wisdom, [the enemy], full of fear and terror, will hear the East resounding with
warlike trumpets,

e	'so vra	gran	de 'strjer	di	'fɛr: ro	a 'dor no
e	**sovra**	**gran**	**destrier**	**di**	**ferro**	**adorno,**
and	upon	great	steed	of	iron	adorned

and [with you] upon a great steed adorned with steel,

di	stu 'por	'mu ti	i	fa re 'tra ti	'ʃi ti	tra	'mil: le	e	'mil: le
di	**stupor**	**muti**	**i**	**faretrati**	**sciti**	**tra**	**mille**	**e**	**mille**
of	stupor	mute	the	quiver-bearing	Turks	among	thousand	and	thousand

in speechless stupor the quiver-bearing Turks, among thousands and thousands of

ka va 'ljɛr	e	'du tʃi	'kar ko	di	'spoʎ: ʎe	o	gran	fer 'nan do	er 'nɛ sto
cavalier	**e**	**duci**	**carco**	**di**	**spoglie,**	**o**	**gran**	**Fernando**	**Ernesto,**
knights	and	captains	loaded	with	spoils	o	great	Fernando	Ernesto

knights and captains laden with spoils, o great Fernando Ernesto,

tiŋ ki ne 'ran: no	'al: la	'tu a	in 'vit: ta	'spa da	'vin ti	tʃe 'dɛn do	le	ko 'ro ne
t'inchineranno	**alla**	**tua**	**invitta**	**spada**	**vinti**	**cedendo**	**le**	**corone**
to you will bow	at the	your	invincible	sword	vanquished	yielding	the	crowns

will bow to your invincible sword, vanquished and yielding their crowns

e	i	'reɲ: ɲi
e	**i**	**regni.**
and	the	kingdoms

and their kingdoms.

GL: **Amor, Istro Real**

☙

Grove notes that this "Lamento d'Olimpia" is no longer thought to be by Monteverdi.

[77]

la 'men to do 'lim pja
Lamento d'Olimpia
Olimpia's Lament

'vɔʎː ʎo	mo 'rir	'vɔʎː ʎo	mo 'ri ɾe	'va nɛl	kon 'fɔr to	'tu o	va 'noɲː ɲi	a 'i ta
Voglio	**morir,**	**voglio**	**morire,**	**van'è'l**	**conforto**	**tuo**	**van'ogni**	**aita.**
I want	to die	I want	to die	in vain is the	comfort	your	in vain every	aid

I want to die, I want to die; useless is your comfort, useless every help.

il	mar 'tir	kon	la	'vi ta	ve 'dra i	ko 'zi	fi 'ni ɾe	'vɔʎː ʎo	mo 'rir	'vɔʎː ʎo	mo 'ri ɾe
Il	**martir**	**con**	**la**	**vita**	**vedrai**	**così**	**finire;**	**voglio**	**morir,**	**voglio**	**morire.**
the	agony	with	the	life	you will see	thus	to end	I want	to die	I want	to die

Thus will you see my agony end with my life; I want to die, I want to die.

o	bi 'ɾe no	'a i	non	pɔsː 'si o	'dir ti	bi 'ɾe no	'mi o	se	per	non	'ɛsː ser
O	**Bireno**	**ahi**	**non**	**poss'io**	**dirti,**	**Bireno**	**mio,**	**se**	**per**	**non**	**esser**
o	Bireno	alas	not	am able I	to say to you	Bireno	mine	if	for	not	to be

'mi o	le	've le	'ʃɔʎː ʎi	e	ti 'par ti	spje 'ta to	e	mi	ti 'tɔʎː ʎi
mio	**le**	**vele**	**sciogli**	**e**	**ti parti**	**spietato**	**e**	**mi**	**ti togli**
mine	the	sails	you unloose	and	you leave	pitiless	and	me	yourself distance

'tor na	o	bi 'ɾe no
torna	**o**	**Bireno.**
come back	o	Bireno

Alas, o Bireno, I cannot say "come back, o Bireno" to you, my Bireno, if you set your sails and leave, pitiless, and distance yourself from me in order not to be mine.

'a i	'ki o	mi 'vɛŋ go 'me no	'trɔpː po	'gwerː ra	kru 'dɛl	mi	'fanː no	al	'kɔ ɾe
Ahi	**ch'io**	**mi vengo meno;**	**troppo**	**guerra**	**crudel**	**mi**	**fanno**	**al**	**core**
alas	[that] I	I am dying	too much	war	cruel	me	make	to the	heart

'te ma	'zdeɲː ɲo	stu 'por	'dɔʎː ʎa	e da 'mo ɾe
tema	**sdegno**	**stupor,**	**doglia**	**ed amore.**
fear	indignation	stupor	sorrow	and love

Alas, I am dying; too much do fear, indignation, stupor, sorrow, and love war cruelly with my heart.

'do ve	vol dʒe 'rɔ	i	'pasː si	'pwɔ i	tu	'duŋ kwe	laʃː 'ʃar mi	kwi	tra
Dove	**volgerò**	**i**	**passi?**	**Puoi**	**tu**	**dunque**	**lasciarmi**	**qui**	**tra**
where	I shall turn	the	steps	are able	you	then	to leave me	here	among

Where shall I go? So you can leave me here amidst

re 'mɔ te	'bal tse	e	al 'pɛ stri	'sasː si	'o ve	'abː bjan	'lem pje	'fɛ ɾe	a	di vo 'rar mi
remote	**balze**	**e**	**alpestri**	**sassi**	**ove**	**abbian**	**l'empie**	**fere**	**a**	**divorarmi;**
remote	cliffs	and	alpine	rocks	where	may have	the cruel	wild beasts	to	to devour me

remote cliffs and mountain rocks, where wild beasts may devour me?

fere = (mod.) fiere

per	te	per 'de il	fra 'tɛlː lo	e	i	dʒe ni 'to ɾi	per 'de i	lo	'sta to
per	**te**	**perdei'l**	**fratello,**	**e**	**i**	**genitori**	**perdei**	**lo**	**stato**
through	you	I lost the	brother	and	the	parents	I lost	the	station

Through you I lost my brother and my parents, and I lost my status;

e	'vɔlː li	la	'tu a	'vi ta	kom 'prar	kon	la	'mi a	'mɔr te
e	**volli**	**la**	**tua**	**vita**	**comprar**	**con**	**la**	**mia**	**morte.**
and	I wanted	the	your	life	to buy	with	the	my	death

and I wanted to purchase your life with my death.

o 'mi a 'mi ze ɾa 'sɔr te o 'ka zo a 'tʃɛr bo del 'reɲ: ɲo 'al to e su 'pɛr bo
O mia misera sorte o caso acerbo del regno alto e superbo.
o my miserable destiny o fate bitter of the kingdom lofty and proud
O my miserable destiny, o bitter fate of the lofty and proud kingdom!

'i o po 'te i pur di 'fri za 'ɛs: ser re 'dʒi na o per te lo spre 'dʒa i
Io potei pur di Frisa esser Regina o per te lo spregiai
I I was able yet of Frisa to be Queen oh for you it I spurned
Yet I was able to be Queen of Frisa; oh, for you I spurned it –

per te kin 'pe ne 'so la mi 'laʃ: ʃi in 'kwe ste 'nu de a 're ne
per te ch'in pene sola mi lasci in queste nude arene.
for you that in sufferings alone me you leave on these bare sands
for you who leave me suffering alone on these bare sands.

o bi 're no dɛ ke non 'mi ɾi e ke non 'mɔ di al 'me no
O Bireno deh che non miri e che non m'odi almeno
o Bireno ah that not you see and that not me you hear at least
O Bireno, ah, could you at least see [me] and hear me,

lab: ban do 'na ta o 'lim pja o se ve 'des: si 'kwan to 'me sta e doʎ: 'ʎo za 'pal: li da
l'abbandonata Olimpia o se vedessi quanto mesta e dogliosa pallida
the abandoned Olimpia oh if you saw how much sad and mournful pale
the abandoned Olimpia; oh, if you saw how sad, mournful, and pale

e la gri 'mo za o bi 're no su 'dis: si o i 'mɛ il 'pjan to
e lagrimosa o Bireno s'udissi ohimè il pianto,
and tearful o Bireno if you would hear alas the weeping
and tearful [her face is]; o Bireno, if you would hear, alas, her weeping

e i 'gra vi o 'me i kwi tor ne 're sti kre 'di o e a 'la u ɾa 'de i so 'spir
e i gravi omei qui torneresti cred'io e a l'aura dei sospir
and the grave laments here you would return believe I and at the breeze of the sighs
and her grevious laments, I think you would return here, and upon the breeze of my sighs

tu sol ke 're sti il mar del 'pjan to 'mi o
tu solcheresti il mar del pianto mio.
you would plough the sea of weeping mine
you would plough the sea of my tears.

ma sen 'por ta no i 'vɛn ti 'lun dʒe 'lwɔ mo spje 'ta to e i 'mjɛ i la 'men ti
Ma sen portano i venti lunge l'uomo spietato, e i miei lamenti
but carry away the winds far the man pitiless and the my laments
But the winds carry the pitiless man far off, with my laments;

e 'de i 'vɔl dʒe la 'prɔ ɾa 'men tre ke pur mi 'laʃ: ʃi
ed ei volge la prora mentre che pur mi lasci
and he turns the prow while that indeed me you leave
and he turns the prow as, indeed, you leave me

in 'du ɾi af: 'fan: ni 'do ve 'pɛr fi do aŋ 'ko ɾa for 'sal tra 'dɔn: na sem pli 'tʃet: ta iŋ 'gan: ni
in duri affanni dove perfido ancora fors'altra donna semplicetta inganni.
in harsh woes where traitorous even perhaps other woman innocent you deceive
with harsh woes while, traitorous, perhaps you are even deceiving another innocent woman.

'an tsi   ke   non   a 'mar mi   'an tsi   ke   'ma i   laʃ: 'ʃar mi   ke   si sa 'ri a   ve 'du to
Anzi   **che**   **non**   **amarmi**   **anzi**   **che**   **mai**   **lasciarmi**   **che**   **si saria**   **veduto**
sooner   than   not   to love me   sooner   than   ever   to leave me   that   it would be   seen

a i 'mɛ   dʒu 'ras: si   far sim: 'mɔ bi le   il   tʃɛl   el   sol   o 'sku ro
ahimè   **giurassi**   **fars' immobile**   **il**   **ciel**   **e'l**   **sol**   **oscuro.**
alas   I would have sworn   to become immobile   the   heaven   and the   sun   obscure
Sooner than not loving me, sooner than ever leaving me, alas, I would have sworn that one would have seen
the heaven stop and the sun darken.

> saria = sarebbe

'a i   'pɛr fi do   'a i   sper 'dʒu ro   e   pur   si 'mɔ vil   tʃɛl   e   'splɛn dil
Ahi   **perfido**   **ahi**   **spergiuro**   **e**   **pur**   **si mov'il**   **ciel**   **e**   **splend'il**
ah   traitor   ah   perjurer   and   yet   itself moves   heaven   and   shines the

'so le   e   non   'ma mi   e   mi   'fud: dʒi   e   mi   'laʃ: ʃi   e
sole,   **e**   **non**   **m'ami**   **e**   **mi**   **fuggi**   **e**   **mi**   **lasci**   **e**
sun   and   not   me you love   and   me   you flee   and   me   you leave   and
Ah, traitor, ah, perjurer! Yet the heaven moves and the sun shines, and you do not love me, and you
flee from me and leave me, and

mi   'strud: dʒi   'a i   bɛn   per   me   pju   non   sad: 'dʒi ra   il   'tʃɛ lo
mi   **struggi:**   **ahi**   **ben**   **per**   **me**   **più**   **non**   **s'aggira**   **il**   **cielo**
me   you destroy   ah   [well]   for   me   more   not   moves around   the   heaven
you destroy me. Ah, no more for me does the heaven revolve;

e   per   me   'sɛm pre   'fi a   ko 'per to   il   sol   di   te ne 'bro zo   've lo
e   **per**   **me**   **sempre**   **fia**   **coperto**   **il**   **sol'**   **di**   **tenebroso**   **velo.**
and   for   me   always   will be   covered   the   sun   with   dark   veil
and for me the sun will always be covered with a dark veil.

> fia =
> (mod.) sarà

ko 'zi   bi 're no   'mi o   ko 'zi   tu   mi   ri 'po ni   'nel: la   'mi a   'rɛd: dʒa
Così   **Bireno**   **mio**   **così**   **tu**   **mi**   **riponi**   **nella**   **mia**   **reggia.**
thus   Bireno   mine   thus   you   me   you put back   in the   my   royal palace
So, Bireno mine, so you put me back in my royal palace.

o   'di o   ko 'zi   tu   miɲ ko 'ro ni   deʎ: 'ʎa vi   'mjɛ i   nel: lo no 'ra ta   'sɛ de
O   **Dio**   **così**   **tu**   **m'incoroni**   **degl'avi**   **miei**   **nell'onorata**   **sede.**
o   God   thus   you   me you crown   of the ancestors   mine   on the honored   seat
O God, so you crown me on the honored throne of my ancestors.

o   'fe de   o   'pu ra   'fe de   o   fe   per   me   sker 'ni ta
O   **fede**   **o**   **pura**   **fede**   **o**   **fé**   **per**   **me**   **schernita**
o   faith   o   pure   faith   o   fidelity   for   me   mocked
O faith, o pure faith, o fidelity for which I am mocked,

o 'lim pja   lu ziɲ 'ga ta   e   al 'fin   tra 'di ta   ɛ   kwi   da   te   laʃ: 'ʃa ta
Olimpia   **lusingata**   **e**   **alfin**   **tradita**   **è**   **qui**   **da**   **te**   **lasciata**
Olimpia   deceived   and   finally   betrayed   is   here   by   you   left
Olimpia – deceived and finally betrayed – is here, left by you

in   mi 'zɛ rja   ka 'de re   per 'ke   'si a   'tʃi bo   al 'fin   'dɔr: ri de   'fɛ re
in   **miseria**   **cadere**   **perché**   **sia**   **cibo**   **alfin**   **d'orride**   **fere.**
in   misery   to fall   so that   she may be   food   in the end   of horrible   wild beasts
to fall in misery so that, in the end, she may be food for horrible wild beasts.

ma   per 'ke   o   tʃɛl   in ven di 'ka to   'las: si   il   tra di 'men to   in 'deɲ: ɲo
Ma   **perché**   **o**   **ciel**   **invendicato**   **lassi**   **il**   **tradimento**   **indegno**
but   why   o   heaven   unrevenged   you leave   the   betrayal   despicable
But why, o heaven, do you leave [this] despicable betrayal unrevenged;

> lassi =
> (mod.) lasci

e	tu	del	'va sto	e	pro tʃel: 'lo zo	'reɲː ɲo	su 'pɛr bo	do ma 'tor
e	**tu**	**del**	**vasto**	**e**	**procelloso**	**regno**	**superbo**	**domator**
and	you	of the	vast	and	tempestuous	realm	proud	dominator

ke	nol	som: 'mer dʒi	'ɛ o lo	ke	non	kom: 'mɔ vi	i	'vɛn ti	al 'tɛ ɾi
che	**no'l**	**sommergi**	**Eolo**	**che**	**non**	**commovi,**	**i**	**venti**	**alteri**
who	not it	you submerge	Aeolus	who	not	you stir	the	winds	haughty

per 'ke	non	li	spri 'dʒo ni	si 'ke	saf: 'fon di	'en tral	vo 'ra tʃe	'se no
perché	**non**	**li**	**sprigioni**	**si ché**	**s'affondi**	**entr'al**	**vorace**	**seno**
why	not	them	you send forth	so that	may sink	within to the	voracious	bosom

il	di zle 'a le	a	me	'kru do	bi 'reno
il	**disleale**	**a**	**me**	**crudo**	**Bireno.**
the	disloyal	to	me	cruel	Bireno

and you, Aeolus, proud dominator of the vast and stormy realm *[the sky]*, why don't you drown him, why don't you move him to pity, why don't you unleash the haughty winds so that the cruel and disloyal Bireno may founder in the voracious deep?

ma	'trɔp: po	'spar go	o i 'mɛ	'du ɾe	kwe 'ɾɛ le	de	ri tor 'na te	a	me	'vo tʃi	se 'ɾe ne
Ma	**troppo**	**spargo**	**ohimè**	**dure**	**querele**	**deh**	**ritornate**	**a**	**me**	**voci**	**serene.**
but	too much	I pour out	alas	harsh	complaints	ah	return	to	me	voices	serene

But, alas, I am pouring out too many harsh complaints; ah, return to me, serene voices.

bi 'reno	o	'mi o	bi 'reno	in	vir 'tu te	da 'mor	se	non	il	'dwɔ lo	le	'mi e
Bireno	**o**	**mio**	**Bireno**	**in**	**virtute**	**d'amor**	**se**	**non**	**il**	**duolo**	**le**	**mie**
Bireno	o	my	Bireno	in	virtue	of love	if	not	the	pain	the	my

> *virtute*
> = *(mod.)*
> *virtù*

dʒu 'sti ɾe	af: 'fre no	per 'do na	o i 'mɛ	per 'kal tro	il	kɔr
giust'ire	**affreno**	**perdona**	**ohimè**	**perch'altro**	**il**	**cor**
legitimate angers	I hold in check	forgive	alas	because other	the	heart

Bireno, o my Bireno, by virtue of love I restrain my just anger, if not my pain; forgive me, alas, because my heart says one thing

'al tro	la	'liŋ gwa	'swɔ na
altro	**la**	**lingua**	**suona.**
other	the	tongue	sounds

and my voice another.

GL: **Bireno, Eolo, Frisa, Olimpia**

☙

[72, 75]

la	'mi a	'tur ka
	La mia turca	
	My Turkish woman	

la	'mi a	'tur ka	ke	da 'mor	non	ha	fe	'tor tʃe	il	pjɛ
La	**mia**	**turca**	**che**	**d'amor**	**non**	**ha**	**fé,**	**torce**	**il**	**piè**
the	my	Turkish woman	who	of love	not	has	faith	turns	the	foot

My Turkish woman, who has no faith in love, turns away

'si o	le	'nar: ro	il	'mi o	do 'lor
s'io	**le**	**narro**	**il**	**mio**	**dolor,**
if I	to her	I relate	the	my	pain

if I tell her of my pain;

'on dal   'dopː pjo   'mi o   mar 'tɔ ɾo   laŋ 'gwɛn do   'mɔ ɾo

Chorus: **ond'al**   **doppio**   **mio**   **martoro**   **languendo**   **moro.**

(first four   from which at the   double   my   martyrdom   languishing   I die

verses)   thus, in double martyrdom, I die languishing.

'po i   ro 'mi ta   se ne 'sta   e   non   vɔl   ke   del   sol

Poi   **romita**   **se ne sta**   **e**   **non**   **vol**   **che**   **del**   **sol**

then   solitary   she remains   and   not   wants   that   of the   sun

> vol =
> (mod.)
> vuole

'gɔ da   pur   di   'su a   bel 'ta

goda   **pur**   **di**   **sua**   **beltà.**

I may take pleasure   even   of   her   beauty

Then she remains aloof and does not even want me to take pleasure in the sunshine of her beauty.

per   la   'kru da   in te ne 'ɾir   non   mi   val   nel   'mi o   mal

Per   **la**   **cruda**   **intenerir**   **non**   **mi**   **val**   **nel**   **mio**   **mal**

in order to   the   cruel one   to soften   not   to me   is of use   in the   my   woe

'prɛ go   'la kri me   o   so 'spir

prego,   **lacrime**   **o**   **sospir.**

entreaty   tears   or   sighs

> prego (lit.) =
> preghiera

To make the cruel one soften neither entreaties, tears, nor sighs are of use in my woe.

di   me   'ri de   e   delː lar 'tʃɛr   ke   nel   sen

Di   **me**   **ride**   **e**   **dell'arcier**   **che**   **nel**   **sen**

of   me   she laughs   and   of the archer   who   in the   breast

di   ve 'len   'tutː ti   'spar se   i   'mjɛ i   pen 'sjɛr

di   **velen**   **tutti**   **sparse**   **i**   **miei**   **pensier.**

with   poison   all   sprinkled   the   my   thoughts

She laughs at me and at the archer *[Cupid]* who sprinkled all the thoughts in my breast with poison.

'prɛn di   'lar ko   in 'vitː to   a 'mor   per   pje 'ta

Prendi   **l'arco**   **invitto**   **Amor,**   **per**   **pietà**

take   the bow   invincible   Love   for   pity

Take your invincible bow, Love; for pity's sake

in   'lɛ i   fa   ke   non   'si a   'tan to   ri 'gor

in   **lei**   **fa**   **che**   **non**   **sia**   **tanto**   **rigor,**

in   her   make   that   not   may be   so much   severity

make her less severe,

'on de   al   'dopː pjo   'mi o   mar 'tɔ ɾo   'i o   pju   non   'mɔ ɾo

onde   **al**   **doppio**   **mio**   **martoro**   **io**   **più**   **non**   **moro.**

from which   at the   double   my   martyrdom   I   more   not   I die

so that, in double martydom, I do not die anymore.

GL: **Amor**

☙

[5, 9, 12, 13, 19, 20, 24, 29, 37, 40, 45, 54, 59, 60, 64, 72, 94] Alternately titled **Lamento d'Arianna.**

from: *L'Arianna (1608)*

character: *Arianna*

Ottavio Rinuccini

laʃː 'ʃa te mi mo 'ri ɾe

Lasciatemi morire

Let me die!

laʃ: 'ʃa te mi   mo 'ri ɾe   e   ke   vo 'le te   ke   mi   kon 'fɔr te
Lasciatemi   morire!   E   che   volete   che   mi   conforte
leave me   to die   and what   you want that   me   it should comfort
Let me die! And what would you have comfort me

> *alt.:* **E chi volete voi...**
> [e ki vo 'le te 'vo i] =
> And who would you have...

> *alt.:* **chi mi conforte...** [ki mi kon 'fɔr te] =
> who should comfort me...

iŋ   ko 'zi   'du ɾa   'sɔɾ te   iŋ   ko 'zi   gran   mar 'ti ɾe   laʃ: 'ʃa te mi   mo 'ri ɾe
in   così   dura   sorte,   in   così   gran   martire?   Lasciatemi   morire.
in   such   hard   fate   in   such   great   suffering   leave me   to die
against such a harsh fate, in such great suffering? Let me die.

> *In* [13], [19], [72], *and* [94] *the scene continues:*

o 'tɛ ze o   'mi o   si   ke   'mi o   ti   vɔ   dir   ke   'mi o   pur   'se i
O Teseo   mio,   sì,   che   mio   ti   vo'   dir,   ché   mio   pur   sei,
o Teseo   mine   yes [that] mine   you I want to say because mine indeed you are
O my Teseo – yes, I want to call you mine because, indeed, you are mine

beŋ 'ke   tin 'vo li   'a i   'kru do   a   ʎi   'ɔk: ki   'mje i
benché   t'involi,   ahi   crudo,   a   gli   occhi   miei.
even though you flee   alas   cruel one from the   eyes   mine
even though you flee, alas, cruel one, from my sight.

> *var.:* **gl'occhi** =
> **gli occhi**

'vɔl dʒi ti   'tɛ ze o   'mi o   o   'di o   'vɔl dʒi ti   in 'dje tra   ri mi 'rar   ko 'le i
Volgiti,   Teseo   mio,   oh   Dio!   Volgiti   indietr'a   rimirar   colei,
turn back   Teseo   mine   oh   God   turn back back to   to see again her who
Turn back, my Teseo. Oh God, turn back to see again her who

> *var.:* **...mio,**
> **volgiti Teseo,**
> **oh Dio.**

> *var.:* **indietro a = indietr'a**

ke   laʃ: 'ʃa to   a   per   te   la   'pa trja   el   'reɲ: ɲo
che   lasciato   ha   per   te   la   patria   e'l   regno,
who   left   has   for   you the homeland and the kingdom
left homeland and kingdom for you,

> *var.:* **e il = e'l**

en   'kwe ste   a 'ɾe ne   aŋ 'ko ɾa   'tʃi bo   di   'fɛ ɾe
e'n   queste   arene   ancora,   cibo   di   fere
and on these   shores   still   food of   wild beasts

> *var.:* **e in = e'n**
> **fere = (mod.) fiere**

di spje 'ta te   e   'kru de   laʃ: ʃe 'ra   'lɔs: sa   iɲ: 'ɲu de
dispietate   e   crude,   lascerà   l'ossa   ignude.
cruel   and   savage   will leave the bones bare
and will leave her bare bones, still on these shores, as food for cruel and savage wild beasts.

> **dispietate = (mod.) spietate**
> *var.:* **lascierà = lascerà**

o   'tɛ ze o   'mi o   se   tu   sa 'pes: si   o   'di o   se   tu   sa 'pes: si   o i 'mɛ
O Teseo   mio,   se   tu   sapessi   o   Dio!   Se   tu   sapessi,   ohimè,
o Teseo   mine   if   you you knew oh   God   if   you   knew   alas
O my Teseo, if you knew – oh God, if you knew, alas,

'ko me   saf: 'fan: na   la   'pɔ ve ɾa   a ri 'an: na   'for se   pen 'ti to   ri vol dʒe 're sti   aŋ 'kor
come   s'affanna   la   povera   Arianna,   forse   pentito   rivolgeresti   ancor
how   is troubled   the poor   Arianna   perhaps repented you would turn again
how poor Arianna is troubled, perhaps, repentant, you would again turn

la   'prɔ ɾa   al   'li to
la   prora   al   lito.
the   prow   to the shore
your prow toward the shore.

> **lito =**
> **(mod.) lido**

ma kon 'la u ɾe   se 'ɾe ne   tu   te ne 'va i   fe 'li tʃe   e 'di o   kwi   'pjaŋ go
Ma con l'aure   serene   tu   te ne vai   felice,   ed io   qui   piango.
but with the breezes   calm   you   you go away   happy   and I   here   I weep
But with the breezes fair you go away happily and I, here, weep.

a   te   pre 'pa ɾa   a 'tɛ ne   'ljɛ te   'pom pe   su 'pɛr be
A   te   prepara   Atene   liete   pompe   superbe,
for   you   prepares   Athens   happy   displays   splendid
For you Athens happily prepares splendid displays,

e 'di o   ri 'maŋ go   'tʃi bo   di   'fɛ ɾe   in   so li 'ta ɾje   a 'ɾe ne
ed io   rimango   cibo   di   fere   in   solitarie   arene.
and I   I remain   food   of   wild beasts   on   solitary   shores
and I remain, on solitary shores, the food of wild beasts.

te   'lu no   e   'lal tro   'tu o   'vek: kjo   pa 'ɾɛn te   strin dʒe 'ran   'ljɛ ti
Te   l'uno   e   l'altro   tuo   vecchio   parente   stringeran   lieti,
you   the one   and   the other   your   old   parent   they will embrace   happy
Both your elderly parents will embrace you happily,

| var.: lieto |
| ['ljɛ to] = |
| happy |

e 'di o   pju   non   ve 'drɔv: vi   o   'ma dre   o   'pa dre   'mi o
ed io   più   non   vedrovvi,   o   madre   o   padre   mio.
and I   more   not   I shall see you   o   mother   o   father   mine
and I shall never again see you, o my mother and father.

'do ve   'do vɛ   la   'fe de   ke   'tan to   mi   dʒu 'ra vi
Dove,   dov'è   la   fede   che   tanto   mi   giuravi?
where   where is   the   faith   which   so much   to me   you swore
Where, where is the faith which you swore to me so much?

ko 'zi   nel: 'lal ta   'sɛ de   tu   mi   ri 'pon   'deʎ: ʎi   'a vi
Così   nell'alta   sede   tu   mi   ripon   degli   avi?
thus   on the high   seat   you   me   you place   of the   ancestors
Is this the way you place me on the lofty seat of my ancestors?

var. in [19]:	in [72]: "fede" is
degl'avi =	no doubt a copying
degli avi	error for "sede"
	ripon = riponi

son   'kwe ste   le   ko 'ro ne   'on de   ma 'dor ni   il   'kri ne
Son   queste   le   corone,   onde   m'adorni   il   crine?
are   these   the   crowns   with which   me you adorn   the   hair
Are these the wreathes with which you adorn my head?

| var.: |
| m'adorn'il = |
| m'adorni il |

'kwe sti   ʎi   'ʃet: tri   'so no   'kwe ste   le   'dʒem: me   e   ʎi   'ɔ ri
Questi   gli   scettri   sono,   queste   le   gemme   e   gli   ori?
these   the   sceptres   are   these   the   gems   and   the   golds (jewels)
Are these the sceptres, these the gems and the jewels,

| var.: e gl'ori |
| = e gli ori |

laʃ: 'ʃar mi   in   ab: ban 'do no   a   'fe ɾa   ke   mi   'strat: tsi   e   mi   di 'vo ɾi
Lasciarmi   in   abbandono   a   fera   che   mi   strazi   e   mi   divori?
to leave me   in   abandonment   to   wild beast   that   me   may tear apart   and   me   may devour
leaving me abandoned for a wild beast to mangle and devour me?

| var. in [54]: Lasciarm'in abbandono |
| var.: stracci ['strat: tʃi] = strazi |

a   'tɛ ze o   'mi o   laʃ: ʃe 'ra i   tu   mo 'ri ɾe   in 'van   pjan 'dʒɛn do   in 'van   gri 'dan do   a 'i ta
Ah   Teseo   mio,   lascerai   tu   morire,   invan   piangendo,   invan   gridando   aita
ah   Teseo   mine   you will let   you   to die   in vain   weeping   in vain   crying   help
Ah, my Teseo, you will let die, weeping in vain, crying in vain for help,

| var. in [19]: gridand'aita |

la	'mi ze ɾa	a ɾi 'an: na	ke	a	te	fi 'dɔs: si	e	ti	'dje	'glɔ rja	e	'vi ta
la	**misera**	**Arianna,**	**che**	**a**	**te**	**fidossi**	**e**	**ti**	**diè**	**gloria**	**e**	**vita?**
the	miserable	Arianna	who to	you		entrusted herself	and	to you	gave	glory	and	life

the miserable Arianna who entrusted herself to you and gave you glory and life?

> *var.: ch'a = che a*

'a i	ke	non	pur	ri 'spon de	'a i	ke	pju	'da spe
Ahi!	**che**	**non**	**pur**	**risponde;**	**ahi!**	**che**	**più**	**d'aspe**
alas	[that]	not	[indeed]	he responds	alas	[that]	more	than snake

> *aspe = (mod.) aspide*

ɛ	'sor do	a	'mjɛ i	la 'men ti
è	**sordo**	**a**	**miei**	**lamenti.**
he is	deaf	to	my	laments

> *var.: d'asp'è sordo a' miei lamenti!*

Alas, he does not answer; alas, he is more deaf than a snake to my laments.

o	'nem bi	o	'tur bi	o	'vɛn ti	som: mer 'dʒe te lo	'vo i	'den tro a	kwel: 'lon de
O	**nembi,**	**o**	**turbi,**	**o**	**venti,**	**sommergetelo**	**voi**	**dentro a**	**quell'onde;**
o	clouds	o	gales	o	winds	submerge him	you	into	that sea

> *var.:*
> *dentr'a =*
> *dentro a*

> *var.:* **dentro quel onde!** (same translation)

O clouds, o gales, o winds, drown him in that sea;

kor: 're te	'ɔr ke	e	ba 'le ne	e	'del: le	'mɛm bra	im: 'mon de
correte,	**orche**	**e**	**balene,**	**e**	**delle**	**membra**	**immonde**
run	sea monsters	and	whales	and	with the	limbs	filthy

em 'pi te	le	vo 'ra dʒi ni	pro 'fon de
empite	**le**	**voragini**	**profonde.**
fill	the	chasms	deep

hurry, sea monsters and whales, and fill your deep insides with his filthy limbs.

ke	'par lo	'a i	ke	va 'ned: dʒo	'mi ze ɾa	o i 'mɛ	ke	'ved: dʒo
Che	**parlo,**	**ahi!**	**che**	**vaneggio?**	**Misera,**	**ohimè!**	**che**	**veggio?**
what	I say	alas	[that]	I rave	miserable	alas	what	I see

> *var.: ...[oimè] che chieggio?*
> [o i 'mɛ ke 'kjed dzo] =
> ...alas, what am I asking?

What am I saying? Alas, am I raving? Miserable, alas, what am I seeing?

o	'tɛ ze o	'mi o	non	son	kwel: 'li o	ke	i	'fɛ ɾi	'det: ti	'ʃɔl se
O	**Teseo**	**mio,**	**non**	**son**	**quell'io,**	**che**	**i**	**feri**	**detti**	**sciolse;**
o	Teseo	mine	not	I am	that I	who	the	cruel	words	uttered

> *var.: ch'i feri*
> *= che i feri*
> *feri = (mod.) fieri*

O my Teseo, I am not that one who uttered the cruel words;

par 'lɔ	laf: 'fan: no	'mi o	par 'lɔ	il	do 'lo ɾe
parlò	**l'affanno**	**mio,**	**parlò**	**il**	**dolore,**
spoke	the woe	mine	spoke	the	grief

> *var.: parlò 'l*
> *= parlò il*

my woe spoke, my grief spoke,

par 'lɔ	la	'liŋ gwa	si	ma	non	dʒa	il	'kɔ ɾe
parlò	**la**	**lingua**	**sì,**	**ma**	**non**	**già**	**il**	**core.**
spoke	the	tongue	yes	but	not	[now]	the	heart

> *var.: già 'l*
> *= già il*

my tongue spoke, yes, but not my heart.

'mi ze ɾa	aŋ 'kor	dɔ 'lɔ ko a	la	tra 'di ta	'spɛ me
Misera,	**ancor**	**dò loco a**	**la**	**tradita**	**speme,**
miserable	yet	I give way to	the	betrayed	hope

> *speme (lit.) = speranze*
> *loco = (mod.) luogo*
> *var.: alla tradita (mod.) = a la tradita*

Miserable, yet I give way to betrayed hope

e	non	si 'speɲ: ɲe	fra	'tan to	'sker no	aŋ 'kor	da 'mor	il	'fɔ ko
e	**non**	**si spegne**	**fra**	**tanto**	**scherno**	**ancor**	**d'amor**	**il**	**foco.**
and	not	burns out	among	so much	scorn	still	of love	the	fire

> *in* [94]*: si spegna*
> [si 'speɲ: ɲa] = may
> [the fire of love]
> [not] burn out.

and, among so much scorn, still the fire of love does not burn out.

> *var.: schern'ancor = scherno ancor*

'speɲ: ɲi   tu   'mɔr te   o 'ma i   le   'fjam: me   in 'deɲ: ɲe
Spegni   **tu,**   **morte,**   **omai**   **le**   **fiamme**   **indegne.**
extinguish   you   death   now   the   flames   unworthy
Now, death, extinguish the unworthy flames.

> *omai (poet.)* = *ormai*

o   'ma dre   o   'pa dre
O   **madre,**   **o**   **padre,**
o   mother   o   father
O mother, o father,

o   del: lan 'ti ko   'reɲ: ɲo   su 'per bi   al 'ber gi   o 'veb: bi   dɔr   la   'ku na
o   **dell'antico**   **regno**   **superbi**   **alberghi,**   **ov'ebbi**   **d'or**   **la**   **cuna;**
o   of the ancient   realm   lofty   refuges   where I had   of gold   the   cradle
o lofty refuges of the ancient realm where I had a golden cradle...

> *in* [94]: *ond'ebbi*
> [on 'dɛb: bi]
> (same translation)
>
> *cuna* = *(mod.) culla*

o   'ser vi   o   'fi di   a 'mi tʃi   'a i   'fa to   in 'deɲ: ɲo
o   **servi,**   **o**   **fidi**   **amici**   **(ahi!**   **fato**   **indegno),**
o   servants   o   faithful   friends   alas   fate   undeserving
o servants, o faithful friends... (alas, fate undeserved!),

mi 'ra te   'o ve   ma   'skɔr to   'em pja   for 'tu na   'mi ra te   di   ke   dwɔl
mirate   **ove**   **m'ha**   **scorto**   **empia**   **fortuna,**   **mirate**   **di**   **che**   **duol**
see   where   me has   escorted   impious   fortune   see   of   what   sorrow
see where impious fortune has led me, see to what sorrow

> *var.:*
> *scort'empia* =
> *scorto empia*
>
> *var.: mi ha = m'ha*

ma   'fat: to   e 'rɛ de   la 'mor   'mi o   la   'mi a   'fe de   e   lal 'tru i   iŋ 'gan: no
m'ha   **fatto**   **erede**   **l'amor**   **mio,**   **la**   **mia**   **fede**   **e**   **l'altrui**   **inganno.**
me has   made   heir   the love   mine   the   my   fidelity   and   the other's   deception
my love, my fidelity, and another's deception have
made me heiress.

> *in* [94]: **m'han fatt'erede** [man 'fat: te 'rɛ de]
> = me have made heir

ko 'zi   va   ki   trɔp: 'pa ma   e   'trɔp: po   'kre de
Così   **va**   **chi**   **tropp'ama**   **e**   **troppo**   **crede.**
thus   it goes   one who   too much loves   and   too much   trusts
So it goes [for] one who loves too much and trusts too much.

[94] *continues further:*

'na kwi   re 'dʒi na   e   del: lan 'ti ka   'krɛ ta   fu   'bɛ lil   'vi ver   'mi o
Nacqui   **regina**   **e**   **dell'antica**   **Creta**   **fu**   **bel' il**   **viver**   **mio**
I was born   queen   and   of the ancient   Crete   was   beautiful the   living   my
I was born a queen, and my life was beautiful in ancient Crete

'men tral   tʃɛl   'pja kwe   'tem po   ɛ   'ki o   'mɔ ra
mentr' al   **ciel**   **piacque;**   **tempo**   **è**   **ch'io**   **mora**
while to the   heaven   it pleased   time   it is   that I   I may die
as long as it pleased heaven. It is time for me to die;

al   'mi o   'vi ver   tak: 'kwe ta
al   **mio**   **viver**   **t'acqueta.**
at the   my   living   resign yourself
resign yourself to the [end of] my life.

> *acqueta: from*
> *"acquetare"* =
> *(mod.) "acquietare"*

'vi vo   'mɔ ro   o   va 'ned: dʒo   o   pur   son   'la u ra   o 'dom bra
Vivo,   **moro,**   **o**   **vaneggio**   **o**   **pur**   **son**   **l'aura,**   **od ombra?**
I live   I die   or   I rave   or   perhaps   I am   the air   or shadow
Am I living, dying, or raving? Or perhaps I am [but] air or shadow?

'las: sa   ke   far   ded: 'dʒi o   ke   'kre der   'dɛd: dʒo
Lassa   che   far   degg'io?   che   creder   deggio?
miserable   what   to do   ought I   what   to believe   I ought
Miserable me, what should I do? What should I believe?

ma   ke   'si a   di   'tɛ ze o   ki   mas: si 'ku ɾa
Ma   che   sia   di   Teseo   chi   m'assicura?
but   what   it may be   of   Teseo   who   me assures
But who can assure me of what happened to Teseo?

aŋ 'kor   'pɛn si   nu 'drir   'ʎa spri   do 'lo ɾi   spe 'ɾan tsa   i 'ni kwa
Ancor   pensi   nudrir   gl'aspri   dolori,   speranza   iniqua!
still   you think   to nourish   the bitter   sorrows   hope   iniquitous
Unjust hope, you still think you will nourish my bitter sorrows!

'a i   'mɔ ɾi   non   tʃer 'kar   a ɾi 'an: na   'al tra   ven 'tu ɾa
Ai   mori,   non   cercar   Arianna   altra   ventura.
alas   die   not   to seek   Arianna   other   fate
Alas, die! Arianna, do not seek a different fate.

> ai =
> (mod.)
> ahi

'I o   son   kon 'tɛn ta   'skor dʒi mi   'o vɛ   a   tɛ   'pja tʃe
Io   son   contenta   scorgimi   ove   a   te   piace;
I   I am   happy   discern me   where   to   you   it pleases
I am happy; see me where you wish.

ke   mi   'las: si   e   'spred: dʒi   or   'tor ni   e
che   mi   lassi   e   spreggi   or   torni   e
that   me   he may leave   and   may spurn   now   may return   and
Whether he leaves me and spurns me, or returns and

> lassi: from
> (mod.) "lasciare"

mi   rak: 'kɔl ga   ɛ   'fɔl: le   'spe me   non   si   'lje vi   i   pen 'sjɛr   'kan dʒa no   i   're dʒi
mi   raccolga   è   folle   speme,   non   sì   lievi   i   pensier   cangiano   i   regi.
me   may pick up   is   foolish   hope   not   so   slight   the thoughts   change   the kings
gathers me up, hope is foolish; kings do not change their minds so easily.

𝒢ℒ: **Arianna, Teseo**

[72, 75, 76]

ma le 'det: to   'si a   la 'spɛt: to
Maledetto sia l'aspetto
Cursed be the face

ma le 'det: to   'si a   la 'spɛt: to   ke   'mar de   'tri sto   me
Maledetto   sia   l'aspetto   che   m'arde,   tristo   me.
cursed   be   the face   which   me inflamed   wretched   me
Cursed be the face which inflamed me, wretched me.

po i 'ki o   'sɛn to   'ri o   tor 'men to   po i 'ki o   'mɔ ɾo
Poich'io   sento   rio   tormento,   poich'io   moro,
since I   I feel   cruel   torment   [since] I   I die

ne   ri 'stɔ ɾo   a   'mi a   fe   sol   per   te
né   ristoro   ha   mia   fé   sol   per   te.
not   consolation   has   my   faith   only   through   you
Because only through you do I feel cruel torment, [and] I am dying, my faith has no consolation.

ma le 'det: ta la sa 'et: ta kim pja 'gɔ ne mor: 'rɔ
Maledetta la saetta ch'impiagò, ne morrò.
cursed the arrow which wounded of it I will die
Cursed [be] the arrow which wounded; I will die from it.

ko 'zi 'vwɔ le il 'mi o 'so le ko 'zi 'bra ma ki di 'za ma 'kwan to pwɔ
Così vuole il mio sole, così brama chi disama quanto può;
thus wants the my sun thus desires she who spurns as much as she can
Thus does my sun *[beloved one]* wish; thus does she who spurns me as much as possible desire.

ke fa 'rɔ
che farò?
what I will do
What shall I do?

'dɔn: na 'ri a 'mɔr te 'mi a vwɔl ko 'zi ki fe 'ri
Donna ria, morte mia vuol così, chi ferì.
lady cruel death mine wants thus who wounded
Thus does the cruel lady who wounded me want my death.

'pren de 'dʒɔ ko del 'mi o 'fɔ ko vwɔl 'ki o 'pe ni ke mi 'zve ni
Prende gioco del mio foco, vuol ch'io peni, che mi sveni;
she takes joke from the my fire she wants that I I may suffer that I may cut my veins
She makes a joke of my passion; she wants me to suffer, to bleed.

mor: 'rɔ kwi 'fjɛ ɾo di
morrò qui, fiero dì.
I will die here cruel day
I shall die here, oh cruel day.

༄

[74]

ma per kwel: 'lam pjo e 'dʒɛ o 'spjɛ gi le 've le
Ma per quell'ampio Egeo spieghi le vele
But you are spreading your sails through that broad Aegean

ma per kwel: 'am pjo e 'dʒɛ o 'spjɛ gi le 've le
Ma per quell'ampio Egeo spieghi le vele
but through that broad Aegean you spread the sails
But you are spreading your sails through that broad Aegean

si dal 'pɔr to lon 'ta no ar 'di to a 'man te
sì dal porto lontano, ardito amante!
so from the port distant daring lover
so far from the port, daring lover!

'rjɛ di ke 'me ko il 'mi o kor 'te ze a 'mi ko 'ved: dʒo ka si gran
Riedi, ché meco il mio cortese amico veggio ch'a sì gran
return because me with the my kind friend I see who at so great
Return, because with me I see my kind friend who, at such a long

*riedi: from
riedere (lit.) =
redire (poet.) =
ritornare*

veggio = (mod.) vedo

'kor so a si gran 'vo lo di 'pal: li do ti 'mor di 'pin dʒe il 'vi zo
corso, a sì gran volo, di pallido timor dipinge il viso.
course at so great flight with pale fear portrays the face
journey, at such a long flight, shows a face [filled with] pale fear.

༄

[74]

'nin fa ke 'skal tsa il 'pjɛ de
Ninfa che, scalza il piede
Nymph, barefooted

'nin fa	ke	'skal tsa	il	'pjɛ de	e	'ʃɔl ta	il	'kri ne	
Ninfa	**che**	**scalza**	**il**	**piede**	**e**	**sciolta**	**il**	**crine**	
nymph	who	barefooted	the	foot	and	loosened	the	head of hair	

Nymph, barefooted and with loosened tresses,

te ne 'va i	di	'dɔʎː ʎa	in	'ban do	per	'kwe ste	'pjadː dʒe	'ljɛ ta	kan 'tan do
te ne vai	**di**	**doglia**	**in**	**bando**	**per**	**queste**	**piaggie**	**lieta**	**cantando**
you leave	of	sorrow	in	exile	through	these	slopes	happy	singing

you go banishing sorrow, happily singing, over these slopes;

e	balː 'lan do	non	'skwɔ ti	a	'lɛr be	le	'fre ske	'bri ne	
e	**ballando**	**non**	**scuoti**	**a**	**l'erbe**	**le**	**fresche**	**brine.**	
and	dancing	not	you shake	from	the grasses	the	new	frost	

and in dancing, you do not [even] shake the new frost from the grass *[because of your light footsteps]*.

[72]

o i 'mɛ 'ki o 'ka do
Ohimè ch'io cado
Alas, I am falling

o i 'mɛ	'ki o	'ka do	o i 'mɛ	kin 'tʃam po	aŋ 'ko ɾa	il	pjɛ	pur	'ko me	'pri a		
Ohimè	**ch'io**	**cado**	**ohimè**	**ch'inciampo**	**ancora**	**il**	**piè**	**pur**	**come**	**pria**		
alas	[that] I	I fall	alas	[that] I stumble	still	the	foot	[yet]	as	before		

Alas, I am falling; alas, my foot is stumbling as before,

pria (poet.) = prima

e	la	sfo 'ɾi ta	'mi a	ka 'du ta	'spɛ me	pur	di 'nɔ vo	ri 'gar	
e	**la**	**sfiorita**	**mia**	**caduta**	**speme**	**pur**	**di novo**	**rigar**	
and	the	wilted	my	fallen	hope	yet	again	to irrigate	

speme (lit.) = speranza; novo = (mod.) nuovo

kon	'fre sko	la kri 'mar	or	mi	kon 'vjɛ ne	
con	**fresco**	**lacrimar**	**or**	**mi**	**conviene.**	
with	fresh	weeping	now	to me	is fitting	

and now it behooves me yet again to water my fallen, wilted hope with fresh tears.

'lasː so	del	'vekː kjo	ar 'dor	ko 'no sko	'lor me	aŋ 'kor	'den tro	nel	'pɛtː to
Lasso	**del**	**vecchio**	**ardor**	**conosco**	**l'orme**	**ancor**	**dentro**	**nel**	**petto,**
alas	of the	old	ardor	I recognize	the marks	still	within	in the	breast

Alas, I recognize the marks of the old passion still within my breast,

ka	'rotː to	il	'va go	a 'spɛtː to	e	i	'gwar di	a 'ma ti
ch'ha	**rotto**	**il**	**vago**	**aspetto**	**e**	**i**	**guardi**	**amati**
because has	broken	the	lovely	appearance	and	the	glances	dear

because the lovely face and the dear glances have shattered

lo	'zmal to	a da man 'tin	on dar 'ma ɾo	il	me 'skin	pen 'sjɛr	dʒe 'la ti	
lo	**smalto**	**adamantin**	**ond'armaro**	**il**	**meschin**	**pensier**	**gelati.**	
the	enamel	adamantine	whence armed	the	wretch	thoughts	frozen	

armaro = amarono

the diamond-hard enamel of frigid thoughts which armed the wretched one *[me]*.

'fɔl: le   kre 'de vo   'i o   pur   da 'ver   'sker mo   si 'kur   da   un   'nu do   ar 'tʃɛ ɾo
Folle   **credevo**   **io**   **pur**   **d'aver**   **schermo**   **sicur**   **da**   **un**   **nudo**   **arciero**
foolish   I believed   I   still   of to have   shield   secure   from   a   naked   archer
Foolish, I still believed I had a safe shield from a naked archer *[Cupid]*,

e   pur   'i o   si   gwer: 'rjɛ ɾo   or   son   ko 'dar do
e   **pur**   **io**   **sì**   **guerriero**   **or**   **son**   **codardo**
and   yet   I   such   warrior   now   I am   coward
and yet I, such a warrior, am now a coward,

ne   'vɔʎ: ʎo   so ste 'ner   il   'kol po   lu ziŋ 'gjer   dun   'so lo   'zgwar do
né   **voglio**   **sostener**   **il**   **colpo**   **lusinghier**   **d'un**   **solo**   **sguardo.**
nor   I wish   to sustain   the   blow   enticing   of a   single   glance
not wishing to sustain the enticing blow of a single glance.

o   kam 'pjon   im: mor 'tal   'zdeɲ: ɲo   'ko me   si   fral   or   'fud: dʒe   in 'djɛ tro
O   **campion**   **immortal**   **sdegno,**   **come**   **sì**   **fral**   **or**   **fugge**   **indietro**
oh   champion   immortal   disdain   how   so   frail   now   flees   back
Oh how disdain, immortal champion, now retreats so frailly.

a   sot: 'tar mi   di   've tro   iŋ 'kan to   er: 'ran te   ma i   kon 'dot: to
A   **sott'armi**   **di**   **vetro**   **incanto**   **errante**   **m'hai**   **condotto**
at   beneath arms   of   glass   enchantment   deceptive   me you have   led

in fe 'del   'kon tro   'spa da   kru 'del   'da spro   di a 'man te
infedel   **contro**   **spada**   **crudel**   **d'aspro**   **diamante.**
infidel   against   sword   cruel   of hard   diamond
In the glass armor of deceptive enchantment you have led me, infidel, against a cruel sword of hard diamond.

o   'ko me   sa   pu 'nir   ti 'ɾan: no   a 'mor   lar 'dir   'dal ma   ru 'bɛl: la
O   **come**   **sa**   **punir**   **tiranno**   **amor**   **l'ardir**   **d'alma**   **rubella!**
oh   how   knows how   to punish   tyrannical   love   the boldness   of soul   rebellious
Oh how tyrannical love knows how to punish the boldness of a rebellious soul!

rubella =
(mod.) ribelle

'u na   'dol tʃe   fa 'vɛl: la   un   se 'ren   'vol to   un   vet: 'tso zo   mi 'ɾar
Una   **dolce**   **favella**   **un**   **seren**   **volto**   **un**   **vezzoso**   **mirar**
A   sweet   speech   a   serene   face   a   charming   looking at
Sweet talk, a serene face, [and] a charming gaze

'sɔʎ: ʎo no   ri le 'gar   un   kɔr   diʃ: 'ʃɔl to
sogliono   **rilegar**   **un**   **cor**   **disciolto.**
are used to   to bind   a   heart   untied
usually mend a broken heart.

'ɔk: ki   'bɛl: li   a   se   fu   'sɛm pre   'bɛl: la   vir 'tu   'dʒu sta   pje 'ta te
Occhi   **belli**   **ah**   **se**   **fu**   **sempre**   **bella**   **virtù**   **giusta**   **pietate,**
eyes   beautiful   ah   if   was   always   beautiful   virtue   just   pity
Beautiful eyes, ah, if a just pity has always been a beautiful virtue,

pietate =
(mod.)
pietà

dɛ   'vo i   non   mi   ne 'ga te   il   'gwar do   e   il   'ri zo
deh,   **voi**   **non**   **mi**   **negate**   **il**   **guardo**   **e**   **il**   **riso,**
ah   you   not   me   deny   the   glance   and   the   laughter
ah, do not deny me your glance and your laughter,

ke   mi   'si a   la   pri 'dʒon   per   si   'bɛl: la   ka 'dʒon   il   pa ɾa 'di zo
che   **mi**   **sia**   **la**   **prigion**   **per**   **sì**   **bella**   **cagion**   **il**   **Paradiso.**
that   to me   may be   the   prison   for   so   beautiful   reason   the   Paradise
so that prison, for such a beautiful cause, may be Paradise for me.

❧

[11]

per 'ke se mo 'dja vi
Perché se m'odiavi
Why, if you hated me

per 'ke	se	mo 'dja vi	mo 'stra vi	da 'mar mi	per	sol	iŋ gan: 'nar mi
Perché	**se**	**m'odiavi**	**mostravi**	**d'amarmi**	**per**	**sol**	**ingannarmi?**
why	if	me you hated	you pretended	of to love me	for	only	to deceive me

Why, if you hated me, did you pretend to love me only to deceive me?

'a i	'stel: la	ti	fe	ko 'zi	'bɛl: la	si	'fjɛ ɾa	si	al 'tɛ ɾa	per	'lal ma	pja 'gar mi
Ahi,	**stella**	**ti**	**fé**	**così**	**bella**	**sì**	**fiera**	**sì**	**altera**	**per**	**l'alma**	**piagarmi.**
alas	star	you	made	so	beautiful	so	cruel	so	proud	for	the soul	to wound me

Alas, a star made you so beautiful, so cruel, so proud, in order to wound my soul.

'i o	ta do 'ra vo	tu	spret: 'tsa vi	me	'em pja	'fil: li	per 'ke
Io	**t'adoravo**	**tu**	**sprezzavi**	**me**	**empia**	**Filli**	**perché?**
I	you adored	you	scorned	me	cruel	Filli	why

I adored you [but] you scorned me, cruel Filli – why?

> *correct modern grammar would be "tu mi sprezzavi, empia…"; this usage of "me" must be an antiquated one…*

ki	sa	'ku na	'vol ta	la	'stɔl ta	fje 'ret: tsa	non	'bra mi	ki	'sprɛt: tsa
Chi	**sa**	**ch'una**	**volta**	**la**	**stolta**	**fierezza**	**non**	**brami**	**chi**	**sprezza.**
who	knows	that one	time	the	foolish	pride	not	may yearn for	the one	it scorns

Who knows if one day your foolish pride may not yearn for the one it scorns.

'a i	'ki o	vɔ	dir	al	kɔr	'mi o	ke	'fug: ga
Ahi,	**ch'io**	**vo'**	**dir**	**al**	**cor**	**mio**	**che**	**fugga**
alas	[that] I	I want	to say	to the	heart	mine	that	it may flee

Alas, I want to tell my heart to flee,

ke	'strug: ga	lin fi 'ni ta	bel: 'let: tsa
che	**strugga**	**l'infinita**	**bellezza.**
that	it may cause pain	the infinite	beauty

to cause pain to the infinite beauty.

'for se	a	te	tok: ke 'ra	a	'kjɛ der	pje 'ta	'em pja	'fil: li	ki	sa
Forse	**a**	**te**	**toccherà**	**a**	**chieder**	**pietà**	**empia**	**Filli**	**chi**	**sa?**
perhaps	to	you	it will befall	to	to beg for	pity	cruel	Filli	who	knows

Perhaps it will befall you to beg for pity, cruel Filli – who knows?

GL: **Filli**

❧

[11]

pju 'ljɛ to il 'gwar do
Più lieto il guardo
[No] more happy the glance

pju	'ljɛ to	il	'gwar do	vɛr	me	non	'dʒi ɾi	'nin fa	ri 'tro za
Più	**lieto**	**il**	**guardo**	**ver'**	**me**	**non**	**giri,**	**ninfa**	**ritrosa**
more	happy	the	glance	toward	me	not	you turn	nymph	reluctant

ne	sɔ	per 'ke
né	**so**	**perché?**
nor	I know	why

You no longer turn your happy glance to me, reluctant nymph, and I know not why.

'tan to	re 'spi ɾi	'kwan to	so 'spi ɾi	ne	pju	ti 'ku ɾi	'del: la	'mi a	fe
Tanto	**respiri**	**quanto**	**sospiri,**	**né**	**più**	**ti curi**	**della**	**mia**	**fé.**
so much	you breathe	as much	you sigh	not	more	you care	of the	my	faithfulness

You sigh as much as you breathe; [but] you do not care about my faithfulness anymore.

'i o	'vi di	at: 'tʃe zo	di	'fjam: mil	'vi zo	kin	pal: li 'det: tsa	'po i	si kan 'dʒɔ
Io	**vidi**	**acceso**	**di**	**fiamm'il**	**viso,**	**ch'in**	**pallidezza**	**poi**	**si cangiò.**
I	I saw	on fire	with	flames the	face	which into	pallor	then	changed

I saw your face burning with flames, then turned to pallor;

e	ap: 'pe na	'ʃɔl si	'da i	'la bri	un	'ri zo	kun	dwɔl	a 'sko zo	lo	raf: fre 'nɔ
E	**appena**	**sciolsi**	**dai**	**labri**	**un**	**riso,**	**ch'un**	**duol**	**ascoso**	**lo**	**raffrenò.**
and	scarcely	released	from the	lips	a	smile	that a	sorrow	hidden	it	restrained

and scarcely was a smile released from your lips when a hidden sorrow restrained it.

| labri = (mod.) labbri | ascoso (lit.) = nascoso = nascosto (from "nascondere") |

'a i	ke	la	'spɛ me	fal: 'la tʃe	e	'ljɛ ve	ra pi da 'men te	a	me	spa 'ri
Ahi	**che**	**la**	**speme**	**fallace**	**e**	**lieve,**	**rapidamente**	**a**	**me**	**sparì.**
alas	[that]	the	hope	vain	and	faint	rapidly	from	me	vanished

Alas, my vain and faint hope quickly vanished.

| speme (lit.) = speranza |

'a i	bɛn	ɛ	've ɾo	kin	'tɛm po	'brɛ ve	ap: 'pe na	'naʃ: ʃe	ke	'mɔ ɾe	il	di
Ahi!	**ben**	**è**	**vero**	**ch'in**	**tempo**	**breve,**	**appena**	**nasce**	**che**	**more**	**il**	**dì.**
alas	well	it is	true	that in	time	brief	scarcely	is born	than	dies	the	day

Alas, how true it is that within a brief time, the day is scarcely born before it dies!

per	'mil: le	'seɲ: ɲi	son	fat: tak: 'kɔr to	ke	'nɔ vo	af: 'fɛt: to
Per	**mille**	**segni**	**son**	**fatt'accorto,**	**che**	**novo**	**affetto**
through	thousand	signs	I am	made aware	that	new	affection

| novo = (mod.) nuovo |

nel	kɔr	ti	sta
nel	**cor**	**ti**	**sta,**
in the	heart	to you	is

Through a thousand signs I have been made aware that a new affection is in your heart;

dʒe 'lo za	'ku 'ɾa	'las: so	ma	'skɔr to	ki	'al tri	min 'vo li	'tu a	gran	bel 'ta
gelosa	**cura**	**lasso**	**m'ha**	**scorto,**	**chi**	**altri**	**m'involi**	**tua**	**gran**	**beltà.**
jealous	concern	unhappy	me has	perceived	who	another	me may steal	your	great	beauty

jealous concern has made unhappy me see that someone else may steal your great beauty from me.

| lasso: inferred is "ahi, lasso!" (= unhappy me, woe is me) |

non	pju	ram: 'men ta	kin	'pjan to	a 'ma ɾo
Non	**più**	**rammenta**	**ch'in**	**pianto**	**amaro,**
not	more	remember	that in	weeping	bitter

Forget that in bitter weeping

'spe zi	i	'bɛ i	'an: ni	di	dʒo ven 'tu
spesi	**i**	**bei**	**anni**	**di**	**gioventù,**
I spent	the	beautiful	years	of	youth

I spent the beautiful years of youth,

ne	kel	'mi o	kɔr	ti	fa	si	'ka ɾo	ne	ke	kwe 'stal ma
né	**ch'el**	**mio**	**cor**	**ti**	**fa**	**sì**	**caro,**	**né**	**che**	**quest'alma**
nor	that the	my	heart	to you	makes	so	dear	nor	that	this soul

| el = (mod.) il |

'sɛn tsa   te   fu
senza   te   fu.
without   you   was

and that your heart is so dear to me, and that this soul was never without you.

[73, 75, 76]

kwel 'zgwar do zdeɲ ɲo 'zet: to
Quel sguardo sdegnosetto
That scornful little glance

kwel   'zgwar do   zdeɲ no 'zet: to   lu 'tʃɛn te   e   mi nat: 'tʃo zo
Quel   sguardo   sdegnosetto   lucente   e   minaccioso,
that   glance   scornful little   bright   and   threatening
That scornful little glance, bright and threatening,

   kwel   'dar do   ve le 'no zo   'vo la   a   fe 'rir mi   il   'pɛt: to
   quel   dardo   velenoso   vola   a   ferirmi   il   petto:
   that   dart   poisonous   flies   to   to wound me   the   breast
   that poison dart, flies to wound my breast.

bel: 'let: tse   on 'di o   tut: 'tar do   e   son   da   me   di 'vi zo
Bellezze   ond'io   tutt'ardo   e   son   da   me   diviso,
beauties   whence I   completely I burn   and   am   from   me   divided
Beauties from which I am all afire and torn apart,

   pja 'ga te mi   kol   'zgwar do   sa 'na te mi   kol   'ri zo
   piagatemi   col   sguardo,   sanatemi   col   riso.
   wound me   with the   glance   heal me   with the   laughter
   wound me with your glance, heal me with your laughter.

ar 'ma te vi   pu 'pil: le   da 'spris: si mo   ri 'go ɾe   ver 'sa te mi   sul   'kɔ ɾe   un   'nem bo
Armatevi   pupille,   d'asprissimo   rigore,   versatemi   su'l   core   un   nembo
arm yourselves   eyes   with harshest   severity   pour to me   upon the   heart   a   shower
Arm yourselves, eyes, with harshest severity; shower my heart

   di   fa 'vil: le   mal   'la bro   non   'si a   'tar do   a   rav: vi 'var mi   ut: 'tʃi zo
   di   faville,   ma'l   labro   non   sia   tardo   a   ravvivarmi   ucciso.
   of   sparks   but the   lip   not   may be   late   to   to revive me   killed
   with sparks, but may your lips not be late in reviving me from death.

> *labro =*
> *(mod.)*
> *labbro*

fe 'ri ska mi   kwel   'zgwar do   ma   'sa ni mi   kwel   'ri zo
Feriscami   quel   sguardo,   ma   sanimi   quel   riso.
let wound me   that   glance   but   let heal me   that   laughter
Let that glance wound me, but let that laughter heal me.

beʎ: 'ʎɔk: ki   a   'lar mi   'i o   vi   pre 'pa ɾo   il   'se no
Begl'occhi   a   l'armi: io   vi   preparo   il   seno;
beautiful eyes   to   the arms   I   for you   I prepare   the   breast
Beautiful eyes, to arms! I ready my breast for you;

   dʒo 'i te   di   pja 'gar mi   in 'sin 'ki o   'veŋ ga 'me no
   gioite   di   piagarmi,   insin ch'io   venga meno.
   delight   in   to wound me   until [that] I   I may swoon
   delight in wounding me until I swoon.

> *in [75] and [76]:*
> *infin[o] = (lit.) insin[o]*

e   se   da   'vɔ stri   'dar di   'i o   re ste 'rɔ   koŋ 'kwi zo
E   se   da'   vostri   dardi   io   resterò   conquiso,
and   if   from the your   darts   I   I will be   conquered

And if I am conquered by your darts,

fe 'ɾi ski no   'kwe i   'zgwar di   ma   'sa na mi   kwel   'ɾi zo
ferischino   quei   sguardi,   ma   sanimi   quel   riso.
let wound   those   glances   but   let heal me   that   laughter

let those glances wound, but let that laughter heal me.

The following is a "lettera amorosa" (love letter), one of the genres of the time. The top of the music page reads: "Lettera amorosa a voce sola in genere rappresentativo e si canta senza battuta." (A love letter for solo voice, composed in expressive, dramatic style [stile rappresentativo] and therefore to be sung without regular measure). (See notes in [73].)

[72, 73]

se i 'laŋ gwi di 'mjɛ i 'zwgar di
Se i languidi miei sguardi
If my languishing glances

se   i   'laŋ gwi di   'mjɛ i   'zwgar di   se   i   so 'spir   in ter: 'rot: ti   se   le
Se   i   languidi   miei   sguardi,   se   i   sospir'   interrotti,   se   le
if   the   languishing   my   glances   if   the   sighs   broken off   if   the

If my languishing glances, if my broken off sighs, if my

'troŋ ke   pa 'rɔ le   non   an   sin 'or   po 'tu to   o   bɛl   'i do lo   'mi o
tronche   parole   non   han   sin or   potuto,   o   bel   idolo   mio,
unfinished   words   not   have so far   been able   o   beautiful   idol   mine

unfinished words have not yet been able, o beautiful idol mine,

'far vi   de   le   'mi e   'fjam: in 'te ɾa   'fe de   led: 'dʒe te   'kwe ste   'nɔ te | in [72]:
farvi   de   le   mie   fiamm' intera   fede: leggete   queste   note, | fiamme intera
to make you   of   the   my   flames whole   faith   read   these   notes | = fiamm' intera

to give you complete faith in my passion, read these notes –

kre 'de te   a   'kwe sta   'kar ta   in   'ku i   'sot: to   'for ma   diŋ 'kjɔ stro   il   kɔr   stil: 'la i
credete   a   questa   carta   in   cui   sotto   forma   d'inchiostro   il   cor   stillai.
believe   in   this   paper   on   which   under   form   of ink   the   heart   I dripped

believe this paper, on which I spilled my heart in the form of ink.

kwi   'sot: to   skor dʒe 'ɾe te   kwel: lin 'tɛr ni   pen 'sjɛ ɾi   ke   kon   'pas: si   da 'mo ɾe | in [72]:
Qui   sotto   scorgerete   quell'interni   pensieri   che   con   passi   d'amore | quelli interni =
here below   discern   those inner   thoughts   which   with   steps   of love | quell'interni

'skor: ron   'la ni ma   'mi a
scorron   l'anima   mia.
flow   the soul   mine

Here below, come to know those inner thoughts which run through my soul on footsteps of love.

'an tsi   av: vam 'par   ve 'dre te   'ko min   'su a   'pro prja   'sfɛ ɾa | in [72]: come in
Anzi   avvampar   vedrete   com'in   sua   propria   sfera | = com' in
in fact   to burn   you will see   how in   its   own   sphere

'nel: le   'vɔ stre   bel: 'let: tse   il   'fɔ ko   'mi o
nelle   vostre   bellezze   il   foco   mio.
in the   your   beauties   the fire   mine

In fact, you will see my fire burning in your beauties as if in its own sphere.

non	ε	dʒa	ˈpar tin	ˈvo i	ke	kon	ˈfɔr tsa	in vi ˈzi bi le	da ˈmo ɾe
Non	è	già	part' in	voi	che	con	forza	invisibile	d'Amore
not	is	[any]	part in	you	that	with	force	invisible	of Love

There is no part in you that, with the invisible force of Love,

ˈtut: ta	se	non	mi	ˈtrag: ga
tutt'a	sé	non	mi	tragga.
everything to	itself	not	me	may draw

in [72]: tutto a se = tutt'a se

does not attract me to you entirely.

ˈal tro	dʒa	non	son	ˈi o	ke	di	ˈvɔ stra	bel ˈta	ˈprɛ da	e	tro ˈfɛ o
Altro	già	non	son	io	che	di	vostra	beltà	preda	e	trofeo.
other	[now]	not	am	I	than	of	your	beauty	prey	and	trophy

I am nothing other than the prey and trophy of your beauty.

a	ˈvo i	mi	ˈvɔl go	o	ˈkjɔ me	ˈka ɾi	ˈmjɛ i	ˈlat: tʃi	ˈdɔ ɾo
A	voi	mi	volgo	o	chiome,	cari	mici	lacci	d'oro.
to	you	me	I turn	o	hair	dear	my	ties	of gold

I turn to you, o tresses, my dear golden ties.

dɛ	ˈko me	ˈma i	po ˈte a	skam ˈpar	si ˈku ɾo	se	ˈko me	ˈlat: tʃi	ˈla ni ma	lɛ ˈgɑ stɛ
Deh,	come	mai	potea	scampar	sicuro,	se	come	lacci	l'anima	legaste,
ah	how	ever	was able	to escape	safe	as	like	ties	the soul	you bound

Ah, however could I escape safely, as you bound my soul like a harness,

potea = poteva

ko ˈmɔ ɾo	la	kom ˈpra ste	ˈvo i	pur	ˈvo i	ˈduŋ kwe	ˈse te
com' oro	la	compraste.	Voi,	pur	voi,	dunque	sete
like gold	it	you bought	you	indeed	you	thus	you are

sete = (mod.) siete
in [72]: come oro = com'oro

[and] you bought it by weight of gold. Indeed, you are thus

de	la	ˈmi a	li ber ˈta	ka ˈte na	e	ˈprɛt: tso
de	la	mia	libertà	catena	e	prezzo.
of	the	my	liberty	chain	and	price

the fetters and the price of my liberty.

ˈsta mi	ˈmjɛ i	pre ˈtsjo zi	ˈbjon de	ˈfi la	di ˈvi ne
Stami	miei	preziosi	bionde	fila	divine,
threads	my	precious	blond	threads	divine

*stame (pl. stami): the thread which connects a human being to life – i.e., "the thread of life" (See **Parca** in the **Glossary**).*

My precious threads, fair threads [hair] divine,

kon	ˈvo i	le ˈtɛr na	ˈpar ka	ˈso vral	ˈfu zo	fa ˈtal	ˈmi a	ˈvi ta	ˈtor tʃe
con	voi	l'eterna	Parca	sovra'l	fuso	fatal	mia	vita	torce.
with	you	the eternal	fate	over the	spindle	fatal	my	life	twists

with you the eternal Fate spins my life around its fateful spindle.

ˈvo i	ka ˈpel: li	ˈdɔ ɾo	ˈvo i	pur	ˈse te	di	ˈlɛ i
Voi,	capelli	d'oro,	voi	pur	sete	di	lei,
you	hair	of gold	you	indeed	are	of	her

sete = (mod.) siete

You, hair of gold – you are indeed of her

ke	ε	ˈtut: ta	ˈfɔ ko	ˈmi o	ˈrad: dʒi	e	fa ˈvil: le
che	è	tutta	foco	mio,	raggi	e	faville.
who	is	all	fire	mine	rays	and	sparks

in [72]: ch'è tutto foco mio = (same translation)

who is all my fire the rays and sparks.

ma   se   fa ˈvil: le   ˈse te   on davˈ vjɛn   ka ˈdoɲ: ɲi   ˈo ɾa
Ma   se   faville   sete,   ond'avvien   ch'ad ogni   ora
but   if   sparks   you are   whence happens   that at every   hour
But if you are sparks, how is it that at every hour,

> in [72]: onde avvien che ad
> = ond' avvien ch'ad

ˈkon tro   ˈlu zo   del   ˈfɔ ko   in ˈdʒu   ʃen ˈde te
contro   l'uso   del   foco   in giù   scendete?
against   the custom   of the   fire   downwards   you descend
contrary to the custom of fire *[which flames upwards]*, you descend?

a   ka   ˈvo i   per   sa ˈlir   ˈʃen der   kon ˈvjɛ ne   ka
Ah,   ch'a   voi   per   salir   scender   conviene,   ch'a
ah   [that] to   you   for   to go up   to descend   is fitting   because to

> in [72]:
> che a voi
> = ch' a voi

la   mad: ˈdʒor   tʃe ˈlɛ ste   ˈo ve   a spi ˈra te   o   ˈsfɛ ra   deʎ: ʎar ˈdo ɾi   o   pa ɾa ˈdi zo
la   maggior   celeste   ove   aspirate,   o   sfera   degl'ardori,   o   Paradiso,
the   greatest   celestial   where   you aspire   either   sphere   of the ardors   or   Paradise
Ah, you must descend in order to ascend, because the greatest celestial sphere – whether that of ardors *[the sphere of fire]*, or Paradise – to which you aspire

> var. in [72]:

kon   la   ma ˈdʒon   tʃe ˈlɛ ste   o va spi ˈra te   o   ˈsfɛ ra   ˈdeʎ: ʎi   ar ˈdo ɾi
con   la   magion   celeste   ov'aspirate   o   sfera   degli   ardori,
with   the   abode   celestial   where you aspire   either   sphere   of the   ardors
[...in order to ascend] with the celestial dwelling to which you aspire – whether the sphere of ardors *[the sphere of fire]*, ...

ɛ   ˈpɔ stin   kwel   bɛl   ˈvi zo
è   post' in   quel   bel   viso.
is   positioned in   that   beautiful   face
is placed in that beautiful face.

> in [72]: posta in
> = post' in

ˈka ɾa   ˈmi a   ˈsel va   ˈdɔ ɾo   ri ˈkis: si mi   ka ˈpel: li   in   ˈvo i   kwel   la bi ˈrin to
Cara   mia   selva   d'oro,   richissimi   capelli,   in   voi   quel   labirinto
dear   my   forest   of gold   richest   hair   in   you   that   labyrinth

> in [72]: laberinto
> = (mod.) labirinto

a ˈmor   in ˈtɛs: se   on duʃ: ˈʃir   non   sa ˈpra   ˈla ni ma   ˈmi a
Amor   intesse,   ond'uscir   non   saprà   l'anima   mia.
Love   weaves   whence to withdraw   not   will know how   the soul   mine
My dear forest of gold, luxuriant tresses, Love weaves in you that labyrinth from which my soul will not know how to withdraw.

ˈtroŋ ki   pur   ˈmɔr ti   ˈra mi   del   pret: ˈtso zo   ˈbo sko
Tronchi   pur   mort' i   rami   del   prezioso   bosco,
may cut off   yet   dead the   branches   of the   precious   woods

> in [72]: morte i
> = mort' i

e   de   la   ˈfra dʒil   ˈkar ne   ˈskwɔ ta   pur   lo   ˈmi o   ˈspir to
e   de   la   fragil   carne   scuota   pur   lo   mio   spirto:
and   of   the   fragile   flesh   may shake   yet   the   my   spirit
May my spirit yet cut off the dead branches of the precious wood, and shake off the frail flesh,

ke   tra   ˈfron de   si   ˈbɛl: le   ˈaŋ ko   re ˈtʃi zo   ri mar: ˈrɔ   pri dʒo ˈnjɛ ɾo
ché   tra   fronde   sì   belle   anco   reciso   rimarrò   prigionero,
because   among   foliage   so   beautiful   even   cut off   I will remain   prisoner
because among foliage so lovely, even cut off, I will remain a prisoner

> in [72]: fra = tra | anco = (mod.) anche

'fat: to   'dʒe li da   'pol ve   e 'dom bra   iɲ: 'ɲu da
fatto   gelida   polve   ed ombra   ignuda.
made   ice-cold   dust   and of shadow   naked
turned into frozen dust and a naked shadow.

> polve = (mod.) polvere

dol 'tʃis: si mi   le 'ga mi   'bɛl: le   'mi e   'pjɔd: dʒe   'dɔ ɾo   kwa 'lor   'ʃɔl te
Dolcissimi   legami,   belle   mie   pioggie   d'oro,   qualor   sciolte
sweetest   ties   beautiful   my   showers   of gold   if   unloosened
Sweetest ties, my beautiful showers of gold, when unloosened

ka 'de te   da   'kwel: le   'rik: ke   'nu bi   'on de   rak: 'kɔl te   'se te
cadete   da   quelle   ricche   nubi,   onde   raccolte   sete,
you fall   from   those   rich   clouds   where   gathered   you are
you fall from those rich clouds where you are gathered

e   ka 'dɛn do   for 'ma te   pret: 'tsjo ze   pro 'tʃɛl: le   'on de   kon   'on de   dɔr
e   cadendo   formate   preziose   procelle,   onde   con   onde   d'or
and   falling   you form   precious   tempests   where   with   waves   of gold
and, falling, you form precious tempests where, with waves of gold,

baɲ: 'ɲan do   an 'da te   'skoʎ: ʎi   di   'lat: te   e   'ri vi   da la 'ba stro
bagnando   andate   scogli   di   latte   e   rivi   d'alabastro,
bathing   you go   rocks   of   milk   and   rivers   of alabaster
you bathe rocks of milk and rivers of alabaster.

'mɔ ɾe   su bi ta 'men te   o   mi 'ra ko le 'tɛr no   da mo 'ro zo   de 'zi o
More   subitamente,   o   miracol' eterno   d'amoroso   desio,
dies   suddenly   o   miracle eternal   of amorous   desire

> more = (mod.) muore

fra   si   'bɛl: le   tem 'pɛ 'star so   il   kɔr   'mi o
fra   sì   belle   tempest' arso   il   cor   mio.
among   such   beautiful   tempests burned   the   heart   mine
My scorched heart suddenly dies, o eternal miracle of amorous desire, among such beautiful storms.

> in [72]: **...tempeste arsi**: possibly = My heart dies suddenly, o eternal miracle of amorous desire; I burned among such beautiful storms.

ma   dʒa   'lo ɾa   min 'vi ta   o   'deʎ: ʎi   af: 'fɛt: ti   'mjɛ i   'nun tsja   fe 'de le
Ma   già   l'ora   m'invita,   o   degli   affetti   miei   nunzia   fedele,
but   already   the hour   me invites   o   of the   affections   mine   messenger   faithful
But already the hour invites me, o faithful messenger of my affections,

'ka ɾa   'kar ta   a mo 'ro za   ke   'dal: la   'pen: na   ti   di 'vi di   o 'ma i
cara   carta   amorosa,   che   dalla   penna   ti   dividi   omai.
dear   paper   amorous   that   from the   pen   you   separate   now
dear loving paper, to part you now from the pen.

> omai (poet.) = ormai

'van: ne   e   sa 'mor   el   'tʃe lo   kor 'te ze   ti   kon 'tʃe de   ke   da   beʎ: 'ʎɔk: ki
Vanne,   e   s'Amor   e'l   Cielo   cortese   ti   concede   che   da   begl'occhi
go away   and   if Love   and the   Heaven   kind   you   grants   that   from   beautiful eyes

non   tat: 'tʃɛn da   il   'rad: dʒo   ri 'ko vra   'en tro   il   bɛl   'se no
non   t'accenda   il   raggio,   ricovra   entro   il   bel   seno.
not   you may enflame   the   ray   take refuge   within   the   beautiful   breast
Go, and if Love and kind heaven will grant you not to be set on fire by the ray of those beautiful eyes, find refuge within the beautiful breast.

> ricovra: from "ricovrare" = (mod.) "ricoverare"

ki   sa   ke   tu   non   'dʒuŋ ga   da   si   fe 'li tʃe   'lɔ ko
Chi   sa   che   tu   non   giunga   da   sì   felice   loco
Who   knows   that   you   not   may reach   from   such   happy   place
Who knows: you may reach, from such a happy place,

per	sen 'tjɛ ri	di	'ne ve	a	un	kɔr	di	'fɔ ko
per	**sentieri**	**di**	**neve**	**a**	**un**	**cor**	**di**	**foco.**
through	paths	of	snow	to	a	heart	of	fire

a heart of fire by way of paths of snow.

GL: **Amor[e], Parca**

            ↫

[43]
from: *L'Incoronazione di Poppea (1643)*
character: *Valletto*   *Giovanni Francesco Busenello*

'sɛn to un 'tʃɛr to non sɔ ke
Sento un certo non so che
I feel a certain I know not what

'sɛn to	un	'tʃɛr to	non	sɔ	ke	ke	mi	'pit: tsi ka	o	di 'lɛt: ta
Sento	**un**	**certo**	**non**	**so**	**che,**	**che**	**mi**	**pizzica**	**o**	**diletta –**
I feel	a	certain	not	I know	what	which	me	stings	or	delights

It seems likely that the correct original was "e" rather than "o" – i.e., "stings and delights me" – (?)

I feel a certain I know not what, which stings or delights me –

'dim: mi	tu	ke	'kɔ za	'eʎ: ʎi	ɛ	da mi 'dʒɛl: la	a mo ro 'zet: ta
dimmi	**tu**	**che**	**cosa**	**egli**	**è,**	**damigella**	**amorosetta!**
tell me	you	what	thing	it	is	damsel	amorous dear one

tell me what it is, dear amorous damsel!

ti	fa 'rɛ i	ti	di 'rɛ i	ma	non	sɔ	kwel	'ki o	vor: 'rɛ i
Ti	**farei,**	**ti**	**direi,**	**ma**	**non**	**so**	**quel**	**ch'io**	**vorrei.**
you	I would do	you	I would tell	but	not	I know	that	which I	I would like

I would show you, I would tell you; but I know not what I want.

se	stɔ	'ke to	il	kɔr	mi	'bat: te
Se	**sto**	**cheto**	**il**	**cor**	**mi**	**batte,**
if	I stay	silent	the	heart	in me	beats

If I stay silent, my heart beats;

se	tu	'par ti	'i o	stɔ	me 'lɛn so
se	**tu**	**parti**	**io**	**sto**	**melenso.**
if	you	part	I	I stay	dumb

if you leave, I am left dumbfounded.

al	'tu o	sen	di	'vi vo	'lat: te	'sɛm pre	a 'spi ro	e	'sɛm pre	'pɛn so
Al	**tuo**	**sen**	**di**	**vivo**	**latte**	**sempre**	**aspiro**	**e**	**sempre**	**penso,**
to the	your	breast	of	alive	milk	always	I aspire to	and	always	I think

I always crave your milky breast, and I always think about it;

ti	fa 'rɛ i	ti	di 'rɛ i	ma	non	sɔ	kwel	'ki o	vor: 'rɛ i
ti	**farei,**	**ti**	**direi,**	**ma**	**non**	**so**	**quel**	**ch'io**	**vorrei.**
you	I would do	you	I would tell	but	not	I know	that	which I	I would like

I would show you, I would tell you; but I know not what I want.

            ↫

[72, 73]

si 'dol tʃe ɛl tor 'men to
Si dolce è'l tormento
So sweet is the torment

si	'dol tʃe	ɛl	tor 'men to	kin	'se no	mi	sta
Si	**dolce**	**è'l**	**tormento**	**ch'in**	**seno**	**mi**	**sta,**
so	sweet	is the	torment	which in	breast	me	is

So sweet is the torment in my breast

in [72]:
*che in =
ch' in*

'ki o	'vi vo	kon 'tɛn to	per	'kru da	bel 'ta
ch'io	**vivo**	**contento**	**per**	**cruda**	**beltà.**
that I	I live	content	for	cruel	beauty

that I live contentedly for cruel beauty.

nel	tʃɛl	di	bel: 'let: tsa	sak: 'kreʃ: ʃi	fje 'ret: tsa	e	'maŋ ki	pje 'ta
Nel	**ciel**	**di**	**bellezza**	**s'accresci**	**fierezza**	**e**	**manchi**	**pietà:**
in the	heaven	of	beauty	may increase	haughtiness	and	may be missing	pity

In the heaven of beauty may haughtiness increase and pity be absent,

ke	'sɛm pre	kwal	'skɔʎ: ʎo	al: 'lon da	dor 'goʎ: ʎo	'mi a	'fe de	sa 'ra
ché	**sempre**	**qual**	**scoglio**	**all'onda**	**d'orgoglio**	**mia**	**fede**	**sarà.**
because	always	like a	rock	in the wave	of pride	my	faith	will be

as my faith will always be like a reef in the path of the waves of pride.

in [72]: *all'onde
(waves) =* same
translation

la	'spɛ me	ɱal: 'la tʃe	ri 'vɔl ga mil	pjɛ
La	**speme**	**fallace**	**rivolgam'il**	**piè.**
the	hope	fallacious	may turn around the	foot

May deceptive hope turn me away.

in [72]: *rivolgami il
= rivolgam'il*
speme (lit.) =
speranza

di 'lɛt: to	ne	'pa tʃe	non	'ʃen da no	a	me
Diletto	**né**	**pace**	**non**	**scendano**	**a**	**me.**
delight	nor	peace	not	may come down	on	me

May neither delight nor peace fall on me.

e	'lem pja	ka 'do ro	mi	'njɛ gi	ri 'stɔ ro	di	'bwɔ na	mer 'tʃe
E	**l'empia**	**ch'adoro**	**mi**	**nieghi**	**ristoro**	**di**	**buona**	**mercé:**
and	the pitiless one	whom I adore	me	may deny	comfort	of	kind	mercy

And may the pitiless one whom I adore deny me the comfort of kind mercy;

*nieghi: from
"niegare" =
(mod.) "negare"

tra	'dɔʎ: ʎa	in fi 'ni ta	tra	'spɛ me	tra 'di ta	vi 'vra	la	'mi a	fe
tra	**doglia**	**infinita,**	**tra**	**speme**	**tradita**	**vivrà**	**la**	**mia**	**fé.**
among	sorrow	infinite	among	hope	betrayed	will live	the	my	faith

my faith will live among infinite sorrow, among betrayed hopes.

per	'fɔ ko	e	per	'dʒe lo	ri 'pɔ zo	non	hɔ
Per	**foco**	**e**	**per**	**gelo**	**riposo**	**non**	**ho.**
through	fire	and	through	ice	repose	not	I have

Through fire and ice I find no repose.

nel	'pɔr to	del	'tʃe lo	ri 'pɔ zo	a 'vrɔ
Nel	**porto**	**del**	**cielo**	**riposo**	**avrò.**
in the	haven	of the	heaven	repose	I shall have

I shall have repose in the haven of heaven.

se	'kol po	mor 'ta le	kon	'ri dʒi do	'stra le	il	kɔr	mim pja 'gɔ
Se	**colpo**	**mortale**	**con**	**rigido**	**strale**	**il**	**cor**	**m'impiagò,**
if	blow	mortal	with	cruel	arrow	the	heart	me wounded

If a mortal blow has wounded my heart with a cruel arrow,

kan 'dʒan do	'mi a	'sɔr te	kol	'dar do	di	'mɔr te	il	kɔr	sa ne 'rɔ
cangiando	**mia**	**sorte**	**col**	**dardo**	**di**	**morte**	**il**	**cor**	**sanerò.**
changing	my	destiny	with the	dart	of	death	the	heart	I will heal

changing my destiny, I will heal my heart with death's dart.

se	'fjam: ma	da 'mo ɾe	dʒa 'ma i	non	'sɛn ti	kwel	'ri dʒi do	'kɔ ɾe	kil
Se	**fiamma**	**d'amore**	**già mai**	**non**	**sentì**	**quel**	**rigido**	**core**	**ch'il**
if	flamme	of love	never	not	felt	that	rigid	heart	that the

in [72]:
che il = ch'il

kɔr	mi	ra 'pi	se	'ne ga	pje 'ta te	la	'kru da	bel 'ta te	ke	'lal ma	in va 'gi
cor	**mi**	**rapì,**	**se**	**nega**	**pietate**	**la**	**cruda**	**beltate**	**che**	**l'alma**	**invaghì,**
heart	me	ravished	if	denies	pity	the	cruel	beauty	who	the soul	infatuated

If that rigid heart which ravished my heart never felt the flame of love,
if the cruel beauty who infatuated my soul denies pity,

pietate = (mod.) pietà
beltade = (mod.) beltà

bɛn	'fi a	ke	do 'lɛn te	pen 'ti ta	e	laŋ 'gwɛn te	so 'spi ɾi mi	un	di
ben	**fia**	**che**	**dolente,**	**pentita**	**e**	**languente**	**sospirimi**	**un**	**dì.**
well	may it be	that	sorrowful	regretful	and	languishing	she may sigh for me	one	day

well may it be that one day, full of sorrow and regret, she will pine for me.

᪥

[95]

Giambattisto Marino

'tɛm pro la 'tʃe tra
Tempro la cetra
I tune my cithara

'tɛm pro	la	'tʃe tra	e	per	kan 'tar	ʎi	o 'no ɾi	di	'mar te
Tempro	**la**	**cetra,**	**e**	**per**	**cantar**	**gli**	**onori**	**di**	**Marte**
I tune	the	cithara	and	for	to sing	the	honors	of	Mars

I tune my cithara, and to sing the praises of Mars

'al tso	ta 'lor	lo	stil	e	i	'kar mi
alzo	**talor**	**lo**	**stil**	**e**	**i**	**carmi.**
I raise	sometimes	the	stylus	and	the	poems

I sometimes take up my stylus and my poems.

ma	in 'van	la	'tɛn to	e	im pos: 'si bil	'par mi
Ma	**invan**	**la**	**tento**	**e**	**impossibil**	**parmi**
but	in vain	it	I try	and	impossible	seems to me

But I try in vain, and it seems impossible to me

'kel: la	dʒa 'ma i	ri 'sɔ ni	'al tro	ka 'mo ɾe
ch'ella	**già mai**	**risoni**	**altro**	**ch'amore.**
that it	never	it may resound	other	than love

that it [my cithara] will ever resound with anything but love.

ko 'zi	pur	tra	la 'ɾe ne	e	pur	tra	'fjo ɾi
Così	**pur**	**tra**	**l'arene**	**e**	**pur**	**tra**	**fiori**
thus	also	among	the sands	and	also	among	flowers

And so from among sands and flowers

'nɔ te	a mo 'ro ze	a 'mor	'tor na	det: 'tar mi	ne	vɔl	'ki o	'prɛn daŋ 'kor
note	**amorose**	**Amor**	**torn'a**	**dettarmi,**	**né**	**vol**	**ch'io**	**prend'ancor**
notes	amorous	Love	returns to	to dictate to me	nor	wishes	that I	take up again

printed on the music page (in error) is "nott'amorose" | *vol[e] (poet.) = vuol[e]*

a	kan 'tar	'dar mi	se	non	di	'kwel: le	on 'deʎ: ʎim 'pja ga	i	'kɔ ɾi
a	**cantar**	**d'armi**	**se**	**non**	**di**	**quelle**	**ond'egl'impiaga**	**i**	**cori.**
to	to sing	of arms	if	not	of	those	whence he wounds	the	hearts

Love returns to dictate amorous notes to me; he does not want me to start singing again about weapons, except for those he uses to wound hearts.

or	'lu mil	'plɛt: tro	e	i	'rod: dzi	at: 'tʃɛn ti	in 'deɲ: ɲi	'mu za	kwal	'djan tʃi
Or	**l'umil**	**plettro**	**e**	**i**	**rozzi**	**accenti**	**indegni,**	**musa,**	**qual**	**dianci**
now	the humble	plectrum	and	the	unrefined	words	unworthy	muse	like	once

ak: 'kɔr da	in 'fin kal	'kan to	de	la	'trom ba	su 'bli me	il	tʃɛl	ti	'deɲ: ɲi
accorda	**in fin ch'al**	**canto**	**de**	**la**	**tromba**	**sublime**	**il**	**Ciel**	**ti**	**degni.**
tune	until to the	song	of	the	trumpet	sublime	the	heaven	you	deigns

Now tune my humble plectrum and my unrefined, unworthy words, o muse, as you once did,
until heaven deigns you worthy of the sublime trumpet's song.

> "la tromba sublime" = the trumpet heralding entrance to Paradise | dianci = (mod.) dianzi

'rje de	ai	'te ne ɾi	'sker tsi	e	'dol tʃe	in 'tan to	lo	'di o	gwer: 'rjɛr
Riede	**ai**	**teneri**	**scherzi**	**e**	**dolce,**	**intanto**	**lo**	**Dio**	**guerrier**
returns	to the	tender	jests	and	sweet	meanwhile	the	god	warrior

> lo = (mod.) il

The warrior god *[Cupid]* meanwhile returns to his tender jests and sweetness,

tem 'pran do	i	'fɛ ɾi	'zdeɲ: ɲi
temprando	**i**	**feri**	**sdegni**
softening	the	harsh	disdains

> feri = (mod.) fieri | The printed "segni" is likely a misprint for "sdegni," which leads to a more reasonable translation in context.

softening his harsh disdain;

in	'grɛm bo	a	tʃi te 'rɛ a	'dɔr mal	'tu o	'kan to
in	**grembo**	**a**	**Citerea**	**dorm'al**	**tuo**	**canto.**
in	bosom	to	Cytherea	may sleep at the	your	song

may he sleep to your song in the lap of Cytherea.

GL: **Amor, Citerea, Marte**

ಜ

[61]
from: *Orfeo (1607)*
character: *Orfeo*

Alessandro Striggio

tu	sɛ	'mɔr ta
Tu se'		**morta**
You are		dead

tu	sɛ	'mɔr ta	'mi a	'vi ta	e 'di o	re 'spi ɾo
Tu	**se'**	**morta,**	**mia**	**vita,**	**ed io**	**respiro.**
you	are	dead	my	life	and I	I breathe

You are dead, my life *[my beloved]*, and I *[still]* breathe.

tu	sɛ	da	me	par 'ti ta	per	'ma i	pju	non	tor 'na ɾe	e 'di o	ri 'maŋ go
Tu	**se'**	**da**	**me**	**partita**	**per**	**mai**	**più**	**non**	**tornare,**	**ed io**	**rimango!**
you	are	from	me	parted	for	never	more	not	to return	and I	I remain

You have left me, never to return, and I remain *[here]*!

nɔ	ke	se	i	'vɛr si	al 'ku na	'kɔ za	'pɔn: no	nan 'drɔ	si 'ku ɾo
No,	**che**	**se**	**i**	**versi**	**alcuna**	**cosa**	**ponno,**	**n'andrò**	**sicuro**
no	[that]	if	the	verses	some	thing	are able	there I will go	confident

> ponno = (mod.) possono

No! If my songs may have effect I will go, confidently,

a	pju	pro 'fon di	a 'bis: si	e	in te ne 'ri to	il	kɔr	del	re	del: 'lom bre
a'	**più**	**profondi**	**abissi**	**e**	**intenerito**	**il**	**cor**	**del**	**re**	**dell'ombre,**
to	most	deep	abysses	and	softened	the	heart	of the	king	of the shades

to the deepest abysses and, having softened the heart of the king of the shades,

'me ko	tra 'rɔt: ti	a	ri ve 'der	le	'stel: le
meco	**trarotti**	**a**	**riveder**	**le**	**stelle,**
with me	I will draw you	to	to see again	the	stars

will draw you with me to see the stars again;

o	se	tʃɔ	ne ge 'ram: mi	'em pjo	de 'sti no
o	**se**	**ciò**	**negherammi**	**empio**	**destino,**
or	if	that	will deny me	pitiless	destiny

or, if pitiless destiny denies me that,

ri mar: 'rɔ	'te ko	in	kom paɲ: 'ɲi a	di	'mɔr te
rimarrò	**teco**	**in**	**compagnia**	**di**	**morte!**
I will remain	you with	in	company	of	death

I will stay with you in the company of death!

ad: 'di o	'ter: ra	ad: 'di o	'tʃɛ lo	e	'so le	ad: 'di o
Addio,	**terra!**	**Addio,**	**cielo**	**e**	**sole!**	**Addio!**
farewell	earth	farewell	sky	and	sun	farewell

Farewell, earth! Farewell, sky and sun! Farewell!

[77]

'vɔʎ: ʎo di 'vi ta uʃ: 'ʃir
Voglio di vita uscir
I want to depart from life

'vɔʎ: ʎo	di	'vi ta	uʃ: 'ʃir	'vɔʎ: ʎo	ke	'ka da no	kwe 'stɔs: sa	in	'pol ve
Voglio	**di**	**vita**	**uscir,**	**voglio**	**che**	**cadano**	**quest'ossa**	**in**	**polve**
I want	from	life	to leave	I want	that	may fall	these bones	in	dust

polve =
(mod.) polvere

I want to depart from life; I want these bones to turn to dust

e	'kwe ste	'mɛm bra	in	'tʃe ne ɾe
e	**queste**	**membra**	**in**	**cenere**
and	these	limbs	in	ashes

and these limbs to ashes,

e	ke	i	siŋ 'gul ti	'mjɛ i	tra	'lom bra	'va da no
e	**che**	**i**	**singulti**	**miei**	**tra**	**l'ombra**	**vadano.**
and	that	the	sobs	mine	among	the shadow	may go

and my sobs to go among the shadows.

dʒa	ke	kwel	pjɛ	kin 'dʒem: ma	'lɛr be	'te ne ɾe	'sem pre	'fud: dʒe	da	me
Già	**che**	**quel**	**piè**	**ch'ingemma**	**l'erbe**	**tenere**	**sempre**	**fugge**	**da**	**me**
now	that	that	foot	which bejewels	the grasses	tender	always	flees	from	me

Now that she whose foot graces the young grass continues to flee from me,

ne	lo	tra 'teŋ go no	i	'lat: tʃi	o i 'mɛ	del	bɛl	fan 'tʃul	di	've ne ɾe
né	**lo**	**tratengono**	**i**	**lacci**	**oimè**	**del**	**bel**	**fanciul**	**di**	**Venere.**
nor	it	restrain	the	snares	alas	of the	beautiful	child	of	Venus

nor, alas, do the snares of Venus' beautiful child *[Cupid]* restrain her,

vɔ	ke	ʎa 'bis: si	il	'mi o	kor 'dɔʎ: ʎo	've da no	e	'la spro	'mi o	mar 'tir
vo'	**che**	**gl'abissi**	**il**	**mio**	**cordoglio**	**vedano**	**e**	**l'aspro**	**mio**	**martir**
I want	that	the abysses	the	my	grief	may see	and	the bitter	my	agony

le	'fu rje	'pjaŋ ga no	e	ke	i	dan: 'na ti	al	'mi o	tor 'men to	'tʃɛ da no
le	**furie**	**piangano**	**e**	**che**	**i**	**dannati**	**al**	**mio**	**tormento**	**cedano.**
the	furies	may weep	and	that	the	damned souls	to	my	torment	may yield

I want the abysses to see my grief, and the furies to weep for my bitter agony, and the damned souls to concede that my suffering is greater than theirs.

a 'di o	kru 'dɛl	ʎor 'gɔʎ: ʎi	'twɔ i	ri 'maŋ ga no	a	iŋ kru de 'lir	kon	'ʎal tri
A Dio	**crudel**	**gl'orgogli**	**tuoi**	**rimangano**	**a**	**incrudelir**	**con**	**gl'altri**
farewell	cruel one	the prides	your	let remain	to	to grow more cruel	with	the others

Farewell, cruel one; let your pride keep growing more cruel with others;

> *A Dio = (mod.) Addio*

a	te	ri 'nun tsjo	ne	vɔ	pju	ke	'mi e	'spɛ me	in	te	si 'fraŋ ga no
a	**te**	**rinunzio**	**né**	**vo'**	**più**	**che**	**mie**	**speme**	**in**	**te**	**si frangano.**
to	you	I renounce	nor	I want	more	that	my	hopes	in	you	themselves may shatter

I renounce you; I do not want my hopes in you to shatter anymore.

> *speme = (lit.) speranze*

'sa pre	la	'tom ba	il	'mi o	mo 'rir	tan: 'nun tʃo	'u na	'la kri ma	'spar dʒi
S'apre	**la**	**tomba**	**il**	**mio**	**morir**	**t'annuncio**	**una**	**lacrima**	**spargi**
opens	the	tomb	the	my	dying	to you I announce	a	tear	shed

My tomb is opening; to you I herald my death. Shed a tear

> *the printed "annuntio" = (mod.) annuncio*

e dal 'fin	'do na mi	di	'tu a	'tar da	pje 'ta de	un	'so lo	'nun tsjo
ed alfin	**donami**	**di**	**tua**	**tarda**	**pietade**	**un**	**solo**	**nunzio**
and at last	give me	of	your	late	pity	a	single	sign

and give me, at last, a single sign of your belated pity;

> *pietade = (mod.) pietà*
>
> *the printed nuntio" = (mod.) nunzio*

e	sa 'man do	tof: 'fe zi	o 'ma i	per 'do na mi
e	**s'amando**	**t'offesi**	**omai**	**perdonami.**
and	if loving	you I offended	now	pardon me

and if in loving you I offended you, now forgive me.

> *omai (poet.) = ormai*

❁ *Obizzi, Domenico (1611/12-after 1630)*

Probably born in Venice, he was employed as a singer at S. Marco there from at least 1627 to 1630. He was connected to influential Venetian patrons; the dedication in his second collection of vocal pieces, *Madrigali et Arie a voce sola*, states that he was fifteen years old at the time of publication, and that from the age of nine he had been living under the protection of the Venetian patrician Lorenzo Loredano. The first of Obizzi's two vocal collections, both published in 1627, was *Madrigali concertati a 2-5 voci con il basso continuo*.

His vocal music suggests a link between the choral madrigal and the forthcoming development of the solo cantata. Paton (see notes in [43]) conjectures that Obizzi may have died in Venice during the great plague of 1630.

---

[43]

'ɛk: ko ke pur ba 'tʃa te
Ecco, che pur baciate
Here indeed you are kissing

'ɛk: ko	ke	pur	ba 'tʃa te	o	'lab: bra	av: ven tu 'ro ze
Ecco,	**che**	**pur**	**baciate,**	**o**	**labbra**	**avventurose,**
here is	[that]	indeed	you kiss	o	lips	adventurous

Here indeed you are kissing, o adventurous lips,

'du na   'bok: ka   dʒen 'til   le   'vi ve   'rɔ ze
d'una   bocca   gentil   le   vive   rose.
of a   mouth   gentle   the   living   roses
the living roses of a gentle mouth.

ma   ke   'pun te   mor 'da tʃi   'men tre   'ki o   'ba tʃo   o i 'mɛ   'pas: sa no   il   'kɔ ɾe
Ma   che   punte   mordaci   mentre   ch'io   bacio   ohimè!   passano   il   core.
but   what   stings   biting   while   that I   I kiss   alas   pass through   the   heart
But what biting stings pass through my heart while I am kissing, alas!

son   'for se   'stra li   i   'ba tʃi
Son   forse   strali   i   baci?
are   perhaps   arrows   the   kisses
Are kisses arrows, perhaps?

a   se   sta   kol   pja 'tʃer   'mi sto   il   do 'lo ɾe
Ah!   se   sta   col   piacer   misto   il   dolore,
ah   if   is   with the   pleasure   mixed   the   pain
Ah, if pain is mingled with pleasure,

a 'ma ɾe   son   le   'tu e   dol 'tʃet: tse   a 'mo ɾe
amare   son   le   tue   dolcezze,   Amore.
bitter   are   the   your   sweetnesses   Love
bitter are your sweetnesses, Love.

GL: **Amore**

❀ *Orlandi, Camillo (fl.1616)*

Born in Verona, he is known to have been in the service of the Archbishop of Salzburg, a devotee of Italian music, in 1616.

Surviving, of his music, is a vocal collection *Arie, Op.2*, which contains dialogues for three characters mostly in recitative style, eight monodies, and six duets.

---

[78]   *Dionisio Lazari*

a   ke   pur 'trɔp: po
Ah che purtroppo
Ah, unfortunately

a   ke   pur 'trɔp: po   ɛ   ver   'fil: li   bɛn   'mi o
Ah   che   purtroppo   è   ver   Filli   ben   mio
ah   [that]   unfortunately   it is   true   Filli   dear one   mine
Ah, unfortunately it is true, Filli, my dear one,

ke   par 'tir   'dɛd: dʒo   e   te   laʃ: 'ʃar   do 'lɛn te
che   partir   deggio   e   te   lasciar   dolente.
that   to depart   I must   and   you   to leave   sorrowful
that I must depart and leave you sorrowful.

ri 'man   fe 'li tʃe   a 'di o   'stel: la   pjan 'dʒen te   ri 'man   fe 'li tʃe   a 'di o   beʎ: 'ʎɔk: ki
Riman   felice   a Dio   stella   piangente,   riman   felice   a Dio   begl'occhi.
remain   happy   farewell   star   weeping   remain   happy   farewell   beautiful eyes
Be happy; farewell, weeping star. Be happy; farewell, beautiful eyes.

| *a Dio =* |
| *(mod.)* |
| *addio* |

'par to   kol   'pjɛ de   se   non   kol   de 'zi o
Parto   co'l   piede   se   non   co'l   desio,
I depart   with the   foot   if   not   with the   desire

I depart bodily, if not by desire;

> *Printed is "si non…" This could intend to be "sì, non…" (= yes, not…); but I've chosen to consider the "si" as a misprint for "se," and have changed it as such.*

e   'sa i   pel   'mi o   par 'tir   'lal ma   laŋ 'gwen te
e   s'hai   pel   mio   partir   l'alma   languente
and   if you have   through the   my   departing   the soul   languishing

and if, because of my departing, your soul languishes,

ti   'fat: tʃo   un   'do no   ir: re vo ka bil 'men te   di   'kwe sto   'ko re   in: na mo 'ra to   aŋ 'ki o
ti   faccio   un   dono   irrevocabilmente   di   questo   core   innamorato   anch'io.
to you   I make   a   gift   irrevocably   of   this   heart   enamored   also I

I, also enamored, irrevocably make a gift to you of this heart.

e   'kwe sti   'ul ti mi   'ba tʃi   e   'kwe ste   e 'strɛ me   'la gri me   kor   ak: 'kɔʎ: ʎo
E   questi   ultimi   baci   e   queste   estreme   lagrime   ch'or   accoglio
and   these   last   kisses   and   these   final   tears   which now   I welcome

And these last kisses and these final tears which I now welcome

in   'kal di   u 'mo ri   da   'ʎɔk: ki   'twɔ i   da   le   'tu e   'la bra   in 'sjɛ me
in   caldi   umori   da   gl'occhi   tuoi   da   le   tue   labra   insieme
in   hot   saps   from   the eyes   your   from   the   your   lips   together

in hot flow from your eyes, and from your lips,

> *da le = (mod.) dalle; labra = (mod.) labbra*

'fi a na   'la ni ma   'mi a   kon 'ti nu i   ar 'do ri
fian' a   l'anima   mia   continui   ardori.
will be to   the soul   mine   continual   ardors

will be continual fuel for my soul.

> *fian[o] = (mod.) saranno*

'fi an   nu tri 'men ti   oɲ: 'ɲor a   la   'mi a   'spɛ me
Fian   nutrimenti   ogn'or a   la   mia   speme,
will be   nourishments   always   to   the   my   hope

They *[the kisses and tears]* will always be sustenance for my hope;

> *speme (lit.) = speranza*

'fi an   per 'pɛ tu e   me 'mɔ rje   on 'di o   ta 'do ri
fian   perpetue   memorie   ond'io   t'adori.
will be   everlasting   memories   from which I   you I may adore

they will be the everlasting memories for which I will adore you.

GL: **Filli**   ☙

[78]

'ka ra gra 'di ta e 'bɛl: la
Cara gradita e bella
Dear, pleasing, and beautiful

'ka ra   gra 'di ta   e   'bɛl: la   'sɛm pre   mi   'fo ste   'fil: li de   'mi a   'stel: la
Cara   gradita   e   bella   sempre   mi   foste   Fillide   mia   stella
dear   pleasing   and   beautiful   always   to me   you were   Fillide   my   star

You were always dear, pleasing, and beautiful to me, Fillide, my star;

ma   'pɔ i ke   'skɔr go   a   'seɲ: ɲi   ke   la 'mor   'mi o   non   'zdeɲ: ɲi
ma   poi che   scorgo   a'   segni   che   l'amor   mio   non   sdegni
but   since   I perceive   at   signs   that   the love   mine   not   you scorn

but since I see by the signs that you do not scorn my love,

> *poi che = (mod.) poiché*

> *"scorno"(= I mock), rather than "scorgo," is printed on the music page; "scorgo," printed in the text at the back of the publication, allows this line to make sense…*

'kwel: la tu 'so la 'sɛ i ke 'gra ta e 'bɛl: la ap: 'pa ɾi a 'ʎɔk: ki 'mjɛ i
quella tu sola sei che grata e bella appari a gl'occhi miei.
that one you alone you are that pleasing and beautiful you appear to the eyes mine
you are the only one who appears pleasing and beautiful to my eyes.

dɛ se pju 'bɛl: la 'bra mi e pju gra 'di ta 'ki o ta 'do ɾi e 'da mi
Deh, se più bella brami e più gradita ch'io t'adori ed ami
ah if more beautiful you desire and more pleasing that I you may adore and may love
Ah, if you wish that I adore you and love you as more beautiful and more pleasing,

'mo stra pju 'vi vo a 'mo ɾe 'ki o ti do ne 'ɾɔ il 'kɔ ɾe
mostra più vivo amore ch'io ti donerò il core,
show more lively love that I you I will give the heart
show [me] more ardent love, and I will give you my heart,

'seɲ: ɲo si 'kur da 'man te non 'fin to ma in a 'mor 'fer mo e kon 'stan te
segno sicur d'amante non finto ma in amor fermo e constante.
sign sure of lover not feigned but in love firm and constant
a sure sign of a lover not false, but firm and constant in love.

*constante =
(mod.) costante*

ma se tu 'for se 'kru da di bel 'ta 'rik: ka e di pje 'ta de iɲ: 'ɲu da
Ma se tu forse cruda di beltà ricca e di pietade ignuda
but if you perhaps cruel of beauty rich and of pity naked
But if you, perhaps cruel, rich in beauty and devoid of pity,

*pietade
= (mod.)
pietà*

pju me ti 'mo stri a 'va ɾa per 'ɛs: ser mi men 'ka ɾa
più me ti mostri avara per essermi men cara,
more to me yourself you show miserly for to be to me less dear
show yourself to be miserly, in order to be less dear to me,

e 'tʃer ki iŋ 'gra ta e 'fɛ ɾa ke 'mil: le e 'mil: le 'vɔl te
e cerchi ingrata e fera che mille, e mille volte
and you seek ungrateful and proud that thousand and thousand times

*fera =
(mod.) fiera*

il 'dʒor no 'i o 'pɛ ɾa
il giorno io pera.
the day I I may perish
and you try, ungrateful and proud, to make me die thousands and thousands of times a day...

*pera (from "perire")
= (mod.) perisca*

non mi fud: 'dʒi ɾe al 'me no se de 'zi o di bel 'ta ti 'pun dʒe il 'se no
Non mi fuggire almeno se desio di beltà ti punge il seno
not me to flee at least if desire of beauty you pricks the breast
Do not flee from me if, at least, the desire for beauty pricks your breast,

per 'ke ne 'swɔ i ver 'dan: ni 'sot: to led: 'dʒa dri 'pan: ni 'tan to 'oɲ: ɲi 'don: na
perché ne' suoi verd'anni sotto leggiadri panni tanto ogni donna
because in her green years beneath pretty clothing so much every woman

ɛ 'bɛl: la 'kwan to da 'mor si 'mo stra 'fi da an 'tʃɛl: la
è bella quanto d'Amor si mostra fida ancella.
is beautiful as much of Love herself shows faithful handmaid
because in her youth, in graceful clothing, every woman is as beautiful as she shows herself to be
a faithful handmaiden to Love.

GL: **Amor, Fillide**

☙

[78]

ke fa 'rɔ 'dɔn: na iŋ 'gra ta
Che farò, donna ingrata
What shall I do, ungrateful woman?

ke	fa 'rɔ	'dɔn: na	iŋ 'gra ta	ti	se gwi 'rɔ	ko 'stan te
Che	**farò,**	**donna**	**ingrata?**	**Ti**	**seguirò**	**costante.**
what	I shall do	woman	ungrateful	you	I will follow	constant

What shall I do, ungrateful woman? I shall follow you faithfully.

del	'tu o	ri 'gor	mal	for tu 'na to	a 'man te	o	mi mo 'rɔ	fra	'kwe sti	'sas: si
Del	**tuo**	**rigor**	**mal**	**fortunato**	**amante**	**o**	**mi morò**	**fra**	**questi**	**sassi**
of the	your	severity	badly	fortunate	lover	oh	I shall die	among	these	rocks

Unfortunate lover of your severity, oh, I shall die among these rocks

> *morò = (mod.) morrò*

on 'di o	tɔ	zmar: 'ri ta	kɔr	'mi o	'ɛk: ko	ri 'spon di	lo	'mi o	'sta to	kon 'siʎ: ʎa
ond'io	**t'ho**	**smarrita**	**cor**	**mio.**	**Ecco**	**rispondi**	**lo**	**mio**	**stato**	**consiglia.**
where I	you I have	lost	heart	mine	behold	respond	the	my	condition	advise

where I lost you, my heart. Look, answer; advise [me about] my condition.

'ɛk: ko	gra 'di ta	o	di	'mɔr te	o	di	'vi ta
Ecco	**gradita**	**o**	**di**	**morte**	**o**	**di**	**vita.**
behold	welcomed	either	of	death	or	of	life

Look: I welcome either death or life.

ke	fa 'rɔ	me	do 'lɛn te	ri ve 'drɔ	'ma i	'fwɔ ra
Che	**farò,**	**me**	**dolente,**	**rivedrò**	**mai**	**fuora**
what	I shall do	me	woeful	I shall see	never	away

What shall I do, sorrowful me? Shall I never see, away

> *fuora (poet.)*
> *= fuori*

del	'gjat: tʃo	'su o	la	'mi a	ne 'vo za	a u 'rɔ ra	o	re ste 'rɔ	'sot: to
del	**ghiaccio**	**suo**	**la**	**mia**	**nevosa**	**aurora?**	**O**	**resterò**	**sotto**
of the	ice	its	the	my	snowy	dawn	oh	I will remain	beneath

from its ice, my snowy dawn? Oh, I shall remain beneath

il	me 'de mo	'tʃɛ lo	'fat: to	'sas: so	al	'tu o	'dʒɛ lo
il	**medemo**	**cielo**	**fatto**	**sasso**	**al**	**tuo**	**gelo.**
the	same	heaven	made	stone	at the	your	ice

> *medemo =*
> *(mod.) medesimo*

the same heaven, made a rock to your ice *[having become indifferent to your coldness]*.

'ɛk: ko	ri 'spon di
Ecco	**rispondi...**
behold	respond

Look, answer...

ke	fa 'rɔ	'duŋ kwe	'a i 'las: so	ti	fud: dʒi 'rɔ	kon 'stret: to
Che	**farò**	**dunque**	**ahi lasso?**	**Ti**	**fuggirò**	**constretto**
what	I shall do	then	alas woe	you	I shall flee	compelled

> *constretto (lit.)*
> *= costretto*

What shall I do, then? Woe is me! I shall flee from you, compelled

del	'tu o	mad: 'dʒor	vo 'ler	del	'tu o	di 'lɛt: to
del	**tuo**	**maggior**	**voler**	**del**	**tuo**	**diletto.**
of the	your	greater	will	of the	your	pleasure

by your stronger will, by your pleasure.

o   mi mo 'rɔ   fra   'kwe sti   'sas: si   on 'di o   tɔ   per 'du to   kɔr   'mi o
O   mi morò   fra   questi   sassi   ond'io   t'ho   perduto   cor   mio.
oh   I will die   among   these   rocks   where I   you I have   lost   heart   mine
Oh, I shall die among these rocks where I lost you, my heart.

'ɛk: ko   ri 'spon di
Ecco   rispondi...
behold   respond
Look, answer...

&

[78]

kru 'dɛl tu 'vwɔi par 'ti ɾe
Crudel, tu vuoi partire
Cruel one, you want to leave

kru 'dɛl   tu   'vwɔ i   par 'ti ɾe   non   mil   ne 'gar   'ki ol   sɔ
Crudel,   tu   vuoi   partire,   non   m'il   negar   ch'io 'l   so
cruel one   you   you want   to depart   not   to me it   to deny   because I it   I know
Cruel one, you want to leave; do not deny it to me, because I know it.

'a i   do 'lor   'a i   mar 'ti ɾe   mar 'tir   on 'di o   mo 'rɔ
Ahi   dolor   ahi   martire,   martir   ond'io   morò.
alas   pain   alas   agony   agony   whence I   I shall die
Alas, [what] pain; alas, [what] agony – agony from which I shall die.

> morò =
> (mod.) morrò

'pɛr fi do   lu ziŋ 'gjɛ ɾo   'do ve   ri 'vɔl dʒi   il   pjɛ
Perfido   lusinghiero   dove   rivolgi   il   piè?
deceptive   flattering   where   you turn   the   step
Deceptive, flattering one, where are you going?

nɔ   non   fu   'ma i   've ɾo   kar 'de sti   'uŋ kwa   per   me
No,   non   fu   mai   vero   ch'ardesti   unqua   per   me.
no   not   was   ever   true   that you burned   ever   for   me
No, it was never true that you ever burned for me.

> unqua (poet.)
> = mai

'las: sa   'ki o   'pjaŋ go   e   'gri do   e 'de i   'ljɛ to   sen va
Lassa   ch'io   piango   e   grido   ed ei   lieto   sen va.
miserable   [that] I   I weep   and   I cry out   and he   happy   goes away
Miserable, I weep and cry out, and he happily goes away.

> ei = egli

'a i   di zle 'al   'a i   in 'fi do   'a i   kɔr   'sɛn tsa   pje 'ta
Ahi   disleal,   ahi   infido,   ahi   cor   senza   pietà.
alas   disloyal   alas   untrustworthy   alas   heart   without   pity
Alas, disloyal one; alas, untrustworthy one; alas, pitiless heart.

'mi ze ɾa   me   'kwa i   'pjan ti   ver 'sai   pju   'vɔl te   il   di
Misera   me   quai   pianti   versai   più   volte   il   dì,
wretched   me   how many   tears   I shed   several   times   the   day
Wretched me; how many tears I shed several times a day,

> *printed is "versar"; more*
> *likely correct is "versai"*
> *printed "misero" should be "misera"*

'kwan ti   so 'spir   e   'kwan ti   dal   kɔr   'spar si   e   per   ki
quanti   sospir   e   quanti   dal   cor   sparsi   e   per   chi?
how many   sighs   and   how many   from the   heart   I shed   and   for   whom
how many, many sighs I poured from my heart, and for whom?

> *printed is "a per chi"; the "a"*
> *must be a misprint for "e"*

non	fur	ve 'ɾa tʃi	'kwe i	'pjan ti	e	'kwe i	so 'spir
Non	**fur**	**veraci**	**quei**	**pianti**	**e**	**quei**	**sospir.**
not	were	truthful	those	tears	and	those	sighs

Those tears and those sighs were not sincere.

fur = furono

'a i	lu ziŋ 'gjeɾ	fal: 'la tʃi	'a i	men 'ti ti	de 'zir
Ahi	**lusinghier**	**fallaci,**	**ahi**	**mentiti**	**desir.**
alas	flattering	deceptive	alas	false	desires

Alas, flattering, deceptive, and false desires.

'ɾɛn di mi	in 'dʒu sto	a 'man te	'ɾɛn di mi	iŋ 'gra to	il	kɔr
Rendimi	**ingiusto**	**amante,**	**rendimi**	**ingrato**	**il**	**cor.**
give back to me	unjust	lover	give back to me	ungrateful one	the	heart

Give me back my heart, unjust lover, ungrateful one.

'fer ma	le	'pjan te	'fam: mi	dʒus 'tit: tʃa	a 'mor
Ferma	**le**	**piante,**	**fammi**	**giustizia**	**Amor.**
stop	the	(soles of) feet	make for me	justice	Love

Stop; give me justice, Love.

per	kwel	'em pjo	e	kru 'dɛ le	ke	di	me	non	cal	pju
Per	**quel**	**empio**	**e**	**crudele**	**che**	**di**	**me**	**non**	**cal**	**più,**
[for]	that	impious	and	cruel one	who	of	me	not	matters	more

That impious and cruel one to whom I no longer matter –

e	'si o	ʎi	'fu i	fe 'de le	a 'mor	lo	'sa i	tu
e	**s'io**	**gli**	**fui**	**fedele**	**Amor**	**lo**	**sai**	**tu.**
[and]	if I	to him	was	faithful	Love	it	you know	you

if I was faithful to him, Love, you know it.

e	se	zveʎ: 'ʎo ti	a 'mo ɾe	'kwal ke	fa 'vil: la	in	sen
E	**se**	**sveglioti**	**Amore**	**qualche**	**favilla**	**in**	**sen**
and	if	stirred in you	Love	some	spark	in	breast

And if Love aroused some spark in your breast,

sveglioti (mod.: svegliotti)
= ti svegliò

da liŋ kon 'stan te	'kɔ ɾe	spi 'ɾɔ	'ko me	ba 'len
dal'inconstante	**core**	**spirò**	**come**	**balen.**
by the inconstant	heart	it expired	like	lightning

it was snuffed out in a flash by your inconstant heart.

inconstante =
(mod.) incostante

a 'mor	'ko mil	kom 'pɔr ti	'ko me	il	kom 'pɔr ti	o	tʃɛl
Amor	**com'il**	**comporti**	**come**	**il**	**comporti**	**o**	**ciel**
Love	how it	you allow	how	it	you allow	o	heaven

Love, how can you allow – how can you allow, o heaven,

kel	tra di 'tor	sen 'pɔr ti	un	kɔr	'tan to	fe 'del
che'l	**traditor**	**sen porti**	**un**	**cor**	**tanto**	**fedel.**
that the	traitor	may take away	a	heart	so	faithful

a traitor to take away so faithful a heart?

'a i	kel	par 'tir	saf: 'fret: ta	e 'di o	ri 'maŋ go	o i 'mɛ
Ahi	**che'l**	**partir**	**s'affretta**	**ed io**	**rimango**	**oimè**
ah	[that] the	departing	hastens	and I	I remain	alas

Ah, the departure is coming quickly; and I remain here, alas,

'mi ze ɾa   dʒo vi 'net: ta   e   ke   sa 'ɾa   di   me
misera   giovinetta,   e   che   sarà   di   me?
miserable   girl   and   what   will be   of   me
miserable girl. And what will become of me?

GL: **Amor[e]**

❧

[78]

dɛ 'ko me in 'van kje 'de te
Deh come in van chiedete
Ah, how you ask in vain

dɛ   'ko me   in   van   kje 'de te   du 'dir   'bɛl: la   si 'ɾɛ na   il   'kan to   'mi o
Deh   come   in   van   chiedete   d'udir   bella   sirena   il   canto   mio.
ah   how   in   vain   you ask   of to hear   beautiful   siren   the   song   mine
Ah, how you ask in vain, beautiful siren, to hear my song.

se   'sor da   'se te   'vo i   'mu to   son   'i o   al   swɔn   de   'vo stri   at: 'tʃɛn ti
Se   sorda   sete   voi   muto   son   io   al   suon   de'   vostri   accenti. | *sete =*
if   deaf   you are   you   mute   am   I   at the   sound   of   your   words | *(mod.) siete*
If you are deaf, I am silent at the sound of your words.

per 'de i   la   'vo tʃe   e   sol   mi   'swɔ na   il   'kɔ ɾe
Perdei   la   voce   e   sol   mi   suona   il   core | *suona = (mod.) sona*
I lost   the   voice   and   only   to me   plays   the   heart

ar mo 'ni a   di   so 'spir   e   di   la 'men ti
armonia   di   sospir   e   di   lamenti.
harmony   of   sighs   and   of   laments
I have lost my voice, and my heart only plays for me a harmony of sighs and laments.

e   sel   'vo stro   ri 'go ɾe   a   'vo i   ne   'tɔʎ: ʎe   il   swɔn
E   se'l   vostro   rigore   a   voi   ne   toglie   il   suon
and   if the   your   rigor   to   you   of it   takes away   the   sound
And if your rigor takes away the sound of it for you,

mi 'ɾa te   il   'pjan to   ke   le   'la gri me   'mi e   'so no   il   'mi o   'kan to
mirate   il   pianto   ché   le   lagrime   mie   sono   il   mio   canto.
see   the   weeping   because   the   tears   mine   are   the   my   song
see my weeping, because my tears are my song.

❧

[78]

o 'va ga e 'bjaŋ ka 'lu na
O vaga e bianca luna
O lovely and pale moon

o   'va ga   e   'bjaŋ ka   'lu na   o   'vo i   'pom pe   del   tʃɛl
O   vaga   e   bianca   luna,   o   voi   pompe   del   ciel
o   lovely   and   white   moon   o   you   pomps   of the   sky

'kja ɾe   e   splen 'dɛn ti   e 'tɛr ne   'stel: le   ar 'dɛn ti   'di te mi   'lu mi   a 'mi tʃi
chiare   e   splendenti   eterne   stelle   ardenti,   ditemi   lumi   amici
clear   and   bright   eternal   stars   ardent   tell me   lights   friendly
O lovely and pale moon, o you glories of the sky, clear and bright, ardent eternal stars,
tell me, friendly lights,

e	'kwan do	'ma i	ve 'de ste		il	pju	ko 'stan te	el	pju	fe 'del	a 'man te
e	**quando**	**mai**	**vedeste**		**il**	**più**	**costante**	**e'l**	**più**	**fedel**	**amante.**
[and]	when	ever	may you have seen		the	more	constant	and the	more	faithful	lover

when you ever may have seen a more constant and faithful lover.

or	'koɲ: ɲi	'kɔ za	ad: dor men 'ta ta	'dʒa tʃe	'sot: to	si 'lɛn tsjo	'vo stro	a 'ma to	e	'ka ɾo
Or	**ch'ogni**	**cosa**	**addormentata**	**giace**	**sotto**	**silenzio**	**vostro**	**amato**	**e**	**caro**
now	that every	thing	sleeping	lies	beneath	silence	your	loved	and	dear

Now that everything sleeps beneath your beloved and dear silence,

'i o	sol	ved: 'dʒar	im 'pa ɾo	'i o	sol	pro 'rom po	in	a mo 'ro zi	'la i
io	**sol**	**veggiar**	**imparo,**	**io**	**sol**	**prorompo**	**in**	**amorosi**	**lai.**
I	alone	to stay awake	I learn	I	alone	I burst forth	in	amorous	lamentations

I alone learn to keep vigil; I alone burst forth with amorous lamentations.

> *veggiar[e] = (mod.) vegliare*
> *lai (poet.) = lamenti*

'dɔr me	ki	ne	ka 'dʒon	a 'skol ta	e	'ta tʃe	'dɔr me	si
Dorme	**chi**	**né**	**cagion**	**ascolta**	**e**	**tace,**	**dorme**	**sì**
sleeps	he who	not	reason	heeds	and	is silent	sleeps	yes

He who does not listen to reason and is silent sleeps, yes,

> *though "né" is printed*
> *without an accent, the*
> *context suggests it*

po i 'ke	'vo i	splen 'de te	'me no	or	ke	di	'vo strɪ	'ra ɪ	'kju zo	εl	se ɾe no
poiché	**voi**	**splendete**	**meno**	**or**	**che**	**di**	**vostri**	**rai**	**chiuso**	**è'l**	**sereno.**
since	you	you shine	less	now	that	of	your	rays	shut off	is the	radiance

as you shine less now that the light of your rays is closed off *[your eyes are shut]*.

[78]

'pjaŋ go no al 'pjan dʒer 'mi o
Piangono al pianger mio
They weep at my tears

'pjaŋ go no	al	'pjan dʒer	'mi o	le	'fε ɾe	e	i	'sas: si
Piangono	**al**	**pianger**	**mio**	**le**	**fere**	**e**	**i**	**sassi,**
weep	at the	weeping	mine	the	wild beasts	and	the	rocks

The wild beasts and the rocks weep at my tears;

> *fere =*
> *(mod.) fiere*

a	'mjε i	'kal di	so 'spir	'tra gon	so 'spi ɾi
a	**miei**	**caldi**	**sospir**	**tragon**	**sospiri.**
at	my	hot	sighs	they draw	sighs

they sigh at my ardent sighs.

'la er	din 'tor no	nu bi 'lo zo	'fas: si	'mɔs: so	aŋ 'keʎ: ʎi
L'aer	**d'intorno**	**nubiloso**	**fassi**	**mosso**	**anch'egli**
the air	around	cloudy	makes itself	moved	even it

> *aer= aere (poet.)*
> *= aria, atmosfera*

a	pje 'ta	de	'mjε i	mar 'ti ɾi
a	**pietà**	**de'**	**miei**	**martiri.**
a	pity	of	my	agonies

The air all around even turns cloudy out of pity for my agonies.

o 'vuŋ kwe	'i o	'pɔ zo	o 'vuŋ kwe	'i o	'vɔl go	i	'pas: si
Ovunque	**io**	**poso**	**ovunque**	**io**	**volgo**	**i**	**passi**
wherever	I	I put down	wherever	I	I turn	the	steps

> *ovunque (lit.)*
> *= dovunque*

Wherever I stop, wherever I turn,

par   ke   di   me   si 'pjaŋ ga   e   si so 'spi ɾi
par   che   di   me   si pianga   e   si sospiri.
it seems   that   of   me   one weeps   and   one sighs
it seems that everything weeps and sighs for me.

par   ke   'di ka   tʃa 'skun   'mɔs: so   al   'mi o   'dwɔ lo
Par   che   dica   ciascun   mosso   al   mio   duolo
it seems   that   says   everyone   moved   at the   my   grief
It seems that everyone, moved by my grief, says

ke   'fa i   tu   kwi   me 'skin   doʎ: 'ʎo zo   e   'so lo
che   fai   tu   qui   meschin   doglioso   e   solo.
what   you do   you   here   wretched one mournful   and   alone
"what are you doing here, wretched one, mournful and alone?"

[78]

tra   'du e   'ne gre   pu pil: 'let: te
Tra due negre pupillette
Between two little black eyes

tra   'du e   'ne gre   pu pil: 'let: te   tra   'du e   'tʃiʎ: ʎa   bru nel: 'let: te
Tra   due   negre   pupillette,   tra   due   ciglia   brunellette
between   two   black   little pupils   among   two   eyelashes   dark
Between two little black eyes and dark eyelashes

negre [negro] =	
(mod.) nere [nero]	

ful mi 'na to   il   kɔr   mi   sta
fulminato   il   cor   mi   sta.
struck by lightning   the   heart to me is
my heart is struck by lightning.

dʒa   le   'su e   'tʃe ne ɾi   a 'du na   'kwel: la   'vi va   'tom ba   e   'bru na
Già   le   sue   ceneri   aduna   quella   viva   tomba   e   bruna
already the   its   ashes   collects   that   living   tomb   and   dark
Already that dark and living tomb is collecting its ashes,

ke   de   'ʎɔk: ki   a 'mor   mi   fa
che   de   gl'occhi   Amor   mi   fa.
which   from   the eyes   Love   to me makes
which Love makes of me from those eyes.

'bɛl: la   'klɔ ɾi   al   'ku i   bɛl   'vi zo   lo   splen 'dor   del   pa ɾa 'di zo
Bella   Clori   al   cui   bel   viso   lo   splendor   del   paradiso
beautiful   Clori   to the whose   beautiful face   the   splendor   of the   paradise
Beautiful Clori, whose beautiful face the splendor of paradise

de gwaʎ: 'ʎar si   'uŋ kwa   non   ɛ
d'eguagliarsi   unqua   non   è,
of to make itself equal never   not   is
never equals,

unqua (poet.)	
= *mai*	

'si o   per   te   son   'dʒun to   a   'mor te   di za 'tʃer ba   la   'mi a   'sɔr te
s'io   per   te   son   giunto   a   morte   disacerba   la   mia   sorte
if I   through   you   am   arrived   at   death   make less bitter   the   my   fate
if I, through you, have arrived at death, make my fate less bitter

kon	un	sol	'tu o	'dol tʃe	o i 'mɛ
con	**un**	**sol**	**tuo**	**dolce**	**oimè.**
with	a	single	your	sweet	alas

with a single sweet "alas" from you.

'om bra	son	'mɛ sta	e	ro 'mi ta	ke	din 'tor no a	la	'mi a	'vi ta
Ombra	**son**	**mesta**	**e**	**romita**	**che**	**d'intorno a**	**la**	**mia**	**vita**
shadow	I am	sad	and	solitary	which	around	the	my	life

> *romita (lit.)*
> *= solitaria*

kin	te	'vis: se	er: 'ran do	vɔ
ch'in	**te**	**visse**	**errando**	**vo,**
which in	you	lived	wandering	I go

I am a sad and solitary shadow which wanders around the life I lived in you.

'prɛn di	in	'pa tʃe	il	'mi o	tor 'men to
Prendi	**in**	**pace**	**il**	**mio**	**tormento,**
take	in	peace	the	my	torment

Quietly accept my torment;

non	zdeɲ: 'ɲar	il	'mi o	la 'men to	'kes: ser	'loŋ ga	o 'ma i	non	pwɔ
non	**sdegnar**	**il**	**mio**	**lamento**	**ch'esser**	**longa**	**omai**	**non**	**può.**
not	to scorn	the	my	lament	that to be	long	now	not	is able

do not scorn my lament, which cannot last much longer now.

> *omai (poet.)*
> *= ormai*
>
> *longa =*
> *(mod.) lunga*

sol ke 'rɔ	'tɔ sto	la 're ne	de	lin 'fɛr no	'sɛn tsa	'spe ne	di	'ma i	pju	ve 'der ti	kwi
Solcherò	**tosto**	**l'arene**	**de**	**l'inferno**	**senza**	**spene**	**di**	**mai**	**più**	**vederti**	**qui**
I will plow	soon	the sands	of	the hell	without	hope	of	ever	more	to see you	here

I will soon plow the sands of hell without the hope of ever seeing you here again;

> *spene (poet.)= speme*
> *= (lit.) speranza*

e	da	'lal me	di spe 'ra te	fa 'rɔ	ke	'pjan te	e da 'ma te
e	**da**	**l'alme**	**disperate**	**farò**	**che**	**piante**	**ed amate**
and	by	the souls	in despair	I will make	that	lamented	and loved

'si an	le	'lu tʃi	on 'di o	mo 'ri
sian	**le**	**luci**	**ond'io**	**morì.**
may be	the	eyes	from which I	I died

and I will make the eyes from which I died be lamented and loved by the despairing souls *[those in hell]*.

GL: **Amor, Clori**

❀ *Orsini, Leonora* (1560?-1634)

Probably born in Florence, she was the daughter of Isabella de' Medici, daughter of the Grand Duke Cosimo de' Medici. Isabella was murdered by her husband Paolo Giordano Orsini, Duke of Bracciano, in 1574. Raised at the court of Francesco de' Medici, Leonora sang, composed, and played various instruments.

By 1588 she had moved to Rome, where she established a musical ensemble of women singers. In 1592 she married and bore eight children; she also, supposedly, took as lover the cardinal Pamphili, future Pope Innocent X. At some point she founded the monastery of Santa Chiara delle Cappuccine in Santa Fiora, and she died in Rome. Her only known composition is in a preserved manuscript of songs compiled by Bottegari known as *The Bottegari Lutebook*. Three of four pieces in that collection which mention her name are dedicated to her, but "Per pianto la mia carne" was probably actually composed by her.

[55, 62]   *Sannazaro*

per 'pjan to la 'mi a 'kar ne
Per pianto la mia carne
Through weeping, my flesh melts

per	'pjan to	la	'mi a	'kar ne	si di 'stil: la
Per	**pianto**	**la**	**mia**	**carne**	**si distilla,**
through	weeping	the	my	flesh	itself falls in drops

Through weeping, my flesh melts

si 'ko mal	sol	la	'ne ve	o	'ko mal	'vɛn to	si di 'sfa	la	'neb: bja
sì com'al	**sol**	**la**	**neve,**	**o**	**com'al**	**vento,**	**si disfa**	**la**	**nebbia.**
like at the	sun	the	snow	or	like at the	wind	is destroyed	the	fog

like the snow does in the sun, or like the fog is dispelled by the wind.

non	sɔ	ke	'far mi	'dɛb: bja
Non	**so**	**che**	**farmi**	**debbia.**
not	I know	what	to do me	I ought

I know not what I should do.

> in [62]: *né so =*
> *non so*

or	pen 'sa tal	'mi o	mal	kwal	'ɛs: ser	'dɛ ve
Or	**pensat' al**	**mio**	**mal**	**qual**	**esser**	**deve.**
now	think of the	my	pain	what	to be	must

Think, now, about what must be my pain.

> in [62]: *qual'esser*
> = *qual[e] esser*

❀ *Pasquini, Bernardo* (1637-1710)

Born in Massa Valdinievole (now Massa e Cozzili) near Lucca, renowned teacher and virtuoso keyboard player, he was employed as an organist in Rome first in 1661, and in 1664 at S. Maria in Aracoeli, which position he held for the rest of his life. His reputation as a keyboard performer led to the patronage of Queen Christina of Sweden, Prince Colonna, Cardinal Ottoboni, Cardinal Pamphili and, most importantly, Prince Giambattista Borghese, whom he served from about 1669 until his death.

Though known as the most important Italian composer of keyboard music between Frescobaldi and Domenico Scarlatti, he was also the leading dramatic composer in Rome during the 1670's *[Grove]*.

Pasquini and Corelli, who was his equal in virtuosity on the violin, performed together in oratorios, operas, and concerts.

Despite Pasquini's fame, little of his music was published and many of his vocal works are lost. He composed some seventeen operas, fourteen oratorios, and more than fifty solo cantatas.

[16, 39]

'bɛl: la 'bok: ka
Bella bocca
Beautiful mouth

'bɛl: la	'bok: ka	mi	'skɔk: ka	pju	'stra li	kon	tʃi 'na bro	dun	'la bro	ri 'dɛn te
Bella	**bocca,**	**mi**	**scocca**	**più**	**strali**	**con**	**cinabro**	**d'un**	**labro**	**ridente,**
beautiful	mouth	to me	shoots	more	arrows	with	cinnabar	of a	lip	laughing

A beautiful mouth shoots more arrows at me with the cinnabar of laughing lips, | *labro* = *(mod.) labbro* |

e	mi	'strin go no	i	'lat: tʃi	fa 'ta li	'lam bre	'fi ne	dun	'kri ne	lu 'tʃen te
e	**mi**	**stringono**	**i**	**lacci**	**fatali,**	**l'ambre**	**fine**	**d'un**	**crine**	**lucente.**
and	me	they clasp	the	ties	fatal	the ambers	delicate	of a	head of hair	shining

and fatal ties clasp me: the delicate amber of resplendent tresses.

❧

[58]

o par go 'let: to ar 'tʃɛ ɾo
O pargoletto arciero
O little archer boy

o	par go 'let: to	ar 'tʃɛ ɾo	non	'ɛs: ser	pju	si	'fjɛ ɾo	'ab: bi	pje 'ta	del	kɔr
O	**pargoletto**	**arciero,**	**non**	**esser**	**più**	**sì**	**fiero,**	**abbi**	**pietà**	**del**	**cor.**
o	baby boy	archer	not	to be	more	so	cruel	have	pity	of the	heart

O little archer boy *[Cupid]*, do not be so cruel anymore; have pity for my heart.

se	've ɾo	'nu me	'sɛ i	ti 'ran: no	'ɛs: ser	non	'dɛ i	ne	'sɛm pre	fe ɾi 'tor
Se	**vero**	**nume**	**sei,**	**tiranno**	**esser**	**non**	**dêi**	**né**	**sempre**	**feritor.**
if	true	deity	you are	tyrant	to be	not	you ought	nor	always	wounder

dêi =
devi

If you are a real god, you ought not be a tyrant, nor always one who wounds.

[1, 2, 15]

'kwan to ɛ 'fɔl: le kwel: la 'man te
Quanto è folle quell'amante
How foolish is that lover

'kwan to	ɛ	'fɔl: le	kwel: la 'man te	ke	pe 'nan do	si di 'spe ɾa
Quanto	**è**	**folle**	**quell'amante,**	**che**	**penando**	**si dispera;**
how much	is	foolish	that lover	who	suffering	gives himself up in despair

How foolish is that lover who, suffering, wastes away in desperation;

la	for 'tu na	ke	iŋ ko 'stan te	'var ja	a 'spɛt: to	e	'kan dʒa	'sfe ɾa
la	**fortuna,**	**ch'è**	**incostante,**	**varia**	**aspetto**	**e**	**cangia**	**sfera.**
the	ʃortune	which is	inconstant	varies	aspect	and	changes	sphere

fortune, which is inconstant, varies its face and changes spheres.

kon	spe 'ran tsa	di	mer 'tʃe de	o sti 'na to	'neʎ: ʎi	a 'mo ɾi
Con	**speranza**	**di**	**mercede,**	**ostinato**	**negli**	**amori**
with	hope	of	reward	obstinate	in the	loves

With the hope of reward, stubborn in my love,

'al: la	'mi a	su 'pɛr ba	'klɔ ɾi	ɔ	dʒu 'ra to	e 'tɛr na	'fe de
alla	**mia**	**superba**	**Clori**	**ho**	**giurato**	**eterna**	**fede!**
to the	my	proud	Clori	I have	sworn	eternal	faith

I have sworn eternal faith to my proud Clori!

GL: **Clori**

[16, 40]

sɔ bɛn 'si o 'pe no
So ben s'io peno
I know well that I suffer

sɔ	bɛn	'si o	'pe no	ben 'ke	spe 'ran tsa	mi	'vi va	in	'se no
So	**ben**	**s'io**	**peno,**	**benché**	**speranza**	**mi**	**viva**	**in**	**seno,**
I know	well	if I	I suffer	even though	hope	to me	may be alive	in	breast

I know well that I suffer; even though hope is alive in my breast,

mag: gjat: tʃa il   'kɔre di   'ri o ti 'mo ɾe 'fred: do ve 'le no

m'agghiaccia il   core di   rio timore freddo veleno.

me freezes the heart with evil fear cold venom

cold venom freezes my heart with heinous fear.

> *rio (lit.) =*
> *reo*

'sɛn to 'ki o 'mɔ ɾo aŋ 'kor ke 'spɛ ɾo il bɛn ka 'do ɾo

Sento ch'io moro, ancor che spero il ben ch'adoro,

I feel that I I die even that I hope the dear one whom I adore

I feel that I am dying, even as I hope for the dear one I adore;

son 'tut: ta 'gwa i ne 'pɔr to 'ma i 'tʃiʎ: ʎo se 'ɾe no

son tutta guai né porto mai ciglio sereno.

I am all woe nor I bear ever brow serene

I am full of woe, and my brow is never serene.

[1, 2]

from: *Erminia in riva del Giordano (1682)* (a Cantata)

character: *Erminia*

Benedetto Pamphili

'ver di 'troŋ ki

Verdi tronchi

Green trees

'ver di 'troŋ ki an: 'no ze 'pjan te 'fo sko a 'zil 'dom bre se 'kre te

Verdi tronchi, annose piante, fosco asil d'ombre secrete,

green tree trunks age-old plants dark asylum of shadows secret

Green trees, age-old plants, dark sanctuary of secret shadows,

> *secrete =*
> *(mod.) segrete*

per pje 'ta kwi rak: koʎ: 'ʎe te del do 'lo ɾe u 'nom bra er: 'ran te

per pietà qui raccogliete del dolore un'ombra errante!

for pity's sake here gather up of the sorrow a shadow wandering

for pity's sake, receive here a wandering shadow of sorrow!

si ke 'lun dʒi dal 'mi o 'so le 'om bra 'mɛ sta il dwɔl mi 'rɛn de

Sì che lungi dal mio sole ombra mesta il duol mi rende;

yes [that] far from the my sun shadow sad the sorrow me renders

Yes, far from my sun *[my beloved]* sorrow makes me a sad phantom;

ma kwel sol ke 'ar der mi 'vwɔ le ɛ spa 'ri to e pur mat: 'tʃɛn de

ma quel sol, che arder mi vuole, è sparito e pur m'accende.

but that sun which to burn me wants is vanished and yet me inflames

but that sun, which wants to burn me, has vanished and yet it inflames me.

Peri, Jacopo (1561-1633)

Nicknamed "Il zazzerino" because of his abundant head of hair, he shares the claim, for his *Dafne (1597)*, with his contemporary rival Giulio Caccini of having composed the first opera in monodic style.

Peri was from a noble Florentine family; organist, chitarrone player, and accomplished singer, he served the Medici court and was active with the *Camerata* group of musicians and literati who met at the home of Count Giovanni de' Bardi, shaping the character of music in the late sixteenth and early seventeenth centuries.

Peri's significant contributions, in addition to *Dafne*, were a second opera, *Euridice (1600)*, and a collection of music for one or more voices with continuo, *Le varie musiche*, published in 1609. Other works have either not survived or exist only in fragments.

[40]

al ˈfon te al ˈpra to
Al fonte, al prato
To the spring, to the meadow

al	ˈfon te	al	ˈpra to	al	ˈbɔ sko	alː ˈlom bra	al	ˈfre sko	ˈfja to
Al	**fonte,**	**al**	**prato,**	**al**	**bosco,**	**all'ombra,**	**al**	**fresco**	**fiato,**
to the	spring	to the	meadow	to the	woods	to the shade	to the	cool	breath of wind

To the spring, to the meadow, to the woods, to the shade, to the cool breath of wind

kel	ˈkal do	ˈzgom bra	pa ˈstor	kor ˈre te
ch'el	**caldo**	**sgombra,**	**pastor**	**correte;**
which the	heat	clears away	shepherd	hurry

which dispels the heat, shepherd, hasten;

el = (mod.) il

tʃa ˈskun	ka	ˈse te	tʃa ˈskun	kɛ	ˈstaŋ ko	ri ˈpɔ zi	il	ˈfjaŋ ko
ciascun	**ch'ha**	**sete,**	**ciascun**	**ch'è**	**stanco**	**riposi**	**il**	**fianco.**
each	who has	thirst	each	who is	tired	let rest	the	flank

let everyone who is thirsty, everyone who is weary, rest!

ˈfuːg ga	la	ˈnɔ ja	ˈfuːg gal	do ˈlo re	il	ˈɾi zo	e	ˈdʒɔ ja
Fugga	**la**	**noia,**	**fugga'l**	**dolore,**	**il**	**riso**	**e**	**gioia**
let flee	the	tedium	let flee the	sorrow	the	laughter	and	joy

Let tedium and sorrow flee; may laughter and joy

sol	ˈka ɾo	a ˈmo ɾe	ˈnɔ sko	sodː ˈdʒor ni	ˈne i	ˈlje ti	ˈdʒor ni
sol	**caro**	**Amore,**	**nosco**	**soggiorni,**	**nei**	**lieti**	**giorni,**
only	dear	Love	with us	may sojourn	in the	happy	days

only, dear Love, stay with us; in the happy days

nosco (poet.) = con noi

ne	ˈsɔ da	ˈma i	kwe ˈrɛ le	o	ˈla i
né	**s'oda**	**mai**	**querele**	**o**	**lai.**
not	may be heard	ever	quarrels	or	lamentations

may quarrels or laments never be heard.

ma	ˈdol tʃe	ˈkan to	di	ˈva gi	utː ˈtʃɛlː li	per	ˈver de	ˈman to	ˈdeʎː ʎi	ar boʃː ˈʃɛlː li
Ma	**dolce**	**canto**	**di**	**vaghi**	**uccelli**	**per**	**verde**	**manto**	**degli**	**arboscelli**
but	sweet	song	of	pretty	birds	through	green	mantle	of the	young trees

a	ˈswɔ ni	ˈsɛm pre	kon	ˈnwɔ ve	ˈtɛm pre	ˈmen tre	kalː ˈlon de	ˈɛkː ko	ri ˈspon de
a	**suoni**	**sempre**	**con**	**nuove**	**tempre,**	**mentre**	**ch'all'onde**	**Ecco**	**risponde.**
at	let sound	always	with	new	timbres	while	[that] to the waves	Echo	answers

Rather, let the sweet song of pretty birds ever resound in the green mantle of the young trees with new tones, while Echo answers the waves.

Ecco = (mod.) Eco

e	ˈmen tre	alː ˈlɛtː ta	ˈkwan to pju ˈpwɔ te	la	tʃi ca ˈlɛtː ta	kon	ˈrɔ ke	ˈnɔ te
E	**mentre**	**alletta**	**quanto più puote**	**la**	**cicaletta**	**con**	**roche**	**note**
and	while	entices	as much as it can	the	little cicada	with	hoarse	notes

puote = (mod.) può

il	ˈsonː no	ˈdol tʃe	kel	ˈkal do	ˈmol tʃe
il	**sonno**	**dolce**	**ch'el**	**caldo**	**molce**
the	slumber	sweet	which the	heat	alleviates

And while the little cicada, with throaty notes, entices as much as it can the sweet slumber which relieves the heat,

e   'no i   pjan 'pja no   kon   'lɛ i   kan 'tja mo
e   **noi**   **pian piano**   **con**   **lei**   **cantiamo.**
[and]   we   very softly   with   her   we sing

we sing very softly with her.

GL: **Amor, Ecco**

&

[48]

bel: 'lis: si ma re 'dʒi na
Bellissima regina
Most beautiful queen

bel: 'lis: si ma   re 'dʒi na   de   'mjɛ i   pen 'sjɛr   di   'fɔ ko
Bellissima   **regina**   **de'**   **miei**   **pensier**   **di**   **foco**
most beautiful   queen   of the   my   thoughts   of   fire

Most beautiful queen of my passionate thoughts,

'dʒun dʒi   a   'mjɛ i   'lab: bri   un   'pɔ ko   la   'bok: ka   ko ɾal: 'li na
giungi   **a'**   **miei**   **labbri**   **un**   **poco**   **la**   **bocca**   **corallina.**
join   to   my   lips   a   little   the   mouth   coral

join your coral mouth to my lips for a little while.

rin 'fre ska   'tan to   ar 'do ɾe   di   'nɛt: ta ɾe   da 'mo ɾe
Rinfresca   **tanto**   **ardore**   **di**   **nettare**   **d'amore.**
cool   so much   passion   with   nectar   of love

Cool my great passion with the nectar of love.

'dʒɛt: ta mi   al   'kɔl: lo   in 'tor no   le   kan di 'det: te   'brat: tʃa
Gettami   **al**   **collo**   **intorno**   **le**   **candidette**   **braccia;**
throw to me   at the   neck   around   the   little snow-white   arms

Throw your delicate snow-white arms around my neck;

'ba tʃa mi   e   non   ti 'spjat: tʃa   ba 'tʃar mi   'nɔt: te   e   'dʒor no
baciami   **e**   **non**   **ti spaccia**   **baciarmi**   **notte**   **e**   **giorno.**
kiss me   and   not   you may it displease   to kiss me   night   and   day

kiss me, and may it not displease you to kiss me night and day.

sol: 'lɛ va   kwel   bɛl   'vi zo   'gwar da mi   'fi zo
Solleva   **quel**   **bel**   **viso,**   **guardami**   **fiso.**
raise   that   beautiful   face   look at me   intently

Lift up that beautiful face of yours; look at me intently.

&

[61]
from: *Euridice (1600)*
character: *Orfeo*

Ottavio Rinuccini

fu 'nɛ ste   'pjad: dʒe
Funeste piaggie
Funereal shores

fu 'ne ste   'pjad: dʒe   om 'bro zi   'ɔr: ri di   'kam pi   ke   di   'stel: le   o   di   'so le
Funeste   **piaggie,**   **ombrosi,**   **orridi**   **campi,**   **che**   **di**   **stelle**   **o**   **di**   **sole**
funereal   shores   dark   horrid   fields   which   of   stars   or   of   sun

non	ve 'de ste	dʒam: 'ma i	ʃin 'til: la	o	'lam pi	rim bom 'ba te	do 'lɛn ti
non	**vedeste**	**giammai**	**scintilla**	**o**	**lampi,**	**rimbombate**	**dolenti**
not	you saw	ever	spark	or	gleams	resound	mournful

Funereal shores, hideous fields, you who have never seen the spark or gleam of stars or sun, resound mournfully

al	swɔn	del: laŋ goʃ: 'ʃo ze	'mi e	pa 'rɔ le	'men tre	kon	'me sti	at: 'tʃɛn ti
al	**suon**	**dell'angosciose**	**mie**	**parole,**	**mentre**	**con**	**mesti**	**accenti**
to the	sound	of the anguished	my	words	while	with	sad	accents

to the anguished sound of my words while, with sad accents,

il	per 'du to	'mi o	bɛn	kon	'vo i	so 'spi ro
il	**perduto**	**mio**	**ben**	**con**	**voi**	**sospiro.**
the	lost	my	dear one	with	you	I sigh

I sigh with you for my lost beloved.

e	'vo i	dɛ	per	pje 'ta	del	'mi o	mar 'ti ro	ke	nel	'mi ze ro	kɔr
E	**voi,**	**deh**	**per**	**pietà**	**del**	**mio**	**martiro,**	**che**	**nel**	**misero**	**cor**
and	you	pray	for	pity	of the	my	agony	which	in the	miserable	heart

di 'mɔ ra	e 'tɛr no	la kri 'ma te	al	'mi o	'pjan to	'om bre	din 'fɛr no
dimora	**eterno,**	**lacrimate**	**al**	**mio**	**pianto,**	**ombre**	**d'inferno!**
dwells	eternal	weep	at the	my	weeping	shades	of hell

And please, with pity for the agony which dwells eternal in my miserable heart,
weep at my tears, you shades *[spirits, souls of the dead]* of hell!

o i 'mɛ	ke	sul: la u 'rɔ ra	'dʒun se	al: lok: 'ka zo	il	sol	deʎ: 'ʎɔk: ki	'mjɛ i
Ohimè!	**che**	**sull'aurora**	**giunse**	**all'occaso**	**il**	**sol**	**degl'occhi**	**miei!**
alas	[that]	upon the dawn	reached	to the west	the	sun	of the eyes	mine

Alas, the light of my eyes reached sunset at the beginning of dawn!

'mi ze ro	e	in su	kwel: 'lo ra	ke	skal 'dar mi	a	'bɛ i	'rad: dʒi
Misero!	**e**	**in su**	**quell'ora,**	**che**	**scaldarmi**	**a'**	**bei**	**raggi**
wretched	and	upwards	that hour	[that]	to warm myself	at	beautiful	rays

'i o	mi kre 'de i	'mɔr te	'spɛn se	il	bɛl	'lu me
io	**mi credei,**	**morte,**	**spense**	**il**	**bel**	**lume,**
I	myself I believed	death	put out	the	beautiful	light

Wretched me! Just when I thought I would bask in the beautiful rays, death extinguished the beautiful light

e	'fred: do	e	'so lo	re 'sta i	fra	il	'pjan to	e	il	'dwɔ lo
e	**freddo**	**e**	**solo**	**restai**	**fra**	**il**	**pianto**	**e**	**il**	**duolo,**
and	cold	and	lonely	I remained	between	the	weeping	and	the	sorrow

and I remained, cold and lonely between weeping and sorrow,

'ko me	'aŋ gwe	swɔl	in	'fred: da	'pjad: dʒa	il	'vɛr no
come	**angue**	**suol**	**in**	**fredda**	**piaggia**	**il**	**verno.**
like	snake	is used to	in	cold	shore	the	winter

like a snake does in a cold place in winter.

> angue = (mod.) serpente
> verno = inverno

la kri 'ma te	al	'mi o	'pjan to	'om bre	din 'fɛr no
Lacrimate	**al**	**mio**	**pianto,**	**ombre**	**d'inferno!**
weep	at the	my	weeping	shades	of hell

Weep at my tears, shades of hell!

❧

[10, 19, 20, 24, 38, 42, 43, 44, 54] Also titled **Invocazione di Orfeo**.
from: *Euridice (1600)*
character: *Orfeo*

Ottavio Rinuccini

dʒo 'i te al 'kan to 'mi o
Gioite al canto mio
Rejoice at my singing

dʒo 'i te	al	'kan to	'mi o	'sel ve	fron 'do ze
Gioite	**al**	**canto**	**mio,**	**selve**	**frondose;**
rejoice	at the	singing	mine	woods	leafy

Rejoice at my singing, leafy woods;

dʒo 'i te	a 'ma ti	'kɔlː li	e	'doɲː ɲin 'tor no
gioite,	**amati**	**colli,**	**e**	**d'ogn'intorno**
rejoice	beloved	hills	and	of everywhere around

rejoice, beloved hills; and all around

'ɛ ko	rim 'bom bi	'dalː le	'valː li	as 'ko ze
eco	**rimbombi**	**dalle**	**valli**	**ascose.**
echo	may resound	from the	valleys	hidden

may an echo resound from the hidden valleys.

> *var.: da le = (mod.) dalle*
> *ascose: from "ascondere"*
> *(lit.) = nascondere*

ri 'sor to	ɛ	il	'mi o	bɛl	sol	di	'radː dʒi	a 'dor no
Risorto	**è**	**il**	**mio**	**bel**	**sol**	**di**	**raggi**	**adorno,**
risen again	is	the	my	beautiful	sun	with	rays	adorned

My beautiful sun *[i.e., Euridice]*, adorned with rays, has risen again;

e	ko	'beʎː ʎi	'ɔkː ki	'on de	fa	'skɔr no	a	'dɛ lo
e	**co'**	**begli**	**occhi,**	**onde**	**fa**	**scorno**	**a**	**Delo,**
and	with	beautiful	eyes	whence	makes	scorn	to	Delos

and with her beautiful eyes with which she puts Delos to shame

> *var.: coi*
> *['ko i] = co'*

radː 'dopː pja	'fwɔ ko	alː 'lal me	e	'lu tʃe	al	'dʒor no
raddoppia	**fuoco**	**all'alme**	**e**	**luce**	**al**	**giorno,**
doubles	fire	in the souls	and	light	to the	day

she doubles the fire in the souls and the light in the day

> *var.: foco ['fɔ ko] = (mod.) fuoco*
> *var.: a l'alme = (mod.) all'alme*

e	fa	'sɛr vi	da 'mor	la	'tɛrː ra	el	'tʃɛ lo
e	**fa**	**servi**	**d'Amor**	**la**	**terra**	**e'l**	**cielo.**
and	makes	servants	of Love	the	earth	and the	heaven

and makes the earth and the heaven servants of Love.

> *vars.: e cielo [e 'tʃɛ lo],*
> *e il cielo [e il 'tʃɛ lo]*
> *= e'l cielo*

𝒢ℒ: **Amor, Delo**

☙

[12, 13, 24, 34, 37] Alternately titled **Nel pur ardor**.
from: *Euridice (1600)*
character: *Tirsi*

Ottavio Rinuccini

nel 'pu ɾo ar 'dor
Nel puro ardor
With pure burning heat

nel	'pu ɾo	ar 'dor	'delː la	pju	'bɛlː la	'stelː la	'a u re a	fa 'tʃɛlː la	di	bɛl
Nel	**puro**	**ardor**	**della**	**più**	**bella**	**stella,**	**aurea**	**facella**	**di**	**bel**
in the	pure	burning heat	of the	most	beautiful	star	golden	torch	of	beautiful

> *var.: pur (or pur') ardor [pu ɾar 'dor] = puro ardor*

'fɔ ko   at: 'tʃɛn di   e   kwi   diʃ: 'ʃen di   su   la u 'ra te   'pju me
foco   accendi,   e   qui   discendi   su   l'aurate   piume,
fire   ignite   and   here   descend   on   the gold-colored   feathers

var.: foc' accendi
= foco accendi

With pure burning heat from the most beautiful star *[the sun]*, ignite a golden torch of beautiful fire
and descend, on golden wing,

dʒo 'kon do   'nu me   e   di   tʃe 'lɛ ste   'fjam: me   'la ni me   in 'fjam: ma
giocondo   nume, e   di   celeste   fiamme   l'anime   infiamma.
joyful   deity   and   with   celestial   flames   the souls   inflame

in [12]: l'anima
= the soul

joyful deity, and inflame souls with heavenly ardor.

'lje to   i me 'nɛ o   'dal ta   dol 'tʃet: tsa   un   'nem bo   tra 'bok: ka   in   'grɛm bo
Lieto   Imeneo,   d'alta   dolcezza   un   nembo   trabocca   in   grembo
happy   Hymen   of great   sweetness   a   shower   overflow   in   lap

Happy Hymen, pour a flood of great sweetness into the laps

'a i   for tu 'na ti   a 'man ti   e   tra   'bɛ i   'kan ti   di   so 'a vi   a 'mo ɾi
ai   fortunati   amanti, e   tra   bei   canti   di   soavi   amori,
to the   lucky   lovers   and   among   beautiful   songs   of   gentle   loves

"a" (instead of "ai"), in a few prints, should be "a'"

of lucky lovers; and, with beautiful songs of gentle love,

'zveʎ: ʎa   'ne i   'kɔ ɾi   'u na   'dol tʃe   'a u ɾa   ɯ   'ɾɪ zo   di   pa ɾa 'di zo
sveglia   nei   cori   una   dolce   aura,   un   riso   di   paradiso.
awaken   in the   hearts   a   sweet   breath   a   smile   of   paradise

stir in their hearts a sweet breath, a smile from paradise.

GL: **Imeneo**

☙

[14, 36]   *Ottavio Rinuccini*

o 'mjɛ i   'dʒor ni   fu 'ga tʃi
O miei giorni fugaci
O my fleeting days

o   'mjɛ i   'dʒor ni   fu 'ga tʃi   o   'brɛ ve   'vi ta   o i 'me   dʒa   'sɛ i   spa 'ɾi ta
O   miei   giorni   fugaci, o   breve   vita,   oimè,   già   sei   sparita.
o   my   days   fleeting   o   brief   life   alas   already   you are   vanished

O my fleeting days, o brief life, alas, you have already vanished.

dʒa   'sɛn to   o   sen 'tir   'par mi   la   ri go 'ro za   'trom ba   da 'van ti a 'te
Già   sento, o   sentir   parmi,   la   rigorosa   tromba   davanti a te
already   I hear   or   to hear   seems to me   the   stern   trumpet   before you

'dʒu sto   siɲ: 'ɲor   kja 'mar mi
giusto   Signor,   chiamarmi.
just   Lord   to call me

Already I hear, or seem to hear, the stern trumpet summoning me to you, righteous Lord.

dʒa   nel   kɔr   mi   rim 'bom ba   il   for mi 'da bil   'swɔ no
Già   nel   cor   mi   rimbomba   il   formidabil   suono,
already   in the   heart   to me   resounds   the   formidable   sound

Already the formidable sound resounds in my heart;

mi ze 'rɛ ɾe   di   me   siɲ: 'ɲor   siɲ: 'ɲor   per 'do no
miserere   di   me,   Signor,   Signor,   perdono!
have mercy   on   me   Lord   Lord   pardon

have mercy on me, Lord; Lord, grant pardon!

☙

[55]
                                                      tu 'dɔr mi
                                                      Tu dormi
                                                      You sleep

tu   'dɔr mi   el   'dol tʃe 'son: no   ti   lu 'ziŋ ga kon   'la li
Tu dormi,   e'l   dolce   sonno   ti   lusinga   con   l'ali.
you   sleep   and the sweet   sleep   you   lures   with   the wings
You sleep, and sweet slumber lures you with its wings.

'a u ɾe   vo 'lan ti   ne   mɔ 'vom bra   dʒam: 'ma i   'ta tʃi   li   'pjan ti
Aure   volanti   né   mov'ombra   giammai,   taci   li   pianti.
breezes   blowing   nor   move shadow   ever   silence   the   tears
No breezes waft or shadows waver; silence your tears.

'i o   ke   non   ɔ   ri 'pɔ zo   se   non   'kwan do   da   'lu mi   'vɛr so   tor: 'rɛn ti   e   'fju mi
Io   che   non   ho   riposo   se   non   quando   da'   lumi   verso   torrenti   e   fiumi,
I   who   not   have rest   if   not   when   from eyes   I shed   torrents   and rivers
I, who do not rest unless I am shedding torrents and rivers [of tears] from my eyes,

     'ɛ skal   not: 'tur no   sol   a   me   dʒo 'jo zo
     esc' al   notturno   sol, a   me   gioioso.
     I go out to the nocturnal   sun   to   me   joyful
     go out in the moonlight, [which is] joyful to me.

tu   lo   splen 'dor   deʎ: ʎar dʒen 'ta ti   'ra i   non   ri 'mi ɾi
Tu   lo   splendor   degl'argentati   rai   non   rimiri,
you   the   splendor   of the silvery   rays   not   you see
You do not see the splendor of the silvery rays,

     e   tu   'sta i   'sor dal   dwɔl   ke   mak: 'kɔ ɾa
     e   tu   stai   sord' al   duol'   che   m'accora;
     and you   you are deaf to the sorrow which me afflicts
     and you are deaf to the sorrow which afflicts me;

     'i o   'sɛn te   'ved: dʒo   oɲ: 'ɲor   'la u ɾa   e   la u 'rɔ ɾa
     io   sent' e   veggio   ogn'or   l'aura   e   l'aurora.
     I   feel and I see   always   the breeze and   the dawn
     I always feel and see the *[nocturnal]* breeze and the dawn.

*veggio =
(mod.) vedo*

tu   'dɔr mi   e   non   a 'skol ti   me   ke   'prɛ go   e   so 'spi ɾo
Tu   dormi,   e   non   ascolti   me   che   prego   e   sospiro,
you   you sleep and   not   you listen to me   that   I beg   and   I sigh
You sleep and do not hear my entreaties and sighs;

     e   'pjaŋ go   e   'bra mo   e   nel: 'lal to   si 'lɛn tsjo   'o ɾa   ti   'kja mo
     e   piango,   e   bramo   e   nell'alto   silenzio   ora   ti   chiamo.
     and I weep   and   I yearn   and   in the high   silence   now   to you I call
     and I weep and yearn and, in the deep silence now I call to you.

bɛn   a   pro 'fon do 'bli o   'fil: li   se 'pol ti   'two i   'sɛn si   vi 'ta li
Ben   ha   profond' oblio,   Filli,   sepolt' i   tuoi   sensi   vitali,
well   has   profound oblivion Filli   buried the your   senses   vital
Profound oblivion has indeed, Filli, buried your sensitivities;

e	'prɔ vin	'va no	de 'star	in	te	pje 'tad:	'dal ma	ke	'mɔ ɾe
e	prov' in	vano	destar	in	te	pietad',	d'alma	che	more.
and	I try in	vain	to awaken	in	you	pity	of soul	that	dies

and I try in vain to awaken in you pity for a dying soul.

pietade = (mod.) pietà

non	ɛ	'fɛ bo	lon 'ta no	vjɛn	'lal ba	ru dʒa 'do za
Non	è	Febo	lontano;	vien	l'alba	rugiadosa.
not	is	Phoebus	far away	comes	the dawn	rosy

Phoebus is not far away; the rosy dawn approaches.

ma ke	'dɔr me	ri 'pɔ za	non	'pjan dʒin 'dar no	i	'swo i	tor 'men ti	il	'kɔ ɾe
Ma che,	dorm' e	riposa,	non	piang' indarno	i	suoi	tormenti	il	core;
but no	sleep and	rest	not	weeps in vain	the	its	torments	the	heart

Go ahead, sleep and rest; my heart does not lament its torments in vain;

indarno (lit.) = invano

Ma che = (mod.) macché

e	se	non	'sɛn ti	tu	mi sɛn ta 'mo ɾe
e	se	non	senti	tu,	mi sent' Amore.
and	if	not	you hear	you	me hears Love

if you do not hear [me], Love hears me.

tu	'dɔr mi	e 'di o	pur	'pjaŋ go	o	'fil: li	o	del	'mi o	kɔr	'dol tʃe	tor 'men to
Tu	dormi,	ed io	pur	piango,	o	Filli,	o	del	mio	cor	dolce	tormento,
you	sleep	and I	yet	I weep	o	Filli	o	of the	my	heart	sweet	torment

You sleep, and still I weep, o Filli, o sweet torment of my heart;

e	kol	'mi o	'pjan to	'i o	'mi ɾil	tʃe lin 'tɛn to
e	co'l	mio	pianto	io	mir' il	ciel' intento.
and	with the	my	weeping	I	gaze at the	sky intently

and in my weeping I gaze intently at the sky.

'en tro	'pju me	do 'do ɾi	tu	ri 'pɔ zil	bɛl	'fjaŋ ko
Entro	piume	d'odori	tu	ripos' il	bel	fianco;
within	feathers	of fragrances	you	reposes the	beautiful	side

In a scented feather-bed reposes your beautiful body;

'i o	fra	'mil: le	do 'lo ɾi	'sɛn to	'sɛn tsa	pje 'ta	ve 'nir mi 'maŋ ko
io,	fra	mille	dolori	sento	senza	pietà	venirmi manco.
I	among	thousand	pains	I feel	without	pity	to die

I, among a thousand pains, am dying pitilessly.

venir[mi] manco = venir[mi] meno

o	'son: no	o	tu	ke	'pɔr ti	'pa tʃe	'a i	'kɔ ɾi
O	sonno,	o	tu	che	porti	pace	ai	cori
o	sleep	o	you	who	you bring	peace	to the	hearts

O sleep, o you who bring peace to hearts

e	le	'men ti	'ɛ gri	kon 'fɔr ti	ti	non	'kja mo	dʒam: mai
e	le	menti	egri	conforti,	ti	non	chiamo	giammai,
and	the	minds	infirm	you comfort	you	not	I call	ever

and comfort infirm minds, I do not invoke you now;

egri (lit.) = infermi

giammai: old, rare meaning = ormai (now)

ma	sol	de 'zi o	ke	'ne i	so 'spi ɾak: 'kwe til	mo 'rir	'mi o
ma	sol	desio	che	nei	sospir' acquet' il	morir	mio.
but	only	I desire	that	in the	sighs you may assuage the	dying	mine

rather, I desire only that you assuage my death with [your] sighs.

desio: from "desiare" (lit.) = "desiderare"

GL: **Amore, Febo, Filli**

&

[40]

un di so 'let: to
Un dì soletto
One day, all alone

un	di	so 'let: to	'vi dil	di 'lɛt: to	on 'dɔ		'tan to	mar 'ti ɾe
Un	**dì**	**soletto**	**vid'il**	**diletto,**	**ond' ho**		**tanto**	**martire,**
one	day	all alone	I saw the	beloved one	from whom I have		so much	suffering

One day I saw my beloved, for whom I suffer so much, all alone;

e	so spi 'ran do	'tut: to	tre 'man do	ko 'zi	le	'pre zi a	'di ɾe
e	**sospirando,**	**tutto**	**tremando,**	**così**	**le**	**presi a**	**dire.**
and	sighing	all	trembling	thus	to her	I began	to speak

and, sighing and all atremble, I began to speak to her like this:

o	tu	ke	'mar di	kon	'dol tʃi	'zgwar di	'ko me	si	'bɛl: la	ap: 'pa ɾi
O,	**tu**	**che**	**m'ardi**	**con**	**dolci**	**sguardi,**	**come**	**sì**	**bella**	**appari!**
o	you	who	me you burn	with	sweet	glances	how	so	beautiful	you appear

O you who set me on fire with sweet glances, how beautiful you look!

'el: la	ve 'lo tʃe	'ʃɔl se	la	'vo tʃe	fra	'va gi	'ri zi	e	'ka ɾi
Ella	**veloce**	**sciolse**	**la**	**voce**	**fra**	**vaghi**	**risi**	**e**	**cari.**
she	quick	loosed	the	voice	among	charming	laughs	and	dear

She quickly let loose her voice *[answered]* in charming and dear laughter.

'el: la	per 'dʒɔ ko	sor: 'ri ze	un	'pɔ ko	'in di	mi	si na 'sko ze
Ella	**per gioco**	**sorrise**	**un**	**poco**	**indi**	**mi**	**si nascose.**
she	for fun	smiled	a	little	then	from me	herself hid

She smiled in fun a little, and then hid herself from me.

e 'di o	do 'lɛn te	pre 'ga va	ar 'dɛn te	ma	pju	non	mi	ri 'spo ze
Ed io	**dolente**	**pregava**	**ardente,**	**ma**	**più**	**non**	**mi**	**rispose.**
and I	aching	I begged	ardently	but	more	not	to me	responded

And I, aching, begged ardently; but she answered me no more.

> *the "a" ending of "pregava" is an antiquated variant of "o" [mod. = pregavo]*

 Perti, Giacomo Antonio *(1661-1756)*

Composer, organist, and teacher born in Crevalcore, near Bologna, he began his music studies at an early age in Bologna with his uncle Lorenzo Perti. At eighteen he contributed the third act to the opera *Atide* performed in Bologna. In 1690 he succeeded his uncle as *maestro di cappella* at the Cathedral of S. Pietro, and in 1696 he became *maestro di cappella* at S. Petronio. Except for some travels to Florence, Rome, and Naples, he spent the rest of his long life in Bologna in that post. He received patronage from Ferdinando III de' Medici and from Emperor Charles VI, who made him a royal councilor in 1740.

Famous in his day as a composer of operas (more than twenty-five), oratorios, psalms, motets, and masses, he also wrote about one hundred and fifty secular cantatas and a collection of *Cantate morali e spirituali,* published in 1688, for one and two voices with violin.

[22, 25, 35]

'beʎ: ʎi 'ɔk: ki
Begli occhi
Beautiful eyes

> *The following Recitative is in [35] but not in [22] or [25]:*

a   'vo i   ke   lat: tʃen 'de ste   rak: ko 'man do   il   'mi o   'fwɔ ko   'ɔk: ki   a do 'ra ti
A   **voi**   **che**   **l'accendeste**   **raccomando**   **il**   **mio**   **fuoco,**   **occhi**   **adorati;**
to   you   who   it kindled   I commend   the   the   my   fire   eyes   adored
To you who kindled it I commend my fire, adored eyes;

in   'vo i   'ko i   'rad: dʒi   a 'ma ti   'dʒɛ mi no   sol   ri 'splen de
in   **voi**   **coi**   **raggi**   **amati**   **gemino**   **sol**   **risplende**
in   you   with the   rays   beloved   *(lit.)* two-fold   sun   shines
in your beloved rays shines a double sun

ke   'lom bra   del   'mi o   dwɔl   di 'le gwa   e   'strud: dʒe
che   **l'ombra**   **del**   **mio**   **duol**   **dilegua**   **e**   **strugge.**
which   the shadow   of the   my   sorrow   dispels   and   destroys
which dispels and destroys the shadow of my sorrow.

> *Following is the Aria, which is the beginning in [22] and [25]:*

'beʎ: ʎi   'ɔk: ki   'i o   non   mi 'pɛn to   da 'ver vi   of: 'fɛr to   il   sen
Begli   **occhi,**   **io**   **non**   **mi pento**   **d'avervi**   **offerto**   **il**   **sen.**
beautiful   eyes   I   not   I regret   of to have you   offered   the   breast; *(fig.)* heart
Beautiful eyes, I do not regret having offered you my heart.

'an tsi   se   le   'mi e   'pe ne   'fos: se ro   'sɛn tsa   'spɛ ne
Anzi   **se**   **le**   **mie**   **pene**   **fossero**   **senza**   **spene,**
on the contrary   if   the   my   sufferings   were   without   hope
On the contrary, if my sufferings were without hope

> *spene (poet.)*
> = *speme (lit.)*
> = *speranza*

'la ni ma   sul   tʃi 'men to   vor: 're i   por 'ta ɾe   al 'men
l'anima   **sul**   **cimento**   **vorrei**   **portare**   **almen.**
the soul   to the   test   I should want   to take   at least
I would at least want to put my soul to the test.

❦

[35, 64]

'dol tʃe   'sker tsa
Dolce scherza
Sweetly plays

'dol tʃe   'sker tsa   e   'dol tʃe   'ri de   'va go   'lab: bro   e   'spi ɾa   a 'mor
Dolce   **scherza**   **e**   **dolce**   **ride**   **vago**   **labbro**   **e**   **spira**   **amor;**
sweet   plays   and   sweet   smiles   charming   lip   and   breathes   love
A charming mouth plays sweetly, smiles sweetly, and breathes love;

ma   tal: 'let: ta   e   'pɔ i   tut: 'tʃi de   ko 'zi   af: 'flid: dʒe   'kwe sto   kɔr
ma   **t'alletta**   **e**   **poi**   **t'uccide**   **così**   **affligge**   **questo**   **cor.**
but   you it entices   and   then   you kills   thus   it afflicts   this   heart
but it entices you and then kills you – that is how it afflicts this heart.

❦

[1, 3, 46]

'i o   son   tsi 'tɛl: la
Io son zitella
I am an old maid

'i o   son   tsi 'tɛl: la   ma   'so no   'skal tra
Io   son   zitella,   ma   sono   scaltra,
I   am   spinster   but   I am   clever
I am an old maid, but I am clever –

   e   'tan to   'skal tra   ke   la   sɔ   'tut: ta
   e   tanto   scaltra,   che   la   so   tutta.
   and   so much   clever   that   it   I know   all
   and so clever that I know it all.

'kwan do   un   a 'man te   kon   te   fa 'vɛl: la
Quando   un   amante   con   te   favella,
when   a   lover   with   you   talks
When a lover talks to you

   tu   'sɛ i   la   'ka ɾa   tu   'sɛ i   la   'bɛl: la
   tu   sei   la   cara,   tu   sei   la   bella.
   you   you are   the   dear one   you   you are   the   beautiful one
   you are the dear one, the beautiful one.

se   da   te   'par te   e   va   da   u 'nal tra   la   'va ga   ɛ   'kwel: la
Se   da   te   parte   e   va   da   un'altra,   la   vaga   è   quella,
If   from   you   leaves   and   goes   to   another one   the   pretty   is   that one
If he leaves you and goes to another, that one is the pretty one,

> *Printed "e quella" must be a mis-copying for "è quella," in the context.*

   tu   'sɛ i   la   'brut: ta
   tu   sei   la   brutta!
   you   you are   the   ugly one
   [and] you are the ugly one!

એ

[12, 40]

'ma i   non   in 'te zi
Mai non intesi
I never perceived

'ma i   non   in 'te zi   per   'al tro   'zgwar do   kwel   'dol tʃe   'stra le   ke   'lal me   im 'pja ga
Mai   non   intesi   per   altro   sguardo   quel   dolce   strale   che   l'alme   impiaga.
ever   not   I perceived   through   other   glance   that   sweet   arrow   which   the souls   wounds
I never felt, through [any] other glance, that sweet arrow which wounds souls.

> *impiagare (lit.) = ferire*

'kwe sto   'ki o   'sɛn to   ɛ   il   'pri mo   'dar do   e   sa 'ɾa   'kwe sta   'lul ti ma   'pja ga
Questo   ch'io   sento   è   il   primo   dardo   e   sarà   questa   l'ultima   piaga.
this one   which I   I feel   is   the   first   dart   and   will be   this   the last   wound
This dart which I feel is the first, and this wound will be the last.

એ

[40]

mi   fa   'vet: tsi
Mi fa vezzi
It caresses me

mi	fa	'vet: tsi	e	vwɔl	'ki o	'ri da	la	ko 'stan tsa	kon	a 'mor
Mi	**fa**	**vezzi**	**e**	**vuol**	**ch'io**	**rida**	**la**	**costanza***	**con**	**amor.**
to me	makes	caresses	and	wants	that I	laugh	the	constancy	with	love

Constancy caresses me and makes me laugh with love.

'i o	non	sɔ	se	'sker tsi	o	'fiŋ ga
Io	**non**	**so,**	**se**	**scherzi**	**o**	**finga,**
I	not	I know	if	it be joking	or	it be pretending

I know not if it is joking or pretending,

mi	lu 'ziŋ ga	e	mi	'bril: la	in	'mɛd: dzo	al	kɔr
mi	**lusinga**	**e**	**mi**	**brilla**	**in**	**mezzo**	**al**	**cor.**
me	it charms	and	to me	it shines	in	middle	to the	heart

[but] it charms me and shines in the depths of my heart.

> *It is possible that "la costanza," though "costanza" was not capitalized in the print, intended to refer to the writer's lover named Costanza: Costanza cuddles...I know not if she is joking...[but] she charms me...of my heart. Or, it could be a "double meaning"(pun).*

[12, 40]

'ʃɔʎ: ʎe	o	'ma i	le	'ne vi
Scioglie	**omai**	**le**	**nevi**

Now melts the snow

'ʃɔʎ: ʎe	o 'ma i	le	'ne vi	e	il	'dʒɛ lo	lo	splen 'dor	ke	il	'mon do	av: 'vi va
Scioglie	**omai**	**le**	**nevi**	**e**	**il**	**gelo**	**lo**	**splendor,**	**che**	**il**	**mondo**	**avviva,**
melts	now	the	snows	and	the	ice	the	splendor	that	the	world	brightens

The splendor that brightens the world now melts the snow and ice;

> omai (poet.) = ormai

e	sa 'dor na	al par del	'tʃe lo	il	ter: 'ren	ke	'pri a	laŋ 'gwi va
e	**s'adorna**	**al par del**	**cielo**	**il**	**terren,**	**che**	**pria**	**languiva.**
and	itself adorns	at equal of	heaven	the	earth	which	before	was languishing

> pria (poet.) = prima

and the earth, which was languishing before, adorns itself on an equal with heaven.

[15, 40]

spe 'rar	'i o	non	do 'vrɛ i
Sperar	**io**	**non**	**dovrei**

I should not hope

spe 'rar	'i o	non	do 'vrɛ i	e	pur	'i o	vɔ	spe 'ran do
Sperar	**io**	**non**	**dovrei,**	**e**	**pur**	**io**	**vo**	**sperando,**
to hope	I	not	I ought	and	yet	I	go	hoping

I should not hope, and yet I am hoping;

'i o	non	do 'vrɛ i	spe 'rar	e	pur	spe 'ran do	vɔ
io	**non**	**dovrei**	**sperar**	**e**	**pur**	**sperando**	**vo.**
I	not	I ought	to hope	and	yet	hoping	I go

I should not hope, and yet I keep hoping.

lu 'ziŋ ga	i	'pjan ti	'mjɛ i	la	'vi sta	del	'mi o	'bɛ ne
Lusinga	**i**	**pianti**	**miei**	**la**	**vista**	**del**	**mio**	**bene,**
gratifies	the	tears	mine	the	sight	of	my	dear one

The sight of my beloved gratifies my tears,

ma	'pa tʃe	in	'tan te	'pe ne	per 'kwan do	tro ve 'rɔ
ma	**pace**	**in**	**tante**	**pene**	**per quando**	**troverò?**
but	peace	in	so many	sufferings	when	I shall find

but when shall I find peace from so much suffering?

�֍ *Pesenti, Martino (c.1600-c.1648)*

Blind from birth, he was born and he died in Venice, where he apparently spent his whole life. Unable to participate in the productions of Venetian churches and theatres due to his blindness, he was nevertheless active as harpsichordist and composer of instrumental works, particularly of dance suites for harpsichord with other instruments. He also composed several volumes of madrigals, canzonettas, and arias.
Pesenti had a private following as well as the patronage of Nicolò de Rossi and Habsburg Archduke Leopold among the nobility.

---

[40]

co 'zi 'ni ljo kan 'tɔ
Così Nilio cantò
Thus sang Nilius

ko 'zi	'ni ljo	kan 'tɔ	fwɔr	'doɲː ɲi	afː 'fanː no	dun	korː 'rɛn te	ruʃː 'ʃɛl
Così	**Nilio**	**cantò,**	**fuor**	**d'ogni**	**affanno,**	**d'un**	**corrente**	**ruscel**
thus	Nilius	sang	far away	from every	trouble	of a	running	brook

'luŋ go	la	'spon da	'nelː la	sta 'dʒon	kɛ	dʒo ven 'tu	delː 'lan no
lungo	**la**	**sponda,**	**nella**	**stagion**	**ch'è**	**gioventù**	**dell'anno,**
along	the	bank	in the	season	which is	youth	of the year

Thus sang Nilius, far from every trouble, along the bank of a running brook in the springtime,

al	mor mo 'rar	delː 'lon da	kaŋ 'kelː la	dir	pa 're a	'ʃɔl ta	dal	'nɔ do
al	**mormorar**	**dell'onda,**	**ch'anch'ella**	**dir**	**parea**	**sciolta**	**dal**	**nodo**
at the	murmuring	of the wave	which also it	to say	seemed	loosed	from the	knot

parea = pareva

dun	'du ro	'gjatː tʃo	e	'gra ve
d'un	**duro**	**ghiaccio**	**e**	**grave:**
of a	hard	ice	and	heavy

in tune with the murmuring of the water, which also seemed to say [that it had been] freed from the knot of a hard and heavy ice:

o	li ber 'ta	li ber 'ta	so 'a ve	aŋ 'ki o	ti	'gɔ do
O	**libertà,**	**libertà**	**soave,**	**anch'io**	**ti**	**godo!**
o	liberty	liberty	sweet	also I	you	I enjoy

O freedom, sweet freedom, I too enjoy you!

ॐ

[36]

e tu 'kre di
E tu credi
And you believe

e	tu	'kre di	e	tu	'pɛn si	o	su 'pɛr bo	'mi o	'kɔ ɾe
E	**tu**	**credi**	**e**	**tu**	**pensi**	**o**	**superbo**	**mio**	**core**
and	you	believe	and	you	think	o	proud	my	heart

And you believe and presume, o proud heart of mine,

di   kot: 'tsar   kon   a 'mo ɾe
di   cozzar   con   Amore?
of   to clash   with   Love
that you will clash with Love

e   da   'kwe i   'nɔ di   im: 'men si   on 'deʎ: ʎi   ti   le 'gɔ   'dʒir te ne   'ʃɔl to
e   da   quei   nodi   immensi   ond'egli   ti   legò   girtene   sciolto?
and   from   those   ties   immeasurable from which he you   he bound to go of them untied
and go on unbridled from those strongest of ties with which he bound you?

o   'fɔl: le   o   'stol to
O   folle,   o   stolto!
o   madman   o   fool
O mad one! O fool!

pju   se 'vɛ ɾo   lo   'zdeɲ: ɲo   'prɔ va   del   'su o   gran   'nu me
Più   severo   lo   sdegno   prova   del   suo   gran   nume
more   severe   the   anger   experiencces of the his   great   god

ki   kon 'tɛn der   pre 'zu me
chi   contender   presume:
he who   to contest   presumes
He who presumes to contest his great god will experience more serious anger from him:

per   fud: 'dʒir   del   'su o   'reɲ: ɲo   un   'pas: so   non   fa 'ɾa i
per   fuggir   del   suo   regno,   un   passo   non   farai
for   to flee   from the his   kingdom   one   step   not   you will make
in fleeing from his kingdom you will not take one step

'ke i   ta 'vra   'kɔl to
ch'ei   t'avrà   colto.
that he   you he will have caught
before he will have caught you.

o   'fɔl: le   o   'stol to
O   folle,   o   stolto!
o   madman   o   fool
O mad one! O fool!

si   kon 'tra ste   'pu ɾe   kon   kwel   gar 'dzon
Sì,   contraste   pure   con   quel   garzon
yes   should you clash [then]   with   that   boy
Yes, if you clash with that boy *[Cupid]*,

ke   'sa i   ke   non   per 'do na   'ma i
che   sai   che   non   perdona   mai:
that   you know   that   not   he pardons   never
you will know that he never forgives:

'kre di   tu   ke   per 'tʃɔ   'si an   men   'du ɾe   le   ka 'te ne
credi   tu   che   perciò   sian   men   dure   le   catene
believe   you   that   therefore may be   less   harsh   the   chains

in   'ku i   ta   in 'vɔl to
in   cui   t'ha   involto?
in   which   you he has   wrapped
Do you think that the chains in which he has entangled you will then become less harsh?

o 'fɔl: le   o 'stol to
O folle,   o stolto!
o madman   o fool
O mad one! O fool!

a 'do ɾa   pur   u 'mi le   la   'tu a   'bɛl: la   ne 'mi ka   'va na   ɛ   'oɲ: 'ɲal tra   fa 'ti ka
Adora   pur   umile   la   tua   bella   nemica,   vana   è   ogn'altra   fatica:
adore   indeed   humble   the   your   beautiful   enemy   vain   is   any other   effort
Indeed, humbly adore your beautiful enemy; any other effort is in vain.

tu   se 'gwir   'al tro   'sti le   tu   'luŋ go   star   po 'tra i
tu   seguir   altro   stile?   Tu   lungo   star   potrai
you   to follow   other   manner   you   distant   to stay   you will be able
Could you follow another path? Will you be able to stay far away

da   kwel   bɛl   'vol to
da   quel   bel   volto?
from   that   beautiful   face
from that beautiful face?

o 'fɔl: le   o 'stol to
O folle,   o stolto!
o madman   o fool
O mad one! O fool!

GL: **Amore**

&

[40]

o bjon 'det: ta laʃ: ʃi 'vet: ta
O biondetta lascivetta
O little, lascivious fair-haired one

o   bjon 'det: ta   laʃ: ʃi 'vet: ta   pa sto 'rel: la   lil: la 'la   pa sto 'rel: la   'tut: ta   'bɛl: la
O   biondetta   lascivetta   pastorella,   (lillala),   pastorella   tutta   bella!
o   little blond   lascivious   sheperdess   tra la la   sheperdess   all   beautiful
O little, lascivious, fair-haired sheperdess – tra la la – utterly beautiful shepherdess!

se   vet: 'tso za   se   fe 'sto za   'i o   ti   'mi ɾo   'a i   so 'spi ɾo
Se   vezzosa,   se   festosa   io   ti   miro,   ahi   sospiro!
if   charming   if   merry   I   you   I see   alas   I sigh
When I see you charming and merry, alas, I sigh!

o   ru 'bɛl: la   'nin fa   'bɛl: la   lil: la 'la   da 'mor   'fre dʒo   da 'mor   'prɛ dʒo
O   rubella   ninfa   bella,   (lillala),   d'amor   fregio,   d'amor   pregio!
o   stubborn   nymph   beautiful   (tra la la)   of love   adornment   of love   prize
O stubborn, beautiful nymph – tra la la – adornment of love, preciousness of love!

*rubella =
(mod.)
ribella*

se   ri 'dɛn te   pur   so 'vɛn te   'i o   ti   'mi ɾo   'a i   so 'spi ɾo
Se   ridente   pur   sovente   io   ti   miro,   ahi   sospiro!
if   smiling   indeed   often   I   you   I see   alas   I sigh
When, indeed often, I see you smiling, alas, I sigh!

o	lil: ˈlet: ta	par go ˈlet: ta	lil: la ˈla	ˈlil: la	a ˈma ta	ˈlil: la	iŋ ˈgra ta
O	**Lilletta**	**pargoletta,**	**(lillala),**	**Lilla**	**amata,**	**Lilla**	**ingrata!**
o	Lilletta	dear child	(tra la la)	Lilla	beloved	Lilla	ungrateful

O dear Lilletta, child – tra la la – beloved Lilla, ungrateful Lilla!

ˈmen tre	iŋ	ˈkan ti	ˈtra ʎi	a ˈman ti	ˈi o	ti	ˈmi ɾo	ˈa i	so ˈspi ɾo
Mentre	**in**	**canti**	**tragli**	**amanti**	**io**	**ti**	**miro,**	**ahi**	**sospiro!**
while	in	songs	among the	lovers	I	you	I see	alas	I sigh

When I see you singing among your lovers, alas, I sigh!

Provenzale, Francesco (c.1626-1704)

Born and died in Naples, he is recognized as one of the founders of the Neapolitan school of opera composers. He may have written at least a half dozen operas; two of them (one being *Difendere l'offensore*, usually known as *La Stellidaura vendicata)*, are extant.

Apparently Provenzale was not engaged in opera after 1678, either because of the flow of other opera composers to Naples, or because he was busy with teaching at the conservatory S. Maria di Loreto and, later, at the conservatory S. Maria della Pietà dei Turchini, where old age forced his retirement in 1701.

He was *maestro di cappella* to the treasury of S. Gennaro in Naples from 1686-99. He was made *maestro onorario* to the viceregal court in Naples in 1680; but when the post of *maestro* was vacated in 1684 and given to the twenty-three-year-old Alessandro Scarlatti, Provenzale resigned in protest. He returned to court service in 1688 as *maestro di cappella di camera* and was reinstated *maestro onorario* in 1690.

[1, 2, 21, 25, 47]
from: *La Stellidaura vendicata (1674)*
character: *Armidoro* *Andrea Perrucci*

dɛ ren ˈde te mi
Deh, rendetemi
Please return to me

dɛ	ren ˈde te mi	ˈom bre	ˈka ɾe	il	ˈmi o	bɛn	ke	mi	ra ˈpi ste
Deh	**rendetemi,**	**ombre**	**care,**	**il**	**mio**	**ben,**	**che**	**mi**	**rapiste!**
pray	return to me	shadows	dear	the	my	dear one	who	from me	you stole

Please return to me, dear shadows, my dear one whom you stole from me!

o	bel: ˈlet: tse	ˈu ni ke	e	ˈra ɾe	ˈa i	da	me	ˈko me	spa ˈɾi ste
O	**bellezze**	**uniche**	**e**	**rare,**	**ahi,**	**da**	**me**	**come**	**spariste!**
o	beauties	unique	and	rare	alas	from	me	how	you vanished

O beauties unique and rare, alas, how you vanished from me!

ri spon ˈde te mi	ˈlar ve	kor ˈte zi	ki	le ˈstin ta	ˈmi a	mi	ru ˈbɔ
Rispondetemi,	**larve**	**cortesi,**	**chi**	**l'estinta**	**mia**	**mi**	**rubò?**
respond to me	spirits	kindly	who	the deceased one	mine	from me	robbed

Answer me, kindly spirits: who robbed me of my deceased one?

dɛ	kwal	ˈnu me	ke	ˈfor se	of: ˈfe zi	ˈda i	ˈmjɛ i	ˈlu mi	lin vo ˈlɔ
Deh!	**qual**	**nume,**	**che**	**forse**	**offesi,**	**dai**	**miei**	**lumi**	**l'involò?**
pray	what	deity	whom	perhaps	I offended	from the	my	eyes	her stole

Pray tell: what deity, whom I perhaps offended, stole her from my eyes?

vars.: ch'io forse offesi [ˈki o ˈfor se of: ˈfe zi] = *che forse offesi; da miei lumi (correct is* da') [da ˈmjɛ i ˈlu mi] = *dai miei lumi*

Quagliati [Quagliato], Paolo (c.1555-1628)

Composer, organist, and cembalist, he was born in Chioggia into a noble family; around 1574 he settled in Rome for the rest of his life. Between 1605 and 1608 he was in the service of Cardinal Odoardo Farnese; during the last years of his life he was in the service of the Ludovisi family, and in 1621 he was appointed private chamberlain to the pope when Cardinal Alessandro Ludovisi became Pope Gregory XV. He was *maestro di capella* at S. Maria Maggiore from 1591 to at least 1621.

In addition to some instrumental and sacred works, and canzonettas and madrigals, Quagliati wrote *Il carro di fedeltà d'amore*, a short festive work which was performed in 1606 on a decorated cart in the streets of Rome during pre-Lenten celebrations, from which "Apra il suo verde seno" is a solo, and *La sfera armoniosa*, a collection of twenty-five solo and duet pieces with a concerted violin part.

[1, 2, 14, 24]   *Pietro Della Valle*

'a pra il 'su o 'ver de 'se no
Apra il suo verde seno
Let open its verdant breast

'a pra	il	'su o	'ver de	'se no	'oɲː ɲi	bɛl	'pra to	a 'mɛ no
Apra	**il**	**suo**	**verde**	**seno**	**ogni**	**bel**	**prato**	**ameno!**
let open	the	its	green	breast	every	beautiful	meadow	delightful

Let every beautiful, delightful meadow open its verdant breast!

'lje ta	e	vet ː'tso za	'ɛ ska	la	'rɔ za	'spi ɾi	'oɲː ɲi	'fjo ɾe	'a u ɾe	da 'mo ɾe
Lieta	**e**	**vezzosa**	**esca**	**la**	**rosa,**	**spiri**	**ogni**	**fiore**	**aure**	**d'amore,**
happy	and	charming	let come out	the	rose	let give forth	every	flower	breezes	of love

Let the rose bloom happily and charmingly, let every flower emanate breaths of love,

a	sa lu 'tar	atː 'tʃin to	'nɔ va	'nin fa	da 'mor	'nɔ vo	dʒa 'tʃin to
a	**salutar**	**accinto**	**nova**	**ninfa**	**d'amor,**	**novo**	**Giacinto!**
to	to greet	ready	new	nymph	of love	new	Hyacinth

novo =
(mod.) nuovo

ready to greet the new nymph of love, the new Hyacinth!

'korː ran	'daʎː ʎi	'al ti	'mon ti	'kja ɾi	kri 'stalː li	e	'fon ti
Corran	**dagli**	**alti**	**monti**	**chiari**	**cristalli**	**e**	**fonti!**
let run	from the	high	mountains	bright	*(poet.)* clear waters	and	springs

Let bright, clear waters and springs flow down from the high mountains!

'a u ɾe	o do 'ra te	or	vakː kor 'da te	kol	mor mo 'ra ɾe	delː 'lak: kwe	'kja ɾe
Aure	**odorate,**	**or**	**v'accordate**	**col**	**mormorare**	**dell'acque**	**chiare,**
breezes	perfumed	now	you attune yourselves	with the	murmuring	of the waters	clear

Perfumed breezes, you now attune yourselves to the murmuring of the clear waters,

or	ke	tra	'fjo ɾi	e	'fron de	'nɔ va	'nin fa	da 'mor	'ɛʃː ʃe	dalː 'lon de
or	**che**	**tra**	**fiori**	**e**	**fronde**	**nova**	**ninfa**	**d'amor**	**esce**	**dall'onde!**
now	that	among	flowers	and	foliage	new	nymph	of love	comes out	from the waves

now that, among flowers and foliage, a new nymph of love appears from the waves!

The following 3ʳᵈ verse is not in [14]:

'vo i	'va gi	e	'pin ti	a u 'dʒɛlː li	a mo ɾo 'zet: ti	e	'znɛlː li
Voi,	**vaghi**	**e**	**pinti**	**augelli,**	**amorosetti**	**e**	**snelli,**
you	lovely	and	decorated	birds	amorous	and	agile

pinti = dipinti
augelli (poet.)
= uccelli

You, lovely and pretty-colored, amorous and agile birds,

nel	'ver de	'pra to	kol	'kan to	a 'ma to	de 'sta te	il	'dʒor no	'va go	e da 'dor no
nel	**verde**	**prato**	**col**	**canto**	**amato**	**destate**	**il**	**giorno**	**vago**	**ed adorno**
in the	green	meadow	with the	singing	beloved	awake	the	day	lovely	adorned

awaken the beautifully adorned day with your beloved singing in the green meadow,

> *in* [25]: **col canto alato** [kol 'kan to a 'la to] = with your winged song

or	ke	dʒa	'spun ta 'fwɔ ɾa	'nɔ va	'nin fa	da 'mor	no 'vɛl: la	a u 'rɔ ɾa
or	**che**	**già**	**spunta fuora**	**nova**	**ninfa**	**d'amor,**	**novella**	**Aurora!**
now	that	already	comes forth	new	nymph	of love	new	Dawn

now that a new nymph of love is already appearing – the new Dawn!

> *fuora (poet.)* = *fuori*

GL: **Aurora, Giacinto**

Quinciani, Lucia (fl.1611)

Virtually nothing is known about Lucia Quinciani (see Candace Smith's notes in [62]). "Udite lagrimosi spirti," below, is her one known composition. It was published in 1611 in a collection of Marc' Antonio Negri, where she is listed as his disciple. As Negri was variously *vicemaestro di cappella* under Monteverdi at S. Marco in Venice and *maestro di cappella* at the cathedral in Verona, Quinciani was likely either Venetian or Veronese.

[62, 96]   *Giovanni Battista Guarini*

u 'di te la gri 'mo zi 'spir ti
Udite lagrimosi spirti
Hear, weeping spirits

u 'di te	la gri 'mo zi	'spir ti	da 'vɛr no
Udite	**lagrimosi**	**spirti**	**d'Averno,**
hear	weeping	spirits	of Avernus

Hear, weeping spirits of Avernus –

u 'di te	'nɔ va	'sɔr te	di	'pe na	e	di	tor 'men to
udite	**nova**	**sorte**	**di**	**pena**	**e**	**di**	**tormento.**
hear	new	fate	of	pain	and	of	torment

hear a new fate of pain and torment.

mi 'ra te	'kru do	af: 'fɛt: to	in	sem 'bjan te	pje 'to zo
Mirate	**crudo**	**affetto**	**in**	**sembiante**	**pietoso**
see	harsh	affection	in	semblance	compassionate

See harsh affection in the semblance of compassion:

la	'mi a	'dɔn: na	kru 'dɛl	pju	del: 'lin 'fɛr no
la	**mia**	**donna**	**crudel**	**più**	**dell'inferno.**
the	my	lady	cruel	more	than hell

my lady, more cruel than hell.

GL: **Averno**

Rasi, Francesco (1574-1621)

Born in Arezzo, he was forbidden ever to return there after being sentenced for the 1610 murder of his stepmother's servant.

Rasi was born into a prominent family; he performed as singer and chitarrone player at the Florentine court and in Rome under the patronage of Grand Duke Ferdinando I of Tuscany. In 1598 he accepted an offer from the Duke of Mantua and probably served the Gonzagas for the rest of his life.

He studied with Caccini in 1594 and was acclaimed as a superior singer; he sang in the first performances of Peri's *Euridice* and probably created the title role in Monteverdi's *Orfeo*.

As a composer, Rasi is important as one of the earliest composers of monodies. His collections *Vaghezze di musica (1608)* and *Madrigali (1610)* contain forty-two pieces, all but two of them for tenor; many of the ornaments are written out as sung by Rasi himself. His *Musica da camera et chiesa* includes five pieces for solo voice, and he also wrote an opera, the music for which has been lost.

He was a poet as well; he published several volumes of poetry and wrote many of his own song texts.

---

[55]   *Francesco Rasi*

'a i fud: dʒi 'ti vo bɛn
Ahi, fuggitivo ben
Ah, dear fugitive one

'a i	fud: dʒi	'ti vo	bɛn	'ko me	si	'tɔ sto	skon so 'la ti	laʃ: 'ʃa sti	i	'mjɛ i	de 'zi ɾi
Ahi,	**fuggitivo**	**ben**	**come**	**sì**	**tosto,**	**sconsolati**	**lasciasti**	**i**	**miei**	**desiri.**
ah	fugitive	dear one	how	so	soon	desolate	you left	the	my	desires

Ah, dear fugitive one, how soon you left my desires desolate.

dɛ	'ko me	'si a	ka	'mjɛ i	do 'lo ɾi	ak: 'kɔ sto
Deh,	**come**	**sia**	**ch'a**	**miei**	**dolori**	**accosto,**
ah	how	it may be	that to	my	sorrows	close

di	'vi ver	'ljɛ ta	pju	'las: sa	de 'zi ɾi
di	**viver**	**lieta**	**più,**	**lassa,**	**desiri?**
of	to live	happy	more	unhappy	you desire

Ah, how can it be that you still desire to live happily – unhappy me – close to my sorrows?

o	'val: li	o	'fju mi	o	'pɔd: dʒi	o	tu	ri 'po sta
O	**valli,**	**o**	**fiumi,**	**o**	**poggi,**	**o,**	**tu**	**riposta,**
o	valleys	o	rivers	o	hills	o	you	refuge

O valleys, o rivers, o hills – o you refuge,

'dol tʃe	'lɔ ko	pje 'to zo	a	'mjɛ i	so 'spi ɾi
dolce	**loco**	**pietoso**	**a'**	**miei**	**sospiri,**
sweet	place	merciful	to	my	sighs

sweet place merciful to my sighs.

se	ri bom 'ba sti	a	'mjɛ i	'gra vi	at: 'tʃɛn ti
se	**rimbombasti**	**a'**	**miei**	**gravi**	**accenti,**
if	you resounded	to	my	somber	words

If you once resounded to my somber words,

u 'di tor	'prɛ go	i	'du ɾi	'mjɛ i	la 'men ti
udit', or	**prego,**	**i**	**duri**	**miei**	**lamenti.**
hear now	I pray	the	bitter	my	laments

hear now, I pray, my bitter laments.

[79]   *Francesco Rasi*

ga la 'tɛ a 'men tre ta 'ma i
Galatea mentre t'amai
Galatea, while I loved you

ga la 'tɛ a	'men tre	ta 'ma i	'tut: to	mi 'dje di	a	la	'tu a	fe
Galatea	**mentre**	**t'amai**	**tutto**	**mi diedi**	**a**	**la**	**tua**	**fé,**
Galatea	while	you I loved	completely	me I devoted	to	the	your	faith

Galatea, while I loved you I devoted myself completely to your faith;

'men tre	'tu o	'no me	in	kɔr	ser 'ba i	'i o	non	ku 'ra i	'nul: la	di	me
mentre	**tuo**	**nome**	**in**	**cor**	**serbai**	**io**	**non**	**curai**	**nulla**	**di**	**me.**
while	your	name	in	heart	I preserved	I	not	I cared	nothing	of	me

while I kept your name in my heart I cared nothing about myself.

po i 'ki o	'vi di	i	'mje i	so 'spi ɾi	'dʒir se ne	al	'vɛn to	a	si	fe 'ri ta
Poich'io	**vidi**	**i**	**miei**	**sospiri**	**girsene**	**al**	**vento**	**a**	**sì**	**ferità**
since I	I saw	the	my	sighs	to go away	at the	wind	at	such	cruelty

ferità (lit.) = crudeltà

girsene (lit.) = andarsene

Since I have seen my sighs fly away with the wind, at such cruelty,

di	pju	non	trar	'pe ne	e	mar 'ti ɾi	'ɛb: bi	de 'zi ɾi	per	'tu e	bel 'ta
di	**più**	**non**	**trar**	**pene**	**e**	**martiri**	**ebbi**	**desiri**	**per**	**tue**	**beltà.**
of	more	not	to draw	pains	and	agonies	I had	desires	for	your	beauty

I have had no more desire to derive pain and agony from your beauty.

o	mer 'tʃe	di	fe 'de le	a 'mo ɾe	o	'lje te	'nɔt: ti	o	'lje ti	di
O	**mercé**	**di**	**fcdclc**	**amore**	**o**	**liete**	**notti**	**o**	**lieti**	**dì,**
o	reward	of	faithful	love	o	happy	nights	o	happy	days

O reward for faithful love, o happy nights, o happy days,

o	'dol tʃe	'spɛ me	del	'mi o	'kɔ ɾe	a	si	'ri o	do 'lo ɾe
o	**dolce**	**speme**	**del**	**mio**	**core, a**		**sì**	**rio**	**dolore**
o	sweet	hope	of the	my	heart	to	such	cruel	sorrow

speme (lit.) = speranza

rio (lit.) = reo

ki	mi	ra 'pi
chi	**mi**	**rapì?**
who	me	robbed

o sweet hope of my heart, who has taken me against my will to such a cruel sorrow?

a ma 'to ɾe	kal 'tjer	ten 'go di	de	le	'mi e	'pe ne	or	'ki o	'mɔ ɾo
Amatore,	**ch'altier**	**ten godi**	**de**	**lc**	**mie**	**pene**	**or**	**ch'io**	**moro**
lover	who proud	you enjoy	of	the	my	sufferings	now	that I	I die

O lover, you who proudly enjoy my suffering now that I am dying,

altier[o] = (mod.) alter[o]

Printed is "morò," which could correctly be "morrò" (I will die) or "moro" (mod.: muoio = I die); I've chosen the latter as most likely. "morò" could also have been penned simply to rhyme with "bramò" at the end of the next line.

e	'sɛ i	le 'ga to	in	'dol tʃi	'mɔ di	per	'ka ɾi	'no di	'kal tri	bra 'mɔ
e	**sei**	**legato**	**in**	**dolci**	**modi**	**per**	**cari**	**nodi**	**ch'altri**	**bramò:**
[and]	you are	joined	in	sweet	ways	through	dear	ties	that another	desired

you are joined in sweet ways with dear ties coveted by someone else:

'al tro	'kɔ ɾe	'kar se	kon 'ten to	e	da 'mor	'lje to	nel	'mon do	fu
Altro	**core**	**ch'arse**	**contento**	**e**	**d'amor**	**lieto**	**nel**	**mondo**	**fu**
other	heart	that burned	content	and	of love	happy	in the	world	was

la	'ku i	dol 'tʃet: tsa	in	un	mo 'men to	kon	'su o	tor 'men to	'tɔl ta	le	fu
la	**cui**	**dolcezza**	**in**	**un**	**momento**	**con**	**suo**	**tormento**	**tolta**	**le**	**fu.**
the	whose	sweetness	in	one	moment	with	its	torment	taken away	from it	was

Another heart that burned contentedly and happy with love was once in the world, whose sweetness was taken from it in one moment, to its torment.

in correct modern grammar, "le" would be "gli"

𝒢𝓛: **Galatea**

[55]   *Gabriello Chiabrera*

in ˈdar no ˈfɛ bo
Indarno Febo
In vain does Phoebus

in ˈdar no	ˈfɛ bo	il	ˈsu o	bɛl	ˈɔ ɾo	e ˈtɛr no
Indarno	**Febo**	**il**	**suo**	**bel**	**oro**	**eterno,**
in vain	Phoebus	the	his	beautiful	gold	eternal

indarno (lit.) =
invano

e	ˈtʃin tsja	mi	di ˈzve la	il	ˈpu ɾo	ar ˈdʒɛn to
e	**Cinzia**	**mi**	**disvela**	**il**	**puro**	**argento,**
and	Cynthia	to me	unveils	the	pure	silver

printed is "Cintia"
= (mod.) Cinzia

In vain does Phoebus reveal to me his beautiful, eternal gold, and Cynthia her pure silver

ˈki o	lon ˈta no	da	ˈvo i	ˈnul: la	non	ˈʃɛr no
ch'io	**lontano**	**da**	**voi**	**nulla**	**non**	**scerno.**
because I	far away	from	you	nothing	not	I discern

scerno (lit.) =
discerno

because, far away from you, I see nothing.

e	ˈmɔ vin ˈdar no	lu ziŋ ˈge vol	ˈvɛn to
E	**mov'indarno**	**lusinghevol**	**vento,**
and	moves in vain	pleasant	wind

mov' [move] = (mod.)
muov' [muove]

And in vain stirs the pleasant wind

e	tra	bɛl: ˈlɛr be	di	ruʃ: ˈʃɛl: lil	ˈswɔ no
e	**tra**	**bell'erbe**	**di**	**ruscell' il**	**suono;**
and	among	beautiful grasses	of	brooks the	sound

and [murmurs] the sound of brooks among the beautiful grasses

ˈki o	lon ˈta no	da	ˈvo i	ˈnul: la	non	ˈsɛn to
ch'io	**lontano**	**da**	**voi**	**nulla**	**non**	**sento.**
because I	far away	from	you	nothing	not	I hear

because, far away from you, I hear nothing.

o i ˈmɛ	del: ˈlɛs: ser	ˈmi o	ˈpɔ ko	ra ˈdʒo no
Oimè,	**dell'esser**	**mio**	**poco**	**ragiono:**
alas,	of the being	mine	little	I reason

Alas, I reflect little on my being

ˈki o	lon ˈta no	da	ˈvo i	ˈnul: la	non	ˈso no
ch'io	**lontano**	**da**	**voi**	**nulla**	**non**	**sono.**
because I	far away	from	you	nothing	not	I am

because, far away from you, I am nothing.

GL: **Cinzia, Febo**

❧

[79]   *Francesco Rasi*

ˈɔk: ki ˈsɛm pre se ˈre ni
Occhi sempre sereni
Eyes ever serene

ˈɔk: ki	ˈsɛm pre	se ˈre ni	per	ˈku i	ˈvi vo	kon ˈtɛn to	lu tʃi ˈdis: si me	ˈstel: le
Occhi	**sempre**	**sereni**	**per**	**cui**	**vivo**	**contento**	**lucidissime**	**stelle**
eyes	always	serene	for	whom	I live	content	most luminous	stars

Eyes ever serene, for whom I live happily, most luminous stars,

ke	non	mi 'ra te	'spɛn to	da	pju	pos: 'sɛn te	'lu me	il	'vɔ stro	'lu me
che	**non**	**mirate**	**spento**	**da**	**più**	**possente**	**lume**	**il**	**vostro**	**lume.**
who	not	you see	extinguished	from	more	powerful	light	the	your	light

you who do not see your light extinguished by a more powerful light *[the sun]...*

'sor ga	'lal ba	e	ri 'me ni	i	'ra i	di	'fɛ bo	at: 'tʃe zi
Sorga	**l'alba**	**e**	**rimeni**	**i**	**rai**	**di**	**Febo**	**accesi,**
may rise	the dawn	and	may bring back	the	rays	of	Phoebus	on fire

May the dawn rise and bring back Phoebus' fiery rays;

'vo i	pju	'kja ɾe	e	pju	'bɛl: le	spje 'ga te	a	me	kor 'te zi
voi	**più**	**chiare**	**e**	**più**	**belle**	**spiegate**	**a**	**me**	**cortesi**
you	more	bright	and	more	beautiful	show		to	me	kind

o you, brighter and more beautiful, kindly show me

pju	bɛl	doɲ: 'ɲal tro	ar 'do ɾe	il	'vɔ stro	ar 'do ɾe
più	**bel**	**d'ogn'altro**	**ardore**	**il**	**vostro**	**ardore.**
more	beautiful	than every other	ardor	the	your	ardor

your ardor, more beautiful than any other ardor.

di	men	'lu tʃi di	'ra i	la	'ka sta	'dɛ a	sap: 'pa gi
Di	**men**	**lucidi**	**rai**	**la**	**casta**	**Dea**	**s'appaghi,**
with	less	shining	rays	the	chaste	goddess	may be satisfied

May the chaste goddess *[Diana (Greek: Artemis), goddess of the moon]* be satisfied with less shining rays;

fre 'dʒar	'lom bre	e	ʎi	or: 'ro ɾi	mo 've te	'vo i	pju	'va gi
fregiar	**l'ombre**	**e**	**gli**	**orrori**	**movete**	**voi**	**più**	**vaghi**
to decorate	the shadows	and	the	horrors	move	you	more	graceful

movete =
(mod.) muovete

de	'bɛ i	tʃe 'lɛ sti	'dʒi ɾi	i	'vɔ stri	'dʒi ɾi
de'	**bei**	**celesti**	**giri**	**i**	**vostri**	**giri.**
than	beautiful	celestial	rotations	the	your	rotations

to beautify the shadows and dark places, you move *[you, eyes]* more gracefully than the beautiful movements of the heavens.

'al tro	'bɛ ne	'ma i	non	bra 'mɔ	la	'mi a	'vi ta
Altro	**bene**	**mai**	**non**	**bramò**	**la**	**mia**	**vita**
other	well-being	ever	not	desired	the	my	life

pju	de	'vɔ stri	splen 'do ɾi	pju	'ka ɾa	e	pju	gra 'di ta
più	**de'**	**vostri**	**splendori,**	**più**	**cara**	**e**	**più**	**gradita**
more	of	your	splendors	more	dear	and	more	welcome

'oɲː ɲi	ter: 're na	'dʒɔ ja	ɛ	'vɔ stra	'dʒɔ ja
d'ogni	**terrena**	**gioia**	**è**	**vostra**	**gioia.**
than every	earthly	joy	is	your	joy

My life never desired another happiness more than your splendor; your joy is more dear and more welcome than any joy of this world.

GL: **Febo**

☙

[79]

Francesco Rasi

per	ki	'mi a	'vo tʃe
Per	**chi**	**mia**	**voce**
For	whomever,	my	voice

per ki	'mi a	'vo tʃe	nan 'dra	ve 'lo tʃe	kol	swɔn	de	'kja ɾi	at: 'tʃɛn ti
Per chi	**mia**	**voce**	**n'andrà**	**veloce;**	**col**	**suon**	**de'**	**chiari**	**accenti**
for whomever	my	voice	will go away	quickly	with the	sound	of	bright	words

For whomever, my voice will fade quickly; with the sound of bright words

non	'fi a	ka 'mo ɾe	mi	'dʒun dʒi	al	'kɔ ɾe	kon	'su e	fa 'vil: lar 'dɛn ti
non	**fia**	**ch'amore**	**mi**	**giungi**	**al**	**core**	**con**	**sue**	**favill' ardenti.**
not	it will be	that love	me	may reach	to the	heart	with	its	sparks burning

love will not reach my heart with its burning sparks.

fia = (mod.) sarà

"giungi" (rather than "giunga"): to avoid two "a"s in a row?...

ma	pur	a 'mo ɾe	mi	'dʒun dʒe	al	'kɔ ɾe	si	'ki o	per	'lu i	so 'spi ɾi
Ma	**pur**	**amore**	**mi**	**giunge**	**al**	**core**	**sì**	**ch'io**	**per**	**lui**	**sospiri**
but	yet	love	me	reaches	at the	heart	so	that I	for	him	I may sigh

But yet love does reach my heart, so that I sigh for him;

'e i	mi	go 'vɛr na	la	'vɔʎ: ʎa	in 'tɛr na	el	fren	de	'mjɛ i	de 'zi ɾi
ei	**mi**	**governa**	**la**	**voglia**	**interna**	**e'l**	**fren**	**de'**	**miei**	**desiri.**
he	me	rules	the	wish	internal	and the	restraint	of	my	desires

he rules my inner wishes and the restraint of my desires.

ei = egli

'em pjo	ti 'ɾan: no	ke	'tan to	af: 'fan: no	kom: 'mɔ vi	'en tro	il	'mi o	'pɛt: to
Empio	**tiranno**	**che**	**tanto**	**affanno**	**commovi**	**entro**	**il**	**mio**	**petto**
impious	tyrant	who	so much	anguish	you stir	within	the	my	breast

Impious tyrant, you who stir so much anguish within my breast,

'kwan do	'fi a	'ma i	ke	'tan ti	'gwa i	si 'kan dʒi no	in	di 'lɛt: to
quando	**fia**	**mai**	**che**	**tanti**	**guai**	**si cangino**	**in**	**diletto?**
when	will be	ever	that	so many	woes	may change	into	pleasure

whenever will it be that so many woes may change into pleasure?

non	'fi a	dʒa 'ma i	ke	'tan ti	'gwa i	'ved: dʒa	dal	kɔr	par 'ti ti
Non	**fia**	**già mai**	**che**	**tanti**	**guai**	**veggia**	**dal**	**cor**	**partiti**
not	will be	ever	that	so many	woes	I may see	from the	heart	departed

I will never see so many troubles having left my heart –

veggia = (mod.) veda

i	'fɔ ki	'twɔ i	'on de	man: 'nɔ i	din 'tʃen di	in fi 'ni ti
i	**fochi**	**tuoi**	**onde**	**m'annoi**	**d'incendi**	**infiniti.**
the	fires	yours	whence	me you bother	of fires	infinite

your passion pesters me with endless fires.

fochi = (mod.) fuochi

❧

[79]   *Francesco Rasi*

un	'gwar do
Un guardo	
One glance	

un	'gwar do	o i 'mɛ	'ki o	'mɔ ɾo	un	'gwar do	'a ni ma	'mi a
Un	**guardo**	**ohimè**	**ch'io**	**moro,**	**un**	**guardo**	**anima**	**mia**
one	glance	alas	that I	I die	one	glance	soul	mine

One glance, alas, as I am dying; one glance, o my soul –

un	'gwar do	'so lo	or	la	'mi a	'vi ta	'si a
un	**guardo**	**solo**	**or**	**la**	**mia**	**vita**	**sia.**
one	glance	only	now	the	my	life	may be

may my life be [contained in] only one glance.

sof: fri 'ra i	tu	kɔr	'mi o	di laʃ: 'ʃar mi	laŋ 'gwi ɾe	di laʃ: 'ʃar mi	mo 'ri ɾe
Soffrirai	**tu**	**cor**	**mio**	**di lasciarmi**	**languire**	**di lasciarmi**	**morire.**
you will suffer	you	heart	mine	of to leave me	to wither	of to leave me	to die

You will suffer, o my beloved, leaving me to languish and die.

un	'gwar do	o i 'mɛ	'ki o	'mɔ ɾun	'gwar do	'so lo	'pri a	ke	'nɛ ska
Un	**guardo**	**ohimè**	**ch'io**	**mor'un**	**guardo**	**solo**	**pria**	**che**	**n'esca**
one	glance	alas	that I	I die one	glance	only	before	that	of it may leave

One glance – alas, I am dying; just one glance before [my soul] leaves

> *pria (poet.) = prima*

dal	kɔr	'pri a	ke	'nɛ ska	dal	kɔr	'la ni ma	'vo lo
dal	**cor,**	**pria**	**che**	**n'esca**	**dal**	**cor**	**l'anim' a**	**volo.**
from the	heart	before	that	of it may leave	from the	heart	the soul in	flight

my heart, before my soul leaves my heart in flight.

✤ *Rigatti, Giovanni Antonio* (c.1613-1648)

Probably born in Venice, he was a choirboy at S. Marco, then *maestro di cappella* at Udine Cathedral, and a teacher at the Conservatorio degl'Incurabili. In 1647 he was appointed a *sottocanonico* of S. Marco.

During his short lifetime he was held in high esteem for his inventiveness and melodic gift, particularly in the composition of church music; nine of his eleven surviving collections of vocal music are of motets, psalms, and masses, most of which include obbligato instruments, usually violins.

Equally notable is his secular collection *Musiche diverse (1641)* for solo voice and continuo, which contains "O biondetta lascivetta pastorella."

---

[27]

o bjon 'det: ta laʃ: ʃi 'vet: ta pa sto 'rel: la
O biondetta lascivetta pastorella
O little blond, lascivious shepherdess

o	bjon 'det: ta	laʃ: ʃi 'vet: ta	pa sto 'rel: la	'tut: ta	'bɛl: la
O	**biondetta**	**lascivetta**	**pastorella**	**tutta**	**bella,**
o	little blond	little lascivious	shepherdess	completely	beautiful

O utterly beautiful little blond, lascivious shepherdess,

se	vet: 'tso za	se	fe 'sto za	'i o	ti	'mi ɾo	'a i	so 'spi ɾo
se	**vezzosa**	**se**	**festosa**	**io**	**ti**	**miro,**	**ahi**	**sospiro.**
if	charming	if	merry	I	you	I see	alas	I sigh

when I see you, charming and merry, alas, I sigh.

o	ru 'bɛl: la	'nin fa	'bɛl: la	da 'mor	'fre dʒo	da 'mor	'prɛ dʒo
O	**rubella**	**ninfa**	**bella**	**d'amor**	**fregio**	**d'amor**	**pregio,**
o	rebellious	nymph	beautiful	of love	adornment	of love	prize

O beautiful, rebellious nymph, adornment of love, prize of love,

> *rubella = (mod.) ribella*
> *pregio = (mod.) premio*

se	ri 'dɛn te	pur	so 'vɛn te	'i o	ti	'mi ɾo	'a i	so 'spi ɾo
se	**ridente**	**pur**	**sovente**	**io**	**ti**	**miro,**	**ahi**	**sospiro.**
if	laughing	indeed	often	I	you	I see	alas	I sigh

When, indeed often, I see you laughing, alas, I sigh.

o	lil:	'let: ta	par go	'let: ta	'lil: la	a 'ma ta	'lil: la	iŋ 'gra ta
O	**Lilletta**		**pargoletta**		**Lilla**	**amata**	**Lilla**	**ingrata,**
o	Lilletta		dear child		Lilla	beloved	Lilla	ungrateful

O dear Lilletta, child – beloved Lilla, ungrateful Lilla,

'men tre	iŋ 'kan ti	tra	ʎi	a 'man ti	'i o	ti	'mi ɾo	e	so 'spi ɾo
mentre	**incanti**	**tra**	**gli**	**amanti**	**io**	**ti**	**miro,**	**e**	**sospiro.**
while	you beguile	among	the	lovers	I	you	I see	and	I sigh

while you beguile your lovers I see you and I sigh.

✻ *Rontani, Raffaello (?-1622)*

In 1610 he was in Florence in the service of Antonio de' Medici; from 1616 until his death he was *maestro di cappella* at S. Giovanni dei Fiorentini in Rome; in Rome he was also *a capo del concerto* for the Duke Sforza.
Though his vocal music is not thought to compare in quality to that of other composers of the time, it was extremely popular in his day; half of his books of *Varie musiche* were reprinted, the first one twice.
His six books contain a total of ninety-seven pieces, some sixty of which are monodies; most are strophic songs, in the later books also including guitar tablatures.

[10, 19, 38, 40]

'kal di so 'spi ɾi
Caldi sospiri
Warm sighs

'kal di	so 'spi ɾi	ke	uʃ: 'ʃi te	dal	'kɔ ɾe
Caldi	**sospiri,**	**che**	**uscite**	**dal**	**core,**
warm	sighs	that	leave	from the	heart

Warm sighs that come from my heart,

> var.: *ch'uscite* = *che uscite*

dɛ	'dʒi te	vo 'lan do	nel	sen	al	'mi o	a 'mo ɾe
deh,	**gite**	**volando**	**nel**	**sen**	**al**	**mio**	**amore.**
pray	go	flying	to the	breast	to the	my	love

please, fly to the breast of my beloved.

> *gite: from "gire"* = *(mod.) "andare"*

'di te	'al: la	'kru da	ke	'la mo	e	la 'do ɾo
Dite	**alla**	**cruda**	**che**	**l'amo**	**e**	**l'adoro,**
say	to the	cruel one	that	her I love	and	her I adore

Tell the cruel one that I love her and adore her,

> *vars.:*   in [40]: *dit'alla* [di 'tal: la] = *dite alla*; *...ch'io l'amo e adoro* ['ki o 'la mo e a 'do ɾo] = that I love and adore her,
> in [19]: *dit'alla cruda ch'io* [printed in error as "s'io"] *l'amo e onoro* [di 'tal: la 'kru da 'ki o 'la mo e o 'no ɾo]
>   = tell the cruel one that I love and honor her,

ke	'mi ɾi	'ki o	'mɔ ɾo	fra	'tan ti	mar 'ti ɾi	o	'kal di	so 'spi ɾi
che	**miri**	**ch'io**	**moro**	**fra**	**tanti**	**martiri,**	**o**	**caldi**	**sospiri!**
that	she may see	that I	I die	among	so many	torments	o	warm	sighs

so she can see that I am dying among so many torments, o warm sighs!

> *In [40] and [10], this line ends with "fra tanti martiri."* | *In [19], "s'io" is printed [in error] instead of "ch'io."*

> *The following verse is not in [10]; the next verse in [10] begins "Caldi sospiri, correte..."*

'kal di   so 'spi ɾi   'si a   'sku do   la   'fe de
Caldi   sospiri,   sia   scudo   la   fede,
warm   sighs   may be   shield   the   fidelity
Warm sighs, may my shield be the fidelity

ke   'las: so   'i o   dʒu 'ra i   a   ki   'mar de   e   nol   'kre de
che,   lasso,   io   giurai   a   chi   m'arde   e   nol   crede!   *nol = non + il*
that   alas   I   I swore   to   the one who   me burns   and   not it   believes
that, alas, I swore to the one who enflames me [but] does not believe it.

in [19]: **che i' lasso io giurai...** *was probably originally* **che ahi lasso...** *(ahi lasso! = miserable me!)*

'sja te   i   gwer: 'rjɛ ɾi   'vo i   'lar me   il   do 'lo ɾe
Siate   i   guerrieri   voi,   l'arme   il   dolore,
be   the   warriors   you   the weapons   the   pain
Be my warriors, my pain the weapons;

fe 'ri te   kwel   'kɔ ɾe   'pri a   'la ni ma   'spi ɾi   *additionally*   o   'kal di   so 'spi ɾi
ferite   quel   core   pria   l'anima   spiri.   *in some prints:*   **O   caldi   sospiri!**
wound   that   heart   before   the soul   may die   o   warm   sighs
wound that heart before my soul dies.   *pria (poet.) = prima*   O warm sighs!

'kal di   so 'spi ɾi   kor: 'rɛ tɛ   da   'klɔ ɾi
Caldi   sospiri,   correte   da   Clori,
warm   sighs   run   to   Clori
Warm sighs, fly to Clori;

pun 'dʒe te   il   bɛl   'pɛt: to   tem 'pra te   i   'mjɛ i   ar 'do ɾi
pungete   il   bel   petto,   temprate   i   miei   ardori.
pierce   the   beautiful   breast   temper   the   my   ardors
penetrate her beautiful breast, temper my ardors.   *in* [40] *and* [19]: **temprat' i mi' ardori** [tem 'pra ti mi ar 'do ɾi]

e   'pɔ i   fe 'li tʃi   kan 'dʒa te vi   iŋ   'kan to
E   poi   felici   cangiatevi   in   canto,
and   then   happy   change yourselves   into   song
And then, happy, change yourselves into song

e   in   'dʒɔ ja   il   'mi o   'pjan to   se   'kan dʒa   de 'zi ɾi   o   'kal di   so 'spi ɾi
e   in   gioia   il   mio   pianto,   se   cangia   desiri,   o   caldi   sospiri!
and   into   joy   the   my   weeping   if   she changes   desires   o   warm   sighs
and my weeping into joy if she changes her wishes, o warm sighs!

in [10]: **È gioia il mio pianto,** [ɛ 'dʒɔ ja il 'mi o 'pjan to] = My weeping will be joy,
In some prints this line ends with "se cangia desiri."

G𝓛: **Clori**

[12, 41] In [41] incorrectly attributed to an "anonymous" composer.   *Giovanni Battista Guarini*
This text is from <u>Il pastor fido</u>, Act IV, Scene 5; Amaryllis is the character speaking.

'ka ɾe   'mi e   'sel ve
Care mie selve
My dear woodlands

'ka ɾe   'mi e   'sel ve   ad: 'di o   ri tʃe 've te   kwes 'tul ti mi   so 'spi ɾi   fiŋ 'ke
Care   mie   selve,   addio;   ricevete   quest'ultimi   sospiri,   finché,
dear   my   woods   farewell   receive   these final   sighs   until
My dear woodlands, farewell; receive these last sighs until,

'ʃɔl ta da 'fɛr: ro in 'dʒu ste 'kru do 'tor ni la 'mi a fred: 'dom bra
sciolta da ferro ingiust'e crudo, torni la mia fredd'ombra
released from chain unjust and cruel may return the my cold shade (spirit)
freed from unjust and cruel shackles, my cold spirit may return

'al: le vɔ 'strom bre a 'ma te ke nel pe 'no zo in 'fɛr no non pwɔ
alle vostr'ombre amate, ché nel penoso inferno non può
to the your shades loved because to the painful hell not is able

gir in: no 'tʃen te ne pwɔ star fra be 'a ti di spe 'ra te do 'lɛn te
gir innocente né può star fra beati, disperat'e dolente.
to go innocent nor is able to be among blessed desperate and sorrowful

gir[e] = girare

to your beloved shade; because an innocent one can not go to painful hell, nor can he, desperate and sorrowful, stay among the blessed.

o mir 'til: lo bɛn fu 'mi ze ro il di ke 'pri a ti 'vi di
O, Mirtillo, ben fu misero il dì che pria ti vidi,
o Mirtillo well was miserable the day that first you I saw

pria (poet.) = prima

O Mirtillo, miserable was the day I first saw you,

el di ke 'pri a ti 'pja kwi
e'l dì che pria ti piacqui.
and the day that first you I pleased
and the day I first pleased you.

po i 'ke la 'vi ta 'mi a pju 'ka ɾa a te ke la 'tu a 'vi ta as: 'sa i
Poiché la vita mia più cara a te che la tua vita assai,
since the life mine more dear to you than the your life much
Since my life [is] much more dear to you than your [own] life,

ko 'zi pur non do 'vri a per 'al tri 'ɛs: ser 'tu a 'vi ta
così pur non dovrìa per altri esser tua vita,
thus still not ought for another to be your life

dovrìa = (mod.) dovrebbe

altri (singular) = another, sombody else

yet, still, your life should not be for another,

ke per 'ɛs: ser ka 'dʒon 'del: la 'mi a 'mɔr te
che per esser cagion della mia morte.
that for to be cause of the my death
except that it be the cause of my death.

G𝓛: **Mirtillo**

☙

[14, 40]   *Giovanni Battista Guarini*
This text is from <u>Il pastor fido</u>, Act III, Scene 1; Mirtillo is the character speaking.

o pri ma 've ɾa
O primavera
O spring

o pri ma 've ɾa dʒo ven 'tu del: 'lan: no 'bɛl: la 'ma dre de 'fjo ɾi
O primavera, gioventù dell'anno, bella madre de' fiori,
o spring youth of the year beautiful mother of (the) flowers
O spring, youth of the year, beautiful mother of the flowers,

'dɛr be no 'vɛl: le e di no 'vɛl: li a 'mo ɾi
d'erbe novelle e di novelli amori!
of grasses new and of new loves
of fresh grasses and new loves!

tu	'tor ni	bɛn	ma	'te ko	non	'tor na no
Tu	**torni**	**ben,**	**ma**	**teco**	**non**	**tornano**
you	you return	indeed	but	you with	not	they return

i	se 'ɾe ni	e	for tu 'na ti	di	'del: le	'mi e	'dʒɔ je
i	**sereni**	**e**	**fortunati**	**dì**	**delle**	**mie**	**gioie.**
the	serene	and	fortunate	days	of the	my	joys

You return, indeed; but the peaceful and happy days of my joy do not return with you.

tu	'tor ni	bɛn	ma	'te ko	'al tro	non	'tor na	ke
Tu	**torni**	**ben,**	**ma**	**teco**	**altro**	**non**	**torna,**	**che**
you	you return	indeed	but	you with	other	not	returns	than

You return, indeed; but with you returns only

del	per 'du to	'mi o	'ka ɾo	te 'zɔ ɾo	la	ri mem 'bran tsa	'mi ze ɾa	e	do 'lɛn te
del	**perduto**	**mio**	**caro**	**tesoro**	**la**	**rimembranza**	**misera**	**e**	**dolente.**
of the	lost	my	dear	treasure	the	rimembrance	miserable	and	sad

the miserable and sad memory of my dear lost treasure.

tu	'kwel: la	'sɛ i	pur	'kwel: la	'kɛ ɾi	pur	'djan tsi
Tu	**quella**	**sei,**	**pur**	**quella**	**ch'eri**	**pur**	**dianzi**
you	that one	you are	still	that one	that you were	then	a short time ago

si	vet: 'tso za	e	'bɛl: la	ma	non	son	'i o	kwel
sì	**vezzosa**	**e**	**bella,**	**ma**	**non**	**son**	**io**	**quel,**
so	charming	and	beautiful	but	not	I am	I am	that one

You are now, as you were a short while ago, so charming and beautiful; but I am not,

ke	dʒa	un	'tɛm po	'fu i	si	'ka ɾo	'aʎ: ʎi	'ɔk: ki	al 'tru i
che	**già**	**un**	**tempo**	**fui,**	**sì**	**caro**	**agli**	**occhi**	**altrui.**
that	before	one	time	I was	so	dear	to the	eyes	another's

as I once was before, so dear in another's *[your]* eyes.

&

[1, 2, 14, 24]

or 'ki o non 'se ɡwo pju

Or ch'io non seguo più

Now that I no longer pursue

or	'ki o	non	'se ɡwo	pju	il	di spje 'ta to	a 'mor	non	'sɛn to	pju	do 'lor
Or	**ch'io**	**non**	**seguo**	**più**	**il**	**dispietato**	**amor,**	**non**	**sento**	**più**	**dolor.**
now	that I	not	I pursue	more	the	merciless	love	not	I feel	more	pain

Now that I no longer pursue merciless love, I no longer feel pain.

> *dispietato (poet.) = spietato*

> *In [1] and [2], "segno" (instead of "seguo") is printed in error.*

e	il	kɔr	ke	in	'doʎ: ʎa	fu	al: 'le ɡro	sta	ke	'vi ve	in	li ber 'ta
E	**il**	**cor,**	**che**	**in**	**doglia**	**fu,**	**allegro**	**sta,**	**ché**	**vive**	**in**	**libertà.**
and	the	heart	which	in	affliction	was	cheerful	is	because	it lives	in	freedom

And my heart, which was afflicted, is cheerful because it lives in freedom.

> *doglia (lit.) = dolore, patimento*

> *Following is the 2ⁿᵈ verse in [1] and [2] but is not included in [14]:*

or	'ki o	non	'a mo	pju	ko 'lɛ i	ke	mi	fe 'ri	fe 'li tʃe	'pas: so	i	di
Or	**ch'io**	**non**	**amo**	**più**	**colei,**	**che**	**mi**	**ferì,**	**felice**	**passo**	**i**	**dì.**
now	that I	not	I love	more	her	who	me	wounded	happy	I pass	the	days

Now that I no longer love her who wounded me, I spend the days happily.

Following is the 3rd verse in [1] and [2], but is not included in [14]:

or	'ki o	non	've d: dʒo	pju	kwel	'vi zo	lu ziŋ 'gjɛr	non	'vi vo	pri dʒo 'njɛr
Or	**ch'io**	**non**	**veggio**	**più**	**quel**	**viso**	**lusinghier,**	**non**	**vivo**	**prigionier.**
now	that I	not	I see	more	that	face	alluring	not	I live	prisoner

Now that I no longer see that alluring face, I do not live a prisoner.

> *veggio (poet.) = vedo*

Following is the 2nd (and last) verse in [14], the 4th (and last) verse in [1] and [2]:

or	'ki o	non	'sen to	pju	i	'fin ti	'swo i	so 'spir	non	'pɔs: so	pju	mo 'rir
Or	**ch'io**	**non**	**sento**	**più**	**i**	**finti**	**suoi**	**sospir,**	**non**	**posso**	**più**	**morir.**
now	that I	not	I hear	more	the	feigned	her	sighs	not	I am able	more	to die

Now that I no longer hear her feigned sighs, I am no longer able to die.

❧

[7]

pe ska 'tri tʃe li gu 'ri na
Pescatrice ligurina
Ligurian fisherwoman

pe ska 'tri tʃe	li gu 'ri na	del	'mi o	kɔr	'dol tʃe	tor 'men to
Pescatrice	**ligurina,**	**del**	**mio**	**cor**	**dolce**	**tormento,**
fisherwoman	Lugurian	of the	my	heart	sweet	torment

Ligurian fisherwoman, sweet torment of my heart,

'pri mo	a 'mor	'del: la	ma 'ri na	ma	fu 'ga tʃe	al par del	'vɛn to
primo	**amor**	**della**	**marina**	**ma**	**fugace**	**al par del**	**vento,**
first	love	of the	(poet.) sea	but	fleeting	like the	wind

first love of the sea but fleeting as the wind,

'fer ma	il	pjɛ	men	'kru do	e	'pɔ i	in	me	'vɔl dʒi	i	'lu mi	'two i
ferma	**il**	**piè**	**men**	**crudo**	**e**	**poi**	**in**	**me**	**volgi**	**i**	**lumi**	**tuoi.**
stop	the	foot	less	cruel	and	then	to	me	turn	the	eyes	your

stop, be less cruel, and then turn your eyes to me.

> *lumi = lights; (poet.) eyes*

in	me	'vɔl dʒi	i	'rad: dʒi	a 'ma ti	de	'bɛʎ: ʎi	'ɔk: ki	on 'di o	so 'spi ro
In	**me**	**volgi**	**i**	**raggi**	**amati**	**de'**	**begli**	**occhi**	**ond'io**	**sospiro;**
to	me	turn	the	rays	beloved	of (the)	beautiful	eyes	for which I	I sigh

Turn to me the beloved rays of your beautiful eyes, for which I sigh –

'ɔk: ki	'ka ri	'ɔk: ki	be 'a ti	'o ve	il	tʃɛl	da 'mor	ri 'mi ro
occhi	**cari,**	**occhi**	**beati**	**ove**	**il**	**ciel**	**d'amor**	**rimiro,**
eyes	dear	eyes	blessed	where	the	heaven	of love	I see

dear blessed eyes, where I see the heaven of love –

'del: le	'grat: tsje	e 'tɛr ni	'ni di	e	del: 'lal me	'ɔk: ki	o mi 'tʃi di
delle	**Grazie**	**eterni**	**nidi**	**e**	**dell'alme**	**occhi**	**omicidi.**
of the	Graces	eternal	nests	and	of the souls	eyes	murderous

home of the eternal Graces, and murderous eyes of the soul.

'ɔk: ki	'vi vi	e	'lu mi	al 'tɛ ri	'lu me	a	'lu me	ar 'dɛn do	u 'ni te
Occhi	**vivi**	**e**	**lumi**	**alteri,**	**lume**	**a**	**lume**	**ardendo**	**unite;**
eyes	bright	and	eyes	proud	eye	to	eye	burning	unite

Eyes bright and eyes proud, unite your burning eyes with mine.

tri on 'fa te	'ɔk: ki	gwer: 'rje ɾi	nel: la 'prir si		me	fe 'ɾi te
Trionfate,	**occhi**	**guerrieri,**	**nell'aprirsi**		**me**	**ferite;**
triumph	eyes	warring	in the opening of yourself		me	you wound

Triumph, warring eyes; when you open, you wound me.

> Assuming a copying error, I've changed the printed "nell'asprissi" to "nell'aprirsi," which makes sense...

> "me" should, gramatically, be "mi"; as the Italian "mi" derives from the Latin "me," the use of "me" here could be an antiquated usage; or, it could simply be a copying error.

tri on 'fa te	or	del	'mi o	'kɔ ɾe	e	kon	'vo i	tri 'on fi	a 'mo ɾe
Trionfate	**or**	**del**	**mio**	**core**	**e**	**con**	**voi**	**trionfi**	**Amore.**
triumph	now	of the	my	heart	and	with	you	may triumph	Love

Triumph now over my heart, and with you may triumph Love.

GL: **Amore, Grazie, Ligurina**

☙

[5, 9, 19, 24]   *Gabriele Chiabrera*

se bɛl 'ri o
Se bel rio
If a beautiful brook

se	bɛl	'ri o	se	bɛl: la u 'ɾet: ta	fra	ler 'bet: ta
Se	**bel**	**rio,**	**se**	**bell'auretta**	**fra**	**l'erbetta**
if	beautiful	brook	if	beautiful breeze	among	the little grasses

> *alt.:*
> tra = fra

	sul	mat: tin	mor mo 'ran 'dɛr: ra
	sul	**mattin**	**mormorand'erra,**
	upon the	morning	murmuring wanders

> *alt.:* mormorando erra = mormorand'erra

If a beautiful brook and a beautiful breeze wander at morn, murmuring, among the new grasses,

	se	di	'fjo ɾi	un	pra ti 'tʃɛl: lo	si fa	'bɛl: lo	'no i	di 'tʃam
	se	**di**	**fiori**	**un**	**praticello**	**si fa**	**bello,**	**noi**	**diciam:**
	if	of	flowers	a	little meadow	makes itself	beautiful	we	we say

if a meadow makes itself beautiful with flowers, we say:

	'ri de	la	'tɛr: ra
	ride	**la**	**terra.**
	smiles	the	earth

the earth is smiling.

> *The following three verses are in different order in different prints; [24] has a total of three verses (not four).*

'kwan do	av: 'vjɛn	ke	un	dzef: fi 'ret: to	per	di 'lɛt: to
Quando	**avvien**	**che**	**un**	**zeffiretto**	**per**	**diletto**
when	it happens	that	a	little breeze	for	pleasure

When it happens that a little breeze, for pleasure,

	'baɲ: ɲi	il	pjɛ	nel: 'lon de	'kja ɾe
	bagni	**il**	**piè**	**nell'onde**	**chiare,**
	may bathe	the	foot	in the waves	clear

bathes its feet in the clear waves

	si: 'ke	'la kwa	su	la 're na	'sker tsi	ap 'pe na
	sì che	**l'acqua**	**su**	**l'arena**	**scherzi**	**appena,**
	so that	the water	upon	the sand	may play	barely

> sì che =
> (mod.) sicché

so that the water plays gently upon the sand,

'no i	di 'tʃam	ke	'ri de	il	'ma ɾe
noi	diciam	che	ride	il	mare.
we	we say	that	smiles	the	sea

we say that the sea is smiling.

se	dʒa 'ma i	tra	fjor	ver 'miʎ: ʎi	se	fra	'dʒiʎ: ʎi
Se	già mai	tra	fior	vermigli,	se	fra	gigli
if	whenever	among	flowers	vermilion	if	among	lilies

Whenever, among vermilion flowers and among lilies,

> già mai = (mod.) giammai

've ste	'lal ba	u 'na u re o	've lo	e	su	'rɔ te	di	dzaf: 'fi ɾo
veste	l'alba	un aureo	velo,	e	su	rote	di	zaffiro
puts on	the dawn	a golden	veil	and	on	wheels	of	sapphire

the dawn puts on a golden veil and, on sapphire wheels

> rote (lit.) = ruote

'mɔ ve	in 'dʒi ɾo	'no i	di 'tʃam	ke	'ri de	il	'tʃɛ lo
move	in giro,	noi	diciam	che	ride	il	cielo.
moves	around	we	we say	that	smiles	the	sky

moves about, we say that the sky is smiling.

> move = (mod.) muove

ben	ɛ	ver	'kwan do	ɛ	dʒo 'kon do	'ri de	il	'mon do
Ben	è	ver:	quando	è	giocondo	ride	il	mondo,
well	it is	true	when	is	cheerful	smiles	the	world

Indeed it is true: when the world is cheerful it smiles,

'ri de	il	tʃɛl	'kwan do	ɛ	dʒo 'jo zo
ride	il	ciel	quando	è	gioioso;
smiles	the	sky	when	it is	joyful

[and] the sky smiles when it is joyful.

bɛn	ɛ	ver	ma	non	san	'pɔ i
Ben	è	ver:	ma	non	san	poi
well	it is	true	but	not	they know how	then

Indeed it is true; but then, they know not how

'ko me	'vo i	'fa ɾe	un	'ri zo	grat: 'tsjo zo
come	voi,	fare	un	riso	grazioso.
like	you	to make	a	smile	charming

to smile as charmingly as you.

✿ *Rosa, Salvator* (1615-1673)

A painter of repute, actor, poet, and satirist, he divided his time from 1635 to 1640 between Rome and Naples; from 1640 to 1649 he was court painter to the Medici in Florence, and then he returned to Rome for the rest of his life. Rosa founded the Accademia dei Percossi, whose members probably included the composer Cesti, for whom he provided texts for at least four cantatas, and for whom Rosa's letters are a major source of biographical information. Also a lutenist and lover of music, Rosa has been credited as a composer of songs, now known to be untrue. Rosa owned a hand-written book of songs (for which he wrote texts) from which excerpts were published, long after his death, attributing him as the composer. The English musicologist Frank Walker examined the book in 1949 and determined that the music was, rather, by well-known composers (Scarlatti, Bononcini, etc.) of the day.

"Star vicino" : see *Anonimo*, page 39

"Vado ben spesso" : see *Bononcini, G.*, page 65

Though the following song is not by Rosa (see biographical sketch), I am including it here because I have not found any information regarding the correct composer. It is attributed to Rosa in [20] and [24].

[20, 24]

'sel ve 'vo i ke le spe 'ran tse
Selve, voi che le speranze
Woodlands, you who [happily preserve] the hopes

'sel ve	'vo i	ke	le	spe 'ran tse	al	dʒo 'ir	'lje te	ser 'ba te
Selve,	**voi,**	**che**	**le**	**speranze**	**al**	**gioir**	**liete**	**serbate,**
woods	you	who	the	hopes	to the	to delight	happy	preserve

Woodlands, you who happily preserve the hopes of delight,

del	pja 'tʃer	'sjɛ te	le	'stan tse	'o ve	pas: 'sar	ded: 'dʒi o	'lo ɾe	be 'a te
del	**piacer**	**siete**	**le**	**stanze,**	**ove**	**passar**	**degg'io**	**l'ore**	**beate!**
of the	pleasure	be	the	rooms	where	to pass	should I	the hours	blessed

be the abode of pleasure where I may pass the blessed hours!

degg'io = (mod.) devo

Rossi, Luigi (1597/1598-1653)

Composer, singer, and organist, he was born near Naples; before the end of 1620 he had moved to Rome, where he joined the service of Marcantonio Borghese, whom he served for sixteen years, and where, in 1633, he became organist at S. Luigi dei Francesi.
In 1636 he left the Borghese and served Cardinal Antonio Barberini, who had become the Cardinal Protector of France. At the Barberini palace in 1642 his first opera, *Il palazzo d'Atlante*, was produced.
When the Barberini were exiled in France because of the persecution of Pope Innocent X, Rossi went to Paris with them and the French prime minister Cardinal Mazarin; in 1647 Rossi's second opera, *Orfeo*, was produced at the Palais Royal, with the support of Mazarin, in a spectacular staging and with great success.
Rossi continued to receive money from Cardinal Antonio Barberini; in 1649 he joined Barberini in Provence for at least a few years. Though away from Rome for many years, he remained famous there, and he died there.
Despite the success of his two operas, he also wrote several oratorios and was most renowned of all for his cantatas, of which he wrote more than a hundred for solo voice and continuo.

[1, 2, 46]

ke sven 'tu ɾa
Che sventura!
What misfortune!

ke	sven 'tu ɾa	son	tan 'tan: ni	'ki o	vi	'sɛr vo	'ki o	va 'do ɾo
Che	**sventura!**	**Son**	**tant'anni,**	**ch'io**	**vi**	**servo,**	**ch'io**	**v'adoro,**
what	misfortune	are	so many years	that I	you	I serve	that I	you I adore

What misfortune! For so many years I have served you, adored you,

ke	laŋ 'gwi sko	ke	mi 'mɔ ɾo	'ɔk: ki	e	'sjɛ te	aŋ 'kor	ti 'ran: ni
che	**languisco,**	**che**	**mi moro,**	**occhi,**	**e**	**siete**	**ancor**	**tiranni!**
that	I languish	that	me I die	eyes	and	you are	still	tyrants

languished and been dying, eyes; and still you are tyrants!

a	'du e	'ra i	ke	at: 'tʃe ze	a 'mo ɾe	'kor: se	in 'trɛ pi da	'u na	'fe de
A	**due**	**rai,**	**che**	**accese**	**Amore,**	**corse**	**intrepida**	**una**	**fede,**
to	two	eyes	which	set on fire	Love	ran	bravely	a	faithfulness

Fidelity, which Love kindled, rushed bravely to two eyes

"corre" (= runs), not "corse," was printed; I changed it to make the tense agree with "trovò" in the next line. If "trovò" were originally "trova," that would work with "corre": ...rushes bravely to two eyes, but finds disdain...

per	a 'ver	'pɔ ka	mer 'tʃe de	ma	tro 'vɔ	'zdeɲː ɲo	e	ri 'go ɾe
per	**aver**	**poca**	**mercede;**	**ma**	**trovò**	**sdegno**	**e**	**rigore.**
in order to	to have	little	reward	but	it found	disdain	and	severity

in order to have some small reward; but it found disdain and severity.

ne	kol	'pjan to	a	'filː li	il	'kɔ ɾe	amː mo 'li	la	'mi a	pu 'pilː la
Né	**col**	**pianto**	**a**	**Filli**	**il**	**core**	**ammolì**	**la**	**mia**	**pupilla;**
nor	with the	weeping	to	Filli	the	heart	softened	the	my	eye

My eyes did not soften the heart of Filli [even] with weeping;

pur	sa	'fran dʒer	'u na	'stilː la	'oɲː ɲi	'pjɛ tra	e	'si a	pur	'du ɾa
pur	**sa**	**franger**	**una**	**stilla**	**ogni**	**pietra,**	**e**	**sia**	**pur**	**dura.**
yet	it knows how	to break	a	drop	every	stone	[and]	may it be	yet	hard

yet a teardrop can break any stone, however hard it may be.

'tur ba	il	'tʃɛ lo	i	'swɔ i	se 're ni	e	kon	'tur bi ni	e	kon	'lam pi
Turba	**il**	**cielo**	**i**	**suoi**	**sereni,**	**e**	**con**	**turbini**	**e**	**con**	**lampi**
disturbs	the	sky	the	its	serenities	and	with	whirlwinds	and	with	lightning flashes

The sky clouds its clearness, and with whirlwinds and lightning

'skwɔ te	'bɔ ɾe a	i	'sal si	'kam pi	ke	di	'kal me	'ɛ ɾan	ri 'pjɛ ni
scuote	**Borea**	**i**	**salsi**	**campi,**	**che**	**di**	**calme**	**eran**	**ripieni.**
shakes	the north wind	the	salty	fields	which	of	calms	were	full

the north wind shakes the seas which were [beforehand] full of calm.

ma	del	tʃɛl	del	mar	i	'se ni	pur	ri 'tor na no	traŋ 'kwilː li
Ma	**del**	**ciel,**	**del**	**mar**	**i**	**seni**	**pur**	**ritornano**	**tranquilli;**
but	of the	sky	of the	sea	the	breasts	then	return	tranquil

But the bosoms of the sky and the sea then become tranquil;

'lal ma	sol	del	'em pja	'filː li	ko 'zi	'fjɛ ɾa	'sɛm pre	'du ɾa
l'alma	**sol**	**del**	**empia**	**Filli**	**così**	**fiera,**	**sempre**	**dura!**
the soul	only	of the	pitiless	Filli	so	cruel	always	endures

only the soul of the pitiless Filli remains so cruel!

GL: **Amore, Borea, Filli**

❧

[58]
from: *Il palazzo d'Atlante [Il palazzo incantato] (1642)*   *Giulio Rospigliosi*

'do ve mi 'spin dʒi a 'mor
Dove mi spingi, Amor
Where are you leading me, Love

'do ve	mi	'spin dʒi	a 'mor	'do ve	o i 'mɛ	'do ve
Dove	**mi**	**spingi,**	**Amor,**	**dove,**	**ohimè,**	**dove?**
where	me	you urge	Love	where	alas	where

Where are you leading me, Love – where, alas, where?

do 'vrɔ	nel	'reɲː ɲo	'tu o	'sɛn tsa	spe 'ɾar	mer 'tʃe	ser 'vir
Dovrò	**nel**	**regno**	**tuo**	**senza**	**sperar**	**merce'**	**servir**
I shall have to	in the	kingdom	your	without	to hope for	recompense	to serve

merce' =
mercede

I shall have to serve in your realm, without hoping for reward,

ki	non	pju	'su o	a 'dal tri	kon sa 'krɔ	'lal ma	e	la	fe
chi	**non**	**più**	**suo**	**ad altri**	**consacrò**	**l'alma**	**e**	**la**	**fe'.**
he who	not	more	hers	to another	dedicated	the soul	and	the	faith

> altri (singular) = another, somebody else

he who, no longer hers *[i.e., mine]*, dedicated his soul and faith to another.

'na ta	'so lo	a	so 'spi ri	laʃː ʃe 'ro	'duŋ kwe	in	'latː tʃi	di	mar 'ti ri
Nata	**solo**	**a'**	**sospiri**	**lascierò**	**dunque**	**in**	**lacci**	**di**	**martiri**
born	only	to	sighs	I will let	therefore	in	knots	of	agonies

'strin dʒer mi	il	pjɛ	'da spre	ri 'tɔr te	e	'nwɔ ve
stringermi	**il**	**piè**	**d'aspre**	**ritorte**	**e**	**nuove.**
to tighten me	the	foot	of harsh	ropes	and	new

Born only to sigh, I will therefore allow my foot to be tied in agonizing knots, with painful and new ropes.

'do ve	mi	'spin dʒi	a 'mor	'do ve	o i 'mɛ	'do ve
Dove	**mi**	**spingi,**	**Amor,**	**dove,**	**ohimè,**	**dove?**
where	me	you urge	Love	where	alas	where

Where are you leading me, Love – where, alas, where?

dal	tʃɛl	di	'va ga	'fron te	'du e	'so li	in	'nɔtː te	il	di
Dal	**ciel**	**di**	**vaga**	**fronte**	**due**	**soli**	**in**	**notte**	**il**	**dì**
from the	heaven	of	charming	forehead	two	only	in	night	the	day

fa 'ran	ka	me	tra 'mon ti	ke	mal	gra 'di to	a 'dal tri	'e i	'splen de	si
faran	**ch'a**	**me**	**tramonti**	**che**	**mal**	**gradito**	**ad altri**	**ei**	**splende**	**sì,**
will make	that to	me	may set	because	badly	welcomed	to another	he	shines	so

From the heaven of a charming face just two [eyes] will turn day into night for me because, unwelcomed, he shines so for another;

> faran = faranno
>
> ei = egli

e	fra	'tɛ ne bre	o 'sku ɾe	po 'tra	il	'mi o	kɔr	ten 'tar	'vi e	mal	si 'ku ɾe
e	**fra**	**tenebre**	**oscure**	**potrà**	**il**	**mio**	**cor**	**tentar**	**vie**	**mal**	**sicure,**
and	among	darkness	gloomy	will be able	the	my	heart	try	ways	badly	safe

and in gloomy darkness will my heart attempt dangerous paths,

ne	dal	'pre zo	kamː 'min	pur	si ri 'mɔ ve
né	**dal**	**preso**	**cammin**	**pur**	**si rimove.**
nor	from the	taken	road	yet	itself removes

not swerving from the road taken.

> rimovere = (mod.) rimuovere

'do ve	mi	'spin dʒi	a 'mor	'do ve	o i 'mɛ	'do ve
Dove	**mi**	**spingi,**	**Amor,**	**dove,**	**ohimè,**	**dove?**
where	me	you urge	Love	where	alas	where

Where are you leading me, Love – where, alas, where?

GL: **Amor**

❧

[30, 45]

fan 'tʃulː la	son	'i o
Fanciulla son io		

I am an innocent young girl

fan 'tʃulː la	son	'i o	ka 'ma ɾe	non	sɔ	'a i	ke	mi mo ɾi 'rɔ
Fanciulla	**son**	**io**	**ch'amare**	**non**	**so,**	**ahi**	**che**	**mi morirò!**
innocent young girl	am	I	who to love	not	I know how	alas	[that]	I shall die

I am an innocent young girl who does not know how to love; alas, I shall die!

se	'vwɔ i	'ki o	ta 'do ɾi	non	'ɛs: ser	kru 'dɛ le
Se	**vuoi**	**ch'io**	**t'adori**	**non**	**esser**	**crudele;**
if	you want	that I	you I may adore	not	to be	cruel

If you want me to adore you, do not be cruel.

tor 'men ti	e	kwe 'ɾɛ le	non	'sɛn te	il	'mi o	'kɔ ɾe
tormenti	**e**	**querele**	**non**	**sente**	**il**	**mio**	**core**
torments	and	complaints	not	hears	the	my	heart

My heart will not feel torments or hear complaints;

nel	'pɛt: to	il	do 'lo ɾe	sof: 'frir	non	po 'trɔ
nel	**petto**	**il**	**dolore**	**soffrir**	**non**	**potrò.**
in the	breast	the	pain	to suffer	not	I will be able

I will not be able to suffer the pain in my breast.

'tu o	'stra le	do 'ɾa to	non	'sar ma	daf: 'fan: ni
Tuo	**strale**	**dorato**	**non**	**s'arma**	**d'affanni,**
your	arrow	golden	not	itself arms	with woes

May your golden arrow not be armed with woes;

ne 'mi ko	a	'mjɛ i	'dan: ni	non	'ɛs: ser	iŋ 'gra to
nemico	**a'**	**miei**	**danni**	**non**	**esser**	**ingrato;**
enemy	to	my	injuries	not	to be	ungrateful

do not be an ungrateful enemy at my expense:

'mi o	'tɛ ne ɾo	'sta to	sof: 'frir	non	lo	pwɔ
mio	**tenero**	**stato**	**soffrir**	**non**	**lo**	**può.**
my	tender	state	to suffer	not	it	is able

my innocence cannot bear it.

kwel	kɔr	ke	tat: 'tʃe ze	e	'lal ma	ti	'djɛ de
Quel	**cor**	**che**	**t'accese**	**e**	**l'alma**	**ti**	**diede**
that	heart	which	you set on fire	and	the soul	you	gave

That heart which set you on fire and gave you its soul

kon	'dol tʃe	mer 'tʃe de	ti	'spɛ ɾa	kor 'te ze
con	**dolce**	**mercede**	**ti**	**spera**	**cortese;**
with	sweet	reward	you	hopes	kind

hopes you will, with sweet reward, be kind;

ol 'trad: dʒi	e dof: 'fe ze	sof: 'fri ɾe	non	pwɔ
oltraggi	**ed offese**	**soffrire**	**non**	**può.**
insults	and offences	to endure	not	it is able

it cannot endure insults and offences.

dɛ	'gwar da	'mi a	'vi ta	dɛ	'sen ti	i	'mjɛ i	'prjɛ gi
Deh	**guarda**	**mia**	**vita,**	**deh**	**senti**	**i**	**miei**	**prieghi,**
ah	watch over	my	life	ah	hear	the	my	pleas

Ah, have respect for my life; ah, hear my pleas.

> *prieghi: plural of*
> *priego = (mod.) prego*
> *= preghiera*

non	'fi a	'ki o	ti	'njɛ gi	mer 'tʃe	pju	gra 'di ta
non	**fia**	**ch'io**	**ti**	**nieghi**	**mercé**	**più**	**gradita;**
not	will be	that I	you	I may deny	favors	more	pleasing

I will not deny you more pleasing favors,

> *nieghi = (mod.) negi,*
> *from "negare"*
> *fia = (mod.) sarà*

e da	pju	fjo 'ri ta	al: 'lor	ti	da 'ɾɔ
ed a	**più**	**fiorita**	**allor**	**ti**	**darò.**
and at	more	flowered	then	to you	I will give

and I will give [them] to you when I am more mature.

❧

Domenico Benigni

[44, 55]

la dʒe lo 'zi a
La gelosia
Jealousy

dʒe lo 'zi a	ke	a 'po ko a 'po ko	nel	'mi o	kɔr	ser 'pɛn do	'va i
Gelosia,	**che**	**a poco a poco**	**nel**	**mio**	**cor**	**serpendo**	**vai,**
jealousy	which	little by little	in the	my	heart	snaking	you go

> *serpendo: from "serpere" = (mod.) serpeggiare*

Jealousy, which little by little snakes into my heart,

non	en 'trar	do 'var de	il	'fɔ ko	've ro	a 'mor	non	'dʒɛ la	'ma i
non	**entrar**	**dov'arde**	**il**	**foco,**	**vero**	**amor**	**non**	**gela**	**mai.**
not	to enter	where burns	the	fire	true	love	not	freezes	ever

do not enter where the fire is burning; true love never becomes cold.

da	me	ke	'bra mi	'for se	'vwɔ i	tu	'ki o	pju	non	'a mi
Da	**me**	**che**	**brami?**	**Forse**	**vuoi**	**tu**	**ch'io**	**più**	**non**	**ami.**
from	me	what	you desire	perhaps	you want	you	that I	more	not	that I love

What do you desire from me? Perhaps you want me not to love anymore.

'fu ɾja	del: 'lal ma	'mi a	non	mi	tor men 'tar	pju	non	pju	'laʃː ʃa mi	dʒe lo 'zi a
Furia	**dell'alma**	**mia!**	**Non**	**mi**	**tormentar**	**più!**	**Non**	**più!**	**Lasciami**	**gelosia!**
fury	of the soul	mine	not	me	to torment	more	not	more	leave me	jealousy

Fury of my soul, torment me no more! No more! Leave me, jealousy!

ma	kru 'dɛl	tu	pur	pjan 'pja no	del	'mi o	kɔr	'sta i	'sulː le	'pɔr te
Ma	**crudel,**	**tu**	**pur**	**pian piano**	**del**	**mio**	**cor**	**stai**	**sulle**	**porte.**
but	cruel	you	yet	gently	of the	my	heart	you lie	at the	gates

But, cruel, you still lie gently at the gates of my heart.

'fud: dʒi	o i 'mɛ	lon 'ta no	del	'tu o	'dʒɛl	ɛ	a 'mor	pju	'for te
Fuggi,	**oimè,**	**lontano;**	**del**	**tuo**	**gel'**	**è**	**Amor**	**più**	**forte.**
flee	alas	far away	than the	your	ice	is	Love	more	strong

> *gel' = gelo in the repeat*

Flee, alas, far from me; Love is stronger than your iciness.

da	me	ke	'bra mi	go 'dɛn do	'i o	sto	de	'mjɛi	pen 'sjɛ ɾi
Da	**me**	**che**	**brami?**	**Godendo**	**io**	**sto**	**de'**	**miei**	**pensieri.**
from	me	what	you desire	enjoying	I	I am	of	my	thoughts

What do you desire from me? I am enjoying my thoughts.

	da	me	ke	'spe ɾi
var. in [44]:	**Da**	**me**	**che**	**speri?**
	from	me	what	you hope

What do you hope from me?

'fu ɾja	del: 'lal ma	'mi a	non	pju	ri 'gor	nɔ	nɔ	'laʃː ʃa mi	dʒe lo 'zi a
Furia	**dell'alma**	**mia!**	**Non**	**più**	**rigor,**	**no,**	**no!**	**Lasciami**	**gelosia!**
fury	of the soul	mine	not	more	cruelty	no	no	leave me	jealousy

Fury of my soul, no more cruelty, no, no! Leave me, jealousy!

GL: Amor

❧

[49]

mut: tʃi 'de te   'beʎ: ʎi 'ɔk: ki

M'uccidete begli occhi
You are killing me, beautiful eyes

mut: tʃi 'de te   'beʎ: ʎi   'ɔk: ki   e   pur   va 'do ɾo
M'uccidete   begli   occhi   e   pur   v'adoro.
me you kill   beautiful   eyes   and   yet   you I adore
You are killing me, beautiful eyes; and yet I adore you.

pju   la   'mɔr te   ke   la   'vi ta   mɛ   gra 'di ta
Più   la   morte   che   la   vita   m'è   gradita
more   the   death   than   the   life   to me is   welcome
Death is more welcome to me than life,

se   per   'vo i   laŋ 'gwi sko   e   'mɔ ɾo
se   per   voi   languisco   e   moro.
if   for   you   I languish   and   I die
as I languish for you and am dying.

nɔ   non   si 'tar di   ɛ   'sɔr te   se   'mɔr te   mav: 'vɛn ta   i   'swɔ i   'dar di
No,   non   si tardi.   È   sorte   se   morte   m'avventa   i   suoi   dardi.
no   not   one may delay   it is   fate   if   death   to me hurls   the   its   darts
No, let's not tarry. It is fate if death hurls its darts at me.

pu 'pil: le   'mi e   'bɛl: le   mo 'ɾir   per   'du e   'stel: le   ɛ   'dol tʃe   mar 'tɔ ɾo
Pupille   mie   belle   morir   per   due   stelle   è   dolce   martoro
eyes   mine   beautiful   to die   for   two   stars   is   sweet   torment

vol 'dʒe te mi   i   'zgwar di
volgetemi   i   sguardi.
turn to me   the   glances
O beautiful eyes mine, to die for two stars *[eyes]* is sweet torment; turn your glances to me.

[1, 2, 46]

non la vo 'le te in 'tɛn de ɾe

Non la volete intendere
You don't want to understand

non   la   vo 'le te   in 'tɛn de ɾe   o sti 'na ti   pen 'sjɛ ɾi   a   'du e   'beʎ: ʎi   'ɔk: ki   'ne ɾi
Non   la   volete   intendere,   ostinati   pensieri,   a   due   begli   occhi   neri,
not   it   you want   to understand   obstinate   thoughts   to   two   beautiful   eyes   dark

si   ke   mi 'vɔʎ: ʎo   'rɛn de ɾe
sì,   che   mi voglio   rendere.
yes   that   I want   to surrender
You don't want to understand, obstinate thoughts, that I want to surrender to two beautiful dark eyes – yes.

ɔ   kom bat: 'tu to   as: 'sa i   'i o   non   ne   'pɔs: so   pju
Ho   combattuto   assai;   io   non   ne   posso   più!
I have   fought   enough   I   not   of it   I can   more
I have fought enough; I've had enough!

a 'mo ɾe   tu   ma 'vra i   kwa 'lo ɾa   ke   'vwɔ i   tu
Amore,   tu   m'avrai,   qualora   che   vuoi   tu!
love   you   me you will have   whenever   [that]   you wish   you
Love, you will have me whenever you wish!

o 'ka ɾa ser vi 'tu   o   ka 'te na   gra 'di ta
O   cara   servitù!   O   catena   gradita!
oh   dear   servitude   oh   chain   welcome
Oh, dear servitude! Oh, welcome chain!

ki   mi   so 'stjɛ ne   in   'vi ta   mi   'prɛ mja   kon   lofː 'fɛn de ɾe
Chi   mi   sostiene   in   vita,   mi   premia   con   l'offendere.
who   me   sustains   in   life   me   rewards   with   the hurting
The one who sustains me in life rewards me by hurting.

'kweʎː ʎi   ke   al   'mon do   'tutː to   'lar te   'tutː te   in seɲː 'ɲɔ
Quegli,   che   al   mondo   tutto   l'arte   tutte   insegnò,
that one   who   to the   world   all   the arts   all   taught

> *Quegli che = Colui che*

kon   'tʃiʎː ʎo   non   aʃː 'ʃutː to   le   'pja ge   'su e   mi 'ɾɔ
con   ciglio   non   asciutto   le   piaghe   sue   mirò.
with   eyelash   not   dry   the   wounds   his   looked at
He who taught the whole world all there is to know *[Cupid]* looked at his wounds and wept.

bel 'ta   'kwan to   'ma i   pwɔ   'kwan to   ɛ   'dol tʃe   ti 'ranː na
Beltà,   quanto   mai   può,   quanto   è   dolce   tiranna!
Beauty   how much   ever   could   how much   it is   sweet   tyrant
How powerful beauty is; what a sweet tyrant it is!

i   pju   sa 'ga tʃi   iŋ 'ganː na   kwan 'dal tri   sa   ri 'prɛn de ɾe
I   più   sagaci   inganna,   quand'altri   sa   riprendere.
the   most   sagacious   it deceives   when another   it knows how   to recapture
It deceives the most sagacious, while it recaptures another.

> *altri (singular) =*
> *another, someone else*

GL: **Amore**

❧

[1, 2, 46]
from: *Il palazzo incantato [Il palazzo d'Atlante] (1642)*
character: *Fiordiligi*

Giulio Rospigliosi

se   mi   'tɔʎː ʎe   'ri a   sven 'tu ɾa
Se mi toglie ria sventura
If cruel misfortune takes from me

se   mi   'tɔʎː ʎe   'ri a   sven 'tu ɾa   ki   le   'fa tʃi   al   kɔr   mi   'de sta
Se   mi   toglie   ria   sventura,   chi   le   faci   al   cor   mi   desta,
if   from me   takes away   cruel   misfortune   he who   the   torches   in the   heart   me   arouses
If cruel misfortune takes away from me the one who arouses the fires in my heart,

> *ria (poet.) = rea*

'lal te   'mu ɾa   kan dʒe 'ɾɔ   kon   la   fo 'ɾɛ sta   'ɛ ko   'rɛ sta
l'alte   mura   cangerò   con   la   foresta,   (Eco:)   resta!
the high   walls   I will change   with   the   forest   (Echo:)   stay
I will exchange the high walls for the forest. *(Echo:)* Stay!

or   'ki o   'prɛn do   'al tro   sen 'tjɛ ro   u 'dir   'par mi   il   'swɔ no   i 'stesː so
Or   ch'io   prendo   altro   sentiero,   udir   parmi   il   suono   istesso
now   that I   I take   other   path   to hear   seems to me   the   sound   itself
Now that I am taking another path, I seem to hear the very sound

del   gwerː 'rjɛ ro   ke   nel   'se no   'i o   'pɔr to   im 'prɛsː so   'ɛ ko   'esː so
del   guerriero,   che   nel   seno   io   porto   impresso,   (Eco:)   esso!
of the   warrior   who   in the   breast   I   I carry   engraved   (Echo:)   him
of the warrior whom I carry engraved in my breast. *(Echo:)* Him!

'la spre   'pe ne   or 'ma i   kon 'so lo   at: ten 'dɛn do   i   di   se 're ni
L'aspre   pene   ormai   consolo   attendendo   i   dì   sereni,
the bitter   pains   now   I console   waiting for   the   days   serene
Now I console my bitter pains by awaiting the peaceful days

se   nel   'dwɔ lo   'fi do   a 'man te   a   me   sov: 'vjɛ ni   'ɛ ko   'vjɛ ni
se   nel   duolo,   fido   amante   a   me   sovvieni,   (Eco:)   vieni!
if   in the   sorrow   faithful   lover   to   me   you give aid   (Echo:)   come
when in my sorrow, faithful lover, you will come to aid me. (*Echo:*) Come!

GL: **Eco**

 ## Sances, Giovanni Felice (c.1600-1679)

Born in Rome, he was a boy soprano at the Collegio Germanico, and in 1614 he participated as "a virtuoso of Cardinal Montalto" *[Grove]* in an opera performance. In 1636 he became a singer in the chapel of Emperor Ferdinand III in Vienna; in 1669 he was appointed *Kapellmeister* at the imperial court there, a post he held until his death.
In addition to about a half dozen operas and as many oratorios, he composed two books of cantatas dedicated to Pio Enea degli Obizzi in 1633. In his songs, Sances used the techniques and styles which characterized early Venetian opera.

[40]

pje 'to zi al: lon ta 'na te vi
Pietosi, allontanatevi
Merciful ones, go away

pje 'to zi   al: lon ta 'na te vi   di spe 'ta ti   se 'gwi te mi
Pietosi,   allontanatevi!   Dispietati,   seguitemi!
merciful ones   distance yourselves   merciless ones   follow me
Merciful ones, go away! Merciless ones, follow me!

e   'vo i   'fu ɾje   et: tʃi 'ta te vi   el   'fjaŋ ko   oɲ: 'ɲor   fe 'ri te mi
E   voi,   furie,   eccitatevi   e'l   fianco   ognor   feritemi!
and   you   furies   rouse yourselves   and the   side   every hour   wound me
And you, furies, rouse yourselves and keep wounding me!

ki   a   per 'du to   il   'su o   'bɛ ne   va   tʃer 'kan do   le   'pe ne
Chi   ha   perduto   il   suo   bene,   va   cercando   le   pene.
one who   has   lost   the   his   dear one   goes   seeking   the   sufferings
One who has lost his beloved seeks suffering.

'sal tri   'da i   'nu mi   la   'mi a   'vi ta   im 'plɔ ɾa
S'altri   dai   numi   la   mia   vita   implora,
if another   from the   gods   the   my   life   implores
If someone else implores the gods for my life,

> *altri:* (singular) =
> *another, someone else*

'tʃen to   'vɔl te   mo 'rir   'pɔs: sa   in   un   'o ɾa
cento   volte   morir   possa   in   un   ora!
hundred   times   to die   may he be able   in   one   hour
may he die a hundred deaths in one hour!

Saracini [Saraceni], Claudio (c.1586-1630)

Born in Siena, he was one of several Claudio Saracinis born there between 1570 and 1590; one cannot be sure which he was. However, from what is documented about this composer, who was referred to as the "nobile senese" *[Grove]*, it is known that he travelled widely in his youth, and that almost his entire output was of monodies in every kind of style of the day; one hundred and thirty-three solo songs are extant. Six (or five, as no.4 is unknown) books of his monodies were printed.

Saracini was a master of declamation, bold and unusual harmonies, and expressive word-painting, showing homage particularly to Monteverdi. He was reputed as a composer only after his death, and his work has recently interested musicologists and performers.

[55]

da te 'par to
Da te parto
I am departing from you

da	te	'par to	kɔr	'mi o	'i o	'va dʊ	'a ni ma	'mi a
Da	**te**	**parto**	**cor**	**mio:**	**io**	**vado,**	**anima**	**mia,**
from	you	I depart	heart	mine	I	I go	soul	mine

I am departing from you, my heart; I go, my soul,

pe ɾe 'grin	sko noʃ: 'ʃu to	diɲ: 'ɲɔ ti	'li di	a bi 'tar	la 'ɾe ne
peregrin	**sconosciuto,**	**d'ignoti**	**lidi**	**abitar**	**l'arene.**
wanderer	unrecognized	of unknown	shores	to inhabit	the sands

an unrecognized wanderer, to inhabit the sands of unknown shores.

> *peregrin[o] =*
> *(mod.) pellegrin[o]*

'er me	kam 'paɲ: ɲe	ab: ban do 'a ti	or: 'ro ɾi	sa 'ran	'del: le	'mi e	'pe ne
Erme	**campagne,**	**abbandonati**	**orrori**	**saran**	**delle**	**mie**	**pene,**
remote	countrysides	forsaken	horrors	will be	of the	my	sufferings

de	'mjɛ i	pas: 'sa ti	ar 'do ɾi	de	'li dol	'mi o	per 'du to
de'	**miei**	**passati**	**ardori**	**de**	**l'idol**	**mio**	**perduto.**
of	my	past	ardors	of	the idol	mine	lost

Remote countrysides will be the forsaken horrors of my sufferings, of my bygone ardors for my lost idol.

'ɛk: ko	'mi ze ɾa	e	'flɛ bi le	e	do 'lɛn te
Ecco	**misera**	**e**	**flebile**	**e**	**dolente,**
here is	miserable	and	mournful	and	sorrowful

Behold, miserable and mournful and sorrowful,

del	'mi o	dwɔl	del	'mi o	ar 'dir	me 'mɔ ɾja	ar 'dɛn te
del	**mio**	**duol,**	**del**	**mio**	**ardir,**	**memoria**	**ardente.**
of the	my	pain	of the	my	boldness	memory	ardent

the ardent memory of my pain, of my boldness.

❧

[55]

'mɔ ɾi mi 'di tʃe
Mori, mi dice
"Die," she says to me

'mɔ ɾi	mi	'di tʃe	e	'men tre	kon	kwel	'gwar do	kru 'dɛl	mo 'rir	mi	'fa i
Mori,	**mi**	**dice,**	**e**	**mentre**	**con**	**quel**	**guardo**	**crudel**	**morir**	**mi**	**fai,**
die	to me	she says	and	while	with	that	glance	cruel	to die	me	you make

"Die," she says to me; and while with that cruel glance you make me die,

> *mori = (mod.) muori*

kon	kwel	'dol tʃe	par 'lar	'vi ta	mi	'da i
con	**quel**	**dolce**	**parlar**	**vita**	**mi**	**dai.**
with	that	sweet	speaking	life	to me	you give

with that sweet voice you give me life.

a	ke	'vi ta	o mi 'tʃi da	ke	mi	tjɛn	'vi vo	sol	per 'ke	man 'tʃi da
Ah,	**che**	**vita**	**omicida,**	**che**	**mi**	**tien**	**vivo**	**sol**	**perché**	**m'ancida!**
ah	what	life	murderous	that	me	keeps	alive	only	so that	me it may kill

Ah, what a murderous life, that keeps me alive only to kill me!   ┌───┐
│ *ancida: from "ancidere" = (mod.) "uccidere"* │
└───┘

'las: so	e	bɛn	'ved: dʒo	o 'ma i	'ko me	neʎ: 'ʎɔk: ki	e	'nel: la	'bok: ka	'pɔr te
Lasso,	**e**	**ben**	**veggio**	**omai**	**come**	**negl'occhi**	**e**	**nella**	**bocca**	**porte,**
woe is me	[and]	well	I see	now	how	in the eyes	and	in the	mouth	bears

┌────────────────────────────┬──┐
│ *veggio = (mod.) vedo*   │ *the "e" ending on "porte" (rather than an "a") is an*   │
│ *omai (poet.) = ormai*   │ *antiquated variant ending (as well as to rhyme with "morte")* │
└────────────────────────────┴──┘

'bɛl: la	'dɔn: na	kru 'dɛl	'vi va	la	'mɔr te
bella	**donna**	**crudel,**	**viva**	**la**	**morte.**
beautiful	woman	cruel	alive	the	death

Woe is me! Well I see now how you, beautiful cruel woman, bear living death in your eyes and on your lips.

✠ *Sartorio, Antonio* (1630-1680)

Born and died in Venice, he was an important composer of operas, esteemed especially for the variety and effect of his arias.

His name first appears in records of the production of his first opera, *Gl'amori infruttuosi di Pirro*, in 1661. He composed about a dozen operas; the best-known one, *Adelaide*, was performed in 1672 and seems to be the first Venetian opera to call for trumpets in its scoring.

In 1666 Sartorio was named *Kapellmeister* to Duke Johann Friedrich of Braunschweig-Lüneburg; he kept this post until 1675, meanwhile making visits to Venice to oversee productions of his operas. Then re-settling in Venice, in 1676 he was appointed *vice-maestro di cappella* at S. Marco, a position he held until his death. He was succeeded at S. Marco by Legrenzi.

In addition to operas, Sartorio composed sacred vocal works and a number of cantatas.

[10, 19, 54] This cantata is also listed in *Grove* among the compositions of Luigi Rossi.

o ke u 'mo ɾe stra va 'gan te
Oh, che umore stravagante
Oh, what a strange temperament

o	o	ke	u 'mo ɾe	stra va 'gan te	kɛ	ko 'lɛ i	ke	'sɛr vo	oɲ: 'ɲoɾa
Oh,	**o**	**che**	**umore**	**stravagante**	**ch'è**	**colei**	**che**	**servo**	**ognora;**
oh	oh	what	temperament	strange	which is	that woman	whom	I serve	always

Oh, oh, what a strange temperament has that woman whom I always serve: ┌──────────────────────────────┐
│ *alt.: ch'umore = che umore* │
├──────────────────────────────┤
│ *in [19]: ogni ora (lit.) = (mod.) ognora* │
└──────────────────────────────┘

or	mi	'sprɛt: tsa	'o ɾa	ma 'do ɾa	a	un	pen 'sjɛr	'sɛm pre	vo 'lan te
or	**mi**	**sprezza**	**ora**	**m'adora;**	**ha**	**un**	**pensier**	**sempre**	**volante,**
now	me	she scorns	now	me she adores	she has	a	thought	always	changeable

now she scorns me, now she adores me. Her thinking is always fickle;

o	ke	u 'mo ɾe	stra va 'gan te
oh	**che**	**umore**	**stravagante!**
oh	what	temperament	strange

oh, what a strange temperament!

un 'dʒor no mi 'dʒu ra 'ki o 'so lo ɔ il 'su o 'kɔ ɾe
Un giorno mi giura ch'io solo ho il suo core
one day to me she swears that I alone I have the her heart
One day she swears to me that I alone have her heart

e ke a 'oɲː ɲi 'al tro ar 'do ɾe et: 'tʃe de il 'mi o 'fɔ ko
e che a ogni altro ardore eccede il mio foco,
and that to every other ardor exceeds the my fire
and that my passion exceeds every other ardor,

> *foco =*
> *(mod.)*
> *fuoco*
>
> *alt. in [19]: ...ch'ogni altro ardore...*

e 'pɔ i di 'li a 'pɔ ko par 'lan do kon me mi 'di tʃe ke afː 'fe
e poi di lì a poco parlando con me, mi dice che affé
and then a little later talking with me me she says that in truth
and then a little later, talking to me, she says that in truth

> *alt.:*
> *ch'affé*

kwel di ve 'du to aŋ 'kor non a il 'su o a 'man te
quel dì veduto ancor non ha il suo amante.
that day seen yet not she has the her lover
she has not yet seen her lover that day.

o ke u 'mo ɾe stra va 'gan te
Oh, che umore stravagante...
oh what temperament strange
Oh, what a strange temperament...

in 'fat: ti ɛ bid: 'dzar: ra e se per for 'tu na iŋ 'ka po a la 'lu na
In fatti è bizzarra, e se per fortuna in capo ha la luna
in fact she is bizarre and if by chance in head she has the moon
In fact, she is bizarre; and if by chance she is in a bad mood,

> *in fatti =*
> *(mod.)*
> *infatti*
>
> *alt.: In fatt'è* | *alt.: in cap' ha*

mi 'sfi da a bat: 'taʎː ʎa
mi sfida a battaglia.
me she challenges to battle
she challenges me to battle.

ma ɛ 'fɔ ko di 'paʎː ʎa 'io 'bɛ ne lo sɔ ke du 'rar non pwɔ
Ma è foco di paglia, io bene lo so che durar non può:
but it is fire of straw I well it I know that to last not it is able
But it is a flash in the pan: I well know that it can not last,

> *in [19]: è un foco di paglia (= same translation)*

per 'ke 'vwɔ le e non vwɔl in u ni 'stan te
perché vuole e non vuol in un instante.
because she wants and not she wants in an instant
because she wants and [then] in an instant, does not want.

o ke u 'mo ɾe stra va 'gan te
Oh, che umore stravagante...
oh what temperament strange
Oh, what a strange temperament...

[57]
from: *La Flora (1681)* (an opera completed after Sartorio's death by Marco Antonio Ziani)   *Novello Bonis*

'sɛ i pur 'bɛlː lo
Sei pur bello
You are indeed handsome

'sɛ i	pur	'bɛl: lo	ma	non	'tan to	'ki o	mi	'vɔʎ: ʎa	di spe 'rar
Sei	pur	bello,	ma	non	tanto	ch'io	mi	voglia	disperar.
you are	indeed	handsome	but	not	so much	that I	myself	I may wish	to despair

You are indeed handsome, but not so much that I wish to despair.

kwel	'tu o	'vet: tso	kwel	'tu o	'bri o	son	bɛn	'va gi
Quel	tuo	vezzo,	quel	tuo	brio	son	ben	vaghi,
that	your	grace	that	your	spirit	are	well	charming

That grace and that spirit of yours are very charming,

ma	il	kɔr	'mi o	non	po 'tran: no	af: 'fe	pja 'gar
ma	il	cor	mio	non	potranno,	affé,	piagar.
but	the	heart	mine	not	they can	in truth	to wound

but they can not, in truth, wound my heart.

'sɛ i	pur	'va go	ma	non	'tan to	'ki o	ti	'dɛd: dʒa	a	'fɔr tsa	a 'mar
Sei	pur	vago,	ma	non	tanto	ch'io	ti	deggia	a	forza	amar.
you are	indeed	charming	but	not	so much	that I	you	I should	by	force	to love

You are indeed charming, but not so much that I am obliged to love you.

'kwel: le	'grat: tsje	del	'tu o	'vol to	son	vet: 'tso ze
Quelle	grazie	del	tuo	volto	son	vezzose,
those	graces	of the	your	face	are	charming

Those pleasing features of your face are charming,

ma	diʃ: 'ʃol to	non	po 'tran: no	il	kɔr	pja 'gar
ma	disciolto	non	potranno	il	cor	piagar.
but	melted	not	they can	the	heart	to wound

but they can not wound my [already] melted heart.

Savioni, Mario (between 1606 and 1608-1685)

Born and died in Rome, he was trained as a choirboy by Vincenzo Ugolini and sang his first opera role (Dorino, in Vitali's *Aretusa*) at a young age.   In 1642 he sang the role of Alceste in Luigi Rossi's first opera *Il palazzo d'Atlante*. During his long career as singer, teacher, and composer, he was director of the Sistine Chapel Choir in Rome from 1659 to 1668.

Though he never achieved the popularity of his contemporaries such as Cesti and Carissimi, Savioni was an important composer of cantatas, of which he is known to have composed almost a hundred and seventy, most of which are for solo soprano. He also composed at least one opera; no evidence of instrumental compositions has been found.

---

[80]

ki	mi	've de	al	sem	'bjan te

ki mi 've de al sem 'bjan te
Chi mi vede al sembiante
Whoever sees my face

ki	mi	've de	al	sem 'bjan te	pjan 'dʒen te	e	sko lo 'ri to	di 'ra	'ki o	'so no	a 'man te
Chi	mi	vede	al	sembiante	piangente	e	scolorito,	dirà	ch'io	sono	amante,
who	me	sees	at the	countenance	weeping	and	colorless	will say	that I	I am	lover

Whoever sees my tearful and pale face will say that I am a lover

ma	o	non	'vi sto	o	non	gra 'di to	e	non	siŋ gan: ne 'ra		po i 'ke
ma	**o**	**non**	**visto**	**o**	**non**	**gradito**	**e**	**non**	**s'ingannerà,**		**poi che**
but	either	not	seen	or	not	welcomed	and	not	will not be mistaken		since

neither noticed nor welcomed, and will not be mistaken, since

la	'mi a	zven 'tu ɾa	fa	de	'troŋ ki	pju	'du ɾa	'ɔd: dʒi
la	**mia**	**sventura**	**fa**	**de'**	**tronchi**	**più**	**dura**	**oggi**
the	my	misfortune	makes	than	tree trunks	more	hard	today

sol	per	'mi o	'dan: no	'u na	bel 'ta
sol	**per**	**mio**	**danno**	**una**	**beltà.**
only	for	my	detriment	a	beauty

today my bad luck makes a beautiful one, to my detriment, harsher than the tree trunks.

'men tre	si sa	ke	'mil: le	'vɔl te	il	di	pur	la	per 'kɔs: se
Mentre	**si sa**	**che**	**mille**	**volte**	**il**	**dì**	**pur**	**la**	**percosse,**
while	one knows	that	thousand	times	the	day	[yet]	her	struck

ko	'swɔ i	'fol go ɾi	ar 'dɛn ti	il	'tʃe ko	'di o	ma	ke	di 'tʃi o
co'	**suoi**	**folgori**	**ardenti**	**il**	**cieco**	**dio,**	**ma**	**che**	**dic' io**
with the	his	arrows	blazing	the	blind	god	but	what	say I

While it is known that the blind god *[Cupid]* has struck her a thousand times a day with his blazing arrows,
– but what am I saying? –

'sel: la	di	'bron dzo	'fos: se	pur	si li kwe fa 'ɾɛb: be	al	'fɔ ko	'mi o
s'ella	**di**	**bronzo**	**fosse**	**pur**	**si liquefarebbe**	**al**	**foco**	**mio.**
if she	of	bronze	were	certainly	would melt	at the	fire	mine

> foco =
> (mod.) *fuoco*

if she were [made] of bronze she would certainly melt from my passion.

'pjɔd: dʒa	da 'ma ɾo	'pjan to	'for mo	do 'vuŋ kwe	'pas: so	ne	dam: mol: 'lir mi	'van to
Pioggia	**d'amaro**	**pianto,**	**formo**	**dovunque**	**passo,**	**né**	**d'ammollirmi**	**vanto,**
rain	of bitter	weeping	I form	wherever	I go	nor	of to soften to me	I boast

I shed a shower of bitter tears wherever I go; but I cannot boast of inciting pity from

ko 'stɛ i	ka	un	sen	di	'lat: te	un	kɔr	di	'sas: so
costei	**ch'a**	**un**	**sen**	**di**	**latte,**	**un**	**cor**	**di**	**sasso.**
that woman	who has	a	breast	of	milk	a	heart	of	stone

that woman who has a milky-white breast [and] a heart of stone.

a	lin 'tɛn do	si	il	'mi o	'pjan to	fu	'so lo	'kwel: lo	ke
Ah'	**l'intendo**	**sì**	**il**	**mio**	**pianto**	**fu**	**solo**	**quello**	**che**
alas	it I understand	yes	the	my	weeping	was	only	that	which

Alas, I understand it, yes: my weeping was only that which,

per	'mi o	'dwɔ lo	din te ne 'rir	la	in 've tʃe	lim pe 'tri
per	**mio**	**duolo**	**d'intenerir**	**la**	**invece**	**l'impetrì.**
through	my	sorrow	of to move to pity	her	instead	her turned to stone

> impetrì: from
> "impetrare"
> (lit.) = "impietrare"

instead of moving her to pity through my sorrow, turned her to stone.

non	ɛ	ko 'zi	il	pen 'sar	ke	'si a	mar 'mɔ		e	va ni 'ta te
Non	**è**	**così,**	**il**	**pensar,**	**che**	**sia**	**marmò,**		**e**	**vanitate,**
not	it is	thus	the	thinking	that	it be	became cold as marble		and	vanity

> vanitate
> = (mod.)
> *vanità*

Let the reasoning not be that she became cold as marble, and [with] vanity;

ke	se	'fos: se	di	'mar mo	al	fin	ko 'ste i	'ko me	o	a 'man te	pen 'sa te
ché	se	fosse	di	marmo	al	fin	costei	come	o	amante	pensate,
because	if	were	of	marble	at the	end	she	how	o	lover	think you

because if in the end she were made of marble, think, o lover, how

da mo 'ro za	pje 'ta te	si ve 'dri a	pur	kwal	ke	ʃin 'til: la	in	'le i
d'amorosa	pietate	si vedria	pur	qual	che	scintilla	in	lei.
of loving	pity	one would see	yet	that	which	sparkles	in	her

one would yet see some spark of loving pity in her.

> pietate =
> (mod.) pietà
>
> vedria (from "vedere") = (mod.) vedrei

&

[80]
from: *La brevità della vita (1600)* (a Cantata)

de spje 'ga te mor 'ta li
Deh spiegate mortali
Ah, o mortals, spread

dɛ	spje 'ga te	mor 'ta li	'de i	pen 'sjɛr	'vɔ stri	il	'vo lo
Deh	spiegate	mortali,	dei	pensier	vostri	il	volo,
ah	unfurl	mortals	of the	thoughts	yours	the	flight

Ah, o mortals, spread the wings of your thoughts,

e	la	vol 'dʒe te	il	'kɔ ɾe	'del: la	'men te	su	'la li	'do ve
e	là	volgete	il	core	della	mente	su	l'ali,	dove,
and	there	turn	the	heart	of the	mind	upon	the wings	where

and turn your heart, on the wings of your mind, to there where,

'tʃin to	di	'glɔ ɾja	e	di	splen 'do ɾe	in	se 'stes: so	se 'kon do
cinto	di	gloria	e	di	splendore	in	sé stesso	secondo,
surrounded	with	glory	and	with	splendor	in	he himself	second

surrounded by glory and splendor second only to himself,

tri pli 'ka to	fjam: 'med: dʒa	il	re	del	'mon do
triplicato	fiammeggia	il	Re	del	mondo.
threefold	blazes	the	King	of the	world

the King of the world blazes in his Trinity.

&

[80]
from: *La brevità della vita (1600)* (a Cantata)

for tu 'na to ki sa
Fortunato chi sa
Fortunate is the one who knows how

for tu 'na to	ki	sa	kon	pjɛ	non	'len to	'kor: rer	le	'vi e	del	'tʃe lo
Fortunato	chi	sa	con	piè	non	lento,	correr	le	vie	del	cielo,
fortunate	who	knows how	with	foot	not	slow	to run	the	paths	of the	heaven

Fortunate is the one who knows how to speedily traverse the pathways of heaven,

'do ve	'pu ɾo	kon 'ten to	di	sem pi 'tɛr ni	ar 'do ɾi	'gɔ don	fe 'li tʃi	in: nam: mo 'ra ti	i	'kɔ ɾi
dove	puro	contento,	di	sempiterni	ardori	godon	felici	innammorati	i	cori.
where	pure	contentment	of	eternal	raptures	enjoy	happy	enamoured	the	hearts

where the happy, enamoured hearts enjoy the pure contentment of eternal raptures.

'kweʎ: ʎi e 'tɛr ni splen 'do ri   'kwel: le so 'a vi ar 'su re ke 'lal me   'oɲ: ɲi or
Quegli   eterni   splendori,   quelle   soavi   arsure   che   l'alme   ogni   or
those   eternal   splendors   those   gentle   fires   which   the souls   every   hour

si dol tʃe 'men te at: 'tʃen do no   'so no   'dʒɔ je si   'pu re
sì   dolcemente   accendono,   sono   gioie   sì   pure,
so   sweetly   inflame   are   joys   so   pure

Those eternal splendors, those gentle fires which always so sweetly inflame the souls, are joys so pure

ke si 'gɔ do no   in tʃɛl   ma   non sin 'tɛn do no
che   si godono   in   ciel   ma   non   s'intendono.
that   are enjoyed   in   heaven   but   not   are understood

that they are enjoyed in heaven but not understood [on earth].

in 'kweʎ: ʎi 'ɔr ti   tʃe 'lɛ sti kon pri ma 'vɛ ra e 'tɛr na 'spun ta no e 'tɛr ne le vi 'ɔ le
In   quegli   orti   celesti   con   primavera   eterna,   spuntano   eterne   le   viole,
in   those   gardens   celestial   with   spring   eternal   grow   eternal   the   violets

In those celestial gardens, with eternal springtime eternal bloom the violets

e i 'dʒiʎ: ʎi la 'su   kon 'fja ti   in 'fɛ sti fra ti 'mo re e pe 'riʎ: ʎi
e   i   gigli,   là su   con   fiati   infesti,   fra   timore   e   perigli,   *là su =*
and   the   lilies   up there   with   breaths   terrible   among   fear   and   perils   *(mod.)*
                                                                                                          lassù

'ma i non 'spi ra a kwi 'lo ne e   'ma i non 'vɛr na
mai   non   spira   aquilone,   e   mai   non   verna.
ever   not   blows   north wind   and   ever   not   storms

and the lilies; up there the north wind never blows, with terrible breaths, among fear and perils; and
it never storms.

o be 'a to o fe 'li tʃe glo 'rjo zo de 'zi o ki   le   spe 'ran tse 'su e ri 'po ne in 'di o
O   beato,   o   felice   glorioso   desio,   chi   le   speranze   sue   ripone   in   Dio.
oh   blessed   oh   happy   glorious   desire   he who   the   hopes   his   places   in   God

Oh [what a] blessed, oh [what a] happy, glorious desire [for] the one who puts his hopes in God.

| For whatever reasons, there is an unusually great number of mispellings, and of |
| missing accents, in the text of the following cantata as printed on the music pages. |

[80]

dʒa kon tʃe 'du to a 've a la li ber 'ta de e u 'ril: lo
Già conceduto avea la libertade Eurillo
Eurillo had already allowed freedom

dʒa kon tʃe 'du to a 've a la   li ber 'ta de e u 'ril: lo al   'su o bɛl 'gred: dʒe   *avea = aveva*
Già   conceduto   avea   la   libertade   Eurillo   al   suo   bel   gregge   *libertade =*
already   allowed   had   the   freedom   Eurillo   to the   his   fine   flock   *(mod.) libertà*

u 'mi le e dʒa   'lje to paʃ: 'ʃe a   'lɛr be   dun 'va go a 'pri le
umile   e   già   lieto   pascea   l'erbe   d'un   vago   aprile,   *pascea =*
meek   and   [already]   happy   was grazing   the grasses   of a   lovely   April   *pasceva*

Eurillo had already put his fine flock out to graze, meekly and happily, upon the grasses of a lovely April

al: 'lo ra ke da 'mo re lin 'tɛr no 'su o do 'lo re per al: le 'vjar nan 'dɔ   'ta tʃi to
allora che   d'amore   l'interno   suo   dolore   per   alleviar   n'andò   tacito,
when   of love   the inner   his   pain   for   to alleviate   went away   silent

when, to alleviate his inner pain of love, he went away silently;

e	'so lo	il	'mɛ sto	pa sto 'rɛl: lo	vi 'tʃi no	a dun	ruʃ: 'ʃɛl: lo
e	solo	il	mesto	pastorello,	vicino	ad un	ruscello
and	alone	the	sad	shepherd	near	to a	brook

and alone, near a brook, the sad shepherd

e	in	'kwe sti	a 'ma ɾi	at: 'tʃen ti	djɛ	pje 'to za	li 'tʃen tsa	a	'swɔ i	la 'men ti
e	in	questi	amari	accenti	die'	pietosa	licenza	a	suoi	lamenti.
[and]	in	these	bitter	words	gave	pitiful	leave	to	his	laments

pitifully expressed his laments in these bitter words:

'ɛʃ: ʃi	o	'fjam: ma	dal	'se no	e	in	'kwe sto	'ri o	dar 'dʒen to
Esci	o	fiamma	dal	seno	e	in	questo	rio	d'argento,
come out	o	flame	from the	breast	and	in	this	brook	of silver

"O flame, leave my breast; and in this silvery brook

rio (poet.) = ruscello

'tɛm pra	il	'mu to	'tu o	ar 'do ɾe	el	'mi o	tor 'men to
tempra	il	muto	tuo	ardore	e'l	mio	tormento.
temper	the	mute	your	ardor	and the	my	torment

temper your mute ardor and my torment.

'ɛʃ: ʃi	ma	non	sko 'pri ɾe	'ɛs: ser	'fjam: ma	da 'mo ɾe	ke	'vi ve	pri dʒo 'nje ɾa
Esci	ma	non	scoprire	esser	fiamma	d'amore,	che	vive	prigioniera
come out	but	not	to reveal	to be	flame	of love	which	lives	prisoner

'en tro	il	'mi o	'kɔ ɾe
entro	il	mio	core.
within	the	my	heart

Leave, but do not reveal [yourself] to be the flame which lives as prisoner in my heart.

'tʃɛs: sa	din tʃe ne 'ri ɾe	'fre na	'lem pjo	de 'zi o
Cessa	d'incenerire	frena	l'empio	desio,
cease	of to burn to ashes	restrain	the impious	desire

Cease burning to ashes, restrain your impious desire,

per 'ke	di	te	non	mor mo 'ras: se	il	'ri o
perché	di	te	non	mormorasse	il	rio.
so that	of	you	not	may have murmured	the	brook

so that the brook will not murmur about you.

uʃ: 'ʃi te	o	so 'spi ɾi	dal	'vɔ stro	ri 'tʃɛt: to	ma	i	'fje ɾi	mar 'ti ɾi
Uscite	o	sospiri	dal	vostro	ricetto	ma	i	fieri	martiri
come out	o	sighs	from the	your	refuge	but	the	cruel	agonies

ta 'tʃe te	del	'pɛt: to
tacete	del	petto.
be silent	of the	breast

Leave your refuge, o sighs; but be silent about the cruel agonies in my breast.

non	'di ɾe	a	kwe 'sta u ɾe	ke	man 'ti tʃi	'vo i	'se te	al	'fɔ ko	'mi o
Non	dire	a	quest'aure,	che	mantici	voi	sete	al	foco	mio,
not	to say	to	these breezes	that	bellows	you	are	to the	fire	mine

Do not tell these breezes that you are the bellows to my fire,

sete = (mod.) siete

foco = (mod.) fuoco

per 'ke	di	'vo i	non	mor mo 'ras: se	il	'ri o
perché	di	voi	non	mormorasse	il	rio.
so that	of	you	not	may have murmured	the	brook

so that the brook will not murmur about you.

a 'ma ɾi 'pjan ti   uʃ: 'ʃi te   da   kwe 'stɔk: ki   do 'lɛn ti   e   i   'du ɾi   'mjɛ i   tor 'men ti
Amari   pianti   uscite   da   quest'occhi   dolenti   e   i   duri   miei   tormenti
bitter   tears   come out   from   these eyes   mournful   and   the   harsh   my   torments

a   pje 'to zi   am: mo 'li te   ma   fer 'ma te vi   'pɔ i   sul   'vol to   'mi o
ah   pietosi   ammolite;   ma   fermatevi   poi   su'l   volto   mio
ah   merciful   mitigate   but   come to a stop   then   upon the   face   mine

Bitter tears, leave these mournful eyes, and – ah, mercifully – lessen my harsh torments;
but then stay upon my face,

per 'ke   di   'vo i   non   mor mo 'ras: se   il   'ri o
perché   di   voi   non   mormoresse   il   rio
so that   of   you   not   may have murmured   the   brook

so that the brook will not murmur about you.

ma   in fe 'li tʃe   o i 'mɛ   ke   'dis: si   dʒa   la   'fjam: ma   i 'nal to   'sa le
Ma   infelice   ohimè   che   dissi: Già   la   fiamma   in alto   sale,
but   unhappy   alas   what   I said   now   the   flame   high up   rises

dʒa   i   so 'spir   'vo lan   'ko i   'vɛn ti   dʒa   le   'la gri me   a   tor: 'rɛn ti
già   i   sospir,   volan   co' i   venti   già   le   lagrime   a   torrenti
now   the   sighs   fly   with the   winds   now   the   tears   in   torrents

'fan: no   un   'fju me   a   me   le 'ta le
fanno   un   fiume   a   me   letale.
make   a   river   to   me   lethal

But, unhappy, alas, what have I said? Now the flame is rising high, now my sighs are flying with the
winds; now my tears, in torrents, are becoming a lethal river for me.

dʒa   sko 'pɛr to   han   kwel: lar 'do ɾe   ke   mi   fe   'vi ver   si   'ljɛ to
Già   scoperto   han'   quell'ardore,   che   mi   fé   viver   sì   lieto.
now   revealed   have   that ardor   which   me   made   to live   so   happy

Now they have revealed that ardor which made me live so happily.

pju   non   vɔ   mer 'tʃe de   o   a 'mo ɾe   sel   'mi o   dwɔl   non   ɛ   se 'gre to
Più   non   vo'   mercede   o   Amore   se'l   mio   duol   non   è   segreto.
more   not   I want   pity   o   Love   if the   my   grief   not   is   secret

I no longer want pity, o Love, if my grief is not kept secret.

ri tor 'na te   o   'mi e   'pe ne   a   la tʃe 'ɾar mi   vi   pro 'met: to   sof: 'fri ɾe   pur 'ke
Ritornate   o   mie   pene   a   lacerarmi,   vi   prometto   soffrire   pur che
return   o   my   pains   to   to tear me apart   you   I promise   to suffer   provided that

Return, o my pains, to rend me; I promise you I will suffer if

'vo i   ri tor 'na te   'oɲ: ɲi   mar 'ti ɾe   ma   'vo i   fud: 'dʒi te   o   'kru de   e
voi   ritornate   ogni   martire;   ma   voi   fuggite,   o   crude,   e
you   return   every   agony   but   you   you flee   o   cruel ones   and

you return every agony; but you flee, o cruel ones, and

mi   'kwi vi   laʃ: 'ʃa te   'mu to   sker 'ni to   e   'so lo   'tut: to   in   'prɛ da al   'mi o 'dwɔ lo
mi   quivi   lasciate   muto   schernito,   e   solo,   tutto   in   preda al   mio duolo.
me   therein   you leave   mute   scorned   and   alone   all   in   prey   to the   my grief

thus you leave me, mute and scorned and alone, entirely a prey to my grief.

se   per 'sɔr te   viɲ kon 'tra te   in   kweʎ: 'ʎɔk: ki   in   'kwe i   'bɛ i   'dʒi ɾi
Se   per sorte   v'incontrate   in   quegl'occhi   in   quei   bei   giri,
if   by chance   you meet up with   in   those eyes   in   those   beautiful   rotations

per   pje 'ta   non   pa le 'za te   i   'mjɛ i   'ta tʃi ti   de 'li ɾi
per   pietà   non   palesate   i   miei   taciti   deliri.
for   pity's sake   not   you reveal   the   my   silent   raptures

If by chance you encounter those beautiful glances in those eyes, for pity's sake do not reveal my silent raptures.

am: mu 'ti te vi   o   'mi e   'pe ne   al   splen 'dor   di   kwel   bɛl   'vi zo
Ammutitevi   o   mie   pene   al   splendor   di   quel   bel   viso
become silent   o   my   pains   to the   splendor   of   that   beautiful face

Be silent, o my pains, at the splendor of that beautiful face,

ke   par 'lar   non   si kon 'vjɛ ne   'ma i   di   'pe ne   in   pa ɾa 'di zo
ché   parlar   non   si conviene   mai   di   pene   in   paradiso.
because   to speak   not   is fitting   ever   of   pains   in   paradise

as one should never speak of pain in paradise."

ko 'zi   e u 'ril: lo   kan 'tɔ   su   'kwe sta   'ver de   'spon da
Così   Eurillo   cantò   su   questa   verde   sponda
thus   Eurillo   sang   upon   this   green   shore

Thus did Eurillo sing upon this verdant shore;

e   per   pje 'ta   da 'mo ɾe   'ta kwe   'la u ɾa   e   'pjan se   'lon da
e   per   pietà   d'Amore   tacque   l'aura   e   pianse   l'onda.
and for   pity   of Love   was silent the air   and wept   the wave

and in sympathy with Love the air was silent and the wave wept.

so spi 'rɔ   e   i   so 'spir   'fu ɾo   si   ar 'dɛn ti   ke   sav: 'vi de   lin fe 'li tʃe
Sospirò,   e   i   sospir   furo   sì   ardenti,   che   s'avvide   l'infelice   *furo = furono*
He sighed   and the sighs   were   so   ardent   that he realized   the unhappy one

He sighed, and his sighs were so ardent that he realized – the unhappy one –

ka 've a   in   'se no   i   'swɔ i   tor 'men ti   'on de   'lje to   del: ler: 'ro ɾe
ch'avea   in   seno   i   suoi   tormenti,   onde   lieto   dell'errore   *avea = aveva*
that he had in   breast   the his   torments   whence   happy   of the error

that he [still] had his torments in his breast; whereupon, happy to realize his error,

al   dʒa   paʃ: 'ʃu to   ar 'men to   se ne tor 'nɔ   kon 'tɛn to
al   già   pasciuto   armento   se ne tornò   contento.
to the   now   grazed   herd   he returned   content

he returned contentedly to his now pastured herd.

GL: **Amore**

❧

[80]

'i o sɔ bɛn dir per 'ke
Io so ben dir perché
I well know why

'i o   sɔ   ben   dir   per 'ke   'maŋ kan   'du e   'stel: le   al   'tʃe lo   a 'mor   di
Io   so   ben   dir   perché   mancan   due   stelle   al   cielo;   Amor   di
I   I know   well   [to say] why   are missing two   stars   in the heaven   Love   from

'tʃin tsja	al	've lo	le	'tɔl se	e	'pɔ i	le	'po ze	in	'fron te	a	te
Cinzia	**al**	**velo**	**le**	**tolse**	**e**	**poi**	**le**	**pose**	**in**	**fronte**	**a**	**te.**
Cynthia	at the	veil	them	took away	and	then	them	placed	on	brow	to	you

printed "Cintia" = (mod.) Cinzia

I well know why two stars are missing from heaven: Love took them
from Cynthia's veil and placed them upon your brow.

	tu	non	mel	'kre di	e	'ri di	'a i	'lu tʃi	'bɛl: le
Chorus:	**Tu**	**non**	**me'l**	**credi**	**e**	**ridi.**	**Ahi**	**luci**	**belle,**
	you	not	me it	you believe	and	you laugh	alas	eyes	beautiful

You don't believe me, and you laugh. Alas, beautiful eyes,

'ko me	'stel: le	non	'se te	se	le	'sɔr ti	pjo 've te
come	**stelle**	**non**	**sete**	**se**	**le**	**sorti**	**piovete.**
like	stars	not	you are	if	the	fortunes	you rain

sete = (mod.) siete

you are not like stars [even] if fortunes pour down from you.

'vo i	'se te	de	'mjɛ i	di	le	'bru ne	e	'kja ɾe	'skɔr te
Voi	**sete**	**de'**	**miei**	**dì**	**le**	**brune**	**e**	**chiare**	**scorte.**
you	are	of	my	days	the	brown	and	clear	escorts

You are the dark, clear guides to my days.

'tut: ta	la	'sɔr te	ke	'go de	il	kɔr	'da i	'vo stri	'zgwar di	uʃ: 'ʃi
Tutta	**la**	**sorte**	**che**	**gode**	**il**	**cor**	**dai**	**vostri**	**sguardi**	**uscì.**
all	the	destiny	which	enjoys	the	heart	from the	your	glances	came out

All the good fortune that my heart enjoys came from your glances.

a	'vo i	'kwan do	mor: 'rɔ	ver: 'ra	lo	'spir to	'mi o
A	**voi**	**quando**	**morrò**	**verrà**	**lo**	**spirto**	**mio.**
to	you	when	I shall die	will come	the	spirit	mine

When I die my spirit will come to you.

pa ɾa 'di zo	na 'ti o	o	pu 'pil: le	a do 'ra te	in	'vo i	go 'drɔ
Paradiso	**natio**	**o**	**pupille**	**adorate**	**in**	**voi**	**godrò.**
paradise	native	o	eyes	adored	in	you	I will enjoy

natio = nativo

I will enjoy a homeland of paradise, o adored eyes, in you.

GL: **Amor, Cinzia**

❧

[80]

'i o	sɔ	kɔ	'pjan to	as: 'sa i
Io	**so**	**ch'ho**	**pianto**	**assai**

I know that I have wept enough

'i o	sɔ	kɔ	'pjan to	as' sa i	'fil: li	non	[ve 'drɔ]	pju
Io	**so**	**ch'ho**	**pianto**	**assai,**	**Filli**	**non**	**[vedrò]**	**più;**
I	I know	that I have	wept	enough	Filli	not	I will see	more

[80] adds "verrò" as a [missing] word; "verrò" (from "venire") makes no sense in context, but "vedrò" is a good possiblity.

I know that I have wept enough; I [will see] Filli no more;

se	'sat: tsja	'fus: si	tu	ko min tʃe 'rɛ i	a	raʃ: ʃu 'gar mi	i	'ra i
se	**sazia**	**fussi**	**tu**	**comincierei**	**a**	**rasciugarmi**	**i**	**rai.**
if	satiated	you may have been	you	I would begin	to	to dry me	the	eyes

printed "satia" = (mod.) sazia

if you were tired of me I would begin to dry my eyes.

sol	le	'la kri me	'mjɛ i	fan	pju	'tor bi do	il	'tɛ bro	a 'ma ro	il	'ma ɾe
Sol	**le**	**lacrime**	**miei**	**fan**	**più**	**torbido**	**il**	**Tebro**	**amaro**	**il**	**mare;**
only	the	tears	mine	make	more	turbid	the	Tiber	bitter	the	sea

Only my tears make the Tiber more turbid, bitter the sea;

e	da	'two i	'lu tʃi	'rje i	'kwa zi	da	un	've tro	la	ka 'dʒon	tra 'spa ɾe
e	**da**	**tuoi**	**luci**	**riei**	**quasi**	**da**	**un**	**vetro**	**la**	**cagion**	**traspare**
and	from	your	eyes	cruel	as if	from	a	glass	the	reason	shines through

and from your cruel eyes the reason shines as if through a glass

> "tui" is printed, instead of "tuoi"

di	kwe 'ston de	ka 'te na	tro 'fɛ i	de	la	bel 'ta	'so no	i	tor 'men ti
di	**quest'onde**	**catena;**	**trofei**	**de**	**la**	**beltà**	**sono**	**i**	**tormenti.**
of	these waves	chain	trophies	of	the	beauty	are	the	torments

[for this] succession of waves; the trophies of beauty are torments.

'kor: re	a	la	'tom ba	il	'pas: so	su	'lor me	de	la	'fe de
Corre	**a**	**la**	**tomba**	**il**	**passo,**	**su**	**l'orme**	**de**	**la**	**fede;**
runs	to	the	tomb	the	step	upon	the footprints	of	the	faith

My steps rush to the grave upon the footprints of faith;

'don ta	ɛ	la	mer 'tʃe de	per 'ke	tʃer 'ka i	din te ne 'ri ɾe	un	'sas: so
[d'on]ta	**è**	**la**	**mercede**	**perché**	**cercai**	**d'intenerire**	**un**	**sasso.**
of shame	is	the	reward	because	I sought	of to soften	a	stone

shame is my reward, because I sought to soften a stone.

'fil: li	dun	'sas: so	'sɛ i	ri 'spon da	nel	'tu o	'se no	'ɛ ko	pje 'to za
Filli	**d'un**	**sasso**	**sei,**	**risponda**	**nel**	**tuo**	**seno**	**eco**	**pietosa.**
Filli	of a	stone	you are	may respond	in the	your	breast	echo	merciful

Filli, you are [made] of stone; may a merciful echo respond in your breast.

ma	non	ros: 'sɔ	ko 'stɛ i	dʒa	'neʎ: ʎi	a 'mo ɾi	'swɔ i	ko 'zi	zdeɲ: 'no za
Ma	**non**	**rossò**	**costei,**	**già**	**negli**	**amori**	**suoi**	**così**	**sdegnosa;**
but	not	blushed	she	already	in the	loves	hers	so	disdainful

But she did not blush, already so disdainful toward her loves;

'far si	'liŋ gwa	a	'u na	'fjɛ ɾa	'pɔ ko	pwɔ	di man 'dar
farsi	**lingua**	**a**	**una**	**fiera**	**poco**	**può**	**dimandar**
to become	tongue	to	a	cruel woman	little	is able	to ask

> dimandar[e] = (mod.) domandar[e]

ki	'nul: la	'spɛ ɾa
chi	**nulla**	**spera.**
he who	nothing	hopes

he who hopes for nothing can ask little of a cruel woman.

GL: **Filli, Tebro**

❧

[80]
from: *La brevità della vita (1660)* (a Cantata)

u 'di te o 'vo i ke del 'mon do fal: 'la tʃe
Udite o voi che del mondo fallace
Lend an ear, o you who of the deceptive world

u 'di te	o	'vo i	ke	del	'mon do	fal: 'la tʃe	fra	'dol tʃi	'sker tsi	e	'kan ti
Udite	**o**	**voi**	**che**	**del**	**mondo**	**fallace**	**fra**	**dolci**	**scherzi**	**e**	**canti**
hear	o	you	who	of the	world	deceptive	among	sweet	jests	and	songs

ma lak: 'kɔr ti   se 'gwi te   i   'pas: si   er: 'ran ti   u 'di te
malaccorti   seguite   i   passi   erranti,   udite.
imprudently   you follow   the   steps   erring   hear

Lend an ear, o you who imprudently follow the errant ways of the deceptive world, among sweet jests and songs – lend an ear!

'brɛ ve   'dʒɔ ja   ke   'pja tʃe   ɛ   di 'lɛt: to   ke   'fud: dʒe   'om bra   men 'da tʃe
Breve   gioia   che   piace   è   diletto   che   fugge,   ombra   mendace.
brief   joy   which   pleases   is   pleasure   that   flees   shadow   false

Brief, pleasing joy is fleeting pleasure, a deceptive shadow.

non   vi   lu 'ziŋ gi   il   'se no   'fra dʒil   'pom pa   mor 'ta le   'lam po   do 'nor   ter: 're no
Non   vi   lusinghi   il   seno   fragil   pompa   mortale,   lampo   d'onor   terreno.
not   you   may lure   the   breast   fragile   pomp   mortal   flash   of honor   terrestrial

Let not worldly pomp, a flash of honor on earth, lure your frail breast.

sol   per   fud: 'dʒir   le   'nɔ stre   'dʒɔ je   an   'la le   kju 'de te   del   'pɛt: to
Sol   per   fuggir   le   nostre   gioie   han   l'ale,   chiudete   del   petto
only   for   to flee   the   our   joys   have   the wings   close   of the   breast

le   'pɔr te   al   di 'lɛt: to   ke   'va no   fal: 'la tʃe   il   'mon do   vi   da
le   porte   al   diletto,   che   vano   fallace   il   mondo   vi   da;
the   doors   to the   pleasure   which   vain   false   the   world   to you   gives

Our joys have wings only in order to flee; close the doors of your breast to the pleasures which the vain and deceptive world offers to you;

par   ke   'ri so   pro 'met: ta   e   'do na   af: 'fan: no
par   che   riso   prometta   e   dona   affanno.
it seems   that   smile   promises   and   gives   woe

it *[the vain and deceptive world]* seems to promise smiles [but] it gives woe.

kre 'de te a   ki   lo   sa
Credete a   chi   lo   sa.
believe   one who   it   knows

Believe one who knows!

non   sa   il   'mon do   al: let: 'tar   ke non   iŋ 'gan: ni   in   sem 'bjan te   dʒɔ 'kon do
Non   sa   il   mondo   allettar   che non   inganni   in   sembiante   giocondo,
not   knows how   the   world   to tempt   only [not]   may deceive   in   semblance   merry

The world only knows how to tempt by deceiving, with the semblance of merriment,

kon   'dol tʃi   'a u re   se 're ne   'kwan do   lu 'ziŋ ga   e   'ri de   'kwe sto   'mo stro
con   dolci   aure   serene,   quando   lusinga   e   ride   questo   mostro
with   sweet   airs   serene   when   entices   and   laughs   this   monster

with sweet, serene airs; when this monster entices and laughs,

se 'kon do di   tor 'men ti   e   di   'pe ne   'fjɛ ɾo   'sɛr pe   tra   fjor
secondo di   tormenti   e   di   pene,   fiero   serpe   tra   fior
depending on   torments   and   on   pains   cruel   snake   among   flowers

> *serpe (lit.)*
> = *serpente*

it produces torment and pain: a cruel snake among the flowers

'la ni me   an 'tʃi de   se   sker 'tsan do   sen va
l'anime   ancide   se   scherzando   sen va.
the souls   kills   as   lightheartedly   goes away

kills the souls as it goes lightheartedly on its way.

kre 'de te a   ki   lo   sa
Credete a   chi   lo   sa.
believe   one who   it   knows

Believe one who knows!

al: 'lor   'tɛs: se   'su e   'frɔ di   'ɔ pra   'swɔ i   'dan: ni
Allor   tesse   sue   frodi,   opra   suoi   danni.
then   weaves   its   deceptions   works   its   damages
Then it weaves its deceptions, works its damage.

> opra: from "oprare"
> (poet.) = (mod.) "operare"

non   sa   il   'mon do   al: let: 'tar   ke non   iŋ 'gan: ni
Non   sa   il   mondo   allettar   che non   inganni.
not   knows how   the   world   to tempt   only [not]   may deceive
The world only knows how to tempt by deceiving.

[80]

'vɔ stro   'so no   o   'mjɛ i   tor 'men ti
Vostro sono, o miei tormenti
I am yours, o my torments

'vɔ stro   'so no   o   'mjɛ i   tor 'men ti   non   'fi a   'ma i   'ki o   vab: ban 'do ni
Vostro   sono,   o   miei   tormenti,   non   fia   mai   ch'io   v'abbandoni;
yours   I am   o   my   torments   not   will be   ever   that I   you I may abandon
I am yours, o my torments; I will never abandon you;

> fia =
> (mod.) sarà

a dun   'rɛ o   non   si per 'do ni   ke   tra 'diʃ: ʃe   i   'swɔ i   kon 'tɛn ti
ad un   reo   non   si perdoni   che   tradisce   i   suoi   contenti.
to a   guilty one   not   one may forgive   that   betrays   the   his   contentments
may a guilty one, who betrays his contentments, not be forgiven.

'kru di   'fa ti   non   dor 'mi te   nɔ   non   dor 'mi te
Crudi   fati   non   dormite,   no,   non   dormite.
cruel   fates   not   sleep you   no   not   sleep you
Cruel fates, do not sleep – no, do not sleep.

su   'tut: ti   a   le   ve 'det: te   le   sa 'et: te   'si an   mor 'ta li   e din fi 'ni te
Su,   tutti   a   le   vedette,   le   saette   sian   mortali   ed infinite.
up   everyone   to   the   lookouts   the   arrows   may be   mortal   and infinite
Come on, everyone, to the lookout; the arrows may be deadly and of infinite number.

'mi e   fe 'ɾi te   non   sa 'ran   'ko me   vɔʎ: 'ʎi o
Mie   ferite   non   saran   come   vogl'io
my   wounds   not   will be   as   wish I
My wounds will not be as I wish,

> saran = saranno

per 'ke   'fɔl: le   il   de 'zir   'mi o   prɛ 'stɔ   'fe de   aŋ 'ko ɾa   a   i   'vɛn ti
perché   folle   il   desir   mio   prestò   fede   ancora   a   i   venti.
because   foolish   the   desire   mine   lent   faith   again   to   the   winds
because my foolish desire again lent its trust to the winds.

✤ *Scarlatti, Alessandro* (1660-1725)

Alessandro Scarlatti was born in Palermo and died in Naples. Father of the celebrated composer of keyboard music Domenico Scarlatti, he was indisputably the most important opera composer of his generation and, indeed, one of the great masters of western music.

At the age of twelve he was sent to Rome, where nothing is known about his musical education; it is conjectured that he studied with Carissimi.

In Rome he became *maestro di cappella* at the court of Queen Cristina of Sweden, patroness of the arts, who had abdicated her Swedish throne in 1654.   He also received patronage from Cardinal Benedetto Pamphili, many of whose texts Scarlatti set to music, and Pietro Ottoboni, also a librettist and named a Cardinal in 1689.

Sometime before 1684 Scarlatti moved to Naples, where he became *maestro di cappella* to the royalty, succeeding Pietro Ziani. His years in Naples were rich in terms of composition as well as in the number of productions of his operas at the Teatro S. Bartolomeo, private theaters, and in other cities.

In 1702 he spent a year in Florence under the patronage of Ferdinando III, but he was not offered a permanent post there.   Returning to Rome, he became assistant *maesto di cappella* at S. Maria Maggiore. In 1708 or 1709 he returned to his former postion in Naples. In 1716, upon the recommendation of Ottoboni, he was knighted as a "Cavaliere" by Pope Clemens XI. From 1718 to 1721 or 1722 he was again in Rome, and in 1722 he returned once more to Naples.

Scarlatti's output was enormous; he composed at least one hundred and fifteen operas, more than a hundred oratorios, and at least six hundred cantatas for solo voice and continuo, as well as a (comparatively) small amount of instrumental music.

---

[97]

a bat: 'taʎ: ʎa pen 'sjɛ ɾi
A battaglia, pensieri
To battle, thoughts

a	bat: 'taʎ: ʎa	pen 'sjɛ ɾi	a	bat: 'taʎ: ʎa	'voʎ: ʎo	'gwɛr: ra	kol	'nu me	da 'mor
A	**battaglia,**	**pensieri**	**a**	**battaglia,**	**voglio**	**guerra**	**col**	**nume**	**d'amor.**
to	battle	thoughts	to	battle	I want	war	with the	god	of love

To battle – thoughts, to battle! I want war with the god of love.

su	fe 'ro tʃi	kwel	'em pjo	at: ter: 'ran te	ven di 'ka te	lof: 'fe ze	del	kɔr
Su,	**feroci,**	**quel**	**empio**	**atterrante**	**vendicate**	**l'offese**	**del**	**cor.**
come on	ferocious	that	pitiless	fearsome	take revenge on	the offences	of the	heart

Come, be ferocious: take revenge for the offences of my heart on that pitiless, fearsome one.

❧

[81]

a ki 'sɛm pre a da pe 'nar
A chi sempre ha da penar
For one who always has to suffer

a	ki	'sɛm pre	a da pe 'nar	ɛ	zven 'tu ɾa
A	**chi**	**sempre**	**ha da penar**	**è**	**sventura**
to	one who	always	has to suffer	it is	misfortune

For one who always has to suffer it is misfortune,

e	non	kon 'fɔr to	il	dar	'lɔ ko	'al: lo	spe 'ɾar
e	**non**	**conforto**	**il**	**dar**	**loco**	**allo**	**sperar,**
and	not	comfort	the	giving	place	to the	hoping

and not comfort, to allow room for hope,

'ko me	a 'punto	in	'mɛd: dzo	al	'ma ɾe	ad: di 'ta ɾe	a	un	'leɲ: ɲo
come	**a punto**	**in**	**mezzo**	**al**	**mare**	**additare**	**a**	**un**	**legno**
like	precisely	in	middle	in the	sea	to point	to	a	ship

just like, in the middle of the sea, pointing a ship

il	'pɔr to	e	'pɔ i	'far lo	'na u fra 'gar
il	**porto**	**e**	**poi**	**farlo**	**naufragar.**
the	port	and	then	to make it	to be shipwrecked

to a harbor and then causing it to sink.

si   per 'ki o   non   'pɔs: so   kan 'dʒar   la   'spɔʎː ʎa   'fra le
Sì,   perch'io   non   posso   cangiar   la   spoglia   frale
yes   because I   not   I am able   to change   the   spoils   corporal
Yes, because I cannot change my human nature,

'vo i   kon   'lu tʃi   di   'frɔ di   e   'kja ɾi   iŋ 'gan: ni
voi   con   luci   di   frodi   e   chiari   inganni
you   with   eyes   of   frauds   and   clear   deceptions

per   me   vi ma ske 'ɾa te   al 'tri   ti 'ɾan: ni
per   me   vi mascherate   altri   tiranni.
for   me   you mask   other   tyrannies
you, with fraudulent eyes and clear deceptions, mask for me other acts of tyranny.

࢙

[57]
from: *La caduta dei Decemviri (1697)*
character: *Valeria*   *Silvio Stampiglia*

a dʒi 'ta to   il   kɔr   mi 'sɛn to
Agitato il cor mi sento
I feel my heart shaken

a dʒi 'ta to   il   kɔr   mi 'sɛn to   'dal: lo   'zdeɲ: ɲo   e   dal: la 'mor
Agitato   il   cor   mi sento   dallo   sdegno   e   dall'amor.
agitated   the   heart   I feel   with the   anger   and   with the love
I feel my heart shaken with anger and with love.

ab: bor: 'ri sko   il   tra di 'men to   e   so 'spi ɾo   il   tra di 'tor
Abborrisco   il   tradimento   e   sospiro   il   traditor.
I abhor   the   treason   and   I long for   the   traitor
I loathe the treason and I long for the traitor.

> *abborrisco: from (mod.) "aborrire"*

࢙

[5, 9, 42]
from: *Tigrane (1715)*   *Domenico Lalli*

al: lak: 'kwi sto   di   'glɔ ɾja
All'acquisto di gloria
To glory and fame

al: lak' 'kwi sto   di   'glɔ ɾja   e   di   'fa ma   tra   'bel: li ke   'skje ɾe
All'acquisto   di   gloria   e   di   fama   tra   belliche   schiere
to the acquisition   of   glory   and   of   fame   among   warring   troops

di   'trom be   gwer: 'rje ɾe   mi   'kja ma   il   fra 'gor
di   trombe   guerriere   mi   chiama   il   fragor.
of   trumpets   warlike   me   calls   the   roar
The resounding of martial trumpets calls me to glory and fame amidst warring troops.

ma   por 'tan do   del   'ka ɾo   'mi o   'bɛ ne   'fis: se   al: 'lal ma
Ma   portando   del   caro   mio   bene   fisse   all'alma
but   carrying   of the   dear   my   dear one   fixed   in the soul
But bearing, fixed in my soul,

> *fisse (lit.): from "figgere"*

le	'gra vi	sven 'tu ɾe	a 'vrɔ	'sɛm pre	'du ɾe	le	'pe ne	nel	kɔr
le	**gravi**	**sventure**	**avrò**	**sempre**	**dure**	**le**	**pene**	**nel**	**cor.**
the	grave	misfortunes	I shall have	always	harsh	the	pains	in the	heart

the grave misfortunes of my beloved one, I shall always have deep pain in my heart.

[34]
from: *Pompeo (1683)*
character: *Claudio*

Nicolò Minato

a 'mor pre 'pa ɾa mi
Amor, preparami
Love, prepare for me

a 'mor	pre 'pa ɾa mi	'al tre	ka 'te ne	ov: 've ɾo	'laʃ: ʃa mi	in	li ber 'ta
Amor,	**preparami**	**altre**	**catene,**	**ovvero**	**lasciami**	**in**	**libertà.**
Love	prepare for me	other	chains	or else	leave me	in	freedom

Love, prepare some other chains for me, or else leave me in freedom.

'i o	vɔ	tʃer 'tis: si mo	kwel	'nɔ do	'fran dʒe ɾe	kin	'lat: tʃo	a 'spris: si mo
Io	**vo'**	**certissimo**	**quel**	**nodo**	**frangere**	**ch'in**	**laccio**	**asprissimo**
I	I want	most certainly	that	knot	to break	which in	tie	most cruel

'stret: to	mi	'tjɛ ne	'sɛn tsa	pje 'ta
stretto	**mi**	**tiene**	**senza**	**pietà.**
tight	me	holds	without	pity

I most certainly want to undo that knot which pitilessly holds me tightly in cruelest ties.

GL: **Amor**

[53]

'ar ma ti
Armati
Arm yourself

'ar ma ti	'mi a	ko 'stan tsa	'se gwi	la	'mi a	spe 'ran tsa	'i o	'vɛŋ go	'te ko	spe 'ran tsa
Armati,	**mia**	**costanza,**	**segui**	**la**	**mia**	**speranza:**	**io**	**vengo**	**teco,**	**speranza.**
arm yourself	my	constancy	follow	the	my	hope	I	I come	you with	hope

Arm yourself, my faith; follow my hope. I am coming with you, hope.

e	tu	ben 'da to	a 'mor	non	'ɛs: ser	'mu to	aŋ 'kor	dʒak: 'ke	'sɛ i	'tʃɛ ko
E	**tu,**	**bendato**	**amor,**	**non**	**esser**	**muto**	**ancor**	**giacché**	**sei**	**cieco.**
and	you	blinfolded	love	not	to be	silent	even	as	you are	blind

And you, blindfolded love *[Cupid]*, be not silent as well as blind.

[18, 39]

bel: 'let: tsa ke 'sa ma
Bellezza, che s'ama
Beauty, when loved

bel: 'let: tsa	ke	'sa ma	ɛ	'dʒɔ ja	del	'kɔ ɾe
Bellezza,	**che**	**s'ama**	**è**	**gioia**	**del**	**core;**
beauty	which	one loves	is	joy	of the	heart

Beauty, when loved, is the heart's joy;

fe 'li tʃe   si 'kja ma   ki   ɛ   'ljɛ to   in   a 'mo ɾe
felice   si chiama,   chi   è   lieto   in   amore.
fortunate   is called   the one who is   happy   in   love
fortunate is the one who is happy in love.

ɛ   'som: mo   pja 'tʃe ɾe   a 'mar   ri a 'ma to
È   sommo   piacere   amar   riamato;
it is   greatest   pleasure   to love   loved in return
It is the greatest pleasure to love [and be] loved in return;

ɛ   'fɔl: le   ki   'bra ma   kon 'tɛn to   mad: 'dʒo ɾe
è   folle,   chi   brama   contento   maggiore.
is   foolish   one who   desires   happiness   greater
anyone who wishes for greater happiness is foolish.

[1, 2, 17, 46]
from: *Il Sedecia, re di Gerusalemme* (an Oratorio)
character: *Ismael*

'kal do   'saŋ gwe
Caldo sangue
Warm blood

'kal do   'saŋ gwe   ke   baɲ: 'ɲan do   il   sen   mi   'va i
Caldo   sangue,   che   bagnando   il   sen   mi   vai
warm   blood   which   bathing   the   breast to me you go
Warm blood which bathes my breast

e   da 'mo ɾe   'fa i   gran   'fe de   al   ge ni 'to ɾe
e   d'amore   fai   gran   fede   al   genitore,
and of love   you make   great   proof   to the   father
and manifests great proof of love for my father,

'fud: dʒi   pur   'fud: dʒi   da   me   'ki o   dja   'mo ɾo   e   'ɾɛ sto   e 'zaŋ gwe
fuggi   pur,   fuggi   da   me,   ch'io   già   moro   e   resto   esangue!
run away   please run away   from   me   because I   already   I die   and   I remain bloodless
run – run from me, please, for I am already dying and bloodless!

'for se   un   di   ri sor dʒe 'ra i   per   ven 'det: ta   'del: la   man   ke   mi   sa 'et: ta
Forse   un   dì   risorgerai   per   vendetta   della   man,   che   mi   saetta;
perhaps   one   day   you will rise again for   revenge   of the   hand   which   me   wounds
Perhaps one day you will rise again, to take revenge on the hand that wounds me;

e   il   vi 'gor   ke   in   me   dʒa   'maŋ ka
e   il   vigor,   che   in   me   già   manca,
and the   strength   which   in   me   now   fails
and the strength which is now failing in me,

'kal do   'saŋ gwe   pas: se 'ra   pju   'sal do   in   te
caldo   sangue,   passerà   più   saldo   in   te.
warm   blood   will pass   more   solid   into you
warm blood, will pass stronger into you.

[18, 39]

'ka ɾa e 'dol tʃe
Cara e dolce
Dear and sweet

'ka ɾa	e	'dol tʃe	dol 'tʃis:	si ma	li ber 'ta	'kwan to	ti	'pjan dʒe	il	'kɔ ɾe
Cara	**e**	**dolce,**	**dolcissima**		**libertà,**	**quanto**	**ti**	**piange**	**il**	**core,**
dear	and	sweet	sweetest		liberty	how much	for you	weeps	the	heart

Dear and sweet, sweetest freedom, how much my heart weeps for you;

fra	i	'lat: tʃi	dun	krin	'dɔ ɾo
fra	**i**	**lacci**	**d'un**	**crin**	**d'oro**
among	the	ties	of a	head of hair	of gold

among the ties of golden tresses

'prɔ va	dun	'tʃiʎ: ʎo	ar 'tʃɛr	la	kru del 'ta
prova	**d'un**	**ciglio**	**arcier**	**la**	**crudeltà.**
feels	from a	brow	archer	the	cruelty

it feels the cruelty of an arrow-hurling *[Cupid's]* brow.

le	'du ɾe	ri 'tɔr te	ke	'ri dʒi da	'sɔr te	mi	da	per	mer 'tʃe
Le	**dure**	**ritorte,**	**che**	**rigida**	**sorte**	**mi**	**dà**	**per**	**mercé**
the	harsh	fetters	which	rigid	fate	to me	gives	for	recompense

The harsh fetters which stern fate gives me as reward

mi	'striŋ go no	il	pje	e	al	'mi o	'luŋ go	pe 'nar	'ne ga no	pje 'ta
mi	**stringono**	**il**	**piè**	**e**	**al**	**mio**	**lungo**	**penar**	**negan**	**pietà.**
to me	tighten	the	foot	and	at the	my	long	suffering	deny	pity

impede my way and deny pity for my long suffering.

☙

[1, 2, 18, 22, 25, 46]

ki 'vwɔ le in: na mo 'rar si
Chi vuole innamorarsi
Whoever wants to fall in love

ki	'vwɔ le	in: na mo 'rar si	tʃi	'de ve	bɛn	pen 'sar
Chi	**vuole**	**innamorarsi,**	**ci**	**deve**	**ben**	**pensar!**
who	wants	to fall in love	of it	ought	well	to think

Whoever wants to fall in love should think about it carefully!

> var.:
> *dee = deve*

a 'mo ɾe	ɛ	un	'tʃer to	'fɔ ko	ke	se	sat: 'tʃen de	un	'pɔ ko	e 'ter no	swɔl	du 'rar
Amore	**è**	**un**	**certo**	**foco,**	**che,**	**se**	**s'accende**	**un**	**poco,**	**eterno**	**suol**	**durar.**
love	is	a	certain	fire	which	if	catches fire	a	little	eternal	is used to	enduring

Love is a certain passion which, if it catches fire briefly, usually lasts forever.

non	ɛ	'ljɛ ve	tor 'men to	a 'ver	pja 'ga to	il	kɔr
Non	**è**	**lieve**	**tormento,**	**aver**	**piagato**	**il**	**cor!**
not	is	light	torment	to have	wounded	the	heart

It is no little torment to have a wounded heart!

sod: 'dʒet: ta	'oɲ: ɲi	vo 'le ɾe	a	'du e	pu 'pil: le	ar 'tʃɛ ɾe	ki	'ser ve	al	'di o	da 'mor
Soggetta	**ogni**	**volere**	**a**	**due**	**pupille**	**arciere,**	**chi**	**serve**	**al**	**dio**	**d'amor.**
subjects	every	wish	to	two	eyes	archer	he who	serves	to the	god	of love

Whoever serves the god of love *[Cupid]* subjects every wish to his archer eyes.

☙

[85]

'klɔ ɾi vet: 'tso za e 'bɛl: la
Clori vezzosa, e bella
Charming and beautiful Clori

'klɔ ɾi	vet: 'tso za	e	'bɛl: la	di	'kwe sta 'man te	'pɛt: to	'so lo	a 'mor	'so la	'dʒɔ ja
Clori	**vezzosa,**	**e**	**bella,**	**di**	**quest'amante**	**petto**	**solo**	**amor**	**sola**	**gioia,**
Clori	charming	and	beautiful	of	this loving	breast	only	love	only	joy

Charming and beautiful Clori, of this loving heart the only love, the only joy,

> Printed is "di questa amante petto"; I'm guessing that the correct original text was "di quest'amante petto,"
> as "questa" needs to agree in (masculine) case with "petto" – i.e., to be either "questo" or "quest'."

e	sol	di 'lɛt: to	per	te	kwe 'stal ma	an 'tʃɛl: la	si 're ze	al	'nu me	in 'fan te
e	**sol**	**diletto,**	**per**	**te**	**quest'alma**	**ancella**	**si rese**	**al**	**nume**	**infante,**
and	only	delight	for	you	this soul	servant	yielded itself	to the	deity	infant

and the only delight, for you this subservient soul yielded to the child god *[Cupid]*,

'sem pre	nel	'su o	de 'zi o	'fer ma	e	ko 'stan te	per	te	'vi vo	pe 'nan do
sempre	**nel**	**suo**	**desio**	**ferma**	**e**	**costante;**	**per**	**te**	**vivo**	**penando**
always	in the	its	desire	firm	and	constant	for	you	I live	suffering

ever firm and constant in its desire. For you I live, suffering

in	'fjɛ ɾi	ar 'do ɾi	'mi a	bel: 'lis: si ma	'klɔ ɾi	e	se	nol	'kre di
in	**fieri**	**ardori**	**mia**	**bellissima**	**Clori,**	**e**	**se**	**nol**	**credi?**
in	cruel	passions	my	most beautiful	Clori	[and	if]	not it	you believe

> *nol =*
> *non + il*

cruel passions, my most beautiful Clori; do you not believe it?

'vɔl dʒi	lo	'zgwar do	e	've di	'pal: li do	e	sko lo 'ri to	il	'mi o	sem 'bjan te
Volgi	**lo**	**sguardo,**	**e**	**vedi**	**pallido,**	**e**	**scolorito**	**il**	**mio**	**sembiante.**
turn	the	glance	and	see	pale	and	colorless	the	my	countenance

Turn your glance [to me] and see my pale and colorless face.

'so no	i	pal: 'lo ɾi	'mjɛ i	'tʃe ne ɾi	di	kwel	'fɔ ko
Sono	**i**	**pallori**	**miei**	**ceneri**	**di**	**quel**	**foco**
are	the	pallors	mine	ashes	of	that	fire

My pallor is the ash of that fire

ke	'strud: dʒe	a 'pɔ ko a 'pɔ ko	il	'kɔ ɾe	a 'man te
che	**strugge,**	**a poco a poco,**	**il**	**core**	**amante.**
which	consumes	little by little	the	heart	loving

which, little by little, consumes my loving heart.

'vi vo	pe 'nan do	ɛ	ver	ma	son	kon 'tɛn to	del: li 'stes: so	tor 'men to	per 'ke	se	'pɛn so
Vivo	**penando,**	**è**	**ver;**	**ma**	**son**	**contento**	**dell'istesso**	**tormento,**	**perché**	**se**	**penso**
I live	suffering	it is true	but	I am	content	with the same	torment	because	if	I think

I live in suffering, it is true; but I am content with that very torment because, when I think

ke	tu	'so la	'sɛ i	ka 'dʒon	di	'tan ti e 'tan ti	af: 'fan: ni	'mjɛ i
che	**tu**	**sola**	**sei**	**cagion**	**di**	**tanti e tanti**	**affanni**	**miei,**
that	you	alone	are	cause	of	so many	anxieties	mine

that you alone are the cause of my many troubles,

di 'vɛn ta	'mi o	dʒo 'i ɾe	la	'pe na	e dil	mar 'ti ɾe
diventa	**mio**	**gioire,**	**la**	**pena**	**ed il**	**martire,**
becomes	my	delight	the	pain	and the	agony

> *martire = (mod.) martirio*

the pain and agony become my pleasure

e	pju	pe 'nar	vor: 're i	per		pa le 'zar ti	pju	ʎaf: 'fɛt: ti	'mjɛ i
e	**più**	**penar**	**vorrei**	**per**		**palesarti**	**più**	**gl'affetti**	**miei.**
and	more	to suffer	I would like	in order to		to reveal	more	the affections	mine

and I would like to suffer more in order to show my affections more.

si	bɛn	'mi o	aŋ kor	vor: 're i	per	te	pju	'pe ne	al	'kɔ ɾe
Sì,	**ben**	**mio,**	**ancor**	**vorrei**	**per**	**te**	**più**	**pene**	**al**	**core.**
yes	dear one	mine	even	I should like	for	you	more	pains	to the	heart

Yes, my beloved, I should like, for you, [to have] even more pain in my heart.

pje 'to za	al	'mi o	do 'lo ɾe	'for se	di 're sti	un	di
Pietosa	**al**	**mio**	**dolore**	**forse**	**diresti**	**un**	**dì:**
merciful	to the	my	sorrow	perhaps	you would say	one	day

Compassionate to my sorrow, perhaps one day you would say:

ki	'vi de	mad: 'dʒor	fe	pju	'fi do	a 'mo ɾe
"chi	**vide**	**maggior**	**fé,**	**più**	**fido**	**amore?"**
who	saw	greater	fidelity	more	devoted	love

"Whoever saw greater fidelity, more devoted love?"

𝒢ℒ: **Clori**

ઈ

[86]

kon 'vo tʃe fe 'sti va
Con voce festiva
With festive voice

kon	'vo tʃe	fe 'sti va	in	'mu zi tʃi	'mɔ di
Con	**voce**	**festiva**	**in**	**musici**	**modi,**
with	voice	festive	in	musical	modes

With festive voice in musical modes

> *musici: form of "musico"(lit.) = musicale*

le 'zal ti	lo	'lɔ di	del	'tɛ bro	la	'ri va
l'esalti,	**lo**	**lodi,**	**del**	**Tebro**	**la**	**riva.**
him may exalt	him	may praise	of the	Tiber	the	bank

may the shores of the Tiber exalt him [and] praise him.

e	'lon da	dʒo 'kon da	kon	'ɛ ko	da 'mo ɾe	ri 'spon da	la	'trom ba
E	**l'onda**	**gioconda**	**con**	**eco**	**d'amore**	**risponda**	**la**	**tromba.**
and	the wave	merry	with	echo	of love	may respond to	the	trumpet

And may the merry wave[s] respond to the trumpet with an echo of love.

> *I'm guessing, in order to make grammatical and contextual sense, that the original was "alla tromba" (or "rispond'alla tromba"), and have translated this line as such.*

dʒo 'i ska	il	'mi o	'kɔ ɾe
Gioisca	**il**	**mio**	**core.**
may rejoice	the	my	heart

May my heart rejoice.

𝒢ℒ: **Tebro**

ઈ

[39]

di 'fe za non a
Difesa non ha
[The heart] has no defense

di 'fe za   non   a   da   un   'gwar do   vet: 'tso zo
Difesa   non   ha   da   un   guardo   vezzoso
defense   not   has   from   a   glance   charming

> guardo (poet.) =
> sguardo

  kwel   kɔr   kɛ   a mo 'ro zo   di   'va ga   bel 'ta
  quel   cor   ch'è   amoroso   di   vaga   beltà.
  that   heart   which is   amorous   of   graceful   beauty

The heart which loves graceful beauty has no defense from a charming glance.

dun   're dʒe   se   il   'kɔ ɾe   'ku pi do   fe 'ɾi
D'un   rege   se   il   core   Cupido   ferì,
of a   king   if   the   heart   Cupid   wounded

If Cupid has wounded the heart of a king,

  so 'dʒɛt: to   ɛ   ben   si   lin: na mo 'ra to   sen   e   'pjan dʒe   'sɛm pre   'sɛm pre
  soggetto   è   ben   sì   l'innamorato   sen   e   piange   sempre   sempre,
  subjected   is   well   thus   the enamored   breast; (fig.) heart   and   weeps   always   always

  his enamored heart is therefore subjected; and always, always he weeps;

  ke   a   'fran dʒer   le   'tɛm pre   di   'ri dʒi do   'fa to
  ché   a   franger   le   tempre   di   rigido   fato,
  because   to   to break   the   hardnesses   of   rigid   fate

  non   'trɔ va   la gri 'man do   al   dwɔl   pje 'ta
  non   trova   lagrimando   al   duol   pietà.
  not   finds   weeping   at the   sorrow   pity

for, [unable] to crush the harshness of rigid fate, he finds no pity for his sorrow in his weeping.

☘

[83]

       e li 'trɔ pjo   da 'mor
       Elitropio d'amor
       Heliotrope of love

e li 'trɔ pjo   da 'mor   'sɛm pre   mad: 'dʒi ɾo   a   va ged: 'dʒar ti   o   'mi o   bɛl
Elitropio   d'amor   sempre   m'aggiro   a   vagheggiarti   o   mio   bel
heliotrope   of love   always   I turn   to   to admire you   o   my   beautiful

> elitropio =
> (mod.)
> eliotropio

Heliotrope of love, I turn always to admire you, o my beautiful

> eliotropio = (lit.) sunflower

> heliotrope [English]: a plant which turns or grows toward the light (such as the sun)

  'so le   al 'tɛ ro   tu   'kwan to   'va go   pju   'tan to   se 'vɛ ro
  sole   altero;   tu   quanto   vago   più   tanto   severo
  sun   proud   you   how much   charming   more   so much   severe

  mi   'rɛn di   per   a 'mor   'dɔʎ: ʎa   e   mar 'ti ɾo
  mi   rendi   per   amor   doglia   e   martiro.
  for me   you make   through   love   suffering   and   agony

> doglia (lit.) = dolore
> martiro = (mod.) martirio

proud sun; because of my love [for you] you cause me suffering and agony, however charming you are [and nonetheless] more severe.

  'bɛl: le   'kjɔ me   i na nel: 'la te   'mɔl: li   'gwan tʃe   im por po 'ra te
  Belle   chiome   inanellate   molli   guancie   imporporate,
  beautiful   hair   curled   soft   cheeks   made crimson

Beautiful curly tresses, soft crimson cheeks,

'i o   vi   'vɔʎː ʎo   i do la 'trar
io   vi   voglio   idolatrar.
I   you   I want   to idolize
I want to idolize you.

kolː lar 'mar vi   di ri 'go ɾe   di fje 'retː tsa   e   di fu 'ro ɾe
Coll'armarvi   di   rigore   di   fierezza   e   di   furore
with the arming yourself   of   severity   of   pride   and   of   fury
The more you arm yourself with severity, pride, and fury,

asː 'sa i   pju   vi   'fa te   a 'mar
assai   più   vi   fate   amar.
much   more   you   you make   to love
the more you make yourself loved.

bɛlː 'li dol   'mi o   da 'mo ɾe   non   'ɛsː ser   si   ri 'tro zo
Bell'idol   mio   d'Amore   non   esser   sì   ritroso;
beautiful idol   mine   of Love   not   to be   so   devious
My beautiful idol of Love, do not be so coy;

non ti   mo 'strar   zdeɲː 'ɲo zo   kon   kɪ   tofː 'fɛr se   in   o lo 'ka u sto   il   'kɔ ɾe
non   ti   mostrar   sdegnoso   con   chi   t'offerse   in   olocausto   il   core.
not   yourself   to show   scornful   with   he who   you offered   in   sacrifice   the   heart
do not be scornful of the one who offered you his heart in sacrifice.

'ka ɾe   'fi la   in   'ku i   da 'mo ɾe   son   tʃi 'fra te   le   ka 'te ne   'sɛm pre 'ma i
Care   fila   in   cui   d'Amore   son   cifrate   le   catene   sempre mai
dear   threads   on   which   of Love   are   embroidered   the   ties   forever
Dear threads with which the ties of Love are embroidered forever,

va do ɾe 'rɔ
v'adorerò.
you I will adore
I will forever adore you.

> *In the repeat of this da capo aria, "v'adorerò" becomes "v'adornerò" [va dor ne 'rɔ]. If intentional, perhaps even in fun, the repeat would translate:* I will forever adorn you.

'kwan to   pju   le 'ga te   il   'kɔ ɾe   e   ak: kreʃː 'ʃe te   le   'mi e   'pe ne
Quanto   più   legate   il   core   e   accrescete   le   mie   pene
how much   more   you bind   the   heart   and   you increase   the   my   pains
The more you bind my heart and increase my pain

pju   fe 'de le   va me 'rɔ
più   fedele   v'amerò.
more   faithful   you I will love
the more faithfully I will love you.

GL: **Amor[e]**

❧

[84]
from: *Scipione nelle Spagne (1714)*   *Apostolo Zeno and N. Serino*

'ɛr dʒi ti a 'mor
Ergiti, amor
Lift your wings, love

'er dʒi ti   a 'mor   'su i   'van: ni   e   'prɛn di   ar 'di to   il   'vo lo
Ergiti,   amor,   sui   vanni   e   prendi   ardito   il   volo
lift up   love   your   wings   and   take   bold   the   flight
Lift your wings, love, and boldly take flight

vanni (poet.) =
ali

sɛn tsab: bas: 'sar ti   pju
senz'abbassarti   più.
without lowering yourself   more
without lowering yourself anymore.

per 'ke   kon   'nuo vi   iŋ 'gan: ni   tu   non   ri 'ka da   al   'swɔ lo,   lo   so ster: 'ra   vir 'tu
Perché   con   nuovi   inganni   tu   non   ricada   al   suolo,   lo   sosterrà   virtù.
so that   with   new   deceptions   you   not   may fall again   to the   ground   it   will sustain   virtue
Virtue will support you so that, from new deceptions, you will not fall again.

❧

[86]

fa 'rɔ la ven 'det: ta
Farò la vendetta
I will take revenge

fa 'rɔ   la   ven 'det: ta   ke   a   me   sa 'spɛt: ta   di   kwel   'pɛr fi do   tra di 'tor
Farò   la   vendetta   che   a   me   s'aspetta   di   quel   perfido   traditor
I will do   the   vengeance   that   to   me   one expects   of   that   perfidious   traitor
I will take the expected revenge on that perfidious traitor

ke   mi   a   si   vi li 'pe za   'fam: mi   star   ko 'zi   so 'spe za
che   mi   ha   sì   vilipesa   fammi   star   così   sospesa
that   me   has   so   scorned   makes me   to be   thus   broken off
who, having so scorned me, thus cuts me off

e da   'da to   a 'dal tri   il   kɔr
ed ha   dato   ad altri   il   cor.
and has   given   to another   the   heart
and has given his heart to another.

printed "à" =
(mod.) ha

altri (singular) = another, someone else

❧

[83]

fer 'ma te o 'ma i fer 'ma te
Fermate omai fermate
Cease – cease now

fer 'ma te   o 'ma i   fer 'ma te   'kan di de   'mi e   ko 'lom be   il   'vo lo   er: 'ran te
Fermate   omai,   fermate   candide   mie   colombe   il   volo   errante
stop   now   stop   white   my   doves   the   flight   wandering
Cease – cease now, my white doves, your wandering flight

omai
(poet.) =
ormai

e   'ʃɔl te   dal   ri 'gor   da u 'ra to   'fre no   'li be ɾe   tra skor: 're te
e   sciolte   dal   rigor   d'aurato   freno   libere   trascorrete
and   loosed   from the   rigor   of (lit.) golden   restraint   free   pass over
and, freed from your golden cage, fly over

di   'ku pi do   il   swɔl   pju   ver ded: 'dʒan te   e   a 'mɛ no
di   Cupido   il   suol   più   verdeggiante   e   ameno.
of   Cupid   the   soil   more   verdant   and   pleasant

the more verdant and pleasant land of Cupid.

per   at: ter: 'rar   lor 'goʎ: ʎo   'du na   bel: 'let: tsa   al 'tɛ ra   'dal: la   pju   'va ga   'sfɛ ɾa
Per   atterrar   l'orgoglio   d'una   bellezza   altera   dalla   più   vaga   sfera
for   to humble   the pride   of a   beauty   haughty   from the   most   lovely   sphere

To crush the pride of a haughty beauty, from the loveliest sphere

kil   'tɛr tso   tʃɛl   di   'bɛl: la   'lu tʃe   in 'do ɾe
ch'il   terzo   ciel   di   bella   luce   indore
which the   third   heaven   of   beautiful   light   gilds

which the third heaven gilds with beautiful light,

> the "e" ending of "indore" is an archaic variant = (mod.) indora

gwi 'da to   'dal: lo   'zdeɲ: ɲo   or   'dʒun dʒe   a 'mo ɾe
guidato   dallo   sdegno   or   giunge   Amore.
guided   by the   anger   now   arrives   Love

guided by anger, Love is now arriving.

se   'kwan do   di   'pa tʃe   'ku pi do   ɛ   fo 'rjɛ ɾo   si   aɾ 'dɛn te   a   la   'ta tʃe
Se   quando   di   pace   Cupido   è   foriero   sì   ardente   ha   la   face,
if   when   of   peace   Cupid   is   herald   so   bright   has   the   torch

If when Cupid is the herald of peace he has such a blazing torch

lo   'stra le   a   si   'fjɛ ɾo   ke   sa 'ra   'kwan do
lo   strale   ha   sì   fiero,   che   sarà   quando
the   arrow   has   so   fierce   what   will be   when

[and] such a fierce arrow, what will happen when

a   far   'gwer: ra   'ʃen de   in   'tɛr: ra   'nu me   i 'ra to   e   'di o   gwer: 'rjɛ ɾo
a   far   guerra   scende   in   terra   nume   irato   e   Dio   guerriero.
to   to make   war   descends   on   earth   deity   angry   and   God   warring

the angry deity and warring God descends to make war on earth?

'duŋ kwe   di   'su a   bel 'ta   'tan to   pre 'zu mi   'psi ke   ke
Dunque   di   sua   beltà   tanto   presumi   Psiche   che
[therefore]   of   her   beauty   so much   you presume   Psyche   that

You presume so much of her beauty, Psyche, that

di   bel: 'let: tsa   ɛ   u 'nom bra   'so la   ke   'al: la   'ma dre   da 'mo ɾe
di   bellezza   è   un'ombra   sola   che   alla   madre   d'amore
of   beauty   it is   a shadow   alone   that   to the   mother   of love

it is only the personification of beauty which, from the mother of love *[Venus]*,

al   pju   bɛl   'nu me   ʎin 'tʃɛn si   u 'zur pa   e   ʎo lo 'ka u sti   in 'vo la
al   più   bel   nume   gl'incensi   usurpa   e   gl'olocausti   invola.
to the   most   beautiful   deity   the perfumes   usurps   and   the sacrifices   steals

the most beautiful deity, usurps the perfumes and robs the sacrifices.

'fjɛ ɾi   'dar di   a 'ku ti   'stra li   a   fe 'rir   vin 'vi ta   un   kɔr
Fieri   dardi   acuti   strali   a   ferir   v'invita   un   cor,
cruel   darts   sharp   arrows   to   to wound   you invites   a   heart

A heart invites wounding by cruel darts and sharp arrows,

ma	kon	'pja ge	'a spre	e	mor 'ta li	di	fje 'ret: tsa	e	non	da 'mor
ma	**con**	**piaghe**	**aspre**	**e**	**mortali**	**di**	**fierezza**	**e**	**non**	**d'Amor.**
but	with	wounds	sharp	and	mortal	of	pride	and	not	of Love

but from sharp, deadly wounds of pride, not from Love.

ben 'ke	'do ɾo	il	'dar do	'mi o	gran	fe 'ri te	'a pre	in	un	sen
Benché	**d'oro**	**il**	**dardo**	**mio**	**gran**	**ferite**	**apre**	**in**	**un**	**sen**
although	of gold	the	dart	mine	great	wounds	opens	in	a	breast

Although golden my dart, it opens deep wounds in a breast;

son	fan 'tʃul: lo	ɛ	ver	ma	'di o	'spar go	net: ɾe	e	ve 'len
son	**fanciullo**	**è**	**ver**	**ma**	**Dio**	**spargo**	**nettare**	**e**	**velen.**
I am	young boy	it is	true	but	God	I scatter	nectar	and	poison

it is true that I *[Cupid]* am [but] a young boy, but as a God I spread [both] nectar and poison.

GL: **Amore, Cupido, Psiche**

☙

[5, 9, 37, 43, 54, 56, 59, 60, 64]
from: *L'honestà negli amori (1680)*
character: *Sandino*

Felice Parnasso (= D. F. Bernini? or Contini)

dʒa il 'so le dal 'gan dʒe
Già il sole dal Gange
Already the sun from the east

dʒa	il	'so le	dal	'gan dʒe	pju	'kja ɾo	sfa 'vil: la
Già	**il**	**sole**	**dal**	**Gange**	**più**	**chiaro**	**sfavilla,**
already	the	sun	from the	Ganges*	more	bright	sparkles

see Glossary

Already the sun from the east is sparkling brighter

e	'tɛr dʒe	'oɲ: ɲi	'stil: la	del: 'lal ba	ke	'pjan dʒe
e	**terge**	**ogni**	**stilla**	**dell'alba**	**che**	**piange.**
and	dries	every	drop	of the dawn	which	weeps

and drying every dewdrop of the weeping dawn.

kol	'rad: dʒo	do 'ra to	in 'dʒɛm: ma	'oɲ: ɲi	'stɛ lo
Col	**raggio**	**dorato**	**ingemma**	**ogni**	**stelo,**
with the	ray	golden	it bejewels	every	stem

> alt. in [37] and [59]: **Con raggio**
> [kon 'rad: dzo] = with ray
> (same translation)

With gilded ray it bejewels every stem

e	ʎi	'a stri	del	'tʃɛ lo	di 'pin dʒe	nel	'pra to
e	**gli**	**astri**	**del**	**cielo**	**dipinge**	**nel**	**prato.**
and	the	stars	of the	heaven	it paints	in the	meadow

and paints the stars of heaven upon the meadow.

GL: **Gange**

☙

[26]

dʒa 'ma i
Già mai
Never

dʒa 'ma i	la	lon ta 'nan tsa	fa 'ra	dal: 'lal ma	'mi a	zva 'nir	si	'dol tʃe	a 'mor
Già mai	**la**	**lontananza**	**farà**	**dall'alma**	**mia**	**svanir**	**sì**	**dolce**	**amor;**
never	the	distance	will make	from the soul	mine	fade away	such	sweet	love

Never will distance make such sweet love fade from my soul;

> *già mai = (mod.) giammai*

e	'lal ta	'mi a	ko 'stan tsa	non	maŋ ke 'ra	se
e	**l'alta**	**mia**	**costanza**	**non**	**mancherà**	**se**
and	the great	my	constancy	not	will fail	if

and my great constancy will not fail if

'pri a	in	me	non	'maŋ ka	il	kɔr
pria	**in**	**me**	**non**	**manca**	**il**	**cor.**
first	in	me	not	fails	the	heart

my heart does not fail me first.

> *pria (poet.) = prima*

&

[55]

go de 'ra i 'sɛm pre kru 'dɛ le
Goderai sempre, crudele
You will always, cruel one, delight

go de 'ra i	'sɛm pre	kru 'dɛ le	a	'mjɛ i	'pjan ti
Goderai	**sempre,**	**crudele,**	**a'**	**miei**	**pianti,**
you will delight	always	cruel one	at	my	tears

You will always, cruel one, delight in my tears,

'al: le	kwe 'rɛ le	dun	a 'man te	ke	ko 'stan te	ta do 'rɔ
alle	**querele**	**d'un**	**amante**	**che**	**costante**	**t'adorò.**
at the	complaints	of a	lover	who	constant	you adored

in the complaints of a lover who adored you faithfully.

'dim: mi	al 'me no	in	ke	pek: 'ka i	ke	se	pɔ i
Dimmi	**almeno**	**in**	**che**	**peccai,**	**che**	**se**	**poi**
tell me	at least	in	what	I sinned	that	if	then

At least tell me how I sinned, for if you then

mɔr te	mi	'dai	'stra li	'dar di	iŋ kon tre 'rɔ
morte	**mi**	**dai,**	**strali,**	**dardi**	**incontrerò.**
death	to me	you give	arrows	darts	encounter

bring me death I will face arrows and darts.

tu	'pjan dʒi	o	stra va 'gan tsa	di	su 'pɛr ba	bel: 'let: tsa
Tu	**piangi,**	**oh**	**stravaganza**	**di**	**superba**	**bellezza!**
you	you weep	oh	extravagant excess	of	proud	beauty

You are weeping – oh extravagant excess of proud beauty!

ki	'ta mi	'fud: dʒi	e	'se gwi	ki	ti	'sprɛt: tsa
Chi	**t'ami**	**fuggi,**	**e**	**segui**	**chi**	**ti**	**sprezza.**
who	you loves	you flee	and	you follow	who	you	scorns

You flee the one who loves you and follow the one who scorns you.

'bɛl: la	se	'bra mi	'pa tʃe	'skat: tʃa	da	'nɔ bil	'kɔ ɾe	kwel: li 'ma go	kru 'dɛ le
Bella,	**se**	**brami**	**pace,**	**scaccia**	**da**	**nobil**	**core**	**quell'imago**	**crudele**
beautiful one	if	you desire	peace	drive	from	noble	heart	that image	cruel

Beautiful one, if you desire peace, drive from your noble heart that cruel image,

> *imago = (mod.) immagine*

ke   'sor da   a   'mjɛ i   kwe 'rɛ le   kol   stral   'kol mo   di   fjɛl   vim 'prɛs: se   a 'mo ɾe
che,   sorda   a   miei   querele,   col   stral   colmo   di   fiel,   v'impresse   Amore.
which   deaf   to   my   complaints   with the   arrow   full   of   gall   there imprinted   Love
deaf to my complaints, which Love imprinted in it with an arrow full of bitterness.

se   'vwɔ i   'pa tʃe   o   di 'lɛt: to   'tor na   kol   'pri mo   af: 'fɛt: to   'mi a   'bɛl: la   a   so spi 'rar
Se   vuoi   pace   o   diletto   torna   col   primo   affetto,   mia   bella,   a   sospirar.
if   you want   peace   or   delight   return   with the   first   affection   my   beauty   to   to sigh
If you want peace or delight, return to sighing with your first love, my beauty.

dɛ   'pjan dʒi   a   'mjɛ i   mar 'ti ɾi   so 'spi ɾa   a   'mjɛ i   so 'spi ɾi
Deh,   piangi   a'   miei   martiri,   sospira   a'   miei   sospiri,
ah   weep   at   my   agonies   sigh   at   my   sighs
Ah, weep at my agony, sigh at my sighing;

ke   tra   le   'dʒɔ je   da 'mor   'dol tʃe   ɛ   il   pe 'nar
che   tra   le   gioie   d'amor   dolce   è   il   penar.
for   among   the   joys   of love   sweet   is   the   suffering
for among the joys of love, suffering is sweet.

a   tu   'par ti   spje 'ta ta   e   a   me   'laʃ: ʃi   doʎ: 'ʎo zo   in   'kwe ste   a 're ne
Ah,   tu   parti,   spietata,   e   a   me   lasci   doglioso   in   queste   arene
ah   you   you depart   pitiless one   and   to   me   you leave   sorrowful   on   these   sands
Ah, you are departing, pitiless one; and you leave me sorrowful on these shores

in   'brat: tʃo   'al: le   'mi e   'pe ne
in   braccio   alle   mie   pene.
in   arm   at the   my   sufferings
in the arms of my sufferings.

al 'men   ko   'two i   'bɛ i   'ra i   'mi ɾa   la   'mɔr te   'mi a   e   'pɔ i   ten 'va i
Almen,   co'   tuoi   bei   rai   mira   la   morte   mia,   e   poi   t'en vai.
at least   with   your   beautiful   eyes   watch   the   death   mine   and   then   go away
At least watch my death with your beautiful eyes, and then leave.

GL: **Amore**

ෂ

[84]
from: *Gerone tiranno di Siracusa (1692)*   *Aurelio Aureli*

ɔ   u 'nal ma
Ho un'alma
I have a soul

ɔ   u 'nal ma   o   'mi o   'nu me   per   'vo i   tut: tar 'dor
Ho   un'alma,   o   mio   nume,   per   voi   tutt'ardor.
I have   a soul   o   my   deity   for   you   all ardor
I have a soul, o divine presence, [which] is all passion for you.

per   le 'gar mi   a   'vo i   'ku pi do   la   'su a   'bɛn da   si zlat: 'tʃɔ
Per   legarmi   a   voi,   Cupido   la   sua   benda   si slacciò,
for   to bind me   to   you   Cupid   the   his   blindfold   untied
In order to bind me to you Cupid untied his blindfold;

ne	'ma i	pwɔ	nɔ	kwel	'lat: tʃo	'fi do	se pa 'rar vi	dal	'mi o	kɔr
né	**mai**	**può,**	**no,**	**quel**	**laccio**	**fido**	**separarvi**	**dal**	**mio**	**cor.**
nor	ever	is able	no	that	tie	faithful	to separate you	from the	my	heart

and that faithful tie can never, no, separate you from my heart.

𝒢ℒ: **Cupido**

☙

[49]

il ro ziɲ: 'ɲwɔ lo
Il rosignuolo
The nightingale

kwi	'do ve	al	fin	mas: 'si do	'ɔ do	'mɛ sto	u ziɲ: 'ɲol	ke	si la 'men ta
Qui	**dove**	**al**	**fin**	**m'assido**	**odo**	**mesto**	**usignol**	**che**	**si lamenta,**
here	where	at the	end	I take my seat	I hear	sad	nightingale	who	laments

Now at the end of my life, I hear the sad nightingale lamenting;

> *rosign[u]olo (lit.) = usign[u]olo*

e	'dor	ke	'so no	in	'kwe sti	or: 'ror	not: 'tur ni
ed	**or**	**che**	**sono**	**in**	**questi**	**orror**	**notturni**
and	now	that	I am	in	these	horrors	nocturnal

and now that I am among these nocturnal horrors

il	do lo 'ro zo	'kan to	'ta tʃi to	e	sol	vɔ ak: kom paɲ: 'ɲar	kol	'pjan to
il	**doloroso**	**canto**	**tacito**	**e**	**sol**	**vo' accompagnar**	**col**	**pianto.**
the	mournful	song	quiet	and	lonely	want to accompany	with the	weeping

I want to accompanying the mournful song, quiet and lonely, with my weeping.

beŋ 'ke	a 'ma ro	si fa	'ka ro	il	pe 'nar	kwan 'dal tri	'pe na
Ben che	**amaro**	**si fa**	**caro**	**il**	**penar**	**quand'altri**	**pena,**
though	bitter	itself makes	dear	the	suffering	when another	suffers

> *ben che (lit.) =*
> *benché; altri =*
> *another, someone else*

Although bitter suffering becomes dear when someone else suffers,

par	ke	'di ka	lal 'tru i	'dwɔ lo	in	pe 'nar	non	'sɛ i	tu	'so lo
par	**che**	**dica**	**l'altrui**	**duolo**	**in**	**penar**	**non**	**sei**	**tu**	**solo.**
it seems	that	says	the other's	sorrow	in	suffering	not	you are	you	alone

it seems that another's sorrows say: in suffering you are not alone.

'dat: ti	'pa tʃe	e	il	dwɔl	raf: 'fre na
Datti	**pace**	**e**	**il**	**duol**	**raffrena.**
give yourself	peace	and	the	sorrow	restrain

Give yourself peace, and restrain the sorrow.

ma	o	'di o	ke	'oɲ: ɲi	do 'lo ɾe	'kwan to	di 'let: ta	pju	'tan tɛ	mad: 'dʒo ɾe
Ma	**oh**	**Dio**	**che**	**ogni**	**dolore**	**quanto**	**diletta**	**più,**	**tant'è**	**maggiore.**
but	oh	God	[that]	every	pain	as much	pleasure	more	so much is	greater

But, oh God, the more every pain gives pleasure, the greater it *[the pain]* is.

lo	sa	pur 'trɔp: po	kwel	'mi ze ɾo	a u dʒe 'let: to	ke	sfo 'gan do	il	'su o	af: 'fɛt: to
Lo	**sa**	**purtroppo**	**quel**	**misero**	**augeletto**	**che**	**sfogando**	**il**	**suo**	**affetto**
it	knows	unfortunately	that	poor	little bird	who	pouring out	the	his	affection

Alas, well it knows that poor little bird, who in pouring its heart out

> *augeletto (poet.) = uccelletto*

di	kwel	dwɔl	ke	lak: 'kɔ ɾa	'sɛm pre	pju	sad: do 'lo ɾa
di	**quel**	**duol**	**che**	**l'accora**	**sempre**	**più**	**s'addolora.**
of	that	pain	which	it breaks his heart	always	more	is afflicted

is hurt more and more by the very pain which breaks his heart.

'lɛn to   'pri ma   iŋ ko 'min tʃa   e   'tut: to   'pɛn de   da   'u na   'trɛ mo la   'vo tʃe
Lento   prima   incomincia   e   tutto   pende   da   una   tremola   voce,
slow   first   begins   and   completely   depends   from   a   tremulant   voice
First he begins slowly, depending completely on a tremulous voice;

e   par   ke   'mɔ ɾa   'kwan do   rin 'fɔr tsa   il   'fja to   e   'prɛ sto   aʃ: 'ʃen de
e   par   che   mora   quando   rinforza   il   fiato   e   presto   ascende,
and   it seems   that   may die   when   reinforces   the   breath   and   quick   rises
and just when it seems that he will die, his breath gains strength and quickly rises;

'tril: la   'ʃɔʎ: ʎe   pju   'nɔ te   e   'pɔ i   so 'spi ɾa
trilla,   scioglie   più   note   e   poi   sospira,
warbles   releases   more   notes   and   then   sighs
he warbles, releases more notes, and then sighs,

'pɔ i   'tʃes: sa   e   si ri 'ti ɾa   mor mo 'ran do   nel   sen   pro 'fun de   'nɔ te
poi   cessa   e   si ritira   mormorando   nel   sen   profunde   note.
then   ceases   and   withdraws   murmuring   in the   breast   deep   notes
then stops and withdraws, deep notes murmuring in his breast.

> profunde = (mod.) profonde

'in di   i 'ɾa to   si 'skwɔ te   si 'sfi da   si ri 'spon de
Indi   irato   si scuote,   si sfida,   si risponde
then   angered   himself shakes   himself challenges   himself answers

> Printed is "si sfeda," which I've changed to "si sfida," which makes sense; no "sfedersi" verb could be found...

e   'pɔ i   sa 'skol ta
e   poi   s'ascolta;
and   then   himself listens to
Then, angered, he shakes himself, challenges himself, answers himself and listens to himself;

e dad dʒi 'tan do   in   'mil: le   'gwi ze   e   'mil: le   la   'go la   ar mo 'njo za
ed agitando   in   mille   guise   e   mille   la   gola   armoniosa
and shaking   in   thousand   ways   and   thousand   the   throat   melodious
and, shaking his melodious throat in thousands and thousands of ways,

ta 'lor   si 'staŋ ka   ma   non   'ma i   ri 'pɔ za
tal or   si stanca   ma   non   mai   riposa.
at times   gets tired   but   not   ever   rests
sometimes he gets tired, but not ever does he rest.

kwel   bɛl   'kan to   ɛ   si   'gra to   ke   al   'mi o   kɔr   la   'pe na   'mol tʃe
Quel   bel   canto   è   sì   grato   che   al   mio   cor   la   pena   molce
that   beautiful   song   is   so   pleasing   that   to the   my   heart   the   suffering   soothes
That beautiful song is so pleasing that it soothes the suffering of my heart

e   ad: dor 'men ta   'oɲ: ɲi   do 'lor
e   addormenta   ogni   dolor.
and   puts to sleep   every   pain
and makes every pain dormant.

pur   de 'li ɾo   e   so 'spi ɾo   ke   kwel   'kan to   kɛ   si   'dol tʃe
Pur   deliro   e   sospiro   ché   quel   canto   ch'è   sì   dolce
yet   I rave   and   I sigh   because   that   song   which is   so   sweet
Yet I rave and sigh, because that song, which is so sweet,

fa   'ki o   'pɛn si   al   'kɔ ɾe   iŋ 'gra to   kil   'mi o   kɔr
fa   ch'io   pensi   al   core   ingrato   ch'il   mio   cor
makes   that I   I may think   to the   heart   ungrateful   that the   my   heart
makes me think of the ungrateful heart: that my dear one

ke	la 'mɔ	'tan to	sol	tra 'di	per	'al tro	a 'mor
che	**l'amò**	**tanto**	**sol**	**tradì**	**per**	**altro**	**amor.**
whom	it loved	so much	only	betrayed	for	other	love

whom it *[my heart]* loved so much only betrayed it for another love.

&

[86]

in 'tɛr: ra la 'gwɛr: ra
In terra la guerra
May war on earth

in	'tɛr: ra	la	'gwɛr: ra	sen 'vo li	fu 'gat ʃe
In	**terra**	**la**	**guerra**	**sen voli**	**fugace;**
on	earth	the	war	may fly away	fleeting

May war on earth fly away;

tʃi	'por ti	kon 'for ti	'da i	'pɔ li	la	'pa tʃe
ci	**porti**	**conforti**	**dai**	**poli**	**la**	**pace.**
to us	may bring	comforts	from the	poles	the	peace

may peace bring us comfort from the ends of the earth.

&

[40]

'i o 'dis: si
Io dissi
I said

'i o	'dis: si	ke	la	'fa tʃe	ke	'mar de	in	sen	per	te
Io	**dissi**	**che**	**la**	**face**	**che**	**m'arde**	**in**	**sen**	**per**	**te,**
I	I said	that	the	torch	which	me burns	in	breast	for	you

I said that the torch which burns in my breast for you

ko 'zi	mat: 'tʃen de	e	'pja tʃe	ke	il: 'lu stra	la	'mi a	fe
così	**m'accende**	**e**	**piace, ché**		**illustra**	**la**	**mia**	**fé.**
thus	me ignites	and	pleases	because	illustrates	the	my	faith

so inflames and pleases me, because it explains my faithfulness.

per 'ke	'kre der	non	'vwɔ i	kru 'dɛl	ke	'si a	ko 'zi
Perché	**creder**	**non**	**vuoi,**	**crudel,**	**che**	**sia**	**così?**
why	to believe	not	you want	cruel one	that	it be	thus

Why do you not want to believe, cruel one, that it is so?

lo	'kjɛ di	'aʎ: ʎi	'ɔk: ki	'two i	ke	ti	di 'ran	di	si
Lo	**chiedi**	**agli**	**occhi**	**tuoi,**	**ché**	**ti**	**diran**	**di**	**sì.**
it	ask	to the	eyes	yours	because	to you	they will say	[of]	yes

Ask your eyes, for they will tell you "yes."

&

[83]

'i o mo ri 'rɛi kon 'tɛn to
Io morirei contento
I would die content

'i o   mo ɾi 'ɾɛ i   kon 'tɛn to   se   il   'mi o   'ka ɾo   te 'zɔ ɾo,   se   'li dol   'mi o
Io   morirei   contento   se   il   mio   caro   tesoro,   se   l'idol   mio
I   I would die   content   if   the   my   dear   treasure   if   the idol   mine

I would die happy if my dear treasure, my idol,

po 'tes: se   kon   le   'su e   'lu tʃi   i 'stes: se   ve 'der   la   fe del 'ta   kon   'ku i
potesse   con   le   sue   luci   istesse   veder   la   fedeltà   con   cui
were able   with   the   her   eyes   themselves   to see   the   faithfulness   with   which

could see with her own eyes the faithfulness with which

mi 'mɔɾo   po 'trɛb: be   al: 'lor   si 'ku ɾa   'vi ver   'la ni ma   'mi a   dal: 'lem pja   dʒe lo 'zi a
mi moro,   potrebbe   allor   sicura   viver   l'anima   mia   dall'empia   gelosia
I die   would be able   then   safe   to live   the soul   mine   from the cruel   jealousy

I am dying; then my soul would be able to live safe from cruel jealousy

e   de 'por: re   'oɲ: ɲi   'ku ɾa   di   ti 'mor   di   so 'spɛt: to   e   di   tor 'men to
e   deporre   ogni   cura   di   timor   di   sospetto   e   di   tormento.
and   to put aside   every   care   of   fear   of   suspicion   and   of   torment

and put aside every care of fear, suspicion, and torment.

'soɲ: ɲi   'fjam: ma   spar 'dʒes: se   fa 'vil: le   'soɲ: ɲi   'bɛl: la   ve 'des: se   lar 'dor
S'ogni   fiamma   spargesse   faville,   s'ogni   bella   vedesse   l'ardor,
if every   flame   would spread   sparks   if every   beauty   would see   the ardor

If every flame were to shed sparks, if every beauty were to see the ardor,

'vo i   sa 'pre ste   a do 'ra te   pu 'pil: le   'kwan to   'va ma   lat: 'tʃe zo   'mi o   kɔr
voi   sapreste   adorate   pupille   quanto   v'ama   l'acceso   mio   cor.
you   would know   adored   eyes   how much   you it loves   the on fire   my   heart

you would know, adored eyes, how much my burning heart loves you.

'soɲ: ɲi   a 'man te   kon   'sal de   ka 'te ne   'das: se   av: 'vin ta   la   'su a   li ber 'ta
S'ogni   amante   con   salde   catene   dasse   avvinta   la   sua   libertà
if every   lover   with   strong   chains   gave   bound   the   his   liberty

If every lover were to bind his freedom with strong chains,

dasse	
(poet.)	
= *desse*	

'vo i   sa 'pre ste   a do 'ra to   'mi o   'bɛ ne   'kwan to   ɛ   'gran de   la   'mi a   fe del 'ta
voi   sapreste   adorato   mio   bene   quanto   è   grande   la   mia   fedeltà.
you   would know   adored   my   dear one   how much   is   great   the   my   faithfulness

you would know, my dear adored one, how great is my faithfulness.

ma   'si a   'kwan to   si 'vɔʎ: ʎa   'a spra   la   'vi a   kal   tʃel   da 'mor   kon 'du tʃe
Ma   sia   quanto   si voglia   aspra   la   via   ch'al   ciel   d'amor   conduce
but   may be   how much   one may wish   harsh   the   way   that to the   heaven   of love   leads

However harsh may be the way leading to the heaven of love,

'sɛm pre   nel   'pɛt: to   'mi o   'kreʃ: ʃe   e   dʒer 'moʎ: ʎa   pju   'fer vi do
sempre   nel   petto   mio   cresce   e   germoglia   più   fervido
always   in the   breast   mine   increases   and   germinates   more   fervid

always in my breast grows and flowers more fervidly

il   de 'zi ɾe   din 'trɛ pi do   se 'gwi ɾe   per   fa ti 'ko zo   'kal: le   in 'tʃer ta   'lu tʃe
il   desire   d'intrepido   seguire   per   faticoso   calle   incerta   luce
the   desire   of fearless   to follow   through   difficult   path   uncertain   light

the desire to follow an uncertain light fearlessly on a difficult path

e   sof: 'frɛn do   e   spe 'ran do   nel   'kol mo   del   pja 'tʃer   'vi ver   pe 'nan do
e   soffrendo   e   sperando   nel   colmo   del   piacer   viver   penando.
and   suffering   and   hoping   in the height   of the pleasure   to live   suffering
and, suffering and hoping, to live, suffering, in the height of pleasure.

'sar mi   pur   'dem pjo   ve 'le no   kwel   bɛl   'se no   'sɛm pre   'tu o   'bɛl: la   sa 'rɔ
S'armi   pur   d'empio   veleno   quel   bel   seno   sempre   tuo,   bella,   sarò.
if it be armed even   of cruel   poison   that   beautiful breast   always   yours   beauty   I will be
Even if your beautiful breast be armed with cruel poison, I will always be yours, beautiful one.

mi   ve 'dra i   pju   'fi do   a 'man te   pju   ko 'stan te   sa 'rɔ   'mɔr to   e   ta me 'rɔ
Mi   vedrai   più   fido   amante   più   costante   sarò   morto   e   t'amerò.
me   you will see most   faithful lover   most   constant   I will be   dead   and   you I will love
You will see me as the most faithful and most constant lover; I will be dead and I will love you.

'vi bri   pur   'liŋ gwa   men 'da tʃe   la   'su a   'fa tʃe   per   dar   'vi ta
Vibri   pur   lingua   mendace   la   sua   face   per   dar   vita
may hurl   [then] tongue   lying   the   its   torch   for   to give life
May your lying tongue hurl its torch to give life

al   'mi o   mar 'tir   'kjɛ de   sʊl   per   'su a   mer 'tʃe de
al   mio   martir   chiede   sol   per   sua   mercede
to the my   martyrdom asks   only for   its   reward
to my martyrdom [which] asks only, as reward,

la   'mi a   'fe de   'dir ti   o   'ka ɾa   e   'po i   mo 'rir
la   mia   fede   dirti   o   cara   e   poi   morir.
the   my   fidelity to say to you   o   dear one   and   then   to die
to tell you of my fidelity, o dear one, and then to die.

si   'fi do   'mi o   'kɔ ɾe   di   se 've ɾa   bɛl: 'let: tsa   lo sti 'na to   ri 'go ɾe
Sì,   fido   mio   core,   di   severa   bellezza   l'ostinato   rigore
yes   faithful my   heart   of   stern   beauty   the obstinate   severity

mer 'tʃe   'dal ta   spe 'ran tsa   tro 'fɛ o   ri mi ɾe 'ra i   di   'tu a   ko 'stan tsa
mercé   d'alta   speranza   trofeo   rimirerai   di   tua   costanza.
recompense   of high   hope   trophy   you will see   of   your   constancy
Yes, my faithful beloved one, you will see the obstinate severity of stern beauty, [the] reward for high hopes, [and the] prize for your constancy.

જ

[81]

'la bra gra 'di te
Labra gradite
Pleasing lips

'la bra   gra 'di te   sɔ   ke   a   me   'di te   'ka ɾo   'mi o   bɛn
Labra   gradite,   so   che   a   me   dite,   caro   mio   ben.
lips   pleasing   I know what   to   me   you say dear   my   dear one
Pleasing lips, I know what you are telling me, my dearly beloved.

| labra (poet.) |
| = labbra |

'on de   kon 'tɛn to   nel   'su o   tor 'men to   'rɛ sta   il   'mi o   sen
Onde   contento   nel   suo   tormento   resta   il   mio   sen.
whence   content   in the its   torment   rests   the   my   breast
Therein is my breast content in its torment.

જ

[85]
'lar mi kru 'dɛ le e 'fjɛ ɾe
L'armi crudele e fiere
Cruel and fierce weapons

'lar mi	kru 'dɛ li	e	'fjɛ ɾe	di	'du e	pu 'pil: le	ar 'tʃɛ ɾe	man	sa et: 'ta to	il	kɔr
L'armi	**crudeli**	**e**	**fiere,**	**di**	**due**	**pupille**	**arciere,**	**m'han**	**saettato**	**il**	**cor.**
the weapons	cruel	and	fierce	of	two	eyes	archer	me have	pierced	the	heart

Cruel and fierce weapons, two arrow-hurling eyes, have pierced my heart.

'po i	'kwel: le	'lu tʃi	iŋ 'gra te	pju	'kru de	e	pju	spje 'ta te	me	lan	ra 'pi to	aŋ kor
Poi	**quelle**	**luci**	**ingrate,**	**più**	**crude**	**e**	**più**	**spietate,**	**me**	**l'han**	**rapito**	**ancor.**
then	those	eyes	ungrateful	more	harsh	and	more	scornful	me	it have	robbed	also

Then those ungrateful eyes, more harsh and scornful, also took it away.

per	far	'kre der	ti 'ɾan: ni	'ʎɔk: ki	'del: la	'mi a	'klɔ ɾi
Per	**far**	**creder**	**tiranni,**	**gl'occhi**	**della**	**mia**	**Clori,**
for	to make	to believe	tyrants	the eyes	of the	my	Clori

To make one believe that the eyes of my Clori are tyrants,

'ba sta	dir	ke	son	'mɔ ɾi
basta	**dir**	**che**	**son**	**mori;**
it is enough	to say	that	are	dark colored

suffice it to say that they are dark;

'bɛ nɛ	kru 'dɛl	'ku pi do	al: 'lor ke	'prɛn de	a	ful mi 'nar	da	i	'lu mi
ben' è	**crudel**	**Cupido**	**allorché**	**prende**	**a**	**fulminar**	**da**	**i**	**lumi,**
well is	cruel	Cupid	(lit.) when	takes	to	fulminating	from	the	eyes

Cupid is very cruel when from his eyes he starts fulminating,

se	ʎin fo 'ka ti	'ra i	fan	ke	ti 'strug: ga	e	non	ri 'pɔ zi	'ma i
se	**gl'infocati**	**rai**	**fan**	**che**	**ti strugga,**	**e**	**non**	**riposi**	**mai.**
if	the fiery	eyes	make	that	you be consumed	and	not	you repose	ever

when his fiery eyes cause you to be consumed and never have repose.

se	un	'vol to	ta 'let: ta	'pɔ i	'tu za	il	ri 'go ɾe	son	'sker tsi
Se	**un**	**volto**	**t'alletta,**	**poi**	**t'usa**	**il**	**rigore,**	**son**	**scherzi,**
if	a	face	you entices	then	to you acts with	the	severity	are	jests

If he entices you [with] a face and then becomes stern, it is in jest

son	'dʒɔ ko	non	ɛ	kru del 'ta
son	**gioco**	**non**	**è**	**crudeltà.**
are	game	not	it is	cruelty

and play, not cruelty.

no' (in the repeat) = non

se	'lɔk: kjo	sa 'et: ta	kon	'zwar di	da 'mo ɾe
Se	**l'occhio**	**saetta**	**con**	**sguardi**	**d'Amore,**
if	the eye	pierces	with	glances	of Love

If he pierces [your] eye with Love's glances,

pe 'nan do	nel	'fɔ ko	'ma i	'trɔ vi	pje 'ta
penando	**nel**	**foco**	**mai**	**trovi**	**pietà.**
suffering	in the	fire	never	you find	pity

you will never find pity, suffering in the fire [of them].

ɛ ver ke pju si 'mi ɾan le pu pil: le pju 'vɔ mi tan fa 'vil: le
È ver, che più si miran le pupille, più vomitan faville.
it is true that more one looks at the eyes more they spew sparks
It is true that the more one looks in the eyes, the more they shoot sparks.

ma 'ko me 'ɛs: ser pwɔ 'ma i ka 'mor da 'ʎɔk: ki
Ma come esser può mai, ch'Amor da gl'occhi,
but how to be is able ever that Love from the eyes

'men trɛ 'tʃɛ ko fan 'tʃul: lo i 'dar di 'skɔk: ki
mentr'è cieco fanciullo, i dardi scocchi?
as he is blind little boy the darts he may shoot
But how ever can it be that Love can shoot darts from his eyes, as he is [but] a blind little boy?

a ke van 'tar ti 'pwɔ i ke 'si an 'ʎɔk: ki da 'mor kweʎ: 'ʎɔk: ki 'two i
Ah, che vantar ti puoi, che sian gl'occhi d'Amor, quegl'occhi tuoi.
ah that to boast to you can that they be the eyes of Love those eyes your
Ah, how can you boast that those eyes of yours are the eyes of Love?

non fu da 'mor la 'fa tʃe 'kwel: la ke mat: 'tʃɛn de fur 'ʎɔk: ki 'bɛl: li
Non fu d'Amor la face quella che m'accende; fur gl'occhi belli.
not was of Love the torch that which me inflames it was the eyes beautiful
What inflamed me was not the torch of Love; it was your beautiful eyes.

> *fur = furono*

ne 'mi tʃi 'al: la 'mi a 'pa tʃe 'sɛm pre li kja me 'rɔ 'lu mi ru 'bɛl: li
Nemici alla mia pace sempre li chiamerò, lumi rubelli.
enemies to the my peace always them I will call eyes rebellious
I will always call them enemies of my peace, rebellious eyes.

> *rubelli = (mod.) ribelli*

𝒢𝓛: **Amor[e], Clori, Cupido**

❧

[39]

la spe 'ran tsa
La speranza
Hope

la spe 'ran tsa mi tra 'diʃ: ʃe mi si 'mo stra e 'pɔ i zva 'niʃ: ʃe
La speranza mi tradisce, mi si mostra e poi svanisce,
the hope me betrays to me itself shows and then vanishes
Hope betrays me; it reveals itself to me and then vanishes,

kwal di 'tan ta lo in fe 'li tʃe 'fud: dʒe 'lon da iŋ gan: na 'tri tʃe
qual di Tantalo infelice fugge l'onda ingannatrice.
like from Tantalus unfortunate flees the wave deceptive
like the deceptive wave eluded the unfortunate Tantalus.

se mi 'naʃ: ʃe 'pit: tʃol 'bɛ ne me lo 'strug: gon 'tʃen to 'pe ne
Se mi nasce picciol bene me lo struggon cento pene;
if to me springs up small happiness to me it destroy hundred pains
If a small happiness comes to me, a hundred sufferings destroy it for me,

ko 'zi il kɔr di 'tit: tsjo aŋ 'ko ɾa 'kreʃ: ʃe sol per 'ke il di 'vo ɾa
così il cor di Tizio ancora cresce sol perché il divora.
thus the heart of Tizio still grows only so that it devours
like Tizio's heart get bigger and bigger only for [the vulture] to devour it.

> *il divora = (mod.) lo divora*
>
> *printed "Titio" = (mod.) Tizio*

𝒢𝓛: **Tantalo, Tizio**

❧

[40]

la 'tu a gra 'di ta fe
La tua gradita fé
Your welcome fidelity

la	'tu a	gra 'di ta	fe	ke	il	'kɔ ɾe	min va 'gi	kwe 'stal ma	a 'do ɾa
La	**tua**	**gradita**	**fé,**	**che**	**il**	**core**	**m'invaghì,**	**quest'alma**	**adora.**
the	your	welcome	faith	which	the	heart	me charmed	this soul	adores

This soul adores your welcome fidelity, which charmed my heart.

pju	stɔ	din 'tor no a	te	il	bɛl	ke	mi	fe 'ɾi	pju	min: na 'mo ɾa
Più	**sto**	**dintorno a**	**te,**	**il**	**bel**	**che**	**mi**	**ferì**	**più**	**m'innamora.**
more	I am	around	you	the	beauty	that	me	wounded	more	me enamors

The more I am around you, the more the beauty that wounded me enamors me.

> dintorno =
> (mod.) intorno

❧

[81]

la 'tu a 'pe na
La tua pena
Your suffering

la	'tu a	'pe na	mi	di 'spja tʃe	'dat: ti	'pa tʃe
La	**tua**	**pena**	**mi**	**dispiace,**	**datti**	**pace.**
the	your	suffering	me	displeases	give yourself	peace

Your suffering displeases me; give yourself peace.

non	sot: 'tjɛ ne	'sɛm pril	'bɛ ne	'kwan do	'pja tʃe	'dat: ti	'pa tʃe
Non	**s'ottiene**	**sempr'il**	**bene**	**quando**	**piace.**	**Datti**	**pace.**
not	one obtains	always the	happiness	when	it pleases	give yourself	peace

One does not always achieve happiness when it pleases. Give yourself peace.

❧

[20, 25, 31, 32, 54, 59, 60, 64]   Alternately titled **Rugiadose, odorose**.
from: *Il Pirro e Demetrio (1694)*
character: *Mario*

Adriano Morselli

le vi o 'let: te
Le violette
The violets

ru dʒa 'do ze	o do 'ro ze	vi o 'let: te	grat: 'tsjo ze	'vo i	vi 'sta te	ver goɲ: 'ɲo ze
Rugiadose,	**odorose,**	**violette**	**graziose,**	**voi**	**vi state**	**vergognose,**
dewy	fragrant	violets	pretty	you	yourselves you stay	shy

Dewy, fragrant, pretty violets, you stay there shyly,

'mɛd: dzo	a 'sko ze	fra	le	'fɔʎ: ʎe	e	zgri 'da te	le	'mi e	'vɔʎ: ʎe
mezzo	**ascose**	**fra**	**le**	**foglie,**	**e**	**sgridate**	**le**	**mie**	**voglie,**
half	hidden	among	the	leaves	and	you rebuke	the	my	wishes

half hidden among the leaves, and rebuke my wishes,

ke	son	'trɔp: po	am bit: 'tsjo ze
che	**son**	**troppo**	**ambiziose.**
which	are	too	ambitious

which are too ambitious.

> alt.: *tropp'ambiziose* ['trɔp: pam bit: 'tsjo ze]
> = *troppo ambiziose*

❧

[98]

lon ˈtan ˈdalː la ˈsu a ˈklɔ ɾi
Lontan dalla sua Clori
Far from his Clori

lon ˈtan   ˈdalː la   ˈsu a   ˈklɔ ɾi   akː ˈkan to   a   un   fju mi ˈtʃɛlː lo
Lontan   dalla   sua   Clori,   accanto   a   un   fiumicello,
far   from the   his   Clori   near   to   a   little river
Far from his Clori, near a little river,

fi ˈle no   il   pa sto ˈɾelː lo   spje ˈga va   in   ˈkwe ste   ˈnɔ te   i   ˈswɔ i   tor ˈmen ti
Fileno   il   pastorello   spiegava   in   queste   note   i   suoi   tormenti
Fileno   the   shepherd   was explaining   in   these   notes   the   his   torments
the shepherd Fileno was describing his torments, in the following way,

ˈa i   ˈtroŋ ki   ˈa i   ˈsasː si   a   kwel   ruʃ ˈʃɛlː lo   ˈa i   ˈven ti
ai   tronchi,   ai   sassi,   a   quel   ruscello,   ai   venti.
to the   tree trunks   to the   stones   to   that   brook   to the   winds
to the trees, the stones, that brook, and the winds.

ˈdo ve   ˈsɛ i   ˈdo ve   ta ˈskon di   ˈka ɾo   e   ˈdol tʃe   ˈmi o   te ˈzɔ ɾo
Dove   sei,   dove   t'ascondi,   caro   e   dolce   mio   tesoro?
where   are you   where   you are hiding   dear   and   sweet   my   treasure
Where are you? Where are you hiding, my dear and sweet treasure?

se   ti   ˈkja mo   e   non   ri ˈspon di   ˈsen to   dʒa   ke   ˈmaŋ ko   e   ˈmɔ ɾo
Se   ti   chiamo   e   non   rispondi   sento   già   che   manco   e   moro.
if   you   I call   and   not   you respond   I feel   [already]   that   I fail   and   I die
If I call you and you do not answer, I feel that I am failing and dying.

kwi   il   ˈtu o   bɛl   ˈvol to   ˈkan di do   e   ver ˈmiʎː ʎo   vin ˈtʃe a   la   ˈrɔ za   e   il   ˈdʒiʎː ʎo
Qui   il   tuo   bel   volto   candido   e   vermiglio   vincea   la   rosa   e   il   giglio,
here   the   your   beautiful   face   white   and   vermilion   conquered   the   rose   and   the   lily
Here your beautiful face was whiter than the lily and rosier than the rose,

vincea = vinceva

e   se   ˈtu a   ˈdol tʃe   ˈbok: ka   il   ˈkan to   so a ˈvisː si mo   ʃoʎː ˈʎe a
e   se   tua   dolce   bocca   il   canto   soavissimo   sciogliea,
and   if   your   sweet   mouth   the   song   most gentle   raised
and when your sweet mouth opened in gentlest song,

sciogliea = scioglieva

ˈla u ɾe   fer ˈmar   fa ˈtʃe a
l'aure   fermar   facea,
the breezes   to stop   it made
it suspended the breezes;

facea = faceva

e   ratː te ˈnɛn do   il   ˈvo lo   vim pa ˈra va   a   kan ˈta ɾe   il   ro ziɲ ˈɲwɔ lo
e   rattenendo   il   volo   v'imparava   a   cantare   il   rosignuolo.
and   restraining   the   flight   there learned   to   to sing   the   nightingale
and, detaining its flight, the nightingale thereby learned to sing.

rattenere (lit.) = trattenere

go ˈde a   ˈkwe sto   ˈlim pi do   ruʃ ˈʃɛlː lo   ˈfar si   ˈspɛkː kjo   al   ˈtu o   ˈbɛlː lo
Godea   questo   limpido   ruscello   farsi   specchio   al   tuo   bello.
delighted in   this   clear   brook   making itself   mirror   at the   your   beauty
This clear brook delighted in reflecting your beauty.

godea = godeva

or	'sek: ko	ɛ	il	'fjo ɾe	e	'lɛr ba	'me sti	ʎi	a u 'dʒɛl: li	in tor bi 'da to	il	'ri o
Or	**secco**	**è**	**il**	**fiore**	**e**	**l'erba,**	**mesti**	**gli**	**augelli,**	**intorbidato**	**il**	**rio.**
now	dry	is	the	flower	and	the grass	sad	the	birds	muddied	the	brook

Now the flowers and grass are dry, the birds sad, the brook muddied.

augelli (poet.) = uccelli

ak: kom 'paɲ: ɲa no	'tut: ti	il	'pjan to	'mi o
Accompagnano	**tutti**	**il**	**pianto**	**mio.**
they accompany	all	the	weeping	mine

They all join in my weeping.

'ko me	o	'di o	non	'vjɛ ni	e	'sɛn ti	i	'mjɛ i	'tri sti	la 'men ti
Come,	**oh**	**Dio,**	**non**	**vieni**	**e**	**senti**	**i**	**miei**	**tristi**	**lamenti,**
how	oh	God	not	you come	and	you hear	the	my	sad	laments

Why, oh God, do you not come and hear my sad laments,

il	'mi o	laŋ 'gwi ɾe
il	**mio**	**languire.**
the	my	languishing

my languishing?

'tor na	'tor na	e	'vo la	se	non	'vwɔ i
Torna,	**torna**	**e**	**vola**	**se**	**non**	**vuoi,**
return	return	and	fly	if	not	you wish

Come back, and quickly, if you do not wish

'lun dʒi	daʎ: 'ʎɔk: ki	'twɔ i	'far mi	mo 'ri ɾe
lungi	**dagl'occhi**	**tuoi**	**farmi**	**morire.**
far away	from the eyes	your	to make me	to die

to make me, far from your eyes, die.

GL: **Clori**

&

[27]

ma	'pri ma	'ki o	'mɔ ɾa
	Ma prima ch'io mora		
	But before I die		

ma	'pri ma	'ki o	'mɔ ɾa	ke	'dʒun ga	kwel: 'lo ɾa
Ma	**prima**	**ch'io**	**mora**	**che**	**giunga**	**quell'ora**
but	before	that I	I may die	that	may arrive	that hour

But before I die, before that hour comes,

dɛ	'sɛn ti	i	la 'men ti	'ki o	'spar go	per	te
deh	**senti**	**i**	**lamenti**	**ch'io**	**spargo**	**per**	**te.**
ah	hear	the	lamentations	that I	I spill	for	you

ah, hear the laments I pour out for you.

'mi o	'bɛ ne	le	'pe ne	del	kɔr	ke	ta 'do ɾa	ti	'nar: ri	'mi a	fe
Mio	**bene**	**le**	**pene**	**del**	**cor**	**che**	**t'adora**	**ti**	**narri**	**mia**	**fé.**
my	dear one	the	suffering	of the	heart	that	you adores	you	may tell	my	faith

My dear one, let my faithfulness tell you the suffering of the heart that adores you.

&

[85]

mi a di ˈvi zo il kɔr
Mi ha diviso il cor
[Destiny] has split my heart

mi	a	di ˈvi zo	il	kɔr	dal	ˈkɔ ɾe
Mi	**ha**	**diviso**	**il**	**cor**	**dal**	**core,**
to me	has	divided	the	heart	from the	heart

kwel	de ˈstin	ke	ˈtrɔp: po	ˈfjɛ ɾo	dal	ˈmi o	bɛn	mi	se pa ˈrɔ
quel	**destin**	**che**	**troppo**	**fiero**	**dal**	**mio**	**ben**	**mi**	**separò.**
that	destiny	which	too	cruel	from the	my	dear one	me	separated

That too cruel destiny which separated me from my dear one has split my heart in two.

ˈi o	lo	ˈse gwo	kol	pen ˈsjɛ ɾo	ma	il	pen ˈsjɛr	non	a	vi ˈgo ɾe
Io	**lo**	**seguo**	**col**	**pensiero**	**ma**	**il**	**pensier**	**non**	**ha**	**vigore**
I	him	I follow	with the	thought	but	the	thought	not	has	strength

I follow him with my thoughts, but my thoughts have not the strength

dar: ɾe ˈstar	ki	se nan ˈdɔ
d'arrestar	**chi**	**se n'andò.**
of to stop	the one who	has gone away

to stop the one who has gone away.

mi	spa ˈri sti	da	ˈʎɔk: ki	ˈi do lo	a ˈma to	ma	nel	ˈmi o	ˈkɔ ɾe	a ˈsko zo
Mi	**sparisti**	**da**	**gl'occhi**	**idolo**	**amato**	**ma**	**nel**	**mio**	**core**	**ascoso**
from me	you disappeared	from	the eyes	idol	beloved	but	in the	my	heart	hidden

You disappeared from my eyes, beloved idol, but deep in my heart

non	mi	ˈlaʃ: ʃi	ri ˈpɔ zo	e	al: ˈlor ke	in ˈvan	ti	ˈtʃer ko
non	**mi**	**lasci**	**riposo**	**e**	**allorché**	**invan**	**ti**	**cerco**
not	to me	you let	repose	and	when	in vain	you	I search for

you allow me no repose; and when in vain I search for you

ˈi o	non	sɔ	ˈko me	mi ri ˈtro vo	sul	ˈla bro	il	ˈtu o	bɛl	ˈno me
io	**non**	**so**	**come**	**mi ritrovo**	**sul**	**labro**	**il**	**tuo**	**bel**	**nome.**
I	not	I know	how	I find again	on the	lip	the	your	beautiful	name

I again find – I know not how – your beautiful name upon my lips.

labro (poet.) = labbro

pur	dal	ˈmi o	ˈpɛt: to	aŋ ˈko ɾa	tu	ˈten ti	di	fud: ˈdʒir
Pur	**dal**	**mio**	**petto**	**ancora**	**tu**	**tenti**	**di**	**fuggir.**
yet	from the	my	breast	still	you	you try	of	to flee

Yet you still try to flee from my breast.

e	per ˈke	af: ˈflit: to	ˈi o	ˈmɔ ɾa	ˈmeʃ: ʃi	daʎ: ˈʎɔk: ki	in	ˈpjan to
E	**perché**	**afflitto**	**io**	**mora**	**m'esci**	**dagl'occhi**	**in**	**pianto**
and	so that	afflicted	I	may die	me you leave	from the eyes	in	weeping

And so that I may die painfully, you leave my eyes through tears,

dal	ˈla bro	ne	so ˈspir
dal	**labro**	**ne'**	**sospir.**
from the	lip	in	sighs

[and] my lips through sighs.

Printed under the music is, variously, "n'è" and "n'e." But in the text-only section of [85] is printed, correctly, "ne'."

ɛ	di ˈvi zo	dal	ˈmon do	il	ˈkli ma	in ˈfi do	ˈdo ve	tu	ˈpɔr ti	il	ˈpjɛ de
È	**diviso**	**dal**	**mondo**	**il**	**clima**	**infido**	**dove**	**tu**	**porti**	**il**	**piede.**
is	divided	from the	world	the	(poet.) climb	treacherous	where	you	take	the	foot

The treacherous slope you are climbing is not of this world.

su   kwel   'bar ba ɾo   'li do   va tʃil: le 'ɾa i   nel: la mo 'ɾo za   'fe de
Su   quel   barbaro   lido   vacillerai   nell'amorosa   fede
on   that   barbarian   shore   you will waver   in the loving   faith
On that barbarian shore you will vacillate about [our] loving faith,

ne   del   'mi o   a 'mor   sa 'ɾan   si 'ku ɾi   i   'pɾɛ gi
né   del   mio   amor   saran   sicuri   i   pregi
nor   of the   my   love   will be   secure   the   rewards
and the rewards of my love will not be certain

'do ve   'sal vi   non   son   sul   'sɔʎ: ʎo   i   'ɾɛ dʒi
dove   salvi   non   son   sul   soglio   i   regi.
where   safe   not   are   on the   throne   the   kings
even where kings are secure on their thrones.

> *regi: plural of*
> *rege (poet.) = re*

'ɛ ɾa   'pɔ ko   al   'mi o   'pɔ ve ɾo   'pɛt: to   il   do 'lor   del: la 'tʃer ba   par 'ti ta
Era   poco   al   mio   povero   petto   il   dolor   dell'acerba   partita,
was   little   to the   my   poor   breast   the   pain   of the bitter   parting
The pain of a bitter parting would have been slight to my poor breast

sun   dʒe 'lo zo   kru 'dɛ le   so 'spɛt: to   non   su 'ni va   a   le 'var mi   la   'vi ta
s'un   geloso   crudele   sospetto   non   s'univa   a   levarmi   la   vita.
if a   jealous   cruel   suspicion   not   united   to   to take away from me   the   life
if a jealous, cruel suspicion had not united with it to take my life away.

ma   non   sɔ   kwal   naʃ: 'ʃe sti
Ma   non   so   qual   nascesti,
but   not   I know   who   you were born
But [though] I know not from whence you came *[i.e., who you are, in birthright]*;

e   un   tal   a 'man te   se   ko 'stan tsa   dʒu 'ɾɔ   'sɛm pre   ɛ   ko 'stan te
e   un   tal   amante   se   costanza   giurò   sempre   è   costante.
[and]   a   such   lover   if   constancy   swore   always   is   constant
such a lover, if she has sworn constancy, is faithful forever.

[86]

'mi o   te 'zɔ ɾo   per   te   'mɔ ɾo
Mio tesoro per te moro
My treasure, for you I am dying

'mi o   te 'zɔ ɾo   per   te   'mɔ ɾo   'vjɛ ni   'pɾe sto   a   kon so 'lar
Mio   tesoro   per   te   moro!   Vieni   presto   a   consolar
my   treasure   for   you   I die   come   quickly   to   to console
My treasure, for you I am dying! Come quickly to console

'kwe sto   kɔr   ke   'tan to   'bra ma   e   ti   'kja ma   a   ri sto 'rar
questo   cor   che   tanto   brama   e   ti   chiama   a   ristorar.
this   heart   which   so much   yearns   and   you   calls to   to   to comfort
this heart which yearns for you so much and calls to you for comfort.

[79]
from: *La fede riconosciuta (1710)*

'mo stri del: 'lɛ re bo
Mostri dell'Erebo
Monsters of Erebus

'mɔ stri	del: 'lɛ re bo	'fu rje	ter: 'ri bi li	di	'zdeɲ: ɲo	ar 'ma te mi
Mostri	**dell'Erebo,**	**furie**	**terribili,**	**di**	**sdegno**	**armatemi,**
monsters	of hell	furies	terrible	of	anger	arm me

Monsters of Erebus, terrible furies, arm me with anger;

in	sen	spi 'ra te mi	'i ra	e	fu 'ror	'zdeɲ: ɲo	'i ra	e	fu 'ror
in	**sen**	**spiratemi**	**ira**	**e**	**furor**	**sdegno,**	**ira,**	**e**	**furor.**
into	breast	breathe to me	rage	and	fury	anger	rage	and	fury

breathe into my breast rage and fury – anger, rage, and fury.

do 'rin da	ɛ	'mɔr ta	e 'di o	vi 'vrɔ
Dorinda	**è**	**morta**	**ed io**	**vivrò?**
Dorinda	is	dead	and I	I will live

Dorinda is dead, and I will live?

non	'vɔʎ: ʎo	nɔ	mo 'rir	ded: 'dʒi o	i 'ni kwo	e	'pɛr fi do	iŋ gan: na 'tor
Non	**voglio,**	**no,**	**morir**	**degg'io,**	**iniquo**	**e**	**perfido**	**ingannator.**
not	I want	no	to die	must I	iniquitous	and	treacherous	deceiver

I do not want [to live]; no, I must die an iniquitous and treacherous deceiver.

GL: **Erebo**

[84]
from: *Griselda (1721)*
character: *Griselda*

nel: 'la spro 'mi o do 'lor
Nell'aspro mio dolor
In my bitter sorrow

nel: 'la spro	'mi o	do 'lor	nɔ	non	ti lu 'ziŋ gi	il	kɔr	'va na	spe 'ran tsa
Nell'aspro	**mio**	**dolor,**	**no,**	**non**	**ti lusinghi**	**il**	**cor,**	**vana**	**speranza.**
in the bitter	my	sorrow	no	not	you may entice	the	heart	vain	hope

In my bitter sorrow, no, do not entice my heart, vain hope.

ve 'dra i	'ki o	son	pju	'fɔr te	'del: la	kru 'dɛl	'mi a	'sɔr te
Vedrai	**ch'io**	**son**	**più**	**forte**	**della**	**crudel**	**mia**	**sorte,**
you will see	that I	am	more	strong	than the	cruel	my	fate

You will see that I am stronger than my cruel fate;

ve 'dra i	ke	a 'mor	mi	'dje de	per	'a ni ma	la	'fe de	e	la	ko 'stan tsa
vedrai	**che**	**amor**	**mi**	**diede**	**per**	**anima**	**la**	**fede**	**e**	**la**	**costanza.**
you will see	that	love	to me	gave	for	soul	the	faith	and	the	constancy

you will see that love gave me a faithful and constant soul.

[81]

ne 'men per 'dʒɔ ko
Né men per gioco
Not even in jest

ne 'men   per   'dʒɔ ko   un   'al tro   'fɔ ko   mat: tʃen de 'ra
Né men   per   gioco   un   altro   foco   m'accenderà.
not even   for   joke   an   other   fire   me will ignite
Not even in jest will another passion inflame me.

> né men[o] =
> (mod.) nemmen[o]

la   'mi a   ko 'stan tsa   'ma i   di   sem 'bjan tsa   si kan dʒe 'ra
La   mia   costanza   mai   di   sembianza   si cangierà.
the   my   constancy   never   of   appearance   will change
My constancy will never change face.

[35, 64]

'ne vi in 'tat: te
Nevi intatte
Untouched snows

'ne vi   in 'tat: te   'vi e   di   'lat: te   del   bɛl   'se no   del   'mi o   bɛn
Nevi   intatte,   vie   di   latte   del   bel   seno   del   mio   ben,
snows   untouched   paths   of   milk   from the   beautiful   breast   of the   my   dear one
Untouched snows, bearers of milk from the beautiful breast of my beloved,*

'ko me   'da te   di spje 'ta te   a   kwes 'ta ni ma   il   ve 'len
come   date,   dispietate   a   quest'anima   il   velen?
how   you give   pitiless   to   this soul   the   poison
how can you, pitiless, give poison to this soul?

> dispietate (poet.) =
> spietate

> *This line is full of images: the snows are the whiteness of the breasts;
> the "vie di latte" are a poetic reference to the Milky Way (la Via lattea).

[61]
from: *La Rosaura (1690)*

Giovanni Battista Lucini

non dar pju 'pe ne o 'ka ro
Non dar più pene, o caro
Do not give more pain, o dear one

non   dar   pju   'pe ne   o   'ka ro   a   ki   ta 'do ra
Non   dar   più   pene,   o   caro,   a   chi   t'adora.
not   to give   more   pains   o   dear   to   who   you adores
Do not give more pain, o dear one, to the one who adores you.

non   mi   maŋ 'kar   di   fe   o   'pri ma   per   mer 'tʃe   'dim: mi   'ki o   'mɔ ra
Non   mi   mancar   di   fé,   o   prima   per   mercé,   dimmi   ch'io   mora.
not   me   to lack   of   fidelity   or   first   for   mercy   tell me   that I   I may die
Do not be unfaithful to me; or first, for mercy's sake, tell me to die.

[84]
from: *La caduta dei Decemviri (1697)*
character: *Valeria*

Silvio Stampiglia

non mi spret: 'tsar
Non mi sprezzar
Do not despise me

non   mi   spret: 'tsar   kru 'dɛ le   non   mi   spret: 'tsar   ko 'zi
Non   mi   sprezzar,   crudele,   non   mi   sprezzar   così.
not   me   to despise   cruel one   not   me   to despise   thus
Do not despise me, cruel one; do not despise me so.

'i o   son   la   'tu a   fe 'de le   e 'di o   pur   'so no   'kwel: la   kaʎ: 'ʎɔk: ki   'two i
Io   son   la   tua   fedele,   ed io   pur   sono   quella   ch'agl'occhi   tuoi
I   am   the   your   faithful one   and I   indeed   I am   that one   who at the eyes   yours
I am your faithful one; and I am, indeed, that one who, in your eyes,

'fu i   'bɛl: la   e   ke   ti   'pja kwi   un   di   kru 'dɛ le
fui   bella   e   che   ti   piacqui   un   dì,   crudele.
was   beautiful   and   who   you   I pleased   one   day   cruel one
was once beautiful and pleasing to you, cruel one.

[84]
from: *Griselda (1721)*
character: *Roberto*

non   vi   vor: 're i   ko 'noʃ: ʃe ɾe
Non vi vorrei conoscere
I wish I didn't know you

non   vi   vor: 're i   ko 'noʃ: ʃe ɾe   bɛʎ: 'ʎɔk: ki   lu ziŋ 'gjɛ ri   per   non   pe 'nar   ko 'zi
Non   vi   vorrei   conoscere,   begl'occhi   lusinghieri,   per   non   penar   così.
not   you   I should wish to know   beautiful eyes   enticing   in order to   not   to suffer   thus
I wish I didn't know you, beautiful, enticing eyes, so as not to suffer so.

ma   dʒak 'ke   'pe no   'tan to   non   vi mo 'stra te   al 'tɛ ri
Ma   giacché   peno   tanto,   non   vi mostrate   alteri,
but   since   I suffer   so much   not   show yourself to be   haughty
But since I suffer so much, do not be haughty;

non   mi   tra 'di te   'vo i   se   il   'fa to   mi   tra 'di
non   mi   tradite   voi   se   il   fato   mi   tradì.
not   me   betray   you   if   the   fate   me   betrayed
do not betray me [even] if fate has betrayed me.

[21, 25]

non   voʎ: 'ʎi o   se   non   ve 'der ti
Non vogl'io se non vederti
I only want to see you

non   voʎ: 'ʎi o   se   non   ve 'der ti   men   kru 'dɛl   'mi o   bɛn   kon   me
Non   vogl'io   se   non   vederti   men   crudel,   mio   ben   con   me.
not   want I   if   not   to see you   less   cruel   my   dear one   with   me
I only want to see you less cruel with me, my dear one.

ti   pro 'met: to   kom pja 'tʃer ti   e   do 'nar mi   'tut: to   a   te
Ti   prometto   compiacerti   e   donarmi   tutto   a   te!
you   I promise   to please you   and   to give myself   all   to   you
I promise to please you and to give myself completely to you!

> *"donormi," rather than (mod.)*
> *"donarmi,"is printed; "donormi"*
> *may be an antiquated verb*
> *form variation of "donerommi"*

'bra mo   sol   di   ri mi 'rar ti   'bɛl: la   'mi a   kon   men   ri 'gor
Bramo   sol   di   rimirarti,   bella   mia,   con   men   rigor;
I long   only   of   to see you   beauty   mine   with   less   severity
I only long to see you, my beauty, with less severity;

mi kon 'tɛn to   da do 'rar ti   'aŋ ko   a 'kɔ sto   del   'mi o   kɔr
Mi contento   d'adorarti   anco   a costo   del   mio   cor.
I am content   of to adore you   even   at the cost   of the   my   heart
I am content to adore you even at the cost of my heart.

> anco =
> (mod.) anche

℞

[4, 6, 8, 20, 25, 32, 38, 39, 54, 59, 60, 64]
from: *Pompeo (1683)*
character: *Sesto*

Nicolò Minato

o tʃes: 'sa te di pja 'gar mi
O cessate di piagarmi
Either stop wounding me

o   tʃes: 'sa te   di   pja 'gar mi   o   laʃ: 'ʃa te mi   mo 'rir
O   cessate   di   piagarmi,   o   lasciatemi   morir,
either   cease   of   to wound me   or   let me   to die
Either stop wounding me, or let me die,

'lu tʃiŋ 'gra te   di spje 'ta te   pju   del   'dʒɛ lo   e   pju   'de i   'mar mi
luc'ingrate,   dispietate,   più   del   gelo   e   più   dei   marmi
eyes ungrateful   pitiless   more   than the   ice   and   more   than the   (marble) stones
ungrateful, pitiless eyes, more than ice and more than stone

> *In [6], [59], and [64]: "del marmi"; in [39]: "di marmi"; correct is "dei (or de') marmi."*

'fred: de   e   'sor de   a   'mjɛ i   mar 'tir
fredde   e   sorde   a'   miei   martir.
cold   and   deaf   to   my   agony
cold and deaf to my suffering.

> alt.: ai = a'
> martir = (mod.) martirio

> [4], [6], [54], [59], *and* [64] *end here; in others there is a 2nd verse:*

pju   dun   'aŋ gwe   pju   dun   'a spe
Più   d'un   angue,   più   d'un   aspe,
more   than a   snake   more   than a   viper

> | angue (lett.) = | aspe = |
> |---|---|
> | serpente | (mod.) aspide |

'kru di   e   'sor di   a   'mjɛ i   so 'spir
crudi   e   sordi   a'   miei   sospir,
cruel   and   deaf   to   my   yearnings
More cruel and deaf to my yearning than a snake or viper,

> *In [25]: printed are "crude" and "sorde"; correct are "crudi" and "sordi," modifying "occhi" in the next line.*

'ɔk: ki   a 'tro tʃi   or goʎ: 'ʎo zi   'vo i   po 'te te   ri sa 'nar mi   e   go 'de te
occhi   atroci,   orgogliosi,   voi   potete   risanarmi   e   godete
eyes   terrible   proud   you   you are able   to heal me   and   you take pleasure
terrible proud eyes, you can heal me and [yet] you take pleasure

al   'mi o   laŋ 'gwir
al   mio   languir.
at the   my   languishing
in my languishing.

> *var. in* [20] *and* [54]:

al   'mi o   sof: 'frir
al   mio   soffrir
at the   my   suffering
in my suffering.

var. in [20] and [32]:

ˈɔk: ki	al ˈtjɛ ɾi	ˈɔk: ki	a ˈtro tʃi	ˈvo i	po ˈte te	ri sa ˈnar mi
occhi	**altieri,**	**occhi**	**atroci,**	**voi**	**potete**	**risanarmi, ...**
eyes	haughty	eyes	terrible	you	are able	to heal me

terrible haughty eyes, you can heal me...

altieri =
(mod.) alteri

var. in [25]:

ˈɔk: ki	al ˈtɛ ɾi	ˈvo i	po ˈte te	ri sa ˈnar mi
occhi	**alteri,**	**voi**	**potete**	**risanarmi, ...**
eyes	haughty	you	are able	to heal me

haughty eyes, you can heal me...

[18, 23, 39]

o dol ˈtʃis: si ma spe ˈran tsa
O dolcissima speranza
O sweetest hope

o	dol ˈtʃis: si ma	spe ˈran tsa	ˈsɛ i	il	ri ˈstɔ ɾo	del	ˈmi o	sen
O	**dolcissima**	**speranza,**	**sei**	**il**	**ristoro**	**del**	**mio**	**sen.**
o	sweetest	hope	you are	the	relief	of the	my	breast; *(fig.)* heart

O sweetest hope, you are the comfort for my heart;

per	e ˈstiŋ gwer	il	ve ˈlen	ˈvjɛ ni	e	as: ˈsi sti	a	ˈmi a	ko ˈstan tsa
Per	**estinguer**	**il**	**velen,**	**vieni**	**e**	**assisti**	**a**	**mia**	**costanza!**
in order to	to extinguish	the	poison	come	and	be witness	at	my	constancy

To nullify the poison, come and witness my fidelity!

[81]

ˈpɛn sa tʃi ˈbɛ ne
Pensaci bene
Think clearly about it

ˈpɛn sa tʃi	ˈbɛ ne	ˈkwe ste	ka ˈte ne	non	son	per	te
Pensaci	**bene**	**queste**	**catene**	**non**	**son**	**per**	**te.**
think of it	well	these	chains	not	are	for	you

Think clearly about it: these ties [of love] are not for you.

[39]

pen ˈsjɛ ɾi
Pensieri
Thoughts

pen ˈsjɛ ɾi	a	ˈdi o	kwal	ˈpe na	in	sem ˈbjan tsa	di	ˈdʒɔ ja	il	sen	maf: ˈfan: na
Pensieri!	**Ah,**	**Dio**	**qual**	**pena**	**in**	**sembianza**	**di**	**gioia**	**il**	**sen**	**m'affanna;**
thoughts	ah	God	what	pain	in	semblance	of	joy	the	breast	me troubles

Thoughts! Oh God, what pain, in the semblance of joy, troubles my breast.

ki	kwe ˈstal ma	kon ˈdan: na	in	so ˈa ve	ka ˈte na	e	kwal	iɲ: ˈɲo to	ˈful mi ne
chi	**quest'alma**	**condanna**	**in**	**soave**	**catena,**	**e**	**qual**	**ignoto**	**fulmine**
who	this soul	condemns	to	sweet	chain	and	what	unknown	thunderbolt

Who condemns this soul to sweet fetters, and what mysterious thunderbolt

gra 'di to vwɔl ke dʒo 'i ska il kɔr 'kwan do ɛ fe 'ri to
gradito vuol che gioisca il cor, quando è ferito?
grateful wants that that it rejoice the heart when it is wounded
wants the heart to be joyfully grateful when it is wounded?

a 'lu tʃi a do 'ra te deʎ: 'ʎa stri da 'mor si 'vo i kan 'dʒa te in 'dʒo ja il do 'lor
Ah luci adorate degl'astri d'Amor, si, voi cangiate in gioia il dolor.
ah lights adored of the stars of Love yes you you change into joy the sorrow
Ah, adored lights of Love's stars, yes, you change sorrow into joy.

fe 'ri te pja 'ga te ke ɛ 'glɔ rja dun kɔr po 'ter vi a do 'ra ɾe
Ferite, piagate ché è gloria d'un cor potervi adorare.
wound pierce because it is glory of a heart to be able you to adore
Wound [me], pierce [me], for it is a heart's bliss to be able to adore you.

ɛ for 'tu na sor 'tir 'pja ge si 'ka ɾe
È fortuna sortir piaghe sì care.
it is fortune to be endowed with wounds so dear
It is [good] fortune to have wounds so dear.

ma 'do ve o i 'mɛ pen 'sje ɾi 'do ve spje 'ga te i nav: ve 'du ti il 'vo lo
Ma dove, ohimè, pensieri, dove spiegate inavveduti il volo;
but where alas thoughts where you unfurl careless the flight
But where, alas, thoughts – where do you carelessly spread your wings?

'vo i tʃer 'ka te pja 'tʃe ɾe ma tro ve 're te 'dwɔ lo e 'kwel kɛ 'pɛd: dʒo
voi cercate piacere, ma troverete duolo, e quelch'è peggio,
you you seek pleasure but you will find grief and that which is worse
You seek pleasure, but you will find grief; and, what is worse,

a 'mjɛ i 'dan: ni pre 'ved: dʒo ke 'lal ma per de 'ra ri 'pɔ zo
a miei danni preveggio, che l'alma perderà riposo.
to my harms I foresee that the soul will lose repose
I foresee, to my detriment, that my soul will lose its repose.

> *preveggio (from "prevedere") =*
> *(mod.) prevedo (from "prevedere")*

ne ʎaf: 'fan: ni ne i tor 'men ti non pa 'vɛn ti ki da 'mor 'sɛr vo si 'fe
Né gl'affanni, né i tormenti, non paventi chi d'Amor servo si fé;
neither the woes nor the torments not may fear he who of Love slave himself made
May the one who has made himself a slave of Love fear neither woes nor torments;

il te 'ner fra 'tʃep: pi il 'pjɛ 'al ma at: 'tʃe za e kɔr pja 'ga to
il tener fra ceppi il piè, alma accesa e cor piagato
the holding among shackles the foot soul on fire and heart wounded
having one's foot in shackles, one's soul on fire, and one's heart wounded

ɛ di 'lɛt: to e par mar 'tir
è diletto e par martir.
is delight and it seems agony
is delight and seems like agony.

> *martir =*
> *martirio*

ɛ ki 'fud: dʒe il 'di o ben 'da to non sa 'ma i ke 'si a dʒo 'ir nɔ
Eh, chi fugge il dio bendato, non sa mai che sia gioir, no!
ah he who flees the god blindfolded not knows ever what be joy no
Ah, he who flees the blindfolded god [Cupid] will never know what joy is – no!

'du e	'bε i	'lu mi	'du e	'bε i	'lab: bri	'so no	'fab: bri	di	dol 'tʃet: tse
Due	**bei**	**lumi,**	**due**	**bei**	**labbri**	**sono**	**fabbri**	**di**	**dolcezze**
two	beautiful	eyes	two	beautiful	lips	are	makers	of	sweetnesses

Two beautiful eyes [and] two beautiful lips are the forgers of sweetnesses

e	di	pja 'tʃer	si	pen 'sje ɾi	vɔ	go 'der	'a i	splen 'do ɾi
e	**di**	**piacer;**	**sì,**	**pensieri,**	**vo'**	**goder**	**ai**	**splendori**
and	of	pleasure	yes	thoughts	I want	to delight	at the	splendors

and pleasure; yes, thoughts, I want to delight in the splendors,

'neʎ: ʎi	ar 'do ɾi	di	si	'nɔ bi le	fa 'tʃɛl: le
negli	**ardori**	**di**	**sì**	**nobile**	**facelle.**
in the	ardors	of	such	noble	torches

in the ardors, of such noble torches.

ε	for 'tu na	sen 'tir	'fjam: me	si	'bɛl: le
È	**fortuna**	**sentir**	**fiamme**	**sì**	**belle!**
it is	fortune	to feel	flames	so	beautiful

It is [good] fortune to feel such beautiful flames!

GL: **Amor**

☙

[35, 64]

per for 'ma ɾe la 'bɛt: ta
Per formare la Betta
To create Betta

per	for 'ma ɾe	la	'bɛt: ta	ke	a 'do ɾo
Per	**formare**	**la**	**Betta**	**che**	**adoro**
for	to form	the	Betta	whom	I adore

To create Betta, whom I adore,

le	'grat: tsje	su 'ni ɾo	al	'va go	la 'vo ɾo
le	**Grazie**	**s'unîro**	**al**	**vago**	**lavoro.**
the	Graces	themselves united	at the	charming	work

the Graces got together for their charming work.

unîro = (mod.) unirono

le	'kja ɾe	pu 'pil: le	son	'kwel: le	ʃin 'til: le	'kaʎ: ʎi	'a stri	ra 'pi ɾo
Le	**chiare**	**pupille**	**son**	**quelle**	**scintille,**	**ch'agli**	**astri**	**rapîro.**
the	bright	eyes	are	those	sparks	which from the	stars	stole away

Those bright eyes are sparks which they stole from the stars.

rapîro = (mod.) rapirono

ma	pju	'lu tʃi di	son	ʎi	'ɔk: ki	ke	am: 'mi ɾo
Ma	**più**	**lucidi**	**son**	**gli**	**occhi**	**che**	**ammiro.**
but	more	shining	are	the	eyes	that	I admire

But more shining are the eyes that I admire.

GL: **Grazie**

☙

[44]

'pɔ ve ɾa pel: le 'gri na
Povera pellegrina
Poor wandering girl

'pɔ ve ɾa   pel: le 'gri na   son   'i o   kɔr   'mi o   per   te
Povera   pellegrina   son   io   cor   mio   per   te.
poor   wandering girl   am   I   heart   mine   through   you
A poor wandering girl am I, my beloved, because of you.

se   iŋ 'kli na   la   'tu a   'ʃel ta   a   'u na   bel 'ta   re 'a le   'laʃ: ʃa mi
Se   inclina   la   tua   scelta   a   una   beltà   reale,   lasciami!
if   inclines   the   your   choice   to   a   beauty   regal   leave me
If your choice leans toward a regal beauty, leave me!

non   son   'kwel: la   'skɔr da ti   il   'mi o   na 'ta le   per   non   maŋ 'kar   di   fe
Non   son   quella;   scordati   il   mio   natale,   per   non   mancar   di   fé
not   I am   that one   forget   the   my   birth   in order   not   to lack   of   faith
I am not such a one; forget that I was ever born, so as not to be [accused of being] unfaithful.

'laʃ: ʃa mi   'skɔr da ti
Lasciami!   Scordati!
leave me   forget
Leave me! Forget!

&

[81]

'pɔ ve ɾe   'mi e   ka 'te ne
Povere mie catene
My miserable shackles

'pɔ ve ɾe   'mi e   ka 'te ne   'pɔ ve ɾa   fe del 'ta
Povere   mie   catene,   povera   fedeltà.
miserable   my   shackles   miserable   fidelity
My miserable shackles, miserable fidelity...

la   'spɛ me   'doɲ: ɲi   'bɛ ne   'per do no   le   'mi e   'pe ne
La   speme   d'ogni   bene   perdono   le   mie   pene,
the   hope   of every   good thing   lose   the   my   sufferings
My sufferings lose every hope of happiness

| speme (poet.) = speranza |

'kwan do   non   ɛ   pju   'mi a   la   li ber 'ta
quando   non   è   più   mia   la   libertà.
when   not   is   more   mine   the   freedom
when freedom is no longer mine.

&

[86]

'rom pe   'sprɛt: tsa
Rompe sprezza
She breaks and scorns

'rom pe   'sprɛt: tsa   kon   un   so 'spir   'oɲ: ɲi   kɔr   beŋ 'ke   di   'pje tra
Rompe   sprezza   con   un   sospir   ogni   cor   benché   di   pietra;
breaks   scorns   with   a   sigh   every   heart   even if   of   stone
With a sigh she breaks [and] scorns every heart, even if it be of stone;

e 'da i	'nu mi	'lal ma	im 'pɛ tra		'oɲː ɲi	'grat: tsja	a	'swɔ i	de 'zir
e dai	**numi**	**l'alma**	**impetra**		**ogni**	**grazia**	**a**	**suoi**	**desir.**
and from the	gods	the soul	obtains through supplication		every	grace	at	her	desires

and she obtains from the gods, through prayer, every grace she desires.

> *About "e dai," above: The editor of [86] notes that the original text reads "e'sai," and changes it to "essa i"; though that is a possibility, I'm choosing to guess that an early copying error of the "s," in "e'sai," for a "d," is likely – hence "e dai."*

ॐ

[10]

se de 'lit: to ɛ la do 'rar ti
Se delitto è l'adorarti
If adoring you is a crime

kwal	'mi a	'kol pa	o	zven 'tu ɾa	ma	ra 'pi to	il	'mi o	bɛn	'li do lo	'mi o
Qual	**mia**	**colpa,**	**o**	**svɛntura**	**m'ha**	**rapito**	**il**	**mio**	**ben**	**l'idolo**	**mio?**
what	my	fault	o	misfortune	me has	robbed	the	my	dear one	the idol	mine

What offence of mine, o misfortune, has robbed me of my dear one, my idol?

'dimː mi	o	'ka ɾo	iɱ ʃe 'del	ke	tɔ	tat: 'ti o
Dimmi,	**o**	**caro**	**infedel,**	**che**	**t'ho**	**fatt'io?**
tell me	o	dear	unfaithful one	what	you I have	done I

Tell me, o dear unfaithful one, what have I done to you?

se	de 'lit: to	ɛ	la do 'rar ti	'i o	son	'rɛ a	dun	'gran de	erː 'ror
Se	**delitto**	**è**	**l'adorarti,**	**io**	**son**	**rea**	**d'un**	**grande**	**error,**
if	crime	it is	the adoring you	I	am	guilty	of a	great	error

If adoring you is a crime, I am guilty of a great error,

tu	siɲː 'ɲor	de	'mjɛ i	vo 'le ɾi	e	ti 'ranː no	di	pen 'sjɛ ɾi
tu	**signor**	**de'**	**miei**	**voleri**	**e**	**tiranno**	**di**	**pensieri;**
you	master	of	my	wishes	and	tyrant	of	thoughts

o you master of my will and tyrant of my thoughts;

'al tra	'kol pa	ke	la 'mar ti	non	ri 'trɔ vo	nel	'mi o	kɔr
altra	**colpa**	**che**	**l'amarti**	**non**	**ritrovo**	**nel**	**mio**	**cor.**
other	fault	than	the loving you	not	I find	in the	my	heart

I find in my heart no fault other than loving you.

ॐ

[4, 6, 8, 59, 60, 64] Titled **Se Florinda è fedele** in [60] – see Editor's notes in [60].
from: *La donna ancora è fedele (1698)*
character: *Alidoro*   *Domenico Filippo Contini*

se flo 'rin do ɛ fe 'de le
Se Florindo è fedele
If Florindo is faithful

se	flo 'rin do	ɛ	fe 'de le	'i o	minː na mo ɾe 'rɔ
Se	**Florindo**	**è**	**fedele**	**io**	**m'innamorerò.**
if	Florindo	is	faithful	I	I will fall in love

If Florindo is faithful, I will fall in love.

po 'tra	ben	'lar ko	'tɛn de ɾe	il	fa ɾe 'tra to		ar 'tʃer
Potrà	**ben**	**l'arco**	**tendere**	**il**	**faretrato**		**arcier,**
will be able	well	the bow	to stretch	the	quiver bearing		archer

The archer *[Cupid]*, armed with quiver, may well draw his bow,

'ki o	mi	sa 'prɔ	di 'fɛn de ɾe	dun	'gwar do	lu ziŋ 'gjer
ch'io	**mi**	**saprò**	**difendere**	**d'un**	**guardo**	**lusinghier.**
because I	myself	I will know how	to defend	from a	glance	flattering

for I will know how to defend myself from a flattering glance.

in [60]: *da un* = *d'un*

'prɛ gi	'pjan ti	e	kwe 'ɾɛ le	'i o	non	a skol te 'rɔ
Preghi,	**pianti**	**e**	**querele**	**io**	**non**	**ascolterò,**
entreaties	tears	and	complaints	I	not	I will listen to

I will not listen to entreaties, grievings and complaints;

ma	se	sa 'ɾa	fe 'de le	'i o	min: na mo ɾe 'rɔ
ma	**se**	**sarà**	**fedele**	**io**	**m'innamorerò.**
but	if	he will be	faithful	I	I will fall in love

but if he is faithful, I will fall in love.

[5, 9, 12, 21, 25, 37, 42, 52, 60]

'sɛn to nel 'kɔ ɾe
Sento nel core
I feel in my heart

'sɛn to	nel	'kɔ ɾe	'tʃer to	do 'lo ɾe	ke	la	'mi a	'pa tʃe	tur 'ban do	va
Sento	**nel**	**core**	**certo**	**dolore,**	**che**	**la**	**mia**	**pace**	**turbando**	**va.**
I feel	in the	heart	certain	pain	which	the	my	peace	disturbing	goes

I feel in my heart a certain pain which disturbs my peace.

'splɛn de	'u na	'fa tʃe	ke	'lal ma	at: 'tʃen de	se	non	ɛ	a 'mo ɾe	a 'mor	sa 'ɾa
Splende	**una**	**face**	**che**	**l'alma**	**accende;**	**se**	**non**	**è**	**amore,**	**amor**	**sarà.**
shines	a	torch	which	the soul	ignites	if	not	is	love	love	will be

A torch shines, which ignites my soul; if it is not love, love it will be.

[4, 6, 8]

se tu 'del: la 'mi a 'mɔr te
Se tu della mia morte
If you of my death

se	tu	'del: la	'mi a	'mɔr te	a	'kwe sta	'dɛ stra	'fɔr te	la	'glɔ ɾja	non	'vwɔ i	dar
Se	**tu**	**della**	**mia**	**morte**	**a**	**questa**	**destra**	**forte**	**la**	**gloria**	**non**	**vuoi**	**dar,**
if	you	of the	my	death	to	this	right hand	strong	the	glory	not	you want	to give

'dal: la	a	'twɔ i	'lu mi
dalla	**a'**	**tuoi**	**lumi,**
give it	to	your	eyes

If you do not want to give the glory of my death to this strong right arm, give it to your eyes,

e	il	'dar do	del	'tu o	'zgwar do	'si a	'kwel: lo	ke	mut: 'tʃi da
e	**il**	**dardo**	**del**	**tuo**	**sguardo**	**sia**	**quello**	**che**	**m'uccida**
and	the	dart	of the	your	glance	may·be	that	which	me may kill

e	mi	kon	'su mi		
e	**mi**	**consumi.**			
and	me	may consume			

and let the thrust of your glance be that which kills me and consumes me.

❧

[84]
from: *L'amor generoso (1714)*   *Silvio Stampiglia*

se 'vwɔ i 'ki o 'vi va
Se vuoi ch'io viva
If you want me to live

se	'vwɔ i	'ki o	'vi va	'ka ɾa	'mi a	'di va
Se	**vuoi**	**ch'io**	**viva,**	**cara**	**mia**	**diva,**
if	you want	that I	may live	dear	my	goddess

> diva (lit.) =
> dea

If you want me to live, my dear goddess,

non	di spret: 'tsar mi	'ki o	vi ve 'ɾɔ	nɔ	nɔ
non	**disprezzarmi**	**ch'io**	**viverò,**	**no,**	**no.**
not	to despise me	that I	I will live	no	no

do not despise me, no, no, so that I will live.

ma	'tut: to	'zdeɲ: ɲo	dun	'vi le	in 'deɲ: ɲo	bɛn	ven di 'kar mi	al: 'lor	sa 'prɔ
Ma	**tutto**	**sdegno,**	**d'un**	**vile**	**indegno**	**ben**	**vendicarmi**	**allor**	**saprò.**
but	all	anger	of a	craven	unworthy one	well	to avenge myself	then	I will know how

But then, full of anger, I will well know how to take revenge on a craven, unworthy one.

❧

[86]

si ri 'skal di il 'tɛ bro
Si riscaldi il Tebro
May the Tiber become warm

si ri 'skal di	il	'tɛ bro	e	'lon da	de	'swo i	'flut: ti	al	mor mo 'ɾar
Si riscaldi	**il**	**Tebro**	**e**	**l'onda**	**de**	**suoi**	**flutti**	**al**	**mormorar.**
may warm up	the	Tiber	and	the water	of	its	waves	at the	murmuring

May the Tiber become warm at the murmuring of the water and its waves.

'kan ti	a	'lu i	'lɔ di	da 'mor
Canti	**a**	**lui**	**lodi**	**d'amor.**
may it sing	to	him	praises	of love

May it sing praises of love to him.

vet: tso 'zet: ta	'po i	ri 'spon da	'kwe sti	'kan ti tʃi	do 'nor	'del: le	a u 'ret: te	al	sus: su 'rar
Vezzosetta	**poi**	**risponda**	**questi**	**cantici**	**d'onor**	**delle**	**aurette**	**al**	**sussurar.**
pretty one	then	may respond to	these	canticles	of honor	of the	breezes	at the	whispering

May the pretty one then respond to these canticles of honor, at the whispering of the breezes.

> *It seems likely that the original was "d'amor," rather than "d'onor," i.e.:* = ...these canticles of love,...

𝒢ℒ: **Tebro**

❧

[81]

si si fe ˈdel
Sì, sì, fedel
Yes, yes, faithful

si   si   fe ˈdel   si   sa ˈɾo
Sì   **sì**   **fedel**   **sì**   **sarò,**
yes   yes   faithful   yes   I will be
Yes, yes – faithful, yes, I will be;

nɔ   nɔ   kɔr   ˈmi o   non   te ˈmer   e   ˈsɛm pre   ta me ˈɾo
no   **no**   **cor**   **mio**   **non**   **temer**   **e**   **sempre**   **t'amerò.**
no   no   heart   mine   not   to fear   [and]   always   you I will love
no, no, my beloved – do not fear; I will love you forever.

ˈka ɾa   ˈbɛl: la   ˈva ga   ˈstel: la   del   ˈmi o   pen ˈsjɛr
Cara,   **bella,**   **vaga**   **stella**   **del**   **mio**   **pensier,**
dear   beautiful   charming   star   of the   my   thought
Dear, beautiful, charming star of my thoughts,

nɔ   nɔ   ti   zdeɲ: ɲe ˈɾo   si   si   ta do ɾe ˈɾo
no   **no**   **ti**   **sdegnerò,**   **sì**   **sì**   **t'adorerò.**
no   no   you   I will scorn   yes   yes   you I will adore
no, no, I will [not] scorn you; yes, yes, I will adore you.

> *Grammatically, this should read "no, non ti sdegnerò,"* (= no, I will not scorn you) *in context of the meaning of the song; the second "no" is taken to be poetic license (if not a misprint) to continue the pattern of "sì sì" and "no no."*

[86]

si ˈswɔ ni la ˈtrom ba
Si suoni la tromba
Sound the trumpet

si ˈswɔ ni   la   ˈtrom ba
Si suoni   **la**   **tromba.**
let one sound   the   trumpet
Sound the trumpet.

ˈmjɛ i   ˈfi di   gwer: ˈrjɛ ɾi   il   ˈkam po   di   ˈfjɛ ɾi   ar ˈma ti   rim ˈbom ba
Miei   **fidi**   **guerrieri,**   **il**   **campo**   **di**   **fieri,**   **armati**   **rimbomba.**
my   faithful   warriors   the   battlefield   of   fierce   armed men   thunders out
My faithful warriors, the battlefield resounds with [the thunder of] fierce soldiers.

> *Printed are "in campo," and "più fieri"; I've changed "in" to "il" and "più" to "di" as being being more plausible grammatically – i.e., as being possible copying errors from the original.*

[4, 6, 8, 54]

son ˈtut: ta ˈdwɔ lo
Son tutta duolo
I am full of grief

son   ˈtut: ta   ˈdwɔ lo   non   ɔ   ke   af: ˈfan: ni
Son   **tutta**   **duolo,**   **non**   **ho**   **che**   **affanni**
I am   all   grief   not   I have   but   woes
I am full of grief; I have only woes,

e	mi	da	'mɔr te	'pe na	kru 'dɛl
e	**mi**	**da**	**morte**	**pena**	**crudel:**
and	to me	gives	death	suffering	cruel

and cruel suffering brings me death.

e	per	me	'so lo	'so no	ti 'ran: ni
e	**per**	**me**	**solo**	**sono**	**tiranni**
and	for	me	only	are	tyrants

ʎi	'a stri	la	'sɔr te	i	'nu mi	il	tʃɛl
gli	**astri,**	**la**	**sorte,**	**i**	**numi,**	**il**	**ciel.**
the	stars	the	fate	the	gods	the	heaven

And only for me are the stars, fate, the gods, and heaven tyrants.

☙

[81]

spe 'ran tsa
Speranza
Hope

spe 'ran tsa	del	'mi o	'kɔ re	il	'ver de	in	'kwe sti	'pra ti
Speranza	**del**	**mio**	**core**	**il**	**verde**	**in**	**questi**	**prati**
hope	of the	my	heart	the	green	on	these	meadows

Hope of my heart, the green in these meadows

si at: 'tɛn de	sat: 'tɛn de	sol	da	te
si attende,	**s'attende**	**sol**	**da**	**te,**
is expected	is expected	only	from	you

is expected – is expected only from you,

se 'pu re	non	at: 'tʃɛn de	del	sen	lim: 'mɛn so	ar 'do re
se pure	**non**	**accende**	**del**	**sen**	**l'immenso**	**ardore**
although	not	enflames	of the	breast	the immense	ardor

although the immense ardor in your breast does not enflame

> se pure =
> (mod.) seppure

i	'fjo ri	al par di	me
i	**fiori**	**al par di**	**me.**
the	flowers	on equal with	me

the flowers as much as it does me.

☙

[83]

spe 'ran tse 'mi e
Speranze mie
My hopes

spe 'ran tse	'mi e	ad: 'di o	'i o	vab: ban 'do no	fra	il	sɔn	di	'kru di	'mar mi
Speranze	**mie,**	**addio;**	**io**	**v'abbandono**	**fra**	**il**	**son**	**di**	**crudi**	**marmi**
hopes	mine	farewell	I	you I abandon	among	the	sound	of	cold	marble stones

Farewell, my hopes; I leave you, among the sound of cold slabs *[sepulchres]*,

> son[o] = (mod.) suon[o]

al: lin 'dʒu rje	de	'tɛm pi	a	'pjan dʒer	'ri e	sven 'tu re
all'ingiurie	**de'**	**tempi,**	**a**	**pianger**	**rie**	**sventure;**
at the ravishes	of the	times	to	to weep	cruel	misfortunes

> rie = plural of
> rio (lit.) = reo

to the ravishes of time, to lament cruel misfortunes;

'i o   mi   di 'pɔr to   a   'ʃeʎː ʎe ɾe   fra   'ru pi   un   bɛl   kon 'fɔr to
io   mi   **diporto**   a   **scegliere**   **fra**   **rupi**   **un**   **bel**   **conforto.**
I   myself   deport   to   to choose   among   cliffs   a   beautiful   comfort

I deport myself, choosing to find among the cliffs a beautiful solace.

> *diporto = (mod.)*
> *deporto (from*
> *"deportare")*

ko 'zi   vwɔl   'delː la   'mi a   'sɔr te   'lem pjo   'fa to   'dar mi   'mɔr te
Così   **vuol**   **della**   **mia**   **sorte**   **l'empio**   **fato**   **darmi**   **morte**
thus   wants   of the   my   destiny   the impious   fate   to give me   death

Thus does the impious fate of my destiny want to give me death,

per 'kil   kɔr   non   'gɔ da   pju   di   fe 'li tʃe   zven tu 'ra ta   'al ma
per ch'il   **cor**   **non**   **goda**   **più**   **di**   **felice**   **sventurata**   **alma**
because the   heart   not   may enjoy   more   of   happy   unlucky   soul

for my heart may no longer enjoy more happiness than [does] an unfortunate soul;

'dʒɛ mi   abː ban do 'na ta   in   si   'kru da   ser vi 'tu
gemi   **abbandonata**   **in**   **sì**   **cruda**   **servitù.**
moan   abandoned   in   such   harsh   servitude

moan, [my soul], abandoned in such dire servitude.

di   don 'dzɛlː le   in fe 'de li   lin si 'djo zi   so 'spi ɾi
Di   **donzelle**   **infedeli**   **l'insidiosi**   **sospiri**
of   damsels   unfaithful   the insidious   sighs

non   u di 'ɾa i   'ma i   pju   'mi o   kɔr   tra 'di to
non   **udirai**   **mai**   **più**   **mio**   **cor**   **tradito.**
not   you will hear   ever   more   my   heart   betrayed

My betrayed heart, you will never again hear the deceptive sighs of unfaithful damsels.

asː 'sa i   'fo sti   sker 'ni to   un   'vi zo   lu zin 'gɛr   pju   non   si 'mi ɾi
Assai   **fosti**   **schernito**   **un**   **viso**   **lusingher**   **più**   **non**   **si miri,**
enough   you were   mocked   a   face   alluring   more   not   may be seen

You have been mocked enough; do not look anymore at an alluring face;

e   per   non   di za 'mar   un   di   in fe 'li tʃe
e   **per**   **non**   **disamar**   **un**   **dì**   **infelice**
[and]   for   not   to not love anymore   one   day   unhappy

sa 'sten ga   oɲː 'ɲun   da 'mar   'trɔpː po   fe 'li tʃe
s'astenga   **ognun**   **d'amar**   **troppo**   **felice.**
let abstain   each one   of loving   too   happy

in order, one unhappy day, to fall out of love, everyone should abstain from loving too happily.

'mjɛ i   afː 'fɛtː ti   'sta te ne   in   'pa tʃe   dʒa   per   'vo i   pje 'ta   non   vɛ   nɔ
Miei   **affetti**   **statene**   **in**   **pace**   **già**   **per**   **voi**   **pietà**   **non**   **v'è,**   **no,**
my   feelings   be you   in   peace   now   for   you   pity   not   there is   no

My feelings, be at peace; now there is no pity for you – no,

ke   a   kwel   sen   ke   a   pju   dun   'pja tʃe   pju   dar   'fe de
ché   **a**   **quel**   **sen**   **che**   **a**   **più**   **d'un**   **piace**   **più**   **dar**   **fede**
because   to   that   breast   which   to   more   than one   is pleasing   more   to give   faith

non   si 'dɛ
non   **si de'.**
not   one ought

> *de' = (mod.) deve*

for one should not trust that breast which pleases more than one [person].

☙

[4, 6, 8, 42, 54]

'spes: so 'vi bra per 'su o 'dʒɔ ko
Spesso vibra per suo gioco
Often hurls, for his amusement

'spes: so	'vi bra	per	'su o	'dʒɔ ko	il	ben 'da to	par go 'let: to	'stra li	'dɔ ɾo
Spesso	**vibra**	**per**	**suo**	**gioco**	**il**	**bendato**	**pargoletto**	**strali**	**d'oro**
often	hurls	for	his	game	the	blindfolded	baby boy	arrows	of gold

The blindfolded boy *[Cupid]*, for his amusement, often hurls arrows of gold

	in	'u mil	'pet: to	stral	di	'fer: ro	in	'nɔ bil	'kɔ ɾe
	in	**umil**	**petto,**	**stral**	**di**	**ferro**	**in**	**nobil**	**core.**
	in	humble	breast	arrows	of	iron	in	noble	heart

var.	in	'nɔ bil	'se no
in the		...in nobil seno.	
repeat:		...to a noble breast.	

to a humble breast, arrows of iron to a noble heart.

'pɔ i	laŋ 'gwɛn do	in 'med: dzo al		'fɔ ko	del	di 'vɛr so	at: 'tʃe zo	'stra le
Poi	**languendo**	**in mezzo al**		**foco**	**del**	**diverso**	**acceso**	**strale**
then	weakening	in the middle of the		fire	of the	different	ignited	arrow

per	od: 'dʒet: to	non	e 'gwa le	'kwe sto	'maŋ ka	e	kwel	vjɛn 'me no
per	**oggetto**	**non**	**eguale**	**questo**	**manca**	**e**	**quel**	**vien meno.**
for	object	not	equal	this one	misses	and	that one	fails

Then, each of the ignited arrows dying in its own fire because its object is not its equal, one misses and the other fails the mark.

☙

[84]
from: *Tigrane (1715)*   *Domenico Lalli*

su sur: 'ran do il ven ti 'tʃɛl: lo
Susurrando il venticello
Whispering, the breeze

su sur: 'ran do	il	ven ti 'tʃɛl: lo	par	ke	'di ka
Susurrando	**il**	**venticello**	**par**	**che**	**dica,**
whispering	the	breeze	it seems	that	it says

Whispering, the breeze seems to say,

ɛ	'ka ɾo	ɛ	'bɛl: lo	il	mo 'ɾi ɾe	per	a 'mor
"È	**caro,**	**è**	**bello**	**il**	**morire**	**per**	**amor."**
it is	dear	it is	beautiful	the	dying	for	love

"Dying for love is dear and beautiful."

pur 'ke	'vi va	il	'mi o	di 'let: to	'del: la	'mɔr te	il	'fjɛ ɾo	a 'spɛt: to
Purché	**viva**	**il**	**mio**	**diletto,**	**della**	**morte**	**il**	**fiero**	**aspetto**
provided that	may live	the	my	beloved	of the	death	the	cruel	face

As long as my beloved one lives, the cruel face of death

sa 'ra	'dʒɔ ja	a	'kwe sto	kɔr
sarà	**gioia**	**a**	**questo**	**cor.**
will be	joy	to	this	heart

will be joy to this heart.

☙

[5, 9]

su ve 'ni te a kon 'siʎ: ʎo
Su, venite a consiglio
Come, come advise me

L'AUTORE (The author):

su	ve ˈni te	a	kon ˈsiʎ: ʎo	o	pen ˈsje ɾi	ko ˈmɛs: ser	ˈma i	pwɔ
Su,	**venite**	**a**	**consiglio,**	**o**	**pensieri.**	**Com'esser**	**mai**	**può**
come on	come	to	counsel	o	thoughts	how to be	ever	can

Come, come advise me, o thoughts.   How ever can it be

ˈki o	ˈsɛr va	a	se ˈmi ɾa	ke	ˈskɔ po	ɛ	del: ˈli ɾa	di ki	min fjam: ˈmɔ	nɔ
ch'io	**serva**	**a**	**Semira,**	**che**	**scopo**	**è**	**dell'ira**	**di chi**	**m'infiammò?**	**No.**
that I	I serve	to	Semira	who	target	is	of the wrath	of the one who	me inflamed	no

that I serve Semira, who is the target of the wrath of the one who inflamed me? No.

I PENSIERI (The thoughts):

ɛ	ˈmeʎ: ʎo	sof: ˈfri ɾe	pe ˈna ɾe	mo ˈri ɾe
È	**meglio**	**soffrire,**	**penare,**	**morire,**
it is	better	to endure	to suffer	to die

It is better to endure, suffer, and die

ke	ˈma i	ri mi ˈra ɾe	od: ˈdʒet: ti	si	ˈfje ɾi
che	**mai**	**rimirare**	**oggetti**	**sì**	**fieri.**
than	ever	to gaze upon	objects	so	cruel

than ever to gaze upon such cruel objects [of love].

L'AUTORE (The author):

ɛ	laʃ: ˈʃa te	i	kon ˈsiʎ: ʎi	o	pen ˈsje ɾi
Eh!	**lasciate**	**i**	**consigli,**	**o**	**pensieri!**
ah	leave	the	counsels	o	thoughts

Ah, stop advising me, o thoughts!

nɔ	tor ˈna te	a	kon ˈsiʎ: ʎo	o	pen ˈsje ɾi	ki	il	ˈse no	ma ˈpri
No,	**tornate**	**a**	**consiglio,**	**o**	**pensieri.**	**Chi**	**il**	**seno**	**m'aprì**
no	return	to	counsel	oh	thoughts	The one who	the	breast	me opened

No, come back to advise me, oh thoughts. The one who opened my breast

kon	ˈdol tʃe	fe ˈri ta	ve ˈdra	ke	ɛ	sker ˈni ta	ˈsu a	ˈfe de	ko ˈzi	si
con	**dolce**	**ferita**	**vedrà**	**che**	**è**	**schernita**	**sua**	**fede**	**così,**	**sì.**
with	sweet	wound	will see	that	is	scorned	her	faith	thus	yes

with a sweet wound will see that her fidelity is thus scorned – yes.

I PENSIERI (The thoughts):

il	ˈtʃe lo	per ˈmet: ta	men	ˈgra ve	ven ˈdet: ta
Il	**cielo**	**permetta**	**men**	**grave**	**vendetta!**
the	heaven	may permit	less	grave	revenge

May heaven permit a less serious revenge!

de ˈstin	pju	so ˈa ve	ɛ	ˈfɔr tsa	ˈki o	ˈspe ɾi
Destin	**più**	**soave**	**è**	**forza**	**ch'io**	**speri.**
destiny	more	sweet	it is	necessity	that I	I should hope for

I must hope for a sweeter destiny.

L'AUTORE (The author):

o	laʃ: ˈʃa te	i	kon ˈsiʎ: ʎi	o	pen ˈsje ɾi
Oh	**lasciate**	**i**	**consigli,**	**o**	**pensieri.**
Oh	leave	the	counsels	o	thoughts

Oh stop advising me, o thoughts.

[10, 18, 34, 38, 39]
from: *Pompeo (1683)*
character: *Mitridate*

Nicolò Minato

toʎː ˈʎe te mi la ˈvi ta aŋ ˈkor
Toglietemi la vita ancor
Take away my life too

toʎː ˈʎe te mi	la	ˈvi ta	aŋ ˈkor	ˈkru dɛ li	ˈtʃɛ li	se	mi	vo ˈle te	ra ˈpir	il	kɔr
Toglietemi	**la**	**vita**	**ancor,**	**crudeli**	**cieli,**	**se**	**mi**	**volete**	**rapir**	**il**	**cor.**
remove from me	the	life	also	cruel	heavens	if	me	you wish	to rob	the	heart

Take away my life too, cruel heavens, if you wish to rob my heart.

in [34]: rapire = rapir[e]

[10] *ends here; in other prints is a 2ⁿᵈ verse:*

ne ˈga te mi	i	ˈra i	del	di	se ˈvɛ ɾe	ˈsfɛ ɾe	se	ˈva ge	ˈsjɛ te	del	ˈmi o	do ˈlor
Negatemi	**i**	**rai**	**del**	**dì,**	**severe**	**sfere,**	**se**	**vaghe**	**siete**	**del**	**mio**	**dolor.**
deny me	the	rays	of the	day	stern	spheres	if	desirous	you are	of the	my	grief

Deny me the light of day, stern stars, if you desire my grief.

in some prints: "il rai";
grammatically correct is "i rai."

ॐ

[7]

tu lo ˈsa i
Tu lo sai
You know it

tu	lo	ˈsa i	ˈkwan to	ta ˈma i	tu	lo	ˈsa i	kru ˈdɛl
Tu	**lo**	**sai**	**quanto**	**t'amai;**	**tu**	**lo**	**sai,**	**crudel.**
you	it	you know	how much	you I loved	you	it	you know	cruel one

You know how much I loved you; you know it, cruel one.

ˈi o	non	ˈbra mo	ˈal tra	mer ˈtʃe
Io	**non**	**bramo**	**altra**	**mercé;**
I	not	I desire	other	reward

I wish for no other reward;

sol	ri ˈkɔr da ti	di	me	e	ˈpo i	ˈsprɛtː tsa	un	in fe ˈdel
sol	**ricordati**	**di**	**me,**	**e**	**poi**	**sprezza**	**un**	**infedel.**
only	may remember you	of	me	and	then	despise	an	unfaithful one

only that you remember me, and then despise an unfaithful one.

ॐ

[61]
from: *La Rosaura (1690)*

Giovanni Battista Lucini

uŋ kɔr da ˈvo i fe ˈri to
Un cor da voi ferito
A heart wounded by you

uŋ	kɔr	da	ˈvo i	fe ˈri to	ˈkjɛ de	mer ˈtʃe	pje ˈta
Un	**cor**	**da**	**voi**	**ferito,**	**chiede**	**mercé,**	**pietà,**
a	heart	by	you	wounded	asks for	mercy	pity

A heart wounded by you asks for mercy [and] pity

e	'spɛ ɾa	'ɛs: ser	gra 'di to	ke	'lal ma	'su a	vi	da
e	spera	esser	gradito	ché	l'alma	sua	vi	da.
and	hopes	to be	pleasing	because	the soul	its	to you	gives

and hopes to be pleasing, as it gives you its soul.

෴

[35, 64]

va per lo 'ma ɾe
Va per lo mare
[The little boat] goes over the sea

va	per	lo	'ma ɾe	ke	la	tʃir 'kon da	'on da	per	'on da	la	na vi 'tʃɛl: la
Va	**per**	**lo**	**mare,**	**che**	**la**	**circonda,**	**onda**	**per**	**onda**	**la**	**navicella.**
goes	through	the	sea	which	it	encircles	wave	through	wave	the	little boat

The little boat goes, wave through wave, over the sea which surrounds it.

> lo = (mod.) il

ko 'zi	il	'mi o	'kɔ ɾe	nel	mar	da 'mo ɾe
Così	**il**	**mio**	**core**	**nel**	**mar**	**d'amore**
thus	the	my	heart	in the	sea	of love

So does my heart, in the sea of love,

or	'ʃen de	or	'sal tsa	'ko me	lo	'zbal tsa	la	'tu a	pro 'tʃɛl: la
or	**scende**	**or**	**s'alza**	**come**	**lo**	**sbalza**	**la**	**tua**	**procella.**
now	sinks	now	rises	like	it	hurls	the	your	tempest

now sink and now rise, as your tempest tosses it about.

෴

[84]
from: *Marco Attilio Regolo (1719)*

vi 'kre do o nɔ
Vi credo, o no
Shall I believe you or not?

vi	'kre do	o	nɔ	spe 'ran tse	a 'ma te	ke	miŋ gan: 'na te
Vi	**credo,**	**o**	**no,**	**speranze**	**amate,**	**che**	**m'ingannate?**
you	I believe	or	no	hopes	loved	which	me deceive

Shall I believe you or not, beloved hopes which deceive me?

aŋ 'kor	pa 'vɛn ta	nel	'pɛt: to	il	kɔr
Ancor	**paventa**	**nel**	**petto**	**il**	**cor.**
still	is afraid	in the	breast	the	heart

The heart in my breast is still afraid.

go 'der	non	sɔ	ke	se	gra 'di te	'spɛ ɾa	mi	'di te
Goder	**non**	**so,**	**ché**	**se**	**gradite**	**spera**	**mi**	**dite,**
to take pleasure	not	I know how	because	if	pleasant	hope	to me	you say

I know not how to have pleasure because, when you pleasingly say to me: "hope,"

pur	mi	tor 'men ta	'fred: do	ti 'mor
pur	**mi**	**tormenta**	**freddo**	**timor.**
yet	me	torments	cold	fear

cold fear nevertheless torments me.

෴

[84]
from: *La Statira (1690)*
character: *Alessandro*

Cardinal Pietro Ottoboni

'vin to 'so no
Vinto sono
I am defeated

'vin to	'so no	e	del	'nu me	ben 'da to	'ba tʃo	'lar ko	e 'da 'do ɾo	ʎi	'stra li
Vinto	**sono,**	**e**	**del**	**nume**	**bendato**	**bacio**	**l'arco**	**ed adoro**	**gli**	**strali,**
defeated	I am	and	of the	deity	blindfolded	I kiss	the bow	and I adore	the	arrows

I am defeated, and I kiss the blindfolded deity's *[Cupid's]* bow and adore his arrows

> *printed is "bagio," an antiquated form of (mod.) "bacio"*

ke	tem 'pra ti	nel	'vol to	a do 'ra to	di	sta 'ti ɾa	fan	'pja ge	mor 'ta li
che	**temprati**	**nel**	**volto**	**adorato**	**di**	**Statira,**	**fan**	**piaghe**	**mortali.**
which	tempered	in the	face	adored	of	Statira	they make	wounds	mortal

which, tempered in the adored face of Statira, produce mortal wounds.

�֎ *Sessa, Claudia (fl. 1613)*

All that is known about Claudia Sessia (see Candace Smith's editorial comments in [62]) is found in Gerolamo Borsieri's *Soplemento* to P. Morigia's *La nobilità di Milano* (1619). Borsieri recounts Sessa's technical and dramatic virtuosity as a singer ("...there was not a singer who could equal her") as well as her modesty ("...some princes who had spoken with her later said that had they not known her to be an angel through her voice, they would have declared her to be an angelic creature in her conduct."). She was a nun at the Milanese convent of S. Maria Annunciata.

Sessa's only extant compositions are the two songs included here, both from the collection *Canoro pianto di Maria Vergine sopra la faccia di Christo estinto* (Venice, 1613), a compilation of poems based on the features of Christ's face set by various composers. Sessa's two songs are dedicated, respectively, to Christ's eyes and ears.

---

[62]

'ɔk: ki 'i o 'vis: si di 'vo i
Occhi, io vissi di voi
Eyes, I lived through you

'ɔk: ki	'i o	'vis: si	di	'vo i	'men tre	'vo i	'fo sti	'vo i	ma	'spɛn ti	'pɔ i
Occhi,	**io**	**vissi**	**di**	**voi**	**mentre**	**voi**	**fosti**	**voi**	**ma**	**spenti**	**poi**
eyes	I	I lived	of	you	while	you	you were	you	but	lifeless	then

Eyes, I lived through you while you were [alive]; but since you are lifeless

'vi vo	di	'vɔ stra	'mɔr te	in	fe 'li tʃe	a li 'men to	ki	me	'nu tre	al	tor 'men to
vivo	**di**	**vostra**	**morte**	**in**	**felice**	**alimento**	**chi**	**mi**	**nutre**	**al**	**tormento**
I live	of	your	death	in	happy	nourishment	who	me	feeds	at the	torment

I live through your death, [you] who feed me with happy nourishment in my torment

e	mi	'maŋ ka	al	dʒo 'i ɾe	per	far	vi 'va tʃe	'mɔr te	al	'mi o	mar 'ti ɾe
e	**mi**	**manca**	**al**	**gioire**	**per**	**far**	**vivace**	**morte**	**al**	**mio**	**martire.**
and	to me	is missing	at the	rejoicing	for	to make	living	death	to the	my	martyrdom

and whom I miss in my joy, in order to giving living death to my martyrdom.

☙

[62]   'vat: te ne pur laʃ: 'ʃi va o 'ɾek: kja u 'ma na
Vattene pur lasciva orecchia umana
Go away, lascivious human ear

'vat: te ne   pur   laʃ: 'ʃi va   o 'ɾek: kja   u 'ma na
Vattene   pur   lasciva   orecchia   umana,
go away   [indeed] lascivious   ear   human
Go away, lascivious human ear,

'tut: ta 'rik: ka   e   pom 'po za di   pen 'dɛn ti   e   di   'rɔ za
tutta   ricca   e   pomposa   di   pendenti   e   di   rosa,
all   rich   and   pompous   with   pendants   and   with   rose
all rich and pompous with pendants and roses

ma   'tut: ta   'sor da   a   'di o   e   'tut: ta   'va na
ma   tutta   sorda   a   Dio   e   tutta   vana.
but   all   deaf   to   God   and   all   vain
but completely deaf to God, and totally vain.

ke   son   del   'mi o   dʒe 'zu   'rɔ ze   e   pen 'dɛn ti
Ché   son   del   mio   Gesù   rose   e   pendenti
because   are   of the   my   Jesus   roses   and   pendants
For the roses and pendants of my Jesus are

i   ru 'bi ni ka 'dɛn ti dal: lo 'ɾek: kje   e   dal   'kri ne
i   rubini   cadenti   dall'orecchie   e   dal   crine,
the   rubies   falling   from the ears   and   from the   head of hair
the rubies *[drops of blood from the crown of thorns]* falling from his ears and locks

in   fjor   ver 'miʎ: ʎi   e din   ver 'miʎ: ʎe   'bri ne
in   fior   vermigli   ed in   vermiglie   brine.
in   flowers   vermilion   and in   vermilion   congealed drops
in vermilion flowers and vermilion drops.

'an tsi   lo 'ɾek: kje   'su e   si   saŋ gwi 'no ze   'al tro   non   son
Anzi   l'orecchie   sue   sì   sanguinose   altro   non   son
In fact   the ears   his   so   bloody   other   not   are
In fact, his ears, so bloody, are none other

ke   'du e   ver 'miʎ: ʎe   'rɔ ze
che   due   vermiglie   rose.
than   two   vermilion   roses
than two vermilion roses.

 Stefani, Giovanni (fl.1618-1626)

Though "Partenza," subtitled *Canzonetta*, is attributed to Stefani (named on the title page in [11] as "Stafani"), he was probably the collector, rather than the composer, of several books of songs with continuo and guitar containing a total of eighty-seven Italian songs, four Sicilian dialect songs and six Spanish songs. *Grove* quotes Stefani, in a preface to the second of three extant song collections, as writing that "his 'feeble talent' allowed him only to collect the songs of others."
He was, at least, a music editor; and there is conjecture that he was, around 1620, organist at the Church of the Graces in Vienna.

[11]

par 'tɛn tsa
Partenza
Parting

mi 'par to	e	nel	par 'tir	ti	'di ko	a 'mo ɾe	kin dʒu sta 'men te
Mi parto	**e**	**nel**	**partir**	**ti**	**dico,**	**amore,**	**ch'ingiustamente**
I depart	and	in the	parting	to you	I say	love,	that unjustly

I am departing; and in parting I say to you, love, that unjustly

tu	mi	'da i	do 'lo ɾe	es: 'sɛn do	'ti o	fe 'de le	'bɔ na 'nɔt: te	kru 'dɛ le
tu	**mi**	**dai**	**dolore,**	**essendo**	**t'io**	**fedele;**	**bona notte**	**crudele.**
you	to me	you give	pain	being	to you I	faithful	good night	cruel one

do you cause me pain, in being faithful to you; good night, cruel one.

> *bona = (mod.) buona*

mi 'par to	e	nel	par 'tir	vɔ	'pas: so 'pas: so	ti	rak: ko 'man do	il	kɔr
Mi parto	**e**	**nel**	**partir**	**vò**	**passo, passo.**	**Ti**	**raccomando**	**il**	**cor**
I depart	and	in the	departing	I go	step by step	to you	I entrust	the	heart

I am departing, and in doing so I go slowly. To you I entrust my heart,

kin	'peɲ: ɲo	'las: so	bɛn	'mi o	'pɔ ke	pa 'rɔ le	'bɔ na 'nɔt: te	'mi o	'so le
ch'in	**pegno**	**lasso,**	**ben**	**mio,**	**poche**	**parole;**	**bona notte**	**mio**	**sole.**
which in	pledge	I leave	dear one	my	few	words	good night	my	sun

which I leave you as a pledge, my dear one, with few words: good night, my sun.

> *lasso = (mod.) lascio*

❀ *Steffani, Agostino* (1654-1728)

Having received his early musical training as a singer in Padua and Rome, Steffani sang in an opera in Venice at the age of eleven.

In 1667 he was taken by the Elector Ferdinand Maria of Bavaria to Munich, where he remained for twenty-one years. In 1680 he was ordained as a priest. After service at the courts of Hanover, Düsseldorf, and Vienna he resumed residence in Hanover in 1709 upon his appointment as Apostolic Vicar in northern Germany.

Steffani was an eminent churchman and diplomat as well as composer and organist. Among his posts prior to that of Apostolic Vicar were court organist and director of chamber music in Munich, Kapellmeister to Duke Ernst August of Hanover, privy councilor and president of the Spiritual Council for the Palatinate in Düsseldorf, and Abbot of Löpsingen.

He is recognized historically as having considerably influenced north German opera (specifically the works of Händel). All of his extant works are vocal works: in addition to some eighteen operas, a large number of vocal duets, a *Stabat Mater*, and collections of motets and chamber cantatas.

---

[87]

ki non 'gɔ de di 'su a 'lɔ de
Chi non gode di sua lode
Whoever does not enjoy praise for himself

ki	non	'gɔ de di	'su a	'lɔ de	ɛ	ti 'ran	del	'prɔ prjo	o 'nor
Chi	**non**	**gode di**	**sua**	**lode**	**è**	**tiran'**	**del**	**proprio**	**onor.**
he who	not	delights in	his	praise	is	tyrant	of the	own	honor

Whoever does not enjoy praise for himself is a tyrant to his own honor.

te	di 'sprɛt: tsi	se	non	'prɛt: tsi	di	'tu o	'no me	il	bɛl	splen 'dor
Te	**disprezzi**	**se**	**non**	**prezzi**	**di**	**tuo**	**nome**	**il**	**bel**	**splendor.**
yourself	you look down on	if	not	you prize	of	your	name	the	fine	splendor

You disparage yourself if you do not value the fine splendor of your name.

ෙ

[87]

ko 'la deʎ: ʎjar 'ka di
Colà degl'Arcadi
Over there [the panpipes] of the Arcadians

ko 'la	deʎ: ʎjar 'ka di	le	'kan: ne	'stri do no						
Colà	**degl'Arcadi**	**le**	**canne**	**stridono.**						
over there	of the Arcadians	the	pipes	shriek						

Over there the panpipes of the Arcadians resound shrilly.

sil 'va ni	e	'dri a di	le	'dan tse	in 'tɛs: so no	ʎar 'tʃe ri	a 'li dʒe ri	'ljɛ ti	ne	'ri do no
Silvani	**e**	**driadi**	**le**	**danze**	**intessono;**	**gl'arcieri**	**aligeri**	**lieti**	**ne**	**ridono.**
sylvans	and	dryads	the	dances	weave	the archers	winged	happy	at them	laugh

Wood nymphs and dryads weave their dances; the winged archers *[Cupids]* laugh happily.

GL: Arcadi

☙

[87]
from: *Briseide (1696)*   *Count Francesco Palmieri*

'dol tʃe a u 'ret: ta
Dolce auretta
Sweet little breeze

'dol tʃe	a u 'ret: ta	ke	si	'gra ta	'spjɛ gin 'tor no	i	'van: ni	dɔr
Dolce	**auretta**	**che**	**si**	**grata**	**spiegh'intorno**	**i**	**vanni**	**d'or,**
sweet	little breeze	who	so	pleasantly	unfurl all around	the	wings	of gold

Sweet little breeze, who unfurl your golden wings so pleasantly,

tu	ti	'ri di	del	'mi o	kɔr
tu	**ti**	**ridi**	**del**	**mio**	**cor.**
you	yourself laugh	at the	my	heart	

you laugh at my heart.

ma	se	'fus: si	in: na mo 'ra ta	o	dun	'dʒɛf: fi ro	o	dun	fjor
Ma	**se**	**fussi**	**innamorata**	**o**	**d'un**	**zeffiro**	**o**	**d'un**	**fior,**
but	if	you were	in love	either	with a	zephyr	or	with a	flower

But if you were in love with a zephyr or a flower

laŋ gwi 'ɾe sti	al	'mi o	do 'lor
languiresti	**al**	**mio**	**dolor.**
you would languish	at the	my	sorrow

you would languish at my sorrow.

☙

[87]

il pa sto 'ɾel: lo
Il pastorello
The shepherd boy

il	pa sto 'ɾel: lo	sen 'dʒa tʃe	af: 'flit: to	'prɛs: so	il	ruʃ: ʃel: lo
Il	**pastorello**	**s'en giace**	**afflitto**	**presso**	**il**	**ruscello**
the	shepherd boy	himself lies down	grieved	near	the	stream

The shepherd boy lies down by the stream, grieving

ke	de zo 'la to	e	dʒa	skon 'fit: to	ɛ	il	'gred: dʒe	a 'ma to
ché	**desolato**	**e**	**già**	**sconfitto**	**è**	**il**	**gregge**	**amato.**
because	desolate	and	already	vanquished	is	the	flock	beloved

because his beloved flock is desolate and vanquished.

'del: la	tsam 'poɲ: ɲa	al	swɔn	fu 'nɛ sto	so 'let: to	e	'mɛ sto
Della	**zampogna**	**al**	**suon**	**funesto**	**soletto**	**e**	**mesto**
of the	bagpipe	at the	sound	mournful	all alone	and	sad

At the mournful sound of the bagpipes, all alone and sad

kan 'tan do	in 'vi ta	a	'pjan dʒer	'se ko	'lon da	e	lo	'spɛ ko
cantando	**invita**	**a**	**pianger**	**seco**	**l'onda**	**e**	**lo**	**speco.**
singing	invites	to	to weep	himself with	the water	and	the	cave

[and] singing, he invites the water and the grotto to weep with him.

e	par	ke	'pɔ i	pjan 'dʒɛn do	'di ka	dɛ	'rjɛ di	a	no i
E	**par**	**che**	**poi**	**piangendo**	**dica:**	**Deh**	**riedi**	**a**	**noi!**
and	it seems	that	then	weeping	he says	please	come back	to	us

And then, weeping, he seems to say, "Please return to us!

dɛ	'rjɛ di	a	'no i	o	'pa tʃe	a 'mi ka	'ɔ tsjo	be 'a to
Deh	**riedi**	**a**	**noi,**	**o**	**pace**	**amica!**	**Ozio**	**beato!**
please	come back	to	us	o	peace	friendly	leisure	blessed

Please come back to us, o friendly peace, blessed leisure!"

❧

[87]

'la gri me do lo 'ro ze
Lagrime dolorose
Sorrowful tears

'la gri me	do lo 'ro ze	da	'ʎɔk: ki	'mjɛ i	ve 'ni ste	kon	'dop: pjo	'fju me
Lagrime	**dolorose,**	**da**	**gl'occhi**	**miei**	**veniste**	**con**	**doppio**	**fiume**
tears	sorrowful	from	the eyes	mine	you came	with	double	river

Sorrowful tears, you flowed from my eyes in a double river

ad	i non 'dar mi	il	'kɔ ɾe
ad	**inondarmi**	**il**	**core.**
to	flood me	the	heart

to flood my heart.

❧

[87]

le 'nin fe pju vet: 'tso ze kon 'pla tʃi do iŋ 'kan to
Le Ninfe più vezzose…Con placido incanto
The most charming nymphs…With peaceful enchantment

le	'nin fe	pju	vet: 'tso ze	'se gwon	la	'bɛl: la	'klɔ ɾi
Le	**ninfe**	**più**	**vezzose**	**seguon**	**la**	**bella**	**Clori**
the	nymphs	most	charming	follow	the	beautiful	Clori

The most charming nymphs follow the beautiful Clori

e	le	'dʒɛm: me	o do 'ɾo ze	'kɛl: la	'spar dʒe	'su i	'kam pi	'ʃel gon
e	le	gemme	odorose	ch'ella	sparge	sui	campi	scelgon
and	the	buds	fragrant	which she	scatters	on the	fields	they choose

and gather the fragrant flowers which she scatters on the fields

per	'far ne	al	krin	'va ɾje	gir 'lan de	'prɛ mi	'po i	di	pa 'sto ɾi
per	farne	al	crin	varie	ghirlande	premi	poi	di	pastori,
for	to make of them	to the	head of hair	various	garlands	rewards	then	of	shepherds

in order to make various garlands which will then be rewards for *[upon the heads of]* shepherds

o	kor: 'ren do	o	lo 'kan do	o	nel	fe 'ri ɾe	le	'bel ve	in si dja 'tri tʃi
o	correndo	o	locando	o	nel	ferire	le	belve	insidiatrici
either	running	or	camping	or	in the	wounding	the	wild beasts	ambushing

[who], whether running or staying in one place, or wounding the ambushing wild beasts

'mo stran	le	'fɔr tse	u 'gwa li	a	un	gran dar 'di ɾe
mostran	le	forze	uguali	a	un	grand'ardire.
they show	the	strengths	equal	to	a	great courage

show a strength equal to their great courage.

kon	'pla tʃi do	iŋ 'kan to	ki	'tɛm pra	il	'su o	'kan to
Con	placido	incanto	chi	tempra	il	suo	canto
with	peaceful	enchantment	he who	tunes	the	his	song

With peaceful enchantment he who tunes his song

> *tempra =*
> *(mod.) tempera*

al	swɔn	'del: le	'tʃe tre	il	'mɔ to	so 'spɛn de	al: 'la u ɾa	e dal	'fon te
al	suon	delle	cetre	il	moto	sospende	all'aura	ed al	fonte,
to the	sound	of the	citharas	the	motion	sospends	to the air	and to the	spring

to the sound of the lyre suspends the movement of air and water

e dal	'mon te	lo	'rɛn de	al	'bɔ sko	'al: le	'pjɛ tre
ed al	monte	lo	rende	al	bosco	alle	pietre.
and to the	mountain	it	renders	to the	woods	to the	rocks

and renders it up to the mountains, woods, and rocks.

> *"le," printed,*
> *must be "lo"*
> *in the context*

G𝓛: Clori

❧

[25]
from: *Marco Aurelio (1681)*   *Ventura Terzago*

'sɛ i si 'ka ɾo
Sei sì caro
You are so dear

'sɛ i	si	'ka ɾo	si	vet: 'tso zo	'a i	nel	'vol to	un	'tʃɛr to	ke
Sei	sì	caro,	sì	vezzoso;	hai	nel	volto	un	certo	che,
you are	so	dear	so	charming	you have	in the	face	a	certain	something

You are so dear, so charming; you have in your countenance a certain something

ke	il	'mi o	kɔr	non	a	ri 'pɔ zo	ne	sa	'vi ver	'sɛn tsa	te
che	il	mio	cor	non	ha	riposo	né	sa	viver	senza	te!
that	the	my	heart	not	has	repose	nor	knows how	to live	without	you

which allows my heart no repose, nor does it know how to live without you!

❧

[87]
from: *Briseide (1696)*   *Count Francesco Palmieri*

un 'kɔ ɾe o 'pjan te o 'sasː si
Un core, o piante, o sassi
[Give] a heart, o trees, o rocks

un	'kɔ ɾe	o	'pjan te	o	'sasː si	'da te	a	kwel	sen	kru 'dɛl
Un	**core,**	**o**	**piante,**	**o**	**sassi,**	**date**	**a**	**quel**	**sen'**	**crudel,**
a	heart	o	trees	o	rocks	give	to	that	breast	cruel

Give a heart, o trees, o rocks, to that cruel breast,

ke	se	del	'vɔ stro	'kɔ ɾe	i mi te 'ral	ri 'go ɾe
che	**se**	**del**	**vostro**	**core**	**imiterà'l**	**rigore,**
that	if	of the	your	heart	it will imitate the	harshness

so that if it will imitate the harshness of your heart

al 'men	'lem pjo	im pa 'rasː si	'dalː la	'vɔ stra	fer 'metː tsa	'dɛsː ser	fe 'del
almen	**l'empio**	**imparassi**	**dalla**	**vostra**	**fermezza**	**d'esser**	**fedel.**
at least	the pitiless one	may learn	from the	your	firmness	of to be	faithful

the pitiless one may at least learn, from your steadfastness, to be faithful.

[87]
from: *Briseide (1696)*   *Count Francesco Palmieri*

'vjɛ ni o 'ka ɾa
Vieni, o cara
Come, o dear

'vjɛ ni	o	'ka ɾa	a 'ma ta	'spɔ za	al	'mi o	kɔr	koɲː 'ɲor	so 'spi ɾa
Vieni,	**o**	**cara**	**amata**	**sposa,**	**al**	**mio**	**cor**	**ch'ognor**	**sospira.**
come	o	dear	beloved	bride	to the	my	heart	which always	sighs

Come, o dear beloved bride, to my heart which is always yearning.

non	a	'pa tʃe	spi ɾe 'ra	se	non	ti	'mi ɾa
Non	**ha**	**pace;**	**spirerà**	**se**	**non**	**ti**	**mira.**
not	has	peace	will expire	if	not	you	it *[my heart]* sees

It has no peace; it will die if I do not see you.

Stradella, Alessandro (1639-1682)

Stradella was born in Nepi, near Viterbo, into an aristocratic family; early facts about his musical education are unclear. Records of his compositions date from 1663 in Rome, where his activities were centered, with interim time spent in Venice and Turin until 1677, when he fled to Bologna after incurring the anger of the family of Cardinal Cibo by falsely arranging a marriage contract for the Cardinal's nephew.

In 1669 Stradella was involved in a plot to steal money from the Roman Catholic Church. All in all, his lifestyle, including liaisons with married women, led to his being fatally stabbed in the back by an assassin in Genoa.

Though he was in the service of the Colonna family in Rome, he composed mostly by commissions rather than under any major royal patronage. He wrote music, both instrumental and vocal, in all the major forms of the time, including at least four operas, prologues and intermezzos in comic style, oratorios, and more than a hundred and fifty cantatas.

His music "constitutes an important link in the period between Cesti and Handel *[Grove]*."

[39]

a por 'fi ɾja vek: kja 'rɛl: la
A Porfiria vecchiarella
Little old Porfiria

a por 'fi ɾja vek: kja 'rɛl: la ke fu 'bɛl: la
A Porfiria vecchiarella, che fu bella,
to Porfiria little old lady who was beautiful
Little old Porfiria, who was once beautiful,

or sod 'dʒa tʃe deʎ: 'ʎan: ni al: 'la spra 'pe na
or soggiace degl'anni all'aspra pena.
now is subjected of the years to the bitter punishment
is now subject to the bitter punishment of the years.

siɲ: 'ɲor dɛ 'fa te dar 'u na ka 'te na
Signor, deh fate dar una catena!
Lord please make to give a (conjugal) tie
Lord, please give her a husband!

❧

[88]
from: *La forza d'amor paterno (1678)*
character: *Lucinda*

Nicolò Minato

ka 'te ne da 'mo ɾe
Catene d'amore
Chains of love

ka 'te ne da 'mo ɾe ke 'lal ma le 'ga te dɛ laʃ: 'ʃa te 'kwe sto 'kɔ ɾe in li ber 'ta
Catene d'amore che l'alma legate, deh, lasciate questo core in libertà,
chains of love that the soul you bind ah leave this heart in freedom
Chains of love that bind the soul, ah, leave this heart in freedom,

kal do 'lo ɾe pju re 'zis te ɾe non sa
ch'al dolore più resistere non sa!
for at the sorrow more to resist not it knows how
for it knows no longer how to resist sorrow!

❧

[1, 2, 21, 25, 46]
from: *Il Floridoro (1695)*
character: *Eurinda*

Flavio Orsini

kol 'mi o 'saŋ gwe kom pre 'rɛ i
Col mio sangue comprerei
I would pay with my blood

kol 'mio 'saŋ gwe kom pre 'rɛ i 'kwel: la 'vi ta a me si 'ka ɾa
Col mio sangue comprerei quella vita a me sì cara,
with my blood I would buy that life to me so dear
I would pay with my blood [to have back] that life so dear to me,

> *alt.: "comprarei" =*
> *an antiquated*
> *variant of "comprerei"*

sa 'u na 'per di ta si a 'ma ɾa son 'du e 'fju mi ʎi 'ɔk: ki 'mjɛ i
s'a una perdita sì amara son due fiumi gli occhi miei.
if at a loss so bitter are two rivers the eyes mine
as my eyes are two rivers [of tears] from such a bitter loss.

[1], [2], *and* [46] *continue with a short Recitative and then an Aria:*

ren 'de te mi	il	'mi o	'bɛ ne	'em pje	'skwa dre	ne 'mi ke
Rendetemi	**il**	**mio**	**bene,**	**empie**	**squadre**	**nemiche,**
give back to me	the	my	dear one	impious	troops	hostile

Give me back my beloved, you impious enemy troops;

'koɲː ɲi	'al tra	ofː 'fe za	'fatː ta	al	'rɛ dʒo	'trɔ no
ch'ogni	**altra**	**offesa,**	**fatta**	**al**	**regio**	**trono,**
that every	other	offence	done	to the	royal	throne

se	fe 'ra spe	ren 'de te	'i o	vi	per 'do no
se	**Feraspe**	**rendete,**	**io**	**vi**	**perdono.**
if	Feraspe	you return	I	you	I pardon

I will pardon every other offence to the royal throne if you return Feraspe.

per pje 'ta	dɛ	'tor na	a	me	a	fe 'ra spe	e	'do ve	'sɛ 1
Per pietà	**deh**	**torna**	**a**	**me;**	**ah,**	**Feraspe,**	**e**	**dove**	**sei?**
for pity's sake	please	come back	to	me	ah	Feraspe	[and]	where	you are

For pity's sake, please come back to me; ah, Feraspe, where are you?

se	do 'lɛn ti	i	'lu mi	'mjɛ i	non	san	'vi ver	'sɛn tsa	te
se	**dolenti**	**i**	**lumi**	**miei**	**non**	**san**	**viver**	**senza**	**te.**
[if]	grieving	the	eyes	mine	not	know how	to live	without	you

Grieving, my eyes do not know how to live without you.

per pje 'ta	dɛ	'tor na	a	me
Per pietà,	**deh**	**torna**	**a**	**me!**
for pity's sake	please	return	to	me

For pity's sake, please return to me!

&

[88]
from: *La forza d'amor paterno (1678)*
character: *Stratonica*

Nicolò Minato

kɔrː 're te	mo 'men ti
Correte, momenti	
Run, time	

kɔrː 're te	mo 'men ti	spa 'ri te	vo 'la te	'fa te vi	al	'mi o	de 'zi re	un	'pun to	'so lo
Correte,	**momenti,**	**sparite,**	**volate,**	**fatevi**	**al**	**mio**	**desire**	**un**	**punto**	**solo.**
run	moments	vanish	fly	make yourselves	at the	my	desire	one	point	only

Run, time – vanish, fly; become, at my desire, one moment only.

son	'lo re	e ter ni 'ta te	'kwan do	si 'vanː no	a	mi zu 'rar	kol	'dwɔ lo
Son	**l'ore**	**eternitate**	**quando**	**si vanno**	**a**	**misurar**	**col**	**duolo.**
are	the hours	eternity	when	they go by	to	to measure	with the	grief

*eternitate =
(mod.)
eternità*

The hours are an eternity when they are measured by grief.

a mo 'ro zo	bar 'lu me	di	'mi e	'prɔ nu be	'fa tʃi	atː 'tʃe ze	il	'lu me
Amoroso	**barlume**	**di**	**mie**	**pronube**	**faci**	**accese**	**il**	**lume,**
amorous	spark	of	my	nuptial	torches	kindled	the	light

A spark of love ignited my hopes of marriage;

ma	di	non	'dʒu sti	afː'fanː ni	'vo i	mi	kol 'ma te	il	'se no	'a stri	ti 'ranː ni
ma	**di**	**non**	**giusti**	**affanni**	**voi**	**mi**	**colmate**	**il**	**seno,**	**astri**	**tiranni.**
but	of	not	rightful	woes	you	me	you fill	the	breast	stars	tyrannical

but you fill my breast with unjust sorrows, tyrannical stars.

❧

[22, 25, 39, 48]

ko 'zi a 'mor mi 'fa i laŋ 'gwir

Così, Amor, mi fai languir

Thus, Love, you make me languish

ko 'zi	a 'mor	mi	'fa i	laŋ 'gwir	non	ɛ	'mi o	tʃɔ	ke	de 'zi o
Così,	**Amor,**	**mi**	**fai**	**languir;**	**non**	**è**	**mio**	**ciò**	**che**	**desio,**
thus	Love	me	you make	to languish	not	is	mine	that	which	I desire

> var. in [22]:
> quel che = ciò
> che; same
> translation

Thus, Love, you make me languish: what I desire is not mine,

ki	mi	'fudː dʒe	se 'gwir	'dɛdː dʒo
chi	**mi**	**fugge**	**seguir**	**deggio,**
who	me	flees	to follow	I must

> var. in [48]: che (= chi) mi fugge

I must follow the one who flees from me,

e	ki	si 'strudː dʒe	nel	'mi o	'fɔ ko	hɔ	da	fudː 'dʒir
e	**chi**	**si strugge**	**nel**	**mio**	**foco**	**ho**	**da**	**fuggir.**
and	who	is consumed	in the	my	fire	I have	to	to flee

and I must flee from the one who is consumed in my passion.

> var. in [48] and [22]: del mio foco = by my passion

ko 'zi	a 'mor	mi	'fa i	pe 'nar	non	mi	'da i	ki	'tan to	a 'ma i
Così,	**Amor,**	**mi**	**fai**	**penar;**	**non**	**mi**	**dai**	**chi**	**tanto**	**amai,**
thus	Love	me	you make	to suffer	not	me	you give	who	so much	I loved

Thus, Love, you make me suffer. You do not give me the one I loved so much;

il	'mi o	'bɛ ne	skatː 'tʃar	'dɛdː dʒo
il	**mio**	**bene**	**scacciar**	**deggio,**
the	my	dear one	to drive away	I ought

I must drive away my beloved

e	mi kon 'vjɛ ne	ki	non	'a mo	pur	a 'mar
e	**mi conviene**	**chi**	**non**	**amo**	**pur**	**amar.**
and	for me is necessary	who	not	I love	yet	to love

> alt.:
> pure ['pu ɾe]
> = pur

and yet I must love the one I do not love.

> var. in [22], [25], and [48]:

ko 'zi	a 'mor	mi	'fa i	pe 'nar	a	mi	'fa i	pe 'nar
Così,	**Amor,**	**mi**	**fai**	**penar,**	**ah!**	**mi**	**fai**	**penar!**
thus	Love	me	you make	to suffer	ah	me	you make	to suffer

Thus, Love, you make me suffer! Ah, you make me suffer!

GL: **Amor**

❧

[88]
from: *La forza d'amor paterno (1678)*
character: *Stratonica*

Nicolò Minato

'fud: dʒi 'fud: dʒi dal 'mi o kɔr
Fuggi, fuggi dal mio cor
Flee, flee from my heart

'fud: dʒi	'fud: dʒi	dal	'mi o	kɔr	im pos: 'si bi le	pen 'sjɛr
Fuggi,	**fuggi**	**dal**	**mio**	**cor,**	**impossibile**	**pensier.**
Flee	flee	from the	my	heart	impossible	thought

Flee; flee from my heart, impossible thought.

non	ɛ	'le tʃi to	vo 'ler	tʃɔ	ke	par	ke	'di ka	a 'mor
Non	**è**	**lecito**	**voler**	**ciò**	**che**	**par**	**che**	**dica**	**Amor.**
not	it is	permitted	to wish	that	which	seems	that	says	Love

It is not right to wish for that which Love seems to say.

'lun dʒi	'lun dʒi	dal	'mi o	sen	im pru 'dɛn te	vo lon 'ta
Lungi,	**lungi**	**dal**	**mio**	**sen,**	**imprudente**	**volontà,**
far	far	from the	my	breast	imprudent	will

Far, far from my breast, imprudent will,

tɔr men 'tar mi	non	sa 'pra	'fjam: ma	iɲ 'dʒu sta	im 'pu ro	ar 'dor	nɔ
tormentarmi	**non**	**saprà**	**fiamma**	**ingiusta,**	**impuro**	**ardor,**	**no.**
to torment me	not	it will know how	flame	unjust	impure	ardor	no

an unjust flame, an impure ardor, will not know how to torment me – no.

GL: **Amor**

&

[57]

'lu tʃi vet: 'tso ze
Luci vezzose
Pretty eyes

'lu tʃi	vet: 'tso ze	nɔ	non	mi	fud: 'dʒi te
Luci	**vezzose,**	**no,**	**non**	**mi**	**fuggite;**
eyes	pretty	no	not	me	you flee

Pretty eyes, no, do not flee from me;

'si a	di	'mɔr te	ter: 'ri bi le	il	'dʒɛ lo	kel	'mi o	a 'mo re	te 'mer lo	non	sa
sia	**di**	**morte**	**terribile**	**il**	**gelo**	**che'l**	**mio**	**amore**	**temerlo**	**non**	**sa;**
be	of	death	terrible	the	chill	for the	my	love	to fear it	not	knows how

let the chill of death be terrible, for my love does not fear it;

e	sa 'ra	pro 'pit: tsjo	il	'tʃɛ lo	se	kon	'vo i	'so lo	mut: 'tʃi de
e	**sarà**	**propizio**	**il**	**cielo**	**se**	**con**	**voi**	**solo**	**m'uccide,**
and	will be	propitious	the	heaven	if	with	you	only	me kills

o mi 'tʃi de	a	me	gra 'di te
omicide	**a**	**me**	**gradite.**
murderers	to	me	welcomed

and heaven will be kind if, together with you, welcomed murderers, it will only kill me.

se	da 'mo re	pro 'pit: tsja	la	'sɔr te	per	'vo i	'so lo	mo 'ri re	mi	fa
Se	**d'amore**	**propizia**	**la**	**sorte**	**per**	**voi**	**solo**	**morire**	**mi**	**fa,**
if	of love	propitious	the	fate	for	you	only	to die	me	makes

If propitious fate makes me die of love just for you,

> *"sole," printed*
> *rather than "solo,"*
> *must be an error*

mi	sa 'ra	'vi ta	la	'mɔr te	ke	per	'ka u za	ko 'zi	'bɛl: la
mi	**sarà**	**vita**	**la**	**morte**	**che**	**per**	**causa**	**così**	**bella**
to me	will be	life	the	death	which	for	cause	so	beautiful

la	'mi a	'stel: la	a	me	di 'spo ze
la	**mia**	**stella**	**a**	**me**	**dispose.**
the	my	star	to	me	arranged

death, which for so beautiful a cause my destiny planned for me, will be life for me.

non	mi	fud: 'dʒi te	nɔ	'lu tʃi	vet: 'tso ze	nɔ	nɔ	'lu tʃi	vet: 'tso ze
Non	**mi**	**fuggite,**	**no,**	**luci**	**vezzose,**	**no,**	**no,**	**luci**	**vezzose.**
not	me	you flee	no	eyes	pretty	no	no	eyes	pretty

Do not flee from me, no, pretty eyes – no, no, pretty eyes.

&

[88]
from: *La forza d'amor paterno (1678)*
character: *Antioco*

Nicolò Minato

mo ri 'rɔ	'stel: le	'pɛr fi de
Morirò, stelle perfide
I will die, perfidious stars

mo ri 'rɔ	'stel: le	'pɛr fi de	si
Morirò,	**stelle**	**perfide,**	**sì.**
I will die	stars	perfidious	yes

I will die, perfidious stars – yes.

se	spa 'ri	da'	'mje i	'lu mi	'oɲ: ɲi	se 'ren	'ʃɔl ga	'mɔr te	o 'ma i
Se	**sparì**	**da'**	**miei**	**lumi**	**ogni**	**seren,**	**sciolga**	**morte**	**omai**
If	vanished	from	my	eyes	every	tranquillity	let release	death	now

> omai
> (poet.) =
> ormai

As every tranquility has vanished from my eyes, let death now release

da	'kwe sto	sen	'ri o	le 'ga me	ke	kwe 'stal ma	im pri dʒo 'nɔ
da	**questo**	**sen**	**rio**	**legame**	**che**	**quest'alma**	**imprigionò.**
from	this	breast	cruel	tie	which	this soul	imprisoned

from this breast the cruel tie which imprisoned this soul.

&

[88]
from: *La forza d'amor paterno (1678)*
character: *Antioco*

'nɔt: te	a 'mi ka	de	ri 'pɔ zi
Notte, amica de' riposi
Night, friend of rest

'nɔt: te	a 'mi ka	de	ri 'pɔ zi	pju	no 'jo zi	a	me	ne 'mi ka
Notte,	**amica**	**de'**	**riposi,**	**più**	**noiosi,**	**a**	**me**	**nemica,**
night	friend	of	reposes	more	annoying	to	me	enemy

i	si 'lɛn tsi	tu	mi	'rɛn di
i	**silenzi**	**tu**	**mi**	**rendi;**
the	silences	you	to me	make

> printed "silenzii" =
> (mod.) "silenzi"

Night, friend of rest, enemy to me, you make silence more annoying for me;

lo 'bli o	ke	al 'tru i	kon 'tʃɛ di	a	me	kon 'tɛn di
l'oblio	**che**	**altrui**	**concedi**	**a**	**me**	**contendi.**
the oblivion	that	others	you grant	to	me	you deny

the oblivion you grant others you deny to me.

'sor dʒi o 'ma i 'dal: le 'pju me   tu   ke il 'lu me
Sorgi **omai** **dalle** **piume,** **tu** **che** **il** **lume**
arise now from the feathers [bed] you who the light

omai
(poet.) =
ormai

e   i   'va gi 'ra i del sol 'bjon do in 'tʃɛ lo ad: 'du tʃi
e **i** **vaghi** **rai** **del** **sol** **biondo** **in** **cielo** **adduci;**
and the lovely rays of the sun golden to heaven you lead

Rise now from sleep, you *[night]* who lead the light and the lovely rays of the golden sun into the sky;

in 'seɲ: ɲa la 'mi a 'lu tʃe a 'kwe ste 'lu tʃi
insegna **la** **mia** **luce** **a** **queste** **luci.**
teach the my eye to these lights

train my eyes to this light.

❧

[39]

'om bre 'vo i ke tʃe 'la te
Ombre, voi che celate
Shadows, you who hide

'om bre 'vo i ke tʃe 'la te del: 'lɛ tra i 'ra i
Ombre, **voi** **che** **celate** **dell'etra** **i** **rai,**
shadows you who you hide of the air the rays

etra (poet.) =
etere, aria

Shadows, you who hide the rays [of light] in the air,

dɛ   per   pje 'ta de al 'me no ren 'de te mi il 'mi o 'so le
deh, **per** **pietade** **almeno** **rendetemi** **il** **mio** **sole,**
ah for pity's sake at least give back to me the my sun

pietade =
(mod.)
pietà

ah, for pity's sake at least give me back my sun;

ren 'de te mi il 'mi o 'bɛ ne op: 'pur non mi vje 'ta te
rendetemi **il** **mio** **bene,** **oppur** **non** **mi** **vietate**
give back to me the my dear one or else not me forbid

printed "o pur" =
(mod.) "oppur[e]"

give me back my beloved, or else do not forbid me

kin   un   'kan di do 'se no pju bɛl del sol aŋ 'kor
ch'in **un** **candido** **seno** **più** **bel** **del** **sol** **ancor,**
that on a white breast more beautiful than the sun even

del   tʃɛl pju a 'dor no 'mi ɾi di 'nɔt: te o 'ma i 'splen de ɾe il 'dʒor no
del **ciel** **più** **adorno** **miri** **di** **notte** **omai** **splendere** **il** **giorno.**
than the sky more lovely I may see at night now to shine the day

to look upon a white breast even more beautiful than the sun, more lovely omai (poet.) = ormai
than the sky, shining now at night as at day.

'fos ke 'lar ve nel sen del 'mi o 'bɛ ne
Fosche **larve,** **nel** **sen** **del** **mio** **bene,**
dark spirits in the breast of the my dear one

Dark spirits, in the breast of my beloved,

or   ke   'dɔr me de 'sta te pje 'ta
or **che** **dorme** **destate** **pietà!**
now that she sleeps awaken pity

now that she is sleeping, awaken pity!

pa le 'za te   la 'tro tʃi   ka 'te ne   kon   ke   a 'mo ɾe   tʃin 'dʒen do   mi   va
Palesate   **l'atroci**   **catene**   **con**   **che**   **Amore**   **cingendo**   **mi**   **va!**
reveal   the dreadful   fetters   with   which   Love   encompassing   me   goes
Reveal the dreadful fetters with which Love enchains me.

'di te   'pu ɾe   kun   sol   ko 'zi   'ka ɾo   'men tre   ot: 'tu zo
Dite   **pure**   **ch'un**   **sol**   **così**   **caro,**   **mentre**   **ottuso**
say   also   that a   sun   so   dear   while   dim

fra   'nu bi   sa 'skon de   'ʎok: ki   'mjɛ i   kon   'tur bi ne   a 'ma ɾo
fra   **nubi**   **s'asconde,**   **gl'occhi**   **miei**   **con**   **turbine**   **amaro**
among   clouds   is hidden   the eyes   mine   with   flood   bitter

> asconde (lit.) = nasconde

'aŋ ke   al   'ma ɾe   fan   'kreʃ: ʃe ɾe   'lon de
anche   **al**   **mare**   **fan**   **crescere**   **l'onde.**
yet   at the   sea   they make   to rise   the waves

> I've changed the printed "san" to "fan," as it's likely that a manuscript "f" was mistaken for an "s," and "fan" makes sense in the context.

Also say that while a sun so dear is hidden among clouds, my eyes, in bitter flood, make the waves of the sea rise.

ko 'zi   'fi do   a vi 'tʃen da   se   fra   ri 'pɔ zi   in 'tan to
Così,   **fido**   **a vicenda:**   **se**   **fra**   **riposi**   **intanto**
thus   faithful   in turn   if   among   resposes   meanwhile
Thus [I am] faithful in turn: if, in resting,

'el: la   'kju de   i   'swɔ i   'lu mi   'i o   'la pro   al   'pjan to
ella   **chiude**   **i**   **suoi**   **lumi,**   **io**   **l'apro**   **al**   **pianto.**
she   closes   the   her   eyes   I   them I open   to the   weeping
she closes her eyes, I open mine to weeping.

'men tre   o   'fil: li   in   'dol tʃe   'son: no   'tɛɲ ɲi   op: 'prɛs: si   i   'two i   pen 'sjɛɾ i
Mentre,   **o**   **Filli,**   **in**   **dolce**   **sonno**   **tegni**   **oppressi**   **i**   **tuoi**   **pensieri,**
while   o   Filli   in   sweet   sleep   you keep   oppressed   the   your   thoughts

> printed "tenghi" = old verb form = tegni = (mod.) tieni

While, o Filli, you keep your thoughts weighed down in sweet slumber,

'lal ma   el   kɔr   do 'lor   si   'fjɛ ɾi   'sen tsa   te   sof: 'frir   non   'pɔn: no
l'alma   **e'l**   **cor**   **dolor**   **sì**   **fieri**   **senza**   **te**   **soffrir**   **non**   **ponno.**
the soul   and the   heart   pain   so   fierce   without   you   to endure   not   they can

> ponno: old verb form = possono

my soul and heart can not endure so fierce a pain without you.

'sor dʒi   'duŋ kwe   'a pri   bɛn   'mi o   'lu tʃi   a   me   si   'ka ɾe   e   'bɛl: le
Sorgi   **dunque,**   **apri,**   **ben**   **mio,**   **luci**   **a**   **me**   **sì**   **care**   **e**   **belle,**
arise   then   open   dear one   mine   eyes   to   me   so   dear   and   beautiful
Get up, then; open, my beloved, your eyes so dear and beautiful to me,

e   kon   'du e   'pla tʃi de   'stel: le   'fu ga   pur   'fa to   si   'ri o
e   **con**   **due**   **placide**   **stelle**   **fuga**   **pur**   **fato**   **sì**   **rio.**
and   with   two   peaceful   eyes   drive away   [indeed]   fate   so   cruel
and with two peaceful eyes dispel a fate so cruel.

o 'ver   se 'gwen do   'lor me   del   'son: no   lu ziŋ 'gjɛr   'om bra   di   'mɔr te
O ver,   **seguendo**   **l'orme**   **del**   **sonno**   **lusinghier:**   **ombra**   **di**   **morte,**
otherwise   following   the footsteps   of the   sleep   enticing   shadow   of   death

> o ver = (mod.) ovver[o]

Otherwise, following in the footsteps of enticing slumber, shadow of death,

mi	pre pa 'rɔ	a	mo 'rir	men 'trel: la	'dɔr me
mi	**preparò**	**a**	**morir,**	**mentr'ella**	**dorme.**
myself	I will prepare	for	to die	while she	sleeps

I will prepare myself to die while she sleeps.

si 'tɔl ga	la	'sal ma	dal	kɔr	tor men 'ta to
Si tolga	**la**	**salma**	**dal**	**cor**	**tormentato,**
let be taken away	the	corpse	from the	heart	tormented

Let my body be taken away from my tormented heart;

se	'la e ɾe	stel: 'la to	mi	'pri va	del: 'lal ma	ko 'zi	'mi o	te 'zɔ ɾo
se	**l'aere**	**stellato**	**mi**	**priva**	**dell'alma**	**così,**	**mio**	**tesoro,**
if	the sky	starry	me	deprives	of the soul	thus	my	treasure

if the star-studded sky thus deprives me of my soul, my treasure,

sjam	'pa ɾi	'al: la	'sɔr te	tu	al	'son: no	'i o	'al: la	'mɔr te
siam	**pari**	**alla**	**sorte,**	**tu**	**al**	**sonno,**	**io**	**alla**	**morte,**
we are	equal	in the	fate	you	to the	sleep	I	to the	death

we will share an equal fate: you to slumber, I to death;

tu	'dɔr mi	'i o	mi	'mɔ ɾo
tu	**dormi,**	**io**	**mi**	**moro.**
you	you sleep	I	me	I die

you will sleep, I will die.

GL: **Amore, Filli**

❧

[88]
from: *La forza d'amor paterno (1678)*
character: *Antioco*

Nicolò Minato

o mo 'ɾi ɾe o li ber 'ta
O morire, o libertà
Either death or freedom

o	mo 'ɾi ɾe	o	li ber 'ta o	o	non	a 'mar
O	**morire**	**o**	**libertà, o...**	**o**	**non**	**amar.**
either	to die	or	freedom or...	or	not	to love

Either death or freedom or... or not to love.

kɔr	do 'lɛn te	'al ma	laŋ 'gwɛn te	'al tro	nɔ	non	si pwɔ far
Cor	**dolente,**	**alma**	**languente,**	**altro,**	**no,**	**non**	**si può far.**
heart	aching	soul	languishing	other	no	not	one can to do

Aching heart, languishing soul, no, there is nothing else to do.

❧

[22, 25]
from: *Il Floridoro (1695)*

Flavio Orsini

per pje 'ta
Per pietà
For pity's sake

per	pje 'ta	dɛ	'tor na	dɛ	'tor na	a	me	a 'mor	'mi o	e	'do ve	'sɛ i
Per	**pietà,**	**deh,**	**torna**	**deh,**	**torna**	**a**	**me!**	**amor**	**mio**	**e**	**dove**	**sei?**
for	pity	ah	return	ah	return	to	me	love	mine	[and]	where	you are

For pity's sake, ah, return to me, my love; where are you?

son do 'lɛn ti   i   'lu mi   'mjɛ i   non   san   'vi ver   'sɛn tsa   te
Son dolenti   i   lumi   miei;   non   san   viver   senza   te.
are   mournful   the   eyes   mine   not   know how   to live   without   you
My eyes are mournful; they do not know how to live without you.

❧

> John Glenn Paton presents evidence that "Pietà, Signore" was actually composed
> by François Joseph Fétis (1784-1871), with a different text. See [60], pg.138.

[25, 29, 43, 54, 59, 60, 64]

pje 'ta   siɲː 'ɲo ɾe
Pietà, Signore
Have pity, Lord

pje 'ta   siɲː 'ɲo ɾe   di   me   do 'lɛn te   siɲː 'ɲor   pje 'ta
Pietà,   Signore,   di   me   dolente;   Signor,   pietà!
pity   Lord   on   me   suffering   Lord   pity
Have pity, Lord, on suffering me; Lord, have pity!

se   a   te   'dʒun dʒe   il   'mi o   pre 'gar
Se   a   te   giunge   il   mio   pregar,
if   to   you   reaches   the   my   praying
If my praying reaches you,

> *alt.: pregare* [pre 'ga ɾe] = *pregar*

non   mi   pu 'ni ska   il   'tu o   ri 'gor
non   mi   punisca   il   tuo   rigor.
not   me   may punish   the   your   severity
may your severity not punish me.

'me no   se 'vɛ ɾi   kle 'mɛn ti   oɲː 'ɲo ɾa   'vɔl dʒi   i   'two i   'zwgar di   'so pra   di   me
Meno   severi,   clementi   ognora,   volgi   i   tuoi   sguardi   sopra   di   me.
less   severe   merciful   always   turn   the   your   glances   over   of   me
Less stern, always merciful, turn your gaze upon me.

> *var.:* **su me** [su me] = same translation
> *in several prints:* ...**deh, volgi...** [dɛ 'vɔl dʒi] = ah, turn...

non   'fi a   'ma i   ke   nelː lin 'fɛr no   'si a   danː 'na to
Non   fia   mai   che   nell'Inferno   sia   dannato
not   will be   ever   that   in the hell   I may be   damned
May it never be that in hell I be damned

> *fia = (mod.) sarà*

nel   'fwɔ ko   e 'tɛr no   dal   'tu o   ri 'gor
nel   fuoco   eterno   dal   tuo   rigor.
to the   fire   eternal   by the   your   severity
to the eternal fire by your severity.

gran   'di o   dʒamː 'ma i   'si a   danː 'na to   nel   'fwɔ ko   e 'tɛr no   dal   'tu o   ri 'gor
Gran   Dio,   giammai,   sia   dannato   nel   fuoco   eterno   dal   tuo   rigor.
great   God   never   I may be   damned   to the   fire   eternal   by the   your   severity
Great God, may I never be damned to the eternal fire by your severity.

❧

[88]
from: *La forza d'amor paterno (1678)*
character: *Stratonica*

Nicolò Minato

'kwan to tar 'da te
Quanto tardate
How much you delay

'kwan to	tar 'da te	o	'kwan to	'dʒɔ je	del: 'lal ma	a	se ɾe 'nar mi	il	sen
Quanto	**tardate,**	**oh,**	**quanto,**	**gioie**	**dell'alma,**	**a**	**serenarmi**	**il**	**sen!**
how much	you delay	oh	how much	joys	of the soul	to	to cheer up me	the	breast

How much you delay – oh, how much, joys of my soul – in cheering my breast!

> *serenare (lit.) = rasserenare*

'kru do	'fa to	al	'mi o	kon 'tɛn to	va	tes: 'sɛn do	il	fu ne 'ral
Crudo	**fato**	**al**	**mio**	**contento**	**va**	**tessendo**	**il**	**funeral;**
cruel	fate	to the	my	happiness	goes	plotting	the	funeral

Cruel fate, to my happiness, plots the funeral;

su	la	'ba ɾa	del	tor 'men to	ʎi	prɛ 'pa ɾa	il	di	fa 'tal
su	**la**	**bara**	**del**	**tormento**	**gli**	**prepara**	**il**	**dì**	**fatal.**
on	the	coffin	of the	torment	to him	it prepares	the	day	fatal

upon the coffin of torment it prepares the fatal day for him.

ॐ

[27]
from: *San Giovanni Battista (1676)* (an Oratorio)
character: *Erodiade*

Abbate Ansaldi

'kwe ste 'la gri me e so 'spi ɾi
Queste lagrime e sospiri
These tears and sighs

'kwe ste	'la gri me	e	so 'spi ɾi	ke	tu	'mi ɾi
Queste	**lagrime**	**e**	**sospiri**	**che**	**tu**	**miri**
these	tears	and	sighs	which	you	look at

These tears and sighs you see

'bra man	'so lo	o	'mi o	gran	re	pur	'pɔ ka	mer 'tʃe
braman	**solo**	**o**	**mio**	**gran**	**re**	**pur**	**poca**	**mercé.**
yearn for	only	o	my	great	king	[indeed]	little	mercy

yearn only, o my great king, for a little mercy.

ॐ

[5, 9, 19, 43] In [43] this song is titled **Io pur seguirò**, and the two sections of text are in reversed order.

ra 'dʒon 'sɛm pre ad: 'di ta
Ragion sempre addita
Reason always guides

ra 'dʒon	'sɛm pre	ad: 'di ta	a 'dal ma	dʒen 'ti le	ke	a 'ma ta	o	sker 'ni ta
Ragion	**sempre**	**addita**	**ad alma**	**gentile**	**che,**	**amata**	**o**	**schernita,**
reason	always	points out	to soul	gentle	that	loved	or	scorned

Reason always guides the gentle soul, whether loved or scorned, so that

lo	'sta bil	'su o	'sti le	non	'kan dʒi	nɔ	nɔ
lo	**stabil**	**suo**	**stile**	**non**	**cangi,**	**no,**	**no!**
the	stable	its	style	not	may change	no	no

its steady path will not change, no, no!

'i o	pur	se gwi 'rɔ	ke	'ʃɔʎː ʎe ɾe	il	pjɛ	'da i	'latː tʃi	di	fe
Io	**pur**	**seguirò,**	**che**	**sciogliere**	**il**	**piè**	**dai**	**lacci**	**di**	**fé**
I	too	I will follow	because	to loosen	the	foot	from the	ties	of	fidelity

non	'tɛn to	non	vɔ	nɔ	non	vɔ
non	**tento,**	**non**	**vò,**	**no,**	**non**	**vò.**
not	I try	not	I wish	no	not	I wish

I too will follow, because I neither try nor wish to loosen the ties of fidelity.

⁂

[5, 9, 19, 55]

se a 'mor manː 'nɔ da il 'pjɛ de

Se amor m'annoda il piede

If love ties me down

se	a 'mor	manː 'nɔ da	il	'pjɛ de	'ko me	'duŋ kwe	fudː dʒi 'rɔ
Se	**amor**	**m'annoda**	**il**	**piede,**	**come**	**dunque**	**fuggirò?**
if	love	me ties	the	foot	how	then	I will flee

If love ties me down, how then will I flee?

alt.: S'amor [sa 'mor...] = *Se amor*

da	kwel	kɔr	ke	non	a	'fe de	li ber 'ta	non	'spe ɾo	nɔ
Da	**quel**	**cor**	**che**	**non**	**ha**	**fede**	**libertà**	**non**	**spero,**	**no.**
from	that	heart	which	not	has	faithfulness	liberty	not	I hope	no

I can not hope for liberty from that unfaithful heart, no.

'si an	pur	'du ɾe	le	ka 'te ne	'kre skan	'sɛm pre	le	'mi e	'pe ne
Sian	**pur**	**dure**	**le**	**catene,**	**crescan**	**sempre**	**le**	**mie**	**pene,**
they may be	[yet]	harsh	the	chains	they may grow	always	the	my	pains

May the chains be harsh, [and] may my pains ever increase,

var. (instead of "crescan sempre le mie pene") in [19] *and* [55]: *dure in sempre le mie pene,* ['du ɾe in 'sɛm pre le 'mi e 'pe ne] = ... [and] always harsh my pains,

kin	ser vi 'tu	co 'stan te	'gɔ de	oɲː 'ɲo ɾa	laŋ 'gwɛn do	un	'kɔ ɾe	a 'man te
ch'in	**servitù**	**costante**	**gode**	**ognora**	**languendo**	**un**	**core**	**amante.**
because in	servitude	constant	enjoys	always	languishing	a	heart	loving

for a loving heart always enjoys languishing in constant servitude.

lo	stral	ke	'pɔr to	al	'kɔ ɾe	dun	bɛl	'gwar do	'kol po	fu
Lo	**stral,**	**che**	**porto**	**al**	**core**	**d'un**	**bel**	**guardo**	**colpo**	**fu.**
the	arrow	which	I carry	in the	heart	from a	beautiful	glance	blow	was

The arrow which I carry in my heart was a stab from a beautiful glance.

in [19] *and* [55]: *ch'io porto* ['ki o 'pɔr to] = *che porto*

pju	non	'ku ɾo	il	'mi o	do 'lo ɾe	'vi vo	'lje to	in	ser vi 'tu
Più	**non**	**curo**	**il**	**mio**	**dolore,**	**vivo**	**lieto**	**in**	**servitù.**
more	not	I care	the	my	sorrow	I live	happy	in	servitude

I care no more about my sorrow; I live happily in servitude.

In [19] *and* [55] *is another verse:*

il	'mi o	kɔr	dʒa	'fatː to	a u 'da tʃe	'sprɛtː tsa	oɲː 'ɲor	lar 'dɛn te	'fa tʃe
Il	**mio**	**cor**	**già**	**fatto**	**audace**	**sprezza**	**ognor**	**l'ardente**	**face,**
the	my	heart	now	made	bold	spurns	always	the burning	torch

My heart, now made bold, always spurns the burning torch,

ke	per	un	'va go	od: 'dʒet: to	oɲ: ɲin 'tʃen djo	da 'mo ɾe	ɛ	'dʒɔ ja	a	un	'pet: to
che	**per**	**un**	**vago**	**oggetto**	**ogn'incendio**	**d'amore**	**è**	**gioia**	**a**	**un**	**petto.**
because	for	a	lovely	object	every fire	of love	is	joy	to	a	breast

because for a lovely object every fire of love is joy to a heart.

> *petto = (fig.) heart*

❧

[10, 19, 23, 26, 38, 39] Alternately titled **Se nel ben** and **Se nel ben sempre incostante**.
from: *Orazio Cocle (1679)*
character: *Elisa*

se nel ben 'sɛm pre
Se nel ben sempre
If in good times

se	nel	ben	'sɛm pre	iŋ ko 'stan te	for 'tu na	va 'gan te
Se	**nel**	**ben**	**sempre**	**incostante**	**fortuna**	**vagante**
if	in the	good	always	inconstant	fortune	wandering

If in good times the always inconstant fortune, wandering,

di	'far si	'sta bi le	'u zo	non	a
di	**farsi**	**stabile**	**uso**	**non**	**ha,**
of	to make itself	steady	custom	not	has

is not used to making itself steady,

'aŋ ko	mu 'ta bi le	nel	mal	sa 'ra
anco	**mutabile**	**nel**	**mal**	**sarà.**
as well	changeable	in the	bad	it will be

it will be changeable in bad times as well.

> *anco = (mod.) anche*

> *In [19] there follows a line sung by the character Orazio:...*

'al ma	pju	'nɔ bi le	ki	tro ve 'ɾa
Alma	**più**	**nobile**	**chi**	**troverà.**
soul	more	noble	who	will find

Who will find a soul more noble!

> *...and then a 2nd verse sung by Elisa:*

se	non	pwɔ	'da stro	iŋ kle 'mɛn te	pu 'pil: la	do 'lɛn te	lo	'zdeɲ: ɲo	'fran dʒe ɾe
Se	**non**	**può**	**d'astro**	**inclemente**	**pupilla**	**dolente**	**lo**	**sdegno**	**frangere**
if	not	is able	of star	inclement	eye	sorrowful	the	scorn	to crush

If scorn is not able to crush the sorrowful eye of an inclement star,

nel	tʃel	mu 'tar	non	'dʒo va	a	'pjan dʒe ɾe	ne	so spi 'rar	nɔ
né 'l	**ciel**	**mutar,**	**non**	**giova**	**a**	**piangere**	**né**	**sospirar,**	**no.**
nor the	heaven	to alter	not	is of avail	to	to weep	nor	to sigh	no

nor to alter heaven, it is of no avail to weep or sigh – no.

❧

[88]
from: *La forza d'amor paterno (1678)*
character: *Arbante*   *Nicolò Minato*

'sɛn tsa spe 'ran tsa o i 'mɛ
Senza speranza, ohimè
Without hope, alas

'sɛn tsa   spe 'ran tsa   o i 'mɛ   'dɛd: dʒo   'duŋ kwe   mo 'rir
Senza   speranza,   ohimè,   deggio   dunque   morir,
without   hope   alas   I must   then   to die
Without hope, alas, then I must die;

deggio =
(mod.)
devo

ne   si 'trɔ va   pje 'ta   de   'mjɛ i   mar 'tir
né   si trova   pietà   de'   miei   martir.
not   is found   pity   of the   my   agonies
no pity is to be found for my agony.

martir[e] =
(mod.)
martirio

'njɛn te   val   fe del 'ta   ne   'dʒo va no   i   so 'spir
Niente   val   fedeltà,   né   giovano   i   sospir.
nothing   is worth   fidelity   nor   avail   the   sighs
Fidelity is worth nothing; sighs are of no avail.

'sɛn tsa   spe 'ran tsa   o i 'mɛ   'dɛ vo   'duŋ kwe   mo 'rir
Senza   speranza,   ohimè,   devo   dunque   morir.
without   hope   alas   I must   then   to die
Without hope, alas, then I must die.

☙

[1, 2, 46]

sɔ bɛn ke mi sa 'et: ta no
So ben, che mi saettano
I well know that they wound me

sɔ   bɛn   ke   mi   sa 'et: ta no   ke   mi   tra 'fig: go no   e   ke   mut: 'tʃi do no
So   ben,   che   mi   saettano,   che   mi   trafiggono   e   che   m'uccidono
I know   well   that   me   they wound with an arrow   that   me   they pierce   and   that   me they kill

ʎi   'zgwar di   del   'mi o   bɛn
gli   sguardi   del   mio   ben.
the   glances   of the   my   dear one
I well know that the glances from my dear one wound me, pierce me, and kill me.

ma   'tan to   mi   di 'lɛt: ta no   'ki o   'lje ta   'vɛn go men
Ma   tanto   mi   dilettano,   ch'io   lieta   vengo men.
but   so much   me   they delight   that I   happy   I swoon
But they delight me so much that I swoon happily.

a 'mor   se   lo   'pwɔ i   'tʃin dʒe ɾe   il   'pjɛ de   le 'ga li   e diŋ ca 'te na lo
Amor,   se   lo   puoi   cingere,   il   piede   legagli   ed incatenalo,
love   if   it   you can   to encircle   the   foot   bind it   and fetter it
Love, if you can encircle it, bind his foot and fetter it

per 'ke   non   'par ta   pju
perché   non   parta   più;
so that   not   may depart   more
so that he may not leave anymore,

dʒak: 'ke   mi   'sɛn to   'strin dʒe ɾe   in   'dol tʃe   ser vi 'tu
già che   mi   sento   stringere   in   dolce   servitù.
since   me   I feel   to clasp   in   sweet   servitude
since I feel enclasped in sweet servitude.

gia che =
(mod.) giacché

GL: **Amor**

Strozzi, Barbara (1619-1677)

Born in Venice, died in Padua, she was the adopted (probably illegitimate) daughter of the poet Giulio Strozzi, with whom she lived until his death; her mother was Isabella Garzoni, Giulio Strozzi's longtime servant. Though Barbara never married, she had four children, and she may have been a courtesan, given letters of the time satirizing her and chastising her morals.

A pupil of Francesco Cavalli, she was a virtuoso singer, often accompanying herself on the lute. Giulio Strozzi founded the "Accademia degli Unisoni," a group of Venetian musicians and literati; Barbara sang at their meetings and participated in their debates.

Barbara Strozzi never wrote an opera, but she was one of the most gifted composers of secular vocal music of the seventeenth century. She published eight books of music in a variety of genres, from simple ariettas to complex cantatas employing recitative, arioso and aria styles, mostly for soprano voice and continuo.

She was imaginative and original in her setting of texts, both dramatic and comic, many of which were by Giulio Strozzi.

[11, 22, 24, 48, 89]

a ˈmor dor miʎ: ˈʎo ne
Amor dormiglione
Sleepy Love

a ˈmor	non	dor ˈmir	pju	su	ˈzveʎ: ʎa ti	o ˈma i
Amor,	**non**	**dormir**	**piu!**	**Su,**	**svegliati**	**omai,**
Love	not	to sleep	more	up	get up	now

Love *[Cupid]*, do not sleep anymore! Come on – get up now,

omai (poet.) = ormai

ke	ˈmen tre	ˈdɔr mi	tu	ˈdor mon	le	ˈdʒɔ je	ˈmi e
che	**mentre**	**dormi**	**tu,**	**dormon**	**le**	**gioie**	**mie,**
because	while	you sleep	you	they sleep	the	joys	mine

because while you are sleeping my joys sleep,

ˈveʎ: ʎa no	i	ˈgwa i	non	ˈɛs: ser	a ˈmor	dap: ˈpɔ ko
vegliano	**i**	**guai.**	**Non**	**esser,**	**Amor,**	**dappoco!**
they are awake	the	troubles	not	to be	Love	worthless

[and] my troubles are awake. Do not be worthless, Love!

ˈstra li	ˈfɔ ko	ˈstra li	su	ˈfɔ ko	su	su
Strali,	**Foco!**	**Strali,**	**su!**	**Foco,**	**su,**	**su!**
arrows	fire	arrows	up	fire	up	up

Arrows, fire – arrows, come on! Fire, come on, come on!

non	dor ˈmir	pju	ˈzveʎ: ʎa ti	su	a ˈmor
Non	**dormir**	**più,**	**svegliati,**	**su,**	**Amor!**
not	to sleep	more	get up	up	Love

Do not sleep anymore; get up, come on, Love!

o	ˈpi gro	o	ˈtar do	tu	non	ˈa i	ˈsɛn so
O	**pigro,**	**o**	**tardo,**	**tu**	**non**	**hai**	**senso!**
oh	lazy one	oh	sluggish one	you	not	you have	sense

Oh lazy one, oh sluggish one, you have no common sense!

a ˈmor	me ˈlɛn so	a ˈmor	ko ˈdar do	a	ˈkwa le	ˈi o	ˈrɛ sto
Amor	**melenso,**	**Amor**	**codardo,**	**ah,**	**quale**	**io**	**resto,**
Love	doltish	Love	cowardly	ah	what	I	remain

Doltish Love, cowardly Love, ah, [see] what a state I am in

alt. for "ah": "ahi" [ˈa i] = alas

ke	nel	'mi o	ar 'do ɾe	tu	'dɔr ma	a 'mo ɾe	maŋ 'ka va	'kwe sto
ché	**nel**	**mio**	**ardore**	**tu**	**dorma,**	**Amore!**	**Mancava**	**questo!**
because	in the	my	ardor	you	may sleep	Love	was missing	this

because you sleep during my passion, Love! I really didn't need this!

var. in [89]:	...**ahi, quale io resto nel mio ardore**... ['a i 'kwa le 'i o 'ɾɛ sto nel 'mi o ar 'do ɾe]
	= ...alas, what a state I am in in my passion...

var. in [11] and [89]:	...**mancava questo ahi! quale io resto.** [maŋ 'ka va 'kwe sto 'a i 'kwa le 'i o 'ɾɛ sto]
	= ...I really didn't need this – alas, what a state I am in!

GL: **Amor[e]**

&

[27]

a 'mo ɾe ɛ ban 'di to
Amore è bandito
Love is banished

a 'mo ɾe	ɛ	ban 'di to	a 'man ti	su
Amore	**è**	**bandito**	**amanti**	**su,**
love	is	banished	lovers	onward

Love is banished; lovers, move on!

ɛ	'fat: to	un	e 'dit: to	ke	a 'mor	non	'si a	pju
è	**fatto**	**un**	**editto**	**che**	**amor**	**non**	**sia**	**più.**
is	made	an	edict	that	love	not	be	more

An edict has been made that love shall be no more.

for 'ni ti	ʎi	a 'mo ɾi	liŋ 'gan: no	e	la	'frɔ de	a	pju	non	'sɔ de
Forniti	**gli**	**amori,**	**l'inganno**	**e**	**la**	**frode**	**ah,**	**più**	**non**	**s'ode**
finished	the	loves	the deception	and	the	fraud	ah	more	not	one hears

Finished are the love affairs; ah, one will no longer hear the deception and the fraud,

tor 'men ti	e	raŋ 'ko ɾi	il	'ka zo	ɛ	spe 'di to
tormenti	**e**	**rancori,**	**il**	**caso**	**è**	**spedito.**
torments	and	grudges	the	case	is	resolved

torments and grudges; the matter is settled.

ki 'mɛ ɾe	al	tʃer 'vɛl: lo	al	kwɔr	dʒe lo 'zi e	a	pas: 'sjo ni	pat: 'tsi e
Chimere	**al**	**cervello,**	**al**	**cuor**	**gelosie**	**ah,**	**passioni,**	**pazzie**
fancies	in the	brain	in the	heart	jealousies	ah	passions	foolishnesses

Ah, dreams of the mind and jealousies of the heart, passions, foolishnesses

son	'dʒi te	al	bor 'dɛl: lo	il	'ka zo	ɛ	spe 'di to
son	**gite**	**al**	**bordello,**	**il**	**caso**	**è**	**spedito**
are	gone	to the	brothel	the	case	is	resolved

have gone to the brothel; the matter is settled.

gite: from gire (lit.) = andare

spe 'ran tsa	e	de 'zi o	kwe 'ɾɛ le	e	so 'spi ɾi	a	siŋ 'gjot: tsi	mar 'ti ɾi
Speranza	**e**	**desio,**	**querele**	**e**	**sospiri**	**ah,**	**singhiozzi,**	**martiri**
hope	and	desire	complaints	and	sighs	ah	sobs	agonies

Ah, hope and desire, complaints and sighs, sobs and agonies

sen 'van: no	al: lob: 'bli o	il	'ka zo	ɛ	spe 'di to
sen vanno	**all'obblio,**	**il**	**caso**	**è**	**spedito**
go away	to the oblivion	the	case	is	resolved

are going to oblivion; the matter is settled.

obblio (lit.) = (mod.) oblio

oɲ: 'ɲun si kon 'fɔr te ral: 'le gre si il 'kɔ re a
Ognun si conforte, rallegresi il core ah,
each one let console himself let be happy the heart [ah]
Let everyone be consoled [and] have happy hearts,

the "e" (rather than "i") verb endings of "conforte" and "rallegre" are archaic/poetic variants

ke il 'ban do da 'mo ɾe ban 'di to a la 'mɔr te
che il bando d'amore bandito ha la morte,
that the ban of love banished has the death
for the banishment of love has banished death.

il 'ka zo ɛ spe 'di to
il caso è spedito.
the case is resolved
The matter is settled.

⁍

[89]

beʎ: 'ʎɔk: ki bɛl 'se no
Begl'occhi, bel seno
Beautiful eyes, beautiful breast

'vo i pur beʎ: 'ʎɔk: ki 'se te 'pɔr te dun pa ɾa 'di zo
Voi pur begl'occhi, sete porte d'un paradiso,
you [indeed] beautiful eyes you are gates of a paradise
You beautiful eyes, you are the gates to a paradise;

sete = (mod.) siete

'vo i tra lo 'sker tso el 'ri zo in 'tʃɛl min tro du 'tʃe te
voi tra lo scherzo e'l riso in ciel m'introducete.
you between the jest and the laugh into heaven me you introduce
between a jest and a laugh you usher me into heaven.

ma 'tan to il kɔr mar 'de te ke dal 'mi o 'fɔ ko e 'tɛr no
Ma tanto il cor m'ardete che dal mio foco eterno
but so much the heart me you burn that from the my fire eternal
But you burn my heart so much that, from my eternal fire,

per le 'pɔr te del tʃɛl 'kor: ro al: lin 'fɛr no
per le porte del ciel, corro all'inferno.
through the gates of the heaven I run to the hell
I run through the gates of heaven into hell.

si bɛl 'se no ke tu 'sɛ i 'u na 'ne ve a ni 'ma ta
Sì, bel seno, che tu sei una neve animata,
yes beautiful breast [that] you you are a snow living
Yes, beautiful breast, you are a living snow;

si ke 'tu a 'dʒɔ dʒa 'gra ta kon 'so la ʎar 'dor 'mjɛ i
sì, che tua giogia grata consola gl'ardor miei.
yes, [that] your joy welcomed consoles the ardors mine
yes, your welcomed joy consoles my ardors.

"giogia" was a problem: I'm guessing that it is a form of (or a misprint for) "gioia"; another possibility of its intention is "giogo" (= yoke): your welcomed yoke...

ma 'tan to al 'fin go 'de i ke 'gran de a 'pɔ ko a 'pɔ ko
Ma tanto alfin godei che grande a poco a poco
but so much eventually I had pleasure that great little by little
But eventually I had such pleasure that, [my ardor] having increased little by little,

fra le 'fal de di dʒɛl 'prɔ vo il 'mi o 'fɔ ko
fra le falde di giel provo il mio foco.
among the flakes of ice I feel the my fire
I feel my fire among the snowflakes.

giel[o]=
(mod.) gelo

'vo i pur 'bɛ i 'kri ni a 'do ɾo 'ka ɾi 'dol tʃi le 'ga mi
Voi pur bei crini, adoro, cari dolci legami,
you too beautiful head of hair I adore dear sweet ties
You too, beautiful hair, dear, sweet ties, I adore –

'vo i pret: 'tsjo zi 'sta mi del 'mi o 'rik: ko te 'zɔ ɾo
voi preziosi stami del mio ricco tesoro.
you precious threads of the my rich treasure
you precious threads of my rich treasure.

ma 'del: la 'sel va 'dɔ ɾo se non mi 'fa te un 'do no
Ma della selva d'oro se non mi fate un dono,
but of the forest of gold if not to me you make a gift
But if you do not make me a gift of the golden forest *[of your hair]*,

fra le mi 'njɛ ɾe dɔr 'pɔ ve ɾo 'i o 'so no
fra le miniere d'or povero io sono.
among the mines of gold poor I I am
I will be poor among the goldmines.

nɔ 'po mi e ɾu 'bi ni ke 'vo i non pa ɾed: 'dʒa te
No, pomi e rubini che voi non pareggiate,
no apples and rubies [that] you not you equal
No, apples and rubies, you do not equal

nɔ di 'kwel: le 'lab: bra a 'ma te i ko 'ɾal: li di 'vi ni
no, di quelle labbra amate i coralli divini.
no of those lips loved the corals divine
the divine corals of those beloved lips – no.

ma non 'ma i ne dʒar 'di ni di 'kwel: la 'bɛl: la 'bok: ka
Ma non mai ne' giardini di quella bella bocca,
but not ever in the gardens of that beautiful mouth
But never, in the gardens of that beautiful mouth,

'koʎ: ʎer 'kwan ti vor: 'rɛ i 'ba tʃi mi 'tok: ka
coglier quanti vorrei baci mi tocca.
to gather how many I should wish kisses to me it happens
will it be for me to gather as many kisses as I should wish.

[7, 89]

Bissari

kja 'ma ta a 'nwɔ vi a 'mo ɾi
Chiamata a nuovi amori
A call to new loves

e	ke	e	ke	'dja vol	sa 'ra	'kwe sto	'sem pre	a 'mar	'duŋ kwe	do 'vrɔ
E	che?	E	che	diavol	sarà	questo,	sempre	amar	dunque	dovrò?
and	what	and	what	devil	will be	this	always	to love	then	I shall have to

What then? What the devil is this: will I always have to love?

or	ke	'ʃol ta	ap: 'pe na	'rɛs to	'nwɔ vo	'lat: tʃo	il	pjɛ	le 'gɔ		a
Or	che	sciolta	appena	resto,	nuovo	laccio	il	piè	legò.	*in* [7]:	Ah!
now	that	released	barely	I remain	new	snare	the	foot	bound		ah

Just having been freed, a new snare has impeded my step.   [Ah!]

non	mi	val	'di ɾe	da 'mor	son	'li be ɾa
Non	mi	val	dire:	d'amor	son	libera,
not	to me	is of use	to say	from love	I am	free

It is no use for me to say, "I am free from love;

'vek: kjo	de 'zi ɾe	pju	non	mi	'la tʃe ɾa
vecchio	desire	più	non	mi	lacera,
old	desire	more	not	me	rends

the old desire doesn't tear me apart anymore,"

ke	se	per	'li djo	non	'sɛn to	ar 'dor
ché	se	per	Lidio	non	sento	ardor,
because	if	for	Lidio	not	I feel	ardor

because, if I don't feel passion for Lidio,

'al tra	bel: 'let: tsa	ri 'toʎ: ʎe mi	il	kɔr
altra	bellezza	ritogliemi	il	cor.
other	handsomeness	takes away again	the	heart

some other handsome man takes my heart away.

ke	mal	ke	ma 'lan: no	a	'me ko	a 'mo ɾe	ke	si 'kre de	al 'fin	di	far
Che	mal!	Che	malanno	ha	meco	Amore,	che	si crede	alfin	di	far?
what	hurt	what	ill will	has	me with	Love	what	himself believes	eventually	of	to do

How painful! What ill will Love has for me; what does he *[Love]* think he is going to do?

se	un	mi	'strus: se	a 'man do	il	'kɔ ɾe	
Se	un	mi	strusse	amando	il	core,	
if	one	me	consumed	loving	the	heart	

If, in loving, one [lover] consumed my heart,

> *in* [89]: S'un
> = Se un

a	ke	'sɛr ve	un	'al tro	a 'mar		a
a	che	serve	un	altro	amar?	*in* [7]:	Ah!
to	what	serves	an	other	loving		ah

what good is loving another one? [Ah!]

ma	il	cat: ti 'vɛl: lo	per 'ki o	non	'fug: ga mi
Ma	il	cattivello,	perch'io	non	fuggami
but	the	naughty boy	so that I	not	me may flee

But the naughty boy *[Cupid]*, so that I will not flee,

vwɔl	ke	il	pju	'bɛl: lo	il	sen	di 'strug: ga mi
vuol	che	il	più	bello	il	sen	distruggami.
wants	that	the	most	handsome one	the	breast; *(fig.)* heart	may destroy me

> *in* [89]:
> ...ch'un' più bello...
> [...kun pju...] = ...a
> most handsome one...

wants the most handsome one to destroy my heart.

se   un   'vi zo   a 'ma bi le   mi   fe   laŋ 'gwir
Se   un   viso   amabile   mi   fe'   languir,
if   a   face   loveable   me   made   to languish

If a loveable face made me languish,

in [89]: *S'un*
= *Se un*

per   'du e   'bɛʎ: ʎi   'ɔk: ki   mi 'sɛn to   mo 'rir
per   due   begli   occhi   mi sento   morir.
for   two   beautiful   eyes   I feel   to die

for two beautiful eyes I feel that I am dying.

in [89]: **begl'occhi**
[bɛʎ: 'ʎɔk: ki]
= *begli occhi*

GL: **Amore**

☙

[11, 89]

Giulio Strozzi

ko 'stu me   de 'gran di
Costume de' grandi
The custom of grandees

go 'de ɾe   e   laʃ: 'ʃa ɾe   ko 'stu man   ʎa 'man ti   bu 'dʒar di   iŋ ko 'stan ti
Godere   e   lasciare   costuman   gl'amanti   bugiardi   incostanti,
to enjoy   and   to leave   are accustomed   the lovers   lying   inconstant

le   'kɔ ze   pju   'ka ɾe
le   cose   più   care.
the   objects   most   dear

Lying and inconstant lovers are accustomed to enjoying and [then] leaving their dearest ones.

'on de   ki   'mɛn te   pju   'spe ɾa   pju   'lɔ de   siŋ 'gan: na   e   si 'gɔ de
Onde   chi   mente   più   spera   più   lode,   s'inganna   e   si gode.
whence   he who   lies   most   hopes   most   praise   himself deceives   and   himself enjoys

Thus he who lies the most hopes for the most praise; he deceives himself and enjoys himself.

kon   'la dri   ko 'man di   si 'ru ba   il   pja 'tʃe ɾe
Con   ladri   comandi   si ruba   il   piacere.
with   thieving   commands   one steals   the   pleasure

One steals pleasure with dishonest words;

spret: 'tsa ɾe   e   go 'de ɾe   ko 'stu me   ɛ   de   'gran di
Sprezzare   e   godere   costume   è   de'   grandi.
scorning   and   taking pleasure   custom   is   of   grandees

scorning and taking pleasure is the custom of grandees.

'on de   ki   'ru ba   pju   'spe ɾa   pju   'lɔ de   siŋ 'gan: na   e   si 'gɔ de
Onde   chi   ruba   più   spera   più   lode,   s'inganna   e   si gode.
whence   he who   robs   most   hopes   most   praise   himself deceives   and   himself enjoys

Thus he who robs the most hopes for the most praise; he deceives himself and enjoys himself.

al   'gran de   e   sa 'pu to   non   'ma i   si kon 'vjɛ ne
Al   grande   e   saputo   non   mai   si conviene
to the   great   and   wise one   not   ever   is expedient

For the great and cunning it is never expedient

go 'de ɾe   e   dir   'bɛ ne   del   bɛn   ka   go 'du to
godere   e   dir   bene   del   ben   ch'a   goduto.
to take pleasure   and   to say   well   of the   well-being   that he has   enjoyed

to take pleasure and [then] to speak well of the happiness he has enjoyed.

'on de   ki   'bjaz ma   pju   'spe ɾa   pju   'lo de   siŋ 'gan: na   e   si 'gɔ de
Onde   chi   biasma   più   spera   più   lode,   s'inganna   e   si gode.
whence   he who   finds fault   most   hopes   most   praise   himself deceives   and   himself enjoys
Thus he who finds fault the most hopes for the most praise; he deceives himself and enjoys himself.

> *biasma: from "biasmare" = (mod.) "biasimare"*

&

[11]

kru 'dɛ le ke non 'sɛn te non 've de non 'par la
Crudele che non sente, non vede, non parla
Cruel one who does not hear, does not see, does not speak

'daʎ: ʎi   a 'bis: si   del   'mi o   'kɔ ɾe   stre pi 'to zi   'ɛ skon   ʎi   at: 'tʃɛn ti
Dagli   abissi   del   mio   core,   strepitosi,   escon   gli   accenti,
from the   abysses   of the my   heart   resounding   come out   the   words
From the depths of my heart come, resounding, the words

a   spje 'gar ti   il   'mi o   do 'lo ɾe   a   nar: 'rar ti   i   'mjɛi   tor 'men ti
a   spiegarti   il   mio   dolore   a   narrarti   i   miei   tormenti.
to   explain to you the   my   sorrow   to   tell you   the   my   torments
to explain my sorrow to you [and] tell you of my torments.

ma   tu   'bɛl: la   kru 'dɛl   'sor da   ti 'fa i
Ma   tu   bella   crudel,   sorda   ti fai,
but   you   beautiful   cruel one   deaf   yourself you make
But you, beautiful cruel one, remain deaf;

o 'ɾek: kja   ke   non   vwɔl   non   'sɛn te   'ma i   nɔ
orecchia   che   non   vuol,   non   sente   mai,   no.
ear   that   not   wants   not   hears   ever   no
the ear which does not want [to hear] never hears – no.

nel: lin 'fɛr no   pju   pro 'fon do   tor men 'ta to   a 'mor   mi   'tjɛ ne
Nell'inferno   più   profondo,   tormentato,   Amor   mi   tiene,
in the inferno   most   deep   tormented   Love   me   holds
In the deepest inferno, Love keeps me tormented.

'doɲ: ɲi   'ma le   a 'tɔr to   ab: 'bon do   son   im: 'mɛn se   le   'mi e   'pe ne
d'ogni   male   a torto   abbondo   son   immense   le   mie   pene.
in every   pain   wrongfully   I abound   are   immense   the   my   sufferings
I am unjustly full of every pain; immense are my sufferings.

ma   tu   'bɛl: la   kru 'dɛl   'tʃɛ ka   ti 'fa i
Ma   tu   bella   crudel,   cieca   ti fai,
but   you   beautiful   cruel one   blind   yourself you make
But you, beautiful cruel one, remain blind;

un   'ɔk: kjo   ke   non   vwɔl   non   've de   'ma i   nɔ
un   occhio   che   non   vuol,   non   vede   mai,   no.
an   eye   that   not   wants   not   sees   ever   no
an eye that does not want [to see] never sees – no.

kon   un   si   po 'tre sti   'so lo   e lo 'kwɛn te   par la 'tri tʃe
Con   un   sì   potresti   solo   eloquente,   parlatrice,
with   one   yes   you would be able   only   eloquent   talker
With only one eloquent "yes" you could, if you would speak –

kon	un	si	'tɔʎ:	ʎer mi		il	'dwɔ lo	kon	un	si	si	'far mi		fe 'li tʃe
con	**un**	**sì**	**togliermi**			**il**	**duolo**	**con**	**un**	**sì,**	**sì,**	**farmi**		**felice.**
with	one	yes	to take away from me			the	sorrow	with	one	yes	yes	to make me		happy

with one "yes" [you could] take away my sorrow; with one "yes" [you could], yes, make me happy.

ma	tu	'bɛl: la	kru 'dɛl	'mu ta	ti 'fa i
Ma	**tu**	**bella**	**crudel,**	**muta**	**ti fai,**
but	you	beautiful	cruel one	silent	yourself you make

But you, beautiful cruel one, remain silent;

la	'bok: ka	ke	non	vwɔl	non	'par la	'ma i	nɔ
la	**bocca**	**che**	**non**	**vuol,**	**non**	**parla**	**mai,**	**no.**
the	mouth	that	not	wants	not	speaks	ever	no

the mouth which does not want [to speak] never speaks – no.

GL: Amor

&

[89]

'dʒu sta ne ga 'ti va
Giusta negativa
Justified refusal

non	mi	'di te	'ki o	'kan ti		po 'ter	da 'mor	per 'ke	di 'rɔ		ke
Non	**mi**	**dite**	**ch'io**	**canti**		**poter**	**d'amor,**	**perché**	**dirò**		**che**
not	me	tell	that I	should sing		power	of love	because	I will say		that

Do not tell me to sing about the power of love, because I will say that

'se te	de	'mu zi tʃi	il	fla 'dʒel: lo	e	'deʎ: ʎi	a 'man ti
sete	**de'**	**musici**	**il**	**flagello**	**e**	**degli**	**amanti.**
you are	of	musicians	the	bane	and	of the	lovers

you are the bane of musicians and of lovers.

> *sete =*
> *(mod.) siete*

nɔ	siɲ: 'ɲor	'bok: ka	non	a pri 'rɔ
No,	**signor,**	**bocca**	**non**	**aprirò.**
no	sir	mouth	non	I will open

No, sir, I will not open my mouth.

a	ki	kan 'tar	de 'vi o	sil	bɛl	'i do lo	'mi o	'lun dʒi	ɛ	da	me
A	**chi**	**cantar**	**dev'io**	**s'il**	**bel**	**idolo**	**mio**	**lungi**	**è**	**da**	**me?**
to	whom	to sing	ought I	if the	beautiful	idol	mine	far away	is	from	me

To whom should I sing if my beautiful idol is far away from me?

'vɛŋ ga	'li do lo	'mi o	'ki o	'kan to	af: 'fe
Venga	**l'idolo**	**mio,**	**ch'io**	**canto**	**affé.**
let come	the idol	mine	that I	I sing	in faith

Let my idol come, and then I will sing, indeed.

non	mi	'di te	'ki o	'swɔ ni	'fɔr tsa	del	tʃɛl
Non	**mi**	**dite**	**ch'io**	**suoni**	**forza**	**del**	**ciel,**
not	me	tell	that I	should play	power	of the	heaven

Do not tell me to play about the power of heaven;

vi	man de 'rɔ	la	'do ve	non	'maŋ ka no	'al tri	a	'vo i	'mu zi tʃi	'bwɔ ni
vi	**manderò**	**là**	**dove**	**non**	**mancano**	**altri**	**a**	**voi**	**musici**	**buoni.**
you	I will send	there	where	not	are lacking	other	than	you	musicians	good

I will send you there where there is no lack of good musicians other than you.

nɔ	siɲː	'ɲor	'ta sto	non	tok: ke 'rɔ
No,	**signor,**	**tasto**	**non**	**toccherò.**	
no	sir	key*	not	I will touch	

No, sir, I will not touch a key.

> * i.e., a key on the keyboard of a musical instrument

a	ki	swo 'nar	de 'vi o	sil	bɛl	'i do lo	'mi o	'lun dʒi	ɛ	da	me
A	**chi**	**suonar**	**dev'io**	**s'il**	**bel**	**idolo**	**mio**	**lungi**	**è**	**da**	**me?**
to	whom	to play	ought I	if the	beautiful	idol	mine	far away	is	from	me

To whom should I play if my beautiful idol is far away from me?

'vɛŋ ga	'li do lo	'mi o	'ki o	'swɔ no	afː 'fe
Venga	**l'idolo**	**mio,**	**ch'io**	**suono**	**affé.**
let come	the idol	mine	that I	I play	in faith

Let my idol come, and then I will play, indeed.

&

[89]

il ro 'mɛ o
Il romeo
The pilgrim

va 'gɔ	men 'di ko	il	'kɔ re	'tutː to	il	'reɲː ɲo	da 'mo re	di man 'dan do	pje 'ta
Vagò	**mendico**	**il**	**core**	**tutto**	**il**	**regno**	**d'amore**	**dimandando**	**pietà,**
roamed	mendicant	the	heart	all	the	realm	of love	asking for	pity

My beggar heart roamed the whole realm of love asking for pity,

> dimandando: from "dimandare" = (mod.) "domandare"

kje 'dɛn do	a 'i ta	nelː lin fe 'li tʃe	'su a	'pɔ ve ra	'vi ta
chiedendo	**aita**	**nell'infelice**	**sua**	**povera**	**vita.**
begging for	help	in the unhappy	its	poor	life

begging for help in its poor, unhappy life.

ne	per	'bɛ ne	'sal da	'fe de	po 'te	tro 'var	mer 'tʃe de
Né	**per**	**bene**	**salda**	**fede**	**poté**	**trovar**	**mercede,**
nor	through	well	solid	faith	was able	to find	reward

It was not able to find reward [even] through very staunch faith,

> the printed "bé" is an antiquated abbreviation = (mod.) bene

ke	di	'kwan te	'eʎː ʎi	a 'mɔ	kru 'dɛ li	a 'tɔr to	kil	fudː 'dʒi
ché	**di**	**quante**	**egli**	**amò**	**crudeli**	**a torto**	**ch'il**	**fuggì,**
because	of	how many	it	loved	cruel ones	wrongfully	that it	fled

because, of the many cruel ones it wrongly loved, some fled it,

kil	tra 'di	kil	'vɔlː le	'mɔr to	ki	kil	'vɔlː le	'mɔr to
ch'il	**tradì,**	**ch'il**	**volle**	**morto,**	**chi,**	**ch'il**	**volle**	**morto.**
that it	betrayed	that it	wanted	dead	those who	that it	wanted	dead

some betrayed it, some wanted it dead.

tor 'nɔ	dal	'su o	kamː 'mi no	il	'mi o	kɔr	pelː le 'gri no
Tornò	**dal**	**suo**	**cammino**	**il**	**mio**	**cor**	**pellegrino,**
it returned	from the	its	journey	the	my	heart	pilgrimaging

My pilgrimaging heart returned from its journey

ne	pje 'to zo	fa 'vor	a	'ma i	tro 'va to	per	il	men 'di ko	'su o	'mi ze ro	'sta to
né	**pietoso**	**favor**	**ha**	**mai**	**trovato**	**per**	**il**	**mendico**	**suo**	**misero**	**stato.**
nor	merciful	kindness	has	ever	found	for	the	mendicant	its	miserable	state

never having found merciful kindness for its miserable, begging state.

fem: mi 'nil	kor te 'zi a	'for tse ke		'spen ta	'si a	'koɲ: ɲi		'rik: ka	bel 'ta	're za	te 'na tʃe
Femminil	**cortesia**	**forz'è che**		**spenta**	**sia,**	**ch'ogni**		**ricca**	**beltà**	**resa**	**tenace**
feminine	courtesy	perforce is that		extinct	it be	because every		rich	beauty	made	resolute

It must be that feminine courtesy is extinct, as every abounding beauty, resolute,

non	lu 'di	nol	mi 'rɔ	lo	man 'dɔ	in	'pa tʃe
non	**l'udì,**	**nol**	**mirò,**	**lo**	**mandò**	**in**	**pace.**
not	it heard	not it	looked at	it	it sent away	in	peace

neither heard it nor looked at it, and sent it away with a blessing.

> nol = non + il

[55]

'la gri me 'mi e
Lagrime mie
My tears

'la gri me	'mi e	a	ke	vi trat: te 'ne te	per 'ke	non	i sfo 'ga te
Lagrime	**mie,**	**a**	**che**	**vi trattenete,**	**perché**	**non**	**isfogate**
tears	mine	to	what	you restrain yourselves	why	not	you give vent to

My tears, why do you restrain yourselves? Why do you not vent

> the "i" in front of "sfogate" was inserted for euphony
>
> lagrime = (mod.) lacrime

il	fjɛr	do 'lo re	ke	mi	'tɔʎ: ʎel	re 'spi ro	e	op: 'pri me	il	'kɔ re
il	**fier**	**dolore,**	**che**	**mi**	**toglie'l**	**respiro**	**e**	**opprime**	**il**	**core.**
the	cruel	sorrow	which	from me	takes away the	breath	and	oppresses	the	heart

the cruel sorrow which takes my breath away and weighs down my heart?

'li dja	ke	'tan ta 'do ro	per 'ke	un	'gwar do	pje 'to zo	a i 'mɛ	mi	do 'nɔ
Lidia,	**che**	**tant'adoro,**	**perché**	**un**	**guardo**	**pietoso,**	**ahimè,**	**mi**	**donò,**
Lidia	whom	so much I adore	because	a	glance	compassionate	alas	to me	gave

Lidia, whom I adore so much because she gave me, alas, a compassionate glance,

il	pa 'tɛr no	ri 'gor	lim pri dʒo 'nɔ
il	**paterno**	**rigor**	**l'imprigionò.**
the	paternal	severity	her imprisoned

has been imprisoned by her father's severity.

tra	'du e	'mu ra	riŋ 'kju za	sta	la	'bɛl: la	in: no 'tʃɛn te	'do ve	'dʒun dʒer	non	pwɔ
Tra	**due**	**mura**	**rinchiusa**	**sta**	**la**	**bella**	**innocente**	**dove**	**giunger**	**non**	**può**
Within	two	walls	locked up	is	the	beautiful	innocent one	where	to reach	not	can

'rad: dʒo	di	'so le	e	kwel	ke	pju	mi	'dwɔ le	e dak: 'kreʃ: ʃil	'mi o	mal
raggio	**di**	**sole,**	**e**	**quel**	**che**	**più**	**mi**	**duole**	**ed accresc'il**	**mio**	**mal,**
ray	of	sun	and	that	which	most	me	pains	and increases the	my	hurt

The beautiful innocent one is shut within walls where no ray of sun can reach;
and what most pains me and increases my hurt,

tor 'men ti	e	'pe ne	ɛ	ke	per 'mi a ka 'dʒo ne	'prɔ va	'ma le	il	'mi o	'bɛ ne
tormenti	**e**	**pene,**	**è**	**che**	**per mia cagione**	**prova**	**male**	**il**	**mio**	**bene.**
torments	and	sufferings	is	that	because of me	experiences	pain	the	my	dear one

torments, and sufferings is that my dear one is experiencing pain because of me.

e	'vo i	'lu mi	do 'lɛn ti	non	pjan 'dʒe te	'la gri me	'mi e	a	ke	vi	trat: te 'ne te
E	**voi**	**lumi**	**dolenti,**	**non**	**piangete!**	**Lagrime**	**mie,**	**a**	**che**	**vi**	**trattenete?**
and	you	eyes	sorrowful	not	you weep	ears	mine	to	what	you	restrain yourselves

And you, sorrowful eyes, do not weep! My tears, why do you restrain yourselves?

'li dja	a i 'mɛ	'veg: go	maŋ 'kar mi		'li dol	'mi o	ke	'tan to	a 'do ro
Lidia,	**ahimè,**	**veggo**	**mancarmi.**		**L'idol**	**mio,**	**che**	**tanto**	**adoro,**
Lidia	alas	I see	to be missing to me		the idol	mine	whom	so much	I adore

Alas, I miss Lidia! My idol, whom I adore so much,

sta	ko 'lɛ i	tra	'du ri	'mar mi	per	'ku i	'spi ro	e	pur	non	'mɔ ro
sta	**colei**	**tra**	**duri**	**marmi**	**per**	**cui**	**spiro**	**e**	**pur**	**non**	**moro.**
remains	she who	within	hard	marbles	for	whom	I expire	and	yet	not	I die

she for whom I am expiring and yet do not die, remains within stone walls.

se	la	'mɔr te	mɛ	gra 'di ta	or	ke	son	'pri va	di	'spɛ ne
Se	**la**	**morte**	**m'è**	**gradita,**	**or**	**che**	**son**	**priva**	**di**	**spene,**
if	the	death	to me is	welcomed	now	that	I am	deprived	of	hope

Since I welcome death, now that I am deprived of hope,

> *spene (poet.) = speme (lit.) = speranza*

dɛ	toʎ: 'ʎe te mi	la	'vi ta	ve ne 'prɛ go	'a spre	'mi e	'pe ne
deh	**toglietemi**	**la**	**vita**	**(ve ne prego)**	**aspre**	**mie**	**pene.**
ah	remove from me	the	life	I beg it of you	bitter	my	sufferings

ah, take away my life, I beg you, my bitter sufferings.

> *printed "dhè," either a misprint or an antiquated spelling, = "deh"*

ma	bɛn	mak: 'kɔr go	ke	per	tor men 'tar mi	mad: dʒor 'men te
Ma	**ben**	**m'accorgo,**	**che**	**per**	**tormentarmi**	**maggiormente,**
but	well	I am aware	that	for	to torment me	even more

But I am well aware that, to torment me even more,

la	'sɔr te	mi	'njɛ ga	'aŋ ko	la	'mɔr te
la	**sorte**	**mi**	**niega**	**anco**	**la**	**morte.**
the	fate	me	denies	even	the	death

fate is denying me even death.

> *niega: from "niegare" = (mod.) "negare"*   *anco = (mod.) anche*

se	'duŋ kwɛ	've ro	o	'di o	ke	sol	del	'pjan to	'mi o
Se	**dunqu'è**	**vero,**	**o**	**Dio,**	**che**	**sol**	**del**	**pianto**	**mio,**
[if]	then it is	true	o	God	that	only	of the	weeping	mine

il	'ri o	de 'sti no	a	'se te
il	**rio**	**destino**	**ha**	**sete.**
the	cruel	destiny	has	thirst

> *rio (lit.) = reo*

Then it is true, o God, that cruel destiny only thirsts for my tears.

❧

[89]

la 'man te bu 'dʒar do
L'amante bugiardo
The lying lover

i	'mjɛ i	'dʒor ni	se 're ni	in 'fɛt: ti	kol	'tu o	'zgwar do
I	**miei**	**giorni**	**sereni**	**infetti**	**col**	**tuo**	**sguardo**
the	my	days	serene	you infect	with the	your	glance

You defile my serene days with your glance

e	kol	so 'spir	bu 'dʒar do	'la ɾja	tu	mav: ve 'le ni
e	**col**	**sospir**	**bugiardo**	**l'aria**	**tu**	**m'avveleni.**
and	with the	sigh	lying	the air	you	me you poison

and you poison the air for me with your lying sighs.

a 'sker tsa e non sker 'ni ɾe a 'mi ɾa e non men 'ti ɾe
Ah, scherza e non schernire, ah, mira e non mentire.
ah joke and not to deride ah look and not to lie
Ah, joke and do not deride; ah, look and do not lie.

Chorus: ma 'fal so e men tsoɲ 'ɲɛr se 'par li o 'ta tʃi
Ma falso e menzogner se parli o taci
but false and untruthful if you speak or you are silent
But, false and untruthful whether speaking or silent,

i 'vet: tsi 'a i 'fin ti e tra di 'to ɾi i 'ba tʃi
i vezzi hai finti e traditori i baci.
the charms you have false and traitors the kisses
you have false charms and kisses that are traitors.

'prɔ vo 'dal: le bu 'dʒi e u 'na ɾja tor men 'ta ta da 'tu e 'frɔ di a bi 'ta ta
Provo dalle bugie un'aria tormentata da tue frodi abitata
I experience by the lies an air tormented by your frauds inhabited
I feel the air tormented by your lies and inhabited by your deceptions

e 'dal: le 'fu ɾje 'mi e
e dalle furie mie.
and by the furies mine
and by my furies.

a 'dʒu ɾa e non men 'ti ɾe a 'ta tʃi e non tra 'di ɾe
Ah, giura e non mentire, ah, taci e non tradire.
ah swear and not to lie ah be silent and not to betray
Ah, swear and do not lie; ah, be silent and do not betray.

ಶ

[89]

la 'man te kon so 'la to
L'amante consolato
The consoled lover

son 'tan to 'i to tʃer 'kan do ke pur al 'fin
Son tanto ito cercando, che pur alfin
I have so much gone searching that [indeed] finally
I searched so much that finally

ito: past participle	
of "ire" = "andare"	

tro 'va i ko 'lɛ i ke de zi 'a i du ɾa 'men te pe 'nan do
trovai colei che desiai duramente penando.
I found that woman whom I desired harshly suffering
I found that woman whom I, deeply suffering, desired.

o 'kwe sta 'vɔl ta si 'ki o non miŋ 'gan: no
O questa volta sì ch'io non m'inganno,
oh this time yes [that] I not myself deceive
Oh yes, this time I am not mistaken;

'si o non 'gɔ do 'mi o 'dan: no
s'io non godo mio danno.
if I not I enjoy the worst for me
if I do not enjoy [this time], woe to me.

son	'ta li	'kwe i	kon 'tɛn ti	ke	pur	al 'fin
Son	**tali**	**quei**	**contenti,**	**che**	**pur**	**alfin**
are	such	those	contentments	which	[indeed]	finally

Such are those contentments that at last

'i o	'prɔ vo	ke	'tut: to	mi ri 'nɔ vo	'dop: po	'luŋ gi	tor 'men ti
io	**provo**	**che**	**tutto**	**mi rinovo**	**doppo**	**lunghi**	**tormenti.**
I	I experience	that	completely	I am renewed	after	long	torments

I feel completely renewed after lengthy torments.

> *doppo =*
> *(mod.) dopo*

> *rinovo: from "rinovare" = (mod.) "rinnovare"*

ma	'tut: ti	ko 'mi o	fɔ	far	non	sa 'pran: no
Ma	**tutti**	**com'io**	**fo**	**far**	**non**	**sapranno**
but	everyone	as I	I do	to do	not	will know how

But not everyone will know how to do as I do;

ki	non	'gɔ de	'su o 'dan: no
chi	**non**	**gode**	**suo danno.**
who	not	enjoys	the worst for him

woe to him who does not enjoy.

&

[89]

la 'man te se 'gre to
L'amante segreto
The secret lover

'vɔʎ: ʎo	mo 'ri ɾe	pjut: 'tɔ sto	kil	'mi o	mal	'vɛŋ ga	a	sko 'pri ɾe
Voglio	**morire,**	**piuttosto**	**ch'il**	**mio**	**mal**	**venga**	**a**	**scoprire.**
I want	to die	rather	than the	my	pain	may come	to	to uncover

I would rather die than have my pain revealed.

o	diz 'grat: tsja	fa 'ta le
O,	**disgrazia**	**fatale!**
oh	disgrace	fatal

Oh, fatal disgrace!

'kwan to	pju	'mi ɾan	'ʎɔk: ki	il	'su o	bɛl	'vol to
Quanto	**più**	**miran**	**gl'occhi**	**il**	**suo**	**bel**	**volto,**
as much	more	they look at	the eyes	the	her	beautiful	face

The more my eyes look at her beautiful face

pju	tjɛn	la	'bok: ka	il	'mi o	de 'zir	se 'pol to
più	**tien**	**la**	**bocca**	**il**	**mio**	**desir**	**sepolto:**
more	holds	the	mouth	the	my	desire	buried

the more my lips keep my desire buried:

ki	ri 'mɛ djo	non	a	'tat: tʃa	il	'su o	'ma le
chi	**rimedio**	**non**	**ha**	**taccia**	**il**	**suo**	**male.**
he who	remedy	not	has	let be silent	the	his	woe

he who has no remedy should be silent about his woe.

non	're sti	di	mi 'ɾar	ki	non	a	'sɔr te
Non	**resti**	**di**	**mirar**	**chi**	**non**	**ha**	**sorte,**
not	may remain	of	to look at	he who	not	has	fortune

He who does not have [good] fortune should not keep looking;

ne   pwɔ   da   si   bɛl   tʃɛl   ve 'nir   la   'mɔr te
né   può   da   sì   bel   ciel   venir   la   morte.
nor   can   from   such   beautiful   heaven   to come   the   death
death cannot come from such a beautiful heaven.

la   'bɛl: la   'dɔn: na   'mi a   so 'vɛn te   'mi ɾo   e 'del: la   a   me   'vɔl dʒe
La   bella   donna   mia   sovente   miro,   ed ella   a   me   volge
the   beautiful   woman   mine   often   I look at   and she   to   me   turns
I often look at my beautiful woman, and she turns to me

pje 'to zo   il   'gwar do   'kwa zi   ke   'vɔʎ: ʎa   'di ɾe   pa 'le za   il   'tu o   mar 'ti ɾe
pietoso   il   guardo,   quasi   che   voglia   dire   "Palesa   il   tuo   martire,"
piteously   the   glance   as if   that   may wish   to say   reveal   the   your   agony
a piteous glance as if wishing to say, "reveal your agony,"

ke   ben   sak: 'kɔr dʒe   ke   mi 'strug: go   e   'ar do
che   ben   s'accorge   che   mi struggo   e   ardo.
because   well   is aware   that   I am consumed   and   I burn
because she is well aware that I am consumed and I burn.

ma   'i o   'vɔʎ: ʎo   mo 'ri ɾe   pjut: 'tɔ sto   kil   'mi o   mal   'vɛŋ ga   a   sko 'pri ɾe
Ma   io   voglio   morire   piuttosto   ch'il   mio   mal   venga   a   scoprire.
but   I   I want   to die   rather   than the   my   pain   may come   to   to uncover
But I would rather die than have my pain revealed.

ler 'bet: ta   kal   'ka der   di   'fred: da   'bri na   'laŋ gwi da   il   'ka po   iŋ 'ki na
L'erbetta   ch'al   cader   di   fredda   brina   languida   il   capo   inchina,
the young grass   which at the   falling   of   cold   frost   languishing   the   head   bows
The young grass which, languishing at the fall of cold frost, bows its head,

al: lap: pa 'rir   del   'so le   'lje ta   ver 'ded: dʒa   pju   di   kwel   ke   'swɔ le
all'apparir   del   sole   lieta   verdeggia   più   di   quel   che   suole:
at the appearing   of the   sun   happy   becomes verdant   more   than   that   which   it is used to
happily becomes, at the appearance of the sun, more verdant than usual;

tal   'i o   sal 'kun   ti 'mor   mi   'dʒɛ la   il   'kɔ ɾe
tal   io,   s'alcun   timor   mi   gela   il   core,
like this   I   if some   fear   me   freezes   the   heart
likewise, if some fear freezes my heart,

al: lap: pa 'rir   di   'lɛ i   'prɛn do   vi 'go ɾe
all'apparir   di   lei   prendo   vigore.
at the appearing   of   her   I take   vigor
I revive when she appears.

ma   'i o   'vɔʎ: ʎo   mo 'ri ɾe   pjut: 'tɔ sto   kil   'mi o   mal   'vɛŋ ga   a   sko 'pri ɾe
Ma   io   voglio   morire   piuttosto   ch'il   mio   mal   venga   a   scoprire.
but   I   I want   to die   rather   than the   my   pain   may come   to   to uncover
But I would rather die than have my pain revealed.

dɛ   'dʒɛt: ta   'lar ko   po de 'ro zo   e   'lar mi   a 'mor
Deh,   getta   l'arco   poderoso   e   l'armi,   Amor,
ah   throw away   the bow   mighty   and   the weapons   Love
Ah, cast aside your mighty bow and weapons, Love,

e   'laʃ: ʃa   o 'ma i   'laʃ: ʃa   di   sa et: 'tar mi
e   lascia   omai,   lascia   di   saettarmi!
and   leave off   now   leave off   of   to shoot me with arrows

and stop piercing me with arrows!

se   non   per   a 'mor   'mi o   'fal: lo   per   o 'nor   'tu o   su 'pɛr bo   'di o
Se   non   per   amor   mio,   fallo   per   onor   tuo,   superbo   dio,
if   not   for   love   mine   do it   for   honor   your   proud   god

Do so, proud god, for your honor if not for love of me,

per 'ke   'glɔ rja   non   ɛ   dun   gwer: 'rjɛr   'fɔr te
perché   gloria   non   è   d'un   guerrier   forte
because   glory   not   it is   of a   warrior   powerful

for it is no glory for a powerful warrior

ut: 'tʃi der   un   ke   sta   vi 'tʃi no   a   'mɔr te
uccider   un   che   sta   vicino   a   morte.
to kill   one   who   is   near   to   death

to kill one who is [already] near death.

GL: **Amor**

☙

[63, 89, 99]   *Giuseppe Artale*

la 'strat: to
L'astratto
The estranged one

'vɔʎ: ʎo   si   vɔ   kan 'tar   'for se   kan 'tan do   tro 'var   'pa tʃe   po 'tes: si
Voglio   sì,   vo'   cantar,   forse   cantando   trovar   pace   potessi
I want   yes   I want   to sing   perhaps   singing   to find   peace   I should be able

al   'mi o   tor 'men to   a   dop: 'pri me ɾe   il   dwɔl   'fɔr tsa   il   kon 'tʃɛn to
al   mio   tormento;   ha   d'opprimere   il   duol   forza   il   concento.
to the   my   torment   has   of to crush   the   grief   power   the   harmony

I want to sing – yes, I want to sing; perhaps I can find solace for my torment by singing;
harmony has the power to overcome grief.

si   si   pen 'sjɛ ro   a 'spɛt: ta   a   so 'nar   ko min 'tʃa mo   e
Sì,   sì,   pensiero   aspetta;   a   sonar   cominciamo,   e
yes   yes   worry   wait   to   to play   let us begin   and

Yes, yes, worries, wait: let us to begin to play, and

> *printed "comintiamo"*
> *= (mod.) "cominciamo"*

a   'nɔ stro   'sɛn so   'u na   kan 'tson   tro 'vja mo
a   nostro   senso   una   canzon   troviamo.
to   our   sense   a   song   let us find

find a song suitable to our mood.

'ɛb: bi   il   'kɔ ɾe   le 'ga to   un   di   dun   bɛl   krin
"Ebbi   il   core   legato   un   dì   d'un   bel   crin..."
I had   the   heart   tied   one   day   of a   beautiful   head of hair

"One day my heart was bound to beautiful tresses..."

la   strat: tʃe 'rɛ i   'su bi to   'ka pro   un   'fɔʎ: ʎo
La   straccerei!   Subito   ch'apro   un   foglio
her   I would tear apart   immediately   that I open   a   page

I would rip her to pieces! The moment I open a book

> *in [89] and [99]: "ch'aspro"*
> *is printed in error*

'sɛn to   ke   mi rak: 'kɔr da   il   'mi o   kor 'dɔʎ: ʎo
sento   **che**   **mi raccorda**   **il**   **mio**   **cordoglio.**
I feel   that   me it reminds   the   my   grief
I feel it reminding me of my grief.

raccorda: from "raccordare"
= (mod.) "ricordare"

fud: 'dʒi a   la   'nɔt: te   e   sol   spje 'ga va   in 'tor no
"Fuggia   **la**   **notte**   **e**   **sol**   **spiegava**   **intorno..."**
was fleeing   the   night   and   sun   was unfolding   around
"The night was fleeing and the sun was unfolding around [us]..."

fuggia = fuggiva

ɛ   si kon 'fon don   kwi   la   'nɔt: tel   'dʒor no
Eh!   **Si confondon**   **qui**   **la**   **nott'e'l**   **giorno.**
ah   they mingle   here   the   night and the   day
Ah, this time night and day are being blurred.

in [89]: "el giorno" =
"e'l giorno," or "il [el
= (mod.) il] giorno"

vo 'la te   o   'fu rje   e   kon du 'tʃe te   un   mi ze 'ra bi le   al   'fɔ ko   e 'tɛr no
"Volate,   **o**   **furie,**   **e**   **conducete**   **un**   **miserabile**   **al**   **foco**   **eterno..."**
fly   o   furies   and   lead   a   miserable one   to the   fire   eternal
"Fly, o furies, and lead a miserable one to the eternal fire..."

foco =
(mod.)
fuoco

ma   ke   fɔ   nel: 'lin 'fɛr no
Ma   **che**   **fo**   **nell'inferno?**
but   what   I do   in the hell
But what am I doing in hell?

in [63]: "à" (rather than "ma"): an error

al   'tu o   tʃɛl   'va go   de 'zi o   'spje ga   'la le   e   'van: ne
"Al   **tuo**   **ciel**   **vago**   **desio,**   **spiega**   **l'ale**   **e**   **vanne..."**
to the   your   heaven   yearning   desire   spread   the wing   and   go
"Toward your heaven, yearning desire, spread your wings and go..."

af: 'fe   ke   kwel   ke   ti   kom 'po ze   'pɔ ko   sa 'pe a   del   a mo 'ro zo   'stra le
Affé   **che**   **quel**   **che**   **ti**   **compose**   **poco**   **sapea**   **del**   **amoroso**   **strale;**
in faith   [that]   the one   who   you   composed   little   knew   of the   amorous   arrow
Truly, the one who composed you knew little about the amorous [Love's] arrow;

sapea = sapeva

de zi 'dɛ rjo   da 'man te   in   tʃɛl   non   'sa le
desiderio   **d'amante,**   **in**   **ciel**   **non**   **sale.**
yearning   of lover   to   heaven   not   goes up
a lover's yearning does not go up to heaven.

go de 'rɔ   'sot: to   la   'lu na
"Goderò   **sotto**   **la**   **luna..."**
I will have pleasure   beneath   the   moon
"I will have pleasure beneath the moon..."

or   'kwe sta   si 'ke   'pɛd: dʒo   sa   il   de 'stin   deʎ: ʎa 'man ti
Or   **questa**   **sì ch'è**   **peggio,**   **sa**   **il**   **destin**   **degl'amanti**
now   this   so that is   worse   knows   the   fate   of the lovers
Now this is [even] worse; she knows the fate of lovers

sì che = (mod.) sicché

e   vwɔl   for 'tu na
e   **vuol**   **fortuna.**
and   wants   (good) fortune
[but yet] wishes for good luck.

'mi ze ɾo   i   'gwa i   man   da   me   'stes: so   a 'strat: to
Misero   i   guai   m'han   da   me   stesso   astratto,
miserable   the   troubles   me have   from   me   myself   abstracted
Miserable me, my troubles have estranged me from myself;

e   tʃer 'kan do   un   sod: 'dʒɛt: to   per   vo 'ler lo   dir
e   cercando   un   soggetto   per   volerlo   dir
and   searching for   a   subject   for   to wish it   to say
and, in seeking a subject to talk about,

sol   'tʃɛn to   nɔ   'det: to
sol   cento   n'ho   detto.
alone   hundred   of them I have   made up
I have made up a mere hundred of them!

ki   nel   'kar tʃe ɾe   dun   'kri ne   i   de 'zi ɾi   a   pri dʒo 'njɛ ɾi
"Chi   nel   carcere   d'un   crine   i   desiri   ha   prigionieri
he who   in the   prison   of a   head of hair   the   desires   has   captive
"For the one whose desires are captive in the prison of tresses,

per   'su e   'krʊ de   'a spre   ru 'i ne   ne 'mɛn   'suɔ i   'so nʊ   i   pen 'sjɛ ɾi
per   sue   crude   aspre   ruine,   ne men   suoi   sono   i   pensieri.
for   his   cruel   bitter   ruin   not even   his   are   the   thoughts
not even his thoughts are his own, to his cruel [and] bitter ruin.

> *ne men =*
> *(mod.)*
> *nemmen*

ki   a dun   'va go   'al to   splen 'do ɾe   diɛ   fe 'del la   li ber 'ta
Chi   ad un   vago   alto   splendore   die'   fedel   la   libertà
he who   to a   lovely   lofty   beauty   gave   faithful   the   freedom
He who faithfully gave up his freedom for a lovely, lofty beauty

> *die' = diede*

'skja vo   al   fin   'tut: to   da 'mo ɾe   ne 'men   'su a   la   'men te   a 'vra
schiavo   al   fin   tutto   d'amore,   ne men   sua   la   mente   avrà."
slave   at the end   completely   of love   not even   his   the   mind   will have
will not even have a mind of his own, being in the end totally a slave to love."

> *in [89]:*
> *" chiavo": a*
> *misprint of*
> *"schiavo"*

kwin 'di o   'mi ze ɾo   e   'stol to   non   vo 'len do   kan 'tar   kan 'ta to   ɔ   'mol to
Quind'io,   misero   e   stolto,   non   volendo   cantar,   cantato   ho   molto.
hence I   miserable   and   foolish   not   wishing   to sing   sung   I have   much
And thus, miserable and foolish, not wishing to sing [anymore], I have sung plenty!

[40, 89] In [40] titled **Soccorrete, luci avare**.

la tra vaʎ: 'ʎa ta
La travagliata
The suffering woman

sok: kor: 're te   'lu tʃi   a 'va ɾe   un   ke   'mwɔ ɾe   di   do 'lo ɾe
Soccorrete,   luci   avare,   un   che   muore   di   dolore
help   eyes   stingy   one   who   dies   of   sorrow
Help, stingy eyes, one who is dying of sorrow,

kon	un	'vɔ stro	'zgwar do	al 'me no
con	**un**	**vostro**	**sguardo**	**almeno!**
with	a	your	glance	at least

with at least a glance from you!

si 'pwɔ	'fa ɾe	del	gwar 'da ɾe	ka ɾi 'ta	ke	'ko sti	'me no
Si può	**fare**	**del**	**guardare**	**carità,**	**che**	**costi**	**meno?**
one can	to make	of the	looking at	charity	what	may cost	less

Can one give an alm that costs less than a look?

pro fe 'ɾi te	'lab: bra	'ka ɾe	'so le	'du e	pa 'ɾɔ le	a	ki	mwɔr	kor 'te zi	al 'me no
Proferite,	**labbra**	**care,**	**sole**	**due**	**parole**	**a**	**chi**	**muor,**	**cortesi**	**almeno.**
utter	lips	dear	only	two	words	to	one who	dies	courteous	at least

Utter, dear lips, just two courteous words, at least, to one who is dying.

si 'pwɔ	'fa ɾe	del	par 'la ɾe	kor te 'zi a	ke	im 'pɔr ti	'me no
Si può	**fare**	**del**	**parlare**	**cortesia,**	**che**	**importi**	**meno?**
one can	to make	of the	speaking	courtesy	what	may be important	less

Can one make, of courtesy, anything less important than a word?

so di 'sfa te	se	vi 'pa ɾe	un	ko 'stan te	'fi do	a 'man te
Sodisfate,	**se**	**vi pare,**	**un**	**costante**	**fido**	**amante**
satisfy	if	you like	a	constant	faithful	lover

> *sodisfate: from "sodisfare" = (mod.) soddisfare*

Satisfy, if you will, a constant and faithful lover

> *var. in [89]:*

	so di 'sfa te	'sɛr vo	a 'man te
	Sodisfate	**servo**	**amante**
	satisfy	servant	lover

Satisfy a servile lover

kon	un	'vɔ stro	ba 'tʃo	al 'me no
con	**un**	**vostro**	**bacio**	**almeno.**
with	a	your	kiss	at least

with at least a kiss from you.

si 'pwɔ	'da ɾe	del	ba 'tʃa ɾe	gwi der 'don	ke	'vaʎ: ʎa	'me no
Si può	**dare**	**del**	**baciare**	**guiderdon,**	**che**	**vaglia**	**meno?**
one can	to give	of the	kissing	reward	what	may be of worth	less

> *vaglia (poet.) = valga (from "valere")*

Can one give a reward that is worth less than kissing?

❧

[89]   *Giulio Strozzi*

la ven 'det: ta
La vendetta
Revenge

la	ven 'det: ta	ɛ	un	'dol tʃe	af: 'fɛt: to	il	di 'spɛt: to	vwɔl	di 'spɛt: to
La	**vendetta**	**è**	**un**	**dolce**	**affetto,**	**il**	**dispetto**	**vuol**	**dispetto,**
the	revenge	is	a	sweet	affection	the	spite	wants	spite

Revenge is a sweet feeling; spite invites spite,

il   ri 'far si   ɛ   un   gran   di 'lɛt: to
il   rifarsi   è   un   gran   diletto.
the   getting even is   a   great   delight
[and] getting even is a great delight.

'va ne   son   'sku ze   e   ra 'dʒo ni   per   pla 'kar   'dɔn: na   ol trad: 'dʒa ta
Vane   son   scuse   e   ragioni   per   placar   donna   oltraggiata,
vain   are   excuses   and reasons   for   to placate woman   outraged
In vain are excuses and reasons, in placating an outraged woman;

non   pen 'sar   ke   ti   per 'do ni
non   pensar   che   ti   perdoni.
not   to think   that you   she may pardon
do not think that she will pardon you.

'dɔn: na   'ma i   non   ven di 'ka ta   'pa tʃe   a   in   'bok: ka   e   'gwɛr: ra   in   'pɛt: to
Donna   mai   non   vendicata   pace   ha   in   bocca   e   guerra   in   petto.
woman   ever   not   avenged   peace   has in   mouth   and war   in   breast
An unavenged woman speaks peace [but] has war in her breast.

non   per 'do na   in   ven di 'kar si   al: la 'man te   pju   gra 'di to
Non   perdona   in   vendicarsi   all'amante   più   gradito
not   she forgives in   avenging herself to the lover   most   agreeable
In avenging herself she does not forgive the most agreeable lover

ke   la 'do ra   e   vwɔl   ri 'far si
che   l'adora   e   vuol   rifarsi;
who   her adores   and wants   the making up
who adores her and wants to make up with her;

'kwan dil   'fjɛ ro   in su per 'bi to   'vɛr so   'lɛ i   'per de   'per dil   ri 'spɛt: to
quand'il   fiero   insuperbito   verso   lei   perde,   perd'il   rispetto.
when the   proud   haughty   way of speaking she   loses   loses the respect
when she loses her proud and haughty posturing, she loses her respect.

&

[89]

le 'ra kli to a mo 'ro zo
L'Eraclito amoroso
The amorous Eraclito

u 'di te   a 'man ti   la   ka 'dʒo ne   o   'di o   ka   la gri 'mar   mi   'pɔr ta
Udite   amanti   la   cagione,   oh   Dio,   ch'a   lagrimar   mi   porta,
hear   lovers   the   reason   oh   God   that to weeping   me   brings
Hear, lovers, the reason that brings me – oh God – to tears:

nel: la do 'ra to   e   'bɛl: lo   'i do lo   'mi o   ke   si   'fi do   kre 'de i
nell'adorato   e   bello   idolo   mio,   che   sì   fido   credei,
in the adored   and beautiful idol   mine   who   so   faithful I believed

la   'fe de   ɛ   'mɔr ta
la   fede   è   morta.
the   faith   is   dead
the faith in my adored and beautiful idol, whom I believed so faithful, is dead.

va 'get: tsa	ɔ	sol	di	'pjan dʒe ɾe	mi 'pa sko	sol	di	'la gri me
Vaghezza	**ho**	**sol**	**di**	**piangere,**	**mi pasco**	**sol**	**di**	**lagrime,**
wish	I have	only	of	to weep	I feed	only	of	tears

The only desire I have is to weep; I feed only on tears;

il	'dwɔ lo	ɛ	'mi a	de 'lit: tsja	e	son	'mi e	'dʒɔ je	i	'dʒe mi ti
il	**duolo**	**è**	**mia**	**delizia,**	**e**	**son**	**mie**	**gioie**	**i**	**gemiti.**
the	sorrow	is	my	delight	and	are	my	joys	the	laments

sorrow is my delight, and laments are my joys.

'oɲ: ɲi	mar 'ti ɾe	aɡ: 'gra da mi	'oɲ: ɲi	do 'lor	di 'let: ta mi
Ogni	**martire**	**aggradami,**	**ogni**	**dolor**	**dilettami.**
every	agony	pleases me	every	pain	delights me

Every agony pleases me; every pain delights me.

i	siŋ 'gul ti	mi	'sa na no	i	so 'spir	mi	kon 'so la no
I	**singulti**	**mi**	**sanano,**	**i**	**sospir**	**mi**	**consolano.**
the	sobs	me	heal	the	sighs	me	console

Sobs heal me; sighs console me.

ma	se	la	'fe de	'ne ga mi	kwel: liŋ ko 'stan te	e	'pɛr fi do
Ma,	**se**	**la**	**fede**	**negami**	**quell'incostante**	**e**	**perfido,**
but	if	the	fidelity	denies me	that inconstant	and	perfidious

But if that inconstant and perfidious one denies me fidelity,

> *Since the writer is a man, one would expect "perfido" to be (feminine) "perfida"; the masculine form could refer gramatically back to "Dio," or to "l'idolo mio."*

al 'men	'fe de	ser 'ba te mi	'si no	'al: la	'mɔr te	o	'la gri me
almen	**fede**	**serbatemi**	**sino**	**alla**	**morte,**	**o**	**lagrime.**
at least	faith	preserve for me	up until	to the	death	o	tears

at least preserve faith for me until death, o tears.

'oɲ: ɲi	tri 'stet: tsa	as: 'sal ga mi	'oɲ: ɲi	kor 'dɔʎ: ʎo	e 'tɛr ni si
Ogni	**tristezza**	**assalgami,**	**ogni**	**cordoglio**	**eternisi,**
every	sadness	let assail me	every	grief	let become immortal

May every sadness assail me, every grief last forever;

'tan to	'oɲ: ɲi	'ma le	af: 'flig: ga mi	ke	mut: 'tʃi da	e	sot: 'tɛr: ri mi
tanto	**ogni**	**male**	**affliggami**	**che**	**m'uccida**	**e**	**sotterrimi.**
so much	every	woe	let grieve me	that	me it may kill	and	it may bury me

may every woe grieve me so much that it may kill me and bury me.

GL: **Eraclito**

❧

[63] I've removed the antiquated "h" from the spelling of the first word of the original title **Hor che Apollo**.

or ke a 'pɔl: lo
Or che Apollo
Now that Apollo

or	ke	a 'pɔl: lo	ɛ	a	'tɛ ti	in	'se no	e	il	'mi o	sol	sta
Or	**che**	**Apollo**	**è**	**a**	**Teti**	**in**	**seno**	**e**	**il**	**mio**	**sol**	**sta**
now	that	Apollo	is	in	Tethys	on	breast	and	the	my	sun	lies

Now that Apollo is upon the breast of Tethys and my sun lies

> *i.e.:* now that it is nighttime...;
> *"my sun"=* my dearest beloved

in 'grɛm bo al   'son: no   or   ka   'lu i   pen 'san 'di o   'i o   'pe no
in grembo al   sonno,   or   ch'a   lui   pensand'io   io   peno
in bosom   of the sleep   now   that to him   thinking I   I   I suffer
in the bosom of sleep... now that, thinking of her, I suffer

> *"lui," grammatically, refers to "il sole," – hence*
> *masculine in gender but idiomatically "her"*

ne   po 'zar 'ʎɔk: ki   'mjɛ i   'pɔn: no   a   'kwe sto   al 'bɛr go
né   posar   gl'occhi miei   ponno,   a   questo   albergo
nor   to rest   the eyes mine   can   to   this   refuge
[and] my eyes cannot rest, to this refuge

per   sfo 'gar il   'dwɔ lo   'vɛŋ go pjan 'dʒɛn te   in: na mo 'ra to   e   'so lo
per   sfogar   il   duolo   vengo   piangente,   innamorato,   e   solo.
in order to to vent the sorrow   I come   weeping   enamored   and   alone
I come weeping, enamored and alone, to vent my sorrow.

si   si   'fil: li   'kwe sto 'kɔ ɾe   ke   per   a 'mor   si   'mɔ ɾe
Sì,   sì,   Filli   questo   core   che   per   amor   si   more,
yes   yes   Filli   this   heart   which for   love   itself dies
Yes, yes, Filli, this heart which is dying of love

a   te   vjɛn   sup: pli 'kan te   de   'two i   'bɛ i   'lu mi   a 'man te
a   te   vien   supplicante,   de'   tuoi   bei   lumi,   amante.
to   you   comes entreating   of   your   beautiful eyes   lover
comes, as lover of your beautiful eyes, to you in supplication.

'mi ɾa al   pjɛ   'tan te   ka 'te ne   lu tʃi 'dis: si ma   'mi a   'stel: la
Mira   al   piè   tante   catene,   lucidissima   mia   stella,
see   at the foot   so many fetters   most shining   my   star
See on my feet the many fetters, my most shining star;

e   se   'dwɔl ti   'ki o   'sti a   in   'pe ne
e   se   duolti   ch'io   stia   in   pene
and   if   you are sorry that I   be   in   sufferings
and if you are sorry that I suffer,

'si i   men   'kru da   o   pur   men   'bɛl: la
sìi   men   cruda   o   pur   men   bella.
be   less   harsh   or   else   less   beautiful
be either less harsh or less beautiful.

se   men   'kru da   pje 'ta de   a 'vrɔ   del   'mi o   ser 'vir
Se   men   cruda   pietade   avrò   del   mio   servir
if   less   harsh   pity   I shall have of the my   serving
If [you are] less harsh, I shall have pity in my servitude –

sa 'prɔ   ke   'ma mi   e   se   men   'bɛl: 'li o   fran 'dʒe 'rɔ   i   le 'ga mi
saprò   che   m'ami,   e   se   men   bell' io   frangerò   i   legami.
I will know that me you love and if   less   beautiful I   I will break   the   ties
I will know that you love me; and if [you are] less beautiful, I will break my ties.

've di   al   'kɔ ɾe   'kwan te   'spi ne   tu   mi   'da i   ver 'miʎ: ʎa   'rɔ za
Vedi   al   core   quante   spine   tu   mi   dai   vermiglia   rosa,
see   to the heart   how many thorns   you to me   you give vermilion   rose
See how many thorns of vermilion rose *[wounds]* you give to my heart;

e	se	'zdɛɲː ɲi	'mi e	ru 'i ne	'si i	men	'fjɛ ɾa	o	men	vet: 'tso za
e	se	**sdegni**	**mie**	**rouine**	**sìi**	**men**	**fiera,**	**o**	**men**	**vezzosa.**
and	if	you disdain	my	ruins	be	less	proud	or	less	charming

and if you disdain my ruin, be less proud or less charming.

rouine =
(mod.)
rovine

ma	i sfo 'ga te vi	spri dʒo 'na te vi	'mjɛ i	so 'spir	'si o	dʒa	kom 'prɛn do
Ma	**isfogatevi,**	**sprigionatevi,**	**miei**	**sospir,**	**s'io**	**già**	**comprendo**
but	vent yourselves	release yourselves	my	sighs	if I	now	I understand

But vent yourselves, release yourselves, my sighs, as I now understand

ke	di	me	'ri de	'fil: li	'aŋ ko	dor 'mɛn do
che	**di**	**me**	**ride**	**Filli**	**anco**	**dormendo.**
that	at	me	laughs	Filli	even	sleeping

that Filli laughs at me even while asleep.

anco =
(mod.) anche

'ri de	de	'mjɛ i	la 'men ti	'tʃɛr to	'kwe sta	'kru dɛ le
Ride	**de'**	**miei**	**lamenti**	**certo,**	**questa**	**crudele**
laughs	at	my	laments	surely	this	cruel one

Surely she laughs at my laments, this cruel one,

e	'sprɛt: tsa	i	'prɛ gi	'mjɛ i	le	'mi e	kwe 'rɛ le
e	**sprezza**	**i**	**preghi**	**miei**	**le**	**mie**	**querele.**
and	scorns	the	entreaties	my	the	my	complaints

and she scorns my entreaties [and] my complaints.

'dɛd: dʒo	per 'tʃɔ	par 'tir	'sɛn tsa	kon 'fɔr to
Deggio	**perciò**	**partir**	**senza**	**conforto**
I must	therefore	to depart	without	consolation

I must therefore depart without consolation;

se	'vi vo	non	mi	'vwɔ i	mi	ve 'dra i	'mɔr to
se	**vivo**	**non**	**mi**	**vuoi,**	**mi**	**vedrai**	**morto.**
if	alive	not	me	you want	me	you will see	dead

if you do not want me alive, you will see me dead.

'men tre	al 'tro ve	il	pjɛ	sin 'vi a	'i o	ti	'laʃː ʃo	in	'dol tʃe	o 'bli o
Mentre	**altrove**	**il**	**piè**	**s'invia,**	**io**	**ti**	**lascio**	**in**	**dolce**	**oblio.**
while	elsewhere	the	foot	itself sends	I	you	I leave	in	sweet	oblivion

While I go elsewhere, I leave you in sweet oblivion.

'par to	'fil: li	'par to	'a ni ma	'mi a	'kwe sto	'si a	'lul ti mo	ad: 'di o
Parto,	**Filli,**	**parto,**	**anima**	**mia,**	**questo**	**sia**	**l'ultimo**	**addio.**
I depart	Filli	I depart	soul	mine	this	may be	the last	farewell

I depart, Filli; I depart, soul of mine. May this be the last farewell.

GL: **Apollo, Filli, Teti**

[15, 40, 89]   In [89] titled **La fanciuletta semplice** (The innocent young girl).   *G. A. Cicognini*

'spes: so per 'en tro al 'pɛt: to
Spesso per entro al petto
Often through my breast

'spes: so	per	'en tro	al	'pɛt: to	mi	'pas: sa	un	non	so	ke
Spesso	**per**	**entro**	**al**	**petto**	**mi**	**passa**	**un**	**non**	**so**	**che,**
often	through	within	to the	breast	to me	passes	a	not	I know	what

Often something – I know not what – passes through my breast;

e	non	so	dir	'seʎ: ʎi	ɛ	o	'mar ti ɾe	o	di 'lɛt: to
e	**non**	**so**	**dir,**	**s'egli**	**è**	**o**	**martire**	**o**	**diletto.**
and	not	I know how	to say	if it	is	either	torment	or	pleasure

and I cannot say if it is pain or pleasure.

ta 'lor	mi 'sɛn to	ut: 'tʃi de ɾe	da	iŋ 'kɔɲ: ɲi to	ri gor
Talor	**mi sento**	**uccidere**	**da**	**incognito**	**rigor;**
at times	I feel myself	to kill	by	unknown	severity

At times I feel like I'm being killed by an unknown severity;

sa 'rɛb: be	pur	da 'ri de ɾe	ke	'fos: se	il	mal	da 'mor
sarebbe	**pur**	**da ridere,**	**che**	**fosse**	**il**	**mal**	**d'amor.**
it would be	however	to be laughed at	that	it were	the	illness	of love

but it would be funny if it were lovesickness.

qwa 'lor	mi	sap: pre 'zɛn ta	di	'klɔ ɾi	il	bɛl	se 'ren
Qualor	**mi**	**s'appresenta**	**di**	**Clori**	**il**	**bel**	**seren**
whenever	to me	presents itself	of	Clori	the	beautiful	clearness

Whenever Clori's sunshine appears before me

mi	'naʃ: ʃe	'fɔ ko	in	sen	ke	'pja tʃe	e	in	un	tor 'men ta
mi	**nasce**	**foco**	**in**	**sen,**	**che**	**piace**	**e**	**in**	**un**	**tormenta.**
to me	is born	fire	in	breast	which	pleases	and	at once		torments

> *in [89]: un foco [un 'fɔ ko] = a fire (springs...)*

fire springs up in my breast which pleases and torments at the same time.

mi 'sɛn to	il	kɔr	di 'vi de ɾe	tra	il	'dʒe lo	e	tra	lar 'dor
Mi sento	**il**	**cor**	**dividere**	**tra**	**il**	**gielo**	**e**	**tra**	**l'ardor;**
I feel	the	heart	to divide	between	the	ice	and	between	the fire

> *gielo (in [89]: giello) = (mod.) gelo*

I feel my heart split between ice and fire;

sa 'rɛb: be	pur	da 'ri de ɾe	ke	'fos: se	il	mal	da 'mor
sarebbe	**pur**	**da ridere,**	**che**	**fosse**	**il**	**mal**	**d'amor.**
it would be	however	to be laughed at	that	it were	the	illness	of love

but it would be funny if it were lovesickness.

> *In [40] and [89] is a 3rd verse:*

i	pju	so 'liŋ gi	or: 'ro ɾi	fre 'kwɛn to	vo lon 'tjer
I	**più**	**solinghi**	**orrori**	**frequento**	**volontier,**
the	most	solitary	abysses	I frequent	voluntarily

> *volontier[o] = volontario*

I don't mind being in the most solitary dark places,

ma	'sɛn to	un	'mi o	pen 'sjɛr	ke	'di tʃe	e	'do ve	ɛ	'klɔ ɾi
ma	**sento**	**un**	**mio**	**pensier,**	**che**	**dice:**	**e**	**dove**	**è**	**Clori?**
but	I hear	a	my	thought	which	says	and	where	is	Clori

but I hear a thought in me saying: "and where is Clori?"

or	ki	mi	sa	de 'tʃi de ɾe	ke	'si a	'kwe sto	fu 'ror
Or	**chi**	**mi**	**sa**	**decidere,**	**che**	**sia**	**questo**	**furor;**
now	who	for me	knows how	to decide	what	be	this	frenzy

Now who can help me decide what this frenzy is?

sa ˈrɛb: be   pur   da ˈri de ɾe   ke   ˈfos: se   il   mal   da ˈmor
sarebbe   pur   da ridere,   che   fosse   il   mal   d'amor.
it would be   indeed   to be laughed at   that   it were   the   illness   of love

It would be funny indeed if it were lovesickness.

*G**L**:* **Clori**

&

[89]   This is titled "A dialogue for one voice..."

tra le spe ˈran tse el ti ˈmo ɾe
Tra le Speranze e'l Timore
Between Hopes and Fear

ti ˈmo ɾe   e   ke   sa ˈra   go ˈdre mo   si   o   nɔ
"Timore,   e   che   sarà?   Godremo   sì   o   nò?"
Fear   and   what   will be   we will take pleasure   yes   or   no

"Fear, what will be? Shall we take pleasure – yes or no?"

ˈda te mi   li ber ˈta   spe ˈran tse   e   vel   di ˈɾɔ
"Datemi   libertà,   Speranze,   e   vel'   dirò:
give me   liberty   Hopes   and   to you it   I will say

"Grant me [the] liberty, Hopes, and I will tell you:

non   sak: ˈkor da no   ˈma i   le   spe ˈran tse   el   ti ˈmor
Non   s'accordano   mai   le   speranze   e'l   timor,
not   come to an agreement   ever   the   hopes   and the   fear

Hopes and fear never agree,

ke   ˈlu no   ˈsoɲː ɲa   ˈgwa i   e   ˈlal tre   at: ˈtʃɛ ka   a ˈmor
ché   l'uno   sogna   guai   e   l'altre   acciecá   Amor. "
because   the one   imagines   troubles   and   the others   blinds   Love

because the one *[fear]* imagines trouble and Love blinds the other *[hopes]*."

> *acciecá: from*
> *"acciecare" =*
> *(mod.) "accecare"*

ti ˈmo ɾe   di   pur   di
"Timore,   di',   pur   di!"
Fear   say   indeed   say

"Fear, tell me – do tell!"

spe ˈran tse   ˈi o   vel   di ˈɾɔ   ma   se   vi   di ˈɾɔ   di   nɔ
"Speranze,   io   vel'   dirò,   ma   se   vi   dirò   di   no,
Hopes   I   to you it   I will say   but   if   to you   I will say   of   no

"Hopes, I will tell you; but if I say 'no' to you

ˈvo i   di ˈɾe te   di   si
voi   direte   di   sì."
you   will say   of   yes

you will [still] say 'yes'."

*G**L**:* **Amor**

 Supriani, *Francesco (?-?)*

No biographical information was found about this composer. The following song has been attributed to him and is included here because it is printed in two collections and is in the style and form of the seventeenth century.

[25, 27]

po ˈtra laʃː ˈʃa ɾe il ˈri o
Potrà lasciare il rio
The brook may cease

po ˈtra	laʃː ˈʃa ɾe	il	ˈri o	di	dar	tri ˈbu to	al	ˈma ɾe
Potrà	**lasciare**	**il**	**rio**	**di**	**dar**	**tributo**	**al**	**mare,**
will be able	to leave off	the	brook	of	to give	tributary	to the	sea

The brook may cease flowing into the sea,

rio (poet.) = ruscello

ma	nɔ	ke	non	pɔsː ˈsi o	laʃː ˈʃar	di	ser ˈbar	fe
ma	**no,**	**che**	**non**	**poss'io**	**lasciar**	**di**	**serbar**	**fé.**
but	no	[that]	not	am able I	to leave off	of	to keep	faith

but no, I cannot cease loving you.

e	ˈpri a	ke	ˈnwɔ vo	a ˈmo ɾe	mi	ˈfatː tʃa	so spi ˈɾa ɾe
E	**pria**	**che**	**nuovo**	**amore**	**mi**	**faccia**	**sospirare,**
and	before	that	new	love	me	may make	to sigh

And before a new love may make me sigh

pria (poet.) = prima

sa ˈpra	kon ˈtɛn to	il	ˈkɔ ɾe	ˈfi do	mo ˈɾir	per	te
saprà	**contento**	**il**	**core**	**fido**	**morir**	**per**	**te.**
will know how	content	the	heart	faithful	to die	for	you

my heart will know, contentedly, how to die faithful to you.

Tarditi, Orazio (1602-1677)

Composer and organist born in Rome, he became a brother in the Camaldolensian order in 1617. Between 1624 and 1637 he was organist at Arezzo Cathedral, then at S. Michele near Venice, and then at Volterra. He was *maestro di cappella* at Forlì Cathedral in 1639, at Jesi Cathedral in 1644, and at Faenza Cathedral from 1647 to 1670. He died in Forlì.

Tarditi was an extremely prolific composer of church music: motets, masses, and psalm settings, of which many books were published. His secular compositions include a book of arias for solo voice and continuo, also with guitar tablature (1628), and a book of solo madrigals (1633).

---

[36]

ki ˈkre de ˈki o ˈva mi
Chi crede ch'io v'ami
Whoever believes that I love you

ki	ˈkre de	ˈki o	ˈva mi	va ˈdo ɾi	ˈmi a	ˈklɔ ɾi
Chi	**crede**	**ch'io**	**v'ami,**	**v'adori,**	**mia**	**Clori,**
who	believes	that I	you I love	you I adore	my	Clori

Whoever believes that I love you [and] adore you, my Clori,

I changed the printed "credi," which makes no sense grammatically, to "crede," assuming a miscopying; possibly the "i" ending was chosen as poetic license to keep the row of "i" endings in the line...

ˈki o	ˈvi va	ʎar ˈdo ɾi	di	ˈvɔ stra	bel ˈta
ch'io	**viva**	**gl'ardori**	**di**	**vostra**	**beltà,**
that I	may live on	the ardors	of	your	beauty

that I live on the ardors of your beauty:

nɔ	ke	nol	ˈkre da	ke	va ni ˈta
no,	**che**	**nol**	**creda**	**che**	**vanità.**
no	[that]	not it	let him believe	what	vanity

no, he should not believe it – what vanity!

nol = non + il

pur	'trɔpː po	dʒa	'kre zi	al	'fal so	sem 'bjan te	ke	'mi ze ɾo	a 'man te
Pur	**troppo**	**già**	**cresi**	**al**	**falso**	**sembiante**	**che**	**misero**	**amante**
yet	too much	before	I believed	in the	false	appearance	which	miserable	lover

Yet once I believed too much in the deceiving looks which a miserable lover

sofː 'fri ɾe	non	pwɔ	nɔ	ke	non	'va mo	nɔ
soffrire	**non**	**può.**	**No,**	**che**	**non**	**v'amo,**	**no.**
to endure	not	is able	no	[that]	not	you I love	no

cannot endure. No, I do not love you, no.

ki	'di tʃe	'ki o	'spar go	so 'spir	e	la 'men ti
Chi	**dice**	**ch'io**	**spargo**	**sospir'**	**e**	**lamenti,**
who	says	that I	I shed	sighs	and	laments

Whoever says that I pour out sighs and laments,

ke	'vi va	in	tor 'men ti	ke	'bra mi	pje 'ta
che	**viva**	**in**	**tormenti,**	**che**	**brami**	**pietà,**
that	I live	in	torments	that	I long for	pity

that I live in torment, that I crave pity:

nɔ	ke	nol	'di kan	ke	va ni 'ta
no,	**che**	**nol**	**dican'**	**che**	**vanità.**
no	[that]	not it	let them say	what	vanity

no, they should not say it – what vanity!

satː 'tʃe zo	il	'mi o	'kɔ ɾe	fu	dʒa	dalː lar 'do ɾe	or	'spɛn to	ɛ	'dʒal	'fɔ ko
S'acceso	**il**	**mio**	**core**	**fu**	**già**	**dall'ardore,**	**or**	**spento**	**è**	**già'l**	**foco**
if ignited	the	my	heart	was	before	of the ardor	now	spent	is	now the	fire

If my heart was once afire with passion, now the fire is extinguished

ne	atː 'tʃɛn der	si 'pwɔ	nɔ	ke	non	'va mo	nɔ
né	**accender**	**si può.**	**No**	**che**	**non**	**v'amo,**	**no.**
nor	to ignite	it is able	no	[that]	not	you I love	no

and cannot be re-kindled. No, I do not love you – no.

> *printed is "acceder,"*
> *a misprint; correct*
> *must be "accender[e]"*

fe 'li tʃe	'mi a	'sɔr te	ke	'ʃol to	da	'latː tʃi	dʒa	son	fwɔr	dim 'patː tʃi
Felice	**mia**	**sorte**	**che,**	**sciolto**	**da**	**lacci,**	**già**	**son**	**fuor**	**d'impacci**
happy	my	fate	that	freed	from	ties	already	I am	far away	from the hindrances

Happy my fate that, free from ties, I am already far away from the hindrances

di	'vɔ stra	bel 'ta	si	kre 'de te	ke	ɛ	va ni 'ta
di	**vostra**	**beltà,**	**sì,**	**credete**	**che**	**è**	**vanità!**
of	your	beauty	yes	believe	that	it is	vanity

of your beauty; yes, you can believe it – what vanity!

e	'ljɛ to	mi 'gɔ do	dʒa	'li be ɾo	e	'ʃol to	dal	'fal so	'su o	'vol to
E	**lieto**	**mi godo**	**già**	**libero**	**e**	**sciolto**	**dal**	**falso**	**suo**	**volto**
and	happy	myself I enjoy	now	free	and	released	from the	false	its	face

And, happy, I am now enjoying myself free and released from its *[your beauty's]* deceitful face,

e	'pe na	non	ɔ	nɔ	ke	non	'va mo	nɔ
e	**pena**	**non**	**ho.**	**No,**	**che**	**non**	**v'amo,**	**no.**
and	pain	not	I have	no	[that]	not	you I love	no

and I have no pain. No, I do not love you – no.

GL: **Clori**

☙

Tenaglia, Antonio Francesco (c.1612-1662 or 1672)

Born in Florence (or Siena?), he was a composer, keyboard virtuoso, and lutenist who spent most of his life in Rome. By 1644 he was in the service of Donna Olimpia Aldobrandini, wife of Camillo Pamphili; later that year he entered the service of Cardinal Antonio Barberini, where he was an associate of Luigi Rossi, whom he emulated. In 1656 his *Il giudizio di Paride* was performed at the Palazzo Pamphili in Rome at festivities honoring Queen Christina of Sweden; he was probably in the service of Prince Ludovisio Pamphili, nephew of Pope Innocent X. In 1661 he became organist of the Basilica S. Giovanni in Laterano, Rome.

Tenaglia wrote two operas, for both of which the music is lost. He was renowned for his many solo cantatas – some sixty-seven, all for soprano voice – which are his only surviving compositions. Many of the anonymous cantatas extant in manuscripts may also have been composed by him.

[10, 24]

'bεʎː ʎi 'ɔkː ki mer 'tʃe,
Begli occhi, mercé
Beautiful eyes, have mercy

'bεʎː ʎi	'ɔkː ki	mer 'tʃe
Begli	**occhi,**	**mercé!**
beautiful	eyes	mercy

Beautiful eyes, have mercy!

dʒa	sulː 'lin di ke	ma 'remː me	non	ti	'kja mo	a	ʃor	le	've le
Già	**sull'indiche**	**maremme**	**non**	**ti**	**chiamo**	**a**	**scior**	**le**	**vele;**
now	over the Indian	marshes	not	you	I call	to	to unfurl	the	sails

> *scior[re] (poet.)*
> *= sciogliere*

I do not call you now to unfurl your sails over the Indian marshes;

> *The marshes on the coast of Africa were thought at the time to be those of India, source of riches – i.e., the jewels mentioned in the last line.*

al	'su o	'dwɔ lo	un	kɔr	fe 'de le
al	**suo**	**duolo**	**un**	**cor**	**fedele**
to the	its	pain	a	heart	faithful

non	de 'zi a	'prε mjo	di	'dʒεmː me	nɔ	nɔ
non	**desia**	**premio**	**di**	**gemme,**	**no,**	**no.**
not	may desire	prize	of	gems	no	no

a faithful heart does not desire a reward of jewels for its pain – no, no.

❧

[5, 9, 19]   The editor of [19] cites *Grove's* article on Tenaglia as attributing this cantata also to Carlo Caproli.

e 'kwan do ve nan 'da te
E quando ve n'andate?
And when will you go away?

e	'kwan do	ve ne an 'da te	spe 'ran tse	a du la 'tri tʃi	'alː la bwɔ 'no ra
E	**quando**	**ve ne andate,**	**speranze**	**adulatrici**	**alla buon'ora?**
and	when	you go away	hopes	flattering	finally

> *alt:*
> *ve ne andate =*
> *ve n'andate*

And when will you finally go away, flattering hopes?

non	vakː kor 'dʒe te	aŋ 'ko ra	o i 'mε	ke	manː no 'ja te
Non	**v'accorgete**	**ancora,**	**ohimè,**	**che**	**m'annoiate?**
not	you realize	yet	alas	that	me you bore

Do you not yet realize, alas, that you bore me?

'i o   pju   'fja to   in   sen   non   ɔ   da   nu 'drir   'vɔ stro   de 'zi ɾe
Io   più   fiato   in   sen   non   ho,   da   nudrir   vostro   desire:
I   more   breath   in   breast   not   I have   for   to nourish   your   desire

> *nudrir[e] =*
> *(mod.) nutrir[e]*

I have no more breath in my breast to feed your desire;

ri sol 've te vi   a   par 'ti ɾe   'ki o   per   'vo i   mo 'rir   non   vɔ
risolvetevi   a   partire,   ch'io   per   voi   morir   non   vo'.
resolve   to   to depart   because I   for   you   to die   not   I want

resolve to leave, because I do not want to die for you.

kwal   ka 'prit: tʃo   vi   man 'dɔ   a   tur 'bar   la   'pa tʃe   'mi a
Qual   capriccio   vi   mandò   a   turbar   la   pace   mia?
what   caprice   you   sent   to   to disturb   the   peace   mine

What caprice sent you to disturb my peace?

'vo i   'sjɛ te   'ar gi   e   pur   la   'vi a   di   par 'tir   non   ri tro 'va te
Voi   siete   Arghi   e   pur   la   via   di   partir   non   ritrovate.
you   are   Arguses   and   yet   the   way   of   to depart   not   you find

You have a hundred eyes, like Argus, and yet you do not find the way to depart.

a   pen 'tir   'duŋ kwe   sa 'vra   la   'mi a   fe   kel   kɔr   va 'pri a
A   pentir   dunque   s'avrà   la   mia   fé   che'l   cor   v'apria?
to   to regret   then   one will have   the   my   faith   which the   heart   to you opened

> *apria =*
> *apriva*

Shall I then have to regret the faith which my heart opened up to you?

dɛ   pren 'dɛn do   un   'dol tʃe   ad: 'di o   'da te   a   me   la   li ber 'ta
Deh,   prendendo   un   dolce   addio,   date   a   me   la   libertà.
ah   taking   a   sweet   farewell   give   to   me   the   liberty

Ah, in taking a sweet farewell, give me liberty.

'i o   da   'vo i   non   'bra mo   dʒa   un   par 'tir   'sɛn tsa   ri 'tor no
Io   da   voi   non   bramo   già   un   partir   senza   ritorno,
I   from   you   not   I desire   now   a   parting   without   return

I do not desire from you now a parting without a returning;

'an tsi   a   far   'nwɔ vo   sod: 'dʒor no   gra di 'rɔ   ke   ri tor 'nja te
anzi   a   far   nuovo   soggiorno   gradirò   che   ritorniate.
rather   to   to make   new   sojourn   I will like   that   you may return

rather, I will be glad when you will be back for a new visit.

> *var. in [19]:*

'nɔ vo   sod: 'dʒor no   go de 'rɔ   ke   ri tor 'na te
novo   soggiorno   goderò   che   ritornate.
new   sojourn   I will enjoy   that   you return

> *novo (poet.) = nuovo*

I will enjoy a new visit upon your return.

GL: **Arghi**

❧

[27]

non   ɛ   'ma i   'sɛn tsa   dwɔl
Non è mai senza duol
He is never without pain

non	ɛ	'ma i	'sɛn tsa	dwɔl	ki	'vi ve	a 'man te
Non	**è**	**mai**	**senza**	**duol**	**chi**	**vive**	**amante.**
not	is	ever	without	pain	he who	lives	lover

He who lives as a lover is never without pain.

'si o	ta do 'ras: si	o	'bɛl: la	'sal: lo	il	tʃɛl
S'io	**t'adorassi**	**o**	**bella**	**sallo**	**il**	**ciel,**
if I	you I loved	o	beautiful one	knows it	the	heaven

Heaven knows if I loved you, o beautiful one;

'sal: lo	a 'mo ɾe	'si o	ti	kja 'mas: si	oɲ: 'ɲor	'mi o	bɛn	'mi a	'stel: la
sallo	**amore**	**s'io**	**ti**	**chiamassi**	**ognor**	**mio**	**ben,**	**mia**	**stella.**
knows it	love	if I	you	I called	always	my	dear one	my	star

love knows if I always called you my dear one, my star.

lo	kon 'fɛs: sa	il	'tu o	'kɔ ɾe	kwal	de i 'ta	pju	'gran de	'so vra di	te	kre 'de vi
Lo	**confessa**	**il**	**tuo**	**core**	**qual**	**deità**	**più**	**grande**	**sovra di**	**te**	**credevi.**
[it]	confesses	the	your	heart	what	deity	more	great	above	you	you believed

Your heart confesses what greater deity you believed to be above you.

> *sovra = (mod.) sopra*

lo	sa 'pe te	'vo i	'tut: ti	'lu mi	da	'kwa li
Lo	**sapete**	**voi**	**tutti**	**lumi**	**da'**	**quali**
[it]	you know	you	all	lights	from the	which

You know, all you lights [of heaven], from which

un	si	bɛl	sol	si 'span de
un	**sì**	**bel**	**sol**	**si spande,**
a	so	beautiful	sun	is shed

such a beautiful sun radiates,

'ken tro	kwel	mor 'tal	've lo	dʒu 'ra i	pju	'du na	'vɔl ta	ak: 'kɔl to	il	'tʃe lo
ch'entro	**quel**	**mortal**	**velo**	**giurai**	**più**	**d'una**	**volta**	**accolto**	**il**	**cielo,**
that within	that	mortal	veil	I swore	more	than one	time	welcomed	the	heaven

that more than once I swore to welcome heaven within my body.

> *"mortal velo" (poet.) = "corpo umano" (human body); the writer is referring to having welcomed death.*

fur	ʎin 'tʃen si	i	so 'spi ɾi	'vit: ti ma	fu	il	'mi o	'pɛt: to	ke
Fur	**gl'incensi,**	**i**	**sospiri**	**vittima**	**fu**	**il**	**mio**	**petto**	**che**
were	(fig.) the flatteries	the	sighs	victim	was	the	my	breast	that

> *fur = furono*

My breast was the victim of the flatteries and sighs which

of: 'fri i	a	te	'kru dɛ le	tra	'fjam: me	di	de 'zi ɾi	sa kri 'fit: tsjo	daf: 'fɛt: to
offrìi	**a**	**te**	**crudele**	**tra**	**fiamme**	**di**	**desiri**	**sacrifizio**	**d'affetto.**
I offered	to	you	cruel one	among	flames	of	desires	sacrifice	of affection

I offered you, cruel one, as a sacrifice of affection among the flames of desire.

> *sacrifizio = (mod.) sacrificio*

lu ziŋ 'ga sti	il	'mi o	'kɔ ɾe	tra 'di sti	la	'mi a	'fe de
Lusingasti	**il**	**mio**	**core,**	**tradisti**	**la**	**mia**	**fede**
you lured	the	my	heart	you betrayed	the	my	faith

You lured my heart, you betrayed my faith;

e	nel	do 'nar	mer 'tʃe de	'em pja	ko 'zi	ti	're ze	il	'tu o	ri 'go ɾe
e	**nel**	**donar**	**mercede**	**empia**	**così**	**ti**	**rese**	**il**	**tuo**	**rigore**
and	in the	giving	reward	pitiless	thus	you	made	the	your	severity

and in giving your reward, your severity made you so pitiless

ke	por 'dʒɛn do mi	a 'i ta	mi	toʎː 'ʎe sti	la	'vi ta
che	**porgendomi**	**aita**	**mi**	**togliesti**	**la**	**vita.**
which	offering me	help	me	you took away	the	life.

that, in offering help, you took my life away.

'do ve	naʃː 'ʃe sti	o	'fɛ ɾa	kwal	ti	nu 'dri	me 'dʒe ɾa
Dove	**nascesti**	**o**	**fera,**	**qual**	**ti**	**nudrì**	**megera,**
where	you were born	o	wild beast	what	you	nourished	shrew

Where were you born, o wild beast? What shrew nourished you?

> fera = (mod.) fiera

'ko me	'den tro	le	'sel ve	in 'mɛdː dzo alː 'lon de	'delː le	'sir ti	pro 'fon de
come	**dentro**	**le**	**selve**	**in mezzo all'onde**	**delle**	**sirti**	**profonde**
how	within	the	forests	in the middle of the waves	of the	shifting sands	deep

How, in the forests, in the midst of the sea's deep shifting sands,

o	tra	lir 'ka ne	'bel ve	im pa 'ra sti	kru 'dɛl	'far ti	o mi 'tʃi da
o	**tra**	**l'Ircane**	**belve**	**imparasti**	**crudel**	**farti**	**omicida?**
or	among	the Ircanian	wild beasts	you learned	cruel	to make yourself	deadly

or among the Ircanian wild beasts, cruel one, did you learn to make yourself deadly?

'mi ze ɾo	ki	si 'fi da	dun	bɛl	'vol to	iŋ ko 'stan te
Misero	**chi**	**si fida**	**d'un**	**bel**	**volto**	**incostante.**
miserable	the one who	trusts	in a	beautiful	face	inconstant

Miserable is the one who trusts a beautiful, inconstant face.

non	ɛ	'ma i	'sɛn tsa	dwɔl	ki	'vi ve	a 'man te
Non	**è**	**mai**	**senza**	**duol**	**chi**	**vive**	**amante.**
not	is	ever	without	pain	he who	lives	lover

He who lives as a lover is never without pain.

GL: **Ircane**

ॐ

[5, 9, 19] The editor of [19] cites *Grove's* article on Tenaglia as listing this cantata of "dubious attribution."

'kwan do sa 'ra kwel di
Quando sarà quel dì?
When will be that day?

kwan do	sa 'ra	kwel	di	'ki o	mi	'vedː dʒa	da	te	fa vo 'ri to	dun	si
Quando	**sarà**	**quel**	**dì**	**ch'io**	**mi**	**veggia**	**da**	**te**	**favorito**	**d'un**	**sì?**
when	will be	that	day	that I	me	may see	from	you	favored	by a	yes

When will that day be when I will see myself favored by a "yes" from you?

'ka ɾa	'bokː ka	'dilː lo	tu	se	a	ka 'ratː te ɾi	di	'ro ze
Cara	**bocca,**	**dillo**	**tu**	**se**	**a'**	**caratteri**	**di**	**rose**
dear	mouth	tell it	you	if	in the	characters (i.e., letters of the alphabet)	of	roses

Dear mouth, tell me if, in the characters made of roses

ke	sul	'labː bro	a 'mor	ti	'po ze	mi	'fa i	'ledː dʒer	ser vi 'tu
che	**sul**	**labbro**	**amor**	**ti**	**pose,**	**mi**	**fai**	**legger:**	**servitù.**
which	on the	lip	love	you	placed	me	you make	to read	servitude

which love placed upon your lips, you will make me read: "servitude."

	ser vi 'tu	per	pje 'ta	ri 'spon di	a	me
additionally in [19]:	**...servitù,**	**per**	**pietà**	**rispondi**	**a**	**me.**
	...servitude	for	pity	respond	to	me

..."servitude"; for pity's sake, answer me.

'kon to	'lo ɾe	a 'du na	a 'du na	'ko me	'fos: ser	'an: ni	in 'te ɾi
Conto	**l'ore**	**ad una**	**ad una**	**come**	**fosser**	**anni**	**interi,**
I count	the hours	at one	by one	like	they were	years	entire

I count the hours, one by one, as though they were whole years;

fosser =
fossero

	ma	nel	'kol mo	'de i	pen 'sjɛ ɾi	'trɔ vo	'skar sa	la	for 'tu na
	ma	**nel**	**colmo**	**dei**	**pensieri**	**trovo**	**scarsa**	**la**	**fortuna.**
	but	at the	height	of the	thoughts	I find	scarce	the	luck

but at the height of my thoughts I find [good] luck scarce.

in [19]:
de' =
dei

e	se	'vi ver	si 'pwɔ	pju	'ka ɾa	'bok: ka	'dil: lo	tu
E	**se**	**viver**	**si può**	**più,**	**cara**	**bocca,**	**dillo**	**tu...**
And	if	to live	it is possible	more	dear	mouth	tell it	you...

And if is is possible to live anymore, dear mouth, tell me...

la	'mi a	'fe de	mas: si 'ku ɾa	ke	par 'lar	'sɛm pre	di	nɔ
La	**mia**	**fede**	**m'assicura**	**che**	**parlar**	**sempre**	**di**	**no**
the	my	faith	me assures	that	to speak	always	of	no

'kwel: la	'dɔn: na	'ma i	non	pwɔ	ke	fe	'bɛl: la	la	na 'tu ɾa
quella	**donna**	**mai**	**non**	**può,**	**che**	**fé**	**bella**	**la**	**natura.**
that	woman	never	not	can	that	made	beautiful	the	nature

My faith assures me that that woman, whom nature made beautiful, cannot always say "no."

🏵 *Torelli, Giuseppe* (1658-1709)

Born in Verona, composer (a pupil of Perti), teacher, and virtuoso violinist, he moved to Bologna around 1684 when accepted as a violinist with the Accademia Filarmonica there; he became a regularly paid member of the *cappella musicale* at the Church of S. Petronio in 1686. When the S. Petronio orchestra was disbanded for economic reasons in 1696 Torelli travelled, performing, and by 1698 he had become *maestro di concerto* for the Margrave of Brandenburg in Ansbach. By 1699 he was in Vienna, and by 1701 he was back in Bologna as a violinist in the re-organized *cappella musicale* at S. Petronio, directed by Perti.

As a composer of instrumental chamber music, Torelli wrote sonatas, sinfonias, concertos, and dance pieces. In his mature style he contributed significantly, along with Stradella and Corelli, to the development of the concerto grosso and the solo concerto.

"Tu lo sai" may not actually have been composed by this Torelli. However, an oratorio, a solo cantata, and "various arias" are listed in *Grove* as vocal works among his output.

[20, 25, 29, 35, 54, 59, 60, 64]

tu lo 'sa i
Tu lo sai
You know it

tu	lo	'sa i	'kwan to	ta 'ma i	tu	lo	'sa i	kru 'dɛl
Tu	**lo**	**sai**	**quanto**	**t'amai;**	**tu**	**lo**	**sai,**	**crudel!**
you	it	you know	how much	you I loved	you	it	you know	cruel one

You know how much I loved you; you know it, cruel one!

'i o	non	'bra mo	'al tra	mer 'tʃe	ma	ri 'kɔr da ti	di	me
Io	**non**	**bramo**	**altra**	**mercé,**	**ma**	**ricordati**	**di**	**me,**
I	not	I desire	other	mercy	but	may remember you	of	me

I wish no other mercy than that you remember me

e   'pɔ i   'sprɛt: tsa   un   in fe 'del
e   poi   sprezza   un   infedel!
and   then   despise   an   unfaithful one
and then despise an unfaithful one!

𝒯*romboncino, Ippolito (fl.1575-1620)*

Little is known about this composer. He is not the Tromboncino (Bartolomeo Tromboncino) who is known as an important sixteenth century composer of frottolas.
Ippolito Tromboncino's only extant songs are preserved in *The Bottegari Lutebook* (see *Bottegari*).

---

[36]

'ak: kwa non ɛ lu 'mor
Acqua non è l'umor
It is not water

'ak: kwa   non   ɛ   lu 'mor   ke   'vɛr san   'ʎɔk: ki
Acqua   non   è   l'umor   che   versan   gl'occhi
water   not   it is the sap   that they shed   the eyes
It is not water the eyes shed

> *printed is "aqua":*
> *antiquated*
> *spelling of*
> *(mod.) "acqua"*

ma   'saŋ gwe   'vi vo   in   kwel   ko 'lor   kon 'vɛr so
ma   sangue   vivo   in   quel   color   converso.
but   blood   living   in   that   color   converted
but living blood, changed in color.

pe 'rɔ   'pal: li do   ɛ   'sɛm pre   un   a ma 'to ɾe   ke   'kwan do   'pjan dʒe
Però   pallido   è   sempre   un   amatore,   ché,   quando   piange,
However   pale   is   always   a   lover   because   when   he weeps
Yet a lover is always pale, because when he weeps,

'saŋ gwe   ɛ   kwel   u 'mo ɾe
sangue   è   quel   umore.
blood   is   that   sap (humour)
he weeps blood.

a 'mor   non   vwɔl   ke   na tu 'ral   tra 'bok: ki
Amor   non   vuol   che   natural   trabocchi,
love   not   wants   that natural   it may overflow
Love does not want it *[the sap]* to overflow naturally,

per 'ke   'fɔ ɾa   spet: 'ta kul   'trɔp: po   av 'vɛr so
perché   fora   spettacul   troppo   avverso
because   it would be   sight   too   adverse
as that would be too unfavorable a sight.

fora =	*spettacul[o] =*
sarebbe	*(mod.) spettacol[o]*

fra   'tan ti   'stra li   e   'tan ti   a 'ku ti   'stɔk: ki
Fra   tanti   strali   e   tanti   acuti   stocchi,
among so many   arrows   and so many   sharp   swords
Among so many wounds from arrows and sharp swords,

in 'oɲː ɲi 'mɔ do   'saŋ gwe   ɛ   kwel   'ki o   'vɛr so
in ogni modo   sangue   è   quel   ch'io   verso.
in   any   case   blood   it is   that   which I   shed
it is always [tears of] blood that I shed.

                         ❧

[55]

                           'i o   son   fe 'ri to
                           Io son ferito
                           I am wounded

'i o   son   fe 'ri to   'a i 'lasː so
Io   son   ferito,   ahi lasso,
I   am   wounded   woe is me
I am wounded – woe is me;

    e   ki   mi   'dje de   akː ku 'zar   pur   vorː 'rɛ i   ma   non   ho   'prɔ va
    e   chi   mi   diede   accusar   pur   vorrei,   ma   non   ho   prova;
    and   the one who   me   gave   to accuse   [indeed]   I should like   but   not   I have   proof
    and I should like to accuse the one who gave me the wound, but I do not have proof;

    ne   sen tsin 'ditː tsjo   al   mal   non   si da   'fe de
    né   senz' indizio   al   mal   non   si da   fede,
    neither   without evidence   to the   wrong   not   one gives   belief
    people do not believe a wrongdoing without evidence,

    ne   'dʒɛtː ta   'saŋ gwe   la   'mi a   'pja ɡa   'nwɔ va
    né   getta   sangue   la   mia   piaga   nuova.
    nor   spouts   blood   the   my   wound   new
    [but] my fresh wound spills no blood.

'i o   'spɛ me   'mɔ ɾo   il   'kol po   non   si 've de
Io   spem' e   moro;   il   colpo   non   si vede,
I   I hope and   I die   the   cut   not   one sees
I hope and die; the wound can not be seen,

    la   'mi a   ne 'mi kar 'ma ta   non   si 'trɔ va
    la   mia   nemic' armata   non   si trova.
    the   my   enemy armed   not   one finds
    [and] my armed enemy can not be found.

ke   'si a   tor 'na ta   'lɛ i   kru 'dɛl   par 'ti to
Che   sia   tornat' a   lei,   crudel   partito,
That   it be   proved to be to   her   cruel   conflict
What a cruel paradox that it be up to her –

    ke   sol   'mabː bja   a   sa 'nar   ki   ma   fe 'ri to
    che   sol   m'abbia   a   sanar   chi   m'ha   ferito.
    that   only   me has   to   to heal   the one   me has   wounded
    that only the one who wounded me can heal me.

Visconti, Domenico (?-1626)

Composer and organist at the Florentine court, he was likely in the service of Antonio de' Medici. He died in Rome about a month after having been appointed organist at S. Maria in Aracoeli.
He was a composer of madrigals, but his best vocal music is found in his published *Il primo libre de arie (1616)*, which contains seventeen solo songs.

[48]

non 'vwɔ i 'ki o 'ta mi
Non vuoi ch'io t'ami?
You do not want me to love you?

non	'vwɔ i	'ki o	'ta mi		non	ta me 'rɔ
Non	**vuoi**	**ch'io**	**t'ami?**		**non**	**t'amerò.**
not	you want	that I	you I may love		not	you I will love

You do not want me to love you? [Then] I will not love you.

'po i	se	mi	'kja mi	non	tu di 'rɔ	tu	liŋ 'gra ta	la	di spje 'ta ta
Poi	**se**	**mi**	**chiami**	**non**	**t'udirò,**	**tu**	**l'ingrata**	**la**	**dispietata**
then	if	me	you call to	not	you I will hear	you	the ungrateful one	the	pitiless one

oɲ: 'ɲor	'det: ta	sa 'ra i		'gwar da	ke	'fa i
ognor	**detta**	**sarai;**		**guarda**	**che**	**fai.**
always	called	you will be		look at	what	you do

Then I will not hear you if you call to me; you will always be called ungrateful and pitiless; mind what you do.

ma	sel	'tu o	'lu me	'dol tʃe	ve 'drɔ	tu	'kwa zi	'nu me	a do re 'rɔ
Ma	**se'l**	**tuo**	**lume**	**dolce**	**vedrò,**	**tu**	**quasi**	**nume**	**adorerò**
but	if the	your	light	sweet	I will see	you	almost	deity	I will adore

But if I will see your sweet light, I will adore you almost as a deity,

e	tu	pje 'to za		e	tu	a mo 'ro za	oɲ: 'ɲor	'det: ta	sa 'ra i
e	**tu**	**pietosa**		**e**	**tu**	**amorosa**	**ognor**	**detta**	**sarai;**
and	you	compassionate		and	you	loving	always	called	you will be

and you will forever be called compassionate and loving;

'gwar da	ke	'fa i
guarda	**che**	**fai.**
look at	what	you do

mind what you do.

Vitali, Filippo (c.1590-1653)

Born in Florence, by 1618 he was in Rome, where his opera *L'Aretusa*, the first secular opera staged in Rome, was performed at the residence of Monsignore Corsini in 1620. In 1621 he was back in Florence, where he composed *intermedi* for Jacopo Cicognini's comedy *La finta mora*, performed at the palace of the Medici in 1622. He returned to Rome in 1631 in the musical service of Cardinal Antonio Barberini, and he sang in the Sistine Chapel choir for fourteen years. From 1648 to 1649 he was *maestro di cappella* at S. Maria Maggiore in Bergamo. He retired to Florence with a benefice and a pension from the Pope, having become a priest sometime before 1631.
The music for a third theatre work, an opera performed in Venice in 1642, has been lost. Otherwise, Vitali published sacred music and several volumes of secular vocal music: arias and madrigals for one to six voices.

[40]

o ˈbɛ i ˈlu mi

O bei lumi

O beautiful eyes

o	ˈbɛ i	ˈlu mi	o	ˈkjɔ me	ˈdɔ ɾo
O	**bei**	**lumi,**	**o**	**chiome**	**d'oro,**
o	beautiful	eyes	o	head of hair	of gold

O beautiful eyes, o golden tresses

on ˈdi o	ˈmɔ ɾo	tra	bɛl	ˈfwɔ ko	e	ˈbɛ i	le ˈga mi
ond'io	**moro**	**tra**	**bel**	**fuoco**	**e**	**bei**	**legami,**
where I	I die	among	beautiful	fire	and	beautiful	ties

wherein I die among beautiful fire and beautiful ties,

ˈfjam: me	e	ˈstra li	rad: dop: ˈpja te	fol go ˈɾa te	per ˈki o	ˈsem pre	avː ˈvam pi
fiamme	**e**	**strali**	**raddoppiate,**	**folgorate**	**per ch'io**	**sempre**	**avvampi**
flames	and	arrows	double	blaze	so that I	always	I may be on fire

e	ˈa mi
e	**ami.**
and	I may love

double your flames and arrows; blaze so that I may burn forever, and love.

a	me	ˈsɛm pre	oɲː ˈɲa spra	ˈsɔr te	ˈka ɾa	ˈmɔr te	ˈfi a	per	ˈvo i	ˈlu tʃi	se ˈɾe ne
A	**me**	**sempre**	**ogn'aspra**	**sorte**	**cara**	**morte**	**fia**	**per**	**voi,**	**luci**	**serene.**
to	me	always	every bitter	fate	dear	death	will be	through	you	eyes	serene

For me every bitter fate and death through you will always be dear, serene eyes.

> fia = (mod.) sarà

ˈkri ni	e	ˈvo i	kil	ˈkɔ ɾe	o ˈno ɾa	ben ˈki o	ˈmɔ ɾa
Crini	**e**	**voi**	**ch'il**	**core**	**onora,**	**ben ch'io**	**mora,**
heads of hair	and	you	which the	heart	honors	even though	I may die

ˈsja te	a	me	ˈdol tʃi	ka ˈte ne
siate	**a**	**me**	**dolci**	**catene!**
be	to	me	sweet	chains

Tresses, you whom my heart honors, although I am dying, be sweet chains for me!

o	se	ˈma i	beʎː ˈʎɔkː ki	al ˈtɛ ɾi	men	se ˈvɛ ɾi
O,	**se**	**mai,**	**begl'occhi**	**alteri,**	**men**	**severi**
oh	if	ever	beautiful eyes	proud	less	severe

vi mo ˈstra ste	a	ˈpre gi	al	ˈpjan to
vi mostraste	**a**	**preghi,**	**al**	**pianto,**
you showed yourselves	at	entreaties	at the	weeping

Oh if ever, beautiful eyes, you proved less refractory to my entreaties [and] my tears,

> preghi (lit.)
> = preghiere

ri di ˈrɛbː be	in	ˈdol tʃi	ˈmɔ di	ˈvɔ stre	ˈlɔ di	ˈkwe sta	ˈtʃe tra	e	ˈkwe sto	ˈkan to
ridirebbe	**in**	**dolci**	**modi**	**vostre**	**lodi,**	**questa**	**cetra**	**e**	**questo**	**canto.**
would repeat	in	sweet	ways	your	praises	this	cither	and	this	song

this cither and this song would repeat your praises in sweet ways.

☙

[7, 41, 44] In [7] titled **Pastorella, ove t'ascondi**.

pa sto 'rɛlː la
Pastorella
Shepherdess

pa sto 'rɛlː la	'o ve	ta 'skon di	'do ve	'fudː dʒi	o i 'mɛ	ke	'fa i
Pastorella	**ove**	**t'ascondi,**	**dove**	**fuggi**	**ohimè,**	**che**	**fai?**
shepherdess	where	you are hiding	where	you flee	alas	what	you do

in [41]: oimè = *(mod.)* ohimè
t'ascondi: from
"ascondersi" = (mod.)
"nascondersi"

Shepherdess, where are you hiding? Whereto are you fleeing?
Alas, what are you doing?

'tor na in 'djɛ tro	al 'men	ri 'spon di	la	ka 'dʒon	per 'ke	ten 'va i
Torna indietro,	**almen**	**rispondi**	**la**	**cagion**	**perché**	**ten' vai!**
return back	at least	answer	the	reason	why	you go away

ten' vai (var.: ten vai)
= te ne vai (from
"andarsene")

Come back; at least tell me the reason you are going away!

in [7]: **Torna indietro o almen...** ['tor na in 'djɛ tro o al 'men...] = Come back, or at least...

'fer ma	il	'pasː so	non	fudː 'dʒi ɾe	non	vo 'ler	'far mi	mo 'ri ɾe
Ferma	**il**	**passo,**	**non**	**fuggire,**	**non**	**voler**	**farmi**	**morire!**
stop	the	step	not	to flee	not	to wish	to make me	to die

Stop; do not flee; do not wish to make me die!

se	tu	'par ti	e	ki	ma 'i ta	se	ten 'va i	ke	mi	kon 'so la
Se	**tu**	**parti**	**e**	**chi**	**m'aita,**	**se**	**ten' vai,**	**chi**	**mi**	**consola?**
if	you	you depart	[and]	who	me helps	if	you go away	who	me	consoles

aita: from
"aitare" =
"aiutare"

If you depart, who will help me? If you go away, who will console me?

ke	sa 'ra	'delː la	'mi a	'vi ta	'sɛn tsa	te	'mi ze ɾa	e	'so la
Che	**sarà**	**della**	**mia**	**vita,**	**senza**	**te**	**misera**	**e**	**sola?**
what	will be	of the	my	life	without	you	miserable	and	lonely

What will become of my life, miserable and lonely without you?

non	par 'ti ɾe	o	'filː li	a 'spɛtː ta	non	fudː 'dʒir	kon	'tan ta	'fretː ta
Non	**partire,**	**o**	**Filli,**	**aspetta,**	**non**	**fuggir**	**con**	**tanta**	**fretta!**
not	to depart	o	Filli	wait	not	to flee	with	such	haste

Do not depart, o Filli; wait – do not flee in such haste!

Following is the 3rd verse in [41]:

o	kru 'dɛ le	ki	pju	'ma i	ta me 'ra	se	me	non	'prɛtː tsi
O	**crudele,**	**chi**	**più**	**mai**	**t'amerà,**	**se**	**me**	**non**	**prezzi?**
o	cruel one	who	more	ever	you will love	if	me	not	you care for

"me," here, rather than "mi,"
either intends "a me" or is an
old usage of "me" from the
Latin = (mod.) "mi."

O cruel one, who will ever love you again, if you do not care for me?

ki	laŋ 'gwi ɾe	a	'two i	'bɛ i	'ra i	verː 'ra	pju	se	me	di 'sprɛtː tsi
Chi	**languire**	**a**	**tuoi**	**bei**	**rai**	**verrà**	**più,**	**se**	**me**	**disprezzi?**
who	to languish	at	your	beautiful	eyes	will come	more	if	me	you spurn

Who will languish in the light of your beautiful eyes again, if you spurn me?

'fudː dʒi	'pu ɾe	un	di	pen 'ti ta	pjan dʒe 'ra i	'kwe sta	par 'ti ta
Fuggi	**pure,**	**un**	**dì**	**pentita**	**piangerai**	**questa**	**partita!**
flee	then	one	day	repentant	you will lament	this	*(lit.)* departure

Flee, then; one day, repentant, you will rue this departure!

Following is the 3rd verse in [7] and [44]:

ma	tu	iŋ ˈgra ta	da	me	ˈfud: dʒi	ne	mi	a ˈskol ti	o	mi	kon ˈso li
Ma	**tu**	**ingrata**	**da**	**me**	**fuggi,**	**né**	**mi**	**ascolti**	**o**	**mi**	**consoli;**
but	you	ungrateful	from	me	you flee	nor	me	you listen to	or	me	you console

But you, ungrateful one – you flee from me and do not listen to me or console me;

ˈsa i	bɛn	tu	ke	mi	di ˈstrud: dʒi	kol		fud: ˈdʒir	e	ˈpo i	ten ˈvo li
sai	**ben**	**tu**	**che**	**mi**	**distruggi**	**col**		**fuggir**	**e**	**poi**	**ten voli.**
you know	well	you	that	me	you destroy	with the		fleeing	and	then	you fly away

you well know that you are destroying me by fleeing, and then you fly away.

> *var. in* [7]: **eppur ten voli** [ep: ˈpur ten ˈvo li] = and nevertheless you fly away.

ˈdim: mi	al ˈme no	o	ˈfil: li	ad: ˈdi o	mor: ˈra	ˈpo i	ˈljɛ to	il	kor	ˈmi o
Dimmi	**almeno,**	**o**	**Filli,**	**addio;**	**morrà**	**poi**	**lieto**	**il**	**cor**	**mio.**
tell me	at least	o	Filli	farewell	will die	then	happy	the	heart	mine

At least say farewell to me, o Filli; then my heart will die happy.

GL: **Filli**

Zaneti, Francesco Maria (?-?)

Jeppesen, in [40], refers to Zaneti as "unknown, probably of the Bolognese School in the second half of the seventeeth century."

Indeed, nothing was found in sources about this composer; perhaps he is actually the "Francesco Zanetti" listed in sources as having been born in 1737. I am including "Avvezzati, mio core" in this volume based on Jeppesen's conjecture.

---

[40]

av: ˈvet: tsa ti ˈmi o ˈkɔ re
Avvezzati, mio core
Become accustomed, my heart

av: ˈvet: tsa ti		ˈmi o	ˈkɔ re	a	so spi ˈrar
Avvezzati,		**mio**	**core,**	**a**	**sospirar!**
become accustomed		my	heart	to	sighing

Become accustomed, my heart, to sighing!

son	da ˈmor	ˈfat: to	un	ve ˈzu vjo
Son	**d'Amor**	**fatto**	**un**	**Vesuvio**
I am	by Love	made	a	Vesuvius

Love has turned me into a Vesuvius,

e	a	di ˈlu vjo	dʒa	mi ˈnon da no	i	tor ˈmen ti
e	**a**	**diluvio**	**già**	**m'inondano**	**i**	**tormenti,**
and	in	deluge	already	me are flooding	the	torments

and torments are already deluging me;

ne	un	sol	ˈrad: dʒo	di	kon ˈtɛn ti	tra	ˈmjɛ i	ˈgwa i	ˈpɔs: so	spe ˈrar
né	**un**	**sol**	**raggio**	**di**	**contenti**	**tra**	**miei**	**guai**	**posso**	**sperar.**
not	a	single	ray	of	contentments	among	my	woes	I am able	to hope for

I cannot hope for a single ray of contentment among my woes.

GL: **Amor, Vesuvio**

Ziani, Marco Antonio (c.1653-1715)

Born in Venice, he may have studied with his uncle, Pietro Andrea Ziani, a composer and organist of great repute, and at the least must have benefitted at the start of his career from his uncle's connections.

While continually active in Venice, where he became a leading composer of opera, in 1686 he became *maestro di cappella di chiesa* to Ferdinando Carlo Gonzaga, the last Duke of Mantua. In 1700 he was appointed *vice-Kapellmeister* to Emperor Leopold I in Vienna, where he had many poets, singers, stage designers, and virtuoso instrumentalists at his disposal, and where he died fifteen years later.

Ziani had a brillant career. He composed, in addition to some thirty-five operas, much sacred music.

[57]
from: *Alessandro Magno in Sidone (1679)*   *Aurelio Aureli*

non 'a mo ma 'bra mo
Non amo, ma bramo
I do not love, but I am longing

non	'a mo	ma	'bra mo	ve 'der	kwel: lod: 'dʒet: to	ke	're ka	di 'lɛt: to	al: 'la ni ma	'mi a
Non	**amo,**	**ma**	**bramo**	**veder**	**quell'oggetto**	**che**	**reca**	**diletto**	**all'anima**	**mia;**
not	I love	but	I long	to see	that object	that	brings	delight	to the soul	mine

I do not love, but I am longing to see the one who brings delight to my soul;

la	'bra ma	kɔ	al	'kɔ ɾe	non	sɔ	se	'si a	a 'mo ɾe
la	**brama**	**ch'ho**	**al**	**core**	**non**	**so**	**se**	**sia**	**amore**
the	yearning	that I have	in the	heart	not	I know	if	it be	love

I do not know if the yearning I have in my heart is love

o	pur	bid: dzar: 'ri a
o	**pur**	**bizzarria.**
or	perhaps	caprice

or perhaps a caprice.

non	'pe no	ma	in	'se no	mi	par	di	sen 'ti ɾe	un	'dol tʃe	de 'zi ɾe
Non	**peno,**	**ma**	**in**	**seno**	**mi**	**par**	**di**	**sentire**	**un**	**dolce**	**desire**
not	I suffer	but	in	breast	to me	seems	of	to feel	a	sweet	desire

I am not suffering, but I seem to feel in my breast a sweet desire

ke	af: 'fan: no	mi	'di a
che	**affanno**	**mi**	**dia.**
that	anxiety	to me	may give

which causes me anxiety.

Glossary

of Names, Places, and Things referred to in the texts

Nouns such as bellezza (= beauty), sorte (= destiny), etc. are frequently capitalized in the texts as personifications addressed by the poets; as such, they are not included in this *Glossary*, and I have often removed their capitalization on my text pages.

Many proper names common in the literature of the time – of shepherds, shepherdesses, nymphs, and satyrs such as Silvio, Silvia, Lidia, Lidio, Fileno, Nice, Lilla, etc. – are not listed here. Neither are the names of characters in the casts of the operas (or oratorios) whose aria texts are included in this volume; in many cases, information about the plots and the characters of the operas (or oratorios) is available in *Grove* and other reference sources.

The numbers in brackets are the page numbers on which the song text containing the *Glossary* reference begins.

Adamo: Adam, of Adam and Eve, the human father of all human beings according to the Book of Genesis.
[1]

Acheronte (Acheron): In the Underworld, one of the two rivers (the other being the Styx) which separated the Underworld from the land of the living. Called the black Acheron, the river of woes. In this text the literary, figurative meaning for "Acheronte" is "l'oltretomba" = the afterlife. (see also **Stigio**).
[173]

Achille (Achilles): Hero of Homer's *Iliad*. The strongest of the Greeks at Troy, he was swift of foot as well as with spear, and known for his courage as well as for his love and compassion. Son of the sea goddess Tethys, as a youth he was turned over to the care of the centaur Chiron, from whom he learned music and archery. Tethys, according to one legend, immersed her son in the river Styx in order to make him immortal, but one of his heels failed to be immersed; Achilles' death came from an arrow which Paris shot into that vulnerable heel.
[157]

Aglaia: Daughter of Zeus and Eurynome, she was the youngest of the three Graces. (see also **Grazie**).
[178]

Amarilli [Amaryllis]: One of the most often named shepherdesses associated with the bucolic setting of Arcadia (see also **Arcadi**) in the *Eclogues* of Virgil and the *Idylls* of Theocritus, as well as in the postclassical era. Amaryllis appears in Tasso's *L'Aminta (1573)*, considered the first true pastoral drama, and as heroine of Guarini's *Il pastor fido (1590)*, a literary landmark reestablishing the popularity of the pastoral form.
[87]

Amor[e] (Greek: Eros; Roman: Cupido, or Amor[e]): One of the earliest gods, and the one most often evoked in these seventeenth century texts. Some sources say he was present at the birth of Aphrodite (Venus) and became her attendant; others describe him as the son of Aphrodite and Ares (Mars), and still others as the son of Iris, goddess of the rainbow, and Zephyr, god of the west wind. Also associated with divine Love, by the Hellenistic period he was often portrayed as a playful and mischievous boy who played tricks on both mortals and gods, armed with bow and arrow. The Roman Cupid, son of Venus, was imagined as a chubby, naked, winged child; and the idea of Cupid as blind or blindfolded became popular from the early Renaissance onward – hence the notion that "Love is blind," striking at random.
[2, 3, 4, 6, 9, 12, 14, 24, 28, 52, 70, 72, 82, 84, 85, 86, 88, 96, 98, 101, 104, 109, 111, 130, 133, 143, 144, 150, 152, 157, 162, 163, 165, 166, 169, 177, 178, 179, 181, 182, 189, 192, 194, 204, 206, 210, 215, 217, 218, 223, 232, 234, 243, 255, 259, 260, 265, 274, 279, 281, 285, 306, 313, 326, 332, 335, 337, 340, 344, 349, 352, 354, 360, 376, 379, 380, 383, 384, 393, 396, 403, 408, 410, 413, 420, 431, 454, 455, 457, 464, 465, 468, 471, 477, 488, 501]

Apollo: Son of Zeus (Roman: Jupiter), one of the twelve Olympian deities and the lord of Parnassus. The sun god, also patron of fine arts, medicine, music, poetry, eloquence, and prophecy. He became a sun god in the fifth century BC, with the epithet "Phoebus" (= "bright, shining"), assuming the powers of Helios, brother of the dawn-goddess Eos (Aurora) and the moon-goddess Selene. Postclassical representations of him often show him driving the sun chariot across the sky, sometimes led by Eos. (see also **Febo**).
[484]

Arcadi: Residents (shepherds, nymphs, demigods and satyrs) of **Arcadia**, a mountainous province in the central Peloponnesus, described by Theocritus and Virgil as a simple pastoral environment but by the late sixteenth century having become a symbol of a pastoral ideal, an idyllic paradise. Arcadia was the setting for bucolic entertainments among the stock characters who later developed into *commedia dell'arte* characters.
[448]

Arghi (Italian plural of "Argo" [Argus]): Argus, son of Arestor, was a monster with a hundred eyes of which only two were closed in sleep at a time. He killed a bull which was ravaging Arcadia, and a satyr who was stealing cattle. Mercury (Hermes) slew him by lulling all his eyes to sleep with the music of the lyre. Juno (Hera) put the eyes of Argus in the tail of a peacock, her favorite bird or, in another version of the legend, turned Argus into that bird.
[491]

Arianna [Ariane] (Ariadne): A daughter of King Minos of Crete, she helped Theseus find his way out of the labyrinth in which he had been intended to be devoured by the Minotaur. She fell in love with Theseus, who took her with him when he left Crete, but she was soon abandoned by him on the island of Naxos (Dia). Dionysus (Bacchus) came to the island to marry her, and they had several children. After her death Dionysus took her to Mount Olympus and set the crown she had been given for her wedding in the heavens as a constellation (the Northern Crown). (see also **Teseo** and **Bacco**).
[314]

Arno: The Arno River, which bisects Florence. Rising on the slopes of Monte Falterona in the Tuscan Apennines, it flows for one hundred and fifty miles to the Ligurian Sea.
[101]

Atlante: Italian name of the Atlas mountains in northern Africa, perhaps referring to the continent as a whole in Frescobaldi's time.
[209]

Atropo [Atropos]: One of the Fates (see **Fati**), she cut the thread of life spun by Clotho.
[229]

Aurora [Eos]: Goddess of the dawn, daughter of the Titan Hyperion and the Titaness Theia, sister of Helios (the Sun) and Selene (the Moon). Every morning she welcomed the arrival of her brother Helios, driving a chariot drawn by her horses Phaethon ("shining") and Lampos ("bright") through the sky with him.
[92, 273, 283, 364]

Averno [Avernus]: A lake (Lake Avernus) near Naples where one of the entrances to Hades, the Underworld, was located. Aeneas entered Hades from a cave in this lake. Entrances to Hades were also believed to be in a cave on Cape Taenarum near Sparta and in the Alcyonian Lake at Lerna.
[218, 365]

Bacco [Bacchus] (Greek: Dionynus): God of wine and nature's fertility as exemplified in the vine, he was the son of Zeus and Semele, a daughter of Cadmus. He married Ariadne after Theseus abandaned her on the island of Naxos. Festivals in his honor were called Bacchanalia.
[181]

Bireno: In Ariosto's *Orlando Furioso (Canto 10),* the husband of Olimpia, Countess of Holland, whom he deserts. Olimpia is bound naked to a rock by pirates, but ultimately rescued by Orlando, who takes her to Ireland, where King Oberto kills Bireno and marries her. (see also **Olimpia** and **Frisa**).
[310]

Borea [Boreas] (Roman: Aquilo): The (harsh) north wind, son of Astraeus and Eos.
[260, 379]

Cinzia (Cynthia): Goddess of the moon, as well as of hunting (Roman: Diana; Greek: Artemis; also known as Delia, Hecate, Luna, Phoebe, and Selene). The name means "she who comes from Mount Cynthus" (on Delos).
[270, 368, 396]

Citerea [Cytherea]: Epithet of Aphrodite (Greek goddess of love and beauty; Roman: Venus), derived from her cult on the island of Cythera.
[332]

Clori [Chloris] (Roman: Flora): A nymph, also goddess of flowers and the personification of spring, and the spouse of Zephyrus.
[3, 14, 41, 106, 165, 167, 344, 347, 372, 406, 420, 423, 449, 486, 489]

Clorida: Variant of the name Clori.
[299]

Cnido [Cnidos, Cnidus]: The ancient city of Caria on the west coast of Asia Minor. The head of Aphrodite (Venus, goddess of love) is the symbol of the city. In its sanctuary of Aphrodite stood the first statue of the goddess in the nude, by Praxiteles, which is known to us only through Roman copies. Praxiteles made two statues, one draped and the other nude; the latter was refused by the Athenians but purchased by the Cnidians.
[255]

Cocito [Cocytus]: The river of wailing, one of the five rivers in Hades across which Charon, the ferryman, brought the souls of the deceased to its gates. (see also **Acheronte** and **Stigio**).
[127, 274]

Colco [Colchis]: An area situated along the southeast coast of the Black Sea, the legendary homeland of Medea, and the destination of the Argonauts' expedition. (see also **Giasone**).
[264]

Cupido: See **Amor[e]** and **Psiche**.
[4, 14, 46, 112, 206, 255, 410, 414, 420]

Delo [Delos]: Sacred island among the Cyclades in the Aegean Sea, the mythological birthplace of the twins Apollo and Artemis born to Leto by Zeus, and one of the main centers of their cult. Poseidon (Greek god of the sea; Roman: Neptune) is said to have fastened the island permanently to the bottom of the sea with a huge pillar. Archeologists have uncovered there a sanctuary of Apollo with temples and halls, a temple of Leto, and numerous pieces of monumental stutuary dating from as early as the seventh century B.C.
[88, 352]

Dido: A legendary princess of Tyre. According to Virgil, her husband Sychaeus (or Sicharbas) was murdered by her brother Pygmailion, who had become king of Tyre, so she fled with her followers to the Libyan coast. She purchased as much land as could be enclosed by a bull's hide cut into one long, thin strip, and thus founded the city of Carthage. She welcomed and fell in love with Aeneas, who was shipwrecked with his crew of Trojan survivors near her palace after the Trojan War. After a year Aeneas left her, urged by Mercury to pursue his journey, and in despair she threw herself into the flames of a funeral pyre.
[282]

Ecco (*mod*: Eco) [Echo]: A nymph whose fate is described variously in different traditions. One says that Pan, enraged because she did not return his love, had her torn apart, preserving only her voice. Another says that Hera deprived her of her voice, except to repeat the last words or syllables she heard spoken, in punishment for promoting love affairs of nymphs with Zeus. And another is that she fell in love with Narcissus (see **Narcisso**) and, because he did not return her love, she pined and wasted away, her bones turned to stone, so that all that was left of her was the echo of her voice.
[86, 349, 385]

Ecuba [Hecuba]: Wife of King Priam of Troy, she became the slave of Odysseus after the fall of Troy when Priam was slain. When she saw on the shore the dead body of her son Polydorus, whom she had entrusted to the king of Chersonnesus, Polymestor, Hecuba took revenge by gouging out Polymestor's eyes and killing his two sons. Just as she was about to be stoned by companions of the king she was changed into a dog and leapt into the sea. (see also **Paride**).
[162]

Elena [Helena]: The daughter of Zeus by Leda, according to legend she was the most beautiful woman in the world. Wife of the Greek King Menelaus, her abduction by Paris (see also **Paride**), son of King Priam of Troy, led to the war in which the Greeks destroyed that city, as recounted in Homer's *Iliad*.
[162]

Elicona: Helicon (Mount Helicon), a mountain in Boeotia sacred to Apollo and the Muses.
[293]

Encelado [Enceladus]: A leader among the Giants, who were a race of mortals born from Gaia (Earth) and the blood of Uranus when he was castrated by Kronos, with bodies half mortal and half serpent. He was struck by Zeus with a thunderbolt in a major war (called the *Gigantomachia)* between the Olympian gods and the Giants, won by the gods. Imprisoned beneath Mount Etna, Enceladus continues to cause earthquakes when he turns over and volcanic eruptions when he hisses and thrusts out his fiery tonge. (see also **Titani**).
[134]

Eolo [Aeolus, also Hippotades]: According to Homer (*Odyssey, Book 10*), a mortal to whom Zeus gave control of the winds. But to Virgil (*Aeneid, Book 1*), he was a god. Aeolus kept the winds in a bag inside a cave on his island (the floating island of Aeolia) and he could release them as he wished or as the gods requested.
[310]

Eraclito [Heraclitus]: Greek philosopher of Ephesus c.500 B.C., he was called the "Obscure Philosopher" and "the Mourner," because he wept at the follies and frailties of human life.
[483]

Erebo [Erebus]. The name means "darkness" and refers to the darkest depths of the Underworld, personified by Hesiod as the son of Chaos. Sometimes it refers to the place in the Underworld through which the souls of the dead must pass to reach Hades, and sometimes to the Underworld itself.
[162, 427]

Erinni (Erinyes) (Roman: Furies): Three sinister, subterranean avenging goddesses who persecuted transgressors, seeking to drive them to insanity or death: Alecto ("the unremitting one"), Megaera ("the envious one"), and Tisiphone ("the avenger of murder").
[279]

Euridice: See **Orfeo**.
[96]

Euro [Euros, Eurus]: The southeast wind; like all winds, thought to be divine beings of a lower order, and understood to be a son of Astraeus and Eos. "Euro" is a literary term in Italian for "scirocco," which in English is "sirocco," a warm and humid southeast wind from the Libyan deserts which blows on the northern Mediterranean coast, chiefly in Italy, Malta, and Sicily.
[282]

Euterpe: The Muse of music and lyric poetry, her name means "gladness," or "agreeable." Some legends say she invented the flute and all other wind instruments. She is associated more with Bacchus (i.e., with wild Bacchanalian music) rather than Apollo (i.e., with orderly, "rational" music). (see also **Musica**).
[98]

Eva: The Eve, of Adam and Eve, in the Book of Genesis, whom Satan in the guise of the serpent encouraged to eat the forbidden fruit.
[78]

Fama [Pheme]: A poetic deity depicted with wings and a trumpet. As a personification of spreading rumor, she was depicted by Virgil as a horrible creature with many jabbering mouths; Ovid represented her as a herald of both truth and falsehood.
[293]

Fati (Fates) (Greek: Moirai; Roman: Parcae): There are three of them, symbolizing through their actions the destiny of mortals: Clotho, who carries the spindle and spins the thread of life, Lachesis, who carries a globe or scroll and determines the length of the thread, and Atropos, who carries shears and cuts the thread.
[234]

Febo [Phoebus]: A name for Apollo as the sun god. Born on Delos, son of Zeus and Leto, he was one of the twelve Olympian gods. As well as sun god, he was variously god of fine arts, medicine, music, poetry, eloquence, purification, and manly youth. As sun god he was depicted as driving a golden chariot drawn by winged horses and accompanied by the Hours and Seasons.
[84, 354, 368]

Fenice (Phoenix): In Egyptian mythology, the phoenix was a bird without a mate, who lived for five hundred years, then burned itself to ashes on a pyre and was reborn from the ashes to live for another such period.
[304]

Fille: Variant of **Filli**.
[19, 59]

Filli (Phyllis): One of the most often mentioned Virgilian shepherdesses (see also **Arcadi**).
[8, 11, 32, 37, 48, 74, 115, 136, 164, 196, 224, 234, 246, 323, 336, 354, 379, 397, 457, 484, 500]

Fillide: Variant of **Filli**.
[94, 112, 224, 337]

Flora: See **Clori**.
[207, 247, 273]

Fortuna: Goddess originally of both good and bad fortune or fate, but later of good fortune only. As the personification of fluctuating fortune she is depicted as standing on a wheel or sphere. She sometimes holds a horn of plenty, symbol of prosperity.
[130, 295]

Frisa (Frisia): The Italian name for (German) Friesland, a historic region of the Netherlands and Germany, bordering the North Sea. West Frisia came under the control of the counts of Holland by 1250, and Olimpia is the daughter of the Count of Holland in Ariosto's *Orlando Furioso (see Books 9-11).* (see also **Bireno** and **Olimpia**).
[310]

Galatea: A sea nymph, daughter of Nereus and Doris, whose name means "milk-white." She fell in love with Acis, son of Faunus (or Pan). In postclassical drama and poetry Galatea had often become a shepherdess or milkmaid, a development deriving from the pastoral settings of her tale as told by Theocritus, Virgil, and Ovid.
[140, 366]

Gange (Ganges): The Ganges River; "dal Gange" means "from the east," the river symbolizing the whole Orient. The figure of speech dates back to Dante's time, the late Middle Ages.
[412]

Giacinto [Hyacintus] (Hyacinth): A handsome young man from Amyclae, he was loved by Apollo, the bard Thamyris, and Zephyr, the west wind. According to Ovid, Apollo was so taken with the young man that he neglected his other duties. While teaching Hyacinth to throw the discus, Apollo accidentally struck and killed him; in another version, it was Zephyr who blew the discus off course out of jealousy. Where Hyacinth's blood spilled, Apollo caused a hyacinth flower to grow.
[364]

Giasone (Jason): Thessalian hero, leader of the Argonauts, the band of heroes who took part in the quest for the Golden Fleece. Jason was to have become the king of Iolchus, but the throne was usurped by Pelias, his father's

half-brother. After bearing reared elsewhere, Jason returned to Iolchus to claim his throne. Pelias assured him that he would relinquish his throne if Jason could recapture the Golden Fleece, believing such a task would be impossible. The fleece of the golden ram hung in Colchis, and Jason was charged with restoring it to its rightful home in Greece. In claiming the Golden Fleece, Jason and fifty of his men were aided by the king's daugher Medea, a sorceress who fell in love with Jason. Jason married Medea on their way back to Iolchus, and Medea killed Pelias when they got there. Jason placed the fleece in the temple of Zeus at Orchomenus, then went with Medea in exile to Corinth. After ten years he divorced Medea to marry King Creon's daughter Glauce (Creusa); in a rage, Medea killed her two children by Jason and then escaped to Athens.
[264]

Giove (Jove, Jupiter) (Greek: Zeus): One of the twelve Olympian deities. Youngest son of the Titans Cronus (Saturn) and Rhea, he defeated his father to become the most powerful and worshipped of all the gods. A sky-god, he was associated with the weather, especially rain and lightning, armed with lightning and thunderbolts as his weapons.
[88]

Grazie (Graces) (Greek: Charities): According to most mythographers the Graces were daughters of Zeus and the Oceanid Eurynome. Typically three in number, they personified grace, charm, and beauty and were named Aglaia (Splendor), Euphrosyne (Mirth), and Thalia (Abundance). Although they usually accompanied the Muses, Aphrodite (Venus), and Eros (Cupid), they could also be found in association with almost any of the Olympian deities.
In the Classical period, the Graces were depicted as clothed young women, but by the Hellenistic era they were frequently nude, a tradition continued by Roman artists. During the Roman era, the Graces (Latin: Gratiae) were also the symbol of gratitude and were called Castitas (Chastity), Voluptas (Pleasure) and Pulchritudo (Beauty).
[178, 376, 433]

Icaro [Icarus]: Son of Daedalus whom Minos had commissioned to construct a labyrinth to contain the flesh-eating Minotaur, and who helped Ariadne arrange Theseus' escape from the labyrinth when he came to Crete to kill the Minotaur. For that treachery Minos shut Daedalus and his son in the labyrinth, and Daedalus made a set of wings, from wax and feathers, so that he and the boy could escape by flying on wings like birds. Despite his father's warning, Icarus flew too high near the sun, which melted the wax of his wings, and fell into the sea which bears his name (the Icarian Sea).
[134]

Imeneo [Hymenaeus] (Hymen): Hymen, god of marriage, was the son of Aphrodite (Venus) and Dionysus (Bacchus), or in some accounts of Apollo and one of the Muses. He was a handsome youth who carried a bridal torch and a garland, and he was frequently associated with Eros (Cupid), god of love. He was invoked at weddings with a hymn called the Hymenaeus.
[352]

Ircana, Ircane: = "of, or from, Ircania" in Italian. Classically spelled "Hyrcania," Ircania was an ancient land in northern Iran, east of the Caspian Sea. In Italian translation the "mare ircana" is the Caspian Sea, and a "tigre ircana" is, figuratively, a hard-hearted person.
[217, 492]

Istro Real: "Istro" comes from the Latin word "Hister," or "Ister," for the Italian "Danubio" (the Danube). A "fiume (river) reale" is a river having tributaries, one which flows into the sea. The Danube is the second longest river in Europe, rising in the Black Forest of Germany and making its way through the southeastern portion of the continent to the Black Sea.
[306]

Lete: Lethe, the river of forgetfulness or oblivion: one of the five rivers which ran through the Underworld ruled by the god Hades (Pluto, or Dis) and his queen Persephone (Proserpine).
[222]

Libra: One of the twelve signs of the zodiac, which the ancients used to tell time and explain changes in the universe. Its symbol is the weighing device known as a balance, and its mythological origin is the scales of Justice. The sun enters Libra on approximately September 23rd.
[271]

Licori [Lycoris]: One of the most often named Virgilian shepherdesses. (see also **Arcadi**).
[217]

Ligurina: From Liguria, a region in northwest Italy bordering the Ligurian Sea and dominated by the Maritime Alps and the Lugurian Apennines. Deriving its name from the Ligurians, its pre-Roman inhabitants, Liguria's city of Genoa became one of the principal maritime and commercial powers of Europe as of about 1400 .
[376]

Maia: A mountain nymph, the oldest and prettiest of the Pleiades (the seven daughters of Atlas, by Pleione, born on Mount Cyllene in Arcadia); after their deaths, the Pleiades were placed in the heavens as a constellation. United with Zeus, she gave birth to Hermes, who is thus "the son of Maia" referred to in the text.
[178]

Maria (Mary): The Virgin Mary.
[78, 82]

Marsia [Marsyas]: A satyr whose prowess with the flute was legendary, he challenged Apollo to a music competition. Apollo agreed, with the stipulation that the winner could punish the loser however he pleased. The contest was judged by the Muses, who granted victory to Apollo. His choice of punishment was to flay the satyr alive. The fauns, satyrs, and nymphs cried so bitterly at Marsyas's suffering that their tears formed a river which bears his name.
[216]

Marte (Mars) (Greek: Ares): The Roman god of power, who evolved into a war god, and the second most important deity, after Jupiter, in the Roman pantheon. He was represented as armed with spear and shield, and warlike exercises were held in his honor. Originally an agricultural god, Mars was associated with spring, regeneration, and growth, but as the Romans became more warlike, so did he.
[235, 332]

Mida [Midas]: One legend concerning King Midas that may be alluded to in Frescobaldi's song text is that at a music contest between Apollo and Pan, he differed with the judge who declared Apollo the winner, saying that Pan was the better musician. Apollo was offended and punished Midas by giving him the ears of a donkey.
[216]

Mirtillo: The lover of Amaryllis in Guarini's *Il pastor fido (1590).* (see also **Amarilli**).
[373]

Musica (Greek: Euterpe): One of the nine muses, who were daughters of Zeus and Mnemosyne or of Uranus and Gaia. They usually lived near springs and brooks, in Pieria east of Mount Olympus, on Mount Helicon in Boeotia, and on Mount Parnassus at Delphi. They were very concerned about their honor and punished any mortal who presumed to equal them in the art of song. (see also **Euterpe**).
[293]

Narcisso [Narciso] (Narcissus): The beautiful son of the river-god Cephissus and the nymph Liriope, Narcissus ignored the love of Echo, for which cruelty Nemesis, goddess of retribution, condemned him to contemplating his own image in the water of a pool on Mount Helicon. Drawn to his own likeness but unable to touch it, he pined away and died, and the gods turned him into the flower that bears his name. According to one account, the rejected Echo also pined away and was changed into a stone which retained the power of speech. (see also **Ecco**).
[118]

Olimpia: The daughter of the Count of Holland, deserted by her husband Bireno, captured and abandoned by pirates, saved by Orlando, and married after Bireno's death to the King of Ireland, in Ariosto's *Orlando Furioso (Canto 10).* (see also **Bireno**).
[310]

Olimpo [Olympus]: Mount Olympus, the highest mountain in ancient Greece (modern-day Macedonia), considered the home of the gods and goddesses because it was thought to reach to Heaven. On the summit, above the clouds, was the palace of Zeus.
[45]

Orcheno = of Orco [Orcus]: The Romans referred to Hades, the god of the dead and ruler of the Underworld, as Orcus. In the context of this Caccini text, however, the word probably refers to the popular legend that Orco was an evil monster who devoured people, especially children.
[101]

Orfeo [Orpheus]: Singer and player of the lyre, and a consummate musician, his music had the power to charm people, animals, and plants, calming and soothing them. He accompanied the Argonauts on their famous voyage, succeeding in calming the storms at sea and preventing his companions from being lured to their death by the Sirens.
He married the dryad Euridice; when she died of a snake bite, he went to the Underworld to beg Hades and Persephone for her return. His wish was granted, because of the beauty of his music, but as he led Euridice out of Hades he disobeyed Persephone's condition that he should not look back along the journey to the world above, and Euridice was lost to him forever, returned to the Underworld. Because of his association with music and poetry, Orpheus became a symbol of the arts in general and, by extenson, social harmony.
[293, 304]

Palla [Pallas]: Another name for Athena, one of the twelve Olympians, who was also called Pallas Athena (and by the Romans, Minerva). Born from the head of Zeus, she was goddess of wisdom and patron of the arts and sciences.
[235]

Parca: See **Fati (Fates).**
[147, 326]

Paride (Paris): A Trojan prince, son of King Priam and Queen Hecuba, he decided the dispute among three god-

desses – Aphrodite, Athena, and Hera – over the golden apple of Eris (Discord) by awarding it to Aphrodite, who had bribed him with the promise of the most beautiful woman in the world. (The episode is often called "The Judgement of Paris.") He deserted his wife, the nymph Oenone, and journeyed to Sparta where he kidnapped Helen, the wife of King Menelaus, or according to some versions persuaded her to elope with him to Troy, thereby making inevitable a war between the Greeks and the Trojans.
[162]

Parma: City in the Emilia-Romagna region of northern Italy, on the Parma River, northwest of Bologna. It was the location of the court of the duchy of Parma and Piacenza created in 1545 by Pope Paul III Farnese and given to his son, whose descendants ruled there until 1731.
[266]

Pasitea [Pasithea]: Another name for **Aglaia**, one of the three Graces. An alternate opinion, and one which makes sense in the context of this da Gagliano song text, is that when *four* Graces are mentioned in mythology, Pasitea is the fourth. (see also **Grazie** and **Agliaia**).
[178]

Penelope: Daughter of Icarius of Sparta, she married King Odysseus of Ithaca (called Ulysses by the Romans) and bore him a son, Telemachus.
During the ten years Odysseus fought in the Trojan War, and for the additional ten years he took to make his way home to Ithaca, Penelope remained faithful to him. However, in his absence, his court was overrun by suitors who, while feasting at Odysseus' expense, tried unsuccessfully to convince her that her husband would never return and that she should choose a new husband from among them.
[295]

Permesso [Permessos]: The "harmonious stream," a river of Beoetia sacred to Apollo and the Muses, rising in Mount Helicon.
[293]

Pindo [Pindus]: A range of mountains northeast of nearby Delphi, including Parnassus, one of the tallest mountains in Greece, sacred to Apollo and the Muses. The cave of the Delphic oracle, Apollo's priest, was located on its slopes, as was the Castalian spring, whose waters were said to have the power of inspiration.
[293]

Priamo (Priam): See **Paride** and **Ecuba.**
[162]

Psiche [Psyche]: A young maiden whose beauty was universally admired, Psyche aroused the jealousy of Venus (Aphrodite), who instructed Cupid (Amor) to make Psyche fall in love with an ugly monster. However, on seeing Psyche, Cupid himself fell in love with her. He had Zephyr carry her to a room in his palace, where he visited her only in the dark and forbade her to look at him. Hearing from her jealous sisters that Cupid was a terrible creature who would devour her, Psyche determined to see him. She stole into the god's chamber while he slept and was struck by his comeliness. A drop of hot oil falling from her lamp awakened him and, angered by her disobedience, he left her.
Pysche wandered the earth in search of Cupid, performing various tasks set for her by Venus. The last of these entailed a journey to the Underworld to retrieve from Persephone a box of beauty. Out of curiosity, Psyche opened the box and found instead a deadly sleep. She quickly fell under its spell until the remorseful Cupid begged Jupiter (Zeus) to allow him to marry her. His wish was granted, and Psyche was brought to Olympus by Mercury (Hermes) to be united with her lover.
The tale of Cupid and Psyche has become an allegory for the voyages of the soul on earth, its trials and tribulations, and its final union with the divine after death. The word "psyche" in Greek means "soul."
[410]

Sisifo [Sisyphus]: Founder of the city of Corinth, known for his cunning. Having observed Zeus's seduction of the nymph Aegina, Sisyphus reported the story to the river-god Asopus, her father. Zeus then punished Sisyphus by sending Thanatos (Death) to claim him. But Sisyphus imprisoned Thanatos in a dungeon from which he was released by Ares, and finally yielded to him only after making his wife, Merope, promise to leave his corpse unburied and to make no offerings for him. In the Underworld, Sisyphus received permission from Hades to return to earth by claiming that he wished to punish Merope for this sacrilege. When he eventually died, the gods punished him by making him perpetually roll a boulder to the top of a hill, only to have it roll back down as it reached the summit – hence the "myth of Sisyphus". In the fine arts he is sometimes grouped with Ixion, Tantalus, and Tityus, known collectively as the Four Blasphemers (or Deceivers, Disgracers, Condemned).
[137]

Stigia. See **Stigio.**
[279]

Stigio = Stygian, of the Styx; Stige = Styx: The river Styx separated the land of the living from the Underworld. The Styx (the river of hate) flowed seven times around the netherworld and the deep, black Acheron (the river of woe). The aged ferryman Charon transported dead souls across the Styx or Acheron into the Underworld, charging them one coin (the *obolus*, placed in the mouth at burial) for the journey. Those who had not received proper

funeral rites were condemned to wait on the shore for a hundred years before Charon would ferry them across the river.
[156]

Tantalo [Tantalus]: A son of Zeus and the Titaness Pluto. A wealthy and powerful king in Lydia, he committed various sins. After he killed his son Pelops and served him in a stew when dining with the gods, apparently to test their divine omniscience, he was punished in Tartarus (one of the parts of the Underworld), condemned to stand chin deep in water that receded when he tried to drink, and with ripe fruit hanging just out of his reach – hence the word "tantalize".
In paintings he is sometimes grouped with Ixion, Sisyphus, and Tityus, known collectively as the Four Blasphemers (or Deceivers, Disgracers, Condemned).
[23, 421]

Tauro [Taurus]: One of the twelve signs of the zodiac, which the ancients used to tell time and explain changes in the universe. The Bull is its symbol, Europa's mount its mythological origin, and the sun enters Taurus on approximately April 20th.
[271]

Tebro: The Tiber (River), the second longest Italian river after the Po; it flows through Rome to enter the Tyrrhenian Sea of the Mediterranean near Ostia Antica.
[397, 407, 437]

Teseo [Theseus]: Son of Aegeus, king of Athens, and Aethra, daughter of Pittheus of Troezen, he was the greatest hero of Athens, and the subject of many adventures.
Each year, as a tribute demanded by King Minos of Crete, fourteen Athenian youths and maidens were sacrificed to the Minotaur. Determined to kill the Minotaur and end the tribute, Theseus traveled to Crete as one of the intended victims. With the help of Minos's daughter Ariadne, who gave him a clew or a skein of thread to trace his path, he was able to find his way through the labyrinth which housed the Minotaur, kill it, and emerge safely. Theseus fled Crete, taking Ariadne with him, but he abandoned her on the island of Naxos. (see also **Arianna**).
[139, 314]

Tessalo: Inhabitant of Tessaglia (Thessaly), a region of east-central Greece between the Pindus mountains and the Aegean Sea.
[264]

Teti [Tethys]: A Titaness and wife (and sister) of Oceanus, she produced with him three thousand daughters, the sea nymphs known as the Oceanids, and an equal number of sons who became river-gods. Deity mother of all rivers, and by extension the personification of all the rivers that surrounded the earth, she was known as the "lovely queen of the sea" and, poetically, as the sea itself.
[224, 484]

Tirsi [Thyrsis, Tyris]: One of the herdsmen (shepherds) mentioned by Virgil and taken up by later poets.
(see also **Arcadi**).
[48, 140]

Titani: Titans, the first race of gods, children of Uranus (Sky) and Gaia (Earth). There were probably twelve of them, as there were twelve Olympian gods and goddesses. They warred for ten years with Zeus, who defeated them with his newly forged thunderbolt and imprisoned them in the depths of the Underworld. By doing so Zeus offended Gaia, who called upon her sons, the Giants, to make war upon the gods, a war called the *Gigantomachia*. (see also **Encelado**).
[134]

Titon [Tithonus]: The handsome Tithonus, a brother of Priam, was loved by the goddess Eos (Aurora) and became her consort. Eos begged Zeus (Jupiter) to make Tithonus immortal, but forgot to ask for him to remain eternally young and beautiful. Zeus granted her wish for his immortality, and Tithonus aged endlessly. When he lost his attractiveness, Eos confined him to a room; only his voice could be heard from within. Eos turned him into a cicada (or in some versions a grasshopper) in order to be able always to enjoy the sound of his chirping.
[92]

Tizio [Tityus]: One of the Four Blasphemers (or Deceivers, Disgracers, Condemned). A son of Zeus and the nymph Elara (or another nymph), he was a Giant. To hide his pregnant mother from Hera's jealousy, Zeus concealed her in the depths of the earth, from which Tityus emerged. When grown, Tityus was incited by Hera to attack Leto, another of Zeus's conquests. He was either struck by an arrow shot by Leto's children, Apollo and Artemis, or struck down by a thunderbolt from Zeus. For his presumption, Tityus was eternally punished in Hades: his body was stretched across nine acres and snakes (or vultures) ate his heart and liver, which process was renewed with the phases of the moon. (see also **Tantalus**).
[421]

Trace: Thrace, a region of the southeast Balkan peninsula. In ancient times it stretched as far north as the Danube river.
[235]

Troia [Troja]: The city of Troy. The Trojan War between the mainland Greeks (Achaeans) and the Trojans of Asia Minor, described in the *Iliad*, was based on what may have been an actual historical event that ended with the destruction of Troy (also known as Ilium) in c.1250 B.C. (see also **Dido**).
[282, 295]

Ulisse [Odysseus] (Ulysses): King of Ithaca, husband of Penelope, and a hero of the Trojan War. The adventures of his voyage home after the Trojan War are the subject of Homer's *Odyssey*.
(see also **Penelope**).
[295]

Vergine [Virgo]: One of the twelve signs of the zodiac, which the ancients used to tell time and explain changes in the universe. The Virgin is its symbol, Astraea its mythological origin, and the sun enters Virgo on approximately August 23rd.
[271]

Vesuvio (Vesuvius): A volcano, the only one still active in Europe, which rises above the Bay of Naples in southern Italy. A great eruption in A.D. 79 buried Pompeii and Stabiae under ashes and Herculaneum under mud flow. Some ten confirmed eruptions occurred between 79 and 1631, when a major eruption destroyed many villages, the lava flow reached the sea, and the skies were darkened for days.
[501]

Virtù [Virtus]: The Romans made deities of all the major virtues. Virtus was the personification of manliness in warfare as well as of integrity and fortitude.
[216]

Vulcano [Volcanus] (Vulcan): Roman god of fire and metalworking, he used his fire to soften metals. With the Cyclopes he established a great forge in the heart of Mount Aetna, where he forged the thunderbolts for Jupiter.
[281]

Zeffiro (Zefiro; Zeffiretto) [Zephyrus]: Zephyr, god of the west wind, according to Hesiod a son of Eos (Aurora), the dawn, and Astraeus. The warm west wind was thought to awaken the cold earth in springtime – hence the word "zephyr," meaning a light, pleasant breeze. Zephyr was sometimes called the husband of Iris, but he is best known as the lover of Flora, goddess of spring, who was transformed from the nymph Chloris by his touch.
[14, 90]

Index

Titles are the first words of the text rather than a generic category (see *Notes about formatting*, pg. iii.).
When the first words of a text are different from a given title, the first words are listed in italics.

A battaglia, pensieri.................................. 401
ABBATINI, ANTONIO MARIA.......................... 1
Accorta lusinghiera.................................. 120
A chi sempre ha da penar......................... 401
Acqua non è l'umor.................................. 496
Adagiati, Poppea...Oblivion soave............ 289
Addio Corino...Vieni, Alidoro.................... 165
Affé, mi fate ridere.................................. 154
Agitato il cor mi sento............................. 402
AGOSTINI, PIETRO SIMONE.......................... 2
Ah che purtroppo.................................... 336
Ahi! dispietato Amor................................ 85
Ahi, fuggitivo ben.................................... 366
Ahimè ch'io moro.................................... 105
Ahi! troppo è duro................................... 289
Ah! quanto è vero.................................... 166
Ah se tu dormi ancora............................. 47
ALBINONI, TOMASO GIOVANNI..................... 2-25
ALDROVANDINI, GIUSEPPE ANTONIO
   VINCENZO.. 25-26
Al fonte, al prato (CACCINI)....................... 86
Al fonte, al prato (PERI)........................... 349
All'acquisto di gloria............................... 402
Alla gloria... 207
All'apparir di risplendente aurora............. 112
Allegrezza del nuovo maggio..................... 266
Alma del core... 110
Amanti, io vi disfido................................ 166
Amar il caro bene.................................... 26
Amarilli... 87
Amarilli mia bella.................................... 87
A' miei pianti... 208
Amor, amor, fammi goder......................... 28
Amor, ch'attendi?.................................... 88
Amor dormiglione................................... 465
Amore è bandito...................................... 466
Amore, ti sento ch'al varco m'attendi........ 206
A morire!... 125
Amor mio, che cosa è questa?.................. 126
Amor, non dormir più!............................ 465
Amorosa pargoletta................................. 253
Amor, preparami..................................... 403
Amor, Sorte, Destino!.............................. 3
ANONIMO... 26-40
A' piè della gran croce............................. 209
A Porfiria vecchiarella.............................. 452
Apra il suo verde seno............................. 364
Apritevi, inferni...................................... 127
Aqua non è l'umor................................... 496
Ardo e scoprir.. 290
Ardo, e taccio il mio mal......................... 210
ARIOSTI, ATTILIO..................................... 41-43
Armati.. 403
Armilla ingrata....................................... 190
A travestirsi... 271
Augellin vago e canoro............................ 244
AUGUSTINI – SEE AGOSTINI

Aur' amorosa.. 89
A voi che l'accendeste............................. 357
Avvezzati, mio core................................. 501
BADALLA, ROSA GIACINTA........................... 43-45
BASSANI, GIOVANNI BATTISTA...................... 45-51
Beato chi può... 154
Begli occhi... 356
Begli occhi, mercé................................... 491
Begl'occhi, ben seno................................ 467
Begl'occhi lucenti.................................... 190
Bella bocca.. 346
Bella Clori... 167
Bella fanciulla.. 191
Bella porta di rubini................................ 192
Belle rose purpurine................................ 90
Bellezza, che s'ama................................. 403
Bellezza tiranna...................................... 242
BELLI, DOMENICO..................................... 51-52
Bellissima regina.................................... 350
Bel tempo per me se n'andò...................... 129
BEMBO, ANTONIA...................................... 52
Benché speranza...................................... 55
Bench'in me giri...................................... 53
Ben veggio... 212
BERTI, GIOVANNI PIETRO............................ 52-53
BIANCOSI, GERARDO.................................. 53-54
BONONCINI, GIOVANNI............................... 54-65
BONONCINI, GIOVANNI MARIA...................... 65-66
BOTTEGARI, COSIMO.................................. 66-68
BRUNI – SEE CAVALLI
BUONONCINI – SEE BONONCINI
BUSATTI, CHERUBINO................................. 69-73
BUZZOLENI, GIOVANNI............................... 73-75
CACCINI, FRANCESCA................................. 75-85
CACCINI, GIULIO...................................... 85-105
CACCINI, SETTIMIA.................................... 106-110
CALDARA, ANTONIO................................... 110-119
Caldi sospiri.. 372
Caldo sangue... 404
CALESTANI, VINCENZO............................... 120-121
CALETTI-BRUNI – SEE CAVALLI
CAMPANA, FRANCESCA................................ 121-123
Cangia, cangia tue voglie.......................... 203
Cantan gl'augelli..................................... 106
CAPROLI, CARLO....................................... 123-125
Cara e dolce... 405
Cara è la rosa, e vaga.............................. 194
Cara gradita e bella................................. 337
Cara mia cetr' andiamo............................ 187
Care mie selve.. 373
CARISSIMI, GIACOMO................................. 125-153
Caro laccio, dolce nodo............................ 245
Caro volto pallidetto................................ 270
Catene d'amore....................................... 452
CAVALIERI – SEE DE' CAVALIERI
CAVALLI, FRANCESCO [CALETTI-BRUNI]........ 153-163
CESARINI, CARLO FRANCESCO..................... 163-165

CESTI, ANTONIO.................................... 165-175
Che angoscia, che affanno!...................... 169
Che farò, donna ingrata.......................... 339
Che fiero costume.................................. 253
Che narri?...Ite, o furie.......................... 45
Che sventura!...................................... 379
Che t'ho fatt'io.................................... 75
Chiamata a nuovi amori............................ 468
Chi crede ch'io v'ami.............................. 489
Chi da' lacci d'Amor.............................. 177
Chi desia di saper................................ 77
Chi è costei...................................... 78
Chi mi confort' ahimè!............................ 92
Chi mi vede al sembiante.......................... 390
Chi non gode di sua lode.......................... 447
Chi non sa quanto inumano......................... 4
Chioma d'oro...................................... 291
Chiome inanellate della sua pargoletta.... 267
Chi si pasce...................................... 155
Chi vuole innamorarsi............................. 405
CIFRA, ANTONIO.................................... 175-177
Cinta di rose..................................... 247
Clori vezzosa, e bella............................ 406
Colà degl'Arcadi.................................. 448
Col mio sangue comprerei.......................... 452
Come raggio di sol................................ 110
Come sete importuni............................... 130
Compatitemi (Filli, Filli...Compatitemi)...... 164
Con che soavità................................... 292
Con ghirlanda di rose............................. 273
Con placido incanto (Le Ninfe più
    vezzose...Con placido incanto)............. 449
Con voce festiva.................................. 407
Core di questo core............................... 107
Correte, momenti.................................. 453
Così, Amor, mi fai languir........................ 454
Così mi disprezzate?.............................. 215
Così Nilio cantò.................................. 360
Così volete, così sara!........................... 131
Costume de' grandi................................ 470
Crudele che non sente, non vede,
    non parla..................................... 471
Crudel, tu vuoi partire........................... 340
Cura, che di timor................................ 274
DA GAGLIANO, MARCO................................ 177-184
Dagli abissi del mio core......................... 471
Dall'arco d'un bel ciglio......................... 6
Dal mio Permesso amato............................ 293
Da procella tempestosa............................ 41
Da te...Se ti piace............................... 55
Da te parto....................................... 387
DE' CAVALIERI, EMILIO............................. 184-186
Degnati, o gran Fernando.......................... 216
Deh come in van chiedete.......................... 342
Deh, contentatevi................................. 132
Deh, dove son fuggiti............................. 93
Deh lascia o core di respirar..................... 56
Deh, lasciatemi il nemico......................... 245
Deh, memoria...................................... 133
Deh, più a me non v'ascondete..................... 56
Deh, rendetemi.................................... 363
Deh! Se tue belle ciglia.......................... 94
Deh spiegate mortali.............................. 392
Del chiaro rio.................................... 8
DEL CAVALIERI — SEE DE' CAVALIERI
Delizie contente.................................. 155
DELLA CIAIA, AZZOLINO BERNARDINO.............. 186

Dell'antro magico................................. 156
DEL LEUTO — SEE LORI
DE LUCA, Non posso disperar — SEE
    BONONCINI, G. 58
DEL VIOLINO, CARLO — SEE CAPROLI
DE ROCHECHOUART, GABRIEL.......................... 186-187
Difesa non ha..................................... 407
Di Licori un guardo altero........................ 217
Di misera regina.................................. 295
Dimmi, Amor....................................... 259
Dimmi cara.. 46
D'INDIA, SIGISMONDO............................... 187-189
Dir ch'io t'ami................................... 261
Dispiegate, guancie amate......................... 79
Disserratevi a me................................. 156
Di stella infesta................................. 25
Dite ch'io canti.................................. 69
Di vostri occhi................................... 51
Dolce Amor, bendato dio........................... 157
Dolce auretta..................................... 448
Dolce scherza..................................... 357
Donna, siam rei di morte.......................... 218
Donn' ingrata..................................... 195
Donzelle, fuggite................................. 158
Dopo sì lungo error............................... 219
Dormi, Amore...................................... 178
Dormi, bella...................................... 46
Dove, dove corri, mio core?....................... 29
Dove, dove, Signor................................ 220
Dove, dove sparir sì ratto........................ 222
Dove mi spingi, Amor.............................. 380
Dove sei gita..................................... 52
Due luci ridenti.................................. 108
Dunque dovrò...................................... 223
È bello l'ardire.................................. 134
Ecco, che pur baciate............................. 335
Ecco ch'io verso il sangue........................ 80
Ecco di dolci raggi............................... 299
Ecco pur ch'a voi ritorno......................... 299
E che? E che diavol sarà questo................... 469
Ed è pur dunque vero.............................. 300
E dove t'aggiri................................... 169
Elitropio d'amor.................................. 408
Entro nave dorata................................. 224
E quando mai cor mio godrai....................... 111
E quando ve n'andate?............................. 491
Ergiti, amor...................................... 409
Eri già tutta mia................................. 302
Et è pur dunque vero.............................. 300
È tornato il mio ben.............................. 70
E tu credi.. 360
FALCONIERI, ANDREA................................ 190-203
Fanciulla son io.................................. 381
Farci pazzo....................................... 255
Farò la vendetta.................................. 410
FASOLO, GIOVANNI BATTISTA......................... 203-205
Fatto bersaglio eterno...In amar bellezza
    altera....................................... 9
FEDELI, RUGGIERO.................................. 205
FEDELLI, RIGGIERO — SEE FEDELI
Fere selvaggie.................................... 94
Ferma, Dorinda mia................................ 121
Fermate omai fermate.............................. 410
Filli, chiedi al mio core......................... 11
Filli, Filli, nol niego...Compatitemi............. 164
Filli mia, se vi pensate.......................... 246
Filli, non t'amo più.............................. 136

Filli vezzosa, Filli amorosa	196
Fortunate passate	41
Fortunato chi sa	392
FRESCHI, DOMENICO	205-206
FRESCOBALDI, GIROLAMO	206-242
Fuggi, fuggi dal mio cor	455
Fuggi, fuggi, fuggi, diletta amante	30
Fuggite, fuggite	137
Funeste piaggie	350
GABRIELLI, DOMENICO	242
GAFFI, (TOMMASO) BERNARDO	243-244
GAGLIANO – SEE DA GAGLIANO	
Galatea mentre t'amai	366
GASPARINI, FRANCESCO	244-246
Gelosia, che a poco a poco	383
GHIVIZZANI, ALESSANDRO	246-247
Già conceduto avea la libertade Eurillo	393
Già il sole dal Gange	412
Già mai	412
Già morta è la fiamma	286
Già sperai	109
Gioite al canto mio	352
Giunto alla cuna	275
Giunto è il giorno fatal	116
Giusta negativa	472
Goderai sempre, crudele	413
Godere e lasciare costuman	470
Gran pazzia	158
Hai core, o crudele	263
Hor che Apollo	484
Ho un'alma	414
Il dannato	183
Il gelsomino	112
Illustratevi, o cieli	304
Il mio core	205
Il mio core non è con me	205
Il pastorello	448
Il romeo	473
Il rosignuolo	415
Il tempo fugge	184
I miei giorni sereni	475
In amar bellezza altera (Fatto bersaglio eterno...In amar bellezza altera)	9
In amor	159
In amor ci vuol ardir	52
Incostante Mustafa?	284
Indarno Febo	368
INDIA – SEE D'INDIA	
Insegnatemi a morire	170
In te la vita	248
In terra la guerra	417
Interrotte speranze	249
Intorno all'idol mio	170
In un fiorito prato	304
In un mar di pensieri	137
Invocazione di Orfeo	352
Io ch'armato sin or	305
Io che nell'ozio naqui e d'ozio vissi	306
Io dissi	417
Io era pargoletta	179
Io morirei contento	417
Io pur seguirò	461
Io so ben dir perché	396
Io so ch'ho pianto assai	397
Io son ferito	497
Io son zitella	357
Ite, o furie (Che narri?...Ite, o furie)	45
KAPSBERGER, JOHANN	247-251
KEISER, REINHARD	251
Labra gradite	419
La fanciuletta semplice	486
La gelosia	383
Lagrime dolorose	449
Lagrime mie	474
L'amante bugiardo	475
L'amante consolato	476
L'amante segreto	477
Lamento d'Arianna	314
Lamento d'Olimpia	310
La mia fede	139
La mia pallida faccia	225
La mia turca	313
LANDI, STEFANO	251-252
LANIER, NICHOLAS	252-253
La pastorella mia	82
L'armi crudele e fiere	420
La rosa	41
Lasciar d'amarti	246
Lasciar d'amarti per non penar	246
Lasciatemi morire	314
La speranza	421
La speranza i cori affida	57
L'astratto	479
La travagliata	481
La tua gradita fé	422
La tua pena	422
La vendetta	482
La violetta	175
LEGRENZI, GIOVANNI	253-258
Le Ninfe più vezzoso...Con placido incanto	449
L'Eraclito amoroso	483
L'esperto nocchiero	57
Le violette	422
LONATI, CARLO AMBROGIO	258
Lontananza crudel	12
Lontan dalla sua Clori	423
L'Orfeo Prologo	293
LORI, ARCANGELO	259-260
LOTTI, ANTONIO	260-261
Luci vezzose (GAFFI)	243
Luci vezzose (STRADELLA)	455
Lungi dall'idol mio	114
Lungi da te	58
Lungi, lungi è amor da me	204
Maddalena alla croce	209
Mai non intesi	358
Maledetto	159
Maledetto sia l'aspetto	319
MANCIA – SEE MANZI	
MANCINI, FRANCESCO	261-262
Ma no, non fuggir	140
MANZI, LUIGI	262-265
MANZIA – SEE MANZI	
MANZOLO, DOMENICO	265
Ma per quell'ampio Egeo spieghi le vele	320
Ma prima ch'io mora	424
Maria, dolce Maria	82
MARINI, BIAGIO	266-269
Ma se tu dormi ancora	47
MATTEIS, NICOLA	270
MAZZAFERRATA, GIOVANNI BATTISTA	271
MAZZOCCHI, DOMENICO	271-283
MELANI, ALESSANDRO	283-284

MELANI, JACOPO.. 284-285
Mentre che'l cor.. 188
Mentre il cor si stilla in piano...................... 262
Mesto in sen... 140
Mi da pena quando spira................................ 14
Mie speranze... 181
Mie speranze lusinghiere................................ 181
Mi fa vezzi.. 358
Mi ha diviso il cor.. 425
MILANUZZI, CARLO... 286-287
MINISCALCHI, GUGLIELMO.................................. 287-288
Mi nudrite di speranza.................................... 256
Mio tesoro per te moro.................................. 426
Mi parto... 66
Mi parto e nel partir ti dico......................... 447
Mirti, faggi... 115
Monologo del "Tempo".................................... 184
MONTEVERDI, CLAUDIO...................................... 288-335
Mori, mi dice.. 387
Morirò, stelle perfide...................................... 456
Morte, da me.. 67
Morte, da me tant' aspettata.......................... 67
Morto son io... 71
Mostri dell'Erebo... 427
M'uccidete begli occhi.................................... 384
Nel camino... 83
Nel cammlno... 83
Nell'aspro mio dolor....................................... 427
Nel pur ardor.. 352
Nel puro ardor.. 352
Né men per gioco... 427
Nevi intatte.. 428
Nina... 31
Ninfa che, scalza il piede................................ 321
Non amo, ma bramo....................................... 502
Non c'è che dire, la voglio così....................... 256
Non dar più pene, o caro................................ 428
Non è mai senza duol..................................... 492
Non è pena maggior.. 68
Non fuggirai.. 73
Non la volete intendere.................................. 384
Non mi dir di palesar...................................... 257
Non mi dite ch'io canti................................. 472
Non mi negate.. 227
Non mi sprezzar.. 428
No, no, mio core... 141
No, no, non si speri!....................................... 142
No, non temete, o pianti.............................. 48
Non piango e non sospiro................................ 96
Non più d'amore... 196
Non posso disperar... 58
Non posso vivere.. 143
Non so come l'alma mia.................................. 2
Non temer, Filli mia.. 32
Non vi vorrei conoscere.................................. 429
Non vogl'io se non vederti.............................. 429
Non vuol ch'io t'ami?...................................... 498
Notte, amica de' riposi................................... 456
Nudo arciero.. 197
O bei lumi.. 499
O bellissimi capelli... 198
O bell'occhi.. 228
O biondetta lascivetta..................................... 362
O biondetta lascivetta pastorella..................... 371
OBIZZI, DOMENICO... 335-336
Oblivion soave (Adagiati, Poppea...
    Oblivion soave).. 289

Occhi belli.. 33
Occhi dell'alma mia... 33
Occhietti amati... 200
Occhi, fonti del core....................................... 34
Occhi, io vissi di voi....................................... 445
Occhi sempre sereni.. 368
O cessate di piagarmi..................................... 430
O, che felice giorno.. 96
O del ben che acquisterò................................ 172
O del Cielo d'Amor... 189
Odi, Euterpe, il dolce canto............................ 98
O dolcissima speranza.................................... 431
O frondoso arboscello..................................... 59
Oh, che umore stravagante.............................. 388
Ohimè, che fur.. 229
Ohimè ch'io cado... 321
Ohimè, se tant' amate.................................... 99
O leggiadri occhi belli..................................... 35
Omai le luci erranti... 277
Ombre, voi che celate..................................... 457
O mia Filli gradita.. 37
O miei giorni fugaci.. 353
O mio cor... 230
O morire, o libertà... 459
O pargoletto arciero....................................... 347
O primavera... 374
Or che Apollo... 484
Or che l'alba.. 266
Or ch'io non seguo più.................................... 375
ORLANDI, CAMILLO... 336-345
ORSINI, LEONORA... 345-346
Oscure selve... 232
O vaga e bianca luna...................................... 342
Ove rivolgo il piede... 16
Parte il piè.. 38
Partenza (CALDARA).. 116
Partenza (STEFANI).. 447
Parti, mi lasci.. 18
PASQUINI, BERNARDO.. 346-348
Pastorella.. 500
Pastorella, ove t'ascondi................................. 500
Pazzarello augellin.. 278
Pensaci bene.. 431
Pensieri... 431
Pensieri quietate.. 38
Perché se m'odiavi.. 323
Per chi mia voce... 369
Per compiacerti, o cara................................... 251
Perfidissimo volto... 99
Perfido, che chiamare..................................... 279
Per formare la Betta....................................... 433
PERI, JACOPO... 348-356
Per la gloria... 61
Per la gloria d'adorarvi.................................... 61
Per la più vaga e bella.................................... 84
Per pianto la mia carne................................... 346
Per pietà... 459
PERTI, GIACOMO ANTONIO................................. 356-360
Pescatrice ligurina... 376
PESENTI, MARTINO... 360-363
Piange il fiore e geme il prato......................... 260
Piangete, ohimè, piangete.............................. 144
Piangete (Piangete aure)................................. 143
Piangete (Piangete, ohimè, piangete)............... 144
Piango invan da[l']idol.................................... 61
Piangono al pianger mio.................................. 343
Pietà, mio caro bene....................................... 65

Pietà, Signore......	460
Pietosi, allontanatevi......	386
Più lieto il guardo......	323
Più non sia......	280
Più non ti voglio credere......	62
Più vaga e vezzosetta......	63
Poiché al vago seren......	19
Posate, dormite......	47
Potrà lasciare il rio......	489
Povera pellegrina......	433
Povere mie catene......	434
Presto io m'innamoro......	271
PROVENZALE, FRANCESCO......	363
Pupille arciere......	182
Pupillette......	72
Pur dicesti, o bocca bella......	260
QUAGLIATI, PAOLO......	364-365
QUAGLIATO – SEE QUAGLIATI	
Qual mia colpa......	435
Quando sarà quel dì?......	494
Quanto è bello il mio diletto......	1
Quanto è folle quell'amante......	347
Quanto tardate......	461
Quel sguardo sdegnosetto......	325
Queste lagrime e sospiri......	461
Questi, ch'al par del ciel......	281
Qui dove al fin m'assido......	415
QUINCIANI, LUCIA......	365
Ragion sempre addita......	461
RASI, FRANCESCO......	365-371
Ricciutella pargoletta......	267
Riedi a me......	21
RIGATTI, GIOVANNI ANTONIO......	371-372
ROCHECHOUART, GABRIEL – SEE DE ROCHECHOUART	
Rompe sprezza......	434
RONTANI, RAFFAELLO......	372-378
ROSA, SALVATOR......	378-379
ROSA, SALVATOR, Star vicino - SEE ANONIMO......	39
ROSA, SALVATOR, Vado ben spesso - SEE BONONCINI, G.	65
ROSSI, LUIGI......	379-386
Rugiadose, odorose......	422
Ruscelletto limpidetto......	22
S'amor m'annoda il piede......	462
SANCES, GIOVANNI FELICE......	386
SARACENI – SEE SARACINI	
SARACINI, CLAUDIO......	387-388
SARTORIO, ANTONIO......	388-390
SAVIONI, MARIO......	390-400
SCARLATTI, ALESSANDRO......	400-445
Scioglie omai le nevi......	359
Scioglietemi pietose......	263
Sconsigliata Doralba, ove t'aggiri?......	285
Se amor m'annoda il piede......	462
Sebben, crudele......	118
Se bel rio......	377
Se delitto è l'adorarti......	435
Se Florinda è fedele......	435
Se Florindo è fedele......	435
Segui, segui, dolente core......	201
Seguita a piangere......	48
Se i languidi miei sguardi......	326
Sei pur bello......	389
Sei sì caro......	450
Se l'aura spira......	233

Se l'onde, ohimè......	234
Selve amiche......	118
Selve, voi che le speranze......	379
Se mai vien tocca......	63
Se mi dicessi, o vaga......	186
Se mi toglie ria sventura......	385
Semplicette verginelle......	268
Semplicetto augellin......	122
Se nel ben......	463
Se nel ben sempre......	463
Se nel ben sempre incostante......	463
Sento nel core......	436
Sento un certo non so che......	330
Senza speranza, ohimè......	463
Se pietade in te non trovi......	265
SESSA, CLAUDIA......	445-446
Se ti piace (Da te...Se ti piace)......	55
Se tu della mia morte......	436
Se voi, luci amate......	187
Se vuoi ch'io viva......	437
Sfogava con le stelle......	100
Sì, che fedele......	64
Sì che morte......	74
Sì dolce è'l tormento......	330
Signor, c'ora fra gli ostri......	235
Si mantiene il mio amor......	173
S'io morrò, che dirà......	39
S'io ti guardo......	123
Si può rimirar......	243
Si riscaldi il Tebro......	437
Sì, sì, fedel......	438
Si suoni la tromba......	438
Sì t'intendo......	118
Sì, voglio morir......	173
So ben, che mi saettano......	464
So ben s'io peno......	347
Soccorrete, luci avare......	481
Soccorretemi, ch'io moro......	146
Son ancor pargoletta......	160
Son ferito......	236
Son povera donzella......	263
Son prigioniero......	262
Son qual Tantalo novello......	23
Son tanto ito cercando......	476
Son tutta duolo......	438
Sospiri di foco......	160
Sospiro, sì......	287
Speranza......	439
Speranze......	161
Speranze mie......	439
Sperar io non dovrei......	359
Spesso per entro al petto......	486
Spesso vibra per suo gioco......	441
Spoglie, che fosti un tempo......	282
Star vicino......	39
STEFANI, GIOVANNI......	446-447
STEFFANI, AGOSTINO......	447-451
STRADELLA, ALESSANDRO......	451-464
STROZZI, BARBARA......	465-488
Suonerà l'ultima tromba......	147
Superbi colli......	252
SUPRIANI, FRANCESCO......	488-489
Susurrando il venticello......	441
Su, venite a consiglio......	441
Sventura, cuor mio......	150
TARDITI, ORAZIO......	489-490
Tempro la cetra......	332

TENAGLIA, ANTONIO FRANCESCO................ 491-495
Ti lascio, anima mia................................. 237
Ti lascio, Eurilla.................................... 49
Timore, e che sarà?............................... 488
Toglietemi la vita ancor.......................... 443
Toglietemi, pietosi................................. 264
TORELLI, GIUSEPPE............................... 495-496
Tra due negre pupillette.......................... 344
Tra le Speranze e'l Timore...................... 488
Tre giorni (Nina).................................... 31
Tremulo spirito...................................... 162
TROMBONCINO, IPPOLITO......................... 496-497
Troppo soavi i gusti................................ 162
Troppo, sotto due stelle.......................... 238
Tu ch'hai le penne, Amore....................... 101
Tu dormi.. 354
Tu lo sai (SCARLATTI)............................. 443
Tu lo sai (TORELLI)................................. 495
Tu mancavi a tormentarmi (CAPROLI)........ 123
Tu mancavi a tormentarmi (CESTI)............ 174
Tu partisti.. 258
Tu sai pur.. 231
Tu se' morta... 333
Udite, amanti.. 104
Udite amanti la cagione.......................... 483
Udite lagrimosi spirti.............................. 365
Udite o voi che del mondo fallace............. 398
Un cor da voi ferito................................ 443
Un core, o piante, o sassi....................... 451
Un dì la bella Clori................................. 165
Un dì soletto... 356
Un guardo.. 370
Un'ombra di pace.................................. 64
Vado ben spesso cangiando loco.............. 65
Vaghe luci.. 119
Vaghe stelle.. 163

Vagò mendico il core.............................. 473
Valli profonde....................................... 183
Vanne, o carta amorosa.......................... 239
Va per lo mare....................................... 444
Vattene pur lasciva orecchia umana.......... 446
Verdi tronchi... 348
Vezzosa Aurora..................................... 283
Vezzosette e care pupillette..................... 202
Vi credo, o no....................................... 444
Vieni, Alidoro (Addio Corindo...Vieni
    Alidoro).. 165
Vieni, o cara... 451
Vieni omai, deh, vieni, o morte................. 175
Vinto sono... 445
VISCONTI, DOMENICO............................. 498
VITALI, FILIPPO..................................... 498-501
Vittoria, mio core!.................................. 152
Vittoria, Vittoria!................................... 152
Vittoria, Vittoria mio core!....................... 152
Vocalizzo... 105
Voglio di vita uscir................................. 334
Voglio farti dire il vero............................ 264
Voglio morire, piuttosto........................... 477
Voglio morir, voglio morire....................... 310
Voglio sì, vo' cantar............................... 479
Voi partite.. 240
Voi pur begl'occhi.................................. 467
Volgimi, o cara Filli................................ 74
Volto caro del mio bel sole...................... 24
Vorrei poter morire................................. 26
Vostro sono, o miei tormenti.................... 400
Vuò cercando.. 43
Vuoi che parta!...................................... 43
ZANETI, FRANCESCO MARIA..................... 501
ZIANI, MARCO ANTONIO........................... 502

Bibliography

with
Numbering Key to sources of texts

ANTHOLOGIES AND MIXED COLLECTIONS

1   *Alte Meister des Bel Canto.* Edited by Ludwig Landshoff. Leipzig: C.F.Peters (Edition Peters No.3348), n.d.

2   *Alte Meister des Bel Canto.* Edited by Ludwig Landshoff. Vol. 1 (No.3348a). Frankfurt: C.F.Peters Corporation, n.d.

3   ——. Vol. 2 (No.3348c).

4   *Anthology of Italian Songs of the Seventeenth and Eighteenth Centuries.* Selected and edited by Alessandro Parisotti. New York: G. Schirmer, Inc., 1894. Book I.

5   ——. Book II. Copyright renewed in 1922 by Theodore Baker.

6   *Anthology of Italian Songs of the 17th and 18th Centuries.* No city: Belwin Mills Publishing Corp. (Kalmus), n.d.

7   *Antiche Gemme Italiane.* Edited by Vittorio Ricci. Reprint, Milan: Casa Ricordi, 1997.

8   *Arie Antiche.* Raccolte ed elaborate da A. Parisotti. Vol. 1. Reprint, Milan: G. Ricordi & C., 1993.

9   ——. Vol. 2.

10   ——. Vol. 3.

11   *Arie Italiane dal XIII al XVIII secolo per basso-baritone.* Elaborazione a cura di Raffaele Mingardo. Milan: Edizioni Suvini Zerboni, 1976.

12   *A Selection of Italian Arias 1600-1800.* Edited by Anthony Lewis. Vol. 1. London: The Associated Board of the Royal Schools of Music, 1983.

13   *Belcanto: 10 Ancient Italian Arias.* Edited by Luciano Tomelleri. Milan: G.Ricordi & C., 1956; reprint, Milan: Casa Ricordi, 1998.

14   *Canzone scordate: An Anthology of Early Songs and Arias.* With piano accompaniments composed by Arne Dørumsgaard. Book 2: *Ten Early Italian Songs.* Huntsville, Tx.: Recital Publications, 1987.

15   ——. Book 3: *Five Early Italian Songs.*

16   ——. Book 4: *Five Early Italian Songs.*

17   ——. Book 5: *Six Early Italian Arias.*

18   ——. Book 6: *Five Scarlatti Songs.*

19   *Celebri Arie Antiche.* Edited by Claudio Dall'Alberto and Marcello Candela. Milan: Rigginenti Editore, 1998.

20   *Classic Italian Songs.* Edited by Mabelle Glenn and Bernard U. Taylor. Vol. 1. Bryn Mawr, Pa.: Oliver Ditson Company, 1936.

21   ——. Vol. 2, 1949.

22   ——. Vol. 3, 1968.

23   *Classic Songs: Italian/French/English.* Compiled and edited by Bernard Taylor. High Voice. Evanston, Illinois: Summy-Birchard Publishing Company, 1959.

24   *Early Italian Songs and Airs.* Edited by Pietro Floridia. Vol. 1, Caccini to Bononcini. Boston: Oliver Ditson Company, 1923.
25   ——. Vol. 2, Provenzale to Supriani. 1924.

26   *Échos d'italie [Les Maîtres Italien des XVII ° et XVIII ° Siècles].* Vol. 6. Paris: A. Durand Fils, n.d.

27   *Eleganti Canzoni ed Arie Italiane del Secolo XVII.* Raccolti, annotati e trascritti per canto e pianoforte da L. Torchi. Milan: G.Ricordi & C., n.d.

28   *Expressive Singing Song Anthology.* By Van A. Christy. Vol. 1. Dubuque, Ia.: Wm. C. Brown Company Publishers, Sixth Printing, 1974.
29   ——. Vol. 2. Fifth Printing, 1974.

30   *Gems of Antiquity.* Edited by Dr. Otto Neitzel. London: The John Church Company, 1909.

31   *German, French and Italian Song Classics.* Edited by Horatio Parker. Cincinnati: The John Church Company, 1912. Volume I, Soprano.
32   ——.   Vol. II, Alto.

33   *Historical Anthology of Music by Women.* Edited by James R. Briscoe. Bloomington, Ind: Indiana University Press, 1987.

34   *Italian Arias of the Baroque and Classical Eras.* Edited by John Glenn Paton. Van Nuys, Ca.: Alfred Publishing Co., Inc., 1994.

35   *Italian Songs of the 18th Century.* Edited by Albert Fuchs. New York: International Music Company, 1954.

36   *Italian Songs of the Renaissance and Baroque periods originally composed for Lute, 5-string Guitar and Clavicembalo.* Edited by John Runge. New York: Hargail Music Press, 1965.

37   *Italian Songs of the 17th and 18th Centuries.* Realization of the Figured Bass and editing by Luigi Dallapiccola. Vol. 1. New York: International Music Company, 1961.
38   ——. Vol. 2.

39   *La Flora (Arie &c. antiche Italiane).* Collected and edited by Knud Jeppesen. Vol. 1. Copenhagen: Wilhelm Hansen, 1949.
40   ——. Vol. 2.
41   ——. Vol. 3.

42   *La gioia di cantare in Italiano.* Compiled by Dietrich Erbelding. Castro Valley, Ca.: Pocket Coach Publications, 1993.

43   *L'aria Barocca.* Realized and Edited, with Introduction, Translations, and Notes by John Glenn Paton. Geneseo, NY: Leyerle Publications, 1985.

44   *Les Gloires de L'Italie.* Recueillis, annotés et transcrits pur Piano et Chant par F. A. Gevaert. Vol. 1. Paris: Heugel & Cie., n.d. [1868?]
45   ——. Vol. 2.

46   *Old Masters of Bel Canto.* Edited by Ludwig Landshoff. Vol. I: Soprano. Boca Raton, Fla.: Masters Music Publications, Inc., 1991.
47   ——. Vol. 3, n.d.

48   *Piccolo Album di Musica Antica.* Collected and transcribed by Alessandro Parisotti. Milan: G.Ricordi & C., 1892.

50   *Songs of the Italian Baroque.* Edited by Frederick F. Polnauer. Bryn Mawr, Pa.: Elkan-Vogel, Inc., 1980.

51   *Songs with Theorbo (ca. 1650-1663).* Edited by Gordon J. Callon. Recent Researches in the Music of the Baroque Era, Vol. 105. Madison, Wi: A-R Editions, 2000.

52   *Steps to Singing for Voice Classes.* Royal Stanton. Belmont, California: Wadsworth Publishing Company, Inc., 1971, 1976.

53   *10 Arie Italiane del Sei e Settecento.* Realizzazione di Vittorio Negri Bryks. Milan: Casa Ricordi, 1983.

54   *THE ARIA Renaissance and Baroque.* Revised by Estelle Liebling, Edited by Ruggero Vené. Low Voice. New York: Franco Colombo, Inc., 1963.

55   *The Solo Song 1580-1730.* A Norton Music Anthology; Edited by Carol MacClintock. New York: W.W.Norton & Company, Inc., 1973.

56   *The Vocal Sound.* Barbara Kinsey Sable. Englewood Cliffs, New Jersey: Prentice-Hall, Inc., 1982.

57   *36 Arie Italiane di 36 diversi autori dei secoli XVII e XVIII per Canto e Pianforte.* Scelta, revisione ed elaborazione di Maffeo Zanon. Reprint, Milan: G.Ricordi & C., 1975.

58   *12 Arie Italiane dei Secoli XVII e XVIII.* Scelta, revisione ed elaborazione di Maffeo Zanon. Milan: G.Ricordi & C., 1953.

59   *Twenty-four Italian Songs and Arias.* New York: G. Schirmer, Inc., 1948. New edition (n.d.) distributed by Hal Leonard Publishing Company.

60   *26 Italian Songs and Arias.* Edited by John Glenn Paton. Van Nuys, Ca.: Alfred Publishing Co., Inc., 1991.

61   *Voices from the Golden Age of Bel Canto.* Collected by Henry Edward Krehbiel, edited by Max Spicker. New York: G.Schirmer, 1910.

62   *Women Composers [Music Through the Ages].* Edited by Sylvia Glickman and Martha Furman Schleifer. Vol. 1: Composers born before 1599. New York: G.K. Hall & Co., 1996.
63   ——. Vol. 2: Composers born 1600-1699. 1996.

64   *World's Favorite Italian Songs and Arias of the 17th and 18th Centuries.* Carlstadt, NJ: Ashley Publications, Inc., 1981.

Collections of Works by a Single Composer

65   Albinoni, Tomaso. *Twelve Cantatas, Op.4.* Edited by Michael Talbot. Recent Researches in the Music of the Baroque Era, Volume 31. Madison, Wisconsin: A-R Editions, Inc., 1979.

66   Caccini, Francesca. *Sonetto spirituali, Madrigale, Aria Romanesca, Motteto, Himno, Canzonetta (soprano and continuo).* Edited by Caroline Cunningham. Bryn Mawr, Pennsylvania: Hildegard Publishing Company, 1998.

67   Caldara, Antonio. *Three Cantatas for Soprano and Continuo.* Edited by Brian Pritchard. Devon, England: Antico Edition, 1996.

68   Carissimi, Giacomo. *Six Solo Cantatas (for High voice and Keyboard).* Edited by Gloria Rose. London: Faber Music Limited, 1969.

69   Frescobaldi, Girolamo. *ARIE MUSICALI per cantarsi nel Gravicimbalo, e Tiorba a una, a due, e a tre voci.* Monumenti Musicali Italiani, Vol.XXI. Edited by Claudio Gallico and Stafano Patuzzi. Milan: Edizioni Suvini Zerboni, 1998.

70   ——. *2 SACRED SONGS.* Realization by Luigi Dallapiccola. New York: International Music Company, 1961.

71   Mazzocchi, D. *Musiche sacre e morali: Sonetti e Arie di più parti a voce sola.* (Airs et Cantates Baroques, volume 3.) Edited by Roger Blanchard. Paris: Bureau de Musique MARIO BOIS (B.M.B.), 1976.

72   Monteverdi, Claudio. *A Voce Sola (Arie, Canzonette e Recitativi).* Edited by G. Francesco Malipiero. Milan: G.Ricordi & Co., 1953; ristampa 1988.
73   ——. *FIVE SONGS.* Edited by George Hunger and Claude Palisca. Bryn Mawr, Pennsylvania: Theodore Presser Company, 1963.
74   ——. *MADRIGALS, Book VIII (Madrigali Guerrieri et Amorosi).* Edited by Gian Francesco Malipiero. New York: Dover Publications, Inc., 1991.
75   ——. *SCHERZI MUSICALI voor hoge stem met basso continuo.* Uitgegeven door Marius Flothuis. Amsterdam: Uitgave Broekmans en van Poppel, [1958?].
76   ——. *SCHERZI MUSICALI.* Revisione e realizzazione del basso continuo di Massimo Lonardi. Milano: Edizioni Suvini Zerboni, 1978.
77   ——. *12 Composizioni Vocali.* A cura di Wolfgang Osthoff. Milano: G.Ricordi & C., 1958.

78   Orlandi, Camillo. Arie a tre, due et voce sola. In Denkmäler der Musik in Salzburg, Band 7. Vorgelegt von Herbert Seifert. Salzburg: Selke Verlag, 1995.

79   Rasi, Francesco. Musiche da camera e chiesa. In Denkmäler der Musik in Salzburg, Band 7. Vorgelegt von Herbert Seifert. Salzburg: Selke Verlag, 1995.

80   Savioni, Mario. *Six Cantatas for one and three voices with continuo.* Santa Barbara, University of California Series of Early Music, Volume 3. Edited by Irving R. Eisley. Bryn Mawr, Pa.: Theodore Presser Co., 1970.

81   Scarlatti, Alessandro. *Ariette.* (Flores Musicae, Vol. IX.) Réalisation de Claude Crussard. Lausanne: Fœtisch Frères S.A., 1958.
82   ——. *Canzone scordate: An Anthology of Early Songs and Arias.* With piano accompaniments composed by Arne Dørumsgaard. Book 6: Five Scarlatti Songs. Huntsville, Tx.: Recital Publications, 1987. **Note:** *The songs in this collection are identified on the text pages as being from [18], listed under "Anthologies and Mixed Collections."*
83   ——. *4 Cantate.* Edited by Giampiero Tintori. Milan: G.Ricordi & C., 1958, 1986, ristampa 1988 and 1997.
84   ——. *TEN ARIAS for High Voice.* Edited by Michael F. Robinson. Schirmer's Library of Musical Classics, Vol.1853. New York: G.Schirmer, Inc., 1967.
85   ——. *Three Cantatas for Voice & Cello with Keyboard.* Nona Pyron, Series Editor. Nutley, NJ: Grancio Editions, 1982.
86   ——. *7 Arie con Tromba Sola.* Edited by Henry Meredith. The Brass Press, 1980.

87   Steffani, Agostino. *Eight Songs (for solo voice, one or two woodwinds and continuo).* Smith College Music Archives, Number XI. Northhampton, Mass.: Smith College, 1950.

88   Stradella, Alessandro. *Sette Arie ed un Recitativo dall'Opera "Forza d'amor paterno."* Elaborazione di Alberto Gentili. Milano: G.Ricordi & C., 1953.

89   Strozzi, Barbara. *14 Arien aus opus II (1651).* Edited by Richard Kolb. Kassel: Furore-Verlag, 1996.

SINGLE PRINTS OF SINGLE WORKS

90   Ariosti, Attilio. *Fortunate passate.* Publication supervised by Wim Thijsse, the Board "Hans Schouwman Society." Amsterdam: Broekmans & van Poppel, 1978.
91   ——. *La Rosa (Cantata for high voice, two violins, and basso continuo).* Edited by Günther Weiß and Theodor Klein. Leipzig: Deutscher Verlag für Musik, 1977.

92   Monteverdi, Claudio. *Ardo e scoprir.* New York: Galaxy Music Corporation, 1954.
93   ——. *Chioma d'oro.* New York: Galaxy Music Corporation, 1954.
94   ——. *Lamento d'Arianna.* Edited by Nicholas Routley. Artarmon, Australia: Saraband Music, n.d.
95   ——. *Tempro la cetra.* Cambs, England: King's Music Gmc, 1992.

96   Quinciani, Lucia. *Udite Lagrimosi Spirti.* Bryn Mawr, Pa.: Hildegard Publishing Company, n.d.

97   Scarlatti, Alessandro. *Arie con Tromba Solo, Nr.9: [Sinfonia &] A battaglia, pensieri.* Edited by Edward H. Tarr. Köln: Haas-Verlag, 1995.
98   ——. *Lontan dalla sua Clori (Solo Cantata for Soprano and Basso continuo).* Edited by Malcolm Boyd. Kassel: Bärenreiter, 1972.

99   Strozzi, Barbara. *L'Astratto.* Edited by Richard Kolb. Kassel: Furore-Verlag, 1996.

DICTIONARIES AND REFERENCE BOOKS

A Handbook of Classical Mythology. By Howe, George and G.A. Harrer. New York: F.S.Crofts & Co., 1929.

Baker's Biographical Dictionary of Musicians. Eighth edition, revised by Nicolas Slonimsky. New York: Schirmer Books, 1992.

Dictionary of Classical Mythology. By J.E. Zimmerman. New York: Harper & Row, 1964.

Dizionario della lingua italiana di Niccolò Tommaseo. Edited by G. Biagi, in 2 volumes, from the 4th edition (1938). La Spezia: Fratelli Melita Editori, 1990.

Dizionario D'Ortografia e di Pronunzia. B. Migliorini, C. Tagliavini, and P. Fiorelli. Torino: ERI/Edizioni RAI Radiotelevisione Italiana, 1969.

Dizionario D'Ortografia e di Pronunzia. B. Migliorini, C. Tagliavini, and P. Fiorelli. Torino: ERI/Edizioni RAI, 1981.

Dizionario Enciclopedico universale della musica e dei musicisti. Le Biografie. Edited by Alberto Basso, in eight volumes. Torino: Unione Tipografico-Editrice Torinese (UTET), 1988.

Dizionario Etimologico Italiano. Battisti, Carlo and Giovanni Alessio. In 5 volumes. Firenze: G. Barbèra Editore, 1975.

Grande Dizionario Inglese-Italiano/Italiano-Inglese. M. Hazon. Milano: Aldo Garzanti Editore, 1975.

Il Nuovo Dizionario Garzanti. Edited by D. Schiannini. Milano: Garzanti Editore, 1985.

Il Nuovo Dizionario Inglese Garzanti. L. I. Caselli. Milano: Garzanti Editore, 1989.

Il Nuovo Zingarelli: Vocabolario della Lingua Italiana di Nicola Zingarelli. 11th Edition; general revision by Miro Dogliotti and Luigi Rosiello. Milano: Zanichelli, 1983.

Italian Dictionary. Third Edition, under the direction of Vladimiro Macchi. Firenze: Sanzoni Editore, 1996.

La Ricerca dell'Infinito. Nel Labirinto dei Verbi: Vol.I, by Alessandra Cattani. Fourth edition. San Francisco: Centro Studi Italiani, 1999.

Roget's International Thesaurus. Fifth Edition, ed. by Robert L. Chapman. New York: HarperCollins Publishers, 1992.

Short Dictionary of Mythology. By P.G. Woodcock. New York: Philosophical Library, 1953.

The Bantam New College Italian & English Dictionary. By Robert C. Melzi. New York: Bantam Books, 1988.

The Cambridge Italian Dictionary. Barbara Reynolds, General editor. Vol.I: Italian-English. Cambridge: Cambridge University Press, 1962.

The Chiron Dictionary of Greek & Roman Mythology. Elizabeth Burr, translator. Wilmette, Illinois: Chiron Publications, 2000.

The Dictionary of Art. Edited by Jane Turner, in thirty-four volumes. (distributed in the US by Grove's Dictionaries, Inc.; New York.) London: C. Macmillan Publishers Limited, 1996.

The New Grove Dictionary of Music & Musicians. Edited by Stanley Sadie, in twenty volumes. London: Macmillan Publishers Limited, 1980; reprinted 1995.

The New GROVE Dictionary of OPERA. Edited by Stanley Sadie, in four volumes. London: Macmillan Press Limited; New York: Grove's Dictionaries of Music Inc., 1992.

The Oxford Guide to Classical Mythology in the Arts, 1300-1990s. Edited by Jane Davidson Reid, in two volumes. New York: Oxford University Press, 1993.

The Ultimate Encyclopedia of Mythology. By Cotterell, Arthur and Rachel Storm. [?]: Anness Publishing Limited (Hermes House), 1999.

Vocabolario Etimologico della Lingua Italiana. O. Pianigiani. Milano: Editrice Sonzonio, 1943.

Webster's Ninth New Collegiate Dictionary. Springfield, Massachusetts: Merriam-Webster Inc., 1987.

INTERNET REFERENCE SITES

britannica.com (Encyclopædia Britannica on line)
grovemusic.com (Grove on line)
loggia.com (Mythography)